Lecture Notes in Computer Science 12551

More information about this subseries at http://www.springer.com/series/7410

Rafael Pass · Krzysztof Pietrzak (Eds.)

Theory
of Cryptography

18th International Conference, TCC 2020
Durham, NC, USA, November 16–19, 2020
Proceedings, Part II

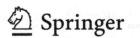 Springer

Editors
Rafael Pass
Cornell Tech
New York, NY, USA

Krzysztof Pietrzak
Institute of Science and Technology Austria
Klosterneuburg, Austria

ISSN 0302-9743   ISSN 1611-3349   (electronic)
Lecture Notes in Computer Science
ISBN 978-3-030-64377-5   ISBN 978-3-030-64378-2   (eBook)
https://doi.org/10.1007/978-3-030-64378-2

LNCS Sublibrary: SL4 – Security and Cryptology

This Springer imprint is published by the registered company Springer Nature Switzerland AG
The registered company address is: Gewerbestrasse 11, 6330 Cham, Switzerland

Preface

The 18th Theory of Cryptography Conference (TCC 2020) was held virtually during November 16–19, 2020. It was sponsored by the International Association for Cryptologic Research (IACR). The general chair of the conference was Alessandra Scafuro.

TCC 2020 was originally planned to be co-located with FOCS 2020 in Durham, North Carolina, USA. Due to the COVID-19 pandemic both events were converted into virtual events, and were held on the same day at the same time. The authors uploaded videos of roughly 20 minutes prior to the conference, and at the conference had a 10-minute window to present a summary of their work and answer questions. The virtual event would not have been possible without the generous help of Kevin and Kay McCurley, and we would like to thank them wholeheartedly.

The conference received 167 submissions, of which the Program Committee (PC) selected 71 for presentation. Each submission was reviewed by at least four PC members. The 39 PC members (including PC chairs), all top researchers in the field, were helped by 226 external reviewers, who were consulted when appropriate. These proceedings consist of the revised version of the 71 accepted papers. The revisions were not reviewed, and the authors bear full responsibility for the content of their papers.

As in previous years, we used Shai Halevi's excellent Web-review software, and are extremely grateful to him for writing it, and for providing fast and reliable technical support whenever we had any questions.

This was the 7th year that TCC presented the Test of Time Award to an outstanding paper that was published at TCC at least eight years ago, making a significant contribution to the theory of cryptography, preferably with influence also in other areas of cryptography, theory, and beyond. This year the Test of Time Award Committee selected the following paper, published at TCC 2008: "Perfectly-Secure MPC with Linear Communication Complexity" by Zuzana Trubini and Martin Hirt. The Award Committee recognized this paper "for introducing hyper-invertible matrices to perfectly secure multiparty computation, thus enabling significant efficiency improvements and, eventually, constructions with minimal communication complexity."

We are greatly indebted to many people who were involved in making TCC 2020 a success. A big thanks to the authors who submitted their papers and to the PC members and external reviewers for their hard work, dedication, and diligence in reviewing the papers, verifying the correctness, and in-depth discussions. A special thanks goes to the general chair Alessandra Scafuro and the TCC Steering Committee.

October 2020

Rafael Pass
Krzysztof Pietrzak

Organization

General Chair

Alessandra Scafuro   North Carolina State University, USA

Program Chairs

Rafael Pass   Cornell Tech, USA
Krzysztof Pietrzak   IST Austria, Austria

Program Committee

Prabhanjan Ananth	University of California, Santa Barbara, USA
Marshall Ball	Columbia University, USA
Sonia Belaïd	CryptoExperts, France
Jeremiah Blocki	Purdue University, USA
Andrej Bogdanov	The Chinese University of Hong Kong, Hong Kong
Chris Brzuszka	Aalto University, Finland
Ignacio Cascudo	IMDEA Software Institute, Spain
Kai-Min Chung	Academia Sinica, Taiwan
Aloni Cohen	Boston University, USA
Ran Cohen	Northeastern University, USA
Nico Dottling	CISPA - Helmholtz Center for Information Security, Germany
Stefan Dziembowski	University of Warsaw, Poland
Oriol Farràs	Universitat Rovira i Virgili, Spain
Georg Fuchsbauer	TU Wien, Austria
Niv Gilboa	Ben-Gurion University of the Negev, Israel
Vipul Goyal	Carnegie Mellon University, USA
Mohammad Hajiabadi	University of California, Berkeley, USA
Justin Holmgren	NTT Research, USA
Zahra Jafargholi	Aarhus University, Denmark
Yael Tauman Kalai	Microsoft Research and MIT, USA
Seny Kamara	Brown University, USA
Dakshita Khurana	University of Illinois Urbana-Champaign, USA
Markulf Kohlweiss	The University of Edinburgh, UK
Ilan Komargodski	NTT Research, USA
Huijia Lin	University of Washington, USA
Mohammad Mahmoody	University of Virginia, USA
Jesper Buus Nielsen	Aarhus University, Denmark
Emmanuela Orsini	KU Leuven, Belgium
Sunoo Park	MIT and Harvard University, USA

Anat Paskin-Cherniavsky	Ariel University, Israel
Oxana Poburinnaya	Simons Institute for the Theory of Computing, USA
Silas Richelson	University of California, Riverside, USA
Alon Rosen	IDC Herzliya, Israel
Abhi Shelat	Northeastern University, USA
Nicholas Spooner	University of California, Berkeley, USA
Uri Stemmer	Ben-Gurion University of the Negev, Israel
Justin Thaler	Georgetown University, USA
Daniel Wichs	Northeastern University and NTT Research, USA
Eylon Yogev	Boston University, USA, and Tel Aviv University, Israel

External Reviewers

Hamza Abusalah
Amit Agarwal
Archita Agarwal
Divesh Aggarwal
Navid Alamati
Younes Talibi Alaoui
Bar Alon
Joel Alwen
Joël Alwen
Miguel Ambrona
Ghous Amjad
Christian Badertscher
Saikrishna
   Badrinarayanan
James Bartusek
Balthazar Bauer
Carsten Baum
Alex Block
Alexander Block
Jonathan Bootle
Adam Bouland
Elette Boyle
Zvika Brakerski
Pedro Branco
Benedikt Bünz
Alper Cakan
Matteo Campanelli
Wouter Castryck
Hubert Chan
Lijie Chen
Yanlin Chen

Yilei Chen
Ilaria Chillotti
Arka Rai Choudhuri
Hao Chung
Michele Ciampi
Katriel Cohn-Gordon
Sandro Coretti
Sandro Coretti-Drayton
Henry Corrigan-Gibbs
Geoffroy Couteau
Dana Dachman-Soled
Hila Dahari
Jost Daniel
Pratish Datta
Bernardo David
Bernardo Machado David
Gareth Davies
Akshay Degwekar
Jack Doerner
Rafael Dowsley
Betul Durak
Betül Durak
Naomi Ephraim
Daniel Escudero
Grzegorz Fabianski
Islam Faisal
Xiong Fan
Song Fang
Antonio Faonio
Prastudy Fauzi
Serge Fehr

Rex Fernando
Ben Fisch
Cody Freitag
Shiuan Fu
Tommaso Gagliardoni
Chaya Ganesh
Sanjam Garg
Romain Gay
Marilyn George
Marios Georgiou
Essam Ghadafi
Alexandru Gheorghiu
Satrajit Ghosh
Aarushi Goel
Sasha Golovnev
Junqing Gong
Rishab Goyal
Daniel Grier
Alex Grilo
Siyao Guo
Iftach Haitner
Britta Hale
Ariel Hamlin
Adam Blatchley Hansen
Alexander Hartl
Carmit Hazay
Javier Herranz
Kyle Hogan
Thibaut Horel
Yao-Ching Hsieh
James Hulett

Shih-Han Hung
Rawane Issa
Håkon Jacobsen
Aayush Jain
Abhishek Jain
Ruta Jawale
Zhengzhong Jin
Fatih Kaleoglu
Chethan Kamath
Simon Holmgaard Kamp
Pihla Karanko
Shuichi Katsumata
Tomasz Kazana
Thomas Kerber
Fuyuki Kitagawa
Susumu Kiyoshima
Michael Klooß
Dima Kogan
Dmitry Kogan
Lisa Kohl
Yash Kondi
Yashvanth Kondi
Venkata Koppula
Ashutosh Kumar
Po-Chun Kuo
Thijs Laarhoven
Fabien Laguillaumie
Kasper Green Larsen
Eysa Lee
Seunghoon Lee
Yi Lee
Tancrède Lepoint
Xiao Liang
Chengyu Lin
Wei-Kai Lin
Yao-Ting Lin
Quanquan Liu
Tianren Liu
Alex Lombardi
Sébastien Lord
Julian Loss
George Lu
Ji Luo
Fermi Ma
Yi-Hsin Ma
Urmila Mahadev

Saeed Mahloujifar
Christian Majenz
Nikolaos Makriyannis
Giulio Malavolta
Mary Maller
Easwar Mangipudi
Nathan Manohar
Jeremias Mechler
Pierre Meyer
Tarik Moataz
Tomoyuki Morimae
Tamer Mour
Marta Mularczyk
Jörn Müller-Quade
Ryo Nishimaki
Olga Nissenbaum
Adam O'Neill
Maciej Obremski
Michele Orrù
Elena Pagnin
Georgios Panagiotakos
Omer Paneth
Alain Passelègue
Sikhar Patranabis
Alice Pellet–Mary
Rafael Del Pino
Rolando La Placa
Antoine Plouviez
Antigoni Polychroniadou
Sihang Pu
Chen Qian
Luowen Qian
Willy Quach
Jordi Ribes-González
Thomas Ricosset
Schuyler Rosefield
Dragos Rotaru
Lior Rotem
Sylvain Ruhault
Alexander Russell
Paul Rösler
Pratik Sarkar
Or Sattath
Sarah Scheffler
Adam Sealfon
Gil Segev

Ido Shahaf
Sina Shiehian
Omri Shmueli
Jad Silbak
Mark Simkin
Luisa Siniscalchi
Marjan Skrobot
Fang Song
Pratik Soni
Akshayaram Srinivasan
Ron Steinfeld
Patrick Struck
Marika Swanberg
Akira Takahashi
Aravind Thyagarajan
Rotem Tsabary
Yiannis Tselekounis
Prashant Vasudevan
Muthuramakrishnan
    Venkitasubramaniam
Daniele Venturi
Mikhail Volkhov
Philip Wadler
Hendrik Waldner
Mingyuan Wang
Tianhao Wang
Rachit Garg and
    Brent Waters
Hoeteck Wee
Weiqiang Wen
Jeroen van Wier
David Wu
Sophia Yakoubov
Takashi Yamakawa
Lisa Yang
Kevin Yeo
Michal Zajac
Mark Zhandry
Bingsheng Zhang
Chen-Da Liu Zhang
Hong-Sheng Zhou
Jiadong Zhu
Vassilis Zikas
Georgios Zirdelis

Contents – Part II

Recursive Proof Composition
from Accumulation Schemes

Benedikt Bünz[1], Alessandro Chiesa[2], Pratyush Mishra[2(✉)], and Nicholas Spooner[2]

[1] Stanford University, Stanford, USA
benedikt@cs.stanford.edu
[2] UC Berkeley, Berkeley, USA
{alexch,pratyush,nick.spooner}@berkeley.edu

Abstract. Recursive proof composition has been shown to lead to powerful primitives such as incrementally-verifiable computation (IVC) and proof-carrying data (PCD). All existing approaches to recursive composition take a succinct non-interactive argument of knowledge (SNARK) and use it to prove a statement about its own verifier. This technique requires that the verifier run in time sublinear in the size of the statement it is checking, a strong requirement that restricts the class of SNARKs from which PCD can be built. This in turn restricts the efficiency and security properties of the resulting scheme.

Bowe, Grigg, and Hopwood (ePrint 2019/1021) outlined a novel approach to recursive composition, and applied it to a particular SNARK construction which does *not* have a sublinear-time verifier. However, they omit details about this approach and do not prove that it satisfies any security property. Nonetheless, schemes based on their ideas have already been implemented in software.

In this work we present a collection of results that establish the theoretical foundations for a generalization of the above approach. We define an *accumulation scheme* for a non-interactive argument, and show that this suffices to construct PCD, even if the argument itself does not have a sublinear-time verifier. Moreover we give constructions of accumulation schemes for SNARKs, which yield PCD schemes with novel efficiency and security features.

Keywords: Succinct arguments · Proof-carrying data · Recursive proof composition

1 Introduction

Proof-carrying data (PCD) [CT10] is a cryptographic primitive that enables mutually distrustful parties to perform distributed computations that run indefinitely, while ensuring that every intermediate state of the computation can be succinctly verified. PCD supports computations defined on (possibly infinite) directed acyclic graphs, with messages passed along directed edges. Verification is facilitated by attaching to each message a succinct proof of correctness. This is a generalization of the notion of *incrementally-verifiable computation* (IVC) due to [Val08], which can be viewed as PCD for the path graph (i.e., for automata). PCD has found applications in enforcing language semantics [CTV13], verifiable MapReduce computations [CTV15], image authentication [NT16], succinct blockchains [Co17, KB20, BMRS20], and others.

© International Association for Cryptologic Research 2020
R. Pass and K. Pietrzak (Eds.): TCC 2020, LNCS 12551, pp. 1–18, 2020.
https://doi.org/10.1007/978-3-030-64378-2_1

Recursive Composition. Prior to this work, the only known method for constructing PCD was from *recursive composition* of succinct non-interactive arguments (SNARGs) [BCCT13, BCTV14, COS20]. This method informally works as follows. A proof that the computation was executed correctly for t steps consists of a proof of the claim "the t-th step of the computation was executed correctly, and there exists a proof that the computation was executed correctly for $t - 1$ steps". The latter part of the claim is expressed using the SNARG verifier itself. This construction yields secure PCD (with IVC as a special case) provided the SNARG satisfies an adaptive knowledge soundness property (i.e., is a SNARK). The efficiency and security properties of the resulting PCD scheme correspond to those of a single invocation of the SNARK.

Limitations of Recursion. Recursion as realized in prior work requires proving a statement that contains a description of the SNARK verifier. In particular, for efficiency, we must ensure that the statement we are proving (essentially) *does not grow* with the number of recursion steps t. For example, if the representation of the verifier were to grow even *linearly* with the statement it is verifying, then the size of the statement to be checked would grow *exponentially* in t. Therefore, prior works have achieved efficiency by focusing on SNARKs which admit sublinear-time verification: either SNARKs for machine computations [BCCT13] or preprocessing SNARKs for circuit computations [BCTV14, COS20]. Requiring sublinear-time verification significantly restricts our choice of SNARK, which limits what we can achieve for PCD.

In addition to the above asymptotic considerations, recursion raises additional considerations concerning concrete efficiency. All SNARK constructions require that statements be encoded as instances of some particular (algebraic) NP-complete problem, and difficulties often arise when encoding the SNARK verifier itself as such an instance. The most well-known example of this is in recursive composition of pairing-based SNARKs, since the verifier performs operations over a finite field that is necessarily different from the field supported "natively" by the NP-complete problem [BCTV14]. This type of problem also appears when recursing SNARKs whose verifiers make heavy use of cryptographic hash functions [COS20].

A New Technique. Bowe, Grigg, and Hopwood [BGH19] suggest an exciting novel approach to recursive composition that replaces the SNARK verifier in the circuit with a simpler algorithm. This algorithm does not itself verify the previous proof π_{t-1}. Instead, it adds the proof to an *accumulator* for verification at the end. The accumulator must not grow in size. A key contribution of [BGH19] is to sketch a mechanism by which this might be achieved for a particular SNARK construction. While they prove this SNARK construction secure, they do not include definitions or proofs of security for their recursive technique. Nonetheless, practitioners have already built software based on these ideas [Halo19, Pickles20].

1.1 Our Contributions

In this work we provide a collection of results that establish the theoretical foundations for the above approach. We introduce the cryptographic object, an *accumulation scheme*, that enables this technique, and prove that it suffices for constructing PCD. We then provide generic tools for building accumulation schemes, as well as several concrete instantiations. Our framework establishes the security of schemes that are already being used by practitioners, and we believe that it will simplify and facilitate further research in this area.

Accumulation Schemes. We introduce the notion of an *accumulation scheme* for a predicate $\Phi\colon X \to \{0,1\}$. This formalizes, and generalizes, an idea outlined in [BGH19]. An accumulation scheme is best understood in the context of the following process. Consider an infinite stream $q_1, q_2, \ldots$ with each $q_i \in X$. We augment this stream with *accumulators* acc_i as follows: at time i, the *accumulation prover* receives (q_i, acc_{i-1}) and computes acc_i; the *accumulation verifier* receives (q_i, acc_{i-1}, acc_i) and checks that acc_{i-1} and q_i were correctly accumulated into acc_i (if not, the process ends). Then at any time t, the *decider* can validate acc_t, which establishes that, for *all* $i \in [t]$, $\Phi(q_i) = 1$. All three algorithms are stateless. To avoid trivial constructions, we want (i) the accumulation verifier to be more efficient than Φ, and (ii) the size of an accumulator (and hence the running time of the three algorithms) does not grow over time. Accumulation schemes are powerful, as we demonstrate next.

Recursion from Accumulation. We say that a SNARK has an accumulation scheme if the predicate corresponding to its verifier has an accumulation scheme (so X is a set of instance-proof pairs). We show that any SNARK having an accumulation scheme where the *accumulation verifier* is sublinear can be used to build a proof-carrying data (PCD) scheme, *even if the SNARK verifier is not itself sublinear.* This broadens the class of SNARKs from which PCD can be built. Similarly to [COS20], we show that if the SNARK and accumulation scheme are post-quantum secure, so is the PCD scheme. (Though it remains an open question whether there are non-trivial accumulation schemes for post-quantum SNARKs.)

Theorem 1 (informal). *There is an efficient transformation that compiles any SNARK with an efficient accumulation scheme into a PCD scheme. If the SNARK and its accumulation scheme are zero knowledge, then the PCD scheme is also zero knowledge. Additionally, if the SNARK and its accumulation scheme are post-quantum secure then the PCD scheme is also post-quantum secure.*

The above theorem holds in the standard model (where all parties have access to a common reference string, but no oracles). Since our construction makes non-black-box use of the accumulation scheme verifier, the theorem does not carry over to the random oracle model (ROM). It remains an intriguing open problem to determine whether or not SNARKs in the ROM imply PCD in the ROM (and if the latter is even possible).

Note that we require a suitable definition of zero knowledge for an accumulation scheme. This is not trivial, and our definition is informed by what is required for Theorem 1 and what our constructions achieve.

Proof-carrying data is a powerful primitive: it implies IVC and, further assuming collision-resistant hash functions, also efficient SNARKs for machine computations. Hence, Theorem 1 may be viewed as an extension of the "bootstrapping" theorem of [BCCT13] to certain non-succinct-verifier SNARKs.

See Sect. 2.1 for a summary of the ideas behind Theorem 1, and the full version for technical details.

Accumulation from Accumulation. Given the above, a natural question is: where do accumulation schemes for SNARKs come from? In [BGH19] it was informally observed that a specific SNARK construction, based on the hardness of the discrete logarithm problem, has an accumulation scheme. To show this, [BGH19] first observe that the verifier in the SNARK construction is sublinear *except for* the evaluation of a certain predicate (checking an opening of a polynomial commitment [KZG10]), then outline a construction which is essentially an accumulation scheme for that predicate.

We prove that this idea is a special case of a general paradigm for building accumulation schemes for SNARKs.

Theorem 2 (informal). *There is an efficient transformation that, given a SNARK whose verifier is succinct when given oracle access to a "simpler" predicate, and an accumulation scheme for that predicate, constructs an accumulation scheme for the SNARK. Moreover, this transformation preserves zero knowledge and post-quantum security of the accumulation scheme.*

The construction underlying Theorem 2 is black-box. In particular, if both the SNARK and the accumulation scheme for the predicate are secure with respect to an oracle, then the resulting accumulation scheme for the SNARK is secure with respect to that oracle.

See Sect. 2.3 for a summary of the ideas behind Theorem 2, and the full version for technical details.

Accumulating Polynomial Commitments. Several works [MBKM19, GWC19, CHM+20] have constructed SNARKs whose verifiers are succinct relative to a specific predicate: checking the opening of a *polynomial commitment* [KZG10]. We prove that two natural polynomial commitment schemes possess accumulation schemes in the random oracle model: PC_{DL}, a scheme based on the security of discrete logarithms [BCC+16, BBB+18, WTS+18]; and PC_{AGM}, a scheme based on knowledge assumptions in bilinear groups [KZG10, CHM+20].

Theorem 3 (informal). *In the random oracle model, there exist (zero knowledge) accumulation schemes for PC_{DL} and PC_{AGM} that achieve the efficiency outlined in the table below (n denotes the number of evaluation proofs, and d denotes the degree of committed polynomials).*

Polynomial commitment	Assumption	Cost to check evaluation proofs	Cost to check an accumulation step	Cost to check final accumulator	Accumulator size
PC_{DL}	DLOG + RO	$\Theta(nd)$ $\mathbb{G}$ mults.	$\Theta(n \log d)$ $\mathbb{G}$ mults.	$\Theta(d)$ $\mathbb{G}$ mults.	$\Theta(\log d)$ $\mathbb{G}$
PC_{AGM}	AGM + RO	$\Theta(n)$ pairings	$\Theta(n)$ $\mathbb{G}_1$ mults.	1 pairing	2 $\mathbb{G}_1$

For both schemes the cost of checking that an accumulation step was performed correctly is *much less* than the cost of checking an evaluation proof. We can apply Theorem 2 to combine either of these accumulation schemes for polynomial commitments with any of the aforementioned predicate-efficient SNARKs, which yields concrete accumulation schemes for these SNARKs with the same efficiency benefits.

We remark that our accumulation scheme for PC_{DL} is a variation of a construction presented in [BGH19], and so our result establishes the security of a type of construction used by practitioners.

We sketch the constructions underlying Theorem 3 in Sect. 2.4, and provide details in the full version of our paper.

New Constructions of PCD. By combining our results, we (heuristically) obtain constructions of PCD that achieve new properties. Namely, starting from either PC_{DL} or PC_{AGM}, we can apply Theorem 2 to a suitable SNARK to obtain a SNARK with an accumulation scheme in the random oracle model. Then we can instantiate the random oracle, obtaining a SNARK and accumulation scheme with *heuristic* security in the standard (CRS) model, to which we apply Theorem 1 to obtain a corresponding PCD scheme. Depending on whether we started with PC_{DL} or PC_{AGM}, we get a PCD scheme with different features, as summarized below.

- *From PC_{DL}: PCD based on discrete logarithms.* We obtain a PCD scheme in the *uniform reference string* model (i.e., without secret parameters) and small argument sizes. In contrast, prior PCD schemes require structured reference strings [BCTV14] or have larger argument sizes [COS20]. Moreover, our PCD scheme can be efficiently instantiated from any cycle of elliptic curves [SS11]. In contrast, prior PCD schemes with small argument size use cycles of pairing-friendly elliptic curves [BCTV14,CCW19], which are more expensive.
- *From PC_{AGM}: lightweight PCD based on bilinear groups.* The recursive statement inside this PCD scheme does not involve checking any pairing computations, because pairings are deferred to a verification that occurs *outside* the recursive statement. In contrast, the recursive statements in prior PCD schemes based on pairing-based SNARKs were more expensive because they checked pairing computations [BCTV14].

Note again that our constructions of PCD are *heuristic* as they involve instantiating the random oracle of certain SNARK constructions with an appropriate hash function. This is because Theorem 3 is proven in the random oracle model, but Theorem 1 is explicitly *not* (as is the case for all prior IVC/PCD constructions [Val08,BCCT13,BCTV14,COS20]). There is evidence that this limitation might be inherent [CL20].

Open Problem: Accumulation in the Standard Model. All known constructions of accumulation schemes for non-interactive arguments make use of either random oracles (as in our constructions) or knowledge assumptions (e.g., the "trivial" construction from succinct-verifier SNARKs). A natural question, then, is whether there exist constructions of accumulation schemes for non-interactive arguments, or any other interesting predicate, from standard assumptions, or any assumptions which are not known to imply SNARKs. A related question is whether there is a black-box impossibility for accumulation schemes similar to the result for SNARGs of [GW11].

1.2 Related Work

Below we survey prior constructions of IVC/PCD.

PCD from SNARKs. Bitansky, Canetti, Chiesa, and Tromer [BCCT13] proved that recursive composition of SNARKs for machine computations implies PCD for constant-depth graphs, and that this in turn implies IVC for polynomial-time machine computations. From the perspective of concrete efficiency, however, one can achieve more efficient recursive composition by using *preprocessing* SNARKs for circuits rather than SNARKs for machines [BCTV14, COS20]; this observation has led to real-world applications [Co17, BMRS20]. The features of the PCD scheme obtained from recursion depend on the features of the underlying preprocessing SNARK. Below we summarize the features of the two known constructions.

- *PCD from Pairing-based SNARKs.* Ben-Sasson, Chiesa, Tromer, and Virza [BCTV14] used pairing-based SNARKs with a special algebraic property to achieve efficient recursive composition with very small argument sizes (linear in the security parameter λ). The use of pairing-based SNARKs has two main downsides. First, they require sampling a *structured reference string* involving secret values ("toxic waste") that, if revealed, compromise security. Second, the verifier performs operations over a finite field that is necessarily different from the field supported "natively" by the statement it is checking. To avoid expensive simulation of field arithmetic, the construction uses *pairing-friendly cycles of elliptic curves*, which severely restricts the choice of field in applications and requires a large base field for security.
- *PCD from IOP-based SNARKs.* Chiesa, Ojha, and Spooner [COS20] used a holographic IOP to construct a preprocessing SNARK that is unconditionally secure in the (quantum) random oracle model, which heuristically implies a post-quantum preprocessing SNARK in the *uniform reference string* model (i.e., without toxic waste). They then proved that any post-quantum SNARK leads to a post-quantum PCD scheme via recursive composition. The downside of this construction is that, given known holographic IOPs, the argument size is larger, currently at $O(\lambda^2 \log^2 N)$ bits for circuits of size N.

IVC from Homomorphic Encryption. Naor, Paneth, and Rothblum [NPR19] obtain a notion of IVC by using somewhat homomorphic encryption and an information-theoretic object called an "incremental PCP". The key feature of their scheme is that security holds under falsifiable assumptions.

There are two drawbacks, however, that restrict the use of the notion of IVC that their scheme achieves.

First, the computation to be verified must be *deterministic* (this appears necessary for schemes based on falsifiable assumptions given known impossibility results [GW11]). Second, and more subtly, completeness holds only in the case where intermediate proofs were honestly generated. This means that the following attack may be possible: an adversary provides an intermediate proof that verifies, but it is impossible for honest parties to generate new proofs for subsequent computations. Our construction of PCD achieves the stronger condition that completeness holds so long as intermediate proofs verify, ruling out this attack.

Both nondeterministic computation and the stronger completeness notion (achieved by all SNARK-based PCD schemes) are necessary for many of the applications of IVC/PCD.

2   Techniques

2.1   PCD from Arguments with Accumulation Schemes

We summarize the main ideas behind Theorem 1, which obtains proof-carrying data (PCD) from any succinct non-interactive argument of knowledge (SNARK) that has an accumulation scheme. For the sake of exposition, in this section we focus on the special case of IVC, which can be viewed as repeated application of a circuit F. Specifically, we wish to check a claim of the form "$F^T(z_0) = z_T$" where F^T denotes F composed with itself T times.

Prior Work: Recursion from Succinct Verification. Recall that in previous approaches to efficient recursive composition [BCTV14, COS20], at each step i we prove a claim of the form "$z_i = F(z_{i-1})$, and there exists a proof π_{i-1} that attests to the correctness of z_{i-1}". This claim is expressed using a circuit R which is the conjunction of F with a circuit representing the SNARK verifier; in particular, the size of the claim is at least the size of the verifier circuit. If the size of the verifier circuit grows linearly (or more) with the size of the claim being checked, then verifying the final proof becomes more costly than the original computation.

For this reason, these works focus on SNARKs with *succinct verification*, where the verifier runs in time *sublinear* in the size of the claim. In this case, the size of the claim essentially *does not grow* with the number of recursive steps, and so checking the final proof costs roughly the same as checking a single step.

Succinct verification is a seemingly paradoxical requirement: the verifier does not even have time to *read* the circuit R. One way to sidestep this issue is *preprocessing*: one designs an algorithm that, at the beginning of the recursion, computes a small cryptographic digest of R, which the recursive verifier can use instead of reading R directly. Because this preprocessing need only be performed once for the given R in an offline phase, it has almost no effect on the performance of each recursive step (in the later online phase).

A New Paradigm: IVC from Accumulation. Even allowing for preprocessing, succinct verification remains a strong requirement, and there are many SNARKs that are not known to satisfy it (e.g., [BCC+16, BBB+18, AHIV17, BCG+17, BCR+19]). Bowe, Grigg, and Hopwood [BGH19] suggested a further relaxation of succinctness that appears to still suffice for recursive composition: a type of "post-processing". Their observation is as follows: if a SNARK is such that we can efficiently "defer" the verification of a claim in a way that does not grow in cost with the number of claims to be checked, then we can hope to achieve recursive composition by deferring the verification of all claims to the end.

In the remainder of this section, we will give an overview of the proof of Theorem 1, our construction of PCD from SNARKs that have this "post-processing" property. We note that this relaxation of requirements is useful because, as suggested in [BGH19], it leads to new constructions of PCD with desirable properties (see discussion at the end of Sect. 1.1). In fact, some of these efficiency features are already being exploited by practitioners working on recursing SNARKs [Halo19, Pickles20].

The specific property we require, which we discuss more formally in the next section, is that the SNARK has an *accumulation scheme*. This is a generalization of the idea described in [BGH19]. Informally, an accumulation scheme consists of three algorithms: an accumulation prover, an accumulation verifier, and a decider. The accumulation prover is tasked with taking an instance-proof pair (z, π) and a previous accumulator acc, and producing a new accumulator acc* that "includes" the new instance. The accumulation verifier, given $((z, \pi), \text{acc}, \text{acc}^*)$, checks that acc* was computed correctly (i.e., that it accumulates (z, π)) into acc). Finally the decider, given a single accumulator acc, performs a single check that simultaneously ensures that *every* instance-proof pair accumulated in acc verifies.[1]

Given such an accumulation scheme, we can construct IVC as follows. Given a previous instance z_i, proof π_i, and accumulator acc_i, the IVC prover first accumulates (z_i, π_i) with acc_i to obtain a new accumulator acc_{i+1}. The IVC prover also generates a SNARK proof π_{i+1} of the claim: "$z_{i+1} = F(z_i)$, and there exist a proof π_i and an accumulator acc_i such that the accumulation verifier accepts $((z_i, \pi_i), \text{acc}_i, \text{acc}_{i+1})$", expressed as a circuit R. The final IVC proof then consists of (π_T, acc_T). The IVC verifier checks such a proof by running the SNARK verifier on π_T and the accumulation scheme decider on acc_T.

Why does this achieve IVC? Throughout the computation we maintain the invariant that if acc_i is a valid accumulator (according to the decider) and π_i is a valid proof, then the computation is correct up to the i-th step. Clearly if this holds at time T then the IVC verifier successfully checks the entire computation. Observe that if we were able to prove that "$z_{i+1} = F(z_i)$, π_i is a valid proof, and acc_i is a valid accumulator", by applying the invariant we would be able to conclude that the computation is correct up to step $i + 1$. Unfortunately we are not able to prove this directly, for two reasons: (i) proving that π_i is a valid proof requires proving a statement about the argument verifier, which may not be sublinear, and (ii) proving that acc_i is a valid accumulator requires proving a statement about the decider, which may not be sublinear.

Instead of proving this claim directly, we "defer" it by having the prover accumulate (z_i, π_i) into acc_i to obtain a new accumulator acc_{i+1}. The soundness property of the accumulation scheme ensures that if acc_{i+1} is valid and the accumulation verifier accepts $((z_i, \pi_i), \text{acc}_i, \text{acc}_{i+1})$, then π_i is a valid proof and acc_i is a valid accumulator. Thus all that remains to maintain the invariant is for the prover to prove that the accumulation verifier accepts; this is possible provided that the *accumulation verifier* is sublinear.

From Sketch to Proof. In the full version of our paper, we give the formal details of our construction and a proof of correctness. In particular, we show how to construct PCD, a more general primitive than IVC. In the PCD setting, rather than each computation step having a single input z_i, it receives m inputs from different nodes. Proving correctness hence requires proving that *all* of these inputs were computed correctly. For our construction, this entails checking m proofs and m accumulators. To do this, we extend the definition of an accumulation scheme to allow accumulating multiple instance-proof pairs and multiple "old" accumulators.

We now informally discuss the properties of our PCD construction.

---

[1] We remark that the notion of an accumulation scheme is *distinct* from the notion of a cryptographic accumulator for a set (e.g., an RSA accumulator), which provides a succinct representation of a large set while supporting membership queries.

- *Efficiency requirements.* Observe that the statement to be proved includes only the *accumulation verifier*, and so the *only* efficiency requirement for obtaining PCD is that this algorithm run in time sublinear in the size of the circuit R. This implies, in particular, that an accumulator must be of size sublinear in the size of R, and hence must not grow with each accumulation step. The SNARK verifier and the decider algorithm need only be efficient in the usual sense (i.e., polynomial-time).
- *Soundness.* We prove that the PCD scheme is sound provided that the SNARK is knowledge sound (i.e., is an adaptively-secure argument of knowledge) and the accumulation scheme is sound (see Sect. 2.2 for more on what this means). We stress that in both cases security should be in the standard (CRS) model, without any random oracles (as in prior PCD constructions).
- *Zero knowledge.* We prove that the PCD scheme is zero knowledge, if the underlying SNARK and accumulation scheme are both zero knowledge (for this part we also formulate a suitable notion of zero knowledge for accumulation schemes as discussed shortly in Sect. 2.2).
- *Post-quantum security.* We also prove that if both the SNARK and accumulation scheme are *post-quantum* secure, then so is the resulting PCD scheme. Here by post-quantum secure we mean that the relevant security properties continue to hold even against polynomial-size *quantum* circuits, as opposed to just polynomial-size *classical* circuits.

2.2 Accumulation Schemes

A significant contribution of this work is formulating a general notion of an accumulation scheme. An accumulation scheme for a non-interactive argument as described above is a particular instance of this definition; in subsequent sections we will apply the definition in other settings.

We first give an informal definition that captures the key features of an accumulation scheme. For clarity this is stated for the (minimal) case of a single predicate input q and a single "old" accumulator acc; we later extend this in the natural way to n predicate inputs and m "old" accumulators.

Definition 1 (informal). *An **accumulation scheme** for a predicate $\Phi\colon X \to \{0,1\}$ consists of a triple of algorithms (P, V, D), known as the prover, verifier, and decider, that satisfies the following properties.*

- Completeness: *For all accumulators* acc *and predicate inputs* $q \in X$, *if* $D(acc) = 1$ *and* $\Phi(q) = 1$, *then for* $acc^\star \leftarrow P(acc, q)$ *it holds that* $V(acc, q, acc^\star) = 1$ *and* $D(acc^\star) = 1$.
- Soundness: *For all efficiently-generated accumulators* $acc, acc^\star$ *and predicate inputs* $q \in X$, *if* $D(acc^\star) = 1$ *and* $V(acc, q, acc^\star) = 1$ *then, with all but negligible probability,* $\Phi(q) = 1$ *and* $D(acc) = 1$.

An accumulation scheme for a SNARK is an accumulation scheme for the predicate induced by the argument verifier; in this case the predicate input q consists of an instance-proof pair $(\mathbb{x}, \pi)$. Note that the completeness requirement does not place any restriction on how the previous accumulator acc is generated; we require that completeness holds for any acc the decider D determines to be valid, and any q for which the predicate Φ holds. This is needed to obtain a similarly strong notion of completeness for PCD, required for applications where accumulation is done by multiple parties that do not trust one another.

Zero Knowledge. For our PCD application, the notion of zero knowledge for an accumulation scheme that we use is the following: one can sample a "fake" accumulator that is indistinguishable from a real accumulator $acc^\star$, *without knowing anything* about the old accumulator acc and predicate input q that were accumulated in $acc^\star$. The existence of the accumulation verifier V complicates matters here: if the adversary knows acc and q, then it is easy to distinguish a real accumulator from a fake one using V. We resolve this issue by modifying Definition 1 to have the accumulation prover P produce a *verification proof* π_V in addition to the new accumulator $acc^\star$. Then V uses π_V in verifying the accumulator, but π_V is *not* required for subsequent accumulation. In our application, the simulator then does *not* have to simulate π_V. This avoids the problem described: even if the adversary knows acc and q, unless π_V is correct, V can simply reject, as it would for a "fake" accumulator. Our informal definition is as follows.

Definition 2. *An accumulation scheme for Φ is **zero knowledge** if there exists an efficient simulator S such that for all accumulators acc and inputs $q \in X$ such that $D(acc) = 1$ and $\Phi(q) = 1$, the distribution of $acc^\star$ when $(acc^\star, \pi_V) \leftarrow P(acc, q)$ is computationally indistinguishable from $acc^\star \leftarrow S(1^\lambda)$.*

Predicate Specification. The above informal definitions omit many important details; we now highlight some of these. Suppose that, as required for IVC/PCD, we have some fixed circuit R for which we want to accumulate pairs (x_i, π_i), where π_i is a SNARK proof that there exists w_i such that $R(x_i, w_i) = 1$. In this case the predicate corresponding to the verifier depends not only on the pair (x_i, π_i), but also on the circuit R, as well as the public parameters of the argument scheme pp and (often) a random oracle ρ.

Moreover, each of these inputs has different security and efficiency considerations. The security of the SNARK (and the accumulation scheme) can only be guaranteed with high probability over public parameters drawn by the generator algorithm of the SNARK, and over the random oracle. The circuit R may be chosen adversarially, but cannot be part of the input q because it is too large; it must be fixed at the beginning.

These considerations lead us to define an accumulation scheme with respect to both a predicate $\Phi \colon \mathcal{U}(*) \times (\{0,1\}^*)^3 \to \{0,1\}$ and a *predicate-specification algorithm* $\mathcal{H}$. We then adapt Definition 1 to hold for the predicate $\Phi(\rho, pp_\Phi, i_\Phi, \cdot)$ where ρ is a random oracle, pp_Φ is output by $\mathcal{H}$, and i_Φ is chosen adversarially. In our SNARK example, $\mathcal{H}$ is equal to the SNARK generator, i_Φ is the circuit R, and $\Phi(\rho, pp, R, (x, \pi)) = \mathcal{V}^\rho(pp, R, x, \pi)$.

Remark 1 (helped verification). We compare accumulation schemes for SNARKs with the notion of "helped verification" [MBKM19]. In a SNARK with helped verification, an untrusted party known as the *helper* can, given n proofs, produce an auxiliary proof that enables checking the n proofs at lower cost than that of checking each proof individually. This batching capability can be viewed as a special case of accumulation, as it applies to n "fresh" proofs only; there is no notion of batching "old" accumulators. It is unclear whether the weaker notion of helped verification alone suffices to construct IVC/PCD schemes.

2.3 Constructing Arguments with Accumulation Schemes

A key ingredient in our construction of PCD is a SNARK that has an accumulation scheme (see Sect. 2.1). Below we summarize the ideas behind Theorem 2, by explaining how to construct accumulation schemes for SNARKs whose verifier is succinct relative to an oracle predicate $\Phi_\circ$ that itself has an accumulation scheme.

Predicate-Efficient SNARKs. We call a SNARK ARG *predicate-efficient* with respect to a predicate $\Phi_\circ$ if its verifier $\mathcal{V}$ operates as follows: (i) run a fast "inner" verifier $\mathcal{V}_{\mathsf{pe}}$ to produce a bit b and query set Q; (ii) accept iff $b = 1$ and for all $\mathsf{q} \in Q$, $\Phi_\circ(\mathsf{q}) = 1$. In essence, $\mathcal{V}$ can be viewed as a circuit with "oracle gates" for $\Phi_\circ$.[2] The aim is for $\mathcal{V}_{\mathsf{pe}}$ to be significantly more efficient than $\mathcal{V}$; that is, the queries to $\Phi_\circ$ capture the "expensive" part of the computation of $\mathcal{V}$.

As noted in Sect. 1.1, one can view recent SNARK constructions [MBKM19, GWC19, CHM+20] as being predicate-efficient with respect to a "polynomial commitment" predicate. We discuss how to construct accumulation schemes for these predicates below in Sect. 2.4.

Accumulation Scheme For Predicate-Efficient SNARKs. Let ARG be a SNARK that is predicate-efficient with respect to a predicate $\Phi_\circ$, and let $\mathsf{AS}_\circ$ be an accumulation scheme for $\Phi_\circ$. To check n proofs, instead of directly invoking the SNARK verifier $\mathcal{V}$, we can first run $\mathcal{V}_{\mathsf{pe}}$ n times to generate n query sets for $\Phi_\circ$, and then, instead of invoking $\Phi_\circ$ on each of these sets, we can accumulate these queries using $\mathsf{AS}_\circ$. Below we sketch the construction of an accumulation scheme $\mathsf{AS}_{\mathsf{ARG}}$ for ARG based on this idea.

To accumulate n instance-proof pairs $[(\mathbb{x}_i, \pi_i)]_{i=1}^n$ starting from an old accumulator acc, the accumulation prover $\mathsf{AS}_{\mathsf{ARG}}.\mathsf{P}$ first invokes the inner verifier $\mathcal{V}_{\mathsf{pe}}$ on each $(\mathbb{x}_i, \pi_i)$ to generate a query set Q_i for $\Phi_\circ$, accumulates their union $Q = \cup_{i=1}^n Q_i$ into acc using $\mathsf{AS}_\circ.\mathsf{P}$, and finally outputs the resulting accumulator $\mathsf{acc}^\star$. To check that $\mathsf{acc}^\star$ indeed accumulates $[(\mathbb{x}_i, \pi_i)]_{i=1}^n$ into acc, the accumulation verifier $\mathsf{AS}_{\mathsf{ARG}}.\mathsf{V}$ first checks, for each i, whether the inner verifier $\mathcal{V}_{\mathsf{pe}}$ accepts $(\mathbb{x}_i, \pi_i)$, and then invokes $\mathsf{AS}_\circ.\mathsf{V}$ to check whether $\mathsf{acc}^\star$ correctly accumulates the query set $Q = \cup_{i=1}^n Q_i$. Finally, to decide whether $\mathsf{acc}^\star$ is a valid accumulator, the accumulation scheme decider $\mathsf{AS}_{\mathsf{ARG}}.\mathsf{D}$ simply invokes $\mathsf{AS}_\circ.\mathsf{D}$.

From Sketch to Proof. The foregoing sketch omits details required to construct a scheme that satisfies the "full" definition of accumulation schemes as stated in the full version of our paper. For instance, as noted in Sect. 2.3, the predicate $\Phi_\circ$ may be an oracle predicate, and could depend on the public parameters of the SNARK ARG. We

---

[2] This is not precisely the case, because the verifier is required to reject immediately if it ever makes a query q with $\Phi_\circ(\mathsf{q}) = 0$.

handle this by requiring that the accumulation scheme for Φ_o uses the SNARK generator $\mathcal{G}$ as its predicate specification algorithm. We also show that zero knowledge and post-quantum security are preserved. See the full version of our paper for a formal treatment of these issues, along with security proofs.

From Predicate-Efficient SNARKs to PCD. In order to build an accumulation scheme $\mathsf{AS_{ARG}}$ that suffices for PCD, ARG and $\mathsf{AS_o}$ must satisfy certain efficiency properties. In particular, when verifying satisfiability for a circuit of size N, the running time of $\mathsf{AS_{ARG}}.\mathsf{V}$ must be sublinear in N, which means in turn that the running times of $\mathcal{V}_{\mathsf{pe}}$ and $\mathsf{AS_o}.\mathsf{V}$, as well as the size of the query set Q, must be sublinear in N. Crucially, however, $\mathsf{AS_o}.\mathsf{D}$ need only run in time polynomial in N.

2.4   Accumulation Schemes for Polynomial Commitments

As noted in Sect. 2.3, several SNARK constructions (e.g., [MBKM19, GWC19, CHM+20]) are predicate-efficient with respect to an underlying *polynomial commitment*, which means that constructing an accumulation scheme for the latter leads (via Theorem 2) to an accumulation scheme for the whole SNARK.

Informally, a polynomial commitment scheme (PC scheme) is a cryptographic primitive that enables one to produce a commitment C to a polynomial p, and then to prove that this committed polynomial evaluates to a claimed value v at a desired point z. An accumulation scheme for a PC scheme thus accumulates claims of the form "C commits to p such that $p(z) = v$" for arbitrary polynomials p and evaluation points z.

In this section, we explain the ideas behind Theorem 3, by sketching how to construct (zero knowledge) accumulation schemes for two popular (hiding) polynomial commitment schemes.

- In Sect. 2.4.1, we sketch our accumulation scheme for $\mathsf{PC_{DL}}$, a polynomial commitment scheme derived from [BCC+16, BBB+18, WTS+18] that is based on the hardness of discrete logarithms.
- In Sect. 2.4.2, we sketch our accumulation scheme for $\mathsf{PC_{AGM}}$, a polynomial commitment scheme based on knowledge assumptions over bilinear groups [KZG10, CHM+20].

In each case, the running time of the accumulation verifier will be sublinear in the degree of the polynomial, and the accumulator itself will not grow with the number of accumulation steps. This allows the schemes to be used, in conjunction with a suitable predicate-efficient SNARK, to construct PCD.

We remark that each of our accumulation schemes is proved secure in the random oracle model by invoking a useful lemma about "zero-finding games" for committed polynomials. Security also requires that the random oracle used for an accumulation scheme for a PC scheme is domain-separated from the random oracle used by the PC scheme itself. See the full version for details.

2.4.1   Accumulation scheme for $\mathsf{PC_{DL}}$

We sketch our accumulation scheme for $\mathsf{PC_{DL}}$. For univariate polynomials of degree less than d, $\mathsf{PC_{DL}}$ achieves evaluation proofs of size $O(\lambda \log d)$ in the random oracle model, and assuming the hardness of the discrete logarithm problem in a prime order group $\mathbb{G}$. In particular, there are no secret parameters (so-called "toxic waste"). However, $\mathsf{PC_{DL}}$ has poor verification complexity: checking an evaluation proof requires $\Omega(d)$ scalar multiplications in $\mathbb{G}$. Bowe, Grigg, and Hopwood [BGH19] suggested a way to amortize this cost across a batch of n proofs. Below we show that their idea leads to an accumulation scheme for $\mathsf{PC_{DL}}$ with an accumulation verifier that uses only $O(n \log d)$ scalar multiplications instead of the naive $\Theta(n \cdot d)$, and with an accumulator of size $O(\log d)$ elements in $\mathbb{G}$.

Summary of $\mathsf{PC_{DL}}$. The committer and receiver both sample (consistently via the random oracle) a list of group elements $\{G_0, G_1, \dots, G_d\} \in \mathbb{G}^{d+1}$ in a group $\mathbb{G}$ of prime order q (written additively). A commitment to a polynomial $p(X) = \sum_{i=0}^{d} a_i X^i \in \mathbb{F}_q^{\leq d}[X]$ is then given by $C := \sum_{i=0}^{d} a_i G_i$. To prove that the committed polynomial p evaluates to v at a given point $z \in \mathbb{F}_q$, it suffices to prove that the triple (C, z, v) satisfies the following NP statement:

$$\exists\, a_0, \dots, a_d \in \mathbb{F} \text{ s.t. } v = \sum_{i=0}^{d} a_i z^i \text{ and } C = \sum_{i=0}^{d} a_i G_i .$$

This is a special case of an *inner product argument* (IPA), as defined in [BCC+16], which proves the inner product of two committed vectors. The receiver simply verifies this inner product argument to check the evaluation. The fact that the vector $(1, z, \dots, z^d)$ is known to the verifier and has a certain structure is exploited in the accumulation scheme that we describe below.

Accumulation Scheme for the IPA. Our accumulation scheme relies on a special structure of the IPA verifier: it generates $O(\log d)$ challenges using the random oracle, then performs cheap checks requiring $O(\log d)$ field and group operations, and finally performs an expensive check requiring $\Omega(d)$ scalar multiplications. This latter check asserts consistency between the challenges and a group element U contained in the proof. Hence, the IPA verifier is succinct *barring the expensive check*, and so constructing an accumulation scheme for the IPA reduces to the task of constructing an accumulation scheme for the expensive check involving U.

To do this, we rely on an idea of Bowe, Grigg, and Hopwood [BGH19], which itself builds on an observation in [BBB+18]. Namely, letting $(\xi_1, \dots, \xi_{\log_2 d})$ be the protocol's challenges, U can be viewed as a commitment to the polynomial $h(X) := \prod_{i=0}^{\log_2(d)-1} (1 + \xi_{\log_2(d)-i} X^{2^i}) \in \mathbb{F}_q^{\leq d}[X]$. This polynomial has the special property that it can be evaluated at any point in just $O(\log d)$ field operations (exponentially smaller than its degree d). This allows transforming the expensive check on U into a check that is amenable to batching: instead of directly checking that U is a commitment to h, one can instead check that the polynomial committed inside U agrees with h at a challenge point z sampled via the random oracle.

We leverage this idea as follows. When accumulating evaluation claims about multiple polynomials $p_1, \dots, p_n$, applying the foregoing transformation results in n checks of the form "check that the polynomial contained in U_i evaluates to $h_i(z)$ at the point z". Because these are all claims for the correct evaluation of the polynomials h_i at *the same point z*, we can accumulate them via standard homomorphic techniques. We now summarize how we apply this idea to construct our accumulation scheme $\mathsf{AS} = (\mathsf{P}, \mathsf{V}, \mathsf{D})$ for $\mathsf{PC}_{\mathsf{DL}}$.

Accumulators in our accumulation scheme have the same form as the instances to be accumulated: they are tuples of the form (C, z, v, π) where π is an evaluation proof for the claim "$p(z) = v$" and p is the polynomial committed in C. For simplicity, below we consider the case of accumulating one old accumulator $\mathsf{acc} = (C_1, z_1, v_1, \pi_1)$ and one instance (C_2, z_2, v_2, π_2) into a new accumulator $\mathsf{acc}^\star = (C, z, v, \pi)$.

Accumulation prover P: compute the new accumulator $\mathsf{acc}^\star = (C, z, v, \pi)$ from the old accumulator $\mathsf{acc} = (C_1, z_1, v_1, \pi_1)$ and the instance (C_2, z_2, v_2, π_2) as follows.

- Compute U_1, U_2 from π_1, π_2 respectively. As described above, these elements can be viewed as commitments to polynomials h_1, h_2 defined by the challenges derived from π_1, π_2.
- Use the random oracle ρ to compute the random challenge $\alpha := \rho([(h_1, U_1), (h_2, U_2)])$.
- Compute $C := U_1 + \alpha U_2$, which is a polynomial commitment to $p(X) := h_1(X) + \alpha h_2(X)$.
- Compute the challenge point $z := \rho(C, p)$, where p is uniquely represented via the tuple $([h_1, h_2], \alpha)$.
- Construct an evaluation proof π for the claim "$p(z) = v$". (This step is the only expensive one.)
- Output the new accumulator $\mathsf{acc}^\star := (C, z, v, \pi)$.

Accumulation verifier V: to check that the new accumulator $\mathsf{acc}^\star = (C, z, v, \pi)$ was correctly generated from the old accumulator $\mathsf{acc} = (C_1, z_1, v_1, \pi_1)$ and the instance (C_2, z_2, v_2, π_2), first compute the challenges α and z from the random oracle as above, and then check that (a) (C_1, z_1, v_1, π_1) and (C_2, z_2, v_2, π_2) pass the cheap checks of the IPA verifier, (b) $C = U_1 + \alpha U_2$, and (c) $h_1(z) + \alpha h_2(z) = v$.

Decider D: on input the (final) accumulator $\mathsf{acc}^\star = (C, z, v, \pi)$, check that π is a valid evaluation proof for the claim that the polynomial committed inside C evaluates to v at the point z.

This construction achieves the efficiency summarized in Theorem 3.

We additionally achieve zero knowledge accumulation for the hiding variant of $\mathsf{PC}_{\mathsf{DL}}$. Informally, the accumulation prover randomizes $\mathsf{acc}^\star$ by including a new random polynomial h_0 in the accumulation step. This ensures that the evaluation claim in $\mathsf{acc}^\star$ is for a random polynomial, thus hiding all information about the original evaluation claims. To allow the accumulation verifier to check that this randomization was performed correctly, the prover includes h_0 in an auxiliary proof π_{V}.

In the full version, we show how to extend the above accumulation scheme to accumulate any number of old accumulators and instances. Our security proof for the resulting accumulation scheme relies on the hardness of zero-finding games, and the security of $\mathsf{PC}_{\mathsf{DL}}$.

2.4.2 Accumulation scheme for $\mathsf{PC}_{\mathsf{AGM}}$

We sketch our accumulation scheme $\mathsf{AS} = (\mathsf{P}, \mathsf{V}, \mathsf{D})$ for $\mathsf{PC}_{\mathsf{AGM}}$. Checking an evaluation proof in $\mathsf{PC}_{\mathsf{AGM}}$ requires 1 pairing, and so checking n evaluation proofs requires n

pairings. AS improves upon this as follows: the accumulation verifier V only performs $O(n)$ scalar multiplications in $\mathbb{G}_1$ in order to check the accumulation of n evaluation proofs, while the decider D performs only a single pairing in order to check the resulting accumulator. This is much cheaper: it reduces the number of pairings from n to 1, and also defers this single pairing to the end of the accumulation (the decider). In particular, when instantiating the PCD construction outlined in Sect. 2.1 with a PC_{AGM}-based SNARK and our accumulation scheme for PC_{AGM}, we can eliminate *all* pairings from the circuit being verified in the PCD construction.

Below we explain how standard techniques for batching pairings using random linear combinations [CHM+20] allow us to realize an accumulation scheme for PC_{AGM} with these desirable properties.

Summary of PC_{AGM}. The committer key ck and receiver key rk for a given maximum degree bound D are group elements from a bilinear group $(\mathbb{G}_1, \mathbb{G}_2, \mathbb{G}_T, q, G, H, e)$: ck $:= \{G, \beta G, \ldots, \beta^D G\} \in \mathbb{G}_1^{D+1}$ consists of group elements encoding powers of a random field element β, while rk $:= (G, H, \beta H) \in \mathbb{G}_1 \times \mathbb{G}_2^2$.

A commitment to a polynomial $p \in \mathbb{F}_q^{\leq D}[X]$ is the group element $C := p(\beta)G \in \mathbb{G}_1$. To prove that p evaluates to v at a given point $z \in \mathbb{F}_q$, the sender computes a "witness polynomial" $w(X) := (p(X) - v)/(X - z)$, and outputs the evaluation proof $\pi := w(\beta)G \in \mathbb{G}_1$. The receiver can check this proof by checking the pairing equation $e(C - vG, H) = e(\pi, \beta H - zH)$. This pairing equation is the focus of our accumulation scheme below. (This summary omits details about degree enforcement and about hiding.)

Accumulation Scheme. We construct an accumulation scheme AS $= (P, V, D)$ for PC_{AGM} by relying on standard techniques for batching pairing equations. Suppose that we wish to simultaneously check the validity of n instances $[(C_i, z_i, v_i, \pi_i)]_{i=1}^n$. First, rewrite the pairing check for the i-th instance as follows:

$$e(C_i - v_i G, H) = e(\pi_i, \beta H - z_i H) \iff e(C_i - v_i G + z_i \pi_i, H) = e(\pi_i, \beta H) . \quad (1)$$

After the rewrite, the $\mathbb{G}_2$ inputs to both pairings do not depend on the claim being checked. This allows batching the pairing checks by taking a random linear combination with respect to a random challenge $r := \rho([C_i, z_i, v_i, \pi_i]_{i=1}^n)$ computed from the random oracle, resulting in the following combined equation:

$$e(\sum_{i=1}^n r^i(C_i - v_i G + z_i \pi_i), H) = e(\sum_{i=1}^n r^i \pi_i, \beta H) . \quad (2)$$

We now have a pairing equation involving an "accumulated commitment" $C^\star := \sum_{i=1}^n r^i(C_i - v_i G + z_i \pi_i)$ and an "accumulated proof" $\pi^\star := \sum_{i=1}^n r^i \pi_i$. This observation leads to the accumulation scheme below.

An accumulator in AS consists of a commitment-proof pair $(C^\star, \pi^\star)$, which the decider D validates by checking that $e(C^\star, H) = e(\pi^\star, \beta H)$. Moreover, observe that by Eq. (1), checking the validity of a claimed evaluation (C, z, v, π) within PC_{AGM} corresponds to checking that the "accumulator" $(C - vG + z\pi, \pi)$ is accepted by the decider D. Thus we can restrict our discussion to accumulating *accumulators*.

The accumulation prover P, on input a list of old accumulators $[\mathsf{acc}_i]_{i=1}^n = [(C_i^\star, \pi_i^\star)]_{i=1}^n$, computes a random challenge $r := \rho([\mathsf{acc}_i]_{i=1}^n)$, constructs $C^\star :=$

$\sum_{i=1}^{n} r^i C_i^\star$ and $\pi^\star := \sum_{i=1}^{n} r^i \pi_i^\star$, and outputs the new accumulator $\mathsf{acc}^\star :=$ $(C^\star, \pi^\star) \in \mathbb{G}_1^2$. To check that $\mathsf{acc}^\star$ accumulates $[\mathsf{acc}_i]_{i=1}^{n}$, the accumulation verifier V simply invokes P and checks that its output matches the claimed new accumulator $\mathsf{acc}^\star$.

To achieve zero knowledge accumulation, the accumulation prover randomizes $\mathsf{acc}^\star$ by including in it an extra "old" accumulator corresponding to a random polynomial, which statistically hides the accumulated claims. To allow the accumulation verifier to check that this randomization was performed correctly, the prover includes this old accumulator in an auxiliary proof π_V.

This construction achieves the efficiency summarized in Theorem 3.

In the full version of our paper, we show how to extend the above accumulation scheme to account for additional features of $\mathsf{PC}_{\mathsf{AGM}}$ (degree enforcement and hiding). Our security proof for the resulting accumulation scheme relies on the hardness of zero-finding games (see full version).

Acknowledgements. The authors thank William Lin for pointing out an error in a prior version of the construction of $\mathsf{PC}_{\mathsf{DL}}$, and Github user 3for for pointing out errors in a prior version of the construction of $\mathsf{PC}_{\mathsf{AGM}}$. This research was supported in part by: the Berkeley Haas Blockchain Initiative and a donation from the Ethereum Foundation. Benedikt Bünz performed part of the work while visiting the Simons Institute for the Theory of Computing.

References

[AHIV17] Scott, A., Carmit, H., Yuval, I., Muthuramakrishnan, V.: Ligero: Lightweight sublinear arguments without a trusted setup. In: Proceedings of the 24th ACM Conference on Computer and Communications Security, CCS 2017, pp. 2087–2104 (2017)

[BBB+18] Bünz, B., Jonathan, B., Dan, B., Andrew, P., Pieter, W., Greg, M.: Bulletproofs: short proofs for confidential transactions and more. In: Proceedings of the 39th IEEE Symposium on Security and Privacy, S&P 2018, pp. 315–334 (2018)

[BCC+16] Bootle, J., Cerulli, A., Chaidos, P., Groth, J., Petit, C.: Efficient zero-knowledge arguments for arithmetic circuits in the discrete log setting. In: Fischlin, M., Coron, J.-S. (eds.) EUROCRYPT 2016. LNCS, vol. 9666, pp. 327–357. Springer, Heidelberg (2016). https://doi.org/10.1007/978-3-662-49896-5_12

[BCCT13] Bitansky, N., Canetti, R., Chiesa, A. and Tromer, E.: Recursive composition and bootstrapping for SNARKs and proof-carrying data. In: Proceedings of the 45th ACM Symposium on the Theory of Computing. STOC 2013, pp. 111–120 (2013)

[BCG+17] Bootle, J., Cerulli, A., Ghadafi, E., Groth, J., Hajiabadi, M., Jakobsen, S.K.: Linear-time zero-knowledge proofs for arithmetic circuit satisfiability. In: Takagi, T., Peyrin, T. (eds.) ASIACRYPT 2017. LNCS, vol. 10626, pp. 336–365. Springer, Cham (2017). https://doi.org/10.1007/978-3-319-70700-6_12

[BCR+19] Ben-Sasson, E., Chiesa, A., Riabzev, M., Spooner, N., Virza, M., Ward, N.P.: Aurora: transparent succinct arguments for R1CS. In: Ishai, Y., Rijmen, V. (eds.) EUROCRYPT 2019. LNCS, vol. 11476, pp. 103–128. Springer, Cham (2019). https://doi.org/10.1007/978-3-030-17653-2_4

[BCTV14] Ben-Sasson, E., Chiesa, A., Tromer, E.: Scalable zero knowledge via cycles of elliptic curves. In: Proceedings of the 34th Annual International Cryptology Conference, CRYPTO 2014, pp. 276–294, (2014)

[BGH19] Sean, B., Jack, G., Daira, H.: Halo: Recursive proof composition without a trusted setup. ePrint Report 2019/1021 (2019)

[BMRS20] Bonneau, J., Meckler, I., Rao, V., Shapiro, E.: Coda: Decentralized cryptocurrency at scale. ePrint Report 2020/352 (2020)

[CCW19] Chiesa, A.: Chua, Lynn, Weidner, Matthew: On cycles of pairing-friendly elliptic curves. SIAM J. Appl. Algebra Geo. **3**(2), 175–192 (2019)

[CHM+20] Chiesa, A., Hu, Y., Maller, M., Mishra, P., Vesely, N., Ward, N.: Marlin: preprocessing zksnarks with universal and updatable SRS. In: Canteaut, A., Ishai, Y. (eds.) EUROCRYPT 2020. LNCS, vol. 12105, pp. 738–768. Springer, Cham (2020). https://doi.org/10.1007/978-3-030-45721-1_26

[CL20] Chiesa, A., Liu, S.: On the impossibility of probabilistic proofs in relativized worlds. In: Proceedings of the 11th Innovations in Theoretical Computer Science Conference, ITCS 2020, pp. 1–30 (2020)

[Co17] O(1) Labs. "Coda Cryptocurrency" (2017) https://codaprotocol.com/

[COS20] Chiesa, A., Ojha, D., Spooner, N.: FRACTAL: post-quantum and transparent recursive proofs from holography. In: Canteaut, A., Ishai, Y. (eds.) EUROCRYPT 2020. LNCS, vol. 12105, pp. 769–793. Springer, Cham (2020). https://doi.org/10.1007/978-3-030-45721-1_27

[CT10] Chiesa, A. and Tromer, E.: Proof-carrying data and hearsay arguments from signature cards. In: Proceedings of the 1st Symposium on Innovations in Computer Science, ICS 2010, pp. 310–331 (2010)

[CTV13] Stephen, C., Eran, T., Jeffrey, A.V.: Enforcing language semantics using proof-carrying data. ePrint Report 2013/513 (2013)

[CTV15] Chiesa, A., Tromer, E., Virza, M.: Cluster computing in zero knowledge. In: Oswald, E., Fischlin, M. (eds.) EUROCRYPT 2015. LNCS, vol. 9057, pp. 371–403. Springer, Heidelberg (2015). https://doi.org/10.1007/978-3-662-46803-6_13

[GW11] Gentry, C., Wichs, D.: Separating succinct non-interactive arguments from all falsifiable assumptions. In: Proceedings of the 43rd Annual ACM Symposium on Theory of Computing, STOC 2011, pp. 99–108 (2011)

[GWC19] Ariel, G., Zachary, J.W., Oana, C.: PLONK: Permutations over lagrange-bases for oecumenical noninteractive arguments of knowledge. ePrint Report 2019/953 (2019)

[Halo19] Sean, B., Jack, G., Daira, H.: Halo (2019) https://github.com/ebfull/halo

[KB20] Assimakis, K., Bonneau, J.: Proof of necessary work: Succinct state verification with fairness guarantees. ePrint Report 2020/190 (2020)

[KZG10] Aniket, K., Gregory, M.Z., Ian, G.: Constant-size commitments to polynomials and their applications. In: Proceedings of the 16th International Conference on the Theory and Application of Cryptology and Information Security, ASIACRYPT 2010, pp. 177–194 (2010)

[MBKM19] Maller, M., Bowe, S., Kohlweiss, M., Meiklejohn, S.: Sonic: Zero-knowledge SNARKs from linear-size universal and updateable structured reference strings. In: Proceedings of the 26th ACM Conference on Computer and Communications Security. CCS 2019 (2019)

[NPR19] Moni, N., Omer, P., Guy, N.R.: Incrementally verifiable computation via incremental pcps. In: Proceedings of the 17th International Conference on the Theory of Cryptography, TCC 2019, pp. 552–576 (2019)

[NT16] Naveh, A., Tromer, E.: PhotoProof: Cryptographic image authentication for any set of permissible transformations. In: Proceedings of the 37th IEEE Symposium on Security and Privacy, S&P 2016, pp. 255–271 (2016)

[Pickles20] O(1) Labs. *Pickles*. https://github.com/o1-labs/marlin

[SS11] Silverman, J.H., Stange, K.E.: Amicable pairs and aliquot cycles for elliptic curves. Exp. Math. **20**(3), 329–357 (2011)

[Val08] Paul, V.: Incrementally verifiable computation or proofs of knowledge imply time/space efficiency. In: Proceedings of the 5th Theory of Cryptography Conference, TCC 2008, pp. 1–18 (2008)

[WTS+18] Wahby, R.S., Tzialla, I., Shelat, A., Thaler, J., Walfish, M.: Doubly-efficient zkSNARKs without trusted setup. In: Proceedings of the 39th IEEE Symposium on Security and Privacy, S&P 2018, pp. 926–943 (2018)

Linear-Time Arguments with Sublinear Verification from Tensor Codes

Jonathan Bootle[1]([✉]), Alessandro Chiesa[1], and Jens Groth[2]

[1] UC Berkeley, Berkeley, USA
{jonathan.bootle,alexch}@berkeley.edu
[2] Dfinity, Zürich, Switzerland
jens@dfinity.org

Abstract. Minimizing the computational cost of the prover is a central goal in the area of succinct arguments. In particular, it remains a challenging open problem to construct a succinct argument where the prover runs in linear time and the verifier runs in polylogarithmic time.

We make progress towards this goal by presenting a new linear-time probabilistic proof. For any fixed $\epsilon > 0$, we construct an interactive oracle proof (IOP) that, when used for the satisfiability of an N-gate arithmetic circuit, has a prover that uses $O(N)$ field operations and a verifier that uses $O(N^\epsilon)$ field operations. The sublinear verifier time is achieved in the holographic setting for every circuit (the verifier has oracle access to a linear-size encoding of the circuit that is computable in linear time).

When combined with a linear-time collision-resistant hash function, our IOP immediately leads to an argument system where the prover performs $O(N)$ field operations and hash computations, and the verifier performs $O(N^\epsilon)$ field operations and hash computations (given a short digest of the N-gate circuit).

Keywords: Interactive oracle proofs · Tensor codes · Succinct arguments

1 Introduction

Succinct arguments are cryptographic proofs for NP in which the number of bits exchanged between the argument prover and the argument verifier is much less than the size of the NP witness (e.g., polylogarithmic in the size of the NP witness). Succinct arguments originate in the seminal works of Kilian [Kil92] and Micali [Mic00], and have now become the subject of intense study from theoreticians and practitioners, with a great deal of effort invested in improving their asymptotic and concrete efficiency.

The main efficiency measures in a succinct argument are communication complexity (the number of bits exchanged between the prover and the verifier), as well as the running time of the prover and the running time of the verifier. Over the last decade there has been much progress in improving the communication complexity and verifier time for succinct arguments whose prover runs in quasilinear time. These advances have, in particular, enabled real-world deployments of succinct arguments as part of security systems where the succinct argument is used to certify correctness of certain medium-size computations (e.g., [Ben+14]).

There are, however, exciting envisioned applications where the succinct argument is used to prove the correctness of large-scale computations (see [OWWB20] and

© International Association for Cryptologic Research 2020
R. Pass and K. Pietrzak (Eds.): TCC 2020, LNCS 12551, pp. 19–46, 2020.
https://doi.org/10.1007/978-3-030-64378-2_2

references therein). While a proving time that is quasilinear is arguably asymptotically efficient, the polylogarithmic overheads severely limit the sizes of computations that can be supported in applications, because proving time quickly becomes a bottleneck.

This state of affairs motivates the fundamental problem of constructing *linear-time succinct arguments*: succinct arguments where the prover runs in linear time and, ideally, also where the verifier runs in sublinear (e.g., polylogarithmic) time. In this paper we present new constructions that make progress on this problem.

Challenges. There are different approaches for constructing succinct arguments, yet essentially all of them follow the same high-level pattern: first, *arithmetize* the computation whose correctness is being proved; second, *probabilistically check* the arithmetized problem via the help of cryptography. Typically, the first step alone already costs more than linear time because it involves, in particular, encoding the computation as a polynomial, an operation that can be performed in quasilinear time thanks to the Fast Fourier Transform (FFT) but is not believed to have a linear-time algorithm. This means that many of the algebraic techniques that have proven useful to construct succinct arguments seem inapplicable in the linear-time regime.

Prior Work. Few works achieve some form of succinct argument without using FFTs, and none of them resolve the problem of constructing linear-time succinct arguments. We briefly review these works below, and also compare their main features in Fig. 1 (alongside the arguments that we construct in this paper).

Several works [BCCGP16, BBBPWM18, WTSTW18, XZZPS19, Set20] forego the use of FFTs by using homomorphic commitments to realize a "cryptographic arithmetization", but in doing so also introduce quasilinear work in the cryptography. In some works the quasilinear costs, due to the cryptography [XZZPS19] or an FFT [ZXZS20], can be isolated to the witness of the non-deterministic computation and thereby achieve linear work if the witness is sufficiently small; but, in general, the witness may be as large as the computation.

While the above works achieve polylogarithmic communication complexity but not linear-time proving, Bootle et al. [BCGGHJ17] achieve linear-time proving with square-root communication complexity (and verification): an argument system for arithmetic circuit satisfiability where, for an N-gate circuit, the prover performs $O(N)$ field operations and hash computations while the verifier performs $O(\sqrt{N})$ field operations and hash computations, with a communication complexity of $O(\sqrt{N})$. Crucially, the hash function is only required to be collision resistant, for which there are linear-time candidates (e.g., assuming the intractability of certain shortest vector problems [AHIKV17]), which leads to a linear-time prover.

Overall, the construction in [BCGGHJ17] remains the only argument system for NP known to date where the prover runs in linear time and where communication complexity is sublinear. Improving on the square-root communication complexity, and ideally also the square-root verifier time, is an open problem.

Linear-time IOPs Suffice. The approach used by Bootle et al. [BCGGHJ17] to obtain their linear-time argument system highlights a natural target for improvement, as we now explain. First, they construct an *interactive oracle proof* (IOP) with prover time $\mathsf{tp} = O(N)$, query complexity $\mathsf{q} = O(\sqrt{N})$, and verifier time $\mathsf{tv} = O(\sqrt{N})$. (An IOP is a "multi-round PCP" [BCS16, RRR16], as we will review later on.) Second, they apply the "commit-then-open" paradigm of Kilian [Kil92], by using a collision-resistant hash function to transform the IOP into an argument system where communication complexity is $O(q \cdot \log N)$. In this latter step, if one can evaluate the hash function in linear time, the resulting argument prover runs in time $O(tp)$ and $O(tv)$. We see here that, given linear-time hash functions, *the problem of constructing linear-time succinct arguments reduces to constructing linear-time IOPs with small query complexity (and verifier time).*

In other words, the target for improvement is the IOP. Our goal in this paper is to construct an IOP with linear-time prover whose query complexity and verifier time improve on the prior art, which would yield an argument system with corresponding improvements. For example, improving query complexity to be polylogarithmic would yield the first linear-time argument with polylogarithmic communication complexity.

We conclude here by noting that the above approach has the additional benefit of being plausibly post-quantum, as the underlying linear-time hash function candidate is based on a lattice problem [AHIKV17].

1.1   Our Results

We construct, for any fixed $\epsilon > 0$, an argument system where the prover performs $O(N)$ field operations and hash computations, communication complexity is $O(N^\epsilon)$, and the verifier performs $O(N^\epsilon)$ field operations and hash computations. We achieve this by improving the state of the art in linear-time IOPs (see Fig. 2): our main result is a public-coin IOP where, for any fixed $\epsilon > 0$, the prover performs $O(N)$ field operations, query complexity is $O(N^\epsilon)$, and the verifier performs $O(N^\epsilon)$ field operations. These costs are when proving the satisfiability of an N-gate arithmetic circuit defined over any field of size $\Omega(N)$.[1]

In more detail, we focus on constructing protocols for *rank-1 constraint satisfiability* (R1CS), a standard generalization of arithmetic circuits where the "circuit description" is given by coefficient matrices.[2]

Definition 1 (informal). *The R1CS problem asks: given a finite field $\mathbb{F}$, coefficient matrices $A, B, C \in \mathbb{F}^{N \times N}$ each containing at most $M = \Omega(N)$ non-zero entries, and an instance vector x over $\mathbb{F}$, is there a witness vector w over $\mathbb{F}$ such that $z := (x, w) \in \mathbb{F}^N$ and $Az \circ Bz = Cz$? (Here "$\circ$" denotes the entry-wise product.)*

Theorem 1 (informal). *For every positive constant $\epsilon > 0$, there is a public-coin holographic IOP for R1CS, over any field of size $\Omega(M)$, with the following parameters:*

– *round complexity is $O(1/\epsilon + \log M)$;*

---

[1] The sublinear time of the argument verifier is achieved in the preprocessing setting, which means that the verifier receives as input a short digest of the circuit that can be derived by anyone (in linear time). Some form of preprocessing is necessary for sublinear verification because the argument verifier just reading the circuit takes linear time. In turn, preprocessing is enabled by the fact that our IOP is holographic, which means that the IOP verifier has oracle access to a linear-size encoding of the circuit that is computable in linear time. See [CHMMVW20, COS20] for more on how holography leads to preprocessing.

[2] Recall that satisfiability of an N-gate arithmetic circuit is reducible, in linear time, to an R1CS instance where the coefficient matrices are $N \times N$ and have $O(N)$ non-zero entries.

- *proof length is $O(M)$ elements in $\mathbb{F}$;*
- *query complexity is $O(M^\epsilon)$;*
- *the prover uses $O(M)$ field operations; and*
- *the verifier uses $O(M^\epsilon)$ field operations, given access to a linear-time encoding of the coefficient matrices.*

Our theorem directly follows from two results of independent interest. First, we construct a proof protocol for R1CS with a linear-time prover, but in an intermediate model that extends the type of queries that the verifier can make in an IOP. Second, we efficiently "implement" this intermediate model via a standard IOP. We summarize each of these two results below. The formal statement of Theorem 1 is given in the full version of this paper .

We remark that our result, unlike many other results about efficient probabilistic proofs, holds over *any* field $\mathbb{F}$ that is large enough (linear in M) without requiring any special structure (e.g., smooth subgroups).

(1) IOP with Tensor Queries for R1CS. We use the notion of a *tensor IOP*, which is an IOP where the verifier can make *tensor queries* to the proof strings sent by the prover, as opposed to just point queries as in a standard IOP. To make a tensor query to one of the received proof strings, the verifier specifies a vector with prescribed tensor structure and receives as answer the inner product of the tensor vector and proof string.

Definition 2 (informal). *A $(\mathbb{F}, k, t)$-tensor IOP modifies the notion of an IOP as follows: (a) the prover message in each round i is a string Π_i in $\mathbb{F}^{\ell_i \cdot k^t}$ for some positive integer ℓ_i; (b) a verifier query may request the value $\langle a_0 \otimes a_1 \otimes \cdots \otimes a_t, \Pi_i \rangle$ for a chosen round i and chosen vectors $a_0 \in \mathbb{F}^{\ell_i}$ and $a_1, \ldots, a_t \in \mathbb{F}^k$.*

The first part to our proof of Theorem 1 is a $(\mathbb{F}, k, t)$-tensor IOP for R1CS with a $O(M)$-time prover, constant query complexity, and a $O(M^{1/t})$-time verifier (who has tensor-query access to the coefficient matrices).

Theorem 2 (informal). *For every finite field $\mathbb{F}$ and positive integers k, t, there is a $(\mathbb{F}, k, t)$-tensor IOP for R1CS that supports coefficient matrices in $\mathbb{F}^{N \times N}$ with $N = k^t$ and up to $M = O(N)$ non-zero entries and has the following parameters:*

- *soundness error is $O(M/|\mathbb{F}|)$;*
- *round complexity is $O(\log N)$;*
- *proof length is $O(N)$ elements in $\mathbb{F}$;*
- *query complexity is $O(1)$;*
- *the prover uses $O(M)$ field operations; and*
- *the verifier uses $O(M^{1/t})$ field operations, given tensor-query access to the coefficient matrices.*

We sketch the ideas behind this result in two steps: in Sect. 2.4 we describe a tensor IOP for R1CS achieving all efficiency parameters except that the verifier explicitly reads the coefficient matrices and uses $O(M)$ field operations; then in Sect. 2.5 we describe how to extend this tensor IOP to the holographic setting, achieving a sublinear verifier time when the verifier is granted tensor-query access to the coefficient matrices. The corresponding technical details are provided in the full version of this paper. From a technical perspective, our construction builds on tools from several papers, such as linear-time scalar products in [BCGGHJ17], linear-time sumchecks in [Tha13, XZZPS19], and linear-time look-ups in [Set20, GW20].

(2) From Tensor Queries to Point Queries. We prove that any tensor IOP can be efficiently implemented as a standard IOP, by way of a subprotocol that "simulates" tensor queries via a collection of point queries.

In more detail, we provide a transformation that receives as input a tensor IOP and any linear code represented via a circuit for its encoding function, and produces as output a point-query IOP that decides the same language as the tensor IOP up to an additional soundness error.

The key efficiency feature of the transformation is that prover complexity is preserved up to the number of tensor queries, the code's rate, and the code's encoding time. In particular, if the prover in the tensor IOP uses a linear number of field operations and the verifier makes a constant number of tensor queries, and the code is linear-time encodable, then the new prover in the standard IOP uses a linear number of field operations. In the following theorem, and throughout the paper, we use "Big O" notation such as $O_a(\cdot)$, which means that the parameter a is treated as a constant.

Theorem 3 (informal). *There is an efficient transformation that takes as input a tensor-query IOP and a linear code, and outputs a point-query IOP that has related complexity parameters, as summarized below.*

- *Input IOP: an $(\mathbb{F}, k, t)$-tensor IOP with soundness error ϵ, round complexity rc, proof length l, query complexity q, prover arithmetic complexity tp, and verifier arithmetic complexity tv.*
- *Input code: a linear code C over $\mathbb{F}$ with rate $\rho = \frac{k}{n}$, relative distance $\delta = \frac{d}{n}$, and encoding time $\theta(k) \cdot k$.*
- *Output IOP: a point-query IOP with soundness error $O_{\delta,t}(\epsilon) + O(d^t/|\mathbb{F}|)$, round complexity $O_t(\text{rc})$, proof length $O_{\rho,t}(q \cdot l)$, query complexity $O_t(k \cdot q)$, prover arithmetic complexity $\text{tp} + O_{\rho,t}(q \cdot l) \cdot \theta(k)$, and verifier arithmetic complexity $\text{tv} + O_t(k \cdot q) \cdot \theta(k)$.*

Moreover, the transformation preserves holography up to the multiplicative overhead θ induced by the encoding function of C and factors that depend on ρ and t.

We stress that the *only* property of the code C used in the above transformation is that it is linear over $\mathbb{F}$, and in particular the code C need not be efficiently decodable, satisfy the multiplication property (entry-wise multiplication of codewords is a codeword in a related code), or even be systematic. We believe that developing techniques that work with a wide range of codes will facilitate further IOP research. For example, known linear-time encodable codes meeting the Gilbert–Varshamov bound are not systematic [DI14]; also, efficient zero knowledge (not a goal in this paper) is typically achieved by using non-systematic codes.

We sketch the ideas behind this result in Sect. 2.2 and 2.3. The technical details are in the full version of this paper. From a technical perspective, our transformation builds on ideas from several papers: the sumcheck protocol for tensor codes in [Mei13]; the ILC-to-IOP compiler in [BCGGHJ17] that works with any linear code; the proximity

	preprocess circuit cost	prover cost	verifier cost	communication complexity	plausibly post-quantum
[BCCGP16] & [BBBPWM18]	n/a	$O(N)$ $\mathbb{F}$-ops $O(N)$ $\mathbb{G}$-exps	$O(N)$ $\mathbb{F}$-ops $O(N)$ $\mathbb{G}$-exps	$O_\lambda(\log N)$	✗
[WTSTW18]	n/a	$O(N)$ $\mathbb{F}$-ops $O(N)$ $\mathbb{G}$-exps	$O(D \log W)$ $\mathbb{F}$-ops $O(N^\epsilon + D \log W)$ $\mathbb{G}$-exps	$O_\lambda(N^{1-\epsilon} + D \log W)$	✗
[XZZPS19]	n/a	$O(N)$ $\mathbb{F}$-ops $O(N)$ $\mathbb{G}$-exps	$O(D \log W)$ $\mathbb{F}$-ops $O(\log W)$ pairings	$O_\lambda(D \log W)$	✗
[Set20]	$O(N)$ $\mathbb{F}$-ops $O(N)$ $\mathbb{G}$-exps	$O(N)$ $\mathbb{F}$-ops $O(N)$ $\mathbb{G}$-exps	$O(\log^2 N)$ $\mathbb{F}$-ops $O(\log^2 N)$ $\mathbb{G}$-exps	$O_\lambda(\log^2 N)$	✗
[BCGGHJ17]	$O(N)$ $\mathbb{F}$-ops $O(N)$ hashes	$O(N)$ $\mathbb{F}$-ops $O(N)$ hashes	$O_\lambda(\sqrt{N})$ $\mathbb{F}$-ops $O_\lambda(\sqrt{N})$ hashes	$O_\lambda(\sqrt{N})$	✓
this work	$O(N)$ $\mathbb{F}$-ops $O(N)$ hashes	$O(N)$ $\mathbb{F}$-ops $O(N)$ hashes	$O_\lambda(N^\epsilon)$ $\mathbb{F}$-ops $O_\lambda(N^\epsilon)$ hashes	$O_\lambda(N^\epsilon)$	✓

Fig. 1. Comparison of several sublinear argument systems that do not use FFTs. The stated costs are for the satisfiability of an N-gate arithmetic circuit over a cryptographically-large field $\mathbb{F}$; for argument systems that achieve sublinear verification we also report the cost to preprocess the circuit. We report separate costs for field operations, group operations, and (collision-resistant) hash invocations; ϵ is any positive constant and λ is the security parameter. Provers for arguments in the top part of the table run in superlinear time. Indeed, $O(N)$ exponentiations in $\mathbb{G}$ result in $\omega(N)$ group operations: $O(\log |\mathbb{F}| \cdot N)$ group operations if performed naively, or else $O(\frac{\log |\mathbb{F}|}{\log \log |\mathbb{F}| + \log N} \cdot N)$ if using Pippenger's algorithm [Pip80]. On the other hand, provers in the bottom part of the table run in linear time. Indeed, as observed in [BCGGHJ17], by using the hash functions of [AHIKV17] one can ensure that $O(N)$ hash invocations are equivalent, up to constants, to $O(N)$ operations in $\mathbb{F}$. The argument systems in [WTSTW18, XZZPS19] specifically require the circuit to be arranged in layers; the reported costs are for a circuit with D layers of width W, in which case $N = D \cdot W$; furthermore the term "$O(D \log W)$ $\mathbb{F}$-ops" in the verifier cost assumes that the circuit is sufficiently uniform and, if not, increases to "$O(N)$ $\mathbb{F}$-ops" (i.e., linear in computation size).

point-query IOPs	encode circuit cost	prover cost	verifier cost	query complexity
[BCGGHJ17]	$O(N)$ $\mathbb{F}$-ops	$O(N)$ $\mathbb{F}$-ops	$O(\sqrt{N})$ $\mathbb{F}$-ops	$O(\sqrt{N})$
this work	$O(N)$ $\mathbb{F}$-ops	$O(N)$ $\mathbb{F}$-ops	$O(N^\epsilon)$ $\mathbb{F}$-ops	$O(N^\epsilon)$

Fig. 2. Comparison of known IOPs with a linear-time prover. The parameters are for an N-gate arithmetic circuit defined over a field $\mathbb{F}$ of size $\Omega(N)$; and ϵ is any positive constant. The sublinear verification in both cases is achieved in the holographic setting (the verifier has oracle access to an encoding of the circuit).

test for the Reed–Solomon code in [BBHR18]; and the code-switching technique in [RR20] for systematic linear codes.

2   Techniques

We summarize the main ideas behind our results. We begin by elaborating on our main result, Theorem 1, which is a new protocol within a proof model called *Interactive Oracle Proof* (IOP) [BCS16, RRR16].

Recall that an IOP is a proof model in which a prover and a verifier interact over multiple rounds, and in each round the prover sends a proof message and the verifier replies with a challenge message. The verifier has query access to all received proof messages, in the sense that it can query any of the proof messages at any desired location. The verifier decides to accept or reject depending on its input, its randomness, and answers to its queries. The main information-theoretic efficiency measures in an IOP are proof length (total size of all proof messages) and query complexity (number of read locations across all proof messages), while the main computational efficiency measures are prover running time and verifier running time.

In this paper we study IOPs because they directly lead to corresponding succinct arguments, via cryptography that introduces only *constant* computational overheads (and in particular preserves linear complexity).[3] Namely, following the paradigm of Kilian [Kil92], any IOP can be "compiled" into a corresponding interactive argument by using a collision-resistant hash function. The argument's communication complexity is $O(q \log l)$, where q and l are the query complexity and the proof length of the IOP.[4] Moreover, with a suitable choice of hash function (e.g., [AHIKV17]), the running times of the argument prover and argument verifier are the same, up to multiplicative constants, as those of the IOP prover and IOP verifier.[5]

The rest of this section summarizes the proof of Theorem 1. We proceed in three steps. First, we describe an intermediate proof model called tensor IOPs; we elaborate on this model in Sect. 2.1. Second, we devise a transformation that, using an arbitrary linear code, efficiently "implements" any tensor IOP as a point-query (standard) IOP; this is our Theorem 3, and we discuss the transformation in Sect. 2.2 and 2.3. Third, we construct a tensor IOP with linear-time prover, constant query complexity, and sublinear-time verifier; this is our Theorem 2, and we discuss this construction in Sect. 2.4 and 2.5.

2.1 IOPs with Tensor Queries

In this work we rely on an intermediate model, informally introduced in Definition 2, called *tensor IOPs*. Below we briefly elaborate on why we introduce this model, and also compare it with other existing models.

Point Queries are for Efficiency. The verifier in an IOP makes *point queries* to proof messages received from the prover: the verifier may specify a round i and a location j

---

[3] We stress that this is a non-trivial property, in the sense that other approaches to construct succinct arguments introduce *super-constant* multiplicative overheads. For example, the transformation from algebraic proofs to succinct arguments in [CHMMVW20] introduces a linear number of exponentiations (which translates to a super-linear number of group operations). These approaches seem unlikely to lead to linear-time succinct arguments, and hence we focus on IOP-based succinct arguments.

[4] The "big O" notation here hides a dependence on the output size of the collision-resistant hash function.

[5] We remark that the more restricted proof model of Probabilistically Checkable Proofs (PCPs) also directly leads to a succinct argument with only constant computational overheads, however the problem of designing linear-time PCPs, with *any* non-trivial query complexity, seems far beyond current techniques.

and then receives as answer $\Pi_i[j]$ (the j-th value of the proof message Π_i sent in round i). Our main result (Theorem 1) is about point-query (standard) IOPs because, as we explained, they lead to succinct arguments via constant computational overheads.

Beyond Point Queries. Researchers have studied variants of the IOP model where the verifier makes other types of queries. For example, Boneh et al. [BBCGI19] study *linear IOPs*, where the verifier may specify a round i and a vector q and then receives as answer the linear combination $\langle q, \Pi_i \rangle$, over a field $\mathbb{F}$. These $\mathbb{F}$-linear queries are a "richer" class because linear combinations can, in particular, select out chosen locations.

From the perspective of this paper, variants such as linear IOPs offer an opportunity to reduce our goal (a certain point-query IOP) into two sub-problems. First, design an efficient IOP with a richer class of queries. Second, devise a way to efficiently "implement" the rich class of queries via only point queries. The former becomes easier as the class of queries becomes richer, while the latter becomes harder. Thus, the class of queries should be chosen to balance the difficulty between the sub-problems, so that both can be solved.

Tensor Queries. In this paper we do not use linear queries because we do not know how to implement linear queries via point queries in the linear-time regime.[6] Nevertheless, we identify a rich-enough sub-class of linear queries for which we are able to solve both of the aforementioned sub-problems: *tensor queries*. These types of linear combinations were used in the sumcheck protocol for tensor codes [Mei13] and also to construct IOPs with proof length approaching witness length [RR20] (the latter work defines an intermediate model that, informally, is an IOP where the verifier is allowed a single tensor query to the witness).

Informally, in a $(\mathbb{F}, k, t)$-tensor IOP, the verifier may specify a round i and a list $(q_0, q_1, \ldots, q_t)$ and then receives as answer the linear combination $\langle q_0 \otimes q_1 \otimes \cdots \otimes q_t, \Pi_i \rangle$, where $q_1, \ldots, q_t \in \mathbb{F}^k$ and the 0-th component q_0 of the tensor vector may be a vector of any length defined over $\mathbb{F}$. The other t components must have fixed lengths k. The fixed lengths impose a recursive structure that we will exploit, while the free length accommodates proof messages of varying sizes. For simplicity, in the rest of the technical overview, we will ignore the 0-th component, assuming that all proof messages have the same length (k^t elements in $\mathbb{F}$).

We formalize the notion of a tensor IOP in the full version of this paper. In fact, we formulate a more general notion of IOP where queries belong to a given query class $\mathcal{Q}$, which specifies which (possibly non-linear) functions of the proof messages are "allowed". Via suitable choices of $\mathcal{Q}$, one can recover the notions of point-query IOPs, linear IOPs, tensor IOPs, and more. Our definitions also account for features such as holography and proximity (both used in this paper). We consider the formulation of IOPs with special queries to be a definitional contribution of independent interest that will help the systematic exploration of other query classes.

---

[6] Bootle et al. [BCGGHJ17] show how to implement the Ideal Linear Commitment (ILC) model in linear time, which is reminiscent of, but distinct from, the linear IOP model. As noted in [BBCGI19], these are reducible to one another, but with losses in parameters. (Applying the transformation of [BCGGHJ17] to an ILC protocol obtained from a linear IOP does *not* preserve linear time.).

2.2 From Tensor Queries to Point Queries

We discuss the main ideas behind Theorem 3, which provides a transformation that takes as input an IOP with tensor queries and a linear code and outputs an IOP with point queries that has related complexity parameters. (Details of the transformation can be found in given in the full version.) The main challenge in designing this transformation is that we need to construct an IOP that efficiently simulates a strong class of queries (tensor queries) by using only a weak class of queries (point queries) and the linearity of the given code. Our transformation combines ideas from several works [Mei13, BCGGHJ17, BBHR18, RR20], as we later explain in Remark 1.

Now we discuss our transformation. Below we denote by $(\mathbf{P}, \mathbf{V})$ the $(\mathbb{F}, k, t)$-tensor IOP that is given as input to the transformation. The other input to the transformation is a linear code $\mathcal{C}$ over the field $\mathbb{F}$ with rate $\rho = k/n$ and relative distance $\delta = d/n$ (the code's message length k and alphabet $\mathbb{F}$ match parameters in the tensor IOP). We denote by $(\hat{\mathbf{P}}, \hat{\mathbf{V}})$ the point-query IOP that we construct as output. This latter has three parts: (1) a *simulation phase*; (2) a *consistency test*; and (3) a *proximity test*. We summarize each in turn below.

Part 1: Simulation Phase. The new prover $\hat{\mathbf{P}}$ and new verifier $\hat{\mathbf{V}}$ simulate $\mathbf{P}$ and $\mathbf{V}$, mediating their interaction with two modifications. First, whenever $\mathbf{P}$ outputs a proof string $\Pi \in \mathbb{F}^{k^t}$ that should be sent to $\mathbf{V}$, $\hat{\mathbf{P}}$ sends to $\hat{\mathbf{V}}$ an encoded proof string $\hat{\Pi} := \mathrm{Enc}(\Pi) \in \mathbb{F}^{n^t}$, for an encoding function $\mathrm{Enc} \colon \mathbb{F}^{k^t} \to \mathbb{F}^{n^t}$ that we discuss shortly. Second, whenever $\mathbf{V}$ outputs a tensor query $q_1 \otimes \cdots \otimes q_t$ for one of the proof strings Π_i, $\hat{\mathbf{V}}$ forwards this query (as a message) to $\hat{\mathbf{P}}$, who replies with a "short" proof message that contains the answer $\langle q_1 \otimes \cdots \otimes q_t, \Pi_i \rangle \in \mathbb{F}$; then $\hat{\mathbf{V}}$ simply reads this value and returns it to $\mathbf{V}$ as the query answer (so $\hat{\mathbf{V}}$ can continue simulating the execution of $\mathbf{V}$).

Observe that if $\hat{\mathbf{P}}$ really answers each tensor query truthfully in the simulation then $\hat{\mathbf{V}}$ inherits the soundness of $\mathbf{V}$, because in this case the tensor IOP $(\mathbf{P}, \mathbf{V})$ is perfectly simulated. However, a malicious $\hat{\mathbf{P}}$ need not answer each tensor query truthfully. The goal of the consistency test and the proximity test (both described below) is to prevent the prover $\hat{\mathbf{P}}$ from misbehaving. Namely, these additional parts of the point-query IOP $(\hat{\mathbf{P}}, \hat{\mathbf{V}})$ will enable $\hat{\mathbf{V}}$ to check that the values received from $\hat{\mathbf{P}}$ as answers to $\mathbf{V}$'s tensor queries are consistent with the received (encoded) proof strings.

On the Encoding Function. The encoding function Enc used in the simulation phase must be chosen to facilitate the design of the consistency proximity tests. We choose $\mathrm{Enc} \colon \mathbb{F}^{k^t} \to \mathbb{F}^{n^t}$ to be the encoding function of the t-wise tensor product $\mathcal{C}^{\otimes t}$ of the "base" linear code $\mathcal{C}$, where t matches the parameter in the tensor IOP. The function Enc is derived from the encoding function $\mathrm{enc} \colon \mathbb{F}^k \to \mathbb{F}^n$ of $\mathcal{C}$. Completeness and soundness of $(\hat{\mathbf{P}}, \hat{\mathbf{V}})$ will ultimately work for *any* linear code $\mathcal{C}$. Crucially to our results on linear-time protocols, prior work [DI14] provides linear-time encodable codes with constant rate over any field $\mathbb{F}$, ensuring that Enc is computable in linear time when t is a constant. Such codes achieving the best known parameters are non-systematic.

Checking the Simulation Phase. In the simulation phase, $\hat{\mathbf{P}}$ has sent several words $\hat{\Pi}_1, \ldots, \hat{\Pi}_\ell \in \mathbb{F}^{n^t}$ that allegedly are codewords in the tensor code $\mathcal{C}^{\otimes t} \subseteq \mathbb{F}^{n^t}$, in which case they encode some proof strings $\Pi_1, \ldots, \Pi_\ell \in \mathbb{F}^{k^t}$. Moreover, $\hat{\mathbf{P}}$ has also claimed that a list of values $(v_q)_{q \in Q}$ are the answers to a corresponding list of tensor queries Q; namely, if $q = (i, q_1, \ldots, q_t)$ then $v_q = \langle q_1 \otimes \cdots \otimes q_t, \Pi_i \rangle$.

Informally, we seek a sub-protocol for $\hat{\mathbf{V}}$ with the following guarantee: (1) if there is a word $\hat{\Pi}_i$ that is far from $\mathcal{C}^{\otimes t}$ then $\hat{\mathbf{V}}$ rejects with high probability; (2) if all words $\hat{\Pi}_1, \ldots, \hat{\Pi}_\ell$ are close to $\mathcal{C}^{\otimes t}$ but one of the answers is inconsistent with the underlying (unique) encoded messages then $\hat{\mathbf{V}}$ also rejects with high probability. A technical contribution of this paper is the design and analysis of such a sub-protocol.

Our sub-protocol is a black-box combination of a consistency test and a proximity test. In the consistency test, the prover $\hat{\mathbf{P}}$ sends, in one round, proof strings that are partial computations of all the tensor queries, and the verifier $\hat{\mathbf{V}}$ leverages these to check that the answers to tensor queries are correct. The consistency test *assumes* that all proof strings are close to certain tensor codes and so, in the proximity test, the prover $\hat{\mathbf{P}}$ and the verifier $\hat{\mathbf{V}}$ interact, over t rounds, in a protocol whose goal is to ensure that all received proof strings are close to the appropriate codes. We now provide more details for each of the two tests.

Part 2: Consistency Test. For simplicity of exposition, we describe the consistency test for the simple case where there is a *single* tensor query or, more generally, a single "extended" tensor query $q_0 \otimes q_1 \otimes \cdots \otimes q_t \in \mathbb{F}^{\ell \cdot k^t}$ to the "stacking" of all proof strings. Namely, $\hat{\mathbf{P}}$ claims that the stacked word $\hat{\Pi} := \mathrm{Stack}(\hat{\Pi}_1, \ldots, \hat{\Pi}_\ell) \in \mathbb{F}^{\ell \cdot n^t}$ can be decoded to some stacked proof string $\Pi := \mathrm{Stack}(\Pi_1, \ldots, \Pi_\ell) \in \mathbb{F}^{\ell \cdot k^t}$ such that $v = \langle q_0 \otimes q_1 \otimes \cdots \otimes q_t, \Pi \rangle$.[7] Below we view Π as a function $\Pi \colon [\ell] \times [k]^t \to \mathbb{F}$, and $\hat{\Pi}$ as a function $\hat{\Pi} \colon [\ell] \times [n]^t \to \mathbb{F}$.

In the special case where the code $\mathcal{C}$ is systematic, the sumcheck protocol for tensor codes [Mei13, RR20] would yield a consistency test that "evaluates" one component of the tensor query at a time. For the general case, where $\mathcal{C}$ can be *any* linear code, we provide a consistency test that consists of a sumcheck-like protocol applied to the "interleaving" of tensor codes. While it is convenient to present the main ideas behind the prover algorithm by speaking of *decoding* (whose cost may exceed our linear-time goal), we stress that the prover need only perform efficient *encoding* operations. We will denote by $(\mathcal{C}^{\otimes t})^\ell$ the ℓ-wise interleaving of the code $\mathcal{C}^{\otimes t}$, where a single symbol of $(\mathcal{C}^{\otimes t})^\ell$ is the concatenation of ℓ symbols of $\mathcal{C}^{\otimes t}$-codewords.

Proof messages. For each $r \in [t]$, the prover $\hat{\mathbf{P}}$ computes and sends words $\{c_r \colon [k] \times [n]^{t-r} \to \mathbb{F}\}_{r \in [t]}$ where c_r is allegedly an interleaved codeword in $(\mathcal{C}^{\otimes t-r})^k$. Intuitively, $c_1, \ldots, c_t$ will help $\hat{\mathbf{V}}$ perform the consistency check that the value $v \in \mathbb{F}$ is the answer to the tensor query $q_0 \otimes q_1 \otimes \cdots \otimes q_t \in \mathbb{F}^{\ell \cdot k^t}$.

- For $r = 1$, the word $c_1 \in (\mathcal{C}^{\otimes t-1})^k$ is derived from $\hat{\Pi} \in \mathcal{C}^{\otimes t}$ via a "fold-then-decode" procedure, which uses the component $q_0 \in \mathbb{F}^\ell$ of the tensor query. For $\gamma \in \mathbb{F}^\ell$, we denote by $\mathrm{Fold}(\hat{\Pi}; \gamma) \colon [n]^t \to \mathbb{F}$ the function $\sum_{i=1}^\ell \gamma_i \cdot \hat{\Pi}_i$ (sum the values of $\hat{\Pi} \colon [\ell] \times [n]^t \to \mathbb{F}$ over the domain $[\ell]$ with coefficients determined by γ). Then, $c_1 \in (\mathcal{C}^{\otimes t-1})^k$ is obtained by partially decoding $\mathrm{Fold}(\hat{\Pi}; q_0)$ (by viewing

---

[7] Extended tensor queries capture tensor queries to specific proof strings: for any desired $i \in [\ell]$, one can choose $q_0 \in \mathbb{F}^\ell$ to be all zeros except for a 1 in the i-th entry so that $\langle q_0 \otimes q_1 \otimes \cdots \otimes q_t, \Pi \rangle = \langle q_1 \otimes \cdots \otimes q_t, \Pi_i \rangle$.

the values of $\mathrm{Fold}(\hat{\Pi}; q_0)\colon [n]^t \to \mathbb{F}$ over the first component $[n]$ of its domain as
$\mathcal{C}$-codewords, and decoding them).
- For each subsequent $r \in \{2, \ldots, t\}$, the word c_r is derived via a similar procedure
  from c_{r-1} and the component $q_{r-1} \in \mathbb{F}^k$ of the tensor query. Namely, c_r is the codeword in $(\mathcal{C}^{\otimes t-r})^k$ obtained by partially decoding $\mathrm{Fold}(c_{r-1}; q_{r-1}) \in \mathcal{C}^{\otimes t-(r-1)}$
  over the first component of its domain as above.

Each round reduces the rank by 1 and, in the last round, the word c_t is a fully decoded
message vector in $\mathbb{F}^k$. The tensor query answer $\langle q_0 \otimes q_1 \otimes \cdots \otimes q_t, \Pi \rangle$ is the successive
folding of Π by components $q_0, \ldots, q_t$. The r-th message c_r is an encoding in $\mathcal{C}^{\otimes t-r}$
of Π after it has been folded up to the r-th component by $q_0, \ldots, q_r$.

Query phase. The verifier $\hat{\mathbf{V}}$ tests the expected relation between messages across rounds
at a random point, and that the execution is consistent with the claimed answer value v.
Namely, since each round's messages are expected to be partial decodings of foldings
of the prior round's messages, for an honest prover $\hat{\mathbf{P}}$ the following equations relate
words across rounds:

- for $r = 1$, $\mathrm{enc}(c_1) = \mathrm{Fold}(\hat{\Pi}; q_0)$;
- for each $r \in \{2, \ldots, t\}$, $\mathrm{enc}(c_r) = \mathrm{Fold}(c_{r-1}; q_{r-1})$.

Above, enc is the encoding function for the base linear code $\mathcal{C}$ applied to the first coordinate of a function with domain $[k] \times [n]^{t-r}$ (for some r), and the identity on all other
coordinates.

The above equations motivate a natural consistency test for the verifier. Namely, $\hat{\mathbf{V}}$
samples a random tuple $(j_1, \ldots, j_t) \in [n]^t$ and checks all of the relevant equations at
this tuple:

- for $r = 1$, $\mathrm{enc}(c_1)(j_1, \ldots, j_t) = \mathrm{Fold}(\hat{\Pi}; q_0)(j_1, \ldots, j_t)$;
- for each $r \in \{2, \ldots, t\}$, $\mathrm{enc}(c_r)(j_r, \ldots, j_t) = \mathrm{Fold}(c_{r-1}; q_{r-1})(j_r, \ldots, j_t)$.

To compute, e.g., $\mathrm{Fold}(c_{r-1}, ; q_{r-1})(j_r, \ldots, j_t)$ and $\mathrm{enc}(c_r)(j_r, \ldots, j_t)$, $\hat{\mathbf{V}}$ makes k
queries to c_{r-1} and c_r.

Finally, $\hat{\mathbf{V}}$ checks consistency with the answer value v via the equation $v = \mathrm{Fold}(c_t; q_t)$.

These consistency checks guarantee that when $\hat{\Pi}, c_1, \ldots, c_{t-1}$ are all codewords
in their respective codes, then they encode consistent partial computations of the tensor
query $q_0 \otimes q_1 \otimes \cdots \otimes q_t \in \mathbb{F}^{\ell \cdot k^t}$ on the message $\Pi \in \mathbb{F}^{\ell \cdot k^t}$ encoded in $\hat{\Pi} \in \mathbb{F}^{\ell \cdot k^t}$.
However, we must ensure that $\hat{\mathbf{V}}$ will reject in the case that any of $\hat{\Pi}, c_1, \ldots, c_{t-1}$ are
far from being codewords. This will be guaranteed by our proximity test.

Part 3: Proximity Test. We discuss the proximity test, again for the simple case of a
single tensor query. In the simulation phase the prover $\hat{\mathbf{P}}$ has sent words $\hat{\Pi}_1, \ldots, \hat{\Pi}_\ell$
allegedly in $\mathcal{C}^{\otimes t}$; this means that $\hat{\Pi} := \mathrm{Stack}(\hat{\Pi}_1, \ldots, \hat{\Pi}_\ell)$ is allegedly in $(\mathcal{C}^{\otimes t})^\ell$. In the
consistency test the prover $\hat{\mathbf{P}}$ has sent words $c_1, \ldots, c_t$ where c_r allegedly is in $(\mathcal{C}^{\otimes t-r})^k$.
The proximity test will ensure that all these words are close to the respective codes.

A reasonable starting point to design such a test is to remember that tensor codes
are locally testable [BS06, Vid15, CMS17]: if a word c is Δ-far from $\mathcal{C}^{\otimes t}$ then a random
axis-parallel line of c fails to be a codeword in $\mathcal{C}$ with probability proportional to Δ.

Since we wish to test *interleaved* tensor codewords, a natural strategy is to apply the axis-parallel test to a random linear combination of the tested words. This strategy does produce a proximity test, but has two drawbacks. First, a calculation shows that the query complexity is non-trivial only for $t > 2$, while we will design a test that is non-trivial for $t > 1$.[8] Second, the axis-parallel test has poor tradeoffs between query complexity and soundness error.[9] Hence we take a different approach inspired by the proximity test for the Reed–Solomon code in [BBHR18]; at a modest increase in proof length, our test will work for any $t > 1$ (and thereby subsume the prior work in [BCGGHJ17]) and will have better query-soundness tradeoffs.

We now describe our proximity test, which has t rounds of interaction, followed by a query phase.

Interactive Phase. In round $r \in [t]$, $\hat{\mathbf{V}}$ sends to $\hat{\mathbf{P}}$ random challenges $\alpha_r, \beta_r \in \mathbb{F}^k$, and $\hat{\mathbf{P}}$ replies with a word $d_r \colon [k] \times [n]^{t-r} \to \mathbb{F}$ (computed as described below) that is allegedly a codeword in $(\mathcal{C}^{\otimes t-r})^k$. Intuitively, for $r \in [t-1]$, the word d_r will be close to a codeword in $\mathcal{C}^{\otimes t-r}$ if and only if c_{r-1} and d_{r-1} are *both* close to codewords in $\mathcal{C}^{\otimes t-(r-1)}$, up to a small error probability.

- In the first round, the word d_1 is derived from $\hat{\Pi}$ via the same "fold-then-decode" procedure that we have already seen. This time, the folding procedure uses the random challenge $\alpha_1 \in \mathbb{F}^\ell$. Then, d_1 is the codeword in $(\mathcal{C}^{\otimes t-1})^k$ obtained by partially decoding $\mathrm{Fold}(\hat{\Pi}; \alpha_1) \in \mathcal{C}^{\otimes t}$.
- In each subsequent round $r = 2, \ldots, t$, the word d_r is derived via a similar procedure from c_{r-1} and d_{r-1}, and the random challenges $\alpha_r, \beta_r \in \mathbb{F}^k$. Namely, d_r is the codeword in $(\mathcal{C}^{\otimes t-r})^k$ obtained by partially decoding $\mathrm{Fold}(c_{r-1}, d_{r-1}; \alpha_r, \beta_r) \in \mathcal{C}^{\otimes t-(r-1)}$.

Each round reduces the rank of the tensor code and, in the last round (when $r = t$), the words c_t and d_t are fully decoded message vectors in $\mathbb{F}^k$.

Query Phase. The verifier $\hat{\mathbf{V}}$ tests the expected relation between messages across rounds at a random point. Since each round's messages are expected to be partial decodings of foldings of the prior round's messages, for an honest prover $\hat{\mathbf{P}}$ the following equations relate words across rounds:

- for $r = 1$, $\mathrm{enc}(d_1) = \mathrm{Fold}(\hat{\Pi}; \alpha_1)$;
- for each $r \in \{2, \ldots, t\}$, $\mathrm{enc}(d_r) = \mathrm{Fold}(c_{r-1}, d_{r-1}; \alpha_r, \beta_r)$.

As in the consistency test, the above equations motivate natural checks for the verifier. Namely, $\hat{\mathbf{V}}$ samples a random tuple $(j_1, \ldots, j_t) \in [n]^t$ and checks all of the relevant equations at this tuple:

---

[8] Query complexity for the strategy using local testing would be $O((\ell + kt) \cdot n)$, while that for our test will be $O(\ell + kt)$.

[9] Let $\delta = d/n$ be the relative distance of $\mathcal{C}$. By incurring a multiplicative increase of λ in query complexity, the strategy using local testing gives a soundness error of, e.g., $O(d^t/|\mathbb{F}|) + (1 - \delta^{O(t)} \cdot \Delta)^\lambda$ when applied to an input of distance Δ from $\mathcal{C}^{\otimes t}$. In contrast, the test in this work will give a soundness error that is (approximately) $O(d^t/|\mathbb{F}|) + (1 - \Delta)^\lambda$.

- for $r = 1$, $\mathrm{enc}(d_1)(j_1, \ldots, j_t) = \mathrm{Fold}(\hat{\Pi}; \alpha_1)(j_1, \ldots, j_t)$;
- for each $r \in \{2, \ldots, t\}$, $\mathrm{enc}(d_r)(j_r, \ldots, j_t) = \mathrm{Fold}(c_{r-1}, d_{r-1}; \alpha_r, \beta_r)$ $(j_r, \ldots, j_t)$.

Similarly to before, to obtain the values needed to perform these checks, $\hat{\mathbf{V}}$ makes ℓ point queries to $\hat{\Pi}$ and k point queries to c_r and d_r for each $r \in [t-1]$.

Efficiency. The tensor IOP $(\mathbf{P}, \mathbf{V})$ given as input to the transformation has proof length l, query complexity q, prover arithmetic complexity tp, and verifier arithmetic complexity tv. Now we discuss the main information-theoretic efficiency measures of the constructed point-query IOP $(\hat{\mathbf{P}}, \hat{\mathbf{V}})$.

- *Proof length* is $O_{\rho,t}(\mathsf{q} \cdot \mathsf{l})$. Indeed, in the simulation phase $\hat{\mathbf{P}}$ encodes and sends all the proof strings produced by $\mathbf{P}$, increasing the number of field elements from $\mathsf{l} = \ell \cdot k^t$ to $\ell \cdot n^t = \frac{n^t}{k^t} \cdot \ell \cdot k^t = \rho^{-t} \cdot \mathsf{l}$. (Plus the q answers to the q tensor queries.) Moreover, in the consistency and proximity tests, $\hat{\mathbf{P}}$ sends, for each of the q queries, $O(n^t)$ field elements in total across t rounds. The sum of these is bounded by $O(\rho^{-t} \cdot \mathsf{q} \cdot \mathsf{l})$.
- *Query complexity* is $O(\ell + t \cdot k \cdot \mathsf{q})$. In the simulation phase, $\hat{\mathbf{V}}$ reads the q answers to the q tensor queries of $\mathbf{V}$ as claimed by $\hat{\mathbf{P}}$. In the consistency and proximity tests, $\hat{\mathbf{V}}$ makes a consistency check that requires point queries on each of the ℓ words $\hat{\Pi}_1, \ldots, \hat{\Pi}_\ell$, plus $O(t \cdot k)$ point queries for each of the q tensor queries. The sum of these is bounded by $O(\ell + t \cdot k \cdot \mathsf{q})$.

Note that the tensor IOP that we construct has query complexity $\mathsf{q} = O(1)$ (see Sect. 2.4), which means that the multiplicative overheads that arise from the number of queries are constant.

Next we discuss computational efficiency measures. These will depend, in particular, on the cost of encoding a message using the base code $\mathcal{C}$. So let $\theta(k)$ be such that $\theta(k) \cdot k$ is the size of an arithmetic circuit that maps a message in $\mathbb{F}^k$ to its codeword in $\mathcal{C}$. In this paper we focus on the case where $\theta(k)$ is a constant.

- *Verifier arithmetic complexity* is $\mathsf{tv} + O_t((\ell + \theta(k) \cdot k) \cdot \mathsf{q})$. The first term is due to $\hat{\mathbf{V}}$ simulating $\mathbf{V}$ in the simulation phase. In addition, in executing the proximity and consistency tests, $\hat{\mathbf{V}}$ makes, for each of q queries and for each of t rounds, an encoding operation that costs $\theta(k) \cdot k$ plus other linear combinations that cost $O(k)$ field operations, and $O(\ell)$ field operations in the first round. Thus in total, $\hat{\mathbf{V}}$ performs $O((\ell + t \cdot \theta(k) \cdot k) \cdot \mathsf{q})$ field operations in the proximity and consistency tests.
- *Prover arithmetic complexity* is $\mathsf{tp} + O_{\rho,t}(\mathsf{q} \cdot \mathsf{l}) \cdot \theta(k)$. The first term is due to $\hat{\mathbf{P}}$ simulating $\mathbf{P}$ in the simulation phase. In the simulation phase, $\hat{\mathbf{P}}$ also has to encode every proof string output by $\mathbf{P}$. This costs $O(\rho^{-t} \cdot \theta(k) \cdot \mathsf{l})$ field operations, as can be seen by observing that the cost of encoding a single proof string $\Pi_i \in \mathbb{F}^{k^t}$ to its corresponding codeword $\hat{\Pi}_i \in \mathbb{F}^{n^t}$ in $\mathcal{C}^{\otimes t}$ is $O(\rho^{-t} \cdot \theta(k) \cdot k^t)$. Establishing a good bound on the cost of $\hat{\mathbf{P}}$ in the consistency and proximity tests requires more care, as we now explain.

In the consistency and proximity tests, $\hat{\mathbf{P}}$ must compute each of the functions $c_1, \ldots, c_t$ and $d_1, \ldots, d_t$. Each c_r and d_r is defined in terms of the previous c_{r-1} and d_{r-1} via a "fold-then-decode" procedure. However, we do *not* wish for $\hat{\mathbf{P}}$ to depend on the cost of decoding the base code $\mathcal{C}$, because for the codes that we eventually use ([DI14]), where θ is constant, *no linear-time error-free decoding algorithm is known*. (Only the error-free case need be considered when designing an honest prover algorithm. Indeed, we never use a decoding algorithm of any sort for $\mathcal{C}$ at any point in this work.) Thankfully, since $\hat{\mathbf{P}}$ knows the message Π encoded in $\hat{\Pi}$, $\hat{\mathbf{P}}$ can compute c_r and d_r for each $r \in [t]$ from scratch from Π by *partially re-encoding*, which contributes an additional term of $O(\rho^{-t} \cdot \theta(k) \cdot k^t)$ per query.

Remark 1. Our construction of a point-query IOP from a tensor IOP and a linear code builds on several prior works. Below, we highlight similarities and differences with each of these works in chronological order.

- The ILC-to-IOP transformation in [BCGGHJ17] shows how any protocol in the Ideal Linear Commitment (ILC) model can be implemented via a point-query IOP, using any given linear code $\mathcal{C}$ as an ingredient. Crucially, if $\mathcal{C}$ has a linear-time encoding procedure, then computational overheads in the transformation are constant. This is what enables [BCGGHJ17] to obtain a linear-time IOP with square-root query complexity.

  Our construction also relies on an arbitrary linear code $\mathcal{C}$ as an ingredient but considers a different implementation problem (tensor queries via point queries), which ultimately enables much smaller query complexity in the resulting point-query IOP. The interactive phase of our construction could be viewed as a recursive variant of the transformation in [BCGGHJ17].

- The "FRI protocol" in [BBHR18] is an IOP for testing proximity of a function to the Reed–Solomon code. The interactive phase consists of a logarithmic number of rounds in which the proximity problem is reduced in size; the reduction relies on a folding operation defined over subgroups that has small locality, and a low probability of distortion. The query phase consists of a correlated consistency check across all rounds.

  Our proximity test could be viewed as an analogue of the FRI protocol for (the interleaving of) tensor codes. Our consistency test could then be viewed as an analogue of using "rational constraints" and the FRI protocol to check the claimed evaluations of the polynomial committed in a Reed–Solomon codeword.

- The sumcheck protocol for the tensor product of *systematic* codes [Mei13] can simulate a tensor query to a proof string via point queries, via the code-switching technique in [RR20]. This preserves the linear time of the prover, and so could be used to prove Theorem 3 for the special case of a systematic code. Our protocol can be viewed as a non-interactive variant that also works for the *interleaving* of codewords from the tensor product of *non*-systematic codes (as required by Theorem 3). As discussed in Sect. 1.1, the ability to freely choose any linear code allows better rate-distance tradeoffs and enables the zero-knowledge property to be achieved more efficiently. Further, at the cost of a moderate increase in proof length, our query complexity and verifier complexity scale better with soundness error when doing soundness amplification.[10]

2.3   On Soundness of the Transformation

The theorem below informally states the security guarantees of the transformation given in the previous section. Details can be found in the full version of this paper. In the rest of this section, we provide some intuition behind the structure of the soundness analysis and the origin of each term in the soundness error.

Theorem 4 (informal). *If $(\mathbf{P}, \mathbf{V})$ is an $(\mathbb{F}, k, t)$-tensor IOP with soundness error ϵ and $\mathcal{C}$ is a linear code with rate $\rho = k/n$ and relative distance $\delta = d/n$, then the point-query IOP $(\hat{\mathbf{P}}, \hat{\mathbf{V}})$ has soundness error*

$$\epsilon + O\left(\frac{d^t}{|\mathbb{F}|}\right) + O\left(\left(1 - \frac{\delta^t}{2}\right)^\lambda\right)$$

when the query phases of the consistency and proximity tests are repeated λ times.

The first term ϵ is inherited from soundness of the original protocol; $\hat{\mathbf{P}}$ may attempt to cheat by accurately simulating a cheating $\mathbf{P}$ in a tensor IOP protocol. The remaining terms are upper bounds on the probability that $\hat{\mathbf{V}}$ will accept when the messages of $\hat{\mathbf{P}}$ fail to accurately simulate tensor queries to $\mathbf{P}$'s messages.

The second term is related to a phenomenon of linear codes known as *distortion*. It is important to consider distortion in the soundness analysis of the proximity test. Given interleaved words $W = (w_1, \ldots, w_\ell) \in \mathbb{F}^{\ell \times n}$ with blockwise distance $e := d(W, \mathcal{C}^\ell)$, we use a result from [AHIV17] that shows that the probability that a random linear combination w of $w_1, \ldots, w_\ell$ satisfies $d(w, \mathcal{C}) < e$ (distortion happens) is $O(d/|\mathbb{F}|)$. In other words, for a random linear combination α, $\text{Fold}(\,\cdot\,; \alpha)$ preserves distance with high probability. The term $O(d^t/|\mathbb{F}|)$ in the soundness error comes from bounding the probability of distortion for each code $\mathcal{C}^{\otimes t-r}$ for $r \in [0, \ldots, t-1]$, which has minimum distance d^{t-r}, as $\hat{\mathbf{P}}$ sends and folds words that are allegedly from each of these codes in the proximity test. Combining the distortion result with a union bound gives probability $O((d^t + d^{t-1} + \cdots + d)/|\mathbb{F}|)$ of distortion occurring anywhere in the protocol. The geometric series is asymptotically dominated by its largest term, hence the bound.

The third term comes from the probability that $\hat{\mathbf{V}}$ rejects in the proximity test, given that $\hat{\mathbf{P}}$ sends c_r or d_r which are far from $\mathcal{C}^{\otimes t-r}$ or that $\hat{\mathbf{V}}$ rejects in the consistency test, given that c_r or d_r contain messages which are inconsistent with earlier c and d words. In either case, the fraction of indices on which the verification equations do not hold is then related to the relative distance of $\mathcal{C}^{\otimes t}$, which is δ^t. Here, λ is the number of entries at which $\hat{\mathbf{V}}$ makes the verification checks in the consistency and proximity tests.

---

[10] Consider the setting in [RR20], which is a single tensor query ($q = 1$) to a single tensor codeword ($\ell = 1$). The sumcheck protocol in [RR20] branches at each recursion, and has query complexity λ^t and verifier time $\text{poly}(\lambda^t, t, k)$ to achieve soundness error $2^{-\Omega(\lambda)}$. By contrast, we achieve query complexity $O(\lambda \cdot kt)$ and verifier time $O(\lambda \cdot \theta kt)$, where θ is a constant.

The above is an intuitive summary, and in the paragraphs below we elaborate further on our analysis.

Soundness Analysis. The proof that our transformation is sound is rather involved, and is a key technical contribution of this paper. The proof is split into two main parts; the analysis of the consistency test and the analysis of the proximity test. The proximity test comprises the most complex part of the analysis.

Our proximity test is recursive, which initially suggests an analysis that recursively applies ideas from [BCGGHJ17]. However, a notable feature of our proximity test is that the verification checks for each $r \in [t]$ are *correlated*. Namely, the verifier $\hat{\mathbf{V}}$ does *not* check e.g. Fold $(c_{r-1}, d_{r-1}; \alpha_r, \beta_r) = \text{enc}(d_r)$ for a random point independently of the other verification equations for other values of r. Rather, $\hat{\mathbf{V}}$ samples $(j_1, \ldots, j_t) \in [n]^t$ and checks whether $\text{Fold}(\hat{\Pi}; \alpha_1)(j_1, \ldots, j_t) = \text{enc}(d_1)(j_1, \ldots, j_t)$. Then, for the verification check that e.g. $\text{Fold}(c_{r-1}, d_{r-1}; \alpha_{r-1}, \beta_{r-1}) = \text{enc}(d_r)$, $\hat{\mathbf{V}}$ will truncate $(j_1, \ldots, j_t)$ to $(j_r, \ldots, j_t)$ and check that $\text{Fold}(c_{r-1}, d_{r-1}; \alpha_{r-1}, \beta_{r-1})(j_r, \ldots, j_t) = \text{enc}(d_r)(j_r, \ldots, j_t)$.

We take inspiration from the soundness analysis for the Reed–Solomon proximity test in [BBHR18]. The analysis in [BBHR18] handles their entire protocol with all correlated consistency checks in one single analysis, and avoids a multiplicative dependence on the number of rounds, which was important in [BBHR18] whose protocol had non-constant round-complexity. The same approach informs our analysis, which has the same structure as that of [BBHR18], but is adapted to the combinatorial setting of tensor codes rather than the algebraic setting of Reed–Solomon codes, and modified to reflect the fact that we wish to perform a proximity test for alleged tensor codewords $\hat{\Pi}, c_1, \ldots, c_{t-1}$ of different ranks in the same protocol (rather that one codeword).

Our analysis is divided into cases, depending on the behavior of a malicious prover $\hat{\mathbf{P}}$.

Proximity Test Soundness. First, suppose that, for some $r \in [t]$, $\hat{\mathbf{P}}$ has sent words c_{r-1} and d_{r-1} that are far from being interleaved $\mathcal{C}^{\otimes t-(r-1)}$-codewords. Yet, through unlucky random choice of α_r or $\beta_r \in \mathbb{F}^k$, one of the intermediate values $\text{Fold}(c_{r-1}, d_{r-1}; \alpha_r, \beta_r)$ is close to $\mathcal{C}^{\otimes t-(r-1)}$. Then, there exists a valid partial decoding d_r that satisfies consistency checks at a large fraction of entries, potentially causing $\hat{\mathbf{V}}$ to accept even though $\hat{\mathbf{P}}$ has not simulated any inner prover $\mathbf{P}$. Since $\text{Fold}(c_{r-1}, d_{r-1}; \alpha_r, \beta_r)$ is a random linear combination of words far from $\mathcal{C}^{\otimes t-(r-1)}$, this implies that distortion has occurred. We apply upper bounds on the probability of distortion.

Second, assume that distortion does not occur in any round. Suppose that the prover $\hat{\mathbf{P}}$ has sent c_{r-1} which is far from being an interleaved $\mathcal{C}^{\otimes t-(r-1)}$-codeword. Consider the latest round r for which $\hat{\mathbf{P}}$ behaves in this way. Then $\text{enc}(d_r)$ is close to $\mathcal{C}^{\otimes t-(r-1)}$, but $\text{Fold}(c_{r-1}, d_{r-1}; \alpha_r, \beta_r)$ is far from $\mathcal{C}^{\otimes t-r}$. Using this fact, the analysis of this case follows from a simpler sub-case. In this sub-case, suppose that $\hat{\mathbf{P}}$ has behaved honestly from the $(r+1)$-th round of the consistency phase onwards, but $\hat{\mathbf{V}}$ makes checks at entries correlated with positions where $\text{Fold}(c_{r-1}, d_{r-1}; \alpha_r, \beta_r)$ is not a $\mathcal{C}^{\otimes t-(r-1)}$-codeword. We show that $\hat{\mathbf{V}}$ will reject.

Consistency Test Soundness. Suppose that the prover $\hat{\mathbf{P}}$ has sent c_{r-1} that is close to an interleaved codeword, but encodes a message that is not consistent with Π. Consider the latest round r for which $\hat{\mathbf{P}}$ behaves in this way. Then, $\mathrm{enc}(c_r)$ and $\mathrm{Fold}(c_{r-1}; q_{r-1})$ are close to different codewords of $\mathcal{C}^{\otimes t-(r-1)}$. This means that for a large fraction of entries $(j_r, \ldots, j_t) \in [n]^{t-r}$ which is related to the relative distance of the code, $\mathrm{Fold}(c_{r-1}; q_{r-1})(j_r, \ldots, j_t) \neq \mathrm{enc}(c_r)(j_r, \ldots, j_t)$, causing $\hat{\mathbf{V}}$ to reject.

Finally, suppose that, for each $r \in [t]$, $\hat{\mathbf{P}}$ has sent c_r that is an interleaved $\mathcal{C}^{\otimes t-r}$-codeword except for noise at a small number of positions, and all encode messages consistent with queries on Π. In this case, $\hat{\mathbf{P}}$ has essentially simulated an inner prover $\mathbf{P}$ correctly, in the sense that an "error-correction" of the words sent by $\hat{\mathbf{P}}$ are a correct simulation. The soundness error is then inherited from the original protocol $(\mathbf{P}, \mathbf{V})$.

2.4 Checking Constraint Systems with Tensor Queries

Our transformation from tensor queries to point queries (Theorem 3) introduces a *multiplicative* blow-up in prover arithmetic complexity (and proof length) that is proportional to the number q of tensor queries. So, for us to ultimately obtain a point-query IOP with linear arithmetic complexity, it is important that the tensor IOP given to the transformation has constant query complexity and a prover with linear arithmetic complexity.

Towards this end, we now turn to Theorem 2, which requires a suitably-efficient tensor IOP for the problem of *rank-1 constraint satisfiability* (R1CS), a generalization of arithmetic circuits given in Definition 1; recall that N is the number of variables and M is the number of coefficients in each coefficient matrix.

A natural starting point would be to build on interactive proofs for evaluating layered arithmetic circuits [GKR08], whose prover can be realized in linear time [Tha13, XZZPS19]. Indeed, the verifier in these protocols only needs to query the low-degree extension of the circuit input, which can be realized via a tensor query to a proof string containing the input sent by the prover. Moreover, the verifier in these protocols is sublinear given oracle access to the low-degree extension of the circuit description. These oracles can be implemented via a sub-protocol if the circuit is sufficiently uniform [GKR08] but, in general, this would require a holographic subprotocol that supports arbitrary circuits (not a goal in those works).

We take a different starting point that is more convenient to describe our holographic tensor IOP for R1CS (and recall that R1CS is a generalization of arithmetic circuits). First, as a warm-up in this section, we discuss a simple construction that fulfills a relaxation of the theorem: a tensor IOP for R1CS with linear proof length $\mathsf{l} = O(N)$, constant query complexity $\mathsf{q} = O(1)$, a prover with linear arithmetic complexity $\mathsf{tp} = O(M)$, and a verifier with linear arithmetic complexity $\mathsf{tv} = O(M)$. After that, in Sect. 2.5, we describe how to modify this simple protocol to additionally achieve sublinear verification time (incurring only minor losses in the other efficiency parameters). Along the way, we uncover new, and perhaps surprising, connections between prior work on linear-time IOPs [BCGGHJ17] and linear-time sumcheck protocols [Tha13].

In the paragraphs below we denote by $(\mathbf{P}, \mathbf{V})$ the $(\mathbb{F}, k, t)$-tensor IOP that we design for R1CS. We outline its high-level structure, and then describe in more detail the main sub-protocol that enables linear arithmetic complexity, which is for a problem that we call *twisted scalar product* (TSP).

High-level Structure. The R1CS problem asks whether, given coefficient matrices $A, B, C \in \mathbb{F}^{N \times N}$ and an instance vector x over $\mathbb{F}$, there exists a witness vector w over $\mathbb{F}$ such that $z := (x, w) \in \mathbb{F}^N$ satisfies $Az \circ Bz = Cz$. Using a similar approach to other proof protocols for R1CS, it suffices for the prover $\mathbf{P}$ to send the full assignment z and its linear combinations $z_A, z_B, z_C \in \mathbb{F}^N$, and convince the verifier $\mathbf{V}$ that $z_A = Az$, $z_B = Bz$, $z_C = Cz$, and $z_A \circ z_B = z_C$ in linear time and using $O(1)$ tensor queries.

To check the first three conditions, the verifier sends a random challenge vector $r \in \mathbb{F}^{n_{\text{row}}}$ with tensor structure. Multiplying on the left by $r^\intercal$ reduces the first three conditions to $\gamma_A = \langle r_A, z \rangle$, $\gamma_B = \langle r_B, z \rangle$, and $\gamma_C = \langle r_C, z \rangle$; here $\gamma_A := \langle r, z_A \rangle$ and $r_A := r^\intercal A$, and similarly for B and C. The verifier can directly obtain the inner products $\gamma_A, \gamma_B, \gamma_C$ through tensor queries to z_A, z_B, z_C. Moreover, both the prover and verifier can locally compute the three vectors r_A, r_B, r_C by right-multiplication by A, B, C respectively, which entails performing a number of arithmetic operations that is linear in the number M of non-zero entries of the matrices.[11] Note that this is the only place where the verifier has to read the entries of A, B, C. The verifier must now check the scalar products $\gamma_A = \langle r_A, z \rangle, \gamma_B = \langle r_B, z \rangle, \gamma_C = \langle r_C, z \rangle$.

Thus, to check R1CS satisfiability, it suffices to check three scalar products and one Hadamard product. (We must also check that $z = (x, w)$, but this is not the main technical challenge.) We solve both scalar and Hadamard products with a common subroutine for twisted scalar products that has a linear-time prover and a constant number of tensor queries, as we discuss below. We refer the reader to the full version of this paper for the details.

Twisted Scalar Products. The main technical contribution in our tensor IOP construction is the design of a protocol for verifying *twisted scalar products* (TSP).

Definition 3. *The* **twisted scalar product** *of two vectors* $u = (u_1, \ldots, u_N)$ *and* $v = (v_1, \ldots, v_N)$ *in* $\mathbb{F}^N$ *with respect to a third vector* $y = (y_1, \ldots, y_N)$ *in* $\mathbb{F}^N$ *is defined to be* $\langle u \circ y, v \rangle = \sum_{i=1}^{N} u_i y_i v_i$. *In other words, the i-th term $u_i v_i$ contributing to the scalar product $\langle u, v \rangle$ has been multiplied, or "twisted", by y_i.*

Standard scalar products (which we need for $\gamma_A = \langle r_A, z \rangle$, $\gamma_B = \langle r_B, z \rangle$, and $\gamma_C = \langle r_C, z \rangle$) follow by setting $y := 1^N$. To handle the Hadamard product $z_A \circ z_B = z_C$, we pick a random vector y, and up to a small error over the random choice of y, checking the Hadamard product is equivalent to checking the twisted scalar product $\langle u \circ y, v \rangle = \tau$ with $u = z_A$, $v = z_B$ and $\tau = \langle z_C, y \rangle$. In sum, to check the R1CS relation we will check four appropriate instances of the twisted scalar product.

Our result for twisted scalar products is as follows.

Lemma 1 (informal). *For every finite field $\mathbb{F}$ and positive integers k, t, there is a $(\mathbb{F}, k, t)$-tensor IOP for twisted scalar products that supports vectors of length $N = k^t$ and twists of the form $y = y_1 \otimes \cdots \otimes y_t$, and has the following parameters:*

---

[11] We remark that one can improve this cost from linear in the number M of non-zero entries in A, B, C to linear in the cost of right multiplication by A, B, C. By the transposition principle (see e.g., [KKB88]), this latter is closely related to the cost E of *left* multiplication by A, B, C, which could be much less than M. For example, if A is the matrix corresponding to a discrete Fourier transform, then $E = O(N \log N)$ is much less than $M = \Theta(N^2)$.

- *soundness error is $O(\frac{\log N}{|\mathbb{F}|})$;*
- *round complexity is $O(\log N)$;*
- *proof length is $O(N)$ elements in $\mathbb{F}$;*
- *query complexity is $O(1)$;*
- *the prover and verifier both use $O(N)$ field operations.*

Lemma 1 follows from prior work: the linear-time sumcheck of [Tha13, XZZPS19] can be applied to the multi-linear extension of the two vectors in the scalar product, and the verifier's queries to those extensions can be implemented as a tensor query. (The twist can also be handled by "folding it" into a tensor query.)

Below we give an alternative proof inspired by the linear-time protocols of [BCGGHJ17], themselves based on [Gro09]. This is interesting because this latter pre-dates [Tha13] and formerly appeared to be a totally distinct design strategy for interactive protocols. In contrast we show a sumcheck-based protocol inspired by these works, and show that they are a different application of the same linear-time sumcheck. From a technical point of view, our scalar-product protocol invokes the linear-time sumcheck on polynomials that encode information in their coefficients rather than in their evaluations (as is usually the case). This leads to modest opportunities for optimization and may have applications when used in combination with polynomial commitments not known to support the Lagrange basis (such as [BFS20]). Below we sketch our construction; details are in the full version of this paper. For simplicity, below we explain the case of scalar products without a twist. Readers who are comfortable with Lemma 1 may skip the rest of this section.

Strawman Construction. Before our construction, we first present a simple linear IOP (an IOP with linear queries as defined in Sect. 2.1) for scalar products, and then high-light the challenges that we need to overcome to obtain our protocol.

The verifier $\mathbf{V}$ has linear query access to two vectors $u = (u_0, \ldots, u_{N-1})$ and $v = (v_0, \ldots, v_{N-1})$ in $\mathbb{F}^N$. The prover $\mathbf{P}$ wishes to convince the verifier $\mathbf{V}$ that $\langle u, v \rangle = \tau$ for a given $\tau \in \mathbb{F}$. Define the two polynomials $U(X) := \sum_{i=0}^{N-1} u_i X^i$ and $V(X) := \sum_{i=0}^{N-1} v_i X^{N-i}$ (the entries of v appear in reverse order in $V(X)$). The product polynomial $W(X) := U(X)V(X)$ has $\langle u, v \rangle$ as the coefficient of X^{N-1}, because for any $i, j \in [N]$, the powers of X associated with u_i and v_j multiply together to give X^{N-1} if and only if $i = j$. With this in mind, $\mathbf{P}$ sends to $\mathbf{V}$ the vector $w := (w_0, \ldots, w_{2N-2})$ of coefficients of $W(X)$.

Next, $\mathbf{V}$ checks the equality $W(X) = U(X) \cdot V(X)$ at a random point: it samples a random $\rho \in \mathbb{F}$; constructs the queries $\nu_1 := (1, \rho, \rho^2, \ldots, \rho^{N-1})$, $\nu_2 := (\rho^{N-1}, \rho^{N-2}, \ldots, 1)$, and $\nu_3 := (1, \rho, \rho^2, \ldots, \rho^{2N-2})$; queries u, v, w respectively at ν_1, ν_2, ν_3 to obtain $\gamma_u = \langle u, \nu_1 \rangle = U(\rho)$, $\gamma_v = \langle v, \nu_2 \rangle = V(\rho)$, $\gamma_w = \langle w, \nu_3 \rangle = W(\rho)$; and checks that $\gamma_u \cdot \gamma_v = \gamma_w$. By the Schwarz–Zippel lemma, this is test is unlikely to pass unless $U(X) \cdot V(X) = W(X)$ as polynomials, and in particular, if the coefficient of X^{N-1} in $W(X)$ is not equal to $\langle u, v \rangle$. Finally, $\mathbf{V}$ constructs the query $\nu_4 := (0, \ldots, 1, 0, \ldots, 0)$, which has a 1 in the N-th position of the vector; then queries w at ν_4 to get $w_{N-1} = \langle w, \nu_4 \rangle$, and checks that it is equal to τ.

This approach gives a linear IOP for verifying scalar products, with $O(1)$ queries and proof length $O(N)$. One can easily convert it into a linear IOP for verifying twisted scalar products by using $\nu_1 \circ y$ instead of ν_1. With additional care, these queries can even be expressed as tensor queries. However, *the main problem with this approach is that* $\mathbf{P}$ *requires* $O(N \log N)$ *operations to compute* $W(X)$ *by multiplying* $U(X)$ *and* $V(X)$.

Scalar Products via Sumcheck. We explain how to obtain a tensor IOP for scalar products where $\mathbf{P}$ uses $O(N)$ operations. First, we explain how to redesign the polynomials $U(X)$ and $V(X)$. Then, we explain how to verify that the scalar product is correct via a sumcheck protocol on the product of these polynomials.

We embed the entries of u and $v \in \mathbb{F}^n$ into *multilinear* polynomials $U(X_1, \ldots, X_l)$ and $V(X_1, \ldots, X_l)$ over $\mathbb{F}$. Namely, in $U(X)$, we replace the monomial X^i, which has coefficient u_i, with a monomial in formal variables $X_1, X_2, \ldots, X_{\log N}$, choosing to include X_j if the j-th binary digit of i is a 1. For example, u_0, u_1, u_2 and u_3 are associated with monomials 1, X_1, X_2, and $X_1 X_2$. Thus, each coefficient u_i is associated with a unique monomial in $X_1, \ldots, X_{\log N}$. As with the strawman solution, the coefficients of $V(X)$ are associated with the same monomials, but in reverse order. For example, v_0 and v_1 are associated with monomials $X_1 X_2 \cdots X_{\log N}$ and $X_2 \cdots X_{\log N}$. This time, the product polynomial $W(X_1, \ldots, X_{\log N}) := U(X_1, \ldots, X_{\log N}) \cdot V(X_1, \ldots, X_{\log N})$ has $\langle u, v \rangle$ as the coefficient of $X_1 X_2 \cdots X_{\log N}$, since for any $i, j \in [N]$ the monomials associated with u_i and v_j multiply together to give $X_1 X_2 \cdots X_{\log N}$ if and only if $i = j$.

Now $\mathbf{V}$ has tensor-query access to u and v, and $\mathbf{P}$ must convince $\mathbf{V}$ that $\langle u, v \rangle = \tau$, which now means checking that $\mathrm{Coeff}_{X_1 \cdots X_l}(W) = \tau$. We turn this latter condition into a sumcheck instance, via a new lemma that relates sums of polynomials over multiplicative subgroups to their coefficients; the lemma extends a result in [BCRSVW19] to the multivariate setting.

Lemma 2 (informal). *Let H be a multiplicative subgroup of $\mathbb{F}$ and $p(X_1, \ldots, X_l)$ a polynomial over $\mathbb{F}$. Then for every integer vector $\vec{j} = (j_1, \ldots, j_l) \in \mathbb{N}^l$,*

$$\sum_{\vec{\omega} = (\omega_1, \ldots, \omega_l) \in H^l} p(\vec{\omega}) \cdot \vec{\omega}^{\vec{j}} = \left(\sum_{\vec{i} + \vec{j} \equiv \vec{0} \bmod |H|} p_{\vec{i}} \right) \cdot |H|^l .$$

Above we denote by $p_{\vec{i}}$ the coefficient of $X_1^{i_1} \cdots X_l^{i_l}$ in p and denote by $\vec{\omega}^{\vec{j}}$ the product $\omega_1^{j_1} \cdots \omega_l^{j_l}$.

Set $H := \{-1, 1\}$, $p := W$, and $\vec{j} := (1, \ldots, 1)$. Since W has degree at most 2 in each variable, the only coefficient contributing to the sum on the right-hand side is the coefficient of $X_1 \cdots X_l$, which is $\langle u, v \rangle$.

In light of the above, the prover $\mathbf{P}$ and the verifier $\mathbf{V}$ engage in a sumcheck protocol for the following claim:

$$\sum_{\vec{\omega} \in \{-1,1\}^l} U(\vec{\omega}) V(\vec{\omega}) \cdot \vec{\omega}^{\vec{1}} = \tau \cdot 2^l .$$

During the sumcheck protocol, over l rounds of interaction, $\mathbf{V}$ will send random challenges $\rho_1, \ldots, \rho_l$. After the interaction, $\mathbf{V}$ needs to obtain the value

$U(\rho_1, \ldots, \rho_l)V(\rho_1, \ldots, \rho_l)$. We show that, in our setting, $\mathbf{V}$ can obtain the two values in this product by making tensor queries to u and v, respectively.

We are left to discuss how $\mathbf{P}$ can be implemented in $O(2^l) = O(N)$ operations.

Recall that the problem in the strawman protocol was that $\mathbf{P}$ had to multiply two polynomials of degree N. Now the problem seems even worse: $\mathbf{P}$ cannot compute W directly as it has a super-linear number of coefficients (W is multi-quadratic in $l = \log N$ variables). However, in the sumcheck protocol, $\mathbf{P}$ *need not compute and send every coefficient of W* and can compute the messages for the sumcheck protocol by using partial evaluations $U(\rho_1, \ldots, \rho_j, X_{j+1}, \ldots, X_{\log N})$ and $V(\rho_1, \ldots, \rho_j, X_{j+1}, \ldots, X_{\log N})$ without ever performing any high-degree polynomial multiplications. This is indeed the logic behind techniques for implementing sumcheck provers in linear time, as discussed in [Tha13, XZZPS19], which, e.g., suffice for sumchecks where the addend is the product of constantly-many multilinear polynomials, as is the case for us.

The full details, which give explicit tensor queries for evaluating U and V, and how to incorporate the "twist" with $y \in \mathbb{F}^N$ into the sumcheck to get our TSP protocol, are given in the full version of this paper.

Remark 2 (binary fields). The astute reader may notice that setting $H = \{-1, 1\}$ in Lemma 2 is only possible when the characteristic of $\mathbb{F}$ is not equal to 2. Nevertheless, a statement similar to Lemma 2 holds for additive subgroups, which in particular we can use in the case of binary fields. Our results then carry over with minor modifications to binary fields as well (and thus all large-enough fields).

2.5 Achieving Holography

Thus far, we have discussed ingredients behind a relaxation of Theorem 1 with no sublinear verification. Namely, (1) an IOP with tensor queries where the verifier receives as *explicit* input the R1CS coefficient matrices A, B, C; and (2) a transformation from this tensor-query IOP to a corresponding point-query IOP.

We now describe how to additionally achieve the sublinear verification in Theorem 1 via holography.

In a holographic IOP for R1CS, the verifier $\mathbf{V}$ no longer receives as explicit input A, B, C. Instead, in addition to the prover $\mathbf{P}$ and the verifier $\mathbf{V}$, a holographic IOP for R1CS includes an additional algorithm, known as the *indexer* and denoted by $\mathbf{I}$, that receives as explicit input A, B, C and outputs an "encoding" of these. The verifier $\mathbf{V}$ then has query access to the output of the indexer $\mathbf{I}$. This potentially enables the verifier $\mathbf{V}$ to run in time that is sublinear in the time to read A, B, C.

Achieving such a verifier speed-up and thereby obtaining Theorem 1, however, requires modifications in both of the aforementioned ingredients. Below we first discuss the modifications to the transformation, as they are relatively straightforward. After that we dedicate the rest of the section to discuss the modifications to the tensor-query IOP, because making it holographic requires several additional ideas.

Preserving Holography in the Transformation. Informally, we want the modified transformation to "preserve holography": if the tensor-query IOP given to the transformation is holographic (the verifier has tensor-query access to the output of an indexer), then the new point-query IOP produced by the transformation is also holographic (the new verifier has point-query access to the output of the new indexer). Moreover, the transformation should introduce only constant multiplicative overheads in the cost of indexing and proving.

So let $\mathbf{I}$ be the indexer of the tensor-query IOP. The new indexer $\hat{\mathbf{I}}$ for the point-query IOP simulates $\mathbf{I}$ and encodes its output using Enc, just as the new prover $\hat{\mathbf{P}}$ encodes the messages from $\mathbf{P}$. (Recall from Sect. 2.2 that Enc is the encoding function for the tensor code $\mathcal{C}^{\otimes t}$.) Subsequently, in the simulation phase of the transformation, whenever the verifier $\mathbf{V}$ wishes to make a tensor query to the output of $\mathbf{I}$, the new verifier $\hat{\mathbf{V}}$ forwards this query to the new prover $\hat{\mathbf{P}}$, who responds with the answer. After that, we extend the consistency and proximity tests in the transformation to also ensure that $\hat{\mathbf{P}}$ answers these additional tensor queries correctly. These tests will require the new verifier $\hat{\mathbf{V}}$ to make point queries to the encoding of the output of $\mathbf{I}$, which is precisely what $\hat{\mathbf{V}}$ has query access to because that is the output of $\hat{\mathbf{I}}$. The constant multiplicative overheads incurred by the transformation still hold after these (relatively minor) modifications.

A Holographic Tensor IOP. In the non-holographic tensor-query IOP outlined in Sect. 2.4, the verifier $\mathbf{V}$, receives as input coefficient matrices A, B, C explicitly, and must perform two types of expensive operations based on these. First, $\mathbf{V}$ expands some random challenges $r_1, \ldots, r_t \in \mathbb{F}^k$ into a vector $r = r_1 \otimes \cdots \otimes r_t \in \mathbb{F}^{k^t}$, which requires $O(k^t)$ arithmetic operations. Second, $\mathbf{V}$ computes the matrix-vector product $r_A := r^\mathsf{T} A$, which in the worst case costs proportionally to the number of non-zero entries of A. Similarly for B and C.

Viewed at a high level, these expensive operations are performed as part of a check that $z_A = Az$ (and similarly for B and C), which has been referred to as a "lincheck" (see e.g. [BCRSVW19]). Thus, it is sufficient to provide a "holographic lincheck" sub-protocol where $\mathbf{V}$ has tensor query access to a matrix U (which is one of A, B, or C), an input vector v, and an output vector v_U, and wishes to check that $v_\mathsf{U} = Uv$.

Challenges to Holography. To illustrate the challenges of obtaining a linear-time holographic lincheck, we first present a simple strawman: a sound protocol that falls (far) short of linear arithmetic complexity. First we describe the indexer, and after that the interaction between the prover and verifier.

- *Indexer.* The indexer receives as input a matrix U over $\mathbb{F}$, which for simplicity we assume has dimension $k^t \times k^t$; we can then identify the rows and columns of U via tuples $(i_1, \ldots, i_t) \in [k]^t$ and $(j_1, \ldots, j_t) \in [k]^t$ respectively. The indexer outputs the vector $u \in \mathbb{F}^{k^{2t}}$ such that $u_{i_1,\ldots,i_t,j_1,\ldots,j_t}$ is the entry of U at row $(i_1, \ldots, i_t)$ and column $(j_1, \ldots, j_t)$. The verifier will have $(\mathbb{F}, k, 2t)$-tensor-query access to u.
- *Prover and Verifier.* To check that $v_\mathsf{U} = Uv$, for the verifier it suffices to check that $\langle r, v_\mathsf{U} \rangle = \langle r^\mathsf{T} U, v \rangle$ for a random $r = r_1 \otimes \cdots \otimes r_t$ in $\mathbb{F}^{k^t}$ (up to a small error over the choice of r). Since $r^\mathsf{T} Uv = \langle r \otimes v, u \rangle$, the verifier wishes to check whether $\langle r, v_\mathsf{U} \rangle = \langle r \otimes v, u \rangle$. The verifier makes the $(\mathbb{F}, k, t)$-tensor query r to v_U to obtain the left hand side. To help the verifier obtain the right hand side, the prover computes $e := r \otimes v \in \mathbb{F}^{2t}$ and sends it to the verifier. Since u need not have a tensor structure, the verifier cannot directly obtain $\langle e, u \rangle$ via a $(\mathbb{F}, k, 2t)$-tensor query to e; instead, the verifier can receive this value from the prover and rely on a

scalar-product protocol to check its correctness. The verifier is thus left to check that indeed $e = r \otimes v$. Note that for any $s = s_1 \otimes \cdots \otimes s_t$ and $s' = s'_1 \otimes \cdots \otimes s'_t$ it holds that $\langle s \otimes s', e \rangle = \langle s, r \rangle \langle s', v \rangle = \langle s_1, r_1 \rangle \cdots \langle s_t, r_t \rangle \langle s', v \rangle$. The verifier checks this equality for random s and s': it directly computes $\langle s_i, r_i \rangle$ for each $i \in [t]$; obtains $\langle s', v \rangle$ via a $(\mathbb{F}, k, t)$-tensor query to v; obtains $\langle s \otimes s', e \rangle$ via a $(\mathbb{F}, k, 2t)$-tensor query to e; and checks the expression.

Crucially, in the protocol described above, the verifier performs only $O(kt)$ field operations. In particular, the verifier did not have to incur the cost of reading the matrix U, which is much greater in general.

However, the foregoing protocol falls (far) short of achieving linear proving time: the indexer outputs a vector u that specifies the matrix U via a *dense* representation of k^{2t} elements, and this leads to the prover having to compute vectors such as $e \in \mathbb{F}^{2t}$, which costs $O(k^{2t})$ operations. On the other hand, in order to represent U, it suffices to specify its *non-zero entries*. Hence, unless U is a dense matrix (with $\Omega(k^{2t})$ non-zero entries), the foregoing protocol does *not* have a linear-time prover (and also does not have a linear-time indexer).

Our goal here is thus a holographic protocol that is efficient relative to a *sparse* representation of the matrix U, for example the triple of vectors $(\mathrm{val}_U, \mathrm{row}_U, \mathrm{col}_U) \in \mathbb{F}^M \times [k^t]^M \times [k^t]^M$ such that val_U is a list of the values of the M non-zero entries of U, and $\mathrm{row}_U, \mathrm{col}_U$ are the indices of these entries in U (i.e., for all $\kappa \in [M]$ it holds that $U(\mathrm{row}_U(\kappa), \mathrm{col}_U(\kappa)) = \mathrm{val}_U(\kappa)$). This is (essentially) the best that we can hope for, as the indexer and the prover must read a description of U.

Efficiency relative to the sparse representation was achieved in [CHMMVW20, COS20], which contributed efficient holographic IOPs for R1CS. However, the prover algorithm in those constructions runs in quasilinear time, and we do not know how to adapt the techniques in these prior works, which are based on univariate polynomials, to our setting (linear-time tensor IOPs). It remains an interesting open problem to build on those techniques to achieve a linear-time holographic lincheck with tensor queries.

Subsequently, Setty [Set20] constructed a preprocessing SNARG for R1CS without FFTs by porting the univariate protocols for R1CS to the multivariate setting (where we have a linear-time sumcheck [Tha13]) and solving the matrix sparsity problem by constructing a polynomial commitment scheme for "sparse multivariate polynomials". His approach to sparsity is combinatorial rather than algebraic: he constructs a linear-size circuit using memory-checking ideas to "load" each non-zero term of the polynomial and add it to a total sum, and then invokes an argument system for uniform circuits that does not use FFTs [WTSTW18]. Since a key component of the construction is a polynomial commitment scheme for (dense) multilinear extensions, and the multilinear extension of a vector is a special case of a tensor query, it is plausible that one could distill a tensor IOP from [Set20] that suits our purposes. However, taking this path is not straightforward given the protocol's complexity, and the informal discussions and proof sketches in [Set20].

Our Approach. To prove our theorem, we build on an earlier protocol of Bootle et al. [BCGJM18] and a recent simplification by Gabizon and Williamson [GW20]. As described below, this leads to a direct and natural construction for a holographic lincheck, which is what we need. The key component in our construction, like the earlier works, is a *look-up protocol*, wherein the prover can convince the verifier that previously-stored values are correctly retrieved. Below we describe how to obtain the lincheck protocol given the look-up protocol as a subroutine, and after that describe the look-up protocol.

As in the strawman protocol, to check that $v_U = Uv$, for the verifier it suffices to check that $\langle r, v_U \rangle = \langle r^\mathsf{T} U, v \rangle$ for a random $r = r_1 \otimes \cdots \otimes r_t$ in $\mathbb{F}^{k^t}$ (up to a small error over r). Again, the verifier can directly obtain the value $\langle r, v_U \rangle$ by querying v_U at the tensor r. The verifier is left to obtain the value of $\langle r^\mathsf{T} U, v \rangle = r^\mathsf{T} U v$, and enlists the prover's help to do so. Therefore, the verifier sends $r_1, \ldots, r_t$ to the prover, who replies with $\gamma := r^\mathsf{T} U v \in \mathbb{F}$. The prover must now convince the verifier that γ is correct.

Towards this, the prover will send partial results in the computation of γ, and the verifier will run sub-protocols to check the correctness of each partial result. To see how to do this, we first re-write the expression $r^\mathsf{T} U v$ in terms of the sparse representation of U:

$$r^\mathsf{T} U v = \sum_{\kappa \in [M]} \mathrm{val}_U(\kappa) \cdot r(\mathrm{row}_U(\kappa)) \cdot v(\mathrm{col}_U(\kappa)) \ . \tag{1}$$

This expression suggests the prover's first message to the verifier, which consists of the following two vectors:

$$r^* := \left(r(\mathrm{row}_U(\kappa)) \right)_{\kappa \in [M]} \quad \text{and} \quad v^* := \left(v(\mathrm{col}_U(\kappa)) \right)_{\kappa \in [M]} \ .$$

Observe that, if the prover was honest, then the right-hand side of Eq. (1) is equal to $\langle \mathrm{val}_U, r^* \circ v^* \rangle$.

Therefore, the verifier is left to check that: (1) $\gamma = \langle \mathrm{val}_U, r^* \circ v^* \rangle$, and (2) r^*, v^* were correctly assembled from the entries of r, v as determined by the indices in $\mathrm{row}_U, \mathrm{col}_U$, respectively.

The verifier can check the first condition via a scalar product subprotocol and a Hadamard product subprotocol (which we have discussed in Sect. 2.4). To check the second condition, the verifier will use a *tensor consistency test* and two *look-up subprotocols*, as we now explain.

Even though the verifier sampled the components $r_1, \ldots, r_t \in \mathbb{F}^k$ that determine the tensor vector $r = r_1 \otimes \cdots \otimes r_t \in \mathbb{F}^{k^t}$, the verifier cannot afford to directly compute r, as this would cost $O(k^t)$ operations. Instead, the prover sends r, and the verifier checks that r was computed correctly from $r_1, \ldots, r_t$ via a simple subprotocol, which we describe in the full version of this paper, that only requires making one tensor query to r and performing $O(tk)$ operations. Now the verifier is in a position to make tensor queries to (the correct) r.

Next, observe that r^* is correct if and only if, for each $\kappa \in [M]$, there is $i \in [k^t]$ such that $(r^*_\kappa, \mathrm{row}_U(\kappa)) = (r_i, i)$. We represent this "look-up" condition via the shorthand $(r^*, \mathrm{row}_U) \subseteq (r, [k^t])$. Similarly, v^* is correct if and only if $(v^*, \mathrm{col}_U) \subseteq (v, [k^t])$. We now discuss a protocol to check such conditions.

Look-ups via tensor queries. A look-up protocol is to check the condition $(c, I) \subseteq (d, [k^t])$, given that the verifier has tensor-query access to the vectors $c \in \mathbb{F}^M$ and $d \in \mathbb{F}^{k^t}$, and also to the index vectors $I \in \mathbb{F}^M$ and $[k^t] \in \mathbb{F}^{k^t}$. (Here we are implicitly associating the integers in $[k^t]$ with an arbitrary k^t-size subset in $\mathbb{F}$.)

Look-up protocols for use in proof systems originate in a work of Bootle et al. [BCGJM18] that aims at low computational overhead for the prover. Their protocol reduces the look-up condition to a univariate polynomial identity, and then the prover helps the verifier to check that the polynomial identity holds when evaluated at a random challenge point. However, the prover in their protocol incurs a logarithmic overhead in the size of the list c, which in our usage would result in a superlinear-time prover.

Gabizon and Williams [GW20] provide a more efficient look-up protocol, which removes the logarithmic overhead by relying on a more expressive *bivariate* polynomial identity. However, they use a different proof model that we do not know how to compile into ours while preserving linear complexity. Our contribution is to give a linear-time tensor IOP for look-ups using their polynomial identity as a starting point.

Below we recall the identity and then summarize our look-up protocol; details can be found in the full version.

First recall that, via a standard use of randomized hashing, we can replace the lookup condition $(c, I) \subseteq (d, [k^t])$ with a simpler *inclusion* condition $a \subseteq b$ for suitable vectors $a \in \mathbb{F}^M$ and $b \in \mathbb{F}^{k^t}$ (each entry in the vector a equals some entry of the vector b). The polynomial identity from [GW20] concerns this latter condition, as we now explain. (We also note that we have modified the polynomial identity to incorporate "wrap-around" in the entries of vectors, to simplify other aspects of our protocols.) Assuming for simplicity that the entries of b are *distinct*, let sort() denote the function that sorts the entries of its input in the order $b_1 \prec b_2 \prec \ldots \prec b_{k^t}$.[12] Let shift() denote a cyclic shift.

Lemma 1 ([GW20]). *Let $a \in \mathbb{F}^M$ and $b \in \mathbb{F}^{k^t}$. Then $a \subseteq b$ if and only if there is $w \in \mathbb{F}^{k^t + M}$ such that*

$$\prod_{j=1}^{M+k^t} (Y(1+Z) + w_j + \mathrm{shift}(w)_j \cdot Z) = (1+Z)^M \prod_{j=1}^{M} (Y + a_j) \prod_{j=1}^{k^t} (Y(1+Z) + b_j + \mathrm{shift}(b)_j \cdot Z) \ .$$

(2)

In the case that $a \subseteq b$, we may take $w = \mathrm{sort}(a, b)$ to satisfy the above equation.

In our look-up protocol, the prover recomputes this polynomial identity at random evaluation points chosen by the verifier and sends intermediate computation steps to the verifier.[13] Both parties run subprotocols to check that the computation was performed correctly and the evaluated polynomial identity holds.

Having sent w to the verifier, the prover also sends the vectors $w_\circlearrowright := \mathrm{shift}(w)$ and $b_\circlearrowright := \mathrm{shift}(b)$. Then after receiving random evaluation points for Y and Z, the prover sends vectors w^*, a^*, b^* containing each evaluated term in the first, second, and third products of Eq. (2) to the verifier, along with the values $\chi_{w^*} := \mathrm{prod}(w^*), \chi_{a^*} := \mathrm{prod}(a^*), \chi_{b^*} := \mathrm{prod}(b^*)$ of each product as non-oracle messages. Here, $\mathrm{prod}()$ denotes the function which takes the product of the entries of its input.

---

[12] When the entries of b are not distinct, one can consider a more complex merge operation; the full version of this paper for details.

[13] One can draw parallels between the combination of randomized hashing and the polynomial identity used in this work, and the combination of randomized and multi-set hashing used in the memory-checking circuit of [Set20]. Conceptually, the [GW20] polynomial identity enforces stronger conditions on w, a and b than a multi-set hash and removes the need for the time-stamping data used in [Set20].

Apart from simple checks that the vectors w^*, a^*, b^* were correctly computed, and using $\chi_{w^*}, \chi_{a^*}, \chi_{b^*}$ to check that Eq. (2) holds, we rely on two additional subprotocols.

- A *cyclic-shift* test to show that e.g. $b_\circlearrowright = \text{shift}(b)$. The polynomial identity $\sum_{i=1}^{k^t} b(i) X^{i-1} - X \cdot \sum_{i=1}^{k^t} b_\circlearrowright(i) X^{i-1} = (1 - X^{k^t}) \cdot b_\circlearrowright(k^t)$ holds if and only if $b_\circlearrowright = \text{shift}(b)$. The verifier uses tensor queries to check that this identity holds at a random point.
- An *entry-product* protocol to show that e.g. $\chi_{w^*} = \text{prod}(w^*)$. This protocol combines a cyclic-shift test with a Hadamard-product protocol in order to verify the correct computation of all partial products leading to the entry product.

The details of both subprotocols can be found in the full version of this paper.

Acknowledgements. We are deeply grateful to Sune K. Jakobsen who was instrumental in the early stages of this research project and provided an initial analysis of a compiler from tensor queries to point queries based on tensor codes. We thank Andrea Cerulli for discussions about error correcting codes.

References

[AHIKV17] Applebaum, B., Haramaty-Krasne, N., Ishai, Y., Kushilevitz, E., Vaikuntanathan, V.: Low-complexity cryptographic hash functions. In: Proceedings of the 8th Innovations in Theoretical Computer Science Conference, ITCS 2017, pp. 1–31, (2017)

[AHIV17] Ames, S., Hazay, C., Ishai, Y., Venkitasubramaniam, M.: Ligero: Lightweight sublinear arguments without a trusted setup. In: Proceedings of the 24th ACM Conference on Computer and Communications Security, CCS 2017, pp. 2087–2104 (2017)

[BBBPWM18] Benedikt, B., Bootle, J., Dan, B., Andrew, P., Pieter, W., Greg, M.: Bulletproofs: short proofs for confidential transactions and more. In: Proceedings of the 39th IEEE Symposium on Security and Privacy, S&P 2018, pp. 315–334 (2018)

[BBCGI19] Boneh, D., Boyle, E., Corrigan-Gibbs, H., Gilboa, N., Ishai, Y.: Zero-knowledge proofs on secret-shared data via fully linear PCPs. In: Boldyreva, A., Micciancio, D. (eds.) CRYPTO 2019. LNCS, vol. 11694, pp. 67–97. Springer, Cham (2019). https://doi.org/10.1007/978-3-030-26954-8_3

[BBHR18] Ben-Sasson, E., Bentov, I., Horesh, Y. and Riabzev, M.: Fast Reed-Solomon interactive oracle proofs of proximity. In: Proceedings of the 45th International Colloquium on Automata, Languages and Programming, ICALP 2018. pp. 1–17 (2018)

[BCCGP16] Bootle, J., Cerulli, A., Chaidos, P., Groth, J., Petit, C.: Efficient zero-knowledge arguments for arithmetic circuits in the discrete log setting. In: Fischlin, M., Coron, J.-S. (eds.) EUROCRYPT 2016. LNCS, vol. 9666, pp. 327–357. Springer, Heidelberg (2016). https://doi.org/10.1007/978-3-662-49896-5_12

[BCGGHJ17] Bootle, J., Cerulli, A., Ghadafi, E., Groth, J., Hajiabadi, M., Jakobsen, S.K.: Linear-time zero-knowledge proofs for arithmetic circuit satisfiability. In: Takagi, T., Peyrin, T. (eds.) ASIACRYPT 2017. LNCS, vol. 10626, pp. 336–365. Springer, Cham (2017). https://doi.org/10.1007/978-3-319-70700-6_12

[BCGJM18] Bootle, J., Cerulli, A., Groth, J., Jakobsen, S., Maller, M.: Arya: nearly linear-time zero-knowledge proofs for correct program execution. In: Peyrin, T., Galbraith, S. (eds.) ASIACRYPT 2018. LNCS, vol. 11272, pp. 595–626. Springer, Cham (2018). https://doi.org/10.1007/978-3-030-03326-2_20

[BCRSVW19] Ben-Sasson, E., Chiesa, A., Riabzev, M., Spooner, N., Virza, M., Ward, N.P.: Aurora: transparent succinct arguments for R1CS. In: Ishai, Y., Rijmen, V. (eds.) EUROCRYPT 2019. LNCS, vol. 11476, pp. 103–128. Springer, Cham (2019). https://doi.org/10.1007/978-3-030-17653-2_4

[BCS16] Ben-Sasson, E., Chiesa, A., Spooner, N.: Interactive oracle proofs. In: Hirt, M., Smith, A. (eds.) TCC 2016. LNCS, vol. 9986, pp. 31–60. Springer, Heidelberg (2016). https://doi.org/10.1007/978-3-662-53644-5_2

[BFS20] Bünz, B., Fisch, B., Szepieniec, A.: Transparent SNARKs from DARK compilers. In: Canteaut, A., Ishai, Y. (eds.) EUROCRYPT 2020. LNCS, vol. 12105, pp. 677–706. Springer, Cham (2020). https://doi.org/10.1007/978-3-030-45721-1_24

[BS06] Ben-Sasson, E.: Sudan, madhu: robust locally testable codes and products of codes. Random Struct. Alg. **28**(4), 387–402 (2006)

[Ben+14] Sasson, E.B., Chiesa, A., Garman, C., Green, M., Miers, I., Tromer, E., Virza, M.: Zerocash: Decentralized anonymous payments from Bitcoin. In: Proceedings of the 2014 IEEE Symposium on Security and Privacy, SP 2014. pp. 459–474, (2014)

[CHMMVW20] Chiesa, A., Hu, Y., Maller, M., Mishra, P., Vesely, N., Ward, N.: Marlin: Preprocessing zksnarks with universal and updatable SRS. In: Canteaut, A., Ishai, Y. (eds.) EUROCRYPT 2020. LNCS, vol. 12105, pp. 738–768. Springer, Cham (2020). https://doi.org/10.1007/978-3-030-45721-1_26

[CMS17] Chiesa, A., Manohar, P., Shinkar, I.: On axis-parallel tests for tensor product codes. In: Proceedings of the 21st International Workshop on Randomization and Computation, RANDOM 2017. pp. 1–22, (2017)

[COS20] Chiesa, A., Ojha, D., Spooner, N.: FRACTAL: Post-quantum and transparent recursive proofs from holography. In: Canteaut, A., Ishai, Y. (eds.) EUROCRYPT 2020. LNCS, vol. 12105, pp. 769–793. Springer, Cham (2020). https://doi.org/10.1007/978-3-030-45721-1_27

[DI14] Druk, E., Ishai, Y.: Linear-time encodable codes meeting the Gilbert-Varshamov bound and their cryptographic applications. In: Proceedings of the 5th Innovations in Theoretical Computer Science Conference, ITCS 2014. pp. 169–182 (2014)

[GKR08] Shafi, G., Yael, T.K., Guy, N.R.: Delegating computation: interactive proofs for Muggles. In: Proceedings of the 40th Annual ACM Symposium on Theory of Computing, STOC 2008. pp. 113–122 (2008)

[GW20] Ariel, G., Zachary J.W.: plookup: A simplified polynomial protocol for lookup tables (2020)

[Gro09] Groth, J.: Linear algebra with sub-linear zero-knowledge arguments. In: Halevi, S. (ed.) CRYPTO 2009. LNCS, vol. 5677, pp. 192–208. Springer, Heidelberg (2009). https://doi.org/10.1007/978-3-642-03356-8_12

[KKB88] Kaminski, M.: Kirkpatrick, David, Bshouty, Nader: addition requirements for matrix and transposed matrix products. J. Alg. **9**(3), 354–364 (1988)

[Kil92] Joe, K.: A note on efficient zero-knowledge proofs and arguments. In: Proceedings of the 24th Annual ACM Symposium on Theory of Computing, STOC 1992. pp. 723–732 (1992)

[Mei13] Meir, O.: IP = PSPACE using error-correcting codes. SIAM J. Comput. **42**(1), 380–403 (2013)

[Mic00] Micali, S.: Computationally sound proofs. SIAM J. Comput. **30**(4), 1253–1298 (2000)

[OWWB20] Ozdemir, A., Wahby, R., Whitehat, B., Boneh, D.: Scaling verifiable computation using efficient set accumulators. In: Proceedings of the 29th USENIX Security Symposium, Security 2020. pp. 2075–2092 (2020)

[Pip80] Pippenger, N.: On the evaluation of powers and monomials. SIAM J. Comput. **9**(2), 230–250 (1980)

[RR20] Ron-Zewi, N., Rothblum, R.: Local proofs approaching the witness length. In: Proceedings of the 61st Annual IEEE Symposium on Foundations of Computer Science FOCS 2020 (2020)

[RRR16] Reingold, O., Rothblum, G.N., Rothblum, R.D.: Constant-round interactive proofs for delegating computation. In: Proceedings of the 48th ACM Symposium on the Theory of Computing, STOC 2016. pp. 49–62 (2016)

[Set20] Setty, S.: Spartan: efficient and general-purpose zksnarks without trusted setup. In: Micciancio, D., Ristenpart, T. (eds.) CRYPTO 2020. LNCS, vol. 12172, pp. 704–737. Springer, Cham (2020). https://doi.org/10.1007/978-3-030-56877-1_25

[Tha13] Thaler, J.: Time-optimal interactive proofs for circuit evaluation. In: Canetti, R., Garay, J.A. (eds.) CRYPTO 2013. LNCS, vol. 8043, pp. 71–89. Springer, Heidelberg (2013). https://doi.org/10.1007/978-3-642-40084-1_5

[Vid15] Viderman, M.: A combination of testability and decodability by tensor products. Random Struct. Alg. **46**(3), 572–598 (2015)

[WTSTW18] Wahby, R.S., Tzialla, I., Shelat, A., Thaler, J, Walfish, M.: Doubly-efficient zkSNARKs without trusted setup. In: Proceedings of the 39th IEEE Symposium on Security and Privacy, S&P 2018, pp. 926–943 (2018)

[XZZPS19] Xie, T., Zhang, J., Zhang, Y., Papamanthou, C., Song, D.: Libra: Succinct zero-knowledge proofs with optimal prover computation. In: Boldyreva, A., Micciancio, D. (eds.) CRYPTO 2019. LNCS, vol. 11694, pp. 733–764. Springer, Cham (2019). https://doi.org/10.1007/978-3-030-26954-8_24

[ZXZS20] Zhang, J., Xie, T., Zhang, Y., Song, D.: Transparent polynomial delegation and its applications to zero knowledge proof. In: Proceedings of the 41st IEEE Symposium on Security and Privacy, S&P 2020. pp. 859–876 (2020)

Barriers for Succinct Arguments in the Random Oracle Model

Alessandro Chiesa[1] and Eylon Yogev[2,3(✉)]

[1] UC Berkeley, Berkeley, USA
[2] Boston University, Boston, USA
eylony@gmail.com
[3] Tel Aviv University, Tel Aviv, Israel

Abstract. We establish barriers on the efficiency of succinct arguments in the random oracle model. We give evidence that, under standard complexity assumptions, there do not exist succinct arguments where the argument verifier makes a small number of queries to the random oracle. The new barriers follow from new insights into how probabilistic proofs play a fundamental role in constructing succinct arguments in the random oracle model.

- *IOPs are necessary for succinctness.* We prove that any succinct argument in the random oracle model can be transformed into a corresponding interactive oracle proof (IOP). The query complexity of the IOP is related to the succinctness of the argument.
- *Algorithms for IOPs.* We prove that if a language has an IOP with good soundness relative to query complexity, then it can be decided via a fast algorithm with small space complexity.

By combining these results we obtain barriers for a large class of deterministic and non-deterministic languages. For example, a succinct argument for 3SAT with few verifier queries implies an IOP with good parameters, which in turn implies a fast algorithm for 3SAT that contradicts the Exponential-Time Hypothesis.

We additionally present results that shed light on the necessity of several features of probabilistic proofs that are typically used to construct succinct arguments, such as holography and state restoration soundness. Our results collectively provide an explanation for "why" known constructions of succinct arguments have a certain structure.

Keywords: Succinct arguments · Interactive oracle proofs

1 Introduction

A succinct argument is a cryptographic proof system for deterministic and non-deterministic languages, whose communication complexity is "succinct" in the sense that it is sublinear in the time to decide the language (for deterministic languages) or witness size (for non-deterministic languages). In the last decade,

© International Association for Cryptologic Research 2020
R. Pass and K. Pietrzak (Eds.): TCC 2020, LNCS 12551, pp. 47–76, 2020.
https://doi.org/10.1007/978-3-030-64378-2_3

succinct arguments have drawn the attention of researchers from multiple communities, being a fundamental cryptographic primitive that has found applications in the real world.

A central goal in the study of succinct arguments is improving their efficiency. An important complexity measure is argument size, which is the number of bits sent from the prover to the verifier. Achieving small argument size is crucial, e.g., in applications where non-interactive succinct arguments are broadcast in a peer-to-peer network and redundantly stored at every node (as in [Ben+14]). Other important complexity measures include the running time of the prover and the running time of the verifier—this latter is the complexity measure that we study in this paper.

There are applications where the running time of the verifier is the main bottleneck and call for verifiers that are *extremely lightweight*. These applications include obfuscating the verifier [Bon+17], or recursive constructions where an outer succinct argument proves that the verifier of an inner succinct argument has accepted [Val08, Bit+13]. In these cases, the circuit (or code) representing the verifier's computation is used in a white-box manner and the verifier's running time dominates the complexity of the final scheme. For instance, in the second example, the running time of the outer prover mainly depends on the running time of the inner verifier.

Our goal is to establish lower bounds on the running time of a succinct argument's verifier.

We focus on the random oracle model. We deliberately restrict our attention to studying succinct arguments that are secure in the *random oracle model* (ROM). This is because the ROM is an elegant information-theoretic model within which we could hope to precisely understand the structure of arbitrary succinct arguments, and prove lower bounds on specific efficiency measures.

Moreover, the ROM supports several well-known constructions of succinct arguments that can be heuristically instantiated via lightweight cryptographic hash functions, are plausibly post-quantum secure [CMS19], and have led to realizations that are useful in practice. These constructions include the Fiat–Shamir transformation [FS86], which applies to public-coin interactive proofs (IPs); the Micali transformation [Mic00], which applies to probabilistically checkable proofs (PCPs); and the BCS transformation [BCS16], which applies to public-coin interactive oracle proofs (IOPs).

How small can verifier query complexity be? As mentioned earlier, the running time of the verifier is a crucial efficiency measure in applications of succinct arguments. While in the ROM each query is considered a constant-time operation, each query actually becomes expensive when the random oracle is heuristically instantiated via a cryptographic hash function. Each query becomes a sub-computation involving very many gates for evaluating the cryptographic hash function, which can dominate the verifier's running time. This, for example, is the case in the recursive construction in [COS20]. In this paper, we ask: how small can the query complexity of a verifier be?

We make our question precise via the notion of bits of security. The soundness error ϵ of a succinct argument in the ROM is a function of several parameters: the instance size, the output size of the random oracle, and the number of queries by the cheating prover to the random oracle. Then we say that a succinct argument provides s *bits of security* if the soundness error ϵ is at most 2^{-s} for every instance size up to 2^s, every prover query complexity up to 2^s, and when the output size of the random oracle is $\Theta(s)$. (See Sect. 3.3 for relevant definitions.)

Known constructions of succinct arguments achieve verifier query complexities that are $\Omega(s)$. This is true even if one were to rely on conjectured "holy grail" probabilistic proofs within these constructions. In particular, no approach is known that could achieve a verifier that makes $o(s)$ queries to the oracle (which would be very desirable).

We are interested in understanding whether small verifier query complexity is possible:

> Do there exist succinct arguments with s bits of security and verifier query complexity $\ll s$?

1.1 Our Contributions

In this paper we contribute new insights into the structure of succinct arguments in the ROM, which we then use to obtain evidence that the answer to the above question is negative. First we prove that IOPs are an inherent ingredient of *any* succinct argument in the ROM. Then we prove limitations of the obtained IOPs, thereby obtaining lower bounds on the number of queries to the random oracle by the verifier in the starting succinct argument. The limitations on IOPs that we prove are rather broad (even when applied to the case of a PCP), and may be of independent interest.

Here we remind the reader that an *interactive oracle proof* (IOP) [BCS16, RRR16] is a proof system that combines the notions of interactive proofs (IP) and probabilistically-checkable proofs (PCPs). Namely, it is an interactive proof where the verifier is granted *oracle access* to the messages sent by the prover and so can probabilistically query them. As opposed to PCPs, IOPs leverage the multiple rounds of communication, which gives them many efficiency improvements in terms of proof size and the running time of the prover. As shown in [BCS16], IOPs with suitable soundness properties can be compiled into non-interactive succinct arguments in the ROM. This, along with the concrete efficiency of IOPs, makes them a central component of many succinct arguments today.

1.1.1 IOPs are Necessary for Succinctness

We prove that IOPs are inherent to succinct arguments in the ROM in a precise sense: *any* succinct argument in the ROM can be generically transformed into an IOP whose query complexity depends on the "succinctness" of the argument. Namely, if the argument prover sends as bits to the argument verifier, then the IOP verifier makes as queries to proof strings sent by the IOP prover.

Moreover, and less intuitively, the IOP verifier makes $O(\mathsf{vq} \cdot \mathsf{a})$ extra queries, where vq is the number of queries made by the argument verifier to the random oracle and a is the number of adaptive rounds of queries by the (honest) argument prover to the random oracle (see Sect. 3.1 for more on adaptivity). The adaptivity parameter a plays a key role in our result, and it is small in all known schemes. (E.g., $\mathsf{a} = O(\log n)$ in succinct arguments obtained via the Micali transformation [Mic00].)

Theorem 1 (informal). *There is an efficient transformation* $\mathbb{T}$ *that satisfies the following. Suppose that* ARG *is a size-*as *argument in the ROM for a language* L *where the honest prover performs* pq *queries in* a *rounds and the verifier performs* vq *queries. Then* IOP $:= \mathbb{T}(\mathsf{ARG})$ *is an IOP for* L *with proof length* $O(\mathsf{pq} + \mathsf{as})$ *and query complexity* $O(\mathsf{as} + \mathsf{vq} \cdot \mathsf{a})$. *Other aspects of* IOP *(such as public coins, soundness, time and space complexities) are essentially the same as in* ARG.

Our result provides a way to construct an IOP by "reverse engineering" an arbitrary succinct argument, leading to a standalone compelling message: succinct arguments in the ROM are "hard to construct" because they must contain non-trivial information-theoretic objects. This holds *regardless* of the complexity of the language proved by the succinct argument. For example, IOPs are inherent even to succinct arguments for deterministic computations (where the primary efficiency goal is an argument verifier that is faster than directly deciding the language). Our necessity result is complementary to a result of Rothblum and Vadhan [RV09], which showed the necessity of PCPs for succinct arguments obtained via blackbox reductions to falsifiable assumptions (see Sect. 1.2). Their result does not apply for succinct arguments in the random oracle model.

In this paper, the necessity of IOPs for succinct arguments in the ROM is more than a compelling message. We demonstrate that the necessity of IOPs is a useful step towards establishing barriers on succinct arguments, because thanks to Theorem 1 we have reduced this problem to establishing barriers on IOPs. Our second main contribution concerns this latter task (see below).

We sketch the ideas behind Theorem 1 in Sect. 2.1; the formal statement of the theorem, which gives a precise accounting of many more parameters, is given and proved in Sect. 4.

1.1.2   From IOPs to Algorithms

We show that IOPs with good parameters (small soundness error relative to query complexity) can be translated to fast algorithms with small space complexity. This translation should be viewed as a tool to establish *barriers* on IOPs: if the language proved by the IOP is hard then the corresponding algorithm may (conjecturally) not exist, contradicting the existence of the IOP to begin with.

Theorem 2 (informal). *Suppose that a language* L *has a public-coin IOP with soundness error* ε, *round complexity* k, *proof length* $\mathsf{l} = \mathrm{poly}(n)$ *over an alphabet* Σ, *query complexity* q, *and verifier space complexity* vs. *If* $\varepsilon = o(2^{-\mathsf{q} \cdot \log \mathsf{l}})$ *then,* *the language L can be decided by a probabilistic algorithm that runs in time exponential in $\widetilde{O}\left(\mathsf{q}\cdot(\log|\varSigma|+\mathsf{k})\right)$ and that runs in space $\widetilde{O}\left(\mathsf{vs}\cdot\mathsf{q}^2\cdot(\log|\varSigma|+\mathsf{k})^2\right)$.*

We sketch the ideas behind Theorem 2 in Sect. 2.2; the formal statement is proved in Sect. 5.

Our result in fact provides a broad generalization of folklore results that impose barriers on IPs and PCPs (both are special cases of IOPs) as we discuss in Sect. 1.2. In particular, the folklore results restrict the verifier and alphabet size, while we do not. For example, Theorem 2 rules out a broader class of PCPs for the "small-query high-soundness" regime than what was previously known: under the (randomized) Exponential-Time Hypothesis (rETH),[1] if the number of queries is constant then the best possible soundness error is $1/\mathrm{poly}(n)$, as long as $\log|\varSigma| \ll n$ (otherwise a trivial PCP exists). We deduce this from the corollary obtained by setting $\mathsf{k}:=1$ in Theorem 2.

Corollary 1 (informal). *Suppose that NP has a PCP with perfect completeness and soundness error ε, and where the verifier tosses r random coins, makes q queries into a proof of length $\mathsf{l} = \mathrm{poly}(n)$ over an alphabet $\varSigma$. Under the rETH assumption, if $\widetilde{O}(\mathsf{q}\log|\varSigma|) = o(n)$, then $\varepsilon \geq 2^{-\mathsf{q}\cdot\log\mathsf{l}}$.*

This yields limitations for PCPs, e.g., in the "cryptographic regime": constant-query PCPs with negligible soundness cannot have polynomial size, even over an exponentially-large alphabet.

1.1.3   Barriers for Succinct Arguments

We now discuss our barriers for succinct arguments, which state that under standard complexity assumptions there are no succinct arguments where the verifier makes a small number of queries to the random oracle, and the honest prover has a small adaptivity parameter a.

Suppose that 3SAT has a succinct argument that provides s bits of security and has argument size as $\ll n$, where n is the number of variables in the 3SAT formula. Suppose that the argument prover makes a adaptive rounds of queries to the random oracle, and the argument verifier makes vq queries to the random oracle. If $\mathsf{vq}\cdot\mathsf{a} \ll s$ then by Theorem 1 we get an IOP with similar efficiency parameters, and with query complexity roughly $o(s)$. Then by Theorem 2 we get an algorithm for 3SAT that runs in time $2^{o(n)}$, contradicting the randomized Exponential Time Hypothesis.

Theorem 3 (informal). *Suppose that 3SAT has a public-coin succinct argument that provides s bits of security and has argument size as $\ll n$, where the prover makes a adaptive rounds of queries to the random oracle and the verifier makes vq queries to the random oracle. If $\mathsf{vq}\cdot\mathsf{a} \ll s$ then rETH is false.*

---

[1] The *randomized Exponential Time Hypothesis* states that there exist $\epsilon > 0$ and $c > 1$ such that 3SAT on n variables and with $c\cdot n$ clauses cannot be solved by probabilistic algorithms that run in time $2^{\epsilon\cdot n}$ [Del+14].

The theorem applies to all constructions, but does not completely answer our motivating question because the theorem has a dependency on the adaptivity parameter a. The question of whether this dependency can be removed remains a challenging open problem. If it turns out that it cannot be removed, then our result suggests a path to construct succinct arguments with more efficient verifiers: the standard Merkle trees (which lead to very small adaptivity) must be replaced with a deeper structure that exploits long adaptive paths of queries. This would be a very exciting development, departing from all paradigms for succinct arguments known to date!

Note that the requirement as $\ll n$ is necessary as if as $= n$ then a trivial argument system, where the prover sends the full satisfying assignment, has no soundness error with no random oracle calls.

We sketch how to derive our barriers in Sect. 2.3; formal statements can be found in Sect. 6, in a more general form that separately considers the case of arbitrary nondeterministic languages (of which 3SAT is an example) and the case of arbitrary deterministic languages.

1.1.4   Additional Applications and Extensions

Our transformation from succinct arguments to IOPs (Sect. 1.1.1) leads to extensions that provide valuable insights into succinct arguments, as we discuss below.

Extension 1: preprocessing implies holography. We now consider succinct arguments in the ROM that have an additional useful feature, known as *preprocessing*. This means that in an offline phase one can produce a short summary for a given circuit and then, in an online phase, one may use this short summary to verify the satisfiability of the circuit with different partial assignments to its inputs.[2] The online phase now can be sublinear in the circuit size *even for arbitrary circuits*.

The BCS transformation extends to obtain preprocessing SNARGs from holographic IOPs [COS20], following a connection between preprocessing and holography introduced in [Chi+20]. Therefore, in light of Theorem 1, it is natural to ask: *do all preprocessing SNARGs in the random oracle model arise from holographic IOPs?* Even if SNARGs "hide" IOPs inside them (due to our result), there may be other approaches to preprocessing beyond holography, at least in principle.

We show that preprocessing *does* arise from holography. We extend the ideas underlying our Theorem 1 to obtain a transformation that given a preprocessing SNARG in the random oracle model outputs a holographic IOP with related complexity measures. This reverse direction strengthens the connection between preprocessing and holography established in [COS20, Chi+20].

Lemma 1. *There is an efficient transformation* $\mathbb{T}$ *that satisfies the following. Suppose that* ARG *is a size-*as **preprocessing** *non-interactive argument in the*

---

[2] Here we focus on succinct arguments for circuit satisfiability for simplicity of exposition. The preprocessing property can be stated more generally, specifically for ternary relations, and we do so in the rest of this paper.

ROM *for an* **indexed** *relation R where the honest prover performs* pq *queries in* a *rounds, the verifier performs* vq *queries, and the indexer outputs a key of size* ivk. *Then* IOP := $\mathbb{T}$(ARG) *is a* **holographic** *IOP for R with proof length* $O(\text{pq} + \text{as})$ *and query complexity* $O(\text{ivk} + \text{as} + \text{vq} \cdot \text{a})$. *Other aspects of* IOP *(such as public coins, soundness, time and space complexities) are essentially the same as in* ARG.

Extension 2: on state restoration soundness. A careful reader may have noticed that our discussion so far did not touch upon a technical, yet important, aspect. Namely, observe that if we applied the transformation in Theorem 1 to a SNARG in the ROM then we would obtain a corresponding public-coin IOP. However, given what we said so far, we are *not* guaranteed that we can compile this IOP back into a SNARG! Indeed, the known approach for constructing SNARGs from IOPs requires the IOP to satisfy a stronger notion of soundness called state restoration soundness [BCS16]. So we should ask: does the IOP output by Theorem 1 satisfy this stronger notion?

We prove that the transformation in Theorem 1 yields an IOP with state-restoration soundness as long as the SNARG had a stronger notion of soundness that we introduce and call *salted soundness*. Informally, this notion allows a cheating SNARG prover to request the random oracle to re-sample the answer for a chosen query (in case the prover did not "like" the prior answer).

Lemma 2 (informal). *The transformation* $\mathbb{T}$ *in Theorem 1 satisfies this additional property: if* ARG *is a SNARG with salted soundness error* $\epsilon_s(t)$ *for query budget t and the prover runs in* a *adaptive rounds then* IOP := $\mathbb{T}$(ARG) *is a public-coin IOP with state restoration soundness error* $\epsilon_s(t \cdot \mathsf{m})$.

This lemma resolves the issue described above because the SNARGs constructed from (state-restoration sound) IOPs in [BCS16] do indeed satisfy the stronger notion of salted soundness (Fig. 1).

1.2   Related Work

Known limitations on IPs and PCPs. Our Theorem 2 implies that IOPs with good parameters can be translated into good algorithms. Below we summarize known facts that impose limitations on restrictions of the IOP model: interactive proofs (IPs) and probabilistically checkable proofs (PCPs).

- **IPs.** The following fact follows from proof techniques in [GH98] (see also [RRR16, Remark 5.1]).

Folklore 1. *If a language L has a public-coin IP where the communication and verifier space complexity are bounded by c, then L can be decided by an algorithm running in space* $O(c)$.

Since it is believed that DTIME$[T] \not\subseteq$ SPACE$[o(T)]$, the above lemma tells us that we should not expect every language in DTIME$[T]$ to have a non-trivial public-coin interactive proof.

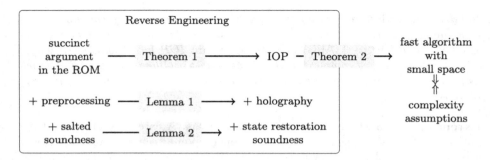

Fig. 1. Summary of our results. The left part shows results related to "reverse engineering" succinct arguments, which derive IOPs with certain properties from succinct arguments with certain properties. The right part depicts the fact that IOPs with good enough parameters lead to algorithms that, for hard enough languages, contradict plausible complexity assumptions.

Both Folklore 1 and our Theorem 2 lead to an algorithm with small space, and the main difference is that our theorem is a statement about IOPs rather than IPs. We note, however, that within the proof of our theorem we prove a lemma (Lemma 3) that can be viewed as a refinement of Folklore 1 as it applies *even when the verifier-to-prover communication is large.*

– **PCPs.** The following fact lower bounds a PCP's soundness error.

Folklore 2. *Suppose that* NP *has a PCP with perfect completeness and soundness error ε, and where the verifier tosses* r *random coins and makes* q *queries into a proof of length* l *over an alphabet Σ. Then the following holds:*

1. *$\varepsilon \geq 2^{-r}$; and*
2. *Under the ETH assumption, if* $r = o(n)$ *and* $q \log |\Sigma| = o(n)$ *then* $\varepsilon \geq 2^{-q \cdot \log |\Sigma|}$.*

In order to understand the implications of the above limitation, we find it helpful to recall a well-known conjecture about possible PCP constructions. The *Sliding Scale Conjecture* states that, for every $\varepsilon \in [1/\text{poly}(n), 1]$, every language in NP has a PCP with perfect completeness and soundness error ε, and where the verifier uses $O(\log n)$ random bits and makes $O(1)$ queries into a proof over an alphabet Σ of size $\text{poly}(1/\varepsilon)$. The conjecture is tight in the sense that we cannot ask for better soundness with the same parameters.

Yet if we allow the verifier to use $\omega(\log n)$ random bits or if $\log |\Sigma| = \omega(\log n)$ then Folklore 2 does not rule out PCPs with soundness error $1/n^{\omega(1)}$. Our Corollary 1 amends this by establishing that one cannot get soundness error better than $1/\text{poly}(n)$ *even if the verifier uses an arbitrary number of random bits and the alphabet is arbitrarily large.*

Probabilistic proofs in succinct arguments. Essentially all known constructions of succinct arguments use some form of probabilistic proof as an ingredient (possibly among other ingredients). Prior to this work, the only known formal statement seeking to explain this phenomenon is a result by Rothblum and Vadhan [RV09] stating that succinct arguments proved secure via a black-box reduction to a falsifiable assumption must "contain" a PCP. This is formalized via a transformation that, given such a succinct argument, outputs a PCP with size and query complexity related to the succinctness of the argument system (and also certain aspects of the security reduction).

Our Theorem 1 is complementary to the result in [RV09], in that we consider succinct arguments that are unconditionally secure in the random oracle model (as opposed to computationally secure in the standard model). Our techniques are also different, in that the technical challenge is to design an efficient sub-protocol to simulate a random oracle (as opposed to detecting if the adversary has "broken cryptography" by using the falsifiability of the cryptographic assumption).

2   Techniques

2.1   IOPs are Necessary for Succinctness

We describe the main ideas behind Theorem 1, which states that any succinct argument in the ROM implies an IOP with related parameters (which in particular demonstrates that IOPs are necessary for succinctness in the ROM). Let P and V be the prover and verifier of an arbitrary succinct argument for a language L (e.g., 3SAT). We seek to "remove" the random oracle from the succinct argument by simulating it via an interactive sub-protocol and ending with an IOP for the same language L. We assume, without loss of generality, that P and V each never query the same element more than once.[3]

Below, we first describe a straightforward approach, then explain problems and challenges on the approach, and finally explain how we overcome the challenges to obtain our result.

A straightforward approach. We can construct an IP with a new prover **P** and a new verifier **V** that respectively simulate the argument prover P and argument verifier V. In addition, we task the IP verifier **V** to simulate the random oracle for *both* P and V, as we explain.

- Whenever the argument prover P wants to query the oracle at an element x, the IP prover **P** forwards the query x to the IP verifier **V**, who replies with a truly random string y that plays the role of the output of the random oracle on x.
- Whenever the argument verifier V queries x, then the IP verifier **V** checks if x had appeared in the transcript as one of the queries and returns the given answer to V if so, or otherwise it feeds V with a truly random value.

---

[3] We can always modify the prover to store previous query answers, so that no query is performed twice. This might increase the space complexity of the prover, but it does not affect the results in this paper.

There is a delicate, yet crucial, issue that needs to be taken care of. A cheating IP prover might query x twice (or more) to get two possible answers for the same query, which might affect the soundness of the IP (and indeed there are succinct arguments where this issue has devastating consequences on the soundness of the IP). Thus, when simulating a verifier query x, the IP verifier $\mathbf{V}$ must assert that x was not issued twice during the protocol (and otherwise reject).

The approach above perfectly removes the random oracle from the succinct argument and yields an IP with similar completeness and soundness. *Henceforth we view the IP constructed above as an IOP whose verifier reads the entire transcript (queries all locations of the exchanged messages).*

The problem. The problem with the IOP described above is its parameters. The argument prover P might perform many queries, and in particular more than the witness size (as is the case in known constructions of succinct arguments). This dominates many parameters of the IOP, including the number of rounds, the number of bits read by the verifier, and its running time—and also yields a trivial IOP for the language. Note that proof length (the number of bits sent by $\mathbf{P}$) is fine, as we do not expect all languages in NP to have an IOP with small proof length, but rather only expect the IOP verifier to read a small number of locations from the prover messages.

Achieving small round complexity. We crucially exploit a parameter of the argument prover P not discussed thus far, namely, its *adaptivity*. We say that P has adaptivity a if it performs a rounds of queries to the random oracle and in each round submits a (possibly long) list of queries and receives corresponding answers. In known constructions, a is very small (e.g., $O(\log n)$). If P has adaptivity a, then the number of rounds in the constructed IOP can be easily reduced to $O(a)$, where the IOP prover $\mathbf{P}$ sends the verifier a list of queries $x_1, \ldots, x_{\mathsf{m}}$, and the IOP verifier $\mathbf{V}$ replies with a list of answers $y_1, \ldots, y_{\mathsf{m}}$, while applying the same logic as before. This reduces the number of rounds of the IOP, but so far has no effect on the number of queries performed by the IOP verifier $\mathbf{V}$, which remains as large as the number of queries performed by the argument prover P.

Perfect hash functions with locality. Our main goal now is to reduce the number of bits read by the IOP verifier $\mathbf{V}$. Consider a query x performed by the argument verifier V. The IOP verifier $\mathbf{V}$ needs to read the transcript to see if the query x was issued and, if so, check that it was issued only once. A simple way to find x in the transcript is to have the IOP prover $\mathbf{P}$ assist with locating x. That is, $\mathbf{P}$ points to the exact location in the transcript for where x was issued. Then $\mathbf{V}$ reads this specific location in the transcript and is assured that x was queried and at the same time reads the corresponding response y. However, how can $\mathbf{V}$ check that x was not issued twice? And how can $\mathbf{P}$ give a proof that the rest of the transcript does *not* contain x?

To deal with these challenges, we use *perfect hash functions*. These are a family of functions $\mathcal{H} = \{h \colon U \to [O(m)]\}$ such that for any S of size m there exists a function $h \in \mathcal{H}$ that is one-to-one on S. Fixing such a family $\mathcal{H}$, we let the IOP prover **P** provide with each set of queries (for each round), a perfect hash function h for the set X of submitted queries and send an array of length $O(m)$ such that element $x \in X$ resides in the cell at index $h(x)$. This way, instead of the IOP verifier **V** scanning (and reading) all prover messages, it suffices for **V** to read the description of h and then query the cell $h(x)$ to determine if x is in the array.

Also, the IOP verifier **V** writes the response y at the same location $h(x)$ in a dedicated array of random values, $Y[h(x)]$. This way, **V** can be convinced that x was *not* issued at a specific round by looking at a single cell $h(x)$ for the array given by **P** at that round. Thus, the query complexity of **V** for simulating a single query of V is mainly determined by the number of rounds of the protocol, which is the rather small value a (the adaptivity of the honest argument prover P). Note that while the entire array Y is sent to the prover, the verifier needs to read only a single location from Y (we elaborate on this further below).

The locality property. Turning the above ideas into our transformation runs into several delicate issues that need to be handled to achieve soundness and good parameters. One issue is that the description of h is, in fact, too large for the verifier to read in its entirety (it is larger than the set itself). However, we observe that **V** need not read the entire function description, but only the parts required for evaluating h at x.

Therefore, we additionally require the perfect hash family to have a *locality property* where, in order to evaluate the hash function h on a single element x, only a relatively small number of bits are required to be read from the description of h. Luckily, several known constructions have this locality property and, specifically, we use the construction of Fredman, Komlós, and Szemerédi [FKS84]. An overview of the [FKS84] construction, its locality property, and a bound on the number of bits required to read are given in Sect. 4.1.

There are additional challenges in realizing the above plan. For example, in terms of soundness, note that a cheating prover might submit a set X and choose a function h that is not perfect for X and contains collision—this could potentially harm soundness. We deal with this and other issues on the way to proving our transformation from succinct arguments to IOPs.

The resulting IOP. This results in an IOP with the following parameters. If the prover had a rounds of adaptivity, then the IOP has $a + 1$ rounds, where the first a rounds are used to simulate the random oracle for the prover, and the last round is dedicated to sending the final output of the prover. The proof length of the IOP (i.e., the total communication of the protocol) is $O(\mathsf{as} + \mathsf{pq})$ symbols where each symbol contains an output of the random oracle. Indeed, for each of the pq queries we an additional $O(1)$ symbols, and for the last round we send the final argument which is as bits (and can be read as a single symbol).

The query complexity is $O(\mathsf{as} + \mathsf{vq} \cdot \mathsf{a})$ as for each of the vq queries of the prover, the verifier needs to scan all a rounds, and performs $O(1)$ queries in each. Then, it reads last prover message entirely which is as bits (which we can view as 1 large symbol of as bits).

The resulting IOP has large communication of randomness from the verifier to the prover. However, the verifier, in order to decide whether to accepts, has to read only a small number of locations, and these are included in the count of the query complexity. Our definition for IOP allows the verifier to have only oracle access to its own randomness and thus the query complexity includes both locations read from the proof and from the randomness. We stress that the compiler of [BCS16] works even for this more general definition of IOP. Therefore, we do not expect to get an IOP with small verifier-to-prover communication as it could be that the succinct argument was constructed from an IOP with large communication (see Sect. 3.4 for the precise definition of IOP and a further discussion on this topic).

See Sect. 4 for further details of the proof.

2.2   Algorithms for IOPs

We describe the main ideas behind Theorem 2, which states that IOPs with good parameters can be translated to fast algorithms with small space complexity. We proceed in two steps.

- *Step 1.* We prove that any IOP can be simulated by an IP (interactive proof) with small prover-to-verifier communication, at the cost of a (large) completeness error that depends on how well one can guess all of the IOP verifier's query locations (the "query entropy" of the IOP).
- *Step 2.* We prove a refinement of a result of Goldreich and Håstad [GH98] that states that languages with public-coin IPs with small prover-to-verifier communication can be decided via fast probabilistic algorithms with small space complexity.

We elaborate on each of these steps in turn below.

Step 1: IOP to laconic IP (Lemma 2 in Lemma 5.1). We prove that any IOP with good enough soundness relative to its *query entropy* can be translated to a laconic IP (an IP with small prover-to-verifier communication). Query entropy is related to the probability of guessing in advance all locations that the IOP verifier will read across the proof strings sent by the IOP prover (see Definition 5 for how query entropy is formally defined). The translation ensures that if the IOP is public coin (as indeed it is in our case) then the IP is also public coin. Moreover, at the cost of an additional completeness error, the IP verifier can be modified so that it makes a single pass on its (large) randomness tape and runs in small space. (This small-space property will be useful later on for establishing barriers on succinct arguments for deterministic languages; see Sect. 2.3.)

We construct the IP as follows. First, the IP prover guesses the locations that the IOP verifier will read. The probability of guessing all locations correctly is 2^{-h}, where h is the query entropy. Assuming a correct guess, the IP prover sends the description of these locations together with corresponding values. If the IOP verifier makes q queries across a proof of length l over an alphabet Σ, then the IP prover sends $q \cdot \log l + q \cdot \log |\Sigma|$ bits. The soundness of the protocol remains the same. What changes is the completeness error, which drastically increases since guessing all locations has a small probability. However, if the soundness error is small enough and as long as there is some difference between completeness and soundness, we get a non-trivial IP. In particular, if the IOP has soundness error $\varepsilon < 2^{-h}$ then the resulting IP has soundness error ε, completeness error $1 - 2^{-h}$, and prover communication $q \cdot \log l + q \cdot \log |\Sigma|$ as mentioned above.

Finally, we show that the IP can be modified (at the expense of the completeness error) to make the IP verifier perform a *single pass* over its randomness tape. Note that the IOP verifier might read the randomness in an arbitrary manner, which would make the IP verifier read it in a similar one. Here, we exploit the fact that the IOP verifier had only *oracle access* to its own random tape, and performed only a limited number of queries. We leverage this and let the IP verifier guess these locations in advance. Then, the verifier reads the randomness tape and stores only the locations it guessed. From here on, the verifier will use only the randomness stored explicitly. Assuming that it guessed correctly, it uses these locations to simulate random access for the IOP verifier. This again adds a large completeness error. However, if the soundness error is small enough, then again the resulting IP is non-trivial and, as discussed above, suffices for our purposes.

Step 2: IP to algorithm (see Lemma 3 in Lemma 5.2). Goldreich and Håstad [GH98] showed that languages with public-coin IPs with small prover-to-verifier communication can be decided via fast probabilistic algorithms. In particular, if L has a public-coin IP where, for an instance of length n, the prover-to-verifier communication is bounded by $c(n)$ and the number of rounds is bounded by $k(n)$ then it holds that

$$L \in \text{BPTIME} \left[2^{O(c(n)+k(n)\cdot \log k(n))} \cdot \text{poly}(n) \right].$$

Their result is shown only for IPs with constant completeness and soundness errors, which is not the case for the IP constructed in Step 1. We stress that the IP constructed Step 1 can be amplified via standard repetition to reach the setting of constant completeness and soundness errors, doing so would increase communication and render the IP not laconic, and hence not useful for us in this paper. Instead, we show a refinement of [GH98] that is suitable to work in the "large-error" regime of IP parameters. Details follow.

We explicitly show the dependency in the completeness and soundness errors, allowing the theorem to apply to IPs with large completeness errors (which we need). This refinement is technical, where we follow the original proof blueprint of [GH98]. We explicitly track the completeness and soundness errors rather than hiding them as constants in the Big-O notation, and adjust other parameters as a function of the completeness and soundness error values. The result is a moderately more involved formula for the running time of the final algorithm, which has these parameters in addition to the communication complexity and the number of rounds.

In particular, we get that if a language L has a public-coin IP with completeness error α, soundness error β, round complexity k, and prover-to-verifier communication c, then it holds that

$$L \in \mathrm{BPTIME}\left[2^{O\left(c(n)+k(n)\cdot\log\frac{k(n)}{1-\alpha(n)-\beta(n)}\right)} \cdot \mathrm{poly}(n)\right].$$

For example, plugging in the IP obtained from Step 1, while assuming that $\varepsilon = o(2^{-q\cdot\log l})$ (and hiding some terms under the $\widetilde{O}$ notation) we get the expression from Theorem 2:

$$L \in \mathrm{BPTIME}\left[2^{\widetilde{O}(q\cdot(\log|\Sigma|+k))}\right].$$

Additionally, we show that if the verifier of the IP reads its randomness *in a single pass*, then the same algorithm can be implemented in small space (the original implementation of [GH98] used space proportional to its running time). Looking ahead, this property is used to achieve the barrier for deterministic languages. We sketch the main idea behind the new algorithm.

The algorithm's main goal is to compute the value of a tree A_x corresponding to (an approximation of) the interaction in the IP protocol. Each node in the tree corresponds to a certain partial transcript of the IP, and computing the value of the tree suffices to decide the language. The straightforward way to compute the value is to compute the value of each node in the tree from the leaves up to the root. This would require space proportional to the size of A_x. Yet, in order to compute the value of the tree it would suffice to store only $\log|A_x|$ values at a time, as for any subtree it suffices to store the value of its root.

There is, however, a major issue with this approach. Namely, the space required to store even a single value of the tree is too large, as writing the location of a node in the tree includes the description of the randomness of the verifier in this partial transcript, which is too large to store explicitly. Here we exploit the fact that the verifier uses a single pass to read its randomness, and show how to compress the description of a node in the tree using the internal memory and state of the verifier, given this partial transcript. This allows us to implicitly store nodes values with small memory. Since it suffices to store only $\log|A_x|$ values at a time we get an algorithm with small memory.

This results in the following conclusion: if the space complexity of the IP verifier is vs when reading its randomness random tape in a single pass then

$$L \in \mathrm{SPACE}\left[O\left(d\cdot(vs+d)\right)\right],$$

where $d = c(n) + k(n)\cdot\log\frac{k(n)}{1-\alpha(n)-\beta(n)}$. Once again, plugging in the IP obtained from Step 1, we get the other expression from Theorem 2:

$$L \in \mathrm{SPACE}\left[\widetilde{O}\left(vs\cdot q^2\cdot(\log|\Sigma|+k)^2\right)\right].$$

2.3   Barriers for Succinct Arguments

Our results provide a methodology for obtaining barriers on succinct arguments for different languages, based on complexity assumptions for the language. We describe this blueprint and give two examples, one for non-deterministic languages and one for deterministic languages, and suggest that additional barriers could be achieved is a similar manner.

This methodology works as follows. Let L be the language for which a barrier is desired, and suppose that one proves (or conjectures) some hardness property about the language L. Now assume that there exists a succinct argument for L with certain efficiency parameters such as soundness, query complexity, prover adaptivity, and so on. First apply Theorem 1 to obtain an IOP with parameters related to the succinct argument, and then apply Theorem 2 to obtain an efficient algorithm for L. If the efficient algorithm violates the hardness of L, then one must conclude that the assumed succinct argument for L does not exist.

Barriers for 3SAT. We apply the above methodology to obtain barriers for succinct arguments for NP based on the Exponential-Time Hypothesis. Suppose that 3SAT over n variables has a succinct argument that provides s bits of security and has argument size $\mathsf{as} \ll n$ (of course, if $\mathsf{as} = n$ then the scheme is trivial). Suppose also that the argument prover makes a adaptive rounds of queries to the random oracle, and the argument verifier makes vq queries to the random oracle.

We apply Theorem 1 to the argument scheme to get a related IOP. Since the argument scheme provides s bits of security, then for any instance $\mathsf{x} \leq 2^s$ and query bound $t \leq 2^s$ and for oracle output size $\lambda = O(s)$ we get that the resulting IOP has soundness $\varepsilon(\mathsf{x}, t, \lambda) \leq 2^{-s}$. Moreover, the verifier reads $O(\mathsf{vq} \cdot \mathsf{a})$ symbols from the transcript, the alphabet size is $|\Sigma| = 2^\lambda$, the number of rounds is $O(\mathsf{a})$, and the proof length is $O(\mathsf{as} + \mathsf{pq})$, which is best to think as $\mathrm{poly}(n)$ for simplicity.

What is important to note here is that if $\mathsf{vq} \cdot \mathsf{a} \ll s$ then the query entropy of the IOP is $2^{-\mathsf{h}} = \mathsf{l}^{-\mathsf{vq} \cdot \mathsf{a}} = \omega(2^{-s})$ and thus $\varepsilon = o(2^{-\mathsf{h}})$. This means that we can apply Step 1 above to get an IP for 3SAT where the prover-to-verifier communication is

$$c(n) = \mathsf{q} \cdot \log \mathsf{l} + \mathsf{q} \cdot \log|\Sigma| = \mathsf{q} \cdot \log n + \mathsf{q} \cdot s = O(s^2),$$

and the difference between the completeness and soundness error is $1 - \alpha(n) - \beta(n) = o(s)$. Then, using Step 2, we get a (randomized) algorithm for 3SAT that runs in time $2^{\tilde{O}(\mathsf{q} \cdot (\log|\Sigma| + \mathsf{k})} = 2^{o(s)} = 2^{o(n)}$, as long as $s^2 \ll n$. This contradicts the (randomized) Exponential Time Hypothesis. Note that the condition that $s^2 \ll n$ is relatively mild, as s is a lower bound for the size of the argument scheme, and the main objective of a succinct argument is to have argument size much smaller than the trivial n bits of communication (sending the satisfying assignment).

The above reasoning can be generalized to any non-deterministic language in NTIME$[T]$, as we work out in detail in Sect. 6.1.

Barriers for DTIME[T]. As a second example of our methodology, we show barriers for deterministic languages. Here, we exploit the fact that the final algorithm obtained in Step 2 has small *space* complexity. Suppose that there is a succinct argument as above for languages in DTIME[T], for some time bound T, with argument size as $\ll T$. Assume that DTIME[T] $\not\subseteq$ SPACE[$o(T)$], a rather unlikely inclusion (which is currently outside of known techniques to either prove or disprove).

As before, if vq $\cdot$ a $\ll s$ then by Theorem 1 we get an IOP with similar efficiency parameters, and with query complexity vq $\cdot$ a $\ll s$. Additionally, if the argument's verifier space complexity is sv $\ll T$ (which is naturally the case with a non-trivial argument scheme) then the verifier of the obtained IOP can be implemented with $O(\mathsf{sv})$ space.

Similar to the analysis we did in the non-deterministic case, here we apply Theorem 2 and get an algorithm for L that runs in space

$$\widetilde{O}(\mathsf{sv} \cdot \mathsf{q}^2 \cdot (\log |\Sigma| + \mathsf{k})^2) = \widetilde{O}(s^4) = o(T),$$

as long as $s^4 \ll T$ (again, a relatively mild condition). This implies that

$$\text{DTIME}[T] \subseteq \text{SPACE}[o(T)],$$

which contradicts the initial conjectured hardness.

Is the dependency on a inherent? Our methodology gives meaningful barriers provided that the adaptivity of the honest prover, a, is somewhat small, e.g., sublinear in the security parameter s. While this is indeed the case for all known constructions, it is not clear if a succinct argument could benefit from large adaptivity. We can thus draw the following conclusion. One possibility is that our results could be improved to eliminate the dependency on a, for example by improving the transformation to IOP to be more efficient and contain queries from several adaptivity rounds to be in the same round of the IOP. Another possibility is that there exist succinct arguments with small verifier query complexity and large prover adaptivity. This latter possibility would be a quite surprising and exciting development, which, in particular, would depart from all paradigms for succinct arguments known to date.

2.4   Additional Results and Applications

Extension 1: preprocessing implies holography. Our Lemma 1 states that we can transform any *preprocessing* succinct argument into a corresponding *holographic* IOP. We do so by extending the transformation that underlies our Theorem 1, and below, we summarize the required changes.

Recall that in a holographic IOP there is an algorithm, known as the *IOP indexer* and denoted **I**, that receives as input, e.g., the circuit whose satisfiability is proved and outputs an encoding of it that will be given as an oracle to the IOP verifier. Our goal here is to construct the IOP indexer by simulating the argument indexer I, which instead relies on the random oracle to output a short digest of the circuit for the argument verifier.

Similarly to the transformation outlined in Sect. 2.1, we need to "remove" the random oracle during the simulation. The IOP indexer uses its randomness ρ_0 to answer any oracle query performed by the argument indexer. Let X_0 be the set of queries performed by the argument indexer. Then, the IOP indexer finds a perfect hash function h_0 for X_0 and creates the corresponding arrays T_0 and Y_0 containing the queried elements and responded positioned according to h_0. Finally, the IOP indexer outputs the string $(\mathsf{ivk}, h_0, T_0, Y_0)$, where ivk is the output of the argument indexer.

We are left to ensure that, during the transformation, any query simulated by the IOP verifier is consistent with the queries performed in the preprocessing step. The IOP prover, uses ρ_0 to simulate, in its head, the above (deterministic) process to get the same output $(\mathsf{ivk}, h_0, T_0, Y_0)$, and thus can act in a consistent way to the queries in X_0.

The IOP verifier reads ivk and uses it to simulate the argument verifier. Recall that for every query x the verifier ensures that x was not issued in any previous round. Here, we modify the verify to search in the array T_0 in addition to the arrays in all the rounds. In this sense, the preprocessing phase acts as "round 0" of the protocol. Completeness and soundness follow in a similar manner to the original transformation.

Extension 2: on state restoration soundness. Our Lemma 2 states that the transformation in Theorem 1 yields an IOP with *state-restoration soundness* when applied to a SNARG that satisfies *salted soundness*, a stronger notion of soundness that we introduce and may be of independent interest. The motivation for this result is that in the "forward" direction we only know how to construct SNARGs from IOPs that *do* satisfy state-restoration soundness [BCS16], which informally means that the IOP prover cannot convince the IOP verifier with high probability even when the IOP prover is allowed to choose from multiple continuations of the interaction up to some budget. We now sketch salted soundness and the ideas behind Lemma 2.

In a succinct argument with salted soundness, the cheating argument prover is allowed to *resample* answers of the random oracle, in a specific way. Suppose the prover queried some element x_1 and got response y_1. If the prover wishes, it may resample x_1 to get a fresh new uniform response y_1'. This process may happen multiple times within the query budget of the algorithm. Then, the prover selects one of these answers, and proceeds to query another element x_2, and so on. The prover is additionally allowed to go back, and change its decision for the value of some x_i. However, this produces a new branch where the values for x_j for $j > i$ have to be resampled. In general, at any step the prover can choose a brach from the set of all branches so far and choose to extend it. Finally, the prover outputs the argument. When the argument verifier queries an element, then it gets a response that is consistent with the branch the prover chose.

We need this security notion to get an IOP with state restoration soundness since this is precisely what a cheating IOP prover can perform within our transformation. In the state-restoration game, the cheating IOP prover can go back to a previous round and ask for new randomness from the IOP verifier.

In our case, the IOP prover will get new randomness for some set of queries. Since these queries simulate a random oracle, it can get fresh randomness for a query intended for a random oracle.

Thus, we show that any cheating prover playing the state-restoration game can be transformed into a cheating prover to the salted soundness game, and yields the desired proof.

3   Definitions

3.1   Random Oracles and Oracle Algorithms

We denote by $\mathcal{U}(\lambda)$ the uniform distribution over all functions $\zeta\colon \{0,1\}^* \to \{0,1\}^\lambda$ (implicitly defined by the probabilistic algorithm that assigns, uniformly and independently at random, a λ-bit string to each new input). If ζ is sampled from $\mathcal{U}(\lambda)$, then we say that ζ is a *random oracle*.

In this paper, we restrict our attention to oracle algorithms that are deterministic. This is without loss of generality as we do not restrict the running of the algorithm in the random oracle model only the number of queries.

Given an oracle algorithm A and an oracle $\zeta \in \mathcal{U}(\lambda)$, $\mathsf{queries}(A, \zeta)$ is the set of oracle queries that A^ζ makes. We say that A is t-query if $|\mathsf{queries}(A, \zeta)| \leq t$ for every $\zeta \in \mathcal{U}(\lambda)$.

Moreover, we consider complexity measures that quantify *how* the algorithm A makes queries: some queries may depend on prior answers while other queries do not. Letting $\zeta^{\mathsf{m}}(x_1, \ldots, x_{\mathsf{m}}) := (\zeta(x_1), \ldots, \zeta(x_{\mathsf{m}}))$, we say that A makes queries in a rounds of width m if there exists an a-query oracle algorithm B such that $B^{\zeta^{\mathsf{m}}} \equiv A^\zeta$ for every $\zeta \in \mathcal{U}(\lambda)$. Note that $t \leq \mathsf{m} \cdot \mathsf{a}$.

Finally, we consider the size of oracle queries, i.e., the number of bits used to specify the query: we say that A has queries of size n if for every $\zeta \in \mathcal{U}(\lambda)$ and $x \in \mathsf{queries}(A, \zeta)$ it holds that $|x| \leq \mathsf{n}$.

We summarize the above via the following definition.

Definition 1. *An oracle algorithm A is $(\mathsf{a}, \mathsf{m}, \mathsf{n})$-query if A makes queries in a rounds of width m, and all queries of A have size at most n.*

3.2   Relations

We consider proof systems for *binary* relations and for *ternary* relations, as we now explain.

- A binary relation R is a set of tuples (x, w) where x is the instance and w the witness. The corresponding language $L = L(R)$ is the set of x for which there exists w such that $(\mathsf{x}, \mathsf{w}) \in R$.
- A ternary relation R is a set of tuples $(\mathsf{i}, \mathsf{x}, \mathsf{w})$ where i is the index, x the instance, and w the witness. The corresponding language $L = L(R)$ is the set of tuples (i, x) for which there exists w such that $(\mathsf{i}, \mathsf{x}, \mathsf{w}) \in R$. To distinguish this case from the above case, we refer to R as an *indexed relation* and L as an *indexed language*.

A binary relation can be viewed as a special case of a ternary relation, where the same index has been fixed for all instances. For example, the indexed relation of satisfiable boolean circuits consists of triples where i is the description of a boolean circuit, x is an assignment to some of the input wires, and w is an assignment to the remaining input wires that makes the circuit output 0. If we restrict this indexed relation by fixing the same circuit for all instances, we obtain a binary relation.

The proof systems that we consider for binary relations are: (a) non-interactive arguments in the random oracle model; and (b) interactive oracle proofs. The proof systems that we consider for indexed (ternary) relations are (a) *preprocessing* non-interactive arguments in the random oracle model; and (b) *holographic* interactive oracle proofs. We will define only the latter two (in Sect. 3.3 and Sect. 3.4 respectively) because the former two can be derived as special cases.

3.3   Non-interactive Arguments in the Random Oracle Model

We consider non-interactive arguments in the random oracle model, where security holds against query-bounded, yet possibly computationally-unbounded, adversaries. Recall that a non-interactive argument typically consists of a prover algorithm and a verifier algorithm that prove and validate statements for a binary relation, which represents the valid instance-witness pairs. Here we define a more general notion known as a *preprocessing* non-interactive argument, which works for indexed relations (see Sect. 3.2). This notion additionally involves an *indexer algorithm*, which receives as input an index and deterministically produces a key pair specialized for producing and validating statements relative to the given index. The usual notion of a non-interactive argument corresponds to a preprocessing non-interactive argument where the indexer algorithm is degenerate (it sets the proving key equal to the index, and similarly sets the verification key equal to the index).

Let $\mathsf{ARG} = (I, P, V)$ be a tuple of (oracle) algorithms, with I deterministic. We say that ARG is a (preprocessing) non-interactive argument, in the random oracle model, for an indexed relation R with (non-adaptive) soundness error ϵ if the following holds.

– **Completeness.** For every $(i, x, w) \in R$ and $\lambda \in \mathbb{N}$,

$$\Pr\left[V^\zeta(\mathsf{ivk}, x, \pi) = 1 \;\middle|\; \begin{array}{c} \zeta \leftarrow \mathcal{U}(\lambda) \\ (\mathsf{ipk}, \mathsf{ivk}) \leftarrow I^\zeta(i) \\ \pi \leftarrow P^\zeta(\mathsf{ipk}, x, w) \end{array} \right] = 1.$$

– **Soundness (non-adaptive).** For every $(i, x) \notin L(R)$, t-query $\tilde{P}$, and $\lambda \in \mathbb{N}$,

$$\Pr\left[V^\zeta(\mathsf{ivk}, x, \pi) = 1 \;\middle|\; \begin{array}{c} \zeta \leftarrow \mathcal{U}(\lambda) \\ (\mathsf{ipk}, \mathsf{ivk}) \leftarrow I^\zeta(i) \\ \pi \leftarrow \tilde{P}^\zeta \end{array} \right] \le \epsilon(i, x, \lambda, t).$$

Complexity measures. We consider several complexity measures beyond soundness error. All of these complexity measures are, implicitly, functions of (i, x) and the security parameter λ.

- *sizes*: proving key size ipks $:= |ipk|$; verification key size ivks $:= |ivk|$; argument size as $:= |\pi|$.
- *times*: the indexer I runs in time it; the prover P runs in time pt; the verifier V runs in time vt.
- *queries*: the indexer I is a iq-query algorithm; the prover P is a (a, m, n)-query algorithm (see Definition 1); the verifier V is a vq-query algorithm.

Bits of security. We are interested to discuss complexity measures, most notably argument size, also as a function of bits of security. Note, though, that we cannot directly equate "bits of security" with $-\log \epsilon(i, x, \lambda, t)$ because this value depends on multiple quantities that we cannot set a priori. Indeed, while we could set the output size λ of the random oracle to be a value of our choice, we may not know which index-instance pairs (i, x) we will consider nor a malicious prover's query bound t. Thus we consider *all* (i, x) and t up to a large size that depends on the desired bits of security, and say that the scheme has s bits of security if $-\log \epsilon(i, x, \lambda, t) \leq s$ for all such i, x, t and where λ is linear in s. This is captured is the following definition.

Definition 2. *We say that* ARG *provides* s **bits of security** *if its soundness error* ϵ *satisfies the following condition with* $\lambda := c \cdot s$ *for some constant* $c > 0$*: for every index-instance pair* $(i, x) \notin L(R)$ *and query bound* $t \in \mathbb{N}$ *with* $\max\{|i| + |x|, t\} \leq 2^s$ *it holds that* $\epsilon(i, x, \lambda, t) \leq 2^{-s}$*.*

The above definition enables us to discuss any complexity measure also, and possibly exclusively, as a function of bits of security as we illustrate in the following definition.

Definition 3. *We say that* ARG *has* **argument size** as(s) *if* ARG *provides* s *bits of security and, moreover,* as(s) *bounds the size of an honestly-generated* π *for any index-instance pair* $(i, x) \in L(R)$ *with* $|i| + |x| \leq 2^s$ *and while setting* $\lambda := \Theta(s)$*.*

3.4   Interactive Oracle Proofs

Interactive Oracle Proofs (IOPs) [BCS16, RRR16] are information-theoretic proof systems that combine aspects of Interactive Proofs [Bab85, GMR89] and Probabilistically Checkable Proofs [Bab+91, Fei+91, AS98, Aro+98], and also generalize the notion of Interactive PCPs [KR08]. Below we describe a generalization of *public-coin* IOPs that is convenient in this paper.

Recall that a k-round public-coin IOP works as follows. For each round $i \in$ [k], the prover sends a proof string Π_i to the verifier; then the verifier sends a uniformly random message ρ_i to the prover. After k rounds of interaction, the verifier makes some queries to the proof strings $\Pi_1, \ldots, \Pi_k$ sent by the prover, and then decides if to accept or to reject.

The definition that we use here generalizes the above notion in two ways.

- *Holography.* The proof system works for indexed relations (see Sect. 3.2), and involves an indexer algorithm that, given an index as input, samples an encoding Π_0 of the index; the randomness ρ_0 used by the indexer to sample the encoding Π_0 is public (known to prover and verifier). The verifier receives oracle access to the encoding Π_0, rather than explicit access to the index.
- *Randomness as oracle.* The verifier has oracle access to its own randomness $\rho_1, \ldots, \rho_k$ and to the indexer's randomness ρ_0. This notion, which naturally arises in our results, is compatible with known compilers, as we explain in Remark 1. We will count verifier queries to the randomness $\rho_0, \rho_1, \ldots, \rho_k$ separately from verifier queries to the encoding Π_0 and proof strings $\Pi_1, \ldots, \Pi_k$.

In more detail, let $\mathsf{IOP} = (\mathbf{I}, \mathbf{P}, \mathbf{V})$ be a tuple where $\mathbf{I}$ is a deterministic algorithm, $\mathbf{P}$ is an interactive algorithm, and $\mathbf{V}$ is an interactive oracle algorithm. We say that IOP is a *public-coin holographic IOP* for an indexed relation R with k rounds and soundness error ε if the following holds.

- **Completeness.** For every $(\mathbb{i}, \mathbb{x}, \mathbb{w}) \in R$,

$$
\Pr_{\rho_0, \rho_1, \ldots, \rho_k} \left[\mathbf{V}^{\Pi_0, \Pi_1, \ldots, \Pi_k, \rho_0, \rho_1, \ldots, \rho_k}(\mathbb{x}) = 1 \;\middle|\;
\begin{array}{l}
\Pi_0 \leftarrow \mathbf{I}(\mathbb{i}, \rho_0) \\
\Pi_1 \leftarrow \mathbf{P}(\mathbb{i}, \mathbb{x}, \mathbb{w}, \rho_0) \\
\Pi_2 \leftarrow \mathbf{P}(\mathbb{i}, \mathbb{x}, \mathbb{w}, \rho_0, \rho_1) \\
\vdots \\
\Pi_k \leftarrow \mathbf{P}(\mathbb{i}, \mathbb{x}, \mathbb{w}, \rho_0, \rho_1, \ldots, \rho_{k-1})
\end{array}
\right] = 1.
$$

- **Soundness.** For every $(\mathbb{i}, \mathbb{x}) \notin L(R)$ and unbounded malicious prover $\tilde{\mathbf{P}}$,

$$
\Pr_{\rho_0, \rho_1, \ldots, \rho_k} \left[\mathbf{V}^{\Pi_0, \tilde{\Pi}_1, \ldots, \tilde{\Pi}_k, \rho_0, \rho_1, \ldots, \rho_k}(\mathbb{x}) = 1 \;\middle|\;
\begin{array}{l}
\Pi_0 \leftarrow \mathbf{I}(\mathbb{i}, \rho_0) \\
\tilde{\Pi}_1 \leftarrow \tilde{\mathbf{P}}(\rho_0) \\
\tilde{\Pi}_2 \leftarrow \tilde{\mathbf{P}}(\rho_0, \rho_1) \\
\vdots \\
\tilde{\Pi}_k \leftarrow \tilde{\mathbf{P}}(\rho_0, \rho_1, \ldots, \rho_{k-1})
\end{array}
\right] \leq \varepsilon(\mathbb{x}).
$$

Complexity measures. We consider several complexity measures beyond soundness error. All of these complexity measures are implicitly functions of the instance $\mathbb{x}$.

- *proof length* l: the total number of bits in $\Pi_0, \Pi_1, \ldots, \Pi_k$.
- *proof queries* q: the number of bits read by the verifier from $\Pi_0, \Pi_1, \ldots, \Pi_k$.
- *randomness length* r: the total number of bits in $\rho_0, \rho_1, \ldots, \rho_k$.
- *randomness queries* $\mathsf{q_r}$: the total number of bits read by the verifier from $\rho_0, \rho_1, \ldots, \rho_k$.
- *indexer time* it: $\mathbf{I}$ runs in time it.
- *prover time* pt: $\mathbf{P}$ runs in time pt.
- *verifier time* vt: $\mathbf{V}$ runs in time vt.

Query entropy. We additionally define a complexity measure called *query entropy* that, informally, captures the entropy of the query locations read by the IOP verifier in an honest execution. In particular, if the query entropy is at most h then the probability of predicting in advance all the locations that the verifier will read at the end of the protocol is at least 2^{-h}, where the probability is taken over the randomness of the IOP verifier and (any) randomness of the honest IOP prover.

Definition 4. *Let X be a random variable. The **sample-entropy** of $x \in \mathsf{supp}(X)$ with respect to X is $H(x) := -\log \Pr[X = x]$. The **min-entropy** of X is $H_{\mathsf{min}}(X) := \min_{x \in \mathsf{supp}(X)} H(x)$.*

Definition 5. *Let $\mathsf{IOP} = (\mathbf{I}, \mathbf{P}, \mathbf{V})$ be an IOP with proof length l for an indexed relation R.*

- *The **query distribution** of IOP for $(\mathtt{i}, \mathtt{x}, \mathtt{w}) \in R$ is the distribution $\mathcal{D}(\mathtt{i}, \mathtt{x}, \mathtt{w})$ over subsets $\mathcal{I} \subseteq [l]$ such that the probability of $\mathcal{I}$ is the probability that the honest IOP verifier $\mathbf{V}$ reads exactly the locations in $\mathcal{I}$ in an honest execution with the IOP prover $\mathbf{P}$ for the triple $(\mathtt{i}, \mathtt{x}, \mathtt{w})$.*
- *The **query entropy** of IOP for an index-instance pair $(\mathtt{i}, \mathtt{x}) \in L(R)$ is*

$$\mathsf{h}(\mathtt{i}, \mathtt{x}) := \max_{\mathtt{w} \ s.t. \ (\mathtt{i}, \mathtt{x}, \mathtt{w}) \in R} H_{\mathsf{min}}(\mathcal{D}(\mathtt{i}, \mathtt{x}, \mathtt{w})) \ .$$

For any IOP with proof length l and query complexity q it holds that for any $(\mathtt{i}, \mathtt{x}, \mathtt{w}) \in R$ the query distribution has no more entropy than the uniform distribution over subsets of size q. Therefore it always holds that $\mathsf{h}(\mathtt{i}, \mathtt{x}) \leq \mathsf{q}(\mathtt{i}, \mathtt{x}) \cdot \log \mathsf{l}(\mathtt{i}, \mathtt{x})$.

Remark 1 (randomness in known compilers). The definition of public-coin (holographic) IOP that we consider additionally grants the verifier oracle access to its own randomness, which in particular, enables the prover to receive much more randomness than allowed by the verifier's running time. We briefly discuss why this feature is motivated by known cryptographic compilers.

First, the size of arguments produced via known cryptographic compilers does not depend on the verifier's randomness complexity. E.g., the Micali compiler [Mic00] maps a PCP into a corresponding non-interactive argument whose size is independent of the PCP verifier's randomness complexity; more generally, the BCS compiler [BCS16] maps a public-coin IOP into a corresponding non-interactive argument whose size is independent of the IOP verifier's randomness complexity.

Second, the running time of the argument verifier produced by these compilers *only* depends on the number of queries to the randomness, *but not on randomness complexity*. Indeed, both in the Micali compiler and in the BCS compiler, the argument prover only needs to invoke the random oracle to answer randomness queries of the underlying PCP/IOP verifier, and in particular, does not have to materialize the unqueried randomness. This is because the random oracle, which serves as a shared randomness resource, enables the argument prover to suitably materialize all the relevant randomness without impacting the argument verifier.

4   From Succinct Arguments to Interactive Oracle Proofs

We formally re-state Theorem 1 and then prove it. The formal theorem statement is somewhat technical, as it contains the precise relationship between parameters of the succinct argument and the corresponding IOP. We advise the reader to first read the informal overview of the proof in Sect. 2.1, as it gives intuition for the relationships between the parameters.

The theorem is stated with respect to a *non-interactive* succinct argument, for the sake of simple presentation. The compiler naturally generalizes to succinct arguments with multiple rounds, and we describe this is Remark 2. We note that we additionally provide the *query entropy* of the compiled IOP (see Definition 5) as it is used later in Theorem 6.

In the theorem below, an $(\mathsf{a}, \mathsf{m}, \mathsf{n})$-query algorithm performs a rounds each containing m queries to a random oracle over defined over $\{0, 1\}^\mathsf{n}$ (see Definition 1).

Theorem 3 (ARG → IOP). *There exists a polynomial-time transformation $\mathbb{T}$ that satisfies the following. If* ARG *is a non-interactive argument in the ROM for a relation R then* IOP $:= \mathbb{T}(\mathsf{ARG})$ *is a public-coin IOP for R, parametrized by a security parameter $\lambda \in \mathbb{N}$, with related complexity as specified below. (All complexity measures take as input an instance $\mathbb{x}$ and the security parameter λ.)*

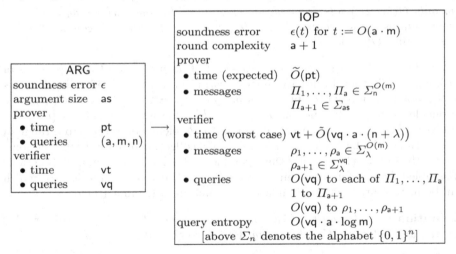

Moreover, the IOP prover and IOP verifier make only black-box use of the argument prover and argument verifier respectively (up to intercepting and answering their queries to the random oracle).

The rest of this section is organized as follows: in Sect. 4.1 we introduce the main tool that we use in our transformation, and in Sect. 4.2 we describe the transformation. Proofs are given in the full version of the paper.

Remark 2 (interactive arguments).   While the focus of this paper is *non-interactive* arguments in the random oracle model (as defined in Sect. 3.3), one could also study *interactive* arguments in the random oracle model. Our proof of Theorem 3 directly extends to give a result also for this more general case, with the main difference being that the round complexity of the IOP increases by the round complexity of the given argument system.

The reason why the proof directly extends is that the main technique for constructing the IOP is a sub-protocol for simulating queries to a random oracle, and this sub-protocol does not "care" if in the meantime the argument prover and argument verifier engage in a conversation. As a result, if the succinct argument has k rounds, then the compiled IOP has k + a rounds.

4.1 Tool: Perfect Hash Functions with Locality

A *perfect hash function* for a set S of size m in a universe U is a function $h: U \to \{1, \ldots, O(m)\}$ that is one-to-one on S. We use a seminal construction of Fredman, Komlós, and Szemerédi [FKS84], observing that it has a certain **locality property** that is crucial for us.

Theorem 4 (follows from [FKS84]). *For any universe U there exist a* $\mathrm{poly}(m, \log |U|)$-*time deterministic algorithm that, given as input a subset $S \subseteq U$ of size m, outputs a perfect hash function $h: U \to \{1, \ldots, O(m)\}$ for S with* $|h| = O(m \cdot \log |U|)$ *bits. In fact, evaluating h on a single input requires reading only $O(\log |U|)$ bits from the description of h, and performing $\tilde{O}(\log |U|)$ bit operations. In alternative to the deterministic algorithm, h can be found in expected time $\tilde{O}(m \cdot \log |U|)$.*

Proof. The FKS construction achieves a perfect hash function h via two levels of hashing. The first level is a hash function $h_0: U \to [m]$ that divides the elements of S among m bins where bin i has b_i elements, with $\sum_{i=1}^{m} b_i^2 = O(m)$. The second level is a hash function $h_i: [m] \to [b_i^2]$, one for each bin $i \in [m]$, that resolves collisions inside bin i by mapping the b_i elements in bin i to a range of size b_i^2. Hence the hash function h consists of a collection of $1+m$ hash functions: one for the first level and m for the second level. Each of the $1+m$ hash functions is sampled from a family of universal hash functions (see Definition 6), which can be instantiated via the standard construction in Lemma 1 below.

Definition 6. *A family $\mathcal{H}$ of hash functions mapping U to $[M]$ is **universal** if for any distinct $x, y \in U$ it holds that $\mathrm{Pr}_{h \leftarrow \mathcal{H}}[h(x) = h(y)] = 1/M$.*

Lemma 1 ([CW79]). *Let p be a prime with $|U| < p \leq \mathrm{poly}(|U|)$. The family $\mathcal{H} = \{h_{a,b}: U \to [M]\}_{a \in \mathbb{F}_p^*, b \in \mathbb{F}_p}$ where $h_{a,b}(x) := (a \cdot x \mod p) \mod M$ is universal. Each $h_{a,b}$ has bit size $O(\log |U|)$ and can be evaluated in $\tilde{O}(\log |U|)$ time.*

The above gives us $|h_0| = O(\log |U|)$ and $|h_i| = O(\log |U|)$ for all $i \in [m]$, and in particular $|h| = O(\sum_{i=0}^{m} |h_i|) = O(m \cdot \log |U|)$.

We now discuss the locality property of the FKS construction. In order to evaluate h on a single element, one needs to use only *two* hash functions among the $1 + m$: the first level hash function h_0 and then the appropriate second level hash function h_i. Thus, to evaluate h on a single element requires reading only the relevant bits of h_0 and h_i from the description of h, which together amount to $O(\log |U|)$ bits. The time to evaluate both h_0 and h_i is $\tilde{O}(\log |U|)$.

We conclude with a discussion of how to find h. Fredman, Komlós, and Szemerédi [FKS84] showed a $\mathrm{poly}(m, \log |U|)$-time deterministic algorithm; Alon and Naor [AN96] showed a faster deterministic algorithm, but the running time remains super-linear. Alternatively, in [FKS84], it was shown that h can be found in expected time $\tilde{O}(m \cdot \log |U|)$. This follows since for a random h_0 it holds that $\sum_{i=1}^{m} b_i^2 = O(m)$ with high probability, and moreover, for a random h_i, the mapping to $[b_i^2]$ is one-to-one with high probability. Thus, in expectation, only a constant number of trials are needed to find h_0 and to find each h_i. □

4.2 The Transformation

Construction 5 (transformation $\mathbb{T}$). *Let* $\mathsf{ARG} = (P, V)$ *be a non-interactive argument in the ROM. We construct a public-coin interactive oracle proof* $\mathsf{IOP} = (\mathbf{P}, \mathbf{V})$, *parametrized by a choice of security parameter* $\lambda \in \mathbb{N}$. *The IOP prover* $\mathbf{P}$ *takes as input an instance* x *and a witness* w, *and will internally simulate the argument prover* P *on input* (x, w), *answering* P's *queries to the random oracle as described below. The IOP verifier* $\mathbf{V}$ *takes as input only the instance* x, *and will simulate the argument verifier* V *on input* x, *answering* V's *queries to the random oracle as described below.*

The interactive phase of the IOP protocol proceeds as follows:

- *For round $j = 1, \ldots, \mathsf{a}$:*
  1. $\mathbf{P}$ *simulates* P *to get its* j-*th query set* $X_j = (x_1, \ldots, x_{\mathsf{m}})$, *and finds a perfect hash function* $h_j \colon \{0, 1\}^{\mathsf{n}} \to [M]$ *for the set* X_j *where* $M = O(\mathsf{m})$. *Then,* $\mathbf{P}$ *creates an* M-*cell array* T_j *such that* $T_j[h_j(x_i)] = x_i$ *for all* $i \in [\mathsf{m}]$, *and all other cells of* T_j *are* $\bot$. *Finally,* $\mathbf{P}$ *sends* $\Pi_j := (h_j, T_j)$ *to* $\mathbf{V}$.
  2. $\mathbf{V}$ *samples* $y_1, \ldots, y_M \in \{0, 1\}^{\lambda}$ *uniformly at random and sends* $\rho_j := (y_1, \ldots, y_M)$ *to* $\mathbf{P}$.
  3. $\mathbf{P}$ *answers* P's *query* x_i *with the value* $\rho_j[h_j(x_i)]$, *for every* $i \in [\mathsf{m}]$.
- $\mathbf{P}$ *simulates* P *until it outputs the non-interactive argument* π; $\mathbf{P}$ *sends* $\Pi_{\mathsf{a}+1} := \pi$ *to* $\mathbf{V}$.

The query phase of the IOP protocol proceeds as follows. The IOP verifier $\mathbf{V}$ *reads the non-interactive argument* π *sent in the last round (the only symbol in* $\Pi_{\mathsf{a}+1}$), *and simulates the argument verifier* V *on input* (x, π), *answering each oracle query* x *with an answer* y *that is derived as follows:*

- $\mathbf{V}$ *reads the necessary bits from* h_j *(in* Π_j*) to evaluate* $h_j(x)$;
- $\mathbf{V}$ *reads* $v_j := T_j[h_j(x)]$ *(in* Π_j*) for all* $j \in [\mathsf{a}]$;
- *if* $v_j \neq x$ *for all* $j \in [\mathsf{a}]$ *then set* y *to be a random value in* $\{0, 1\}^{\lambda}$;
- *if there exists* $j \neq j'$ *such that* $v_j = x$ *and* $v_{j'} = x$ *then halt and reject;*
- *let* j *be the unique value such that* $v_j = x$, *and set* $y := \rho_j[h_j(x)]$.

If each query was answered successfully, **V** *rules according to the output of V. (Note that, formally, the randomness used by the IOP verifier* **V** *to answer queries of the argument verifier V that were not also asked by the argument prover P should be treated as a last verifier message* ρ_{a+1} *consisting of* vq *random* λ*-bit strings. The IOP verifier will then "consume" this randomness as needed.)*

The proof appears in the full version of the paper.

5   From Interactive Oracle Proofs to Algorithms

We formally re-state and prove Theorem 2, which states that IOPs with good parameters (small soundness error relative to soundness error or, more precisely, query entropy) can be translated to good algorithms (fast algorithms with small space complexity). We use this transformation in Sect. 6 to show that, for certain languages, if the IOP parameters are "too good" then the resulting algorithms contradict standard complexity assumptions (and therefore cannot exist).

Theorem 6 (IOP to algorithm). *Suppose that a language L has a public-coin IOP with completeness error* c, *soundness error* ε, *round complexity* k, *proof length* l *over an alphabet* Σ, *query complexity* q, *and query entropy* h. *If* $\delta := (1 - \text{c}) \cdot 2^{-\text{h}} - \varepsilon > 0$ *then, for* $c := \text{q} \cdot \log \text{l} + \text{q} \cdot \log |\Sigma|$ *the language L is in*

$$\text{BPTIME} \left[2^{O\left(c(n) + \text{k}(n) \cdot \log \frac{\text{k}(n)}{\delta(n)}\right)} \cdot \text{poly}(n) \right].$$

Let the verifier space complexity be vs, *randomness length* r *(over* Σ*) and randomness query complexity* q_r. *If* $\delta' := (1 - \text{c}) \cdot 2^{-\text{h}} \cdot \text{r}^{-\text{q}_\text{r}} - \varepsilon > 0$ *then the same algorithm can be implemented in space*

$$O \left(\text{vs} \cdot \left(c(n) + \text{k}(n) \cdot \log \frac{\text{k}(n)}{\delta'(n)} \right)^2 \right).$$

(Above it suffices to take c to be the number of bits to specify the set of queries by the IOP verifier and their corresponding answers. This is useful when queries are correlated or answers are from different alphabets.)

The proof appears in the full version of the paper.

5.1   IOP to Laconic IP

The lemma below states that any IOP with good enough soundness relative to its *query entropy* can be translated to a laconic IP (an IP with small prover-to-verifier communication). Query entropy is the probability of guessing in advance the exact locations that the IOP verifier will read across the proof strings sent by the IOP prover; see Definition 5 for how query entropy is formally defined.

Lemma 2 (IOP to laconic IP). *Suppose that a language L has an IOP with completeness error* c, *soundness error* ε, *round complexity* k, *proof length* l *over an alphabet* Σ, *query complexity* q, *and query entropy* h. *If* $\varepsilon < (1 - c) \cdot 2^{-h}$ *then* L *has an IP with completeness error* $1 - (1 - c) \cdot 2^{-h}$, *soundness error* ε, *round complexity* k, *and prover-to-verifier communication* $q \cdot \log l + q \cdot \log |\Sigma|$. *(More generally, communication is bounded by the number of bits to specify the set of queries by the IOP verifier and their corresponding answers.) If the IOP is public-coin then the IP is public-coin.*

Moreover, the IP can be modified so that the IP verifier performs a single pass over the randomness tape, with completeness error $1 - (1 - c) \cdot 2^{-h} \cdot r^{-q_r}$, *and space complexity* $O(vs + q_r \cdot \log r + q_r \log |\Sigma|))$ *where* vs *is the space complexity of the IOP verifier.*

The proof appears in the full version of the paper.

5.2 IP to Algorithm

Goldreich and Håstad [GH98] have shown that languages with public-coin IPs with small prover-to-verifier communication can be decided via fast probabilistic algorithms. Their result is shown for IPs with constant completeness and soundness errors. Below we show a refinement of their theorem, where we explicitly provide the dependency in the completeness and soundness errors, which allows supporting IPs with large completeness errors (which we need). Moreover, we note that if the IP verifier reads its randomness in a single pass, the probabilistic algorithm for deciding the language can be implemented in small space (which we also need).

Lemma 3 (IP to algorithm). *Suppose that a language L has a public-coin IP with completeness error* α, *soundness error* β, *round complexity* k, *and prover-to-verifier communication* c. *Then, for* $d(n) := c(n) + k(n) \cdot \log \frac{k(n)}{1 - \alpha(n) - \beta(n)}$ *the language L is in*

$$\text{BPTIME} \left[2^{O(d)} \cdot \text{poly}(n) \right].$$

Moreover, if the space complexity of the IP verifier is vs *when reading its randomness random tape in a single pass then the language L is in*

$$\text{SPACE} \left[O \left(d \cdot (vs + d) \right) \right].$$

The proof appears in the full version of the paper.

6 Barriers for Succinct Arguments

We prove that, under plausible complexity assumptions, there do not exist succinct arguments where the argument verifier makes a small number of queries to the random oracle and the honest argument prover has a small adaptivity parameter. We separately consider that case of succinct arguments for nondeterministic languages (NTIME) in Sect. 6.1, and the case of deterministic languages (DTIME) in Sect. 6.2.

In both cases our approach consists of the following steps: (1) we use Theorem 3 to transform the succinct argument into a corresponding IOP; then, (2) we use Theorem 6 to transform the IOP into an algorithm with certain time and space complexity; finally, (3) we argue that, under standard complexity assumptions, such an algorithm does not exist.

6.1   The Case of Nondeterministic Languages

Theorem 7. *Suppose that* NTIME[T] *has a non-interactive argument* ARG *that provides s bits of security and has argument size* as $= o(T)$ *(see Definitions 2 and 3), where the prover makes* a *adaptive rounds of* m *queries to the random oracle, and the verifier makes* vq *queries to the random oracle. If (1)* vq $\cdot$ a $\cdot$ log(m) $= o(s)$; *and (2)* $\log n \leq s \leq o(T^{1/2})$, *then* NTIME[$T(n)$] $\subseteq$ BPTIME[$2^{o(T(n))}$] *(an unlikely inclusion).*

Remark 3 (s vs. T). If as $= \Omega(T)$ then the trivial scheme of sending the T bits of a valid witness yields a non-interactive argument (indeed, proof), and so we consider the case as $= o(T)$. For technical reasons, we also need that $s = o(T^{1/2})$, a rather weak condition. Additionally, we restrict the instance size to be at most exponential in s, and therefore assume that $\log n \leq s$.

Remark 4 ("a" in known compilers). In the Micali transformation [Mic00], the argument prover performs a $= \Theta(\log l)$ rounds of queries to the random oracle (one round for each level of a Merkle tree over a PCP of size l), whereas the argument verifier performs vq $= \Theta(q \cdot \log l + r)$ queries to the random oracle. When using known or conjectured PCPs in the Micali transformation, we get vq $= \Omega(s)$. In particular, the hypothesis vq $\cdot$ a $\cdot$ log(m) $= o(s)$ does not apply, and as expected does not lead to the inclusion stated in the theorem.

Remark 5 (interactive argument). Similar to the way Theorem 3 is presented, to get a simple presentation, we state the above theorem for non-interactive succinct arguments. We note, however, that the theorem naturally generalizes to any *public-coin* succinct argument with k rounds (note that always k $\leq$ as), as long as $s^2 \cdot$ k $= o(T)$.

6.2   The Case of Deterministic Languages

Theorem 8. *Suppose that* DTIME[T] *has a non-interactive argument* ARG *that provides s bits of security and has argument size* as $= o(T)$ *(see Definitions 2 and 3), where the prover makes* a *adaptive rounds of* m *queries to the random oracle, and the verifier makes* vq *queries to the random oracle and has space complexity* sv. *If (1)* vq $\cdot$ a $\cdot$ log(a $\cdot$ m) $= o(s)$; *(2)* sv $\cdot (s^4 + $ as$^2) = o(T)$; *and (3)* $\log n \leq s$ *then* DTIME[$T(n)$] $\subseteq$ SPACE[$o(T(n))$] *(an unlikely inclusion).*

The proof appears in the full version of the paper.

Acknowledgments. We thank Amey Bhangale, Karthik C. S., and Inbal Livni Navon for fruitful discussions regarding PCPs and the sliding scale conjecture.

Alessandro Chiesa is funded by the Ethereum Foundation and Eylon Yogev is funded by the ISF grants 484/18, 1789/19, Len Blavatnik and the Blavatnik Foundation, and The Blavatnik Interdisciplinary Cyber Research Center at Tel Aviv University. This work was done (in part) while the second author was visiting the Simons Institute for the Theory of Computing.

References

[AN96] Alon, N., Naor, M.: Derandomization, witnesses for boolean matrix multiplication and construction of perfect hash functions. Algorithmica **16**(4/5), 434–449 (1996)

[Aro+98] Arora, S., Lund, C., Motwani, R., Sudan, M., Szegedy, M.: Proof verification and the hardness of approximation problems. J. ACM **45**(3), 501–555 (1998). Preliminary version in FOCS '92

[AS98] Arora, S., Safra, S.: Probabilistic checking of proofs: a new characterization of NP. J. ACM **45**(1), 70–122 (1998). Preliminary version in FOCS '92

[Bab+91] Babai, L., Fortnow, L., Levin, L.A., Szegedy, M.: Checking computations in polylogarithmic time. In: Proceedings of the 23rd Annual ACM Symposium on Theory of Computing, STOC 1991, pp. 21–32 (1991)

[Bab85] Babai, L.: Trading group theory for randomness. In: Proceedings of the 17th Annual ACM Symposium on Theory of Computing, STOC 1985, pp. 421–429 (1985)

[BCS16] Ben-Sasson, E., Chiesa, A., Spooner, N.: Interactive oracle proofs. In: Proceedings of the 14th Theory of Cryptography Conference, TCC 2016-B, pp. 31–60 (2016)

[Bit+13] Bitansky, N., Canetti, R., Chiesa, A., Tromer, E.: Recursive composition and bootstrapping for SNARKs and proof-carrying data. In: Proceedings of the 45th ACM Symposium on the Theory of Computing, STOC 2013, pp. 111–120 (2013)

[Bon+17] Boneh, D., Ishai, Y., Sahai, A., Wu, D.J.: Lattice-based SNARGs and their application to more efficient obfuscation. In: Coron, J.-S., Nielsen, J.B. (eds.) EUROCRYPT 2017. LNCS, vol. 10212, pp. 247–277. Springer, Cham (2017). https://doi.org/10.1007/978-3-319-56617-7_9

[Chi+20] Chiesa, A., Hu, Y., Maller, M., Mishra, P., Vesely, N., Ward, N.: Marlin: preprocessing zkSNARKs with universal and updatable SRS. In: Canteaut, A., Ishai, Y. (eds.) EUROCRYPT 2020. LNCS, vol. 12105, pp. 738–768. Springer, Cham (2020). https://doi.org/10.1007/978-3-030-45721-1_26

[CMS19] Chiesa, A., Manohar, P., Spooner, N.: Succinct arguments in the quantum random oracle model. In: Hofheinz, D., Rosen, A. (eds.) TCC 2019. LNCS, vol. 11892, pp. 1–29. Springer, Cham (2019). https://doi.org/10.1007/978-3-030-36033-7_1

[COS20] Chiesa, A., Ojha, D., Spooner, N.: FRACTAL: post-quantum and transparent recursive proofs from holography. In: Canteaut, A., Ishai, Y. (eds.) EUROCRYPT 2020. LNCS, vol. 12105, pp. 769–793. Springer, Cham (2020). https://doi.org/10.1007/978-3-030-45721-1_27

[CW79]   Carter, L., Wegman, M.N.: Universal classes of hash functions. J. Comput. Syst. Sci. **18**(2), 143–154 (1979)

[Del+14] Dell, H., Husfeldt, T., Marx, D., Taslaman, N., Wahlén, M.: Exponential time complexity of the permanent and the Tutte polynomial. ACM Trans. Algorithms **10**(4), Art. 21, 32 (2014)

[Fei+91] Feige, U., Goldwasser, S., Lovász, L., Safra, S., Szegedy, M.: Approximating clique is almost NP-complete (preliminary version). In: Proceedings of the 32nd Annual Symposium on Foundations of Computer Science, SFCS 1991, pp. 2–12 (1991)

[FKS84] Fredman, M.L., Komlós, J., Szemerédi, E.: Storing a sparse table with 0(1) worst case access time. J. ACM **31**(3), 538–544 (1984)

[FS86]   Fiat, A., Shamir, A.: How to prove yourself: practical solutions to identification and signature problems. In: Odlyzko, A.M. (ed.) CRYPTO 1986. LNCS, vol. 263, pp. 186–194. Springer, Heidelberg (1987). https://doi.org/10.1007/3-540-47721-7_12

[GH98]   Goldreich, O., Håstad, J.: On the complexity of interactive proofs with bounded communication. Inf. Process. Lett. **67**(4), 205–214 (1998)

[GMR89] Goldwasser, S., Micali, S., Rackoff, C.: The knowledge complexity of interactive proof systems. SIAM J. Comput. **18**(1), 186–208 (1989). Preliminary version appeared in STOC '85

[KR08]   Kalai, Y.T., Raz, R.: Interactive PCP. In: Aceto, L., Damgård, I., Goldberg, L.A., Halldórsson, M.M., Ingólfsdóttir, A., Walukiewicz, I. (eds.) ICALP 2008. LNCS, vol. 5126, pp. 536–547. Springer, Heidelberg (2008). https://doi.org/10.1007/978-3-540-70583-3_44

[Mic00] Micali, S.: Computationally sound proofs. SIAM J. Comput. **30**(4), 1253–1298 (2000). Preliminary version appeared in FOCS '94

[RRR16] Reingold, O., Rothblum, R., Rothblum, G.: Constant-round interactive proofs for delegating computation. In: Proceedings of the 48th ACM Symposium on the Theory of Computing, STOC 2016, pp. 49–62 (2016)

[RV09]   Rothblum, G.N., Vadhan, S.: Are PCPs inherent in efficient arguments? In: Proceedings of the 24th IEEE Annual Conference on Computational Complexity, CCC 2009, pp. 81–92 (2009)

[Val08] Valiant, P.: Incrementally verifiable computation or proofs of knowledge imply time/space efficiency. In: Canetti, R. (ed.) TCC 2008. LNCS, vol. 4948, pp. 1–18. Springer, Heidelberg (2008). https://doi.org/10.1007/978-3-540-78524-8_1

[Ben+14] Ben-Sasson, E., et al.: Zerocash: decentralized anonymous payments from Bitcoin. In: Proceedings of the 2014 IEEE Symposium on Security and Privacy, SP 2014, pp. 459–474 (2014)

Accumulators in (and Beyond) Generic Groups: Non-trivial Batch Verification Requires Interaction

Gili Schul-Ganz and Gil Segev[✉]

School of Computer Science and Engineering,
Hebrew University of Jerusalem, 91904 Jerusalem, Israel
{gili.schul,segev}@cs.huji.ac.il

Abstract. We prove a tight lower bound on the number of group operations required for batch verification by any generic-group accumulator that stores a less-than-trivial amount of information. Specifically, we show that $\Omega(t \cdot (\lambda / \log \lambda))$ group operations are required for the batch verification of any subset of $t \geq 1$ elements, where $\lambda \in \mathbb{N}$ is the security parameter, thus ruling out non-trivial batch verification in the standard non-interactive manner.

Our lower bound applies already to the most basic form of accumulators (i.e., static accumulators that support membership proofs), and holds both for known-order (and even multilinear) groups and for unknown-order groups, where it matches the asymptotic performance of the known bilinear and RSA accumulators, respectively. In addition, it complements the techniques underlying the generic-group accumulators of Boneh, Bünz and Fisch (CRYPTO '19) and Thakur (ePrint '19) by justifying their application of the Fiat-Shamir heuristic for transforming their interactive batch-verification protocols into non-interactive procedures.

Moreover, motivated by a fundamental challenge introduced by Aggarwal and Maurer (EUROCRYPT '09), we propose an extension of the generic-group model that enables us to capture a bounded amount of arbitrary non-generic information (e.g., least-significant bits or Jacobi symbols that are hard to compute generically but are easy to compute non-generically). We prove our lower bound within this extended model, which may be of independent interest for strengthening the implications of impossibility results in idealized models.

1 Introduction

Cryptographic accumulators [BdM93], in their most basic form, generate a short commitment to a given set of elements while supporting non-interactive and publicly-verifiable membership proofs. Such accumulators, as well as ones that

G. Schul-Ganz and G. Segev—Supported by the European Union's Horizon 2020 Framework Program (H2020) via an ERC Grant (Grant No. 714253).

R. Pass and K. Pietrzak (Eds.): TCC 2020, LNCS 12551, pp. 77–107, 2020.
https://doi.org/10.1007/978-3-030-64378-2_4

offer more advanced features (e.g., non-membership proofs, aggregation of proofs and batch verification) have been studied extensively given their wide applicability to authenticating remotely-stored data (see, for example, [BdM93, ST99, BLL00, CL02, NN98, CJ10, ABC+12, Sla12, MGG+13, CF14, GGM14, PS14] and the references therein).

Known constructions of accumulators can be roughly classified into two categories: hash-based constructions and group-based constructions. Hash-based constructions generate a short commitment via a Merkle tree [Mer87, CHK+08], where the length of the resulting commitment is independent of the number of accumulated elements, and the length of membership proofs and the verification time are both logarithmic in the number of accumulated elements. Group-based constructions, exploiting the *structure* provided by their underlying groups, lead to accumulators in which the length of the commitment, the length of membership proofs and the verification time are all independent of the number of accumulated elements. Such accumulators have been constructed in RSA groups [BP97, CL02, LLX07, Lip12] and in bilinear groups [Ngu05, DT08, CKS09]. In both cases the constructions do not exploit any particular property of the representation of the underlying groups, and are thus generic-group constructions [Nec94, BL96, Sho97, MW98, DK02, Mau05, JS08, JR10, JS13, FKL18].[1]

Accumulators with Batch Verification. Motivated by recent applications of accumulators to stateless blockchains and interactive oracle proofs [Tod16, BCS16, AHI+17, BSBH+18, BCR+19], Boneh, Bünz and Fisch [BBF19] developed techniques for the aggregation of membership proofs (and even of non-membership proofs) and for their batch verification. Given that hash-based accumulators seem less suitable for offering such advanced features [OWW+20], Boneh et al. exploited the structure provided by RSA groups, and more generally by unknown-order groups such as the class group of an imaginary quadratic number field.

Specifically, Boneh et al. showed that membership proofs and non-membership proofs for any subset of t elements can be aggregated into a single proof whose length is independent of t. Then, by relying on the techniques of Wesolowski [Wes19], they showed that such aggregated proofs can be verified via an *interactive* protocol, where the number of group operations performed by the verifier is nearly independent of t (instead of growing with t in a multiplicative manner as in the verification of t separate proofs). By applying the Fiat-Shamir transform with a hash function that produces random primes, Boneh et al. showed that their interactive verification protocol yields a *non-interactive publicly-verifiable* verification procedure. Analogous results were subsequently obtained in bilinear groups by Thakur [Tha19], who extended the techniques

---

[1] We note that the RSA-based accumulator hashes the elements into primes before accumulating them. This is captured within the generic-group model since the accumulated elements are provided explicitly as bit-strings (i.e., they are not group elements and therefore such hashing can be performed by generic algorithms). Equivalently, the RSA-based accumulator can be viewed as a generic-group accumulator that accumulates prime numbers.

of Boneh et al. and Wesolowski to such groups based on the constructions of Nguyen [Ngu05] and of Damgård and Triandopoulos [DT08].

Non-trivial Batch Verification vs. Interaction. Other than applying the Fiat-Shamir transform for obtaining a non-interactive verification procedure, the constructions of Boneh et al. and Thakur are generic-group constructions, relying on the existing generic-group accumulators in RSA groups [BP97, CL02, LLX07] and in bilinear groups [Ngu05, DT08]. This introduces a substantial gap between generic-group accumulators that support non-trivial batch verification and generic-group accumulators that support only trivial batch verification (i.e., via the verification of individual proofs). Given the key importance of non-interactive verification in most applications that involve accumulators, this leads to the following fundamental question:

> *Does non-trivial batch verification in generic-group*
> *accumulators require interaction?*

This question is of significant importance not only from the foundational perspective of obtaining a better understanding of the feasibility and efficiency of supporting advanced cryptographic features, but also from the practical perspective. Specifically, following Wesolowski [Wes19], Boneh et al. implement the Fiat-Shamir transform using a hash function that produces random primes. As discussed by Boneh et al. [BBF19] and by Ozdemir, Wahby, Whitehat and Boneh [OWW+20], who proposed various potential realizations for such a hash function, this affects the efficiency, the correctness and the security of the resulting accumulator. More generally, and even when implementing the Fiat-Shamir transform via any standard hash function, in many cases the transformation violates the elegant algebraic structure of the underlying interactive protocol, leading to potentially-substantial overheads when implemented within larger systems (e.g., systems that rely on efficient algebraic proof systems).

1.1 Our Contributions

We prove a tight lower bound on the number of group operations performed during batch verification by any generic-group accumulator that uses less-than-trivial space. In particular, we show that no such accumulator can support non-trivial batch verification in the standard non-interactive manner. Our lower bound applies already to the most basic form of accumulators (i.e., static accumulators that support membership proofs), and holds both for known-order (and even multilinear) groups and for unknown-order groups, where it matches the asymptotic performance of the known bilinear and RSA accumulators, respectively.[2]

Moreover, motivated by a fundamental challenge introduced by Aggarwal and Maurer [AM09]), we propose an extension of the generic-group model that

---

[2] Our results hold also for the more restrictive notion of vector commitments [CF13, BBF19, LM19], which provide the same functionality as accumulators, but for ordered lists instead of sets.

enables us to capture a bounded amount of arbitrary non-generic information (e.g., least significant bits or Jacobi symbols that are hard to compute generically but are easy to compute non-generically [AM09, JS13]). We prove our lower bound within this extended model, where we measure efficiency in terms of the number of group operations and in terms of the amount of non-generic information. This extension of the generic-group model may be of independent interest for strengthening the implications of impossibility results in idealized models.

In what follows we state our results somewhat informally in order to avoid introducing the entire list of parameters with which we capture the efficiency of generic-group accumulators (we refer the reader to Sect. 2.2 for our formal definitions). Here we will focus on the following three main parameters, n_{Acc}, ℓ_{Acc} and q, that are associated with an accumulator $\mathcal{ACC}$, where we denote by $\lambda \in \mathbb{N}$ the security parameter:

- $n_{\mathsf{Acc}}(\lambda, k)$ and $\ell_{\mathsf{Acc}}(\lambda, k)$ are the number of group elements and the bit-length of the explicit string, respectively, stored by the accumulator when accumulating k elements.
- $q(\lambda, t, k)$ is the number of group-operation queries issued by the accumulator's verification procedure when verifying a membership proof for t out of k elements.

Our Main Result. Our main result is a tight bound on the trade-off between the amount of information that an accumulator stores when accumulating $k \geq 1$ elements and its number of group operations when verifying a membership proof for $1 \leq t \leq k$ elements. We prove that this number of group operations must scale multiplicatively with t, thus ruling out non-trivial batch verification. This is captured by the following theorem which applies both to known-order groups and to unknown-order groups.[3]

Theorem 1.1 (Simplified). *For any generic-group accumulator $\mathcal{ACC}$ over a domain $\mathcal{X} = \{\mathcal{X}_\lambda\}_{\lambda \in \mathbb{N}}$ it holds that*

$$q(\lambda, t, k) = \Omega \left(t \cdot \frac{\log_2 \binom{|\mathcal{X}_\lambda|}{k} - \left[n_{\mathsf{Acc}} \cdot \log_2(n_{\mathsf{Acc}} + 1) + \ell_{\mathsf{Acc}} \right]}{k} \cdot \frac{1}{\log \lambda} \right)$$

for all sufficiently large $\lambda \in \mathbb{N}$. In particular, if $|\mathcal{X}_\lambda| = 2^{\Omega(\lambda)}$ then for any $0 < \epsilon < 1$ either

$$n_{\mathsf{Acc}} \cdot \log_2(n_{\mathsf{Acc}} + 1) + \ell_{\mathsf{Acc}} \geq (1 - \epsilon) \cdot \log_2 \binom{|\mathcal{X}_\lambda|}{k}$$

or

$$q(\lambda, k, t) = \Omega \left(t \cdot \frac{\epsilon \lambda}{\log \lambda} \right).$$

---

[3] We note that all logarithms in this paper are to the base of 2, which we omit whenever used within asymptotic expressions in a multiplicative manner.

For interpreting our main theorem, note that $\log_2 \binom{|\mathcal{X}_\lambda|}{k}$ is the expected number of bits required for an exact representation of k elements, and that $n_{\text{Acc}} \cdot \log_2(n_{\text{Acc}} + 1) + \ell_{\text{Acc}}$ is the amount of information that is actually stored by a generic-group accumulator from its verification algorithm's point of view: $n_{\text{Acc}} \cdot \log_2(n_{\text{Acc}}+1)$ bits of information resulting from the equality pattern among the n_{Acc} stored group elements, and ℓ_{Acc} additional explicit bits of information. Thus, the expression

$$\frac{\log_2 \binom{|\mathcal{X}_\lambda|}{k} - \left[n_{\text{Acc}} \cdot \log_2(n_{\text{Acc}} + 1) + \ell_{\text{Acc}} \right]}{k}$$

captures the average information loss per accumulated element. Our theorem shows that as long as the amount of information stored by an accumulator is bounded away from the information-theoretic amount that is required for an exact representation, then non-trivial batch verification is impossible.

Our lower bound on the efficiency of batch verification matches the performance of the RSA accumulator considered by Boneh et al. [BBF19] in which $n_{\text{Acc}} = 1$ and $\ell_{\text{Acc}} = 0$ (i.e., the accumulator stores just a single group element), and $|\mathcal{X}_\lambda| = 2^{\Omega(\lambda)}$. In this accumulator, batch verification of t elements can be computed via a single exponentiation in the group $\mathbb{Z}_N^*$, where the exponent is the product of t numbers, each of which is of length λ bits. Since the order of the group is unknown, it seems that the exponent cannot be reduced modulo the group order prior to the exponentiation, and therefore this computation requires $\Omega(t \cdot \lambda)$ group operations, or $\Omega\left(t \cdot \frac{\lambda}{\log \lambda} \right)$ group operations with preprocessing [BGM+92] – thus matching our lower bound.[4]

Moreover, we show that our result holds even in the generic d-linear group model for any $d \geq 2$. We generalize Theorem 1.1 and similarly show that $\Omega\left(t \cdot \frac{\lambda}{\log \lambda} \cdot \frac{1}{d} \right)$ group operations are required for batch verifying a membership proof for t elements. This matches the performance of the bilinear accumulator constructed by Nguyen [Ngu05] in which $n_{\text{Acc}} = 1$ and $\ell_{\text{Acc}} = 0$ (i.e., the accumulator stores just a single group element), and $|\mathcal{X}_\lambda| = 2^{\Omega(\lambda)}$. In this accumulator, trivial batch verification of t elements consists of computing t exponentiations, translating to $\Omega(t \cdot \lambda)$ group operations, or to $\Omega\left(t \cdot \frac{\lambda}{\log \lambda} \right)$ group operations with preprocessing as above. This once again matches our lower bound, showing that trivial batch verification is indeed optimal for this accumulator.

Beyond Generic Groups. Lower bounds in idealized models shed substantial insight on our understanding of a wide range of both hardness assumptions and cryptographic constructions. For example, such lower bounds apply to a wide range of algorithms and constructions, and thus help directing cryptanalytic efforts and candidate constructions away from generic impossibility results.

---

[4] The additional information resulting from such preprocessing can be included with the information stored by the accumulator. This amount of information is independent of the number of accumulated elements, and thus does not influence our result.

However, despite their importance, a major drawback of such lower bounds is clearly their restriction to idealized models. This drawback was discussed by Aggarwal and Maurer [AM09], noting that there are certain computations that are hard with respect to generic algorithms but are extremely simple with respect to non-generic ones. Two important examples for such computations are computing the least significant bit [AM09] or the Jacobi symbol of a random group element [JS13]. Motivated by this major drawback, Aggarwal and Maurer proposed the problem of considering more general and realistic models where all algorithms are given access, for example, to least significant bits or Jacobi symbols of elements.

Addressing the challenge introduced by Aggarwal and Maurer, we show that our techniques are applicable even in an extended model that enables us to capture a bounded amount of non-generic information. Specifically, for any family Φ of predicates $\phi(\cdot, \cdot)$ that take as input the group order and a group element, we equip all algorithms with access to an oracle that responds to Φ-queries: On input a query of the form $(\phi, \widehat{x})$, where $\phi \in \Phi$ and $\widehat{x}$ is an implicit representation of a group element x, the oracle returns $\phi(N, x)$ where N is the order of the group. We refer to this extension as the Φ-augmented generic-group model, and note that the family Φ may be tailored to the specific non-generic structure of any underlying group. This model, allowing a bounded amount of non-generic information, can be viewed as an intermediate model between the generic-group model that does not allow any non-generic information, and the algebraic-group model [FKL18, MTT19, AHK20, FPS20] that allows direct access to the representation of the underlying group.

At a high-level, we prove that our result still holds for any family Φ of polynomially-many predicates (in particular, it still holds for the case $|\Phi| = 2$ that enables to compute least significant bits and Jacobi symbols). More specifically, letting $q(\lambda, t, k)$ denote the number of group-operation queries and Φ-queries issued by an accumulator's verification procedure when verifying a membership proof for t out of k elements, and considering also predicate families Φ of super-polynomial size, we prove the following theorem (which again applies both to known-order groups and to unknown-order groups).

Theorem 1.2 (Simplified). *For any predicate family Φ and for any Φ-augmented generic-group accumulator $\mathcal{ACC}$ over a domain $\mathcal{X} = \{\mathcal{X}_\lambda\}_{\lambda \in \mathbb{N}}$ it holds that*

$$q(\lambda, t, k) = \Omega \left(t \cdot \frac{\log_2 \binom{|\mathcal{X}_\lambda|}{k} - \left[n_{\mathsf{Acc}} \cdot \log_2(n_{\mathsf{Acc}} + 1) + \ell_{\mathsf{Acc}} \right]}{k} \cdot \frac{1}{\log \lambda + \log |\Phi|} \right)$$

for all sufficiently large $\lambda \in \mathbb{N}$. In particular, if $|\mathcal{X}_\lambda| = 2^{\Omega(\lambda)}$ then for any $0 < \epsilon < 1$ either

$$n_{\mathsf{Acc}} \cdot \log_2(n_{\mathsf{Acc}} + 1) + \ell_{\mathsf{Acc}} \geq (1 - \epsilon) \cdot \log_2 \binom{|\mathcal{X}_\lambda|}{k}$$

or

$$q(\lambda, k, t) = \Omega\left(t \cdot \frac{\epsilon\lambda}{\log \lambda + \log |\Phi|}\right).$$

It should be noted that our result in this augmented model do not contradict the highly-efficient non-interactive batch verification procedures of the accumulators constructed by Boneh, Bünz and Fisch [BBF19] and by Thakur [Tha19]. Their verification procedures are obtained by applying the (non-generic) Fiat-Shamir transform to interactive verification protocols. Although our augmented model does allow any predicate family Φ, the trade-off resulting from Theorem 1.2 becomes meaningless when instantiated with the parameters that are required for accommodating the Fiat-Shamir transform.

For example, it is possible to consider a predicate family Φ that consists of predicates ϕ_i that output the i-th output bit of any given collection of hash functions. However, within our model, the family Φ has to be fixed ahead of time, whereas the soundness of the Fiat-Shamir transform relies on the hash function being completely random. This means that realizing the Fiat-Shamir transform within our augmented model requires including such a predicate $\phi_{h,i}$ for every function h mapping group elements to, say, λ bits, as this would then enable sampling a random function. However, in this case, the size $|\Phi|$ of the family Φ becomes too large for our trade-off to be meaningful. An additional example is a predicate family Φ that consists of predicates ϕ_i that directly output the i-th bit of a group element. Applying these predicates to all group elements in the view of the verification algorithm increases the number q of queries that are issued by the verification algorithm at least by a multiplicative factor of λ (i.e., λ queries for each group element), and then once again our trade-off is no longer meaningful – and thus does not contradict the known non-generic constructions.

1.2   Overview of Our Approach

The Framework. We prove our result within the generic-group model introduced by Maurer [Mau05], which together with the incomparable model introduced by Shoup [Sho97], seem to be the most commonly used approaches for capturing generic-group computations. At a high level, in both models algorithms have access to an oracle for performing the group operation and for testing whether two group elements are equal. The difference between the two models is in the way that algorithms specify their queries to the oracle. In Maurer's model algorithms specify their queries by pointing to two group elements that have appeared in the computation so far (e.g., the 4th and the 7th group elements), whereas in Shoup's model group elements have an explicit representation (sampled uniformly at random from the set of all injective mappings from the group to sufficiently long strings) and algorithms specify their queries by providing two strings that have appeared in the computation so far as encodings of group elements.

Jager and Schwenk [JS08] proved that the complexity of any computational problem that is defined in a manner that is independent of the representation of the underlying group (e.g., computing discrete logarithms) in one model is essentially equivalent to its complexity in the other model. However, not all generic cryptographic constructions are independent of the underlying representation.

More generally, these two models are rather incomparable. On one hand, the class of cryptographic schemes that are captured by Maurer's model is a subclass of that of Shoup's model – although as demonstrated by Maurer his model still captures all schemes that only use the abstract group operation and test whether two group elements are equal. On the other hand, the same holds also for the class of adversaries, and thus in Maurer's model we have to break the security of a given scheme using an adversary that is more restricted when compared to adversaries in Shoup's model. We refer the reader to Sect. 2.1 for a formal description of Maurer's generic-group model.[5]

Generic-Group Accumulators. A generic-group accumulator $\mathcal{ACC}$ consists of three algorithms, denoted Setup, Prove and Vrfy. Informally (and very briefly), the algorithm Setup receives as input a set $X \subseteq \mathcal{X}$ of elements to accumulate and produces a representation Acc together with a secret state, where $\mathcal{X}$ is the universe of all possible elements. The algorithm Prove receives as input the secret state and a set $S \subseteq X$, and outputs a membership proof π, which can then be verified by the algorithm Vrfy. Note that the case $|S| = 1$ captures standard verification of individual elements, whereas the case $|S| > 1$ captures batch verification (i.e., simultaneous verification of sets of elements). Each of these algorithms may receive as input and return as output a combination of group elements and explicit strings.

We consider the standard notion of security for accumulators when naturally extended to consider batch verification. That is, we consider an adversary who specifies a set $X \subseteq \mathcal{X}$ of elements, receives an accumulator Acc that is honestly generated for X, and can then ask for honestly-generated membership proofs for sets $S \subseteq X$ (in fact, the adversary we present for proving our result does not require such *adaptive* and *post-challenge* access to honestly-generated proofs). Then, the adversary aims at outputting a pair (S^*, π^*) that is accepted by the verification algorithm as a valid membership proof for the set S^* with respect to the accumulator Acc although $S^* \nsubseteq X$. We refer the reader to Sect. 2.2 for formal definitions.

From Capturing Information Loss to Exploiting it. We prove our result by presenting a generic-group adversary that attacks any generic-group accumulator. Our attacker is successful against any accumulator that does not satisfy the trade-off stated in Theorem 1.1 between the amount of information that the accumulator stores and the number of group-operation queries issued by its verification algorithm. The main idea underlying our approach can be summarized via the following two key steps:

---

[5] In fact, we consider two different flavors of Maurer's model, for capturing both known-order and unknown-order groups. The reader is referred to Sect. 2.1 for an in-depth discussion of these two flavors and of the extent to which each of them captures group-based cryptographic constructions.

- **Step I: Capturing the information loss.** We identify and account for the total amount of information on a random set X of accumulated elements from the point of view of a generic-group verification algorithm.
- **Step II: Exploiting the information loss.** We show that any gap between this amount of information and the amount of information that is required for an exact representation of such a set X can be exploited by a generic-group attacker for generating a false batch-membership proof.

In what follows we elaborate on these two steps, first focusing on our main result and then discussing its extensions. Let $\mathcal{ACC} = (\mathsf{Setup}, \mathsf{Prove}, \mathsf{Vrfy})$ be a generic-group accumulator, and consider the view of its verification algorithm Vrfy on input an accumulator Acc, a set S, and a membership proof π for the fact that all elements of S have been accumulated within Acc. For simplicity, we assume here that Acc and π consist only of group elements, and we note that our proof in fact considers the more general case where they may consist of both group elements and explicit strings. Then, the view of the verification algorithm consists of the following ingredients:

- The accumulator Acc consists of group elements, and therefore the verification algorithm essentially only observes the equality pattern among these elements, and does not observe the elements themselves. This enables us to upper bound the amount of information provided by Acc by upper bounding the number of possible equality patterns among the group elements that are included in Acc.
- Once the computation starts, the verification algorithm generates a sequence of group-operation queries, where each such query is specified by pointing to two group elements that have appeared in the computation so far (we allow the verification algorithm to issue all possible equality queries). The following two observations enable us to upper bound the amount of information provided by this computation by upper bounding the number of possible query patterns that the verification algorithm observes, together with the number of possible equality patterns among the group elements included in the proof π and among the responses to the queries: (1) There are only polynomially-many possibilities for the two pointers included in each query (since queries are specified by pointing to two group elements that have appeared in the computation so far), and (2) we can effectively upper bound the number of possible query patterns induced by the proof and the responses using the number of queries issued by the verification algorithm instead of using the length of the proof π (which may be significantly larger).

This accounts for the total amount of information that is available to the verification algorithm from a single execution. However, different executions of the verification algorithm may be highly correlated via Acc and via the membership proofs (which are all generated from the secret state). Therefore, in order to capture the total amount of information that is available on the entire accumulated set X, our attacker $\mathcal{A}$ gathers this information as follows. First, it chooses a random set $X \subseteq \mathcal{X}$ of k elements for which the setup algorithm Setup will honestly generate an accumulator Acc. Then, $\mathcal{A}$ partitions X into subsets of size t, and asks for an honestly-generated batch-membership proof for each such subset. Next, $\mathcal{A}$ executes the verification algorithm to verify each of these k/t proofs, and records the above information for all of the subsets.

At this point we show that the information recorded from these k/t batch verifications must be at least the amount of information that is required for representing a random set X of size k. This is done by proving that, with high probability over the choice of X, this information can be exploited for forging a batch-membership proof for a set $S^* \nsubseteq X$ of size t. The most subtle part of our proof is in tailoring the set S^* and its false proof in a manner that is indistinguishable to the verification algorithm from those of at least one of the k/t subsets of X, and we refer the reader to Sect. 3 for the details of this part of our attack.

Extensions. As discussed above, we extend our result to accumulators in generic d-linear groups and to accumulators that rely on a bounded amount of non-generic information. Both of these extensions essentially rely on the same basic idea, which is the observation that each query issued by the verification algorithm can be fully represented in a somewhat succinct manner. Specifically, each such query is determined by: (1) Pointers to its inputs (where the number of inputs may now range from 2 to d), (2) the type of query (e.g., addition or subtraction queries in $\mathbb{Z}_N$, multilinear queries, or any other type of non-generic query $\phi \in \Phi$), and (3) the contribution of its response to the equality pattern among all group elements involved in the computation, or the contribution of its explicit response to the overall amount of information in the case of non-generic queries. For each of these two extensions, we first adapt our proof to identify and account for the total amount of information on a random set X of accumulated elements from the verification algorithm's point of view. Then, we accordingly adapt our tailored set S^* and its false proof in a manner that remains indistinguishable to the verification algorithm even when equipped with more expressive queries.

1.3 Related Work

In addition to the above-discussed motivation underlying our work, the problem we consider can be viewed as inspired by a long line of research on proving efficiency trade-offs for various primitives that are constructed in a black-box manner in the standard model (see, for example, [KST99, GGK+05, BM07, Wee07, BM09, HK10, HHR+15] and the many references therein). Despite the similarity in terms of the goal of proving efficiency trade-offs, there are several fundamental differences between this line of research and our work, as we now discuss.

Conceptually, results in this line of research provide lower bounds for constructions that are based on specific and somewhat weak assumptions, such as the existence of one-way functions or permutations. Our work provides a lower bound for any generic-group scheme, capturing assumptions that seem significantly stronger than the existence of minimal cryptographic primitives. As a consequence, our lower bound applies to a wide variety of practical constructions, instead of somewhat theoretical constructions that are based on minimal assumptions.

Generally speaking, it is more challenging to prove lower bounds for schemes in the generic-group model when compared to lower bounds for black-box constructions based on minimal assumptions. One-way functions or permutations are typically modeled via random functions or permutations, which admit very little structure that can be utilized by cryptographic constructions. This stands in complete contrast to generic-group constructions that exploit the algebraic structure of the underlying groups. The prime example for this substantial gap is the fact that key-agreement protocols do not exist relative to a random function or permutation, but do exist based on the decisional Diffie-Hellman assumption and thus in the generic-group model [DH76, IR89, BM09].

Technically, out of this long line of research, the result that is closest to the problem we consider is that of Horvitz and Katz [HK10]. They proved a lower bound on the efficiency of statistically-binding commitment schemes based on one-way permutations, in terms of the number of invocations of the one-way permutation during the commit stage. In addition to the above-discussed differences between this line of research and our work, here we would like to point out two more differences. First, Horvitz and Katz proved a lower bound for a primitive with statistical soundness, whereas we consider a primitive with standard computational soundness[6]. Second, and much more crucial, they proved a lower bound on the efficiency of the *commit* stage, whereas we prove a lower bound on the efficiency of *verification*. This is especially crucial given that accumulators can be viewed as commitments with short local openings, and thus in general a lower bound on the efficiency of the commit stage does not seem to imply any meaningful lower bound on the efficiency of the decommit stage.

1.4 Paper Organization

The remainder of this paper is organized as follows. First, in Sect. 2 we present the basic notation used throughout the paper, and formally describe the framework of generic-group accumulators. In Sect. 3 we prove our main result in the generic-group model, and in Sect. 4 we briefly discuss several open problems that arise from this work. Due to space limitations we refer the reader to the full version of this work for the extension of our result to the generic multilinear-group model and to its extension beyond the generic-group model.

2 Preliminaries

In this section we present the basic notions and standard cryptographic tools that are used in this work. For a distribution X we denote by $x \leftarrow X$ the process

---

[6] When interpreted in our setting of the generic-group model (where algorithms are unbounded in their internal computation), computational soundness considers adversaries that issue a polynomial bounded of group-operation queries, whereas statistical soundness considers adversaries that may issue an unbounded number of such queries.

of sampling a value x from the distribution X. Similarly, for a set $\mathcal{X}$ we denote by $x \leftarrow \mathcal{X}$ the process of sampling a value x from the uniform distribution over $\mathcal{X}$. For an integer $n \in \mathbb{N}$ we denote by $[n]$ the set $\{1, \ldots, n\}$. For a vector $v \in \mathcal{X}^k$, where $\mathcal{X}$ is a set and $k \in \mathbb{N}$, and for any $j \in [k]$, we denote by $(v)_j$ the jth coordinate of v. For a set $\mathcal{J} \subseteq \mathbb{Z}$ and an integer $i \in \mathbb{Z}$ we let $i + \mathcal{J} = \{i + j | j \in \mathcal{J}\}$. A function $\nu : \mathbb{N} \to \mathbb{R}^+$ is *negligible* if for any polynomial $p(\cdot)$ there exists an integer N such that for all $n > N$ it holds that $\nu(n) \leq 1/p(n)$.

2.1   Generic Groups and Algorithms

We prove our results within the generic-group model introduced by Maurer [Mau05]. We consider computations in cyclic groups of order N (all of which are isomorphic to $\mathbb{Z}_N$ with respect to addition modulo N), for a λ-bit integer N that is generated by an order-generation algorithm $\mathsf{OrderGen}(1^\lambda)$, where $\lambda \in \mathbb{N}$ is the security parameter (and N may or may not be prime).

When considering such groups, each computation in Maurer's model is associated with a table $\mathbf{B}$. Each entry of this table stores an element of $\mathbb{Z}_N$, and we denote by V_i the group element that is stored in the ith entry. Generic algorithms access this table via an oracle $\mathcal{O}$, providing black-box access to $\mathbf{B}$ as follows. A generic algorithm $\mathcal{A}$ that takes d group elements as input (along with an optional bit-string) does not receive an explicit representation of these group elements, but instead, has oracle access to the table $\mathbf{B}$, whose first d entries store the $\mathbb{Z}_N$ elements corresponding to the d group element in $\mathcal{A}$'s input. That is, if the input of an algorithm $\mathcal{A}$ is a tuple $(g_1, \ldots, g_d, x)$, where $g_1, \ldots, g_d$ are group elements and x is an arbitrary string, then from $\mathcal{A}$'s point of view the input is the tuple $(\widehat{g_1}, \ldots, \widehat{g_d}, x)$, where $\widehat{g_1}, \ldots, \widehat{g_d}$ are pointers to the group elements $g_1, \ldots, g_d$ (these group elements are stored in the table $\mathbf{B}$), and x is given explicitly. All generic algorithms in this paper will receive as their first input a generator of the group; we capture this fact by always assuming that the first entry of $\mathbf{B}$ is occupied by $1 \in \mathbb{Z}_N$, and we will sometimes forgo noting this explicitly. The oracle $\mathcal{O}$ allows for two types of queries:

- **Group-operation queries:** On input $(i, j, \circ)$ for $i, j \in \mathbb{N}$ and $\circ \in \{+, -\}$, the oracle checks that the ith and jth entries of the table $\mathbf{B}$ are not empty, computes $V_i \circ V_j \bmod N$ and stores the result in the next available entry. If either the ith or the jth entries are empty, the oracle ignores the query.
- **Equality queries:** On input $(i, j, =)$ for $i, j \in \mathbb{N}$, the oracle checks that the ith and jth entries of the table $\mathbf{B}$ are not empty, and then returns 1 if $V_i = V_j$ and 0 otherwise. If either the ith or the jth entries are empty, the oracle ignores the query.

In this paper we consider interactive computations in which multiple algorithms pass group elements (as well as non-group elements) as inputs to one another. This is naturally supported by the model as follows: When a generic algorithm $\mathcal{A}$ outputs k group elements (along with a potential bit-string σ), it outputs the indices of k (non-empty) entries in the table $\mathbf{B}$ (together with σ).

When these outputs (or some of them) are passed on as inputs to a generic algorithm $\mathcal{C}$, the table **B** is re-initialized, and these values (and possibly additional group elements that $\mathcal{C}$ receives as input) are placed in the first entries of the table. Additionally, we rely on the following conventions:

1. Throughout the paper we refer to values as either "explicit" ones or "implicit" ones. Explicit values are all values whose representation (e.g., binary strings of a certain length) is explicitly provided to the generic algorithms under consideration. Implicit values are all values that correspond to group elements and that are stored in the table **B** – thus generic algorithms can access them only via oracle queries. We will sometimes interchange between providing group elements as input to generic algorithms implicitly, and providing them explicitly. Note that moving from the former to the latter is well defined, since a generic algorithm $\mathcal{A}$ that receives some of its input group elements explicitly can always simulate the computation as if they were received as part of the table **B**.

2. For a group element g, we will differentiate between the case where g is provided explicitly and the case where it is provided implicitly via the table **B**, using the notation g in the former case, and the notation $\widehat{g}$ in the latter. Additionally, we extend this notation to a vector v of group elements, which may be provided either explicitly (denoted v) or implicitly via the table **B** (denoted $\widehat{v}$).

Known-Order vs. Unknown-Order Generic Groups. We consider two flavors of generic groups: groups of known orders and groups of unknown orders. In the case of known-order groups, as discussed above we prove our results within Maurer's generic-group model [Mau05] that lets all algorithms receive the order of the underlying group as an explicit input.

In the case of unknown-order groups, we prove our results in a natural variant of Maurer's model by following the approach of Damgård and Koprowski [DK02]. They considered a variant of Shoup's "random-encoding" model [Sho97] where the order of the underlying group is not included as an explicit input to all algorithms (still, however, the corresponding order-generation algorithm OrderGen is publicly known). We consider the exact same variant of Maurer's model (i.e., Maurer's model where the order of the underlying group is not included as an explicit input to all algorithms) for proving our results for unknown-order groups.

The known-order and unknown-order flavors of generic groups are incomparable for analyzing the security of cryptographic constructions. In the known-order variant, constructions can explicitly rely on the order of the underlying group, but this holds for attackers as well. In the unknown-order variant, neither constructions or attackers can explicitly rely on the order of the underlying group.

Finally, it should be noted that these two flavors of generic groups seem to somewhat differ in the extents in which they capture group-based constructions of cryptographic primitives. While the known-order flavor seems to capture quite accurately generic computations in prime-order cyclic groups and multilinear groups, the unknown-order flavor seems somewhat less accurate in capturing generic computations in RSA groups. Specifically, in the unknown-order flavor, the order of the underlying group is hidden in an information-theoretic manner and generic algorithm are unbounded in their internal computation. However, in "natural" RSA-based constructions, the order of the underlying group is only computationally hidden (i.e., the modulus $N = P \cdot Q$ is known but the order of the multiplicative group $\mathbb{Z}_N^*$ is unknown based on the factoring assumption), and algorithms are polynomially-bounded in their computation.

Addressing these differences, Aggarwal and Maurer [AM09] proposed the incomparable generic-ring model, where algorithms are provided with the modulus N but are restricted in their computation. A interesting open problem for future research is whether or not our techniques extend to other idealized models such as the generic-ring model. Despite any potential differences between the various models, impossibility results in any idealized model direct cryptanalytic efforts and candidate constructions away from generic impossibility results, and serve as a necessary step towards proving such results within less-idealized models.

2.2   Generic-Group Accumulators

For concreteness, we frame the following definition for known-order generic groups, noting that the analogous definition for unknown-order generic groups is obtained by not providing the order N of the underlying group as an input to any of the algorithms. Our definition is parameterized by 5 functions corresponding to the measures of efficiency that are considered in our work, and we refer the reader to Table 1 for the list of all the parameters used in the following definition.

Definition 2.1. A generic-group $(n_{\mathsf{Acc}}, \ell_{\mathsf{Acc}}, n_\pi, \ell_\pi, q)$-accumulator over a domain $\mathcal{X} = \{\mathcal{X}_\lambda\}_{\lambda \in \mathbb{N}}$ is a triplet $\mathcal{ACC} = (\mathsf{Setup}, \mathsf{Prove}, \mathsf{Vrfy})$ of generic algorithms defined as follows:

- The algorithm Setup is a probabilistic algorithm that receives as input the security parameter $\lambda \in \mathbb{N}$, the group order N and a set $X \subseteq \mathcal{X}_\lambda$. It outputs an accumulator $\mathsf{Acc} = (\widehat{\mathsf{Acc}_\mathsf{G}}, \mathsf{Acc}_\mathsf{str})$ and a state $\mathsf{state} \in \{0,1\}^*$, where Acc_G is a sequence of $n_{\mathsf{Acc}}(\lambda, |X|)$ group elements, and $\mathsf{Acc}_\mathsf{str} \in \{0,1\}^{\ell_{\mathsf{Acc}}(\lambda, |X|)}$.
- The algorithm Prove is a probabilistic algorithm that receives as input an accumulator Acc, a state $\mathsf{state} \in \{0,1\}^*$ and a set $S \subseteq \mathcal{X}_\lambda$, and outputs a proof $\pi = (\widehat{\pi_G}, \pi_\mathsf{str})$, where π_G is a sequence of $n_\pi(\lambda, |S|, k)$ group elements, $\pi_\mathsf{str} \in \{0,1\}^{\ell_\pi(\lambda, |S|, k)}$ is an explicit string, and k is the number of elements that have been accumulated by Acc.
- The algorithm Vrfy is a deterministic algorithm that receives as input an accumulator Acc, a set $S \subseteq \mathcal{X}_\lambda$ and a proof π, issues an arbitrary number of *equality* queries and at most $q(\lambda, |S|, k)$ *group-operation* queries and outputs a bit $b \in \{0,1\}$, where k is the number of elements that have been accumulated by Acc. Note that we do not restrict the number of equality queries that

Table 1. The parameters considered in Definition 2.1.

λ	The security parameter
$k(\lambda)$	The number of accumulated elements (i.e., $k = |X|$)
$t(\lambda)$	The number of elements for which a batch membership proof is generated and then verified (i.e., $t = |S|$ where $S \subseteq X$)
$n_{\mathsf{Acc}}(\lambda, k)$	The number of group elements produced by Setup when accumulating a set of k elements
$\ell_{\mathsf{Acc}}(\lambda, k)$	The bit-length of the explicit string produced by Setup when accumulating a set of k elements
$n_\pi(\lambda, t, k)$	The number of group elements produced by Prove when proving membership of a set of t elements out of k accumulated elements
$\ell_\pi(\lambda, t, k)$	The bit-length of the explicit string produced by Prove when proving membership of a set of t elements out of k accumulated elements
$q(\lambda, t, k)$	The number of *group-operation* queries issued by Vrfy when verifying a membership proof for a set of t elements out of k accumulated elements (we prove our lower bound even for verification algorithms that issue an arbitrary number of *equality* queries)

are issued by the verification algorithm and this only makes our lower bound stronger (i.e., our lower bound on the number of group-operation queries holds even for accumulators in which the verification algorithm issues all possible equality queries).

Correctness. The correctness requirement for this most basic form of accumulators is quite natural: For any set $X \subseteq \mathcal{X}_\lambda$ of accumulated elements, any membership proof that is generated by the algorithm Prove for any set $S \subseteq X$ should be accepted by the algorithm Vrfy. More formally:

Definition 2.2. A generic-group accumulator $\mathcal{ACC} = (\mathsf{Setup}, \mathsf{Prove}, \mathsf{Vrfy})$ over a domain $\mathcal{X} = \{\mathcal{X}_\lambda\}_{\lambda \in \mathbb{N}}$ is correct with respect to an order-generation algorithm OrderGen if for any $\lambda \in \mathbb{N}$ and for any two sets $S \subseteq X \subseteq \mathcal{X}_\lambda$, it holds that

$$\Pr\left[\mathsf{Vrfy}^{\mathcal{O}}\left(\mathsf{Acc}, S, \pi\right) = 1\right] = 1$$

where $N \leftarrow \mathsf{OrderGen}(1^\lambda)$, $(\mathsf{Acc}, \mathsf{state}) \leftarrow \mathsf{Setup}^{\mathcal{O}}(\lambda, N, X)$ and $\pi \leftarrow \mathsf{Prove}^{\mathcal{O}}(\mathsf{Acc}, \mathsf{state}, S)$, and the probability is taken over the internal randomness of all algorithms.

Security. We extend the standard notion of security for accumulators to consider batch verification (i.e., supporting the simultaneous verification of sets of elements instead of individual elements). Our notion of security considers an adversary who specifies a set $X \subseteq \mathcal{X}_\lambda$ of elements, receives an accumulator Acc that is honestly generated for X, and can then ask for honestly-generated membership proofs for sets $S \subseteq X$. Then, the adversary aims at outputting a pair (S^*, π^*), where $S^* \subseteq \mathcal{X}_\lambda$, that is accepted by the verification algorithm as a valid membership proof for the set S^* with respect to the accumulator Acc although $S^* \nsubseteq X$.

Definition 2.3. A generic-group accumulator $\mathcal{ACC} = (\mathsf{Setup}, \mathsf{Prove}, \mathsf{Vrfy})$ over a domain $\mathcal{X} = \{\mathcal{X}_\lambda\}_{\lambda \in \mathbb{N}}$ is secure with respect to an order-generation algorithm OrderGen if for any algorithm $\mathcal{A} = (\mathcal{A}_0, \mathcal{A}_1)$ that issues a polynomial number of queries there exists a negligible function $\nu(\lambda)$ such that

$$\Pr\left[\mathsf{Expt}_{\mathcal{ACC},\mathcal{A}}(\lambda) = 1\right] \leq \nu(\lambda)$$

for all sufficiently large $\lambda \in \mathbb{N}$, where the experiment $\mathsf{Expt}_{\mathcal{ACC},\mathcal{A}}(\lambda)$ is defined as follows:

1. $N \leftarrow \mathsf{OrderGen}(1^\lambda)$.
2. $X \leftarrow \mathcal{A}_0^{\mathcal{O}}(1^\lambda, N)$ where $X \subseteq \mathcal{X}_\lambda$.
3. $(\mathsf{Acc}, \mathsf{state}) \leftarrow \mathsf{Setup}^{\mathcal{O}}(1^\lambda, N, X)$.
4. $(S^*, \pi^*) \leftarrow \mathcal{A}_1^{\mathcal{O}, \mathsf{Prove}^{\mathcal{O}}(\mathsf{Acc}, \mathsf{state}, \cdot)}(1^\lambda, N, \mathsf{Acc})$ where $S^* \subseteq \mathcal{X}_\lambda$.
5. If $\mathsf{Vrfy}^{\mathcal{O}}(\mathsf{Acc}, S^*, \pi^*) = 1$ and $S^* \nsubseteq X$ then output 1, and otherwise output 0.

Note that the above definition provides the algorithm $\mathcal{A}_1$ with *adaptive* and *post-challenge* access to the oracle $\mathsf{Prove}^{\mathcal{O}}(\mathsf{Acc}, \mathsf{state}, \cdot)$. In fact, the adversaries we present for proving our results do not require such a strong form of access to honestly-generated proofs. Specifically, already our algorithm $\mathcal{A}_0$ can specify a list of queries to this oracle, in a completely non-adaptive manner and independently of the challenge accumulator Acc. That is, our results apply already for a seemingly much weaker notion of security.

In addition, note that the output of the setup algorithm consists of two values: A public value Acc (the accumulator itself) that is used by both the Prove algorithm and the Vrfy algorithm, and a private state state that is used only by the Prove algorithm (the private state may include, for example, the randomness that was used by the Setup algorithm, for generating the accumulator).

Finally, as standard in the generic-group model, the above definition restricts only the number of queries issued by the adversary, and does not restrict the adversary's internal computation (i.e., the definition considers computationally-unbounded adversaries). As a consequence, note that without loss of generality such an adversary $\mathcal{A} = (\mathcal{A}_0, \mathcal{A}_1)$ is deterministic, and there is no need to transfer any state information from $\mathcal{A}_0$ to $\mathcal{A}_1$ (this can at most double the number of queries issued by $\mathcal{A}$).

3 Our Lower Bound in the Generic-Group Model

In this section we prove our main technical result, providing a lower bound on the number of group-operation queries required for batch verification. We prove the following theorem.

Theorem 3.1. *Let $\mathcal{ACC}$ be an $(n_{\mathsf{Acc}}, \ell_{\mathsf{Acc}}, n_\pi, \ell_\pi, q)$-accumulator in the generic-group model over a domain $\mathcal{X} = \{\mathcal{X}_\lambda\}_{\lambda \in \mathbb{N}}$, for some polynomials $n_{\mathsf{Acc}} = n_{\mathsf{Acc}}(\lambda, k)$, $\ell_{\mathsf{Acc}} = \ell_{\mathsf{Acc}}(\lambda, k)$, $n_\pi = n_\pi(\lambda, k, t)$, $\ell_\pi = \ell_\pi(\lambda, k, t)$ and $q = q(\lambda, k, t)$, and let $\mathsf{OrderGen}$ be an order-generation algorithm. If $\mathcal{ACC}$ is secure with respect to $\mathsf{OrderGen}$, then for any polynomials $k = k(\lambda) \geq 1$ and $t = t(\lambda) \leq k$ and for all sufficiently large $\lambda \in \mathbb{N}$ it holds that*

$$q(\lambda, t, k) = \Omega\left(t \cdot \frac{\log_2 \binom{|\mathcal{X}_\lambda|}{k} - \left[n_{\mathsf{Acc}} \cdot \log_2(n_{\mathsf{Acc}} + 1) + \ell_{\mathsf{Acc}} \right]}{k} \cdot \frac{1}{\log \lambda}\right).$$

As discussed in Sect. 1.1, recall that $\log_2 \binom{|\mathcal{X}_\lambda|}{k}$ is the expected number of bits required for an exact representation of k elements, and that $n_{\mathsf{Acc}} \cdot \log_2(n_{\mathsf{Acc}} + 1) + \ell_{\mathsf{Acc}}$ is the amount of information that is actually stored by a generic-group accumulator from its verification algorithm's point of view. The following corollary of Theorem 3.1 shows that as long as the amount of information stored by an accumulator is bounded away from the information-theoretic amount that is required for an exact representation, then non-trivial batch verification is impossible.

Corollary 3.2. *Let $\mathcal{ACC}$ be an $(n_{\mathsf{Acc}}, \ell_{\mathsf{Acc}}, n_\pi, \ell_\pi, q)$-accumulator in the generic-group model over a domain $\mathcal{X} = \{\mathcal{X}_\lambda\}_{\lambda \in \mathbb{N}}$, for some polynomials $n_{\mathsf{Acc}} = n_{\mathsf{Acc}}(\lambda, k)$, $\ell_{\mathsf{Acc}} = \ell_{\mathsf{Acc}}(\lambda, k)$, $n_\pi = n_\pi(\lambda, k, t)$, $\ell_\pi = \ell_\pi(\lambda, k, t)$ and $q = q(\lambda, k, t)$, and let $\mathsf{OrderGen}$ be an order-generation algorithm. If $\mathcal{ACC}$ is secure with respect to $\mathsf{OrderGen}$ and $|\mathcal{X}_\lambda| = 2^{\Omega(\lambda)}$, then for any polynomials $k = k(\lambda) \geq 1$ and $t = t(\lambda) \leq k$, for any $0 < \epsilon < 1$ and for all sufficiently large $\lambda \in \mathbb{N}$, either*

$$n_{\mathsf{Acc}} \cdot \log_2(n_{\mathsf{Acc}} + 1) + \ell_{\mathsf{Acc}} \geq (1 - \epsilon) \cdot \log_2 \binom{|\mathcal{X}_\lambda|}{k}$$

or

$$q(\lambda, k, t) = \Omega\left(t \cdot \frac{\epsilon \lambda}{\log \lambda}\right).$$

We prove the following lemma from which we then derive Theorem 3.1 and Corollary 3.2.

Lemma 3.3. *Let $\mathcal{ACC}$ be an $(n_{\mathsf{Acc}}, \ell_{\mathsf{Acc}}, n_\pi, \ell_\pi, q)$-accumulator in the generic-group model over a domain $\mathcal{X} = \{\mathcal{X}_\lambda\}_{\lambda \in \mathbb{N}}$, for some polynomials $n_{\mathsf{Acc}} = n_{\mathsf{Acc}}(\lambda, k)$, $\ell_{\mathsf{Acc}} = \ell_{\mathsf{Acc}}(\lambda, k)$, $n_\pi = n_\pi(\lambda, k, t)$, $\ell_\pi = \ell_\pi(\lambda, k, t)$ and $q = q(\lambda, k, t)$, and let $\mathsf{OrderGen}$ be an order-generation algorithm. If $\mathcal{ACC}$ is secure with respect to $\mathsf{OrderGen}$ then for any polynomials $k = k(\lambda) \geq 1$ and $t = t(\lambda) \leq k$ and for all sufficiently large $\lambda \in \mathbb{N}$ it holds that*

$$\frac{1}{2} \cdot \binom{|\mathcal{X}_\lambda|}{k} < (n_{\mathsf{Acc}} + 1)^{n_{\mathsf{Acc}}} \cdot 2^{\ell_{\mathsf{Acc}}} \cdot (n_{\mathsf{Acc}} + n_\pi + 3q + 1)^{6q \cdot \lceil k/t \rceil} \qquad (1)$$

In what follows, in Sect. 3.1 we prove Lemma 3.3, and then in Sect. 3.2 we rely on Lemma 3.3 for deriving the proofs of Theorem 3.1 and Corollary 3.2.

3.1   Proof of Lemma 3.3

For simplicity, we first prove the lemma for the case of known-order groups, and then show that the proof extends to unknown-order groups. The proof of Lemma 3.3 relies on the following notation given an $(n_{Acc}, \ell_{Acc}, n_\pi, \ell_\pi, q)$-generic-group accumulator $\mathcal{ACC} = (\mathsf{Setup}, \mathsf{Prove}, \mathsf{Vrfy})$ over a domain $\mathcal{X} = \{\mathcal{X}_\lambda\}_{\lambda \in \mathbb{N}}$ (recall Definition 2.1):

- In any execution of the verification algorithm $\mathsf{Vrfy}^{\mathcal{O}}(\mathsf{Acc}, S, \pi)$, note that the table $\mathbf{B}$ which stores group elements (and to which the oracle $\mathcal{O}$ provide black-box access – as described in Sect. 2.1) consists of at most $n_{Acc} + n_\pi + q + 1$ entries: The table contains the generator $1 \in \mathbb{Z}_N$ in its first entry (as standard for all computations in this model), then it contains the n_{Acc} group elements that are part of the accumulator Acc, the n_π group elements that are part of the proof π, and finally at most q additional group elements that result from the group-operation queries issued by the verification algorithm. In addition, recall that each such query can be specified by providing a pair of indices to entries in the table together with the query type (i.e., the group operation $+$ or the group operation $-$). Therefore, each query has at most $2(n_{Acc} + n_\pi + q + 1)^2$ possibilities. We let $\mathsf{VrfyQueries}_{\mathsf{Acc}, S, \pi}$ denote the concatenation of the encodings of all queries made during the computation $\mathsf{Vrfy}^{\mathcal{O}}(\mathsf{Acc}, S, \pi)$ (in the order in which the queries were issued). Thus, the total number of possibilities for $\mathsf{VrfyQueries}_{\mathsf{Acc}, S, \pi}$ is at most

$$\left(2 \cdot (n_{Acc} + n_\pi + q + 1)^2\right)^q \leq (n_{Acc} + n_\pi + q + 1)^{3q},$$

  since $2 \leq n_{Acc} + n_\pi + q + 1$.
- In any execution of the verification algorithm $\mathsf{Vrfy}^{\mathcal{O}}(\mathsf{Acc}, S, \pi)$ we would also like to encode the equality pattern of all group elements in the table $\mathbf{B}$. Recall that the table contains the generator $1 \in \mathbb{Z}_N$, the n_{Acc} group elements that are part of the accumulator Acc, the n_π group elements that are part of the proof π, and then at most q additional group elements that result from the group-operation queries issued by the verification algorithm. We split this encoding into the following three ingredients:
  - The equality pattern for the generator $1 \in \mathbb{Z}_N$ and the n_{Acc} group elements that are part of the accumulator Acc (i.e., for the $n_{Acc} + 1$ first entries of the table) can be encoded as follows: For each of the n_{Acc} group elements that are part of the accumulator Acc we encode the index of the minimal entry among the first $n_{Acc} + 1$ entries of the table that contains the same group element (independently of whether a corresponding equality query was explicitly issued by the verification algorithm). We denote this encoding by $\mathsf{AccEqualities}_{\mathsf{Acc}}$. There are at most $(n_{Acc} + 1)^{n_{Acc}}$ possibilities for $\mathsf{AccEqualities}_{\mathsf{Acc}}$.
  - The equality pattern for the n_π group elements that are part of the proof π (i.e., for the next n_π entries of the table) can be similarly encoded which results in at most $(n_{Acc} + n_\pi + 1)^{n_\pi}$ possibilities. However, n_π can

be significantly larger than q, and this may potentially lead to a too-long encoding for the purpose of our proof.

Thus, instead of encoding the equality pattern among all n_π group elements that are part of the proof π, it is in fact sufficient for us to encode the equality pattern only among those elements that are involved in the group-operation queries that are issued during the computation $\mathsf{Vrfy}^{\mathcal{O}}(\mathsf{Acc}, S, \pi)$. There are at most q such queries, and therefore we need to encode the equality pattern only among at most $2q$ elements out of the n_π group elements that are part of the proof π. For each such element we encode the index of the minimal entry among the first $n_{\mathsf{Acc}}+2q+1$ entries of the table that contains the same group element (not including the entries that are not involved in any of the group-operation queries). The number of possibilities for $\mathsf{ProofEqualities}_{\mathsf{Acc},S,\pi}$, is at most $(n_{\mathsf{Acc}} + 2q + 1)^{2q}$.

- The equality pattern for the (at most) q group elements that result from the group-operation queries issued by the verification algorithm (i.e., for the last q entries of the table) can be encoded the same way (while again not including the entries of the proof π that are not involved in any of the group-operation queries) resulting in at most $(n_{\mathsf{Acc}} + 2q + q + 1)^q$ possibilities. We denote this encoding by $\mathsf{QueriesEqualities}_{\mathsf{Acc},S,\pi}$.

Equipped with the above notation, we now prove Lemma 3.3.

Proof of Lemma 3.3. Let $\mathcal{ACC} = (\mathsf{Setup}, \mathsf{Prove}, \mathsf{Vrfy})$ be an $(n_{\mathsf{Acc}}, \ell_{\mathsf{Acc}}, n_\pi, \ell_\pi, q)$-generic-group accumulator for some $n_{\mathsf{Acc}} = n_{\mathsf{Acc}}(\lambda, k)$, $\ell_{\mathsf{Acc}} = \ell_{\mathsf{Acc}}(\lambda, k)$, $n_\pi = n_\pi(\lambda, k, t)$, $\ell_\pi = \ell_\pi(\lambda, k, t)$ and $q = q(\lambda, k, t)$, and let $\mathsf{OrderGen}$ be an order-generation algorithm. Fix any polynomials $k = k(\lambda) \geq 1$ and $t = t(\lambda) \leq k$. We show that if Eq. (1) does not hold for infinitely many values of $\lambda \in \mathbb{N}$, then there exists a generic-group attacker $\mathcal{A}$ that issues a polynomial number of queries for which $\Pr[\mathsf{Expt}_{\mathcal{ACC},\mathcal{A}}(\lambda) = 1]$ is non-negligible in the security parameter $\lambda \in \mathbb{N}$ (recall that the experiment $\mathsf{Expt}_{\mathcal{ACC},\mathcal{A}}(\lambda)$ was defined in Definition 2.3 for capturing the security of generic-group accumulators).

At a high level, for any security parameter $\lambda \in \mathbb{N}$ our attacker $\mathcal{A}$, participating in the experiment $\mathsf{Expt}_{\mathcal{ACC},\mathcal{A}}(\lambda)$, will choose a random set $X \subseteq \mathcal{X}_\lambda$ of k elements for which the setup algorithm Setup will honestly generate an accumulator. Then, $\mathcal{A}$ will partition S into subsets of size t, and ask for an honestly-generated batch membership proof for each such subset. Then, with high probability, this will allow $\mathcal{A}$ to forge a batch membership proof for a set $S^* \nsubseteq X$ of size t.

In what follows we first describe the attacker $\mathcal{A}$ and then analyze its success probability. For simplicity we assume throughout the proof that t divide k, and we let $v = k/t$ (this is not essential and can be trivially avoided at the cost of somewhat degrading the readability of the proof). In addition, we let $<$ denote any ordering of the elements of the set $\mathcal{X} = \{\mathcal{X}_\lambda\}_{n \in \mathbb{N}}$ (e.g., the lexicographic order). As discussed in Sect. 2.1, recall that for a group element g and for a vector of group elements v, we will differentiate between the case where g and v are provided explicitly and the case where they are provided implicitly via the table **B**, using the notation g and v in the former case, and the notation $\hat{g}$ and $\hat{v}$ in the latter.

The attacker $\mathcal{A} = (\mathcal{A}_0, \mathcal{A}_1)$

The algorithm $\mathcal{A}_0$. On input $(1^\lambda, N)$ and oracle access to $\mathcal{O}(\cdot)$, the algorithm $\mathcal{A}_0$ samples a uniformly distributed set $X \subseteq \mathcal{X}_\lambda$ that consists of k distinct elements $x_1 < \cdots < x_k$. It then outputs the set X, and also passes it as its internal state to the algorithm $\mathcal{A}_1$.

The algorithm $\mathcal{A}_1$. On input $(1^\lambda, N, \mathsf{Acc}, X)$ and oracle access to $\mathcal{O}(\cdot)$ and to $\mathsf{Prove}^{\mathcal{O}}(\mathsf{Acc}, \mathsf{state}, \cdot)$, where $(\mathsf{Acc}, \mathsf{state}) \leftarrow \mathsf{Setup}^{\mathcal{O}}(1^\lambda, N, X)$ is honestly-generated within the experiment $\mathsf{Expt}_{ACC,\mathcal{A}}(\lambda)$, the algorithm $\mathcal{A}_1$ is defined as follows:

1. The algorithm $\mathcal{A}_1$ computes the equality pattern $\mathsf{AccEqualities}_{\mathsf{Acc}}$ by issuing equality queries (recall that $\mathsf{Acc} = (\widehat{\mathsf{Acc}_\mathsf{G}}, \mathsf{Acc}_\mathsf{str})$, where Acc_G is a sequence of $n_\mathsf{Acc}(\lambda, k)$ group elements that can be accessed indirectly via oracle queries, and $\mathsf{Acc}_\mathsf{str} \in \{0,1\}^{\ell_\mathsf{Acc}(\lambda, k)}$ is an explicit string that can be accessed directly).

2. For every $i \in [v]$ the algorithm $\mathcal{A}_1$ queries the oracle $\mathsf{Prove}^{\mathcal{O}}(\mathsf{Acc}, \mathsf{state}, \cdot)$ with the set $S_i = \{x_{(i-1)\cdot t+1}, \ldots, x_{i\cdot t}\}$ to obtain a proof $\pi_i \leftarrow \mathsf{Prove}^{\mathcal{O}}(\mathsf{Acc}, \mathsf{state}, S_i)$. We denote $\pi_i = (\widehat{\pi_{i,G}}, \pi_{i,\mathsf{str}})$, where $\pi_{i,G}$ is a sequence of $n_\pi(\lambda, t, k)$ group elements that can be accessed indirectly via oracle queries and $\pi_{i,\mathsf{str}} \in \{0,1\}^{\ell_\pi(\lambda, t, k)}$ is an explicit string that can be accessed directly.

   Then, the algorithm $\mathcal{A}_1$ executes $\mathsf{Vrfy}^{\mathcal{O}}(\mathsf{Acc}, S_i, \pi_i)$ for obtaining the query pattern $\mathsf{VrfyQueries}_{\mathsf{Acc}, S_i, \pi_i}$ by forwarding the queries issued by Vrfy to the oracle $\mathcal{O}$, and issues additional equality queries for computing the equality patterns $\mathsf{ProofEqualities}_{\mathsf{Acc}, S_i, \pi_i}$ and $\mathsf{QueriesEqualities}_{\mathsf{Acc}, S_i, \pi_i}$.

3. The algorithm $\mathcal{A}_1$ finds a set $X' \subseteq \mathcal{X}_\lambda$ that consists of k distinct elements $x'_1 < \cdots < x'_k$, and strings $r', r'_1, \ldots, r'_v \in \{0,1\}^*$ satisfying the following requirements:

   - $X' \neq X$.
   - $\mathsf{AccEqualities}_{\mathsf{Acc}'} = \mathsf{AccEqualities}_{\mathsf{Acc}}$ and $\mathsf{Acc}'_\mathsf{str} = \mathsf{Acc}_\mathsf{str}$, where $(\mathsf{Acc}', \mathsf{state}') = \mathsf{Setup}(1^\lambda, N, X'; r')$ and $\mathsf{Acc}' = (\mathsf{Acc}'_\mathsf{G}, \mathsf{Acc}_\mathsf{str})$. Note that all inputs to the computation $\mathsf{Setup}(1^\lambda, N, X'; r')$ are explicitly known to $\mathcal{A}_1$, and therefore this computation can be internally emulated without any oracle queries.
   - For every $i \in [v]$ it holds that

     $$\mathsf{VrfyQueries}_{\mathsf{Acc}', S'_i, \pi'_i} = \mathsf{VrfyQueries}_{\mathsf{Acc}, S_i, \pi_i}$$
     $$\mathsf{ProofEqualities}_{\mathsf{Acc}', S'_i, \pi'_i} = \mathsf{ProofEqualities}_{\mathsf{Acc}, S_i, \pi_i}$$
     $$\mathsf{QueriesEqualities}_{\mathsf{Acc}', S'_i, \pi'_i} = \mathsf{QueriesEqualities}_{\mathsf{Acc}, S_i, \pi_i}$$

     where $\pi'_i = \mathsf{Prove}(\mathsf{Acc}', \mathsf{state}', S'_i; r'_i)$ and $S'_i = \{x'_{(i-1)\cdot t+1}, \ldots, x'_{i\cdot t}\}$.

   If such a set X' and strings $r', r'_1, \ldots, r'_v \in \{0,1\}^*$ do not exist, then the algorithm $\mathcal{A}_1$ aborts the experiment.

4. Let $i^* \in [v]$ be any index such that $S'_{i^*} \not\subseteq X$ (e.g., the smallest one), then the algorithm $\mathcal{A}_1$ outputs $S^* = S'_{i^*}$ and $\pi^* = (\widehat{\pi^*_G}, \pi^*_\mathsf{str})$, where π^*_G is a sequence of n_π group elements that are defined below and $\pi^*_\mathsf{str} = \pi'_{i^*, \mathsf{str}}$ is an explicit string.

(a) Let $\mathcal{J} \subseteq [n_\pi]$ be the positions of the group elements that are part of the proof π_{i^*} which are accessed by the group-operation queries issued during the computation $\mathsf{Vrfy}^{\mathcal{O}}(\mathsf{Acc}, S_{i^*}, \pi_{i^*})$.

(b) For every $j \in \mathcal{J}$ we define $(\pi_G^*)_j = (\pi_{i^*,G})_j$ (i.e., we set π_G^* to agree with $\pi_{i^*,G}$ on the group elements in the positions included in $\mathcal{J}$).

(c) Let $T = 1 + n_{\mathsf{Acc}} + n_\pi + q$, and for every $j \in [T]$ we denote by V_j and V_j' the group element at the jth entry of the table $\mathbf{B}$ in the computations $\mathsf{Vrfy}^{\mathcal{O}}(\mathsf{Acc}, S_{i^*}, \pi_{i^*})$ and $\mathsf{Vrfy}^{\mathcal{O}}(\mathsf{Acc}', S_{i^*}', \pi_{i^*}')$, respectively. Note that $T = 1 + n_{\mathsf{Acc}} + n_\pi + q$ is indeed an upper bound on the number of entries in the table $\mathbf{B}$ in these computations: The first entry contains the element $1 \in \mathbb{Z}_N$, the next n_{Acc} entries contain the group elements of the given accumulator, the next n_π entries contains the group elements of the given proof, and then there are at most q entries that result from the group-operation queries issued by the verification algorithm. Let $\mathcal{I} = \{1, \ldots, 1 + n_{\mathsf{Acc}}\} \cup (1 + n_{\mathsf{Acc}} + \mathcal{J}) \cup \{1 + n_{\mathsf{Acc}} + n_\pi + 1, \ldots, 1 + n_{\mathsf{Acc}} + n_\pi + q\} \subseteq [T]$. [Recall that $1 + n_{\mathsf{Acc}} + \mathcal{J} = \{1 + n_{\mathsf{Acc}} + j | j \in \mathcal{J}\}$.]

(d) For every $j \in [n_\pi] \setminus \mathcal{J}$ in increasing order we define $(\pi_G^*)_j$ as follows:

   i. If there exists a position $w \in \mathcal{I}$ such that $(\pi_{i^*,G}')_j = V_w'$, then we define $(\pi_G^*)_j = V_w$.

   ii. Otherwise, if for all positions $w \in \mathcal{I}$ it holds that $(\pi_{i^*,G}')_j \neq V_w'$ then
      A. If there exists some $k \in [n_\pi] \setminus \mathcal{J}$ such that $k < j$ and $(\pi_{i^*,G}')_j = (\pi_{i^*,G}')_k$, then define $(\pi_G^*)_j = (\pi_G^*)_k$ (note that $(\pi_G^*)_k$ is already defined in this stage since $k < j$).
      B. Otherwise, we define $(\pi_G^*)_j$ arbitrarily such that $(\pi_G^*)_j \neq V_w$ for all $w \in \mathcal{I}$ and $(\pi_G^*)_j \neq (\pi_G^*)_k$ for all $k \in [n_\pi] \setminus \mathcal{J}$ such that $k < j$.

At this point, after having described our attacker $\mathcal{A}$, we are ready to analyze its success probability: In Claim 3.4 we prove that $\mathcal{A}$ aborts with probability at most $1/2$, and in Claim 3.5 we prove that any execution in which $\mathcal{A}$ does not abort results in a successful forgery. First, however, we observe that the query complexity of our attacker is polynomial in $k(\lambda)$, $n_{\mathsf{Acc}}(\lambda, k)$, $n_\pi(\lambda, k, t)$ and $q(\lambda, k, t)$, and thus polynomial in the security parameter $\lambda \in \mathbb{N}$. Specifically, the algorithm $\mathcal{A}_0$ does not issue any queries, and the algorithm $\mathcal{A}_1$ issues the following queries:

- Step 1: This step requires at most $(n_{\mathsf{Acc}}(\lambda, k))^2$ queries for computing the equality pattern $\mathsf{AccEqualities}_{\mathsf{Acc}}$ among the group elements Acc_G of the given accumulator Acc.

- Step 2: This step requires v queries for obtaining the proofs $\pi_1, \ldots, \pi_v$, and at most $v \cdot (n_\pi(\lambda, t, k) + n_{\mathsf{Acc}}(\lambda, k))^2$ queries for computing the equality patterns $\mathsf{ProofEqualities}_{\mathsf{Acc}, S_i, \pi_i}$ among the group elements $\pi_{i,G}$ of the proofs $\pi_1, \ldots, \pi_v$. In addition, this step requires at most $v \cdot q(\lambda, t, k) + v \cdot (q(\lambda, t, k) + n_\pi(\lambda, t, k) + n_{\mathsf{Acc}}(\lambda, k))^2$ queries for computing the query patterns $\mathsf{VrfyQueries}_{\mathsf{Acc}, S_1, \pi_1}, \ldots,$ $\mathsf{VrfyQueries}_{\mathsf{Acc}, S_v, \pi_v}$ and the query equality patterns $\mathsf{QueriesEqualities}_{\mathsf{Acc}, S_1, \pi_1},$ $\ldots, \mathsf{QueriesEqualities}_{\mathsf{Acc}, S_v, \pi_v}$.

- Step 3: No queries. All inputs to the relevant computations are explicitly known to $\mathcal{A}_1$, and therefore these computations can be internally emulated without any oracle queries.

– Step 4: The sub-steps 4(a) – 4(c) do not require any queries, whereas sub-step 4(d) does require issuing both group-operation queries and equality queries. Specifically, in sub-step 4(d).ii.B. the attacker defines $(\pi_G^*)_j$ arbitrarily such that $(\pi_G^*)_j \neq V_w$ for all $w \in \mathcal{I}$ and $(\pi_G^*)_j \neq (\pi_G^*)_k$ for all $k \in [n_\pi] \setminus \mathcal{J}$ such that $k < j$. This can be done, for example, by adding $1 \in \mathbb{Z}_N$ to $(\pi_G^*)_j$ in an iterative manner until $(\pi_G^*)_j \neq V_w$ for all $w \in \mathcal{I}$ and $(\pi_G^*)_j \neq (\pi_G^*)_k$ for all $k \in [n_\pi] \setminus \mathcal{J}$ such that $k < j$. The number of such iterations is upper bounded by the number of distinct elements in the table $\mathbf{B}$, which is at most $1 + n_{\mathsf{Acc}}(\lambda, k) + n_\pi(\lambda, t, k) + q(\lambda, t, k)$ (the number of entries in $\mathbf{B}$).

Claim 3.4. For any $\lambda \in \mathbb{N}$, if

$$\frac{1}{2} \cdot \binom{|\mathcal{X}_\lambda|}{k} \geq (n_{\mathsf{Acc}} + 1)^{n_{\mathsf{Acc}}} \cdot 2^{\ell_{\mathsf{Acc}}} \cdot (n_{\mathsf{Acc}} + n_\pi + 3q + 1)^{6q \cdot \lceil k/t \rceil} \tag{2}$$

then $\Pr[\mathcal{A} \text{ aborts}] < 1/2$.

Proof of Claim 3.4. We show that if Eq. (2) holds then with probability at least $1/2$ the attacker is able to find a set $X' \subseteq \mathcal{X}_\lambda$ that consists of k distinct elements $x_1' < \cdots < x_k'$, and strings $\vec{r}' = (r', r_1', \ldots, r_v') \in \{0, 1\}^*$, that satisfy the requirements specified in Step 3. Denote by $r \in \{0, 1\}^*$ the randomness used by the algorithm Setup in the experiment $\mathsf{Expt}_{\mathcal{ACC}, \mathcal{A}}(\lambda)$ (i.e., $(\mathsf{Acc}, \mathsf{state}) = \mathsf{Setup}^{\mathcal{O}}(1^\lambda, N, X; r)$). In addition, for every $i \in [v]$ denote by $r_i \in \{0, 1\}^*$ the randomness used by the oracle $\mathsf{Prove}^{\mathcal{O}}(\mathsf{Acc}, \mathsf{state}, \cdot)$ when computing a batch membership proof for the set S_i in the experiment $\mathsf{Expt}_{\mathcal{ACC}, \mathcal{A}}(\lambda)$ (i.e., $\pi_i = \mathsf{Prove}^{\mathcal{O}}(\mathsf{Acc}, \mathsf{state}, S_i; r_i)$), and let $\vec{r} = (r, r_1, \ldots, r_v)$. We show that even when restricting the attacker to choose $\vec{r}' = \vec{r}$ there is still a set X' that satisfies the requirements specified in Step 3 with probability at least $1/2$ over the choice of X.

Consider the function $F_{\vec{r}}$ that takes as input a set $X \subseteq \mathcal{X}_\lambda$ of k distinct elements $x_1 < \cdots < x_k$, and returns as output the following values:

$$F_{\vec{r}}(X) = \Big(\mathsf{AccEqualities}_{\mathsf{Acc}}, \mathsf{Acc}_{\mathsf{str}},$$

$$\mathsf{VrfyQueries}_{\mathsf{Acc}, S_1, \pi_1}, \ldots, \mathsf{VrfyQueries}_{\mathsf{Acc}, S_v, \pi_v},$$

$$\mathsf{ProofEqualities}_{\mathsf{Acc}, S_1, \pi_1}, \ldots, \mathsf{ProofEqualities}_{\mathsf{Acc}, S_v, \pi_v},$$

$$\mathsf{QueriesEqualities}_{\mathsf{Acc}, S_1, \pi_1} \ldots, \mathsf{QueriesEqualities}_{\mathsf{Acc}, S_v, \pi_v} \Big)$$

where $S_i = \{x_{(i-1) \cdot t + 1}, \ldots, x_{i \cdot t}\}$ for every $i \in [v]$, $(\mathsf{Acc}, \mathsf{sk}) \leftarrow \mathsf{Setup}^{\mathcal{O}}(\lambda, N, X; r)$, and $\pi_i \leftarrow \mathsf{Prove}(\mathsf{Acc}, \mathsf{sk}, S_i; r_i)$ for every $i \in [v]$. Our goal is to prove that with probability at least $1/2$ over the choice of X there exists a set $X' \neq X$ such that $F_{\vec{r}}(X') = F_{\vec{r}}(X)$. We prove this claim by showing that the size of the image of the function $F_{\vec{r}}$, denoted $\mathsf{Image}(F_{\vec{r}})$, is at most half the size of its domain (this guarantees that with probability at least $1/2$ over the choice of X there exists a set $X' \neq X$ as required).

The domain of the function $F_{\vec{r}}$ is of size $\binom{|\mathcal{X}_\lambda|}{k}$. The number of possibilities for an output of the function $F_{\vec{r}}$ is the product of the following quantities (as discussed above when defining $\mathsf{AccEqualities}_{\mathsf{Acc}}$, $\mathsf{VrfyQueries}_{\mathsf{Acc},S_i,\pi_i}$, $\mathsf{ProofEqualities}_{\mathsf{Acc},S_i,\pi_i}$ and $\mathsf{QueriesEqualities}_{\mathsf{Acc},S_i,\pi_i}$):

– $\mathsf{AccEqualities}_{\mathsf{Acc}}$ and $\mathsf{Acc}_{\mathsf{str}}$ have $(n_{\mathsf{Acc}}+1)^{n_{\mathsf{Acc}}}$ and $2^{\ell_{\mathsf{Acc}}}$ possibilities, respectively.
– $\mathsf{VrfyQueries}_{\mathsf{Acc},S_i,\pi_i}$ for every $i \in [v]$ has $(n_{\mathsf{Acc}}+n_\pi+q+1)^{3q}$ possibilities.
– $\mathsf{ProofEqualities}_{\mathsf{Acc},S_i,\pi_i}$ for every $i \in [v]$ has $(n_{\mathsf{Acc}}+2q+1)^{2q}$ possibilities.
– $\mathsf{QueriesEqualities}_{\mathsf{Acc},S_i,\pi_i}$ for every $i \in [v]$ has $(n_{\mathsf{Acc}}+3q+1)^{q}$ possibilities.

Thus, the size of the image of the function $F_{\vec{r}}$ can be upper bounded via

$$|\mathsf{Image}(F_{\vec{r}})| \leq (n_{\mathsf{Acc}}+1)^{n_{\mathsf{Acc}}} \cdot 2^{\ell_{\mathsf{Acc}}} \cdot (n_{\mathsf{Acc}}+n_\pi+3q+1)^{6q \cdot \lceil k/t \rceil}.$$

We assume that Eq. (2) holds, and therefore the size of the image of the function $F_{\vec{r}}$ is at most half the size of its domain, and the claim follows.

Claim 3.5. For any $\lambda \in \mathbb{N}$ it holds that

$$\Pr\left[\mathsf{Expt}_{ACC,\mathcal{A}}(\lambda) = 1 \big| \mathcal{A} \text{does not abort}\right] = 1.$$

Proof of Claim 3.5. Assuming that $\mathcal{A}$ does not abort we prove that $\mathsf{Vrfy}^{\mathcal{O}}(\mathsf{Acc}, S'_{i^*}, \pi^*) = 1$. Together with the fact that $S'_{i^*} \not\subseteq X$, this implies that $\mathsf{Expt}_{ACC,\mathcal{A}}(\lambda) = 1$. Recall that the proof $\pi^* = \left(\widehat{\pi^*_G}, \pi^*_{\mathsf{str}}\right)$ is constructed using the two proofs π_{i^*} and π'_{i^*}, where:

– $\mathcal{A}$ queried the oracle $\mathsf{Prove}^{\mathcal{O}}(\mathsf{Acc}, \mathsf{state}, \cdot)$ with the set S_{i^*} to obtain $\pi_{i^*} = \left(\widehat{\pi_{i^*,G}}, \pi_{i^*,\mathsf{str}}\right) \leftarrow \mathsf{Prove}^{\mathcal{O}}(\mathsf{Acc}, \mathsf{state}, S_{i^*})$, where $\pi_{i^*,G}$ is a sequence of group elements and $\pi_{i^*,\mathsf{str}}$ is an explicit string.
– $\mathcal{A}$ generated $\pi'_{i^*} = \left(\widehat{\pi'_{i^*,G}}, \pi'_{i^*,\mathsf{str}}\right) \leftarrow \mathsf{Prove}(\mathsf{Acc}', \mathsf{state}', S'_i; r'_i)$ subject to the requirements specified in the description of the attack, where $\pi'_{i^*,G}$ is a sequence of group elements and $\pi'_{i^*,\mathsf{str}}$ is an explicit string.

The correctness of the accumulator guarantees that $\mathsf{Vrfy}^{\mathcal{O}}(\mathsf{Acc}, S_{i^*}, \pi_{i^*}) = 1$ and $\mathsf{Vrfy}(\mathsf{Acc}', S'_{i^*}, \pi'_{i^*}) = 1$, and we show that $\mathsf{Vrfy}^{\mathcal{O}}(\mathsf{Acc}, S_{i^*}, \pi^*) = 1$. This will follow from the fact that the computation of the verification algorithm, which can access group elements only via the oracle $\mathcal{O}$, cannot distinguish between the two inputs $(\mathsf{Acc}', S'_{i^*}, \pi'_{i^*})$ and $(\mathsf{Acc}, S'_{i^*}, \pi^*)$.

Recall that each computation is associated with a table $\mathbf{B}$, where each entry of this table stores an element of $\mathbb{Z}_N$, and that the oracle $\mathcal{O}$ provides black-box access to $\mathbf{B}$ via group operations and equality queries. Let $T = 1 + n_{\mathsf{Acc}} + n_\pi + q$, and for every $j \in [T]$ we denote by V_j, V'_j and V^*_j the $\mathbb{Z}_N$ element that is located at the jth entry of the table $\mathbf{B}$ in the computations $\mathsf{Vrfy}^{\mathcal{O}}(\mathsf{Acc}, S_{i^*}, \pi_{i^*})$, $\mathsf{Vrfy}(\mathsf{Acc}', S'_{i^*}, \pi'_{i^*})$ and $\mathsf{Vrfy}^{\mathcal{O}}(\mathsf{Acc}, S'_{i^*}, \pi^*)$, respectively.

Recall that we denoted by $\mathcal{J} \subseteq [n_\pi]$ the positions of the group elements that are part of the proof π_{i*} which are accessed by the group-operation queries issued during the computation $\mathsf{Vrfy}^{\mathcal{O}}(\mathsf{Acc}, S_{i*}, \pi_{i*})$. Recall also that we defined $\mathcal{I} = \{1, \ldots, 1 + n_{\mathsf{Acc}}\} \cup (1 + n_{\mathsf{Acc}} + \mathcal{J}) \cup \{1 + n_{\mathsf{Acc}} + n_\pi + 1, \ldots, 1 + n_{\mathsf{Acc}} + n_\pi + q\} \subseteq [T]$. Observe that $(V_1, \ldots, V_T)$ and $(V_1', \ldots, V_T')$, have the same equality pattern when restricted to the position included in $\mathcal{I}$ (although they may correspond to different $\mathbb{Z}_N$ elements), since based on the description of our attacker it holds that

$$\mathsf{AccEqualities}_{\mathsf{Acc}'} = \mathsf{AccEqualities}_{\mathsf{Acc}}$$

$$\mathsf{ProofEqualities}_{\mathsf{Acc}', S_{i*}', \pi_{i*}'} = \mathsf{ProofEqualities}_{\mathsf{Acc}, S_{i*}, \pi_{i*}}$$

$$\mathsf{QueriesEqualities}_{\mathsf{Acc}', S_{i*}', \pi_{i*}'} = \mathsf{QueriesEqualities}_{\mathsf{Acc}, S_{i*}, \pi_{i*}}.$$

In addition, the same queries are issued in the computations $\mathsf{Vrfy}^{\mathcal{O}}(\mathsf{Acc}, S_{i*}, \pi_{i*})$ and $\mathsf{Vrfy}(\mathsf{Acc}', S_{i*}', \pi_{i*}')$, as $\mathsf{VrfyQueries}_{\mathsf{Acc}', S_{i*}', \pi_{i*}'} = \mathsf{VrfyQueries}_{\mathsf{Acc}, S_{i*}, \pi_{i*}}$.

Recall that for every $j \in \mathcal{J}$ we defined $(\pi_G^*)_j = (\pi_{i*, G})_j$. Note that the first $1 + n_{\mathsf{Acc}} + n_\pi$ entries of the table $\mathbf{B}$ are the $\mathbb{Z}_N$ elements corresponding to the group elements that are provided as part of the inputs to the computation. In both the computations $\mathsf{Vrfy}^{\mathcal{O}}(\mathsf{Acc}, S_{i*}, \pi_{i*})$ and $\mathsf{Vrfy}^{\mathcal{O}}(\mathsf{Acc}, S_{i*}', \pi^*)$ the first $1 + n_{\mathsf{Acc}} + n_\pi$ entries of the table $\mathbf{B}$ are the elements $(1, \mathsf{Acc}_G, \pi_{i*, G})$ and $(1, \mathsf{Acc}_G, \pi_G^*)$ respectively. Therefore, for every $w \in \mathcal{I} \cap [1 + n_{\mathsf{Acc}} + n_\pi]$ it holds that $V_w^* = V_w$. Since $(V_1, \ldots, V_T)$ and $(V_1', \ldots, V_T')$, have the same equality pattern on the indices in $\mathcal{I}$, we get that $(V_1', \ldots, V_{1 + n_{\mathsf{Acc}} + n_\pi}')$ and $(V_1^*, \ldots, V_{1 + n_{\mathsf{Acc}} + n_\pi}^*)$ have the same equality pattern on the indices in $\mathcal{I}$. Recall also that for every $j \in [n_\pi] \setminus \mathcal{J}$ we defined $(\pi_G^*)_j$ according to the equalities in $(V_1', \ldots, V_T')$ using the elements in $(V_1, \ldots, V_T)$ or new element when needed. So $(V_1^*, \ldots, V_{1 + n_{\mathsf{Acc}} + n_\pi}^*)$ and $(V_1', \ldots, V_{1 + n_{\mathsf{Acc}} + n_\pi}')$ have the same equality pattern everywhere (i.e., not only when restricted to the positions included in $\mathcal{I}$).

In what follows we prove that $(V_1^*, \ldots, V_T^*)$ and $(V_1', \ldots, V_T')$ have the same equality pattern everywhere (although they may correspond to different $\mathbb{Z}_N$ elements). Together with the fact that the explicit inputs to their respective computations, $\mathsf{Vrfy}^{\mathcal{O}}(\mathsf{Acc}, S_{i*}', \pi^*)$ and $\mathsf{Vrfy}(\mathsf{Acc}', S_{i*}', \pi_{i*}')$, are the same (these are the explicit bit-strings $\mathsf{Acc}_{\mathsf{str}}$, S_{i*}' and $\pi_{i*, \mathsf{str}}'$), we obtain that $\mathsf{Vrfy}^{\mathcal{O}}(\mathsf{Acc}, S_{i*}', \pi^*) = \mathsf{Vrfy}(\mathsf{Acc}', S_{i*}', \pi_{i*}')$ as required.

We prove, via induction on $j \in \{0, \ldots, q\}$, that (1) for every $w \in \mathcal{I} \cap [1 + n_{\mathsf{Acc}} + n_\pi + j]$ it holds that $V_w^* = V_w$, and (2) $(V_1^*, \ldots, V_{1 + n_{\mathsf{Acc}} + n_\pi + j}^*)$ and $(V_1', \ldots, V_{1 + n_{\mathsf{Acc}} + n_\pi + j}')$ have the same equality pattern. For the case $j = 0$ this has already been established above.

Now assume that for some $j \in \{0, \ldots, q - 1\}$ we have that for every $w \in \mathcal{I} \cap [1 + n_{\mathsf{Acc}} + n_\pi + j]$ it holds that $V_w^* = V_w$, and that $(V_1^*, \ldots, V_{1 + n_{\mathsf{Acc}} + n_\pi + j}^*)$ and $(V_1', \ldots, V_{1 + n_{\mathsf{Acc}} + n_\pi + j}')$ have the same equality pattern. We would like to argue that the same holds for $j + 1$ as well. The entries $V_{1 + n_{\mathsf{Acc}} + n_\pi + j + 1}^*$ and $V_{1 + n_{\mathsf{Acc}} + n_\pi + j + 1}$ contain the result of the next group-operation query in the computations $\mathsf{Vrfy}^{\mathcal{O}}(\mathsf{Acc}, S_{i*}', \pi^*)$ and $\mathsf{Vrfy}^{\mathcal{O}}(\mathsf{Acc}, S_{i*}, \pi_{i*})$. The next group-operation query in the computation $\mathsf{Vrfy}^{\mathcal{O}}(\mathsf{Acc}, S_{i*}', \pi^*)$ is identical to that of the computation $\mathsf{Vrfy}(\mathsf{Acc}', S'_{i*}, \pi'_{i*})$ (since both computations have the same explicit inputs and so far have the same equality patterns in their tables), and the next group-operation query in the computation $\mathsf{Vrfy}(\mathsf{Acc}', S'_{i*}, \pi'_{i*})$ is identical to that of the computation $\mathsf{Vrfy}^{\mathcal{O}}(\mathsf{Acc}, S_{i*}, \pi_{i*})$ (since we required $\mathsf{VrfyQueries}_{\mathsf{Acc}', S'_{i*}, \pi'_{i*}} = \mathsf{VrfyQueries}_{\mathsf{Acc}, S_{i*}, \pi_{i*}}$). Therefore, the next group-operation query in the computation $\mathsf{Vrfy}^{\mathcal{O}}(\mathsf{Acc}, S'_{i*}, \pi^*)$ is identical to that of the computation $\mathsf{Vrfy}^{\mathcal{O}}(\mathsf{Acc}, S_{i*}, \pi_{i*})$. Since the two tables $(V_1^*, \dots, V_{1+n_{\mathsf{Acc}}+n_\pi+j}^*)$ and $(V_1, \dots, V_{1+n_{\mathsf{Acc}}+n_\pi+j})$ are identical on the indices in $\mathcal{I}$, which contain the indices of the queries of Vrfy, this implies that $(V_1^*, \dots, V_{1+n_{\mathsf{Acc}}+n_\pi+j+1}^*)$ and $(V_1, \dots, V_{1+n_{\mathsf{Acc}}+n_\pi+j+1})$ are identical on the indices in $\mathcal{I}$ (which proves part (1)).

Note that $(V_1, \dots, V_{1+n_{\mathsf{Acc}}+n_\pi+j+1})$ and $(V_1', \dots, V_{1+n_{\mathsf{Acc}}+n_\pi+j+1}')$ have the same equality pattern on the indices in $\mathcal{I}$ (by the description of our attacker), and therefore $(V_1^*, \dots, V_{1+n_{\mathsf{Acc}}+n_\pi+j+1}^*)$ and $(V_1', \dots, V_{1+n_{\mathsf{Acc}}+n_\pi+j+1}')$ have the same equality pattern on the indices in $\mathcal{I}$. In addition, the elements $(\pi_G^*)_j$ of π_G^* for all $j \in [n_\pi] \setminus \mathcal{J}$ are chosen to agree with the equality pattern of $(V_1', \dots, V_T')$. Thus, $(V_1^*, \dots, V_{1+n_{\mathsf{Acc}}+n_\pi+j+1}^*)$ and $(V_1', \dots, V_{1+n_{\mathsf{Acc}}+n_\pi+j+1}')$ have the same equality pattern. ∎

This settles the proof of Lemma 3.3. ∎

Extension to Unknown-Order Groups. As discussed in Sect. 2.1, we consider two different flavors of generic groups: groups of known orders and groups of unknown orders. When modeling known-order generic groups then all algorithms receive the order of the underlying group as an explicit input, and when modeling unknown-order generic groups then the order is not provided (still, however, the corresponding order-generation algorithm $\mathsf{OrderGen}$ is publicly known). In our case, this difference corresponds to whether or not the accumulator's procedures Setup, Prove and Vrfy, and our attacker $\mathcal{A}$ receive the order of the group as input, and the above proof of Lemma 3.3 assumes that they do.

This proof easily extends to the case where the accumulator's procedures and our attacker do not receive the order of the group as input. Specifically, note that our attacker uses the order N of the group only in Step 3 of the algorithm $\mathcal{A}_1$, for finding a set $X' \subseteq \mathcal{X}_\lambda$ and randomness $\vec{r'} = (r', r_1', \dots, r_v')$ that satisfy the prescribed requirements (finding these values requires $\mathcal{A}_1$ to internally perform computations modulo N). However, if the accumulator's procedures do not receive the order of the group as input, then we can modify the algorithm $\mathcal{A}_1$ to find in Step 3, together with X' and $\vec{r'}$, an integer N' in the support of the computation $\mathsf{OrderGen}(1^\lambda)$ such that the exact same conditions are satisfied (while performing the required internal computations modulo N').

The proof of Claim 3.4 is essentially unchanged, now showing that even when restricting the attacker to choose $\vec{r'} = \vec{r}$ and $N' = N$ there is still a set X' that satisfies the prescribed requirements with probability at least $1/2$ over the choice of X (i.e., there exists at least one suitable choice of $\vec{r'}$ and N' exactly as before). The proof of Claim 3.5 is completely unchanged, since the accumulator's procedures do not receive the order of the group as input, the exact same proof shows that the verification algorithm, which can access group elements only via the oracle $\mathcal{O}$, cannot distinguish between the two inputs $(\mathsf{Acc}', S'_{i*}, \pi'_{i*})$ and $(\mathsf{Acc}, S'_{i*}, \pi^*)$.

3.2 Proofs of Theorem 3.1 and Corollary 3.2

Equipped with Lemma 3.3 we now derive Theorem 3.1 and Corollary 3.2.

Proof of Theorem 3.1. Lemma 3.3 implies that for all sufficiently large $\lambda \in \mathbb{N}$ it holds that

$$
\begin{aligned}
\log_2 \binom{|\mathcal{X}_\lambda|}{k} &< n_{\mathsf{Acc}} \cdot \log_2(n_{\mathsf{Acc}} + 1) + \ell_{\mathsf{Acc}} \\
&\quad + \left\lceil \frac{k}{t} \right\rceil \cdot 6q \cdot \log_2(n_{\mathsf{Acc}} + n_\pi + 3q + 1) + 1 \\
&\leq n_{\mathsf{Acc}} \cdot \log_2(n_{\mathsf{Acc}} + 1) + \ell_{\mathsf{Acc}} \\
&\quad + \frac{2k}{t} \cdot 6q \cdot \log_2(n_{\mathsf{Acc}} + n_\pi + 3q + 1) + 1.
\end{aligned}
$$

Therefore, using the fact that $t \leq k$ and $q \geq 1$ we obtain

$$
\begin{aligned}
t \cdot \frac{\log_2 \binom{|\mathcal{X}_\lambda|}{k} - \left[n_{\mathsf{Acc}} \cdot \log_2(n_{\mathsf{Acc}} + 1) + \ell_{\mathsf{Acc}} \right]}{k} &\leq 12q \log_2(n_{\mathsf{Acc}} + n_\pi + 3q + 1) + \frac{t}{k} \\
&\leq 12q \log_2(n_{\mathsf{Acc}} + n_\pi + 3q + 1) + 1 \\
&\leq 13q \log_2(n_{\mathsf{Acc}} + n_\pi + 3q + 1).
\end{aligned}
$$

Since the functions n_{Acc}, n_π and q are all polynomials in the security parameter $\lambda \in \mathbb{N}$, then $\log_2(n_{\mathsf{Acc}} + n_\pi + 3q + 1) = O(\log_2 \lambda)$, and therefore

$$
q = \Omega \left(t \cdot \frac{\log_2 \binom{|\mathcal{X}_\lambda|}{k} - \left[n_{\mathsf{Acc}} \cdot \log_2(n_{\mathsf{Acc}} + 1) + \ell_{\mathsf{Acc}} \right]}{k} \cdot \frac{1}{\log \lambda} \right).
$$

∎

Proof of Corollary 3.2. If we assume that

$$
n_{\mathsf{Acc}} \cdot \log_2(n_{\mathsf{Acc}} + 1) + \ell_{\mathsf{Acc}} < (1 - \epsilon) \cdot \log_2 \binom{|\mathcal{X}_\lambda|}{k}
$$

then

$$
\begin{aligned}
\log_2 \binom{|\mathcal{X}_\lambda|}{k} - \left[n_{\mathsf{Acc}} \cdot \log_2(n_{\mathsf{Acc}} + 1) + \ell_{\mathsf{Acc}} \right] &> \epsilon \cdot \log_2 \binom{|\mathcal{X}_\lambda|}{k} \\
&\geq \epsilon k \cdot \log_2 \left(\frac{|\mathcal{X}_\lambda|}{k} \right) \\
&= \epsilon k \cdot \Omega(\lambda),
\end{aligned}
\tag{3}
$$

where Eq. (3) follows from the assumption that $|\mathcal{X}_\lambda| \geq 2^{\Omega(\lambda)}$ and the fact that $k = k(\lambda)$ is polynomial in the security parameter $\lambda \in \mathbb{N}$. Therefore,

$$q = \Omega \left(t \cdot \frac{\log_2 \binom{|\mathcal{X}_\lambda|}{k} - \left[n_{\mathsf{Acc}} \cdot \log_2(n_{\mathsf{Acc}} + 1) + \ell_{\mathsf{Acc}} \right]}{k} \cdot \frac{1}{\log \lambda} \right)$$

$$= \Omega \left(t \cdot \frac{\epsilon \lambda}{\log \lambda} \right). \qquad \blacksquare$$

4 Open Problems

In this section we briefly discuss several open problems that arise from this work.

Randomized Verification and Imperfect Correctness. Our work considers accumulators with deterministic verification procedures and perfect correctness, as noted in Sect. 2.2. Although this seems to be the case with the known accumulators, the more general case of accumulators with randomized verification procedures and imperfect correctness (i.e., valid proofs are accepted with all but a negligible probability) is clearly fundamental, and thus an interesting direction for future research.

Non-trivial Non-interactive Batch Verification in Shoup's Model. As discussed in Sect. 1.2, we prove our result within the generic-group model introduced by Maurer [Mau05], which together with the incomparable model introduced by Shoup [Sho97], seem to be the most commonly used approaches for capturing generic-group computations. A natural open problem is whether our result can be either proved or circumvented within Shoup's model.

One should note that our result can be circumvented by applying the Fiat-Shamir transform [BBF19, Tha19], and that the random injective mapping used in Shoup's model for explicitly representing group elements may potentially be exploited towards this goal. Although, this can perhaps be viewed as somewhat abusing Shoup's model by relying on the randomness provided by the injective mapping (which does not actually exist in concrete implementation of cryptographic groups) instead of relying on the algebraic structure of the group.

The Efficiency of Batch Verification in Other Settings. Our work considers the efficiency of batch verification in the specific setting of accumulators. More generally, however, the efficiency of batch verification may be interesting to study in other settings as well. One such setting is the general one of non-interactive arguments, and specifically that of succinct non-interactive arguments [Mic94] (which seem tightly related to accumulators as succinct non-interactive arguments may be used to provide, for example, short membership proofs for accumulated values).

References

[ABC+12] Ahn, J.H., Boneh, D., Camenisch, J., Hohenberger, S., Shelat, A., Waters, B.: Computing on authenticated data. In: Cramer, R. (ed.) TCC 2012. LNCS, vol. 7194, pp. 1–20. Springer, Heidelberg (2012). https://doi.org/10.1007/978-3-642-28914-9_1

[AHI+17] Ames, S., Hazay, C., Ishai, Y., Venkitasubramaniam, M.: Ligero: lightweight sublinear arguments without a trusted setup. In: Proceedings of the 2017 ACM SIGSAC Conference on Computer and Communications Security, pp. 2087–2104 (2017)

[AHK20] Agrikola, T., Hofheinz, D., Kastner, J.: On instantiating the algebraic group model from falsifiable assumptions. In: Canteaut, A., Ishai, Y. (eds.) EUROCRYPT 2020. LNCS, vol. 12106, pp. 96–126. Springer, Cham (2020). https://doi.org/10.1007/978-3-030-45724-2_4

[AM09] Aggarwal, D., Maurer, U.: Breaking RSA generically is equivalent to factoring. In: Joux, A. (ed.) EUROCRYPT 2009. LNCS, vol. 5479, pp. 36–53. Springer, Heidelberg (2009). https://doi.org/10.1007/978-3-642-01001-9_2

[BBF19] Boneh, D., Bünz, B., Fisch, B.: Batching techniques for accumulators with applications to IOPs and stateless blockchains. In: Boldyreva, A., Micciancio, D. (eds.) CRYPTO 2019. LNCS, vol. 11692, pp. 561–586. Springer, Cham (2019). https://doi.org/10.1007/978-3-030-26948-7_20

[BCR+19] Ben-Sasson, E., Chiesa, A., Riabzev, M., Spooner, N., Virza, M., Ward, N.P.: Aurora: transparent succinct arguments for R1CS. In: Ishai, Y., Rijmen, V. (eds.) EUROCRYPT 2019. LNCS, vol. 11476, pp. 103–128. Springer, Cham (2019). https://doi.org/10.1007/978-3-030-17653-2_4

[BCS16] Ben-Sasson, E., Chiesa, A., Spooner, N.: Interactive oracle proofs. In: Hirt, M., Smith, A. (eds.) TCC 2016. LNCS, vol. 9986, pp. 31–60. Springer, Heidelberg (2016). https://doi.org/10.1007/978-3-662-53644-5_2

[BdM93] Benaloh, J., de Mare, M.: One-way accumulators: a decentralized alternative to digital signatures. In: Helleseth, T. (ed.) EUROCRYPT 1993. LNCS, vol. 765, pp. 274–285. Springer, Heidelberg (1994). https://doi.org/10.1007/3-540-48285-7_24

[BGM+92] Brickell, E.F., Gordon, D.M., McCurley, K.S., Wilson, D.B.: Fast exponentiation with precomputation. In: Rueppel, R.A. (ed.) EUROCRYPT 1992. LNCS, vol. 658, pp. 200–207. Springer, Heidelberg (1993). https://doi.org/10.1007/3-540-47555-9_18

[BL96] Boneh, D., Lipton, R.J.: Algorithms for black-box fields and their application to cryptography. In: Koblitz, N. (ed.) CRYPTO 1996. LNCS, vol. 1109, pp. 283–297. Springer, Heidelberg (1996). https://doi.org/10.1007/3-540-68697-5_22

[BLL00] Buldas, A., Laud, P., Lipmaa, H.: Accountable certificate management using undeniable attestations. In: Proceedings of the 7th ACM Conference on Computer and Communications Security, pp. 9–17 (2000)

[BM07] Barak, B., Mahmoody-Ghidary, M.: Lower bounds on signatures from symmetric primitives. In: Proceedings of the 48th Annual IEEE Symposium on Foundations of Computer Science, pp. 680–688 (2007)

[BM09] Barak, B., Mahmoody-Ghidary, M.: Merkle puzzles are optimal — an $O(n^2)$-query attack on any key exchange from a random oracle. In: Halevi, S. (ed.) CRYPTO 2009. LNCS, vol. 5677, pp. 374–390. Springer, Heidelberg (2009). https://doi.org/10.1007/978-3-642-03356-8_22

[BP97]   Barić, N., Pfitzmann, B.: Collision-free accumulators and fail-stop signature schemes without trees. In: Fumy, W. (ed.) EUROCRYPT 1997. LNCS, vol. 1233, pp. 480–494. Springer, Heidelberg (1997). https://doi.org/10.1007/3-540-69053-0_33

[BSBH+18] Ben-Sasson, E., Bentov, I., Horesh, Y., Riabzev, M.: Scalable, transparent, and post-quantum secure computational integrity. Cryptology ePrint Archive, Report 2018/046 (2018). https://eprint.iacr.org/2018/046

[CF13]   Catalano, D., Fiore, D.: Vector commitments and their applications. In: Kurosawa, K., Hanaoka, G. (eds.) PKC 2013. LNCS, vol. 7778, pp. 55–72. Springer, Heidelberg (2013). https://doi.org/10.1007/978-3-642-36362-7_5

[CF14]   Yakoubov, S., Fromknecht, C., Velicanu, D.: A decentralized public key infrastructure with identity retention. Cryptology ePrint Archive, Report 2014/803 (2014). https://eprint.iacr.org/2014/803

[CHK+08] Camacho, P., Hevia, A., Kiwi, M., Opazo, R.: Strong accumulators from collision-resistant hashing. In: Wu, T.-C., Lei, C.-L., Rijmen, V., Lee, D.-T. (eds.) ISC 2008. LNCS, vol. 5222, pp. 471–486. Springer, Heidelberg (2008). https://doi.org/10.1007/978-3-540-85886-7_32

[CJ10]   Canard, S., Jambert, A.: On extended sanitizable signature schemes. In: Pieprzyk, J. (ed.) CT-RSA 2010. LNCS, vol. 5985, pp. 179–194. Springer, Heidelberg (2010). https://doi.org/10.1007/978-3-642-11925-5_13

[CKS09]   Camenisch, J., Kohlweiss, M., Soriente, C.: An accumulator based on bilinear maps and efficient revocation for anonymous credentials. In: Jarecki, S., Tsudik, G. (eds.) PKC 2009. LNCS, vol. 5443, pp. 481–500. Springer, Heidelberg (2009). https://doi.org/10.1007/978-3-642-00468-1_27

[CL02]   Camenisch, J., Lysyanskaya, A.: Dynamic accumulators and application to efficient revocation of anonymous credentials. In: Yung, M. (ed.) CRYPTO 2002. LNCS, vol. 2442, pp. 61–76. Springer, Heidelberg (2002). https://doi.org/10.1007/3-540-45708-9_5

[DH76]   Diffie, W., Hellman, M.E.: New directions in cryptography. IEEE Trans. Inf. Theory 22(6), 644–654 (1976)

[DK02]   Damgård, I., Koprowski, M.: Generic lower bounds for root extraction and signature schemes in general groups. In: Knudsen, L.R. (ed.) EUROCRYPT 2002. LNCS, vol. 2332, pp. 256–271. Springer, Heidelberg (2002). https://doi.org/10.1007/3-540-46035-7_17

[DT08]   Damgård, I., Triandopoulos, N.: Supporting non-membership proofs with bilinear-map accumulators. Cryptology ePrint Archive, Report 2008/538 (2008). https://eprint.iacr.org/2008/538

[FKL18]   Fuchsbauer, G., Kiltz, E., Loss, J.: The algebraic group model and its applications. In: Shacham, H., Boldyreva, A. (eds.) CRYPTO 2018. LNCS, vol. 10992, pp. 33–62. Springer, Cham (2018). https://doi.org/10.1007/978-3-319-96881-0_2

[FPS20]   Fuchsbauer, G., Plouviez, A., Seurin, Y.: Blind Schnorr signatures and signed ElGamal encryption in the algebraic group model. In: Canteaut, A., Ishai, Y. (eds.) EUROCRYPT 2020. LNCS, vol. 12106, pp. 63–95. Springer, Cham (2020). https://doi.org/10.1007/978-3-030-45724-2_3

[GGK+05] Gennaro, R., Gertner, Y., Katz, J., Trevisan, L.: Bounds on the efficiency of generic cryptographic constructions. SIAM J. Comput. 35(1), 217–246 (2005)

[GGM14]   Garman, C., Green, M., Miers, I.: Decentralized anonymous credentials. In: Proceedings of the 21st Annual Network and Distributed System Security Symposium (NDSS) (2014)

[HHR+15] Haitner, I., Hoch, J.J., Reingold, O., Segev, G.: Finding collisions in interactive protocols - tight lower bounds on the round and communication complexities of statistically hiding commitments. SIAM J. Comput. **44**(1), 193–242 (2015)

[HK10] Horvitz, O., Katz, J.: Bounds on the efficiency of black-box commitment schemes. Theor. Comput. Sci. **411**(10), 1251–1260 (2010)

[IR89] Impagliazzo, R., Rudich, S.: Limits on the provable consequences of one-way permutations. In: Proceedings of the 21st Annual ACM Symposium on Theory of Computing, pp. 44–61 (1989)

[JR10] Jager, T., Rupp, A.: The semi-generic group model and applications to pairing-based cryptography. In: Abe, M. (ed.) ASIACRYPT 2010. LNCS, vol. 6477, pp. 539–556. Springer, Heidelberg (2010). https://doi.org/10.1007/978-3-642-17373-8_31

[JS08] Jager, T., Schwenk, J.: On the equivalence of generic group models. In: Baek, J., Bao, F., Chen, K., Lai, X. (eds.) ProvSec 2008. LNCS, vol. 5324, pp. 200–209. Springer, Heidelberg (2008). https://doi.org/10.1007/978-3-540-88733-1_14

[JS13] Jager, T., Schwenk, J.: On the analysis of cryptographic assumptions in the generic ring model. J. Cryptol. **26**(2), 225–245 (2013)

[KST99] Kim, J.H., Simon, D.R., Tetali, P.: Limits on the efficiency of one-way permutation-based hash functions. In: Proceedings of the 40th Annual IEEE Symposium on Foundations of Computer Science, pp. 535–542 (1999)

[Lip12] Lipmaa, H.: Secure accumulators from Euclidean rings without trusted setup. In: Bao, F., Samarati, P., Zhou, J. (eds.) ACNS 2012. LNCS, vol. 7341, pp. 224–240. Springer, Heidelberg (2012). https://doi.org/10.1007/978-3-642-31284-7_14

[LLX07] Li, J., Li, N., Xue, R.: Universal accumulators with efficient nonmembership proofs. In: Katz, J., Yung, M. (eds.) ACNS 2007. LNCS, vol. 4521, pp. 253–269. Springer, Heidelberg (2007). https://doi.org/10.1007/978-3-540-72738-5_17

[LM19] Lai, R.W.F., Malavolta, G.: Subvector commitments with application to succinct arguments. In: Boldyreva, A., Micciancio, D. (eds.) CRYPTO 2019. LNCS, vol. 11692, pp. 530–560. Springer, Cham (2019). https://doi.org/10.1007/978-3-030-26948-7_19

[Mau05] Maurer, U.: Abstract models of computation in cryptography. In: Smart, N.P. (ed.) Cryptography and Coding 2005. LNCS, vol. 3796, pp. 1–12. Springer, Heidelberg (2005). https://doi.org/10.1007/11586821_1

[Mer87] Merkle, R.C.: A digital signature based on a conventional encryption function. In: Pomerance, C. (ed.) CRYPTO 1987. LNCS, vol. 293, pp. 369–378. Springer, Heidelberg (1988). https://doi.org/10.1007/3-540-48184-2_32

[MGG+13] Miers, I., Garman, C., Green, M., Rubin, A.D.: Zerocoin: anonymous distributed e-cash from bitcoin. In: Proceeding of the 2013 IEEE Symposium on Security and Privacy, pp. 397–411 (2013)

[Mic94] Micali, S.: CS proofs. In: Proceedings of the 35th Annual IEEE Symposium on the Foundations of Computer Science, pp. 436–453 (1994)

[MTT19] Mizuide, T., Takayasu, A., Takagi, T.: Tight reductions for Diffie-Hellman variants in the algebraic group model. In: Matsui, M. (ed.) CT-RSA 2019. LNCS, vol. 11405, pp. 169–188. Springer, Cham (2019). https://doi.org/10.1007/978-3-030-12612-4_9

[MW98]   Maurer, U., Wolf, S.: Lower bounds on generic algorithms in groups. In: Nyberg, K. (ed.) EUROCRYPT 1998. LNCS, vol. 1403, pp. 72–84. Springer, Heidelberg (1998). https://doi.org/10.1007/BFb0054118

[Nec94] Nechaev, V.I.: Complexity of a determinate algorithm for the discrete logarithm. Math. Notes **55**(2), 91–101 (1994)

[Ngu05] Nguyen, L.: Accumulators from bilinear pairings and applications. In: Menezes, A. (ed.) CT-RSA 2005. LNCS, vol. 3376, pp. 275–292. Springer, Heidelberg (2005). https://doi.org/10.1007/978-3-540-30574-3_19

[NN98]   Nissim, K., Naor, M.: Certificate revocation and certificate update. In: Proceedings of the 7th USENIX Security Symposium (1998)

[OWW+20] Ozdemir, A., Wahby, R.S., Whitehat, B., Boneh, D.: Scaling verifiable computation using efficient set accumulators. In: Proceedings of the 29th USENIX Security Symposium, pp. 2075–2092 (2020)

[PS14]   Pöhls, H.C., Samelin, K.: On updatable redactable signatures. In: Boureanu, I., Owesarski, P., Vaudenay, S. (eds.) ACNS 2014. LNCS, vol. 8479, pp. 457–475. Springer, Cham (2014). https://doi.org/10.1007/978-3-319-07536-5_27

[Sho97] Shoup, V.: Lower bounds for discrete logarithms and related problems. In: Fumy, W. (ed.) EUROCRYPT 1997. LNCS, vol. 1233, pp. 256–266. Springer, Heidelberg (1997). https://doi.org/10.1007/3-540-69053-0_18

[Sla12] Slamanig, D.: Dynamic accumulator based discretionary access control for outsourced storage with unlinkable access. In: Keromytis, A.D. (ed.) FC 2012. LNCS, vol. 7397, pp. 215–222. Springer, Heidelberg (2012). https://doi.org/10.1007/978-3-642-32946-3_16

[ST99]   Sander, T., Ta-Shma, A.: Flow control: a new approach for anonymity control in electronic cash systems. In: Franklin, M. (ed.) FC 1999. LNCS, vol. 1648, pp. 46–61. Springer, Heidelberg (1999). https://doi.org/10.1007/3-540-48390-X_4

[Tha19] Thakur, S.: Batching non-membership proofs with bilinear accumulators. Cryptology ePrint Archive, Report 2019/1147 (2019). https://eprint.iacr.org/2019/1147

[Tod16] Todd, P.: Making UTXO set growth irrelevant with low-latency delayed TXO commitments (2016). https://petertodd.org/2016/delayed-txo-commitments

[Wee07] Wee, H.: One-way permutations, interactive hashing and statistically hiding commitments. In: Vadhan, S.P. (ed.) TCC 2007. LNCS, vol. 4392, pp. 419–433. Springer, Heidelberg (2007). https://doi.org/10.1007/978-3-540-70936-7_23

[Wes19] Wesolowski, B.: Efficient verifiable delay functions. In: Ishai, Y., Rijmen, V. (eds.) EUROCRYPT 2019. LNCS, vol. 11478, pp. 379–407. Springer, Cham (2019). https://doi.org/10.1007/978-3-030-17659-4_13

Batch Verification and Proofs of Proximity with Polylog Overhead

Guy N. Rothblum[1]([✉]) and Ron D. Rothblum[2]([✉])

[1] Weizmann Institute, Rehovot, Israel
rothblum@alum.mit.edu
[2] Technion - Israel Institute of Technology, Haifa, Israel
rothblum@cs.technion.ac.il

In Memoriam: Uriel G. Rothblum

Abstract. Suppose Alice wants to convince Bob of the correctness of k NP statements. Alice could send k witnesses to Bob, but as k grows the communication becomes prohibitive. Is it possible to convince Bob using smaller communication (without making cryptographic assumptions or bounding the computational power of a malicious Alice)? This is the question of *batch verification* for NP statements. Our main result is a new interactive proof protocol for verifying the correctness of k UP statements (NP statements with a unique witness) using communication that is *poly-logarithmic* in k (and a fixed polynomial in the length of a single witness).

This result is obtained by making progress on a different question in the study of interactive proofs. Suppose Alice wants to convince Bob that a huge dataset has some property. Can this be done if Bob can't even read the entire input? In other words, what properties can be verified in *sublinear* time? An Interactive Proof of Proximity guarantees that Bob accepts if the input has the property, and rejects if the input is far (say in Hamming distance) from having the property. Two central complexity measures of such a protocol are the query and communication complexities (which should both be sublinear). For every query parameter q, and for every language in logspace uniform NC, we construct an interactive proof of proximity with query complexity q and communication complexity $(n/q) \cdot \mathsf{polylog}(n)$.

Both results are optimal up to poly-logarithmic factors, under reasonable complexity-theoretic or cryptographic assumptions. The second result, which is our main technical contribution, builds on a distance amplification technique introduced in a beautiful recent work of Ben-Sasson, Kopparty and Saraf [CCC 2018].

1 Introduction

The power of efficiently verifiable proof-systems is a central question in the study of computation. It has been the focus of a rich literature spanning cryptography and complexity theory. This literature has put forth and studied different notions of proof systems and different notions of efficient verification.

© International Association for Cryptologic Research 2020
R. Pass and K. Pietrzak (Eds.): TCC 2020, LNCS 12551, pp. 108–138, 2020.
https://doi.org/10.1007/978-3-030-64378-2_5

Interactive proofs, introduced in the seminal work of Goldwasser, Micali and Rackoff [GMR89], are one of the most fundamental notions in this field. An interactive proof is an interactive protocol between a randomized verifier and an untrusted prover. The prover convinces the verifier of the validity of a computational statement, usually framed as membership of an input x in a language $\mathcal{L}$. Soundness is unconditional. Namely, if the input is not in the language, then no matter what (unbounded and adaptive) strategy a cheating prover might employ, the verifier should reject with high probability over its own coin tosses. Interactive proofs have had a dramatic impact on complexity theory and on cryptography. Opening the door to randomized and interactive verification led to revolutionary notions of proof verification, such as zero knowledge interactive proofs [GMR89, GMW91] and probabilistically checkable proofs (PCPs) [BGKW88, FRS94, BFL91, BFLS91, FGL+96, AS92, ALM+98]. Interactive proof-systems also allow for more efficient verification of larger classes of computations (compared with NP proof systems), as demonstrated in the celebrated IP = PSPACE Theorem [LFKN92, Sha92].

Still, foundational questions about the power of interactive proof systems have remained open. Our work studies two such questions:

1.1 Batch Verification

Can interactive proofs allow for more efficient *batch verification* of a collection of NP statements?

Question 1:
How efficiently can an untrusted prover convince a verifier of the correctness of
k NP statements?

A naive solution is sending the k witnesses in their entirety. An honest prover, who knows the witnesses, runs in polynomial time, but the communication grows linearly with k. For the case of UP statements—NP statements with a unique witness—we show a protocol where the communication complexity grows polylogarithmically with k (and the honest prover remains efficient):

Theorem 1 (Informally Stated, see Theorems 4.2 **and** 4.1**).** *Let $\mathcal{L} \in$ UP with witnesses of length $m = m(n)$. There exists an interactive proof for verifying that k instances $x_1, \ldots, x_k$, each of length n, all belong to $\mathcal{L}$. The communication complexity is $\mathsf{poly}(\log(k), m)$, where poly refers to a fixed polynomial that depends only on the language $\mathcal{L}$. The number of rounds is $\mathsf{polylog}(k)$. The verifier runs in time $\tilde{O}(k \cdot n) + \mathsf{polylog}(k) \cdot \mathsf{poly}(m)$, where n is the length of each of the instances. The honest prover runs in time $\mathsf{poly}(k, n, m)$ given the k unique witnesses.*

This resolves the communication complexity of batch verification for UP up to $\mathsf{poly}(\log(k), m)$ factors: under complexity-theoretic assumptions, even for $k = 1$ there are UP languages (e.g. unique SAT) for which every interactive proof system requires communication complexity $\Omega(m)$ [GH98, GVW02]. When the number of instances k is large, this can be a significant improvement over the naive solution in which the prover sends over all k witnesses.

We note that for UP relations that are checkable in log-space uniform NC, we can reduce the communication complexity to $m \cdot \mathsf{polylog}(k, m)$. As discussed above, this is tight up to $\mathsf{polylog}(k)$ factors (under complexity assumptions). We also note that, assuming the existence of one-way functions, our batch verification protocol (which is public coin) can be made zero-knowledge using standard techniques [BGG+88].

Comparison to Prior Work. A different solution can be obtained via the IP = PSPACE theorem, by observing that the membership of k inputs in an NP language can be decided in space $O(\log k + m \cdot \mathsf{poly}(n))$, where n is the length of a single input and m is the length of a single NP witness. Thus, by the IP = PSPACE Theorem, there is an interactive proof for batch verification with communication complexity $\mathsf{poly}(\log k, n, m)$. A major caveat, however, is that the complexity of proving correctness (the running time of the *honest* prover) is *exponential in* $\mathsf{poly}(n, m)$. We, on the other hand, focus on batch verification where the honest prover runs in *polynomial time* given the k NP witnesses. We refer to such an interactive proof as having an *efficient prover*.[1] Another significant drawback of this solution is that the number of rounds becomes $\mathsf{poly}(m, \log k)$.

Two recent works have constructed protocols for efficient batch verification of UP statements. Reingold, Rothblum and Rothblum [RRR16] gave a protocol with communication complexity $\mathsf{polylog}(k) \cdot \mathsf{poly}(m) + k \cdot \mathsf{polylog}(m)$. In a subsequent work [RRR18] they eliminated the additive k factor but increased the multiplicative factor, by showing a (constant-round) protocol with communication complexity $k^{\varepsilon} \cdot \mathsf{poly}(m)$, for any $\varepsilon > 0$. Our main result achieves the best of both worlds: eliminating the additive linear factor while preserving the polylogarithmic multiplicative factor (although our protocol has a larger number of rounds than that of [RRR18]).

1.2   Interactive Proofs of Proximity

A different question (which turns out to be related) asks which statements can be verified in *sublinear* time, i.e. without even reading the entire input. This immediately raises the question of what computational model is used to capture "sublinear time". Drawing inspiration from the literature on sublinear *algorithms*, a natural choice is to adopt the perspective of property testing, a study initiated by Rubinfeld and Sudan [RS96] and Goldreich, Goldwasser and Ron [GGR98], which considers highly-efficient randomized algorithms that solve approximate decision problems, while only inspecting a small fraction of the input. Such algorithms, commonly referred to as property testers for a set S (say the set of objects with some property), are given query access to an input, and are required to determine whether the input is in S (has the property), or is far (say, in Hamming distance) from every string in S (far from having the property). A rich literature has put forward property testers for many natural properties.

---

[1] Efficiency of the honest prover (given an NP witness) has been central in the study of zero-knowledge interactive proofs [GMR89, GMW91]. It has also been central to the study of efficient batch verification in recent works [RRR16, RRR18].

Analogously, in the proof verification setting, Interactive Proofs of Proximity (IPPs) aim to verify that a given input is close to a set (or a property). Given a desired proximity parameter $\delta \in (0, 1]$, the soundness condition of standard interactive proofs is relaxed: it should be impossible to convince the verifier to accept statements that are δ-far (in fractional Hamming distance) from true statements (except with small probability). Such proof-systems were first introduced by Ergün, Kumar and Rubinfeld [EKR04] and were more recently further studied by Rothblum, Vadhan and Wigderson [RVW13] and by Gur and Rothblum [GR13]. The verifier's query complexity and running time, as well as the communication, should all be sublinear in the input length. Other parameters of interest include the (honest) prover's running time and the number of rounds.

The hope is that IPPs can overcome inherent limitations of property testing: for example, demonstrating specific properties where verifying proximity can be significantly faster than the time needed to test (without a prover). Another goal is showing that sublinear-time verification is possible for much richer families of properties than those for which property testers exist. In particular, research on property testing has focused on constructing testers for languages based on their combinatorial or algebraic structure. This limitation seems inherent, because there exist simple and natural languages for which (provably) no sublinear time property testers exist. In contrast, it is known that highly non-trivial IPPs exist for every language that can be decided in bounded-polynomial depth or space [RVW13, RRR16]. However, the optimal tradeoffs between the query and communication complexities needed for proof verification were not known, and this is the second foundational question we study:

Question 2:
What are the possible tradeoffs between the query and communication complexities in interactive proofs of proximity, and for which statements?

For the case of languages in (uniform) NC—languages that can be decided by polynomial-sized circuits of polylogarithmic depth—we show that the product of the query and communication complexities can be quasi-linear.

Theorem 2 (Informally Stated, see Theorem 4.1). *Let $t = t(n) \leq n$ be a parameter. For every $\delta \leq \frac{t \cdot \mathsf{polylog}(n)}{n}$ and every language $\mathcal{L}$ in log-space uniform NC, there exists an IPP for $\mathcal{L}$ with respect to proximity parameter δ, with communication complexity $t \cdot \mathsf{polylog}(n)$ and query complexity $O(1/\delta)$. The verifier runs in time $\tilde{O}(t + n/t)$ and the prover runs in time $\mathsf{poly}(n)$.*

For example, by setting $t(n) = \sqrt{n}$ we obtain an IPP for NC with query, communication and verification complexity all $\tilde{O}(\sqrt{n})$. This result resolves the question for such languages, up to polylogarithmic factors, as Kalai and Rothblum [KR15] showed that (under a reasonable cryptographic assumption) there exists a language in NC^1 for which the product of the query and communication complexities cannot be sublinear.

Comparison and Relationship to [RVW13]. Theorem 2 shows that the product of the query complexity and the communication can be quasi-linear (for a distance parameter that is the inverse of the query complexity). Rothblum, Vadhan and Wigderson [RVW13] showed a similar statement, but the product of the query and communication complexities was $n^{1+o(1)}$.

Our protocol builds on the framework developed in their work, introducing several new ideas and using a key distance amplification technique from a beautiful recent work of Ben-Sasson, Kopparty and Saraf [BKS18]. We find the improvement from $n^{1+o(1)}$ to $\tilde{O}(n)$ to be significant: beyond the fact that it provides a nearly-optimal (up to polylog(n) factors) trade-off for a foundational problem, it allows for IPPs with polylog(n) communication and sublinear query complexity. In prior work, achieving sublinear query complexity (for NC) required $n^{o(1)}$ communication. The importance of this distinction is exemplified in the application of IPPs towards batch verification for UP [RRR18]. That construction repeatedly uses IPPs with slightly-sublinear query complexity. The communication of the resulting batch verification protocol is dominated by the communication complexity of the IPPs. Indeed, the improved IPP of Theorem 2 is the key component behind the improved UP batch verification protocol of Theorem 1.

1.3   Related Works

Batch Verification with Computational Soundness. If one is willing to settle for *computational* soundness (i.e., soundness holds only against polynomial-time cheating strategies) and to use cryptographic assumptions, then efficient batch verification is possible for all of NP. In particular, Kilian [Kil92] gave an interactive argument-system for all of NP based on collision-resistant hash functions with only poly-logarithmic communication complexity. Since verifying the membership of k instances in an NP language is itself an NP problem, we immediately obtain a batch verification protocol with communication complexity poly(log(n), log(k), κ), where κ is a cryptographic security parameter.

More recently, Brakerski, Holmgren and Kalai [BHK17] obtained an efficient *non-interactive* batch-verification protocol assuming the existence of a computational private information retrieval scheme. Non-interactive batch verification protocols also follow from the existence of *succinct non-interactive zero-knowledge arguments (zkSNARGs)*, which are known to exist under certain strong, and non-falsifiable, assumptions (see, e.g. [Ish], for a recent survey).

We emphasize that the batch verification protocols of both [Kil92] and [BHK17] only provide computational soundness and are based on unproven cryptographic assumptions. In contrast, the result of Theorem 1 offers statistical soundness and is unconditional.

Interactive Proofs of Proximity. Beyond the works [EKR04, RVW13, GR13] that were mentioned above, interactive proofs of proximity have drawn considerable attention [FGL14, GGR15, KR15, RRR16, GR17, BRV18, RRR18, CG18, GLR18, RR19, GRSY20].

In particular, we mention that a recent work of Ron-Zewi and Rothblum [RR19, Theorem 3, see also Remark 1.3] shows that for every constant ϵ, every language computable in polynomial-time and bounded polynomial space has an IPP with communication complexity $\epsilon \cdot n$ and constant query complexity. Note that the product between the query and communication complexity in their result is $O(n)$, rather than $n \cdot \mathsf{polylog}(n)$ as in Theorem 2. However, in constrast to Theorem 2, their result is restricted to the regime of constant query complexity and only yields communication complexity that is smaller by a constant factor than that of the trivial solution (see Proposition 3.3).

1.4   Organization

Section 2 contains a technical overview of our techniques. In Sect. 3 we provide preliminaries and our main results are stated in Sect. 4. In Sect. 5 we introduce the PVAL problem and show how to amplify its distance. Our efficient PVAL IPP is in Sect. 6. Lastly, in Sect. 7 we use the results established in the prior sections to prove Theorem 1 and Theorem 2.

2   Technical Overview

To prove Theorem 1 we rely on a recent result of Reingold et $al.$ [RRR18] who showed how to reduce the construction of UP batch verification protocol to that of constructing efficient IPPs. In particular, via the connection established in [RRR18], in order to prove Theorem 1, it suffices to prove Theorem 2 with respect to $cc = \mathsf{polylog}(n)$.

Thus, in this overview we focus on proving Theorem 2. Our starting point for the proof of Theorem 2 is the IPP construction for NC from [RVW13] (which achieves weaker parameters than those of Theorem 2).

The [RVW13] protocol is centered around a parameterized problem called PVAL, which stands for "Polynomial eVALuation" and is defined next. A key step in the [RVW13] proof is showing that PVAL is "complete" for constructing IPPs for NC. In more detail, for every language $\mathcal{L} \in$ NC, [RVW13] show an $interactive$ reduction, in which the verifier $makes$ no $queries$ to its $input$. At the end of the reduction, the verifier generates a "parameterization" of the PVAL problem so that if the original input x belonged to $\mathcal{L}$ then x belongs to PVAL, whereas if x was far from $\mathcal{L}$ then, with high probability, x is also far from PVAL.

Thus, an efficient IPP for PVAL immediately yields an efficient IPP for $\mathcal{L}$ as follows: the prover and verifier first engage in the interactive reduction to obtain a parameterization of the PVAL problem. Then, the two parties run the efficient IPP protocol to check proximity to the newly generated PVAL instance.

In this work we follow the same strategy. We do not modify the interactive reduction step from [RVW13]. Our improved efficiency stems from a more efficient IPP for PVAL (than that of [RVW13]), which suffices to obtain our main results.

We start by defining a specific variant[2] of the PVAL problem that suffices for our purposes.

The PVAL *Problem.* Let $\mathbb{F}$ be a (sufficiently large) finite field. The PVAL problem is parameterized by an integer $t \in \mathbb{N}$, which we refer to as the *arity*, and a *dimension* $m \in \mathbb{N}$. In addition the problem is parameterized by t vectors $\mathbf{j} = (\mathbf{j}_1, \ldots, \mathbf{j}_t) \in (\mathbb{F}^m)^t$ and t scalars $\mathbf{v} = (v_1, \ldots, v_t) \in \mathbb{F}^t$. The main input to PVAL$(t, \mathbf{j}, \mathbf{v})$ is the truth table of a function $f : \{0,1\}^m \to \mathbb{F}$. We say that $f \in$ PVAL$(t, \mathbf{j}, \mathbf{v})$ if it holds that $\hat{f}(\mathbf{j}_i) = v_i$, for every $i \in [t]$, where $\hat{f} : \mathbb{F}^m \to \mathbb{F}$ is the multi-linear extension of f.[3] Thus, the goal of the PVAL verifier is to distinguish the case that (1) the multilinear extension $\hat{f}$ of the input function f is equal, at t given points, to t corresponding values, or (2) is far from any such function. Note that the verifier is only allowed to make a sub-linear (i.e., $\ll 2^m$) number of queries to f, but is allowed to communicate with the (untrusted) prover who has full access to f.

Our main technical contribution is an IPP for checking δ-proximity to PVAL$(t, \mathbf{j}, \mathbf{v})$ with communication complexity roughly $t \cdot \text{poly}(m)$ and query complexity $O(1/\delta)$ (see Theorem 6.1 for the formal statement). (Note that setting $\delta = 2^m \cdot \text{poly}(m)/t$ results in the product of the query and communication complexities being $\tilde{O}(2^m)$, which is quasi-linear in the input length.) We proceed to describe the new IPP for PVAL.

Attempt 1: Divide and Conquer. Fix a parameterization $(t, \mathbf{j}, \mathbf{v})$ for PVAL, where $\mathbf{j} = (\mathbf{j}_1, \ldots, \mathbf{j}_t)$ and $\mathbf{v} = (v_1, \ldots, v_t)$, and consider a given input $f : \{0,1\}^m \to \mathbb{F}$. Following [RVW13], we would like to first decompose the t claims that we are given about f into claims about the underlying functions $f_0, f_1 : \{0,1\}^{m-1} \to \mathbb{F}$, where $f_0(\cdot) \equiv f(0, \cdot)$ and $f_1(\cdot) \equiv f(1, \cdot)$. To do so, the verifier asks the prover to provide the contributions of f_0 and f_1 to the linear claims $\hat{f}(\mathbf{j}_i) = v_i$, for all $i \in [t]$. In more detail, let us view each vector $\mathbf{j}_i$ as $\mathbf{j}_i = (\chi_i, \mathbf{j}'_i)$ where $\chi_i \in \mathbb{F}$ and $\mathbf{j}'_i \in \mathbb{F}^{m-1}$ (i.e., we isolate the first component of $\mathbf{j}_i$ as χ_i and the remaining components as an $(m-1)$-dimensional vector $\mathbf{j}'_i$). The prover sends the vectors $\mathbf{v}_0, \mathbf{v}_1 \in \mathbb{F}^{m-1}$, where $\mathbf{v}_0 = \hat{f}_0|_{\mathbf{j}'}$ and $\mathbf{v}_1 = \hat{f}_1|_{\mathbf{j}'}$. Note that the prover cannot send arbitrary vectors since the verifier can check (and indeed *does* check) that $\mathbf{v}_0$ and $\mathbf{v}_1$ are consistent with $\mathbf{v}$. (I.e., that $\mathbf{v} = (1-\bar{\chi}) \cdot \mathbf{v}_0 + \bar{\chi} \cdot \mathbf{v}_1$, where $\bar{\chi} = (\chi_1, \ldots, \chi_t)$ and the multiplication is pointwise.) See Fig. 1 for an illustration.

A natural idea at this point, is to try to combine f_0 and f_1 (and the corresponding claims that we have about them) into a single $m - 1$ variate function on which we can recurse. For example, we can take a random linear combination of the two functions as follows: the verifier chooses random coefficients

---

[2] In particular, for simplicity and since it is sufficient for our results we consider a variant of PVAL with respect to the *multi-linear* extension rather than a more general low degree extension considered in [RVW13].

[3] Recall that the multilinear extension $\hat{f} : \mathbb{F}^m \to \mathbb{F}$ of $f : \{0,1\}^m \to \mathbb{F}$ is the unique multilinear polynomial that agrees with f on $\{0,1\}^m$. See Sect. 3.1 for details.

$$\mathbb{F}^{m-1}$$

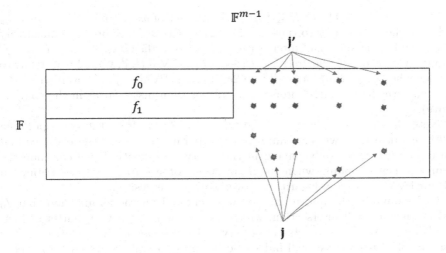

Fig. 1. Decomposing the claims $f|_\mathbf{j} = \mathbf{v}$.

$c^{(0)}, c^{(1)} \in \mathbb{F}$, sends them to the prover. The two parties then recurse on the input $f' = c^{(0)} \cdot f_0 + c^{(1)} \cdot f_1$ wrt the claims $\hat{f}'|_{\mathbf{j}'} = \mathbf{v}'$, with $\mathbf{v}' = c^{(0)} \cdot \mathbf{v}_0 + c^{(1)} \cdot \mathbf{v}_1$.[4]

Note that the input has shrunk by a factor of 2 and it is not too diffi-cult to argue that if f was δ-far from $\mathsf{PVAL}(t, \mathbf{j}, \mathbf{v})$ then f' is about δ-far from $\mathsf{PVAL}(t, \mathbf{j}', \mathbf{v}')$. Thus, with very little communication (i.e., $O(t \cdot \log(|\mathbb{F}|))$ we have reduced the input size by half and preserved the distance. We can continue recursing as such until the input reaches a sufficiently small size so that the verifier can solve the problem by itself (or, rather, verifier can employ a "trivial" protocol, with $1/\delta$ query complexity and linear communication in the size of the final input).

The problem with this approach is that while the input size has shrunk by half, as we recurse we will need to emulate each query to f' by using two queries to f. Thus, while the input length has shrunk by half, the query complexity has doubled and essentially no progress has been made. Indeed, if we unwind the recursion, we see that the total query complexity in the proposed protocol is linear in the input length.

Doubling the Distance: A Pipe Dream? For every $b \in \{0, 1\}$, let δ_b be the distance of f_b from $\mathsf{PVAL}(t, \mathbf{j}, \mathbf{v}_b)$ and let $P_b \in \mathsf{PVAL}(t, \mathbf{j}, \mathbf{v}_b)$ such that $\Delta(f_b, P_b) = \delta_b$ (without getting into the details we remark that P_0 and P_1 will be unique in our regime of parameters). Note that if f is δ-far from PVAL then $\delta_0 + \delta_1 \geq 2\delta$, since otherwise f is δ-close to the function $P \in \mathsf{PVAL}(t, \mathbf{j}, \mathbf{v})$ defined as $P(\sigma, \mathbf{x}) = (1 - \sigma) \cdot P_0(\mathbf{x}) + \sigma \cdot P_1(\mathbf{x})$.

---

[4] Intuitively, the reason to use a *random* linear combination rather than some fixed combination such as $f_0 + f_1$ is avoiding (w.h.p) the possibility that the differences of f_0 and f_1 from their corresponding PVAL instances (i.e. the 0/1 vectors that can be added to f_0 and f_1 to reach vectors in PVAL) cancel each other out.

For every $b \in \{0,1\}$, let $I_b \subseteq \{0,1\}^m$ be the set of $\delta_b \cdot 2^m$ points on which P_b and f_b disagree (we refer to these as the "error pattern"). Suppose momentarily that I_0 and I_1 have a small intersection (or are even disjoint). In such a case, f' is roughly $\delta_0 + \delta_1 \geq 2\delta$ far from $c_0 \cdot P_0 + c_1 \cdot P_1 \in \mathsf{PVAL}(t, \mathbf{j}', \mathbf{v}')$. This leads us to wonder whether f' could actually be 2δ far from $\mathsf{PVAL}(t, \mathbf{j}', \mathbf{v}')$ even when the error patterns have a large intersection (rather than just δ far as in the analysis above).

Note that if it is indeed the case that f' is 2δ far from the corresponding PVAL instance then we have improved two parameters: both the distance and the input size, while only paying in the query complexity. If we continue the recursion now (stopping when the input size is of size roughly t) we obtain an IPP for PVAL with poly-logarithmic overhead, as we desired.

Unfortunately, the above analysis was centered on the assumption that I_0 and I_1 have a small intersection, which we cannot justify. As a matter of fact, for all we know, the two sets could very well be *identical*. In such a case, the distance of f' from PVAL will indeed be (roughly) δ and we are back to square one.

See Fig. 2 for an illustration for the possible "error patterns" of f_0 and f_1 and how they affect the "error patterns" of f'.

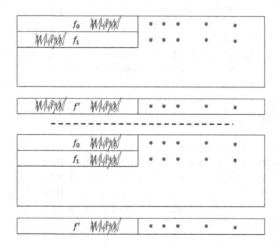

Fig. 2. Possible alignments of the "Noise"

We pause here for a detour, recalling the approach of [RVW13] (this is not essential for understanding our construction and can be skipped). They observe that if δ_0 and δ_1 are roughly equal, then the verifier can simply recurse on one of them. This roughly maintains the distance, while avoiding doubling the query complexity. On the other hand, if say $\delta_0 \gg \delta_1$, they show that the random linear combination technique described above does increase the distance (intuitively, the row with smaller distance cannot "cancel out" the error pattern of the row with larger distance). We remark that they lose a constant multiplicative factor in this argument, which leads them to consider a decomposition into polylog(n) many rows, rather than 2. Of course, the verifier does not know whether $\delta_0 \approx \delta_1$ or $\delta_0 \gg \delta_1$. However, they show that the verifier can "cover its bases" by considering a small number of (approximations to the) decompositions of the distance across rows. This results in the creation of $O(\log \log n)$ smaller recursive instances, where the product of the new distance and the new effective query complexity of at least one of these instances is "good" (the definition of "good" allows for losing super-constant multiplicative factors). Over the course of $\Omega(\log n/\log \log n)$ recursive steps, the losses and the ballooning number of recursive instances add up, and result in a roughly $2^{\log n/\log \log n} = n^{o(1)}$ overhead in the product between the final query and communication complexities.

Reducing the Intersection Size. A key new ingredient in our protocol is randomly permuting the truth tables of the functions f_0 and f_1, in order to make the sets I_0 and I_1 (pseudo-)random, and therefore likely to have a small intersection. This is inspired by the beautiful recent result of Ben Sasson, Kopparty and Saraf [BKS18] on amplifying distances from the Reed-Solomon code. More precisely, the verifier chooses random permutations $\pi_0, \pi_1 : \{0, 1\}^m \to \{0, 1\}^m$ (from a suitable family of permutations, to be discussed below). We consider the new functions $f_0 \circ \pi_0$ and $f_1 \circ \pi_1$. The hope is that the entropy induced by these permutations will make the error patterns in $f_0 \circ \pi_0$ and in $f_1 \circ \pi_1$ have a small intersection. Then, rather than recursing on $c_0 \cdot f_0 + c_1 \cdot f_1$, we will aim to recurse on $f' = c_0 \cdot (f_0 \circ \pi_0) + c_1 \cdot (f_1 \circ \pi_1)$.

To make this approach work we have to overcome several difficulties. First, we need to ensure that we can translate the claims that we have about $\hat{f}_0$ and $\hat{f}_1$ into claims about $\widehat{f_0 \circ \pi_0}$ and $\widehat{f_1 \circ \pi_1}$. We do so by choosing π_0 and π_1 as random *affine* maps over $\mathbb{F}^m$, while ensuring that the restriction of these maps to $\{0, 1\}^m$ forms a permutation. We argue that this ensures that:

$$\widehat{f_0 \circ \pi_0} \equiv \hat{f}_0 \circ \pi_0, \tag{1}$$

and similarly for f_1. To see that Eq. (1) holds, observe that if π_0 is an affine function, then both sides of the equation are multilinear polynomials that agree on $\{0, 1\}^m$. Therefore they must also agree on $\mathbb{F}^m$.

Equation (1) implies that the claims that we have about the multi-linear extensions of $f_0 \circ \pi_0$ and $f_1 \circ \pi_1$ are simply permutations of the claims about f_0 and f_1, respectively.

A second difficulty that arises at this point is that the claims that we have about $f_0 \circ \pi_0$ and $f_1 \circ \pi_1$ are not "aligned". The former claims are about positions $\pi_0^{-1}(\mathbf{j}')$ and the latter about $\pi_1^{-1}(\mathbf{j}')$ (in the multi-linear extensions of $f_0 \circ \pi_0$ and $f_1 \circ \pi_1$, respectively). Since the claims are not aligned, it unclear how to combine them to get t claims about the input f'.

As our first step toward resolving this difficulty, we have the prover "complete the picture" by providing the verifier also with the (alleged) values of $\hat{f}_0 \circ \pi_0$ at positions $\pi_1^{-1}(\mathbf{j}')$ and those of $\hat{f}_1 \circ \pi_1$ at positions $\pi_0^{-1}(\mathbf{j}')$.

Note that the prover can cheat to its heart's desire about these claims, but the point is that we now have a single set $I = \pi_0^{-1}(\mathbf{j}') \cup \pi_1^{-1}(\mathbf{j}')$ so that each function f_b is still δ_b far from the claims that we have about $f_b|_I$. Since the claims are now properly aligned, we can derive a new sequence of claims about f'. More importantly, we prove a technical lemma (building on the result of Ben Sasson *et al.* [BKS18]), showing that if f is δ-far from PVAL$(t, \mathbf{j}, \mathbf{v})$ then, with high probability, f' is roughly 2δ-far from the corresponding PVAL instance (induced by the prover's new claims).

To summarize, the approach so far lets us double the distance in each iteration as we desired. Unfortunately, it also raises a new problem: the arity of the new PVAL instance that we generated has doubled - rather than just having t claims we now have roughly $2t$ claims (corresponding to the size of the set I). See Fig. 3 for an illustration.

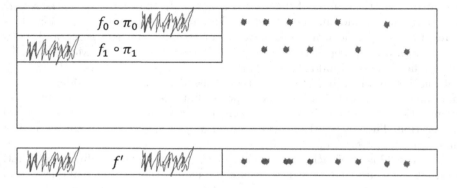

Fig. 3. Permuting the inputs and resulting arity growth

Arity Reduction Step. We resolve this final difficulty by once more employing interaction, and using the prover in order to reduce the $2t$ claims that we have about $f_0 \circ \pi_0$ and $f_1 \circ \pi_1$ to just t (aligned) claims each, while preserving the distance.

The idea here is to consider a degree $O(t)$ curve $\mathcal{C} : \mathbb{F} \to \mathbb{F}^m$ passing through the set of points I. The prover sends to the verifier the values of $\hat{f}_0 \circ \pi_0|_{\mathcal{C}}$ and $\hat{f}_1 \circ \pi_1|_{\mathcal{C}}$. The verifier checks that that the provided values lie on a degree $O(t)$ univariate polynomial (since $\hat{f}_b \circ \pi_b \circ \mathcal{C}$ has low degree, for both $b \in \{0, 1\}$). The verifier also checks that the values that correspond to points in the set I, are consistent with the claims that it has. The verifier now chooses a set of t random points $\rho = (\rho_1, \dots, \rho_t)$ on the curve. The new claims about $\hat{f}_0$ and $\hat{f}_1$ are those that correspond to the set of points in ρ. In particular, this lets us reduce the number of claims from $2t$ to t.

We want to argue that this arity-reduction sub-protocol preserves the distance. This is accomplished by taking a union bound over all inputs that are (roughly) 2δ-close to f', and showing that for each of them, the probability that it satisfies the new claim is tiny. We conclude that f' is indeed (roughly) 2δ-far from the resulting PVAL instance (a similar idea was used in the proof that PVAL is complete [RVW13]).

3 Preliminaries

For a string $x \in \Sigma^n$ and an index $i \in [n]$, we denote by $x_i \in \Sigma$ the ith entry in x. If $I \subseteq [n]$ is a set then we denote by $x|_I$ the sequence of entries in x corresponding to coordinates in I.

Let $x, y \in \Sigma^n$ be two strings of length $n \in \mathbb{N}$ over a (finite) alphabet Σ. We define the (relative Hamming) distance of x and y as $\Delta(x, y) \stackrel{\text{def}}{=} |\{x_i \neq y_i : i \in [n]\}| / n$. If $\Delta(x, y) \leq \varepsilon$, then we say that x is ε-close to y, and otherwise we say that x is ε-far from y. We define the distance of x from a (non-empty) set $S \subseteq \Sigma^n$ as $\Delta(x, S) \stackrel{\text{def}}{=} \min_{y \in S} \Delta(x, y)$. If $\Delta(x, S) \leq \varepsilon$, then we say that x is ε-close to S and otherwise we say that x is ε-far from S. We extend these definitions from strings to functions by identifying a function with its truth table. For a set S, take its minimum distance to be the minimum, over all distinct vectors $x, y \in S$ of $\Delta(x, y)$. We use $\Delta(S)$ to denote the minimum distance of S. Fixing a vector space, for a set S and a vector x, we denote $(x + S) = \{x + y : y \in S\}$. For a scalar c, we denote $(c \cdot S) = \{c \cdot y : y \in S\}$.

3.1 Multivariate Polynomials and Low Degree Extensions

We recall some important facts on multivariate polynomials (see [Sud95] for a far more detailed introduction). A basic fact, captured by the Schwartz-Zippel lemma is that low degree polynomials cannot have too many roots.

Lemma 3.1 (Schwartz-Zippel Lemma). *Let* $P : \mathbb{F}^m \to \mathbb{F}$ *be a non-zero polynomial of total degree* d. *Then,*

$$\Pr_{x \in \mathbb{F}^m} [P(x) = 0] \leq \frac{d}{|\mathbb{F}|}.$$

An immediate corollary of the Schwartz-Zippel Lemma is that two distinct polynomials $P, Q : \mathbb{F}^m \to \mathbb{F}$ of total degree d may agree on at most a $\frac{d}{|\mathbb{F}|}$-fraction of their domain $\mathbb{F}^m$.

Throughout this work we consider fields in which operations can be implemented efficiently (i.e., in poly-logarithmic time in the field size). Formally we define such fields as follows.

Definition 3.1. *We say that an ensemble of finite fields* $\mathbb{F} = (\mathbb{F}_n)_{n \in \mathbb{N}}$ *is constructible if elements in* $\mathbb{F}_n$ *can be represented by* $O(\log(|\mathbb{F}_n|))$ *bits and field operations (i.e., addition, subtraction, multiplication, inversion and sampling random elements) can all be performed in* polylog$(|\mathbb{F}_n|)$ *time given this representation.*

A well known fact is that for every $S = S(n)$, there exists a *constructible field ensemble* of size $O(S)$ and its representation can be found in $\mathsf{polylog}(S)$ time (see, e.g., [Gol08, Appendix G.3] for details).

Let $\mathbb{H}$ be a finite field and $\mathbb{F} \supseteq \mathbb{H}$ be an extension field of $\mathbb{H}$. Fix an integer $m \in \mathbb{N}$. A basic fact is that for every function $\phi : \mathbb{H}^m \to \mathbb{F}$, there exists a unique extension of ϕ into a function $\hat{\phi} : \mathbb{F}^m \to \mathbb{F}$ (which agrees with ϕ on $\mathbb{H}^m$; i.e., $\hat{\phi}|_{\mathbb{H}^m} \equiv \phi$), such that $\hat{\phi}$ is an m-variate polynomial of individual degree at most $|\mathbb{H}| - 1$. Moreover, there exists a collection of $|\mathbb{H}|^m$ functions $\{\hat{\tau}_x\}_{x \in \mathbb{H}^m}$ such that each $\hat{\tau}_x : \mathbb{F}^m \to \mathbb{F}$ is the m-variate polynomial of degree $|\mathbb{H}| - 1$ in each variable defined as:

$$\hat{\tau}_x(z) \overset{\text{def}}{=} \prod_{i \in [m]} \prod_{h \in \mathbb{H} \setminus \{x_i\}} \frac{z_i - h}{x_i - h}.$$

and for every function $\phi : \mathbb{H}^m \to \mathbb{F}$ it holds that

$$\hat{\phi}(z_1, \ldots, z_m) = \sum_{x \in \mathbb{H}^m} \hat{\tau}_x(z_1, \ldots, z_m) \cdot \phi(x).$$

The function $\hat{\phi}$ is called the *low degree extension* of ϕ (with respect to $\mathbb{F}$, $\mathbb{H}$ and m). In the special case in which $\mathbb{H} = \mathrm{GF}(2)$, the function $\hat{\phi}$ (which has individual degree 1) is called the *multilinear extension* of ϕ (with respect to $\mathbb{F}|$ and m).

3.2   A Useful Permutation Family

Let $m \in \mathbb{N}$. For every $a \in \mathrm{GF}(2^m)$, let $f_a : (\mathrm{GF}(2))^m \to (\mathrm{GF}(2))^m$ be defined as $f_a(x) = a \cdot x$, where we identify elements in $\mathrm{GF}(2^m)$ with vectors in $(\mathrm{GF}(2))^m$ in the natural way. Thus, for every $a \in (\mathrm{GF}(2))^m$, there exists a matrix $M_a \in (\mathrm{GF}(2))^{m \times m}$ such that $f(x) = M_a \cdot x$. Note that if $a \neq 0$ then the matrix M_a is invertible, and its inverse is given by $M_{a^{-1}}$.

Let $\mathbb{F}$ be a finite field that is an extension field of $\mathrm{GF}(2)$. For every $a, b \in (\mathrm{GF}(2))^m$ consider the function $\pi_{a,b} : \mathbb{F}^m \to \mathbb{F}^m$ defined as: $\pi_{a,b}(x) = M_a \cdot x + b$. Let $\pi_{a,b}|_{(\mathrm{GF}(2))^m}$ denote the restriction of $\pi_{a,b}$ to the domain $(\mathrm{GF}(2))^m$ and let $\Pi_m = \{\pi_{a,b} : a, b \in (\mathrm{GF}(2))^m, a \neq 0\}$.

Proposition 3.1. *The following holds for every $a, b \in (\mathrm{GF}(2))^m$:*

1. *The function $\pi_{a,b}$ is an affine map over $\mathbb{F}$.*
2. *If $a \neq 0$ then the function $\pi_{a,b}$ forms a permutation over $\mathbb{F}^m$ and $\pi_{a,b}|_{(\mathrm{GF}(2))^m}$ forms a permutation over $(\mathrm{GF}(2))^m$.*
3. *The function family $\{\pi_{a,b}|_{(\mathrm{GF}(2))^m}\}_{a,b \in (\mathrm{GF}(2))^m}$ is pairwise independent.*
4. *If $\mathbb{F}$ and $\mathrm{GF}(2^m)$ are constructible, then given $a, b \in (\mathrm{GF}(2))^m$ and $x \in \mathbb{F}^m$ it is possible to compute $\pi_{a,b}(x)$ in time $\mathsf{poly}(m, \log(|\mathbb{F}|))$.*

Proof. Item 1 is evident from the construction. For Item 2, let $a \neq 0$ and take any $x, x' \in \mathbb{F}^m$. Observe that if $M_a \cdot x + b = M_a \cdot x' + b$ then $M_a \cdot (x - x') = \mathbf{0}$. Multiplying both sides on the left by $M_{a^{-1}}$ (a matrix in $\mathrm{GF}(2)^{m \times m} \subseteq \mathbb{F}^{m \times m}$)

we get that $x = x'$. Thus, $\pi_{a,b}$ is a permutation over $\mathbb{F}^m$. Since the image of $\pi_{a,b}|_{(\mathrm{GF}(2))^m}$ lies in $(\mathrm{GF}(2))^m$ this also means that $\pi_{a,b}|_{(\mathrm{GF}(2))^m}$ is a permutation over $(\mathrm{GF}(2))^m$.

For Item 3, let $x_1, x_2, y_1, y_2 \in (\mathrm{GF}(2))^m$ with $x_1 \neq x_2$. Then:

$$\Pr_{a,b}[M_a \cdot x_1 + b = y_1 \wedge M_a \cdot x_2 + b = y_2] = \Pr_{a,b}[a \cdot x_1 + b = y_1 \wedge a \cdot x_2 + b = y_2]$$

$$= \Pr_{a,b}\left[\begin{pmatrix} a \\ b \end{pmatrix} \cdot \begin{pmatrix} x_1 & 1 \\ x_2 & 1 \end{pmatrix} = \begin{pmatrix} y_1 \\ y_2 \end{pmatrix}\right]$$

$$= 2^{-2m},$$

where in the first expression the arithmetic is over the field $\mathrm{GF}(2)$ and in the second and third expressions the arithmetic is over $\mathrm{GF}(2^m)$, and the last equality follows from the fact that $\det\begin{pmatrix} x_1 & 1 \\ x_2 & 1 \end{pmatrix} = x_1 - x_2 \neq 0$.

Lastly, for Item 4, observe that M_a can be generated in $\mathsf{poly}(m)$ time by taking the product of a with a basis of $(\mathrm{GF}(2))^m$. Given the full description of M_a, the product $M_a \cdot x + b$ can be computed in $\mathsf{poly}(m, \log(|\mathbb{F}|))$ time.

Proposition 3.2. *Let $\phi : (\mathrm{GF}(2))^m \to \mathbb{F}$ and let $\hat{\phi} : \mathbb{F}^m \to \mathbb{F}$ be its multilinear extension. Let $\psi = \phi \circ (\pi_{a,b}|_{(\mathrm{GF}(2))^m})$ (a function over $(\mathrm{GF}(2))^m$), and let $\hat{\psi}$ be the multilinear extension of ψ. Then:*

$$\forall x \in \mathbb{F}^m, \ (\hat{\phi} \circ \pi_{a,b})(x) = \hat{\psi}(x).$$

Proof. By Proposition 3.1, the function $\pi_{a,b}$ is an affine map over $\mathbb{F}$. Thus, $(\hat{\phi} \circ \pi_{a,b})$ is multilinear. By definition, $\hat{\psi}$ is also multilinear (since it is a low degree extension). We have that $\hat{\psi}$ and $\hat{\phi} \circ \pi_{a,b}$ are both multilinear, and they agree over $(\mathrm{GF}(2))^m$. By uniqueness of the multilinear extension, they must also agree over $\mathbb{F}^m$. $\blacksquare$

3.3   Succinct Descriptions

Throughout this work we use NC^1 to refer to the class of logspace uniform Boolean circuits of logarithmic depth and constant fan-in. Namely, $\mathcal{L} \in \mathsf{NC}^1$ if there exists a logspace Turing machine M that on input 1^n outputs a full description of a logarithmic depth circuit $C : \{0,1\}^n \to \{0,1\}$ such that for every $x \in \{0,1\}^n$ it holds that $C(x) = 1$ if and only if $x \in \mathcal{L}$.

We next define a notion of succinct representation of circuits. Loosely speaking, a function $f : \{0,1\}^n \to \{0,1\}$ has a succinct representation if there is a short string $\langle f \rangle$, of poly-logarithmic length, that describes f. That is, $\langle f \rangle$ can be expanded to a full description of f. The actual technical definition is slightly more involved and in particular requires that the full description of f be an NC_1 (i.e., logarithmic depth) circuit:

Definition 3.2 (Succinct Description of Functions). *We say that a function $f : \{0,1\}^n \to \{0,1\}$ of size s has a* succinct description *if there exists a* *string $\langle f \rangle$ of length* polylog(n) *and a logspace Turing machine M (of constant size, independent of n) such that on input 1^n, the machine M outputs a full description of an* NC^1 *circuit C such that for every $x \in \{0,1\}^n$ it holds that $C(\langle f \rangle, x) = f(x)$. We refer to $\langle f \rangle$ as the succinct description of f.*

We also define succinct representation for sets $S \subseteq [k]$. Roughly speaking this means that the set can be described by a string of length polylog(k). The formal definition is somewhat more involved:

Definition 3.3 (Succinct Description of Sets). *We say that a set $S \subseteq [k]$ of size s has a succinct description if there exists a string $\langle S \rangle$ of length* polylog(k) *and a logspace Turing machine M such that on input 1^k, the machine M outputs a full description of a depth* polylog(k) *and size* poly$(s, \log k)$ *circuit (of constant fan-in) that on input $\langle S \rangle$ outputs all the elements of S as a list (of length $s \cdot \log(k)$).*

We emphasize that the size of the circuit that M outputs is proportional to the actual size of the set S, rather than the universe size k.

3.4   Interactive Proofs of Proximity

Loosely speaking, IPPs are interactive proofs in which the verifier runs in sub-linear time in the input length, where the soundness requirement is relaxed to rejecting inputs that are *far* from the language w.h.p. (for inputs that are not in the language, but are close to it, no requirement is made). Actually, we will think of the input of the verifier as being composed of two parts: an *explicit* input $x \in \{0,1\}^n$ to which the verifier has direct access, and an *implicit* (longer) input $y \in \{0,1\}^m$ to which the verifier has oracle access. The goal is for the verifier to run in time that is sub-linear in m and to verify that y is far from any y' such that the pair (x, y') are in the language. Since such languages are composed of input pairs, we refer to them as *pair languages*.

Definition 3.4 (Interactive Proof of Proximity (IPP) [EKR04,RVW13]). *An* interactive proof of proximity *(IPP) for the pair language $\mathcal{L}$ is an interactive protocol with two parties: a (computationally unbounded) prover $\mathcal{P}$ and a computationally bounded verifier $\mathcal{V}$. Both parties get as input $x \in \{0,1\}^n$ and a proximity parameter $\varepsilon > 0$. The verifier also gets oracle access to $y \in \{0,1\}^m$ whereas the prover has full access to y. At the end of the interaction, the following two conditions are satisfied:*

1. **Completeness:** *For every pair $(x, y) \in \mathcal{L}$, and proximity parameter $\varepsilon > 0$ it holds that*
$$\Pr\left[(\mathcal{P}(y), \mathcal{V}^y)(x, |y|, \varepsilon) = 1 \right] = 1.$$

2. **Soundness:** *For every $\varepsilon > 0$, $x \in \{0,1\}^n$ and y that is ε-far from the set $\{y' : (x, y') \in \mathcal{L}\}$, and for every computationally unbounded (cheating) prover $\mathcal{P}^*$ it holds that*
$$\Pr\left[(\mathcal{P}^*(y), \mathcal{V}^y)(x, |y|, \varepsilon) = 1 \right] \leq 1/2.$$

An IPP for $\mathcal{L}$ is said to have **query complexity** $q = q(n, m, \varepsilon)$ if, for every $\varepsilon > 0$ and $(x, y) \in \mathcal{L}$, the verifier $\mathcal{V}$ makes at most $q(|x|, |y|, \varepsilon)$ queries to y when interacting with $\mathcal{P}$. The IPP is said to have **communication complexity** $cc = cc(n, m, \varepsilon)$ if, for every $\varepsilon > 0$ and pair $(x, y) \in \mathcal{L}$, the communication between $\mathcal{V}$ and $\mathcal{P}$ consists of at most $cc(|x|, |y|, \varepsilon)$ bits. If the honest prover's running time is polynomial in n and m, then we way that the IPP is *doubly-efficient*.

The special case of IPPs in which the entire interaction consists of a single message sent from the prover to the verifier is called MAPs (in analogy to the complexity class MA) and was studied in [GR17, GGR15]. We will use the following simple observation:

Proposition 3.3 (See, e.g., [GR17]). *Every $\mathcal{L} \in \mathsf{DTIME}(t)$ has an MAP with respect to proximity parameter $\delta \in (0, 1)$ with communication complexity n and query complexity $O(1/\delta)$. The verifier runs in time $t + n + O(\log(n)/\varepsilon)$. The prover runs in time $O(n)$*

Proof (Proof Sketch). The prover sends to the verifier a full description of the input x (i.e., an n bit string). Given the message x' received from the prover (allegedly equal to the input x), the verifier first checks that $x' \in \mathcal{L}$ (this step requires no queries to x). The verifier further checks that x and x' agree on a random set of $O(1/\delta)$ coordinates.

Completeness is immediate, whereas to see that soundness holds, observe that the prover must send $x' \in \mathcal{L}$, since otherwise the verifier rejects. If x is δ-far from $\mathcal{L}$ then x and x' disagree on a at least δ fraction of their coordinates and so the verifier accepts with probability at most $(1 - \delta)^{O(1/\delta)} = 1/2$.

4   Our Results

Our first main result is an IPP for any language in NC with optimal query/communication tradeoff (up to poly-logarithmic factors).

Theorem 4.1. *Let $\delta = \delta(n) \in (0, 1)$ be a proximity parameter and let $\mathcal{L}$ be a pair language that is computable by logspace-uniform Boolean circuits of depth $D = D(n) \geq \log n$ and size $S = S(n) \geq n$ with fan-in 2 (where n denotes the implicit input and n_{exp} denotes the explicit input). Then, $\mathcal{L}$ has a public-coin IPP for δ-proximity with perfect completeness and the following parameters:*

- *Soundness Error: $1/2$.*
- *Query complexity: $q = O(1/\delta)$.*
- *Communication Complexity: $cc = \delta \cdot n \cdot D \cdot \mathsf{poly}\log(S)$.*
- *Round Complexity: $D \cdot \mathsf{polylog}(S)$.*
- *Verifier Running Time: $\delta \cdot n \cdot n_{exp}\mathsf{poly}(D, \log(S)) + (1/\delta) \cdot \mathsf{polylog}(n)$.*
- *Prover Running Time: $\mathsf{poly}(S)$.*

Furthermore, the verification procedure can be described succinctly as follows. At the end of the interaction either the verifier rejects or in time $\delta \cdot n \cdot \mathsf{poly}(D, \log(S))$ it outputs a succinct description $\langle Q \rangle$ of a set $Q \subseteq [n]$ of size q and a succinct description $\langle \phi \rangle$ of a predicate $\phi : \{0, 1\}^q \to \{0, 1\}$ so that its decision predicate given an input function f is equal to $\phi(f|Q)$.

Our second main result (which relies on Theorem 4.1) is an interactive proof for batch verification of any UP language, with communication complexity that is optimal up to poly-logarithmic factors.

Theorem 4.2. *For every* UP *language $\mathcal{L}$ with witness length $m = m(n)$, whose witness relation can be computed in logspace-uniform* NC, *there exists a public-coin interactive proof (with perfect completeness) for verifying that k instances $x_1, \ldots, x_k$, each of length $n \leq \mathsf{poly}(m)$, are all in $\mathcal{L}$. The complexity of the protocol is as follows:*

- *Communication complexity: $m \cdot \mathsf{polylog}(k, m)$.*
- *Number of rounds: $\mathsf{polylog}(k, m)$.*
- *Verifier runtime: $(n \cdot k + m) \cdot \mathsf{polylog}(k, m)$.*
- *The honest prover, given the k unique witnesses, runs in time $\mathsf{poly}(m, k)$.*

Using the Cook-Levin reduction, any UP language can be reduced to Unique-SAT which is a UP language whose witness relation can be computed in logspace-uniform NC, with only a $\mathsf{poly}(n, m)$ blowup to the witness size. Hence, Theorem 4.2 yields the following corollary.

Corollary 4.1. *For every* UP *language $\mathcal{L}$ with witness length $m = m(n)$, there exists a public-coin interactive proof (with perfect completeness) for verifying that k instances $x_1, \ldots, x_k$, each of length $n \leq \mathsf{poly}(m)$, are all in $\mathcal{L}$. The complexity of the protocol is as follows:*

- *Communication complexity: $\mathsf{poly}(m, \log(k))$.*
- *Number of rounds: $\mathsf{polylog}(m, k)$.*
- *Verifier runtime: $(n \cdot k) \cdot \mathsf{polylog}(m, k) + \mathsf{poly}(m, \log k)$.*
- *The honest prover, given the k unique witnesses, runs in time $\mathsf{poly}(m, k)$.*

5   The PVAL Problem

In this section we define the PVAL problem and state properties related to it that we will need in our proof. Due to lack of space, all proofs in this section are deferred to the full version.

Let $\mathbb{F}$ be a finite field, $\mathbb{H} \subseteq \mathbb{F}$ and $m \in \mathbb{N}$ be an integer.

Definition 5.1. *The PVAL problem is parameterized by an ensemble $(\mathbb{F}, \mathbb{H}, m)_n$. The explicit input to the problem is $(n, t, \mathbf{j}, \mathbf{v})$, where $t \in \mathbb{N}$, $\mathbf{j} = (j_1, \ldots, j_t) \in (\mathbb{F}^m)^t$ and $\mathbf{v} = v_1, \ldots, v_t \in \mathbb{F}^t$. The implicit input is a function $f : \mathbb{H}^m \to \mathbb{F}$. YES instances of the problems are all functions $f : \mathbb{H}^m \to \mathbb{F}$ such that for every $i \in [t]$ it holds that $\hat{f}(j_i) = v_i$, where $\hat{f}$ is the low degree extension of f.*

Since the low-degree extension is an error correcting code with high distance, for sufficiently large randomly chosen location sets $\mathbf{j}$, the induced PVAL problem has large minimum distance:

Proposition 5.1 (PVAL on random locations has large distance). *Let* $\mathbb{H} \subseteq \mathbb{F}$ *be finite fields, and let* m, d *be integers s.t.* $|\mathbb{F}| \geq 2m|\mathbb{H}|$. *For* $t \geq (d \cdot \log(|\mathbb{H}|^m \cdot |\mathbb{F}|) + \kappa)$ *it is the case that:*

$$\Pr_{\mathbf{j} \in (\mathbb{F}^m)^t} \left[\Delta(\mathsf{PVAL}(t, \mathbf{j}, \mathbf{0})) \leq \frac{d}{|\mathbb{H}|^m} \right] < 2^{-\kappa}.$$

The following key lemma builds on the distance amplification theorem for Reed Solomon codes of Ben-Sasson, Kopparty and Saraf [BKS18].

Lemma 5.1. *Fix a finite field* $\mathbb{F}$ *of characteristic 2 and integers* $m, t > 0$. *For* $\mathbf{j} \in (\mathbb{F}^m)^t$, *suppose that* $\mathsf{PVAL}(t, \mathbf{j}, \mathbf{0})$ *has size strictly larger than 1 and minimal distance* λ. *Let* $\mathbf{v}', \mathbf{v}'' \in \mathbb{F}^t$ *be vectors s.t. both* $\mathsf{PVAL}(t, \mathbf{j}, \mathbf{v}')$ *and* $\mathsf{PVAL}(t, \mathbf{j}, \mathbf{v}'')$ *are non-empty. Let* $f' : \{0,1\}^m \to \mathbb{F}$ *be at distance* δ' *from* $\mathsf{PVAL}(t, \mathbf{j}, \mathbf{v}')$, *and let* $f'' : \{0,1\}^m \to \mathbb{F}$ *be at distance* δ'' *from* $\mathsf{PVAL}(t, \mathbf{j}, \mathbf{v}'')$. *Consider permutations* $\sigma, \pi \in \Pi$, *where* Π *is the useful collection of permutations over* $\mathbb{F}^m$ *defined in Sect. 3.2. For scalars* $c', c'' \in \mathbb{F}$, *define:*

$$f \triangleq c' \cdot (f' \circ \sigma) + c'' \cdot (f'' \circ \pi),$$

and let $S_{\sigma, \pi} \subseteq \mathbb{F}^{2t}$ *be the set of pairs of vectors* $(\mathbf{u}, \mathbf{w})$ *s.t. the sets* $\mathsf{PVAL}\left(2t, (\sigma^{-1}(\mathbf{j}), \pi^{-1}(\mathbf{j})), (\mathbf{v}', \mathbf{u})\right)$ *and* $\mathsf{PVAL}\left(2t, (\sigma^{-1}(\mathbf{j}), \pi^{-1}(\mathbf{j})), (\mathbf{w}, \mathbf{v}'')\right)$ *are non-empty. For* $(\mathbf{u}, \mathbf{w}) \in S_{\sigma, \pi}$, *define:*

$$\delta_{\sigma, \pi, c', c'', \mathbf{u}, \mathbf{w}} = \Delta\left(f, \mathsf{PVAL}\left(2t, (\sigma^{-1}(\mathbf{j}), \pi^{-1}(\mathbf{j})), (c' \cdot (\mathbf{v}', \mathbf{u}) + c'' \cdot (\mathbf{w}, \mathbf{v}''))\right)\right).$$

Then for every $\varepsilon \in [0, 1/2]$, *taking*

$$\delta = \max \left(\frac{\delta' + \delta''}{2}, \min(\delta' + \delta'' - \delta'\delta'' - 2\varepsilon, \lambda/3 - 3\varepsilon) \right),$$

it is the case that:

$$\Pr_{\sigma, \pi \leftarrow \Pi} \left[\exists (\mathbf{u}, \mathbf{w}) \in S_{\sigma, \pi} \text{ s.t. } \Pr_{c', c'' \leftarrow \mathbb{F}} [\delta_{\sigma, \pi, c', c'', \mathbf{u}, \mathbf{w}} < \delta] > \frac{1}{\varepsilon|\mathbb{F}|} + \frac{1}{|\mathbb{F}|} \right] < \frac{\min(\delta', \delta'')}{\varepsilon^2 \cdot 2^m} + \frac{2}{2^m}$$

$$(2)$$

5.1 Interactive Proof for **PVAL** Emptiness

Our PVAL IPP will also utilize the following (standard) interactive proof for checking whether a given PVAL instance (specified by the vector sequence $\mathbf{j}$) is empty.

Lemma 5.2. *Let* $t, m \in \mathbb{N}$ *and* $\mathbb{F}$ *a finite field. There is a public-coin interactive proof for the language* $\mathcal{L} = \{ \mathbf{j} \in (\mathbb{F}^m)^t : \mathsf{PVAL}(t, \mathbf{j}, \mathbf{0}) \neq \emptyset \}$ *with perfect completeness and the following parameters:*

- *Communication complexity:* $\mathsf{poly}(m, \log(t))$.
- *Round Complexity:* $\mathsf{poly}(m, \log(t))$.
- *Verifier running time:* $t \cdot \mathsf{poly}(m, log(|\mathbb{F}|))$.
- *Prover running time:* $\mathsf{poly}(2^m, t)$.

6   Efficient IPP for PVAL

In this section we show our efficient IPP protocol for the PVAL problem.

Theorem 6.1 (IPP for PVAL). *Let $t, m \in \mathbb{N}$ such that $m \in [\log(t), \frac{t^{1/5}}{14}]$. Let $\mathbb{F}$ be a constructible finite field ensemble of characteristic 2 such that $|\mathbb{F}| = \Theta\left(2^m \cdot t^2 \cdot m^2\right)$. Let $\mathbf{j} = (\mathbf{j}_1, \dots, \mathbf{j}_t) \in (\mathbb{F}^m)^t$ and $\mathbf{v} = (v_1, \dots, v_t) \in \mathbb{F}^t$ such that $\Delta(\mathsf{PVAL}(t, \mathbf{j}, \mathbf{0})) \geq (t/2^m) \cdot \frac{1}{14m^2}$.*

Then, for every proximity parameter $\delta \geq \frac{200m^3}{2^m}$ the set $\mathsf{PVAL}(t, \mathbf{j}, \mathbf{v})$ has a public-coin IPP with respect to proximity parameter δ, with perfect completeness and the following parameters:

- *Soundness Error:* $1/2$.
- *Query complexity:* $q = O\left(\max\left(1/\delta, \frac{2^m}{t} \cdot \mathsf{poly}(m)\right)\right)$.
- *Round complexity:* $\mathsf{poly}(m)$.
- *Communication Complexity:* $cc = t \cdot \mathsf{poly}(m)$.
- *Verifier Running Time:* $(t + q) \cdot \mathsf{poly}(m)$.
- *Prover Running Time:* $\mathsf{poly}(2^m)$.

Furthermore, if $\delta > (t/2^m) \cdot \frac{1}{\mathsf{poly}(m)}$ then, the entire verification procedure can be described succinctly as follows. At the end of the interaction either the verifier rejects or in time $\mathsf{poly}(m)$ it outputs a succinct description $\langle Q \rangle$ of a set $Q \subseteq [|2^m|]$ of size q and a succinct description $\langle \phi \rangle$ of a predicate $\phi : \{0, 1\}^q \to \{0, 1\}$ so that its decision predicate given an input function f is equal to $\phi(f|Q)$.

The rest of this section is devoted to the proof of Theorem 6.1.

The IPP protocol for PVAL is recursive. In each step we reduce the dimension m by 1 (which shrinks the input size by half), while simultaneously (roughly) doubling the distance of the problem from the relevant PVAL instance but also doubling the query complexity.

We denote the starting dimension by m_0 whereas the current dimension (within the recursion) is denoted by m (initially we set $m = m_0$. With that notation, the efficient IPP protocol for PVAL is presented in Fig. 4. Its completeness, soundness and complexity are analyzed in the subsequent subsections.

6.1   Completeness

We prove that completeness holds by induction on m. The base case (i.e., $m \leq \log(t)$) follows from Step 1 in the protocol (while relying on Proposition 3.3). We proceed to analyze the case $m > \log(t)$ (under the inductive hypothesis that the protocol is complete for dimension $m - 1$).

Efficient IPP for PVAL

Fixed parameters (unchanged in the recursion): PVAL arity parameter $t \in \mathbb{N}$, a maximal dimension $m_0 \in [\log(t), t^{1/5}/14]$. A finite field $\mathbb{F}$ of characteristic 2 such that $|\mathbb{F}| = \Theta\left(2^{m_0} \cdot t^2 \cdot m_0^2\right)$.

Parameters (modified in the recursion): dimension $m \in [\log(t), m_0]$, proximity parameter $\delta \in (0, 1)$. A sequence of vectors $\mathbf{j} = (\mathbf{j}_1, \ldots, \mathbf{j}_t) \in (\mathbb{F}^m)^t$ and field elements $\mathbf{v} = (v_1, \ldots, v_t) \in \mathbb{F}^t$.

Invariants: let $\lambda = \Delta(\text{PVAL}(t, \mathbf{j}, 0))$. We require that $\delta \geq \frac{200 m_0^3}{2^m} \cdot (1 - \frac{2}{m_0})^{m_0 - m}$, and that $\lambda \geq (t/2^m) \cdot \frac{1}{14 m_0^2}$.

Verifier Input: oracle access to $f : \{0, 1\}^m \to \mathbb{F}$.

Prover Input: direct access to f.

Goal: verify that $\forall i \in [t]$, $\hat{f}(\mathbf{j}_i) = v_i$ (recall that $\hat{f} : \mathbb{F}^m \to \mathbb{F}$ is the multilinear extension of f).

The Protocol:

1. (Base Case:) If $m \leq \log(t)$, then the prover and verifier simply emulate the trivial MAP protocol of Proposition 3.3 (with soundness error $1/100$). The verifier accepts if the underlying MAP verifier accepts and otherwise it rejects.
2. Otherwise (i.e., if $m > \log(t)$), the protocol proceeds as follows.
3. For every $i \in [t]$, decompose $\mathbf{j}_i$ into $\mathbf{j}_i = (\chi_i, \mathbf{j}_i') \in \mathbb{F} \times \mathbb{F}^{m-1}$.
4. For every $i \in [t]$ and $b \in \{0, 1\}$, the prover computes and sends $\zeta_i^{(b)} = \hat{f}(b, \mathbf{j}_i')$.
5. The verifier receives $\left(\tilde{\zeta}_i^{(b)}\right)_{b \in \{0,1\}, i \in [t]}$ and checks $v_i = (1 - \chi_i) \cdot \tilde{\zeta}_i^{(0)} + \chi_i \cdot \tilde{\zeta}_i^{(1)}$, $\forall i \in [t]$.
6. The verifier random permutations $\pi^{(0)}, \pi^{(1)} \leftarrow \Pi_{m-1}$, where Π_{m-1} is the useful collection of permutations over $\mathbb{F}^{m-1}$ defined in Section 3.2. The verifier sends $\pi^{(0)}$ and $\pi^{(1)}$.
7. The verifier chooses t random points $\rho_1, \ldots, \rho_t \in \mathbb{F}^{m-1}$. Let $\mathcal{C} : \mathbb{F} \to \mathbb{F}^{m-1}$ be a low degree curve passing through the set of $3t$ points $\left\{(\pi^{(b)})^{-1}(\mathbf{j}_i')\right\}_{b \in \{0,1\}, i \in [t]} \cup \{\rho_1, \ldots, \rho_t\}$.
   In more detail, fix a canonical set of distinct field elements $\{\lambda_i^{(b)}\}_{b \in \{0,1,\perp\}, i \in [t]} \subset \mathbb{F}$. Let $\mathcal{C} : \mathbb{F} \to \mathbb{F}^{m-1}$ be the unique degree $3t - 1$ curve such that $\mathcal{C}(\lambda_i^{(b)}) = (\pi^{(b)})^{-1}(\mathbf{j}_i')$, for every $i \in [t]$ and $b \in \{0, 1\}$, and $\mathcal{C}(\lambda_i^{(\perp)}) = \rho_i$, for every $i \in [t]$ (such a curve can be found by interpolation). The verifier sends the values $\rho_1, \ldots, \rho_t$ (which determine $\mathcal{C}$) to the prover.
8. The prover sends to the verifier the degree $O(m \cdot t)$ univariate polynomials $g^{(0)}$ and $g^{(1)}$, where $g^{(b)}(\cdot) = \hat{f}\left(b, \pi^{(b)}(\mathcal{C}(\cdot))\right)$, e.g., by sending their coefficient representations.
9. For every $b \in \{0, 1\}$, the verifier receives $\tilde{g}^{(b)}$ from the prover. The verifer checks that for every $b \in \{0, 1\}$ and $i \in [t]$, it holds that $\tilde{g}^{(b)}(\lambda_i^{(b)}) = \tilde{\zeta}_i^{(b)}$. The prover and verifier also run the interactive proof of Lemma 5.2, with soundness error $\frac{1}{100 m_0}$ to check that
   $$\text{PVAL}\left(2t, \{\lambda_i^{(b)}\}_{b \in \{0,1\}, i \in [t]}, \{\tilde{g}^{(b')}(\lambda_i^{(b)})\}_{b \in \{0,1\}, i \in [t]}\right) \neq \emptyset, \text{ for both } b' \in \{0, 1\}.$$
10. The verifier chooses at random $\xi_1, \ldots, \xi_t \in \mathbb{F}$ and $c^{(0)}, c^{(1)} \in \mathbb{F}$.
11. The parties recurse on the implicit input function $f' : \{0, 1\}^{m-1} \to \mathbb{F}$ defined as $f'(\mathbf{x}) = c^{(0)} \cdot f(0, \pi^{(0)}(\mathbf{x})) + c^{(1)} \cdot f(1, \pi^{(1)}(\mathbf{x}))$ and the claim that for all $i \in [t]$, it holds that $\hat{f}'(\mathcal{C}(\xi_i)) = c^{(0)} \cdot \tilde{g}^{(0)}(\xi_i) + c^{(1)} \cdot \tilde{g}^{(1)}(\xi_i)$ (a PVAL instance of dimension $m - 1$). Each of the verifier's queries to f' in the recursion are emulated by making 2 queries to f. The proximity parameter in the recursion is set to be $\delta' = \min\left(2\delta \cdot (1 - \frac{2}{m_0}), (t/2^m) \cdot \frac{1}{1400 m_0^2}\right)$
12. If any of the verifier's checks failed then it rejects, otherwise it accepts.

Fig. 4. Efficient IPP for PVAL

Let $\mathbf{j} = (\mathbf{j}_1, \ldots, \mathbf{j}_t) \in (\mathbb{F}^m)^t$ and $\mathbf{v} = (v_1, \ldots, v_t) \in \mathbb{F}^t$. Suppose that $f \in$ PVAL$(t, \mathbf{j}, \mathbf{v})$. As in the protocol, for every $i \in [t]$, decompose $\mathbf{j}_i$ into $\mathbf{j}_i = (\chi_i, \mathbf{j}'_i) \in \mathbb{F} \times \mathbb{F}^{m-1}$. Let $\mathbf{j}' \stackrel{\text{def}}{=} (\mathbf{j}'_1, \ldots, \mathbf{j}'_t) \in (\mathbb{F}^{m-1})^t$.

We show that all the checks made by the verifier in the protocol pass (when interacting with the honest prover):

1. In Step 5, for every $i \in [t]$:

$$(1 - \chi_i) \cdot \zeta_i^{(b)} + \chi_i \cdot \zeta_i^{(1)} = (1 - \chi_i) \cdot \hat{f}(0, \mathbf{j}'_i) + \chi_i \cdot \hat{f}(1, \mathbf{j}'_i) = \hat{f}(\mathbf{j}_i) = v_i,$$

as required.

2. In Step 9, for every $i \in [t]$ and $b \in \{0, 1\}$:

$$g^{(b)}\left(\lambda_i^{(b)}\right) = \hat{f}\left(b, \pi^{(b)}\left(c\left(\lambda_i^{(b)}\right)\right)\right) = \hat{f}\left(b, \pi^{(b)}\left((\pi^{(b)})^{-1}\left(\mathbf{j}'_i\right)\right)\right) = \hat{f}(b, \mathbf{j}'_i) = \zeta_i^{(b)},$$

as required.

3. For Step 11, for every $i \in [t]$, it holds that:

$$\hat{f}'(C(\xi_i)) = c^{(0)} \cdot \hat{f}(0, \pi^{(0)} \cdot C(\xi_i)) + c^{(1)} \cdot \hat{f}(1, \pi^{(1)}(C(\xi_i))) = c^{(0)} \cdot g^{(0)}(\xi_i) + c^{(1)} \cdot g^{(1)}(\xi_i),$$

where the first equality follows from Proposition 3.2.

Since all the verifier's checks pass, it accepts, and completeness follows.

6.2   Soundness

We prove, by induction on m, that the soundness error of the protocol is at most $\frac{m}{10m_0} + \frac{1}{100}$. The base case (i.e., $m \leq \log(t)$) is immediate from Step 1 (while relying on Proposition 3.3). We proceed to analyze the case that $m > \log(t)$ (under the inductive hypothesis that the protocol has soundness error at most $\frac{m-1}{10m_0}$ for dimension $m - 1$).

Let $\mathbf{j} = (\mathbf{j}_1, \ldots, \mathbf{j}_t) \in (\mathbb{F}^m)^t$ and $\mathbf{v} = (v_1, \ldots, v_t) \in \mathbb{F}^t$. Let $\delta = \Delta(f, \text{PVAL}(t, \mathbf{j}, \mathbf{v}))$. Fix a cheating prover strategy $\tilde{P}$. Assume without loss of generality that $\tilde{P}$ is deterministic (otherwise fix its best choice of randomness).

We start by defining several important values that will be used in the analysis. Let $\left(\tilde{\zeta}_i^{(b)}\right)_{b \in \{0,1\}, i \in [t]}$ be the (fixed) values sent by $\tilde{P}$ as its first message (i.e., in Step 4). We may assume that

$$(1 - \chi_i) \cdot \tilde{\zeta}_i^{(0)} + \chi_i \cdot \tilde{\zeta}_i^{(1)} = v_i, \tag{3}$$

for every $i \in [t]$, since otherwise the verifier rejects in Step 5.

Define $\mathbf{v}^{(b)} \stackrel{\text{def}}{=} \left(\tilde{\zeta}_1^{(b)}, \ldots, \tilde{\zeta}_t^{(b)}\right) \in \mathbb{F}^t$. Also, for every $i \in [t]$, decompose $\mathbf{j}_i$ into $\mathbf{j}_i = (\chi_i, \mathbf{j}'_i) \in \mathbb{F} \times \mathbb{F}^{m-1}$. Let $\mathbf{j}' \stackrel{\text{def}}{=} (\mathbf{j}'_1, \ldots, \mathbf{j}'_t) \in (\mathbb{F}^{m-1})^t$. Lastly, for every $b \in \{0, 1\}$, let $f^{(b)}(\cdot) \stackrel{\text{def}}{=} f(b, \cdot)$ and let $\delta^{(b)} \stackrel{\text{def}}{=} \Delta\left(f^{(b)}, \text{PVAL}\left(t, \mathbf{j}', \mathbf{v}^{(b)}\right)\right)$.

Our goal will be to show that the input f' for the recursive step (i.e., Step 11) has distance roughly 2δ from the corresponding PVAL instance (i.e., the distance doubles). This is done in two steps: showing that f' has distance roughly $\delta^{(0)} + \delta^{(1)}$, and that this quantity is lower bounded by 2δ. Since it is simpler, we start with the latter step.

Claim 6.2

$$\delta^{(0)} + \delta^{(1)} \geq 2\delta.$$

Proof. For every $b \in \{0,1\}$, let $P^{(b)} : \{0,1\}^{m-1} \to \mathbb{F}$ such that $P^{(b)} \in \mathsf{PVAL}\left(t, \mathbf{j}', \mathbf{v}^{(b)}\right)$ and $\Delta\left(P^{(b)}, f^{(b)}\right) = \delta^{(b)}$. Such a $P^{(b)}$ exists as long as $\mathsf{PVAL}\left(t, \mathbf{j}', \mathbf{v}^{(b)}\right) \neq \emptyset$ and note that otherwise $\delta^{(b)}$ is infinite and the claim clearly holds).

Consider the function $P : \{0,1\}^m \to \mathbb{F}$ defined as $P(b, \mathbf{x}) = P^{(b)}(\mathbf{x})$. Observe that $\Delta(P, f) = \frac{\delta^{(0)} + \delta^{(1)}}{2}$. On the other hand, for every $i \in [t]$, $b \in \{0,1\}$ and $(j_1, \ldots, j_m) \in \mathbb{F}^m$:

$$\hat{P}(j_1, \ldots, j_m) = (1 - j_1) \cdot \hat{P}(0, j_2, \ldots, j_m) + j_1 \cdot \hat{P}(1, j_2, \ldots, j_m)$$
$$= (1 - j_1) \cdot \hat{P}^{(0)}(j_2, \ldots, j_m) + j_1 \cdot \hat{P}^{(1)}(j_2, \ldots, j_m), \qquad (4)$$

where both equalities can be verified by observing that they hold for all $(j_1, \ldots, j_m) \in \{0,1\}^m$, and therefore hold also for all $(j_1, \ldots, j_m) \in \mathbb{F}^m$ (since two multilinear polynomials that agree on the Boolean hypercube agree everywhere).

Thus, for every $i \in [t]$, it holds that

$$\hat{P}(\mathbf{j}_i) = (1 - \chi_i) \cdot \hat{P}^{(0)}(\mathbf{j}_i') + \chi_i \cdot \hat{P}^{(1)}(\mathbf{j}_i')$$
$$= (1 - \chi_i) \cdot \tilde{\zeta}_i^{(0)} + \chi \cdot \tilde{\zeta}_i^{(1)}$$
$$= v_i,$$

where the first equality is by Eq. (4), the second equality follows from the fact that $P^{(b)} \in \mathsf{PVAL}\left(t, \mathbf{j}', \mathbf{v}^{(b)}\right)$ and the third equality from Eq. (3).

We conclude that f is $\left(\frac{\delta^{(0)} + \delta^{(1)}}{2}\right)$-close to $\mathsf{PVAL}(t, \mathbf{j}, \mathbf{v})$ and so $\frac{\delta^{(0)} + \delta^{(1)}}{2} \geq \delta$. □

Now, let $\pi^{(0)}, \pi^{(1)} \leftarrow \Pi$ be the permutations sampled randomly by the verifier in Step 6 and let $\rho_1, \ldots, \rho_t \in \mathbb{F}$ be the random values sampled in Step 7. As in the protocol, let $\mathcal{C} : \mathbb{F} \to \mathbb{F}^{m-1}$ be the unique degree $3t - 1$ curve such that $\mathcal{C}(\lambda_i^{(b)}) = (\pi^{(b)})^{-1}(\mathbf{j}_i')$, for every $i \in [t]$ and $b \in \{0,1\}$, and $\mathcal{C}(\lambda_i^{(\perp)}) = \rho_i$, for every $i \in [t]$. Let $\tilde{g}^{(0)}$ and $\tilde{g}^{(1)}$ be the degree $O(m \cdot t)$ univariate polynomials sent by $\tilde{P}$ in Step 8. Note that $\mathcal{C}$, $\tilde{g}^{(0)}$ and $\tilde{g}^{(1)}$ are all random variables that depend on $\pi^{(0)}, \pi^{(1)}$ and $\rho_1, \ldots, \rho_t$.

We may assume without loss of generality that for every choice of $\pi^{(0)}, \pi^{(1)}, \rho_1, \ldots, \rho_t$ made by the verifier it holds that

$$\forall i \in [t], \ b \in \{0,1\} : \quad \tilde{g}_i^{(b)}(\lambda_i^{(b)}) = \tilde{\zeta}_i^{(b)}, \qquad (5)$$

since otherwise the verifier immediately rejects in Step 9. Thus, we can modify the prover $\check{P}$ to *always* send polynomials satisfying Eq. (5) without decreasing $\check{P}$'s success probability.

For every $c^{(0)}, c^{(1)} \in \mathbb{F}$, define the function $f'_{\pi^{(0)}, \pi^{(1)}, c^{(0)}, c^{(1)}} : \{0, 1\}^{m-1} \to \mathbb{F}$ as $f'_{\pi^{(0)}, \pi^{(1)}, c^{(0)}, c^{(1)}}(\mathbf{x}) = c^{(0)} \cdot f(0, \pi^{(0)}(\mathbf{x})) + c^{(1)} \cdot f(1, \pi^{(1)}(\mathbf{x}))$.

Recall that $\delta^{(b)} = \Delta\left(f^{(b)}, \mathsf{PVAL}\left(t, \mathbf{j}', \mathbf{v}^{(b)}\right)\right)$. We now invoke Lemma 5.1 on $f^{(0)}$ and $f^{(1)}$ with $\varepsilon \overset{\text{def}}{=} \delta_{\text{avg}}/m_0$, where $\delta_{\text{avg}} = (\delta^{(0)} + \delta^{(1)})/2$. We obtain that:

$$\Pr_{\pi^{(0)}, \pi^{(1)} \leftarrow \Pi}\left[\exists \mathbf{u}, \mathbf{w} \in S_{\pi^{(0)}, \pi^{(1)}} \text{ s.t. } \Pr_{c^{(0)}, c^{(1)} \in \mathbb{F}}\left[\delta_{\pi^{(0)}, \pi^{(1)}, c^{(0)}, c^{(1)}, \mathbf{u}, \mathbf{w}} < \delta^*\right] > \frac{1}{\varepsilon |\mathbb{F}|} + \frac{1}{|\mathbb{F}|}\right] \tag{6}$$

is less than $\frac{\min(\delta^{(0)}, \delta^{(1)})}{\varepsilon^2 \cdot 2^m} + \frac{2}{2^m}$, where $\delta_{\pi^{(0)}, \pi^{(1)}, c^{(0)}, c^{(1)}, \mathbf{u}, \mathbf{w}}$ is defined as the distance of $f'_{\pi^{(0)}, \pi^{(1)}, c^{(0)}, c^{(1)}}$ from

$$\mathsf{PVAL}\left(2t, \left((\pi^{(0)})^{-1}(\mathbf{j}'), (\pi^{(1)})^{-1}(\mathbf{j}')\right), \left(c^{(0)} \cdot (\mathbf{v}^{(0)}, \mathbf{u}) + c^{(1)} \cdot (\mathbf{w}, \mathbf{v}^{(1)})\right)\right),$$

and

$$\delta^* \overset{\text{def}}{=} \max\left(\delta_{\text{avg}}, \min\left(\delta^{(0)} + \delta^{(1)} - \delta^{(0)} \cdot \delta^{(1)} - 2\varepsilon, \lambda/3 - 3\varepsilon\right)\right), \tag{7}$$

and $S_{\pi^{(0)}, \pi^{(1)}} \subseteq \mathbb{F}^{2t}$ is the set of pairs of vectors $(\mathbf{u}, \mathbf{w})$ such that the sets $\mathsf{PVAL}(2t, ((\pi^{(0)})^{-1}(\mathbf{j}'), (\pi^{(1)})^{-1}(\mathbf{j}')), (\mathbf{v}^{(0)}, \mathbf{u}))$ and $\mathsf{PVAL}(2t, ((\pi^{(0)})^{-1}(\mathbf{j}'), (\pi^{(1)})^{-1}(\mathbf{j}')), (\mathbf{w}, \mathbf{v}^{(1)}))$ are non-empty.

We have that $\frac{\min(\delta^{(0)}, \delta^{(1)})}{\varepsilon^2 \cdot 2^m} + \frac{2}{2^m} \leq \frac{\delta_{\text{avg}}}{\varepsilon^2 \cdot 2^m} + \frac{2}{2^m} = \frac{m_0^2}{\delta_{\text{avg}} \cdot 2^m} + \frac{2}{2^m} \leq \frac{1}{50 m_0}$ and that $\frac{1}{\varepsilon |\mathbb{F}|} + \frac{1}{|\mathbb{F}|} \leq \frac{m_0}{\delta_{\text{avg}} \cdot 2 m_0} + \frac{1}{2 m_0} \leq \frac{m_0}{\delta_{\text{avg}} \cdot 2^m} + \frac{1}{2^m} \leq \frac{1}{100 m_0}$, where for both we used the fact that $\delta_{\text{avg}} \geq \delta \geq \frac{100 m_0^3}{2^m}$ (by Claim 6.2 and our invariant on δ) and our setting of $|\mathbb{F}|$ and m. Thus, Eq. (6) implies that:

$$\Pr_{\pi^{(0)}, \pi^{(1)} \leftarrow \Pi}\left[\exists \mathbf{u}, \mathbf{w} \in S_{\pi^{(0)}, \pi^{(1)}} \text{ s.t. } \Pr_{c^{(0)}, c^{(1)} \in \mathbb{F}}\left[\delta_{\pi^{(0)}, \pi^{(1)}, c^{(0)}, c^{(1)}, \mathbf{u}, \mathbf{w}} < \delta^*\right] > \frac{1}{100 m_0}\right] \tag{8}$$

is less than $\frac{1}{50 m_0}$. We proceed to show that δ^* is lower bounded by (roughly) 2δ.

Proposition 6.1. $\delta^* \geq \min\left(2\delta \cdot (1 - \frac{2}{m_0}), \lambda/100\right)$.

Proof. Recall that $\delta^* \geq \delta_{\text{avg}}$ and that $\delta^* \geq \min(\lambda/3 - 3\varepsilon, \delta^{(0)} + \delta^{(1)} - \delta^{(0)} \cdot \delta^{(1)} - 2\varepsilon)$ (see Eq. (7)). The proof of the proposition is based on a (somewhat tedious) case analysis.

Suppose first that $\delta^* \geq \delta^{(0)} + \delta^{(1)} - \delta^{(0)} \cdot \delta^{(1)} - 2\varepsilon$. In this case the proposition follows from the following claim:

Claim 6.3. $\delta^{(0)} + \delta^{(1)} - \delta^{(0)} \cdot \delta^{(1)} - 2\varepsilon \geq 2\delta \cdot (1 - \frac{2}{m_0})$.

Proof. By the AM-GM inequality it holds that:

$$\delta^{(0)} + \delta^{(1)} - \delta^{(0)} \cdot \delta^{(1)} \geq 2\delta_{\mathrm{avg}} - \delta_{\mathrm{avg}}^2.$$

We consider two cases. Suppose first that $\delta_{\mathrm{avg}} \leq 2/m_0$. Then,

$$2\delta_{\mathrm{avg}} - \delta_{\mathrm{avg}}^2 - 2\varepsilon = 2\delta_{\mathrm{avg}} - \delta_{\mathrm{avg}}^2 - 2\delta_{\mathrm{avg}}/m_0 \geq 2\delta \cdot (1 - 2/m_0),$$

where the inequality is based on Claim 6.2 and our presumed upper bound on δ_{avg}. Thus, we may assume that $\delta_{\mathrm{avg}} \geq 2/m_0$. Then,

$$2\delta_{\mathrm{avg}} - \delta_{\mathrm{avg}}^2 - 2\varepsilon \geq \delta_{\mathrm{avg}}/2 \geq 1/m_0 \geq 2\delta \cdot (1 - 2/m_0),$$

where the first inequality holds for sufficiently large m_0 and using the fact that $\delta_{\mathrm{avg}} \leq 1$ and the last inequality from the fact that $\delta < \frac{1}{100m_0}$.

Thus, we may assume that $\delta^* \geq \lambda/3 - 3\varepsilon$.

Suppose now that $\varepsilon < \lambda/300$. Then, we have that $\delta \geq \lambda/3 - 3\varepsilon \geq \lambda/100$ and we are done. Thus, we may assume that $\lambda/300 \leq \varepsilon = \delta_{\mathrm{avg}}/m_0$. On the other hand, we have that $\delta^* \geq \delta_{\mathrm{avg}} \geq \frac{m_0}{300} \cdot \lambda \geq \lambda/100$, for sufficiently large m_0.

This concludes the proof of Proposition 6.1.

Fix $\pi^{(0)}$ and $\pi^{(1)}$ such that the event specified in Eq. (8) does not hold. That is, for every $\mathbf{u}, \mathbf{w} \in S_{\pi^{(0)}, \pi^{(1)}}$ it holds that

$$\Pr_{c^{(0)}, c^{(1)} \in \mathbb{F}} \left[\delta_{\pi^{(0)}, \pi^{(1)}, c^{(0)}, c^{(1)}, \mathbf{u}, \mathbf{w}} < \delta^* \right] \leq \frac{1}{100m_0}.$$

Let $\mathbf{u} = \left(\tilde{g}^{(0)}(\lambda_1^{(1)}), \ldots, \tilde{g}^{(0)}(\lambda_t^{(1)}) \right)$ and $\mathbf{w} = \left(\tilde{g}^{(1)}(\lambda_1^{(0)}), \ldots, \tilde{g}^{(1)}(\lambda_t^{(0)}) \right)$. Suppose that $\mathbf{u}, \mathbf{w} \notin S_{\pi^{(0)}, \pi^{(1)}}$ then $\mathsf{PVAL}\left(2t, \{\lambda^{(b)}\}_{b \in \{0,1\}, i \in [t]}, \{\tilde{g}^{(b')} (\lambda_i^{(b)})\}_{b \in \{0,1\}, i \in [t]} \right) = \emptyset$, for either $b' = 0$ or $b' = 1$. In Step 9 the verifier and prover run an interactive proof to check that this is not the case and so the verifier rejects in this case with probability at least $1 - \frac{1}{100m_0}$. Thus, we may assume that $\mathbf{u}, \mathbf{w} \in S_{\pi^{(0)}, \pi^{(1)}}$.

In particular, this means that for all but $\frac{1}{100m_0}$ fraction of $c^{(0)}, c^{(1)} \in \mathbb{F}$, it holds that $f'_{\pi^{(0)}, \pi^{(1)}, c^{(0)}, c^{(1)}}$ is at distance at least δ^* from

$$\mathsf{PVAL}\left(2t, \left((\pi^{(0)})^{-1}(\mathbf{j}'), (\pi^{(1)})^{-1}(\mathbf{j}') \right), (\omega_k)_{k \in [2t]} \right),$$

where $\omega_{b \cdot t + i} = c^{(0)} \cdot \tilde{g}_i^{(0)}(\lambda_i^{(b)}) + c^{(1)} \cdot \tilde{g}_i^{(1)}(\lambda_i^{(b)})$.

Let us fix $c^{(0)}$ and $c^{(1)}$ such that the foregoing statement holds. Let

$$\delta' \stackrel{\mathrm{def}}{=} \min \left(2\delta \cdot (1 - \frac{2}{m_0}), (t/2^m) \cdot \frac{1}{1400m_0^2} \right) \tag{9}$$

and observe that by Proposition 6.1 (and the invariant lower bound on λ), it holds that $\delta' \leq \delta^*$.

Claim 6.4. *With all but* $\frac{1}{100m_0}$ *probability over the choice of* $\xi_1, \ldots, \xi_t \in \mathbb{F}$ *it holds that the function* $f'_{\pi^{(0)}, \pi^{(1)}, c^{(0)}, c^{(1)}}$ *is at distance at least* δ' *from the set*

$$\mathsf{PVAL}\left(t, (\mathcal{C}(\xi_i))_{i \in [t]}, \left(c^{(0)} \cdot \tilde{g}_i^{(0)}(\xi_i) + c^{(1)} \cdot \tilde{g}_i^{(1)}(\xi_i)\right)_{i \in [t]}\right).$$

Proof. Fix some $h : \{0,1\}^{m-1} \to \mathbb{F}$ at relative distance $\leq \delta' \leq \delta^*$ from $f'_{\pi^{(0)}, \pi^{(1)}, c^{(0)}, c^{(1)}}$. By our assumption on $c^{(0)}$ and $c^{(1)}$ we have $h \notin$ $\mathsf{PVAL}\left(2t, ((\pi^{(0)})^{-1}(\mathbf{j'}), (\pi^{(1)})^{-1}(\mathbf{j'})), (\omega_k)_{k \in [2t]}\right)$, where $\omega_{b \cdot t + i} = c^{(0)} \cdot \tilde{g}_i^{(0)}(\lambda_i^{(b)}) + c^{(1)} \cdot \tilde{g}_i^{(1)}(\lambda_i^{(b)})$. In particular, this means that there exists some $b \in \{0,1\}$ and $i \in [t]$ such that:

$$\hat{h}\left(\mathcal{C}(\lambda_i^{(b)})\right) \neq c^{(0)} \cdot \tilde{g}_i^{(0)}(\lambda_i^{(b)}) + c^{(1)} \cdot \tilde{g}_i^{(1)}(\lambda_i^{(b)}).$$

The functions $\hat{h} \circ \mathcal{C}$ and $c^{(0)} \cdot \tilde{g}^{(0)}(\cdot) + c^{(1)} \cdot \tilde{g}^{(1)}(\cdot)$ are therefore *different* polynomials of degree $O(m \cdot t)$. Thus, the probability over a random $\xi \in \mathbb{F}^{m-1}$ that $\hat{h}(\mathcal{C}(\xi)) = \tilde{g}^{(0)}(\xi) + c \cdot \tilde{g}^{(1)}(\xi)$ is at most $O(m \cdot t / |\mathbb{F}|) \leq 1/2$. Therefore, the probability that $h \in \mathsf{PVAL}\left(t, (\mathcal{C}(\xi_i))_{i \in [t]}, \left(\tilde{g}_i^{(0)}(\xi_i) + c \cdot \tilde{g}_i^{(1)}(\xi_i)\right)_{i \in [t]}\right)$ is at most 2^{-t}.

The number of functions $h : \{0,1\}^{m-1} \to |\mathbb{F}|$ that are δ'-close to $f'_{\pi,c}$ is upper bounded by $(2^{m-1} \cdot |\mathbb{F}|)^{\delta' \cdot 2^{m-1}} \leq 2^{\delta' \cdot 2^m \cdot m \cdot \log(|\mathbb{F}|)}$. Therefore, by a union bound, we have that $f'_{\pi,c}$ is δ'-far from $\mathsf{PVAL}\left(t, (\mathcal{C}(\xi_i))_{i \in [t]}, c^{(0)} \cdot \left(\tilde{g}_i^{(0)}(\xi_i) + c^{(1)} \cdot \tilde{g}_i^{(1)}(\xi_i)\right)_{i \in [t]}\right)$, with all but $2^{\delta' \cdot 2^m \cdot m \cdot \log(|\mathbb{F}|) - t}$ probability. Since $\delta' \leq (t/2^m) \cdot \frac{1}{1400m_0^2}$, we have that this probability is upper bounded by $\frac{1}{100m_0}$. $\blacksquare$

Assuming that the event stated in Claim 6.4 holds, the protocol is run recursively on input $f'_{\pi^{(0)}, \pi^{(1)}, c^{(0)}, c^{(1)}}$ that is at least δ'-far from the relevant PVAL instance. At this point we would like to argue that by the inductive hypothesis, the verifier rejects with high probability. However, to do so, we still need to argue that the recursive invocation satisfies all the prescribed invariants.

Claim 6.5. $\delta' \geq \frac{200m_0^3}{2^{m-1}} \cdot (1 - \frac{2}{m_0})^{m_0 - (m-1)}$.

Proof. We consider two cases. If $\delta' = 2\delta \cdot (1 - \frac{2}{m_0})$ then:

$$\delta' \geq 2\left(\frac{200m_0^3}{2^m} \cdot (1 - \frac{2}{m_0})^{m_0 - m}\right) \cdot (1 - \frac{2}{m_0}) = \frac{200m_0^3}{2^{m-1}} \cdot (1 - \frac{2}{m_0})^{m_0 - (m-1)},$$

as required. Otherwise,

$$\delta' = (t/2^m) \cdot \frac{1}{1400m_0^2} \geq \frac{200m_0^3}{2^{m-1}} \geq \frac{200m_0^3}{2^{m-1}} \cdot (1 - \frac{2}{m_0})^{m_0 - (m-1)},$$

where the first inequality follows from the fact that $m_0 \leq t^{1/5}/14$.

Claim 6.6. *With all but* $\frac{1}{100m_0}$ *probability over the choice of* $\rho_1, \ldots, \rho_t$ *and* $\xi_1, \ldots, \xi_t$, *it holds that* $\lambda' \geq (t/2^{m-1}) \cdot \frac{1}{14m_0^2}$, *where* $\lambda' = \Delta(\mathsf{PVAL}(t, \mathbf{j}', \mathbf{0}))$.

Proof. Observe that $\xi_1, \ldots, \xi_t \notin \{\lambda_i^{(b)}\}_{b \in \{0,1\}, i \in [t]}$ with probability $1 - \frac{2t^2}{|\mathbb{F}|} \geq 1 - \frac{1}{200m_0}$.

Since the curve $\mathcal{C}$ passes through t random points (i.e., $\rho_1, \ldots, \rho_t$), the distribution over points through which the curve $\mathcal{C}$ passes is t-wise independent, other than at the fixed points $\{\lambda_i^{(b)}\}_{b \in \{0,1\}, i \in [t]}$. Putting the above two facts together, we obtain that with all but $\frac{1}{200m_0}$ probability, the set of points $\mathbf{j}' = (\mathcal{C}(\xi_1), \ldots, \mathcal{C}(\xi_t))$ is uniformly distributed in $(\mathbb{F}^{m-1})^t$.

Recall that $\lambda' = \Delta(\mathsf{PVAL}(t, \mathbf{j}', \mathbf{0}))$. By Proposition 5.1, since $t \geq \frac{t}{14m_0^2} \cdot \log(2^m \cdot |\mathbb{F}|) + \log(200m_0)$,

$$\Pr\left[\lambda' \leq (t/2^{m-1}) \cdot \frac{1}{14m_0^2}\right] < \frac{1}{200m_0},$$

and the claim follows.

Thus, the invariants for the recursive step are satisfied and so the verifier accepts in the recursion with probability at most $\frac{m-1}{10m_0} + 1/100$. Overall, by accounting for all of the bad events in the analysis above, we get that the verifier accepts with probability at most:

$$\frac{m-1}{10m_0} + 1/100 + 5 \cdot \frac{1}{100m_0} \leq \frac{m}{10m_0} + 1/100$$

as required.

6.3   Complexity

Communication Complexity. We first analyze the complexity of a single iteration (i.e., excluding the recursion). The verifier only sends to the prover a specification of the permutations $\pi^{(0)}$ and $\pi^{(1)}$ (which take $2m$ bits each), the values $\rho_1, \ldots, \rho_t$, $\xi_1, \ldots, \xi_t \in \mathbb{F}$ and $c^{(0)}, c^{(1)} \in \mathbb{F}$. Overall the verifier-to-prover communication is $2m + (2t + 1) \cdot \log_2(|\mathbb{F}|)$. The prover in turn sends $(\zeta_i^{(b)})_{i \in [t], b \in \{0,1\}}$ and the polynomials $\tilde{g}^{(0)}$ and $\tilde{g}^{(1)}$ (of degree $O(t \cdot m)$). Thus, the total prover to verifier communication is $O(t \cdot m \cdot \log(|\mathbb{F}|))$.

Thus, the overall communication complexity is given by $cc(m)$ where $cc(m) = O(t \cdot m \cdot \log(|\mathbb{F}|)) + cc(m-1)$ if $m > \log(t)$ and $cc(m) = 2^m \cdot \log(|\mathbb{F}|)$ otherwise. Overall we have $cc(m) \leq O(m^2 \cdot t \cdot \log(|\mathbb{F}|))$.

Query Complexity. Denote the query complexity by $q(m, \delta)$. Note that if $m \leq \log(t)$ then $q(m, \delta) = O(1/\delta)$ and otherwise $q(m, \delta) = 2 \cdot q(m-1, \delta') = 2q\left(m - 1, \min\left(2\delta \cdot (1 - \frac{2}{m_0}), (t/2^m) \cdot \frac{1}{1400m_0^2}\right)\right)$. The stated query complexity follows from the following claim.

Claim 6.7. *There exists a fixed constant c such that for every m and δ it holds that $q(m, \delta) \leq c \cdot (1 - \frac{2}{m_0})^{-m} \cdot \max\left(\frac{1}{\delta}, \frac{2800 \cdot 2^m \cdot m_0^2}{t}\right)$.*

Proof. We prove by induction on m. The base case $m = \log(t)$ is immediate. Suppose that the claim holds for $m - 1$. Then:

$$q(m, \delta) = 2q\left(m - 1, \min\left(2\delta \cdot (1 - \frac{2}{m_0}), (t/2^m) \cdot \frac{1}{1400m_0^2}\right)\right)$$

Suppose first that $2\delta \cdot (1 - \frac{2}{m_0}) < (t/2^m) \cdot \frac{1}{1400m_0^2}$. Then,

$$q(m, \delta) = 2q\left(m - 1, 2\delta \cdot (1 - \frac{2}{m_0})\right)$$

$$\leq 2c \cdot (1 - \frac{2}{m_0})^{-(m-1)} \cdot \max\left(\frac{1}{2\delta \cdot (1 - \frac{2}{m_0})}, \frac{2^{m-1} \cdot m_0^2}{t}\right)$$

$$= c \cdot (1 - \frac{2}{m_0})^{-m} \cdot \max\left(\frac{1}{\delta}, \frac{2^m \cdot m_0^2}{t}\right)$$

as required. Otherwise, $2\delta \cdot (1 - \frac{2}{m_0}) \geq (t/2^m) \cdot \frac{1}{1400m_0^2}$ and we have that:

$$q(m, \delta) = 2q\left(m - 1, (t/2^m) \cdot \frac{1}{1400m_0^2}\right)$$

$$\leq 2c \cdot (1 - \frac{2}{m_0})^{-(m-1)} \cdot \max\left(\frac{1400 \cdot 2^m \cdot m_0^2}{t}, \frac{2800 \cdot 2^{m-1} \cdot m_0^2}{t}\right)$$

$$\leq c \cdot (1 - \frac{2}{m_0})^{-m} \cdot \frac{2800 \cdot 2^m \cdot m_0^2}{t}$$

$$\leq c \cdot (1 - \frac{2}{m_0})^{-m} \cdot \max\left(\frac{1}{\delta}, \frac{2800 \cdot 2^m \cdot m_0^2}{t}\right).$$

Prover Runtime. In every iteration, the prover only does elementary manipulations of the truth table of f (and never needs to fully materialize the truth table of $\hat{f}$). It also runs the prover of Lemma 5.2. Overall its running time is $\mathsf{poly}(2^m, m_0, \log(|\mathbb{F}|), t) = \mathsf{poly}(2^{m_0})$.

Verifier Runtime and Succinct Description. The queries made by the verifier can be succinctly specified by the permutations $\pi^{(0)}$ and $\pi^{(1)}$ used through the recursion as well as the random locations that it queries in the base case. The total number of bits needed to describe the permutations is at most $2(m_0)^2$. The number of bits needed in the base case is equal to the total number of queries divided by $2^{m_0}/t$ (since in each of the $m_0 - \log(t)$ iterations the number of queries doubled) and multiplied by $\log(2^m) = m$ (to specify the location). By the above analysis this quantity is therefore upper bounded by $O\left(\frac{t \cdot m_0}{2^{m_0}} \cdot \max\left(1/\delta, \frac{2^{m_0}}{t}\right)\right. \cdot$
$\left. \mathsf{poly}(m)\right) = O(\mathsf{poly}(m) + \frac{t \cdot m_0}{2^{m_0}}) \cdot (1/\delta))$. If $\delta > (t/2^{m_0}) \cdot \frac{1}{\mathsf{poly}(m)}$ this string has $\mathsf{poly}(m)$ length as required.

Given the set of base points we can generate the list of q queries by repeatedly applying the two permutations that we have for each level of the recursion. Since the permutations can be computed in $\mathsf{poly}(m)$ time (see Proposition 3.1), we obtain that a logspace Turing machine can generate a $\mathsf{poly}(m)$ depth circuit that outputs the entire set of q query locations.

As for the succinct description of the verification predicate, observe that all of the verifier's checks that do not involve the input can be implemented in time $\mathsf{poly}(t, m_0, \log(|\mathbb{F}|)) = \mathsf{poly}(t)$. The testing of the actual input only happens in the case in which the prover sends over the alleged actual input $\tilde{f}_\perp$ (which at the end of the recursion has length $t \cdot \log(|\mathbb{F}|)$). This string $\tilde{f}_\perp$ is part of the description of the verification predicate, together also with all of the $c^{(0)}, c^{(1)}$ values generated in the recursion. Using these values it is possible to construct a $q \cdot \mathsf{poly}(m_0, \log(|\mathbb{F}|))$ size depth $\mathsf{poly}(m_0)$ circuit that given the query answers checks their consistency with $\tilde{f}_\perp$.

7   Proving Theorem 4.1 and Theorem 4.2

Theorem 4.1 follows immediately by combining [RVW13, Theorem 1.3] with Theorem 6.1, while setting $t = \delta \cdot n \cdot \mathsf{polylog}(n)$.

In order to prove Theorem 4.2 we utilize an idea from the work of Reingold *et al.* [RRR18] who used known IPP protocols to achieve batch verification for UP languages. We restate a more general form of their reduction below. In the interest of directness, we avoid defining or using Interactive Witness Verification protocols, as they did. Instead, we use IPPs for pair languages:

Theorem 7.1 (From IPPs to UP batch verification (generalization of [RRR18, Theorem 3.3])). *Suppose that for every query parameter $q = q(n) \in \{1, \ldots, m\}$, and for every pair languages $\mathcal{L}$ that can be computed by log-space uniform polynomial-size circuits with fan-in 2 and depth $D = D(n)$, there exists an interactive proof of proximity where the verifier is public-coin and, on input (x, y), at the end of the interaction either the verifier rejects, or it outputs a succinct description $\langle Q \rangle$ of a set $Q \subseteq [|y|]$ of size q and succinct description $\langle \phi \rangle$ of a predicate $\phi : \{0, 1\}^q \to \{0, 1\}$, and for every input pair (x, y):*

– **Completeness:** *If $(x, y) \in \mathcal{L}$ then*

$$\Pr\left[\mathcal{V} \text{ does not reject and } \phi(y_Q) = 1\right] = 1.$$

– **Soundness:** *If $\mathcal{L}(x) = \emptyset$ (there is no y' s.t. $(x, y') \in \mathcal{L}$), then for every prover $\mathcal{P}^*$:*

$$\Pr\left[\mathcal{V} \text{ does not reject and } \phi(y_Q) = 1\right] \le 1/2.$$

Let $\mathsf{cc} = \mathsf{cc}(q, D, n, m)$ be the communication complexity, $r = r(q, D, n, m)$ the number of rounds, $\mathcal{V}\mathsf{time}(q, D, n, m)$ the verifier's runtime, and assume that the honest prover runs in polynomial time.

Then, for every UP language $\mathcal{L}$ with witness length $m = m(n)$, whose witness relation can be computed in NC, there exists a public-coin interactive proof (with *perfect completeness) for verifying that k instances $x_1, \ldots, x_k$, each of length n, are all in $\mathcal{L}$. Taking $D' = \mathsf{polylog}(n, k)$ and $m' = k \cdot m$, the complexity of the protocol is as follows:*

- *Communication complexity: $O\left(m + \sum_{i=1}^{\log k} \mathsf{cc}(\frac{k}{2^i}, D', \frac{n'}{2^i}, \frac{m'}{2^i})\right)$.*
- *Number of rounds: $O\left(\sum_{i=1}^{\log k} r(\frac{k}{2^i}, D', \frac{n'}{2^i}, \frac{m'}{2^i})\right)$.*
- *Verifier runtime: $O\left(m \log n + \sum_{i=1}^{\log k} \mathcal{V}\mathsf{time}(\frac{k}{2^i}, D', \frac{n'}{2^i}, \frac{m'}{2^i})\right)$.*
- *The honest prover, given the k unique witnesses, runs in polynomial time.*

Theorem 4.2 now follows from Theorem 7.1 by utilizing the efficient IPPs for NC given in Theorem 4.1.

Acknowledgments. We thank Oded Goldreich and Omer Reingold for helpful and illuminating discussions on these topics. We thank the TCC revewiers for their careful reading of the manuscript and useful comments.

Guy Rothblum has received funding from the European Research Council (ERC) under the European Union's Horizon 2020 research and innovation programme (grant agreement No. 819702). Research also supported by the Israel Science Foundation (grant number 5219/17) and an Amazon Research Award.

Ron Rothblum was supported in part by a Milgrom family grant, by the Israeli Science Foundation (Grants No. 1262/18 and 2137/19), and the Technion Hiroshi Fujiwara cyber security research center and Israel cyber directorate.

References

[ALM+98] Arora, S., Lund, C., Motwani, R., Sudan, M., Szegedy, M.: Proof verification and the hardness of approximation problems. J. ACM **45**(3), 501–555 (1998)

[AS92] Arora, S., Safra, S.: Probabilistic checking of proofs; A new characterization of NP. In: 33rd Annual Symposium on Foundations of Computer Science, Pittsburgh, Pennsylvania, USA, 24–27 October 1992, pp. 2–13 (1992)

[BFL91] Babai, L., Fortnow, L., Lund, C.: Non-deterministic exponential time has two-prover interactive protocols. Comput. Complex. **1**, 3–40 (1991)

[BFLS91] Babai, L., Fortnow, L., Levin, L.A., Szegedy, M.: Checking computations in polylogarithmic time. In: Proceedings of the 23rd Annual ACM Symposium on Theory of Computing, New Orleans, Louisiana, USA, 5–8 May 1991, pp. 21–31 (1991)

[BGG+88] Ben-Or, M., et al.: Everything provable is provable in zero-knowledge. In: Goldwasser, S. (ed.) CRYPTO 1988. LNCS, vol. 403, pp. 37–56. Springer, New York (1990). https://doi.org/10.1007/0-387-34799-2_4

[BGKW88] Ben-Or, M., Goldwasser, S., Kilian, J., Wigderson, A.: Multi-prover interactive proofs: how to remove intractability assumptions. In: Proceedings of the 20th Annual ACM Symposium on Theory of Computing, Chicago, Illinois, USA, 2–4 May 1988, pp. 113–131 (1988)

[BHK17] Brakerski, Z., Holmgren, J., Kalai, Y.T.: Non-interactive delegation and batch NP verification from standard computational assumptions. In: Proceedings of the 49th Annual ACM SIGACT Symposium on Theory of Computing, STOC 2017, Montreal, QC, Canada, 19–23 June 2017, pp. 474–482 (2017)

[BKS18] Ben-Sasson, E., Kopparty, S., Saraf, S.: Worst-case to average case reductions for the distance to a code. In: 33rd Computational Complexity Conference, CCC 2018, San Diego, CA, USA, 22–24 June 2018, pp. 24:1–24:23 (2018)

[BRV18] Berman, I., Rothblum, R.D., Vaikuntanathan, V.: Zero-knowledge proofs of proximity. In: 9th Innovations in Theoretical Computer Science Conference, ITCS 2018, Cambridge, MA, USA, 11–14 January 2018, pp. 19:1–19:20 (2018)

[CG18] Chiesa, A., Gur, T.: Proofs of proximity for distribution testing. In: 9th Innovations in Theoretical Computer Science Conference, ITCS 2018, Cambridge, MA, USA, 11–14 January 2018, pp. 53:1–53:14 (2018)

[EKR04] Ergün, F., Kumar, R., Rubinfeld, R.: Fast approximate probabilistically checkable proofs. Inf. Comput. **189**(2), 135–159 (2004)

[FGL+96] Feige, U., Goldwasser, S., Lovász, L., Safra, S., Szegedy, M.: Interactive proofs and the hardness of approximating cliques. J. ACM **43**(2), 268–292 (1996)

[FGL14] Fischer, E., Goldhirsh, Y., Lachish, O.: Partial tests, universal tests and decomposability. In: ITCS, pp. 483–500 (2014)

[FRS94] Fortnow, L., Rompel, J., Sipser, M.: On the power of multi-prover interactive protocols. Theor. Comput. Sci. **134**(2), 545–557 (1994)

[GGR98] Goldreich, O., Goldwasser, S., Ron, D.: Property testing and its connection to learning and approximation. J. ACM (JACM) **45**(4), 653–750 (1998)

[GGR15] Goldreich, O., Gur, T., Rothblum, R.D.: Proofs of proximity for context-free languages and read-once branching programs. In: Halldórsson, M.M., Iwama, K., Kobayashi, N., Speckmann, B. (eds.) ICALP 2015. LNCS, vol. 9134, pp. 666–677. Springer, Heidelberg (2015). https://doi.org/10.1007/978-3-662-47672-7_54

[GH98] Goldreich, O., Håstad, J.: On the complexity of interactive proofs with bounded communication. Inf. Process. Lett. **67**(4), 205–214 (1998)

[GLR18] Gur, T., Liu, Y.P., Rothblum, R.D.: An exponential separation between MA and AM proofs of proximity. In: Chatzigiannakis, I., Kaklamanis, C., Marx, D., Sannella, D. (eds.) 45th International Colloquium on Automata, Languages, and Programming, ICALP 2018, Prague, Czech Republic, 9–13 July 2018. LIPIcs, vol. 107, pp. 73:1–73:15. Schloss Dagstuhl - Leibniz-Zentrum für Informatik (2018)

[GMR89] Goldwasser, S., Micali, S., Rackoff, C.: The knowledge complexity of interactive proof systems. SIAM J. Comput. **18**(1), 186–208 (1989)

[GMW91] Goldreich, O., Micali, S., Wigderson, A.: Proofs that yield nothing but their validity for all languages in NP have zero-knowledge proof systems. J. ACM **38**(3), 691–729 (1991)

[Gol08] Goldreich, O.: Computational Complexity - A Conceptual Perspective. Cambridge University Press, Cambridge (2008)

[GR13] Gur, T., Rothblum, R.D.: Non-interactive proofs of proximity. In: Electronic Colloquium on Computational Complexity (ECCC), vol. 20, p. 78 (2013)

[GR17] Gur, T., Rothblum, R.D.: A hierarchy theorem for interactive proofs of proximity. In: 8th Innovations in Theoretical Computer Science Conference, ITCS 2017, Berkeley, CA, USA, 9–11 January 2017, pp. 39:1–39:43 (2017)

[GRSY20] Goldwasser, S., Rothblum, G.N., Shafer, J., Yehudayoff, A.: Interactive proofs for verifying machine learning. In: Electronic Colloquium on Computational Complexity (ECCC), vol. 27, p. 58 (2020)

[GVW02] Goldreich, O., Vadhan, S.P., Wigderson, A.: On interactive proofs with a laconic prover. Comput. Complex. **11**(1–2), 1–53 (2002)

[Ish] Ishai, Y.: Zero-knowledge proofs from information-theoretic proof systems. https://zkproof.org/2020/08/12/information-theoretic-proof-systems/

[Kil92] Kilian, J.: A note on efficient zero-knowledge proofs and arguments (extended abstract). In: STOC, pp. 723–732 (1992)

[KR15] Kalai, Y.T., Rothblum, R.D.: Arguments of proximity. In: Gennaro, R., Robshaw, M. (eds.) CRYPTO 2015, Part II. LNCS, vol. 9216, pp. 422–442. Springer, Heidelberg (2015). https://doi.org/10.1007/978-3-662-48000-7_21

[LFKN92] Lund, C., Fortnow, L., Karloff, H.J., Nisan, N.: Algebraic methods for interactive proof systems. J. ACM **39**(4), 859–868 (1992)

[RR19] Ron-Zewi, N., Rothblum, R.: Local proofs approaching the witness length. In: Electronic Colloquium on Computational Complexity (ECCC), vol. 26, p. 127 (2019)

[RRR16] Reingold, O., Rothblum, G.N., Rothblum, R.D.: Constant-round interactive proofs for delegating computation. In: Proceedings of the 48th Annual ACM SIGACT Symposium on Theory of Computing, STOC 2016, Cambridge, MA, USA, 18–21 June 2016, pp. 49–62 (2016)

[RRR18] Reingold, O., Rothblum, G.N., Rothblum, R.D.: Efficient batch verification for UP. In: 33rd Computational Complexity Conference, CCC 2018, San Diego, CA, USA, 22–24 June 2018, pp. 22:1–22:23 (2018)

[RS96] Rubinfeld, R., Sudan, M.: Robust characterizations of polynomials with applications to program testing. SIAM J. Comput. **25**(2), 252–271 (1996)

[RVW13] Rothblum, G.N., Vadhan, S., Wigderson, A.: Interactive proofs of proximity: delegating computation in sublinear time. In: STOC, pp. 793–802 (2013)

[Sha92] Shamir, A.: IP = PSPACE. J. ACM **39**(4), 869–877 (1992)

[Sud95] Sudan, M. (ed.): Efficient Checking of Polynomials and Proofs and the Hardness of Appoximation Problems. LNCS, vol. 1001. Springer, Heidelberg (1995). https://doi.org/10.1007/3-540-60615-7

Batch Verification for Statistical Zero Knowledge Proofs

Inbar Kaslasi[1]([✉]), Guy N. Rothblum[2], Ron D. Rothblum[1], Adam Sealfon[3], and Prashant Nalini Vasudevan[3]

[1] Technion - Israel Institute of Technology, Haifa, Israel
{inbark,rothblum}@cs.technion.ac.il
[2] Weizmann Institute, Rehovot, Israel
rothblum@alum.mit.edu
[3] UC Berkeley, Berkeley, USA
{asealfon,prashvas}@berkeley.edu

Abstract. A statistical zero-knowledge proof (SZK) for a problem Π enables a computationally unbounded prover to convince a polynomial-time verifier that $x \in \Pi$ without revealing any additional information about x to the verifier, in a strong information-theoretic sense.

Suppose, however, that the prover wishes to convince the verifier that k separate inputs $x_1, \ldots, x_k$ all belong to Π (without revealing anything else). A naive way of doing so is to simply run the SZK protocol separately for each input. In this work we ask whether one can do better – that is, is efficient *batch verification* possible for SZK?

We give a partial positive answer to this question by constructing a batch verification protocol for a natural and important subclass of SZK – all problems Π that have a *non-interactive* SZK protocol (in the common random string model). More specifically, we show that, for every such problem Π, there exists an honest-verifier SZK protocol for batch verification of k instances, with communication complexity $\mathsf{poly}(n) + k \cdot \mathsf{poly}(\log n, \log k)$, where poly refers to a fixed polynomial that depends only on Π (and not on k). This result should be contrasted with the naive solution, which has communication complexity $k \cdot \mathsf{poly}(n)$.

Our proof leverages a new NISZK-complete problem, called *Approximate Injectivity*, that we find to be of independent interest. The goal in this problem is to distinguish circuits that are nearly injective, from those that are non-injective on almost all inputs.

1 Introduction

Zero-knowledge proofs, introduced in the seminal work of Goldwasser, Micali and Rackoff [GMR89], are a remarkable and incredibly influential notion. Loosely speaking, a zero-knowledge proof lets a prover P convince a verifier V of the validity of some statement without revealing any additional information.

In this work we focus on *statistical zero-knowledge proofs*. These proof-systems simultaneously provide unconditional *soundness* and *zero-knowledge*:

The full version is available on ECCC [KRR+20].

© International Association for Cryptologic Research 2020
R. Pass and K. Pietrzak (Eds.): TCC 2020, LNCS 12551, pp. 139–167, 2020.
https://doi.org/10.1007/978-3-030-64378-2_6

- Even a *computationally unbounded* prover P^* cannot convince V to accept a false statement (except with some negligible probability).
- Any efficient, but potentially malicious, verifier V^* learns nothing in the interaction (beyond the validity of the statement) in the following strong, statistical, sense: there exists an algorithm, called the simulator, which can efficiently simulate the entire interaction between V^* and P based only on the input x, so that the simulation is indistinguishable from the real interaction even to a *computationally unbounded* distinguisher.

The class of promise problems[1] having a statistical zero-knowledge proof is denoted by SZK. This class contains many natural problems, including many of the problems on which modern cryptography is based, such as (relaxations of) integer factoring [GMR89], discrete logarithm [GK93, CP92] and lattice problems [GG00, MV03, PV08, APS18].

Since the study of SZK was initiated in the early 80's many surprising and useful structural properties of this class have been discovered (see, e.g., [For89, AH91, Oka00, SV03, GSV98, GV99, NV06, OV08]), and several applications have been found for hard problems in this (and related) classes (for example, see [Ost91, OW93, BDRV18a, BDRV18b, KY18, BBD+20]). It is known to be connected to various cryptographic primitives [BL13, KMN+14, LV16, PPS15] and algorithmic and complexity-theoretic concepts [Dru15], and has consequently been used to show conditional impossiblility results. In particular, a notable and highly influential development was the discovery of natural complete problems for SZK [SV03, GV99].

In this work we are interested in the following natural question. Suppose that a particular problem Π has an SZK protocol. This means that there is a way to efficiently prove that $x \in \Pi$ in zero-knowledge. However, in many scenarios, one wants to be convinced not only that a single instance belongs to Π but rather that k different inputs $x_1, \ldots, x_k$ all belong to Π. One way to do so is to simply run the underlying protocol for Π k times, in sequence, once for each input x_i.[2] However, it is natural to ask whether one can do better. In particular, assuming that the SZK protocol for Π has communication complexity m, can one prove (in statistical zero-knowledge) that $x_1, \ldots, x_k \in \Pi$ with communication complexity $\ll k \cdot m$? We refer to this problem as *batch verification for* SZK.

We view batch verification of SZK as being of intrinsic interest, and potentially of use in the study of the structure of SZK. Beyond that, batch verification of SZK may be useful to perform various cryptographic tasks, such as batch verification of digital signature schemes [NMVR94, BGR98, CHP12] or batch verification of well-formedness of public keys (see, e.g., [GMR98]).

---

[1] Recall that a promise problem Π consists of two ensembles of sets YES = $(\text{YES}_n)_{n \in \mathbb{N}}$ and $(\text{NO}_n)_{n \in \mathbb{N}}$, such that the YES_n's and NO_n's are disjoint. Instances in YES are called YES instances and those in NO are called NO instances.

[2] The resulting protocol can be shown to be zero-knowledge (analogously to the fact that *sequential* repetition preserves statistical zero-knowledge).

1.1   Our Results

We show that non-trivial batch verification is possible for a large and natural subset of languages in SZK. Specifically, we consider the class of promise problems having *non-interactive statistical zero-knowledge proofs*. A non-interactive statistical zero-knowledge proof [BFM88] is a variant of SZK in which the verifier and the prover are given access to a uniformly random *common random string* (CRS). Given this CRS and an input x, the prover generates a proof string π which it sends to the verifier. The verifier, given x, the CRS, and the proof string π, then decides whether to accept or reject. In particular, no additional interaction is allowed other than the proof π. Zero-knowledge means that it is possible to simulate the verifier's view (which consists of the CRS and proof π) so that the simulation is *statistically* indistinguishable from the real interaction. The corresponding class of promise problems is abbreviated as NISZK.

Remark 1.1. *An* NISZK *for a problem Π is equivalent to a two-round public-coin honest-verifier* SZK *protocol. Recall that* honest-verifier *zero-knowledge, means that the* honest verifier *learns essentially nothing in the interaction, but a* malicious verifier *may be able to learn non-trivial information.*

The class NISZK contains many natural and basic problems such as: variants of the quadratic residuosity problem [BSMP91, DSCP94], lattice problems [PV08, APS18], etc. It is also known to contain *complete* problems [SCPY98, GSV99], related to the known complete problems for SZK.

Our main result is an honest-verifier statistical zero-knowledge protocol for batch verification of any problem in NISZK. In order to state the result more precisely, we introduce the following definition.

Definition 1.2. *Let $\Pi = (\text{YES}, \text{NO})$ be a promise problem, where* YES $=$ $(\text{YES}_n)_{n \in \mathbb{N}}$ *and* NO $= (\text{NO}_n)_{n \in \mathbb{N}}$, *and let $k = k(n) \in \mathbb{N}$. We define the promise problem $\Pi^{\otimes k} = (\text{YES}^{\otimes k}, \text{NO}^{\otimes k})$, where* $\text{YES}^{\otimes k} = (\text{YES}_n^{\otimes k})_{n \in \mathbb{N}}$, $\text{NO}^{\otimes k} =$ $(\text{NO}_n^{\otimes k})_{n \in \mathbb{N}}$ *and*

$$\text{YES}_n^{\otimes k} = (\text{YES}_n)^k$$

and

$$\text{NO}_n^{\otimes k} = (\text{YES}_n \cup \text{NO}_n)^k \setminus (\text{YES}_n)^k .$$

That is, instances of $\Pi^{\otimes k}$ are k instances of Π, where the YES instances are all in YES and the NO instances consist of at least one NO instances for Π.[3]

With the definition of $\Pi^{\otimes k}$ in hand, we are now ready to formally state our main result:

---

[3] This notion of composition is to be contrasted with that employed in the closure theorems for SZK under composition with formulas [SV03]. There, a composite problem similar to $\Pi^{\otimes k}$ is considered that does not require in its NO sets that all k instances satisfy the promise, but instead just that at least one of the instances is a NO instance of Π.

Theorem 1.3 (Informally Stated, see Theorem 3.1). *Suppose that $\Pi \in$* NISZK. *Then, for every $k = k(n) \in \mathbb{N}$, there exists an (interactive)* honest-verifier SZK *protocol for $\Pi^{\otimes k}$ with communication complexity* $\text{poly}(n) + k \cdot \text{poly}(\log n, \log k)$, *where n refers to the length of a single instance and* poly *refers to a fixed polynomial independent of k.*

The verifier's running time is $k \cdot \text{poly}(n)$ and the number of rounds is $O(k)$.

We emphasize that our protocol for $\Pi^{\otimes k}$ is interactive and *honest-verifier* statistical zero-knowledge (HVSZK). Since we start with an NISZK protocol (which as mentioned above is a special case of HVSZK), it is somewhat expected that the resulting batch verification protocol is only HVSZK. Still, obtaining a similar result to Theorem 1.3 that achieves *malicious-verifier* statistical zero-knowledge is a fascinating open problem (see Sect. 1.4 for additional open problems). We mention that while it is known [GSV98] how to transform any HVSZK protocol into a full-fledged SZK protocol (i.e., one that is zero-knowledge even wrt a malicious verifier), this transformation incurs a polynomial overhead that we cannot afford.

1.2   Related Works

Batch Verification via **IP** = PSPACE. A domain in which batch computing is particularly easy is bounded space computation - if a language $\mathcal{L}$ can be decided in space s then k instances of $\mathcal{L}$ can be solved in space $s + \log(k)$ (by reusing space). Using this observation, the **IP** = PSPACE theorem [LFKN92, Sha92] yields an efficient interactive proof for batch verification of any problem in PSPACE. However, the resulting protocol has several major drawbacks. In particular, it does not seem to preserve zero-knowledge, which makes it unsuitable for the purposes of our work.

Batch Verification with Efficient Prover. Another caveat of the **IP** = PSPACE approach is that it does not preserve the efficiency of the prover. That is, even if we started with a problem that has an interactive proof with an *efficient prover*, the batch verification protocol stemming from the **IP** = PSPACE theorem has an *inefficient* prover.

Reingold *et al.* [RRR16, RRR18] considered the question of whether batch verification of NP proofs with an efficiency prover is possible, assuming that the prover is given the NP witnesses as an auxiliary input. These works construct such an interactive batch verification protocol for all problems in UP $\subseteq$ NP (i.e., languages in NP in which YES instances have a unique proof). In particular, the work of [RRR18] yields a batch verification protocol for UP with communication complexity $k^{\delta} \cdot \text{poly}(m)$, where m is the original UP witness length and $\delta > 0$ is any constant.

Note that it seems unlikely that the [RRR16, RRR18] protocols preserve zero-knowledge. Indeed, these protocols fundamentally rely on the so-called *unambiguity* (see [RRR16]) of the underlying UP protocol, which, at least intuitively, seems at odds with zero-knowledge.

Batch Verification with Computational Soundness. Focusing on protocols achieving only *computational soundness*, we remark that interactive batch verification can be obtained directly from Kilian's [Kil92] highly efficient protocol for all of NP (assuming collision resistant hash functions). A *non-interactive* batch verification protocol was given by Brakerski *et al.* [BHK17] assuming the hardness of learning with errors. Non-interactive batch verification protocols also follow from the existence of *succinct non-interactive zero-knowledge arguments (zkSNARGs)*, which are known to exist under certain strong, and non-falsifiable, assumptions (see, e.g. [Ish], for a recent survey).

Randomized Iterates. The *randomized iterate* is a concept introduced by Goldreich, Krawczyk, and Luby [GKL93], and further developed by later work [HHR11, YGLW15], who used it to construct pseudorandom generators from regular one-way functions. Given a function f, its randomized iterate is computed on an input x and descriptions of hash functions $h_1, \ldots, h_m$ by starting with $x_0 = f(x)$ and iteratively computing $x_i = f(h_i(x_{i-1}))$. The hardcore bits of these iterates were then used to obtain pseudorandomness. While the randomized iterate was used for a very different purpose, this process of alternating the evaluation of a given function with injection of randomness (which is what the hash functions were for) is strongly reminiscent of our techniques. It would be very interesting if there is a deeper connection between our techniques and the usage of these iterates in relation to pseudorandom generators.

1.3   Technical Overview

Batch Verification for Permutations. As an initial toy example, we first consider batch verification for a specific problem in NISZK. Let PERM be the promise problem defined as follows. The input to PERM is a description of a Boolean circuit $C : \{0,1\}^n \to \{0,1\}^n$. The YES inputs consist of circuits that define permutations over $\{0,1\}^n$ whereas the NO inputs are circuits so that every element in the image has at least two preimages.[4] It is straightforward to see that PERM $\in$ NISZK.[5]

Our goal is, given as input k circuits $C_1, \ldots, C_k$, to distinguish (via a zero-knowledge proof) the case that all of the circuits are permutations from the case

---

[4] PERM can be thought of as a variant of the *collision problem* (see [Aar04, Chapter 6]) in which the goal is to distinguish a permutation from a 2-to-1 function.

[5] A two round public-coin honest-verifier *perfect* zero-knowledge protocol for PERM can be constructed as follows. The verifier sends a random string $y \in \{0,1\}^n$ and the prover sends $x = C^{-1}(y)$. The verifier needs to check that indeed $y = C(x)$. It is straightforward to check that this protocol is *honest-verifier* perfect zero-knowledge and has soundness $1/2$, which can be amplified by parallel repetition (while noting that honest-verifier zero-knowledge is preserved under parallel repetition).

This protocol can be viewed as a NIPZK by viewing the verifier's coins as the common random string. On the other hand, assuming that NISZK $\neq$ NIPZK, PERM is not NISZK-complete.

that one or more is 2-to-1. Such a protocol can be constructed as follows: the verifier chooses at random $x_1 \in \{0,1\}^n$, computes $x_{k+1} = C_k(C_{k-1}(\ldots C_1(x_1)\ldots))$ and sends x_{k+1} to the prover. The prover now responds with the preimage $x_1' = C_1^{-1}(C_2^{-1}(\ldots C_k^{-1}(x_{k+1})\ldots))$. The verifier checks that $x_1 = x_1'$ and if so it accepts, otherwise it rejects.[6]

Completeness follows from the fact that the circuits define permutations and so $x_1 = x_1'$. For soundness, observe that for a NO instance, x_{k+1} has at least two preimages under the composed circuit $C_k \circ \cdots \circ C_1$. Therefore, a cheating prover can guess the correct preimage x_0 with probability at most $1/2$ (and the soundness error can be reduced by repetition). Lastly observe that the protocol is (perfect) honest-verifier zero-knowledge: the simulator simply emulates the verifier while setting $x_1' = x_1$.

The Approximate Injectivity Problem. Unfortunately, as mentioned above, PERM is presumably not NISZK-complete and so we cannot directly use the above protocol to perform batch verification for arbitrary problems in NISZK. Instead, our approach is to identify a relaxation of PERM that is both NISZK-complete and amenable to batch verification, albeit via a significantly more complicated protocol.

More specifically, we consider the *Approximate Injectivity* (promise) problem. The goal here is to distinguish circuits that are almost injective, from ones that are highly non-injective. In more detail, let $\delta \in [0,1]$ be a parameter. We define AI_δ to be a promise problem in which the input is again a description of a Boolean circuit C mapping n input bits to $m \geq n$ output bits. YES instances are those circuits for which all but δ fraction of the inputs x have no collisions (i.e., $\Pr_x[|C^{-1}(C(x))| > 1] < \delta$). NO instances are circuits for which all but δ fraction of the inputs have at least one colliding input (i.e., $\Pr_x[|C^{-1}(C(x))| = 1] < \delta$).

Our protocol for batch verification of any problem $\Pi \in \mathsf{NISZK}$ consists of two main steps:

- First, we show that AI_δ is NISZK-hard: i.e., there exists an efficient Karp reduction from Π to AI_δ.
- Our second main step is showing an efficient HVSZK batch verification protocol for AI_δ. In particular, the communication complexity of the protocol scales (roughly) additively with the number of instances k.

Equipped with the above, an HVSZK protocol follows by having the prover and verifier reduce the instances $x_1, \ldots, x_k$ for Π to instances $C_1, \ldots, C_k$ for AI_δ, and then engage in the batch verification protocol for AI_δ on common input $(C_1, \ldots, C_k)$.

---

[6] A related but slightly different protocol, which will be less useful in our eventual construction, can be obtained by observing that (1) the mapping $(C_1, \ldots, C_k) \mapsto C_k \circ \cdots \circ C_1$ is a Karp-reduction from an instance of $\mathsf{PERM}^{\otimes k}$ to an instance of PERM with n input/output bits, and (2) that PERM has an NISZK protocol with communication complexity that depends only on n.

Before describing these two steps in detail, we remark that we find the identification of AI_δ as being NISZK-hard (in fact, NISZK-complete) to be of independent interest. In particular, while AI_δ bears some resemblance to problems that were already known to be NISZK-complete, the special almost-injective nature of the YES instances of AI_δ seems very useful. Indeed, this additional structure is crucial for our batch verification protocol.

AI_δ *is* NISZK-*hard.* We show that AI_δ is NISZK-hard by reducing to it from the Entropy Approximation problem (EA), which is known to be complete for NISZK [GSV99].[7] An instance of EA is a circuit C along with a threshold $k \in \mathbb{R}^+$, and the problem is to decide whether the Shannon entropy of the output distribution of C when given uniformly random inputs (denoted $H(C)$) is more than $k + 10$ or less than $k - 10$.[8]

For simplicity, suppose we had a stronger promise on the output distribution of C — that it is a flat distribution (in other words, it is uniform over some subset of its range). In this case, for any output y of C, the promise of EA tells us something about the *number of pre-images* of y. To illustrate, suppose C takes n bits of input. Then, in a YES instance of EA, the size of the set $\left|C^{-1}(y)\right|$ is at most $2^{n-(k+10)}$, and in the NO case it is at least $2^{n-(k-10)}$. Recall that for a reduction to AI_δ, we need to make the sizes of most inverse sets 1 for YES instances and more than 1 for NO instances. This can now be done by using a hash function to shatter the inverse sets of C.

That is, consider the circuit $\widehat{C}$ that takes as input an x and also the description of a hash function h from, say, a pairwise-independent hash family H, and outputs $(C(x), h, h(x))$. If we pick H so that its hash functions have output length $(n - k)$, then out of any set of inputs of size $2^{n-(k+10)}$, all but a small constant fraction will be mapped injectively by a random h from H. On the other hand, out of any set of inputs of size $2^{n-(k-10)}$, only a small constant fraction will be mapped injectively by a random h. Thus, in the YES case, it may be argued that all but a small constant fraction of inputs (x, h) are mapped injectively by $\widehat{C}$, and in the NO case only a small constant fraction of inputs are. So for some constant δ, this is indeed a valid reduction from EA to AI_δ. For smaller functions δ, the reduction is performed by first amplifying the gap in the promise of EA and then proceeding as above.

Finally, we can relax the simplifying assumption of flatness using the asymptotic equipartition property of distributions. In this case, this property states that, however unstructured C may be, its t-fold repetition $C^{\otimes t}$ (that takes an input tuple $(x_1, \ldots, x_t)$ and outputs $(C(x_1), \ldots, C(x_t))$) is "approximately flat" for large enough t. That is, with increasingly high probability over the output distribution of $C^{\otimes t}$, a sample from it will have a pre-image set of size close to its expectation, which is $2^{t \cdot (n - H(C))}$. Such techniques have been previously used for similar purposes in the SZK literature and elsewhere, for example as the

---

[7] In fact, we also show that AI_δ is in NISZK, and thus is NISZK-complete, by reducing back from it to EA.

[8] In the standard definition of EA [GSV99], the promise is that $H(C)$ is either more than $k + 1$ or less than $k - 1$, but this gap can be amplified easily by repetition of C.

flattening lemma of Goldreich *et al.* [GSV99] (see the full version for details and the proof).

Batch Verification for Exact Injectivity. For sake of simplicity, for this overview we focus on batch verification of the *exact* variant of AI_δ, that is, when $\delta = 0$. In other words, distinguishing circuits that are truly injective from those in which every image y has at least two preimages (with no exceptions allowed). We refer to this promise problem as INJ. Modulo some technical details, the batch verification protocol for INJ, presented next, captures most of the difficulty in our batch verification protocol for AI_δ.

Before proceeding we mention that the key difference between INJ and PERM is that YES instances of the former are merely injective whereas for the latter they are permutations. Interestingly, this seemingly minor difference causes significant complications.

Our new goal is, given as input circuits $C_1, \ldots, C_k : \{0,1\}^n \to \{0,1\}^m$, with $m \geq n$, to distinguish the case that all of the circuits are injective from the case that at least one is entirely non-injective.

Inspired by the batch verification protocol for PERM, a reasonable approach is to choose x_1 at random but then try to hash the output $y_i = C_i(x_i) \in \{0,1\}^m$, of each circuit C_i, into an input $x_{i+1} \in \{0,1\}^n$ for C_{i+1}. If a hash function could be found that was injective on the image of C_i then we would be done. However, it seems that finding such a hash function is, in general, extremely difficult.

Rather, we will hash each y_i by choosing a random hash function from a small hash function family. More specifically, for every iteration $i \in [k]$ we choose a random seed z_i for a (seeded) randomness extractor $\mathsf{Ext} : \{0,1\}^m \times \{0,1\}^d \to \{0,1\}^n$ and compute $x_{i+1} = \mathsf{Ext}(y_i, z_i)$. See Fig. 1 for a diagram describing this sampling process.

In case all the circuits are injective (i.e., a YES instance), a simple inductive argument can be used to show that each y_i is (close to) a distribution having min-entropy n, and therefore the output $x_{i+1} = \mathsf{Ext}(y_i, z_i)$ of the extractor is close to uniform in $\{0,1\}^n$. Note that for this to be true, we need a very good extractor that essentially extracts *all of the entropy*. Luckily, constructions of such extractors with a merely poly-logarithmic seed length are known [GUV07].

This idea leads us to consider the following strawman protocol. The verifier chooses at random $x_1 \in \{0,1\}^n$ and k seeds $z_1, \ldots, z_k$. The verifier then computes inductively: $y_i = C_i(x_i)$ and $x_{i+1} = \mathsf{Ext}(y_i, z_i)$, for every $i \in [k]$. The verifier sends $(x_{k+1}, z_1, \ldots, z_k)$ to the prover, who in turn needs to guess the value of x_1.

The major difficulty that arises in this protocol is in completeness: the honest prover's probability of predicting x_1 is very small. To see this, suppose that all of the circuits $C_1, \ldots, C_k$ are injective. Consider the job of the honest prover: given $(x_{k+1}, z_1, \ldots, z_k)$ the prover needs to find x_1. The difficulty is that x_{k+1} is likely to have many preimages under $\mathsf{Ext}(\cdot, z_k)$. While this statement depends on the specific structure of the extractor, note that even in a "dream scenario" in which $\mathsf{Ext}(\cdot, z_k)$ were a random function, a constant fraction of x_{k+1}'s would have more than one preimage (in the image of C_k).

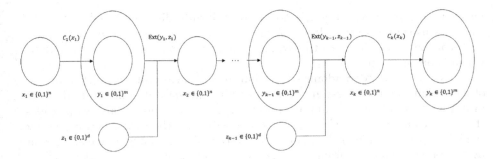

Fig. 1. The sampling process

A similar type of collision in the extractor is likely to occur in most of the steps $i \in [k]$. Therefore, the overall number of preimages x_1' that are consistent with $(x_{k+1}, z_1, \ldots, z_k)$ is likely to be $2^{\Omega(k)}$ and the prover has no way to guess the correct one among them. The natural remedy for this is to give the prover some additional information, such as a hash of x_1, in order to help pick it correctly among the various possible options. However, doing so also helps a cheating prover find x_1 in the case where one of the circuits is non-injective. And it turns out that the distribution of the number of x_1's in the two cases – where all the C_i's are injective and where one is non-injective – are similar enough that it is not clear how to make this approach work as is.

Isolating Preimages via Interaction. We circumvent the issue discussed above by employing *interaction*. The key observation is that, even though the number of pre-images x_1 of the composition of all k circuits is somewhat similar in the case of all YES instance and the case of one NO instance among them, if we look at this composition circuit-by-circuit, the number of pre-images in an injective circuit is clearly different from that in a non-injective circuit. In order to exploit this, we have the verifier *gradually* reveal the y_i's rather than revealing them all at once.

Taking a step back, let us consider the following naive protocol:

1. For $i = k, \ldots, 1$:
   (a) The verifier chooses at random $x_i \in \{0, 1\}^n$ and sends $y_i = C_i(x_i)$ to the prover.
   (b) The (honest) prover responds with $x_i' = C_i^{-1}(y_i)$.
   (c) The verifier immediately rejects if the prover answered incorrectly (i.e., $x_i' \neq x_i$).

It is not difficult to argue that this protocol is indeed an HVSZK protocol (with soundness error $1/2$, which can be reduced by repetition). Alas, the communication complexity is at least $k \cdot n$, which is too large.

However, a key observation is that this protocol still works even if we generate the y_i's as in the strawman protocol. Namely, $x_{i+1} = \mathsf{Ext}(y_i, z_i)$ and $y_i = C_i(x_i)$, for every $i \in [k]$, where the z_i's are fresh uniformly distributed (short) seeds. This lets us significantly reduce the *randomness complexity* of the above naive protocol. Later we shall use this to also reduce the *communication complexity*, which is our main goal.

To see that the "derandomized" variant of the naive protocol works, we first observe that completeness and zero-knowledge indeed still hold. Indeed, since in a YES case all the circuits are injective, the honest prover always provides the correct answer - i.e., $x'_i = x_i$. Thus, not only does the verifier always accept (which implies completeness), but it can also easily simulate the messages sent by the prover (which guarantees honest-verifier statistical zero-knowledge).[9]

Arguing soundness is slightly more tricky. Let $i^* \in [k]$ be the smallest integer so that C_{i^*} is a NO instance. Recall that in the i^*-th iteration of the protocol, the prover is given y_{i^*} and needs to predict x_{i^*}. If we can argue that x_{i^*} is (close to) uniformly distributed then (constant) soundness follows, since C_{i^*} is a NO instance and therefore non-injective on every input.

We argue that x_{i^*} is close to uniform by induction. For the base case $i = 1$ this is obviously true since x_1 is sampled uniformly at random. For the inductive step, assume that x_{i-1} is close to uniform, with $i \leq i^*$. Since C_{i-1} is injective (since $i - 1 < i^*$), this means that $y_{i-1} = C_{i-1}(x_{i-1})$ is close to uniform in the image of C_1, a set of size 2^n. Thus, $\mathsf{Ext}(y_{i-1}, z_{i-1})$ is applied to a source (that is close to a distribution) with min-entropy n. Since Ext is an extractor, this means that x_i is close to uniform, concluding the induction.

Reducing Communication Complexity via Hashing. Although we have reduced the *randomness complexity* of the protocol, we have not reduced the *communication complexity* (which is still $k \cdot n$). We shall do so by, once more, appealing to hashing.

Let us first consider the verifier to prover communication. Using hashing, we show how the verifier can specify each y_i to the prover by transmitting only a *poly-logarithmic* number of bits. Consider, for example, the second iteration of the protocol. In this iteration the verifier is supposed to send y_{k-1} to the prover but can no longer afford to do so. Notice however that at this point the prover already knows x_k. We show that with all but negligible probability, the number of candidate pairs (y_{k-1}, z_{k-1}) that are consistent with x_k (and so that y_{k-1} is in the image of C_{i-1}) is very small. This fact (shown in Proposition 4.4 in Sect. 4), follows from the fact that Ext is an extractor with small seed length.[10] In more detail, we show that with all but negligible probability, the number of candidates is roughly (quasi-)polynomial. Thus, it suffices for the verifier to send a hash of poly-logarithmic length (e.g., using a pairwise independent hash

---

[9] Actually the protocol as described achieves perfect completeness and perfect honest-verifier zero-knowledge. However, the more general AI_δ problem will introduce some (negligible) statistical errors.

[10] This observation is simple in hindsight but we nevertheless find it somewhat surprising. In particular, it cannot be shown by bounding the expected number of collisions and applying Markov's inequality since the *expected* number of collisions in Ext is very large (see [Vad12, Problem 6.4]).

function) to specify the correct pair (y_{k-1}, z_{k-1}). This idea extends readily to all subsequent iterations.

Thus, we are only left with the task of reducing the communication from the prover to the verifier (which is currently $n \cdot k$). We yet again employ hashing. The observation is that rather than sending x_i in its entirety in each iteration, it suffices for the prover to send a short hash of x_i. The reason is that, in the case of soundness, when we reach iteration i^*, we know that y_i has two preimages: $x_i^{(0)}$ and $x_i^{(1)}$. The prover at this point has no idea which of the two is the correct one and so as long as the hashes of $x_i^{(0)}$ and $x_i^{(1)}$ differ, the prover will only succeed with probability $1/2$. Thus, it suffices to use a pairwise independent hash function.

To summarize, after an initial setup phase in which the verifier specifies y_k and the different hash functions, the protocol simply consists of a "ping pong" of hash values between the verifier and the prover. In each iteration the verifier first reveals a hash of the pair (y_i, z_i), which suffices for the prover to fully recover y_i. In response, the prover sends a hash of x_i, which suffices to prove that the prover knows the correct preimage of y_i. For further details, a formal description of the protocol, and the proof, see Sect. 4.

1.4 Discussion and Open Problems

Theorem 1.3 gives a non-trivial batch verification protocol for any problem in NISZK. However, we believe that it is only the first step in the study of batch verification of SZK. In particular, and in addition to the question of obtaining *malicious verifier* zero-knowledge that was already mentioned, we point out several natural research directions:

1. As already pointed out, Theorem 1.3 only gives a batch verification protocol for problems in NISZK. Can one obtain a similar result for all of SZK?
   As a special interesting case, consider the problem of batch verification for the graph non-isomorphism problem: deciding whether or not there exists a pair of isomorphic graphs among k such pairs. Theorem 1.3 yields an efficient batch verification protocol for this problem under the assumption that the graphs have no non-trivial automorphisms. Handling the general case remains open and seems like a good starting point for a potential generalization of Theorem 1.3 to all of SZK.
2. Even though we started off with an NISZK protocol for Π, the protocol for $\Pi^{\otimes k}$ is highly interactive. As a matter of fact, the number of rounds is $O(k)$. Is there an NISZK batch verification protocol for any $\Pi \in$ NISZK?
3. While the communication complexity in the protocol for $\Pi^{\otimes k}$ only depends (roughly) *additively* on k, this additive dependence is still linear. Is a similar result possible with a sub-linear dependence on k?[11] For example, with $\mathsf{poly}(n, \log k)$ communication?

---

[11] While a linear dependence on k seems potentially avoidable, we note that a polynomial dependence on n seems inherent (even for just a single instance, i.e., when $k = 1$).

4. A different line of questioning follows from looking at prover efficiency. While in general one cannot expect provers in interactive proofs to be efficient, it is known that any problem in SZK ∩ NP has an SZK protocol where the honest prover runs in polynomial-time given the NP witness for the statement being proven [NV06]. Our transformations, however, make the prover quite inefficient. This raises the interesting question of whether there are batch verification protocols for languages in SZK ∩ NP (or even NISZK ∩ NP) that are zero-knowledge and also preserve the prover efficiency. This could have interesting applications in, say, cryptographic protocols where the honest prover is the party that generated the instance in the first place and so has a witness for it (e.g., in a signature scheme where the signer wishes to prove the validity of several signatures jointly).

While the above list already raises many concrete directions for future work, one fascinating high-level research agenda that our work motivates is a *fine-grained* study of SZK. In particular, optimizing and improving our understanding of the concrete polynomial overheads in structural study of SZK.

Remark 1.4 (Using circuits beyond random sampling). *To the best of our knowledge, all prior works studying complete problems for SZK and NISZK only make a very restricted usage of the given input circuits. Specifically, all that is needed is the ability to generate random samples of the form $(r, C(r))$, where r is uniformly distributed random string and C is the given circuit (describing a probability distribution).*

In contrast, our protocol leverages the ability to feed a (hash of an) output of one circuit as an input to the next circuit. This type of adaptive usage escapes the "random sampling paradigm" described above. In particular, our technique goes beyond the (restrictive) black box model of Holenstein and Renner [HR05], who showed limitations for statistical distance polarization within this model (see also [BDRV19]).

1.5   Organization

We start with preliminaries in Sect. 2. The batch verification result for NISZK is formally stated in Sect. 3 and proved therein, based on results that are proved in the subsequent sections. In Sect. 4 we show a batch verification protocol for AI_δ. Due to lack of space, we defer the proof that AI_δ is NISZK-complete to the full version.

2   Preliminaries

2.1   Probability Theory Notation and Background

Given a random variable X, we write $x \leftarrow X$ to indicate that x is sampled according to X. Similarly, given a finite set S, we let $s \leftarrow S$ denote that s is selected according to the uniform distribution on S. We adopt the convention that when the same random variable occurs several times in an expression, all occurrences refer to a single sample. For example, $\Pr[f(X) = X]$ is defined to be the probability that when $x \leftarrow X$, we have $f(x) = x$. We write U_n to denote the random variable distributed uniformly over $\{0, 1\}^n$. The support of a distribution D over a finite set U, denoted $Supp(D)$, is defined as $\{u \in U : D(u) > 0\}$.

The *statistical distance* of two distributions P and Q over a finite set U, denoted as $\Delta(P, Q)$, is defined as $\max_{S \subseteq U}(P(S) - Q(S)) = \frac{1}{2} \sum_{u \in U} |P(u) - Q(u)|$.

We recall some standard basic facts about statistical distance.

Fact 2.1 (Data processing inequality for statistical distance). *For any two distributions X and Y, and every (possibly randomized) process f:*

$$\Delta(f(X), f(Y)) \leq \Delta(X, Y)$$

Fact 2.2. *For any two distributions X and Y, and event E:*

$$\Delta(X, Y) \leq \Delta(X|_E, Y) + \Pr_X[\neg E],$$

where $X|_E$ denotes the distribution of X conditioned on E.

Proof. Let $p_u = \Pr[X = u]$ and $q_u = \Pr[Y = u]$. Also, let $p_{u|E} = \Pr_X[X = u|E]$ and $p_{u|\neg E} = \Pr_X[X = u|\neg E]$.

$$\Delta(X, Y) = \frac{1}{2} \sum_u |p_u - q_u|$$

$$= \frac{1}{2} \sum_u \left| \Pr_X[E] \cdot p_{u|E} + \Pr_X[\neg E] \cdot p_{u|\neg E} - \Pr_X[E] \cdot q_u - \Pr_X[\neg E] \cdot q_u \right|$$

$$\leq \frac{1}{2} \sum_u \left(\left| \Pr_X[E] \cdot p_{u|E} - \Pr_X[E] \cdot q_u \right| + \left| \Pr_X[\neg E] \cdot p_{u|\neg E} - \Pr_X[\neg E] \cdot q_u \right| \right)$$

$$= \Pr_X[E] \cdot \Delta(X|_E, Y) + \Pr_X[\neg E] \cdot \Delta(X|_{\neg E}, Y)$$

$$\leq \Delta(X|_E, Y) + \Pr_X[\neg E].$$

We also recall Chebyshev's inequality.

Lemma 2.3 (Chebyshev's inequality). *Let X be a random variable. Then, for every $\alpha > 0$:*

$$\Pr\left[|X - E[X]| \geq \alpha\right] \leq \frac{Var[X]}{\alpha^2}.$$

2.2 Zero-Knowledge Proofs

We use $(P, V)(x)$ to refer to the *transcript* of an execution of an interactive protocol with prover P and verifier V on common input x. The transcript includes the input x, all messages sent by P to V in the protocol and the verifier's random coin tosses. We say that the transcript $\tau = (P, V)(x)$ is accepting if at the end of the corresponding interaction, the verifier accepts.

Definition 2.4 (HVSZK). *Let* $c = c(n) \in [0,1]$, $s = s(n) \in [0,1]$ *and* $z = z(n) \in [0,1]$. *An* Honest Verifier SZK Proof-System (HVSZK) *with completeness error* c, *soundness error* s *and zero-knowledge error* z *for a promise problem* $\Pi = (\Pi_{\text{YES}}, \Pi_{\text{NO}})$, *consists of a probabilistic polynomial-time verifier* V *and a computationally unbounded prover* P *such that following properties hold:*

- **Completeness:** *For any* $x \in \Pi_{\text{YES}}$:

$$\Pr\left[(\mathsf{P}, \mathsf{V})(x) \text{ is accepting}\right] \geq 1 - c(|x|).$$

- **Soundness:** *For any (computationally unbounded) cheating prover* P^* *and any* $x \in \Pi_{\text{NO}}$:

$$\Pr\left[(\mathsf{P}^*, \mathsf{V})(x) \text{ is accepting}\right] \leq s(|x|).$$

- **Honest Verifier Statistical Zero Knowledge:** *There is a probabilistic polynomial-time algorithm* Sim *(called the* simulator*) such that for any* $x \in \Pi_{\text{YES}}$:

$$\Delta\left((\mathsf{P}, \mathsf{V})(x), \mathsf{Sim}(x)\right) \leq z(|x|).$$

If the completeness, soundness and zero-knowledge errors are all negligible, we simply say that Π has an HVSZK protocol. We also use HVSZK to denote the class of promise problems having such an HVSZK protocol.

We also define *non-interactive zero knowledge proofs* as follows.

Definition 2.5 (NISZK). *Let* $c = c(n) \in [0,1]$, $s = s(n) \in [0,1]$ *and* $z = z(n) \in [0,1]$. *An* non-interactive statistical zero-knowledge proof (NISZK) *with completeness error* c, *soundness error* s *andzero-knowledge error* z *for a promise problem* $\Pi = (\Pi_{\text{YES}}, \Pi_{\text{NO}})$, *consists of a probabilistic polynomial-time verifier* V, *a computationally unbounded prover* P *and a polynomial* $\ell = \ell(n)$ *such that following properties hold:*

- **Completeness:** *For any* $x \in \Pi_{\text{YES}}$:

$$\Pr_{r \in \{0,1\}^{\ell(|x|)}} \left[\mathsf{V}(x, r, \pi) \text{ accepts}\right] \geq 1 - c(|x|),$$

where $\pi = \mathsf{P}(x, r)$.

- **Soundness:** *For any* $x \in \Pi_{\text{NO}}$:

$$\Pr_{r \in \{0,1\}^{\ell(|x|)}} \left[\exists \pi^* \text{ s.t. } \mathsf{V}(x, r, \pi^*) \text{ accepts}\right] \leq s(|x|).$$

- **Honest Verifier Statistical Zero Knowledge:** *There is a probabilistic polynomial-time algorithm* Sim *(called the* simulator*) such that for any* $x \in \Pi_{\text{YES}}$:

$$\Delta\left((U_\ell, \mathsf{P}(x, U_\ell)), \mathsf{Sim}(x)\right) \leq z(|x|).$$

As above, if the errors are negligible, we say that Π has a NISZK protocol and use NISZK to denote the class of all such promise problems.

2.3   Many-Wise Independent Hashing

Hash functions offering bounded independence are used extensively in the literature. We use a popular variant in which the output of the hash function is *almost* uniformly distributed on the different points. This relaxation allows us to save on the representation length of functions in the family.

Definition 2.6 (δ-almost ℓ-wise Independent Hash Functions). *For $\ell = \ell(n) \in \mathbb{N}$, $m = m(n) \in \mathbb{N}$ and $\delta = \delta(n) > 0$, a family of functions $\mathcal{F} = (\mathcal{F}_n)_n$, where $\mathcal{F}_n = \{f : \{0,1\}^m \to \{0,1\}^n\}$ is δ-almost ℓ-wise independent if for every $n \in \mathbb{N}$ and distinct $x_1, x_2, \ldots, x_\ell \in \{0,1\}^m$ the distributions:*

- *$(f(x_1), \ldots, f(x_\ell))$, where $f \leftarrow \mathcal{F}_n$; and*
- *The uniform distribution over $(\{0,1\}^n)^\ell$,*

are δ-close in statistical distance.

When $\delta = 0$ we simply say that the hash function family is ℓ-wise independent. Constructions of (efficiently computable) many-wise hash function families with a very succinct representation are well known. In particular, when $\delta = 0$ we have the following well-known construction:

Lemma 2.7 (See, e.g., [Vad12, Section 3.5.5]). *For every $\ell = \ell(n) \in \mathbb{N}$ and $m = m(n) \in \mathbb{N}$ there exists a family of ℓ-wise independent hash functions $\mathcal{F}_{n,m}^{(\ell)} = \{f : \{0,1\}^m \to \{0,1\}^n\}$ where a random function from $\mathcal{F}_{n,m}^{(\ell)}$ can be selected using $O(\ell \cdot \max(n,m))$ bits, and given a description of $f \in \mathcal{F}_{n,m}^{(\ell)}$ and $x \in \{0,1\}^m$, the value $f(x)$ can be computed in time $\mathsf{poly}(n,m,\ell)$.*

For $\delta > 0$, the seminal work of Naor and Naor [NN93] yields a highly succinct construction.

Lemma 2.8 ([NN93, Lemma 4.2]). *For every $\ell = \ell(n) \in \mathbb{N}$, $m = m(n) \in \mathbb{N}$ and $\delta = \delta(n) > 0$, there exists a family of δ-almost ℓ-wise independent hash functions $\mathcal{F}_{n,m}^{(\ell)} = \{f : \{0,1\}^m \to \{0,1\}^n\}$ where a random function from $\mathcal{F}_{n,m}^{(\ell)}$ can be selected using $O(\ell \cdot n + \log(m) + \log(1/\delta))$ bits, and given a description of $f \in \mathcal{F}_{n,m}^{(\ell)}$ and $x \in \{0,1\}^m$, the value $f(x)$ can be computed in time $\mathsf{poly}(n,m,\ell,\log(1/\delta))$.*

2.4   Seeded Extractors

The min-entropy of a distribution X over a set $\mathcal{X}$ is defined as $H_\infty(X) = \min_{x \in \mathcal{X}} \log(1/\Pr[X = x])$. In particular, if $H_\infty(X) = k$ then, $\Pr[X = x] \leq 2^{-k}$, for every $x \in \mathcal{X}$.

Definition 2.9 ([NZ96]). *Let $k = k(n) \in \mathbb{N}$, $m = m(n) \in \mathbb{N}$, $d = d(n)$ and $\epsilon = \epsilon(n) \in [0,1]$. We say that the family of functions $\mathsf{Ext} = (\mathsf{Ext}_n)_{n \in \mathbb{N}}$, where $\mathsf{Ext}_n : \{0,1\}^n \times \{0,1\}^d \to \{0,1\}^m$, is a (k,ϵ)-extractor if for every $n \in \mathbb{N}$ and distribution X supported on $\{0,1\}^n$ with $H_\infty(X) \geq k$, it holds that $\Delta(\mathsf{Ext}(X, U_d), U_m) \leq \epsilon$, where U_d (resp., U_m) denotes the uniform distribution on d (resp., m) bit strings.*

Lemma 2.10 ([GUV07, Theorem 4.21]). *Let $k = k(n) \in \mathbb{N}$, $m = m(n) \in \mathbb{N}$ and $\epsilon = \epsilon(n) \in [0,1]$ such that $k \leq n$, $m \leq k + d - 2\log(1/\epsilon) - O(1)$, $d = \log(n) + O(\log(k) \cdot \log(k/\epsilon))$ and the functions k, m and ϵ are computable in $\mathsf{poly}(n)$ time. Then, there exists a polynomial-time computable (k, ϵ)-extractor $\mathsf{Ext} = (\mathsf{Ext}_n)_{n \in \mathbb{N}}$ such that $\mathsf{Ext}_n : \{0,1\}^n \times \{0,1\}^d \to \{0,1\}^m$.*

3   Batch Verification for NISZK

In this section we formally state and prove our main result.

Theorem 3.1. *Let $\Pi \in \mathsf{NISZK}$ and $k = k(n) \in \mathbb{N}$ such that $k(n) = 2^{n^{o(1)}}$. Then, $\Pi^{\otimes k}$ has an $O(k)$-round HVSZK protocol with communication complexity $k \cdot \mathsf{poly}(\log n, \log k) + \mathsf{poly}(n)$ and verifier running time $k \cdot \mathsf{poly}(n)$.*

The proof of Theorem 3.1 is divided into two main steps:

1. As our first main step, we introduce a new NISZK-hard problem, called *approximate injectivity*. The problem is defined formally in Definition 3.2 below and its NISZK hardness is established by Lemma 3.3. Due to space restrictions, the proof of Lemma 3.3 is deferred to the full version.
2. The second step is constructing a batch verification protocol for approximate injectivity, as given in Theorem 3.4. The proof of Theorem 3.4 appears in Sect. 4.

We proceed to define the approximate injectivity problem and state its NISZK-hardness.

Definition 3.2. *Let $\delta = \delta(n) \to [0,1]$ be a function computable in $\mathsf{poly}(n)$ time. The Approximate Injectivity problem with approximation δ, denoted by AI_δ, is a promise problem* (YES, NO), *where* YES $= (\mathrm{YES}_n)_{n \in \mathbb{N}}$ *and* NO $= (\mathrm{NO}_n)_{n \in \mathbb{N}}$ *are sets defined as follows:*

$$\mathrm{YES}_n = \left\{ (1^n, C) \; : \; \Pr_{x \leftarrow \{0,1\}^n} \left[|C^{-1}(C(x))| > 1 \right] < \delta(n) \right\}$$

$$\mathrm{NO}_n = \left\{ (1^n, C) \; : \; \Pr_{x \leftarrow \{0,1\}^n} \left[|C^{-1}(C(x))| > 1 \right] > 1 - \delta(n) \right\}$$

where, in both cases, C is a circuit that takes n bits as input. The size of an instance $(1^n, C)$ is n.

Lemma 3.3. *Let $\delta = \delta(n) \in [0,1]$ be a non-increasing function such that $\delta(n) > 2^{-o(n^{1/4})}$. Then, AI_δ is NISZK-hard.*

As mentioned above, the proof of Lemma 3.3 appears in the full version. Our main technical result is a batch verification protocol for AI_δ.

Theorem 3.4. *For any $k = k(n) \in \mathbb{N}$, $\delta = \delta(n) \in [0, \frac{1}{100k^2}]$ and security parameter $\lambda = \lambda(n)$, the problem $\mathsf{AI}_\delta^{\otimes k}$ has an HVSZK protocol with communication complexity $O(n)+k \cdot \mathsf{poly}(\lambda, \log N, \log k)$, where N is an upper bound on the size of each of the given circuits (on n input bits). The completeness and zero-knowledge errors are $O(k^2 \cdot \delta + 2^{-\lambda})$ and the soundness error is a constant bounded away from 1.*

The verifier running time is $k \cdot \mathsf{poly}(N, \log k, \lambda)$ and the number of rounds is $O(k)$.

The proof of Theorem 3.4 appears in Sect. 4. With Lemma 3.3 and Theorem 3.4 in hand, the proof of Theorem 3.1 is now routine.

Proof (Proof of Theorem 3.1). Let $\Pi \in \mathsf{NISZK}$. We construct an HVSZK protocol for $\Pi^{\otimes k}$ as follows. Given as common input $(x_1, \ldots, x_k)$, the prover and verifier each first employ the Karp reduction of Lemma 3.3 to each instance to obtain circuits $(C_1, \ldots, C_k)$ wrt $\delta = \frac{1}{2^{\mathsf{poly}(\log n, \log k)}}$. The size of each circuit, as well as the number of inputs bits, is $\mathsf{poly}(n)$.

The parties then emulate a $\mathsf{poly}(\log n, \log k)$ parallel repetition of the SZK protocol of Theorem 3.4 on input $(C_1, \ldots, C_k)$ and security parameter $\lambda = \mathsf{poly}(\log n, \log k)$. Completeness, soundness and honest-verifier zero-knowledge follow directly from Lemma 3.3 and Theorem 3.4, with error $O(k \cdot \delta + 2^{-\lambda}) = negl(n, k)$, where we also use the fact that parallel repetition of interactive proofs reduces the soundness error at an exponential rate, and that parallel repetition preserves *honest verifier* zero-knowledge.

To analyze the communication complexity and verifier running time, observe that the instances C_i that the reduction of Lemma 3.3 generates have size $\mathsf{poly}(n)$. The batch verification protocol of Theorem 3.4 therefore has communication complexity $\mathsf{poly}(n) + k \cdot \mathsf{poly}(\log n, \log k)$ and verifier running time $k \cdot \mathsf{poly}(n)$.

4 Batch Verification for AI

In this section we prove Theorem 3.4 by constructing an HVSZK protocol for batch verification of the approximate injectivity problem AI_δ (see Definition 3.2 for the definition of AI_δ). For convenience, we restate Theorem 3.4 next.

Theorem 3.4. *For any $k = k(n) \in \mathbb{N}$, $\delta = \delta(n) \in [0, \frac{1}{100k^2}]$ and security parameter $\lambda = \lambda(n)$, the problem $\mathsf{AI}_\delta^{\otimes k}$ has an HVSZK protocol with communication complexity $O(n)+k \, \mathsf{poly} \, (\lambda, \log N, \log k)$, where N is an upper bound on the size of each of the given circuits (on n input bits). The completeness and zero-knowledge errors are $O(k^2 \cdot \delta + 2^{-\lambda})$ and the soundness error is a constant bounded away from 1.*

The verifier running time is $k \cdot \mathsf{poly}(N, \log k, \lambda)$ and the number of rounds is $O(k)$.

HVSZK Batch Verification Protocol for Al_δ

INPUT: Circuits $C_1, \ldots, C_k : \{0,1\}^n \to \{0,1\}^m$ and security parameter λ, where all circuits have size at most N, input length n, and output length $m \leq N$.

- Wlog we assume that all the circuits have the same output length $m \leq N$. This can be achieved by padding.

INGREDIENTS:

- Let $\mathsf{Ext} = \mathsf{Ext}_n$ be the explicit extractor from Lemma 2.10, where $\mathsf{Ext}_n : \{0,1\}^m \times \{0,1\}^d \to \{0,1\}^n$, so that Ext_n supports min-entropy $n-1$, has error $\epsilon = \frac{1}{k^2 \cdot 2^\lambda}$ and the seed length d is as guaranteed by Lemma 2.10.
- Let H_n be the explicit family of $\frac{1}{2^{2\lambda+d+2\log k}}$-almost pairwise-independent hash functions of Lemma 2.8, where $H_n : \{0,1\}^m \times \{0,1\}^d \to \{0,1\}^{2\lambda+d+2\log k}$ and d is the seed length of the extractor as specified above.
- Let G_n be the explicit family of pairwise-independent hash functions of Lemma 2.7, where $G_n : \{0,1\}^n \to \{0,1\}^\ell$ and $\ell = O(1)$ (e.g., $\ell = 3$ suffices).

THE PROTOCOL:

1. Setup for V:
   (a) Sample $h \leftarrow H_n$ and $g \leftarrow G_n$.
   (b) Sample $x_1 \leftarrow \{0,1\}^n$.
   (c) For $i = 1, \ldots, k$:
      i. Compute $y_i = C_i(x_i)$.
      ii. Sample $z_i \leftarrow \{0,1\}^d$.
      iii. Compute $x_{i+1} = \mathsf{Ext}(y_i, z_i)$.
2. V sends h, g, and x_{k+1} to P.
3. P sets $x'_{k+1} = x_{k+1}$.
4. For $i = k, \ldots, 1$:
   (a) V sends $\beta_i = h(y_i, z_i)$ to P.
   (b) P computes y'_i by finding the unique pair (y'_i, z'_i) s.t. $\mathsf{Ext}(y'_i, z'_i) = x'_{i+1}$ and $h(y'_i, z'_i) = \beta_i$. If such a pair (y'_i, z'_i) does not exist or is not unique, P sends a special abort symbol to V.
   (c) P computes x'_i by inverting C_i at y'_i and sends $\alpha_i = g(x'_i)$ to V. If an inverse of y'_i does not exist or is not unique, P sends a special abort symbol to V.
   (d) If V got an abort symbol or if $\alpha_i \neq g(x_i)$, then it rejects and aborts.
5. If all previous tests passed then V accepts.

Fig. 2. A batch SZK protocol for Al

Let k, δ and λ be as in the statement of Theorem 3.4. In order to prove the theorem we need to present an HVSZK protocol for $\mathsf{AI}_\delta^{\otimes k}$ with the specified parameters. The protocol is presented in Fig. 2. The rest of this section is devoted to proving that the protocol indeed satisfies the requirements of Theorem 3.4.

Section Organization. First, in Sect. 4.1 we prove several lemmas that will be useful throughout the analysis of the protocol. Using these lemmas, in Sects. 4.2 and 4.4, we, respectively, establish the completeness, honest-verifier statistical zero-knowledge and soundness properties of the protocol. Lastly, in Sect. 4.5 we analyze the communication complexity and verifier runtime.

4.1 Useful Lemmas

Let $C_1, \ldots, C_k : \{0,1\}^n \to \{0,1\}^m$ be the given input circuits (these can correspond to either a YES or NO instance of AI_δ). Throughout the proof we use $i^* \in [k+1]$ to denote the index of the first NO instance circuit, if such a circuit exists, and $i^* = k+1$ otherwise. That is, $i^* = \min\left(\{k+1\} \cup \{i \in [k] : C_i \text{ is a NO instance}\}\right)$.

For every $i \in [k]$ we introduce the following notations:

- We denote by X_i the distribution over the string $x_i \in \{0,1\}^n$ as sampled in the verifier's setup phase. That is, $X_1 = U_n$ and for every $i \in [k]$, it holds that $Y_i = C_i(X_i)$ and $X_{i+1} = \mathsf{Ext}(Y_i, Z_i)$, where each Z_i is an iid copy of U_d.
- We denote the subset of strings in $\{0,1\}^m$ having a unique preimage under C_i by S_i (i.e., $S_i = \{y_i : |C_i^{-1}(y_i)| = 1\}$). Abusing notation, we also use S_i to refer to the uniform distribution over the corresponding set.

For a function f, we define ν_f as $\nu_f(x) = |\{x' : f(x') = f(x)\}|$. We say that $x \in \{0,1\}^n$ has siblings under f, if $\nu_f(x) > 1$. When f is clear from the context, we omit it from the notation.

Lemma 4.1. *For every $i \leq i^*$ it holds that* $\Delta\left(X_i, U_n\right) \leq \frac{1}{k \cdot 2^\lambda} + k \cdot \delta$.

Proof. We show by induction on i that $\Delta\left(X_i, U_n\right) \leq (i-1) \cdot \left(\frac{1}{k^2 \cdot 2^\lambda} + \delta\right)$. The lemma follows by the fact that $i \leq k$.

For the base case (i.e., $i = 1$), since X_1 is uniform in $\{0,1\}^n$ we have that $\Delta\left(X_1, U_n\right) = 0$. Let $1 < i \leq i^*$ and suppose that the claim holds for $i-1$. Note that $i-1 < i^*$ and so C_{i-1} is a YES instance circuit.

Claim 4.1.1. $\Delta\left(\mathsf{Ext}(S_{i-1}, U_d), U_n\right) \leq \frac{1}{k^2 \cdot 2^\lambda}$.

Proof. By definition of AI_δ, the set S_{i-1} has cardinality at least $(1-\delta) \cdot 2^n$. Since $\delta < 1/2$, this means that the min-entropy of (the uniform distribution over) S_i is at least $n-1$. The claim follows by the fact that Ext is an extractor for min-entropy $n-1$ with error $\epsilon = \frac{1}{k^2 \cdot 2^\lambda}$.

We denote by W_i the distribution obtained by selecting (x_{i-1}, z_{i-1}) uniformly in $\{0,1\}^n \times \{0,1\}^d$ and outputting $\mathsf{Ext}\left(C_{i-1}(x_{i-1}), z_{i-1}\right)$.

Claim 4.1.2. $\Delta(W_i, U_n) \leq \frac{1}{k^2 \cdot 2^\lambda} + \delta$.

Proof. Consider the event that X_{i-1} has a sibling (under C_{i-1}). Since C_{i-1} is a YES instance, this event happens with probability at most δ. On the other hand, the distribution of $C_i(X_{i-1})$, conditioned on X_{i-1} not having a sibling, is simply uniform in S_i. The claim now follows by Claim 4.1.1 and Fact 2.2.

We are now ready to bound $\Delta(X_i, U_n)$, as follows:

$$\Delta(X_i, U_n) \leq \Delta(X_i, W_i) + \Delta(W_i, U_n)$$
$$= \Delta\Big(\mathsf{Ext}(C_{i-1}(X_{i-1}), U_d), \mathsf{Ext}(C_{i-1}(U_n), U_d)\Big) + \Delta(W_i, U_n)$$
$$\leq \Delta(X_{i-1}, U_n) + \frac{1}{k^2 \cdot 2^\lambda} + \delta$$
$$\leq (i-1) \cdot \left(\frac{1}{k^2 \cdot 2^\lambda} + \delta\right),$$

where the first inequality is by the triangle inequality, the second inequality is by Fact 2.1 and Claim 4.1.2 and the third inequality is by the inductive hypothesis.

Definition 4.2. *We say that the tuple* $(x_1, h, z_1, ...z_k)$ *is* good *if the following holds, where we recursively define* $y_i = C_i(x_i)$ *and* $x_{i+1} = \mathsf{Ext}(y_i, z_i)$, *for every* $i < i^*$:

1. *For every* $i < i^*$, *there does not exist* $x_i' \neq x_i$ *s.t.* $C_i(x_i) = C_i(x_i')$ *(i.e.,* x_i *has no siblings).*
2. *For every* $i < i^*$, *there does not exist* $(y_i', z_i') \neq (y_i, z_i)$ *such that* $y_i' \in S_i$, $\mathsf{Ext}(y_i', z_i') = \mathsf{Ext}(y_i, z_i)$ *and* $h(y_i', z_i') = h(y_i, z_i)$.

Lemma 4.3. *The tuple* $(x_1, h, z_1, ...z_k)$ *sampled by the verifier* V *is good with probability at least* $1 - O(k^2 \cdot \delta + 2^{-\lambda})$.

In order to prove Lemma 4.3, we first establish the following proposition, which bounds the number of preimages of a random output of the extractor.

Proposition 4.4. *For any* $S \subseteq \{0,1\}^m$ *with* $2^{n-1} \leq |S| \leq 2^n$ *and any security parameter* $\lambda > 1$, *it holds that:*

$$\Pr_{y \leftarrow S, z \leftarrow U_d}\big[\nu_{\mathsf{Ext}}(y, z) > 2^{d+\lambda}\big] \leq \epsilon + \frac{1}{2^\lambda}.$$

Proof. Throughout the current proof we use ν as a shorthand for ν_{Ext}. Abusing notation, we also use S to refer to the uniform distribution over the set S.

For a given security parameter $\lambda > 1$, denote by H (for "heavy") the set of all $(y, z) \in S \times \{0,1\}^d$ that have $\nu(y, z) > |S| \cdot 2^{d-n+\lambda}$, and by $\mathsf{Ext}(H)$ the set $\{\mathsf{Ext}(y, z) : (y, z) \in H\}$. By definition, for any $z \in \mathsf{Ext}(H)$, we have that $\Pr[\mathsf{Ext}(S, U_d) = z] > 2^{-n+\lambda}$. This implies that:

$$|\mathsf{Ext}(H)| < 2^{n-\lambda}.$$

Note again that for any $z \in \mathsf{Ext}(H)$, the above probability is more than 2^{-n}, which is the probability assigned to z by the uniform distribution U_n. It then follows from the definition of statistical distance that:

$$\Delta\left(\mathsf{Ext}(S,U_d),U_n\right) \geq \sum_{z \in \mathsf{Ext}(H)} \left(\Pr\left[\mathsf{Ext}(S,U_d) = z\right] - 2^{-n}\right)$$

$$= \Pr\left[\mathsf{Ext}(S,U_d) \in \mathsf{Ext}(H)\right] - |\mathsf{Ext}(H)| \cdot 2^{-n}$$

$$> \Pr\left[\mathsf{Ext}(S,U_d) \in \mathsf{Ext}(H)\right] - 2^{-\lambda}.$$

Since $|S| \geq 2^{n-1}$, the min entropy of S is at least $n-1$, and therefore, it holds that $\Delta\left(\mathsf{Ext}(S,U_d),U_n\right) \leq \epsilon$. Together with the fact that $\Pr\left[\mathsf{Ext}(S,U_d) \in \mathsf{Ext}(H)\right] = \Pr\left[(S,U_d) \in H\right]$, we have:

$$\Pr_{y \leftarrow S, z \leftarrow U_d}\left[\nu(y,z) > |S| \cdot 2^{d-n+\lambda}\right] \leq \epsilon + \frac{1}{2^{\lambda}}.$$

And since $|S| \leq 2^n$ we have

$$\Pr_{y \leftarrow S, z \leftarrow U_d}\left[\nu(y,z) > 2^{d+\lambda}\right] \leq \epsilon + \frac{1}{2^{\lambda}}.$$

Using Proposition 4.4 we are now ready to prove Lemma 4.3.

Proof (Proof of Lemma 4.3). For any $i < i^*$, let E_i denote the event that *either* (1) there exists $x_i' \neq x_i$ such that $C_i(x_i) = C_i(x_i')$, or (2) there exists $(y_i',z_i') \neq (y_i,z_i)$ such that $y_i' \in S_i$, $\mathsf{Ext}(y_i',z_i') = \mathsf{Ext}(y_i,z_i)$ and $h(y_i',z_i') = h(y_i,z_i)$, where $(x_1,\ldots,x_{k+1},y_1,\ldots,y_k,z_1,\ldots,z_k)$ are as sampled by the verifier.

Lemma 4.3 follows from the following claim, and a union bound over all $i \in [k]$.

Claim 4.4.1. $\Pr[E_i] \leq (k+1) \cdot \delta + \frac{4}{k \cdot 2^{\lambda}}$, for every $i \in [k]$.

Proof. We first analyze the probability for the event E_i when x_i is sampled uniformly at random. By definition of AI_{δ}:

$$\Pr_{x_i \leftarrow U_n}\left[x_i \text{ has siblings }\right] \leq \delta.$$

Let us condition on x_i with no siblings being chosen. Under this conditioning, $C_i(x_i)$ is uniform in S_i. We note that $|S_i| \geq (1-\delta) \cdot 2^n \geq 2^{n-1}$ and $|S_i| \leq 2^n$. Thus, by Proposition 4.4 (using security parameter $\lambda + \log k$) it holds that:

$$\Pr_{y_i \leftarrow S_i, z \leftarrow U_d}\left[\nu_{\mathsf{Ext}}(y,z) > k \cdot 2^{\lambda+d}\right] \leq \epsilon + \frac{1}{k \cdot 2^{\lambda}} \leq \frac{2}{k \cdot 2^{\lambda}},$$

where the last inequality follows from the fact that $\epsilon = \frac{1}{k^2 \cdot 2^{\lambda}}$.

Let us therefore assume that the pair (y_i,z_i) has at most $k \cdot 2^{\lambda+d}$ siblings under Ext. We wish to bound the probability that there exists a preimage that collides with (y_i,z_i) under h. Since h is $2^{-(2\lambda+d+2\log k)}$-almost pairwise-independent (into a range of size $2^{2\lambda+d+2\log k}$), for any pair (y', z'), the probability that it collides with (y_i, z_i) under h is at most $\frac{2}{2^{2\lambda+d+2\log k}}$. Since y_i has at most $k \cdot 2^{\lambda+d}$ siblings (under Ext), by a union bound, the probability that any of them collide with (y_i, z_i) (under h) is at most $k \cdot 2^{\lambda+d} \cdot 2^{-(2\lambda+d+2\log k)} = \frac{1}{k \cdot 2^{\lambda}}$.

Thus, when x_i is sampled uniformly at random, the probability that it has a sibling (under C_i) or that there exist (y', z') such that $\mathsf{Ext}(y', z') = \mathsf{Ext}(y_i, z_i)$, where $y'_i \in S_i$ and $h(y', z') = h(y_i, z_i)$, is at most:

$$\delta + \frac{2}{k \cdot 2^{\lambda}} + \frac{1}{k \cdot 2^{\lambda}} = \delta + \frac{3}{k \cdot 2^{\lambda}}.$$

The claim follows by the fact that, by Lemma 4.1, the actual distribution of x_i is $\left(\frac{1}{k \cdot 2^{\lambda}} + k \cdot \delta\right)$-close to uniform.

This concludes the proof of Lemma 4.3.

4.2 Completeness

Let $C_1, \ldots, C_k \in \mathsf{AI}_\delta$. Assume first that V generates a *good* tuple $(x_1, h, z_1, \ldots, z_k)$ (as per Definition 4.2). Observe that in such a case, by construction of the protocol, it holds that $x'_i = x_i$ and $y'_i = y_i$, for every $i \in [k]$. Therefore, the verifier accepts in such a case (with probability 1).

By Lemma 4.3, the tuple $(x_1, h, g, z_1, \ldots, z_k)$ is good with all but $O\left(k^2 \cdot \delta + 2^{-\lambda}\right)$ probability. Thus, the completeness error is upper bounded by $O\left(k^2 \cdot \delta + 2^{-\lambda}\right)$.

4.3 Honest-Verifier Statistical Zero-Knowledge

The simulator is presented in Fig. 3.

The generation of $(x_1, h, g, z_1, \ldots, z_k)$ is identical for the verifier and for the simulator. Assuming that the tuple $(x_1, h, z_1, \ldots, z_k)$ is good, by construction the prover does not abort in the honest execution (as in the case of completeness). Moreover, in this case, each x'_i (resp., (y'_i, z'_i)) found by the prover is equal to x_i (resp., (y_i, z_i)) chosen by the verifier. Therefore, conditioned on the tuple $(x_1, h, z_1, \ldots, z_k)$ being good, the distributions of (1) the transcript generated in the honest execution, and (2) the simulated transcript are identically distributed. The fact that the protocol is honest-verifier statistical zero-knowledge now follows from Lemma 4.3, and by applying Fact 2.2 twice.

4.4 Soundness

Let $C_1, \ldots, C_k : \{0,1\}^n \to \{0,1\}^m$ be such that one of them is a NO instance of AI_δ. Recall that $i^* \in [k]$ denotes the index of the first such NO instance circuit (i.e., C_{i^*} is a NO instance of AI_δ but for every $i < i^*$, it holds that C_i is a YES instance).

We first make two simplifying assumptions. First, recall that value of y_{i^*} is specified by the verifier by having it send $x_{k+1}, \beta_k, \ldots, \beta_{i^*}$ to the prover. Instead,

---

Simulator for the AI_δ Batch Verification Protocol

INPUT: $C_1, \ldots, C_k$

THE SIMULATOR:

1. Sample $h \leftarrow H_n$, $g \leftarrow G_n$ and $x_1 \in \{0,1\}^n$.
2. For $i = 1, \ldots, k$:
   (a) Compute $y_i = C_i(x_i)$.
   (b) Sample $z_i \leftarrow \{0,1\}^d$.
   (c) Compute $\alpha_i = g(x_i)$.
   (d) Compute $\beta_i = h(y_i, z_i)$.
   (e) Compute $x_{i+1} = \text{Ext}(y_i, z_i)$.
3. Output $\text{transcript} = \Big((C_1, \ldots, C_k), (x_1, z_1, \ldots, z_k, h, g), (\alpha_k, \ldots, \alpha_1)\Big)$.

Fig. 3. Simulator for AI_δ batch verification

we will simply assume that the verifier sends y_{i^*} directly to the prover. Since y_{i^*} can be used to generate the verifier's distribution consistently, revealing y_{i^*} only makes the prover's job harder and therefore can only increase the soundness error. Second, we modify the protocol so that the verifier merely checks that $\alpha_{i^*} = g(x_{i^*})$ – if so it accepts and otherwise it rejects. Once again having removed the verifier's other tests can only increase the soundness error.

Thus, it suffices to bound the soundness error of the following protocol. The verifier samples x_{i^*} as in the real protocol, sends $y_{i^*} = C_{i^*}(x_{i^*})$ and the hash function g to the prover and expects to get in response $g(x_{i^*})$. We show that the prover's probability of making the verifier accept is bounded by a constant.

In order to bound the prover's success probability in the foregoing experiment, we first give an upper bound assuming that x_{i^*} is uniform in $\{0,1\}^n$, rather than as specified by the protocol (and, as usual, $y_{i^*} = C_{i^*}(x_{i^*})$). Later we shall remove this assumption using Lemma 4.1, which guarantees that x_{i^*} is actually *close* to uniform.

Let P^* be the optimal prover strategy. Namely, given g and y_{i^*}, the prover P^* outputs the hash value $\alpha_{i^*} \in \{0,1\}^\ell$ with the largest probability mass (i.e., that maximizes $|C_{i^*}^{-1}(y_{i^*}) \cap g^{-1}(\alpha)|$).

Let $\widehat{Y}_{i^*}$ denote the distribution obtained by sampling $x \in \{0,1\}^n$ uniformly at random, conditioned on x have a sibling under C_{i^*} and outputting $C_{i^*}(x)$. Using elementary probability theory we have that:

$$\Pr_{\substack{g \leftarrow G_n \\ x_{i^*} \leftarrow \{0,1\}^n}} \left[P^*(g, y_{i^*}) = g(x_{i^*}) \right] \leq \Pr_{\substack{g \leftarrow G_n \\ x_{i^*} \leftarrow \{0,1\}^n}} \left[P^*(g, y_{i^*}) = g(x_{i^*}) \mid x_{i^*} \text{ has siblings} \right]$$

$$+ \Pr[x_{i^*} \text{ has no siblings}]$$

$$\leq \Pr_{\substack{g \leftarrow G_n \\ y_{i^*} \leftarrow \widehat{Y}_{i^*} \\ x_{i^*} \leftarrow C_{i^*}^{-1}(y_{i^*})}} \left[P^*(g, y_{i^*}) = g(x_{i^*}) \right] + \delta$$

$$= E_{y_{i^*} \leftarrow \widehat{Y}_{i^*}} \left[\Pr_{\substack{g \leftarrow G_n \\ x_{i^*} \leftarrow C_{i^*}^{-1}(y_{i^*})}} \left[P^*(g, y_{i^*}) = g(x_{i^*}) \right] \right] + \delta, \tag{1}$$

where the second inequality follows from the fact that C_{i^*} is a NO instance.

Fix y_{i^*} in the support of $\widehat{Y}_{i^*}$ (i.e., $|C_{i^*}^{-1}(y_{i^*})| \geq 2$) and let $u = |C_{i^*}^{-1}(y_{i^*})|$. We show that $\Pr_{g \in G^n, x_{i^*} \leftarrow C_{i^*}^{-1}(y_{i^*})} \left[P^*(g, y_{i^*}) = g(x_{i^*}) \right]$ is upper bounded by a constant.

Let E be the event (defined only over the choice of g) that for every hash value $\alpha \in \{0,1\}^\ell$, it holds that $|C_{i^*}^{-1}(y_{i^*}) \cap g^{-1}(\alpha)| \leq \frac{7}{8}u$. That is, the event E means that no hash value has more than 7/8 fraction of the probability mass (when sampling x_{i^*} uniformly in $C_{i^*}^{-1}(y_{i^*})$ and outputting $g(x_{i^*})$).[12]

Claim 4.4.2. The event E occurs with probability a least $1/10$.

Proof. Fix a hash value $\alpha \in \{0,1\}^\ell$, and let $X = |C_{i^*}^{-1}(y_{i^*}) \cap g^{-1}(\alpha)|$ be a random variable (over the randomness of g). Observe that X can be expressed as a sum of u pairwise independent Bernoulli random variables, each of which is 1 with probability $2^{-\ell}$ and 0 otherwise. Thus, the expectation of X is $u/2^\ell$ and the variance is $u \cdot 2^{-\ell} \cdot (1 - 2^{-\ell}) \leq u \cdot 2^{-\ell}$. By Chebyshev's inequality (Lemma 2.3), it holds that

$$\Pr \left[X > \frac{7}{8}u \right] \leq \Pr \left[\left| X - \frac{u}{2^\ell} \right| > \frac{3}{4}u \right]$$

$$\leq \frac{Var\,[X]}{(3/4)^2 \cdot u^2}$$

$$\leq \frac{16}{9u} \cdot \frac{1}{2^\ell},$$

where the first inequality follows from the fact that ℓ is a sufficiently large constant. Taking a union bound over all α's we have that the probability that there exists some α with more than 7/8 fraction of the preimages in U (under g) is less than $\frac{16}{9u} < 0.9$, where we use the fact that $u \geq 2$.

---

[12] We remark that the choice of 7/8 is somewhat but not entirely arbitrary. In particular, in case u is very small (e.g., $u = 2$) there may very well be a hash value that has 50% of the probability mass.

Observe that conditioned on the event E, the probability (over $x_{i^*} \leftarrow C_{i^*}^{-1}(y_{i^*})$) that $\mathsf{P}^*(g, y_{i^*}) = g(x_{i^*})$ is at most $7/8$. Thus, by Claim 4.4.2 we obtain that:

$$\Pr_{g, x_{i^*} \leftarrow C_{i^*}^{-1}(y_{i^*})}[\mathsf{P}^*(g, y_{i^*}) \neq g(x_{i^*})] \geq \Pr[E] \cdot \Pr_{g, x_{i^*} \leftarrow C_{i^*}^{-1}(y_{i^*})}[\mathsf{P}^*(g, y_{i^*}) \neq g(x_{i^*})|E] \geq 1/80.$$

Plugging this into Eq. (1), we have that the prover convinces the verifier to accept with probability at most $1 - \frac{1}{80} + \delta$, when x_{i^*} is sampled uniformly at random in $\{0,1\}^n$.

By Lemma 4.1 it holds that $\Delta\left(X_{i^*}, U_n\right) \leq \frac{1}{k \cdot 2^\lambda} + k \cdot \delta$. Therefore (using Fact 2.2), the probability that the verifier accepts when x_{i^*} is sampled as in the protocol is at most $1 - \frac{1}{80} + \frac{1}{k \cdot 2^\lambda} + (k + 1) \cdot \delta$, which is bounded away from 1 since $\delta < \frac{1}{100k^2}$ and λ is sufficiently large.

4.5   Communication Complexity and Verifier Run Time

We first bound the amount of bits sent during the interaction:

- Sending x_{k+1} costs n bits.
- By Lemma 2.10, the seed length of the extractor is $d = \log(m) + O(\log n \cdot \log(\frac{n}{\epsilon})) = \log(N) + \lambda \cdot polylog(n, k)$ and therefore, the cost of sending $z_1, ..., z_k$ is $k \cdot (\log(N) + \lambda \cdot polylog(n, k))$.
- By Lemma 2.8, the description length of $h : \{0,1\}^m \times \{0,1\}^d \to \{0,1\}^{2\lambda+d+2\log k}$, a $\frac{1}{2^{2\lambda+d+2\log k}}$-almost pairwise-independent hash function, is $O(\log(N) + \lambda + polylog(k))$. The cost of sending the hashes $\beta_1, ..., \beta_k$ is $k \cdot O(\lambda + d + \log k) = k \cdot (\log(N) + \lambda \cdot polylog(n, k))$.
- By Lemma 2.7, the description length of $g \in \{0,1\}^n \to \{0,1\}^\ell$, a pairwise independent hash function, is $O(n)$. The cost of sending the hashes $\alpha_1, ..., \alpha_k$ is $O(k)$.

In total, the communication complexity is $O(n) + k \cdot (\log(N) + \lambda \cdot polylog(n, k))$. As for the verifier run time, For each iteration i the verifier running time is as follows:

- Evaluating the circuit C_i takes time $\mathsf{poly}(N)$.
- By Lemma 2.10, evaluating Ext takes time $\mathsf{poly}(m, d) = \mathsf{poly}(N, \log k, \lambda)$.
- By Lemma 2.8, evaluating h on an input of size $m + d$ takes time $\mathsf{poly}(N, \log k, \lambda)$.
- By Lemma 2.7, evaluating g on an input of size n takes time $\mathsf{poly}(n)$.

In total, the verifier running time is $k \cdot \mathsf{poly}(N, \log k, \lambda)$.

Acknowledgments. We thank an anonymous TCC reviewer for pointing that our techniques fall outside the scope of the Holenstein-Renner [HR05] blackbox model (see Remark 1.4).

Inbar Kaslasi and Ron Rothblum were supported in part by a Milgrom family grant, by the Israeli Science Foundation (Grants No. 1262/18 and 2137/19), and the Technion Hiroshi Fujiwara cyber security research center and Israel cyber directorate.

Guy Rothblum has received funding from the European Research Council (ERC) under the European Union's Horizon 2020 research and innovation programme (grant agreement No. 819702).

Adam Sealfon was a PhD student at MIT for part of the duration of this project, and was supported in part by NSF CNS-1413920, Sloan/NJIT 996698, MIT/IBM W1771646, and NSF CNS-1804794.

Prashant Vasudevan was supported in part by AFOSR Award FA9550-19-1-0200, AFOSR YIP Award, NSF CNS Award 1936826, DARPA and SPAWAR under contract N66001-15-C-4065, a Hellman Award and research grants by the Okawa Foundation, Visa Inc., and Center for Long-Term Cybersecurity (CLTC, UC Berkeley). The views expressed are those of the authors and do not reflect the official policy or position of the funding agencies.

References

[Aar04] Aaronson, S.: Limits on efficient computation in the physical world. CoRR, abs/quant-ph/0412143 (2004)

[AH91] Aiello, W., Hastad, J.: Statistical zero-knowledge languages can be recognized in two rounds. J. Comput. Syst. Sci. **42**(3), 327–345 (1991)

[APS18] Alamati, N., Peikert, C., Stephens-Davidowitz, N.: New (and Old) Proof Systems for Lattice Problems. In: Abdalla, M., Dahab, R. (eds.) PKC 2018, Part II. LNCS, vol. 10770, pp. 619–643. Springer, Cham (2018). https://doi.org/10.1007/978-3-319-76581-5_21

[BBD+20] Ball, M., et al.: Cryptography from information loss. In: Vidick, T. (ed.) 11th Innovations in Theoretical Computer Science Conference, ITCS 2020, Seattle, Washington, USA, 12–14 January 2020. LIPIcs, vol. 151, pp. 81:1–81:27. Schloss Dagstuhl - Leibniz-Zentrum für Informatik (2020)

[BDRV18a] Berman, I., Degwekar, A., Rothblum, R.D., Vasudevan, P.N.: From laconic zero-knowledge to public-key cryptography. In: Shacham, H., Boldyreva, A. (eds.) CRYPTO 2018, Part III. LNCS, vol. 10993, pp. 674–697. Springer, Cham (2018). https://doi.org/10.1007/978-3-319-96878-0_23

[BDRV18b] Berman, I., Degwekar, A., Rothblum, R.D., Vasudevan, P.N.: Multicollision resistant hash functions and their applications. In: Nielsen, J.B., Rijmen, V. (eds.) EUROCRYPT 2018, Part II. LNCS, vol. 10821, pp. 133–161. Springer, Cham (2018). https://doi.org/10.1007/978-3-319-78375-8_5

[BDRV19] Berman, I., Degwekar, A., Rothblum, R.D., Vasudevan, P.N.: Statistical difference beyond the polarizing regime. In: Hofheinz, D., Rosen, A. (eds.) TCC 2019, Part II. LNCS, vol. 11892, pp. 311–332. Springer, Cham (2019). https://doi.org/10.1007/978-3-030-36033-7_12

[BFM88] Blum, M., Feldman, P., Micali, S.: Non-interactive zero-knowledge and its applications (extended abstract). In: Proceedings of the 20th Annual ACM Symposium on Theory of Computing, Chicago, Illinois, USA, 2–4 May 1988, pp. 103–112 (1988)

[BGR98] Bellare, M., Garay, J.A., Rabin, T.: Fast batch verification for modular exponentiation and digital signatures. In: Nyberg, K. (ed.) EUROCRYPT 1998. LNCS, vol. 1403, pp. 236–250. Springer, Heidelberg (1998). https://doi.org/10.1007/BFb0054130

[BHK17] Brakerski, Z., Holmgren, J., Kalai, Y.: Non-interactive delegation and batch NP verification from standard computational assumptions. In: Hatami, H., McKenzie, P., King, V. (eds.) Proceedings of the 49th Annual ACM SIGACT Symposium on Theory of Computing, STOC 2017, Montreal, QC, Canada, 19–23 June 2017, pp. 474–482. ACM (2017)

[BL13] Bogdanov, A., Lee, C.H.: Limits of provable security for homomorphic encryption. In: Canetti, R., Garay, J.A. (eds.) CRYPTO 2013, Part I. LNCS, vol. 8042, pp. 111–128. Springer, Heidelberg (2013). https://doi.org/10.1007/978-3-642-40041-4_7

[BSMP91] Blum, M., De Santis, A., Micali, S., Persiano, G.: Noninteractive zero-knowledge. SIAM J. Comput. 20(6), 1084–1118 (1991)

[CHP12] Camenisch, J., Hohenberger, S., Pedersen, M.Ø.: Batch verification of short signatures. J. Cryptol. 25(4), 723–747 (2012)

[CP92] Chaum, D., Pedersen, T.P.: Wallet databases with observers. In: Brickell, E.F. (ed.) CRYPTO 1992. LNCS, vol. 740, pp. 89–105. Springer, Heidelberg (1993). https://doi.org/10.1007/3-540-48071-4_7

[Dru15] Drucker, A.: New limits to classical and quantum instance compression. SIAM J. Comput. 44(5), 1443–1479 (2015)

[DSCP94] De Santis, A., Di Crescenzo, G., Persiano, G.: The knowledge complexity of quadratic residuosity languages. Theor. Comput. Sci. 132(2), 291–317 (1994)

[For89] Fortnow, L.J.: Complexity-theoretic aspects of interactive proof systems. Ph.D. thesis, Massachusetts Institute of Technology (1989)

[GG00] Goldreich, O., Goldwasser, S.: On the limits of nonapproximability of lattice problems. J. Comput. Syst. Sci. 60(3), 540–563 (2000)

[GK93] Goldreich, O., Kushilevitz, E.: A perfect zero-knowledge proof system for a problem equivalent to the discrete logarithm. J. Cryptol. 6(2), 97–116 (1993)

[GKL93] Goldreich, O., Krawczyk, H., Luby, M.: On the existence of pseudorandom generators. SIAM J. Comput. 22(6), 1163–1175 (1993)

[GMR89] Goldwasser, S., Micali, S., Rackoff, C.: The knowledge complexity of interactive proof systems. SIAM J. Comput. 18(1), 186–208 (1989)

[GMR98] Gennaro, R., Micciancio, D., Rabin, T.: An efficient non-interactive statistical zero-knowledge proof system for quasi-safe prime products. In: Gong, L., Reiter, M.K. (eds.) CCS 1998, Proceedings of the 5th ACM Conference on Computer and Communications Security, San Francisco, CA, USA, 3–5 November 1998, pp. 67–72. ACM (1998)

[GSV98] Goldreich, O., Sahai, A., Vadhan, S.: Honest-verifier statistical zero-knowledge equals general statistical zero-knowledge. In: STOC (1998)

[GSV99] Goldreich, O., Sahai, A., Vadhan, S.: Can statistical zero knowledge be made non-interactive? or on the relationship of SZK and NISZK. In: Wiener, M. (ed.) CRYPTO 1999. LNCS, vol. 1666, pp. 467–484. Springer, Heidelberg (1999). https://doi.org/10.1007/3-540-48405-1_30

[GUV07] Guruswami, V., Umans, C., Vadhan, S.P.: Unbalanced expanders and randomness extractors from parvaresh-vardy codes. In: 22nd Annual IEEE Conference on Computational Complexity (CCC 2007), San Diego, California, USA, 13–16 June 2007, pp. 96–108. IEEE Computer Society (2007)

[GV99] Goldreich, O., Vadhan, S.P.: Comparing entropies in statistical zero knowledge with applications to the structure of SZK. In: CCC (1999)

[HHR11] Haitner, I., Harnik, D., Reingold, O.: On the power of the randomized iterate. SIAM J. Comput. 40(6), 1486–1528 (2011)

[HR05] Holenstein, T., Renner, R.: One-way secret-key agreement and applications to circuit polarization and immunization of public-key encryption. In: Shoup, V. (ed.) CRYPTO 2005. LNCS, vol. 3621, pp. 478–493. Springer, Heidelberg (2005). https://doi.org/10.1007/11535218_29

[Ish] Ishai, Y.: Zero-knowledge proofs from information-theoretic proof systems. https://zkproof.org/2020/08/12/information-theoretic-proof-systems/

[Kil92] Kilian, J.: A note on efficient zero-knowledge proofs and arguments (extended abstract). In: Kosaraju, S.R., Fellows, M., Wigderson, A., Ellis, J.A. (eds.) Proceedings of the 24th Annual ACM Symposium on Theory of Computing, Victoria, British Columbia, Canada, 4–6 May 1992, pp. 723–732. ACM (1992)

[KMN+14] Komargodski, I., Moran, T., Naor, M., Pass, R., Rosen, A., Yogev, E.: One-way functions and (im)perfect obfuscation. In: 55th IEEE Annual Symposium on Foundations of Computer Science, FOCS 2014, Philadelphia, PA, USA, 18–21 October 2014, pp. 374–383. IEEE Computer Society (2014)

[KRR+20] Kaslasi, I., Rothblum, G.N., Rothblum, R.D., Sealfon, A., Vasudevan, P.N.: Batch verification for statistical zero knowledge proofs. In: Electronic Colloquium on Computational Complexity (ECCC) (2020)

[KY18] Komargodski, I., Yogev, E.: On distributional collision resistant hashing. In: Shacham, H., Boldyreva, A. (eds.) CRYPTO 2018, Part II. LNCS, vol. 10992, pp. 303–327. Springer, Cham (2018). https://doi.org/10.1007/978-3-319-96881-0_11

[LFKN92] Lund, C., Fortnow, L., Karloff, H.J., Nisan, N.: Algebraic methods for interactive proof systems. J. ACM 39(4), 859–868 (1992)

[LV16] Liu, T., Vaikuntanathan, V.: On Basing Private Information Retrieval on NP-Hardness. In: Kushilevitz, E., Malkin, T. (eds.) TCC 2016, Part I. LNCS, vol. 9562, pp. 372–386. Springer, Heidelberg (2016). https://doi.org/10.1007/978-3-662-49096-9_16

[MV03] Micciancio, D., Vadhan, S.P.: Statistical zero-knowledge proofs with efficient provers: lattice problems and more. In: Boneh, D. (ed.) CRYPTO 2003. LNCS, vol. 2729, pp. 282–298. Springer, Heidelberg (2003). https://doi.org/10.1007/978-3-540-45146-4_17

[NMVR94] Naccache, D., M'Rahi, D., Vaudenay, S., Raphaeli, D.: Can D.S.A. be improved? — complexity trade-offs with the digital signature standard. In: De Santis, A. (ed.) EUROCRYPT 1994. LNCS, vol. 950, pp. 77–85. Springer, Heidelberg (1995). https://doi.org/10.1007/BFb0053426

[NN93] Naor, J., Naor, M.: Small-bias probability spaces: Efficient constructions and applications. SIAM J. Comput. 22(4), 838–856 (1993)

[NV06] Nguyen, M.-H., Vadhan, S.P.: Zero knowledge with efficient provers. In: Proceedings of the 38th Annual ACM Symposium on Theory of Computing, Seattle, WA, USA, 21–23 May 2006, pp. 287–295 (2006)

[NZ96] Nisan, N., Zuckerman, D.: Randomness is linear in space. J. Comput. Syst. Sci. 52(1), 43–52 (1996)

[Oka00] Okamoto, T.: On relationships between statistical zero-knowledge proofs. J. Comput. Syst. Sci. 60(1), 47–108 (2000)

[Ost91] Ostrovsky, R.: One-way functions, hard on average problems, and statistical zero-knowledge proofs. In: Structure in Complexity Theory Conference, pp. 133–138 (1991)

[OV08]   Ong, S.J., Vadhan, S.: An equivalence between zero knowledge and commitments. In: Canetti, R. (ed.) TCC 2008. LNCS, vol. 4948, pp. 482–500. Springer, Heidelberg (2008). https://doi.org/10.1007/978-3-540-78524-8_27

[OW93]   Ostrovsky, R., Wigderson, A.: One-way fuctions are essential for nontrivial zero-knowledge. In: ISTCS, pp. 3–17 (1993)

[PPS15]   Pandey, O., Prabhakaran, M., Sahai, A.: Obfuscation-based non-blackbox simulation and four message concurrent zero knowledge for NP. In: Dodis, Y., Nielsen, J.B. (eds.) TCC 2015, Part II. LNCS, vol. 9015, pp. 638–667. Springer, Heidelberg (2015). https://doi.org/10.1007/978-3-662-46497-7_25

[PV08]   Peikert, C., Vaikuntanathan, V.: Noninteractive statistical zero-knowledge proofs for lattice problems. In: Wagner, D. (ed.) CRYPTO 2008. LNCS, vol. 5157, pp. 536–553. Springer, Heidelberg (2008). https://doi.org/10.1007/978-3-540-85174-5_30

[RRR16]   Reingold, O., Rothblum, G.N., Rothblum, R.D.: Constant-round interactive proofs for delegating computation. In: Proceedings of the 48th Annual ACM SIGACT Symposium on Theory of Computing, STOC 2016, Cambridge, MA, USA, 18–21 June 2016, pp. 49–62 (2016)

[RRR18]   Reingold, O., Rothblum, G.N., Rothblum, R.D.: Efficient batch verification for UP. In: 33rd Computational Complexity Conference, CCC 2018, San Diego, CA, USA, 22–24 June 2018, pp. 22:1–22:23 (2018)

[SCPY98]   De Santis, A., Di Crescenzo, G., Persiano, G., Yung, M.: Image density is complete for non-interactive-SZK. In: Larsen, K.G., Skyum, S., Winskel, G. (eds.) ICALP 1998. LNCS, vol. 1443, pp. 784–795. Springer, Heidelberg (1998). https://doi.org/10.1007/BFb0055102

[Sha92]   Shamir, A.: IP = PSPACE. J. ACM 39(4), 869–877 (1992)

[SV03]   Sahai, A., Vadhan, S.: A complete problem for statistical zero knowledge. J. ACM (JACM) 50(2), 196–249 (2003)

[Vad12]   Vadhan, S.P.: Pseudorandomness. Found. Trends Theor. Comput. Sci. 7(1–3), 1–336 (2012)

[YGLW15]   Yu, Yu., Gu, D., Li, X., Weng, J.: The randomized iterate, revisited - almost linear seed length PRGs from a broader class of one-way functions. In: Dodis, Y., Nielsen, J.B. (eds.) TCC 2015, Part I. LNCS, vol. 9014, pp. 7–35. Springer, Heidelberg (2015). https://doi.org/10.1007/978-3-662-46494-6_2

Public-Coin Zero-Knowledge Arguments with (almost) Minimal Time and Space Overheads

Alexander R. Block[1]([✉]), Justin Holmgren[2], Alon Rosen[3], Ron D. Rothblum[4], and Pratik Soni[5]

[1] Purdue University, West Lafayette, USA
block9@purdue.edu
[2] NTT Research, East Palo Alto, USA
justin.holmgren@ntt-research.com
[3] IDC Herzliya, Herzliya, Israel
alon.rosen@idc.ac.il
[4] Technion, Haifa, Israel
rothblum@cs.technion.ac.il
[5] University of California, Santa Barbara, Santa Barbara, USA
pratik_soni@cs.ucsb.edu

Abstract. Zero-knowledge protocols enable the truth of a mathematical statement to be certified by a verifier without revealing any other information. Such protocols are a cornerstone of modern cryptography and recently are becoming more and more practical. However, a major bottleneck in deployment is the efficiency of the prover and, in particular, the space-efficiency of the protocol.

For every NP relation that can be verified in time T and space S, we construct a public-coin zero-knowledge argument in which the prover runs in time $T \cdot \mathrm{polylog}(T)$ and space $S \cdot \mathrm{polylog}(T)$. Our proofs have length $\mathrm{polylog}(T)$ and the verifier runs in time $T \cdot \mathrm{polylog}(T)$ (and space $\mathrm{polylog}(T)$). Our scheme is in the random oracle model and relies on the hardness of discrete log in prime-order groups.

Our main technical contribution is a new space efficient *polynomial commitment scheme* for multi-linear polynomials. Recall that in such a scheme, a sender commits to a given multi-linear polynomial $P : \mathbb{F}^n \to \mathbb{F}$ so that later on it can prove to a receiver statements of the form "$P(x) = y$". In our scheme, which builds on commitments schemes of Bootle et al. (Eurocrypt 2016) and Bünz et al. (S&P 2018), we assume that the sender is given multi-pass streaming access to the evaluations of P on the Boolean hypercube and we show how to implement both the sender and receiver in roughly time 2^n and space n and with communication complexity roughly n.

1 Introduction

Zero-knowledge protocols are a cornerstone of modern cryptography, enabling the truth of a mathematical statement to be certified by a prover to a verifier

R. Pass and K. Pietrzak (Eds.): TCC 2020, LNCS 12551, pp. 168–197, 2020.
https://doi.org/10.1007/978-3-030-64378-2_7

without revealing any other information. First conceived by Goldwasser, Micali, and Rackoff [27], zero knowledge has myriad applications in both theory and practice and is a thriving research area today. Theoretical work primarily investigates the complexity tradeoffs inherent in zero-knowledge protocols:

- the number of rounds of interaction,
- the number of bits exchanged between the prover and verifier
- the computational complexity of the prover and verifier (e.g. running time, space usage)
- the degree of soundness—in particular, soundness can be statistical or computational, and the protocol may or may not be a proof of knowledge.

ZK-SNARKs (Zero-Knowledge Succinct Non-interactive ARguments of Knowledge) are protocols that achieve particularly appealing parameters: they are *non-interactive* protocols in which to certify an NP statement x with witness w, the prover sends a proof string π of length $|\pi| \ll |w|$. Such proof systems require setup (namely, a common reference string) and (under widely believed complexity-theoretic assumptions [24,25]) are limited to achieving computational soundness.

One of the main bottlenecks limiting the scalability of ZK-SNARKs is the high computational complexity of generating proof strings. In particular, a major problem is that even for the lowest-overhead ZK-SNARKs (see e.g. [4,22,39] and follow-up works), the prover requires $\Omega(T)$ *space* to certify correctness of a time-T computation, even if that computation uses space $S \ll T$.

As typical computations require much less space than time, such space usage can easily become a hard bottleneck. While it is straight-forward to run a program for as long as one's patience allows, a computer's memory cannot be expanded without purchasing additional hardware. Moreover, the memory architecture of modern computer systems is hierarchical, consisting of different tiers (various cache levels, RAM, and nonvolatile storage), with latencies and capacities that increase by orders of magnitude at each successive level. In other words, high space usage can also incur a heavy penalty in running time.

In this work, we focus on uniform non-deterministic computations—that is, proving that a nondeterministic time-T space-S Turing machine accepts an input x. Our objective is to obtain "complexity-preserving" (ZK-)SNARKs [10] for such computations, i.e., SNARKs in which the prover runs in time roughly T and space roughly S. Relatively efficient *privately verifiable* solutions are known [11,29]. In such schemes the verifier holds some secret state that, if leaked, compromises soundness. However, many applications (such as cryptocurrencies or other massively decentralized protocols) require public verifiability, which is the emphasis of our work.

To date, *publicly verifiable* complexity-preserving SNARKs are known only via recursive composition [9,47]. This approach indeed yields SNARKs with prover running time $\tilde{O}(T)$ and space usage $S \cdot \mathrm{polylog}(T)$, but with significant concrete overheads. Recursively composed SNARKs require both the prover and verifier to make non-black-box usage of an "inner" verifier for a different SNARK, leading to enormous computational overhead in practice.

Several recent works [14,16,18] attempt to solve the inefficiency problems with recursive composition, but the protocols in these works rely on heuristic and poorly understood assumptions to justify their soundness. While any SNARK (with a black-box security reduction) inherently relies on non-falsifiable assumptions [23], these SNARKs possess additional troubling features. They rely on hash functions that are modeled as random oracles in the security proof, despite being used in a non-black-box way by the honest parties. Security thus cannot be reduced to a simple computational hardness assumption, even in the random oracle model. Moreover, the practicality of the schemes crucially requires usage of a novel hash function (e.g., Rescue [1]) with algebraic structure designed to maximize the *efficiency* of non-black-box operations. Such hash functions have endured far less scrutiny than standard SHA hash functions, and the algebraic structure could potentially lead to a security vulnerability.

In this work, we ask:

Can we devise a complexity-preserving ZK-SNARK in the random oracle model based on standard cryptographic assumptions?

1.1 Our Results

Our main result is an affirmative answer to this question.

Theorem 1. *Assume that the discrete-log problem is hard in obliviously sampleable[1] prime-order groups. Then, for every* NP *relation that can be verified by a random access machine in time T and space S, there exists a publicly verifiable ZK-SNARK, in the random oracle model, in which both the prover and verifier run in time $T \cdot \mathrm{polylog}(T)$, the prover uses space $S \cdot \mathrm{polylog}(T)$, and the verifier uses space $\mathrm{polylog}(T)$. The proof length is poly-logarithmic in T.*

We emphasize that the verifier in our protocol has similar running time to that of the prover, in contrast to other schemes in the literature that offer *poly-logarithmic* time verification. While this limits the usefulness of our scheme in delegating (deterministic) computations, our scheme is well-geared towards *zero-knowledge* applications in which the prover and verifier are likely to have similar computational resources.

At the heart of our ZK-SNARK for NP relations verifiable by time-T space-S random access machine (RAM) is a new public-coin *interactive* argument of knowledge, in the random oracle model, for the same relation where the prover runs in time $T \cdot \mathrm{polylog}(T)$ and requires space $S \cdot \mathrm{polylog}(T)$. We make this argument zero-knowledge by using standard techniques which incurs minimal

---

[1] By *obliviously sampleable* we mean that there exist algorithms S and S^{-1} such that on input random coins r, the algorithm S samples a uniformly random group element g, whereas on input g, the algorithm S^{-1} samples random coins r that are consistent with the choice of g. In other words, if S uses ℓ random bits then the joint distributions $(U_\ell, S(U_\ell))$ and $(S^{-1}(S(U_\ell)), S(U_\ell))$ are identically distributed, where U_ℓ denotes the uniform distribution on ℓ bit strings..

asymptotic blow-up in the efficiency of the argument [2,20,48]. Finally, applying the Fiat-Shamir transformation [21] to our public-coin zero-knowledge argument yields Theorem 1.

Space-Efficient Polynomial Commitment for Multi-linear Polynomials. The key ingredient in our public-coin interactive argument of knowledge is a new space efficient *polynomial commitment scheme,* which we describe next.

Polynomial commitment schemes were introduced by Kate et al. [32] and have since received much attention [3,7,17,33,49,50], in particular due to their usage in the construction of efficient zero-knowledge arguments. Informally, a polynomial commitment scheme is a cryptographic primitive that allows a committer to send to a receiver a commitment to an n-variate polynomial $Q : \mathbb{F}^n \to \mathbb{F}$, over some finite field $\mathbb{F}$, and later reveal evaluations y of Q on a point $\mathbf{x} \in \mathbb{F}^n$ of the receiver's choice along with a proof that indeed $y = Q(\mathbf{x})$.

In this work we construct polynomial commitment schemes where the space complexity is (roughly) *logarithmic* in the description size of the polynomial. In order to state this result more precisely, we must first determine the type of access that the committer has to the polynomial.

We first note that in this work we restrict our attention to *multi-linear* polynomials (i.e., polynomials which have individual degree 1). Note that such a polynomial $Q : \mathbb{F}^n \to \mathbb{F}$ is uniquely determined by its evaluations on the Boolean hybercube, that is, $\big(Q(0), \ldots, Q(2^n - 1)\big)$, where the integers in $\mathbb{Z}_{2^n}$ are associated with vectors in $\{0, 1\}^n$ in the natural way.

Towards achieving our space efficient implementation, and motivated by our application to the construction of an efficient argument-scheme, we assume that the committer has *multi-pass streaming access* to the evaluations of the polynomial on the Boolean hypercube. Such an access pattern can be modeled by giving the committer access to a read-only tape that is pre-initialized with the values $\big(Q(0), \ldots, Q(2^n - 1)\big)$. At every time-step the committer is allowed to either move the machine head to the right or to restart its position to 0.

Theorem 2 (Informal, see Theorem 5). *Let $\mathbb{G}$ be an obliviously sampleable group of prime-order p and let $Q : \mathbb{F}^n \to \mathbb{F}$ be some n-variate multi-linear polynomial. Assuming the hardness of discrete-log over $\mathbb{G}$ and multi-pass streaming access to the sequence $(Q(0), \ldots, Q(2^n - 1))$, there exists a polynomial commitment scheme for Q in the random oracle model such that*

1. *The commitment consists of one group element, evaluation proofs consist of $O(n)$ group and field elements,*
2. *The committer and receiver perform $\tilde{O}(2^n)$ group and field operations, make $\tilde{O}(2^n)$ queries to the random oracle, and store only $O(n)$ group and field elements, and*
3. *The committer makes $O(n)$ passes over $(Q(0), \ldots, Q(2^n - 1))$.*

Following [32], a number of works have focussed on achieving asymptotically optimal proof sizes (more generally, communication), and time complexity for both committer and receiver. However, the space complexity of the committer has been largely ignored; naively it is lower-bounded by the size of the committer's input (which is a description of the polynomial). As mentioned above, we believe that obtaining a space-efficient polynomial commitment scheme in the streaming model to be of independent interest and may even eventually lead to significantly improved performance of interactive oracle proofs, SNARKS, and related primitives in practice.

We also mention that the streaming model is especially well-suited to our application of building space-efficient SNARKs. The reason is that in such schemes, the prover typically uses a polynomial commitment scheme to commit to a low-degree extension of the transcript of a RAM program, which, naturally, can be generated as a stream in space that is proportional to the space complexity of the underlying RAM program.

At a high level, we use an algebraic homomorphic commitment (e.g., Pedersen commitment [40]) to succinctly commit to the polynomial Q (by committing to the sequence $(Q(0), \ldots, Q(2^n - 1))$). Next, to provide evaluation proofs, our scheme leverages the fact that evaluating Q on point $\mathbf{x}$ reduces to computing an inner-product between $(Q(0), \ldots, Q(2^n - 1))$ and the sequence of Lagrange coefficients defined by the evaluation point $\mathbf{x}$. Relying on the homomorphic properties of our commitment, the basic step of our evaluation protocol is a 2-move (randomized) reduction step which allows the committer to "fold" a statement of size 2^n into a statement of size $2^n/2$. Our scheme is inspired from the "inner-product argument" of Bootle et al. [13] (and its variants [15,48]) but differs in the 2-move reduction step. More specifically, their reduction step folds the left half of $(Q(0), \ldots, Q(2^n - 1))$ with its right half (referred to as msb-based folding as the index of the elements that are folded differ in the most significant bit). This, unfortunately, is not compatible with our streaming model (we explain this shortly). We instead perform the more natural *lsb-based folding* which, indeed, is compatible with the streaming model. We additionally exploit random access to the inner-product argument's setup parameters (defined by the random oracle) and the fact that any component of the coefficient sequence can be computed in polylogarithmic time, i.e. $\mathsf{poly}(n)$ time. We give a high level overview of our scheme in Sect. 2.1.

1.2   Prior Work

Complexity Preserving ZK-SNARKs. Bitansky and Chiesa [11] proposed to construct complexity preserving ZK-SNARKS by first constructing complexity preserving multi-prover interactive proof (MIPs) and then compile them using cryptographic techniques. While our techniques share the same high-level approach, our compilation with a polynomial-commitment scheme yields a publicly verifiable scheme whereas [11] only obtain a designated verifier scheme.

Blumberg et al. [12] give a 2-prover complexity preserving MIP of knowledge, improving (concretely) on the complexity preserving MIP of [11] (who obtain a 2-prover MIP via a reduction from their many-prover MIP). Both Bitansky and Chiesa and Blumberg et al. obtain their MIPs from reducing RAMs to circuits via the reduction of Ben-Sasson et al. [5], then appropriately arithmetize the circuit into an algebraic constraint satisfaction problem. Holmgren and Rothblum [29] obtain a non-interactive protocol based on standard (falsifiable assumptions) by also constructing a complexity preserving MIP for RAMs (achieving no-signaling soundness) and compiling it into an argument using fully-homomorphic encryption (á la [8,30,31]). We remark that [29] reduce a RAM directly to algebraic constraints via a different encoding of the RAM transcript, thereby avoiding the reduction to circuits entirely.

Another direction for obtaining complexity preserving ZK-SNARKS is via recursive composition [9,47], or "bootstrapping". Here, one begins with an "inefficient" SNARK and bootstraps it recursively to produce publicly verifiable complexity preserving SNARKs. While these constructions yield good asymptotics, these approaches require running the inefficient SNARK on many sub-computations. Recent works [14,16,18] describe a novel approach to recursive composition which attempt to solve the inefficiencies of the aforementioned recursive compositions, though at a cost to the theoretical basis for the soundness of their scheme (as discussed above).

Interactive Oracle Proofs. Interactive oracle proofs (IOPs), introduced by Ben-Sasson et al. [6] and independently by Reingold et al. [41], are interactive protocols where a verifier has oracle access to all prover messages. IOPs capture (and generalize), both interactive proofs and PCPs.

A recent line of work [5,12,19,26,42,44,46,48] follows the framework of Kilian [34] and Micali [37] to obtain efficient arguments by constructing efficient IOPs and compiling them into interactive arguments using collision resistant hashing [6,34] or the random oracle model [6,37].

Polynomial Commitments. Polynomial commitment schemes were introduced by Kate et al. [32] and have since been an active area of research. Lines of research for construction polynomial commitment schemes include privately verifiable schemes [32,38], publicly-verifiable schemes with trusted setup [17], and zero-knowledge schemes [49]. More recently, much focus has been on obtaining publicly-verifiable schemes without a trusted setup [3,7,17,33,49,50]. We note that in all prior works on polynomial commitments, the space complexity of the sender is proportional to the description size of the polynomial, whereas we achieve *poly-logarithmic* space complexity.

2   Technical Overview

As mentioned above, the key component in our construction is that of a public-coin interactive argument for RAM computations. The latter construction itself consists of two key technical ingredients. First, we construct a *polynomial interactive oracle proof* (polynomial IOP) for time-T space-S RAM computations in which the prover runs in time $T \cdot \text{polylog}(T)$ and space $S \cdot \text{polylog}(T)$. We note that this ingredient is a conceptual contribution which formalizes prior work in the language of polynomial IOPs. Second, we compile this IOP with a space-efficient extractable *polynomial commitment scheme* where the prover has multi-pass streaming access to the polynomial to which it is committing—a property that plays nicely with the streaming nature of RAM computations. We emphasize that the construction of the space-efficient polynomial commitment scheme is our main technical contribution, and describe our scheme in more detail next.

2.1   Polynomial Commitment to Multi-linear Polynomials in the Streaming Model

Fix a finite field $\mathbb{F}$ of prime order p. Also fix an obliviously sampleable (see Footnote 1) group $\mathbb{G}$ of order p in which the discrete logarithm is hard. Let $H : \{0,1\}^* \to \mathbb{G}$ be the random oracle.

In order to describe our polynomial commitment scheme, we start with some notation. Let n be a positive integer and set $N = 2^n$. We will be considering N-dimensional vectors over $\mathbb{F}$ and will index such vectors using n dimensional binary vectors. For example, if $\mathbf{b} \in \mathbb{F}^{2^6}$ then $\mathbf{b}_{000101} = b_5$. For convenience, we will denote $\mathbf{b} \in \mathbb{F}^N$ by $(b_{\mathbf{c}} : \mathbf{c} \in \{0,1\}^n)$ where $b_{\mathbf{c}}$ is the $\mathbf{c}$-th element of $\mathbf{b}$. For $\mathbf{b} = (b_n, \ldots, b_1) \in \{0,1\}^n$ we refer to b_1 as the least-significant bit (lsb) of $\mathbf{b}$. Finally, for $\mathbf{b} \in \mathbb{F}^N$, we denote by $\mathbf{b}_e$ the restriction of $\mathbf{b}$ to the even indices, that is, $\mathbf{b}_e = (b_{\mathbf{c}0} : \mathbf{c} \in \{0,1\}^{n-1})$. Similarly, we denote by $\mathbf{b}_o = (b_{\mathbf{c}1} : \mathbf{c} \in \{0,1\}^{n-1})$ the restriction of $\mathbf{b}$ to odd indices.

Let $Q : \mathbb{F}^n \to \mathbb{F}$ be a multi-linear polynomial. Recall that such a polynomial can be fully described by the sequence of its evaluations over the Boolean hypercube. More specifically, for any $\mathbf{x} \in \mathbb{F}^n$, the evaluation of Q on $\mathbf{x}$ can be expressed as

$$Q(\mathbf{x}) = \sum_{\mathbf{b} \in \{0,1\}^n} Q(\mathbf{b}) \cdot z(\mathbf{x}, \mathbf{b}), \tag{1}$$

where $z(\mathbf{x}, \mathbf{b}) = \prod_{i \in [n]} \left(b_i \cdot x_i + (1 - b_i) \cdot (1 - x_i) \right)$. We use $\mathbf{Q} \in \mathbb{F}^N$ to denote the restriction of Q to the Boolean hybercube (i.e., $\mathbf{Q} = (Q(\mathbf{b}) : \mathbf{b} \in \{0,1\}^n)$).

Next, we describe the our commitment scheme which has three phases: (a) Setup, (b) Commit and (c) Evaluation.

Setup and Commit Phase. During setup, the committer and receiver both consistently define a sequence of N generators for $\mathbb{G}$ using the random oracle, that is, $\mathbf{g} = (g_{\mathbf{b}} = H(\mathbf{b}) : \mathbf{b} \in \{0,1\}^n)$. Then, given streaming access to $\mathbf{Q}$, the committer computes the Pedersen multi-commitment [40] C defined as

$$C = \prod_{\mathbf{b} \in \{0,1\}^n} (g_{\mathbf{b}})^{Q_{\mathbf{b}}}. \tag{2}$$

For $\mathbf{g} \in \mathbb{G}^{2^n}$ and $\mathbf{Q} \in \mathbb{F}^{2^n}$, we use $\mathbf{g}^{\mathbf{Q}}$ as a shorthand to denote the value $\prod_{\mathbf{b} \in \{0,1\}^n} (g_{\mathbf{b}})^{Q_{\mathbf{b}}}$. Assuming the hardness of discrete-log for $\mathbb{G}$, we note that C in Eq. (2) is a binding commitment to $\mathbf{Q}$ under generators $\mathbf{g}$. Note that the committer only needs to perform a single-pass over $\mathbf{Q}$ and performs N exponentiations to compute C while storing only $O(1)$ number of group and field elements.[2]

Evaluation Phase. On input an evaluation point $\mathbf{x} \in \mathbb{F}^n$, the committer computes and sends $y = Q(\mathbf{x})$ and defines the auxiliary commitment $C_y \leftarrow C \cdot g^y$ for some receiver chosen generator g. Then, both engage in an argument (of knowledge) for the following NP statement which we refer to as the "inner-product" statement:

$$\exists \mathbf{Q} \in \mathbb{Z}_p^N \; : \; y = \langle \mathbf{Q}, \mathbf{z} \rangle \text{ and } C_y = g^y \cdot \mathbf{g}^{\mathbf{Q}} \, , \tag{3}$$

where $\mathbf{z} = (z(\mathbf{x}, \mathbf{b}) : \mathbf{b} \in \{0, 1\}^n)$ as defined in Eq. (1). This step can be viewed as proving knowledge of the decommitment $\mathbf{Q}$ of the commitment C_y, which furthermore is consistent with the inner-product claim that $y = \langle \mathbf{Q}, \mathbf{z} \rangle$.

Inner-product Argument. A basic step in the argument for the above inner-product statement is a 2-move randomized reduction step which allows the prover to decompose the N-sized statement $(C_y, \mathbf{z}, y)$ into two $N/2$-sized statements and then "fold" them into a single $N/2$-sized statement $(\bar{C}_{\bar{y}}, \bar{\mathbf{z}} = (\bar{z}_\mathbf{c} : \mathbf{c} \in \{0, 1\}^{n-1}), \bar{y})$ using the verifier's random challenge. We explain the two steps below (as well as in Fig. 1).

1. Committer computes the cross-product $y_e = \langle \mathbf{Q}_e, \mathbf{z}_o \rangle$ between the even-indexed elements $\mathbf{Q}_e$ with the odd-indexed vectors $\mathbf{z}_o$. Furthermore, it computes a binding commitment C_e that binds y_e (with g) and $\mathbf{Q}_e$ (with $\mathbf{g}_o$). That is,

$$C_e = g^{y_e} \cdot \mathbf{g}_o^{\mathbf{Q}_e} \, , \tag{4}$$

where recall that for $\mathbf{g} = (g_1, \ldots, g_t)$ and $\mathbf{x} = (x_1, \ldots, x_t)$ the expression $\mathbf{g}^{\mathbf{x}} = \prod_{i \in [t]} g_i^{x_i}$. This results in an $N/2$-sized statement $(C_e, \mathbf{z}_o, y_e)$ with witness $\mathbf{Q}_e$. Similarly, as in Fig. 1 it computes the second $N/2$-sized statement $(C_o, \mathbf{z}_e, y_o)$ with witness $\mathbf{Q}_o$. The committer sends (y_e, y_o, C_e, C_o) to the receiver.
2. After receiving a random challenge $\alpha \in \mathbb{F}^*$, committer folds its witness $\mathbf{Q}$ into an $N/2$-sized vector $\bar{\mathbf{Q}} = \alpha \cdot \mathbf{Q}_e + \alpha^{-1} \cdot \mathbf{Q}_o$. More specifically, for every $\mathbf{c} \in \{0, 1\}^{n-1}$,

$$\bar{Q}_\mathbf{c} = \alpha \cdot Q_{\mathbf{c}0} + \alpha^{-1} \cdot Q_{\mathbf{c}1} \, . \tag{5}$$

Similarly, the committer and receiver both compute the rest of the folded statement $(\bar{C}_{\bar{y}}, \bar{\mathbf{z}}, \bar{y})$ as shown in Fig. 1.

Relying on the homomorphic properties of Pedersen commitments, it can be shown that if $\mathbf{Q}$ were a witness to $(C_y, \mathbf{z}, y)$ then $\bar{\mathbf{Q}}$ is a witness for $(\bar{C}_{\bar{y}}, \bar{\mathbf{z}}, \bar{y})$.[3] In the actual protocol, the parties then recurse on smaller statements $(\bar{C}_{\bar{y}}, \bar{\mathbf{z}}, \bar{y})$

---

[2] Here, we treat exponentiation as an atomic operation but note that computing g^α for $\alpha \in \mathbb{Z}_p$ can be emulated, via repeated squarings, by $O(\log p)$ group multiplications while storing only $O(1)$ number of group and field elements.

[3] Albeit under different set of generators but we ignore this for now.

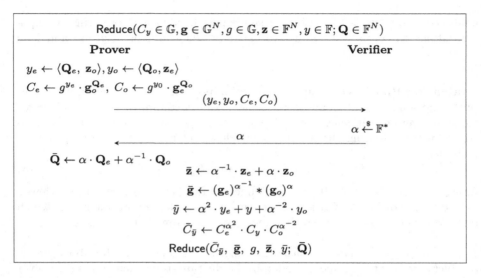

Fig. 1. Our 2-move randomized reduction step for the inner-product protocol where recall that for any $\mathbf{Q} \in \mathbb{F}^N$, we denote by $\mathbf{Q}_e$ the elements of $\mathbf{Q}$ indexed by even numbers where $\mathbf{Q}_o$ denotes the elements with odd indices. On input a statement of size $N > 1$, Reduce results in a statement of size $N/2$.

forming a recursion tree. After $\log N$ steps, the statement is of size 1 in which case the committer sends its witness which is a single field element. This gives an overall communication of $O(\log N)$ field and group elements. Next we briefly discuss the efficiency of the scheme.

Efficiency. For the purpose of this overview, we focus only on the time and space efficiency of the committer in the inner-product argument (the analysis for the receiver is analogous). Recall that in a particular step of the recursion, suppose we are recursing on the $N/2$-sized statement $(\bar{C}_{\bar{y}}, \bar{\mathbf{z}}, \bar{y})$ with witness $\bar{\mathbf{Q}}$, the committer's computation includes computing (a) the cross-product $\langle \bar{\mathbf{Q}}_e, \bar{\mathbf{z}}_o \rangle$ between the even half of $\bar{\mathbf{Q}}$ and the odd half of $\bar{\mathbf{z}}$, and (b) the "cross-exponentiation" $\bar{\mathbf{g}}_o^{\bar{\mathbf{Q}}_e}$ of the even half of $\bar{\mathbf{Q}}$ with the odd half of the generators $\bar{\mathbf{g}}$.[4]

A straightforward approach to compute (a) is to have $\bar{\mathbf{Q}}$ (and $\bar{\mathbf{z}}$) in memory, but this requires the committer to have $\Omega(N)$ space which we want to avoid. Towards a space efficient implementation, first note every element of $\bar{\mathbf{Q}}$ depends on only two, more importantly, consecutive elements of $\mathbf{Q}$. This coupled with streaming access to $\mathbf{Q}$ is sufficient to simulate streaming access to $\bar{\mathbf{Q}}$ while making only **one** pass over $\mathbf{Q}$. Secondly, by definition, computing any element of $\mathbf{z}$ requires only $O(\log N)$ field operations while storing only $O(n)$ field elements This then allows to compute any element of $\bar{\mathbf{z}}$ on the fly with $\mathrm{polylog}(N)$ operations. Given the simulated streaming access to $\bar{\mathbf{Q}}$ along with

---

[4] Efficiency for $\langle \bar{\mathbf{Q}}_o, \bar{\mathbf{z}}_e \rangle$ and $\bar{\mathbf{g}}_e^{\bar{\mathbf{Q}}_o}$ can be argued similarly.

Scheme	[13,15] (msb-based)	This work (lsb-based)
$\bar{Q}_{\mathbf{b}}$	$\alpha \cdot Q_{0\mathbf{b}} + \alpha^{-1} \cdot Q_{1\mathbf{b}}$	$\alpha \cdot Q_{\mathbf{b}0} + \alpha^{-1} \cdot Q_{\mathbf{b}1}$
$\bar{z}_{\mathbf{b}}$	$\alpha^{-1} \cdot z_{0\mathbf{b}} + \alpha \cdot z_{1\mathbf{b}}$	$\alpha^{-1} \cdot z_{\mathbf{b}0} + \alpha \cdot z_{\mathbf{b}1}$
$\bar{g}_{\mathbf{b}}$	$(g_{0\mathbf{b}})^{\alpha^{-1}} * (g_{1\mathbf{b}})^{\alpha}$	$(g_{\mathbf{b}0})^{\alpha^{-1}} * (g_{\mathbf{b}1})^{\alpha}$

Fig. 2. Table highlights the differences between the 2-move randomized reduction steps of the inner-product argument of [13,15] (second column) and our scheme (third column). Specifically, given $\mathbf{Q}, \mathbf{z}, \mathbf{g}$ of size 2^n, the rows describe the definition of the $2^n/2$ sized vectors $\bar{\mathbf{Q}}, \bar{\mathbf{z}}, \bar{\mathbf{g}}$ respectively where $\mathbf{b} \in \{0,1\}^{n-1}$.

the ability to compute any element of $\bar{\mathbf{z}}$ on the fly is sufficient to compute the $\langle \bar{\mathbf{Q}}_e, \bar{\mathbf{z}}_o \rangle$. Note this step, overall, requires performing only a single pass over $\mathbf{Q}$ and $N \cdot \text{polylog} N$ operations, and storing only the evaluation point $\mathbf{x}$ and verifier challenge α (along with some book-keeping). The computation of (b) is handled similarly, except that here we crucially leverage the fact that $\mathbf{g}$ is defined using the random oracle, and hence the committer has random access to all of the generators in $\mathbf{g}$. Relying on similar ideas as in (a), the committer can compute $\bar{\mathbf{g}}_o^{\bar{\mathbf{Q}}_e}$ while additionally making $O(N)$ queries to the random oracle. Overall, this gives the required prover efficiency. Please see Sect. 4.3 for a full discussion on the efficiency.

Comparison with the 2-move Reduction Step of [13,48]. In their protocol, a major difference is in how the folding is performed (Step 2, Fig. 1). We list concrete differences in Fig. 2. But at a high level, since they fold the first element $Q_{00^{n-1}}$ with the $N/2$-nd element $Q_{10^{n-1}}$, it takes at least a one pass over $\mathbf{Q}$ to even compute the first element of $\bar{\mathbf{Q}}$, thereby requiring $\Omega(N)$ passes over $\mathbf{Q}$ which is undesirable.[5] Although we differ in the 2-move reduction steps, the security of our scheme follows from ideas similar to [13,48].

2.2 Polynomial IOPs for RAM Programs

The second ingredient we use to obtain space-efficient interactive arguments for NP relations verifiable by time-T space-S RAMs is a space-efficient *polynomial interactive oracle proof system* [6,17,41]. Informally, an interactive oracle proof (IOP) is an interactive protocol such that in each round the verifier sends a message to the prover, and the prover responds with proof string that the verifier can query in only a few locations. A polynomial IOP is an IOP where the proof string sent by the prover is a polynomial (i.e, all evaluations of a polynomial on a domain), and if a cheating prover successfully convinces a verifier then the proof string is consistent with some polynomial.

---

[5] When a polynomial commitment is used in building arguments, it takes $O(N)$ time to stream $\mathbf{Q}$, and requiring $\Omega(N)$ passes results in a prover that runs in quadratic time.

We consider a variant of the polynomial IOP model in which the prover sends messages which are encoded by the channel; in particular, the time and space complexity of the encoding computed by the channel do not factor into the complexity of the prover. For our purposes, we use the polynomial IOP that is implicit in [12] and consider it with a channel which computes multi-linear extensions of the prover messages. We briefly describe the IOP construction for completeness (see Sect. 5 for more details). The polynomial IOP at its core first leverages the space-efficient RAM to arithmetic circuit satisfiability reduction of [12] (adapting techniques of [5]). This reduction transforms a time-T space-S RAM into a circuit of size $T \cdot \mathrm{polylog}(T)$ and has the desirable property (for our purposes) that the circuit can be accessed by the prover in a streaming manner: the assignment of gate values in the circuit can be streamed "gate-by-gate" in time $T \cdot \mathrm{polylog}(T)$ and space $S \cdot \mathrm{polylog}(T)$, which, in particular, allows a prover to compute a correct transcript of the circuit in time $T \cdot \mathrm{polylog}(T)$ and space $S \cdot \mathrm{polylog}(T)$.

The prover sends the verifier an oracle that is the multi-linear extension of the gate values (i.e., the transcript), where we remark that this extension is computed by the channel. The correctness of the computation is reduced to an algebraic claim about a low degree polynomial which is identically 0 on the Boolean hypercube if and only if the circuit is satisfied by the given witness. Finally, the prover and verifier engage in the classical sum-check protocol [36, 45] to verify that the constructed polynomial indeed vanishes on the Boolean hypercube.

Theorem 3. *There exists a public-coin polynomial IOP over a channel which encodes prover messages as multi-linear extensions for* NP *relations verifiable by a time-T space-S random access machine M such that if $y = M(x; w)$ then*

1. *The* IOP *has perfect completeness and statistical soundness, and has $O(\log(T))$ rounds;*
2. *The prover runs in time $T \cdot \mathrm{polylog}(T)$ and space $S \cdot \mathrm{polylog}(T)$ (not including the space required for the oracle) when given input-witness pair $(x; w)$ for M, sends a single polynomial oracle in the first round, and has $\mathrm{polylog}(T)$ communication in all subsequent rounds; and*
3. *The verifier runs in time $(|x| + |y|) \cdot \mathrm{polylog}(T)$, space $\mathrm{polylog}(T)$, and has query complexity 3.*

2.3 Obtaining Space-Efficient Interactive Arguments

We compile Theorem 3 and Theorem 2 into a space-efficient interactive argument scheme for NP relations verifiable by RAM computations.

Theorem 4 (Informal, see Theorem 6). *There exists a public-coin inter-active argument for* NP *relations verifiable by a time-T space-S random access machine M, in the random oracle model, under the hardness of discrete-log in obliviously sampleable prime-order groups such that:*

1. *The prover runs in time $T \cdot \mathrm{polylog}(T)$ and space $S \cdot \mathrm{polylog}(T)$;*

2. *The verifier runs in time $T \cdot \text{polylog}(T)$ and space $\text{polylog}(T)$; and*
3. *The round complexity is $O(\log T)$ and the communication complexity is $\text{polylog}(T)$.*

The interactive argument of Theorem 4 is obtained by modifying the polynomial IOP of Theorem 3 with the commitment scheme of Theorem 2 in the following manner. First, the prover uses the polynomial commitment scheme to send a commitment to the multi-linear extension of the gate values rather than an oracle. This is possible to do in a space-efficient manner because of the streaming nature of RAM computations and the streaming nature of the IOP. Second, the verifier oracle querie are replaced with the prover and verifier engaging in the evaluation protocol of the polynomial commitment scheme. The remainder of the IOP protocol remains unchanged. Thus we obtain Theorem 4. We obtain Theorem 1 by transforming the interactive argument to a zero-knowledge interactive argument using standard techniques, then apply the Fiat-Shamir transformation [21].

3   Preliminaries

We let λ denote the security parameter, let $n \in \mathbb{N}$ and $N = 2^n$. For a finite, non-empty set S, we let $x \xleftarrow{\$} S$ denote sampling element x from S uniformly at random. We let $\text{Primes}(1^\lambda)$ denote the set of all λ-bit primes. We let $\mathbb{F}_p$ denote a finite field of prime cardinality p, often use lower-case Greek letters to denote elements of $\mathbb{F}$, e.g., $\alpha \in \mathbb{F}$. For a group $\mathbb{G}$, we denote elements of $\mathbb{G}$ with sans-serif font; e.g., $\mathsf{g} \in \mathbb{G}$. We use boldface lowercase letters to denote binary vectors, e.g. $\mathbf{b} \in \{0,1\}^n$. We assume for a bit string $(b_n, \ldots, b_1) = \mathbf{b} \in \{0,1\}^n$ that b_n is the most significant bit and b_1 is the least significant bit. For bit string $\mathbf{b} \in \{0,1\}^n$ and $b \in \{0,1\}$ we let $b\mathbf{b}$ (resp., $\mathbf{b}b$) denote the string $(b \circ \mathbf{b}) \in \{0,1\}^{n+1}$ (resp.,$(\mathbf{b} \circ b) \in \{0,1\}^{n+1}$), where "$\circ$" is the string concatenation operator. We use boldface lowercase Greek denotes $\mathbb{F}$ vectors, e.g., $\boldsymbol{\alpha} \in \mathbb{F}^n$, and let $\boldsymbol{\alpha} = (\alpha_n, \ldots, \alpha_1)$ for $\alpha_i \in \mathbb{F}$. We let uppercase letters denote sequences and let corresponding lowercase letters to denote its elements, e.g., $Y = (y_{\mathbf{b}} \in \mathbb{F} : \mathbf{b} \in \{0,1\}^n)$ is a sequence of 2^n elements in $\mathbb{F}$. We denote by $\mathbb{F}^N$ the set of all sequences over $\mathbb{F}$ of size N.

Random Oracle. We let $\mathcal{U}(\lambda)$ denote the set of all functions that map $\{0,1\}^*$ to $\{0,1\}^\lambda$. A random oracle with security parameter λ is a function $H : \{0,1\}^* \rightarrow \{0,1\}^\lambda$ sampled uniformly at random from $\mathcal{U}(\lambda)$.

3.1   The Discrete-Log Relation Assumption

Let GGen be an algorithm that on input $1^\lambda \in \mathbb{N}$ returns $(\mathbb{G}, p, \mathsf{g})$ such that $\mathbb{G}$ is the description of a finite cyclic group of prime order p, where p has length λ, and g is a generator of $\mathbb{G}$.

Assumption 1 (Discrete-log Assumption). *The Discrete-log Assumption holds for* GGen *if for all PPT adversaries A there exists a negligible function* $\mu(\lambda)$ *such that*

$$\Pr\left[\alpha' = \alpha : (\mathbb{G}, \mathsf{g}, p) \xleftarrow{\$} \mathsf{GGen}(1^\lambda),\ \alpha \xleftarrow{\$} \mathbb{Z}_p, \alpha' \xleftarrow{\$} A(\mathbb{G}, \mathsf{g}, \mathsf{g}^\alpha)\right] \le \mu(\lambda)\ .$$

For our purposes, we use the following variant of the discrete-log assumption which is equivalent to Assumption 1.

Assumption 2 (Discrete-log Relation Assumption [13]). *The Discrete-log Relation Assumption holds for* GGen *if for all PPT adversaries A and for all* $n \ge 2$ *there exists a negligible function* $\mu(\lambda)$ *such that*

$$\Pr\left[\exists \alpha_i \ne 0 \wedge \prod_{i=1}^n \mathsf{g}_i^{\alpha_i} = 1 : \begin{array}{l} (\mathbb{G}, \mathsf{g}, p) \xleftarrow{\$} \mathsf{GGen}(1^\lambda),\ \mathsf{g}_1, \ldots, \mathsf{g}_n \xleftarrow{\$} \mathbb{G}\ , \\ (\alpha_1, \ldots, \alpha_n) \in \mathbb{Z}_p^n \xleftarrow{\$} A(\mathbb{G}, \mathsf{g}_1, \ldots, \mathsf{g}_n)\ . \end{array}\right] \le \mu(\lambda)\ .$$

We say $\prod_{i=1}^n \mathsf{g}_i^{\alpha_i} = 1$ is a non-trivial discrete log relation between $\mathsf{g}_1, \ldots, \mathsf{g}_n$. The Discrete Log Relation assumption states that an adversary can't find a non-trivial relation between randomly chosen group elements.

3.2 Interactive Arguments of Knowledge in ROM

Definition 1 (Witness Relation Ensemble). *A* witness relation ensemble *or* relation ensemble *is a ternary relation* $\mathcal{R}_L$ *that is polynomially bounded, polynomial time recognizable and defines a language* $\mathcal{L} = \{(pp, x) : \exists w \text{ s.t. } (pp, x, w) \in \mathcal{R}_\mathcal{L}\}$. *We omit pp when considering languages recognized by binary relations.*

Definition 2 (Interactive Arguments [27]). *Let* $\mathcal{R}$ *be some relation ensemble. Let* (P, V) *denote a pair of PPT interactive algorithms and* Setup *denote a non-interactive setup algorithm that outputs public parameters pp given security parameter* 1^λ. *Let* $\langle P(pp, x, w), V(pp, x) \rangle$ *denote the output of V's interaction with P on common inputs public parameter pp and statement x where additionally P has the witness w. The triple* (Setup, P, V) *is an* argument *for* $\mathcal{R}$ *in the* random oracle model (ROM) *if*

1. *Perfect Completeness. For any adversary A*

$$\Pr\left[(x, w) \notin \mathcal{R} \text{ or } \langle P^H(pp, x, w), V^H(pp, x) \rangle = 1\right] = 1\ ,$$

   where probability is taken over $H \xleftarrow{\$} \mathcal{U}(\lambda), pp \xleftarrow{\$} \mathsf{Setup}^H(1^\lambda), (x, w) \xleftarrow{\$} A^H(pp)$.

2. *Computational Soundness. For any non-uniform PPT adversary A*

$$\Pr\left[\forall w\ (x, w) \notin \mathcal{R} \text{ and } \langle A^H(pp, x, st), V^H(pp, x) \rangle = 1\right] \le \mathsf{negl}(\lambda)\ ,$$

   where probability is taken over $H \xleftarrow{\$} \mathcal{U}(\lambda), pp \xleftarrow{\$} \mathsf{Setup}^H(1^\lambda), (x, st) \xleftarrow{\$} A^H(pp)$.

Remark 1. Usually completeness is required to hold for all $(x, w) \in \mathcal{R}$. However, for the argument systems used in this work, statements x depends on pp output by Setup and the random oracle H. We model this by asking for completeness to hold for statements sampled by an adversary A, that is, for $(x, w) \xleftarrow{\$} A(pp)$.

For our applications, we will need (Setup, P, V) to be an argument of knowledge. Informally, in an argument of knowledge for $\mathcal{R}$, the prover convinces the verifier that it "knows" a witness w for x such that $(x, w) \in \mathcal{R}$. In this paper, knowledge means that the argument has *witness-extended emulation* [28,35].

Definition 3 (Witness-Extended Emulation). *Given a public-coin interactive argument tuple* (Setup, P, V) *and some arbitrary prover algorithm* P^*, *let* Record(P^*, pp, x, st) *denote the message transcript between* P^* *and* V *on shared input* x, *initial prover state* st, *and* pp *generated by* Setup. *Furthermore, let* $\mathsf{E}^{\mathsf{Record}(P^*, pp, x, st)}$ *denote a machine* E *with a transcript oracle for this interaction that can be rewound to any round and run again on fresh verifier randomness. The tuple* (Setup, P, V) *has witness-extended emulation if for every deterministic polynomial-time* P^* *there exists an expected polynomial-time emulator* E *such that for all non-uniform polynomial-time adversaries* A *the following holds:*

$$\Pr\left[A^H(tr) = 1 : \begin{array}{c} H \xleftarrow{\$} \mathcal{U}(\lambda), \ pp \xleftarrow{\$} \mathsf{Setup}^H(1^\lambda), \\ (x, st) \xleftarrow{\$} A^H(pp), \ tr \xleftarrow{\$} \mathsf{Record}^H(P^*, pp, x, st) \end{array}\right]$$

$$\approx \Pr\left[\begin{array}{c} A^H(tr) = 1 \ and \\ tr \ accepting \implies (x, w) \in \mathcal{R} \end{array} : \begin{array}{c} H \xleftarrow{\$} \mathcal{U}(\lambda), \ pp \xleftarrow{\$} \mathsf{Setup}^H(1^\lambda), \\ (x, st) \xleftarrow{\$} A^H(pp), \\ (tr, w) \xleftarrow{\$} \mathsf{E}^{H, \mathsf{Record}^H(P^*, pp, x, st)}(pp, x) \end{array}\right]$$

It was shown in [13,17] that witness-extended emulation is implied by an extractor that can extract the witness given a tree of accepting transcripts. For completeness we state this—dubbed Generalized Forking Lemma—more formally below but refer to [17] for the proof.

Definition 4 (Tree of Accepting Transcripts). *An* $(n_1, \ldots, n_r)$*-tree of accepting transcripts for an interactive argument on input* x *is defined as follows: The root of the tree is labelled with the statement* x. *The tree has* r *depth. Each node at depth* $i < r$ *has* n_i *children, and each child is labeled with a distinct value for the* i*-th challenge. An edge from a parent node to a child node is labeled with a message from* P *to* V. *Every path from the root to a leaf corresponds to an accepting transcript, hence there are* $\prod_{i=1}^{r} n_i$ *distinct accepting transcripts overall.*

Lemma 1 (Generalized Forking Lemma [13,17]). *Let* (Setup, P, V) *be an* r*-round public-coin interactive argument system for a relation* $\mathcal{R}$. *Let* T *be a tree-finder algorithm that, given access to a* Record($\cdot$) *oracle with rewinding capability, runs in polynomial time and outputs an* $(n_1, \ldots, n_r)$*-tree of accepting transcripts with overwhelming probability. Let* Ext *be a deterministic polynomial-time extractor algorithm that, given access to* T*'s output, outputs a witness* w *for the statement* x *with overwhelming probability over the coins of* T. *Then,* (P, V) *has witness-extended emulation.*

Definition 5 (Public-coin). *An argument of knowledge is called public-coin if all messages sent from the verifier to the prover are chosen uniformly at random and independently of the prover's messages, i.e., the challenges correspond to the verifier's randomness* H.

Zero-Knowledge. We also need our argument of knowledge to be zero-knowledge, that is, to not leak partial information about w apart from what can be deduced from $(x, w) \in \mathcal{R}$.

Definition 6 (Zero-knowledge Arguments). *Let* (Setup, P, V) *be an public-coin interactive argument system for witness relation ensemble* $\mathcal{R}$*. Then,* (Setup, P, V) *has computational zero-knowledge with respect to an auxiliary input if for every PPT interactive machine* V^**, there exists a PPT algorithm* S*, called the simulator, running in time polynomial in the length of its first input, such that for every* $(x, w) \in \mathcal{R}$ *and any* $z \in \{0, 1\}^*$:

$$View(\langle P(w), V^*(z) \rangle(x)) \approx_c S(x, z),$$

where $View(\langle P(w), V^*(z) \rangle(x))$ *denotes the distribution of the transcript of interaction between* P *and* V^**, and* $\approx_c$ *denotes that the two quantities are computationally indistinguishable. If the statistical distance between the two distributions is negligible then the interactive argument is said to be statistical zero-knowledge. If the simulatro is allowed to abort with probability at most* $1/2$*, but the distribution of its output conditioned on not aborting is identically distributed to* $View(\langle P(w), V^*(z) \rangle(x))$*, then the interactive argument is called perfect zero-knowledge.*

3.3   Multi-linear Extensions

Definition 7 (Multi-linear Extensions). *Let* $n \in \mathbb{N}$*,* $\mathbb{F}$ *be some finite field and let* $W : \{0, 1\}^n \to \mathbb{F}$*. Then, the multi-linear extension of* W *(denoted as* $\mathsf{MLE}(W, \cdot) : \mathbb{F}^n \to \mathbb{F}$*) is the (unique) multi-linear polynomial that agrees with* W *on* $\{0, 1\}^n$*. Equivalently,*

$$\mathsf{MLE}(W, \boldsymbol{\zeta} \in \mathbb{F}^n) = \sum_{\mathbf{b} \in \{0,1\}^n} W(\mathbf{b}) \cdot \prod_{i=1}^{n} \beta(b_i, \zeta_i) \, ,$$

where $\beta(b, \zeta) = b \cdot \zeta + (1 - b) \cdot (1 - \zeta)$.

For notational convenience, we denote $\prod_{i=1}^{k} \beta(b_i, \zeta_i)$ by $\overline{\beta}(\mathbf{b}, \boldsymbol{\zeta})$.

Remark 2. There is a bijective mapping between the set of all functions from $\{0, 1\}^n \to \mathbb{F}$ to the set of all n-variate multi-linear polynomials over $\mathbb{F}$. More specifically, as seen above every function $W : \{0, 1\}^n \to \mathbb{F}$ defines a (unique) multi-linear polynomial. Furthermore, every multi-linear polynomial $Q : \mathbb{F}^n \to \mathbb{F}$ is, in fact, the multi-linear extension of the function that maps $\mathbf{b} \in \{0, 1\}^n \to Q(\mathbf{b})$.

Streaming Access to Multi-linear Polynomials. For our commitment scheme, we assume that the committer will have *multi-pass streaming* access to the function table of W (which defines the multi-linear polynomial) in the lexicographic ordering. Specifically, the committer will be given access to a read-only tape that is pre-initialized with the sequence $W = (w_{\mathbf{b}} = W(\mathbf{b}) : \mathbf{b} \in \{0,1\}^n)$. At every time-step the committer is allowed to either move the machine head to the right or to restart its position to 0.

With the above notation, we can now view $\mathsf{MLE}(W, \boldsymbol{\zeta} \in \mathbb{F}^n)$ as an inner-product between W and $Z = (z_{\mathbf{b}} = \overline{\beta}(\mathbf{b}, \boldsymbol{\zeta}) : \mathbf{b} \in \{0,1\}^n)$ where computing $z_{\mathbf{b}}$ requires $O(n = \log N)$ field multiplications for fixed $\boldsymbol{\zeta}$ any $\mathbf{b} \in \{0,1\}^n$.

3.4 Polynomial Commitment Scheme to Multi-linear Extensions

Polynomial commitment schemes, introduced by Kate et al. [32] and generalized in [17,44,48], are a cryptographic primitive that allows one to commit to a multivariate polynomial of bounded degree and later provably reveal evaluations of the committed polynomial. Since we consider only multi-linear polynomials, we tailor our definition to them.

Convention. In defining the syntax of various protocols, we use the following convention for any list of arguments or returned tuple $(a, b, c; d, e)$ – variables listed before semicolon are known both to the prover and verifier whereas the ones after are only known to the prover. In this case, a, b, c are public whereas d, e are secret. In the absence of secret information the semicolon is omitted.

Definition 8 (Commitment to Multi-linear Extensions). *A polynomial commitment to multi-linear extensions is a tuple of protocols* (Setup, Com, Open, Eval)*:*

1. *$pp \xleftarrow{\$} \mathsf{Setup}^H(1^\lambda, 1^N)$ takes as input the unary representations of security parameter $\lambda \in \mathbb{N}$ and size parameter $N = 2^n$ corresponding to $n \in \mathbb{N}$, and produces public parameter pp. We allow pp to contain the description of the field $\mathbb{F}$ over which the multi-linear polynomials will be defined.*
2. *$(\mathsf{C}; d) \xleftarrow{\$} \mathsf{Com}^H(pp, Y)$ takes as input public parameter pp and sequence $Y = (y_{\mathbf{b}} : \mathbf{b} \in \{0,1\}^n) \in \mathbb{F}^N$ that defines the multi-linear polynomial to be committed, and outputs public commitment C and secret decommitment d.*
3. *$b \leftarrow \mathsf{Open}^H(pp, \mathsf{C}, Y, d)$ takes as input pp, a commitment C, sequence committed Y and a decommitment d and returns a decision bit $b \in \{0,1\}$.*
4. *$\mathsf{Eval}^H(pp, \mathsf{C}, \boldsymbol{\zeta}, \gamma; Y, d)$ is a public-coin interactive protocol between a prover P and a verifer V with common inputs—public parameter pp, commitment C, evaluation point $\boldsymbol{\zeta} \in \mathbb{F}^n$ and claimed evaluation $\gamma \in \mathbb{F}$, and prover has secret inputs Y and d. The prover then engages with the verifier in an interactive argument system for the relation*

$$\mathcal{R}_{\mathsf{mle}}(pp) = \left\{ (\mathsf{C}, \boldsymbol{\zeta}, \gamma; Y, d) : \mathsf{Open}^H(pp, \mathsf{C}, Y, d) = 1 \wedge \gamma = \mathsf{MLE}(Y, \boldsymbol{\zeta}) \right\}. \quad (6)$$

The output of V is the output of Eval *protocol.*

Furthermore, we require the following three properties.

1. *Computational Binding.* For all PPT adversaries A and $n \in \mathbb{N}$

$$\Pr\left[b_0 = b_1 \neq 0 \land Y_0 \neq Y_1 : \begin{array}{c} H \xleftarrow{\$} \mathcal{U}(\lambda), \ pp \xleftarrow{\$} \mathsf{Setup}^H(1^\lambda, 1^N) \\ (\mathsf{C}, Y_0, Y_1, d_0, d_1) \xleftarrow{\$} A^H(pp) \\ b_0 \leftarrow \mathsf{Open}^H(pp, \mathsf{C}, Y_0, d_0) \\ b_1 \leftarrow \mathsf{Open}^H(pp, \mathsf{C}, Y_1, d_1) \end{array} \right] \leq \mathsf{negl}(\lambda) \ .$$

2. *Perfect Correctness.* For all $n, \lambda \in \mathbb{N}$ and all $Y \in \mathbb{F}^N$ and $\zeta \in \mathbb{F}^n$,

$$\Pr\left[1 = \mathsf{Eval}^H(pp, \mathsf{C}, Z, \gamma; Y, d) : \begin{array}{c} H \xleftarrow{\$} \mathcal{U}(\lambda), \ pp \xleftarrow{\$} \mathsf{Setup}^H(1^\lambda, 1^N), \\ (\mathsf{C}; d) \xleftarrow{\$} \mathsf{Com}^H(pp, Y), \ \gamma = \mathsf{MLE}(Y, \zeta) \end{array} \right] = 1 \ .$$

3. *Witness-extended Emulation.* We say that the polynomial commitment scheme has witness-extended emulation if Eval has a witness-extended emulation as an interactive argument for the relation ensemble $\{\mathcal{R}_{\mathsf{mle}}(pp)\}_{pp}$ (Eq. (6)) except with negligible probability over the choice of H and coins of $pp \xleftarrow{\$} \mathsf{Setup}^H(1^\lambda, 1^N)$.

4   Space-Efficient Commitment for Multi-linear Extensions

In this section we describe our polynomial commitment scheme for multilinear extensions, a high level overview of which was provided in Sect. 2.1. We dedicate the remainder of the section to proving our main theorem:

Theorem 5. *Let* GGen *be a generator of obliviously sampleable, prime-order groups. Assuming the hardness of discrete logarithm problem for* GGen, *the scheme* $(\mathsf{Setup}, \mathsf{Com}, \mathsf{Open}, \mathsf{Eval})$ *defined in Sect. 4.1 is a polynomial commitment scheme to multi-linear extensions with witness-extended emulation in the random oracle model. Furthermore, for every* $N \in \mathbb{N}$ *and sequence* $Y \in \mathbb{F}^N$, *the committer/prover has multi-pass streaming access to* Y *and*

1. Com *performs* $O(N \log p)$ *group operations, stores* $O(1)$ *field and group elements, requires one pass over* Y, *makes* N *queries to the random oracle, and outputs a single group element. Evaluating* $\mathsf{MLE}(Y, \cdot)$ *requires* $O(N)$ *field operations, storing* $O(1)$ *field elements and requires one pass over* Y.
2. Eval *is public-coin and has* $O(\log N)$ *rounds with* $O(1)$ *group elements sent in every round. Furthermore,*
   - *Prover performs* $O(N \cdot (\log^2 N) \cdot \log p)$ *field and group operations,* $O(N \log N)$ *queries to the random oracle, requires* $O(\log N)$ *passes over* Y *and stores* $O(\log N)$ *field and group elements.*
   - *Verifier performs* $O(N \cdot (\log N) \cdot \log p)$ *field and group operations,* $O(N)$ *queries to the random oracle, and stores* $O(\log N)$ *field and group elements.*

Section 4.1 describes our scheme, Sect. 4.2 and Sect. 4.3 establish its security and efficiency.

Eval$(pp, \mathsf{C}, \zeta, \gamma; Y)$

1:   V samples and sends $\mathbf{g} \xleftarrow{\$} \mathbb{G}$

2:   P and V define $\mathsf{C}_\gamma \leftarrow \mathsf{C} \cdot \mathbf{g}^\gamma$

3:   P and V define the sequence $Z = \left(z_{\mathbf{b}} = \prod_{i=1}^{n} \beta(b_i, \zeta_i) : \mathbf{b} \in \{0,1\}^{n-1} \right)$

4:   P and V engage in $\mathsf{EvalReduce}(\mathsf{C}_\gamma, Z, \gamma, \mathbf{g}, \mathbf{g}; Y)$

EvalReduce$(\mathsf{C}_\gamma \in \mathbb{G}, Z = (z_{\mathbf{b}}), \gamma \in \mathbb{F}, \mathbf{g} = (g_{\mathbf{b}}), \mathbf{g}; Y = (y_{\mathbf{b}}))$

proves knowledge of Y such that: $\mathsf{C}_\gamma = \mathsf{Com}(\mathbf{g}, Y) \cdot \mathbf{g}^\gamma$ and $\langle Y, Z \rangle = \gamma$.

1:   $N \leftarrow |Z|, n \leftarrow \log N$

2:   **if** $N = 1$: **then**

3:       Let $\mathbf{g} = (g'), Z = (z), Y = (y)$

4:       P sends y to V who accepts iff $\mathsf{C}_\gamma = g'^y \cdot \mathbf{g}^{y \cdot z}$

5:   **else**

6:       P computes γ_L and γ_R where

$$\gamma_L \leftarrow \sum_{\mathbf{b} \in \{0,1\}^{n-1}} y_{\mathbf{b}0} \cdot z_{\mathbf{b}1} \; ; \; \gamma_R \leftarrow \sum_{\mathbf{b} \in \{0,1\}^{n-1}} y_{\mathbf{b}1} \cdot z_{\mathbf{b}0}.$$

7:       P computes and sends C_L and C_R where

$$\mathsf{C}_L \leftarrow \mathbf{g}^{\gamma_L} \cdot \prod_{\mathbf{b} \in \{0,1\}^{n-1}} (g_{\mathbf{b}1})^{y_{\mathbf{b}0}} \; ; \; \mathsf{C}_R \leftarrow \mathbf{g}^{\gamma_R} \cdot \prod_{\mathbf{b} \in \{0,1\}^{n-1}} (g_{\mathbf{b}0})^{y_{\mathbf{b}1}}.$$

8:       V samples $\alpha \xleftarrow{\$} \mathbb{F}$ and sends it to P.

9:       P computes and sends $\gamma' = \alpha^2 \cdot \gamma_L + \gamma + \alpha^{-2} \cdot \gamma_R$.

10:      P and V both compute

$$\mathsf{C}'_{\gamma'} \leftarrow (\mathsf{C}_L)^{\alpha^2} \cdot \mathsf{C}_\gamma \cdot (\mathsf{C}_R)^{\alpha^{-2}},$$

$$Z' = \left(z'_{\mathbf{b}} = \alpha^{-1} \cdot z_{\mathbf{b}0} + \alpha \cdot z_{\mathbf{b}1} \right)_{\mathbf{b} \in \{0,1\}^{n-1}},$$

$$\mathbf{g}' = \left(g'_{\mathbf{b}} = (g_{\mathbf{b}0})^{\alpha^{-1}} \cdot (g_{\mathbf{b}1})^{\alpha} \right)_{\mathbf{b} \in \{0,1\}^{n-1}}.$$

11:      P computes $Y' = \left(y'_{\mathbf{b}} = \alpha \cdot y_{\mathbf{b}0} + \alpha^{-1} \cdot y_{\mathbf{b}1} \right)_{\mathbf{b} \in \{0,1\}^{n-1}}.$

12:      **return** $\mathsf{EvalReduce}(\mathsf{C}'_{\gamma'}, Z', \gamma', \mathbf{g}', \mathbf{g}; Y')$

Fig. 3. Eval protocol for the commitment scheme from Sect. 4.1.

4.1   Commitment Scheme

We describe a commitment scheme $(\mathsf{Setup}, \mathsf{Com}, \mathsf{Open}, \mathsf{Eval})$ to multi-linear extensions below.

1. $\mathsf{Setup}^H(1^\lambda, 1^N)$: On inputs security parameter 1^λ and size parameter $N = 2^n$ and access to H, Setup samples $(\mathbb{G}, p, \mathbf{g}) \xleftarrow{\$} \mathsf{GGen}(1^\lambda)$, sets $\mathbb{F} = \mathbb{F}_p$ and returns

$pp = (\mathbb{G}, \mathbb{F}, N, p)$. Furthermore, it implicitly defines a sequence of generators $\mathbf{g} = (g_{\mathbf{b}} = H(\mathbf{b}) : \mathbf{b} \in \{0,1\}^n)$.

2. $\mathsf{Com}^H(pp, Y)$ returns $\mathsf{C} \in \mathbb{G}$ as the commitment and Y as the decommitment where

$$\mathsf{C} \leftarrow \prod_{\mathbf{b} \in \{0,1\}^n} (g_{\mathbf{b}})^{y_{\mathbf{b}}} .$$

3. $\mathsf{Open}^H(pp, \mathsf{C}, Y)$ returns 1 iff $\mathsf{C} = \mathsf{Com}^H(pp, Y)$.

4. $\mathsf{Eval}^H(pp, \mathsf{C}, \boldsymbol{\zeta}, \gamma; Y)$ is an interactive protocol $\langle P, V \rangle$ that begins with V sending a random $\mathbf{g} \xleftarrow{\$} \mathbb{G}$. Then, both P and V compute the commitment $\mathsf{C}_\gamma \leftarrow \mathsf{C} \cdot \mathbf{g}^\gamma$ to additionally bind the claimed evaluation γ. Then, P and V engage in an interactive protocol $\mathsf{EvalReduce}$ on input $(\mathsf{C}_\gamma, Z, \mathbf{g}, \mathbf{g}, \gamma; Y)$ where the prover proves knowledge of Y such that

$$\mathsf{C}_\gamma = \mathsf{Com}(\mathbf{g}, Y) \cdot \mathbf{g}^\gamma \wedge \langle Y, Z \rangle = \gamma,$$

where $Z = (z_{\mathbf{b}} = \bar{\beta}(\mathbf{b}, \boldsymbol{\zeta}) : \mathbf{b} \in \{0,1\}^n)$. We define the protocol in Fig. 3.

Remark 3. In fact, our scheme readily extends to proving any linear relation $\boldsymbol{\alpha}$ about a committed sequence Y (i.e., the value $\langle \boldsymbol{\alpha}, Y \rangle$), as long as each element of $\boldsymbol{\alpha}$ can be generated in poly-logarithmic time.

4.2 Correctness and Security

Lemma 2. *The scheme from Sect. 4.1 is perfectly correct, computationally binding and* Eval *has witness-extended emulation under the hardness of the discrete logarithm problem for groups sampled by* GGen *in the random oracle model.*

The perfect correctness of the scheme follows from the correctness of $\mathsf{EvalReduce}$ protocol, which we prove in Lemma 3, computationally binding follows from that of Pedersen multi-commitments which follows from the hardness of discrete-log (in the random oracle model). The witness-extended emulation of Eval follows from the witness-extended emulation of the inner-product protocol in [15]. At a high level, we make two changes to their inner-product protocol: (1) sample the generators using the random oracle H, (2) perform the 2-move reduction step using the lsb-based folding approach (see Sect. 2.1 for a discussion). At a high level, given a witness Y for the inner-product statement $(\mathsf{C}_\gamma, \mathbf{g}, Z, \gamma)$, one can compute a witness for the permuted statement $(\mathsf{C}_\gamma, \pi(\mathbf{g}), \pi(Z), \gamma)$ for any efficiently computable/invertible public permutation π. Choosing π as the permutation that reverses its input allows us, in principle, to base the extractability of our scheme (lsb-based folding) to the original scheme of [15]. We provide a formal proof in the full version. Due to (1) our scheme enjoys security only in the random-oracle model.

Lemma 3. *Let* $(\mathsf{C}_\gamma, Z, \gamma, \mathbf{g}, \mathbf{g}; Y)$ *be inputs to* $\mathsf{EvalReduce}$ *and let* $(\mathsf{C}'_{\gamma'}, Z', \gamma', \mathbf{g}', \mathbf{g}; Y')$ *be generated as in Fig. 3. Then,*

$$\begin{array}{ccc} \mathsf{C}_\gamma = \mathsf{Com}(\mathbf{g}, Y) \cdot \mathbf{g}^\gamma & & \mathsf{C}'_{\gamma'} = \mathsf{Com}(\mathbf{g}', Y') \cdot \mathbf{g}^{\gamma'} \\ \wedge & \implies & \wedge \\ \langle Y, Z \rangle = \gamma & & \langle Y', Z' \rangle = \gamma' \end{array} .$$

Proof. Let $N = |Z|$ and let $n = \log N$. Then,

1. To show $\gamma' = \langle Y', Z' \rangle$:

$$\langle Y', Z' \rangle = \sum_{\mathbf{b} \in \{0,1\}^{n-1}} y'_{\mathbf{b}} \cdot z'_{\mathbf{b}},$$

$$= \sum_{\mathbf{b} \in \{0,1\}^{n-1}} (\alpha \cdot y_{\mathbf{b}0} + \alpha^{-1} \cdot y_{\mathbf{b}1}) \cdot (\alpha^{-1} \cdot z_{\mathbf{b}0} + \alpha \cdot z_{\mathbf{b}1}),$$

$$= \sum_{\mathbf{b} \in \{0,1\}^{n-1}} y_{\mathbf{b}0} \cdot z_{\mathbf{b}0} + \alpha^2 \cdot y_{\mathbf{b}0} \cdot z_{\mathbf{b}1} + y_{\mathbf{b}1} \cdot z_{\mathbf{b}1} + \alpha^{-2} \cdot y_{\mathbf{b}1} \cdot z_{\mathbf{b}1},$$

$$= \gamma + \alpha^2 \cdot \gamma_\mathsf{L} + \alpha^{-2} \cdot \gamma_\mathsf{R} = \gamma'.$$

2. $\underline{C'_{\gamma'} = \mathsf{Com}(\mathbf{g}', Y') \cdot \mathbf{g}^{\gamma'}}$:

$$\mathsf{Com}(\mathbf{g}', Y') = \prod_{\mathbf{b} \in \{0,1\}^{n-1}} (g'_{\mathbf{b}})^{y'_{\mathbf{b}}} , = \prod_{\mathbf{b} \in \{0,1\}^{n-1}} \left(g_{\mathbf{b}0}^{\alpha^{-1}} \cdot g_{\mathbf{b}1}^{\alpha} \right)^{\alpha \cdot y_{\mathbf{b}0} + \alpha^{-1} \cdot y_{\mathbf{b}1}},$$

$$= \prod_{\mathbf{b} \in \{0,1\}^{n-1}} \left(g_{\mathbf{b}0}^{y_{\mathbf{b}0}} \cdot g_{\mathbf{b}0}^{\alpha^{-2} \cdot y_{\mathbf{b}1}} \cdot g_{\mathbf{b}1}^{\alpha^2 \cdot y_{\mathbf{b}0}} \cdot g_{\mathbf{b}1}^{y_{\mathbf{b}1}} \right),$$

$$= \prod_{\mathbf{b} \in \{0,1\}^{n-1}} (g_{\mathbf{b}0}^{y_{\mathbf{b}1}})^{\alpha^{-2}} \cdot g_{\mathbf{b}0}^{y_{\mathbf{b}0}} \cdot g_{\mathbf{b}1}^{y_{\mathbf{b}1}} \cdot (g_{\mathbf{b}1}^{y_{\mathbf{b}0}})^{\alpha^2}.$$

Then, above with the definition of γ' implies that $C'_{\gamma'} = \mathsf{Com}(\mathbf{g}', Y') \cdot \mathbf{g}^{\gamma'}$.

4.3 Efficiency

In this section we discuss the efficiency aspects of each of the protocols defined in Sect. 4.1 with respect to four complexity measures: (1) queries to the random oracle H, (2) field/group operations performed, (3) field/group elements stored and (4) number of passes over the stream Y.

For the rest of this section, we fix $n, N = 2^n, H, \mathbb{G}, \mathbb{F}, \zeta \in \mathbb{F}^n$ and furthermore fix $Y = (y_\mathbf{b} : \mathbf{b} \in \{0,1\}^n)$, $\mathbf{g} = (g_\mathbf{b} = H(\mathbf{b}) : \mathbf{b} \in \{0,1\}^n)$ and $Z = (z_\mathbf{b} = \bar\beta(\mathbf{b}, \zeta) : \mathbf{b} \in \{0,1\}^n)$. Note given ζ, any $z_\mathbf{b}$ can be computed by performing $O(n)$ field operations.

First, consider the prover P of Eval protocol (Fig. 3). Given the inputs $(C, Z, \gamma, \mathbf{g}, g; Y)$, P and V call the recursive protocol EvalReduce on the N sized statement $(C_\gamma, Z, \gamma, \mathbf{g}, g; Y)$ where $C_\gamma = C \cdot g^\gamma$. The prover's computation in this call to EvalReduce is dictated by computing (a) $\gamma_\mathsf{L}, \gamma_\mathsf{R}$ (line 6), (2) $C_\mathsf{L}, C_\mathsf{R}$ (line 7) and (c) inputs for the next recursive call on EvalReduce with $N/2$ sized statement $(C'_{\gamma'}, Z', \gamma', \mathbf{g}', g; Y')$ (line 9,11). The rest of its computation requires $O(1)$ number of operations. The recursion ends on the n-th call with statement of size 1. For $k \in \{0, \ldots, n\}$, the inputs at the k-th depth of the recursion be denoted with superscript k, that is, $C^{(k)}, \gamma^{(k)}, Z^{(k)}, \mathbf{g}^{(k)}, Y^{(k)}$. For example,

Computez$(k, \mathbf{c}, \boldsymbol{\zeta}, \boldsymbol{\alpha})$	Computeg$^H(k, \mathbf{c}, \boldsymbol{\alpha})$
1: $\quad z_{\mathbf{c}}^{(k)} \leftarrow 0$	1: $\quad g_{\mathbf{c}}^{(k)} \leftarrow 0$
2: $\quad$ **foreach** $\mathbf{a} \in \{0,1\}^k$ **do**	2: $\quad$ **foreach** $\mathbf{a} \in \{0,1\}^k$ **do**
3: $\quad\quad$ temp $\leftarrow 1_{\mathbb{F}}$	3: $\quad\quad$ temp $\leftarrow 1_{\mathbb{F}}$
4: $\quad\quad$ **foreach** $j \in \{1,\dots,k\}$ **do**	4: $\quad\quad$ **foreach** $j \in \{1,\dots,k\}$ **do**
5: $\quad\quad\quad$ temp $\leftarrow$ temp $\cdot$ coeff$(\alpha^{(j-1)}, a_j)$	5: $\quad\quad\quad$ temp $\leftarrow$ temp $\cdot$ coeff$(\alpha^{(j-1)}, a_j)$
6: $\quad\quad$ $z_{\mathbf{c}}^{(k)} \leftarrow$ temp $\cdot \beta(\mathbf{c} \circ \mathbf{a}, \boldsymbol{\zeta})$	6: $\quad\quad$ $g_{\mathbf{c}}^{(k)} \leftarrow H(\mathbf{c} \circ \mathbf{a})^{\text{temp}}$
7: $\quad$ **return** $z_{\mathbf{c}}^{(k)}$	7: $\quad$ **return** $g_{\mathbf{c}}^{(k)}$

Fig. 4. Algorithms for computing $z_{\mathbf{b}}^{(k)}$ and $g_{\mathbf{b}}^{(k)}$. In both algorithms $\mathbf{c} \in \{0,1\}^{n-k}$ and $\boldsymbol{\alpha} = (\alpha^{(0)}, \dots, \alpha^{(k-1)})$, where $\beta(\mathbf{b}, \boldsymbol{\zeta}) = \prod_{i=1}^{n} \beta(b_i, \zeta_i)$ for $\mathbf{b} = \mathbf{c} \circ \mathbf{a}$ and $\mathsf{coeff}(\alpha, c) = \alpha \cdot c + \alpha^{-1} \cdot (1-c)$.

$Z^{(0)} = Z$, $Y^{(0)} = Y$ denote the initial inputs (at depth 0) where prover computes $\gamma_L^{(0)}, \gamma_R^{(0)}, C_L^{(0)}, C_R^{(0)}$ with verifier challenge $\alpha^{(0)}$. The sequences $Z^{(k)}, Y^{(k)}$ and $g^{(k)}$ are of size 2^{n-k}.

At a high level, we ask prover to never explicitly compute the sequences $\mathbf{g}^{(k)}, Z^{(k)}, Y^{(k)}$ (item (c) above) but instead compute elements $g_{\mathbf{b}}^{(k)}, z_{\mathbf{b}}^{(k)}, y_{\mathbf{b}}^{(k)}$, of the respective sequences, on demand, which then can be used to compute $\gamma_L^{(k)}, \gamma_R^{(k)}, C_L^{(k)}, C_R^{(k)}$ in required time and space. For this, first it will be useful to see how the elements of sequences $Z^{(k)}, Y^{(k)}, \mathbf{g}^{(k)}$ depend on the initial (i.e., depth-0) sequence $Z^{(0)}, Y^{(0)}, \mathbf{g}^{(0)}$.

Relating $Y^{(k)}$ with $Y^{(0)}$. First, lets consider $Y^{(k)} = (y_{\mathbf{b}}^{(k)} : \mathbf{b} \in \{0,1\}^{n-k})$ at depth $k \in \{0, \dots, n\}$. Let $(\alpha^{(0)}, \dots, \alpha^{(k-1)})$ be the verifier's challenges sent in all prior rounds.

Lemma 4 (Streaming of $Y^{(k)}$). *For every $\mathbf{b} \in \{0,1\}^{n-k}$,*

$$y_{\mathbf{b}}^{(k)} = \sum_{\mathbf{c} \in \{0,1\}^k} \left(\prod_{j=1}^{k} \mathsf{coeff}(\alpha^{(j-1)}, c_j) \right) \cdot y_{\mathbf{b} \circ \mathbf{c}}, \tag{7}$$

where $\mathsf{coeff}(\alpha, c) = \alpha \cdot (1-c) + \alpha^{-1} \cdot c$.

The proof follows by induction on depth k. Lemma 4 allows us to simulate the stream $Y^{(k)}$ with **one** pass over the initial sequence Y, additionally performing $O(N \cdot k)$ multiplications to compute appropriate coeff functions.

Relating $Z^{(k)}$ with $Z^{(0)}$. Next, consider $Z^{(k)} = (z_{\mathbf{b}}^{(k)} : \mathbf{b} \in \{0,1\}^{n-k})$ at depth $k \in \{0, \dots, n\}$.

Lemma 5 (Computing $z_{\mathbf{b}}^{(k)}$). *For every* $\mathbf{b} \in \{0,1\}^{n-k}$,

$$z_{\mathbf{b}}^{(k)} = \sum_{\mathbf{c} \in \{0,1\}^k} \left(\prod_{j=1}^{k} \mathsf{coeff}(\alpha^{(j-1)}, c_j) \right) \cdot z_{\mathbf{boc}}, \tag{8}$$

where $\mathsf{coeff}(\alpha, c) = \alpha \cdot c + \alpha^{-1} \cdot (1 - c)$. *Furthermore, computing* $z_{\mathbf{b}}^{(k)}$ *requires* $O(2^k \cdot n)$ *field multiplications and storing* $O(n)$ *elements (see algorithm* Computez *in Fig. 4).*

Relating $\mathrm{g}^{(k)}$ *with* $\mathrm{g}^{(0)}$. Finally, consider $\mathbf{g}^{(k)} = (\mathbf{g}_{\mathbf{b}}^{(k)} : \mathbf{b} \in \{0,1\}^{n-k})$ at depth $k \in \{0, \ldots, n\}$.

Lemma 6 (Computing $\mathbf{g}_{\mathbf{b}}^{(k)}$). *For every* $\mathbf{b} \in \{0,1\}^{n-k}$,

$$\mathbf{g}_{\mathbf{b}}^{(k)} = \prod_{\mathbf{c} \in \{0,1\}^k} \mathbf{g}_{\mathbf{boc}}^{\mathsf{coeff}(\alpha, \mathbf{c})} \; ; \; \mathsf{coeff}(\alpha, \mathbf{c}) = \prod_{i=1}^{k} \alpha^{(j-1)} \cdot c_j + (\alpha^{(j-1)})^{-1} \cdot (1 - c_j). \tag{9}$$

Furthermore, computing $\mathbf{g}_{\mathbf{b}}^{(k)}$ *requires* $2^k \cdot k$ *field multiplications,* 2^k *queries to* H, 2^k *group multiplications and exponentiations, and storing* $O(k)$ *elements (see algorithm* Computeg *in Fig. 4).*

We now discuss the efficiency of the commitment scheme.

Commitment Phase. We first note that Com^H on input pp and given streaming access to Y can compute the commitment $\mathsf{C} = \prod_{\mathbf{b}}(H(\mathbf{b}))^{y_{\mathbf{b}}}$ for $\mathbf{b} \in \{0,1\}^n$ making N queries to H, performing N group exponentiations and a single pass over Y. Furthermore, requires storing only a single group element.

Note that a single group exponentiation $\mathbf{g}^{\alpha}$ can be emulated while performing $O(\log p)$ group multiplications while storing $O(1)$ group and field elements. Since, $\mathbb{G}, \mathbb{F}$ are of order p, field and group operations can, furthermore, be performed in $\mathrm{polylog}(p(\lambda))$ time.

Evaluating $\mathsf{MLE}(Y, \zeta)$. The honest prover (when used in higher level protocols) needs to evaluate $\mathsf{MLE}(Y, \zeta)$ which requires performing $O(N \log N)$ field operations overall and a single pass over stream Y.

Prover Efficiency. For every depth-k of the recursion, it is sufficient to discuss the efficiency of computing $\gamma_{\mathsf{L}}^{(k)}, \gamma_{\mathsf{R}}^{(k)}, \mathsf{C}_{\mathsf{L}}^{(k)}, \mathsf{C}_{\mathsf{R}}^{(k)}$. We argue the complexity of computing $\gamma_{\mathsf{L}}^{(k)}$ and $\mathsf{C}_{\mathsf{L}}^{(k)}$ and the analysis for the remaining is similar. We give a formal algorithm Prover in Fig. 5.

Computing $\gamma_{\mathsf{L}}^{(k)}$. Recall that $\gamma_{\mathsf{L}}^{(k)} = \sum_{\mathbf{b}} y_{\mathbf{b}0}^{(k)} \cdot z_{\mathbf{b}1}^{(k)}$ for $\mathbf{b} \in \{0,1\}^{n-k-1}$. To compute $\gamma_{\mathsf{L}}^{(k)}$ we stream the initial N-sized sequence Y and generate elements of

$$
\begin{array}{ll}
\multicolumn{2}{l}{\mathsf{Prover}^H(pp, k, Y, \zeta, \mathbf{g}, \alpha^{(0)}, \ldots, \alpha^{(k-1)})} \\
\hline
1: & \gamma_\mathsf{L}, \gamma_\mathsf{R}, y^{(k)} \leftarrow 0_\mathbb{F}, \mathbf{g}^{(k)}, \mathsf{C}_\mathsf{L}, \mathsf{C}_\mathsf{R} \leftarrow 1_\mathbb{G}, count \leftarrow 0 \\
2: & \textbf{foreach } \mathbf{b} = (b_n, \ldots, b_1) \in \{0,1\}^n \textbf{ do} \\
3: & \quad temp \leftarrow 1_\mathbb{F} \\
4: & \quad \textbf{foreach } j \in \{1, \ldots, k\} \textbf{ do} \\
5: & \qquad temp \leftarrow temp \cdot \mathsf{coeff}(\alpha^{(j-1)}, b_j) \\
6: & \quad y^{(k)} \leftarrow y^{(k)} + temp \cdot y_\mathbf{b} \\
7: & \quad count \leftarrow count + 1 \\
8: & \quad \textbf{if } count == 2^k \textbf{ then} \\
9: & \qquad z^{(k)} \leftarrow \mathsf{Computez}(k, (b_n, \ldots, b_{n-k+1}, 1 - b_{n-k}), \zeta, \alpha^{(0)}, \ldots, \alpha^{(k-1)}) \\
10: & \qquad \mathbf{g}^{(k)} \leftarrow \mathsf{Computeg}^H(k, (b_n, \ldots, b_{n-k+1}, 1 - b_{n-k}), \alpha^{(0)}, \ldots, \alpha^{(k-1)}) \\
11: & \qquad \textbf{if } b_{n-k} == 0 \textbf{ then} \\
12: & \qquad\quad \gamma_\mathsf{L} \leftarrow \gamma_\mathsf{L} + z^{(k)} \cdot y^{(k)} \ ; \ \mathsf{C}_\mathsf{L} \leftarrow \mathsf{C}_\mathsf{L} \cdot (\mathbf{g}^{(k)})^{y^{(k)}} \\
13: & \qquad \textbf{else} \\
14: & \qquad\quad \gamma_\mathsf{R} \leftarrow \gamma_\mathsf{R} + z^{(k)} \cdot y^{(k)} \ ; \ \mathsf{C}_\mathsf{R} \leftarrow \mathsf{C}_\mathsf{R} \cdot (\mathbf{g}^{(k)})^{y^{(k)}} \\
15: & \qquad y^{(k)} \leftarrow 0_\mathbb{F}; \ \mathbf{g}^{(k)} \leftarrow 1_\mathbb{G}; \ count \leftarrow 0 \\
16: & \mathsf{C}_\mathsf{L} \leftarrow \mathsf{C}_\mathsf{L} \cdot \mathbf{g}^{\gamma_\mathsf{L}} \ ; \ \mathsf{C}_\mathsf{R} \leftarrow \mathsf{C}_\mathsf{R} \cdot \mathbf{g}^{\gamma_\mathsf{R}} \\
17: & \textbf{return } (\gamma_\mathsf{L}, \mathsf{C}_\mathsf{L}, \gamma_\mathsf{R}, \mathsf{C}_\mathsf{R})
\end{array}
$$

Fig. 5. Space-efficient prover

the sequence $(y_{\mathbf{b}0}^{(k)} : \mathbf{b} \in \{0,1\}^{n-k-1})$ in a streaming manner. Since each $y_{\mathbf{b}0}^{(k)}$ depends on a contiguous block of 2^k elements in the initial stream Y, we can compute $y_{\mathbf{b}0}^{(k)}$ by performing $2^k \cdot k$ field operations (lines 2–7 in Fig. 5). For every $\mathbf{b} \in \{0,1\}^{n-k-1}$, after computing $y_{\mathbf{b}0}^{(k)}$, we leverage "random access" to Z and compute $z_{\mathbf{b}1}^{(k)}$ (Lemma 5) which requires $O(2^k \cdot k)$ field operations. Overall, $\gamma_\mathsf{L}^{(k)}$ can be computed in $O(N \cdot k)$ field operations and a single pass over Y.

Computing $\mathsf{C}_\mathsf{L}^{(k)}$. The two differences in computing $\mathsf{C}_\mathsf{L}^{(k)}$ (see Fig. 3 for the definition) is that (a) we need to compute $\mathbf{g}_{\mathbf{b}1}^{(k)}$ instead of computing $z_{\mathbf{b}1}^{(k)}$ and (b) perform group exponentiations, that is, $\mathbf{g}_{\mathbf{b}1}^{(k)}{}^{y_{\mathbf{b}0}^{(k)}}$ as opposed to group multiplications as in the computation of $\gamma_\mathsf{L}^{(k)}$. Both steps overall can be implemented in $O(N \cdot k \cdot \log p)$ field and group operations and N queries to H (Lemma 6). Overall, at depth k the prover (1) makes $O(N)$ queries to H, (2) performs $O(N \cdot k \cdot \log(p))$ field and group operations and (3) requires a single pass over Y.

Therefore, the entire prover computation (over all calls to EvalReduce) requires $O(\log N)$ passes over Y, makes $O(N \log N)$ queries to H and performs $O(N \cdot \log^2 N \cdot \log p)$ field/group operations. Furthermore, this requires storing only $O(\log N)$ field and group elements.

Verifier Efficiency. V only needs to compute folded sequence $Z^{(n)}$ and folded generators $g^{(n)}$ at depth-n of the recursion. These can computed by invoking Computez and Computeg (Fig. 4) with $k = n$ and require $O(N \cdot \log(N, p))$ field and group operations, $O(N)$ queries to H and storing $O(\log N)$ field and group elements.

Lemma 7. *The time and space efficiency of each of the phases of the protocols are listed below[6]:*

Computation	H queries	Y passes	$\mathbb{F}/\mathbb{G}$ ops	$\mathbb{G}/\mathbb{F}$ elements
Com	N	1	$O(N)$	$O(1)$
$\mathsf{MLE}(Y, \zeta)$	0	1	$O(N \log N)$	$O(1)$
P (in Eval)	$O(N \log N)$	$O(\log N)$	$O(N \log^2 N)$	$O(\log N)$
V (in Eval)	$O(N)$	0	$O(N \log N)$	$O(\log N)$

Finally, Theorem 5 follows directly from Lemma 2 and Lemma 7.

5   A Polynomial IOP for Random Access Machines

We obtain space efficient arguments for any NP relation verifiable by time-T space-S RAM computations by compiling our polynomial commitment scheme with a suitable space-efficient *polynomial interactive oracle proof* (IOP) [6,17,41]. Informally, a polynomial IOP is a multi-round interactive PCP such that in each round the verifier sends a message to the prover and the prover responds with a proof oracle that the verifier can query via random access, with the additional property that the proof oracle is a polynomial.

We dedicate the remainder of this section to giving a high-level overview our polynomial IOP (PIOP), presented in Fig. 6, which realizes Theorem 3. Full details are deferred to the full-version. We first recall that we consider a variant of the polynomial IOP model in which all prover messages are encoded by a channel and that the prover does not incur the cost of this encoding in its time and space complexity. In particular, we consider a channel which computes the multi-linear extension of the prover messages. Our space-efficient PIOP leverages the RAM to circuit satisfiability reduction of [12]: this RAM to circuit reduction outputs an arithmetic circuit of size $T \cdot \text{polylog}(T)$, which we denote as C_M, over finite field $\mathbb{F}$ of size $\text{polylog}(T)$. The circuit is defined such that such that $C_M(x) = y$ if and only if $M(x; w) = y$ for auxiliary input w. Further, the circuit has a "streaming" property: the string of gate assignments W of C_M on input x can be computed "gate-by-gate" in time $T \cdot \text{polylog}(T)$ and space $S \cdot \text{polylog}(T)$. In our model, this allows our prover to stream its message through the encoding channel in time $T \cdot \text{polylog}(T)$ and space $S \cdot \text{polylog}(T)$ and send the verifier

---

[6] $\log(p)$ factors are omitted.

PIOP$(M, x, T, S; w)$

1 : P compiles circuit C_M and transcript W via the reduction of [12].

2 : P provides V with an oracle for $\overline{W}$.

3 : V samples $\tau \xleftarrow{\$} \mathbb{F}^{3s}$ and sends τ to P.

4 : P computes polynomial h_τ and sets $\gamma \leftarrow 0$. P sends γ to V.

5 : V sets $\gamma' \leftarrow \gamma$.

6 :   **foreach** $j \in \{1, \ldots, 3s\}$ **do** // sum-check

7 : P sends $h_\tau^{(j)}(X_j)$ to V, where $h_\tau^{(j)}(X_j) \leftarrow \displaystyle\sum_{c' \in \{0,1\}^{3s-j}} h_\tau(\alpha_1, \ldots, \alpha_{j-1}, X_j, c')$.

8 : V checks $\gamma' \stackrel{?}{=} h_\tau^{(j)}(0) + h_\tau^{(j)}(1)$, rejecting if equality doesn't hold.

9 : V samples $\alpha_j \xleftarrow{\$} \mathbb{F}$ and sets $\gamma' \leftarrow h_\tau^{(j)}(\alpha_j)$.

10 :   **if** $j < 3s$ **then** V sends α_j to P **endif**

11 : V queries the oracle $\overline{W}$ and obtains $\gamma_i \leftarrow \overline{W}(\alpha^{(i)})$ for $i \in \{1, 2, 3\}$, where $\alpha^{(i)} \leftarrow (\alpha_{i\cdot 1}, \ldots, \alpha_{i\cdot s})$.

12 : V computes $h_\tau(\alpha)$ using oracle queries γ_i and accepts if and only if $\gamma' = h_\tau(\alpha)$.

Fig. 6. Our Polynomial IOP for time-T space-S RAM computations.

with an oracle to the *multi-linear extension* of W, denoted as $\overline{W}$. We emphasize that $\overline{W}$ is the only oracle sent by the prover to the verifier, and that this and the streaming property of W are key to the composition of our PIOP with the polynomial commitment scheme of Theorem 5.

The circuit satisfiability instance (C_M, x, y) is next reduced to an algebraic claim about a constant-degree polynomial $F_{x,y}$ whose structure depends on the wiring pattern of C_M, x and y, and the oracle $\overline{W}$. The polynomial $F_{x,y}$ has the property that it is the 0-polynomial if and only if $\overline{W}$ is a multi-linear extension of a correct transcript; i.e., that W is a witness for $C_M(x) = y$. A verifier is convinced that $F_{x,y}$ is the 0-polynomial if $F_{x,y}(\tau) = 0$ for uniformly random $\mathbb{F}$-vector τ. $F_{x,y}$ is suitably structured such that a prover can convince a verifier that $F_{x,y}(\tau) = 0$ via the classical sum-check protocol [36, 45]. In particular, the value $F_{x,y}(\tau)$ is expressed as a summation of some constant-degree polynomial h_τ over the Boolean hypercube:

$$F_{x,y}(\tau) = \sum_{c \in \{0,1\}^n} h_\tau(c) .$$

The polynomial h_τ has the following two key efficiency properties: (1) the prover's messages in the sum-check that depend on h_τ are computable in $T \cdot \text{polylog}(T)$ time and space $S \cdot \text{polylog}(T)$ (see [12, Lemma 4.2], full details deferred to the full-version); and (2) given oracle $\overline{W}$ the verifier in time $\text{polylog}(T)$ can evaluate h_τ at any point without explicit access to the circuit C_M (see [12, Theorem 4.1 and Lemma 4.2], full details deferred to the full-version).

6   Time- and Space-Efficient Arguments for RAM

We obtain space-efficient arguments $\langle P_{\mathsf{arg}}, V_{\mathsf{arg}} \rangle$ for NP relations that can be verified by time-T space-S RAMs by composing the polynomial commitment scheme of Theorem 5 and the polynomial IOP of Fig. 6. Specifically, the prover P_{arg} and V_{arg} runs the prover and the verifier of the underlying PIOP except two changes: (1) P_{arg} (line 2, Fig. 6) instead provides V_{arg} with a commitment to the multilinear extension of the circuit transcript W. Here P_{arg} crucially relies on streaming access to W to compute the commitment in small-space using Com. (2) P_{arg} and V_{arg} run the protocol Eval in place of all verifier queries to the oracle $\overline{W}$ (line 11, Fig. 6). We state the formal theorem and defer its proof to the full-version.

Theorem 6 (Small-Space Arguments for RAMs). *There exists a public-coin interactive argument for* NP *relations verifiable by time-T space-S random access machines M, in the random oracle model, under the hardness of discrete-log in obliviously sampleable prime-order groups with the following complexity.*

1. *The protocol has perfect completeness, has $O(\log(T))$ rounds and $\mathrm{polylog}(T)$ communication, and has witness-extended emulation.*
2. *The prover runs in time $T \cdot \mathrm{polylog}(T)$ and space $S \cdot \mathrm{polylog}(T)$ given input-witness pair $(x; w)$ for M; and*
3. *The verifier runs in time $T \cdot \mathrm{polylog}(T)$ and space $\mathrm{polylog}(T)$.*

We discuss how we modify our interactive argument of knowledge from Theorem 6 to satisfy zero-knowledge and then make the resulting argument non-interactive, thus obtaining Theorem 1.

Zero-Knowledge. We use commit-and-prove techniques introduced in [2,20] and later implemented in [48]. At a high level, this requires making two changes in our base protocols: (1) modify polynomial commitment from Sect. 4 to satisfy zero-knowledge—we modify all commitments sent in both Com and Eval protocols (Fig. 3) to additionally include blinding factors. For example, commitment to $x \in \mathbb{F}$ under generator $g \in \mathbb{G}$ is changed from g^x to $g^x \cdot h^r$ for some randomly sampled $h \xleftarrow{\$} \mathbb{G}$ and $r \xleftarrow{\$} \mathbb{F}$. Further, at the end of the EvalReduce protocol when $N = 1$, prover instead of sending the witness in the clear instead engages with the verifier in Schnorr's zero-knowledge proof of dot-product protocol [43]. This along with hiding of the commitments now ensure that the resulting polynomial commitment is zero-knowledge. (2) We replace all messages sent in the argument Theorem 6 in the clear with Pedersen hiding commitments and use techniques developed in [48] to ensure verifier checks go through. We emphasize that these changes do not asymptotically blow up the complexity of the protocol and, in particular, keep the space-complexity low. Furthermore, this transformation preserves the knowledge-soundness and public-coin features of the underlying argument [48].

Non-interactivity. We apply the Fiat-Shamir (FS) transform [21] to our zero-knowledge argument of knowledge, thereby obtaining a non-interactive, zero-knowledge argument of knowledge. However, note that it is folklore that applying FS to a t-round public-coin argument of knowledge yields a non-interactive argument of knowledge where the extractor runs in time exponential in t. Since our protocol has $O(\log T)$ rounds our extractor runs in $\mathsf{poly}(T)$-time.

Acknowledgements. This work was done in part while Alexander R. Block and Pratik Soni were visiting the FACT Research Center at IDC Herzliya, Israel. Ron Rothblum was supported in part by a Milgrom family grant, by the Israeli Science Foundation (Grants No. 1262/18 and 2137/19), and the Technion Hiroshi Fujiwara cyber security research center and Israel cyber directorate. Alon Rosen is supported in part by ISF grant No. 1399/17 and Project PROMETHEUS (Grant 780701). Pratik Soni was supported in part by NSF grants CNS-1528178, CNS-1929901 and CNS-1936825 (CAREER), Glen and Susanne Culler Chair, ISF grant 1861/16 and AFOSR Award FA9550-17-1-0069. Alexander R. Block was supported in part by NSF grant CCF-1910659.

References

1. Aly, A., Ashur, T., Ben-Sasson, E., Dhooghe, S., Szepieniec, A.: Design of symmetric-key primitives for advanced cryptographic protocols. Cryptology ePrint Archive, Report 2019/426 (2019). https://eprint.iacr.org/2019/426
2. Ben-Or, M., et al.: Everything provable is provable in zero-knowledge. In: Goldwasser, S. (ed.) CRYPTO 1988. LNCS, vol. 403, pp. 37–56. Springer, New York (1990). https://doi.org/10.1007/0-387-34799-2_4
3. Ben-Sasson, E., Bentov, I., Horesh, Y., Riabzev, M.: Fast reed-solomon interactive oracle proofs of proximity. In: Chatzigiannakis, I., Kaklamanis, C., Marx, D., Sannella, D. (eds.) ICALP 2018. LIPIcs, vol. 107, pp. 14:1–14:17. Schloss Dagstuhl (2018). https://doi.org/10.4230/LIPIcs.ICALP.2018.14
4. Ben-Sasson, E., Bentov, I., Horesh, Y., Riabzev, M.: Scalable zero knowledge with no trusted setup. In: Boldyreva, A., Micciancio, D. (eds.) CRYPTO 2019, Part III. LNCS, vol. 11694, pp. 701–732. Springer, Cham (2019). https://doi.org/10.1007/978-3-030-26954-8_23
5. Ben-Sasson, E., Chiesa, A., Genkin, D., Tromer, E.: Fast reductions from RAMs to delegatable succinct constraint satisfaction problems: extended abstract. In: Kleinberg, R.D. (ed.) ITCS 2013, pp. 401–414. ACM (2013). https://doi.org/10.1145/2422436.2422481
6. Ben-Sasson, E., Chiesa, A., Spooner, N.: Interactive oracle proofs. In: Hirt, M., Smith, A. (eds.) TCC 2016, Part II. LNCS, vol. 9986, pp. 31–60. Springer, Heidelberg (2016). https://doi.org/10.1007/978-3-662-53644-5_2
7. Ben-Sasson, E., Goldberg, L., Kopparty, S., Saraf, S.: DEEP-FRI: sampling outside the box improves soundness. Cryptology ePrint Archive, Report 2019/336 (2019). https://eprint.iacr.org/2019/336
8. Biehl, I., Meyer, B., Wetzel, S.: Ensuring the integrity of agent-based computations by short proofs. In: Rothermel, K., Hohl, F. (eds.) MA 1998. LNCS, vol. 1477, pp. 183–194. Springer, Heidelberg (1998). https://doi.org/10.1007/BFb0057658

9. Bitansky, N., Canetti, R., Chiesa, A., Tromer, E.: Recursive composition and bootstrapping for SNARKS and proof-carrying data. In: Boneh, D., Roughgarden, T., Feigenbaum, J. (eds.) 45th ACM STOC, pp. 111–120. ACM Press (2013). https://doi.org/10.1145/2488608.2488623

10. Bitansky, N., Chiesa, A.: Succinct arguments from multi-prover interactive proofs and their efficiency benefits. Cryptology ePrint Archive, Report 2012/461 (2012). http://eprint.iacr.org/2012/461

11. Bitansky, N., Chiesa, A.: Succinct arguments from multi-prover interactive proofs and their efficiency benefits. In: Safavi-Naini, R., Canetti, R. (eds.) CRYPTO 2012. LNCS, vol. 7417, pp. 255–272. Springer, Heidelberg (2012). https://doi.org/10.1007/978-3-642-32009-5_16

12. Blumberg, A.J., Thaler, J., Vu, V., Walfish, M.: Verifiable computation using multiple provers. Cryptology ePrint Archive, Report 2014/846 (2014). http://eprint.iacr.org/2014/846

13. Bootle, J., Cerulli, A., Chaidos, P., Groth, J., Petit, C.: Efficient zero-knowledge arguments for arithmetic circuits in the discrete log setting. In: Fischlin, M., Coron, J.-S. (eds.) EUROCRYPT 2016, Part II. LNCS, vol. 9666, pp. 327–357. Springer, Heidelberg (2016). https://doi.org/10.1007/978-3-662-49896-5_12

14. Bowe, S., Grigg, J., Hopwood, D.: Halo: recursive proof composition without a trusted setup. Cryptology ePrint Archive, Report 2019/1021 (2019). https://eprint.iacr.org/2019/1021

15. Bünz, B., Bootle, J., Boneh, D., Poelstra, A., Wuille, P., Maxwell, G.: Bulletproofs: short proofs for confidential transactions and more. In: 2018 IEEE Symposium on Security and Privacy, pp. 315–334. IEEE Computer Society Press (2018). https://doi.org/10.1109/SP.2018.00020

16. Bünz, B., Chiesa, A., Mishra, P., Spooner, N.: Proof-carrying data from accumulation schemes. Cryptology ePrint Archive, Report 2020/499 (2020). https://eprint.iacr.org/2020/499

17. Bünz, B., Fisch, B., Szepieniec, A.: Transparent SNARKs from DARK compilers. In: Canteaut, A., Ishai, Y. (eds.) EUROCRYPT 2020, Part I. LNCS, vol. 12105, pp. 677–706. Springer, Cham (2020). https://doi.org/10.1007/978-3-030-45721-1_24

18. Chiesa, A., Ojha, D., Spooner, N.: FRACTAL: post-quantum and transparent recursive proofs from holography. In: Canteaut, A., Ishai, Y. (eds.) EUROCRYPT 2020, Part I. LNCS, vol. 12105, pp. 769–793. Springer, Cham (2020). https://doi.org/10.1007/978-3-030-45721-1_27

19. Cormode, G., Mitzenmacher, M., Thaler, J.: Practical verified computation with streaming interactive proofs. In: Goldwasser, S. (ed.) ITCS 2012, pp. 90–112. ACM (2012). https://doi.org/10.1145/2090236.2090245

20. Cramer, R., Damgård, I.: Zero-knowledge proofs for finite field arithmetic, or: can zero-knowledge be for free? In: Krawczyk, H. (ed.) CRYPTO 1998. LNCS, vol. 1462, pp. 424–441. Springer, Heidelberg (1998). https://doi.org/10.1007/BFb0055745

21. Fiat, A., Shamir, A.: How to prove yourself: practical solutions to identification and signature problems. In: Odlyzko, A.M. (ed.) CRYPTO 1986. LNCS, vol. 263, pp. 186–194. Springer, Heidelberg (1987). https://doi.org/10.1007/3-540-47721-7_12

22. Gennaro, R., Gentry, C., Parno, B., Raykova, M.: Quadratic span programs and succinct NIZKs without PCPs. In: Johansson, T., Nguyen, P.Q. (eds.) EUROCRYPT 2013. LNCS, vol. 7881, pp. 626–645. Springer, Heidelberg (2013). https://doi.org/10.1007/978-3-642-38348-9_37

23. Gentry, C., Wichs, D.: Separating succinct non-interactive arguments from all falsifiable assumptions. In: Fortnow, L., Vadhan, S.P. (eds.) 43rd ACM STOC, pp. 99–108. ACM Press (2011). https://doi.org/10.1145/1993636.1993651
24. Goldreich, O., Håstad, J.: On the complexity of interactive proofs with bounded communication. Inf. Process. Lett. **67**(4), 205–214 (1998)
25. Goldreich, O., Vadhan, S.P., Wigderson, A.: On interactive proofs with a laconic prover. Comput. Complex. **11**(1–2), 1–53 (2002)
26. Goldwasser, S., Kalai, Y.T., Rothblum, G.N.: Delegating computation: interactive proofs for muggles. In: Ladner, R.E., Dwork, C. (eds.) 40th ACM STOC, pp. 113–122. ACM Press (2008). https://doi.org/10.1145/1374376.1374396
27. Goldwasser, S., Micali, S., Rackoff, C.: The knowledge complexity of interactive proof systems. SIAM J. Comput. **18**(1), 186–208 (1989). https://doi.org/10.1137/0218012
28. Groth, J., Ishai, Y.: Sub-linear zero-knowledge argument for correctness of a shuffle. In: Smart, N. (ed.) EUROCRYPT 2008. LNCS, vol. 4965, pp. 379–396. Springer, Heidelberg (2008). https://doi.org/10.1007/978-3-540-78967-3_22
29. Holmgren, J., Rothblum, R.: Delegating computations with (almost) minimal time and space overhead. In: Thorup, M. (ed.) 59th FOCS, pp. 124–135. IEEE Computer Society Press (2018). https://doi.org/10.1109/FOCS.2018.00021
30. Kalai, Y.T., Raz, R.: Probabilistically checkable arguments. In: Halevi, S. (ed.) CRYPTO 2009. LNCS, vol. 5677, pp. 143–159. Springer, Heidelberg (2009). https://doi.org/10.1007/978-3-642-03356-8_9
31. Kalai, Y.T., Raz, R., Rothblum, R.D.: Delegation for bounded space. In: Boneh, D., Roughgarden, T., Feigenbaum, J. (eds.) 45th ACM STOC, pp. 565–574. ACM Press (2013). https://doi.org/10.1145/2488608.2488679
32. Kate, A., Zaverucha, G.M., Goldberg, I.: Constant-size commitments to polynomials and their applications. In: Abe, M. (ed.) ASIACRYPT 2010. LNCS, vol. 6477, pp. 177–194. Springer, Heidelberg (2010). https://doi.org/10.1007/978-3-642-17373-8_11
33. Kattis, A., Panarin, K., Vlasov, A.: RedShift: transparent SNARKs from list polynomial commitment IOPs. Cryptology ePrint Archive, Report 2019/1400 (2019). https://eprint.iacr.org/2019/1400
34. Kilian, J.: A note on efficient zero-knowledge proofs and arguments (extended abstract). In: 24th ACM STOC, pp. 723–732. ACM Press (1992). https://doi.org/10.1145/129712.129782
35. Lindell, Y.: Parallel coin-tossing and constant-round secure two-party computation. J. Cryptol. **16**(3), 143–184 (2003). https://doi.org/10.1007/s00145-002-0143-7
36. Lund, C., Fortnow, L., Karloff, H.J., Nisan, N.: Algebraic methods for interactive proof systems. In: 31st FOCS, pp. 2–10. IEEE Computer Society Press (1990). https://doi.org/10.1109/FSCS.1990.89518
37. Micali, S.: CS proofs (extended abstracts). In: 35th FOCS, pp. 436–453. IEEE Computer Society Press (1994). https://doi.org/10.1109/SFCS.1994.365746
38. Papamanthou, C., Shi, E., Tamassia, R.: Signatures of correct computation. In: Sahai, A. (ed.) TCC 2013. LNCS, vol. 7785, pp. 222–242. Springer, Heidelberg (2013). https://doi.org/10.1007/978-3-642-36594-2_13
39. Parno, B., Howell, J., Gentry, C., Raykova, M.: Pinocchio: nearly practical verifiable computation. In: 2013 IEEE Symposium on Security and Privacy, pp. 238–252. IEEE Computer Society Press (2013). https://doi.org/10.1109/SP.2013.47
40. Pedersen, T.P.: Non-interactive and information-theoretic secure verifiable secret sharing. In: Feigenbaum, J. (ed.) CRYPTO 1991. LNCS, vol. 576, pp. 129–140. Springer, Heidelberg (1992). https://doi.org/10.1007/3-540-46766-1_9

41. Reingold, O., Rothblum, G.N., Rothblum, R.D.: Constant-round interactive proofs for delegating computation. In: Wichs, D., Mansour, Y. (eds.) 48th ACM STOC, pp. 49–62. ACM Press (2016). https://doi.org/10.1145/2897518.2897652
42. Ron-Zewi, N., Rothblum, R.: Local proofs approaching the witness length. Electron. Colloquium Comput. Complex. **26**, 127 (2019). https://eccc.weizmann.ac.il/report/2019/127
43. Schnorr, C.P.: Efficient signature generation by smart cards. J. Cryptol. **4**(3), 161–174 (1991). https://doi.org/10.1007/BF00196725
44. Setty, S.: Spartan: efficient and general-purpose zkSNARKs without trusted setup. In: Micciancio, D., Ristenpart, T. (eds.) CRYPTO 2020, Part III. LNCS, vol. 12172, pp. 704–737. Springer, Cham (2020). https://doi.org/10.1007/978-3-030-56877-1_25
45. Shamir, A.: IP=PSPACE. In: 31st FOCS, pp. 11–15. IEEE Computer Society Press (1990). https://doi.org/10.1109/FSCS.1990.89519
46. Thaler, J.: Time-optimal interactive proofs for circuit evaluation. In: Canetti, R., Garay, J.A. (eds.) CRYPTO 2013, Part II. LNCS, vol. 8043, pp. 71–89. Springer, Heidelberg (2013). https://doi.org/10.1007/978-3-642-40084-1_5
47. Valiant, P.: Incrementally verifiable computation or proofs of knowledge imply time/space efficiency. In: Canetti, R. (ed.) TCC 2008. LNCS, vol. 4948, pp. 1–18. Springer, Heidelberg (2008). https://doi.org/10.1007/978-3-540-78524-8_1
48. Wahby, R.S., Tzialla, I., shelat, a., Thaler, J., Walfish, M.: Doubly-efficient zkSNARKs without trusted setup. In: 2018 IEEE Symposium on Security and Privacy, pp. 926–943. IEEE Computer Society Press (2018). https://doi.org/10.1109/SP.2018.00060
49. Wijesekera, P., et al.: The feasibility of dynamically granted permissions: aligning mobile privacy with user preferences. In: 2017 IEEE Symposium on Security and Privacy, pp. 1077–1093. IEEE Computer Society Press (2017). https://doi.org/10.1109/SP.2017.51
50. Zhang, J., Xie, T., Zhang, Y., Song, D.: Transparent polynomial delegation and its applications to zero knowledge proof. In: 2020 IEEE Symposium on Security and Privacy, pp. 859–876. IEEE Computer Society Press (2020). https://doi.org/10.1109/SP40000.2020.00052

On the Price of Concurrency in Group Ratcheting Protocols

Alexander Bienstock[1], Yevgeniy Dodis[1], and Paul Rösler[2(✉)]

[1] New York University, New York, USA
{abienstock,dodis}@cs.nyu.edu
[2] Chair for Network and Data Security, Ruhr University Bochum, Bochum, Germany
paul.roesler@rub.de

Abstract. *Post-Compromise Security*, or PCS, refers to the ability of a given protocol to recover—by means of normal protocol operations—from the exposure of local states of its (otherwise honest) participants. While PCS in the two-party setting has attracted a lot of attention recently, the problem of achieving PCS in the group setting—called *group ratcheting* here—is much less understood. On the one hand, one can achieve excellent security by simply executing, in parallel, a two-party ratcheting protocol (e.g., Signal) for each pair of members in a group. However, this incurs $\mathcal{O}(n)$ communication overhead for every message sent, where n is the group size. On the other hand, several related protocols were recently developed in the context of the IETF Messaging Layer Security (MLS) effort that improve the communication overhead per message to $\mathcal{O}(\log n)$. However, this reduction of communication overhead involves a great restriction: group members are not allowed to send and recover from exposures concurrently such that reaching PCS is delayed up to n communication time slots (potentially even more).

In this work we formally study the trade-off between PCS, concurrency, and communication overhead in the context of group ratcheting. Since our main result is a lower bound, we define the cleanest and most restrictive setting where the tension already occurs: *static* groups equipped with a *synchronous* (and authenticated) broadcast channel, where up to t arbitrary parties can concurrently send messages in any given round. Already in this setting, we show in a symbolic execution model that PCS requires $\Omega(t)$ communication overhead per message. Our symbolic model permits as building blocks black-box use of (even "dual") PRFs, (even key-updatable) PKE (which in our symbolic definition is at least as strong as HIBE), and broadcast encryption, covering all tools used in previous constructions, but prohibiting the use of exotic primitives.

To complement our result, we also prove an almost matching upper bound of $\mathcal{O}(t \cdot (1 + \log(n/t)))$, which smoothly increases from $\mathcal{O}(\log n)$ with no concurrency, to $\mathcal{O}(n)$ with unbounded concurrency, matching the previously known protocols.

The full version [11] of this extended abstract is available as entry 2020/1171 in the IACR eprint archive.

R. Pass and K. Pietrzak (Eds.): TCC 2020, LNCS 12551, pp. 198–228, 2020.
https://doi.org/10.1007/978-3-030-64378-2_8

1   Introduction

POST-COMPROMISE SECURITY.   End-to-end (E2E) encrypted messaging systems including WhatsApp, Signal, and Facebook Messenger have increased in popularity. In these systems, intermediaries including the messaging service provider should not be able to read or modify messages. Moreover, as typical sessions in such E2E systems can last for a very long time, state compromise of some of the participants is becoming a real concern to the deployment of such systems. To address this security concern, modern E2E systems fulfill a novel property called *Post-Compromise Security* [16], which refers to the ability of a given protocol to recover—by means of normal protocol operations—from the exposure of local states of its (otherwise honest) participants. For example, the famous two-party Signal [28] protocol achieves PCS by having parties continuously run fresh sessions of Diffie-Hellman key agreement "in the background".

GROUP MESSAGING.   By now, the setting of PCS-secure two-party encrypted messaging systems is relatively well understood [2,10,15,19,23,24,30]. In contrast, the setting of PCS-secure *group* messaging is much less understood. On the one extreme, several systems, including Signal Messenger itself, achieve PCS in groups by simply executing, in parallel, a two-party PCS-secure protocol (e.g., Signal) for each pair of members in a group. In addition to achieving PCS, this simple technique is also extremely resilient to asynchrony and concurrency: people can send messages concurrently, receive them out-of-order, or be off-line for extended periods of time. However, it comes at a steep communication overhead $\mathcal{O}(n)$ for every message sent, where n is the group size.

On the other hand, several related protocols [3–5,14] (some of them introduced under the term *continuous group key agreement (CGKA)*[1]) were recently developed in the context of the IETF Message Layer Security (MLS) initiative for group messaging [7]. One of the main goals of this initiative was to achieve PCS with a significantly lower communication overhead. And, indeed, for static groups, these protocols improve this overhead per message to $\mathcal{O}(\log n)$. More precisely, these protocols separate protocol messages into two categories: *Payload* messages, used to actually encrypt messages, have no overhead, but also do not help in establishing PCS. In contrast, *update* messages carry no payload, but exclusively establish PCS: intuitively, an update message from user A refreshes all cryptographic material held by A. These update messages have size proportional to $\mathcal{O}(\log n)$ in MLS-related protocols, which is a significant saving for large groups, compared to the pairwise-Signal protocol.

CONCURRENCY.   Unfortunately, this reduction of communication overhead for MLS-related protocols involves a great restriction: *all update messages must be generated and processed one-by-one in the same order by all the group members.*

---

[1] By distinguishing between "CGKA" and "group ratcheting", these works differentiate between the asymmetric cryptographic parts of the protocols and the entire key establishment procedure, respectively [5]. In order to avoid this strict distinction, we call it "group ratcheting" here.

We stress that this does not just mean that update messages can be prepared concurrently, but processed in some fixed order. Instead, fresh update message cannot be *prepared* until all previous update messages are *processed*. In particular, it is critical to somehow implement what these protocols call a "delivery server", whose task is to reject all-but-one of the concurrently prepared update messages, and then to ensure that all group members process the "accepted updates" in the same correct order. Implementing such a delivery server poses a significant burden not only in terms of usability (which is clear), but also for *security* of these protocols, as it delays reaching PCS up to n communication time slots (potentially more in asynchronous settings, such as messaging). Indeed, the concurrency restriction of MLS is currently one of the biggest criticisms and hurdles towards its wide-spread use and adoption (see [3] for extensive discussion of this). In contrast, pairwise Signal does not have any such concurrency restriction, albeit with a much higher communication overhead. See Sect. 4 and Table 1 for more detailed comparison of various existing methods for group ratcheting.

OUR MAIN QUESTION. This brings us to the main question we study in this work:

What is the trade-off between PCS, concurrent sending and low communication complexity in encrypted group messaging protocols?

For our lower bound, we define the cleanest and most restrictive setting where the tension already occurs: *static* groups equipped with a *synchronous* (and authenticated) broadcast channel, where up to t arbitrary users can concurrently send messages in any given round. In particular, $t = 1$ corresponds to the restrictive MLS setting which, we term "no concurrency", and $t = n$ corresponds to unrestricted setting achieved by pairwise Signal, which we term "full concurrency". Also, without loss of generality, and following the convention already established in MLS-related protocols, we focus on the "key encapsulation" mechanism of group messaging protocols. Namely, our model is the following:

We have a static group of n members whose goal is to continuously share a group key k. Group members have private states st, and communicate in rounds over a public broadcast channel. Each round refreshes the current group key k into the next group key k' as follows: 1. At the beginning of a round, an arbitrary subset of up to t group members is selected by the adversary to update the current group key k. These groups members are called *senders* (of a given round). 2. During each round, each sender—*unaware of the identities of other senders*—tosses fresh random coins, sends a ciphertext c over the broadcast channel, and updates its private state st. 3. At the end of each round, all (up to t) ciphertexts c are received by all n users, who use them to update their state st, and output a new group key k'. 4. At the end of each round, the adversary can learn the current group key k', and is also allowed to expose an arbitrary number of group member states st.

For our lower bound, we will demand the following, rather weak, PCS guarantee. A key k after round i (not directly revealed to the attacker) is secure if: (a) no user is exposed in round $i' \geq i$; (b) all users sent at least one update ciphertext between their latest exposure and round $i-1$; and (c) after all exposed users sent once without being exposed again, at least one user additionally sent in round $j \leq i$. Condition (a) will only be used in our lower bound (to make it stronger), to ensure that our lower bound is only due to the PCS, but not a complementary property called *forward*-secrecy, which states that past round keys cannot be compromised upon current state exposure. However, our upper bound will achieve forward-secrecy, dropping (a).

Condition (b) is the heart of PCS, demanding that security should be eventually restored once every exposed user updated its state. Condition (c) permits a one-round delay before PCS takes place. While not theoretically needed, avoiding this extra round seems to require some sort of multiparty non-interactive key exchange for *concurrent* state updates, which currently requires exotic cryptographic assumptions, such as multi-linear maps [12,13]. In contrast, the extra round allows to use traditional public-key cryptography techniques, such as the exposed user sending fresh public-keys, and future senders using these keys in the extra round to send fresh secret(s) to this user. While condition (c) strengthens our lower bound, our upper bound construction can be minimally adjusted to achieve PCS for *non-concurrent* state updates even without this "extra round".

For conciseness, we call any protocol in our model a *group ratcheting* scheme, taking inspiration from the "double ratchet" paradigm used in design of the Signal protocol [28].

OUR UPPER BOUND. We show nearly matching lower and upper bounds on the efficiency of t-concurrent, PCS-secure group ratcheting schemes. With our upper bound we provide a group ratcheting scheme with message overhead $\mathcal{O}(t \cdot (1 + \log(n/t)))$, which smoothly increases from $\mathcal{O}(\log n)$ with no concurrency, to $\mathcal{O}(n)$ with unbounded concurrency, matching the upper bounds of the previously known protocols. Our upper bound is proven in the standard computational model. For the weak notion of PCS alone sketched above (i.e., conditions (a)–(c)), we only need public-key encryption (PKE) and pseudorandom functions (PRFs). Our construction carefully borrows elements from the complete subtree method of [27] used in the context of broadcast encryption (BE), and the TreeKEM protocol of the MLS standard [3,7] used in the context of non-concurrent group ratcheting. Similarly, one can view our construction as an adapted combination of components from Tainted TreeKEM [4] and the most recent MLS draft (verion-09) [8] with its propose-then-commit technique. By itself, none of these constructions is enough to do what we want: BE scheme of [27] allows to send a fresh secret to all-but-t senders from the previous round (this is needed for PCS), but needs centralized distribution of correlated secret keys to various users, while the TreeKEM schemes no longer need a group manager, but do not withstand concurrency of updates in a rather critical way. Finally, the propose-then-commit technique, when naively combined with (Tainted) TreeKEM as in MLS [8], in the worst case induces an overhead linear in the group size, and still does not completely achieve our desired concurrency and PCS guarantees. Nevertheless, we show how to combine these structures together—in a very concrete and non-black-box way—to obtain our scheme with overhead $\mathcal{O}(t \cdot (1 + \log(n/t)))$.

Moreover, we can easily achieve forward-security in addition to PCS (i.e., drop restriction (a) on the attacker), by using the recent technique of [3,24], which basically replaces traditional PKE with so called *updatable* PKE (uPKE). Informally, such PKE is *stateful*, and only works if all the senders are synchronized with the recipient (which can be enforced in our model, even with concurrency). Intuitively, each uPKE ciphertext updates the public and secret keys in a correlated way, so that future ciphertexts (produced with new public key) can be decrypted with the new secret key, but old ciphertexts cannot be decrypted with the new secret key. Hence, uPKE provides an efficient and practical mechanism for forward-secrecy in such a synchronized setting, without the need of heavy, less efficient tools, such as hierarchical identity based encryption (HIBE), directly used as a building block for strongly secure group ratcheting [5], or used as an intermediary component to build stronger *key-updatable* PKE (kuPKE)[2] for secure two-party messaging [23,30].

OUR LOWER BOUND. We prove a lower bound $\Omega(t)$ on the efficiency of any group ratcheting protocol which only uses "realistic" tools, such as (possibly key-updatable (See footnote 2)) PKE, (possibly so called "dual") PRFs, and general BE (see Sect. 2 for explaining these terms). We define our symbolic notion of key-updatable PKE so that it even captures functionality and security guarantees at least as strong as one expects from HIBE. To the best of our knowledge, these primitives include all known tools used in all "practical" results on group ratcheting (including our upper bound). Thus, our result nearly matches our upper bound, and shows that the $\Omega(n)$ *overheard of pairwise Signal protocol is optimal for unbounded concurrency*, at least within our model.

To motivate our model for the lower bound, group ratcheting would be "easy" if we could use "exotic" tools, such as multiparty non-interactive key agreement (mNIKE), multi-linear maps, or general-purpose obfuscation. For example, using general mNIKE, one can easily achieve PCS and unbounded concurrency, by having each member simply broadcast its new public key, without any knowledge of other senders: at the end of each round, the union of latest keys of all the group members magically (and non-interactively) updates the previous group key to a new, unrelated value. Of course, we currently don't have any even remotely practical mNIKE protocols, so it seems natural that we must define a model which only permits the use of "realistic" tools, such as (ku)PKE, (dual) PRFs, BE, (HIBE,) etc.

To formally address this challenge, we use a *symbolic* modeling framework inspired by the elegant work of Micciancio and Panjwani [26], who used it to derive a lower bound for the efficiency of multi-cast encryption. Symbolic models treat all elements as symbols whose algebraic structure is entirely disregarded,

---

[2] While for our upper bound construction weaker and more efficient uPKE (based on DH groups) suffices as in [3,24], to strengthen our lower bound we allow constructions to use stronger and less efficient key-updatable PKE (thus far based on HIBE) as in [6,23,30].

and which can be used only as intended. E.g., a symbolic public key can be defined to only encrypt messages, and the only way to decrypt the resulting ciphertext is to have another symbol corresponding to the associated secret key. In particular, one cannot perform any other operations with the symbolic public key, such as verifying a signature, using it for a Diffie-Hellman key exchange, etc.

We use such a symbolic model to precisely define the primitives we allow, including the grammar of symbols and valid derivation rules between them (see Fig. 1). We then formalize the intuition for our lower bound in Sect. 5 (that we formally prove in the full version [11]). Our bound is actually very strong: it is the *best-case* lower bound, which holds for any execution schedule of group ratcheting protocols within our model, and which is proven against highly restricted adversaries for extremely little security requirements. Specifically, we show that each sender for round i must send at least one fresh message over the broadcast channel "specific" to every sender of the previous round $i - 1$.[3] While intuitively simple, the exact formalization of this result is non-trivial, in part due to the rather advanced nature of the underlying primitives we allow. For example, we must show that no matter what shared infrastructure was established before round $(i - 1)$, and no matter what information a sender A sent in round $i - 1$, there is no way for A to always recover at round i from potential exposure at round $(i - 2)$, unless every sender B in round i sends some message "only to A".

PERSPECTIVE. To put our symbolic result in perspective, early use of symbolic models in cryptography date to the Dolev-Yao model [18], and were used to prove "upper bounds", meaning security of protocols which were too complex to analyze in the standard "computational model" (with reductions to well established simpler primitives or assumptions). In contrast, Micciancio and Panjwani [26] observed that symbolic models can also be used in a different way to prove impossibility results (i.e., *lower* bounds) on the efficiency of building various primitives using a fixed set of (symbolic) building blocks. This is interesting because we do not have many other compelling techniques to prove such lower bounds.

To the best of our knowledge, the only other technique we know is that of "black-box separations" [22]. While originally used for black-box impossibility results [22], Gennaro and Trevisan [20] adapted this technique to proving efficiency limitations of black-box reductions, such as building psedorandom generators from one-way permutations. However, black-box separation lower bounds are not only complex (which to some extent is true for symbolic lower bounds as well), but also become exponentially harder, as the primitive in question becomes more complex to define, or more diverse building blocks are allowed. In particular, to the best of our knowledge, the setting of group ratcheting using kuPKE, HIBE, dual PRFs, and BE used in this paper, appears several orders of magnitude more complex than what can be done with the state-of-the-art black-box lower bounds.

---

[3] Except for itself, if the sender was active in the prior round. This intuitively explains why our "best-case" lower bound is actually $(t - 1)$ and not t.

Thus, we hope that our paper renews the interests in symbolic lower bounds, and that our techniques would prove useful to study other settings where such lower bounds could be proven.

2   Preliminaries

We shortly introduce our notation as well as the syntax of the most important cryptographic building blocks. We also sketch their security guarantees that we formally define along the full proofs in our full version [11].

Notation. We distinguish between deterministic and probabilistic assignments with symbols $\leftarrow$ and $\leftarrow_\$$, respectively; the latter denotes sampling of an element x from the uniform distribution over a set $\mathcal{X}$ ($x \leftarrow_\$ \mathcal{X}$) and invoking a probabilistic algorithm alg on input a with output x ($x \leftarrow_\$ \mathrm{alg}(a)$). In order to make the used random coins r of an invocation explicit (and turning it into a deterministic invocation), we write $x \leftarrow \mathrm{alg}(a; r)$. We denote the cardinality of a set $\mathcal{X}$ or the length of a string s with symbols $|\mathcal{X}|$ and $|s|$. Concatenations of two bit-strings s_1, s_2 is written as $s_1 \| s_2$.

Adversaries $\mathcal{A}$ in our computational models are probabilistic algorithms invoked in a security experiment denoted by the term **Game**. Therein they can call oracles, denoted by term **Oracle**.

In our symbolic model we describe grammar rules as follows. For three types of symbols X, Y, and Z, $X \mapsto Y|Z$ denotes that symbols of type X can be parsed as symbols of type Y or type Z. A type that cannot be parsed further is called *terminal type*. Using these grammar rules, we define derivation rules that describe how symbols can be derived from sets of (other) symbols. For a symbol m and set of symbols $\boldsymbol{M}$, $\boldsymbol{M} \vdash m$ means that m can be derived from the symbols in set $\boldsymbol{M}$ by using the grammar and derivation rules that we specify in our symbolic model.

(Dual) Pseudo-random Function. A pseudo-random function prf takes a symmetric key and some associated data, and outputs another symmetric key such that for sets $\mathcal{K}, \mathcal{AD}$: $\mathrm{prf}(k, ad) \to k'$ with $k, k' \in \mathcal{K}$ and $ad \in \mathcal{AD}$. A dual pseudo-random function dprf takes two symmetric keys and outputs another symmetric key such that for set $\mathcal{K}$: $\mathrm{dprf}(\{k_1, k_2\}) \to k'$ with $k_1, k_2, k' \in \mathcal{K}$ with the added property that $\mathrm{dprf}(k_1, k_2) = \mathrm{dprf}(k_2, k_1) = k'$. For simplicity (in our proof), we only consider symmetric dual PRFs [9].

A secure PRF outputs a key that is *secret*[4] if the input key is secret as well. A dual PRF additionally achieves secrecy of the output key in case at most one of the two input keys is known by an attacker.

---

[4] Where *secrecy* means indistinguishable from a random key in the computational model and underivable from public symbols in the symbolic execution model.

Key-Updatable Public Key Encryption. Key-updatable public key encryption (kuPKE) is an extension of public key encryption that allows for independent updates of public and secret key with respect to some associated data. This primitive has been used in constructions of two-party ratcheting (e.g., [23,25,29, 30]). Furthermore, a work by Balli et al. [6] recently showed that it is actually necessary for building optimally secure two-party ratcheting.

A kuPKE scheme UE is a tuple of algorithms UE = (gen, up, enc, dec) where up takes some associated data together with either a public key or a secret key and produces a new public key or secret key respectively such that for sets $\mathcal{SK}, \mathcal{PK}, \mathcal{C}, \mathcal{M}, \mathcal{AD}$: $\mathrm{gen}(sk) \to pk$, $\mathrm{up}(sk, ad) \to sk'$, $\mathrm{up}(pk, ad) \to pk'$, $\mathrm{enc}(pk, m) \to_\$ c$, and $\mathrm{dec}(sk, c) \to m$ with $sk, sk' \in \mathcal{SK}$, $pk, pk' \in \mathcal{PK}$, $ad \in \mathcal{AD}$, $m \in \mathcal{M}$, and $c \in \mathcal{C}$. A kuPKE scheme UE is correct if for synchronously updated public key and secret key, the latter can decrypt ciphertexts produced with the former: $\Pr[\forall n \in \mathbb{N} \ \mathrm{dec}(sk_n, \mathrm{enc}(pk_n, m)) = m : sk_0 \leftarrow_\$ \mathcal{SK}, pk_0 = \mathrm{gen}(sk_0), \forall i \in [n] \ ad_i \leftarrow_\$ \mathcal{AD}, pk_{i+1} = \mathrm{up}(pk_i, ad_i), sk_{i+1} = \mathrm{up}(sk_i, ad_i), m \leftarrow_\$ \mathcal{M}] = 1$.

A secure kuPKE scheme intuitively guarantees that a message, encrypted to public key pk' that was derived from another public key pk via sequential updates under associated-data from vector $ad \in \mathcal{AD}^*$, cannot be decrypted by a (computationally bounded, or symbolic) adversary even with access to any secret keys, derived via updates from pk's secret key sk under an associated-data vector $ad' \in \mathcal{AD}^*$ such that ad' is not a prefix of ad. Note that this intuitive security notion matches security of HIBE when associated data is being parsed as identity strings.

Broadcast Encryption. A broadcast encryption (BE) scheme BE is a tuple of four algorithms BE = (gen, reg, enc, dec) where reg takes a (main) secret key and an integer and produces an accordingly *registered* secret key, enc takes, in addition to public key and message, a set of integers to indicate which registered secret keys must be unable to decrypt the message such that for sets $\mathcal{MSK}, \mathcal{SK}, \mathcal{MPK}, \mathcal{C}, \mathcal{M}$: $\mathrm{gen}(msk) \to mpk$, $\mathrm{reg}(msk, u) \to_\$ sk$, $\mathrm{enc}(mpk, \boldsymbol{RM}, m) \to_\$ c$, and $\mathrm{dec}(sk, c) \to m$ with $msk \in \mathcal{MSK}$, $mpk \in \mathcal{MPK}$, $u \in \mathbb{N}$, $sk \in \mathcal{SK}$, $\boldsymbol{RM} \subset \mathbb{N}$, $m \in \mathcal{M}$, and $c \in \mathcal{C}$. A broadcast encryption scheme BE is correct if all registered secret keys that were not excluded when encrypting with the public key can decrypt the corresponding encrypted message: $\Pr[\mathrm{dec}(sk, \mathrm{enc}(mpk, \boldsymbol{RM}, m)) = m : msk \leftarrow_\$ \mathcal{MSK}, mpk = \mathrm{gen}(msk), u \leftarrow_\$ \mathbb{N}, sk \leftarrow_\$ \mathrm{reg}(msk, u), \boldsymbol{RM} \subset \mathbb{N} \backslash \{u\}] = 1$.

A secure BE scheme intuitively guarantees that a message, encrypted to a (main) public key mpk with a set of removed users $\boldsymbol{RM}$, cannot be decrypted by a (computationally bounded, or symbolic) adversary even with access to any secret keys, registered under mpk's main secret key msk for numbers $u \in \boldsymbol{RM}$.

3   Security of Concurrent Group Ratcheting

In this work we consider an abstraction of group ratcheting under significant relaxations and restrictions with respect to the real-world. The purpose of this approach is to disregard irrelevant aspects in order to highlight the immediate effects of concurrent state updates in group ratcheting.

In the following, we define syntax and (restricted) security of ratcheting in static groups against computationally bounded adversaries. We assume in our model that all group members have access to a round-based reliable and authenticated broadcast. Additionally, since our focus are concurrent operations in an initialized group, we consider an abstract initialization algorithm for deriving initial user states.[5]

Syntax. A static group ratcheting protocol is a tuple of three algorithms $\mathsf{GR} = (\mathsf{init}, \mathsf{snd}, \mathsf{rcv})$ such that for sets $\mathcal{ST}_{\mathsf{GR}}, \mathcal{C}_{\mathsf{GR}}, \mathcal{K}_{\mathsf{GR}}, \mathcal{R}$:

- $\mathsf{init}(n; r) \rightarrow (st_1, \ldots, st_n)$ with $n \in \mathbb{N}$, $r \in \mathcal{R}$, and $st_1, \ldots, st_n \in \mathcal{ST}_{\mathsf{GR}}$; creates an initial local state for every participating group member.
- $\mathsf{snd}(st; r) \rightarrow (st', c)$ with $st, st' \in \mathcal{ST}_{\mathsf{GR}}$, $r \in \mathcal{R}$, and $c \in \mathcal{C}_{\mathsf{GR}}$; takes the current state of an instance (in addition to freshly sampled random coins) and outputs the updated state and update information within a ciphertext that is to be sent via the broadcast.
- $\mathsf{rcv}(st, c) \rightarrow (st', k)$ with $st, st' \in \mathcal{ST}_{\mathsf{GR}}$, $c \subset \mathcal{C}_{\mathsf{GR}}$, and $k \in \mathcal{K}_{\mathsf{GR}}$; takes the current state of an instance and a set of update ciphertexts (e.g., all broadcast ciphertexts since this instance's last receiving), and outputs the updated state and the current (joint) group key.

Security. Security experiments $\mathsf{KIND}^b_{\mathsf{GR}}$ in which adversary $\mathcal{A}$ attacks scheme GR proceed as follows:

1. $\mathcal{A}$ determines the number of group members n. Afterwards the challenger invokes the init algorithm to generate initial secret states for all members. Then the security experiment continues in rounds. In every round i
   - adversary $\mathcal{A}$ chooses set $\boldsymbol{U}^i_{\mathsf{S}}$ of senders. For each sender $u \in \boldsymbol{U}^i_{\mathsf{S}}$ algorithm snd is invoked. All resulting ciphertexts are both given to $\mathcal{A}$ and received by all group members via invocations of algorithm rcv.
   - adversary $\mathcal{A}$ chooses set $\boldsymbol{U}^i_{\mathsf{X}}$ of exposed users. The local state of each user $u \in \boldsymbol{U}^i_{\mathsf{X}}$ after receiving in round i is given to $\mathcal{A}$.
2. During the entire security experiment, $\mathcal{A}$ can challenge group keys established in any round i^*. $\mathcal{A}$ either obtains a random key (if $b = 0$) or the actual group key from round i^* (if $b = 1$) in response.
3. When terminating, $\mathcal{A}$ returns a guess b' such that it wins if $b = b'$ and for all challenged group keys it holds that:
   (a) no user was exposed after a challenged group key was computed,
   (b) every user sent at least once after being exposed and before a challenged group key was computed, and

---

[5] We note that we only consider a single independently established group session. For protocols in which participants use the same secrets simultaneously across multiple (thereby dependent) sessions, we refer the reader to a work by Cremers et al. [17]. Both the problems and the solutions for these two considerations appear to be entirely distinct.

(c) after all exposed users sent once without being exposed again, at least one user additionally sent before a challenged group key was computed.

Group keys for which conditions 3a–3c hold are marked *secure*.

We restrict the adversary with condition (3a) only because the resulting weaker security definition already suffices to prove our *lower* bound of communication complexity. For our full model in which we prove the construction of our *upper* bound secure, we strengthen adversaries by lifting restriction (3a). This reflects that our upper bound construction achieves immediate forward-secrecy while our lower bound already holds without requiring any form of forward-secrecy.

Condition (3b) models that a user who was exposed must generate fresh secrets and send the respective public values to the group before it can receive confidential information for establishing new secure group keys. After all exposed users recovered by sending subsequently, their sent contribution must be used effectively to establish a new secret group key. Therefore, condition (3c) additionally requires one further response from a user as a reaction to all newly contributed public values.

For removing condition (3c) either 1. The last users who recovered did so concurrently at most as a pair of two (such that their new public contributions can be merged into a shared group key non-interactively with NIKE mechanisms), or 2. Multiparty NIKE schemes exist (for resolving cases of more concurrently recovering users). In order to simplify our security definition by not introducing an according case distinction tracing occurrences of case 1, we generally restrict the adversary with condition (3c). We note that for proving our lower bound, restricting the adversary by this condition strengthens our result.

Intuitively, a group ratcheting scheme is secure if no adversary $\mathcal{A}$ exists that wins the above defined security experiment with probability non-negligibly higher than $1/2$.

Restrictions of the Model. With the following abstractions, simplifications, and restrictions, we support clarity and comprehensibility of our results and strengthen the statement of our lower bound. We consider: 1. A round-based communication setting, 2. Static groups, 3. All group members receive in every round, 4. Only passive adversaries 5. Adversaries can expose users only after receiving, and 6. Adversaries cannot attack used randomness. As we do not aim to develop a functional and secure group messenger but to theoretically analyze the foundations of concurrent group ratcheting, we believe this is justified.

4   Deficiencies of Existing Protocols

The problem of constructing group ratcheting could be solved trivially if efficient *multiparty non-interactive key exchange* schemes existed. Especially for the concurrent recovery from state exposures in group ratcheting, the lack of this tool appears to be crucial: Due to not being able to combine independently

proposed fresh public key material, existing efficient group ratcheting constructions cannot process concurrent operations as we will explain in this section. In
Table 1 we summarize the characteristics of previous group ratcheting schemes
in comparison to our construction and the lower bound.

Table 1. Properties of group ratcheting constructions and our lower bound. $t = |U_{\mathsf{S}}^{i-1}|$ is the number of members who sent concurrently in the previous round. For
the overhead we consider a worst-case scenario in a constant size group. Constructions
denoted with '◐'/'◑' provide PCS under no concurrency and can handle concurrent
state updates without reaching PCS with them.

	PCS	Concurrency	Overhead
Sender Key Mechanism [31]	○	●	1
Parallel Pairwise Signal [2,15,31]	●	●	n
Asynchronous Ratcheting Trees [14]	●	○	$\log(n)$
Causal TreeKEM [32]	◐	◑	$\log(n)$
TreeKEM Familiy [3,4]	●	○	$\log(n)$
MLS Draft-09 [8]	◐	◑	n
Optimally Secure Tainted TreeKEM [5]	◐	◑	$\log(n)$
Our Construction	●	●	$t \cdot (1 + \log(n/t))$
Our Lower Bound	●	●	$t - 1$

Sender Key Mechanism. WhatsApp uses the so called *sender key mechanism* for
implementing group chats [31]. This mechanism distributes a symmetric *sender
key* for each member in a group. When sending a group message, the sender
protects the payload with its own sender key, transmits the resulting (single)
ciphertext, and hashes the used sender key to obtain its next sender key. The
receivers decrypt the ciphertext with the sender's sender key and also update
the sender's sender key by hashing it.

While the deterministic derivation of sender keys induces no communication
overhead after the initial distribution of sender keys, it implies the reveal of
all future sender keys as soon as a member state is exposed (breaking post-
compromise security). However, as each group member's key material is processed and used independently, concurrently initiated group operations can be
processed naturally.

Parallel Execution of Pairwise Signal. The group ratcheting mechanism implemented in the Signal messenger bases on parallel executions of the two-
party Double Ratchet Algorithm [2,15,28] between each pair of members in a
group [31]. Due to splitting the group of size n into its n^2 independent pairwise
components, this construction can naturally handle concurrency. At the same
time, this approach induces a communication overhead of $\mathcal{O}(n)$ ciphertexts per
sent group payload.

Since the Double Ratchet Algorithm reaches post-compromise security (PCS) for each pair of members, also its parallel execution achieves this goal for the group against passive adversaries or if the member set remains static. Rösler et al. [31] describe an active attack against PCS in dynamic groups that exploits the implemented decentralized membership management. Furthermore, the delayed recovery from state exposures in the Double Ratchet Algorithm due to a strictly alternating update schedule between protocol participants (cf. analysis and fix in [2]) lets recoveries from state exposures in the group become effective only after every group member sent once at worst. With stronger two-party ratcheting protocols (e.g., [2,23,24,29,30]) this problem can be solved.

Asynchronous Ratcheting Tree. While the two above described approaches compute and use multiple symmetric keys in parallel for protecting communication in groups, the following constructions do so by deriving a single shared group key at each step of the group's lifetime. Therefore they arrange asymmetric key material on nodes in a tree structure in which each leaf represents a group member and the common root represents the shared group secret. Every group member stores the asymmetric secrets on the path from its leaf to the common root in its local state. For updating the local state, in order to recover from an adversarial exposure, all constructions let the updating member generate new asymmetric secrets for each node on their path to the root.

In the Asynchronous Ratcheting Trees (ART) design [14], these asymmetric secrets are exponents in a Diffie–Hellman (DH) group. State updates of a member's path is conducted as follows: the updating member freshly samples a new secret exponent for its own leaf and then deterministically derives every ancestor node's secret exponent as the shared DH key from its two children's public DH shares. All resulting new public DH shares on the path are sent to the group, inducing a communication overhead of $\mathcal{O}(\log(n))$ per update operation. Other members perform the same derivations for updated nodes on their own paths to the root to obtain the new exponents. Since all secrets in the updating member's local state are renewed based on fresh random coins, this mechanism achieves PCS.

The reason for ART not being able to process concurrent update operations is that simultaneous updates of nodes in the tree with independently computed DH exponents cannot be merged into a joint tree structure while reaching PCS. For t concurrent updates, a t-party NIKE would be needed to combine the resulting t new proposed DH shares into a shared secret exponent for the ancestor node at which all updating members' paths to the root join together. (As mentioned before, if multiparty NIKE existed, group ratcheting can be solved trivially without complex tree structures.)

Causal TreeKEM. As in the ART design [14], Causal TreeKEM [32] uses exponents in a DH group as asymmetric secrets on nodes in the tree. Also the update procedure is conceptually the same. However, in case of concurrently proposed path updates, the conflicting new exponents on a node are combined via exponent-addition and the conflicting public DH shares on a node are combined via multiplying these group elements.

Although this merge-mechanism resolves conflicts caused by concurrency, the combination of updated path secrets is not post-compromise secure: the old exponents of two nodes (from which their updating users A and B aimed to recover), whose common parent was updated via a combination of concurrent path updates, suffice to derive their parent's resulting new exponent. (The new exponent is the old exponent mixed with random values from A and B that they encrypt to the other's old node key.)

TreeKEM Family. In the family of TreeKEM constructions [3,4], the asymmetric key material of nodes in the tree are key encapsulation mechanism (KEM) key pairs or, in forward-secure TreeKEM, updatable KEM key pairs. For updating its local state, a group member samples a fresh secret from which it deterministically derives seeds for each node on its path to the root, such that all ancestor seeds can be derived from their descendant seeds (but not vice versa). The updating member generates the new key pair for each updated node from its seed deterministically, and encapsulates the node's seed to the public key of the child which is not on the member's path to the root. This mechanism achieves PCS and induces a communication overhead of $\mathcal{O}(\log(n))$ per update.

The idea of recovery from exposures is undermined in case of concurrency, since updating members send their new seeds for a node on their path to public keys of siblings, simultaneously being updated and replaced by new key material of members who concurrently update: the potentially exposed secrets *from which* one updating member aims to recover can then be used to obtain the new secrets *with which* the other updating user aims to recover (as in the case of Causal TreeKEM). Consequently, concurrent updates in TreeKEM are essentially ineffective with respect to PCS.

Forward-secure TreeKEM [3] uses an updatable KEM for enhancing forward-security guarantees of the above described mechanism. Tainted TreeKEM [4] enhances PCS guarantees with respect to dynamic membership changes in groups. Neither of these changes affect the trade-offs discussed here.

MLS Draft-09. Based on TreeKEM, the most recent draft of MLS [8] distinguishes between two state update variants: (a) In an *update proposal* a member refreshes only its own leaf key pair, removes all other nodes on the path from this leaf to the root, and makes the root parent of all nodes that thereby became parentless. (b) In a *commit* a member combines previous update proposals and refreshes all key pairs on the path from its own leaf to the root (matching the normal TreeKEM update as described in the last paragraph).

In principle, both update variants achieve PCS for respective the sender. However, for simultaneously sent *commits*, all but one are rejected (e.g., by a central server) meaning that PCS under concurrency is not achieved for rejected updating commits. Furthermore, while *update proposals* can be processed concurrently, they eventually let the tree's depth degrade to 1, inducing a worst-case overhead of $\mathcal{O}(n)$ for later commits.[6]

Optimally Secure Tainted TreeKEM. Recently and concurrent to our work, an optimally secure variant of group ratcheting, based on a combination of Tainted TreeKEM and MLS draft-09, was proposed by Alwen et al. [5]. In addition to authentication guarantees (which is independent of our focus), their protocol achieves strong security guarantees for group partitions due to concurrency: instead of assuming that a (consensus) mechanism rejects conflicting commits as in MLS, they anticipate that different sub-groups of group members may process different of these commits such that the overall perspective on the group diverges. Their protocol guarantees that, after diverging, exposing states of one sub-group's members does not affect the security of another sub-groups' secrets. Intuitively, this is achieved by using HIBE key pairs on the tree's nodes that are regularly updated via secret-key-delegation based on identity strings that reflect the current perspective on the group. (For details, we refer the interested reader to [5].)

While these changes increase security with respect to some form of forward-secrecy under group partitions, they do not entirely solve the issue of conflicting commits as in MLS: committed state updates still only have an effect in a sub-group that processes the commit such that only one user at a time can update secrets on the path from its leave to the root whereas other user's path updates remain ineffective.

Our construction from Sect. 6 bypasses the issue of concurrently generated, incompatible path proposals by postponing the update of affected nodes in the tree by one communication round. However, "immediate" PCS can still be reached for non-concurrent updates by composing our construction with one of the above described ones without loss in efficiency. We note that some of the above constructions provide strong security guarantees with respect to active adversaries, dynamic groups, entirely asynchronous communication, or weak randomness, which is out (and partially independent) of our consideration's scope.

5   Intuition for Lower Bound

Our lower bound proof intuitively says that every group ratcheting scheme with better communication complexity than this bound is either insecure, or not correct, or cannot be built from the building blocks we consider. In the following, we first list these considered building blocks and argue why the selection of those is indeed justified (and not too restrictive). We then abstractly explain the symbolic security definition of group ratcheting, and finally sketch the steps of our proof that is formally given in the full version [11].

---

[6] Consider, for example, a scenario in which the same majority of members always sends update proposals and a fixed disjoint set of few members always commits. In this case, the overhead of commits for these few members converges to $\mathcal{O}(n)$.

5.1 Symbolic Building Blocks

The selection of primitives which a group ratcheting construction may use to reach minimal communication complexity in our symbolic model is inspired by the work of Micciancio and Panjwani [26]. For their lower bound of communication complexity in multi-cast encryption—which can also be understood as group key exchange—, Micciancio and Panjwani allow constructions to use pseudorandom generators, secret sharing, and symmetric encryption. We instead consider 1. *(dual) pseudo-random functions*, 2. *key-updatable public key encryption* (with functionality and symbolic security guarantees at least as strong as those of *hierarchical identity based encryption*), and 3. *broadcast encryption* and thereby significantly extend the power of available building blocks. As secret sharing appears to be rather irrelevant in our setting—as well as it is irrelevant in their setting—, we neglect it to achieve better clarity in model and proof.

Bulding Blocks in Related Work. To support the justification of our selection, we note that all previous constructions of group ratcheting base on less powerful building blocks than we consider here: The ART construction [14] relies on a combination of dual PRF and Diffie-Hellman (DH) group. The actual properties used from the DH group can also be achieved by using generic public key encryption (PKE)—as demonstrated by its following successors. TreeKEM as proposed in the MLS initiative [3,8] relies on a PRG and a PKE scheme. TreeKEM with extended forward-secrecy [3] relies on a PRG and an updatable PKE scheme. The syntax of the latter in combination with the respective computational security guarantees can be considered weaker than our according symbolic variant of kuPKE. Tainted TreeKEM [4] relies on a PKE scheme in the random oracle model. Optimally secure Tainted TreeKEM [5] relies on an HIBE scheme in the random oracle model. As noted before, functionality and security guarantees of HIBE are captured in our symbolic notion of kuPKE. The property of the random oracle that allows for mixing multiple input values of which at least one is confidential to derive a confidential random output can be achieved similarly by using (a cascade of) dual PRF invocations.[7]

Only the post-compromise *insecure* merge-mechanism of DH shares from Causal TreeKEM [32] is not captured in our symbolic model. However, turning this mechanism post-compromise *secure* results in multi-party NIKE, which we intentionally exclude.

Grammar. The grammar definition of the considered building blocks bases on five types of symbols: messages M, secret keys SK, symmetric keys K, public keys PK, and random coins R (which is a terminal type). These types and their relation are specified in the lower right corner of Fig. 1. For simplicity

---

[7] If the constructions in [4,5] would rely on stronger (security) guarantees of the random oracle model, their practicability might be questionable.

Derivation of protected values:	Derivation of secret keys:
a) $m \in M \implies M \vdash m$	e) $M \vdash sk \implies \forall ad \ M \vdash \mathrm{up}(sk, ad)$
b) $M \vdash k \implies \forall ad \ M \vdash \mathrm{prf}(k, ad)$	f) $M \vdash sk \implies \forall u \ M \vdash \mathrm{reg}(sk, u)$
c) $M \vdash k_1, k_2 \implies M \vdash \mathrm{dprf}(\{k_1, k_2\})$	

Derivation of protected values (cont.):	Grammar rules:
d) $M \vdash \mathrm{enc}(pk, RM, m), sk :$	
$\quad \mathrm{Fit}(pk, RM, sk) \implies M \vdash m$	1. $M \mapsto SK \mid PK \mid \mathrm{enc}(PK, \mathcal{S}(\mathbb{N}), M)$
Derivation of public values:	2. $SK \mapsto K \mid \mathrm{up}(SK, M) \mid \mathrm{reg}(SK, \mathbb{N})$
g) $M \vdash sk \implies M \vdash \mathrm{gen}(sk)$	3. $K \mapsto R \mid \mathrm{prf}(K, M) \mid \mathrm{dprf}(\{K, K\})$
h) $M \vdash pk \implies \forall ad \ M \vdash \mathrm{up}(pk, ad)$	4. $PK \mapsto \mathrm{gen}(SK) \mid \mathrm{up}(PK, M)$
i) $M \vdash pk, m \implies \forall RM \ M \vdash \mathrm{enc}(pk, RM, m)$	

Fig. 1. Grammar and derivation rules of building blocks in the symbolic model.

(and in order to strengthen our lower bound result), we consider algorithms gen and enc interoperable for kuPKE and BE.[8]

Derivation Rules. Symbolic security for the building blocks is defined via derivation rules that describe the conditions under which symbols can be derived from sets of (other) symbols. These rules are defined in Fig. 1 clustered into those with which protected values can be obtained, with which secret keys can be updated or registered, and with which public values can be obtained.

Rules b) and c) describe the security of (dual) PRFs, rules d), e), and g) to i) describe the security and functionality of kuPKE (and HIBE), and rules d), f), g), and i) describe the security and functionality of BE.

Rule d), describing the conditions under which a ciphertext can be decrypted, uses predicate Fit that validates the compatibility of public key and secret key (and set of removed registered users). Intuitively, a secret key sk is compatible with a public key pk if all updates for obtaining sk correspond to updates for obtaining pk in the same order and under the same associated data with respect to an initial key pair, or if the former was registered under the main secret key of the latter.

5.2 Symbolic Group Ratcheting

The syntax of group ratcheting was introduced in Sect. 3. In the following we map this syntax to the grammar definition above, and shortly give an intuition for the correctness and security of group ratcheting in the symbolic model.

Inputs and outputs of group ratcheting algorithms init, snd, and rcv are random coins $\mathcal{R}$, local user states $\mathcal{ST}_{\mathsf{GR}}$, ciphertexts $\mathcal{C}_{\mathsf{GR}}$, and group keys $\mathcal{K}_{\mathsf{GR}}$. In our grammar these random coins are sets of type R symbols, local states and ciphertexts are sets of type M symbols, and group keys are symbols of type K.

According to this grammar, we require from symbolic constructions of group ratcheting for being *correct* that 1. all outputs of a group ratcheting algorithm

---

[8] As a simplification we use $\mathbb{N}$ to denote the user input symbol of BE, $\mathcal{S}(\cdot)$ to denote an unordered compilation of multiple such symbols, and $\{\cdot, \cdot\}$ to denote an unordered compilation of two key symbols. For kuPKE encryptions the second parameter in our symbolic model can be ignored.

invocation can be derived from its inputs via the derivation rules defined above and 2. in each round the group keys, computed by all users, are equal. The first condition is necessary to allow for symbolic adversaries. We note that this condition furthermore implies "inverse derivation guarantees", meaning that symbols can *only* be obtained via our derivation rules. For example, for inputs IN and outputs OUT of an algorithm invocation, output $k' \in$ OUT with $\text{prf}(k, ad) = k'$ is either also element of set IN (i.e., $k' \in$ IN), or k' is encrypted in a ciphertext contained in set IN, or IN $\vdash k$ holds. We explicitly provide these inverse derivation guarantees in our full version [11].

Security. To transfer the computational security experiment from Sect. 3 to the execution of symbolic attackers against group ratcheting, only few small changes are necessary: 1. a symbolic adversary $\mathcal{A}$ follows the above defined derivation rules for an unbounded time, 2. the target of $\mathcal{A}$ is not to distinguish *securely* marked real group keys from random ones but to derive such *securely* marked keys from the ciphertexts, sent in each round, and the states, exposed at the end of each round, with these derivation rules.

A group ratcheting scheme is *secure in the symbolic model* if an unbounded adversary cannot derive any of the securely marked group keys from the combination of all rounds' ciphertexts and exposed states via the above defined rules. The fully formal variant of this definition is in Fig. 2.

Game $\text{SYM}_{\text{GR}}(n, U_{\mathbf{X}}^0,$	**Proc** Round(U)	**Proc** Expose(U)
$\quad U_{\mathbf{S}}^1, U_{\mathbf{X}}^1, \dots, U_{\mathbf{S}}^q, U_{\mathbf{X}}^q)$	13 Require $U \subseteq [n]$	25 Require $U \subseteq [n]$
00 $\mathbf{XU} \leftarrow \emptyset;\ \mathbf{SEC} \leftarrow \emptyset$	14 For all $u \in U$:	26 $\mathbf{XU} \leftarrow \mathbf{XU} \cup U$
01 $\mathbf{XST} \leftarrow \emptyset;\ \mathbf{C} \leftarrow \emptyset$	15 $\quad r_u \leftarrow_\$ \mathcal{R}$	27 $XST[i] \leftarrow \bigcup_{u \in U} st_u$
02 $XST[\cdot] \leftarrow \emptyset;\ C[\cdot] \leftarrow \emptyset$	16 $\quad (st_u, c_u) \leftarrow \text{snd}(st_u; r_u)$	28 $\mathbf{XST} \leftarrow \mathbf{XST} \cup XST[i]$
03 $K[\cdot] \leftarrow \perp;\ r \leftarrow_\$ \mathcal{R}$	17 $C[i] \leftarrow \bigcup_{u \in U} c_u$	29 $\mathbf{SEC} \leftarrow \mathbf{SEC} \setminus [i-1]$
04 $(st_1, \dots, st_n) \leftarrow \text{init}(n; r)$	18 For all $u \in [n]$:	30 Return
05 Call Expose($U_{\mathbf{X}}^0$)	19 $\quad (st_u, k_u) \leftarrow \text{rcv}(st_u, C[i])$	
06 For i from 1 to q:	20 If $\mathbf{XU} = \emptyset \wedge (U \neq \emptyset)$	
07 $\quad$ Call Round($U_{\mathbf{S}}^i$)	$\quad \vee i - 1 \in \mathbf{SEC}$):	
08 $\quad$ Call Expose($U_{\mathbf{X}}^i$)	21 $\quad \mathbf{SEC} \leftarrow \{i\}$	
09 $\mathbf{C} \leftarrow \bigcup_{j \in [q]} C[i]$	22 $\quad \mathbf{XU} \leftarrow \mathbf{XU} \setminus U$	
10 If $\exists i' \in \mathbf{SEC}$:	23 $\quad K[i] \leftarrow k_1$	
$\quad K[i'] \in \text{Der}(\mathbf{C} \cup \mathbf{XST})$:	24 Return	
11 $\quad$ Stop with 1		
12 Stop with 0		

Fig. 2. Security definition of concurrent group ratcheting in our symbolic model.

5.3 Lower Bound

Using this symbolic framework, we formulate (a sketched variant of) the lower bound of communication complexity for secure (and correct) group ratcheting constructions:

Let GR *be a secure and correct group ratcheting scheme. For every round* i *in a symbolic execution of* GR *with senders* U_S^i *and exposed users* U_X^i, *the number of sent symbols is* $|C[i]| \geq |U_S^i| \cdot (|U_S^{i-1}| - 1)$.

For our proof, we consider a symbolic adversary that proceeds as follows:

1. In round $i - 2$ a set of members $U_X^{i-2} \subseteq [n]$ with $|U_X^{i-2}| > 1$ is exposed.
2. In subsequent round $i - 1$ these exposed users send (i.e., $U_S^{i-1} := U_X^{i-2}$).
3. In round i a non-empty set of members $\emptyset \neq U_S^i \subseteq [n]$ sends.

Assuming no user was exposed in any round before or after $i - 2$, our symbolic security definition requires the group key in round i to be secure (i.e., not derivable from exposed states and sent ciphertexts up to round i). In order to show that each sender in round i must send at least $|U_S^{i-1}| - 1$ ciphertexts to establish this secure group key, we analyze the effects of exposures in round $i - 2$, sending in round $i - 1$, and sending in round i in the following paragraphs.

At the end of round $i - 2$ any symbol derivable by users in set U_X^{i-2} is also derivable by the adversary. After generating new secret random coins at the beginning of round $i - 1$, users in set U_S^{i-1} can derive symbols, that the adversary cannot derive, from these new random coins and public symbols from their (exposed) state. We call such derivable symbols of types SK, K, and R that the adversary cannot derive *useful secrets*. Symbols of these types that are derivable by the adversary are called *useless secrets* (resulting in two complementary sets). Before sending in round $i - 1$, new useful secrets of a user $u^* \in U_S^{i-1}$ are only derivable for u^* itself but not for any other user $u \in [n] \backslash \{u^*\}$. This is because the origin of these new useful secrets are the new secret random coins generated at the beginning of round $i - 1$ and no communication took place after their generation yet. Hence, at sending in round $i - 1$ users in set U_S^{i-1} share no *compatible* useful secrets with other users. Secrets are called *compatible* if they are equal or if they are registered via rule f) under the same (main) secret key.

We formulate three observations: I) For deriving a public key pk from a set of type R symbols it is necessary according to grammar rule 4. and derivation rules g) and h) (with their inverse derivation guarantees) that its secret key sk (or one of its update-ancestors' secret key sk) is derivable from this set as well. II) For deriving a ciphertext c, encrypted to a public key pk, from a set of type R symbols it is necessary according to grammar rule 1. and derivation rule i) (with its inverse derivation guarantees) that this public key pk is derivable from it as well. III) Unifying all random coins generated by all users up to (including) round $i - 1$ except those generated by user $u^* \in U_S^{i-1}$ in round $i - 1$ forms a set of type R symbols from which all useful secrets at the beginning of round $i - 1$ can be derived except those that are new to user u^* at that point. Combining these observations shows that at the beginning of round $i - 1$ no user $u \neq u^*$ can derive public keys to useful secrets of user $u^* \in U_S^{i-1}$. This further implies that user u cannot derive ciphertexts encrypted to such public keys. As a result, the set of symbols sent by one user $u \in U_S^{i-1}$ in round $i - 1$ contains no ciphertexts directed to useful secrets derivable by another user $u^* \in U_S^{i-1} \backslash \{u\}$ that would transport useful secrets between such users.

We further observe: According to the inverse derivation guarantees of rule c), both inputs to a dual PRF invocation must be derivable for deriving its output. As this requires a shared useful secret on input for deriving a shared useful secret as output, also a dual PRF establishes no shared (compatible) useful secrets in round $i - 1$. All remaining derivation rules either output no secrets, or are *unidimensional*, meaning that they only immediately derive one (useful) secret from another. As a result, also after receiving in round $i - 1$ users in set $U_{\mathbf{S}}^{i-1}$ share no compatible useful secrets.

Sampling random coins before sending in round i again produces no shared compatible useful secrets between users that shared none before. Hence, also before receiving in round i, users in set $U_{\mathbf{S}}^{i-1}$ share no compatible useful secrets. We remark that our symbolic correctness and security definition requires for the given adversary that the shared group key derived in round i (after receiving) is a *useful secret*.

For quantifying the number of ciphertexts sent in round i, we define two *key graphs* $\mathcal{G}_i^{\text{before}}$ and $\mathcal{G}_i^{\text{after}}$ that represent useful secrets as nodes and derivations among them as edges. Secret y being derivable from secret x is represented by a directed edge from x to y. Although inspired by the proof technique of Micciancio and Panjwani [26], the use of key (derivation) graphs in our proof is entirely new.

Graph $\mathcal{G}_i^{\text{before}}$ includes a node for each useful secret that exists after receiving in round i and an edge for each derivation among them except for derivations possible only due to ciphertexts sent in round i. Graph $\mathcal{G}_i^{\text{after}}$ contains $\mathcal{G}_i^{\text{before}}$ and additionally includes edges for derivations possible due to ciphertexts sent in round i. Thus, the number of additional edges in $\mathcal{G}_i^{\text{after}}$ equals the number of sent ciphertexts in round i. Mapping our derivation rules to edges is highly non-trivial (e.g., each sent ciphertext must appear at most once). All details are in the full version [11].

The fact that users in set $U_{\mathbf{S}}^{i-1}$ share no compatible useful secrets before receiving in round i finds expression in graph $\mathcal{G}_i^{\text{before}}$ as follows: Every such user $u \in U_{\mathbf{S}}^{i-1}$ is represented by nodes in a set $\mathcal{V}_u^i$ that stand for its useful secret random coins from rounds $i - 1$ and i (the latter only if u also sent in round i). For every pair of users $u_1, u_2 \in U_{\mathbf{S}}^{i-1}$ with $u_1 \neq u_2$ there exists no node in graph $\mathcal{G}_i^{\text{before}}$ that is reachable via a path from a node in set $\mathcal{V}_{u_1}^i$ and a path from a node in set $\mathcal{V}_{u_2}^i$ simultaneously (including trivial paths). In contrast, every set $\mathcal{V}_u^i$ with $u \in U_{\mathbf{S}}^{i-1}$ must contain a node from which a path in graph $\mathcal{G}_i^{\text{after}}$ reaches node v^* that represents the group key in round i.

In graph $\mathcal{G}_i^{\text{before}}$ node v^* was reachable via a path from nodes $\mathcal{V}_u^i$ of at most one user $u \in U_{\mathbf{S}}^{i-1}$. Otherwise v^* would have been a compatible useful secret for two users in set $U_{\mathbf{S}}^{i-1}$ before receiving in round i. Consequently, at least one edge per user $u^* \in U_{\mathbf{S}}^{i-1} \backslash \{u\}$ must be included in $\mathcal{G}_i^{\text{after}}$ in addition to those contained in $\mathcal{G}_i^{\text{before}}$. Hence, $\mathcal{G}_i^{\text{after}}$ contains at least $|U_{\mathbf{S}}^{i-1}| - 1$ more edges than $\mathcal{G}_i^{\text{before}}$, implying that at least $|U_{\mathbf{S}}^{i-1}| - 1$ ciphertexts were sent in round i.

We now observe that invocations of algorithm snd in every round are independent of sets $U_{\mathbf{X}}^j$ for all j, and invocations of algorithm snd in round i are independent of set $U_{\mathbf{S}}^i$. As a consequence, every sender $u \in U_{\mathbf{S}}^i$ must send $|U_{\mathbf{S}}^{i-1}| - 1$

ciphertexts, anticipating the worst case that it is the only sender in that round. Therefore, $|U_{\mathsf{S}}^{i}| \cdot (|U_{\mathsf{S}}^{i-1}| - 1)$ ciphertexts are sent in (every) round i.

Interpretation. This lower bound, formally proved in the full version of this article [11], describes the best case of communication complexity both within our model but partially also with respect to the real-world: it holds against very weak adversaries for significantly reduced functionality requirements of group ratcheting without any form of required forward-secrecy. Lower bounds, induced by forward-secrecy for group key exchange [26], may furthermore apply to practical group ratcheting and therefore increase necessary communication complexity thereof.[9] We note that our result even applies to any two rounds between which no user sent.

Bypassing our lower bound is possible for constructions that exploit the algebraic structure of elements (which is forbidden in symbolic models), base on building blocks that we do not allow here (e.g., multiparty NIKE), or provide weaker security guarantees (e.g., recover from state exposures only with an additional delay in rounds).

For clarity we note that the key graph concept used here is independent of the tree structure of keys within our upper bound construction in Sect. 6.

6   Upper Bound of Communication Complexity

In order to overcome the deficiencies of existing protocols, we postpone the refresh of parts of the key material in the group by one operation. The resulting construction closely (up to a factor of $\approx \log(n/t)$) meets our communication complexity lower bound.

For computational security of group ratcheting, games $\mathrm{KIND}_{\mathsf{GR}}^{b}$ from Sect. 3 are slightly adapted to additionally require immediate forward-secrecy. We note that the use of (a weak form of) kuPKE instead of standard PKE in our construction is only due to required forward-secrecy. Furthermore, the weak kuPKE used can be efficiently built from standard assumptions (see e.g., a construction from DDH in [24]).

6.1   Construction

Our construction uses ideas from the complete subtree method of broadcast encryption [27] and resembles concepts from TreeKEM [3,4]. More specifically, the construction bases on a static complete (directed) binary tree structure τ with n leaves (i.e., one leaf per group member), on top of which at every node, there is an evolving kuPKE key pair. The secret key at each of the n leaves is known only by the unique user that occupies that leaf. For the remaining nodes

---

[9] We observe that if a group-ratcheting-pendant of the amortized $\log(n)$ lower bound for forward-secure group key exchange by Micciancio and Panjwani [26] applies as a factor on our lower bound, then our construction from Sect. 6 has optimal communication complexity.

we maintain the invariant that the only secret keys in a user's state at a given time are those that are at nodes along the direct path of its corresponding leaf to the root of the tree.

We refer to the children of a node v in a tree as $v.c_0$ (left child) and $v.c_1$ (right child), and its parent as $v.p$. Furthermore we let $i, j, i > j$ be two rounds in which the set of sending group members is non-empty and there is no intermediate round l, $i > l > j$, with non-empty sending set. For simplicity in the description we define $j := i - 1$.

Sending. To recover from state exposures, our construction lets senders in round $i-1$ refresh only their own individual leaf key pair. Senders in round i then refresh all remaining secret keys stored in the local states of round $i - 1$ senders (i.e., for nodes on their direct paths to the root) on their behalf. This is illustrated in Fig. 3. Note that (as explained below in paragraph *Receiving*) all group members collect the senders of round $i - 1$ into a set U_{i-1} in the rcv algorithm of round $i - 1$. Our construction, formally defined in Fig. 4, accordingly lets all senders in a round perform five tasks:

1) To refresh their own individual secret key: Generate a fresh secret key for their corresponding leaf and send the respective public key to the group (lines 42–43, 63).
2) To refresh and rebuild direct paths of last round's senders: Sample a new seed for the leaf of each sender of the last round and encrypt it to the respective sender's (refreshed) leaf public key (lines 46–49). Then derive a seed for each non-leaf node on the direct paths from these leaves to the root using the new seeds at the leaves (line 50). Each seed will be used to deterministically generate a fresh key pair for its node.
3) To share refreshed secrets with members who did not send in the last round: Encrypt the new seed of each refreshed non-leaf node to the public key of its child from which it was not derived (lines 52–55, 58–61). Update the used public keys via kuPKE algorithm up (lines 56, 62).
4) To inform the group of changed public keys: Send all changed public keys to the group, including those for which seeds were renewed, and those that were updated via kuPKE (lines 50, 56, 62, 63).
5) Sample and encrypt a group key k for the round to all other users in the group (lines 44, 48, 54, 63).

In step 2), one seed is individually encrypted to each user in set U_{i-1} via public key encryption, which will allow them to reconstruct their direct path in the tree. The purpose of this individual encryption is to let the recent senders forget their old (potentially exposed) secrets and use their fresh secret (which they generated during their last sending) to obtain new, secure secrets on their direct path.

We now describe how all remaining group members are able to rebuild the tree in their view. The reader is invited to follow the explanation and focus their attention on the tree in the lower right corner of Fig. 3. In this tree, directed edges represent the derivation of a seed at a node from one of its children (dotted) or

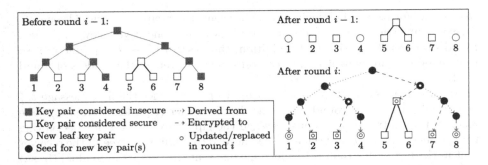

Fig. 3. Example tree for two rounds $i-1$ and i with $n = 8$, $U_{i-1} = \{1,4,8\}$, and $U_i \neq \emptyset$. In round $i-1$, senders generate new key pairs for their leaves. In round i, senders generate seeds for all nodes considered insecure from round $i-1$ and replace leaf key pairs for round $i-1$ senders, as shown in the bottom-right corner.

encryption of a seed at a node to one of its children (dashed). We consider the Steiner Tree $ST(U_{i-1})$ induced by the set of leaves of users in U_{i-1}. $ST(U_{i-1})$ is the minimal subtree of the full tree that connects all of the leaves of U_{i-1} and the root; in the lower right corner tree of Fig. 3, $ST(U_{i-1})$ is the subtree of blue filled circles and edges between them. For each *degree-one node* v of $ST(U_{i-1})$ (i.e., nodes with only one child in the Steiner Tree), its seed is encrypted to the public key of its child which is not in $ST(U_{i-1})$. This seed can be used to derive some (possibly all) of the secret keys for the nodes on the direct path of v, including v itself (lines 51–56). We denote the set of such degree one nodes of the Streiner Tree as $ST(U_{i-1})_1$ and the child of a node v in $ST(U_{i-1})_1$ that is not in the Steiner Tree as $v.c_{\notin ST(U_{i-1})}$.[10] For each *degree-two node* v of $ST(U_{i-1})$ (i.e., nodes with two children in the Steiner Tree), its seed is encrypted to the public key of its right child (lines 57–62). We denote the set of such degree-two nodes of the Steiner Tree as $ST(U_{i-1})_2$. All of these encrypted seeds are derived from the fresh leaf seeds of users in set U_{i-1} via prf computations, as explained below in paragraph *Construction Subroutines*.

Alongside the seeds, some randomly sampled associated data ad is also encrypted in the ciphertexts of the above paragraph (lines 52, 58). Public keys used for the encryption are afterwards updated with this associated data ad (lines 56, 62). Upon receipt, this associated data is used correspondingly to update the secret keys as well. Due to this mechanism, immediate forward-secrecy is achieved since secret keys stored in users' local states are updated as soon as they are used for decryption.

We refer to the union of nodes that are in the Steiner Tree with nodes that are children of degree-one nodes in the Steiner Tree as $CST = \{v : v \in ST(U_{i-1}) \vee v = w.c_{\notin ST(U_{i-1})} \forall w \in ST(U_{i-1})_1\}$. For step 4) above, senders must publish the new public keys corresponding to all nodes of $CST(U_{i-1})$ (lines 50, 56, 62, 63).

---

[10] We overload the set theoretic symbol $\notin$ here for brevity.

Receiving. For rounds in which no member sent, the recipients forward-securely derive symmetric keys (one <u>out</u>put group key, and one <u>saved</u> key) from last round's secrets (lines 87–88). In addition, they assign $U_i \leftarrow U_{i-1}$ (line 68), so that senders of subsequent rounds can refresh the secrets of the senders of round $i - 1$.

In case members sent in a round, a receiver determines the first message bc^* among all sent in this round, via some definite order (e.g., lexicographic). The receiver then retrieves from this message the ciphertext set CT for decrypting the symmetric secret k and the first seed needed to rebuild the tree: If the receiver sent in the last active round (in which anyone sent), it uses its individual (fresh) secret key (lines 74–75). Otherwise, it uses the secret key of the first node on its direct path that is the child of some node in $ST(U_{i-1})$ (lines 76–79). The decrypted seed, as well as the rest of CT, and the public keys of the Steiner Tree within bc^* are then used to rebuild the secret path for the receiver, as well as the public key tree, as described below in paragraph *Construction Subroutines* (line 81). The resulting symmetric secret is then used to derive the output group key and a new saved key (as described above for rounds without ciphertexts).

Additionally, secret keys used to decrypt ciphertexts (including those as described in the *Construction Subroutines* paragraph below), are updated with the associated data that was also decrypted from the respective ciphertexts (lines 79, 80, 111, 112). Finally, all senders of the round are collected into U_i and their new public keys are saved (lines 82–85) in order to later achieve post-compromise security.

Construction Subroutines. In the common state initialization algorithm init, a complete binary tree of n leaves with a public key at each node is initialized using a list of corresponding secret keys SK_{init} with procedure $PK_\tau \leftarrow$ genPKTree(SK_{init}) (line 34). Also, the secret keys along the direct path to the root of leaf u for each user are retrieved for that user, using $SK_u \leftarrow$ getSKPath(SK_{init}, u).

Figure 5 details the subroutines for genSTree and Rebuild (lines 50 and 81). Subroutine genSTree is used in the snd algorithm to compute the seeds and public keys at each node of the Steiner tree $ST(U_{i-1})$ using the seeds $DK[v]$ sampled for the leaves $v \in U_{i-1}$ (lines 46–49). For each $v \in U_{i-1}$, the receiver uses $DK[v]$ to compute the node's secret key, public key, and (possibly) the seed to be used for its parent (lines 97–100), continuing up the tree until there has already been a seed generated for some node w on the path.

Rebuild is used in the rcv algorithm, by each user u to rebuild its "secret key path" as well as the "public key tree" using the public keys of the Steiner Tree $PK_{ST(U_{i-1})}$, the set of ciphertexts CT, and the seed k_{der} obtained from CT corresponding to a node v^* in the tree. First, for every $v \in CST(U_{i-1})$, the receiver sets its public key to that which is in the dictionary $PK_{ST(U_{i-1})}$ (lines 104–105). Then, starting from node v^* using k_{der}, the receiver derives the secret key for v^* and a new seed for its parent if the node is the left child of its parent. Otherwise the receiver uses the secret key just derived to decrypt the

```
Proc init(n)                                          Proc rcv(st, BC)
31  i ← 1, U_0 ← ∅                                    66  (u, i, PK_τ, SK_u, U_{i-1}, sk^0, sk^1, k_sav) ← st
32  m ← CBT(n)                                        67  If BC = ∅:
33  SK_init ←$ SK^m                                   68    U_i ← U_{i-1}
34  PK_τ ← genPKTree(SK_init)                         69    skip to line 87
35  k_sav ←$ K                                        70  U_i ← ∅
36  For u from 1 to n:                                71  Let bc* ∈ BC be first in some definite
37    SK_u ← getSKPath(SK_init, u)                          order
38    sk^0 ← ⊥; sk^1 ← ⊥                              72  (v, pk', CT, PK_{ST(U_{i-1})}) ← bc*
39    st_u ← (u, i, PK_τ, SK_u, U_0, sk^0, sk^1, k_sav)  73  If u ∈ U_{i-1}:
40  Return (st_1, ..., st_n)                          74    k_der||k ← dec(sk^0, CT[u])
                                                      75    v* ← u
Proc snd(st)                                          76  Else:
41  (u, i, PK_τ, SK_u, U_{i-1}, sk^0, sk^1, k_sav) ← st  77    v* ← getSNode(u, ST(U_{i-1}))
42  sk' ←$ SK                                         78    sk ← SK_u[v*.c_{∉ST(U_{i-1})}]
43  pk' ← gen(sk')                                    79    k_der||ad||k ← dec(sk, CT[v*])
44  k ←$ K ∩ M                                        80    SK_u[v*.c_{∉ST(U_{i-1})}] ← up(sk, ad)
45  DK[·] ← ⊥                                         81  (SK'_u, PK'_τ) ←
46  For each v ∈ U_{i-1}:                                   Rebuild(st, PK_{ST(U_{i-1})}, CT, k_der, v*)
47    DK[v] ←$ K ∩ M                                  82  For all bc ∈ BC:
48    ct ←$ enc(PK_τ[v], DK[v]||k)                    83    (v, pk', CT, PK_{ST(U_{i-1})}) ← bc
49    CT[v] ← ct                                      84    U_i ← U_i ∪ {v}
50  (DK_{ST(U_{i-1})}, PK_{ST(U_{i-1})}) ←            85    PK'_τ[v] ← pk'
        genSTree(DK, U_{i-1})                         86    k_sav ← k
51  For each v ∈ ST(U_{i-1})_1:                       87  k_out ← prf(k_sav, out)
52    ad ←$ AD ∩ M                                    88  k_sav ← prf(k_sav, sav)
53    pk ← PK_τ[v.c_{∉ST(U_{i-1})}]                   89  sk^0 ← sk^1
54    ct ←$ enc(pk, DK_{ST(U_{i-1})}[v]||ad||k)       90  i' ← i + 1
55    CT[v] ← ct                                      91  st ← (u, i', PK'_τ, SK'_u, U_i, sk^0, sk^1, k_sav)
56    PK_{ST(U_{i-1})}[v.c_{∉ST(U_{i-1})}] ← up(pk, ad)  92  Return (st, k_out)
57  For each v ∈ ST(U_{i-1})_2:
58    ad ←$ AD ∩ M
59    pk ← PK_{ST(U_{i-1})}[v.c_1]
60    ct ←$ enc(pk, DK_{ST(U_{i-1})}[v]||ad)
61    CT[v] ← ct
62    PK_{ST(U_{i-1})}[v.c_1] ← up(pk, ad)
63  bc ← (u, pk', CT, PK_{ST(U_{i-1})})
64  st ← (u, i, PK_τ, SK_u, U_{i-1}, sk^0, sk', k_sav)
65  Return (st, bc)
```

Fig. 4. Construction of concurrent group ratcheting in the computational model. $CBT(n)$ calculates the number of nodes in a complete binary tree with n leaves. $getSNode(u, ST(U_{i-1}))$ finds the first node v on the direct path of u that is in $ST(U_{i-1})$.

seed to be used at its parent (lines 107–113). The receiver continues up the tree until the root is reached.

Efficiency. We here provide a short and simple proof of our communication complexity upper bound.[11]

---

[11] One might observe that using ideas from the Layered Subset Difference BE method [21] could lower the communication complexity of our construction, however we failed to do so due to potential security issues.

Proc genSTree(DK, U_{i-1})	**Proc** Rebuild(st, $PK_{ST(U_{i-1})}$, CT, k_{der}, v^*)
93 $DK_{ST(U_{i-1})}[\cdot] \leftarrow \perp; PK_{ST(U_{i-1})}[\cdot] \leftarrow \perp$	102 $(u, i, PK_\tau, SK_u, U_{i-1}, sk^0, sk^1, k_{sav}) \leftarrow st$
94 For each $v \in U_{i-1}$ from left to right:	103 $PK'_\tau \leftarrow PK_\tau; SK'_u \leftarrow SK_u$
95 $\quad k_{der} \leftarrow DK[v]$	104 For each $v \in CST(U_{i-1})$:
96 $\quad$ While $DK_{ST(U_{i-1})}[v] = \perp$ and $v \neq r$:	105 $\quad PK_\tau[v]' \leftarrow PK_{ST(U_{i-1})}[v]$
97 $\quad\quad DK_{ST(U_{i-1})}[v] \leftarrow k_{der}$	106 $v \leftarrow v^*$
98 $\quad\quad k'_{der}\|sk^v \leftarrow \mathrm{prf}(k_{der}, \mathbf{der})$	107 While $v \neq r$:
99 $\quad\quad PK_{ST(U_{i-1})}[v] \leftarrow \mathrm{gen}(sk^v)$	108 $\quad k'_{der}\|sk^v \leftarrow \mathrm{prf}(k_{der}, \mathbf{der})$
100 $\quad\quad v \leftarrow v.p, k_{der} \leftarrow k'_{der}$	109 $\quad SK'_u[v] \leftarrow sk^v$
101 Return $(DK_{ST(U_{i-1})}, PK_{ST(U_{i-1})})$	110 $\quad$ If $\deg(v.p) = 2$ and $v = v.p.c_1$:
	111 $\quad\quad k'_{der}\|ad \leftarrow \mathrm{dec}(sk^v, CT[v.p])$
	112 $\quad\quad SK'_u[v] \leftarrow \mathrm{up}(sk^v, ad)$
	113 $\quad v \leftarrow v.p, k_{der} \leftarrow k'_{der}$
	114 Return (PK'_τ, SK'_u)

Fig. 5. Subroutines for construction upper bound. $\deg(v)$ refers to the degree of a node v in a tree, i.e. number of children.

Lemma 1. *For every round* $i \in [q]$, *the communication costs in an execution* $(n, U_X^0, U_S^1, U_X^1, \ldots, U_S^1, U_X^q)$ *are*

$$|C[i]| = \mathcal{O}\left(|U_S^i| \cdot |U_S^{i-1}| \cdot \left(1 + \log\left(\frac{n}{|U_S^{i-1}|}\right)\right)\right).$$

We note that $|C[i]|$ denotes the number of sent items (i.e., ciphertexts and public keys) per round. Their individual length depends on the respectively deployed kuPKE scheme. (In a setting that defines a *security parameter*, the factor with which the communication costs are multiplied is (asymptotically) constant in this security parameter.)

Proof. We track communication of each user $u \in U_S^i$ that sends in round i. From this, the result follows easily. In round i, user u sends one ciphertext and one public key for each $v \in ST(U_S^{i-1})$ (plus an additional public key for at most one child c_v of each v). It is shown in [27] that $|ST(U_S^{i-1})_1| = \mathcal{O}\left(|U_S^{i-1}| \cdot \log\left(\frac{n}{|U_S^{i-1}|}\right)\right)$. Moreover, it follows from the analysis in [27] that $|ST(U_S^{i-1})_2| + |U_S^{i-1}| = \mathcal{O}\left(|U_S^{i-1}|\right)$. Since $ST(U_S^{i-1}) = ST(U_S^{i-1})_1 \cup ST(U_S^{i-1})_2 \cup U_S^{i-1},$[12] we have accounted for each node $v \in ST(U_S^{i-1})$.

Therefore, each user $u \in U_S^i$ communicates $\mathcal{O}\left(|U_S^{i-1}| \cdot \left(1 + \log\left(\frac{n}{|U_S^{i-1}|}\right)\right)\right)$ information. □

Theorem 1 (informal). *Assuming secure kuPKE (as proposed in [3, 24]) and PRF constructions, the construction of Fig. 4 is a secure group ratcheting scheme according to the forward-secure variant of game* KIND_{GR}^b *from Sect. 3, with security loss at most* $(q_{Round} + 1) \cdot ((\lceil \log(n) \rceil + 1) \cdot \mathrm{Adv}_{PR}^{\mathrm{prfind}}(\mathcal{B}_{PR}) + \lceil \log(n) \rceil \cdot$

---

[12] We overload U_S^{i-1} to also refer to the set of leaves corresponding to the users $u' \in U_S^{i-1}$.

$\mathsf{Adv}_{\mathsf{UE}}^{\mathsf{kind}}(\mathcal{B}_{\mathsf{UE}}))$, *where n is the number of group members, q_{Round} is the number of executed rounds, and $\mathsf{Adv}_{\mathsf{PR}}^{\mathsf{prfind}}(\mathcal{B}_{\mathsf{PR}})$, $\mathsf{Adv}_{\mathsf{UE}}^{\mathsf{kind}}(\mathcal{B}_{\mathsf{UE}})$ are upper bounds on the advantage of any adversaries $\mathcal{B}_{\mathsf{PR}}$, $\mathcal{B}_{\mathsf{UE}}$ against the security of PRF and kuPKE, respectively.*

For the formal version of this theorem and the full security proof, we refer the reader to our full version [11]. Below we provide a proof sketch that intuitively summarizes our proof idea.

Proof (sketch). Recall that in our construction, for each round i (with senders) initiated by the adversary, the initial secret key generated at each node in the Steiner Tree $ST(U_{i-1})$ is derived via a PRF computation (lines 98, 108). The key idea behind our proof is that we slowly replace these initial secret keys with keys that are drawn uniformly from the space of secret keys. Then, we replace all encryptions to such keys (lines 48, 54, 60) with fake ciphertexts that are independent of the actual contents of the message. Furthermore, in the rcv() algorithm of our hybrid experiments, we hardcode the associated data to be used to update the secret key to which it is encrypted (lines 80, 112), so that all users maintain consistent views of the key pairs at each node v in τ, despite the fake ciphertexts.

However, we must be careful to only replace the secret keys and ciphertexts which the adversary cannot compute directly because of the corruption of some user $u \in [n]$. Specifically, after corruption of a user $u \in [n]$, we generate the secret keys along their direct path in τ as well as any ciphertexts encrypted to these secret keys as in Fig. 4. For any node v in τ, we then wait until each of the corrupted users corresponding to the leaves of the subtree rooted at v send in a subsequent round. It is not until this point that we can again replace any of the secret keys and ciphertexts in our hybrids. This does not violate security because if some corrupted user u in the subtree rooted at v has not yet refreshed their leaf key pair in some round i, the adversary can trivially compute the secret key at v, as well as the output group secret of that round. Thus, the output group secret is not considered secure for round i anyway. Moreover, by forward secrecy of the kuPKE scheme's updates, any ciphertexts encrypted to *previous* versions of the key pair (i.e., before the latest update) of a node along the direct path of a corrupted user u are still secure. Thus all previous secret keys along the direct path of u and any previous output group secrets are still secure (provided that no other users were corrupted).

Now recall that the secret key of an interior node v in $ST(U_{i-1})$ for some round i is generated via a PRF computation on a key output at one of the children of v (lines 98–100). Therefore, our hybrid experiments must proceed by first replacing the secret keys (resp. subsequent encryptions to them) of leaves in $ST(U_{i-1})$ with uniformly random (resp. fake) values, followed by the secret keys of their parents, and so on, until we reach the root. When we reach the hybrids corresponding to the root, for all rounds in which the adversary cannot anyway trivially compute the uniformly random key encrypted to all users that will be used to derive the output group secret, all ciphertexts broadcast are independent of it. We finally add hybrids replacing the output group secret keys (line 87) and any intermediate saved keys for rounds with no senders (line 88) with uniformly random keys. Therefore, in our final hybrid, the output group secrets for non-trivially attackable rounds are uniformly random and independent of all ciphertexts broadcast throughout the protocol.   □

6.2   Discussion

We shortly reflect on our construction, compare it to previous works, discuss its limitations with respect to the security model, and propose possible efficiency improvements.

The main purpose of our protocol is to give an upper bound that confirms our lower bound, but not to provide optimal security and maximal functionality under concurrency. Nevertheless, our construction provides the same security as parallel pairwise Signal executions, i.e. FS and PCS one round with non-empty sender set after all exposed users updated their states. In addition, it provides full concurrency for user updates unlike those in [3–5,8,14,32].

When using a variant of our construction for dynamic groups, removed members in such groups may maliciously store secrets that they saw during their membership for breaking confidentiality of group secrets after their membership. Effectively solving this problem—discussed as "double-join"—could be achieved by using ideas from protocols constructed for dynamic groups, such as MLS and Tainted TreeKEM. Without these ideas, it would be required that siblings of all removed users that are still in the group issue state updates before any removed user would be unable to derive the output secrets. Yet, as we discuss below, dynamic member changes appear to happen rather seldom in many practical applications such that this restriction might be insignificant.

Our security model is somewhat weak: we require an honest (but curious) mechanism that clocks rounds, we do not allow the adversary access to random coins used by senders in a round that are not saved to their state, and we do not allow the adversary to alter broadcast messages. Clock synchronization could, however, be rather coarse (resulting in long round periods) as our protocol's speedup in reaching PCS, compared to non-concurrent alternatives that require members to update their states one after another, is already significant. Furthermore, we note that all members processing all ciphertexts in a round (as defined in our model) is not mandatory but allows for immediate forward-secrecy due to kuPKE key pair updates. Processing all previous ciphertexts before sending is usually also unproblematic as sending anyways requires a user to come online, such that all cryptographic operations can be executed at that moment. Especially for reaching authentication and handling out-of-order receipts, tools that are independent of our core state update mechanism can be added (maybe even generically) to our construction. The problem of weak random coins is indeed an open problem for concurrent group ratcheting that we leave for future research.

As stated earlier, it is not ultimately clear whether our lower bound or upper bound is loose (or even both of them). One technique to improve our upper bound would be to utilize more sophisticated broadcast encryption methods

than the Complete Subtree method [27], such as the Layered Subset Difference method [21] or techniques from the recently proposed optimal broadcast
encryption scheme [1], while still preserving security. Additionally, if one allows
a slight relaxation in the model by allowing for delayed PCS, i.e. PCS in some
$\Delta > 1$ rounds, then better communication complexity could be achieved. This
is because if users update their state in a given round i by publishing a fresh
public key, other users could send secrets to these users to help them recover in
all rounds $i' \in \{i + 1, i + 2, \ldots, i + \Delta\}$, spreading out the communication costs
across these rounds and allowing for some adaptivity between senders therein.

6.3   Insights for Practice

We shortly summarize concepts from our construction that could enhance, and
insights from our lower bound that could influence real-world protocols (like the
MLS initiative's design).

Almost-Immediate PCS. As mentioned many times before, immediate PCS
under t-concurrency appears to require t-party NIKE (which is currently inaccessible). Postponing the update of *shared* secrets to a reaction in the next protocol execution step, as implemented in our construction, bypasses this problem.
The major advantages of this bypass are a significant speedup for PCS, compared to sequential state updates, and a maintained balanced tree structure,
compared to tree modifications, resulting in a reduced tree depth, or group partitions. An open question remains to analyze our scheme's resilience against weak
randomness.

Static Groups are Practical. Some deficiencies of our protocol are only relevant
in dynamic settings. In contrast, constant groups can benefit from this construction significantly as it maintains communication complexity in all cases nearly
optimally. We emphasize that many groups in real-world applications indeed seldom or never change the set of members (e.g., family groups, friendship group,
smaller working groups, etc.).

To resolve issues with respect to membership changes, the mechanism proposed in Tainted TreeKEM [4] could be applied on path updates in our protocol.
Thereby, the "double-join"-problem could be prevented.

Better Solutions. In the light of our lower bound, finding better solutions for
reaching PCS under concurrency seems very complicated, if not unlikely. The
set of permitted building blocks in our symbolic model is very powerful, the
functionality required by constructions in this setting is very restricted, and the
adversarial power in the lower bound security definition is very limited. Hence,
it seems necessary to utilize "more exotic" primitives or relax the required PCS
guarantees for obtaining better constructions.

References

1. Agrawal, S., Yamada, S.: Optimal broadcast encryption from pairings and LWE. In: Canteaut, A., Ishai, Y. (eds.) EUROCRYPT 2020, Part I. LNCS, vol. 12105, pp. 13–43. Springer, Cham (2020). https://doi.org/10.1007/978-3-030-45721-1_2
2. Alwen, J., Coretti, S., Dodis, Y.: The double ratchet: security notions, proofs, and modularization for the signal protocol. In: Ishai, Y., Rijmen, V. (eds.) EURO-CRYPT 2019, Part I. LNCS, vol. 11476, pp. 129–158. Springer, Cham (2019). https://doi.org/10.1007/978-3-030-17653-2_5
3. Alwen, J., Coretti, S., Dodis, Y., Tselekounis, Y.: Security analysis and improvements for the IETF MLS standard for group messaging. In: Micciancio, D., Ristenpart, T. (eds.) CRYPTO 2020, Part I. LNCS, vol. 12170, pp. 248–277. Springer, Cham (2020). https://doi.org/10.1007/978-3-030-56784-2_9
4. Alwen, J., et al.: Keep the dirt: tainted TreeKEM, an efficient and provably secure continuous group key agreement protocol. Cryptology ePrint Archive, report 2019/1489 (2019). https://eprint.iacr.org/2019/1489
5. Alwen, J., Coretti, S., Jost, D., Mularczyk, M.: Continuous group key agreement with active security. In: Pass, R., Pietrzak, K. (eds.) TCC 2020. LNCS, vol. 12551, pp. 261–290. Springer, Cham (2020)
6. Balli, F., Rösler, P., Vaudenay, S.: Determining the core primitive for optimally secure ratcheting. In: Advances in Cryptology. ASIACRYPT 2020–Proceedings of the 26th International Conference on the Theory and Application of Cryptology and Information Security, Virtual. LNCS, 7–11 December 2020 (2020)
7. Barnes, R., Beurdouche, B., Millican, J., Omara, E., Cohn-Gordon, K., Robert, R.: The messaging layer security (MLS) protocol (2020). https://datatracker.ietf.org/doc/draft-ietf-mls-protocol/
8. Barnes, R., Beurdouche, B., Millican, J., Omara, E., Cohn-Gordon, K., Robert, R.: The messaging layer security (MLS) protocol draft-ietf-mls-protocol-09. Internet-draft, September 2020. https://www.ietf.org/archive/id/draft-ietf-mls-protocol-09.txt
9. Bellare, M., Lysyanskaya, A.: Symmetric and dual PRFs from standard assumptions: a generic validation of an HMAC assumption. Cryptology ePrint Archive, report 2015/1198 (2015). http://eprint.iacr.org/2015/1198
10. Bellare, M., Singh, A.C., Jaeger, J., Nyayapati, M., Stepanovs, I.: Ratcheted encryption and key exchange: the security of messaging. In: Katz, J., Shacham, H. (eds.) CRYPTO 2017, Part III. LNCS, vol. 10403, pp. 619–650. Springer, Cham (2017). https://doi.org/10.1007/978-3-319-63697-9_21
11. Bienstock, A., Dodis, Y., Rösler, P.: On the price of concurrency in group ratcheting protocols. Cryptology ePrint Archive, report 2020/1171 (2020). https://eprint.iacr.org/2020/1171
12. Boneh, D., et al.: Multiparty non-interactive key exchange and more from isogenies on elliptic curves. Cryptology ePrint Archive, report 2018/665 (2018). https://eprint.iacr.org/2018/665
13. Boneh, D., Silverberg, A.: Applications of multilinear forms to cryptography. Cryptology ePrint Archive, report 2002/080 (2002). http://eprint.iacr.org/2002/080

14. Cohn-Gordon, K., Cremers, C., Garratt, L., Millican, J., Milner, K.: On ends-to-ends encryption: asynchronous group messaging with strong security guarantees. In: Lie, D., Mannan, M., Backes, M., Wang, X. (eds.) ACM CCS 2018, pp. 1802–1819. ACM Press, October 2018

15. Cohn-Gordon, K., Cremers, C.J.F., Dowling, B., Garratt, L., Stebila, D.: A formal security analysis of the signal messaging protocol. In: 2017 IEEE European Symposium on Security and Privacy, EuroS&P 2017, Paris, France, 26–28 April 2017, pp. 451–466. IEEE (2017)

16. Cohn-Gordon, K., Cremers, C.J.F., Garratt, L.: On post-compromise security. In: IEEE 29th Computer Security Foundations Symposium, CSF 2016, Lisbon, Portugal, 27 June–1 July 2016, pp. 164–178. IEEE Computer Society (2016)

17. Cremers, C., Hale, B., Kohbrok, K.: Efficient post-compromise security beyond one group. Cryptology ePrint Archive, report 2019/477 (2019). https://eprint.iacr.org/2019/477

18. Dolev, D., Yao, A.C.C.: On the security of public key protocols (extended abstract). In: 22nd FOCS, pp. 350–357. IEEE Computer Society Press, October 1981

19. Durak, F.B., Vaudenay, S.: Bidirectional asynchronous ratcheted key agreement with linear complexity. In: Attrapadung, N., Yagi, T. (eds.) IWSEC 2019. LNCS, vol. 11689, pp. 343–362. Springer, Cham (2019). https://doi.org/10.1007/978-3-030-26834-3_20

20. Gennaro, R., Trevisan, L.: Lower bounds on the efficiency of generic cryptographic constructions. In: 41st FOCS, pp. 305–313. IEEE Computer Society Press, November 2000

21. Halevy, D., Shamir, A.: The LSD broadcast encryption scheme. In: Yung, M. (ed.) CRYPTO 2002. LNCS, vol. 2442, pp. 47–60. Springer, Heidelberg (2002). https://doi.org/10.1007/3-540-45708-9_4

22. Impagliazzo, R., Rudich, S.: Limits on the provable consequences of one-way permutations. In: 21st ACM STOC, pp. 44–61. ACM Press, May 1989

23. Jaeger, J., Stepanovs, I.: Optimal channel security against fine-grained state compromise: the safety of messaging. In: Shacham, H., Boldyreva, A. (eds.) CRYPTO 2018, Part I. LNCS, vol. 10991, pp. 33–62. Springer, Cham (2018). https://doi.org/10.1007/978-3-319-96884-1_2

24. Jost, D., Maurer, U., Mularczyk, M.: Efficient ratcheting: almost-optimal guarantees for secure messaging. In: Ishai, Y., Rijmen, V. (eds.) EUROCRYPT 2019, Part I. LNCS, vol. 11476, pp. 159–188. Springer, Cham (2019). https://doi.org/10.1007/978-3-030-17653-2_6

25. Jost, D., Maurer, U., Mularczyk, M.: A unified and composable take on ratcheting. In: Hofheinz, D., Rosen, A. (eds.) TCC 2019, Part II. LNCS, vol. 11892, pp. 180–210. Springer, Cham (2019). https://doi.org/10.1007/978-3-030-36033-7_7

26. Micciancio, D., Panjwani, S.: Optimal communication complexity of generic multicast key distribution. In: Cachin, C., Camenisch, J.L. (eds.) EUROCRYPT 2004. LNCS, vol. 3027, pp. 153–170. Springer, Heidelberg (2004). https://doi.org/10.1007/978-3-540-24676-3_10

27. Naor, D., Naor, M., Lotspiech, J.: Revocation and tracing schemes for stateless receivers. In: Kilian, J. (ed.) CRYPTO 2001. LNCS, vol. 2139, pp. 41–62. Springer, Heidelberg (2001). https://doi.org/10.1007/3-540-44647-8_3

28. Perrin, T., Marlinspike, M.: The double ratchet algorithm (2016). https://signal.org/docs/specifications/doubleratchet/

29. Poettering, B., Rösler, P.: Asynchronous ratcheted key exchange. Cryptology ePrint Archive, report 2018/296 (2018). https://eprint.iacr.org/2018/296

30. Poettering, B., Rösler, P.: Towards bidirectional ratcheted key exchange. In: Shacham, H., Boldyreva, A. (eds.) CRYPTO 2018, Part I. LNCS, vol. 10991, pp. 3–32. Springer, Cham (2018). https://doi.org/10.1007/978-3-319-96884-1_1
31. Rösler, P., Mainka, C., Schwenk, J.: More is less: on the end-to-end security of group chats in Signal, WhatsApp, and Threema. In: 2018 IEEE European Symposium on Security and Privacy (EuroS&P), pp. 415–429. IEEE (2018)
32. Weidner, M.: Group messaging for secure asynchronous collaboration. Ph.D. thesis, MPhil dissertation (2019). Advisors: A. Beresford and M. Kleppmann. https://mattweidner.com/acs-dissertation.pdf

Stronger Security and Constructions of Multi-designated Verifier Signatures

Ivan Damgård[1], Helene Haagh[1], Rebekah Mercer[2], Anca Nitulescu[1(✉)],
Claudio Orlandi[1], and Sophia Yakoubov[1]

[1] Aarhus University, Aarhus, Denmark
{ivan,orlandi,sophia.yakoubov}@cs.au.dk, helenehaagh@gmail.com,
anca.nitulesc@gmail.com
[2] O(1) Labs, San Francisco, USA
rebekah@o1labs.org

Abstract. Off-the-Record (OTR) messaging is a two-party message authentication protocol that also provides plausible deniability: there is no record that can later convince a third party what messages were actually sent. The challenge in *group OTR*, is to enable the sender to sign his messages so that group members can verify who sent a message (signatures should be *unforgeable*, even by group members). Also, we want the off-the-record property: even if some verifiers are corrupt and collude, they should not be able to prove the authenticity of a message to any outsider. Finally, we need *consistency*, meaning that if any group member accepts a signature, then all of them do.

To achieve these properties it is natural to consider Multi-Designated Verifier Signatures (MDVS). However, existing literature defines and builds only limited notions of MDVS, where (a) the off-the-record property (*source hiding*) only holds when *all* verifiers could conceivably collude, and (b) the consistency property is not considered.

The contributions of this paper are two-fold: stronger definitions for MDVS, and new constructions meeting those definitions. We strengthen source-hiding to support any subset of corrupt verifiers, and give the first formal definition of consistency. We build three new MDVS: one from generic standard primitives (PRF, key agreement, NIZK), one with concrete efficiency and one from functional encryption.

1 Introduction

Encrypted and authenticated messaging has experienced widespread adoption in recent years, due to the attractive combination of properties offered by, for

This research was supported by: the Concordium Blockhain Research Center, Aarhus University, Denmark; the Carlsberg Foundation under the Semper Ardens Research Project CF18-112 (BCM); the European Research Council (ERC) under the European Unions's Horizon 2020 research and innovation programme under grant agreement No 669255 (MPCPRO) and No 803096 (SPEC); the Danish Independent Research Council under Grant-ID DFF-6108-00169 (FoCC); the NSF MACS project.

R. Pass and K. Pietrzak (Eds.): TCC 2020, LNCS 12551, pp. 229–260, 2020.
https://doi.org/10.1007/978-3-030-64378-2_9

example, the Signal protocol [Mar13]. With so many conversations happening over the internet, there is a growing need for protocols offering security to conversation participants. Encryption can be used to guarantee privacy of message contents, but authenticating messages while maintaining the properties of an in person conversation is more involved. There are two properties of in person conversations related to authenticity that we wish to emulate in the context of digital conversations:

- *Unforgeability*, meaning that the receiver should be convinced that the message actually came from the sender in question, and
- *Off-the-record* or *deniability*, meaning that the receiver cannot later prove to a third party that the message came from the sender.

Off-the-record (OTR) messaging offers a solution to this in the two-party case, enabling authentication of messages such that participants can convincingly deny having made certain statements, or even having taken part in the conversation at all [BGB04]. The protocol deals with encrypted messages accompanied by a message authentication code (MAC) constructed with a shared key. MACs work well in two-party conversations, because for parties S(ender) and R(eciever) with a shared secret key, a MAC attests 'this message comes from S or R'. MACs provide unforgeability, since a party R receiving a message authenticated with such a MAC knows that if this MAC verifies, the message came from S. MACs provide off-the-record (deniable) communication as R cannot convince a third party that a message and MAC originally came from S (since R could have produced it just as easily). More generally, tools that provide unforgeable, off-the-record two-party communication are known as *Designated Verifier Signatures* (DVSs, proposed by [JSI96] and [Cha96]).

When there are multiple recipients, for example in group messaging, the situation becomes more complicated. The need for unforgeability can be generalized as the need for all parties in the group to agree on a conversation transcript. There are two components to this: unforgeability, as before, and *consistency*, which requires that if one recipient can verify a signature, they all can. Without the consistency property, a signer could send a message that only one recipient could verify; that recipient would then be unable to convince the rest to accept that message, and would disagree with them about the transcript of the conversation.

DVSs have been extended to the multiparty setting under the name of *Multi-Designated Verifier Signatures (MDVSs)* (we give a number of references in Fig. 1). One might hope that these schemes would work for off-the record group messaging; however, it turns out that existing MDVS definitions and schemes do not have the properties one would naturally ask for. In the following section, we give a motivating example illustrating which properties we should actually ask from an MDVS scheme, and we explain how existing schemes fall short of providing them.

1.1   A Motivating Example for MDVS

Imagine a government official Sophia who wants to blow the whistle on some corrupt government activity; e.g., perhaps her colleague, $\mathcal{A}$aron, accepted a bribe.[1] She wants to send a message describing this corruption to Robert, Rachel and Rebekah, who are all Reporters at national newspapers.

Naturally, Sophia wants the Reporters to be convinced that she is the true sender of the message. Otherwise, they would have no reason to believe—or print—the story.

Goal 1 (Unforgeability). *It is vital that each of the Reporters be able to authenticate that the message came from Sophia.*

In order to achieve unforgeability, Sophia produces a signature σ using an MDVS scheme, and attaches it to her message. (In such a scheme, each sender has a private signing key and each recipient has a private verification key.) However, blowing the whistle and reporting on $\mathcal{A}$aron's corrupt activity could put Sophia in danger. If any of Robert, Rachel or Rebekah could use σ to demonstrate to $\mathcal{A}$aron that Sophia blew the whistle on him, she could lose her position, or face other grave consequences.

Goal 2 (Source-Hiding/Off-the-Record). *It is vital that the Reporters be unable to prove to an outsider ($\mathcal{A}$aron) that the message came from Sophia.*

One way to guarantee that the Reporters cannot link Sophia to the message is to require that the Reporters can *simulate* a signature σ themselves. Then, if they try to implicate Sophia by showing σ to $\mathcal{A}$aron, he would have no reason to believe them; as far as he is concerned, the Reporters could have produced σ to try to frame Sophia.

All previous constructions only support off-the-record in the limited sense that *all* of the Reporters must collaborate in order to produce a simulated signature.[2] However, this is insufficient. Suppose, for instance, that $\mathcal{A}$aron knows Rachel was undercover—and thus unreachable—for the entire time between the bribery taking place, and Robert and Rebekah bringing σ to $\mathcal{A}$aron. Then he

---

[1] Ring signatures [RST01] can be similarly used in this context; Sophia could use a ring signature scheme to sign in such a way that anyone could verify that the signature came from someone in her organization, but not that it came from her, specifically. However, MDVS has an advantage here, since it is possible that $\mathcal{A}$aron only doubts the trustworthiness of one of his colleagues; if Sophia uses a ring signature, that signature would convince $\mathcal{A}$aron that she was the signer, but if she uses an MDVS signature, $\mathcal{A}$aron wouldn't know whether she was the true signer, or whether the signature was just a simulation (even if Sophia was his only suspect).

In the context of a group off-the-record conversation, MDVS signatures are clearly the right tool, as members of the group should learn the identity of the sender of each message.

[2] One previous work [Tia12] allows a single verifier to simulate a signature. However, in this construction a simulated signature created by a malicious verifier will look like a real signature for all other designated verifiers, violating unforgeability.

would conclude that Rachel could not have collaborated in simulating σ, and so it must be genuine. Even with the off-the-record definition used in prior works, it is still possible that some subset of the Reporters would be able to implicate Sophia in the eyes of $\mathcal{A}$aron. We therefore need a stronger off-the-record defintion.

Contribution 1 (Off-The-Record For Any Subset). *We give a stronger definition of the off-the-record property, where any subset of Reporters must be able to simulate a signature. A simulation looks like a genuine signature to an outsider, even given the verification keys of the subset that produced it (as well as a number of other signatures that are guaranteed to be genuine).*

Under our stronger definition, no set of Reporters is able to use σ to provably tie Sophia to the message *even if $\mathcal{A}$aron has side information about communication amongst the Reporters* as well as guaranteed-to-be-genuine signatures.

Remark 1 (The Tension Between Off-The-Record and Unforgeability). Note that, if Rachel did not participate in Robert and Rebekah's signature simulation (e.g. if she was undercover at the time), she will later be able to distinguish the simulation from a real signature produced by Sophia. Otherwise, Robert and Rebekah would have succeeded in producing a forgery that fools Rachel.

This means that under a sufficiently strong model of attack, we cannot have unforgeability and off-the-record at the same time. Namely, suppose $\mathcal{A}$aron first gets a signature σ from Robert and Rebekah, while preventing them from communicating with Rachel. Then he coerces Rachel into giving him her secret verification key. By the unforgeability property, he can use this key to tell if σ is a simulation. (Note that $\mathcal{A}$aron will be able to tell whether Rachel gives him her true verification key, since he may have other signatures from Sophia that he knows are genuine that he can use to test it. So, she has no choice but to hand over her real verification key.)

Given this observation, we choose to explore the model where the secret keys of all coerced/corrupted verifiers (but not honest ones) can be used to simulate a signature, as this is the strongest model of attack in which both unforgeability and off-the-record can be achieved. As we shall see, even in this model, achieving both properties requires highly non-trivial constructions and implies a lower bound on the size of signatures.

Finally, let us fast forward to the moment when Robert, Rachel and Rebekah receive Sophia's message. They want to print this high-profile story as soon as possible, but of course they want to be sure they won't make themselves look foolish by printing the story if their colleagues—the other well-respected Reporters listed as recipients—don't believe it actually came from Sophia. The concern here is that Sophia could be dishonest and her actual goal could be to discredit the Reporters. Hence we need another property—consistency, or designated verifier transferability.

Goal 3 (Consistency/Designated Verifier Transferability). *It is desirable that, even if Sophia is malicious, if one of the Reporters can authenticate that the message came from Sophia, all of them can.*

Contribution 2. *We provide the first formal definition of consistency.*

Now that we have covered the basic storyline, let us consider a few possible plot-twists. First, what if Aaron is tapping the wires connecting the government building to the outside world? Then he will see Sophia's message—together with her signature σ—as she sends it to the Reporters. In such a situation, we would want the signature σ not to give Sophia—or the Reporters—away.

Goal 4 (Privacy of Identities). *It is desirable that σ shouldn't reveal Sophia's or the Reporters' identities[3]. When only the signer's—Sophia's—identity is hidden, this property is called* privacy of signer identity (PSI).

Next, what if, at the time at which Sophia has the opportunity to send out her message, she cannot look up Rebekah's public key securely—perhaps because Rebekah has not yet set up an account on the secure messaging system Sophia uses? Then, it would be ideal for Sophia to need nothing other than Rebekah's identity (and some global public parameters) in order to include her as a designated verifier. Rebekah would then be able to get the appropriate key from a trusted authority such as the International Press Institute[4] (having proved that she is, in fact, Rebekah), and would be able to use that key to verify Sophia's signature.

Goal 5 (Verifier-Identity-Based (VIB) Signing). *It is desirable that Sophia should only need the Reporters' identities, not their public keys, in order to produce her designated verifier signature.*

Contribution 3. *We give the first three constructions that achieve unforgeability, off-the-record with any-subset simulation, and consistency. One of them additionally achieves privacy of identities and verifier-identity-based signing.*

The third construction achieves privacy of verifiers identities (PVI) even if the secret signing key is leaked (but not the random coins used to produce the signature). This is a stronger flavor of the PVI notion with more possible applications, such as *Post-Compromise Anonymity* guarantees.

---

[3] Note that privacy of identities is related to—but very different from—off-the-record. Neither of these definitions is strictly stronger than the other. *Privacy of identities* is weaker in that it assumes that none of the Reporters help in identifying Sophia as the sender, while *off-the-record* makes no such assumptions. However, *privacy of identities* is stronger in that it requires that σ alone reveal nothing about Sophia's identity to anyone other than the Reporters; *off-the-record* allows such leakage, as long as it is not provable.

[4] This trusted authority can also be distributed; perhaps the master secret is secret-shared across several different institutions, who must collaborate in order to produce a secret verification key.

This last construction, may, at first glance, seem strictly better; however, the price it pays is two-fold: It uses functional encryption (which requires strong computational assumptions), and it requires an involved trusted setup in which a master secret is used to derive verifier keys. Note that such a trusted setup is clearly necessary in order to achieve verifier-identity-based signing.

In contrast, our first two constructions can be instantiated either in the random oracle model, or with a common reference string—in both cases avoiding the need for a master secret key. They use only standard primitives such as pseudorandom functions, pseudorandom generators, key agreement and NIZKs. The first construction uses these primitives in a black-box way; the second construction uses specific instances of these primitives, for concrete efficiency.

In the following subsections, we give an overview of previous work and then discuss our results in more detail. The main challenge of building stronger MDVS schemes is combining the three core properties we strive for: unforgeability, off-the-record for any subset, and consistency. This is highly non-trivial.

1.2   Flavors of Multi-designated Verifier Signatures

There are many ways to define MDVS and its properties. Figure 1 summarizes the approaches taken by prior work, compared to our own.

Verification. There are several different flavors of verification. In some MDVS schemes, even a single designated verifier cannot link a signature to the signer; the designated verifiers need to work together in order to verify a signature. Thus, we have two notions of verification: *local* verification and *cooperative* verification (where *all* designated verifiers need to cooperate in order to verify the signature).

Remark 2. In the schemes with cooperative verification, we need not additionally require consistency, since we have it implicitly: verifiers will agree on the verification decision they reach together. The notion of consistency is non-interactive, and more challenging to achieve in schemes with local verification.

Simulation. Recall that the off-the-record property states that an outsider cannot determine whether a given signature was created by the signer or simulated by the designated verifiers. We have three flavors of such simulateability: *one* designated verifier (out of n) can by himself simulate a signature (as done by [Tia12])[5], *all* designated verifiers need to collude in order to simulate a signature (all other works on MDVS), or *any subset* of the designated verifiers can simulate a signature (this paper). Of course, the simulated signature should remain indistinguishable from a real one even in the presence of the secrets held by the simulating parties.

---

[5] If *only* one designated verifier can simulate a signature, it must be distinguishable from a real signature by other verifiers (by the strong unforgeability property). Two colluding verifiers would be able to prove to an outsider that a given signature is not a simulation by showing that it verifiers for both of them. So, any-subset simulation gives strictly stronger off-the-record guarantees than one-verifier simulation.

Unforgeability. There is also the standard security property of signature schemes, which is *unforgeability*; no one (except the signer) should be able to construct a signature that any verifier will accept as a valid signature from that signer. There are two flavors of unforgeability. The first is *weak* unforgeability, where designated verifiers can forge, but others cannot. The second is *strong* unforgeability, where a designated verifier can distinguish between real signatures and signatures simulated by other verifiers; that is, even other designated verifiers cannot fool a verifier into accepting a simulated signature.[6] (In the weak unforgeability game, the adversary does not have access to any designated verifier keys; in the strong unforgeability game, the adversary is allowed access to some such keys.) Since strong unforgeability is the notion of unforgeability we require, in the rest of this paper, *unforgeability* refers to *strong* unforgeability (unless otherwise specified).

Schemes	PSI	Verification	Simulation	Unforgeability	Signature Size	Consistency
[JSI96,Ver06]	No	All	All	Weak	$O(1)$	N/A
[Cho08]	No	Local	All	Weak	$O(1)$	Yes
[LSMP07]	No	Local	All	Weak	$O(1)$	No
[ZAYS12]	No	Local	All	Strong	$O(1)$	Yes
Our work, from standard primitives	No	Local	Any subset $\mathcal{C}$	Strong	$O(|\mathcal{D}|)$	Yes
[NSM05,Cho06]	Yes	All	All	Weak	$O(|\mathcal{D}|)$	N/A
[MW08,SHCL08,Cha11]	Yes	All	All	Weak	$O(1)$	N/A
[LV04]	Yes	Local	All	Weak	$O(1)$	Yes
[SKS06]	Yes	Local	All	Weak	$O(|\mathcal{D}|)$	No
[Ver06,LV07]	Yes	Local	All	Weak	$O(|\mathcal{D}|)$	Yes
[ZAYS12]	Yes	Local	All	Strong	$O(|\mathcal{D}|)$	Yes
[Tia12]	Yes	Local	One	Weak	$O(1)$	Yes
Our work, from FE	Yes	Local	Any subset $\mathcal{C}$ of size up to t	Strong	$O(t)$	Yes

Fig. 1. MDVS constructions and their properties. Let $\mathcal{D}$ be the set of designated verifiers, and $t \leq |\mathcal{D}|$ be an upper bound on the set of colluding designated verifiers $\mathcal{C} \subseteq \mathcal{D}$.

1.3 Our Contributions

We propose formal definitions of all the relevant security properties of MDVS in the strongest flavor, including the definition of off-the-record with any-subset simulation. We also give the first formal (game based) definition of consistency, where a corrupt signer can collude with some of the designated verifiers to create an inconsistent signature.

---

[6] Note that when all designated verifiers are needed for the simulation, then a designated verifier will be able to distinguish a simulation from a real signature based on whether he participated in the simulation of the signature. However, if this is the only way he can distinguish, then the signature scheme has *weak* unforgeability, since the simulated signature is still a valid forgery.

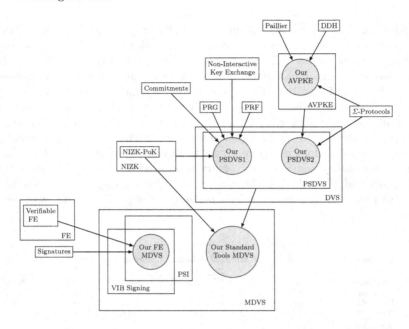

Fig. 2. Our MDVS Constructions and Building Blocks

We then give several different constructions of MDVS that achieve these properties, including local verification, off-the-record with any-subset simulation, and strong unforgeability. Our constructions, and the tools they require, are mapped out in Fig. 2. In particular, these are the first constructions that combine any-subset simulation and with strong unforgeability, as described in Fig. 1. We get these results at the expense of signature sizes that are larger than in some of the earlier constructions. However, this is unavoidable, as shown in Theorem 1 below.

Theorem 1. *Any MDVS with any-subset simulation and strong unforgeability must have signature size $\Omega(|\mathcal{D}|)$.*

Remark 3. It may seem from the table that our functional encryption based scheme contradicts the theorem, but this is not the case. It can be instantiated such that signatures can be simulated by collusions up to a certain maximal size t, and then signatures will be of size $\Omega(|\mathcal{C}|)$. However, if we want *any* subset to be able to simulate, the signature size is $\Omega(|\mathcal{D}|)$, in accordance with the theorem.

Proof. Imagine that we give all the verifiers' keys to a sender and a receiver; the sender can now encode an arbitrary subset $\mathcal{C} \subseteq \mathcal{D}$ by letting $\mathcal{C}$ construct a simulated signature σ on some default message, and sending it to the receiver. The receiver can infer $\mathcal{C}$ from σ: by strong unforgeability, all verifiers' keys outside $\mathcal{C}$ will reject σ, whereas keys in $\mathcal{C}$ will accept, since we require the simulation to look convincing even given the secret keys in $\mathcal{C}$. It follows that σ must consist of enough bits to determine $\mathcal{C}$, which is $\log_2(2^{|\mathcal{D}|}) = |\mathcal{D}|$. □

Why First Ideas Fail

Using MACs. Black-box usage of a standard MAC scheme cannot help us combine unforgeability with consistency.[7] There are two straightforward ways to use a standard MAC scheme in this context: sharing a MAC key among the entire group, and sharing MAC keys pairwise. Sharing a single key does not provide the desired notion of unforgeability, since any member of the group can forge messages from any other member. Sharing keys pairwise does not provide the desired notion of consistency. If recipients R_1 and R_2 are the chosen recipients of a message, and R_1 receives a message he accepts as coming from S, he cannot be sure that R_2 would also accept that message: If S is corrupt, he could include a valid MAC for R_1 and an invalid MAC for R_2.

Using Proofs of Knowledge. A standard technique for making designated verifier signatures for a single verifier is to start from an interactive protocol that proves knowledge of either the signer's or the verifier's secret key, and turn this into a signature scheme using the Fiat-Shamir paradigm. It may seem natural to try to build an MDVS from this. However, it turns out to be challenging to achieve strong unforgeability using this technique; a signature cannot consist of a proof of knowledge of the signer's or one of the verifiers' secret keys, since any verifier will be able to convince other verifiers to accept a signature that did not come from the signer. For the same reason, a signature cannot consist of a proof of knowledge of the signer's secret key or some subset of the verifiers' secret keys.

MDVS from Standard Primitives. Our first class of MDVS constructions is based only on standard primitives. With one exception specified below, all of these constructions can be instantiated in the random oracle model with no trusted setup. (Without random oracles, we would need to set up a common reference string.)

The idea is that the signer creates a DVS signature for each verifier individually, and then proves the consistency of those signatures.[8] To support such proofs, we define a new primitive called Publicly Simulatable Designated Verifier Signatures (PSDVS) in Sect. 3.1, which is a single-verifier DVS equipped with extra properties. We then show, in Sect. 3.2, that a PSDVS together with a non-interactive zero knowledge proof of knowledge (NIZK-PoK) imply an MDVS for any number of signers and verifiers. Finally, we give some constructions of PSDVS. Our first PSDVS construction (in Sect. 3.3) uses only generic tools, namely pseudorandom functions, non-interactive key exchange (such as Diffie-Hellman), and non-interactive zero-knowledge proofs of knowledge. Our second PSDVS construction (in Sect. 3.4) aims at better concrete efficiency. It is based

---

[7] Note that our construction from standard primitives does make use of MAC schemes; however, it does so in a complex, non-black-box way.

[8] Simply proving that all of the signatures verify would violate the off-the-record property; instead, the signer proves that either all of the signatures are real, or they are all simulated, as described in Sect. 3.

on DDH, strong RSA and Paillier encryption, is secure in the random oracle model, and requires a constant number of exponentiations for all operations. This scheme requires the trusted generation of an RSA modulus so that the factorization remains unknown. We also sketc.h a variant that requires no trusted setup, is secure in the random oracle model, and only requires (a variant of) the DDH assumption. However, this version requires double discrete log proofs, and therefore requires a non-constant number of exponentiations.

In order to support one of our constructions in which the signer sends an encrypted MAC key, we introduce a new tool we call Authenticated and Verifiable Encryption (AVPKE), which may be of independent interest. This is a variant of Paillier encryption with built-in authentication, and as such it is related to the known primitive "signcryption" [Zhe97]. However, our AVPKE scheme has the additional property that we can give efficient zero-knowledge proofs involving the encrypted message, using the algebraic properties of Paillier encryption.

To sign in our PSDVS schemes, the signer and verifiers first must establish a shared symmetric key k. In some cases they can do this non-interactively, using their secret and public keys, while in other cases the signer must send an encrypted key alongside the signature. After this, the signer sends a MAC on the message under key k; this MAC is based on a pseudorandom function.

MDVS from Functional Encryption. Our last construction is based on Verifiable Functional Encryption (VFE). It has the advantages of additionally meeting the privacy of identities and verifier-identity-based signing properties. Additionally, it can be set up to have smaller signatures if we are willing to make a stronger assumption on the number of colluding verifiers. Namely, the signature size is $O(t)$, where t is the size of the largest number of colluding verifiers we want to tolerate. The downsides are that, with current state of the art, VFE requires non-standard computational assumptions and a trusted setup.

Remark 4. If we are going to put a bound on the size of a collusion, it may seem we can use bounded collusion FE, which can be realized from standard assumptions [GVW12, AV19], and then there is no need for our other constructions from standard primitives. However, this is not true. Bounded collusion FE requires us to fix the bound on collusion size at key generation time; a bound that may later turn out to be too small. Additionally, ciphertext sizes in bounded collusion FE depend on the bound; thus, choosing a large bound to make sure we can handle the application implies a cost in efficiency. The MDVS signature sizes would depend on some upper bound on number of corrupt parties in the *system*, as opposed to on the number of recipients for the signature in question, which may be orders of magnitude smaller.

In a nutshell, the idea behind the functional encryption based construction is to do the proof of knowledge of one of the relevant secret keys "inside the ciphertext". In a little more detail, the idea is to encrypt a list of t *standard* signatures, where t is the maximal size of collusion we want to protect against (that is, $t \geq |\mathcal{C}|$), and the MDVS signature will simply be this ciphertext. To sign, the signer will generate their own standard signature σ_S on the message, and then encrypt a list a signatures consisting of σ_S followed by $t-1$ dummy values. To verify a signature, a verifier R gets a functional decryption key that will look at the list of signatures inside the ciphertext and output accept or reject. It will accept if the list contains a valid signature from S or a valid signature from R. Now, if a corrupt set of verifiers $\mathcal{C}$ wants to simulate a signature, they will all sign the message and encrypt the list of these signatures. By security of the encryption scheme, this looks like a real signature, and will indeed verify under all verification keys belonging to verifiers in $\mathcal{C}$. However, no honest verifier will accept it as a signature from S, so we have strong unforgeability.

2 Multi-designated Verifier Signatures

MDVS Algorithms. A *multi-designated verifier signature* (MDVS) scheme is defined by the following probabilistic polynomial-time algorithms:

Setup$(1^\kappa) \to (pp, msk)$: On input the security parameter $\kappa \in \mathbb{N}$, outputs public parameters pp and the master secret key msk.

SignKeyGen$(pp, msk) \to (spk, ssk)$: On input the public parameter pp and the master secret key msk, outputs the public key spk and secret key ssk for a signer.

VerKeyGen$(pp, msk) \to (vpk, vsk)$: On input the public parameter pp and the master secret key msk, outputs the public key vpk and secret key vsk for a verifier.

Sign$(pp, ssk_i, \{vpk_j\}_{j \in \mathcal{D}}, m) \to \sigma$: On input the public parameters pp, a secret signing key ssk_i, the public keys of the designated verifiers $\{vpk_j\}_{j \in \mathcal{D}}$, and a message m, outputs a signature σ.

Verify$(pp, spk_i, vsk_j, \{vpk_{j'}\}_{j' \in \mathcal{D}}, m, \sigma) \to d$: On input the public parameters pp, a public verification key spk_i, a secret key vsk_j of a verifier such that $j \in \mathcal{D}$, the public keys of the designated verifiers $\{vpk_j\}_{j \in \mathcal{D}}$, a message m, and a signature σ, outputs a boolean decision d: $d = 1$ (accept) or $d = 0$ (reject).

Sim$(pp, spk_i, \{vpk_j\}_{j \in \mathcal{D}}, \{vsk_j\}_{j \in \mathcal{C}}, m) \to \sigma'$: On input public parameters pp, a public verification key spk_i, the public keys of the designated verifiers $\{vpk_j\}_{j \in \mathcal{D}}$, the secret keys of the corrupt designated verifiers $\{vsk_j\}_{j \in \mathcal{C}}$, and a message m, outputs a simulated signature σ'.

The different algorithms take many different inputs, which are not all needed for all of our constructions. Thus, to simplify the notation we exclude these inputs in later sections whenever they are not needed.

MDVS Properties. Let σ be a signature from signer i on message m and designated for verifiers $\mathcal{D}$. We ask for the following (informal) properties:

Correctness: All verifiers $j \in \mathcal{D}$ are able to verify an honestly generated signature σ.

Consistency: If there exists one verifier $j \in \mathcal{D}$ that accepts the signature σ, then all other designated verifiers (i.e. all $j' \in \mathcal{D}\backslash\{j\}$) also accept σ.

Unforgeability: An adversary without knowledge of the secret key ssk_i for signer i cannot create a signature σ' that is accepted by any designated verifier as a signature from signer i.

Off-The-Record: Given a signature σ, any malicious subset of the designated verifiers $\mathcal{C} \subseteq \mathcal{D}$ cannot convince any outsider that σ is a signature from signer i (i.e. the malicious set could have simulated the signature themselves).

(Optionally) Privacy of Identities: Any outsider (without colluding with any designated verifiers) cannot determine the identity of the signer and/or the identities of the designated verifiers.

(Optionally) Verifier-Identity-Based Signing: The signer should be able to produce a signature for a set of designated verifiers without requiring any information about them apart from their identities. In other words, we should have $vpk_j = j$ for a verifier with identity j.

Throughout our formal definitions we use the following six oracles:

Signer Key Generation Oracle: $\mathcal{O}_{SK}(i)$
1. If a signer key generation query has previously been performed for i, look up and return the previously generated key.
2. Otherwise, output and store $(spk_i, ssk_i) \leftarrow \mathsf{SignKeyGen}(pp, msk)$.

Verifier Key Generation Oracle: $\mathcal{O}_{VK}(j)$
1. If a verifier key generation query has previously been performed for j, look up and return the previously generated key.
2. Otherwise, output and store $(vpk_j, vsk_j) \leftarrow \mathsf{VerKeyGen}(pp, msk)$.

Public Signer Key Generation Oracle: $\mathcal{O}_{SPK}(i)$
1. $(spk_i, ssk_i) \leftarrow \mathcal{O}_{SK}(i)$.
2. Output spk_i.

Public Verifier Key Generation Oracle: $\mathcal{O}_{VPK}(j)$
1. $(vpk_j, vsk_j) \leftarrow \mathcal{O}_{VK}(j)$.
2. Output vpk_j.

Signing Oracle: $\mathcal{O}_S(i, \mathcal{D}, m)$
1. $(spk_i, ssk_i) \leftarrow \mathcal{O}_{SK}(i)$.
2. For all $j \in \mathcal{D}$: $vpk_j \leftarrow \mathcal{O}_{VPK}(j)$.
3. Output $\sigma \leftarrow \mathsf{Sign}(pp, ssk_i, \{vpk_j\}_{j \in \mathcal{D}}, m)$.

Verification Oracle: $\mathcal{O}_V(i, j, \mathcal{D}, m, \sigma)$
1. $spk_i \leftarrow \mathcal{O}_{SPK}(i)$.
2. $(vpk_j, vsk_j) \leftarrow \mathcal{O}_{VK}(j)$.
3. Output $d \leftarrow \mathsf{Verify}(pp, spk_i, vsk_j, \{vpk_{j'}\}_{j' \in \mathcal{D}}, m, \sigma)$.

Definition 1 (Correctness). *Let $\kappa \in \mathbb{N}$ be the security parameter, and let* $\mathsf{MDVS} = (\mathsf{Setup}, \mathsf{SignKeyGen}, \mathsf{VerKeyGen}, \mathsf{Sign}, \mathsf{Verify}, \mathsf{Sim})$ *be an MDVS scheme.* MDVS *is correct if for all signer identities i, messages m, verifier identity sets $\mathcal{D}$ and $j \in \mathcal{D}$, it holds that*

$$\Pr\left[\mathsf{Verify}(pp, spk_i, vsk_j, \{vpk_{j'}\}_{j' \in \mathcal{D}}, m, \sigma) \neq 1\right] = 0,$$

where the inputs to Verify *are generated as follows:*

- $(pp, msk) \leftarrow$ Setup(1^κ);
- $(spk_i, ssk_i) \leftarrow$ SignKeyGen(pp, msk, i);
- $(vpk_j, vsk_j) \leftarrow$ VerKeyGen(pp, msk, j) *for* $j \in \mathcal{D}$;
- $\sigma \leftarrow$ Sign$(pp, ssk_i, \{vpk_j\}_{j \in \mathcal{D}}, m)$.

In Definition 1, we require that all the designated verifiers can verify the signature, without considering what happens for parties that are not designated verifiers (i.e. parties who should not be able to verify the signature). Parties that are not designated verifiers are accounted for by the off-the-record property.

Definition 2 (Consistency). *Let* $\kappa \in \mathbb{N}$ *be the security parameter, and let* MDVS = (Setup, SignKeyGen, VerKeyGen, Sign, Verify, Sim) *be an MDVS scheme. Consider the following game between a challenger and an adversary* $\mathcal{A}$:

$$\text{Game}^{con}_{\text{MDVS}, \mathcal{A}}(\kappa)$$

1. $(pp, msk) \leftarrow$ Setup(1^κ)
2. $(m^*, i^*, \mathcal{D}^*, \sigma^*) \leftarrow \mathcal{A}^{\mathcal{O}_{SK}, \mathcal{O}_{VK}, \mathcal{O}_{SPK}, \mathcal{O}_{VPK}, \mathcal{O}_V}(pp)$

We say that $\mathcal{A}$ *wins the game if there exist verifiers* $j_0, j_1 \in \mathcal{D}^*$ *such that:*

$$\text{Verify}(pp, spk_{i^*}, vsk_{j_0}, \{vpk_{j'}\}_{j' \in \mathcal{D}^*}, m^*, \sigma^*) = 0,$$
$$\text{Verify}(pp, spk_{i^*}, vsk_{j_1}, \{vpk_{j'}\}_{j' \in \mathcal{D}^*}, m^*, \sigma^*) = 1,$$

where all keys are the honestly generated outputs of the key generation oracles, and $\mathcal{O}_{VK}$ *is never queried on* j_0 *or* j_1.
MDVS *is* consistent *if, for all PPT adversaries* $\mathcal{A}$,

$$\text{adv}^{con}_{\text{MDVS}, \mathcal{A}}(\kappa) = \Pr\left[\mathcal{A} \text{ wins } \text{Game}^{con}_{\text{MDVS}, \mathcal{A}}(\kappa)\right] \leq \text{negl}(\kappa).$$

Definition 2 states that even a valid signer (i.e. someone who knows a secret signing key) cannot create an inconsistent signature that will be accepted by some designated verifiers and rejected by others. By the correctness property, an honestly generated signature is accepted by all designated verifiers. By design, corrupt designated verifiers can construct an inconsistent signature, since some verifiers will accept it (i.e. those verifiers that created it), while the remaining honest designated verifiers will reject the simulated signature. Thus, we need to ask for $j \neq j_0, j_1$ for all queries j to the oracle $\mathcal{O}_{VK}$.

Definition 3 (Existential Unforgeability). *Let* $\kappa \in \mathbb{N}$ *be the security parameter, and let* MDVS = (Setup, SignKeyGen, VerKeyGen, Sign, Verify, Sim) *be an MDVS scheme. Consider the following game between a challenger and an adversary* $\mathcal{A}$:

$$\mathsf{Game}^{euf}_{\mathsf{MDVS},\mathcal{A}}(\kappa)$$

1. $(pp, msk) \leftarrow \mathsf{Setup}(1^\kappa)$
2. $(m^*, i^*, \mathcal{D}^*, \sigma^*) \leftarrow \mathcal{A}^{\mathcal{O}_{SK}, \mathcal{O}_{VK}, \mathcal{O}_{SPK}, \mathcal{O}_{VPK}, \mathcal{O}_S}(pp)$

We say that $\mathcal{A}$ wins the game if we have all of the following:

- for all queries i to oracle $\mathcal{O}_{SK}$, it holds that $i^* \neq i$;
- for all queries $(i, \mathcal{D}, m)$ to oracle $\mathcal{O}_S$ that result in signature σ, it holds that $(i^*, \mathcal{D}^*, m^*) \neq (i, \mathcal{D}, m)$;
- there exists a verifier $j' \in \mathcal{D}^*$ such that for all queries j to oracle $\mathcal{O}_{VK}$, it holds that $j' \neq j$ and

$$\mathsf{Verify}(pp, spk_{i^*}, vsk_{j'}, \{vpk_{j''}\}_{j'' \in \mathcal{D}^*}, m^*, \sigma^*) = 1,$$

where all keys are honestly generated outputs of the key generation oracles.

MDVS is existentially unforgeable if, for all PPT adversaries $\mathcal{A}$,

$$\mathsf{adv}^{euf}_{\mathsf{MDVS},\mathcal{A}}(\kappa) = \Pr\left[\mathcal{A} \text{ wins } \mathsf{Game}^{euf}_{\mathsf{MDVS},\mathcal{A}}(\kappa)\right] \leq \mathsf{negl}(\kappa).$$

Definition 3 states that an adversary cannot create a signature that any honest verifier will accept as coming from a signer whose secret signing key the adversary does not know. The adversary will always get the public keys of the involved parties, i.e. signer with identity i^* and the designated verifiers $\mathcal{D}$, through the key generation oracles. He is also allowed to obtain the secret keys of every party except the signer i^* and at least one designated verifier. The reason why we need at least one honest verifier is that corrupt verifiers can create a simulated signature that will look like a real signature with respect to their own verifier secret keys. However, this simulation will be rejected by any honest designated verifier, i.e. the simulation will be a valid forgery for the corrupt verifiers, but not for the honest verifiers.

Definition 4 (Off-The-Record). *Let $\kappa \in \mathbb{N}$ be the security parameter, let MDVS = (Setup, SignKeyGen, VerKeyGen, Sign, Verify, Sim) be an MDVS scheme, and let t be an upper bound on the number of verifiers an adversary $\mathcal{A}$ can corrupt. Consider the following game between a challenger and a stateful adversary $\mathcal{A}$, where all keys are honestly generated outputs of the key generation oracles:*

$$\mathsf{Game}^{otr}_{\mathsf{MDVS},\mathsf{Sim},\mathcal{A}}(\kappa)$$

1. $(pp, msk) \leftarrow \mathsf{Setup}(1^\kappa)$
2. $(i^*, \mathcal{D}^*, m^*, \mathcal{C}^*) \leftarrow \mathcal{A}^{\mathcal{O}_{SK}, \mathcal{O}_{VK}, \mathcal{O}_{SPK}, \mathcal{O}_{VPK}, \mathcal{O}_S, \mathcal{O}_V}(pp)$
3. $b \leftarrow \{0, 1\}$
4. $\sigma_0 \leftarrow \mathsf{Sign}(pp, ssk_{i^*}, \{vpk_j\}_{j \in \mathcal{D}^*}, m^*)$
5. $\sigma_1 \leftarrow \mathsf{Sim}(pp, spk_{i^*}, \{vpk_j\}_{j \in \mathcal{D}^*}, \{vsk_j\}_{j \in \mathcal{C}^*}, m^*)$
6. $b' \leftarrow \mathcal{A}^{\mathcal{O}_{SK}, \mathcal{O}_{VK}, \mathcal{O}_{SPK}, \mathcal{O}_{VPK}, \mathcal{O}_S, \mathcal{O}_V}(\sigma_b)$

We say that $\mathcal{A}$ wins the game if $b' = b$, and all of the following hold:

- $|\mathcal{C}^*| \leq t$ and $\mathcal{C}^* \subseteq \mathcal{D}^*$;
- *for all queries i to oracle $\mathcal{O}_{SK}$ it holds that $i^* \neq i$;*
- *for all queries j to oracle $\mathcal{O}_{VK}$ it holds that $j \notin \mathcal{D}^* \backslash \mathcal{C}^*$;*
- *for all queries $(i, j, \mathcal{D}, m, \sigma)$ to $\mathcal{O}_V$ it holds that $\sigma_b \neq \sigma$.*

We say that an MDVS scheme is t-off-the-record if, for all PPT adversaries $\mathcal{A}$,

$$\mathsf{adv}_{\mathsf{MDVS},\mathsf{Sim},\mathcal{A}}^{otr}(\kappa) = \Pr\left[\mathcal{A} \text{ wins } \mathsf{Game}_{\mathsf{MDVS},\mathsf{Sim},\mathcal{A}}^{otr}(\kappa)\right] - \frac{1}{2} \leq \mathsf{negl}(\kappa).$$

If a scheme supports $t = |\mathcal{D}|$, we say that it is off-the-record.

Definition 4 states that any adversary that corrupts a subset (of size t) of the designated verifiers $\mathcal{C}^*$ cannot determine whether the received signature was created by real signer i^* or simulated by the corrupt verifiers $\mathcal{C}^*$. The adversary is not allowed to see the secret keys for the designated verifiers that are in $\mathcal{D}^* \backslash \mathcal{C}^*$. If the adversary was allowed to get secret keys of additional parties in $\mathcal{D}^*$ (which are not in $\mathcal{C}^*$), then he would be able to distinguish trivially, since any honest designated verifiers (i.e. any $j \in \mathcal{D}^* \backslash \mathcal{C}^*$) can distinguish simulated signatures from real signatures (from the unforgeability property).

Definition 5 (Privacy of Identities). *Let $\kappa \in \mathbb{N}$ be the security parameter, and let MDVS = (Setup, SignKeyGen, VerKeyGen, Sign, Verify, Sim) be an MDVS scheme. Consider the following game between a challenger and a stateful adversary $\mathcal{A}$, where all keys are the honestly generated outputs of the key generation oracles:*

$$\mathsf{Game}_{\mathsf{MDVS},\mathcal{A}}^{pri}(\kappa)$$

1. $(pp, msk) \leftarrow \mathsf{Setup}(1^\kappa)$
2. $(m^*, i_0, i_1, \mathcal{D}_0, \mathcal{D}_1) \leftarrow \mathcal{A}^{\mathcal{O}_{SK}, \mathcal{O}_{VK}, \mathcal{O}_{SPK}, \mathcal{O}_{VPK}, \mathcal{O}_S, \mathcal{O}_V}(pp)$
3. $b \leftarrow \{0, 1\}$
4. $\sigma^* \leftarrow \mathsf{Sign}(pp, ssk_{i_b}, \{vpk_j\}_{j \in \mathcal{D}_b}, m^*)$
5. $b' \leftarrow \mathcal{A}^{\mathcal{O}_{SK}, \mathcal{O}_{VK}, \mathcal{O}_{SPK}, \mathcal{O}_{VPK}, \mathcal{O}_S, \mathcal{O}_V}(\sigma^*)$

We say that $\mathcal{A}$ wins the game if $b = b'$, and all of the following hold:

- $|\mathcal{D}_0| = |\mathcal{D}_1|$;
- *for all queries i to $\mathcal{O}_{SK}$, it holds that $i \notin \{i_0, i_1\}$;*
- *for all queries j to $\mathcal{O}_{VK}$, it holds that $j \notin \mathcal{D}_0 \cup \mathcal{D}_1$;*
- *for all queries $(i, j, \mathcal{D}, m, \sigma)$ to $\mathcal{O}_V$, it holds that $\sigma^* \neq \sigma$.*

MDVS *has* privacy of identities *if, for all PPT adversaries $\mathcal{A}$,*

$$\mathsf{adv}_{\mathsf{MDVS},\mathcal{A}}^{pri}(\kappa) = \Pr\left[\mathcal{A} \text{ wins } \mathsf{Game}_{\mathsf{MDVS},\mathcal{A}}^{pri}(\kappa)\right] - \frac{1}{2} \leq \mathsf{negl}(\kappa).$$

We say that MDVS has additional properties as follows:

- *privacy of the signer's identity (PSI) if we make the restriction that $\mathcal{D}_0 = \mathcal{D}_1$;*

- *privacy of the designated verifiers' identities (PVI)* if we make the restriction that $i_0 = i_1$.

Definition 5 states that an adversary cannot distinguish between signatures from two different signers (PSI) if he does not know the secret key of any of the signers or designated verifiers (as designated verifiers *are* allowed to identify the signer). Furthermore, it should not help him to see other signatures that he knows are from the signers in question.

In addition, if we vary the verifier sets ($\mathcal{D}_0 \neq \mathcal{D}_1$), then the MDVS scheme has privacy of designated verifier's identities (PVI), which means that any outsider without knowledge of any secret keys cannot distinguish between signatures meant for different verifiers.

Definition 6 (Verifier-Identity-Based Signing). *We say that an MDVS scheme has* verifier-identity-based signing *if for honestly generated verifier keys* (vsk_j, vpk_j) *for verifier with identity j, we have* $vpk_j = j$.

Note that, in order to achieve verifier-identity-based signing, verifier key generation must require a master secret key msk. Otherwise, any outsider would be able to generate a verification key for verifier j, and use it to verify signatures meant only for that verifier.

Relation to Previous Definitions. Our definition of MDVS is consistent with previous work in this area, but with some differences. Our MDVS syntax closely follows the one introduced by [LV04], but we allow for a master secret key in the case where the keys are generated by a trusted party (like in our construction based on functional encryption). Our security definitions are adapted from those in [LV04, ZAYS12] to capture the flexibility introduced by allowing any subset of designated verifiers to simulate a signature, thus providing better deniability properties. Finally, we formalize consistency as an additional and desirable requirement.

3   Standard Primitive-Based MDVS Constructions

In this section we show how to create an MDVS scheme that uses only standard primitives, such as key exchange, commitments, pseudorandom functions and generators, and non-interactive zero knowledge proofs.

On a high level, one way to build an MDVS is for the signer to use a separate DVS with each verifier; the MDVS signature would then consist of a vector of individual DVS signatures. This gives us almost everything we need—the remaining issue is consistency. Each verifier can verify one of the DVS signatures, but is not convinced that all of the other verifiers will come to the same conclusion.

A solution to this consistency issue is to include as part of the MDVS signature a zero knowledge proof that all of the DVS signatures verify. However, this introduces a new issue with off-the-record. Now, a colluding set of verifiers will not be able to simulate a signature unless *all* of the verifiers collude. In order to produce such a convincing zero knowledge proof as part of the signature, they would need to forge signatures for the other verifiers in the underlying DVS scheme, which they should not be able to do.

So, instead of using a zero knowledge proof of knowledge that all of the DVS signatures verify, we use a proof that *either* all of the DVS signatures verify, *or they are all simulated*. Then, a corrupt set of verifiers can simulate all of the underlying DVS signatures—with the caveat that the signatures they simulate for themselves should be convincing simulations even in the presence of their secret keys—and, instead of proving that all of the signatures verify, they prove that all of the signatures are simulations.

3.1   New Primitive: Provably Simulatable Designated-Verifier Signatures (PSDVS)

Designated Verifier Signatures (DVS) have a simulation algorithm Sim which is used to satisfy the off-the-record property. Given the signer's public key, the verifier's secret key and a message m, Sim should return a signature which is indistinguishable from a real signature. A *Provably Simulatable DVS (PSDVS)* has some additional properties:

Definition 7. *A PSDVS must satisfy the standard notions of correctness and existential unforgeability. Additionally, it should satisfy* PubSigSim *indstinguishability (Definition 8),* PubSigSim *correctness (Definition 9),* PubSigSim *soundness (Definition 10),* VerSigSim *indstinguishability (Definition 11),* VerSigSim *correctness (Definition 12),* VerSigSim *soundness (Definition 13), provable signing correctness (Definition 14), and provable signing soundness (Definition 15).*

Provable Public Simulation. As in *PSI* (Definition 5), anyone should be able to produce a signature that is indistinguishable from a real signature. Additionally, the party simulating the signature should be able to produce a proof that this is *not* a real signature. This proof will be incorporated into the MDVS proof of consistency; the colluding verifiers, when producing a simulation, need to prove that all underlying PSDVS signatures are real, or that they are all fake.

In other words, we require two additional algorithms, as follows:

1. $\mathsf{PubSigSim}(pp, spk, vpk, m) \to (\sigma, \pi)$
2. $\mathsf{PubSigVal}(pp, spk, vpk, m, \sigma, \pi) \to d \in \{0, 1\}$

The colluding verifiers will produce a public simulation in the underlying PSDVS for verifiers outside their coalition, and use $\mathsf{PubSigSim}$ to prove that this simulation is not a real signature. π will not be explicitly included in the proof of "the underlying PSDVS signatures are all real or all fake," of course, as it would give away the fact that all underlying signatures are fake, as opposed to all being real; rather, it will be wrapped in a larger zero knowledge proof.

Definition 8 (PubSigSim Indistinguishability). *We say that the PSDVS has* PubSigSim *Indistinguishability if* PubSigSim *produces a signature* σ *that is indistinguishable from real. More formally, an adversary should not be able to win the following game with probability non-negligibly more than half:*

$$\text{Game}_{\text{PVDVS},\mathcal{A}}^{PubSigSim\text{-}Ind}(\kappa)$$

1. $pp \leftarrow \text{Setup}(1^{\kappa})$
2. $(spk, ssk) \leftarrow \text{SignKeyGen}(pp)$
3. $(vpk, vsk) \leftarrow \text{VerKeyGen}(pp)$
4. $m^* \leftarrow \mathcal{A}^{\mathcal{O}_S,\mathcal{O}_V}(spk, vpk)$
5. $b \leftarrow \{0, 1\}$
6. $\sigma_0 \leftarrow \text{Sign}(pp, ssk, vpk, m^*)$
7. $(\sigma_1, \pi) \leftarrow \text{PubSigSim}(pp, spk, vpk, m^*)$
8. $b' \leftarrow \mathcal{A}^{\mathcal{O}_S,\mathcal{O}_V}(pp, spk, vpk, m^*, \sigma_b)$

We say that $\mathcal{A}$ *wins the* PubSigSim-Ind *game if* $b = b'$ *and for all queries* (m, σ) *to* $\mathcal{O}_V$, *it holds that* $(m, \sigma) \neq (m^*, \sigma_b)$.

Definition 9 (PubSigSim Correctness). *We say that the PSDVS has* Pub-SigSim *Correctness if for all* $pp \leftarrow \text{Setup}(1^{\kappa})$; $(spk, ssk) \leftarrow \text{SignKeyGen}(pp)$; $(vpk, vsk) \leftarrow \text{VerKeyGen}(pp)$; $m \in \{0, 1\}^*$; $(\sigma, \pi) \leftarrow \text{PubSigSim}(pp, spk, vpk, m)$;

$$\Pr[\text{PubSigVal}(pp, spk, vpk, m, \sigma, \pi) = 1] = 1.$$

Definition 10 (PubSigSim Soundness). *We say that the PSDVS has* Pub-SigSim *Soundness if it is hard to construct a signature* σ *which is accepted by the verifier algorithm and at the same time can be proven to be a simulated signature. More formally, an adversary should not be able to win the following game with non-negligible probability:*

$$\text{Game}_{\text{PVDVS},\mathcal{A}}^{PubSigSim\text{-}Sound}(\kappa)$$

1. $pp \leftarrow \text{Setup}(1^{\kappa})$
2. $(spk, ssk) \leftarrow \text{SignKeyGen}(pp)$
3. $(vpk, vsk) \leftarrow \text{VerKeyGen}(pp)$
4. $(m^*, \sigma^*, \pi^*) \leftarrow \mathcal{A}(pp, ssk, spk, vpk)$

We say that $\mathcal{A}$ *wins the* PubSigSim-Sound *game if* $\text{Verify}(pp, vsk, m^*, \sigma^*) = 1$ *and* $\text{PubSigVal}(pp, spk, vpk, m^*, \sigma^*, \pi^*) = 1$.

Provable Verifier Simulation. As in *off-the-record* (Definition 4), a verifier should be able to produce a signature that is indistinguishable from a real signature, *even given its secret key*. Additionally, the verifier should be able to produce a proof that the signature is *not* a real signature (that is, that the verifier, and not the signer, produced it). This proof will be incorporated into the MDVS proof of consistency.

In other words, we require two additional algorithms, as follows:

1. $\text{VerSigSim}(pp, spk, vpk, vsk, m) \rightarrow (\sigma, \pi)$
2. $\text{VerSigVal}(pp, spk, vpk, m, \sigma, \pi) \rightarrow d \in \{0, 1\}$

The colluding verifiers will produce a verifier simulation in the underlying PSDVS for verifiers *inside* their coalition, and use VerSigSim to prove that this simulation is not a real signature.

Definition 11 (VerSigSim Indistinguishability). *We say that the PSDVS has* VerSigSim *Indistinguishability if* VerSigSim *produces a signature σ that is indistinguishable from real. More formally, an adversary should not be able to win the following game with probability non-negligibly more than half:*

$$\text{Game}_{\text{PVDVS},\mathcal{A}}^{VerSigSim\text{-}Ind}(\kappa)$$

1. $pp \leftarrow \text{Setup}(1^\kappa)$
2. $(spk, ssk) \leftarrow \text{SignKeyGen}(pp)$
3. $(vpk, vsk) \leftarrow \text{VerKeyGen}(pp)$
4. $m^* \leftarrow \mathcal{A}^{\mathcal{O}_S}(pp, spk, vpk, vsk)$
5. $b \leftarrow_\$ \{0, 1\}$
6. $\sigma_0 \leftarrow \text{Sign}(pp, ssk, vpk, m^*)$
7. $(\sigma_1, \pi) \leftarrow \text{VerSigSim}(pp, spk, vsk, m^*)$
8. $b' \leftarrow \mathcal{A}^{\mathcal{O}_S}(pp, spk, vpk, vsk, m^*, \sigma_b)$

We say that $\mathcal{A}$ wins the VerSigSim-Ind *game if $b = b'$.*

Definition 12 (VerSigSim Correctness). *We say that the PSDVS has* VerSigSim *Correctness if for all $pp \leftarrow \text{Setup}(1^\kappa)$, $(spk, ssk) \leftarrow \text{SignKeyGen}(pp)$, $(vpk, vsk) \leftarrow \text{VerKeyGen}(pp)$, $m \in \{0,1\}^*$, $(\sigma, \pi) \leftarrow \text{VerSigSim}(pp, spk, vpk, vsk, m)$,*

$$\Pr[\text{VerSigVal}(pp, spk, vpk, m, \sigma, \pi) = 1] = 1.$$

Definition 13 (VerSigSim Soundness). *We say that the PSDVS has* Ver-SigSim Soundness *if the signer is not able to produce σ and π that pass the validation check* VerSigVal, *i.e. π is a proof that σ was not produced by the signer. More formally, an adversary should not be able to win the following game with non-negligible probability:*

$$\text{Game}_{\text{PVDVS},\mathcal{A}}^{VerSigSim\text{-}Sound}(\kappa)$$

1. $pp \leftarrow \text{Setup}(1^\kappa)$
2. $(spk, ssk) \leftarrow \text{SignKeyGen}(pp)$
3. $(vpk, vsk) \leftarrow \text{VerKeyGen}(pp)$
4. $(m^*, \sigma^*, \pi^*) \leftarrow \mathcal{A}(pp, ssk, spk, vpk)$

$\mathcal{A}$ wins the VerSigSim-Sound *game if* VerSigVal$(pp, spk, vpk, m^*, \sigma^*, \pi^*) = 1$.

Provable Signing. Lastly, we require a provable variant of signing, so that the signer is able to produce a proof that a signature is real. In other words, we require the signing algorithm $\text{Sign}(pp, spk, ssk, vpk, m) \to (\sigma, \pi)$ to output π as well. We also require one additional validation algorithm, as follows:

$$\text{RealSigVal}(pp, spk, vpk, m, \sigma, \pi) \to d \in \{0, 1\}$$

Definition 14 (Provable Signing Correctness). *We say that the PSDVS has* Provable Signing Correctness *if* $\forall pp \leftarrow$ Setup(1^κ), $(spk, ssk) \leftarrow$ SignKeyGen (pp), $(vpk, vsk) \leftarrow$ VerKeyGen(pp), $m \in \{0,1\}^*$, $(\sigma, \pi) \leftarrow$ Sign(pp, spk, ssk, vpk, m),
$$\Pr[\mathsf{RealSigVal}(pp, spk, vpk, m, \sigma, \pi) = 1] = 1.$$

Definition 15 (Provable Signing Soundness). *We say that the PSDVS has* Provable Signing Soundness *if the proof of correctness* π *produced by* Sign *does not verify unless* σ *verifies. More formally, an adversary should not be able to win the following game with non-negligible probability:*

$$\mathsf{Game}_{\mathsf{PVDVS},\mathcal{A}}^{Sign\text{-}Sound}(\kappa)$$

1. $pp \leftarrow$ Setup(1^κ)
2. $(spk, ssk) \leftarrow$ SignKeyGen(pp)
3. $(vpk, vsk) \leftarrow$ VerKeyGen(pp)
4. $(m^*, \sigma^*, \pi^*) \leftarrow \mathcal{A}(pp, ssk, spk, vpk)$

We say that $\mathcal{A}$ *wins the* Sign-Sound *game if* RealSigVal$(pp, spk, vpk, m^*, \sigma^*, \pi^*) = 1$ *and* Verify$(pp, spk, vsk, m^*, \sigma^*) = 0$.

Note that none of these proofs π are parts of the signature. If included in the signature, such proofs would allow an adversary to distinguish a simulation from a real signature.

3.2 Standard Primitive-Based MDVS Construction

Given a PSDVS, as defined in Sect. 3.1, we can build an MDVS. The transformation is straightforward: the signer uses the PSDVS to sign a message for each verifier, and proves consistency using a non-interactive zero knowledge proof of knowledge. The proof of consistency will claim that either all of the PSDVS signatures verify, or all of them are simulated.

Construction 1. *Let* PSDVS = (Setup, SignKeyGen, VerKeyGen, Sign, Verify, RealSigVal, PubSigSim, PubSigVal, VerSigSim, VerSigVal) *be a provably simulatable designated verifier signature scheme, and* NIZK-PoK = (Setup, Prove, Verify) *be a non-interactive zero knowledge proof of knowledge system and* $\mathcal{R}_{cons}$ *a relation that we will define later in the protocol.*

Setup(1^κ):
    1. $crs \leftarrow$ NIZK-PoK.Setup$(1^\kappa, \mathcal{R}_{cons})$.
    2. PSDVS.$pp \leftarrow$ PSDVS.Setup(1^κ).
    Output $(crs, \mathsf{PSDVS}.pp)$ as the public parameters pp.
SignKeyGen(pp): $(spk_i, ssk_i) \leftarrow$ PSDVS.SignKeyGen(PSDVS.pp).
    Output (spk_i, ssk_i) as signer i's public/secret key pair.
VerKeyGen(pp): $(vpk_j, vsk_j) \leftarrow$ PSDVS.VerKeyGen(PSDVS.pp).
    Output (vpk_j, vsk_j) as verifier j's public/secret key pair.
Sign$(pp, ssk_i, \{vpk_j\}_{j \in \mathcal{D}}, m)$:

1. For every verifier $j \in \mathcal{D}$, compute a signature and proof of signature validity as $(\sigma_j, \pi_j) \leftarrow \mathsf{PSDVS.Sign}(\mathsf{PSDVS}.pp, ssk_i, vpk_j, m)$.
2. Create a proof π of consistency, i.e a proof of knowledge of $\{\pi_j\}_{j \in \mathcal{D}}$ such that either all signatures are real (as demonstrated by $\{\pi_j\}_{j \in \mathcal{D}}$), or all signatures are fake (as could be demonstrated by the proofs produced by $\mathsf{PSDVS.PubSigSim}$ or $\mathsf{PSDVS.VerSigSim}$).
3. $\sigma = (\{\sigma_j\}_{j \in \mathcal{D}}, \pi)$.

Output σ as the signature.

$\mathsf{Verify}(pp, spk_i, vsk_j, m, \sigma = (\{\sigma_j\}_{j \in \mathcal{D}}, \pi))$:

1. Let $d_\pi \leftarrow \mathsf{NIZK\text{-}PoK.Verify}(crs, u = (\mathsf{PSDVS}.pp, spk_i, \{vpk_j\}_{j \in \mathcal{D}}, \{\sigma_j\}_{j \in \mathcal{D}}), \pi)$.
2. Let $d \leftarrow \mathsf{PSDVS.Verify}(\mathsf{PSDVS}.pp, spk_i, vsk_j, m, \sigma_j) \wedge d_\pi$.

Output d as the verification decision.

$\mathsf{Sim}(pp, spk_i, \{vpk_j\}_{j \in \mathcal{D}}, \{vsk_j\}_{j \in \mathcal{C}}, m)$:

1. For $j \in \mathcal{D} \cap \mathcal{C}$: $(\sigma_j, \pi_j) \leftarrow \mathsf{VerSigSim}(\mathsf{PSDVS}.pp, spk_i, vpk_j, vsk_j, m)$.
2. For $j \in \mathcal{D} \backslash \mathcal{C}$: $(\sigma_j, \pi_j) \leftarrow \mathsf{PubSigSim}(\mathsf{PSDVS}.pp, spk_i, vpk_j, m)$.
3. Use these signatures and proofs to produce the NIZK π for consistency.
4. $\sigma = (\{\sigma_j\}_{j \in \mathcal{D}}, \pi)$.

Output σ as the signature.

Theorem 2. *Assume* PSDVS *is a secure provably simulatable designated verifier signature scheme and* $\mathsf{NIZK\text{-}PoK}$ *is a secure non-interactive zero knowledge proof of knowledge system. Then Construction 1 is a correct and secure MDVS scheme (without privacy of identities (Definition 5)).*

Due to space limitations, the proof of Theorem 2 is deferred to the full version.

3.3   Standard Primitive-Based PSDVS Construction

We can build a PSDVS from a special message authentication code (MAC) which looks uniformly random without knowledge of the secret MAC key—such a MAC can be built from any pseudorandom function. A signature on a message m will be a MAC on (m, t), where t is some random tag. Proving that the signature is real simply involves proving knowledge of a MAC key that is consistent with the MAC and some global public commitment to the MAC key. A public proof that the signature is simulated and does not verify would involve proving that the MAC was pseudorandomly generated. A verifier's proof that the signature is simulated would involve proving that the tag was generated in a way that only the verifier could use (e.g. from a PRF to which only the verifier knows the key).

Of course, this is not ideal, since MACs require knowledge of a shared key; in order to use MACs, we would need to set up shared keys between every possible pair of signer and verifier. However, we can get around this using non-interactive key exchange (NIKE). Each signer and verifier publishes a public key, and any pair of them can agree on a shared secret key by simply using their own secret key and the other's public key. The construction is as follows:

Construction 2. *Let:*

- COMM = (Setup, Commit, Open) *be a commitment scheme,*
- PRF = (KeyGen, Compute) *be a length-preserving pseudorandom function,*
- PRG *be a length-doubling pseudorandom generator,*
- NIZK = (Setup, Prove, Verify) *be a non-interactive zero knowledge proof system, and*
- NIKE = (KeyGen, KeyExtract, KeyMatch) *be a non-interactive key exchange protocol. KeyMatch is an additional algorithm that checks if a public key and a secret key match. KeyMatch is not typically defined as a part of a NIKE scheme; however, such an algorithm always exists.*

Setup(1^κ):
1. $crs_i \leftarrow$ NIZK.Setup($1^\kappa, \mathcal{R}_i$), $i = 1, 2, 3$.
2. $ck \leftarrow$ COMM.Setup(1^κ).
Output $(\{crs_1, crs_2, crs_3\}, ck)$ as the public parameters pp.
SignKeyGen(pp):
1. (NIKE.pk_S, NIKE.sk_S) $\leftarrow$ NIKE.KeyGen(1^κ).
2. $ssk =$ NIKE.sk_S.
3. $spk =$ NIKE.pk_S.
Output ssk as the signer's secret key and spk as the signer's public key.
VerKeyGen(pp):
1. (NIKE.pk_R, NIKE.sk_R) $\leftarrow$ NIKE.KeyGen(1^κ).
2. $k_R \leftarrow$ PRF.KeyGen(1^κ). (Informally, this key will be used by the verifier to simulate signatures using VerSigSim.)
3. Choose randomness (i.e. decommitment value) r_R at random.
4. $c_R =$ COMM.Commit($ck, k_R; r_R$). (Informally, this commitment will be used by the verifier to support its proofs of fake-ness.)
5. $vsk = ($NIKE.$sk_R, k_R, r_R)$.
6. $vpk = ($NIKE.$pk_R, c_R)$.
Output vsk as the verifier's secret key and vpk as the verifier's public key.
Sign($pp, ssk =$ NIKE.$sk_S, vpk = ($NIKE.$pk_R, c_R), m$):
The signer computes a shared key with the designated verifier and proceeds to sign the message m:
1. $k_{shared} =$ NIKE.KeyExtract(NIKE.sk_S, NIKE.pk_R). (Informally, this key will be used as a MAC key.)
2. Choose t at random.
3. $\sigma = (\sigma_1, \sigma_2) \leftarrow (t, \mathsf{PRF}_{k_{shared}}((m, t)))$.
4. $\pi \leftarrow$ NIZK.Prove(crs_1, u, w) where $u = ((\sigma_1, \sigma_2),$ NIKE.pk_S, NIKE.$pk_R, m)$ and $w = ($NIKE.$sk_S, k_{shared})$
We define the relation $\mathcal{R}_1$ indexed by NIKE public parameters and PRF for a statement u and witness w:

$$\mathcal{R}_1 = \{(u = (\sigma_1, \sigma_2, \text{NIKE}.pk_S, \text{NIKE}.pk_R, m), w = (\text{NIKE}.sk_S, k_{shared})) :$$
$$\mathsf{KeyMatch}(\text{NIKE}.pk_S, \text{NIKE}.sk_S) = 1$$
$$\wedge\ k_{shared} = \text{NIKE.KeyExtract}(\text{NIKE}.sk_S, \text{NIKE}.pk_R)$$
$$\wedge\ \sigma_2 = \mathsf{PRF}_{k_{shared}}((m, \sigma_1))\}$$

Output σ as the signature, and π as the proof of real-ness.

Verify($pp, spk = $ NIKE.$pk_S, vsk = ($NIKE.$sk_R, k_R, r_R), m, \sigma = (\sigma_1, \sigma_2)$):

1. k_{shared} = NIKE.KeyExtract(NIKE.sk_R, NIKE.pk_S). (Informally, this key will be used as a MAC key.)
2. If PRF$_{k_{shared}}((m, \sigma_1)) = \sigma_2$, set $d = 1$. Otherwise, set $d = 0$.

Output d as the verification decision.

RealSigVal($pp, spk, vpk, m, \sigma, \pi$):

Output $d \leftarrow$ NIZK.Verify(crs_1, σ, π) as the validation decision.

PubSigSim(pp, m):

1. Choose a PRG seed seed.
2. Choose σ_1 and σ_2 pseudorandomly by running PRG on seed.
3. $\sigma \leftarrow (\sigma_1, \sigma_2)$.
4. Let $\pi \leftarrow$ NIZK.Prove($crs_2, u = \sigma, w = $ seed).
   We define the relation $\tilde{\mathcal{R}}_2$ indexed by the PRG for a statement $u = (\sigma = (\sigma_1, \sigma_2))$ and the witnesses $w = $ seed:

$$\tilde{\mathcal{R}}_2 = \{(u = \sigma; w = \text{seed}) : u = \text{PRG}(w)\} \tag{1}$$

Output σ as the simulated signature, and π as the proof of fake-ness.

PubSigVal($pp, spk, vpk, m, \sigma = (\sigma_1, \sigma_2), \pi$):

Output $d \leftarrow$ NIZK.Verify(crs_2, σ, π) as the validation decision.

VerSigSim($pp, spk = $ NIKE.$pk_S, vpk = ($NIKE.$pk_R, c_R), vsk = ($NIKE.$sk_R, k_R, r_R), m$):

The verifier can fake a signature using its PRF key k_R.

1. $k_{shared} = $ NIKE.KeyExtract(NIKE.sk_R, NIKE.pk_S).
2. Choose r at random.
3. $t \leftarrow$ PRF$_{k_R}(r)$.
4. $\sigma \leftarrow (t, \text{PRF}_{k_{shared}}((m, t)))$.
5. Let $\pi \leftarrow$ NIZK.Prove($crs_3, u = (c_R, \sigma_1), w = (k_R, r_R, r)$).
   We define the relation $\tilde{\mathcal{R}}_3$ indexed by the c public parameters and PRF for statements u and witnesses w:

$$\tilde{\mathcal{R}}_3 = \{(u = (c_R, \sigma_1), w = (k_R, r_R, r)) : k_R = \text{COMM.Open}(c_R, r_R) \wedge \sigma_1 = \text{PRF}_{k_R}(r)\}$$

Output σ as the simulated signature and π as the proof of fake-ness.

VerSigVal($pp, spk, vpk, m, \sigma, \pi$):

Output $d \leftarrow$ NIZK.Verify($crs_3, (c_R, \sigma_1), \pi$) as the validation decision.

Theorem 3. *If the schemes* COMM, PRF, PRG, NIZK, NIKE *are secure, then Construction 2 is a correct and secure PSDVS scheme as per Definition 7.*

Due to space limitations, the proof of Theorem 3 is deferred to the full version.

3.4   DDH and Paillier-Based PSDVS Construction

The goal of this section is to construct a PSDVS scheme based on DDH and the security of Paillier encryption. The idea in the PSDVS construction is that the authenticator for a message m will be $\mathsf{H}(m, t)^k$ in a group G where t is a nonce, k is a key known to both parties and H is a hash function modeled as a random oracle. The construction requires that certain properties of the key can be proved in zero-knowledge, and we can do this efficiently using standard Σ-protocols because the key is in the exponent. However, naive use of this idea would mean that a sender needs to store a key for every verifier he talks to, and the set-up must generate correlated secret keys for the parties. To get around this, we will instead let the sender choose k on the fly and send it to the verifier, encrypted using a new variant of Paillier encryption. In the following subsection we describe and prove this new encryption scheme, and then we specify the actual PSDVS construction. Paillier-style encryption comes in handy since its algebraic properties are useful in making our zero knowledge proofs efficient.

Paillier-Based Authenticated and Verifiable Encryption. An authenticated and verifiable encryption scheme (AVPKE) involves a sender S and a receiver R. Such a scheme comes with the following polynomial time algorithms:

$\mathsf{Setup}(1^\kappa) \to pp$: A probabilistic algorithm for setup which outputs public parameters.

$\mathsf{KeyGen}_\mathsf{S}(pp) \to (sk_\mathsf{S}, pk_\mathsf{S})$: A probabilistic sender key generation algorithm.

$\mathsf{KeyGen}_\mathsf{R}(pp) \to (sk_\mathsf{R}, pk_\mathsf{R})$: A probabilistic receiver key generation algorithm.

$\mathsf{Enc}_{pp, sk_\mathsf{S}, pk_\mathsf{R}}(k) \to c$: A probabilistic encryption algorithm for message k.

$\mathsf{Dec}_{pp, sk_\mathsf{R}, pk_\mathsf{S}}(c) \to \{k, \bot\}$: A decryption algorithm that outputs either reject or a message.

We require, of course, that $\mathsf{Dec}_{pp, sk_\mathsf{R}, pk_\mathsf{S}}(\mathsf{Enc}_{pp, sk_\mathsf{S}, pk_\mathsf{R}}(k)) = k$ for all messages k.

Intuitively, the idea is that given only the receiver public key pk_R and his own secret key sk_S, the sender S can encrypt a message k in such a way that on receiving the ciphertext, R can check that k comes from S, no third party knows k and finally, the encryption is verifiable in that it allows S to efficiently prove in zero-knowledge that k satisfies certain properties.

Our AVPKE scheme adds an authentication mechanism on top of Paillier encryption:

Construction 3. *Let:*

- Ggen *be a Group Generator, a probabilistic polynomial time algorithm which on input 1^κ outputs the description of a cyclic group G and a generator g, such that the order of G is a random κ-bit RSA modulus n, which is the product of so-called safe primes. (That is, $n = pq$ where $p = 2p' + 1, q = 2q' + 1$ and p', q' are also primes.) Finally, we need the algorithm to output an element $\hat{g} \in \mathbb{Z}_n^*$ of order $p'q'$.*

– NIZK = (Setup, Prove, Verify) *be a simulation-sound non-interactive zero knowledge proof system. In this section, we will use Σ-protocols made non-interactive using the Fiat-Shamir heuristic, so in this case* Setup *is empty and there is no common reference string.*

Ggen *can be constructed using standard techniques. For instance, first gener-ate n using standard techniques, then repeatedly choose a small random number r until $P = 2rn + 1$ is a prime. Let g' be a generator of $\mathbb{Z}_P^*$. Then let G be the subgroup of $\mathbb{Z}_P^*$ generated by $g = g'^{2r} \bmod P$.[9] Finally, to construct the element $\hat{g}$, let $u \in_R \mathbb{Z}_n$ and set $\hat{g} = u^2 \bmod n$. Indeed, this is a random square, and since the subgroup of squares modulo n has only large prime factors in its order (p' and q'), a random element is a generator with overwhelming probability[10].*

Setup(1^κ): *Run* Ggen *to generate a modulus n and $\hat{g} \in \mathbb{Z}_n^*$ as explained above. Output $pp = (n, \hat{g})$.*
KeyGen$_S$(pp): *Pick $sk_S \in_R \mathbb{Z}_n$, and set $pk_S = \hat{g}^{sk_S}$. Output (sk_S, pk_S).*
KeyGen$_R$(pp): *Pick $\alpha_1, \alpha_2 \in_R \mathbb{Z}_n$, set $sk_R = (\alpha_1, \alpha_2)$, and set $pk_R = (\beta_1, \beta_2) = (\hat{g}^{\alpha_1}, \hat{g}^{\alpha_2})$.*

The public key values are statistically indistinguishable from random elements in the group generated by $\hat{g}$ since n is a sufficiently good "approximation" to the order $p'q'$ of $\hat{g}$.

Enc$_{pp, sk_S, pk_R}(k; r, b_1, b_2)$:
1. *The randomness should have been picked as follows: $r \in_R \mathbb{Z}_n$ and $b_1, b_2 \in_R \{0, 1\}$.*
2. *Set $c_1 = (-1)^{b_1} \hat{g}^r \bmod n$.*
3. *Set $c_2 = (n + 1)^k ((-1)^{b_2} \beta_1^{sk_S} \beta_2^r \bmod n)^n \bmod n^2$.*
4. *Let π_{valid} be a non-interactive zero-knowledge proof of knowledge wherein given public data $(n, \hat{g}, (c_1, c_2))$, the prover shows knowledge of a witness $w = (k, r, b_1, v)$ such that $c_1 = (-1)^{b_1} \hat{g}^r$ and $c_2 = (n + 1)^k v^n \bmod n^2$. An honest prover can use $v = (-1)^{b_2} \beta_1^{sk_S} \beta_2^r \bmod n$. The factor $(-1)^{b_1}$ is only in the ciphertext for technical reasons: it allows π_{valid} to be efficient.*
   Output $c = (c_1, c_2, \pi_{valid})$.
Dec$_{pp, sk_R = (\alpha_1, \alpha_2), pk_S}(c = (c_1, c_2, \pi_{valid}))$:
1. *Check that c_1, c_2 have Jacobi symbol 1 modulo n, and check π_{valid}. Output reject if either check fails.*
2. *Let $u = pk_S^{\alpha_1} c_1^{\alpha_2} \bmod n$ and check that $(c_2 u^{-n})^n \bmod n^2 = \pm 1$. $\mathbb{Z}_{n^2}^*$ con-tains a unique subgroup of order n, generated by $n + 1$. So here we are verifying that – up to a sign difference – $c_2 u^{-n} \bmod n^2$ is in the subgroup generated by $n + 1$. If the check fails, output reject.*
3. *Otherwise, compute k such that $(n + 1)^k = \pm c_2 u^{-n} \bmod n^2$.[11]*

---

[9] The group G will be used in the construction of the PSDVS scheme.
[10] This set-up need to keep the factorization of n secret. Hence, to avoid relying on a trusted party, the parties can use an interactive protocol to generate n securely, there are several quite efficient examples in the literature.
[11] k can be computed using the standard "discrete log" algorithm from Paillier decryp-tion.

An AVPKE scheme should allow anyone to make "fake" ciphertexts that look indistinguishable from real encryptions, given only the system parameters. Furthermore, the receiver R should be able to use his own secret key sk_R and the public key pk_S of the sender to make ciphertexts with exactly the same distribution as real ones. This is indeed true for our scheme:

Fake Encryption: Let $r \in_R \mathbb{Z}_n, b, b' \in_R \{0, 1\}$ and $v \in \mathbb{Z}_n^*$ be a random square.

Then, $\mathsf{Enc}_{pp,fake}(k; r, b, b', v) = ((-1)^b \hat{g}^r \bmod n, (n + 1)^k ((-1)^{b'} v)^n \bmod n^2), \pi_{valid}$ where π_{valid} is constructed following the NIZK prover algorithm.

R's Equivalent Encryption: $\mathsf{Enc}_{pp,sk_R,pk_S}(k; r, b_1, b_2) = ((-1)^{b_1} \hat{g}^r \bmod n, (n + 1)^k (-1)^{b_2} (pk_S^{\alpha_1} \hat{g}^{r\alpha_2} \bmod n)^n \bmod n^2), \pi_{valid}$
where $r \in_R \mathbb{Z}_n, b_1, b_2 \in_R \{0, 1\}$ and π_{valid} is constructed following the NIZK prover algorithm.

In the following, we will sometimes suppress the randomness from the notation and just write, e.g., $\mathsf{Enc}_{pp,sk_S,pk_R}(k)$.

By simple inspection of the scheme it can be seen that:

Lemma 1. *For all k, $\mathsf{Dec}_{pp,sk_R,pk_S}(\mathsf{Enc}_{pp,sk_S,pk_R}(k)) = k$. Furthermore, encryption by S and by R returns the same ciphertexts: for all messages k and randomness r, b_1, b_2, we have $\mathsf{Enc}_{pp,sk_S,pk_R}(k; r, b_1, b_2) = \mathsf{Enc}_{pp,sk_R,pk_S}(k; r, b_1, b_2)$.*

Lemma 2. *If DDH in $\langle \hat{g} \rangle$ is hard, then $(k, \mathsf{Enc}_{pp,sk_S,pk_R}(k; r, b_1, b_2))$ is computationally indistinguishable from $(k, \mathsf{Enc}_{pp,fake}(k; r', b, b', v))$ for any fixed message k and randomness $r, b_1, b_2, r', b, b', v$, as long as the discrete log of β_2 to the base $\hat{g}$ is unknown.*

Definition 16. *Consider the following experiment for an AVPKE scheme and a probabilistic polynomial time adversary $\mathcal{A}$: Run the set-up and key generation and run $\mathcal{A}^{\mathcal{O}_E, \mathcal{O}_D}(pp, pk_R, pk_S)$. Here, $\mathcal{O}_E$ takes a message k as input and returns $\mathsf{Enc}_{pp,sk_S,pk_R}(k)$, while $\mathcal{O}_D$ takes a ciphertext and returns the result of decrypting it under pk_S, sk_R (which will be either reject or a message). $\mathcal{A}$ wins if it makes $\mathcal{O}_D$ accept a ciphertext that was not obtained from $\mathcal{O}_E$. The scheme is authentic if any PPT $\mathcal{A}$ wins with negligible probability.*

Lemma 3. *If the DDH problem in $\langle \hat{g} \rangle$ is hard, the AVPKE scheme defined above is authentic.*

Due to space limitations, the proof of Lemma 3 is deferred to the full version.

We proceed to show that the AVPKE scheme hides the message encrypted even if adversary knows the secret key of the sender, and even if a decryption oracle is given. This is essentially standard CCA security.

Definition 17. *Consider the following experiment for an AVPKE scheme and a probabilistic polynomial time adversary $\mathcal{A}$: Run the set-up and key generation and run $\mathcal{A}^{\mathcal{O}_E}(pp, pk_R, sk_S)$. Here, $\mathcal{O}_E$ takes two messages k_0, k_1 as input, selects a bit η at random and returns $c^* = \mathsf{Enc}_{pp,sk_S,pk_R}(k_\eta)$. $\mathcal{O}_D$ takes a ciphertext and returns the result of decrypting it under pk_S, sk_R (which will be either reject or* *a message). A may submit anything other than c^* to $\mathcal{O}_D$, and must output a bit η' at the end. It wins if $\eta' = \eta$. The scheme is* private *if any PPT $\mathcal{A}$ wins with negligible advantage over $\frac{1}{2}$.*

In the following we will use the assumption underlying the Paillier encryption scheme, sometimes known as the *composite degree residuosity assumption* (CDRA): a random element x in $\mathbb{Z}_{n^2}^*$ where $x \bmod n$ has Jacobi symbol 1 is computationally indistinguishable from $y^n \bmod n^2$ where $y \in \mathbb{Z}_n^*$ is random of Jacobi symbol 1[12].)

Lemma 4. *Assume that DDH in $\langle \hat{g} \rangle$ is hard and that CDRA holds. Then the AVPKE scheme satisfies Definition 17.*

Due to space limitations, the proof of Lemma 4 is deferred to the full version.

We say that an AVPKE scheme is *secure* if it is authentic, private, supports equivalent encryption by R and indistinguishable fake encryption.

Construction 4 (PSDVS Scheme). *Let:*

- Ggen *be a Group Generator, a probabilistic polynomial time algorithm which on input 1^κ outputs $G, g, n, \hat{g}$ exactly as in the previous AVPKE construction.*
- H *be a hash function which we model as a random oracle. We assume it maps onto the group G.*
- NIZK = (Setup, Prove, Verify) *be a simulation-sound non-interactive zero knowledge proof system. In this section, we will use Σ-protocols made non-interactive using the Fiat-Shamir heuristic, so in this case* Setup *is empty and there is no common reference string.*

Setup(1^κ): Let $(G, g, \hat{g}, n) \leftarrow$ Ggen(1^κ) and let $h \in_R G$. Set $pp = (G, g, \hat{g}, n, h)$. Return pp as the public parameters.

SignKeyGen(pp): Run key generation for the AVPKE scheme as defined above to get keys $ssk = sk_S, spk = pk_S$ for the signer S. Output ssk as the signer's secret key and spk as the signer's public key.

VerKeyGen(pp):
1. Run key generation for the AVPKE scheme as defined above to get keys sk_R, pk_R for the verifier R. (These keys will be used to sign messages and verify signatures.)
2. Choose $k_R \in_R \mathbb{Z}_n$. (This key will be used by the verifier to simulate signatures using VerSigSim.)
3. Choose $r_R \in_R \mathbb{Z}_n$ and let $c_R = g^{k_R} h^{r_R}$. (This commitment will be used by the verifier to support its proofs of fake-ness.)
4. $vsk = (sk_R, k_R, r_R)$, $vpk = (pk_R, c_R)$.

Output vsk as the verifier's secret key and vpk as the verifier's public key.

---

[12] The original CDRA assumption does not have the restriction to Jacobi symbol 1, but since the Jacobi symbol is easy to compute without the factors of n, the two versions are equivalent.

$\mathsf{Sign}(pp, ssk = sk_S, pk_R, m)$:

1. Choose $t \in_R G, r \in_R \mathbb{Z}_n, b_1, b_2 \in_R \{0, 1\}, s \in_R \mathbb{Z}_n^*, k_s \in_R \mathbb{Z}_n$.
2. Let $\sigma \leftarrow (t, \mathsf{H}(m, t)^{k_s}, \mathsf{Enc}_{pp, sk_S, pk_R}(k_s; r, b_1, b_2))$.
3. $\pi \leftarrow \mathsf{NIZK.Prove}(u = (\sigma = (\sigma_1, \sigma_2, \sigma_3), pk_V, pk_S, m), w = (sk_S, k_s, r, b_1, b_2))$ be a zero knowledge proof of knowledge of witness w such that:

$$\sigma_2 = \mathsf{H}(m, \sigma_1)^{k_s} \wedge \sigma_3 = \mathsf{Enc}_{pp, sk_S, pk_R}(k_s; r, b_1, b_2)$$

Output σ as the signature, and π as the proof of real-ness.

$\mathsf{Verify}(pp, spk = pk_S, vsk = (sk_R, k_R, r_R), m, \sigma = (\sigma_1, \sigma_2, \sigma_3))$:

1. Decrypt σ_3 as $k_s = \mathsf{Dec}_{pp, sk_R, pk_S}(\sigma_3)$. If this fails, set $d = 0$ and abort.
2. If $\sigma_2 = \mathsf{H}(m, \sigma_1)^{k_s}$, set $d = 1$. Otherwise, set $d = 0$.

Output d as the verification decision.

$\mathsf{PubSigSim}(pp, m)$:

1. Choose $k, k' \in_R \mathbb{Z}_n$, such that $k \neq k'$.
2. Choose $t \in_R G, r \in_R \mathbb{Z}_n, b, b' \in_R \{0, 1\}, v \in_R \mathbb{Z}_n$, such that v has Jacobi symbol 1.
3. $\sigma \leftarrow (t, \mathsf{H}(m, t)^k, \mathsf{Enc}_{pp, fake}(k'; r, b, b', v))$.
4. Let $\pi \leftarrow \mathsf{NIZK.Prove}(u = \sigma = (\sigma_1, \sigma_2, \sigma_3), w = (k, k'))$ be a zero-knowledge proof of knowledge such that:

$$\sigma_2 = \mathsf{H}(m, \sigma_1)^k \wedge \sigma_3 = \mathsf{Enc}_{pp, fake}(k'; \cdot, \cdot, \cdot, \cdot) \wedge k \neq k'.$$

Output σ as the simulated signature, and π as the proof of fake-ness. The notation $\mathsf{Enc}_{pp, fake}(k'; \cdot, \cdot, \cdot, \cdot)$ means that the proof only has to establish that the plaintext inside the encryption is some value k' different from k.

$\mathsf{VerSigSim}(pp, spk = pk_S, vpk = (pk_R, c_R), vsk = (sk_R, k_R, r_R), m)$:

1. Choose $r_t \in_R \mathbb{Z}_n, t = g^{k_R} h^{r_t}, k_s \in_R \mathbb{Z}_n, b_1, b_2 \in_R \{0, 1\}$ and $v \in_R \mathbb{Z}_n^*$ of Jacobi symbol 1.
2. $\sigma \leftarrow (t, \mathsf{H}(m, t)^{k_s}, \mathsf{Enc}_{pp, sk_R, pk_S}(k_s; r, b_1, b_2))$.
3. Let $\pi \leftarrow \mathsf{NIZK.Prove}(u = ((\sigma_1, \sigma_2, \sigma_3), c_R, m), w = (k_R, r_R, r_t))$ be a zero-knowledge proof of knowledge of witness $w = (k_R, r_R, r_t)$ such that:

$$\sigma_1 = g^{k_R} h^{r_t} \wedge c_R = g^{k_R} h^{r_R}.$$

Output σ as the simulated signature and π as the proof of fake-ness.

Theorem 4. *If the AVPKE scheme is secure, and under the DDH assumption, Construction 4 is a secure PSDVS scheme.*

Due to space limitations, the proof of Theorem 4 is deferred to the full version. In the full version we describe a PSDVS scheme based on prime order groups. It gets around the need to generate a Paillier modulus securely, at the cost of requiring double discrete log proofs.

4   FE-Based Construction

In this section, we present an MDVS scheme based on functional encryption. One disadvantage of this scheme is that it requires a trusted setup; secret verification keys must be derived from a master secret key. However, the accompanying advantage is that this scheme has verifier-identity-based signing; verifiers' public keys consist simply of their identity, allowing any signer to encrypt to any set of verifiers without needing to retrieve their keys from some PKI first.

At a high level, we are first given a digital signature scheme (DS) and a functional encryption scheme (FE). The keys of the signer with identity i are a secret DS signing key sk_i and corresponding public DS verification key vk_i. An MDVS signature c is a FE ciphertext obtained by encrypting the plaintext that consists of the message m, the signer's DS verification key vk_i, a set of designated verifier identities $\mathcal{D}$, and the signer's DS signature σ on the message using the secret DS signing key sk_i. That is, $c = \mathsf{FE.Enc}(pp, (m, vk_i, \mathcal{D}, \sigma))$. Verifier j's public key is simply their identity j (that is, $vpk_j = j$). Their secret key consists of a DS key pair (sk_j, vk_j), and an FE secret key dk_j. dk_j is the secret key for a function that checks whether j is among the specified designated verifiers, and then checks whether the DS signature σ inside the ciphertext c is either a valid signature under the signer's verification key vk_i, or under the verifier's verification key vk_j. However, this basic scheme does not give us the off-the-record property; we therefore tweak it slightly, as we describe below.

From One to Many DS Signatures. In order to ensure that any subset of valid verifiers cannot convince an outsider of the origin of the MDVS signature, we need to replace the one DS signature in the ciphertext with a set of DS signatures. The reason is that, if only one signature is contained in the ciphertext, any designated verifier can prove to an outsider that "it was either me or the signer that constructed the signature". If more than one verifier proves this about the same MDVS signature, then the signature must have come from the signer.

To prevent this kind of "intersection attack", we allow the ciphertext to contain a set Σ of DS signatures, and change the corresponding FE secret keys to check if there exists a DS signature in the set that either verifies under the signer's or the verifier's DS verification key. Now, an outsider will no longer be convinced that it was the signer who constructed the MDVS signature, since each of the colluding verifiers could have constructed a DS signature that verifies under their own verification key, and then encrypted this set together with the public verification key of the signer.

Achieving Consistency. In order to achieve consistency, we need security against malicious encryption in the underlying FE scheme. We need to ensure that any (possibly maliciously generated) ciphertext is consistent with one specific message across decryption with different functions. Otherwise, a malicious MDVS signer may be able to construct a ciphertext (i.e. a signature) that will be valid for one designated verifier but not valid for another, thereby breaking the consistency property. Security against a malicious encryption is a property of verifiable functional encryption (VFE), which was introduced by Badrinarayanan et al. [BGJS16]. However, it turns out that we do not need the full power of VFE, which also includes precautions against a malicious setup. Thus, we define a weaker notion of VFE, and substitute the standard FE scheme with this new scheme allowing us to achieve the MDVS consistency property.

4.1   Ciphertext Verifiable Functional Encryption

The formal definition of Functional Encryption and Ciphertext Verifiable FE and the security notions can be found in the full version. Informally, the ciphertext verifiability property states that for all ciphertexts c, it must hold that if c passes the verification algorithm, then there exists a unique plaintext x asociated with c, meaning that for all functions $f \in \mathcal{F}$ the decryption of c will yield $f(x)$.

4.2   The MDVS Construction

Construction 5. *Let* SIGN $=$ (KeyGen, Sign, Verify) *be a standard digital signature scheme and let* VFE $=$ (Setup, KeyGen, Enc, Dec, Verify) *be a functional encryption scheme secure with ciphertext verifiability. Then we define a MDVS scheme* FEMDVS $=$ (Setup, KeyGen, Sign, Verify, Sim) *as follows:*

Setup(1^κ): $(pp^{\mathsf{FE}}, msk^{\mathsf{FE}}) \leftarrow$ VFE.Setup(1^κ).
    Output public parameter $pp = pp^{\mathsf{FE}}$ and master secret key $msk = msk^{\mathsf{FE}}$.
SignKeyGen(i): $(sk_i, vk_i) \leftarrow$ SIGN.KeyGen(1^κ).
    Output the signer's secret key $ssk_i = sk_i$ and public key $spk_i = vk_i$.[13]
VerKeyGen(msk, j):
    1. $vpk_j = j$,
    2. $(sk_j, vk_j) \leftarrow$ SIGN.KeyGen(1^κ),
    3. $dk_j \leftarrow$ VFE.KeyGen(msk^{FE}, f_j), where f_j is defined as follows.

Function f_j
Input: $m, vk_i, \{vpk_{j'}\}_{j' \in \mathcal{D}}, \Sigma$;
Const: vpk_j, vk_j;
1. If $vpk_j \notin \{vpk_{j'}\}_{j' \in \mathcal{D}}$: output $\perp$;
2. If $\exists \sigma \in \Sigma$: SIGN.Verify(vk_i, m, σ) $= 1$ OR SIGN.Verify(vk_j, m, σ) $= 1$:
output $(m, vk_i, \{vpk_{j'}\}_{j' \in \mathcal{D}})$;
3. Else: output $\perp$

Output the verifiers secret key $vsk_j = (sk_j, dk_j)$ and public key $vpk_j = j$.[14]

---

[13] We assume that the mapping $i \rightarrow (ssk_i, spk_i)$ is unique in the system. This can be achieved without loss of generality by pseudorandomly generating the randomness required in the key generation process from the identity i and the master secret key.

[14] We assume that the mapping $j \rightarrow (vsk_j, vpk_j)$ is unique in the system. This can be achieved wlog by pseudorandomly generating the randomness required in the key generation process from the identity j and the master secret key.

$\mathsf{Sign}(pp, ssk_i, \{vpk_j\}_{j \in \mathcal{D}}, m)$:
1. $\sigma \leftarrow \mathsf{SIGN.Sign}(sk_i, m)$.
2. Output $c = \mathsf{VFE.Enc}(pp^{\mathsf{FE}}, (m, vk_i, \{vpk_j\}_{j \in \mathcal{D}}, \{\sigma, \bot, \cdots, \bot\}))$.

$\mathsf{Verify}(pp, spk_i, vsk_j, \{vpk_j\}_{j \in \mathcal{D}}, m, c)$:
1. Check whether $\mathsf{VFE.Verify}(pp^{\mathsf{FE}}, c) = 1$. If not, output 0.
2. Compute $(m', vk_i', \{vpk_j\}_{j \in \mathcal{D}'}) \backslash \bot \leftarrow \mathsf{VFE.Dec}(dk_j, c)$. If the output is $\bot$, output 0.
3. Check $m' = m$, $vk_i' = vk_i$ (with $spk_i = vk_i$), and $\mathcal{D}' = \mathcal{D}$. If all hold, output 1. Otherwise output 0.

$\mathsf{Sim}(pp, spk_i, \{vpk_j\}_{j \in \mathcal{D}}, \{vsk_j\}_{j \in \mathcal{C}}, m)$:
1. For each $j \in \mathcal{C}$, $vsk_j = (sk_j, dk_j)$.
2. Compute $\sigma_j \leftarrow \mathsf{SIGN.Sign}(sk_j, m^*)$.
3. Let $\Sigma = \{\sigma_j\}_{j \in \mathcal{C}^*}$, add default values to get the required size.
4. Output $c = \mathsf{VFE.Enc}(pp^{\mathsf{FE}}, (m^*, spk_i, \{vpk_j\}_{j \in \mathcal{D}}, \Sigma))$.

Theorem 5. *Assume that* VFE *is an IND-CPA secure functional encryption scheme with ciphertext verifiability, and* SIGN *is an existential unforgeable digital signature scheme. Then Construction 5 is a correct and secure MDVS scheme with privacy of identities and verifier-identity-based signing.*

Due to space limitations, the proof of Theorem 5 is deferred to the full version.

References

[AV19]   Ananth, P., Vaikuntanathan, V.: Optimal bounded-collusion secure functional encryption. In: Hofheinz, D., Rosen, A. (eds.) TCC 2019. LNCS, vol. 11891, pp. 174–198. Springer, Cham (2019). https://doi.org/10.1007/978-3-030-36030-6_8

[BGB04]   Borisov, N., Goldberg, I., Brewer, E.: Off-the-record communication, or, why not to use PGP. In: Proceedings of the 2004 ACM Workshop on Privacy in the Electronic Society, pp. 77–84. ACM (2004)

[BGJS16]   Badrinarayanan, S., Goyal, V., Jain, A., Sahai, A.: Verifiable functional encryption. In: Cheon, J.H., Takagi, T. (eds.) ASIACRYPT 2016. LNCS, vol. 10032, pp. 557–587. Springer, Heidelberg (2016). https://doi.org/10.1007/978-3-662-53890-6_19

[Cha96]   Chaum, D.: Private signature and proof systems. US Patent 5,493,614 (1996)

[Cha11]   Chang, T.Y.: An ID-based multi-signer universal designated multi-verifier signature scheme. Inf. Comput. **209**(7), 1007–1015 (2011)

[Cho06]   Chow, S.S.M.: Identity-based strong multi-designated verifiers signatures. In: Atzeni, A.S., Lioy, A. (eds.) EuroPKI 2006. LNCS, vol. 4043, pp. 257–259. Springer, Heidelberg (2006). https://doi.org/10.1007/11774716_23

[Cho08]   Chow, S.S.M.: Multi-designated verifiers signatures revisited. IJ Netw. Secur. **7**(3), 348–357 (2008)

[GVW12]   Gorbunov, S., Vaikuntanathan, V., Wee, H.: Functional encryption with bounded collusions via multi-party computation. In: Safavi-Naini, R., Canetti, R. (eds.) CRYPTO 2012. LNCS, vol. 7417, pp. 162–179. Springer, Heidelberg (2012). https://doi.org/10.1007/978-3-642-32009-5_11

[JSI96]   Jakobsson, M., Sako, K., Impagliazzo, R.: Designated verifier proofs and their applications. In: Maurer, U. (ed.) EUROCRYPT 1996. LNCS, vol. 1070, pp. 143–154. Springer, Heidelberg (1996). https://doi.org/10.1007/3-540-68339-9_13

[LSMP07] Li, Y., Susilo, W., Mu, Y., Pei, D.: Designated verifier signature: definition, framework and new constructions. In: Indulska, J., Ma, J., Yang, L.T., Ungerer, T., Cao, J. (eds.) UIC 2007. LNCS, vol. 4611, pp. 1191–1200. Springer, Heidelberg (2007). https://doi.org/10.1007/978-3-540-73549-6_116

[LV04]   Laguillaumie, F., Vergnaud, D.: Multi-designated verifiers signatures. In: Lopez, J., Qing, S., Okamoto, E. (eds.) ICICS 2004. LNCS, vol. 3269, pp. 495–507. Springer, Heidelberg (2004). https://doi.org/10.1007/978-3-540-30191-2_38

[LV07]   Laguillaumie, F., Vergnaud, D.: Multi-designated verifiers signatures: anonymity without encryption. Inf. Process. Lett. 102(2–3), 127–132 (2007)

[Mar13]   Marlinspike, M.: Advanced cryptographic ratcheting (2013)

[MW08]   Ming, Y., Wang, Y.: Universal designated multi verifier signature scheme without random oracles. Wuhan Univ. J. Nat. Sci. 13(6), 685–691 (2008). https://doi.org/10.1007/s11859-008-0610-6

[NSM05]   Ng, C.Y., Susilo, W., Mu, Y.: Universal designated multi verifier signature schemes. In: 11th International Conference on Parallel and Distributed Systems, ICPADS 2005, Fuduoka, Japan, 20–22 July 2005, pp. 305–309 (2005)

[RST01]   Rivest, R.L., Shamir, A., Tauman, Y.: How to leak a secret. In: Boyd, C. (ed.) ASIACRYPT 2001. LNCS, vol. 2248, pp. 552–565. Springer, Heidelberg (2001). https://doi.org/10.1007/3-540-45682-1_32

[SHCL08] Seo, S.-H., Hwang, J.Y., Choi, K.Y., Lee, D.H.: Identity-based universal designated multi-verifiers signature schemes. Comput. Stand. Interfaces 30(5), 288–295 (2008)

[SKS06]   Shailaja, G., Kumar, K.P., Saxena, A.: Universal designated multi verifier signature without random oracles. In: 9th International Conference in Information Technology, ICIT 2006, Bhubaneswar, Orissa, India, 18–21 December 2006, pp. 168–171 (2006)

[Tia12]   Tian, H.: A new strong multiple designated verifiers signature. IJGUC 3(1), 1–11 (2012)

[Ver06]   Vergnaud, D.: New extensions of pairing-based signatures into universal designated verifier signatures. In: Bugliesi, M., Preneel, B., Sassone, V., Wegener, I. (eds.) ICALP 2006. LNCS, vol. 4052, pp. 58–69. Springer, Heidelberg (2006). https://doi.org/10.1007/11787006_6

[ZAYS12] Zhang, Y., Au, M.H., Yang, G., Susilo, W.: (Strong) multi-designated verifiers signatures secure against rogue key attack. In: Xu, L., Bertino, E., Mu, Y. (eds.) NSS 2012. LNCS, vol. 7645, pp. 334–347. Springer, Heidelberg (2012). https://doi.org/10.1007/978-3-642-34601-9_25

[Zhe97]   Zheng, Y.: Digital signcryption or how to achieve cost(signature & encryption) $\ll$ cost(signature) + cost(encryption). In: Kaliski, B.S. (ed.) CRYPTO 1997. LNCS, vol. 1294, pp. 165–179. Springer, Heidelberg (1997). https://doi.org/10.1007/BFb0052234

Continuous Group Key Agreement
with Active Security

Joël Alwen[1], Sandro Coretti[2], Daniel Jost[3], and Marta Mularczyk[3(✉)]

[1] Wickr, San Francisco, USA
jalwen@wickr.com
[2] IOHK, Hong Kong, Hong Kong
sandro.coretti@iohk.io
[3] ETH Zurich, Zurich, Switzerland
{dajost,mumarta}@inf.ethz.ch

Abstract. A *continuous group key agreement* (CGKA) protocol allows a long-lived group of parties to agree on a continuous stream of fresh secret key material. CGKA protocols allow parties to join and leave mid-session but may neither rely on special group managers, trusted third parties, nor on any assumptions about if, when, or for how long members are online. CGKA captures the core of an emerging generation of highly practical end-to-end secure group messaging (SGM) protocols.

In light of their practical origins, past work on CGKA protocols have been subject to stringent engineering and efficiency constraints at the cost of diminished security properties. In this work, we somewhat relax those constraints, instead considering progressively more powerful adversaries.

To that end, we present 3 new security notions of increasing strength. Already the weakest of the 3 (*passive* security) captures attacks to which all prior CGKA constructions are vulnerable. Moreover, the 2 stronger (*active* security) notions even allow the adversary to use parties' exposed states combined with full network control to mount attacks. In particular, this is closely related to so-called *insider attacks* which involve malicious group members actively deviating from the protocol. Although insiders are of explicit interest to practical CGKA/SGM designers, our understanding of this class of attackers is still quite nascent. Indeed, we believe ours to be the first security notions in the literature to precisely formulate meaningful guarantees against (a broad class of) insiders.

For each of the 3 new security notions we give a new CGKA scheme enjoying sub-linear (potentially even logarithmic) communication complexity in the number of group members (on par with the asymptotics of state-of-the-art practical constructions). We prove each scheme *optimally* secure, in the sense that the only security violations possible are those necessarily implied by correctness.

M. Mularczyk—Research supported by the Zurich Information Security and Privacy Center (ZISC).

R. Pass and K. Pietrzak (Eds.): TCC 2020, LNCS 12551, pp. 261–290, 2020.
https://doi.org/10.1007/978-3-030-64378-2_10

1   Introduction

1.1   Overview and Motivation

A *continuous group key agreement* (CGKA) protocol allows a long-lived dynamic group to agree on a continuous stream of fresh secret group keys. In CGKA new parties may join and existing members may leave the group at any point mid-session. In contrast to standard (dynamic) GKA, the CGKA protocols are *asynchronous* in that they make no assumptions about if, when, or for how long members are online.[1] Moreover, unlike, say, broadcast encryption, the protocol may not rely on a (trusted) group manager or any other designated party. Due to a session's potentially very long life-time (e.g., years), CGKA protocols must ensure a property called *post-compromise forward security (PCFS)*. PCFS strengthens the two standard notions of *forward security (FS)* (the keys output must remain secure even if some party's state is compromised in the future) and *post-compromise security (PCS)* (parties recover from state compromise after exchanging a few messages and the keys become secure again) in that it requires them to hold *simultaneously*.

The first CGKA protocol was introduced by Cohn-Gordon et al. in [15] although CGKA as a (term and) generic stand-alone primitive was only later introduced by Alwen et al. in [4]. To motivate the new primitive [4] puts forth the intuition that CGKA abstracts the cryptographic core of an "MLS-like" approach to SGM protocol design in much the same way that CKA (the 2-party analogue of CGKA) abstracts the asymmetric core of a double-ratchet based 2-party secure messaging protocol [1]. Indeed, MLS's computational and communication complexities, support for dynamic groups, it's asynchronous nature, trust assumptions and it's basic security guarantees are naturally inherited from the underlying TreeKEM CGKA sub-protocol. Finally, we believe that the fundamental nature of key agreement and the increasing focus on highly distributed practical cryptographic protocols surely allows for further interesting applications of CGKA beyond SGM.

In [4] the authors analyzed (a version of) the *TreeKEM* CGKA protocol [12]; the core cryptographic component in the *scalable* end-to-end *secure group messaging (SGM)* protocol *MLS*, currently under development by the eponymous Messaging Layer Security working group of the IETF [10].

An SGM protocol is an asynchronous (in the above sense) protocol enabling a dynamic group of parties to privately exchange messages over the Internet. While such protocols initially relied on a service provider acting as a trusted third party, nowadays end-to-end security is increasingly the norm and provider merely act as untrusted delivery services. SGM protocols are expected to provide PCFS for messages (defined analogously to CGKA).[2] The proliferation of SGM protocols in practice has been extensive with more than 2 billion users today.

---

[1] Instead, the protocol must allow parties that come online to immediately derive all new key material agreed upon in their absence simply by locally processing all protocol messages sent to the group during the interim. Conversely, any operations they wish to perform must be implemented non-interactively by producing a single message to be broadcasted to the group.

[2] As for CGKA, PCFS is *strictly* stronger than the "non-simultaneous" combination of FS and PCS. That is, there are protocols that individually satisfy FS and PCS, but not PCFS [4].

For both CGKA and SGM, the main bottleneck in scaling to larger groups is the communication and computational complexity of performing a group operation (e.g. agree on a new group key, add or remove a party, etc.). Almost all protocols, in particular all those used in practice today, have complexity $\Omega(n)$ for groups of size n (e.g. [20,24] for sending a message and [26] for removing a party). This is an unfortunate side effect of them being built black-box on top of 2-party secure messaging (SM) protocols. The first (CGKA) protocol to break this mold, thereby achieving "fair-weather" complexity of $O(\log(n))$, is the ART protocol of [15]. Soon to follow were the TreeKEM family of protocols including those in [2,4,12] and their variations (implicit) in successive iterations of MLS. By *fair-weather* complexity we informally mean that the cost of the next operation in a session can range from $\Theta(\log(n))$ to $\Theta(n)$ depending on the exact sequence of preceding operations. However, under quite mild assumptions about the online/offline behaviour of participants, the complexity can be kept in the $O(\log(n))$ range.

The Security of CGKA. To achieve PCFS, TreeKEM (and thus MLS) allows a party to perform an "update" operation. These refresh the parties state so as to heal in case of past compromises but come at the price of necessitating a broadcast to the group. The current design of MLS (and, consequently, the analysis by [4]) does not prevent attackers from successfully forging communication from compromised parties in the time period *a state compromise of the party and their next update*. The assumption that attackers won't attempt such forgeries—henceforth referred to as the *cannot-inject assumption (CIA)*—prevents adversaries from, say, *destroying* the group's state by sending maliciously crafted broadcasts. Thus it is closely related to *insider security*, i.e., security against group members who actively deviate from the prescribed protocol, which has hitherto been a mostly open problem and remains an ongoing concern for the MLS working group.[3]

A second assumption that underlies prior work on secure group messaging is the *no-splitting assumption (NSA)*: When multiple parties propose a change to the group state simultaneously, the delivery service (and, hence, the attacker) is assumed to mediate and choose the change initiated by *one* of the parties and deliver the corresponding protocol message to all group members. This (artificially) bars the attacker from splitting the group into subgroups (unaware of each other) and thereby potentially breaking protocol security. As such, the NSA represents a serious limitation of the security model.

Contributions. At a high level, this paper makes 2 types of contributions: (1) we introduce *optimal* CGKA security definitions that avoid the CIA and the NSA, where "optimality" requires that each produced key be secure unless it can be *trivially*—due to the correctness of the protocol—computed using the information leaked to the attacker via corruption; (2) we provide protocols satisfying the proposed definitions. These contributions are discussed in Sects. 1.2 and 1.3, respectively.

---

[3] Note that the Signal [24] 2-party SM protocol is not secure without CIA.

1.2 Defining Optimally Secure CGKA

Overview. This work proposes the first security definitions in the realm of secure group messaging that do not impose any unrealistic restrictions on adversarial capabilities. The definitions allow the adversary to control the communication network, including the delivery service, as well as to corrupt parties by leaking their states and/or controlling their randomness. Furthermore, two settings, called the *passive setting* and the *active setting*, are considered: The passive setting only makes the CIA (but not the NSA) and hence corresponds to a passive network adversary (or authenticated channels). It should be considered a stepping stone to the active setting, where attackers are limited by neither CIA nor NSA. We note that [2,3,15] have also considered the setting without the NSA.

While the active setting does not, per se, formally model malicious parties, it does allow the adversary to send arbitrary messages on behalf of parties whose states leaked.[4] Thus, the new security definition goes a long way towards considering the insider attacks mentioned above.

Flexible Security Definitions. The security definitions in this work are flexible in that several crucial parts of the definitions are generic. Most importantly, following the definitional paradigm of [3], they are parameterized by a so-called *safety predicate*, encoding which keys are expected to be secure in any given execution. *Optimal* security notions are obtained if the safety predicate marks as insecure only those keys that are trivially computable by the adversary due to the correctness of the protocol. While the constructions in this work all achieve optimal security (in different settings), sub-optimal but meaningful security notions may also be of interest (e.g., for admitting more efficient protocols) and can be obtained by appropriately weakening the security predicate.

History Graphs. The central formal tool used to capture CGKA security are so-called *history graphs*, introduced in [3]. A history graph is a symbolic representation of the semantics of a given CGKA session's history. It is entirely agnostic to the details of a construction and depends only on the high-level inputs to the CGKA protocol and the actions of the adversary.

More concretely, a history graph is an annotated tree, in which each node represents a fixed group state (including a group key). A node v is annotated with (the semantics of) the group operations that took place when transitioning from the parent node to v, e.g., "Alice was added using public key epk. Bob was removed. Charlie updated his slice of the distributed group state." The node is further annotated to record certain events, e.g., that bad randomness was used in the transition or that parties' local states leaked to the adversary while they are in group state v. To this end, for each party the history graph maintains a pointer indicating which group state the party is (meant) to be in.

---

[4] For example, the adversary is allowed to "bypass" the PKI and add new members with arbitrary keys.

Active Case: Dealing with Injections. Probably the greatest challenge in defining security for the *active* setting is how to sensibly model injected messages in a way that maintains consistency with a real world protocol, yet provides interesting security guarantees. In more detail, by using the leaked protocol state of a party and fixing their randomness, the attacker can "run ahead" to predict the exact protocol messages a party will produce for future operations. In particular, it may use an injection to invite new members to join the group at a future history graph node which does not even exist yet in the experiment. Yet, an existing member might eventually catch up to the new member at which point their real world protocols will have consistent states (in particular, a consistent group key).

More fundamentally, the security definition can no longer rely on 2 assumptions which have significantly simplified past security notions (and proofs) for CGKA. Namely, (A) that injections are never accepted by their receiver and (B) that each new protocol message by an honest party always defines a fresh group state (i.e. history graph node).

Hence, to begin modeling injections, we create new "adversarial" history graph nodes for parties to transition to when they join a group by processing an injected message. This means that, in the active setting, the history graph is really a forest, not a tree. We restrict our security experiment to a single "Create Group" operation so there is (at most) 1 tree rooted at a node *not* created by an injection. We call this tree the *honest group* and it is for this group that we want to provide security guarantees.

The above solution is incomplete, as it leaves open the question of how to model delivery of injected protocol messages to members already in a group (honest or otherwise). To this end, the functionality relies on 2 reasonable properties of a protocol:

1. Protocol messages are unique across the whole execution and can be used to identify nodes. This means that any pair of parties that accept a protocol message will agree on all (security relevant) aspects of their new group states, e.g., the group key and group membership.
2. Every protocol message w welcoming a new member to a group in state (i.e., node) v_i must uniquely identify the corresponding protocol message c updating existing group members to v_i.

The net result is that we can now reasonably model meaningful expectations for how a protocol handles injections. In particular, suppose an existing group member id_1 at a node v_1 accepts an injected protocol message c. If another party id_2 already processed c, then we simply move id_1 to the same node as id_2. Otherwise, we check if c was previously assigned to a welcome message w injected to some id_3. If so, we can safely attach the node v_3 created for w as a child of v_1 and transition id_1 to v_3. With the two properties above, we can require that id_1 and id_2 (in the first case) or id_1 and id_3 (the second case) end up in consistent states.

Finally, if neither c nor a matching w has appeared before then we can safely create a fresh "adversarial" node for id_1 as a child of v_1. We give no guarantees for keys in adversarial nodes (as secrecy is anyway inherently lost). Still, we require that they do not affect honest nodes.

Composable and Simulation-Based Security. This work formalizes CGKA security by considering appropriate functionalities in the UC framework [13]. Since universal composition is an extremely strong guarantee and seems to be impossible for CGKA in the standard model (for reasons similar to the impossibility of UC-secure key exchange under adaptive corruptions [18]), this work also considers a weaker definition in which, similarly to [7] and [23], the environment is constrained to not perform corruptions that would cause the so-called *commitment problem*. In particular, the weaker statement is still (at least) as strong as a natural game-based definition (as used by related work) that would exclude some corruptions as "trivial wins." In other words, restricting the environment only impacts composition guarantees, which are not the main aspect of this work. Nevertheless, we believe that our statements are a solid indication for multi-group security (see th full version [5] for more discussion).

A simulation-based security notion also provides a neat solution for deciding how adversarially injected packets should affect the history graph. That is, it provides a clean separation of concerns, dealing with the protocol specific aspects in the simulator, while keeping the definition protocol independent.

CGKA Functionalities. As mentioned above, the approach taken in this work is to formalize CGKA security in the UC framework via ideal CGKA functionalities, which maintain the history graph as the session evolves. A reader familiar with the use of UC security (in the context of secure multi-party computation) might expect passive and active security to be captured by considering protocol executions over an authenticated and an insecure network, respectively.

As we strive to treat CGKA as a primitive, however, and not directly enforce how it is used, we design our CGKA UC functionalities as "idealized CGKA services" (much in the way that PKE models an idealized PKE service in [13,14]) instead. Thus, they offer the parties interfaces for performing all group operations, but then simply hand out the corresponding idealized protocol message back to the environment. The attacker gets to choose an arbitrary string to represent the idealized protocol message that would be created for that same operation in the real world. This encodes that no guarantees are made about protocol messages beyond their semantic effects as captured by the history graph.

Just as for PKE, this approach further means that it is up to the environment to "deliver" the idealized messages from the party that initiated an operation to all other group members. This carries the additional benefit that it allows to formalize correctness, whereas typical UC definitions often admit "trivial" protocols simply rejecting all messages (with the simulator not delivering them in the ideal world).

The passive setting is then modeled by restricting the environment to only deliver messages previously chosen to represent a group operation. Meanwhile, in the active setting, the restriction is dropped instead allowing injections; that is delivery of new messages.

Relation to Full Insider Security. We model active corruptions as leaking a party's state, intercepting all their communication, and injecting arbitrary messages on there behalf. While this allows the adversary to emulate the party in essentially every respect it does leave one last capability out of reach to the adversary; namely interactions with the PKI. A malicious insider might, say, register malformed or copied public keys as their own in the PKI. In contrast, an active adversary may not register keys even on behalf of corrupt parties. At most they can leak the secret components of honestly generated key pairs.

While one might conceivably implement such strong PKI in certain real world settings we believe that closing this gap remains an important open problem for future work.

1.3   Protocols with Optimal Security

Overview. We put forth three protocols, all with the same (fair-weather) asymptotic efficiency as the best CGKA protocols in the literature.

Interestingly, even in the passive case, optimal security is not achieved by any existing protocol—not even inefficient solutions based on pairwise channels. Instead, we adapt the "key-evolving" techniques of [21] to the group setting to obtain Protocol P-Pas enjoying optimal security for the passive setting; i.e., against passive but adaptive adversaries.[5]

Next, we augment P-Pas to obtain two more protocols geared to the active setting and meeting incomparable security notions. Specifically, Protocol P-Act provides security against both active and adaptive adversaries but at the cost of a slightly less than ideal "robustness" guarantees. More precisely, the adversary can use leaked states of parties to inject messages that are processed correctly by some parties, but rejected by others.

Meanwhile, the protocol P-Act-Rob uses non-interactive zero-knowledge proofs (NIZKs) to provide the stronger guarantee that if one party accepts a message, then all other parties do but therefore only against active but static adversaries.

For protocols P-Pas and P-Act we prove security with respect to two models. First, in a relaxation of the UC framework with restricted environments (this notion achieves restricted composition and is analogous to game-based notions), we prove security in the non-programmable random oracle model. Second, we prove full UC security in the programmable random oracle model. For the third protocol P-Act-Rob, we consider the standard model, but only achieve semi-static security (the environment is restricted to commit ahead of time to certain information—but not to all inputs).

Techniques Used in the Protocols. Our protocol P-Pas for the passive setting is an adaptation of the TTKEM protocol, a variant of the TreeKEM protocol introduced in [2] which we have adapted to the propose-and-commit syntax of MLS (draft 9). Next we use hierarchical identity based encryption (HIBE) in

---

[5] We do place some restrictions on their adaptivity described bellow in the paragraph on the commitment problem.

lieu of regular public-key encryption and ensures that *all* keys are updated with every operation. This helps in avoiding group-splitting attacks, as it ensures that different subgroups use keys for different HIBE identities.

In the active setting, there are two difficulties to solve. First, to prevent injecting messages from uncorrupted parties, we use key-updating signatures [21] that prevent injections using state from another subgroup after a split.

Second, we have to ensure that the adversary cannot use leaked secrets (including signing keys) to craft a message that processed by two parties makes them transition to incompatible states. In other words, a message should prove to a party that any other party processing it ends up in a compatible state. A natural attempt to solve this would be a generic compiler inspired by GMW [19], where the committer provides a non-interactive zero knowledge (NIZK) proof that it executed the protocol correctly. Unfortunately, the GMW approach requires each part to commit to the whole randomness at the beginning of the protocol.[6] which is incompatible with PCS, since healing from corruption requires fresh randomness.

Hence, we instead propose two non-black-box modifications of P-Pas. First, th protocol P-Act uses a simple solution based on a hash function. The mechanism guarantees that all partitions that accept a message also end up with a consistent state. However, parties may not agree on whether to accept or reject the injection. So our second protocol P-Act-Rob implements the consistency using a NIZK proof attached to each message proving its consistency. As a price, we can no longer model a key part of the consistency relation via a random oracle which means our proof technique for adaptive adversaries no longer applies. Thus, for P-Act-Rob, we only prove a type of static security.

1.4 Related Work

2-Party Ratcheting. 2-party Ratcheting is a similar primitive to CKA (the 2-party analogue of CGKA), both originally designed with secure messaging protocols in mind. (Indeed, the terms are sometimes used interchangeably.)

Ratcheting was first investigated as a stand-alone primitive by Bellare et al. [11]. That work was soon followed by the works of [25] and [21] who considered active security for Ratcheting (the later in the context of an SM protocol). In particular, the work of Poettring and Rösler [25] can be viewed as doing for Ratcheting what our work does for the past CGKA results. In contrast, [16,22] looked at strong security notions for Ratcheting achievable using practically efficient constructions, albeit at the cost of losing message-loss resilience. In recent work, Balli et al. [8] showed that for such strong security notions imply a weak version of HIBE. Two-party continuous key agreement (CKA) was first defined in [1] where it was used build a family of SM protocols generalizing Signal's messaging protocol [24].

---

[6] The NIZK is with respect to th committed randomness. The randomness is sampled jointly using an MPC protocol.

CGKA. In comparison to the 2-party primitives, SGM and CGKA have received less attention. In practice, SGM protocols make black-box use of 2-party SM (or at least 2-party Ratcheting) which results in $\Omega(n)$ computational and communication complexity in the group size n for certain operations [17,20,24,26]. The first CGKA with logarithmic fair-weather complexity (defined above) was introduced ART protocol by Cohn-Gordon et al. in [15]. This was soon followed by (several variant of) the TreeKEM CGKA [12]. The RTreeKEM (for "re-randomized TreeKEM") introduced and analyzed in [3] greatly improves the FS properties of TreeKEM and ART. However, security is only proven using both the CIA and NSA and results in a quasi-polynomial loss for adaptive security. Meanwhile, the TTKEM construction (i.e. "Tainted TreeKEM") in [2] has the first adaptive security proof with *polynomial* loss and only uses the CIA (although it does not achieve optimal security). Finally, the CGKA in the current MLS draft [9] represents a significant evolution of the above constructions in that it introduces the "propose and commit" paradigm used in this work and in [4]. Our construction build on TTKEM, RTreeKEM and the propose-and-commit version of TreeKEM.

Modeling CGKA. From a definitional point of view, we build on the history graph paradigm of [3]. That work, in turn, can be seen as a generalization of the model introduced by Alwen et al. [4]. To avoid the commitment problem we adopt the restrictions of environments by Backes et al. [7] to the UC framework. A similar approach has also been used by Jost, Maurer, and Mularczyk [23] in the realm of secure messaging.

2 Continuous Group Key Agreement

2.1 CGKA Schemes

A CGKA scheme aims at providing a steady stream of shared (symmetric) secret keys for a dynamically evolving set of parties. Those two aspects are tied together by so-called *epochs*: each epoch provides a (fresh) group key to a (for this epoch) fixed set of participants. CGKA schemes are *non-interactive*—a party creates a new epoch by broadcasting a single message, which can then be processed by the other members to move along. Rather than relying on an actual broadcast scheme, CCKA schemes however merely assume an untrusted (or partially trusted) delivery service. As multiple parties might try to initiate a new epoch simultaneously, the delivery service's main job is to determine the successful one by picking an order. As a consequence, a party trying to initiate a new epoch itself cannot immediately move forward to it but rather has to wait until its message is confirmed by the delivery service. For simplicity, we assume that the party then just processes it the same way as any other member.

Evolving the Member Set: Add and Remove Proposals. During each epoch, the parties propose to add or remove members by broadcasting a corresponding *proposal.* To create a new epoch, a party then selects an (ordered) list thereof to be applied. We say that the party *commits* those proposals, and thus call the respective message the *commit message* and the creator thereof the committer.

Group Policies. A higher-level application using a CGKA scheme may impose various restrictions on who is allowed to perform which operations (e.g. restricting commits to administrators or restricting valid proposal vectors within a commit). In this work, we consider a very permissive setting. It is easy to see that any result in the permissive setting carries over to a more restrictive setting.

PKI. CGKA schemes in many aspects represent a generalization of non-interactive key exchange (NIKE) to groups. Indeed, adding a new member must be possible without this party participating in the protocol. Rather, the party should be able to join the group by receiving a single *welcome message* that was generated alongside the commit message. Hence, CGKA schemes rely on a PKI that provides some initial key material for new members. This work assumes a simple PKI functionality for this purpose, described in Sect. 3.

State Compromises and Forward Security. CGKA schemes are designed with exposures of parties' states in mind. In particular, they strive to provide FS: exposing a party's state in some epoch should not reveal the group keys of past epochs. This also implies, that once removed, a party's state should reveal nothing about the group keys.

Post-compromise Security and Update Proposals. In addition, CGKA schemes should also provide PCS. For this, parties regularly send *update proposals*, which roughly suggest removing the sender and immediately adding him with a fresh key (analogous to the one from PKI). In addition, the committer always implicitly updates himself.

2.2 CGKA Syntax

A *continuous group key-agreement scheme* is a tuple of algorithms CGKA = (kg, create, join, add, rem, upd, commit, proc, key) with the following syntax. To simplify notation, we assume that all algorithms implicitly know ID of the party running them.

- **Group Creation:** $\gamma \leftarrow$ create() takes no input and returns a fresh protocol state for a group containing only the user party running the algorithm. In particular, this represents the first *epoch* of a new session.[7]
- **Key Generation:** $(\mathsf{pk}, \mathsf{sk}) \leftarrow \mathsf{kg}()$ samples a fresh public/secret key pair (which will be sent to the PKI).
- **Add Proposal:** $(\gamma', p) \leftarrow \mathsf{add}(\gamma, \mathsf{id}_t, \mathsf{pk}_t)$ proposes adding a new member to the group. On input a protocol state, identity of the new member and his public key (generated by kg), it outputs an updated state and *add proposal message*.

---

[7] To create a group, a party adds the other members using individual add proposals.

- **Remove Proposal:** $(\gamma', p) \leftarrow \mathsf{rem}(\gamma, \mathsf{id}_t)$ proposes removing a member from the group. On input a protocol state and identity, it outputs an updated state and *remove proposal message*.
- **Update Proposal:** $(\gamma', p) \leftarrow \mathsf{upd}(\gamma)$ proposes updating the member's key material. It outputs an updated state and an *update proposal message*.
- **Join A Group:** $(\gamma', \mathsf{roster}, \mathsf{id}_i) \leftarrow \mathsf{join}(\mathsf{sk}, w)$ allows a party with secret key sk (generated by kg) to join a group with a welcome message w. The outputs are: an updated protocol state, a group *roster* (i.e. a set of IDs listing the group members), and the ID of the inviter (i.e. the party that created the welcome message).
- **Commit:** $(\gamma, c, w) \leftarrow \mathsf{commit}(\gamma, \vec{p})$ applies (a.k.a. *commits*) a vector of proposals to a group. The output consists of an updated protocol state, *commit message* and a (potentially empty) *welcome message* (depending on if any add proposal messages where included in $\vec{p}$).[8]
- **Process:** $(\gamma', \mathsf{info}) \leftarrow \mathsf{proc}(\gamma, c, \vec{p})$ processes an incoming commit message and the corresponding proposals to output a *commit info message* info and an updated group state which represents a new epoch in the ongoing CGKA session. The commit info message captures the semantics of the processed commit and it has the form:

$$\mathsf{info} = (\mathsf{id}, (\mathsf{propSem}_1, \dots, \mathsf{propSem}_z))$$

where id is the ID sender of the commit message the vector conveys the semantics of the committed add and remove proposals via triples of the form $\mathsf{propSem} = (\mathsf{id}_s, \mathsf{op}, \mathsf{id}_t)$. Here, id_s denotes the identity of the proposal's sender, $\mathsf{op} \in \{\texttt{"addP"}, \texttt{"remP"}\}$ is the proposal's type and id_t is the identity of the proposal's target (i.e. the partying being added or removed).
- **Get Group Key:** $(\gamma', K) \leftarrow \mathsf{key}(\gamma)$ outputs the current group key for use by a higher-level application, and deletes it from the state.

3 UC Security of CGKA

This section outlines the basic UC security statements of CGKA schemes we use throughout the remaining part of this work. The concrete functionalities $\mathcal{F}_{\mathrm{CGKA-AUTH}}$ and $\mathcal{F}_{\mathrm{CGKA}}$, formalizing the guarantees in the passive and active setting, are then introduced in Sects. 4 and 5, respectively.

The CGKA Functionalities. This paper captures security of CGKA schemes by comparing the UC protocol based on CGKA to an ideal functionality. Recall that we model the functionalities as idealized "CGKA services". For example, when a party wishes to commit proposals, it has to input (an idealized version of) those proposals $\vec{p}$ to the functionality. The functionality then outputs an idealized control message c (and potentially a welcome message w), chosen by

---

[8] For simplicity, we do assume a global welcome message sent to all joining parties, rather than individual ones (which could result in lower overall communication).

the simulator. The functionality does not concern itself with the delivery of control messages c; this must be accomplished by a higher-level protocol.

Our functionalities encode the following basic assumptions: (1) Only group members allowed to create proposals and commit to sequences thereof. (2) We require that every proposal individually makes sense, i.e., a party is only allowed to propose to remove or add a party that is currently in, respectively not in the group. When committing to a sequence of proposals where some are no longer applicable (e.g., due to first including a removal proposal and then one that updates the same party) the offending one is ignored (here the update). More restrictive policies can of course be enforced by the higher-level application making use of the CGKA functionality.

Finally, to simplify definitions, the functionality identify epochs by the control messages c creating them.

PKI. CGKA protocols rely on a service that distributes so-called key bundles used to add new members to the group. (Using the syntax of Sect. 2, a key bundle is the public key output by kg.) In order not to distract from the main results, this work uses a simplified PKI service that generates one key pair for each identity, making the public keys available to all users. This guarantees to the user proposing to add someone to the group that the new member's key is available, authentic, and honestly generated.

Our PKI is defined by the functionality $\mathcal{F}_{\mathrm{PKI}}$, and our CGKA protocols are analyzed in the $\mathcal{F}_{\mathrm{PKI}}$-hybrid model. Concretely, $\mathcal{F}_{\mathrm{PKI}}$ securely stores key bundle secret keys until fetched by their owner. For a formal description of $\mathcal{F}_{\mathrm{PKI}}$ is presented in the full version [5]. We there also discuss the rationale of our PKI model and how it relates to how comparable PKI are thought of in practice.

CGKA as a UC Protocol. In order to assess the security of CGKA scheme as defined in Sect. 2 relative to an ideal functionality, the CGKA scheme is translated into a CGKA *protocol* where a user id accepts the following inputs:

- **Create**: If the party is the designated group creator,[9] then the protocol initializes γ using create().
- (**Propose**, act), act $\in \{\mathsf{up}, \mathsf{add\text{-}id}_t, \mathsf{rem\text{-}id}_t\}$: If id is not part of the group, the protocol simply returns $\perp$. Otherwise, it invokes the corresponding algorithm add, rem, or upd using the currently stored state γ. For add, it first fetc.hes pk_t for id_t from $\mathcal{F}_{\mathrm{PKI}}$. The protocol then outputs p to the environment, and stores the updated state γ' (deleting the old one).
- (**Join**, w): If id is already in the group, the protocol returns $\perp$. Otherwise, it fetches sk and fresh randomness r from $\mathcal{F}_{\mathrm{PKI}}$, invokes join($\mathsf{sk}, w; r$), stores γ, and outputs the remaining results (or an error $\perp$).
- (**Commit**, $\vec{p}$) and (**Process**, $c, \vec{p}$) and **Key**: If id is not part of the group, the protocol returns $\perp$. Otherwise, it invokes the corresponding algorithm using the current γ, stores γ', and outputs the remaining results (or $\perp$) to the environment.

---

[9] Formally, the creator is encoded as part of the SID; upon calling **Create**, a party checks whether it is the designated one, and otherwise just ignores the invocation.

Modeling Corruptions. We start with the (non-standard for UC but common for messaging) corruption model with both continuous state leakage (in UC terms, transient passive corruptions) and adversarially chosen randomness (this resembles the semi-malicious model of [6]). Roughly, we model this in UC as follows. The adversary repeatedly corrupts parties by sending them two types of corruption messages: (1) a message **Expose** causes the party to send its entire state to the adversary (once), (2) a message (**CorrRand**, b) sets the party's rand-corrupted flag to b. If this flag is set, the party's randomness-sampling algorithm is replaced by asking the adversary to choose the random values. Ideal functionalities are activated upon corruptions and can adjust their behavior accordingly. We give a formal description of the corruption model in the full version [5].

Restricted Environments. Recall that in the passive setting we assume that the adversary does not inject messages, which corresponds to authenticated network. However, with the above modeling, one obviously cannot assume authenticated channels. Instead, we consider a weakened variant of UC security, where statements quantify over a restricted class of *admissible* environments, e.g. those that only deliver control messages outputted by the CGKA functionality, and provide no guarantees otherwise. Whether an environment is admissible or not is defined by the ideal functionality $\mathcal{F}$. Concretely, the pseudo-code description of $\mathcal{F}$ can contain statements of the form **req** *cond* and an environment is called admissible (for $\mathcal{F}$), if it has negligible probability of violating any such *cond* when interacting with $\mathcal{F}$. See the full version [5] for a formal definition.

Apart from modeling authenticated channels, we also use this mechanism to avoid the so-called commitment problem (there, we restrict the environment not to corrupt parties at certain times, roughly corresponding to "trivial wins" in the game-based language). We always define two versions of our functionalities, with and without this restriction.

4 Security of CGKA in the Passive Setting

The History Graph. CGKA functionalities keep track of group evolution using so-called *history graphs* (cf. Fig. 1), a formalism introduced in [3]. The nodes in a history graph correspond either to group creation, to commits, or to proposals. Nodes of the first two categories correspond to particular group states and form a tree. The root of the tree is a (in fact, the only) group-creation node, and each commit node is a child of the node corresponding to the group state from which it was created. Similarly, proposal nodes point to the commit node that corresponds to the group state from which they created.

Any commit node is created from a (ordered) subset of the proposals of the parent node; which subset is chosen is up to the party creating the commit. Observe that it is possible for commit nodes to "fork," which happens when parties simultaneously create commits from the same node.

For each party, the functionality also maintains a pointer Ptr[id] indicating the current group state of the party. This pointer has two special states: before

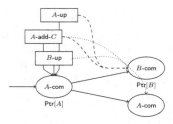

Fig. 1. A graphical representation of a history graph with three commit nodes (circles) and proposal nodes (rectangles), respectively.

joining the pointer is set to fresh and after leaving the group to removed. Note that a party's pointer does not move upon creation of a new commit node. Rather, the pointer is only moved once the corresponding control message is input by the party. This models, e.g., the existence of a delivery service that resolves forks by choosing between control messages that correspond to nodes with the same parent.[10]

CGKA functionalities identify commit resp. proposal nodes by the corresponding (unique) control messages c resp. proposal messages p (chosen by the simulator). The arrays Node[·] resp. Prop[·] map control messages c resp. proposal messages p to commit resp. proposal nodes. Moreover, for a welcome message w, array Wel[w] stores the commit node to which joining the group via w leads. Nodes in the history graph store the following values:

- orig: the party whose action created the node
- par: the parent commit node
- stat $\in$ {good, bad}: a status flag indicating whether secret information corresponding to the node is known to the adversary (e.g., by having corrupted its creator or the creator having used bad randomness).

Proposal nodes further store the following value:

- lbl $\in$ {up, add-id$'$, rem-id$'$}: the proposed action

Commit nodes further store the following values:

- pro: the ordered list of committed proposals,
- mem: the group members,
- key: the group key,
- chall: a flag set to true if a random group key has been generated for this node, and to false if the key was set by the adversary (or not generated);
- exp: a set keeping track of parties corrupted in this node, including whether only their secret state used to process the next commit message or also the key leaked.

---

[10] Note, however, that such behavior is not imposed by the functionality; it is entirely possible that group members follow different paths.

The CGKA Functionality $\mathcal{F}_{\text{CGKA-AUTH}}$. The remainder of this section introduces and explains functionality $\mathcal{F}_{\text{CGKA-AUTH}}$, which deals with *passive* network adversaries, i.e., adversaries who do not create their own control messages (nor proposals) and who deliver them in the correct order. It is described in Fig. 2 with some bookkeeping functions outsourced to Fig. 3.

Interaction with Parties. The inputs with which uncorrupted parties interact with $\mathcal{F}_{\text{CGKA-AUTH}}$ are described first; the boxed content in Fig. 2 is related to corruption and described later. Initially, the history graph is empty and the only possible action is for a designated party $\text{id}_{\text{creator}}$ to create a new group with itself in it.

The input **Propose** allows parties to create new proposals. $\mathcal{F}_{\text{CGKA-AUTH}}$ ensures that only parties that are currently in the group can create proposals (line [a]). Recall that the proposal identifier p is chosen by the simulator (line [b]) but guaranteed to be unique (line [c]). The identifier is returned to the calling party.

Parties create new commits using the input **Commit**. As part of the input, the calling party has to provide an ordered list of proposals to commit to. All proposals have to be well-defined, belong to the party's current commit node, and are valid with respect to its member set (line [d]). Moreover, a party is not allowed to commit to a proposal that removes the party from the group (line [e]). Once more, the simulator chooses the identifier c for the commit, and, if a new party is added in one of the proposals, the attacker also choses the welcome message w (line [b]). Both c and w must be unique (line [c]).

A current group member can move their pointer to a child node c of their current state by calling $(\textbf{Process}, c, \boldsymbol{p})$ (in case the proposals $\boldsymbol{p}$ in c removes the group member, their pointer is set to $\perp$ instead). The functionality ensures a party always inputs the correct proposal array (line [d]). Moreover, it imposes *correctness*: while the simulator is notified of the action (line [f]), the pointer is moved to c and the helper **get-output-process** returns the proposals true interpretations irrespective of the simulator's actions.

A new member can join the group at node $\text{Wel}[w]$ via $(\textbf{Join}, w)$. The value $\text{Wel}[w]$ must exist and correspond to a commit node for which the calling party is in the group (line [g]).

Finally, **Key** outputs the group key for the party's current node. The keys are selected via the function **set-key**(c), which either returns a random key or lets the simulator pick the key if information about it has been leaked due to corruption or the use of bad randomness (see below).

Corruptions and Bad Randomness. Generally, keys provided by $\mathcal{F}_{\text{CGKA-AUTH}}$ are always uniformly random and independent unless the information the adversary has obtained via corruption would trivially allow to compute them (as a consequence of protocol correctness). In order to stay on top of this issue, the functionality must do some bookkeeping, which is used by the predicate **safe** to determine whether a key would be known to the adversary.

First, when a party id is exposed via $(\textbf{Expose}, \text{id})$, the following from id's state that becomes available to the adversary:

Functionality $\mathcal{F}_{\text{CGKA-AUTH}}$

The group creator $\text{id}_{\text{creator}}$ is encoded as part of sid. The functionality is parameterized in:
- the predicate **safe**, specifying which keys are leaked via corruptions
- the flag **restrict-corruptions**, denoting whether it provides full adaptive security.

Initialization

Ptr$[\cdot] \leftarrow$ fresh
Node$[\cdot]$, Prop$[\cdot]$, Wel$[\cdot] \leftarrow \perp$
$\boxed{\text{RndCor}[\cdot], \text{RndPool}[\cdot] \leftarrow \text{good}}$
HasKey$[\cdot] \leftarrow$ false

Inputs from $\text{id}_{\text{creator}}$

Input Create

if Ptr$[\text{id}_{\text{creator}}] \neq$ fresh then return $\perp$
$\boxed{\text{stat} \leftarrow \textbf{rand-stat}(\text{id}_{\text{creator}})}$
Node$[\epsilon] \leftarrow \textbf{create-root}(\text{id}_{\text{creator}}, \boxed{\text{stat}})$
HasKey$[\text{id}_{\text{creator}}] \leftarrow$ true
Ptr$[\text{id}_{\text{creator}}] \leftarrow \epsilon$

Inputs from a party id

Input (Propose, act), act $\in \{\text{up}, \text{add-id}', \text{rem-id}'\}$

a: if Ptr$[\text{id}] \in \{\text{fresh}, \text{removed}\}$ then return $\perp$
b: Send (Propose, id, act) to the adversary and receive p.
c: **assert** Prop$[p] = \perp$
    $\boxed{\begin{array}{l} \text{stat} \leftarrow \text{good} \\ \text{if act} = \text{up then} \\ \quad \text{stat} \leftarrow \textbf{rand-stat}(\text{id}) \end{array}}$
    Prop$[p] \leftarrow \textbf{create-prop}(\text{Ptr}[\text{id}], \text{id}, \text{act}, \boxed{\text{stat}})$
    return p

Input (Commit, $\vec{p}$) p

a: if Ptr$[\text{id}] \in \{\text{fresh}, \text{removed}\}$ then return $\perp$
d: **req** $\forall p \in \vec{p}$: ($\text{Prop}[p] \neq \perp \wedge$ **valid-proposal**(c, p))
    mem $\leftarrow$ **members**$(\text{Ptr}[\text{id}], \vec{p})$
e: **req** id $\in$ mem
b: Send (Commit, id, $\vec{p}$) to the adversary and receive (c, w).
c: **assert** Node$[c] = \perp$
    $\boxed{\text{stat} \leftarrow \textbf{rand-stat}(\text{id})}$
    Node$[c] \leftarrow \textbf{create-child}(\text{Ptr}[\text{id}], \text{id}, \vec{p}, \text{mem}, \boxed{\text{stat}})$
    assert $w \neq \perp$ **iff** (mem $\setminus$ Node$[\text{Ptr}[\text{id}]]$.mem) $\neq \varnothing$
    if $w \neq \perp$ then
c: **assert** Wel$[w] = \perp$
    Wel$[w] \leftarrow c$
    return (c, w)

Input Key

a: if Ptr$[\text{id}] \in \{\text{fresh}, \text{removed}\} \vee \neg$HasKey$[\text{id}]$ then
    return $\perp$
    if Node$[\text{Ptr}[\text{id}]]$.key $= \perp$ then
    set-key$(\text{Ptr}[\text{id}])$
    HasKey$[\text{id}] \leftarrow$ false
    return Node$[\text{Ptr}[\text{id}]]$.key

Input (Process, $c, \vec{p}$)

a: if Ptr$[\text{id}] \in \{\text{fresh}, \text{removed}\}$ then return $\perp$
d: **req** Node$[c] \neq \perp \wedge$ Node$[c]$.par $=$ Ptr$[\text{id}]$
    $\wedge$ Node$[c]$.pro $= \vec{p}$
f: Send (Process, id, $c, \vec{p}$) to the adversary.
    if $\exists p \in \vec{p}$:Prop$[p]$.act $=$ rem-id then
    Ptr$[\text{id}] \leftarrow$ removed
    else
    Ptr$[\text{id}] \leftarrow c$
    $\boxed{\textbf{rand-stat}(\text{id})}$
    HasKey$[\text{id}] \leftarrow$ true
    return **get-output-process**(c)

Input (Join, w)

    if Ptr$[\text{id}] \notin \{\text{fresh}, \text{removed}\}$ then return $\perp$
    $c \leftarrow$ Wel$[w]$
g: **req** $c \neq \perp \wedge$ Node$[c] \neq \perp \wedge$ id $\in$ Node$[c]$.mem
    Send (Join, id, w) to the adversary
        and receive ack.
    if Ptr$[\text{id}] =$ fresh $\vee$ ack then
    Ptr$[\text{id}] \leftarrow c$
    $\boxed{\textbf{rand-stat}(\text{id})}$
    HasKey$[\text{id}] \leftarrow$ true
    return **get-output-join**(c)
    else
    return $\perp$

Corruptions

Input (Expose, id)

$\boxed{\begin{array}{l} \text{if Ptr}[\text{id}] \in \{\text{fresh}, \text{removed}\} \text{ then} \\ \quad \text{return} \\ \text{Node}[\text{Ptr}[\text{id}]].\text{exp} \leftarrow \text{Node}[\text{Ptr}[\text{id}]].\text{exp} \\ \qquad\qquad\qquad \cup \{(\text{id}, \text{HasKey}[\text{id}])\} \\ \textbf{update-status-after-expose}(\text{id}) \\ \text{RndPool}[\text{id}] \leftarrow \text{bad} \\ \hdashline \text{if restrict-corruptions then} \\ \quad \textbf{req } \forall c, \text{ if Node}[c].\text{chall} = \text{true then } \textbf{safe}(c) \\ \text{else} \\ \quad \text{Send to the adversary} \\ \qquad\qquad \{(c, \text{Node}[c].\text{key}) : \neg\textbf{safe}(c)\}. \end{array}}$

Input (CorrRand, id, b), $b \in \{\text{good}, \text{bad}\}$

$\boxed{\text{RndCor}[\text{id}] \leftarrow b}$

Fig. 2. The ideal CGKA functionality for the passive setting. The behavior related to corruptions is marked in $\boxed{\text{boxes.}}$ The helper functions are defined in Fig. 3 and the optimal predicate safe used in this paper is defined in Fig. 4.

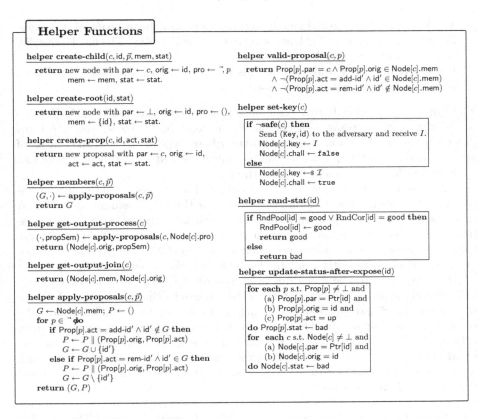

Fig. 3. The helper functions for the CGKA functionality, defined in Fig. 2. The behavior related to corruptions is marked in boxes.

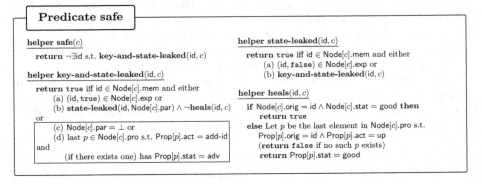

Fig. 4. The predicate safe, that determines if the key in a node c is secure. The part in the box is only relevant in the active setting (Sect. 4).

- Any key material id stored locally in order to process future control messages.
- The current group key, if id has not retrieved it yet via Key. The flag HasKey[id] indicates if id currently holds the key.
- The key material for update proposals and commits that id has created from its current epoch (but not processed yet).

The functionality records this symbolically as follows: the pair (id, HasKey[id]) is added to the "corrupted set" exp of id's current node. To address the third point, the helper function **update-status-after-expose**(id) sets the status of all child nodes (update proposals and commits) created by id to stat = bad, i.e., they are marked as no longer healing the party.

The second avenue for the attacker to obtain information about group keys is when the parties use bad randomness. Note that this work assumes that CGKA schemes use their own randomness pool, which is refreshed with randomness from the underlying operating system (OS) before every use. This guarantees that a party uses good randomness whenever (1) the OS supplies random values or (2) the pool is currently random (from the attacker's perspective).

In $\mathcal{F}_{\text{CGKA-AUTH}}$, the flag RndCor[id] records for each party id whether id's OS currently supplies good randomness; the flag can be changed by the adversary at will via CorrRand. Moreover, for each party id, the functionality stores the status of its randomness pool in RndPool[id]. Whenever id executes a randomized action, the functionality checks whether id uses good randomness by calling **rand-stat**(id) and stores the result as the stat flag of the created history graph node. As a side effect, **rand-stat**(id) updates the pool status to good if good fresh OS randomness is used.

The Safety Predicate. The predicate **safe**(c) is defined as follows: The key corresponding to c is secure if and only if it has not been exposed via one of the parties. This can happen in two situations: either if the party's state has been exposed in this particular state c while the party still stored the key ((id, true) ∈ Node[c].exp), or its previous state (not necessary with the key) is known to the adversary and c did not heal the party. This can also be interpreted as a reachability condition: the key is exposed if the party has been corrupted in any ancestor of c and there is no "healing" commit in between.

The commit c is said to be healing, iff it contains an update by id with good randomness or id is the committer and used good randomness. Observe that this is optimal as those are the only operations, that by definition of a CGKA scheme, are supposed to affect the party's own key material.

Adaptive Corruptions. Exposing a party's state may trigger some keys that were already output as secure (i.e., random) now to become insecure. Unfortunately, this is a stereotypical situation of the so-called commitment problem[11] of simulation-based security. Hence, we define two variants of $\mathcal{F}_{\text{CGKA-AUTH}}$, which

---

[11] Roughly, the simulator, having already outputted a commit message that "binds" him to the group key, now has to produce a secret state, such that processing this message results in the (random) key from the functionality.

differ in the behavior upon exposure (see the part in the ⌐dashed box¬)—in the
weaker notion (**restrict-corruptions** = true), the environment is restricted
not to corrupt a party if it would cause a challenged key to become insecure,
while in the stronger notion the adversary is simply given all now insecure keys.

5   Security of CGKA in the Active Setting

This section introduces the functionality $\mathcal{F}_{CGKA}$, which deals with active network adversaries, i.e., it allows the environment to input arbitrary messages. It
is defined in Fig. 5, and the differences from $\mathcal{F}_{CGKA-AUTH}$ are marked in boxes.
  On a high level, the main difficulty compared to the passive setting is that
$\mathcal{F}_{CGKA}$ has to account for inherent injections of valid control messages, where the
adversary uses leaked states of parties. To this end, $\mathcal{F}_{CGKA}$ marks history graph
nodes created by the adversary via injections by a special status flag stat = adv.
It maintains the following *history graph invariant*, formally defined in Fig. 7:

1. Adversarially created nodes only occur if inherent, that is, their (claimed)
   creator's state must have leaked in the parent node. (We explain the special
   case of creating orphan nodes later.)
2. The history graph is consistent.

The invariant is checked at the end of every action potentially violating it
(cf. lines [g]). We now describe the changes and additional checks in more detail.

Injected Proposals and Commits. First, consider the case where a party calls
commit with an injected proposal p (i.e., Prop[p] = $\bot$). In such case, the simulator is allowed to reject the input (if it is invalid) by sending ack = false.
Otherwise, $\mathcal{F}_{CGKA}$ asks the simulator to interpret the missing proposals by providing properties (action etc.) for new proposal nodes (line [d]) and marks them
as adversarial by setting their status to adv. (Those interpretations must be valid
with respect to the corresponding actions, cf. line [e], as otherwise the simulator
must reject the input.) The behavior of $\mathcal{F}_{CGKA}$ in case a party calls process with
an injected commit or proposal message is analogous, except that the simulator
also interprets the commit message, creating a new commit node (line [h]).
  While in the authentic-network setting we could enforce that each honest
propose and commit call results in a unique proposal or commit message, this
is no longer the case when taking injections into account. For example, add
proposals are deterministic, so if the adversary uses a leaked state to deliver an
add proposal p, then the next add proposal computed by the party is p as well.
The same can happen with randomized actions where the adversary controls
the randomness. Accordingly, we modify the behavior of $\mathcal{F}_{CGKA}$ on propose and
commit inputs and allow outputting messages corresponding to existing nodes,
as long as this is consistent. That is, in addition to the invariant, $\mathcal{F}_{CGKA}$ at this
point also needs to enforce that the values stored as part of the preexisting node
correspond to the intended action, and that this does not happen for randomized
actions with fresh randomness (see lines [a]). If all those checks succeed, the node
is treated as non-adversarial and we adjust its status accordingly (see lines [b]).

Functionality $\mathcal{F}_{\text{CGKA}}$

The functionality expects as part of the instance's session identifier sid the group creator's identity $\text{id}_{\text{creator}}$. It is parameterized in:

- the predicate **safe**, specifying which keys are leaked via corruptions
- the flag **restrict-corruptions**, indicating if it restricts the environment (avoiding the commitment problem), or if it provides full adaptive security
- the flag **robust**, indicating that parties must be able to process "honest" messages.

Initialization and input Create **from** $\text{id}_{\text{creator}}$

This is the same as in $\mathcal{F}_{\text{CGKA-AUTH}}$ in Fig. 2.

Inputs from a party id

Input (Propose, act), act $\in$ {up, add-id$'$, rem-id$'$}

    if Ptr[id] $\in$ {fresh, removed} then return $\perp$
    Send (Propose, id, act) to the adversary; receive p.
    stat $\leftarrow$ good
    if act = up then
        stat $\leftarrow$ **rand-stat**(id)
    if Prop[p] = $\perp$ then
        Prop[p] $\leftarrow$ **create-prop**(Ptr[id], id, act, stat)
    else
a: $\boxed{\textbf{check-prop-consistency}(p, \text{id}, \text{act}, \text{stat})}$
b: $\boxed{\text{Prop}[p].\text{stat} \leftarrow \text{stat}}$
    return p

Input (Commit, $\vec{p}$)

    if Ptr[id] $\in$ {fresh, removed} then return $\perp$
    Send (Commit, id, $\vec{p}$) to the adversary
           and receive ($\boxed{ack}, c, w$).
c: $\boxed{\text{if \textbf{valid-comm-by-correctness}}(\text{id}, \vec{p}) \vee ack \text{ then}}$
d: $\boxed{\textbf{fill-proposals}(\text{id}, \vec{p})}$
e: $\boxed{\forall p \in \vec{p} : \textbf{assert valid-proposal}(\text{Ptr}[\text{id}], p)}$
    stat $\leftarrow$ **rand-stat**(id)
    mem $\leftarrow$ **members**(Ptr[id], $\vec{p}$)
    assert id $\in$ mem
    if Node[c] = $\perp$ then
        Node[c] $\leftarrow$ **create-child**(Ptr[id], id, $\vec{p}$, mem, stat)
    else
a: $\boxed{\begin{array}{l}\textbf{check-comm-consistency}(c, \text{id}, \vec{p}, \text{stat}, \text{mem}) \\ \text{Node}[c].\text{stat} \leftarrow \text{stat}\end{array}}$
f: if Node[c].par = $\perp$ then **attach**(c, id, $\vec{p}$)
    assert $w \neq \perp$ **iff** (mem \ Node[Ptr[id]].mem) $\neq \varnothing$
    if $w \neq \perp$ then
        assert Wel[w] $\in \{\perp, c\}$
        Wel[w] $\leftarrow c$
g: $\boxed{\textbf{assert invariant}}$
    return (c, w)
    $\boxed{\textbf{else return } \perp}$

Input Key

    if Ptr[id] $\in$ {fresh, removed} $\vee \neg$HasKey[id] then
        return $\perp$
    if Node[Ptr[id]].key = $\perp$ then
        set-key(Ptr[id])
    HasKey[id] $\leftarrow$ false
    return Node[Ptr[id]].key

Input (Process, $c, \vec{p}$)

    if Ptr[id] $\in$ {fresh, removed} then return $\perp$
    Send (Process, id, $c, \vec{p}$) to the adversary
          $\boxed{\text{and receive } (ack, \text{orig}').}$
c: $\boxed{\text{if \textbf{valid-proc-by-correctness}}(\text{id}, c, \vec{p}) \vee ack \text{ then}}$
d: $\boxed{\textbf{fill-proposals}(\text{id}, \vec{p})}$
e: $\boxed{\forall p \in \vec{p} : \textbf{assert valid-proposal}(\text{Ptr}[\text{id}], p)}$
    mem $\leftarrow$ **members**(Ptr[id], $\vec{p}$)
    if Node[c] = $\perp$ then
h: Node[c] $\leftarrow$ **create-child**(
             Ptr[id], orig$'$, $\vec{p}$, mem, adv)
    else
i: **check-valid-successor**(c, id, $\vec{p}$, mem)
f: if Node[c].par = $\perp$ then **attach**(c, id, $\vec{p}$)
    if $\exists p \in \vec{p}$:Prop[p].act = rem-id then
        Ptr[id] $\leftarrow$ removed
    else
        Ptr[id] $\leftarrow c$
        rand-stat(id)
        HasKey[id] $\leftarrow$ true
g: $\boxed{\textbf{assert invariant}}$
    return **get-output-process**(c)
    $\boxed{\textbf{else return } \perp}$

Input (Join, w)

    if Ptr[id] $\neq$ {fresh, removed} then return $\perp$
    Send (Join, id, w) to the adversary
          $\boxed{\text{and receive } (ack, c', \text{orig}', \text{mem}').}$
c: $\boxed{\text{if \textbf{valid-join-by-correctness}}(\text{id}, w) \vee ack \text{ then}}$
    $c \leftarrow$ Wel[w]
    if $c = \perp$ then
        $c \leftarrow c'$
j: Wel[w] $\leftarrow c$
    if Node[c] = $\perp$ then
k: Node[c] $\leftarrow$ **create-child**($\perp$, orig$'$, $\perp$, mem$'$, adv)
    Ptr[id] $\leftarrow c$
    rand-stat(id)
    HasKey[id] $\leftarrow$ true
g: $\boxed{\textbf{assert invariant}}$
    return **get-output-join**(c)
    $\boxed{\textbf{else return } \perp}$

Corruptions

This is the same as in $\mathcal{F}_{\text{CGKA-AUTH}}$ in Fig. 2.

Fig. 5. The ideal CGKA functionality for the active setting. The behavior related to injections is marked in boxes. The corresponding helper functions are defined in Figs. 3 and 6, the invariant in Fig. 7, and the optimal predicate **safe** in Fig. 4.

Helper Functions

helper fill-proposals$(\text{id}, \vec{p})$

  for $p \in \vec{p}$ s.t. Prop$[p] = \bot$ **do**
    Send (Proposal, p) to the adversary
        and receive (orig, act).
    Prop$[p] \leftarrow$ create-prop(Ptr[id], orig, act, adv)

helper check-prop-consistency$(p, \text{id}, \text{act}, \text{stat})$

  // Preexisting p valid for id proposing act?
  assert Prop$[p]$.orig = id $\wedge$ Prop$[p]$.act = act
      $\wedge$ Prop$[p]$.par = Ptr[id] $\wedge$ Prop$[p]$.stat = adv
  if act = up **then**
    assert stat $\neq$ good

helper check-comm-consistency$(c, \text{id}, \vec{p}, \text{stat}, \text{mem})$

  // Preexisting c valid for id committing $\vec{\cdot}p$
  check-valid-successor$(c, \text{id}, \vec{p}, \text{mem})$
  assert stat $\neq$ good $\wedge$ Node$[c]$.stat = adv
      $\wedge$ Node$[c]$.orig = id

helper check-valid-successor$(c, \text{id}, \vec{p}, \text{mem})$

  // Preexisting node valid for id processing $(c, \vec{\cdot}p$
  assert Node$[c]$.mem = mem $\wedge$ Node$[c]$.pro $\in \{\bot, \vec{p}\}$
      $\wedge$ Node$[c]$.par $\in \{\bot, \text{Ptr[id]}\}$

helper attach$(c, \text{id}, \vec{p})$

  // Attach (detached) node c as successor of id's current
  // node with proposals $\vec{\cdot}p$
  Node$[c]$.par $\leftarrow$ Ptr[id]; Node$[c]$.pro $\leftarrow \vec{\cdot}p$

helper valid-comm-by-correctness$(\text{id}, \vec{p})$

  // Does correctness enforce the commit-call to succeed?
  return $\forall p \in \vec{\cdot}p$:Prop$[p] \neq \bot \wedge$ **valid-proposal**(Ptr[id], p)
      $\wedge$ id $\in$ **members**(Ptr[id], $\vec{p}$)

helper valid-proc-by-correctness$(\text{id}, c, \vec{p})$

  // Does correctness enforce the process-call to succeed?
  if Node$[c] = \bot \vee$ Node$[c]$.par $\neq$ Ptr[id] $\vee$ Node$[c]$.pro $\neq \vec{\cdot}p$
  then return false
  else if robust **then**
    return $\neg$(Node$[c]$.orig = id $\wedge$ Node$[c]$.stat = adv)
      $\wedge \neg$(last $p \in \vec{\cdot}$pt. Prop$[p]$.orig = id$\wedge$
        Prop$[p]$.act = up exists and has Prop$[p]$.stat = adv)
  else
    return Node$[c]$.stat $\neq$ adv $\wedge$ $\forall p \in \vec{\cdot}p$:Prop$[p]$.stat $\neq$ adv

helper valid-join-by-correctness(id, w)

  // Does correctness enforce the join-call to succeed?
  $c \leftarrow$ Wel[w]
  return robust $\wedge$ Ptr[id] = fresh $\wedge c \neq \bot \wedge$ Node$[c] \neq \bot$
      $\wedge$ Node$[c]$.stat $\neq$ adv
      $\wedge$ id $\in$ (Node$[c]$.mem \ Node$[c]$.par.mem)

Fig. 6. The additional helper functions for $\mathcal{F}_{\text{CGKA}}$, defined in Fig. 5.

Injected Welcome Messages. If a party calls join with an injected welcome message, we again ask the simulator to interpret the injected welcome message by providing the corresponding commit message c (line [j]), which can either refer to an existing node or a new one the simulator is allowed to set the corresponding values for (line [k]). The main difficulty compared to injected proposals and commits, however, is that sometimes this node's position in the history graph cannot be determined. For example, consider an adversary who welcomes a party id to a node at the end of a path that he created in his head, by advancing the protocol a number of steps from a leaked state. Unless welcome messages contain the whole conversation history (and not just e.g. a constant size transcript hash thereof), it is impossible for any efficient simulator to determine the path.

As a result, $\mathcal{F}_{\text{CGKA}}$ deals with an injected welcome message w as follows: if the commit node to which w leads does not exist (c is provided by the simulator), then a new detached node is created, with all values (except parent and proposals) determined by the simulator. The new member can call propose, commit and process from this detached node as from any other node, creating an alternative history graph rooted at the detached node. Moreover, new members can join the alternative graph. The node, together with its alternative subtree, can be attached to the main tree when the commit message c is generated or successfully processed by a party from the main tree. The function

---

Predicate invariant

Return true if all of the following are true:

- *adversarial nodes created only by corrupted parties:*
  - $\forall c$, if Node[c].stat = adv then **state-leaked**(Node[c].par, Node[c].orig)
    or Node[c].par = $\bot$
  - $\forall p$, if Prop[p].stat = adv then **state-leaked**(Prop[p].par, Prop[p].orig)
- *the history graph's state is consistent:* $\forall c$ s.t. Node[c].par $\neq \bot$:
  - Node[c].pro $\neq \bot$ and $\forall p \in$ Node[c].pro Prop[p].par = Node[c].par
  - Node[c].mem = **members**(Node[c].par, Node[c].pro)
- *pointers consistent:* $\forall$id s.t. Ptr[id] $\notin$ {fresh, removed} : id $\in$ Node[Ptr[id]].mem
- *the graph contains no cycles*

Fig. 7. The graph invariant. The predicate **state-leaked** is defined as part of the predicate **safe** in Fig. 4.

check-valid-successor, invoked during commit and process (lines [i,a]) verifies if attaching is allowed.

Security. So far we have explained how the CGKA functionality maintains a consistent history graph, even when allowing (inherent) injections. It remains to consider how such adversarially generated nodes affect the secrecy of group keys. First, obviously an adversarial commit or update does not heal the corresponding party. Note that **heals** from the safe predicate (cf. Fig. 4) already handles this by checking for stat = good. Second, for adversarial add proposals we have to assume that the contained public-key was chosen such that the adversary knows the corresponding secret key, implying that the adversary can read its welcome message. Hence, both secret state of the added party and the new group key are considered exposed (see the part (d) in Fig. 4 marked with a $\boxed{box}$).

Finally, consider a detached node created by an injected welcome message. Recall that new members join using a welcome message, containing all the relevant information about the group. Since our model does not include any long-term PKI, this welcome message is the only information about the group available to them and we cannot hope for a protocol that detects injected welcome messages. Moreover, we don't know where in the history graph a detached node belongs, and in particular whether it is a descendant of a node where another party is exposed or not. This means that we cannot guarantee secrecy for keys in detached nodes or their children (the part (c) of in Fig. 4 marked with a $\boxed{box}$). Still, we can at least express that this does not affect the guarantees of existing group members, and can start considering the subtree's security once it is attached to the main tree (e.g. by a party from the main tree moving there).

Robustness. Finally, we consider robustness, i.e., correctness guarantees with respect to honestly generated ciphertext when parties might have processed adversarially generated ones beforehand. We define two variants of $\mathcal{F}_{\text{CGKA}}$, differing in the level of robustness. Intuitively, the stronger variant (**robust** = **true**) requires that honestly generated ciphertexts can always be processed by the intended recipients, while in the weaker variant (**robust** = `false`) the adversary can inject ciphertexts resulting parties to reject subsequent honest ones.

6   Construction for the Passive Setting

We now introduce the protocol P-Pas for the authenticated setting. A formal description can be found in the full version [5]. The protocol P-Pas is a modification of the TTKEM protocol [2] when executed in a propose-and-commit manner. We thus first briefly describe TTKEM and its vulnerability to cross-group attacks.

6.1   TTKEM

The (distributed) group state consists primarily of a *labeled left-balanced binary tree* (LT) τ, where each group member is assigned one of the leafs. All nodes (except the root that stores the group key) have labels epk and esk, denoting the public and secret key of a PKE scheme, respectively. The public key and the overall structure of the tree is considered public information, whereas the secret keys are only known by the members whose leaf is in the corresponding sub-tree.

Proposals represent suggestions for modifying the current LT. More concretely, a *Remove* proposal deletes all the labels of the specified member's leaf, an *Add* proposal adds a new leaf assigned to the new member id_t where epk is fetched from the PKI, and an *Update* proposal suggests replacing esk and epk in a member's leaf by a fresh pair, with the public key specified in the proposal.

The proposals are applied upon creating or processing a commit message, to derive the new state of the tree. When applying the proposals, some of the keys stored at intermediate leafs can no longer be used: to achieve PCS in case of updates a party all nodes (potentially) known to that party, and analogously for removals. Moreover, for freshly added parties it cannot be assumed that they know the keys on their direct path (to the root). TreeKEM deals with those issues by *blanking* all those nodes. TTKEM, on the other hand, simply lets the committer choose fresh keys for all those nodes and marks them as *tainted* (i.e., sampled) by the committer via an additional public taintedby label. In particular, those keys now in turn must be assumed to be known to that party[12], and thus when committing one of his updates, also needs to be replaced in turn.

The commit message must allows all other group members to compute their respective views of the new LT, i.e., to learn all new public keys but also all replaced secret keys on their direct path. To simplify this, the commit algorithm generates the keys by first partitioning the to be re-keyed nodes into a number of path segments from a start node u to one of its ancestors v. Each of this segment is then re-keyed by "hashing up the path". Namely, it chooses a random secret s and iterates over the nodes in $(u \leadsto v)$. At each step it derives a new key pair

---

[12] While the party does not need to store any secret keys off his direct path, they might still have leaked to the adversary e.g. when using adversarially chosen randomness.

for the node using random coins $H_2(s)$ and updates the secret for use with the next node on the path by setting $s \leftarrow H_1(s)$.

Hence, each user only needs to learn one ciphertext for each segment: the seed for where the path first meets the user's direct path. Thus, the protocol simply encrypts each fresh key it to all its children's secrets that are not replaced as well. Care has to be taken where two different segments meet, i.e., where a one's segment's node is the parent of another segment's node. There, we still have to encrypt the node to the child, yet ensure that the child node's new key is used (for PCS). This can be done by processing the segments from "lower" to "higher", according to the depth of their end point.

Most users then process the above commit message in the obvious way. The only exception is the committer himself, which for PCS cannot decrypt the commit using any of his state. He can, however, simply stores the new ratchet tree at the time of creating it.

A welcome message prepared by the committer contains the public part of the (new) LT τ'. Additionally, for each freshly added member, the welcome message contains the secret labels of all nodes on the new member's direct path (except the leaf) encrypted under a second public key epk' stored as part of the add proposal. (An add proposal in TTKEM contains two public keys epk and epk'.)

Cross-Group Attacks. The TTKEM protocol is vulnerable against so-called cross-group attacks. Intuitively, those attacks are possible against protocols where commits affect only part of the group state. Consider the following example:

1. Create a group with A, B and C. Move all parties to the same node $\mathsf{Node}[c_0]$.
2. Make A send a commit c_1 and B send a commit c_2, neither containing an update for C.
3. Move C to $\mathsf{Node}[c_1]$, and A and B to $\mathsf{Node}[c_2]$.
4. Expose C's secret state.

In an optimally secure protocol, the two sub-groups should evolve independently, without the exposure of C in the one branch affecting the security of the other branch. In case of TTKEM, however, the group states in epochs c_0, c_1 and c_2 all share the same key pair for C's leaf. Moreover, if C is added last, then his node in the tree will be the direct right child of the root. Thus, when generating c_1 and c_2, both A and B encrypt the new root secret under C's leaf public key.[13] Hence, the adversary can derive the group key of $\mathsf{Node}[c_2]$ by using C's leaked secret key to decrypt the corresponding ciphertext in c_2.

We note that this cannot be easily fixed by just mixing the old group key into the new one. For this, we modify the above attack and corrupt B after Step 1. This leaks the old group key. Still, by PCS the key in c_2 should be secure.

---

[13] This attack can be easily extended to C's leaf not being a direct child of the root.

6.2   The Protocol P-Pas

To avoid cross-group attacks, we modify TTKEM so that a commit evolves all key pairs in the LT. For this, we first replace the standard encryption scheme by HIBE. That is, each node, instead of labels epk and esk, has two public mpk and id, as well as one private label hsk. In the order listed, these labels contain a (master) HIBE public key, and a HIBE identity vector and the corresponding HIBE secret key for identity id. Encryption for a node is done with mpk and id. Whenever a new key pair is created for an internal node (e.g. during rekeying), the node's id is initialized to the empty string. For leaf nodes, the first ID in the vector id is set to the ID of the user assigned to that leaf.

Second, we can now evolve all keys with every commit: For nodes whose keys does not get replaced with the commit, we simply append the hash of the commit message $H_3(c)$ to the HIBE ID vectors, and update all secret keys on the processor's direct path accordingly.

Intuitively, this provides forward secrecy for individual HIBE keys in the LT. First, HIBE schemes ensure that secret keys for an ID vector can not be used to derive secrets for prefixes of that ID vector. So, the HIBE key of a node can not be used to derive its keys from previous epochs. Second, this guarantees in the event the group is split into parallel epochs (by delivering different commit messages to different group members) that the keys of a node in one epoch can not be used to derive the keys for that node in any parallel epochs. That is because, more generally, HIBE schemes ensure that secret keys for an ID vector id can not be used to derive keys for any other ID vector id' unless id is a prefix of id'. But as soon as parallel epochs are created, the resulting ID vectors of any given node in both LTs have different commit messages in them at the same coordinate ensuring that no such vector is a prefix of another.

We prove two statements about P-Pas. First, if the hash functions are modeled as non-programmable random oracles, then the protocol realizes the relaxed functionality that restricts the environment not to perform certain corruptions. Second, for programmable random oracles it achieves full UC security. Formally, we obtain the following theorems, proven in the full version [5].

Theorem 1. *Assuming that* HIBE *and* PKE *are* IND-CPA *secure, the protocol* P-Pas *realizes* $\mathcal{F}_{\text{CGKA-AUTH}}$ *with* **restrict-corruptions** = true *in the* $(\mathcal{F}_{\text{PKI}},$ $\mathcal{G}_{RO})$*-hybrid model, where* $\mathcal{G}_{RO}$ *denotes the global random oracle, calls to hash functions* H_i *are replaced by calls to* $\mathcal{G}_{RO}$ *with prefix* H_i *and calls to* PRG.eval *are replaced by calls to* $\mathcal{G}_{RO}$ *with prefix* PRG.

Theorem 2. *Assuming that* HIBE *and* PKE *are* IND-CPA *secure, the protocol* P-Pas *realizes* $\mathcal{F}_{\text{CGKA-AUTH}}$ *with* **restrict-corruptions** = false *in the* $(\mathcal{F}_{\text{PKI}},$ $\mathcal{F}_{RO})$*-hybrid model, where* $\mathcal{F}_{RO}$ *denotes the (local) random oracle, calls to hash functions* H_i *are replaced by calls to* $\mathcal{G}_{RO}$ *with prefix* H_i *and calls to* PRG.eval *are replaced by calls to* $\mathcal{G}_{RO}$ *with prefix* PRG.

7   Constructions for the Active Setting

This section explains how to gradually enhance our protocol with passive security from Sect. 6 to deal with active network adversaries.

7.1   Basic Modifications of the Passive Protocol

Authentication. The goal of the first modification is to prevent injections whenever they are not inherent given correctness, i.e., the adversary should be able to make some party accept a message as coming from id in epoch c only if id's state in c is exposed (in the sense of the safe predicate). We achieve this using key-updatable signatures (KUS) [21], a signature analog on of HIBE, where verification additionally takes an identity vector and signing keys can be updated to lower-level ones, for longer identity vectors.

To this end, we modify the group state with each leaf in the LT getting two additional labels: a KUS verification key spk and a corresponding signing key ssk for the leafs identity vector id (the same one as for HIBE). The leaf's KUS keys live alongside its HIBE keys: each update and commit of the user id assigned to the leaf contains a fresh spk, and whenever id processes a commit message c, he updates ssk using the identity c. All messages sent by id are signed with his current signing key and verified by receiving parties respectively. Accordingly, the PKI key generation outputs an additional KUS key pair for the new member.

Binding Control Messages to Epochs. The actively secure protocols have to ensure that control messages are not used of context, e.g., trying to process a commit message that does not originate from the current state, or using a proposal belonging to a different epoch in a commit message. This is achieved by each control message (commit or proposal) contains an epoch id epid, which is simply a hash of the last commit message, and additionally each commit message containing a hash of the list of committed proposals.

Proposal Validation. For active security, the commit and proc algorithms have to check that all proposals being committed to were created by a current member of the group, that add- and remove-proposals only add and remove parties that are currently not yet in the group, respectively already in the group, and that the proposals don't remove the party executing commit from the group (as this party chooses the next group key).

Validating the Public State in Welcome Messages. Recall that $\mathcal{F}_{\text{CGKA}}$ allows the environment to inject a welcome message, making a party join a detached node. If afterwards the environment makes a different party process the corresponding commit message, the node is attached to its parent. $\mathcal{F}_{\text{CGKA}}$ requires that in such case the joining and the processing party end up in a consistent state (e.g. they agree on the member set). Our protocol guarantees this by 1) including in a commit message a hash $\mathsf{H}_5(\tau_{pub})$, where τ_{pub} is the public part of the LT in the new epoch, and 2) including the whole commit c in the welcome message.

If after processing a commit c the resulting LT doesn't match the hash, the protocol returns $\bot$. The joining party verifies that τ_{pub} in the welcome message matches the hash in the commit c and computes epid as hash of c.[14]

7.2   The Non-Robust Protocol

Well-Formedness via Hashing. The next goal is to prevent the adversary from successfully injecting (using leaked states) malformed control messages. This is not a problem for our proposal messages, since they only contain public information, which can be easily verified.[15] However, commit and welcome messages both contain a number of ciphertexts of (supposedly) related data, only part of which can be decrypted by a given party. The following simple solution to this problem provides security, but not robustness.

Consider first commit messages, which contain a number of public keys and a number of ciphertexts, used by a party to derive his slice of corresponding secret keys and the new group key. While validity of derived secret keys can be verified against the public keys, this is not the case for the group key. Hence, we add to the message an analogue of a public-key for the group key—we use hash functions H_6 and H_7 and whenever a party is ready to send a commit c creating an LT τ, it attaches to c a *confirmation key* $H_6(c, \tau.\text{grpkey})$ (recall that grpkey is the label in the root of τ) with which grpkey can be validated. The actual group key for the new epoch is then defined to be $H_7(\tau.\text{grpkey})$.

Second, a welcome message contains the public part of the LT τ_{pub}, encryption of the new member's slice of the secret part and the commit message c. The join algorithm performs the same checks as proc: it verifies the decrypted secret keys against the public keys in τ_{pub} and the decrypted $\tau.\text{grpkey}$ against the confirmation key in c.

Putting it All Together. Combining the above techniques results in our first protocol, P-Act. In particular, a commit in P-Act is computed as follows: (1) Generate the message c as in the protocol with passive security (taking into account the additional KUS labels). (2) Add the hash of the public state and epoch id: $c \leftarrow (c, \text{epid}, H_5(\tau_{pub}))$. (3) Compute the confirmation key as conf-key $= H_6(c, \tau.\text{grpkey})$. (4) Output $(c, \text{conf-key})$, signed with the current KUS secret key. (We note that we use KUS with unique signatures).

Security. We note that the confirmation key has in fact two functions. Apart from guaranteeing that parties end up with the same group keys, in the random oracle model, it also constitutes a proof of knowledge of the group key with respect to the commit message. This prevents the adversary from copying parts of commits sent by honest parties, where he does not know the secrets, into

---

[14] Recall that the functionality identifies epochs by c, so in order for the simulator to determine the epoch for injected welcome messages, it has to contain the whole c.

[15] Note that the validity of the public-key contained in add-proposals cannot be verified as our model does not consider an identity PKI.

his injected commits (he cannot copy the honest committer's confirmation key, because the control message c no longer matches).

As in the case of protocols with passive security, we prove two statements: if the hash functions are modeled as non-programmable random oracles, then we achieve security with respect to a restricted class of environments, while if the random oracles are programmable, we achieve full UC security. Both theorems are proven in the full version [5].

Theorem 3. *Assuming that* HIBE *and* PKE *are* IND-CCA *secure, and* KUS *is* EUF-CMA *secure the non-robust protocol* P-Act *realizes* $\mathcal{F}_{\text{CGKA}}$ *with* **robust** $=$ **false** *and* **restrict-corruptions** $=$ **true** *in the* $(\mathcal{F}_{\text{PKI}}, \mathcal{G}_{RO})$-*hybrid model, where* $\mathcal{G}_{RO}$ *denotes the global random oracle, calls to hash functions* H_i *are replaced by calls to* $\mathcal{G}_{RO}$ *with prefix* H_i *and calls to* PRG.eval *are replaced by calls to* $\mathcal{G}_{RO}$ *with prefix* PRG.

Theorem 4. *Assuming that* HIBE *and* PKE *are* IND-CCA *secure, and* KUS *is* EUF-CMA *secure the non-robust protocol* P-Act *realizes* $\mathcal{F}_{\text{CGKA}}$ *with* **robust** $=$ **false** *and* **restrict-corruptions** $=$ **true** *in the* $(\mathcal{F}_{\text{PKI}}, \mathcal{F}_{RO})$-*hybrid model, where* $\mathcal{F}_{RO}$ *denotes the (local) random oracle, calls to hash functions* H_i *are replaced by calls to* $\mathcal{G}_{RO}$ *with prefix* H_i *and calls to* PRG.eval *are replaced by calls to* $\mathcal{G}_{RO}$ *with prefix* PRG.

7.3 The Robust Protocol Using NIZKs

Unfortunately, the solution with the confirmation key not provide robustness, since a party cannot verify all ciphertexts, and so it may accept a commit message that will be rejected by another party. In order to provide robustness, we need a mechanism that allows parties to verify well-formedness of all ciphertexts in a commit message. For this, we replace the simple method of well-formedness verification via hashing by a non-interactive zero-knowledge argument (NIZK). In particular, in our robust protocol P-Act-Rob a commit message contains a NIZK of knowledge of randomness r and secret state γ such that (1) running th commit of P-Pas with r and γ results in the given message and (2) secret keys in γ match the public keys in the receiver's ratchet tree. Intuitively, this is secure since P-Pas is already secure against adversarial randomness, and since r and γ can be extracted from the NIZK of knowledge.

For lack of space, we leave details and the security proof to the full version [5]. The statement we prove is that P-Act-Rob realizes in the *standard model* a static version of $\mathcal{F}_{\text{CGKA}}$, where, whenever an id commits, the environment must specify if the key in the new node should be secure, in which case certain corruptions are disabled, or not. The reason for using a different type of statement than for other protocols is that P-Act-Rob uses a NIZK for a statement involving hash evaluations. On the other hand, our proofs of adaptive security require modeling the hash as a random oracle.

References

1. Alwen, J., Coretti, S., Dodis, Y.: The double ratchet: security notions, proofs, and modularization for the signal protocol. In: Ishai, Y., Rijmen, V. (eds.) EURO-CRYPT 2019. LNCS, vol. 11476, pp. 129–158. Springer, Cham (2019). https://doi.org/10.1007/978-3-030-17653-2_5

2. Alwen, J., et al.: Keep the dirt: tainted treekem, an efficient and provably secure continuous group key agreement protocol. Cryptology ePrint Archive, Report 2019/1489 (2019). https://eprint.iacr.org/2019/1489

3. Alwen, J., Coretti, S., Dodis, Y., Tselekounis, Y.: Modular design of secure group messaging. Private Communication 32 (2020)

4. Alwen, J., Coretti, S., Dodis, Y., Tselekounis, Y.: Security analysis and improvements for the IETF MLS standard for group messaging. In: Micciancio, D., Ristenpart, T. (eds.) CRYPTO 2020. LNCS, vol. 12170, pp. 248–277. Springer, Cham (2020). https://doi.org/10.1007/978-3-030-56784-2_9

5. Alwen, J., Coretti, S., Jost, D., Mularczyk, M.: Continuous group key agreement with active security. Cryptology ePrint Archive, Report 2020/752 (2020). https://eprint.iacr.org/2020/752

6. Asharov, G., Jain, A., López-Alt, A., Tromer, E., Vaikuntanathan, V., Wichs, D.: Multiparty computation with low communication, computation and interaction via threshold FHE. In: Pointcheval, D., Johansson, T. (eds.) EUROCRYPT 2012. LNCS, vol. 7237, pp. 483–501. Springer, Heidelberg (2012). https://doi.org/10.1007/978-3-642-29011-4_29

7. Backes, M., Dürmuth, M., Hofheinz, D., Küsters, R.: Conditional reactive simulatability. In: Gollmann, D., Meier, J., Sabelfeld, A. (eds.) ESORICS 2006. LNCS, vol. 4189, pp. 424–443. Springer, Heidelberg (2006). https://doi.org/10.1007/11863908_26

8. Balli, F., Rösler, P., Vaudenay, S.: Determining the core primitive for optimally secure ratcheting. In: Advances in Cryptology–ASIACRYPT 2020 (2020), to appear

9. Barnes, R., Beurdouche, B., Millican, J., Omara, E., Cohn-Gordon, K., Robert, R.: The messaging layer security (MLS) protocol (draft-ietf-mls-protocol-09). Technical report IETF, March 2020. https://datatracker.ietf.org/doc/draft-ietf-mls-protocol/

10. Barnes, R., Millican, J., Omara, E., Cohn-Gordon, K., Robert, R.: Message layer security (MLS) WG. https://datatracker.ietf.org/wg/mls/about/

11. Bellare, M., Singh, A.C., Jaeger, J., Nyayapati, M., Stepanovs, I.: Ratcheted encryption and key exchange: the security of messaging. In: Katz, J., Shacham, H. (eds.) CRYPTO 2017. LNCS, vol. 10403, pp. 619–650. Springer, Cham (2017). https://doi.org/10.1007/978-3-319-63697-9_21

12. Bhargavan, K., Barnes, R., Rescorla, E.: Treekem: asynchronous decentralized key-management for large dynamic groups, May 2018

13. Canetti, R.: Universally composable security: a new paradigm for cryptographic protocols. In: 42nd Annual Symposium on Foundations of Computer Science, pp. 136–145. IEEE Computer Society Press, October 2001. https://doi.org/10.1109/SFCS.2001.959888

14. Canetti, R., Krawczyk, H., Nielsen, J.B.: Relaxing chosen-ciphertext security. In: Boneh, D. (ed.) CRYPTO 2003. LNCS, vol. 2729, pp. 565–582. Springer, Heidelberg (2003). https://doi.org/10.1007/978-3-540-45146-4_33

15. Cohn-Gordon, K., Cremers, C., Garratt, L., Millican, J., Milner, K.: On ends-to-ends encryption: asynchronous group messaging with strong security guarantees. In: Lie, D., Mannan, M., Backes, M., Wang, X. (eds.) ACM CCS 2018: 25th Conference on Computer and Communications Security, pp. 1802–1819. ACM Press, October 2018. https://doi.org/10.1145/3243734.3243747

16. Durak, F.B., Vaudenay, S.: Bidirectional asynchronous ratcheted key agreement with linear complexity. In: Attrapadung, N., Yagi, T. (eds.) IWSEC 2019. LNCS, vol. 11689, pp. 343–362. Springer, Cham (2019). https://doi.org/10.1007/978-3-030-26834-3_20

17. Facebook: Messenger secret conversations (technical whitepaper version 2.0) (2016). Accessed May 2020. https://fbnewsroomus.files.wordpress.com/2016/07/messenger-secret-conversations-technical-whitepaper.pdf

18. Freire, E.S.V., Hesse, J., Hofheinz, D.: Universally composable non-interactive key exchange. In: Abdalla, M., De Prisco, R. (eds.) SCN 2014. LNCS, vol. 8642, pp. 1–20. Springer, Cham (2014). https://doi.org/10.1007/978-3-319-10879-7_1

19. Goldreich, O., Micali, S., Wigderson, A.: How to play any mental game or a completeness theorem for protocols with honest majority. In: Aho, A. (ed.) 19th Annual ACM Symposium on Theory of Computing, pp. 218–229. ACM Press, May 1987. https://doi.org/10.1145/28395.28420

20. Howell, C., Leavy, T., Alwen, J.: Wickr messaging protocol : Technical paper (2019). https://1c9n2u3hx1x732fbvk1ype2x-wpengine.netdna-ssl.com/wp-content/uploads/2019/12/WhitePaper_WickrMessagingProtocol.pdf

21. Jaeger, J., Stepanovs, I.: Optimal channel security against fine-grained state compromise: the safety of messaging. In: Shacham, H., Boldyreva, A. (eds.) CRYPTO 2018. LNCS, vol. 10991, pp. 33–62. Springer, Cham (2018). https://doi.org/10.1007/978-3-319-96884-1_2

22. Jost, D., Maurer, U., Mularczyk, M.: Efficient ratcheting: almost-optimal guarantees for secure messaging. In: Ishai, Y., Rijmen, V. (eds.) EUROCRYPT 2019. LNCS, vol. 11476, pp. 159–188. Springer, Cham (2019). https://doi.org/10.1007/978-3-030-17653-2_6

23. Jost, D., Maurer, U., Mularczyk, M.: A unified and composable take on ratcheting. In: Hofheinz, D., Rosen, A. (eds.) TCC 2019. LNCS, vol. 11892, pp. 180–210. Springer, Cham (2019). https://doi.org/10.1007/978-3-030-36033-7_7

24. Marlinspike, M., Perrin, T.: The double ratchet algorithm, November 2016. https://whispersystems.org/docs/specifications/doubleratchet/doubleratchet.pdf

25. Poettering, B., Rösler, P.: Towards bidirectional ratcheted key exchange. In: Shacham, H., Boldyreva, A. (eds.) CRYPTO 2018. LNCS, vol. 10991, pp. 3–32. Springer, Cham (2018). https://doi.org/10.1007/978-3-319-96884-1_1

26. WhatsApp: Whatsapp encryption overview (2017). Accessed May 2020. https://www.whatsapp.com/security/WhatsApp-Security-Whitepaper.pdf

Round Optimal Secure Multiparty Computation from Minimal Assumptions

Arka Rai Choudhuri[1(✉)] 🔟, Michele Ciampi[2], Vipul Goyal[3,4], Abhishek Jain[1],
and Rafail Ostrovsky[5]

[1] Johns Hopkins University, Baltimore, USA
{achoud,abhishek}@cs.jhu.edu
[2] The University of Edinburgh, Edinburgh, UK
mciampi@ed.ac.uk
[3] Carnegie Mellon University, Pittsburgh, USA
goyal@cs.cmu.edu
[4] NTT Research, East Palo Alto, USA
[5] University of California, Los Angeles, USA
rafail@cs.ucla.edu

Abstract. We construct a four round secure multiparty computation (MPC) protocol in the plain model that achieves security against any dishonest majority. The security of our protocol relies only on the existence of four round oblivious transfer. This culminates the long line of research on constructing round-efficient MPC from minimal assumptions (at least w.r.t. black-box simulation).

1 Introduction

The ability to securely compute on private datasets of individuals has wide applications of tremendous benefits to society. Secure multiparty computation (MPC) [18,37] provides a solution to the problem of computing on private data by allowing a group of parties to jointly evaluate any function over their private inputs in such a manner that no one learns anything beyond the output of the function.

Since its introduction nearly three decades ago, MPC has been extensively studied along two fundamental lines: necessary *assumptions* [18,26,30], and *round complexity* [2,4,6,8,9,13,18,21,28,29,32,33,36].[1] Even for the case of malicious adversaries who may corrupt any number of parties, both of these topics, individually, are by now pretty well understood:

- It is well known that oblivious transfer (OT) is both necessary and sufficient [26,30] for MPC.
- A recent sequence of works have established that *four rounds* are both necessary [13] and sufficient [2,3,6,25] for MPC (with respect to black-box simulation). However, the assumptions required by these works are far from optimal, ranging from subexponential hardness assumptions [2,6] to polynomial hardness of specific forms of encryption schemes [25] or specific number-theoretic assumptions [3].

---

[1] A detailed discussion on related works can be found in the full version.

© International Association for Cryptologic Research 2020
R. Pass and K. Pietrzak (Eds.): TCC 2020, LNCS 12551, pp. 291–319, 2020.
https://doi.org/10.1007/978-3-030-64378-2_11

In this work, we consider the well studied goal of building round-efficient MPC while minimizing the underlying cryptographic assumptions. Namely:

Can we construct round optimal MPC from minimal assumptions?

Precisely, we ask whether it is possible to construct four round MPC from four round OT. This was explicitly left as an open problem in the elegant work of Benhamouda and Lin [5] who constructed k-round MPC from k-round OT for $k \geq 5$.

1.1   Our Results

In this work, we resolve the above question in the affirmative. Namely, we construct four round malicious-secure MPC based only on four round (malicious-secure) OT. Our protocol admits black-box simulation and achieves security against malicious adversaries in the dishonest majority setting.

Theorem 1 (Informal). *Assuming the existence of four round OT, there exists a four round MPC protocol for any efficiently computable functionality in the plain model.*

This settles the long line of research on constructing round efficient MPC from minimal cryptographic assumptions.

Our Approach. To obtain our result, we take a conceptually different approach from the works of [2,3,6,25] for enforcing honest behavior on (possibly malicious) protocol participants. Unlike these works, we do not require the parties to give an *explicit* proof of honest behavior within the first three rounds of the protocol. Instead, we devise a *multiparty conditional disclosure of secrets* mechanism that ensures that the final round messages of the honest parties become "opaque" if even a single participant behaved maliciously. A key property of this mechanism is that it allows for each party to obtain a *public* witness that attests to honest behavior of all the parties, without compromising the security of any party. We refer the reader to Sect. 2 for details.

On the Minimal Assumptions. We study MPC in the standard broadcast communication model, where in each round, every party broadcasts a message to the other parties. In this model, k-round MPC implies k-round *bidirectional* OT, where each round consists of messages from both the OT sender and the receiver. However, it is not immediately clear whether it also implies k-round OT in the standard, *alternating-message* model for two-party protocols where each round consists of a message from only one of the two parties. As such, the minimal assumption for k-round MPC is, in fact, k-round bidirectional OT (as opposed to alternating-message OT).

Towards establishing the optimality of Theorem 1, we observe that k-round bidirectional OT implies k-round alternating-message OT.

Theorem 2. *k-round bidirectional OT implies k-round alternating-message OT.*

Our transformation is unconditional and generalizes a message rescheduling strategy previously considered by Garg et al. [13] for the specific case of three round coin-tossing protocols. In fact, this transformation is even more general and applies to any two-party functionality, with the restriction that only one party learns the output in the alternating- essage protocol.

An important corollary of Theorem 2 is that it establishes the missing piece from the result of Benhamouda and Lin [5] who constructed k-round MPC from any k-round alternating-message OT for $k \geq 5$. Their result, put together with our main result in Theorem 1 provides a *full resolution* of the fundamental question of basing round efficient MPC on minimal assumptions.

In the sequel, for simplicity of exposition, we refer to alternating-message OT as simply OT.

2   Technical Overview

Before we dive into the technical contributions of our work, for the uninitiated reader, we provide a brief summary of the key challenges that arise in the design of a four round MPC protocol and the high-level strategies adopted in prior works for addressing them. We group these challenges into three broad categories, and will follow the same structure in the remainder of the section.

Enforcing Honest Behavior. A natural idea, adopted in prior works, is to start with a protocol that achieves security against semi-malicious[2] adversaries and compile it using zero-knowledge (ZK) proofs [20] à la GMW compiler [19] to achieve security against malicious adversaries. This is not easy, however, since we are constrained by the number of rounds. As observed in prior works, when the underlying protocol is *delayed* semi-malicious[3] [2,5], we can forego establishing honest behavior in the first two rounds. In particular, it suffices to establish honest behavior in the third and fourth rounds. The main challenge that still persists, however, is that ZK proofs – the standard tool for enforcing honest behavior – are impossible in three rounds w.r.t. black-box simulation [17]. Thus, an alternative mechanism is required for establishing honest behavior in the third round.

Need for Rewind Security. Due to the constraint on the number of rounds, all prior works utilize design templates where multiple sub-protocols are executed in *parallel*. This creates a challenge when devising a black-box simulation strategy that works by rewinding the adversary. In particular, if the simulator rewinds the adversary (say) during second and third round of the protocol, e.g., to extract its input, we can no longer rely on stand-alone security of sub-protocols used in those rounds. This motivates the

---

[2] Roughly speaking, such adversaries behave like semi-honest adversaries, except that they may choose arbitrary random tapes.

[3] Roughly speaking, a delayed semi-malicious adversary is similar to semi-malicious adversary, except that in the second last round of a k-round protocol, it is required to output (on a special tape) a witness (namely, its input and randomness) that establishes its honest behavior in all the rounds so far.

use of sub-protocols that retain their security even in the presence of some number of rewinds. Indeed, much work is done in all prior works to address this challenge.

Non-malleability. For similar reasons as above, we can no longer rely on standard soundness guarantee of ZK proofs (which only hold in the stand-alone setting). All prior works address this challenge via a careful use of some non-malleable primitive such as non-malleable commitments [10] in order to "bootstrap non-malleability" in the entire protocol. This leads to an involved security analysis.

Our primary technical contribution is in addressing the first two issues. We largely follow the template of prior works in addressing non-malleability challenges. As such, In the remainder of this technical overview, we focus on the first two issues, and defer discussion on non-malleability to the full version.

Organization. We describe our key ideas for tackling the first and second issues in Sects. 2.1 and 2.2, respectively. We conclude by providing a summary of our protocol in Sect. 2.3.

Full Version. Due to space constraints, preliminaries, details of the proofs, and complexity calculations have been omitted from this manuscript, and can be found in the full version of the paper [7].

2.1   Enforcing Honest Behavior

In any four round protocol, a rushing adversary may always choose to *abort* after receiving the messages of honest parties in the last round. At this point, the adversary has already received enough information to obtain the output of the function being computed. This suggests that we must enforce "honest behavior" on the protocol participants *within the first three rounds* in order to achieve security against malicious adversaries. Indeed, without any such safeguard, a malicious adversary may be able learn the inputs of the honest parties, e.g., by acting maliciously so as to change the functionality being computed to the identity function.

Since three-round ZK proofs with black-box simulation are known to be impossible, all recent works on four round MPC devise non-trivial strategies that only utilize weaker notions of ZK (that are achievable in three or less rounds) to enforce honest behavior within the first three rounds of the MPC protocol. However, all of these approaches end up relying on assumptions that are far from optimal: [2] and [6] use super-polynomial-time hardness assumptions, [25] use Zaps [11] and affine-homomorphic encryption schemes, and [3] use a new notion of promise ZK together with three round strong WI [27], both of which require specific number-theoretic assumptions.

A Deferred Verification Approach. We use a different approach to address the above challenge. We do not require the parties to give an explicit proof of honest behavior within the first three rounds. Of course, this immediately opens up the possibility for an adversary to cheat in the first three rounds in such a manner that by observing the messages of the honest parties in the fourth round, it can completely break privacy. To prevent such an attack, we require the parties to "encrypt" their last round message in such a manner that it can only be decrypted by using a "witness" that establishes honest behavior in the first three rounds. In other words, the verification check for honest behavior is deferred to the fourth round.

In the literature, the above idea is referred to as conditional disclosure of secrets (CDS) [1]. Typically, however, CDS is defined and constructed as a two-party protocol involving a single encryptor – who encrypts a secret message w.r.t. some statement – and a single decryptor who presumably holds a witness that allows for decryption.[4]

This does not suffice in the multiparty setting due to the following challenges:

- The multiparty setting involves multiple decryptors as opposed to a single decryptor. A naive way to address this would be to simply run multiple executions of two-party CDS in parallel, each involving a different decryptor, such that the ith execution allows party i to decrypt by using a witness that establishes its own honest behavior earlier in the protocol. However, consider the case where the adversary corrupts at least two parties. In the above implementation, a corrupted party who behaved honestly during the first three rounds would be able to decrypt the honest party message in the last round even if another corrupted party behaved maliciously. This would clearly violate security. As such, we need a mechanism to *jointly* certify honest behavior of *all* the parties (as opposed to a single party).
- In the two-party setting, the input and randomness of the decryptor constitutes a natural witness for attesting its honest behavior. In the multiparty setting, however, it is not clear how an individual decryptor can obtain such a witness that establishes honest behavior of all the parties without trivially violating privacy of other parties.

We address these challenges by implementing a *multiparty conditional disclosure of secrets* (MCDS) mechanism. Informally speaking, an MCDS scheme can be viewed as a tuple of (possibly interactive) algorithms (Gen, Enc, Dec): (a) Gen takes as input an instance and witness pair (x, w) and outputs a "public" witness π. (b) Enc takes as input n statements $(x_1, \ldots, x_n)$ and a message m and outputs an encryption c of m. (c) Dec takes as input a ciphertext c and tuples $(x_1, \pi_1), \ldots, (x_n, \pi_n)$ and outputs m or $\bot$. We require the following properties:

- **Correctness:** If all the instances $(x_1, \ldots, x_n)$ are true, then dec outputs m.
- **Message Privacy:** If at least one instance is false, then c is semantically secure.
- **Witness Privacy:** There exists a simulator algorithm that can simulate the output π of Gen without using the private witness w.

The security properties of MCDS allow us to overcome the aforementioned challenges. In particular, the witness privacy guarantee allows the parties to publicly release the witnesses $(\pi_1, \ldots, \pi_n)$ while maintaining privacy of their inputs and randomness.

In order to construct MCDS with witness privacy guarantee, we look towards ZK proof systems. As a first attempt, we could implement public witnesses via a delayed-input[5] four round ZK proof system. Specifically, each party i is required to give a ZK

---

[4] There are some exceptions; we refer the reader to the full version for discussion on other models.

[5] A proof system is said to be delayed input if the instance is only required for computing the last round of the proof.

proof for x_i such that the last round of the proof constitutes a public witness π_i. Further, a simple, non-interactive method to implement the encryption and the decryption mechanism is witness encryption [12]. However, presently witness encryption is only known from non-standard assumptions (let alone OT).

To achieve our result from minimal assumptions, we instead use garbled circuits [37] and four round OT to implement MCDS. Namely, each party i garbles a circuit that contains hardwired the entire transcript of the first three rounds of the underlying MPC, as well the fourth round message of the MPC of party i. Upon receiving as input a witness $\pi_1, \ldots, \pi_n$, where π_j is a witness for honest behavior of party j, the garbled circuit outputs the fourth round message. Each party j can encode its witness π_j in the OT receiver messages, where the corresponding sender inputs will be the wire labels of the garbled circuit. Party j then release its private randomness used inside OT in the fourth round so that any other party j' can use it to compute the output of the OT, thereby learning the necessary wire labels for evaluating the garbled circuit sent by party i. For security, it is imperative the witness π_j remains hidden until the randomness is revealed in the fourth round.

A problem with the above strategy is that in a four round OT, the receiver's input must be fixed by the third round. This means that we can no longer use four round ZK proofs, and instead must use *three round* proofs to create public witnesses of honest behavior. But which three round proofs must we use? Towards this, we look to the weaker notion of *promise* ZK introduced by [3]. Roughly, promise ZK relaxes the standard notion of ZK by guaranteeing security only against malicious verifiers who do *not* abort. Importantly, unlike standard ZK, distributional[6] promise ZK can be achieved in only three rounds with black-box simulation in the bidirectional message model. This raises two questions – is promise ZK sufficient for our purposes, and what assumptions are required for three round promise ZK?

Promise ZK Under the Hood. Let us start with the first question. An immediate challenge with using promise ZK is that it provides no security in the case where the verifier always aborts. In application to four round MPC, this corresponds to the case where the (rushing) adversary always aborts in the third round. Since the partial transcript at the end of third round (necessarily) contains inputs of honest parties, we still need to argue security in this case. The work of [3] addressed this problem by using a "hybrid" ZK protocol that achieves the promise ZK property when the adversary is non-aborting, and strong witness-indistinguishability (WI) property against aborting adversaries. The idea is that by relying on strong WI property (only in the case where adversary aborts in the third round), we can switch from using real inputs of honest parties to input 0. However, three round strong WI is only known based on specific number-theoretic assumptions [27].

To minimize our use of assumptions, we do *not* use strong WI, and instead devise a hybrid argument strategy – similar to that achieved via strong WI – by using promise ZK *under the hood*. Recall that since we use the third round prover message of promise ZK as a witness for conditional decryption, it is not given in the clear, but is instead "encrypted" inside the OT receiver messages in the third round. This has the positive effect of shielding promise ZK from the case where the adversary always aborts in the

---

[6] That is, where the instances are sampled from a public distribution.

third round.[7] In particular, we can use the following strategy for arguing security against aborting adversaries: we first switch from using promise ZK third round prover message to simply using 0's as the OT receiver's inputs. Now, we can replace the honest parties' inputs with 0 inputs by relying on the security of the sub-protocols used within the first three rounds. Next, we can switch back to using honestly computed promise ZK third round prover message as the OT receiver's inputs.

Let us now consider the second question, namely, the assumptions required for three round promise ZK. The work of [3] used specific number-theoretic assumptions to construct three round (distributional) promise ZK. However, we only wish to rely on the use of four round OT. Towards this, we note that the main ingredient in the construction of promise ZK by [3] that necessitated the use of number-theoretic assumptions is a three round WI proof system that achieves "bounded-rewind-security." Roughly, this means that the WI property holds even against verifiers who can rewind the prover an a priori bounded number of times.

Towards minimizing assumptions, we note that a very recent work of [23] provides a construction of such a WI based only on non-interactive commitments. By using their result, we can obtain three round promise ZK based on non-interactive commitments, which in turn can be obtained from four round OT using the recent observation of Lombardi and Schaeffer [31].

2.2 Rewinding Related Challenges

While the above ideas form the basis of our approach, we run into several obstacles during implementation due to rewinding-related issues that we mentioned earlier. In order to explain these challenges and our solution ideas, we first describe a high-level template of our four round MPC protocol based on the ideas discussed so far. To narrow the focus of the discussion on the challenges unique to the present work, we ignore some details for now and discuss them later.

An Initial Protocol Template. We devise a compiler from four round delayed semi-malicious MPC protocols of a special form to a four round malicious-secure MPC protocol. Specifically, we use a four round delayed semi-malicious protocol Π obtained by plugging in a four-round malicious-secure (which implies delayed semi-malicious security) OT in the k-round semi-malicious MPC protocol of [5, 14] based on k-round semi-malicious OT. An important property of this protocol that we rely upon is that it consists only of OT messages in the first $k - 2$ rounds. Further, we also rely upon the random self-reducibility of OT, which implies that the first two rounds do not depend on the OT receiver's input, and the first three rounds do not depend on the sender's input.[8]

To achieve malicious security, similar to prior works, our compiler uses several building blocks (see Sect. 2.3 for a detailed discussion). One prominent building block is a three-round extractable commitment scheme that is executed in *parallel* with the first three rounds of the delayed semi-malicious MPC. The extractable commitment

---

[7] Note that if the protocol does progress to the fourth round, then we do not need to shield promise ZK anymore.

[8] We note that this property was also used by [5] in their construction of k-round malicious-secure MPC.

scheme is used by the parties to commit to their inputs and randomness. This allows the simulator for our protocol to extract the adversary's inputs and randomness *by rewinding the second and third rounds*, and then use them to simulate the delayed semi-malicious MPC.

Bounded-Rewind-Secure OT. The above template poses an immediate challenge in proving security of the protocol. Since the simulator rewinds the second and third rounds in order to extract the adversary's inputs, this means that the second and third round messages of the delayed semi-malicious MPC also get rewound. For this reason, we cannot simply rely upon delayed semi-malicious security of the MPC. Instead, we need the MPC protocol to remain secure *even when it is being rewound*. More specifically, since we are using an MPC protocol where the first two rounds only consist of OT messages, we need a *four round rewind-secure OT protocol*. Since the third round of a four round OT only contains a message from the OT receiver, we need the following form of rewind security property: an adversarial sender cannot determine the input bit used by the receiver even if it can rewind the receiver during the second and third round.

Clearly, an OT protocol with black-box simulation cannot be secure against an arbitrary number of rewinds. In particular, the best we can hope for is security against an a priori *bounded* number of rewinds. Following observations from [3], we note that bounded-rewind security of OT is, in fact, *sufficient* for our purposes. Roughly, the main idea is that the rewind-security of OT is invoked to argue indistinguishability of two consecutive hybrids inside our security proof. In order to establish indistinguishability by contradiction, it suffices to build an adversary that breaks OT security with some non-negligible probability (as opposed to overwhelming probability). This, in turn means that the reduction only needs to extract the adversary's input required for generating its view with non-negligible probability. By using a specific extractable commitment scheme, we can ensure that the number of rewinds necessary for this task are a priori bounded.

Standard OT protocols, however, do not guarantee any form of bounded-rewind security. Towards this, we provide a generic construction of a four round bounded-rewind secure OT starting from any four round OT, which may be of independent interest. Our transformation is in fact more general and works for any $k \geq 4$ round OT, when rewinding is restricted to rounds $k - 2$ and $k - 1$. For simplicity, we describe our ideas for the case where we need security against *one* rewind; our transformation easily extends to handle more rewinds.

A natural idea to achieve one-rewind security for receivers, previously considered in [5], is the following: run two copies of an OT protocol in parallel for the first $k - 2$ rounds. In round $k - 1$, the receiver randomly chooses one of the two copies and only continues that OT execution, while the sender continues both the OT executions. In the last round, the parties only complete the OT execution that was selected by the receiver in round $k - 1$. Now, suppose that an adversarial sender rewinds the receiver in rounds $k - 2$ and $k - 1$. Then, if the receiver selects different OT copies on the "main" execution thread and the "rewound" execution thread, we can easily reduce one-rewind security of this protocol to stand-alone security of the underlying OT.

The above idea suffers from a subtle issue. Note that the above strategy for dealing with rewinds is inherently *biased*, namely, the choice made by the receiver on the rewound thread is *not* random, and is instead correlated with its choice on the main thread. If we use this protocol in the design of our MPC protocol, it leads to the following issue during simulation: consider an adversary who chooses a random z and then always aborts if the receiver selects the z-th OT copy. Clearly, this adversary only aborts with probability $1/2$ in an honest execution. Now, consider the high-level simulation strategy for our MPC protocol discussed earlier, where the simulator rewinds the second and third rounds to extract the adversary's inputs. In order to ensure rewind security of the OT, this simulator, with overall probability $1/2$, will select the z-th OT copy on *all* the rewound execution threads. However, in this case, the simulator will always *fail* in extracting the adversary's inputs no matter how many times it rewinds.

We address the above problem via a secret-sharing approach to eliminate the bias. Instead of simply running two copies of OT, we run $\ell \cdot n$ copies in parallel during the first $k - 2$ rounds. These $\ell \cdot n$ copies can be divided into n tuples, each consisting of ℓ copies. In round $k - 1$, the receiver selects a single copy from each of the n tuples at random. It then uses n-out-of-n secret sharing to divide its input bit b into n shares $b_1, \ldots, b_n$, and then uses share b_i in the OT copy selected from the i-th tuple. In the last round, sender now additionally sends a garbled circuit (GC) that contains its input (x_0, x_1) hardwired. The GC takes as input all the bits $b_1, \ldots, b_n$, reconstructs b and then outputs x_b. The sender uses the labels of the GC as its inputs in the OT executions. Intuitively, by setting ℓ appropriately, we can ensure that for at least one tuple i, the OT copies randomly selected by the receiver on the main thread and the rewound threads are different, which ensures that b_i (and thereby, b) remains hidden. We refer the reader to the technical section for more details.

Proofs Of Proofs. We now describe another challenge in implementing our template of four round MPC. As discussed earlier, we use a three round extractable commitment scheme to enable extraction of the adversary's inputs and randomness. For reasons similar to those as for the case of OT, we actually use an extractable commitment scheme that achieves bounded-rewind security. Specifically, we use a simplified variant of the three-round commitment scheme constructed by [3].[9]

A specific property of this commitment scheme is that in order to achieve rewind security, it is designed such that the third round message of the committer is not "verifiable." This means that the committer may be able to send a malformed message without being detected by the receiver. For this reason, we require each party to prove the "well-formedness" of its commitment via promise ZK. This, however, poses the following challenge during simulation: since the third round prover message of promise ZK is encrypted inside OT receiver message, the simulator doesn't know whether the adversary's commitment is well-formed or not. In particular, if the adversary's commitment is not well-formed, the simulator may end up running *forever*, in its attempt to extract the adversary's input via rewinding.

---

[9] The commitment scheme of [3] also achieves some security properties, in addition to bounded rewind security, that are not required by our compiler. Hence, we use a simplified variant of their scheme.

One natural idea to deal with this issue is to first extract adversary's promise ZK message from the OT executions via rewinding, and then decide whether or not to attempt extracting the adversary's input. However, since we are using an *arbitrary* (malicious-secure) OT, we do *not* know in advance the number of rewinds required for extracting the receiver's input. This in turn means that we cannot correctly set the rewind security of the sub-protocols used in our final MPC protocol appropriately in advance.

We address this issue via the following strategy. We use *another* three round (delayed-input) extractable commitment scheme [34] (ecom) as well as another copy of promise ZK. This copy of promise ZK proves honest behavior in the first three rounds, and its third message is committed inside the extractable commitment. Further, the third round message of this extractable commitment is such that it allows for polynomial-time extraction (with the possibility of "over-extraction"[10]). This, however, comes at the cost that this extractable commitment does not achieve any rewind security. Interestingly, stand-alone security of this scheme suffices for our purposes since we only use it in the case where the adversary always aborts in the third round (and therefore, no rewinds are performed).

The main idea is that by using such a special-purpose extractable commitment scheme, we can ensure that an a priori fixed constant number of rewinds are sufficient for extracting the committed value, namely, the promise ZK third round prover message, with noticeable probability. This, in turn, allows us to set the rewind security of other sub-protocols used in our MPC protocol in advance to specific constants.

Of course, the adversary may always choose to commit to malformed promise ZK messages within the extractable commitment scheme. In this case, our simulator may always decide not to extract adversary's input, *even if the adversary was behaving honestly otherwise*. This obviously would lead to a view that is distinguishable from the real world. To address this issue, we use a *proofs of proofs* strategy. Namely, we require the first copy of promise ZK, which is encrypted inside OT, to prove that the second copy of promise ZK is "accepting". In this case, if the adversary commits malformed promise ZK messages within the extractable commitment, the promise ZK message inside OT will not be accepting. This, in turn, means that due to the security of garbled circuits, the fourth round messages of the parties will become "opaque".

Finally, we remark that for technical reasons, we do extract the promise ZK encrypted inside the OT receiver message in our *final* hybrid. However, in this particular hybrid, the number of rewinds required for extraction do not matter since in this hybrid, we only make change inside a *non-interactive* primitive (specifically, garbled circuit) that is trivially secure against an *unbounded* polynomial number of rewinds.

2.3 Protocol Design Summary

Putting all the various pieces together, we describe the overall structure of the protocol at a high level to demonstrate the purpose of its various components in the context of the protocol.

---

[10] This means the extractor can output a non $\bot$ value if the commitment has no valid opening.

For simplicity we consider the messages sent from P_i to P_j. Note that even though P_j is the intended recipient for the messages in a two party sub-protocol, the messages are broadcast to all parties.

Delayed Semi-malicious MPC (blue). P_i uses input x and randomness r to compute the messages msg_k for the bounded rewind secure four-round delayed semi malicious protocol Π.

Multiparty Conditional Disclosure of Secrets (red). As discussed earlier, the last message of Π is not sent in the clear but instead sent inside a garbled circuit GC used to implement MCDS. We use a four-round oblivious transfer protocol ot_k to allow the parties to obtain garbled circuit wire labels corresponding to their witnesses. We defer the discussion on the witness for MCDS below.

Rewind Secure Extractable commitment (green). The same input and randomness used to compute messages for Π is committed via an extractable commitment $recom_k$. This is done to enable the simulator to extract the inputs and randomness of the adversary for simulation. As discussed earlier, we use a three round extractable commitment that achieves bounded rewind security.

Promise ZK (purple). We use promise ZK in a non-black box manner in our protocol. Specifically, it consists of a trapdoor generation phase td_k, and a bounded rewind secure witness indistinguishable proof rwi_k. As discussed in our *proofs of proofs* strategy, we actually use two copies of the promise ZK (indexed by subscripts a and b in the figure), but both of these copies will share a single instance of the trapdoor generation. At a high level, both rwis prove that either the claim is true or "I committed to the trapdoor in the non-malleable commitment" (see below). We also note that one of the rwi copies, specifically, the copy indexed with subscript b is used as a witness for the MCDS mechanism.

Witness Indistinguishable Proof (orange). We also use a regular witness indistinguishable proof wi (without any rewind security) to establish honest behavior of the parties in the last round of the protocol. This effectively involves proving that either the last round message was computed honestly or "I committed to the trapdoor in the non-malleable commitment" (see below).

Extractable Commitment (brown). As discussed earlier, we use an extractable commitment ecom (without rewind security) to implement our *proofs of proofs* strategy to enable simulation.

Non-malleability (dark blue). We bootstrap non-malleability in our protocol using non-malleable commitments ncom in a similar manner to prior works [2,3]. Specifically, in the honest execution of the protocol, the parties simply commit to a random value $\tilde{r}$. We rely on specific properties of the ncom, which we do not discuss here and refer the reader to the technical sections.

Finally, we note that our protocol design uses multiple sub-protocols with bounded rewind security. We do not discuss how the bounds for the sub-protocols are set here, and instead defer this discussion to Sect. 5.

Complexity of the Protocol Description. One might wonder why our construction is so involved and whether there is a simpler construction. This is an important question that needs to be addressed. Unfortunately, our current understanding of the problem does not allow for a protocol that is easier to describe, but we believe that our solution is less complex than the prior state-of-the-art solutions [3,25].

3 Preliminaries

We present the syntax and informal definitions of some preliminaries below. Additional preliminaries, and the full definitions can be found in the full version.

3.1 Extractable Commitments with Bounded Rewinding Security

In this section, we describe an extractable commitment protocol that is additionally secure against a bounded number of rewinds. Since we are interested in the three round protocol, we limit our discussion in this section to this setting. A simple extractable commitment is a commitment protocol between a sender (with input x) and a receiver which allows an extractor, with the ability to rewind the sender via the second and third round of the protocol, to extract the sender's committed value. Several constructions of three round extractable commitment schemes are known in the literature (see, e.g., [34,35]).

When we additionally require bounded rewind security, we shall parameterize this bound by B_{recom}. Roughly this means that the value committed by a sender in an execution of the commitment protocol remains hidden even if a malicious receiver can rewind the sender back to the start of the second round of the protocol an a priori bounded B_{recom} number of times. Extraction will then necessarily require strictly larger than B_{recom} rewinds.

In the remainder of the section, we describe a construction of a three round extractable commitment protocol with bounded rewind security $\mathsf{RECom} = (S, R)$. The construction is adapted from the construction presented in [3], and simplified for our setting since we do not require the stronger notion of "reusability", as defined in their work.

In our application, we set $B_{\mathsf{recom}} = 4$; however, our construction also supports larger values of B_{recom}. For technical reasons, we don't define or prove B_{recom}-rewinding security property and reusability property for our extractable commitment protocol. Instead, this is done inline in our four round MPC protocol.

Construction. Let Com denote a non-interactive perfectly binding commitment scheme based on injective one-way functions. Let N and B_{recom} be positive integers such that $N - B_{\mathsf{recom}} - 1 \geq \frac{N}{2} + 1$. For $B_{\mathsf{recom}} = 4$, it suffices to set $N = 12$. The three round extractable commitment protocol RECom is described in Fig. 1.

Sender S has input x.

Commitment Phase:

1. **Round 1:** S does the following:
   - Pick N random degree B_{recom} polynomials $\mathsf{p}_1, \ldots, \mathsf{p}_N$ over $\mathbb{Z}_q$, where q is a prime larger than 2^λ.
   - Compute $\mathsf{recom}_{1,\ell}^{S \to R} \leftarrow \mathsf{Com}(\mathsf{p}_\ell; r_\ell)$ using a random string r_ℓ, for every $\ell \in [N]$.
   - Send $\mathsf{recom}_1^{S \to R} = (\mathsf{recom}_{1,1}^{S \to R}, \ldots, \mathsf{recom}_{1,N}^{S \to R})$ to R.
2. **Round 2:** R does the following:
   - Pick random values $z_\ell \leftarrow_{\$} \mathbb{Z}_q$ for every $\ell \in [N]$.
   - Send $\mathsf{recom}_2^{R \to S} = (z_1, \ldots, z_N)$ to S.
3. **Round 3:** S does the following:
   - Compute $\mathsf{recom}_{3,\ell}^{S \to R} \leftarrow (x \oplus \mathsf{p}_\ell(0), \mathsf{p}_\ell(z_\ell))$ for all $\ell \in [N]$.
   - Send $\mathsf{recom}_3^{S \to R} = (\mathsf{recom}_{3,1}^{S \to R}, \ldots, \mathsf{recom}_{3,N}^{S \to R})$ to R.

Decommitment Phase:

1. S outputs $\mathsf{p}_1, \ldots, \mathsf{p}_N$ together with the randomness $r_1, \ldots, r_N$ used in the first round commitments.
2. R first verifies the following:
   - For each $\ell \in [N]$, $\mathsf{recom}_{1,\ell}^{S \to R} = \mathsf{Com}(\mathsf{p}_\ell; r_\ell)$.
   - Parse $\mathsf{recom}_{3,\ell}^{S \to R} = (\alpha_\ell, \beta_\ell)$. Verify that $\beta_\ell = \mathsf{p}_\ell(z_\ell)$.
   - For each $\ell \in [N]$, compute $x_\ell = \mathsf{p}_\ell(0) \oplus \alpha_\ell$. Verify that all the x_ℓ values are equal.
   If any of the above verifications fail, R outputs $\perp$. Otherwise, R outputs x.

Fig. 1. Extractable commitment scheme recom.

The corresponding properties for the above construction is presented in the full version.

3.2 Trapdoor Generation Protocol with Bounded Rewind Security

This section, we discuss the syntax and provide an intuitive definition, along with a sketched construction, for a Trapdoor Generation Protocol with Bounded Rewind Security [3]. The complete definition along with the construction is provided in the full version.

In a Trapdoor Generation Protocol, without bounded rewind security, a sender S (a.k.a. trapdoor generator) communicates with a receiver R. The protocol itself has no output, and the receiver has no input. The goal is for the sender to establish a trapdoor upon completion. On the one hand, the trapdoor can be extracted via a special extraction algorithm that has the ability to rewind the sender. On the other hand, no cheating receiver should be able to recover the trapdoor.

Syntax. A trapdoor generation protocol $\mathsf{TDGen} = (\mathsf{TDGen}_1, \mathsf{TDGen}_2, \mathsf{TDGen}_3,$ $\mathsf{TDOut}, \mathsf{TDValid}, \mathsf{TDExt})$ is a three round protocol between two parties - a sender (trapdoor generator) S and receiver R that proceeds as below.

1. **Round 1** - $\mathsf{TDGen}_1(\cdot)$: S computes and sends $\mathsf{td}_1^{S \to R} \leftarrow \mathsf{TDGen}_1(r_S)$ using a random string r_S.
2. **Round 2** - $\mathsf{TDGen}_2(\cdot)$: R computes and sends $\mathsf{td}_2^{R \to S} \leftarrow \mathsf{TDGen}_2(\mathsf{td}_1^{S \to R}; r_R)$ using randomness r_R.
3. **Round 3** - $\mathsf{TDGen}_3(\cdot)$: S computes and sends $\mathsf{td}_3^{S \to R} \leftarrow \mathsf{TDGen}_3(\mathsf{td}_2^{R \to S}; r_S)$
4. **Output** - $\mathsf{TDOut}(\cdot)$ The receiver R outputs $\mathsf{TDOut}(\mathsf{td}_1^{S \to R}, \mathsf{td}_2^{R \to S}, \mathsf{td}_3^{S \to R})$.
5. **Trapdoor Validation Algorithm** - $\mathsf{TDValid}(\cdot)$: Given input $(\mathsf{t}, \mathsf{td}_1^{S \to R})$, output a single bit 0 or 1 that determines whether the value t is a valid trapdoor corresponding to the message td_1 sent in the first round of the trapdoor generation protocol.

In what follows, for brevity, we set td_1 to be $\mathsf{td}_1^{S \to R}$. Similarly we use td_2 and td_3 instead of $\mathsf{td}_2^{R \to S}$ and $\mathsf{td}_3^{S \to R}$, respectively. Note that the algorithm $\mathsf{TDValid}$ does not form a part of the interaction between the trapdoor generator and the receiver. It is, in fact, a public algorithm that enables public verification of whether a value t is a valid trapdoor for a first round message td_1.

The protocol satisfies two properties: (i) Sender security, i.e., no cheating PPT receiver can learn a valid trapdoor, and (ii) Extraction, i.e., there exists an expected PPT algorithm (a.k.a. extractor) that can extract a trapdoor from an adversarial sender via rewinding.

Extraction. There exists a PPT extractor algorithm TDExt that, given a set of values[11] $(\mathsf{td}_1, \{\mathsf{td}_2^i, \mathsf{td}_3^i\}_{i=1}^3)$ such that $\mathsf{td}_2^1, \mathsf{td}_2^2, \mathsf{td}_2^3$ are distinct and $\mathsf{TDOut}(\mathsf{td}_1, \mathsf{td}_2^i, \mathsf{td}_3^i) = 1$ for all $i \in [3]$, outputs a trapdoor t such that $\mathsf{TDValid}(\mathsf{t}, \mathsf{td}_1) = 1$.

1-Rewind Security. Intuitively, a Trapdoor Generation protocol is 1-rewind secure if it protects a sender against a (possibly cheating) receiver that has the ability to rewind it once. Specifically, the receiver is allowed to query the sender on two (possibly adaptive) different second round messages, thereby receiving two different third round responses from the sender. It should be the case that the trapdoor still remains hidden to the receiver.

Construction Based on One-way Functions. We sketch here the simple construction based on any signature scheme. In the first round, the sender samples a signing key pair and sends the verification key to the receiver. The receiver queries a random message in the second round, and the sender responds with the corresponding signature in the third. The trapdoor is defined to be 3 distinct (message, signature) pairs. It is easy to see that both extraction and 1-rewind security are satisfied for this construction.

---

[11] These values can be obtained from the malicious sender via an expected PPT rewinding procedure. The expected PPT simulator in our applications performs the necessary rewindings and then feeds these values to the extractor TDExt.

3.3   Witness Indistinguishable Proofs with Bounded Rewinding Security

In this section we discuss the informal definition of a delayed input witness indistinguishable arguments (WI) to additionally satisfy B_{rwi}-bounded rewinding security, where the same statement is proven across all the rewinds. We refer to such primitives as B_{rwi}-bounded rewind secure WI.

B_{rwi}-**Bounded Rewinding Security.** The intuition for the definition is similar to that of the trapdoor generation protocol as described in the previous section. Here, for the three round delayed-input witness indistinguishable argument we want witness indistinguishability to be preserved as long as the verifier is restricted to rewinding the prover B_{rwi}-1 times. Specifically, the prover sends its first round message to the verifier, who then chooses (i) a triple consisting of a statement, and any two corresponding witnesses w_0 and w_1; (ii) B_{rwi}-1 s round verifier messages for the single first round prover message. The prover then completes the protocol, responding to each of the B_{rwi}-1 verifier messages, using either witness w_0 or w_1 for *every* response.

We refer the reader to the full version for the formal definitions of both, a delayed input WI, and the B_{rwi}-bounded rewind secure WI.

It was recently shown in [24] that there exists such WI arguments assuming non-interactive commitments. For further details, see the full version. We will use their scheme in our protocol.

3.4   Special Non-Malleable Commitments

In this work we make use of a commitment scheme that is non-malleable, non-malleable with respect to extraction and enjoys some additional properties. We refer to such a commitment scheme as a *special non-malleable commitment scheme*. We refer the reader to the full version for the basic definitions of non-malleable commitments. In the full version we also briefly detail the non-malleable commitment scheme of [22] and show that it is a special non-malleable commitment scheme.

4   Oblivious Transfer with Bounded Rewind Security

In this section we define, and then construct, a strengthening of regular oblivious transfer. We construct a rewinding secure Oblivious Transfer (OT) assuming the existence of four round OT protocol. For an OT protocol to be rewind secure, we require security against an adversary who is allowed to re-execute the second and third round of the protocol multiple times. But the first and fourth round are executed only once.

4.1   Definition

We start by formalizing the notion of a rewind secure oblivious transfer protocol. We shall denote by $out_R \langle S(x), R(y) \rangle$ the output of the receiver R on execution of the protocol between R with input y, and sender S with input x. The four round oblivious transfer protocol is specified by four algorithms OT_j for $j \in [4]$; and the corresponding output protocol message is denoted by ot_j. We consider a delayed receiver input notion of the protocol where the receiver input is only required for the computation of ot_3.

Definition 1. *An interactive protocol (S, R) between a polynomial time sender S with inputs s_0, s_1 and polynomial time receiver R with input b, is a four round bounded rewind secure oblivious transfer (OT) if the following properties hold:*

- **Correctness.** *For any selection bit b, for any messages $s_0, s_1 \in \{0, 1\}$, it holds that*

$$\Pr\left[out_R \langle S(s_0, s_1), R(b)\rangle = s_b\right] = 1$$

  where the probability is over the random coins of the sender S and receiver R.
- **Security against Malicious Sender with B rewinds.** *Here, we require indistinguishability security against a malicious sender where the receiver uses input $b[k]$ in the k-th rewound execution of the second and third round. Specifically, consider the experiment described below.* $\forall \left\{b^0[k], b^1[k]\right\}_{k \in [B]} \in \{0, 1\}$ *where*

  Experiment E^σ:
  1. Run OT_1 to obtain ot_1 which is independent of the receiver input. Send to $\mathcal{A}$.
  2. $\mathcal{A}$ then returns $\{ot_2[j]\}_{j \in [B]}$ messages.
  3. For each $j \in [B]$, run OT_3 on $(ot_1, ot_2[j], b^\sigma[j])$ and send the response to $\mathcal{A}$.
  4. The output of the experiment is the entire transcript.
  We say that the scheme is secure against malicious senders with B rewinds if the experiments E^0 and E^1 are indistinguishable.

4.2 Construction

We describe below the protocol Π^R which achieves rewind security against malicious senders. The Sender S's input is $s_0, s_1 \in \{0, 1\}$ while the receiver R's input is $b \in \{0, 1\}$.

Components. We require the following two components:

- $n \cdot B_{OT}$ instances of a 4 round OT protocol which achieves indistinguishability security against malicious senders.
- $GC = (Garble, Eval)$ is a secure garbling scheme.

Protocol. The basic idea is to split the receiver input across multiple different OT executions such that during any rewind, a different set of OTs will be selected to proceed with the execution thereby preserving the security of the receiver's input. The sender constructs a garbled circuit which is used to internally recombine the various inputs shares and only return the appropriate output. The protocol is described below.

Round 1. (Π_1^R) : The receiver R computes the first round message of all the OTs. $\forall i \in [n], k \in [\mathsf{B_{OT}}]$, $\mathsf{ot}_1^{i,k} := \mathsf{OT}_1\left(1^\lambda; r_R\right)$ and send $\left\{\mathsf{ot}_1^{i,k}\right\}_{i \in [n], k \in [\mathsf{B_{OT}}]}$ to S. We refer to index i as the outer index, and k as the inner index.

Round 2. (Π_2^R) : The sender S responds to all of the OT messages. $\forall i \in [n], k \in [\mathsf{B_{OT}}]$, compute $\mathsf{ot}_2^{i,k} := \mathsf{OT}_2\left(\mathsf{ot}_1^{i,k}; r_S\right)$ and sends $\left\{\mathsf{ot}_2^{i,k}\right\}_{i \in [n], k \in [\mathsf{B_{OT}}]}$ to R.

Round 3. (Π_3^R) : The receiver now selects only a single OT to continue for i. It then encodes its input b by computing n additive shares and using each share as an input to a separate OT. Specifically, receiver R does the following:

- Compute n additive shares of b. Specifically, sample the first $n-1$ shares at random $\forall \ell \in [n-1]$ $b_\ell \leftarrow_\$ \{0,1\}$ and set the last share $b_n := b \bigoplus_{\ell=1}^{n-1} b_j$.
- Sample within each tuple, the index for which to continue the OT. $\forall i \in [n]$, $\sigma_i \leftarrow_\$ [\mathsf{B_{OT}}]$.
- Use input b_i to compute the receiver message for $\mathsf{ot}_3^{i,\sigma_i}$. The other OTs are discontinued. Specifically, $\forall i \in [n]$, compute $\mathsf{ot}_3^{i,\sigma_i} \leftarrow \mathsf{OT}_3\left(b_i, \mathsf{ot}_1^{i,\sigma_i}, \mathsf{ot}_2^{i,\sigma_i}; r_R\right)$ and send $\left\{\mathsf{ot}_3^{i,\sigma_i}, \sigma_i\right\}_{i \in [n]}$ to S.

Round 4. (Π_4^R) : The sender encodes its inputs (s_0, s_1) in a garbled circuit and uses the corresponding labels to complete the OT protocol.

- Compute garbled circuit: $\left(\overline{C}_{\mathsf{ot}}, \overline{\mathsf{lab}}\right) := \mathsf{Garble}\left(C_{\mathsf{ot}}[s_0, s_1]; r_{\mathsf{gc},i}\right)$, where Circuit $C_{\mathsf{ot}}[s_0, s_1]$ on input $b_1, \ldots, b_n$ outputs s_b where $b := \bigoplus_{i=1}^n b_i$.
- For $i \in [n]$, compute $\mathsf{ot}_4^{i,\sigma_i} := \mathsf{OT}_4\left(\mathsf{lab}_{i,0}, \mathsf{lab}_{i,1}, \mathsf{ot}_1^{i,\sigma_i}, \mathsf{ot}_2^{i,\sigma_i}, \mathsf{ot}_3^{i,\sigma_i}; r_S\right)$ and send $\left\{\mathsf{ot}_4^{i,\sigma_i}\right\}_{i \in [n]}$ to R.

Evaluation. (OTEval') : The receiver R now evaluates the OT protocol to obtain labels needed to evaluate the output of the garbled circuit.

- For $i \in [n]$, compute $\widehat{\mathsf{lab}}_i := \mathsf{OTEval}\left(b_i, \mathsf{ot}_1^{i,\sigma_i}, \mathsf{ot}_2^{i,\sigma_i}, \mathsf{ot}_3^{i,\sigma_i}, \mathsf{ot}_4^{i,\sigma_i}; r_R\right)$
- Output $s' := \mathsf{Eval}\left(\overline{C}_{\mathsf{ot}}, \left\{\widehat{\mathsf{lab}}_i\right\}_{i \in [n]}\right)$

We now have the corresponding Lemma, which we prove in the full version.

Lemma 1. *Assuming receiver indistinguishability of* OT *against malicious senders, the receiver input in* Π^R *remains indistinguishable under* $\mathsf{B_{OT}}$-*rewinds.*

Remark 1. We note that while our construction is proved against malicious senders, for our application it suffices to have the following two properties:

- bounded rewind security against semi malicious senders.
- standalone security against receivers.

Remark 2. While not relevant to the bounded rewind security of the scheme, we note that in our applications, a malicious sender might compute the garbled circuit incorrectly. This stems from the fact that there will be multiple participants evaluating the garbled circuit to compute the OT output. We will therefore have to prove that the messages of the protocol were in fact computed correctly.

4.3   Four Round Delayed Input Multiparty Computation with Bounded Rewind Security

Looking ahead, for our main result, we will compile an underlying semi-malicious protocol to achieve malicious security. In order to use the underlying semi-malicious protocol in a black-box manner, we will require the protocol to satisfy bounded rewind security. We start with an intuitive definition which we follow by formalizing the intuition.

To start with, we consider a four round delayed input semi-malicious protocols satisfying the following additional properties, where we denote by msg_k the messages of all parties output in the k-th round by Π.

1. **Property 1:** msg_1 and msg_2 of Π contain only messages of OT instances.
2. **Property 2:** msg_1 and msg_2 of Π do not depend on the input. The input is used only in the computation of msg_3 and msg_4.
3. **Property 3:** The simulator S simulates the honest parties' messages msg_1 and msg_2 via S_1 and S_2 by simply running the honest OT sender and receiver algorithms.
4. **Property 4:** msg_3 can be divided into two parts: (i) components independent of the OT messages; and (ii) OT messages.

Here we clarify what it means for a component of a message to be independent of OT messages. We say a component of msg_3 is independent of OT messages if its computation in the third round is independent of the both the private and public state of OT.

The recent works of [5,14] construct two round semi-malicious protocols. Both protocols when instantiated with a four round OT protocol, satisfy the above structure. This follows from the fact that when their protocols are instantiated with a four round OT protocol, the non-OT components of their protocol are executed only in round 3.

The bounded rewind security notion follows in similar vein to the bounded rewind secure primitives we have previously defined. Note that the primary difference here stems from the fact that the protocol we consider is in the simultaneous message model. We say that a protocol satisfying the above properties is bounded rewind secure if the protocol remains secure in the presence of an that adversary is able to rewind the honest parties in the second and third round of the execution. Specifically, an adversary is allowed to: (a) initially query $B - 1$ many distinct second round messages and receive third round messages in response; (b) in the last (B-th) query, the adversary also includes inputs for the honest parties. The adversary should then be unable to distinguish between the case that the protocol completes from the B-th query onward, where the last round was either completed with honest inputs provided by the adversary, or simulated.

Instantiation. On plugging in the bounded rewind-secure OT constructed in the previous section into the semi-malicious protocols of [5, 14] gives us the required delayed input MPC protocol with bounded rewind security.

5   Four Round MPC

Building Blocks. We list below all the building blocks of our protocol.

- **Trapdoor Generation Protocol:** $\mathsf{TDGen} = (\mathsf{TDGen}_1, \mathsf{TDGen}_2, \mathsf{TDGen}_3, \mathsf{TDOut}, \mathsf{TDValid}, \mathsf{TDExt})$ is a three round B_{td}-rewind secure trapdoor generation protocol based on one-way functions (see Sect. 3.2). We set B_{td} to be 2.
  In our MPC construction, we use a "multi-receiver" version of TDGen that works as follows: whenever a sender party i sends its first round message td_1, *all* of the other $(n-1)$ parties send a second round receiver message $\mathsf{td}_{2,i}$. The sender now prepares $\mathsf{td}_2 = (\mathsf{td}_{2,1}|| \ldots ||\mathsf{td}_{2,n-1})$, and then uses it to compute td_3. All the $(n-1)$ receivers individually verify the validity of td_3.
- **Delayed-Input WI Argument:** $\mathsf{WI} = (\mathsf{WI}_1, \mathsf{WI}_2, \mathsf{WI}_3, \mathsf{WI}_4)$ is a three round delayed-input witness indistinguishable proof system (see Sect. 3.3), where WI_4 is used to compute the decision of the verifier.
- **Bounded-Rewind Secure WI Argument:** $\mathsf{RWI} = (\mathsf{RWI}_1, \mathsf{RWI}_2, \mathsf{RWI}_3, \mathsf{RWI}_4)$ is a three round delayed-input witness-indistinguishable proof with B_{rwi_a}-rewind security (see Sect. 3.3). RWI_4 is used to compute the decision of the verifier. We will use two different instances of RWI that we will refer to as RWI_a and RWI_b, where the subscripts a and b denote the different instances. We set their respective rewind security parameters B_{rwi_a} and B_{rwi_b} to be some fixed polynomial.
- **Special Non-malleable Commitment:** $\mathsf{NMCom} = \big(\mathsf{NMCom}_1, \mathsf{NMCom}_2,$ $\mathsf{NMCom}_3\big)$ is a three round special non-malleable commitment scheme. Let $\mathsf{Ext}_{\mathsf{NMCom}}$ denote the extractor associated with NMCom.
- **Bounded-Rewind Secure Extractable Commitment:** $\mathsf{RECom} = (\mathsf{RECom}_1, \mathsf{RECom}_2, \mathsf{RECom}_3)$ is the three round B_{recom}-rewind secure delayed-input extractable commitment based on non-interactive commitments (see Section 3.1). We set rewinding security parameter B_{recom} to be 4. $\mathsf{Ext}_{\mathsf{RECom}}$ is the extractor associated with RECom.
- **Extractable Commitment:** $\mathsf{Ecom} = (\mathsf{Ecom}_1, \mathsf{Ecom}_2, \mathsf{Ecom}_3, \mathsf{Ext}_{\mathsf{Ecom}})$ is the three round delayed-input extractable commitment scheme based on statistically binding commitment schemes. They satisfy the 2-extraction property.
- **Delayed Semi-Malicious MPC:** Π is a four round B_Π-bounded rewind secure delayed input MPC protocol based on oblivious transfer (see Sect. 4.3). We set B_Π to be 9.
- **Garbled Circuits:** $\mathsf{GC} = (\mathsf{Garble}, \mathsf{Eval})$ is a secure garbling scheme. We denote the labels $\{\mathsf{lab}_{i,0}, \mathsf{lab}_{i,1}\}_{i \in [L]}$ by $\overline{\mathsf{lab}}$. We will often partition the labels of the garbled circuit to indicate the party providing the input corresponding to the label indices, and denote this by $\overline{\mathsf{lab}}_{|_j}$ for party j.

- **Oblivious Transfer:** $\mathsf{OT} = (\mathsf{OT}_1, \mathsf{OT}_2, \mathsf{OT}_3, \mathsf{OT}_4)$ is a four round oblivious transfer protocol. We abuse notation slightly and use this as implementing parallel OT executions where the receiver's input is a string of length ℓ and the sender now has ℓ pairs of inputs. We require regular indistinguishability security against a malicious sender. In addition, we require extraction of the receiver's input bit.

Levels of Rewind Security. We recall the notion of bounded-rewind security and the need for levels of rewind security. Bounded-rewind security, as in [3], is used in the security proof to argue indistinguishability in intermediate hybrids. The main idea is that when arguing indistinguishability of two hybrids, to derive a contradiction it suffices to build an adversary with non-negligible success probability. As such, as long as the adversary does not abort with some non-negligible probability (which is indeed true), a small constant number of rewinds are sufficient for extracting with non-negligible probability. The exact bounded-rewind security constants for various primitives are carefully set to establish various "levels" of security.

For primitives with bounded rewind security, we require

$$B_{\mathsf{rwi}_a}, B_{\mathsf{rwi}_b}, B_\Pi > B_{\mathsf{recom}} > B_{\mathsf{td}}$$

where they denote the total number of rewinds (including the main thread) that they are secure against. In addition, we require all of them to be larger than the number of threads required to extract from NMCom and Ecom. For the above primitives, we have $B_{\mathsf{rwi}_a} = B_{\mathsf{rwi}_b} = \mathsf{poly}(\lambda)$ (for some fixed polynomial), $B_\Pi = 9$, $B_{\mathsf{recom}} = 4$ and $B_{\mathsf{td}} = 2$ thus satisfying our requirements.

Notation for Transcripts. We introduce a common notation that we shall use to denote *partial* transcripts of an execution of different protocols that we use in our MPC construction. For any execution of protocol X, we use $\mathbf{T}_X[\ell]$ to denote the transcript of the first ℓ rounds.

NP Languages. We define the NP languages used for the three different proof systems that we use in our protocol. We denote statements and witnesses as st and w, respectively.

1. RWI_a: We use RWI_a for language L_a, which is characterized by the following relation R_a:

$$\mathsf{st} := \left(\mathbf{T}_\Pi[2], \left\{ \mathbf{T}_{\mathsf{recom}}^j[3] \right\}_{j \in [n]}, \{\mathsf{msg}_\ell\}_{\ell \in [3]}, \mathbf{T}_{\mathsf{ncom}}[3], \mathsf{td}_1 \right)$$

$$\mathsf{w} := \left(\mathsf{inp}, \mathsf{r}, \left\{ \mathsf{r}_{\mathsf{recom}}^j \right\}_{j \in [n]}, \mathsf{t}, \mathsf{r}_{\mathsf{ncom}} \right)$$

$R_a(\mathsf{st}, \mathsf{w}) = 1$ if *either* of the following conditions is satisfied:

(a) **Honest:** *all* of the following conditions hold:
  - $\forall j$, $\mathbf{T}_{\mathsf{recom}}^j[3]$ is a well-formed transcript of RECom w.r.t. input $(\mathsf{inp}, \mathsf{r})$ and randomness $\mathsf{r}_{\mathsf{recom}}^j$.
  - for every $\ell \leq 3$, msg_ℓ is an honestly computed ℓ^{th} round message in the protocol Π w.r.t. input inp, randomness r and the first $(\ell - 1)$ round protocol transcript $\mathbf{T}_\Pi[\ell - 1]$.

(b) **Trapdoor:** $\mathbf{T}_{\mathsf{ncom}}[3]$ is an honest transcript of NMCom w.r.t. input t and randomness $\mathsf{r}_{\mathsf{ncom}}$ (AND) t is a valid trapdoor w.r.t. td_1

---

2. RWI_b: We use RWI_b for language L_b, which is characterized by the following relation R_b:

$$\mathsf{st} := \left(\left\{ \mathbf{T}^j_{\mathsf{rwi}_a}[2], \mathsf{st}^j_a, \mathbf{T}^j_{\mathsf{ecom}}[3] \right\}_{j \in [n]}, \mathbf{T}_{\mathsf{ncom}}[3], \mathsf{td}_1 \right)$$

$$\mathsf{w} := \left(\left\{ r^j_{\mathsf{rwi}_a}, w^j_a, \mathsf{rwi}^j_{3,a}, r^j_{\mathsf{ecom}} \right\}_{j \in [n]}, \mathsf{t}, r_{\mathsf{ncom}} \right).$$

$R_b(\mathsf{st}, \mathsf{w}) = 1$ if *either* of the following conditions is satisfied:

(a) **Honest:** *all* of the following conditions hold:
   - $\forall j$, $\mathbf{T}^j_{\mathsf{ecom}}[3]$ is a well-formed transcript of Ecom w.r.t. input $\left\{ \mathsf{rwi}^k_{3,a} \right\}_{k \in [n]}$ and randomness r^j_{ecom}.
   - $\forall j$, $\mathbf{T}^j_{\mathsf{rwi}_a}[2] \| \mathsf{rwi}^j_{3,a}$ is an honestly computed transcript of RWI_a for L_a with statement st^j_a, witness w^j_a and randomness $r^j_{\mathsf{rwi}_a}$.[a]

(b) **Trapdoor:** $\mathbf{T}_{\mathsf{ncom}}[3]$ is an honest transcript of NMCom w.r.t. input t and randomness r_{ncom} (AND) t is a valid trapdoor w.r.t. td_1

---

[a] Since RWI is not publicly verifiable, the relation establishes that the RWI prover messages were computed honestly w.r.t. the witness and randomness for the statement.

---

3. WI: We use WI for language L_c, which is characterized by the following relation R_c:

$$\mathsf{st} := \left(\left\{ \mathsf{msg}_i, \mathsf{ncom}_i \right\}_{i \in [3]}, \left\{ \mathsf{recom}^j_i \right\}_{i \in [3], j \in [n]}, \left\{ \mathsf{rwi}^j_i \right\}_{i \in [2], j \in [n]}, \right.$$
$$\left. \mathsf{Trans}_3, \left\{ \mathsf{ot}^j_i \right\}_{i \in [4], j \in [n]}, \left\{ \mathsf{st}^j \right\}_{j \in [n]}, \widetilde{\mathsf{C}}, \mathsf{td}_1, \mathbf{T}_{\mathsf{NMCom}}[3] \right)$$

$$\mathsf{w} := \left(\mathsf{inp}, \mathsf{r}, \left\{ r^j_{\mathsf{recom}}, r^j_{\mathsf{ot}}, r^j_{\mathsf{rwi}} \right\}_{j \in [n]}, \mathsf{msg}_4, r_{\mathsf{gc}}, \mathsf{t}, r_{\mathsf{ncom}} \right)$$

$R_c(\mathsf{st}, \mathsf{w}) = 1$ if *either* of the following conditions is satisfied:

(a) **Honest:** For every j, *all* of the following conditions hold:
   - $\mathbf{T}^j_{\mathsf{recom}}[3]$ is a well-formed transcript of RECom w.r.t. input $(\mathsf{inp}, \mathsf{r})$ and randomness r^j_{recom}.
   - msg_4 is honestly computed round 4 message of Π w.r.t. inp, randomness r and transcript $\mathbf{T}_\Pi[3]$.
   - $(\widetilde{\mathsf{C}}, \overline{\mathsf{lab}})$ is honest garbling of C that contains hardwired values $\mathsf{msg}_4, \left\{ \mathbf{T}^j_{\mathsf{rwi}}[2], \mathsf{st}^j, r^j_{\mathsf{rwi}} \right\}_{j \in [n]}$, using randomness r_{gc}. (See Figure 2.)
   - ot^j_4 is honestly computed using $\overline{\mathsf{lab}}_{|_j}$, randomness r^j_{ot} and transcript $\mathbf{T}^j_{\mathsf{ot}}[3]$. $(\mathbf{T}^j_{\mathsf{ot}}[4] = \mathbf{T}^j_{\mathsf{ot}}[3] \| \mathsf{ot}^j_4)$.

(b) **Trapdoor:** $\mathbf{T}_{\mathsf{ncom}}[3]$ is an honest transcript of NMCom w.r.t. input t and randomness r_{ncom} (AND) t is a valid trapdoor w.r.t. td_1

$$\mathsf{C}\left[\mathsf{msg}_4, \left\{ \mathbf{T}^j_{\mathsf{rwi}_b}[2], \mathsf{st}^j_b, r^j_{\mathsf{rwi}_b} \right\}_{j \in [n]} \right]$$

Input: $\{\mathsf{rwi}^j_{3,b}\}_{j \in [n]}$

- If for every $j \neq i$, $\mathsf{RWI}_4\left(\mathsf{st}^j_b, \mathbf{T}^j_{\mathsf{rwi}_b}[2] \| \mathsf{rwi}^j_{3,b}; r^j_{\mathsf{rwi}_b} \right) = 1$, **output** msg_4;
- Else, **output** $\perp$.

Fig. 2. Circuit C

5.1 The Protocol

In this section, we describe our four round MPC protocol between n players $P_1, \cdots, P_n$. Let x_i denote the input of party P_i. At the start of the protocol, each party samples a sufficiently long random tape to use in the various sub-protocols; let r_X denote the randomness used in sub-protocol X.

Notational Conventions. We establish some conventions for simplifying notation in the protocol description. We only indicate randomness as an explicit input for computing the first round message of a sub-protocol; for subsequent computations, we assume it to be an implicit input. Similarly, we assume that any next-message of a sub-protocol takes as input a partial transcript of the "previous" rounds, and do not write it explicitly. Whenever necessary, we augment our notation with superscript $i \rightarrow j$ to indicate the a instance of an execution of a sub-protocol between a "sender" i and "receiver" j (where sometimes, the sender is a prover and receiver is a verifier). When the specific instance is clear from context, we shall drop the superscript. When we wish to refer to multiple instances involving a party i, we will use the shorthand superscript $i \rightarrow \bullet$ or $\bullet \rightarrow i$, depending upon whether i is the sender or the receiver. For example, $\mathbf{T}^{i \rightarrow \bullet}_X[\ell]$ will be a shorthand to indicate $\left\{ \mathbf{T}^{i \rightarrow j}_X[\ell] \right\}_{j \in [n]}$.

We will sometimes use explanatory comments within the protocol description, denoted as //comment. Finally, we note that all messages in the protocol are broadcast; if any party aborts during the first three rounds of the protocol, it broadcasts an abort in the subsequent round. We do not write this explicitly in the protocol, and assume it to be implicit. We now proceed to describe the protocol.

Round 1: P_i computes and broadcasts the *first* round messages of the following protocols:

1. Delayed semi-malicious MPC Π: $\mathsf{msg}_{1,i} \leftarrow \Pi_1(r_i)$.
2. Sender message of TDGen: $\mathsf{td}_{1,i} \leftarrow \mathsf{TDGen}_1(r_{\mathsf{td},i})$.

For every $j \neq i$:

3. Prover message of the three delayed-input WI argument systems
   - WI: $\mathsf{wi}_1^{i \to j} \leftarrow \mathsf{WI}_1(r_{\mathsf{wi}}^{i \to j})$.
   - RWI_a: $\mathsf{rwi}_{a,1}^{i \to j} \leftarrow \mathsf{RWI}_1(r_{\mathsf{rwi}_a}^{i \to j})$.
   - RWI_b: $\mathsf{rwi}_{b,1}^{i \to j} \leftarrow \mathsf{RWI}_1(r_{\mathsf{rwi}_b}^{i \to j})$.

4. Sender message of the three delayed-input commitment schemes
   - Ecom: $\mathsf{ecom}_1^{i \to j} \leftarrow \mathsf{Ecom}_1(r_{\mathsf{ecom}}^{i \to j})$.
   - RECom: $\mathsf{recom}_1^{i \to j} \leftarrow \mathsf{RECom}_1(r_{\mathsf{recom}}^{i \to j})$.
   - NMCom: $\mathsf{ncom}_1^{i \to j} \leftarrow \mathsf{NMCom}_1(r_{\mathsf{ncom}}^{i \to j})$.
5. Receiver message of OT: $\mathsf{ot}_1^{j \to i} \leftarrow \mathsf{OT}_1(r_{\mathsf{ot}}^{j \to i})$.

Round 2: P_i computes and broadcasts the *second* round messages of the following protocols:

1. Delayed semi-malicious MPC Π: $\mathsf{msg}_{2,i} \leftarrow \Pi_2$.

For every $j \neq i$:

2. Receiver message of TDGen: $\mathsf{td}_2^{i \to j} \leftarrow \mathsf{TDGen}_2$.
3. Verifier message of the three delayed-input WI argument systems
   - WI: $\mathsf{wi}_2^{j \to i} \leftarrow \mathsf{WI}_2$
   - RWI_a: $\mathsf{rwi}_{a,2}^{j \to i} \leftarrow \mathsf{RWI}_2$
   - RWI_b: $\mathsf{rwi}_{b,2}^{j \to i} \leftarrow \mathsf{RWI}_2$
4. Receiver message of the three delayed-input commitment schemes
   - Ecom: $\mathsf{ecom}_2^{j \to i} \leftarrow \mathsf{Ecom}_2$.
   - RECom: $\mathsf{recom}_2^{j \to i} \leftarrow \mathsf{RECom}_2$.
   - NMCom: $\mathsf{ncom}_2^{j \to i} \leftarrow \mathsf{NMCom}_2$.
5. Sender message of OT: $\mathsf{ot}_2^{i \to j} \leftarrow \mathsf{OT}_2$.

Round 3: P_i computes and broadcasts the *third* round messages of the following protocols:

1. Delayed semi-malicious Π: $\mathsf{msg}_{3,i} \leftarrow \Pi_3(x_i)$ using input x_i. //First step where P_i is using its input.
2. TDGen: $\mathsf{td}_{3,i} \leftarrow \mathsf{TDGen}_3$.

For every $j \neq i$:

3. NMCom: $\mathsf{ncom}_3^{i \to j} \leftarrow \mathsf{NMCom}_3(\tilde{r}_j)$ to commit to a random $\tilde{r}_j$.
4. RECom: $\mathsf{recom}_3^{i \to j} \leftarrow \mathsf{RECom}_3(x_i, r_i)$ to commit to (x_i, r_i).
5. RWI: $\mathsf{rwi}_{a,3}^{i \to j} \leftarrow \mathsf{RWI}_3(\mathsf{st}_a^{i \to j}, w_a^{i \to j})$ to prove that $R_a(\mathsf{st}_a^{i \to j}, w_a^{i \to j}) = 1$, where

   $$\text{Statement } \mathsf{st}_a^{i \to j} := (\mathbf{T}_{\Pi}[2], \mathbf{T}_{\mathsf{recom}}^{i \to \bullet}[3], \{\mathsf{msg}_{\ell,i}\}_{\ell \in [3]}, \mathbf{T}_{\mathsf{ncom}}^{i \to j}[3], \mathsf{td}_{1,j})$$

   "Honest" witness $w_a^{i \to j} := (x_i, r_i, r_{\mathsf{recom}}^{i \to \bullet})$

6. Ecom: $\mathsf{ecom}_3^{i \to j} \leftarrow \mathsf{Ecom}_3(\mathsf{rwi}_{a,3}^{i \to \bullet})$ to commit to $\mathsf{rwi}_{a,3}^{i \to \bullet}$.
7. RWI_b: $\mathsf{rwi}_{b,3}^{i \to j} \leftarrow \mathsf{RWI}_3(\mathsf{st}_b^{i \to j}, w_b^{i \to j})$ to prove that $R_b(\mathsf{st}_b^{i \to j}, w_b^{i \to j}) = 1$, where

   $$\text{Statement } \mathsf{st}_b^{i \to j} := (\mathbf{T}_{\mathsf{rwi}_a}^{i \to \bullet}[2], \mathsf{st}_a^{i \to \bullet}, \mathbf{T}_{\mathsf{ecom}}^{i \to \bullet}[3], \mathbf{T}_{\mathsf{ncom}}^{i \to j}[3], \mathsf{td}_{1,j})$$

   "Honest" witness $w_b^{i \to j} := (r_{\mathsf{rwi}_a}^{i \to \bullet}, w_a^{i \to \bullet}, \mathsf{rwi}_{a,3}^{i \to \bullet}, r_{\mathsf{ecom}}^{i \to \bullet})$

8. OT: Receiver message $\mathsf{ot}_3^{j \to i} \leftarrow \mathsf{OT}_3(\mathsf{rwi}_{b,3}^{i \to j})$ using input $\mathsf{rwi}_{b,3}^{i \to j}$.

Round 4: P_i computes and broadcasts the following messages:

1. If $\exists j \neq i$ such that $\mathsf{TDValid}(\mathsf{td}_{1,j}, \mathsf{td}_{2,j}, \mathsf{td}_{3,j}) \neq 1$, **abort**.
   //where $\mathsf{td}_{2,j} := (\mathsf{td}_2^{1 \to j} || \cdots || \mathsf{td}_2^{n \to j})$.

2. Delayed semi-malicious MPC Π: Fourth round message $\mathsf{msg}_{4,i} \leftarrow \Pi_4$.

3. Garbled Circuit: $\overline{\mathsf{C}}_i$, where $(\overline{\mathsf{C}}_i, \overline{\mathsf{lab}}_i) \leftarrow \mathsf{Garble}(\mathsf{C}[\mathsf{msg}_{4,i}, \mathbf{T}_{\mathsf{rwi}_b}^{\bullet \to i}[2], \mathsf{st}_b^{\bullet \to i}, \mathsf{r}_{\mathsf{rwi}_b}^{\bullet \to i}]; \mathsf{r}_{\mathsf{gc},i})$.
   Circuit C is defined in Figure 2.

For every $j \neq i$:

4. OT: Fourth round sender message $\mathsf{ot}_4^{i \to j} \leftarrow \mathsf{OT}_4\left(\overline{\mathsf{lab}}_{i|_j}\right)$ using input $\overline{\mathsf{lab}}_{i|_j}$.
   //$\overline{\mathsf{lab}}_{i|_j}$ denotes labels corresponding to the input wires for P_j's input.

5. OT: Receiver randomness $\mathsf{r}_{\mathsf{ot}}^{j \to i}$. //This is used by other parties to compute OT output.

6. WI: $\mathsf{wi}_3^{i \to j} \leftarrow \mathsf{WI}_3\left(\mathsf{st}_c^{i \to j}, \mathsf{w}_c^{i \to j}\right)$, to prove that $R_c(\mathsf{st}_c^{i \to j}, \mathsf{w}_c^{i \to j}) = 1$, where
   Statement $\mathsf{st}_c^{i \to j} := (\mathbf{T}_{\Pi}[3], \mathbf{T}_{\mathsf{recom}}^{i \to \bullet}[3], \mathbf{T}_{\mathsf{rwi}_b}^{\bullet \to i}[2], \mathsf{st}_b^{\bullet \to i}, \mathbf{T}_{\mathsf{ot}}^{\bullet \to i}[4], \overline{\mathsf{C}}_i, \mathbf{T}_{\mathsf{ncom}}^{i \to j}[3], \mathsf{td}_{1,j})$
   "Honest" witness $\mathsf{w}_c^{i \to j} := (\mathsf{x}_i, \mathsf{r}_i, \mathsf{r}_{\mathsf{recom}}^{i \to \bullet}, \mathsf{r}_{\mathsf{ot}}^{i \to \bullet}, \mathsf{r}_{\mathsf{rwi}_b}^{\bullet \to i}, \mathsf{msg}_{4,i}, \mathsf{r}_{\mathsf{gc},i})$

Output Computation: P_i computes the following:

1. If $\exists j \neq i$, s.t. $\mathsf{WI}_4(\mathsf{st}_c^{j \to i}, \mathbf{T}_{\mathsf{wi}}^{j \to i}[3]) \neq 1$, output $\bot$ and **abort**.

2. Compute OT outputs: $\forall j \neq i, \forall k \neq \{i, j\}$,
   $\widehat{\mathsf{lab}}_{j|_k} \leftarrow \mathsf{OTEval}(\mathbf{T}_{\mathsf{ot}}^{j \to k}[4]; \mathsf{r}_{\mathsf{ot}}^{j \to k})$

3. Evaluate garbled circuits: $\forall j \neq i$, $\widehat{\mathsf{msg}}_{4,j} \leftarrow \mathsf{Eval}(\overline{\mathsf{C}}_j, \widehat{\mathsf{lab}}_j)$, where $\widehat{\mathsf{lab}}_j := (\widehat{\mathsf{lab}}_{j|_1} || \cdots || \widehat{\mathsf{lab}}_{j|_n})$.
   If any evaluation returns $\bot$, then output $\bot$ and **abort**.

4. Output $y_i \leftarrow \mathsf{OUT}(\mathsf{x}_i, \mathbf{T}_{\Pi}[4]; \mathsf{r}_i)$, where $\mathbf{T}_{\Pi}[4]$ includes $\mathbf{T}_{\Pi}[3]$ and $\widehat{\mathsf{msg}}_{4,j}$ for every j.

Our main result is stated in the following theorem.

Theorem 3. *Assuming the hiding property of oblivious transfer, the hiding property of extractable commitment, the hiding property of extractable commitment with bounded rewind security, delayed semi malicious protocol with bounded rewind security computing any function $\mathcal{F}$, special non-malleable commitments, witness indistinguishable proofs with bounded rewind security, security of garbled circuits, trapdoor generation protocol with bounded rewind security, in addition to the correctness of these primitives, then the presented protocol is a four round protocol for $\mathcal{F}$ secure against a malicious dishonest majority.*

Remark 3. All the above primitives can be based on one-way functions, non-interactive commitments and oblivious transfer (OT). In a recent note by Lombardi and Schaeffer [31], they give a construction of a perfectly binding non-interactive commitment based on perfectly correct key agreement. As they point out, such key agreement schemes can be based on perfectly correct oblivious transfer [15]. This gives us both a non-interactive commitment schemes, and one-way functions, based on perfectly correct oblivious transfer. Thus it suffices to instantiate all our primitives using just oblivious transfer.

We thus have the following corollary.

Corollary 1. *Assuming polynomially secure oblivious transfer with perfect correctness, our constructed protocol is a four round multiparty computation protocol for any function $\mathcal{F}$.*

The complete security analysis of the above protocol is presented in the full version. Below we present a high level description of the main ideas of the proof and how the bounded rewind-security parameters are set.

5.2 Security

We emphasize that our discussion below is informal, and not a complete picture of the simulator and hybrids. Our intent is to give an outline of the key hybrids and simulation steps to convey the main ideas. This will already highlight the need for various levels of rewind security, one of the main challenges in proving security. There are lots of other challenges that we do not discuss here, and similar to prior works, the full security analysis is much more complex and we refer the reader to the full version for the analysis.

One particular challenge that we ignore is that of an aborting adversary, either implicitly or explicitly, in the first three rounds of the protocol. The case of an explicitly aborting adversary is dealt with in a similar manner to [3, 16] by initially sampling a partial transcript, using dummy inputs, to determine if the adversary aborts, and then re-sampling the transcript in case the adversary does not abort. For an implicitly aborting adversary, the simulator (via extraction) can determine if the adversary aborted, but honest parties are not aware of this in the first three rounds of the protocol. This case relies on the security of the multi-party CDS (via OT and garbled circuits) to deal with the implicit aborts. Stepping around these challenges, the main steps in the simulation involve (a) rewinding the adversary to extract the trapdoor and inputs; (b) completing the witness indistinguishable arguments using the extracted trapdoor; (c) simulating the underlying protocol using the output obtained from the ideal functionality.

Key Hybrid Components. We give below a high level overview of some key hybrids in keeping with our simplified description of the simulator above. This will allow us to discuss our specific choices for the level of rewinds.

- The first hybrid is identical to the real protocol execution. Each witness indistinguishable (WI) argument in our protocol allows for a *trapdoor witness*, arising from the trapdoor generation protocol and the non-malleable commitment (NMCom). We would like it to be the case that a simulator is able to derive the trapdoor and produce a simulated transcript via the *trapdoor witness*, an adversary should not be in possession of a *trapdoor witness* thereby forcing honest behavior if the witness indistinguishable argument is accepting.

  In order to argue that the adversary is not in possession of the *trapdoor witness*, we need to ensure the following *invariant*: the adversary does not commit to the trapdoor inside of the NMCom.

  In order to do so in this hybrid, we rely on the rewind security of the trapdoor generation protocol. Specifically, we extract from the NMCom by rewinding the adversary once in the second and third round (two total executions of the second and third round). If indeed the adversary was committing to the trapdoor, the extraction is successful with some noticeable probability and thereby breaking the rewind security of the trapdoor generation protocol. Note, as observed in [3], to arrive at a contradiction via reduction it is sufficient to extract with noticeable (as opposed to overwhelming) probability. This explains why we require $B_{td} \geq 2$.

For each change that we subsequently make through the various primitives, we will bootstrap the above technique, and argue that this invariant continues to hold. Specifically, in order to arrive at a contradiction, we will extract from the NMCom to break the security property of the corresponding primitive if the *invariant* ceases to hold. This already gives us a flavor for primitives to be secure against (at least) two rewinds needed for the extraction from the NMCom.

- In this hybrid, the simulator creates sufficient rewind execution threads in order to extract the adversary's input and the trapdoors needed to prove the WI using the *trapdoor witness*. These rewind threads have the same first round messages as the "main" execution thread, but the second and third round messages are computed in each rewind thread with fresh randomness. The rewind threads terminate on completion of the third round of the protocol.

- In the previous hybrid, the simulator is still using the honest inputs in the rewind threads. In this hybrid the rewind threads are switched from using the honest party's inputs, to an honest execution with input 0. Note that these threads finish by the end of the third round.

While the changes made in this hybrid are done in a sequence of steps, and needs to be argued carefully, the sequence closely resembles the changes that will be made in the main execution thread below. Therefore, we primarily focus on the hybrids pertaining to the main execution thread.

- In this hybrid, the simulator uses the trapdoors extracted from the rewind threads to commit to the trapdoor inside the NMCom on the main execution thread. In order to argue indistinguishability, we perform a reduction to an external NMCom challenger. In order to generate the transcript internally, and complete the reduction, we need to rewind the adversary to get the trapdoor and inputs. But this causes a problem since the rewind threads might require responses to challenges that are meant for the external challenger. Here, we rely on the fact that the third round of our instantiated NMCom has pseudorandom messages, allowing us to respond to adversarial queries in the third round, that cannot be forwarded to the external NMCom challenger. This prevents the need for bounded rewind security from the NMCom.

- In a sequence of sub-hybrids, the simulator uses the extracted trapdoor to complete both the bounded rewind secure witness indistinguishable arguments using the *trapdoor witness*. As seen above, for the reduction we will need to rewind the adversary to extract, thereby rewinding the external challenger. Since we require extraction of the adversary's inputs, the parameter for the bounded rewind secure witness indistinguishable argument needs to satisfy $B_{rwi} > B_{recom}$.

- In this hybrid, the simulator uses the extracted trapdoor to complete the witness indistinguishable argument. Since the third round of this protocol is completed in the fourth round of our compiled protocol, rewinding the adversary to extract the trapdoor and input in the second and third round circumvents issues discussed above. Therefore, we don't require this primitive to be rewind secure.

- In this hybrid, the simulator switches to committing to 0 inside the rewind secure extractable commitment (RECom). Unlike the previous cases, this is potentially circularity since the arguments above do not directly extend. This is because it cannot be the case that the external challenger remains secure if we rewind the adversary B_{recom} times to extract its input.

Instead, this is argued carefully where initially we argue that switching to a commitment of a "junk" value in the third round of the RECom doesn't affect our ability to extract from the adversary. This "junk" commitment can be made without knowledge of any randomness of the specific RECom instance. To argue this, we rely on the bounded rewind security of the extractable commitment, while still extracting the trapdoor to complete the transcript. This gives us the requirement that $B_{\mathsf{recom}} > B_{\mathsf{td}}$. This then allows for extraction of input in the reduction without violating rewinding circularity since, on the look ahead threads to extract, we can commit to junk without affecting input extraction.

- In this hybrid, the simulator simulates the transcript of the underlying bounded rewind secure protocol Π. Here too, we require extracting the inputs in order to send it to the ideal functionality. Therefore, we require $B_\Pi > B_{\mathsf{recom}}$.

Acknowledgments. We would like to thank Alex Lombardi and Luke Schaeffer for pointing out to us that any OT with perfect completeness implies non-interactive commitment schemes, and, for suggesting to us to revise our theorem statements to reflect this observation. Vipul Goyal is supported in part by the NSF award 1916939, a gift from Ripple, a JP Morgan Faculty Fellowship, a PNC center for financial services innovation award, and a Cylab seed funding award. Arka Rai Choudhuri and Abhishek Jain are supported in part by DARPA/ARL Safeware Grant W911NF-15-C-0213, NSF CNS-1814919, NSF CAREER 1942789, Samsung Global Research Outreach award and Johns Hopkins University Catalyst award. Arka Rai Choudhuri is also supported by NSF Grants CNS-1908181, CNS-1414023, and the Office of Naval Research Grant N00014-19-1-2294. Rafail Ostrovsky is supported in part by NSF-BSF Grant 1619348, DARPA/SPAWAR N66001-15-C-4065, ODNI/IARPA 2019-1902070008 US-Israel BSF grant 2012366, JP Morgan Faculty Award, Google Faculty Research Award, OKAWA Foundation Research Award, IBM Faculty Research Award, Xerox Faculty Research Award, B. John Garrick Foundation Award, Teradata Research Award, and Lockheed-Martin Corporation Research Award. The views and conclusions contained herein are those of the authors and should not be interpreted as necessarily representing the official views or policies, either expressed or implied, of the Department of Defense, DARPA, ODNI, IARPA, or the U.S. Government. The U.S. Government is authorized to reproduce and distribute reprints for governmental purposes notwithstanding any copyright annotation therein. Michele Ciampi was partially supported by H2020 project PRIVILEDGE #780477.

References

1. Aiello, B., Ishai, Y., Reingold, O.: Priced oblivious transfer: how to sell digital goods. In: Pfitzmann, B. (ed.) EUROCRYPT 2001. LNCS, vol. 2045, pp. 119–135. Springer, Heidelberg (2001). https://doi.org/10.1007/3-540-44987-6_8

2. Ananth, P., Choudhuri, A.R., Jain, A.: A new approach to round-optimal secure multiparty computation. In: Katz, J., Shacham, H. (eds.) CRYPTO 2017. LNCS, vol. 10401, pp. 468–499. Springer, Cham (2017). https://doi.org/10.1007/978-3-319-63688-7_16

3. Badrinarayanan, S., Goyal, V., Jain, A., Kalai, Y.T., Khurana, D., Sahai, A.: Promise zero knowledge and its applications to round optimal MPC. In: Shacham, H., Boldyreva, A. (eds.) CRYPTO 2018. LNCS, vol. 10992, pp. 459–487. Springer, Cham (2018). https://doi.org/10.1007/978-3-319-96881-0_16

4. Beaver, D., Micali, S., Rogaway, P.: The round complexity of secure protocols (extended abstract). In: 22nd ACM STOC, pp. 503–513. ACM Press, May 1990. https://doi.org/10.1145/100216.100287

5. Benhamouda, F., Lin, H.: k-round multiparty computation from k-round oblivious transfer via garbled interactive circuits. In: Nielsen, J.B., Rijmen, V. (eds.) EUROCRYPT 2018. LNCS, vol. 10821, pp. 500–532. Springer, Cham (2018). https://doi.org/10.1007/978-3-319-78375-8_17

6. Brakerski, Z., Halevi, S., Polychroniadou, A.: Four round secure computation without setup. In: Kalai, Y., Reyzin, L. (eds.) TCC 2017. LNCS, vol. 10677, pp. 645–677. Springer, Cham (2017). https://doi.org/10.1007/978-3-319-70500-2_22

7. Choudhuri, A.R., Ciampi, M., Goyal, V., Jain, A., Ostrovsky, R.: Round optimal secure multiparty computation from minimal assumptions. Cryptology ePrint Archive, Report 2019/216 (2019). https://eprint.iacr.org/2019/216

8. Ciampi, M., Ostrovsky, R., Siniscalchi, L., Visconti, I.: Delayed-input non-malleable zero knowledge and multi-party coin tossing in four rounds. In: Kalai, Y., Reyzin, L. (eds.) TCC 2017. LNCS, vol. 10677, pp. 711–742. Springer, Cham (2017). https://doi.org/10.1007/978-3-319-70500-2_24

9. Ciampi, M., Ostrovsky, R., Siniscalchi, L., Visconti, I.: Round-optimal secure two-party computation from trapdoor permutations. In: Kalai, Y., Reyzin, L. (eds.) TCC 2017. LNCS, vol. 10677, pp. 678–710. Springer, Cham (2017). https://doi.org/10.1007/978-3-319-70500-2_23

10. Dolev, D., Dwork, C., Naor, M.: Non-malleable cryptography (extended abstract). In: 23rd ACM STOC, pp. 542–552. ACM Press, May 1991. https://doi.org/10.1145/103418.103474

11. Dwork, C., Naor, M.: Zaps and their applications. In: 41st FOCS, pp. 283–293. IEEE Computer Society Press, November 2000. https://doi.org/10.1109/SFCS.2000.892117

12. Garg, S., Gentry, C., Sahai, A., Waters, B.: Witness encryption and its applications. In: Boneh, D., Roughgarden, T., Feigenbaum, J. (eds.) 45th ACM STOC, pp. 467–476. ACM Press, June 2013. https://doi.org/10.1145/2488608.2488667

13. Garg, S., Mukherjee, P., Pandey, O., Polychroniadou, A.: The exact round complexity of secure computation. In: Fischlin, M., Coron, J.-S. (eds.) EUROCRYPT 2016. LNCS, vol. 9666, pp. 448–476. Springer, Heidelberg (2016). https://doi.org/10.1007/978-3-662-49896-5_16

14. Garg, S., Srinivasan, A.: Two-round multiparty secure computation from minimal assumptions. In: Nielsen, J.B., Rijmen, V. (eds.) EUROCRYPT 2018. LNCS, vol. 10821, pp. 468–499. Springer, Cham (2018). https://doi.org/10.1007/978-3-319-78375-8_16

15. Gertner, Y., Kannan, S., Malkin, T., Reingold, O., Viswanathan, M.: The relationship between public key encryption and oblivious transfer. In: 41st FOCS, pp. 325–335. IEEE Computer Society Press, November 2000. https://doi.org/10.1109/SFCS.2000.892121

16. Goldreich, O., Kahan, A.: How to construct constant-round zero-knowledge proof systems for NP. J. Cryptol. **9**(3), 167–189 (1996). https://doi.org/10.1007/BF00208001

17. Goldreich, O., Krawczyk, H.: On the composition of zero-knowledge proof systems. SIAM J. Comput. **25**(1), 169–192 (1996). https://doi.org/10.1137/S0097539791220688

18. Goldreich, O., Micali, S., Wigderson, A.: How to play any mental game or A completeness theorem for protocols with honest majority. In: Aho, A. (ed.) 19th ACM STOC, pp. 218–229. ACM Press (May 1987). https://doi.org/10.1145/28395.28420

19. Goldreich, O., Micali, S., Wigderson, A.: How to prove all NP statements in zero-knowledge and a methodology of cryptographic protocol design (extended abstract). In: Odlyzko, A.M. (ed.) CRYPTO 1986. LNCS, vol. 263, pp. 171–185. Springer, Heidelberg (1987). https://doi.org/10.1007/3-540-47721-7_11

20. Goldwasser, S., Micali, S., Rackoff, C.: The knowledge complexity of interactive proof systems. SIAM J. Comput. **18**(1), 186–208 (1989)

21. Goyal, V.: Constant round non-malleable protocols using one way functions. In: Fortnow, L., Vadhan, S.P. (eds.) 43rd ACM STOC, pp. 695–704. ACM Press, June 2011. https://doi.org/10.1145/1993636.1993729

22. Goyal, V., Pandey, O., Richelson, S.: Textbook non-malleable commitments. In: Wichs, D., Mansour, Y. (eds.) 48th ACM STOC, pp. 1128–1141. ACM Press, June 2016. https://doi.org/10.1145/2897518.2897657

23. Goyal, V., Richelson, S.: Non-malleable commitments using Goldreich-Levin list decoding. In: Zuckerman, D. (ed.) 60th FOCS, pp. 686–699. IEEE Computer Society Press, November 2019. https://doi.org/10.1109/FOCS.2019.00047

24. Goyal, V., Richelson, S.: Non-malleable commitments using goldreich-levin list decoding. In: FOCS (2019)

25. Halevi, S., Hazay, C., Polychroniadou, A., Venkitasubramaniam, M.: Round-optimal secure multi-party computation. In: Shacham, H., Boldyreva, A. (eds.) CRYPTO 2018. LNCS, vol. 10992, pp. 488–520. Springer, Cham (2018). https://doi.org/10.1007/978-3-319-96881-0_17

26. Ishai, Y., Prabhakaran, M., Sahai, A.: Founding cryptography on oblivious transfer – efficiently. In: Wagner, D. (ed.) CRYPTO 2008. LNCS, vol. 5157, pp. 572–591. Springer, Heidelberg (2008). https://doi.org/10.1007/978-3-540-85174-5_32

27. Jain, A., Kalai, Y.T., Khurana, D., Rothblum, R.: Distinguisher-dependent simulation in two rounds and its applications. In: Katz, J., Shacham, H. (eds.) CRYPTO 2017. LNCS, vol. 10402, pp. 158–189. Springer, Cham (2017). https://doi.org/10.1007/978-3-319-63715-0_6

28. Katz, J., Ostrovsky, R.: Round-optimal secure two-party computation. In: Franklin, M. (ed.) CRYPTO 2004. LNCS, vol. 3152, pp. 335–354. Springer, Heidelberg (2004). https://doi.org/10.1007/978-3-540-28628-8_21

29. Katz, J., Ostrovsky, R., Smith, A.: Round efficiency of multi-party computation with a dishonest majority. In: Biham, E. (ed.) EUROCRYPT 2003. LNCS, vol. 2656, pp. 578–595. Springer, Heidelberg (2003). https://doi.org/10.1007/3-540-39200-9_36

30. Kilian, J.: Founding cryptography on oblivious transfer. In: 20th ACM STOC, pp. 20–31. ACM Press, May 1988. https://doi.org/10.1145/62212.62215

31. Lombardi, A., Schaeffer, L.: A note on key agreement and non-interactive commitments. Cryptology ePrint Archive, Report 2019/279 (2019). https://eprint.iacr.org/2019/279

32. Pass, R.: Bounded-concurrent secure multi-party computation with a dishonest majority. In: Babai, L. (ed.) 36th ACM STOC, pp. 232–241. ACM Press, June 2004. https://doi.org/10.1145/1007352.1007393

33. Pass, R., Wee, H.: Constant-round non-malleable commitments from sub-exponential one-way functions. In: Gilbert, H. (ed.) EUROCRYPT 2010. LNCS, vol. 6110, pp. 638–655. Springer, Heidelberg (2010). https://doi.org/10.1007/978-3-642-13190-5_32

34. Prabhakaran, M., Rosen, A., Sahai, A.: Concurrent zero knowledge with logarithmic round-complexity. In: 43rd FOCS, pp. 366–375. IEEE Computer Society Press, November 2002. https://doi.org/10.1109/SFCS.2002.1181961

35. Rosen, A.: A note on constant-round zero-knowledge proofs for NP. In: Naor, M. (ed.) TCC 2004. LNCS, vol. 2951, pp. 191–202. Springer, Heidelberg (2004). https://doi.org/10.1007/978-3-540-24638-1_11

36. Wee, H.: Black-box, round-efficient secure computation via non-malleability amplification. In: 51st FOCS, pp. 531–540. IEEE Computer Society Press, October 2010. https://doi.org/10.1109/FOCS.2010.87

37. Yao, A.C.C.: How to generate and exchange secrets (extended abstract). In: 27th FOCS, pp. 162–167. IEEE Computer Society Press, October 1986. https://doi.org/10.1109/SFCS.1986.25

Reusable Two-Round MPC from DDH

James Bartusek[1]([✉]), Sanjam Garg[1], Daniel Masny[2], and Pratyay Mukherjee[2]

[1] University of California, Berkeley, USA
{jamesbartusek,sanjamg}@berkeley.edu
[2] Visa Research, Palo Alto, USA
{dmasny,pratmukh}@visa.com

Abstract. We present a reusable two-round multi-party computation (MPC) protocol from the Decisional Diffie Hellman assumption (DDH). In particular, we show how to upgrade *any* secure two-round MPC protocol to allow reusability of its first message across multiple computations, using Homomorphic Secret Sharing (HSS) and pseudorandom functions in NC^1— each of which can be instantiated from DDH.

In our construction, if the underlying two-round MPC protocol is secure against semi-honest adversaries (in the plain model) then so is our reusable two-round MPC protocol. Similarly, if the underlying two-round MPC protocol is secure against malicious adversaries (in the common random/reference string model) then so is our reusable two-round MPC protocol.

Previously, such reusable two-round MPC protocols were only known under assumptions on lattices. At a technical level, we show how to upgrade any two-round MPC protocol to a *first message succinct* two-round MPC protocol, where the first message of the protocol is generated *independently* of the computed circuit (though it is not reusable). This step uses homomorphic secret sharing (HSS) and low-depth pseudorandom functions. Next, we show a generic transformation that upgrades any first message succinct two-round MPC to allow for reusability of its first message.

1 Introduction

Motivating Scenario. Consider the following setting: a set of n hospitals publish encryptions of their sensitive patient information $x_1, \ldots, x_n$. At a later stage, for the purposes of medical research, they wish to securely evaluate a circuit C_1 on their joint data by publishing just one additional message - that is, they wish to jointly compute $C_1(x_1, \ldots, x_n)$ by each broadcasting a single message, without revealing anything more than the output of the computation. Can they do so? Furthermore, what if they want to additionally compute circuits $C_2, C_3 \ldots$ at a later point on the same set of inputs?

Supported in part from AFOSR Award FA9550-19-1-0200, NSF CNS Award 1936826, DARPA SIEVE Award, and research grants by the Sloan Foundation, Visa Inc., and Center for Long-Term Cybersecurity (CLTC, UC Berkeley). Any opinions, findings and conclusions or recommendations expressed in this material are those of the author(s) and do not necessarily reflect the views of the funding agencies.

© International Association for Cryptologic Research 2020
R. Pass and K. Pietrzak (Eds.): TCC 2020, LNCS 12551, pp. 320–348, 2020.
https://doi.org/10.1007/978-3-030-64378-2_12

Seminal results on secure multi-party computation (MPC) left quite a bit to be desired when considering the above potential application. In particular, the initial construction of secure multi-party computation by Goldreich, Micali and Wigderson [GMW87] required parties to interact over a large number of rounds. Even though the round complexity was soon reduced to a constant by Beaver, Micali and Rogaway [BMR90], these protocols fall short of achieving the above vision, where interaction is reduced to the absolute minimum.

Making progress towards this goal, Garg et al. [GGHR14] gave the first constructions of *two-round* MPC protocols, assuming indistinguishability obfuscation [GGH+13] (or, witness encryption [GLS15, GGSW13]) and one-way functions.[1] A very nice feature of the Garg et al. construction is that the first round message is indeed reusable across multiple executions, thereby achieving the above vision. Follow up works realized two-round MPC protocols based on significantly weaker computational assumptions. In particular, two-round MPC protocols based on LWE were obtained [MW16, BP16, PS16], followed by a protocol based on bilinear maps [GS17, BF01, Jou04]. Finally, this line of work culminated with the recent works of Benmahouda and Lin [BL18] and Garg and Srinivasan [GS18], who gave constructions based on the minimal assumption that two-round oblivious transfer (OT) exists.

However, in these efforts targeting two-round MPC protocols with security based on weaker computational assumptions, compromises were made in terms of reusability. In particular, among the above mentioned results only the obfuscation based protocol of Garg et al. [GGHR14] and the lattice based protocols [MW16, BP16, PS16] offer reusability of the first message across multiple executions. Reusability of the first round message is quite desirable. In fact, even in the two-party setting, this problem has received significant attention and has been studied under the notion of non-interactive secure computation [IKO+11, AMPR14, MR17, BJOV18, CDI+19]. In this setting, a receiver first publishes an encryption of its input and later, any sender may send a single message (based on an arbitrary circuit) allowing the receiver to learn the output of the circuit on its input. The multiparty case, which we study in this work, can be seen as a natural generalization of the problem of non-interactive secure computation. In this work we ask:

Can we obtain reusable two-round MPC protocols from assumptions not based on lattices?

1.1   Our Result

In this work, we answer the above question by presenting a general compiler that obtains reusable two-round MPC, starting from any two-round MPC and using homomorphic secret sharing (HSS) [BGI16] and pseudorandom functions in NC^1. In a bit more detail, our main theorem is:

---

[1] The Garg et al. paper required other assumptions. However, since then they have all been shown to be implied by indistinguishability obfuscation and one-way functions.

Theorem 1 (Main Theorem). *Let* $\mathcal{X} \in \{$*semi-honest in plain model, malicious in common random/reference sting model*$\}$*. Assuming the existence of a two-round* $\mathcal{X}$*-MPC protocol, an HSS scheme, and pseudorandom functions in* NC^1*, there exists a* reusable *two-round* $\mathcal{X}$*-MPC protocol.*

We consider the setting where an adversary can corrupt an arbitrary number of parties. We assume that parties have access to a broadcast channel.

Benmahouda and Lin [BL18] and Garg and Srinivasan [GS18] showed how to build a two-round MPC protocol from the DDH assumption. The works of Boyle et al. [BGI16, BGI17] constructed an HSS scheme assuming DDH. Instantiating the primitives in the above theorem, we get the following corollary:

Corollary 2. *Let* $\mathcal{X} \in \{$*semi-honest in plain model, malicious in common random/reference sting model*$\}$*. Assuming DDH, there exists a* reusable *two-round* $\mathcal{X}$*-MPC protocol.*

Previously, constructions of reusable two-round MPC were only known assuming indistinguishability obfuscation [GGHR14, GS17] (or, witness encryption [GLS15, GGSW13]) or were based on multi-key fully-homomorphic encryption (FHE) [MW16, PS16, BP16]. Furthermore, one limitation of the FHE-based protocols is that they are in the CRS model even for the setting of semi-honest adversaries.

We note that the two-round MPC protocols cited above additionally achieve overall communication independent of the computed circuit. This is not the focus of this work. Instead, the aim of this work is to realize two-round MPC with reusability, without relying on lattices. As per our current understanding, MPC protocols with communication independent of the computed circuit are only known using lattice techniques (i.e., FHE [Gen09]). Interestingly, we use HSS, which was originally developed to improve communication efficiency in two-party secure computation protocols, to obtain reusability.

First Message Succinct Two-Round MPC. At the heart of this work is a construction of a *first message succinct* (FMS) two-round MPC protocol— that is, a two-round MPC protocol where the first message of the protocol is computed independently of the circuit being evaluated. In particular, the parties do not need to know the description of the circuit that will eventually be computed over their inputs in the second round. Furthermore, parties do not even need to know the *size* of the circuit to be computed in the second round.[2] This allows parties to publish their first round messages and later compute any arbitrary circuit on their inputs. Formally, we show the following:

Theorem 3. *Let* $\mathcal{X} \in \{$*semi-honest in plain model, malicious in common random/reference sting model*$\}$*. Assuming DDH, there exists a first message succinct two-round* $\mathcal{X}$*-MPC protocol.*

---

[2] Note that this requirement is more stringent than just requiring that the size of the first round message is independent of the computed circuit, which can be achieved using laconic OT [CDG+17] for any two-round MPC protocol.

Such protocols were previously only known based on iO [GGHR14, DHRW16] or assumptions currently needed to realize FHE [MW16, BP16, PS16, ABJ+19]. Note that for the learning-with-errors (LWE) based versions of these protocols, the first message can only be computed knowing the depth (or, an upper bound on the maximum depth) of the circuit to be computed. We find the notion of first message succinct two-round MPC quite natural and expect it be relevant for several other applications. In addition to using HSS in a novel manner, our construction benefits from the powerful garbling techniques realized in recent works [LO13, GHL+14, GLOS15, GLO15, CDG+17, DG17b].

From First Message Succinctness to Reusability. On first thought, the notion of first message succinctness might seem like a minor enhancement. However, we show that this "minor looking" enhancement is sufficient to enable reusable two-round MPC (supporting arbitrary number of computations) generically. More formally:

Theorem 4. *Let $\mathcal{X} \in \{semi\text{-}honest\ in\ plain\ model,\ malicious\ in\ common\ random/reference\ sting\ model\}$. Assuming a first message succinct two-round MPC protocol, there exists a reusable two-round $\mathcal{X}$-MPC protocol.*

Two recent independent works have also explicitly studied reusable two-round MPC, obtaining a variety of results. First, Benhamouda and Lin [BL20] construct reusable two-round MPC from assumptions on bilinear maps. Their techniques are quite different than those used in this paper and, while they need stronger assumptions than us, their protocol does have the advantage that the number of parties participating in the second round need not be known when generating first round messages. In our protocol, the number of parties in the system is a parameter used to generate the first round messages. Second, Ananth et al. [AJJ20] construct semi-honest reusable two-round MPC from lattices in the plain model. Prior work from lattices [MW16] required a CRS even in the semi-honest setting. The work of Ananth et al. [AJJ20] includes essentially the same transformation from "first message succinct" MPC to reusable MPC that constitutes the third step of our construction (see Sect. 2.3).

2 Technical Overview

In this section, we highlight our main ideas for obtaining reusability in two-round MPC. Our construction is achieved in three steps. Our starting point is the recently developed primitive of Homomorphic Secret Sharing (HSS), which realizes the following scenario. A secret s is shared among two parties, who can then non-interactively evaluate a function f over their respective shares, and finally combine the results to learn $f(s)$, but nothing more.

2.1 Step 1: Overview of the scHSS Construction

First, we show how to use a "standard" HSS (for only two parties, and where the reconstruction algorithm is simply addition) to obtain a new kind of HSS, which we call *sharing compact HSS* (scHSS). The main property we achieve with scHSS is the ability to share a secret among n parties, for any n, while maintainting compactness of the share size. In particular, as in standard HSS, the sharing algorithm will be independent of the circuit that will be computed on the shares. We actually obtain a few other advantages over constructions of standard HSS [BGI16, BGI17], namely, we get negligible rather than inverse polynomial evaluation error, and we can support computations of any polynomial-size circuit. To achieve this, we sacrifice compactness of the *evaluated* shares, simplicity of the reconstruction algorithm, and security for multiple evaluations. However, it will only be crucial for us that multiple parties can participate, and that the *sharing* algorithm is compact.

The approach: A sharing-compact HSS scheme consists of three algorithms, Share, Eval, and Dec. Our construction follows the compiler of [GS18] that takes an arbitrary MPC protocol and squishes it to two rounds. At a high level, to share a secret x among n parties, we have the Share algorithm first compute an n-party additive secret sharing $x_1, \ldots, x_n$ of x. Then, it runs the first round of the squished n-party protocol on behalf of each party j with input x_j.[3] Finally, it sets the j'th share to be all of the first round messages, plus the secret state of the j'th party. The Eval algorithm run by party j will simply run the second round of the MPC, and output the resulting message. The Dec algorithm takes all second round messages and reconstructs the output.

Recall that we aim for a sharing-compact HSS, which in particular means that the Share algorithm must be independent of the computation supported during the Eval phase. Thus, the first observation that makes the above approach viable is that the first round of the two-round protocol that results from the [GS18] compiler is *independent* of the particular circuit being computed. Unfortunately, it is *not* generated independently of the *size* of the circuit to be computed, so we must introduce new ideas to remove this size dependence.

The [GS18] compiler: Before further discussing the size dependence issue, we recall the [GS18] compiler. The compiler is applied to any *conforming* MPC protocol, a notion defined in [GS18].[4] Roughly, a conforming protocol operates via a sequence of actions $\phi_1, \ldots, \phi_T$. At the beginning of the protocol, each party j broadcasts a one-time pad of their input, and additionally generates some secret state v_j. The encrypted inputs are arranged into a global public state st, which will be updated throughout the protocol. At each step t, the action $\phi_t = (j, f, g, h)$ is carried out by having party j broadcast the bit $\gamma_t := \mathsf{NAND}(\mathsf{st}_f \oplus v_{j,f}, \mathsf{st}_g \oplus v_{j,g}) \oplus v_{j,h}$. Everybody then updates the global state by setting $\mathsf{st}_h := \gamma_t$. We require that the transcript of the protocol is publicly decodable, so that after the T actions are performed, anybody can learn the (shared) output by inspecting st.

---

[3] Actually, we use an $n\lambda$-party MPC protocol, for reasons that will become clear later in this overview.

[4] We tweak the notion slightly here, so readers familiar with [GS18] may notice some differences in this overview.

Now, the [GS18] compiler works as follows. In the first round of the compiled protocol, each party runs the first round of the conforming protocol and broadcasts a one-time pad of their input. In the second round, each party generates a set of garbled circuits that non-interactively implement the computation phase of the conforming protocol. In particular, this means that an evaluator can use the garbled circuits output by each party to carry out each action $\phi_1, \ldots, \phi_T$, learn the resulting final st, and recover the output. The garbled circuits operate as follows. Each garbled circuit for party j takes as input the public state st, and outputs information that allows recovery of input labels for party j's next garbled circuit, corresponding to an updated version of the public state. To facilitate this, the initial private state of each party must be hard-coded into each of their garbled circuits.

In more detail, consider a particular round t and action $\phi_t = (j^*, f, g, h)$. Each party will output a garbled circuit for this round. We refer to party j^* as the "speaking" party for this round. Party j^*'s garbled circuit will simply use its private state to compute the appropriate NAND gate and update the public state accordingly, outputting the correct labels for party j^*'s next garbled circuit, and the bit γ_t to be broadcast. It remains to show how the garbled circuit of each party $j \neq j^*$ can incorporate this bit γ_t, revealing the correct input label for $their$ next garbled circuit. We refer to party j as the "listening" party. In [GS18], this was facilitated by the use of a two-round oblivious transfer (OT). In the first round, each pair of parties (j, j^*) engages in the first round of multiple OT protocols with j acting as the sender and j^* acting as the receiver. Specifically, j^* sends a set of receiver messages to party j. Then during action t, party j's garbled circuit responds with j's sender message, where the sender's two strings are garbled input labels $\mathsf{lab}_0, \mathsf{lab}_1$ of party j's next garbled circuit. Party j^*'s garbled circuit reveals the randomness used to produce the receiver's message with the appropriate receiver bit γ_t. This allows for public recovery of the label lab_{γ_t}.

However, note that each of the T actions requires its own set of OTs to be generated in the first round. Each is then "used up" in the second round, as the receiver's randomness is revealed in the clear. This is precisely what makes the first round of the resulting MPC protocol depend on the $size$ of the circuit to be computed: the parties must engage in the first round of $\Omega(T)$ oblivious transfers during the first round of the MPC protocol.

Pair-Wise Correlations: As observed also in [GIS18], the point of the first round OT messages was to set up pair-wise correlations between parties that were then exploited in the second round to facilitate the transfer of a bit from party j^*'s garbled circuit to party j's garbled circuit. For simplicity, assume for now that when generating the first round, the parties j and j^* already know the bit γ_t that is to be communicated during action t. This is clearly not the case, but this issue is addressed in [GS18, GIS18] (and here) by generating four sets of correlations, corresponding to each of the four possible settings of the two bits of the public state (α, β) at the indices (f, g) corresponding to action $\phi_t = (j^*, f, g, h)$.

Now observe that the following correlated randomness suffices for this task. Party j receives uniformly random strings $z^{(0)}, z^{(1)} \in \{0,1\}^\lambda$, and party j^* receives the string $z^{(*)} := z^{(\gamma_t)}$. Recall that party j has in mind garbled input labels $\mathsf{lab}_0, \mathsf{lab}_1$ for its next garbled circuit, and wants to reveal lab_{γ_t} in the clear, while keeping $\mathsf{lab}_{1-\gamma_t}$ hidden. Thus, party j's garbled circuit will simply output $(\mathsf{lab}_0 \oplus z^{(0)}, \mathsf{lab}_1 \oplus z^{(1)})$, and party j^*'s garbled circuit outputs $z^{(*)}$. Now, instead of generating first round OT messages, the Share algorithm could simply generate all of the pair-wise correlations and include them as part of the shares. Of course, the number of correlations necessary still depends on T, so we will need the Share algorithm to produce *compact* representations of these correlations.

Compressing Using Constrained PRFs: Consider a pair of parties (j, j^*), and let T_{j^*} be the set of actions where j^* is the speaking party. We need the output of Share to (implicitly) include random strings $\{z_t^{(0)}, z_t^{(1)}\}_{t \in T_{j^*}}$ in j's share and $\{z_t^{(\gamma_t)}\}_{t \in T_{j^*}}$ in j^*'s share. The first set of strings would be easy to represent compactly with a PRF key k_j, letting $z_t^{(b)} := \mathsf{PRF}(k_j, (t, b))$. However, giving the key k_j to party j^* would reveal too much, as it is imperative that we keep $\{z_t^{(1-\gamma_t)}\}_{t \in T_{j^*}}$ hidden from party j^*'s view. We could instead give party j^* a *constrained* version of the key k_j that only allows j^* to evaluate $\mathsf{PRF}(k_j, \cdot)$ on points (t, γ_t). We expect that this idea can be made to work, and one could hope to present a construction based on the security of (single-key) constrained PRFs for constraints in NC^1 (plus a standard PRF computable in NC^1). Such a primitive was achieved in [AMN+18] based on assumptions in a traditional group, however, we aim for a construction from weaker assumptions.

Utilizing HSS: Inspired by [BCGI18, BCG+19], we take a different approach based on HSS. Consider sharing the PRF key k_j between parties j and j^*, producing shares sh_j and sh_{j^*}, and additionally giving party j the key k_j in the clear. During action t, we have parties j and j^* (rather, their garbled circuits) evaluate the following function on their respective shares: if $\gamma_t = 0$, output 0^λ and otherwise, output $\mathsf{PRF}(k_j, t)$. Assuming that the HSS evaluation is correct, and using the fact that HSS reconstruction is *additive* (over $\mathbb{Z}_2$), this produces a pair of outputs (y_j, y_{j^*}) such that if $\gamma_t = 0$, $y_j \oplus y_{j^*} = 0^\lambda$, and if $\gamma_t = 1$, $y_j \oplus y_{j^*} = \mathsf{PRF}(k_j, t)$. Now party j sets $z_t^{(0)} := y_j$ and $z_t^{(1)} := y_j \oplus \mathsf{PRF}(k_j, t)$, and party j^* sets $z_t^{(*)} := y_{j^*}$. This guarantees that $z_t^{(*)} = z_t^{(\gamma_t)}$ and that $z_t^{(1-\gamma_t)} = z_t^{(*)} \oplus \mathsf{PRF}(k_j, t)$, which should be indistinguishable from random to party j^*, who doesn't have k_j in the clear.

Tying Loose Ends: This approach works, except that, as alluded to before, party j's garbled circuit will not necessarily know the bit γ_t when evaluating its HSS share. This is handled by deriving γ_t based on public information (some bits α, β of the public shared state), and the private state of party j^*. Since party j^*'s private state cannot be public information, this derivation must happen within the HSS evaluation, and in particular, the secret randomness that generates j^*'s private state must be part of the secret shared via HSS. In our construction, we compile a conforming protocol where each party j^*'s randomness can be generated by a PRF with key s_{j^*}. Thus, we can share the keys (k_j, s_{j^*}) between parties j and j^*, allowing them to compute output shares with respect to the correct γ_t. Finally, note that the computation performed by HSS essentially only consists of PRF evaluations. Thus, assuming a PRF in NC1 (which follows from DDH [NR97]), we only need to make use of HSS that supports evaluating circuits in NC1, which also follows from DDH [BGI16,BGI17].

Dealing with the $1 - 1/Poly$ Correctness of HSS: We are not quite done, since the [BGI16,BGI17] constructions of HSS only achieve correctness with $1 - 1/\text{poly}$ probability. At first glance, this appears to be straightforward to fix. To complete action $\phi_t = (j^*, f, g, h)$, simply repeat the above λ times, now generating sets $\{z_{t,p}^{(0)}, z_{t,p}^{(1)}\}_{p \in [\lambda]}$ and $\{z_{t,p}^{(*)}\}_{p \in [\lambda]}$, using the values $\{\text{PRF}(k_j, (t, p))\}_{p \in [\lambda]}$. Party j now masks the same labels $\text{lab}_0, \text{lab}_1$ with λ different masks, and to recover lab_{γ_t}, one can unmask each value and take the most frequently occurring string to be the correct label. This does ensure that our scHSS scheme is correct except with negligible probability.

Unfortunately, the $1/\text{poly}$ correctness actually translates to a *security* issue with the resulting scHSS scheme. In particular, it implies that an honest party's evaluated share is indistinguishable from a simulated evaluated share with probability only $1 - 1/\text{poly}$. To remedy this, we actually use an $n\lambda$-party MPC protocol, and refer to each of the $n\lambda$ parties as a "virtual" party. The Share algorithm now additively secret shares the secret x into $n\lambda$ parts, and each of the n real parties participating in the scHSS receives the share of λ virtual parties. We are then able to show that for any set of honest parties, with overwhelming probability, there will exist at least one corresponding virtual party that is "simulatable". The existence of a single simulatable virtual party is enough to prove the security of our construction.

At this point it is important to point out that, while the above strategy suffices to prove our construction secure for a single evaluation (where the circuit evaluated can be of any arbitrary polynomial size), it does *not* imply that our construction achieves reusability, in the sense that the shares output by Share may be used to evaluate any unbounded polynomial number of circuits. Despite the fact that the PRF keys shared via HSS should enable the parties to generate an unbounded polynomial number of pair-wise correlations, the $1/\text{poly}$ evaluation error of the HSS will eventually break simulation security. Fortunately, as alluded to before, the property of sharing-compactness actually turns out to be enough to bootstrap our scheme into a truly reusable MPC protocol. The key ideas that allow for this will be discussed in Sect. 2.3.

2.2   Step 2: From scHSS to FMS MPC

In the second step, we use a scHSS scheme to construct a first message succinct two-round MPC protocol (in the rest of this overview we will call it FMS MPC). The main feature of a scHSS scheme is that its Share algorithm is independent of the computation that will be performed on the shares. Intuitively, this is very similar to the main feature offered by a FMS MPC protocol, in that the first round is independent of the circuit to be computed. Now, suppose that we have an imaginary trusted entity that learns everyone's input $(x_1, \ldots, x_n)$ and then gives each party i a share sh_i computed as $(\mathsf{sh}_1, \ldots, \mathsf{sh}_n) \leftarrow \mathsf{Share}(x_1 \| \ldots \| x_n)$. Note that, due to sharing-compactness this step is independent of the circuit C to be computed by the FMS MPC protocol. After receiving their shares, each party i runs the scHSS evaluation circuit $\mathsf{Eval}(i, \mathsf{C}, \mathsf{sh}_i)$ to obtain their own output share y_i, and then broadcasts y_i . Finally, on receiving all the output shares $(y_1, \ldots, y_n)$, everyone computes $y := \mathsf{C}(x_1, \ldots x_n)$ by running the decoding procedure of scHSS: $y := \mathsf{Dec}(y_1, \ldots, y_n)$.

A Straightforward *Three*-Round Protocol. Unfortunately, we do *not* have such a trusted entity available in the setting of FMS MPC. A natural approach to resolve this would be to use any standard two-round MPC protocol (from now on we refer to such a protocol as vanilla MPC) to realize the Share functionality in a distributed manner. However, since the vanilla MPC protocol would require at least two rounds to complete, this straightforward approach would incur one additional round. This is inevitable, because the parties receive their shares only at the end of the second round. Therefore, an additional round of communication (for broadcasting the output shares y_i) would be required to complete the final protocol.

Garbled Circuits to the Rescue. Using garbled circuits, we are able to squish the above protocol to operate in only *two* rounds. The main idea is to have each party i additionally send a garbled circuit $\widetilde{\mathsf{C}}_i$ in the second round. Each $\widetilde{\mathsf{C}}_i$ garbles a circuit that implements $\mathsf{Eval}(i, \mathsf{C}, \cdot)$. Given the labels for sh_i, $\widetilde{\mathsf{C}}_i$ can be evaluated to output $y_i \leftarrow \mathsf{Eval}(i, \mathsf{C}, \mathsf{sh}_i)$. Note that, if it is ensured that every party receives all the garbled circuits *and* all the correct labels after the second round, they can obtain all $(y_1, \ldots, y_n)$, and compute the final output y without further communication. The only question left now is how the correct labels are communicated within two rounds.

Tweaking Vanilla MPC to Output Labels. For communicating the correct labels, we slightly tweak the functionality computed by the vanilla MPC protocol. In particular, instead of using it just to compute the shares $(\mathsf{sh}_1, \ldots, \mathsf{sh}_n)$, we have the vanilla MPC protocol compute a slightly different functionality that first computes the shares, and rather than outputting them directly, outputs the corresponding correct labels for everyone's shares.[5] This is enabled by having each party provide a random value r_i, which is used to generate the labels, as an additional input to D. Therefore, everyone's correct labels are now available after the completion of the second round of the vanilla MPC protocol. Recall that parties also broadcast their garbled circuits along with the second round of

---

[5] It is important to note that the set of garbled labels corresponding to some input x hides the actual string x. Hence, outputting all the labels instead of specific shares enables everyone to obtain the desired output without any further communication, but also does not compromise security.

the vanilla MPC. Each party i, on receiving all $\widetilde{C}_1, \ldots \widetilde{C}_n$ and all correct labels, evaluates to obtain $(y_1, \ldots, y_n)$ and then computes the final output y.[6]

2.3 Step 3: From FMS MPC to Reusable MPC

Finally, in this third step, we show how FMS MPC can be used to construct *reusable* two-round MPC, where the first message of the protocol can be reused across multiple computations.

We start with the observation that a two-round FMS MPC protocol allows us to compute arbitrary sized circuits after completion of the first round. This offers a limited form of (bounded) reusability, in that all the circuits to be computed could be computed together as a single circuit. However, once the second round is completed, no further computation is possible. Thus, the main challenge is how to leverage the ability to compute a single circuit of unbounded size to achieve *unbounded* reusability. Inspired by ideas from [DG17b], we address this challenge by using the ideas explained in Step 2 (above) repeatedly. For the purposes of this overview, we first explain a simpler version of our final protocol, in which the second round is expanded into multiple rounds. A key property of this protocol is that, using garbled circuits, those expanded rounds can be squished back into just one round (just like we did in Step 2) while preserving reusability.

Towards Reusability: A Multi-round Protocol. The fact that FMS MPC does not already achieve reusability can be re-stated as follows: the first round of FMS MPC (computed using an algorithm MPC_1) can only be used for a single second round execution (using an algorithm MPC_2). To resolve this issue, we build a GGM-like [GGM84] tree-based mechanism that generates a *fresh* FMS first round message for each circuit to be computed, while ensuring that no FMS first round message is reused.

The first round of our final two-round reusable protocol, as well the multi-round simplified version, simply consists of the first round message corresponding to the *root* level (of the GGM tree) instance of the FMS protocol. We now describe the subsequent rounds (to be squished to a single second round later) of our multi-round protocol.

Intuitively, parties iteratively use an FMS instance at a particular level of the binary tree (starting from the root) to generate two new first-round FMS messages corresponding to the next level of the tree. The leaf FMS protocol instances will be used to compute the actual circuits. The root to leaf path traversed to compute a circuit C is decided based on the description of the circuit C itself.[7]

---

[6] We remark that, in the actual protocol each party i sends their labels, encrypted, along with the garbled circuit $\widetilde{C}_i$ in the second round. The vanilla MPC protocol outputs the correct sets of decryption keys based on the shares, which allows everyone to obtain the correct sets of labels, while the other labels remain hidden.

[7] We actually use the string whose first λ bits are the *size* of C, and the remaining bits are the description of C. This is to account for the possibility that one circuit may be a prefix of another.

In more detail, parties first send the second round message of the root (0'th) level FMS protocol instance for a fixed circuit N (independent of the circuit C to be computed) that samples and outputs "left" and "right" MPC_1 messages using the same inputs that were used in the root level FMS. Now, depending on the first bit of the circuit description, parties choose either the left (if the first bit is 0) or the right (if the first bit is 1) MPC_1 messages for the next (1st) level. Now using the chosen FMS messages, parties generate the MPC_2 message for the same circuit N as above. This results in two more fresh instances of the MPC_1 messages for the next (2nd) level. As mentioned before, this procedure is continued until the leaf node is reached. At that point the MPC_2 messages are generated for the circuit C that the parties are interested in computing.

Note that, during the evaluation of two different circuits (each associated with a different leaf node), a certain number of FMS protocol instances might get *re-executed*. However, our construction ensures that this is merely a re-execution of a fixed circuit with the exact same input/output behavior each time. This guarantees that no FMS message is reused (even though it might be re-executed). Finally, observe that this process of iteratively computing more and more MPC_1 messages for the FMS protocol is only possible because the generation of the first message of an FMS protocol can be performed independently of the circuit that gets computed in the second round. In particular, the circuit N computes two more MPC_1 messages on behalf of each party.

Squishing the Multiple Rounds: Using Ideas in Step 2 Iteratively. We take an approach similar to Step 2, but now starting with a two-round FMS MPC (instead of a vanilla MPC). In the second round, each party will send a sequence of garbled circuits where each garbled circuit will complete one instance of an FMS MPC which generates labels for the next garbled circuit. This effectively emulates the execution of the same FMS MPC instance in the multi-round protocol, but without requiring any additional round. Now, the only thing left to address is how to communicate the correct labels.

Communicating the Labels for Each Party's Garbled Circuit. The trick here is (again very similar to step 2) to tweak the circuit N, in that instead of outputting the two MPC_1 messages for the next level, N (with an additional random input r_i from each party i) now outputs labels corresponding to the messages.[8]

For security reasons, it is not possible to include the same randomness r_i in the input to each subsequent FMS instance. Thus, we use a carefully constructed tree-based PRF, following the GGM [GGM84] construction and pass along *not* the key of the PRF but a careful derivative that is sufficient for functionality and does not interfere with security.

Adaptivity in the Choice of Circuit. Our reusable two-round MPC protocol satisfies a strong adaptive security guarantee. In particular, the adversary

---

[8] Again, the actual protocol is slightly different, in that all labels are encrypted and sent along with the garbled circuits, and N outputs decryption keys corresponding to the correct labels.

may choose any circuit to compute after seeing the first round messages (and even after seeing the second round messages for other circuits computed on the same inputs). This stronger security is achieved based on the structure of our construction, since the first round messages of the FMS MPC used to compute the actual circuit are only revealed when the actual execution happens in the second round of the reusable protocol. In particular, we do not even have to rely on "adaptive" security of the underlying FMS protocol to achieve this property.[9]

3 Preliminaries

For standard cryptographic preliminaries, see the full version [BGMM20].

3.1 Two-Round MPC

Throughout this work, we will focus on two-round MPC protocols. We now define the syntax we follow for a two-round MPC protocol.

Definition 5 (Two-Round MPC Procotol). An n-party two-round MPC protocol is described by a triplet of PPT algorithms $(\mathsf{MPC}_1, \mathsf{MPC}_2, \mathsf{MPC}_3)$ with the following syntax.

- $\mathsf{MPC}_1(1^\lambda, \mathsf{CRS}, \mathsf{C}, i, x_i; r_i) =: (\mathsf{st}_i^{(1)}, \mathsf{msg}_i^{(1)})$: Takes as input 1^λ, a common random/reference string CRS, (the description of) a circuit C to be computed, identity of a party $i \in [n]$, input $x_i \in \{0,1\}^*$ and randomness $r_i \in \{0,1\}^\lambda$ (we drop mentioning the randomness explicitly when it is not needed). It outputs party i's first message $\mathsf{msg}_i^{(1)}$ and its private state $\mathsf{st}_i^{(1)}$.
- $\mathsf{MPC}_2(\mathsf{C}, \mathsf{st}_i^{(1)}, \{\mathsf{msg}_j^{(1)}\}_{j \in [n]}) \to (\mathsf{st}_i^{(2)}, \mathsf{msg}_i^{(2)})$: Takes as input (the description of) a circuit[10] C to be computed, the state[11] of a party $\mathsf{st}_i^{(1)}$, and the first round messages of all the parties $\{\mathsf{msg}_j^{(1)}\}_{j \in [n]}$. It outputs party i's second round message $\mathsf{msg}_i^{(2)}$ and its private state $\mathsf{st}_i^{(2)}$.
- $\mathsf{MPC}_3(\mathsf{st}_i^{(2)}, \{\mathsf{msg}_j^{(2)}\}_{j \in [n]}) =: y_i$: Takes as input the state of a party $\mathsf{st}_i^{(2)}$, and the second round messages of all the parties $\{\mathsf{msg}_j^{(2)}\}_{j \in [n]}$. It outputs the ith party's output y_i.

Each party runs the first algorithm MPC_1 to generate the first round message of the protocol, the second algorithm MPC_2 to generate the second round message

---

[9] This is for reasons very similar to those in [DG17a].

[10] It might seem unnatural to include C in the input of MPC_2 when it was already used as an input for MPC_1. This is done to keep the notation consistent with a stronger notion of two-round MPC where C will be dropped from the input of MPC_1.

[11] Without loss of generality we may assume that the MPC_2 algorithm is deterministic given the state $\mathsf{st}_i^{(1)}$. Any randomness needed for the second round could be included in $\mathsf{st}_i^{(1)}$. Even in the reusable (defined later) case, it is possible to use a PRF computed on the input circuit to provide the needed randomness for the execution of MPC_2.

of the protocol and finally, the third algorithm MPC_3 to compute the output. The messages are broadcasted after executing the first two algorithms, whereas the state is kept private.

The formal security definition is provided in the full version [BGMM20].

First Message Succinct Two-Round MPC. We next define the notion of a first message succinct (FMS) two-round MPC protocol. This notion is a strengthening (in terms of efficiency) of the above described notion of (vanilla) two-round MPC. Informally, a two-round MPC protocol is first message succinct if the first round messages of all the parties can be computed without knowledge of the circuit being evaluated on the inputs. This allows parties to compute their first message independent of the circuit (in particular, independent also of its size) that will be computed in the second round.

Definition 6 (First Message Succinct Two-Round MPC). *Let* $\pi = (\mathsf{MPC}_1, \mathsf{MPC}_2, \mathsf{MPC}_3)$ *be a two-round MPC protocol. Protocol* π *is said to be first message succinct if algorithm* MPC_1 *does not take as input the circuit* C *being computed. More specifically, it takes an input of the form* $(1^\lambda, \mathsf{CRS}, i, x_i; r_i)$.

Note that a first message succinct two-round MPC satisfies the same correctness and security properties as the (vanilla) two-round MPC.[12]

Reusable Two-Round MPC. We next define the notion of a *reusable* two-round MPC protocol, which can be seen as a strengthening of the security of a first message succinct two-round MPC protocol. Informally, reusability requires that the parties should be able to *reuse* the same first round message to securely evaluate an *unbounded* polynomially number of circuits $\mathsf{C}_1, \ldots, \mathsf{C}_\ell$, where ℓ is a polynomial (in λ) that is independent of any other parameter in the protocol. That is, for each circuit C_i, the parties can just run the second round of the protocol each time (using exactly the same first round messages) allowing the parties to evaluate the circuit on the *same inputs*. Note that each of these circuits can be of size an arbitrary polynomial in λ.

Very roughly, security requires that the transcript of all these executions along with the set of outputs should not reveal anything more than the inputs of the corrupted parties and the computed outputs.

We again formalize security (and correctness) via the real/ideal world paradigm. Consider n parties $P_1, \ldots, P_n$ with inputs $x_1, \ldots, x_n$ respectively. Also, consider an adversary $\mathcal{A}$ corrupting a set $I \subset [n]$ of parties.

The Real Execution. In the real execution, the n-party first message succinct two-round MPC protocol $\pi = (\mathsf{MPC}_1, \mathsf{MPC}_2, \mathsf{MPC}_3)$ is executed in the presence of an adversary $\mathcal{A}$. The adversary $\mathcal{A}$ takes as input the security parameter λ and an auxiliary input z. The execution proceeds in two phases:

---

[12] In particular, for an FMS two-round MPC protocol, its first message is succinct but may not be reusable.

- **Phase I:** All the honest parties $i \notin I$ execute the first round of the protocol by running the algorithm MPC_1 using their respective input x_i. They broadcast their first round message $\mathsf{msg}_i^{(1)}$ and preserve their secret state $\mathsf{st}_i^{(1)}$. Then the adversary $\mathcal{A}$ sends the first round messages on behalf of the corrupted parties following any arbitrary (polynomial-time computable) strategy (a semi-honest adversary follows the protocol behavior honestly and runs the algorithm $\mathsf{MPC}_1(\cdot)$).
- **Phase II (Reusable):** The adversary outputs a circuit C, which is provided to all parties.

  Next, each honest party computes the algorithm MPC_2 using this circuit C (and its secret state $\mathsf{st}_i^{(1)}$ generated as the output of MPC_1 in Phase I). Again, adversary $\mathcal{A}$ sends arbitrarily computed (in PPT) second round messages on behalf of the corrupt parties. The honest parties return the output of MPC_3 executed on their secret state and the received second round messages.

  The adversary $\mathcal{A}$ decides whether to continue the execution of a different computation. If yes, then the computation returns to the beginning of phase II. In the other case, phase II ends.

The interaction of $\mathcal{A}$ in the above protocol π defines a random variable $\mathsf{REAL}_{\pi,\mathcal{A}}(\lambda, \boldsymbol{x}, z, I)$ whose distribution is determined by the coin tosses of the adversary and the honest parties. This random variable contains the output of the adversary (which may be an arbitrary function of its view) as well as the output recovered by each honest party.

The Ideal Execution. In the ideal execution, an ideal world adversary Sim interacts with a trusted party. The ideal execution proceeds as follows:

1. **Send inputs to the trusted party:** Each honest party sends its input to the trusted party. Each corrupt party P_i, (controlled by Sim) may either send its input x_i or send some other input of the same length to the trusted party. Let x_i' denote the value sent by party P_i. Note that for a semi-honest adversary, $x_i' = x_i$ always.
2. **Adversary picks circuit:** Sim sends a circuit C to the ideal functionality which is also then forwarded to the honest parties.
3. **Trusted party sends output to the adversary:** The trusted party computes $\mathsf{C}(x_1', \ldots, x_n') = (y_1, \ldots, y_n)$ and sends $\{y_i\}_{i \in I}$ to the adversary.
4. **Adversary instructs trusted party to abort or continue:** This is formalized by having the adversary Sim send either a continue or abort message to the trusted party. (A semi-honest adversary never aborts.) In the latter case, the trusted party sends to each uncorrupted party P_i its output value y_i. In the former case, the trusted party sends the special symbol $\perp$ to each uncorrupted party.
5. **Reuse:** The adversary decides whether to continue the execution of a different computation. In the yes case, the ideal world returns to the start of Step 2.
6. **Outputs:** Sim outputs an arbitrary function of its view, and the honest parties output the values obtained from the trusted party.

Sim's interaction with the trusted party defines a random variable $\mathsf{IDEAL}_{\mathsf{Sim}}(\lambda, \boldsymbol{x}, z, I)$. Having defined the real and the ideal worlds, we now proceed to define our notion of security.

Definition 7. *Let λ be the security parameter. Let π be an n-party two-round protocol, for $n \in \mathsf{N}$. We say that π is a reusable two-round MPC protocol in the presence of malicious (resp., semi-honest) adversaries if for every PPT real world adversary (resp., semi-honest adversary) $\mathcal{A}$ there exists a PPT ideal world adversary (resp., semi-honest adversary) Sim such that for any $\boldsymbol{x} = \{x_i\}_{i \in [n]} \in (\{0,1\}^*)^n$, any $z \in \{0,1\}^*$, any $I \subset [n]$ and any PPT distinguisher $\mathcal{D}$, we have that*

$$|Pr[\mathcal{D}(\mathsf{REAL}_{\pi,\mathcal{A}}(\lambda, \boldsymbol{x}, z, I)) = 1] - Pr[\mathcal{D}(\mathsf{IDEAL}_{\mathsf{Sim}}(\lambda, \boldsymbol{x}, z, I)) = 1]|$$

is negligible in λ.

4 Step 1: Constructing Sharing-Compact HSS from HSS

In this section, we start by recalling the notion of homomorphic secret sharing (HSS) and defining our notion of *sharing-compact* HSS. We use the standard notion of HSS, which supports two parties and features additive reconstruction. In contrast, our notion of sharing compactness is for the multi-party case, but does not come with the typical bells and whistles of a standard HSS scheme—specifically, it features compactness *only* of the sharing algorithm and *without* additive reconstruction. For brevity, we refer to this notion of HSS as sharing-compact HSS (scHSS). In what follows, we give a construction of sharing-compact HSS and prove its security.

4.1 Sharing-Compact Homomorphic Secret Sharing

We continue with our definition of sharing-compact HSS, which differs from HSS in various ways:

- we support sharing among an arbitrary number of parties (in particular, more than 2);
- we have a simulation-based security definition;
- we support a notion of *robustness*;
- we have negligible correctness error;
- our reconstruction procedure is not necessarily additive;
- we require security for only *one* evaluation.

We do preserve the property that the sharing algorithm, and in particular, the size of the shares, is independent of the size of the program to be computed.

Definition 8 (Sharing-compact Homomorphic Secret Sharing (scHSS)). *A scHSS scheme for a class of programs $\mathcal{P}$ is a triple of PPT algorithms (Share, Eval, Dec) with the following syntax:*

Share$(1^\lambda, n, x)$: *Takes as input a security parameter 1^λ, a number of parties n, and a secret $x \in \{0,1\}^*$, and outputs shares $(x_1, \ldots, x_n)$.*
Eval(j, P, x_j): *Takes as input a party index $j \in [n]$, a program P, and share x_j, and outputs a string $y_j \in \{0,1\}^*$.*
Dec$(y_1, \ldots, y_n)$: *Takes as input all evaluated shares $(y_1, \ldots, y_n)$ and outputs $y \in \{0,1\}^*$.*

The algorithms satisfy the following properties.

- **Correctness:** *For any program $P \in \mathcal{P}$ and secret x,*

$$\Pr\left[\text{Dec}(y_1, \ldots, y_n) = P(x) : \begin{array}{c} (x_1, \ldots, x_n) \leftarrow \text{Share}(1^\lambda, x) \\ \forall j, y_j \leftarrow \text{Eval}(j, P, x_j) \end{array}\right] = 1 - \text{negl}(\lambda).$$

- **Robustness:** *For any non-empty set of honest parties $H \subseteq [n]$, program $P \in \mathcal{P}$, secret x, and PPT adversary $\mathcal{A}$,*

$$\Pr\left[\text{Dec}(y_1, \ldots, y_n) \in \{P(x), \bot\} : \begin{array}{c} (x_1, \ldots, x_n) \leftarrow \text{Share}(1^\lambda, x) \\ \forall j \in H, y_j \leftarrow \text{Eval}(j, P, x_j) \\ \{y_j\}_{j \in [n] \setminus H} \leftarrow \mathcal{A}(\{x_j\}_{j \in [n] \setminus H}, \{y_j\}_{j \in H}) \end{array}\right] = 1 - \text{negl}(\lambda).$$

- **Security:** *There exists a PPT simulator $\mathcal{S}$ such that for any program $P \in \mathcal{P}$, any secret x, and any set of honest parties $H \subseteq [n]$ we have that:*

$$\left\{ \{x_i\}_{i \in [n] \setminus H}, \{y_i\}_{i \in H} : \begin{array}{c} (x_1, \ldots, x_n) \leftarrow \text{Share}(1^\lambda, n, x), \\ \forall i \in H, y_i \leftarrow \text{Eval}(i, P, x_i) \end{array}\right\} \stackrel{c}{\approx} \left\{ \mathcal{S}(1^\lambda, P, n, H, P(x)) \right\}.$$

4.2 Conforming Protocol

In our construction, we need a modification of the notion of conforming MPC protocol from [GS18]. Consider an MPC protocol Φ between parties $P_1, \ldots, P_n$. For each $i \in [n]$, we let $x_i \in \{0,1\}^m$ denote the input of party P_i. We consider any random coins used by a party to be part of its input (we can assume each party uses at most λ bits of randomness, and expands as necessary with a PRF). A conforming protocol Φ is defined by functions inpgen, gen, post, and computation steps or what we call *actions* $\phi_1, \cdots \phi_T$. The protocol Φ proceeds in three stages: the input sharing stage, the computation stage, and the output stage. For those familiar with the notion of conforming protocol from [GS18, GIS18], we outline the differences here.

- We split their function pre into (inpgen, gen), where inpgen is universal, in the sense that it only depends on the input length m (and in particular, not the function to be computed).
- We explicitly maintain a single public global state st that is updated one bit at a time. Each party's private state is maintained implicitly via their random coins s_i chosen during the input sharing phase.
- We require the transcript (which is fixed by the value of st at the end of the protocol) to be *publicly decodable*.

Next, we give our description of a conforming protocol.

- **Input sharing phase**: Each party i chooses random coins $s_i \leftarrow \{0,1\}^\lambda$, computes $(w_i, r_i) := \mathsf{inpgen}(x_i, s_i)$ where $w_i = x_i \oplus r_i$, and broadcasts w_i. Looking ahead to the proof of Lemma 9, we will take s_i to be the seed of a $\mathsf{PRF}(s_i, \cdot) : \{0,1\}^* \to \{0,1\}$.
- **Computation phase**: Let T be a parameter that depends on the circuit C to be computed. Each party sets the global public state

$$\mathsf{st} := (w_1 \| 0^{T/n} \| w_2 \| 0^{T/n} \| \cdots \| w_n \| 0^{T/n}),$$

and generates their secret state $v_i := \mathsf{gen}(i, s_i)$.[13] Let ℓ be the length of st or v_i (st and v_i will be of the same length). We will also use the notation that for index $f \in [\ell]$, $v_{i,f} := \mathsf{gen}_f(i, s_i)$.

For each $t \in \{1 \cdots T\}$ parties proceed as follows:
  1. Parse action ϕ_t as (i, f, g, h) where $i \in [n]$ and $f, g, h \in [\ell]$.
  2. Party P_i computes *one* NAND gate as

$$\gamma_t = \mathsf{NAND}(\mathsf{st}_f \oplus v_{i,f}, \mathsf{st}_g \oplus v_{i,g}) \oplus v_{i,h}$$

  and broadcasts γ_t to every other party.
  3. Every party updates st_h to the bit value γ_t received from P_i.

We require that for all $t, t' \in [T]$ such that $t \neq t'$, we have that if $\phi_t = (\cdot, \cdot, \cdot, h)$ and $\phi_{t'} = (\cdot, \cdot, \cdot, h')$ then $h \neq h'$ (this ensures that no state bit is ever overwritten).
- **Output phase**: Denote by $\Gamma = (\gamma_1, \ldots, \gamma_T)$ the transcript of the protocol, and output $\mathsf{post}(\Gamma)$.

Lemma 9. *For any input length m, there exists a function inpgen such that any n party MPC protocol Π (where each party has an input of length at most m) can be written as a conforming protocol $\Phi = (\mathsf{inpgen}, \mathsf{gen}, \mathsf{post}, \{\phi_t\}_{t \in T})$ while inheriting the correctness and the security of the original protocol.*

The proof of this lemma is very similar to the proof provided in [GS18], and is deferred to the full version [BGMM20].

4.3 Our Construction

We describe a sharing-compact HSS scheme for sharing an input $x \in \{0,1\}^m$ among n parties.

Ingredients: We use the following ingredients in our construction.

- An $n\lambda$-party conforming MPC protocol Φ (for computing an arbitrary functionality) with functions $\mathsf{inpgen}, \mathsf{gen}$, and post.

---

[13] Technically, gen should also take the parameters n, T as input, but we leave these implicit.

- A homomorphic secret sharing scheme (HSS.Share, HSS.Eval) supporting evaluations of circuits in NC^1. To ease notation in the description of our protocol, we will generally leave the party index, identifier, and error parameter δ implicit. The party index will be clear from context, the identifier can be the description of the function to be evaluated, and the error parameter will be fixed once and for all by the parties.
- A garbling scheme for circuits (Garble, GEval).
- A robust private-key encryption scheme (rob.enc, rob.dec).
- A PRF that can be computed in NC^1.

Theorem 10. *Assuming a semi-honest MPC protocol (with any number of rounds) that can compute any polynomial-size functionality, a homomorphic secret sharing scheme supporting evaluations of circuits in NC^1, and a PRF that can be computed in NC^1, there exists a sharing-compact homomorphic secret sharing scheme supporting the evaluation of any polynomial-size circuit.*

Notation: As explained in Sect. 2, our construction at a high level follows the template of [GS18] (which we refer to as the GS protocol). In the evaluation step of our construction, each party generates a sequence of garbled circuits, one for each action step of the conforming protocol. For each of these action steps, the garbled circuit of one party speaks and the garbled circuits of the rest listen. We start by describing three circuits that aid this process: (i) circuit F (described in Fig. 1), which includes the HSS evaluations enabling the speaking/listening mechanism, (ii) circuit P* (described in Fig. 2) garbled by the speaking party, and (iii) circuit P (described in Fig. 3) garbled by the listening party.

(i) Circuit F. The speaking garbled circuit and the listening garbled circuit need shared secrets for communication. Using HSS, F provides an interface for setting up these shared secrets. More specifically, consider a speaking party j^* and a listening party $j \neq j^*$ during action t. In our construction, the parties j, j^* will be provided with HSS shares of their secrets $\{s_j, s_{j^*}\}, \{k_j, k_{j^*}\}$. Note that the order of s_j and s_{j^*} in $\{s_j, s_{j^*}\}$ and the order of k_j and k_{j^*} in $\{k_j, k_{j^*}\}$ is irrelevant. All of the secret information used by party j^* in computation of its conforming protocol messages is based on s_{j^*}. Also, during action t, party j's garbled circuit will need to output encrypted labels for its next garbled circuit. Secret k_j is used to generate any keys needed for encrypting garbled circuit labels. Concretely, in the circuit G (used inside F), observe that s_{j^*} is used to perform the computation of γ, and k_j is used to compute the "difference value", explained below.

Both party j and party j^* can compute F on their individual share of $\{s_j, s_{j^*}\}, \{k_j, k_{j^*}\}$. They either obtain the same output value (in the case that party j^*'s message bit for the tth action is 0) or they obtain outputs that differ by a pseudorandom *difference* value known only to party j (in the case that party j^*'s message bit for the tth action is 1). This difference value is equal to $\mathsf{PRF}(k_j, (t, \alpha, \beta, p))$, where t, α, β and p denote various parameters of the protocol.

$$F[t, \alpha, \beta, p](\mathsf{sh})$$

Input: sh.
Hardcoded: The action number $t \in [T]$, bits α, β, and index $p \in [\lambda]$.

1. Let $\phi_t = (j^*, f, g, h)$.
2. Let $G[t, \alpha, \beta, p, f, g, h]$ be the circuit that on input $\{s_j, s_{j^*}\}, \{k_j, k_{j^*}\}$:
   (a) Set $\gamma := \mathsf{NAND}\left(\alpha \oplus \mathsf{gen}_f(j^*, s_{j^*}), \beta \oplus \mathsf{gen}_g(j^*, s_{j^*})\right) \oplus \mathsf{gen}_h(j^*, s_{j^*})$.
   (b) If $\gamma = 0$, output 0^λ, else output $\mathsf{PRF}(k_j, (t, \alpha, \beta, p))$.

Output: HSS.Eval(sh, $G[t, \alpha, \beta, p, f, g, h]$).

Fig. 1. The Circuit F.

Next, we'll see how the circuit F enables communication between garbled circuits. In our construction the speaking party will just output the evaluation of F on its share (for appropriate choices of t, α, β and p). On the other hand, party j will encrypt the zero-label for its next garbled circuit using the output of the evaluation of F on its share (for appropriate choices of t, α, β and p) and will encrypt the one-label for its next garbled circuit using the exclusive or of this value and the difference value. Observe that the output of the speaking circuit will be exactly the key used to encrypt the label corresponding to the bit sent by j^* in the tth action.

Finally, we need to ensure that each circuit G evaluated under the HSS can be computed in NC^1. Observe that G essentially only computes $\mathsf{gen}_f(j^*, s_{j^*})$ evaluations and $\mathsf{PRF}(k_j, \cdot)$ evaluations. The proof of Lemma 9 shows that $\mathsf{gen}_f(j^*, s_{j^*})$ may be computed with a single PRF evaluation using key s_{j^*}. Thus, if we take each s_j, k_j to be keys for a PRF computable in NC^1, it follows that G will be in NC^1.

(ii) The Speaking Circuit P^*. The construction of the speaking circuit is quite simple. The speaking circuit for the party j^* corresponding to action t computes the updated global state and the bit γ sent out in action t. However, it must somehow communicate γ to the garbled circuit of each $j \neq j^*$. This effect is achieved by having P^* return the output of F (on relevant inputs as explained above). However, technical requirements in the security proof preclude party j^* from hard-coding its HSS share sh into P^*, and having P^* compute on this share. Thus, we instead hard-code the outputs of F on all relevant inputs. More specifically, we hard-code $\left\{z_{j,p}^{(\alpha,\beta)}\right\}_{\substack{\alpha,\beta \in \{0,1\}, \\ j \in [n']\setminus\{j^*\}, \\ p \in [\lambda]}}$, where $z_{j,p}^{(\alpha,\beta)}$ is obtained as the output $F[t, \alpha, \beta, p](\mathsf{sh})$.

$$\mathsf{P^*}\left[j^*, \left\{ z_{j,p}^{(\alpha,\beta)} \right\}_{\substack{\alpha,\beta\in\{0,1\}, \\ j\in[n']\setminus\{j^*\}, \\ p\in[\lambda]}}, (v_f, v_g, v_h), \overline{\mathsf{lab}} \right] (\mathsf{st})$$

Input: st.

Hardcoded: A (virtual) party index j^*, a set of strings $\left\{ z_{j,p}^{(\alpha,\beta)} \right\}_{\substack{\alpha,\beta\in\{0,1\}, \\ j\in[n']\setminus\{j^*\}, \\ p\in[\lambda]}}$,

three bits (v_f, v_g, v_h), and a set of labels $\overline{\mathsf{lab}} = \{\mathsf{lab}_{k,0}, \mathsf{lab}_{k,1}\}_{k\in[\ell]}$.

1. Compute $\gamma := \mathsf{NAND}(\mathsf{st}_f \oplus v_f, \mathsf{st}_g \oplus v_g) \oplus v_h$.
2. Set $\mathsf{st}_h := \gamma$.

Output: $\left(\gamma, \left\{ z_{j,p}^{(\mathsf{st}_f, \mathsf{st}_g)} \right\}_{\substack{j\in[n']\setminus\{j^*\}, \\ p\in[\lambda]}}, \{\mathsf{lab}_{k,\mathsf{st}_k}\}_{k\in[\ell]} \right).$

Fig. 2. The Speaking Circuit P^*.

(iii) The Listening Circuit P. The construction of the listening circuit mirrors that of the speaking circuit. The listening circuit outputs the labels for all wires except the hth wire that it is listening on. For the hth wire, the listening circuit outputs encryptions of the two labels under two distinct keys, where one of them will be output by the speaking circuit during this action. As in the case of speaking circuits, for technical reasons in the proof, we cannot have the listening circuit compute these value but must instead hard-code them. More specifically, we hard code $\left\{ z_{p,0}^{(\alpha,\beta)}, z_{p,1}^{(\alpha,\beta)} \right\}_{\substack{\alpha,\beta\in\{0,1\}, \\ p\in[\lambda]}}$, where $z_{p,0}^{(\alpha,\beta)}$ is obtained as $\mathsf{F}[t,\alpha,\beta,p](\mathsf{sh})$ and $z_{p,1}^{(\alpha,\beta)}$ is obtained as $z_{p,0}^{(\alpha,\beta)} \oplus \mathsf{PRF}\left(k_j, (t,\alpha,\beta,p)\right)$.

$$\mathsf{P}\left[j, \left\{ z_{p,0}^{(\alpha,\beta)}, z_{p,1}^{(\alpha,\beta)} \right\}_{\substack{\alpha,\beta\in\{0,1\}, \\ p\in[\lambda]}}, (f,g,h), \overline{\mathsf{lab}} \right] (\mathsf{st})$$

Input: st.

Hardcoded. A (virtual) party index j, set of strings $\left\{ z_{p,0}^{(\alpha,\beta)}, z_{p,1}^{(\alpha,\beta)} \right\}_{\substack{\alpha,\beta\in\{0,1\}, \\ p\in[\lambda]}}$,

three indices (f, g, h), and a set of labels $\overline{\mathsf{lab}} = \{\mathsf{lab}_{k,0}, \mathsf{lab}_{k,1}\}_{k\in[\ell]}$.

Output: $\left(\left\{ \mathsf{rob.enc}\left(z_{p,b}^{(\mathsf{st}_f, \mathsf{st}_g)}, \mathsf{lab}_{h,b} \right), \right\}_{b\in\{0,1\}, p\in[\lambda]}, \{\mathsf{lab}_{k,\mathsf{st}_k}\}_{k\in[\ell]\setminus\{h\}} \right).$

Fig. 3. The Listening Circuit P.

The Construction Itself: The foundation of a sharing-compact HSS for evaluating circuit C is a conforming protocol Φ (as described earlier in Sect. 4.2) computing the circuit C. Very roughly (and the details will become clear as we go along), in our construction, the Share algorithm will generate secret shares of the input x for the n parties. Additionally, the share algorithm generates the first round GS MPC messages on behalf of each party. The Eval algorithm will roughly correspond to the generation of the second round messages of the GS MPC protocol. Finally, the Dec algorithm will perform the reconstruction, which corresponds to the output computation step in GS after all the second round messages have been sent out.

The Sharing Algorithm: Because of the inverse polynomial error probability in HSS (hinted at in Sect. 2 and explained in the proof), we need to use an $n' = n\lambda$ (virtual) party protocol rather than just an n party protocol. Each of the n parties actually messages for λ virtual parties. Barring this technicality and given our understanding of what needs to be shared to enable the communication between garbled circuits, the sharing is quite natural.

On input x, the share algorithm generates a secret sharing of x (along with the randomness needed for the execution of Φ) to obtain a share x_j for each virtual party $j \in [n']$. In addition, two PRF keys s_j, k_j for each virtual party $j \in [n']$ are sampled. Now, the heart of the sharing algorithm is the generation of HSS shares of $\{s_j, s_{j'}\}, \{k_j, k_{j'}\}$ for every pair of $j \neq j' \in [n']$, which are then provided to parties j and j'. Specifically, the algorithm computes shares $\mathsf{sh}_j^{\{j,j'\}}$ and $\mathsf{sh}_{j'}^{\{j,j'\}}$ as the output of $\mathsf{HSS.Share}\left(1^\lambda, (\{s_j, s_{j'}\}, \{k_j, k_{j'}\})\right)$. Note that we generate only one set of shares for each j, j' and the ordering of j and j' is irrelevant (we use the set notation to signify this).

$\mathsf{Share}(1^\lambda, n, x)$:

1. Let $n' = n\lambda$, $m' = m+\lambda$, and $x_1 := (z_1 \| \rho_1) \in \{0,1\}^{m'}, \ldots, x_{n'} := (z_{n'} \| \rho_{n'}) \in \{0,1\}^{m'}$, where $z_1, \ldots, z_{n'}$ is an additive secret sharing of x, and each $\rho_i \in \{0,1\}^\lambda$ is uniformly random. The ρ_i are the random coins used by each party in the MPC protocol Π underlying the conforming protocol Φ.
2. For each $j \in [n']$:
   (a) Draw PRF keys $s_j, k_j \leftarrow \{0,1\}^\lambda$, so that $\mathsf{PRF}(s_j, \cdot) : \{0,1\}^* \to \{0,1\}$ and $\mathsf{PRF}(k_j, \cdot) : \{0,1\}^* \to \{0,1\}^\lambda$, where both of these pseudorandom functions can be computed by NC^1 circuits.
   (b) Compute $(w_j, r_j) := \mathsf{inpgen}(x_j, s_j)$.
3. For each $j \neq j' \in [n']$, compute $\left(\mathsf{sh}_j^{\{j,j'\}}, \mathsf{sh}_{j'}^{\{j,j'\}}\right) \leftarrow \mathsf{HSS.Share}\left(1^\lambda, \left(\{s_j, s_{j'}\}, \{k_j, k_{j'}\}\right)\right)$.
4. Let $\overline{\mathsf{sh}}_j = \left(x_j, s_j, k_j, \left\{\mathsf{sh}_j^{\{j,j'\}}\right\}_{j' \in [n'] \setminus \{j\}}\right)$.
5. For each $i \in [n]$, output party i's share $\mathsf{sh}_i := \left(\{w_j\}_{j \in [n']}, \left\{\overline{\mathsf{sh}}_j\right\}_{j \in [(i-1)\lambda+1, \cdots, i\lambda]}\right)$.

The Evaluation Algorithm: Observe that the sharing algorithm is independent of the conforming protocol Φ (and the circuit C to be computed), thus achieving sharing compactness. This is due to the fact that the function inpgen is *universal* for conforming protocols Φ (as explained in Sect. 4.2).

In contrast, the evaluation algorithm will emulate the entire protocol Φ. First, it will set the error parameter δ for HSS, depending on the protocol Φ. Then, each virtual party j (where each party controls λ virtual parties) generates a garbled circuit for each action of the conforming protocol. For each action, the speaking party uses the speaking circuit P* and the rest of the parties use the listening circuit P.

$\mathsf{Eval}(i, \mathsf{C}, \mathsf{sh}_i)$:

1. Parse sh_i as $\left(\{w_j\}_{j \in [n']}, \{\overline{\mathsf{sh}}_j\}_{j \in [(i-1)\lambda+1, \cdots, i\lambda]} \right)$, let T be a parameter[14] of the conforming protocol Φ computing C, and set the HSS error parameter $\delta = 1/8\lambda^2 T$.

2. Set $\mathsf{st} := (w_1 \| 0^{T/n'} \| w_2 \| 0^{T/n'} \| \cdots \| w_{n'} \| 0^{T/n'})$.

3. For each $j \in [(i-1)\lambda+1, \cdots, i\lambda]$, run the following procedure. $\mathsf{VirtualEval}(j, \mathsf{C}, \overline{\mathsf{sh}}_j)$:

   (a) Parse $\overline{\mathsf{sh}}_j$ as $\left(x_j, s_j, k_j, \left\{ \mathsf{sh}_j^{\{j,j'\}} \right\}_{j' \in [n'] \setminus \{j\}} \right)$.

   (b) Compute $v_j := \mathsf{gen}(j, s_j)$.

   (c) Set $\overline{\mathsf{lab}}^{j,T+1} := \left\{ \mathsf{lab}_{k,0}^{j,T+1}, \mathsf{lab}_{k,1}^{j,T+1} \right\}_{k \in [\ell]}$ where for each $k \in [\ell]$ and $b \in \{0,1\}$, $\mathsf{lab}_{k,b}^{j,T+1} := 0^\lambda$.

   (d) For each t from T down to 1:
      i. Parse ϕ_t as (j^*, f, g, h).
      ii. If $j = j^*$, compute (where P* is described in Fig. 2 and F is described in Fig. 1)

$$\mathsf{arg}_1 := \left\{ \mathsf{F}[t, \alpha, \beta, p] \left(\mathsf{sh}_{j^*}^{\{j^*,j\}} \right) \right\}_{\substack{j \in [n'] \setminus \{j^*\}, \\ \alpha,\beta \in \{0,1\}, \\ p \in [\lambda]}}$$

$$\mathsf{arg}_2 := (v_{j^*,f}, v_{j^*,g}, v_{j^*,h})$$

$$\left(\widetilde{\mathsf{P}}^{j^*,t}, \overline{\mathsf{lab}}^{j^*,t} \right) \leftarrow \mathsf{Garble} \left(1^\lambda, \mathsf{P}^* \left[j^*, \mathsf{arg}_1, \mathsf{arg}_2, \overline{\mathsf{lab}}^{j^*,t+1} \right] \right).$$

   iii. If $j \neq j^*$, compute (where P is described in Fig. 3 and F is described in Fig. 1)

$$\mathsf{arg}_1 := \left\{ \begin{array}{c} \mathsf{F}[t, \alpha, \beta, p] \left(\mathsf{sh}_j^{\{j^*,j\}} \right), \\ \mathsf{F}[t, \alpha, \beta, p] \left(\mathsf{sh}_j^{\{j^*,j\}} \right) \oplus \mathsf{PRF}\left(k_j, (t, \alpha, \beta, p) \right) \end{array} \right\}_{\substack{\alpha,\beta \in \{0,1\}, \\ p \in [\lambda]}}$$

$$\mathsf{arg}_2 := (f, g, h)$$

$$\left(\widetilde{\mathsf{P}}^{j,t}, \overline{\mathsf{lab}}^{j,t} \right) \leftarrow \mathsf{Garble} \left(1^\lambda, \mathsf{P} \left[j, \mathsf{arg}_1, \mathsf{arg}_2, \overline{\mathsf{lab}}^{j,t+1} \right] \right).$$

---

[14] Recall that T is the number of actions to be taken.

(e) Set $\overline{y}_j := \left(\left\{ \widetilde{\mathsf{P}}^{j,t} \right\}_{t \in [T]}, \left\{ \mathsf{lab}_{k,\mathsf{st}_k}^{j,1} \right\}_{k \in [\ell]} \right)$. Recall st was defined in step 2.

4. Output $y_i := \left\{ \overline{y}_j \right\}_{j \in [(i-1)\lambda+1, \cdots, i\lambda]}$.

The Decoding Algorithm: The decoding algorithm is quite natural given what we have seen so far. Garbled circuits from each virtual party are executed sequentially, communicating among themselves. This results in an evaluation of the conforming protocol Φ and the final output can be computed using the post algorithm.

$\mathsf{Dec}(y_1, \ldots, y_n)$:

1. For each $i \in [n]$, parse y_i as $\left\{ \left(\left\{ \widetilde{\mathsf{P}}^{j,t} \right\}_{t \in [T]}, \left\{ \mathsf{lab}_k^{j,1} \right\}_{k \in [\ell]} \right) \right\}_{j \in [(i-1)\lambda+1, \cdots, i\lambda]}$.

2. For each $j \in [n']$, let $\widetilde{\mathsf{lab}}^{j,1} := \left\{ \mathsf{lab}_k^{j,1} \right\}_{k \in [\ell]}$.

3. For each t from 1 to T,
    (a) Parse ϕ_t as (j^*, f, g, h).
    (b) Compute $\left(\gamma_t, \{z_{j,p}^*\}_{\substack{j \in [n'] \setminus \{j^*\} \\ p \in [\lambda]}}, \widetilde{\mathsf{lab}}^{j^*, t+1} \right) := \mathsf{GEval} \left(\widetilde{\mathsf{P}}^{j^*, t}, \widetilde{\mathsf{lab}}^{j^*, t} \right)$.
    (c) For each $j \neq j^*$:
        i. Compute $\left(\{\mathsf{elab}_{p,0}, \mathsf{elab}_{p,1}\}_{p \in [\lambda]}, \left\{ \mathsf{lab}_k^{j,t+1} \right\}_{k \in [\ell] \setminus \{h\}} \right) := \mathsf{GEval} \big(\widetilde{\mathsf{P}}^{j,t},$ $\widetilde{\mathsf{lab}}^{j,t} \big)$.
        ii. If there exists $p \in [\lambda]$, such that $\mathsf{rob.dec} \left(z_{j,p}^*, \mathsf{elab}_{p,\gamma_t} \right) \neq \perp$, then set the result to $\mathsf{lab}_h^{j,t+1}$. If all λ decryptions give $\perp$, then output $\perp$ and abort.
        iii. Set $\widetilde{\mathsf{lab}}^{j,t+1} := \left\{ \mathsf{lab}_k^{j,t+1} \right\}_{k \in [\ell]}$.
4. Set $\Gamma = (\gamma_1, \ldots, \gamma_T)$ and output $\mathsf{post}(\Gamma)$.

The proof of correctness, security and robustness can be found in the full version [BGMM20].

5   Step 2: FMS MPC from Sharing-Compact HSS

In this section, we use a sharing-compact HSS scheme to construct a *first message succinct* two-round MPC protocol that securely computes any polynomial-size circuit. We refer to Sect. 2.2 for a high-level overview of the construction. For modularity of presentation, we begin by defining a label encryption scheme.

Label Encryption. This is an encryption scheme designed specifically for encrypting a grid of $2 \times \ell$ garbled input labels corresponding to a garbled circuit with input length ℓ. The encryption algorithm takes as input a $2 \times \ell$ grid of strings (labels) along with a $2 \times \ell$ grid of keys. It encrypts each label using each corresponding key, making use of a *robust* private-key encryption scheme

---

A first message succinct MPC protocol (FMS.MPC$_1$, FMS.MPC$_2$, FMS.MPC$_3$)

Main Ingredients:
  - A (vanilla) two-round MPC protocol (MPC$_1$, MPC$_2$, MPC$_3$).
  - A scHSS scheme (Share, Eval, Dec).
  - A garbled circuit scheme (Garble, GEval).
  - A label encryption scheme (LabEnc, LabDec).

FMS.MPC$_1$(1^λ, CRS, i, x_i):
  1. Draw $r_i \leftarrow \{0,1\}^\lambda$, and compute $(\mathsf{st}_i^{(1)}, \mathsf{msg}_i^{(1)}) \leftarrow \mathsf{MPC}_1(1^\lambda, \mathsf{CRS}, \mathsf{D}, i, (x_i, r_i))$.
  2. Output FMS.$\mathsf{st}_i^{(1)} := (\mathsf{st}_i^{(1)}, r_i)$ and FMS.$\mathsf{msg}_i^{(1)} := \mathsf{msg}_i^{(1)}$.

FMS.MPC$_2$(C, FMS.$\mathsf{st}_i^{(1)}$, $\{$FMS.$\mathsf{msg}_j^{(1)}\}_{j \in [n]}$):
  1. Compute $(\mathsf{st}_i^{(2)}, \mathsf{msg}_i^{(2)}) \leftarrow \mathsf{MPC}_2(\mathsf{D}, \mathsf{st}_i^{(1)}, \{\mathsf{msg}_j^{(1)}\}_{j \in [n]})$.
  2. Compute $(\tilde{\mathsf{C}}, \overline{\mathsf{lab}}) \leftarrow \mathsf{Garble}(1^\lambda, \mathsf{Eval}(i, \mathsf{C}, \cdot))$.
  3. Compute $\overline{\mathsf{elab}} \leftarrow \mathsf{LabEnc}(\overline{K}, \overline{\mathsf{lab}})$ where $\overline{K} = \{\mathsf{PRF}(r_i, (t, b))\}_{t \in [\ell], b \in \{0,1\}}$.
  4. Output FMS.$\mathsf{st}_i^{(2)} := \mathsf{st}_i^{(2)}$ and FMS.$\mathsf{msg}_i^{(2)} := (\mathsf{msg}_i^{(2)}, \tilde{\mathsf{C}}, \overline{\mathsf{elab}})$.

FMS.MPC$_3$(FMS.$\mathsf{st}_i^{(2)}$, $\{$FMS.$\mathsf{msg}_j^{(2)}\}_{j \in [n]}$):
  1. Compute $\{\widehat{K}_j\}_{j \in [n]} := \mathsf{MPC}_3(\mathsf{st}_i^{(2)}, \{\mathsf{msg}_j^{(2)}\}_{j \in [n]})$.
  2. For each $j \in [n]$:
      (a) Compute $\widehat{\mathsf{lab}}_j := \mathsf{LabDec}(\widehat{K}_j, \overline{\mathsf{elab}}_j)$.
      (b) Compute $Y_j := \mathsf{GEval}(\tilde{\mathsf{C}}_j, \widehat{\mathsf{lab}}_j)$.
  3. Output $y := \mathsf{Dec}(Y_1, \ldots, Y_n)$.

Fig. 4. A first message succinct MPC protocol (FMS.MPC$_1$, FMS.MPC$_2$, FMS.MPC$_3$)

Circuit D

Input: $(x_1, r_1), \ldots, (x_n, r_n)$

  1. $(\mathsf{csh}_1, \ldots, \mathsf{csh}_n) \leftarrow \mathsf{Share}(1^\lambda, n, (x_1 || \ldots || x_n))$.
  2. For each $i \in [n]$:
      (a) For each $t \in [\ell]$, set $K_{i,t} := \mathsf{PRF}(r_i, (t, \mathsf{csh}_i[t]))$.
      (b) Set $\widehat{K}_i := \{K_{i,t}\}_{t \in [\ell]}$.

Output: $(\widehat{K}_1 \ldots \widehat{K}_n)$

Fig. 5. The (randomized) circuit D

(rob.enc, rob.dec). It then randomly permutes each pair (column) of ciphertexts, and outputs the resulting $2 \times \ell$ grid. On the other hand, decryption only takes as input a set of ℓ keys, that presumably correspond to exactly one ciphertext per column, or, exactly one input to the garbled circuit. The decryption algorithm uses the keys to decrypt exactly one label per column, with the robustness of (rob.enc, rob.dec) ensuring that indeed only one ciphertext per column is able to be decrypted. The random permutations that occur during encryption ensure that a decryptor will recover a valid set of input labels *without knowing* which input they actually correspond to. This will be crucial in our construction.

LabEnc($\overline{K}, \overline{\text{lab}}$) : On input a key $\overline{K} = \{K_{i,b}\}_{i \in [\ell], b \in \{0,1\}}$ and $\overline{\text{lab}} = \{\text{lab}_{i,b}\}_{i \in [\ell], b \in \{0,1\}}$ (where $K_{i,b}, \text{lab}_{i,b} \in \{0,1\}^{\lambda}$), LabEnc draws n random bits $b'_i \leftarrow \{0,1\}$ and outputs $\overline{\text{elab}} = \{\text{elab}_{i,b}\}_{i \in [\ell], b \in \{0,1\}}$, where $\text{elab}_{i,b} := \text{rob.enc}(K_{i,b \oplus b'_i}, \text{lab}_{i,b \oplus b'_i})$.

LabDec($\widehat{K}, \overline{\text{elab}}$): On input a key $\widehat{K} = \{K_i\}_{i \in [\ell]}$ and $\overline{\text{elab}} = \{\text{elab}_{i,b}\}_{i \in [\ell], b \in \{0,1\}}$, for each $i \in [\ell]$ output $\text{rob.dec}(K_i, \text{elab}_{i,0})$ if it is not $\perp$ and $\text{rob.dec}(K_i, \text{elab}_{i,1})$ otherwise.

We present the formal construction in Fig. 4. It is given for functionalities C where every party receives the same output, which is without loss of generality. Throughout, we will denote by ℓ the length of each party's scHSS share. Note that the circuit D used by the construction is defined immediately after in Fig. 5. Finally, $p[t]$ denotes the t'th bit of a string $p \in \{0,1\}^*$.

Theorem 11. *Let $\mathcal{X} \in \{$semi-honest in the plain model, semi-honest in the common random/reference string model, malicious in the common random/reference string model$\}$. Assuming a (vanilla) $\mathcal{X}$ two-round MPC protocol and a scHSS scheme for polynomial-size circuits, there exists an $\mathcal{X}$ first message succinct two-round MPC protocol.*

The proof of Theorem 11 can be found in the full version [BGMM20].

6 Step 3: Two-Round Reusable MPC from FMS MPC

We start by giving a high-level overview of the reusable MPC, which we call r.MPC. Recall from Sect. 2.3 that round one of r.MPC essentially just consists of round one of an FMS.MPC instance computing the circuit N. We refer to this as the 0'th (instance of) MPC. Now fix a circuit C to be computed in round two, and its representative string $p := \langle C \rangle$, which we'll take to be length m. This string p fixes a root-to-leaf path in a binary tree of MPCs that the parties will compute. In round two, the parties compute round two of the 0'th MPC, plus m (garbled circuit, encrypted labels) pairs. Each of these is used to compute an MPC in the output phase of r.MPC. The first $m - 1$ of these MPCs compute N, and the m'th MPC computes C.

In the first round of r.MPC, each party i also chooses randomness r_i, which will serve as the root for a binary tree of random values generated as in [GGM84] by a PRG (G_0, G_1). Below, we set $r_{i,0} := r_i$, where the 0 refers to the fact that the 0'th MPC will be computing the circuit N on input that includes $\{r_{i,0}\}_{i \in [n]}$. The string p then generates a sequence of values $r_{i,1}, \ldots, r_{i,m}$ by $r_{i,d} := G_{p[d]}(r_{i,d-1})$. The d'th MPC will be computing the circuit N on input that includes $\{r_{i,d}\}_{i \in [n]}$.

Now, it remains to show how the m (garbled circuit, encrypted labels) pairs output by each party in round two can be used to reconstruct each of the m MPC outputs, culminating in C. We use a repeated application of the mechanism developed in the last section. In particular, the d'th garbled circuit output by party i computes their second round message of the d'th MPC. The input labels are encrypted using randomness derived from party i's root randomness r_i. Specifically, as in last section, we use a PRF to compute a $2 \times \ell$ grid of keys, which will be used to LabEnc the $2 \times \ell$ grid of input labels. The key to this PRF will be generated by a PRG $(\mathsf{H}_0, \mathsf{H}_1)$ applied to $r_{i,d-1}$. Since we are branching based on the bit $p[d]$, the key will be set to $\mathsf{H}_{p[d]}(r_{i,d-1})$.

Likewise, the d'th MPC (for $d < m$), using inputs $\{r_{i,d}\}_{i \in [n]}$, computes two instances of the first round of the $d + 1$'st MPC, the "left child" using inputs $\{\mathsf{G}_0(r_{i,d})\}_{i \in [n]}$ and the "right child" using inputs $\{\mathsf{G}_1(r_{i,d})\}_{i \in [n]}$. It then uses the PRF key $\mathsf{H}_0(r_{i,d})$ to output the ℓ keys corresponding to party i's left child first round message, and the key $\mathsf{H}_1(r_{i,d})$ to output the ℓ keys corresponding to party i's right child first round message.

Finally, in the output phase of r.MPC, all parties can recover party i's second round message of the d'th MPC, by first using the output of the $d - 1$'st MPC to decrypt party i's input labels corresponding to its first round message of the d'th MPC, and then using those labels to evaluate its d'th garbled circuit, finally recovering the second round message. Once all of the d'th second round messages have been recovered, the output may be reconstructed. Note that this output is exactly the set of keys necessary to repeat the process for the $d + 1$'st MPC. Eventually, the parties will arrive at the m'th MPC, which allows them to recover the final output $\mathsf{C}(x_1, \ldots, x_n)$. One final technicality is that each party's second round message for each MPC may be generated along with a secret state. We cannot leak this state to other parties in the output phase, so in the second round of r.MPC, parties will actually garble circuits that compute their second round (state, message) pair, encrypt the state with their own secret key, and then output the encrypted state plus the message in the clear. In the output phase, each party i can decrypt their own state, (but not anyone else's) and use their state to reconstruct the output of each MPC.

The formal construction and the proof of the following theorem are deferred to the full version [BGMM20].

Theorem 12. *Let $\mathcal{X} \in \{$semi-honest in the plain or CRS model, malicious in the CRS model$\}$. Assuming a first message succinct $\mathcal{X}$ two-round MPC protocol, there exists an $\mathcal{X}$ reusable two-round MPC protocol.*

Acknowledgements. We thank Saikrishna Badrinarayanan for valuable contributions while collaborating during the early stages of this work.

References

[ABJ+19] Ananth, P., Badrinarayanan, S., Jain, A., Manohar, N., Sahai, A.: From fe combiners to secure mpc and back. In: Hofheinz, D., Rosen, A. (eds.) TCC 2019. LNCS, vol. 11891, pp. 199–228. Springer, Cham (2019). https://doi.org/10.1007/978-3-030-36030-6_9

[AJJ20] Prabhanjan, A., Abhishek, J., Zhengzhong, J.: Multiparty homomorphic encryption (or: On removing setup in multi-key fhe). Cryptology ePrint Archive, Report 2020/169 (2020). https://eprint.iacr.org/2020/169

[AMN+18] Attrapadung, N., Matsuda, T., Nishimaki, R., Yamada, S., Yamakawa, T.: Constrained PRFs for NC^1 in traditional groups. In: Shacham, H., Boldyreva, A. (eds.) CRYPTO 2018. Part II, volume 10992 of LNCS, pp. 543–574. Springer, Heidelberg (2018)

[AMPR14] Afshar, A., Mohassel, P., Pinkas, B., Riva, B.: Non-interactive secure computation based on cut-and-choose. In: Nguyen, P.Q., Oswald, E. (eds.) EUROCRYPT 2014. LNCS, vol. 8441, pp. 387–404. Springer, Heidelberg (2014). https://doi.org/10.1007/978-3-642-55220-5_22

[BCG+19] Boyle, E., Couteau, G., Gilboa, N., Ishai, Y., Kohl, L., Scholl, P.: Efficient pseudorandom correlation generators: silent ot extension and more. In: Boldyreva, A., Micciancio, D. (eds.) CRYPTO 2019. LNCS, vol. 11694, pp. 489–518. Springer, Cham (2019). https://doi.org/10.1007/978-3-030-26954-8_16

[BCGI18] Elette, B., Geoffroy, C., Niv, G., Yuval, I.: Compressing vector OLE. In: David, L., Mohammad, M., Michael, B., XiaoFeng, W., (eds.), ACM CCS 2018, pp. 896–912. ACM Press (2018)

[BF01] Boneh, D., Franklin, M.: Identity-based encryption from the weil pairing. In: Kilian, J. (ed.) CRYPTO 2001. LNCS, vol. 2139, pp. 213–229. Springer, Heidelberg (2001). https://doi.org/10.1007/3-540-44647-8_13

[BGI16] Boyle, E., Gilboa, N., Ishai, Y.: Breaking the circuit size barrier for secure computation under ddh. In: Robshaw, M., Katz, J. (eds.) CRYPTO 2016. LNCS, vol. 9814, pp. 509–539. Springer, Heidelberg (2016). https://doi.org/10.1007/978-3-662-53018-4_19

[BGI17] Boyle, E., Gilboa, N., Ishai, Y.: Group-based secure computation: optimizing rounds, communication, and computation. In: Coron, J.-S., Nielsen, J.B. (eds.) EUROCRYPT 2017. LNCS, vol. 10211, pp. 163–193. Springer, Cham (2017). https://doi.org/10.1007/978-3-319-56614-6_6

[BGMM20] Bartusek, J., Garg, S., Masny, D. and Muhkerjee, P.: Reusable two-round mpc from ddh. Cryptology ePrint Archive, Report 2020/170 (2020). https://eprint.iacr.org/2020/170

[BJOV18] Badrinarayanan, S., Jain, A., Ostrovsky, R., Visconti, I.: Non-interactive secure computation from one-way functions. In: Peyrin, T., Galbraith, S. (eds.) ASIACRYPT 2018. LNCS, vol. 11274, pp. 118–138. Springer, Cham (2018). https://doi.org/10.1007/978-3-030-03332-3_5

[BL18] Benhamouda, F., Lin, H.: k-Round multiparty computation from k-round oblivious transfer via garbled interactive circuits. In: Nielsen, J.B., Rijmen, V. (eds.) EUROCRYPT 2018. LNCS, vol. 10821, pp. 500–532. Springer, Cham (2018). https://doi.org/10.1007/978-3-319-78375-8_17

[BL20] Fabrice, B., Huijia, L.: Multiparty reusable non-interactive secure computation. Cryptology ePrint Archive, Report 2020/221 (2020). http://eprint.iacr.org/2020/221

[BMR90] Donald, B., Silvio, M., Phillip, R.: The round complexity of secure protocols (extended abstract). In: 22nd ACM STOC, pp. 503–513. ACM Press (1990)

[BP16] Brakerski, Z., Perlman, R.: Lattice-based fully dynamic multi-key fhe with short ciphertexts. In: Robshaw, M., Katz, J. (eds.) CRYPTO 2016. LNCS, vol. 9814, pp. 190–213. Springer, Heidelberg (2016). https://doi.org/10.1007/978-3-662-53018-4_8

[CDG+17] Cho, C., Döttling, N., Garg, S., Gupta, D., Miao, P., Polychroniadou, A.: Laconic oblivious transfer and its applications. In: Katz, J., Shacham, H. (eds.) CRYPTO 2017. LNCS, vol. 10402, pp. 33–65. Springer, Cham (2017). https://doi.org/10.1007/978-3-319-63715-0_2

[CDI+19] Chase, M., et al.: Reusable non-interactive secure computation. In: Boldyreva, A., Micciancio, D. (eds.) CRYPTO 2019. LNCS, vol. 11694, pp. 462–488. Springer, Cham (2019). https://doi.org/10.1007/978-3-030-26954-8_15

[DG17a] Döttling, N., Garg, S.: From selective IBE to full IBE and selective HIBE. In: Kalai, Y., Reyzin, L. (eds.) TCC 2017. LNCS, vol. 10677, pp. 372–408. Springer, Cham (2017). https://doi.org/10.1007/978-3-319-70500-2_13

[DG17b] Döttling, N., Garg, S.: Identity-Based encryption from the diffie-hellman assumption. In: Katz, J., Shacham, H. (eds.) CRYPTO 2017. LNCS, vol. 10401, pp. 537–569. Springer, Cham (2017). https://doi.org/10.1007/978-3-319-63688-7_18

[DHRW16] Dodis, Y., Halevi, S., Rothblum, R.D., Wichs, D.: Spooky encryption and its applications. In: Robshaw, M., Katz, J. (eds.) CRYPTO 2016. LNCS, vol. 9816, pp. 93–122. Springer, Heidelberg (2016). https://doi.org/10.1007/978-3-662-53015-3_4

[Gen09] Craig, G.: Fully homomorphic encryption using ideal lattices. In: Michael, M., editor, 41st ACM STOC, pp. 169–178. ACM Press (2009)

[GGH+13] Sanjam, G., Craig, G., Shai, H., Mariana, R., Amit, S., Brent, W.: Candidate indistinguishability obfuscation and functional encryption for all circuits. In: 54th FOCS, pp. 40–49. IEEE Computer Society Press (2013)

[GGHR14] Garg, S., Gentry, C., Halevi, S., Raykova, M.: Two-round secure MPC from indistinguishability obfuscation. In: Lindell, Y. (ed.) TCC 2014. LNCS, vol. 8349, pp. 74–94. Springer, Heidelberg (2014)

[GGM84] Oded, G., Shafi, G., Silvio, M.: How to construct random functions (extended abstract). In: 25th FOCS, pp. 464–479. IEEE Computer Society Press (1984)

[GGSW13] Sanjam, G., Craig, G., Amit, S., Brent, W.: Witness encryption and its applications. In: Dan, B., Tim, R., Joan, F., (eds.), 45th ACM STOC, pp. 467–476. ACM Press (2013)

[GHL+14] Gentry, C., Halevi, S., Lu, S., Ostrovsky, R., Raykova, M., Wichs, D.: Garbled RAM revisited. In: Nguyen, P.Q., Oswald, E. (eds.) EUROCRYPT 2014. LNCS, vol. 8441, pp. 405–422. Springer, Heidelberg (2014). https://doi.org/10.1007/978-3-642-55220-5_23

[GIS18] Garg, S., Ishai, Y., Srinivasan, A.: Two-round mpc: information-theoretic and black-box. In: Beimel, A., Dziembowski, S. (eds.) TCC 2018. Part I, volume 11239 of LNCS, pp. 123–151. Springer, Heidelberg (2018)

[GLO15] Sanjam, G., Steve, L., Rafail, O.: Black-box garbled RAM. In Venkatesan, G., (eds.), 56th FOCS, pp. 210–229. IEEE Computer Society Press (2015)

[GLOS15] Sanjam G., Steve, L., Rafail, O., Alessandra, S.: Garbled RAM from one-way functions. In Rocco, A.S., Ronitt, R., (eds.), 47th ACM STOC, pp. 449–458. ACM Press (2015)

[GLS15] Dov Gordon, S., Liu, F.-H., Shi, E.: Constant-round mpc with fairness and guarantee of output delivery. In: Gennaro, R., Robshaw, M. (eds.) CRYPTO 2015. LNCS, vol. 9216, pp. 63–82. Springer, Heidelberg (2015). https://doi.org/10.1007/978-3-662-48000-7_4

[GMW87] Oded, G., Silvio, M., Avi, W.: How to play any mental game or A completeness theorem for protocols with honest majority. In: Alfred, A., (eds.), 19th ACM STOC, pp. 218–229. ACM Press (1987)

[GS17] Sanjam, G., Akshayaram S.: Garbled protocols and two-round MPC from bilinear maps. In: 58th FOCS, pp. 588–599. IEEE Computer Society Press (2017)

[GS18] Garg, S., Srinivasan, A.: Two-round multiparty secure computation from minimal assumptions. In: Nielsen, J.B., Rijmen, V. (eds.) EUROCRYPT 2018. LNCS, vol. 10821, pp. 468–499. Springer, Cham (2018). https://doi.org/10.1007/978-3-319-78375-8_16

[IKO+11] Ishai, Y., Kushilevitz, E., Ostrovsky, R., Prabhakaran, M., Sahai, A.: Efficient non-interactive secure computation. In: Paterson, K.G. (ed.) EUROCRYPT 2011. LNCS, vol. 6632, pp. 406–425. Springer, Heidelberg (2011). https://doi.org/10.1007/978-3-642-20465-4_23

[Jou04] Joux, A.: A one round protocol for tripartite Diffie-Hellman. J. Cryptol. **17**(4), 263–276 (2004)

[LO13] Steve, L., Ostrovsky, R.: How to garble RAM programs. In: Johansson, T., Nguyen, P.Q. (eds.) EUROCRYPT 2013. LNCS, vol. 7881, pp. 719–734. Springer, Heidelberg (2013)

[MR17] Mohassel, P., Rosulek, M.: Non-interactive secure 2pc in the offline/online and batch settings. In: Coron, J.-S., Nielsen, J.B. (eds.) EUROCRYPT 2017. LNCS, vol. 10212, pp. 425–455. Springer, Cham (2017). https://doi.org/10.1007/978-3-319-56617-7_15

[MW16] Mukherjee, P., Wichs, D.: Two round multiparty computation via multi-key fhe. In: Fischlin, M., Coron, J.-S. (eds.) EUROCRYPT 2016. LNCS, vol. 9666, pp. 735–763. Springer, Heidelberg (2016). https://doi.org/10.1007/978-3-662-49896-5_26

[NR97] Moni, N., Omer, R.: Number-theoretic constructions of efficient pseudorandom functions. In: 38th FOCS, pp. 8–467. IEEE Computer Society Press (1997)

[PS16] Peikert, C., Shiehian, S.: Multi-key fhe from lwe, revisited. In: Hirt, M., Smith, A. (eds.) TCC 2016. LNCS, vol. 9986, pp. 217–238. Springer, Heidelberg (2016). https://doi.org/10.1007/978-3-662-53644-5_9

Mr NISC: Multiparty Reusable Non-Interactive Secure Computation

Fabrice Benhamouda[1]($\boxtimes$) and Huijia Lin[2]($\boxtimes$)

[1] Algorand Foundation, New York, USA
fabrice.benhamouda@normalesup.org
[2] University of Washington, Seattle, USA
rachel@cs.washington.edu

Abstract. Reducing interaction in Multiparty Computation (MPC) is a highly desirable goal in cryptography. It is known that 2-round MPC can be based on the minimal assumption of 2-round Oblivious Transfer (OT) [Benhamouda and Lin, Garg and Srinivasan, EC 2018], and 1-round MPC is impossible in general. In this work, we propose a natural "hybrid" model, called *multiparty reusable Non-Interactive Secure Computation (mrNISC)*. In this model, parties publish encodings of their private inputs x_i on a public bulletin board, once and for all. Later, any subset I of them can compute *on-the-fly* a function f on their inputs $\boldsymbol{x}_I = \{x_i\}_{i \in I}$ by just sending a single message to a stateless evaluator, conveying the result $f(\boldsymbol{x}_I)$ and nothing else. Importantly, the input encodings can be *reused* in any number of on-the-fly computations, and the same classical simulation security guaranteed by multi-round MPC, is achieved. In short, mrNISC has a minimal yet "tractable" interaction pattern.

We initiate the study of mrNISC on several fronts. First, we formalize the model of mrNISC protocols, and present both a UC security definition and a game-based security definition. Second, we construct mrNISC protocols in the plain model with semi-honest and semi-malicious security based on pairing groups. Third, we demonstrate the power of mrNISC by showing two applications: non-interactive MPC (NIMPC) with reusable setup and a distributed version of program obfuscation.

At the core of our construction of mrNISC is a witness encryption scheme for a special language that verifies Non-Interactive Zero-Knowledge (NIZK) proofs of the validity of computations over committed values, which is of independent interest.

1 Introduction

Reducing interaction in Multiparty Computation (MPC) is a highly desirable goal in cryptography, both because each round of communication is expensive and because the liveness of parties is hard to guarantee, especially when the number of participants is large. Contrary to throughput, latency is now essentially limited by physical constraints, and the time taken by a round of communication cannot be significantly reduced anymore. Moreover, non-interactive primitives are more versatile and more amenable to be used as powerful building blocks.

© International Association for Cryptologic Research 2020
R. Pass and K. Pietrzak (Eds.): TCC 2020, LNCS 12551, pp. 349–378, 2020.
https://doi.org/10.1007/978-3-030-64378-2_13

Recent works [7, 21] constructed 2-round MPC protocols from the minimal primitive of 2-round Oblivious Transfer (OT), where in each round all participants simultaneously broadcast one message. Is it possible to further reduce interaction? The answer is no in general as any non-interactive (i.e., one-round) protocol is susceptible to the so-called residual attack, and cannot achieve the classical simulation security.

In this work, we introduce and study a natural "hybrid" model, between the 2-round and the 1-round settings, which gets us close to having non-interactive protocols while still providing classical security guarantees. We call this model **multiparty reusable Non-Interactive Secure Computation (mrNISC)**. In this model, parties publish encodings of their private inputs x_i on a public bulletin board, once and for all. Later, any subset I of them can compute *on-the-fly* a function f on their inputs $x_I = \{x_i\}_{i \in I}$ by just sending a single public message to a stateless evaluator, conveying the result $f(x_I)$ and nothing else. Importantly, the input encodings are reusable across any number of computation sessions, and are generated independently of any information of later computation sessions—each later computation can evaluate any polynomial-time function, among any polynomial-size subset of participants. Figure 1 depicts the setting. The security guarantee is that an adversary corrupting a subset of parties, chosen statically at the beginning, learns no information about the private inputs of honest parties, beyond the outputs of the computations they participated in. This holds for any polynomial number of computation sessions.

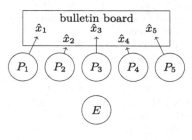

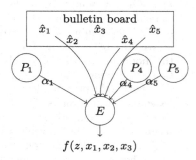

(a) Parties P_i publish the encodings $\hat{x}_i$ of their inputs x_i. (Step done a single time, usable for multiple computations.)

(b) Parties P_1, P_4, P_5 want to let the evaluator E compute $f(z, x_1, x_4, x_5)$ by each sending a single message α_i.

Fig. 1. mrNISC market (z is a public input to the function)

Our Contributions. We initiate the study of mrNISC at the following fronts:

Modeling: We introduce the mrNISC model and formalize both UC security through an ideal mrNISC functionality, and a simpler game-based security notion that implies UC security. Our model aims for maximal flexibility. Consider the simplest form of 2-round MPC with reusable first messages, where the first messages could potentially depend on the number of parties, complexity of the computations, and potentially all parties must participate in all computations. mrNISC does not have such restriction. In addition, our model allows adaptive choices of inputs and computations, uses weak communication channels, and allows honest parties to individually opt out of computations.

Construction: We construct the first mrNISC protocols based on SXDH in asymmetric (prime-order) pairing groups. Our protocols are in the plain-model (without any trusted setup), and satisfies semi-honest, and semi-malicious security. For malicious security, reliance on some trusted setups is inevitable. We use a CRS.

Techniques: At the core of our construction is a witness encryption (WE) scheme for a special language that verifies non-interactive zero-knowledge (NIZK) proofs of the validity of computations over committed values. We construct it from bilinear groups. This significantly extends the range of languages for which we know how to construct WE from standard assumptions, which is a result of independent interest.

Applications: We demonstrate the power of mrNISC protocols in two cryptographic applications. First mrNISC allows to generically transform non-interactive MPC protocols [5] using correlated randomness into non-interactive MPC protocols in the PKI plus CRS model. Second, mrNISC enables a secret-sharing analogue of Virtual Black-Box program obfuscation [4]—called secret sharing VBB.

Comparing with previous models of MPC with minimal interaction, mrNISC naturally generalizes the beautiful notion of reusable NISC by Ishai et al. [30] from two party to multiple parties. It differs from the notions of non-interactive MPC (NIMPC) [5] and Private Simultaneous Messages (PSM) [17,29] which achieves weaker security or restricts the corruption pattern.

It is very plausible that multi-key fully-homomorphic encryption (MKFHE) with threshold decryption, which implies 2-round MPC [2,13,33], is sufficient for mrNISC. However, proving it is not straightforward. For instance, the current definitions of threshold decryption e.g., [3,33] are insufficient for constructing mrNISC, as simulatability only ensures that a single partial decryption can be simulated (hence this definition does not allow to re-use ciphertexts.)

Organization of the Paper. Next we start with giving more details of our results. In Sect. 2, we formally define mrNISC schemes, and provide an overview of our construction of mrNISC from bilinear maps; the technical bulk of the construction is constructing WE for NIZK of commitments. Next, we define witness encryption for NIZK of commitments, and construct a scheme for NC^1 in Sect. 3. Due to the lack of space, we refer the reader to the full version [8] for the following: 1) Bootstrapping WE for NIZK of commitments for NC^1 to a scheme for P, 2) the UC definition of mrNISC protocols, 3) The formal constructions of UC-secure mrNISC protocols from mrNISC schemes, 4) the applications of mrNISC, and 5) more detailed comparison with related works.

1.1   Our Results in More Detail

Definition. We start with defining a mrNISC scheme, consisting of an input encoding Com, computation Encode, and output Eval algorithms. An mrNISC scheme immediately yields an MPC protocol with minimal interaction pattern, called an mrNISC protocol. We formalize a game-based security notion for mrNISC scheme, as well as UC-security for mrNISC protocols, and show that the former implies the latter. We have both definitions since they each has its own advantage: UC security is the strongest security notion for MPC protocols, and implies security under composition. The ideal mrNISC functionality we define provides a simple interface for using our protocols in bigger systems. On the other hand, the game-based security notion is more succinct and easier to manipulate. By showing that game-based security implies UC security, we have the best of both sides.

mrNISC Scheme. A mrNISC scheme is defined by:

- Input Encoding: A party P_i encodes its private input x_i by invoking $(\hat{x}_i, s_i) \leftarrow$ Com$(1^\lambda, x_i)$. It then publishes the encoding $\hat{x}_i$ and keeps the secret state s_i.
- Computation: In order for a subset of parties $\{P_i\}_{i \in I}$ to compute the functionality f on their private inputs $\boldsymbol{x}_I$ and a public input z, each party in I generates a computation encoding $\alpha_i \leftarrow$ Encode$(z, \{\hat{x}_j\}_{j \in I}, s_i)$ and sends it to the evaluator. Here, z can be viewed as part of the description of the function $f(z, \star)$ that is computed.
- Output: The evaluator reconstructs the output $y =$ Eval$(z, \{\hat{x}_i\}_{i \in I}, \{\alpha_i\}_{i \in I})$. (Note that reconstruction is *public* as the evaluator has no secret state.) Correctness requires that $y = f(z, \{x_i\}_{i \in I})$ when everything is honestly computed.

It is easy to see that an mrNISC scheme for f immediately gives an mrNISC protocol for f. Simulation-security requires that the view of an adversary corrupting the evaluator and any subset of parties, can be simulated using just the outputs of the computations that honest parties participate in. We consider static corruption: The set of corrupted parties C are chosen at the beginning and fixed; later, in a computation involving parties I, the corrupted and honest parties are respectively $I \cap C$ and $I \cap \bar{C}$.

The same security intuition can be formalized with different degree of flexibility. In the simplest *selective setting*, where the function f, parties' inputs $x_1, \ldots, x_m$, and $(z^1, I^1), \ldots, (z^K, I^K)$ for different computations are all chosen selectively at the beginning, the view of corrupted parties in C is simulatable by a universal simulator $\mathcal{S}$ as follows.

Selective Security: $\quad \Big\{ \{x_i, r_i\}_{i \in C}, \ \{\hat{x}_i\}_{i \in \bar{C}}, \ \{\alpha_i^1\}_{i \in I^1 \cap \bar{C}}, \ \ldots, \ \{\alpha_i^K\}_{i \in I^K \cap \bar{C}} \Big\}$

$$\approx \Big\{ \mathcal{S}\left(\{x_i\}_{i \in C}, \ \left(y^1, z^1, I^1\right), \ldots, \left(y^K, z^K, I^K\right) \right) \Big\}$$

$$y^k = f(z^k, \boldsymbol{x}_{I^k}), \ \forall k \in [K]$$

where $\{x_i, r_i\}_{i \in C}$ are the inputs and randomness of corrupted parties, $\hat{x}_i$ is the input encoding of an honest party P_i, and α_i^k the computation encoding from an honest party P_i in session k. The above definition captures *semi-honest* security. In the stronger *semi-malicious* security [2], the corrupted parties still follow the protocol specification but are allowed to choose the randomness arbitrarily.

Dynamics in the mrNISC. The simple selective setting has several drawbacks undesirable for capturing a dynamic mrNISC setting we envision. Instead, in mrNISC, we have:

- *Adaptive Choices:* Each party's input x_i is chosen adaptively. Each computation specified by (z, I) is chosen adaptively, before it starts. Different computation can use the same z and/or I, or different ones. Parties outside I are not involved in and not even aware of computation (z, I). $f(z, \star)$ can be any polynomial time computable function, and I any polynomial size subset.
- *Asynchronous P2P Communication:* Parties have access to a common public bulletin board, but otherwise should only use asynchronous point-to-point authenticated channels. We do not assume any broadcast channel.
- *Optional Participation:* In a computation session (z^k, I^k), honest parties in I^k may opt in or out of any computation. We do not require all honest parties to participate. Furthermore, the output of a computation is revealed only after all parties in I^k send their computation encoding. (This means that, in any computation session, the simulation of all but the last honest computation encoding must be done without knowing the output of the computation.)

Our mrNISC ideal functionality in the UC framework [11] captures all above features. Clearly, selective security is insufficient for implementing the mrNISC ideal functionality. We thus formalize a game-based adaptive-security of mrNISC schemes, Definition 3 in the overview (Sect. 2.1) and we show that it implies UC-security. We emphasize that our adaptive security does not mean security against adaptive corruptions.

Lemma 1 (Informal). *An mrNISC scheme for a function f satisfying adaptive semi-malicious (or semi-honest) privacy implies a protocol that UC-implements the mrNISC ideal functionality for f in the plain model with semi-malicious (or semi-honest) security.*

Following standard techniques [2], semi-malicious UC protocols in the plain model can be transformed into malicious UC protocols in the CRS model using malicious UC-NIZK.

Plain-Model mrNISC from Bilinear Groups. We construct mrNISC schemes for polynomial time computable functions in the plain model from bilinear maps.

Theorem 1 (Informal). *There is an mrNISC scheme in the plain model for any function in P, satisfying adaptive semi-malicious security, based on the SXDH assumption on asymmetric bilinear groups.*

Our construction builds upon the construction of 2-round MPC protocols using general purpose WE and NIZK [24], which in turn improves upon the protocols of [18] based on indistinguishability obfuscation. (Unfortunately, follow-up works based on standard assumptions [7,20,21] do not have reusable first messages.)

So far, known WE schemes can be split into two categories. The first is WE for general NP language from very strong obfuscation-like assumptions, e.g., [19]. The second is WE from standard assumptions, but for very specific languages, such as, language of commitment (or hashes) of a given message, like in [15,16], and languages of commitments that commit to value satisfying up to quadratic equations, like in [20,21]. These functionality, however, is too weak for constructing 2-round MPC.

WE for NIZK of Com. We observe that it suffices to have witness encryption for a language that verifies NIZK proofs for the validity of computation over committed values. We then construct a commitment scheme Com, a NIZK proof system NIZK, and a WE scheme for the language $\mathcal{L}_{WE}$ of statements of form $X_{WE} = (crs, c_1, \ldots, c_m, G, y)$ (where crs is a CRS of NIZK, every c_i is a commitment of Com, and G is an arbitrary polynomial-sized circuit). The statement is true if and only if there exists a NIZK proof π (i.e., the witness) proving w.r.t. crs that G evaluated on the values $v_1, \ldots, v_m$ committed in $c_1, \ldots, c_m$ through Com outputs y, i.e., $G(v_1, \ldots, v_m) = y$. More precisely, the witness relations for WE and NIZK proof are:

$$\mathcal{R}_{WE}(X_{WE} = (crs, c_1, \ldots, c_m, G, y), \ \pi) = 1 \ \text{ iff } \ \mathsf{NIZKVer}(crs, X_{NIZK}, \pi) = 1 \quad (1)$$

$$\mathcal{R}_{NIZK}(X_{NIZK} = (c_1, \ldots, c_m, G, y), \ ((v_1, \rho_1), \ldots, (v_m, \rho_m))) = 1$$
$$\text{iff } \forall i \in [m], \ (v_i, \rho_i) \text{ is a valid opening of } c_i \text{ and } G(v_1, \ldots, v_m) = y \quad (2)$$

We call such a triple (Com, NIZK, WE) as WE for NIZK of commitments and construct it from bilinear pairing groups.

Theorem 2 (Informal). *There is a WE for NIZK of commitments* (Com, NIZK, WE) *based on SXDH over asymmetric bilinear pairing groups.*

We remark that our construction co-designs (Com, NIZK, WE) together. It significantly extends the range of statements that WE supports, and is based on standard assumptions, which is of independent interest.

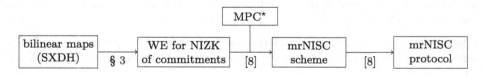

Fig. 2. Construction of mrNISC schemes and protocols (mrNISC protocols implement the mrNISC ideal functionality; MPC* is an MPC with some special properties). Citation [8] is the full version of the paper.

Applications. We show two applications of mrNISC. A summary of the applications is in Fig. 3.

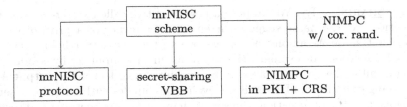

Fig. 3. Applications of mrNISC schemes (mrNISC protocols implement the mrNISC ideal functionality). See the full version [8].

NON-INTERACTIVE MPC WITH REUSABLE SETUP [5] proposed the model of non-interactive MPC (NIMPC), where to jointly compute a function, each party sends a single message to an evaluator, **without** *initially committing to their inputs*. In this setting, adversaries can always evaluate the residual function $f|_{H,\{x_i\}_{i\in H}}$ where the inputs of the honest parties are fixed, on all possible inputs of the corrupted parties, a.k.a. the *residual attack*. Thus, NIMPC aims at achieving the best-possible security that the only information of honest parties' inputs revealed is the residual function $f|_{H,\{x_i\}_{i\in H}}$. NIMPC is a powerful and flexible concept equivalent, under different corruption models (i.e., what set C of parties can be corrupted), to garbled circuits, Private Simultaneous Messages [17,29] protocols, and program obfuscation. Almost all NIMPC protocols are constructed in a model where parties receive *correlated randomness* sampled by a trusted third party from some distribution. However, correlated randomness is not reusable, and must be re-sampled independently for each computation session. So far, the only construction of NIMPC protocols with reusable setups is by [28], which makes use of a (reusable) PKI plus CRS, but is based on the sub-exponential security of IO and DDH. Using mrNISC, we give a generic transformation from any NIMPC protocols using correlated randomness to ones in the PKI plus CRS model.

Corollary 1. *Applying our transformation to known NIMPC protocols [5,6], gives the following NIMPC protocols in the PKI plus CRS model assuming mrNISC for P and UC-NIZK for NP.*

1. *NIMPC for the iterated product function $f(x_1, \ldots, x_n) = x_1 \cdots x_n$ over a group, against any number of corruption.*
2. *NIMPC for P from multi-input functional encryption, against any number of corruption.*
3. *NIMPC for P, against a constant number of corruption (each holding a $O(1)$-bit input).*

The first and third bullets are achieved for the first time, using only reusable setups. We weaken the assumption needed for the second bullet from sub-exponentially secure IO in [28] to polynomially secure IO, equivalent to multi-input functional encryption [23], which is a necessary assumption.

SECRET-SHARING VBB We propose a new primitive called *secret-sharing VBB* obfuscation. As the name suggests, it enables the owner of a private program M to secret share M among N servers, where the i'th server holds share M_i. Later, the servers can evaluate the program on any input x, by sending one message, called the output shares, to an evaluator who learns the output $M(x)$ and nothing else; this holds even if the evaluator colludes with all but one server. Analogous to VBB obfuscation, the secret shares of M are reusable and security is simulation-based. While VBB is impossible in general, secret-sharing VBB can be implemented using mrNISC in a simple way. Though the construction from mrNISC is simple, we found secret-sharing VBB conceptually interesting and it can be readily used to turn applications of VBB into their secret-sharing counterparts. For instance, for cryptographic primitives, such as, IBE, ABE, PE, and FE, where a central trusted authority issues secret keys for identities, key policies, and functions respectively, we can decentralize the trusted authority by creating a secret-sharing VBB obfuscation of the key generation algorithm among multiple servers. Importantly, the servers do not need to communicate with each other and only need to send a single message to the inquirer of a key.

The notion of secret-sharing VBB appears similar to the notions of Homomorphic Secret Sharing and Function Secret Sharing (HSS/FSS) [9, 10]. The main difference is that in secret-sharing VBB the evaluator may collude with all but one servers, whereas in HSS/FSS the evaluator is honest. Consequently, the security of secret-sharing VBB must hold even when all output shares are made public, whereas HSS/FSS does not guarantee security in this setting. Another similar notion is bit-fixing homomorphic sharing proposed in [31], which is tailor made for the construction there. Secret sharing VBB is simpler and more natural.

2 Technical Overview

2.1 Security Definition of mrNISC Schemes

We now present the game-based definition of adaptive security of mrNISC scheme. In the full version [8], we present the ideal mrNISC functionality and show that the definition below implies UC-security.

Definition 3 (Adaptive Security). An mrNISC scheme mrNISC for f is semi-honest (or semi-malicious) private if there exists a PPT simulator $\mathcal{S}$, such that, for all PPT adversary $\mathcal{A}$, the views of $\mathcal{A}$ in the following experiments $\mathsf{Exp}_{\mathcal{A},\mathcal{S}}(\mathsf{Real}, \lambda, f)$ and $\mathsf{Exp}_{\mathcal{A},\mathcal{S}}(\mathsf{Ideal}, \lambda, f)$ are indistinguishable.

Experiment $\mathsf{Exp}_{\mathcal{A},\mathcal{S}}(\mathsf{Real}, \lambda, f)$: $\mathcal{A}$ chooses the number of parties M and the set of honest parties $H \subseteq [M]$; the set of corrupted parties is $\bar{H}$. It interacts with a challenger in an arbitrary number of iterations till it terminates. In every iteration k, it can submit *one query* of one of the following three types.

CORRUPT INPUT ENCODING: Upon $\mathcal{A}$ sending a query $(\mathsf{input}, P_i, x_i, \rho_i)$ for a corrupt party $i \in \bar{H}$, record $\hat{x}_i$ generated by $(\hat{x}_i, s_i) = \mathsf{Com}(1^\lambda, x_i; \rho_i)$. In the semi-honest case, ρ_i is randomly sampled, whereas in the semi-malicious case, it is chosen by $\mathcal{A}$.

HONEST INPUT ENCODING: Upon $\mathcal{A}$ choosing the input (input, P_i, x_i) of an honest party $i \in H$, generate $(\hat{x}_i, s_i) \leftarrow \mathsf{Com}(1^\lambda, x_i)$ and send $\hat{x}_i$ to $\mathcal{A}$.
$\mathcal{A}$ is restricted to submit one input query for each party P_i.

HONEST COMPUTATION ENCODING: Upon $\mathcal{A}$ querying (compute, P_i, z, I) for an honest party $i \in H \cap I$, if the input encodings $\{\hat{x}_j\}_{j \in I}$ of all parties in $H \cap I$ have been generated, send $\mathcal{A}$ the computation encoding $\alpha_i \leftarrow$ $\mathsf{Encode}(z, \{\hat{x}_j\}_{j \in I}, s_i)$. $((z, I)$ is the unique identifier of a computation.)

Experiment $\mathsf{Exp}_{\mathcal{A}, \mathcal{S}}(\mathsf{Ideal}, \lambda, f)$: Same as the above experiment, except: Invoke $\mathcal{S}(1^\lambda, f)$.

CORRUPT INPUT ENCODING: Additionally send query (input, P_i, x_i, ρ_i) to $\mathcal{S}$.

HONEST INPUT ENCODING: Upon $\mathcal{A}$ choosing (input, P_i, x_i) for $i \in H$, send query (input, P_i) to $\mathcal{S}$ who generates a simulated input encoding $\tilde{x}_i$ for Adv.

HONEST COMPUTATION ENCODING: Upon $\mathcal{A}$ choosing (compute, P_i, z, I), if this is the last honest computation encoding to be generated for computation (z, I) (i.e., $\forall\, j \neq i \in I \cap H$, $\mathcal{A}$ has queried (compute, P_j, z, I) before), send $\mathcal{S}$ the query (compute, P_i, z, I) and the output $y = f(z, \{x_t\}_{t \in I})$; otherwise, send $\mathcal{S}$ the query (compute, P_i, z, I) without y. $\mathcal{S}$ generates a simulated computation encoding $\tilde{\alpha}_i$ for Adv.

We emphasize that the definition above captures all dynamic choices described in the introduction. For instance, in the ideal world, for each computation session, simulation of all but the last honest computation encoding do not use the output of that session, ensuring that the output remains hidden until all honest computation encodings are sent.

2.2   Overview of Our mrNISC Scheme

Our construction of mrNISC scheme follows the round collapsing approach for constructing 2-round MPC protocols started in [18]; in particular, we build on the work of [24].

The Round Collapsing Approach. The *round-collapsing* approach collapses a inner MPC protocol with a polynomial L number of rounds into a 2-round outer MPC protocol as follows. Assume that each party P_i in the inner MPC broadcast one message m_i^ℓ in each round ℓ. In the first round of outer MPC, each party P_i commits $c_i \leftarrow \mathsf{COM}(x_i, r_i)$ to its input x_i and some random tape r_i to be used to execute the inner MPC protocol. In the second round, each party P_i sends one garbled circuit $\hat{\mathsf{F}}_i^\ell$ per round $\ell \in [L]$ of the inner MPC protocol corresponding to the next message function F_i^ℓ of P_i. This garbled circuit takes as input all the messages $\boldsymbol{m}^{<\ell} = \{m_j^l\}_{l < \ell, j \in [n]}$ sent in previous rounds, and outputs the next message m_i^ℓ of P_i of the inner MPC (or the output for the last round $\ell = L$).

To compute the output from all garbled circuits $\{\hat{\mathsf{F}}_i^\ell\}_{\ell \in [L], i \in [n]}$, each P_i needs to provide a way to compute the labels of its garbled circuits $\hat{\mathsf{F}}_i^\ell$ that correspond to the correct messages of the inner MPC, where a message m_j^l is correct if it is computed from P_j's input and randomness (x_j, r_j) committed to in the first round. For this, [24] proposed the following mechanism using a general purpose WE and NIZK. Let k_0, k_1 be two labels of P_i's garbled circuit $\hat{\mathsf{F}}_i^\ell$ for an input wire that takes in the t'th bit $y = m_{j,t}^l$ of a message from P_j. Recall that m_j^l is output by P_j's garbled circuit $\hat{\mathsf{F}}_j^l$. The goal is translating the valid bit y to the corresponding label k_y—that is "let $\hat{\mathsf{F}}_j^l$ communicate y to $\hat{\mathsf{F}}_i^{\ell}$". [24] modifies the garbled circuits as follows.

- To "receive" y, $\hat{\mathsf{F}}_i^{\ell-1}$ *for round* $\ell-1$ additionally outputs $\mathsf{ct}_y \leftarrow \mathsf{WEnc}(X_y, k_y)$ for $y \in \{0, 1\}$, under the statement X_y that there is a NIZK proof π_y proving that $y = m_{j,t}^l$ is computed correctly from P_j's input and randomness (x_j, r_j) committed in c_j, according to the protocol specification and the partial transcript of messages $\boldsymbol{m}^{<l}$ before round l.
- To "send" y, $\hat{\mathsf{F}}_j^l$ additionally outputs a NIZK proof π that $y = m_{j,t}^l$ is computed correctly from (x_j, r_j) committed in c_j.

For correctness, decrypting ct_y using π as a witness reveals k_y. For security, k_{1-y} remains hidden, thanks to the security of WE and soundness NIZK. Moreover, the ZK property of NIZK ensures that P_j's committed input and randomness (x_j, r_j) remains hidden, protecting P_j's privacy.

Observe that the first messages of the [24] protocol consist of a commitment to parties' input x_i and randomness r_i. We show (as a corollary of our mrNISC construction) that the first messages can be made reusable if we replace r_i with a PRF seed s_i which can generate pseudo-random tapes for an unbounded number of computations.

Challenge and Our Method. The problem is we do not have general purpose WE from standard assumptions. Previous 2-round MPC constructions from standard assumptions circumvent this problem using weaker tools, namely functional commitment with witness encryption from OT in [7], or homomorphic proof commitment with encryption from bilinear pairing groups in [20], or achieving its effect using OT in [21]. Unfortunately, as we explain shortly, using these weaker tools kills the reusability of the first messages.

We restore the reusability of first messages using **WE for NIZK of commitments**, which suffices for the purpose of [24]. WE for NIZK of commitments is a triple (Com, NIZK, WE) of commitment, NIZK, and WE schemes. It allows to commit to any values $c_1 \leftarrow \mathsf{Com}(v_1) \ldots c_m \leftarrow \mathsf{Com}(v_m)$ and later reveal multiple NIZK proofs π^k w.r.t. a crs that $G^k(v_1 \ldots v_m) = y^k$ for multiple polynomial-size circuits G^k and outputs y^k. In addition, the proofs π^k can be used to decrypt ciphertexts $\mathsf{ct} \leftarrow \mathsf{WEnc}((\mathsf{crs}, c_1 \ldots c_m, G^k, y^k), \mathsf{m})$ tied to a statement $X^k = (\mathsf{crs}, c_1 \ldots c_m, G^k, y^k)$, so that, the message m is recovered if and only if π^k is an accepting proof that $G^k(v_1 \ldots v_m) = y^k$ w.r.t. crs. The formal witness relation for WE is in Eq. (1) and that for NIZK in Eq. (2).

The two key properties of WE for NIZK of commitments are *i) reusability* of commitments – one can generate an unbounded number of NIZK proofs and WE ciphertexts w.r.t. them while keeping committed values hidden (only information in the statements is revealed), and *ii) support for* P *computation –* the statements $X^k = (c, G, y)$ are about the correctness of arbitrary polynomial-sized circuits. These two properties are crucial for achieving the reusability of MPC first messages. Our specific definition and construction of WE for NIZK of commitments has an additional bonus feature that it is "dual-mode" in the sense that in a binding mode, binding of commitments, soundness of NIZK, and semantic security of WE are all information theoretic and perfect, and in a simulation mode, the commitments are perfectly equivocable, NIZK perfectly zero-knowledge. These two modes are controlled by how the CRS is sampled and are indistinguishable. The "dual-mode" feature is not necessary for mrNISC, but might be useful for other applications. We give an overview of our WE for NIZK of commitments in Sect. 2.3, and formal construction for NC^1 in Sect. 3 and for P in the full version [8].

Combined with the round-collapsing approach of [24], we obtain semi-honest, in fact semi-malicious, mrNISC protocols in the CRS model from pairing groups. We can further remove the CRS, by letting each party P_i sample a CRS in the binding mode for generating its own commitments and NIZK proofs, while generating WE ciphertexts w.r.t. other parties' CRS, yielding protocols in the plain model. This does not hurt security because for every correctly generated binding CRS, the binding of commitments and the soundness of NIZK hold information theoretically; hence semi-malicious corrupted parties can't cheat and the WE ciphertexts they receive are information theoretically secure. The simulator on the other hand can sample honest parties' CRS in the simulation mode to simulate their commitments and NIZK proofs.

Implementing Additional Features in mrNISC. Beyond making the first messages reusable, we carefully implement features in mrNISC—namely, adaptive choices of inputs and computations, asynchronous P2P communication, and optional participation of honest parties. Technically, this means simulation of a message can only use information that is available to the simulator at the moment, e.g., only the last delivered honest message in a session can be simulated using the output of that session, all other honest messages are simulated with no information. We show this can be achieved if the inner MPC satisfies *output-delayed simulatability*—all but the last message from honest parties can be simulated without the output, which is the case w.r.t. the GMW protocol [22]. We then show that the resulting collapsed protocols achieves dynamics in mrNISC.

Comparison with Homomorphic Proof Commitments with Encryption. The homomorphic proof commitment with encryption of [20,21] can be viewed as a WE for NIZK of the statement that (a linear combination of) committed values is 0 or 1. This in turns gives WE for NIZK of NAND, which verifies NIZK proofs that c_1, c_2, c_3 commit to three values v_1, v_2, v_3 such that $v_3 = \text{NAND}(v_1, v_2)$. The acute reader may remark that being able to prove NAND relations between committed values allow to prove any statement $X^k = (c, G^k, y^k)$, by including, in the NIZK proof, commitments to intermediate values in the computation of G^k, and proofs of correctness of every NAND gate computation w.r.t. them. This is the whole idea of GOS NIZK [25], on which

[20] is based. However, we do not know how to construct WE for verifying such NIZK proofs, because checking these proofs require verifying *quadratic* relations among (committed) elements in the proof. The essence of the problem is that we do not how to construct WE verifying quadratic relations in the *witness* (i.e., the NIZK proof here); if we knew, we would have obtained general purpose WE. This should be distinguished from checking quadratic relations between (committed) elements in the *statement*. The latter is the case in [20] and is easier, because the WE encryption procedure knows the statement and can use it to create the ciphertext, but it cannot do the same with the witness.

2.3   Construction of WE for NIZK of Commitments

Key Ideas. Our key idea is to design NIZK proofs π that can be verified by a linear equation, so that we can construct WE for verifying the proofs using a *WE for linear languages*, which are essentially hash proof systems (see, e.g., [1]). More specifically, we want to turn verifying a NIZK proof π of a statement $X = (c, G, y)$ into verifying a system of linear equations $\theta = \Gamma\pi$. Crucially, θ and Γ, which describe the linear equations, must depend only on the statement X (independent of π). As such, θ, π are known at WE encryption time, and we can use hash proof systems to generate a WE ciphertext that reveals the message given a witness π satisfying the linear system, and information theoretically hides the message if no such witness exists. More precisely, commitments and NIZKs are pairing group elements, and the linear equations are on values in the exponent; at the moment, we ignore this detail.

Unfortunately, verifying known NIZK proofs requires verifying quadratic relations between elements in the proof—the proof contains intermediate computation values, and verification checks the correctness of computation of each gate, which is quadratic. Designing WE for checking quadratic relations between elements in the witness is a barrier, which would give general purpose WE. Our next idea is leveraging that NC^1 circuits can be represented as *restricted multiplication straight-line* (RMS) programs, where multiplication occurs between intermediate values and input elements; importantly, the latter are committed in c contained in the statement X. This asymmetry in multiplication allows to design NIZK proofs π verified by a *linear* system θ, Γ defined by the statement. Roughly speaking, the proof π contain (encodings of) intermediate values, while θ, Γ contain (encodings of) inputs elements. Then, multiplication between Γ and π captures multiplication between input elements and intermediate values in RMS programs. Hence, we can use WE for linear language to obtain WE for NIZK of commitments for NC^1. Finally, we present a generic bootstrapping technique for lifting from a scheme for NC^1, to a scheme for all polynomial-size circuits P.

Our NIZK for NC^1 with linear verification equations makes use of the homomorphic commitment schemes developed in existing NIZK proofs and some of the ideas behind these proofs [25, 27]. For simplicity, our description below uses GOS homomorphic proof commitments which are based on composite-order bilinear groups. Our final solution in Sect. 3 uses the same ideas but is based on the Groth and Sahai NIZK [27] which uses prime order bilinear groups.

WE for Linear Languages. We start with witness encryption for linear languages. A linear language over $\mathbb{Z}_p$ consists of tuples of a matrix $\Gamma \in \mathbb{Z}_p^{K \times k}$ and a vector $\boldsymbol{\theta} \in \mathbb{Z}_p^K$ in the column span of Γ. A witness for $(\boldsymbol{\theta}, \Gamma)$ is a vector $\boldsymbol{\pi}$ s.t. $\boldsymbol{\theta} = \Gamma \boldsymbol{\pi}$. There is an extremely simple WE scheme for linear language: A ciphertext encrypting $m \in \mathbb{Z}_p$ consists of $\boldsymbol{\alpha}^T \Gamma$ and $\boldsymbol{\alpha}^T \boldsymbol{\theta} + m$ for a random row vector $\boldsymbol{\alpha}^T$. When the statement is false, that is, $\boldsymbol{\theta}$ is outside the column span of Γ, $\boldsymbol{\alpha}^T \Gamma$ contains no information of $\boldsymbol{\alpha}^T \boldsymbol{\theta}$, which hides m.

$$\text{Linear WE} \qquad \mathsf{LWEnc}((\boldsymbol{\theta}, \Gamma), \mathsf{m}) : \ \boldsymbol{\alpha} \leftarrow \mathbb{Z}_p^K, \ \ \mathsf{ct} = \boldsymbol{\alpha}^T \boldsymbol{\theta} + \mathsf{m}, \boldsymbol{\alpha}^T \Gamma$$

Can we use linear WE to verify a complex computation $G(v) = y$ over committed values v? If we had a fully homomorphic commitment scheme for which verification of the opening (i.e., decommitment) is linear, we would solve the problem. Verifying that "c opens to v and $G(v) = y$" is equivalent to that "c' opens to y" w.r.t. c' obtained from homomorphic evaluation of G on c. Now a message m can be encrypted using linear WE w.r.t. c', y (which decides $\boldsymbol{\theta}, \Gamma$) and a proof π is simply an opening of c' (ignoring ZK for now). Unfortunately, we do not know how to construct such commitment scheme.

Linear Proof for One Multiplication. GOS [25] constructed a commitment scheme with linear opening that can do one homomorphic multiplication, using pairing groups.

Let $(N, \mathbb{G}_1, \mathbb{G}_2, \mathbb{G}_t, e, g_1, g_2)$ describe a bilinear group of order N. We use the bracket notation $[a]_b := g_b^a$ in G_b for $a \in \mathbb{Z}_N$ – referred to as an encoding of a, and write $a[a']_b = [aa']_b$ as applying group exponentiation in G_b and $[aa']_t = [a]_1[a']_2$ as applying the pairing operation. GOS uses a composite order $N = pq$ symmetric bilinear group, where the two source groups are the same $\mathbb{G} = \mathbb{G}_1 = \mathbb{G}_2$; we simply write $[a]$ as a source group element.

The CRS of the commitment scheme contains $[h]$ for a random element in $\mathbb{Z}_N$ of *order q*. A commitment to v in $\mathbb{Z}_p$ is simply $[c] = [rh + v]$ using a random scalar $r \leftarrow \mathbb{Z}_N$. Such a commitment is perfectly binding, because h has order q, and v is in $\mathbb{Z}_p$. Given two commitments $[c_1] = [r_1 h + v_1]$ and $[c_2] = [r_2 h + v_2]$, we can compute a commitment of the product in the target group. Furthermore, we can prove that the product $v_1 v_2$ is equal to some value v_{12}, and the verification is linear in the proof π:

$$\text{One Multiplication} \quad [c_1 c_2]_t = [c_1][c_2] = [(r_1 r_2 h + r_1 v_2 + r_2 v_1)\, h + v_1 v_2]_t$$

$$\text{Proof} \quad [\pi] := [t_1 + t_2 h] \quad \text{for } t_1 = r_1 v_2 + r_2 v_1, \ t_2 = r_1 r_2$$

$$\text{Verification} \quad 0 \overset{?}{=} [c_1][c_2] - [h][\pi] - [1][v_{12}]$$

In other words, the last equation shows that $[\pi] = [t_1 + t_2 h]$ is a proof for the statement "$[c_1]$ and $[c_2]$ commits to values v_1 and v_2 so that $v_1 v_2 = v_{12}$."

Since the verification is linear, combined with WE for linear language, this immediately gives a WE for NIZK of correctness of one multiplication. This approach was exploited in [20] for obtaining WE for NIZK of correctness of one NAND.

Going beyond one Multiplication (Step 1). The main issue of the above construction is that a GOS commitment only allows for the evaluation of a single multiplication gate (or equivalently a single NAND), as $[c_1 c_2]_t$ is now in the target group. To evaluate more complex functions G, we need to be able to make further multiplications. The idea is that the prover can commit to $v_1 v_2$ in the source group: $[c_\times] = [r_\times h + v_1 v_2]$ and then prove that $[c_\times]$ indeed commits to the same value as $[c_1 c_2]_t$:

Multiplication $\quad [c_\times - c_1 c_2]_t = [1][c_\times] - [c_1][c_2] = [(-r_1 r_2 h + r_\times - r_1 v_2 - r_2 v_1) h]_t$

Proof $\quad [\pi_\times] := [t_1 + t_2 h] \quad$ for $t_1 = r_\times - r_1 v_2 - r_2 v_1, \ t_2 = -r_1 r_2$ $\qquad$ (3)

Verification $\quad 0 \overset{?}{=} [1][c_\times] - [c_1][c_2] - [h][\pi_\times]$ $\qquad$ (4)

Furthermore, by linearity of the GOS commitment, it is also possible to prove that a commitment $[c_+] = [r_+ h + v_+]$ commits to a value v_+ that is a linear combination of values v_1 and v_2 committed in $[c_1]$ and $[c_2]$: $v_+ = \mu_1 v_1 + \mu_2 v_2$ (for some public scalars μ_1, μ_2).

Linear $\quad [c_+ - \mu_1 c_1 - \mu_2 c_2]_t = [c_+] - \mu_1[c_1] - \mu_2[c_2] = [(r_+ - \mu_1 r_1 - \mu_2 r_2) h]_t$

Proof $\quad [\pi_+] := r_+ - \mu_1 r_1 - \mu_2 r_2$ $\qquad$ (5)

Verification $\quad 0 \overset{?}{=} [c_+] - \mu_1[c_1] - \mu_2[c_2] - [h][\pi_+]$ $\qquad$ (6)

To extend to proving P computations, we can proceed as follows. To commit a bitstring v, we commit each bit individually as a GOS commitment: $[c_i] = [r_i h + v_i]$. Then, to prove that $G(v) = y$, we represent G as a sequence of linear operations and multiplications, and introduce an intermediate commitment for each intermediate result. The proof consists of these intermediate commitments $[c'_j]$, intermediate proofs that they were computed properly (using Eq. (3) or Eq. (5)) and the opening r'_o of the commitment $[c'_o] = [r'_o h + y]$ corresponding to the output of G. Verification would consist of verifying the intermediate proofs (using Eqs. (4) and (6)) and the opening of the output commitment.

The final proof would actually be a zero-knowledge proof and would in essence be a GOS or a Groth-Sahai proof [25, 27]. The zero-knowledge property comes from the following two facts: (1) if h is chosen to be of order N (instead of q), commitments are fully equivocable, and (2) there is a single proof $[\pi_\times]$ (resp., $[\pi_+]$) satisfying the verification Eq. 3 (resp., Eq. (5)). Leveraging these two facts, a ZK simulator for a proof of, say one multiplication, can equivocate $c_1, c_2, c_\times$ to any values satisfying $\tilde{v}_\times = \tilde{v}_1 \tilde{v}_2$, the equivocation gives a fake witness for computing the unique proof.

Unfortunately, the final proof verification is not linear: if two intermediate values v_1, v_2 need to be multiplied, Eq. (4) would involve a product of the corresponding two commitments c_1, c_2, which is quadratic in the final proof.

Restricted Multiplication Program (Step 2). To keep verification linear in the final proof, we remark that we just need to ensure that every multiplication involves at least one input commitment, but never two intermediate commitments (which are part of the final proof). In that case Eq. (4) becomes linear in the intermediate commitment. Hence, we can use the above ideas to verify any restricted multiplication straight-line (RMS) computation [10,14], which includes all NC^1 computations. Indeed, in an RMS program, the only allowed operations are linear operations over inputs or intermediate values, and multiplications of one intermediate value v'_j with one input v_i (but not of two intermediate values).

Improved NC^1 Scheme Based on SXDH. The above construction of WE for NIZK of commitments for NC^1 uses composite group order with pairings which are notoriously inefficient. In Sect. 3, we propose a construction solely based on the standard assumption SXDH over asymmetric prime order pairing groups. The construction follows the same ideas described above, but is based on the Groth-Sahai NIZK proofs, which use vector subspaces to implement features of the subgroup structure. The scheme becomes more complex. That's why we explain our ideas w.r.t. the simpler GOS NIZK system.

Polynomial-Size Circuits. We now present a generic bootstrapping technique from a WE scheme for NIZK of commitments for RMS to one for P. We can encode any polynomial-size computation $y = G(v)$ into a randomized encoding $o = \mathsf{RE}(G, v; \mathsf{PRF}(k))$ that reveals only y (with randomness expanded from a seed k using a PRF). Since both RE and PRF are computable in NC^1, our RMS-scheme can verify whether o is correctly computed from v, k committed in some commitments c, but cannot verify that o indeed decodes to y (which belongs to P). Instead, we use a garbled circuit to verify the latter and use WE to ensure that only labels corresponding to the correct RE encoding o are revealed. More precisely, a WE ciphertext of m w.r.t. (G, c, y) for a polynomial-size circuit G contains 1) a garbled circuit $\widehat{F}_{y,m}$ of $F_{y,m}$ that outputs m iff given an input o' that decodes to y, and 2) WE encryption (using the RMS-scheme) of labels under statements that verify the computation of o from (k, v) committed in c. Decryption requires NIZK proofs certifying the correctness of o, which allows recovering labels for o, and then m.

Applications. Due to the lack of space, we refer the reader to the full version [8] for applications of mrNISC. At a very high-level, in scenarios where a set of parties need many copies of freshly sampled correlated randomness, we can use mrNISC to replace correlated randomness with reusable PKI and CRS setup: Parties' public key in the PKI is simply an encoding of their private PRF key, later on, they can jointly run mrNISC to sample fresh correlated randomness using the pseudorandom coins generated from all parties' PRF keys. In NIMPC, sampling correlated randomness and generating NIMPC message using this correlated randomness can be combined in one mrNISC computation.

3   WE for NIZK of Commitments: NC^1

In this section, we define and construct our new primitive: witness encryption (WE) for NIZK of commitments (for the complexity class P), which is the main component for the construction of our mrNISC scheme.

As explained in Sect. 2.3, from a high-level point of view, WE for NIZK of commitments combines the properties of homomorphic proof commitments with encryption [20] and of functional commitments with witness selector [7]. Compared with the former, it supports general statements in P (instead of a single NAND gate evaluation). Compared with the latter, it allows for zero-knowledge to hold when multiple NIZK proofs are generated.

3.1   Definition of Witness Encryption for NIZK of Commitments

We start by defining dual-mode commitment schemes (a.k.a., hybrid commitments [12]), where the CRS can be generated in two computationally indistinguishable ways: one yielding perfectly binding commitments and one yielding equivocal (a.k.a., simulatable or trapdoor) commitments. The term "dual-mode commitment" comes from [32].

We may not need dual-mode commitments to construct mrNISC, but just simulatable/equivocal commitments (without a perfectly binding setup). However using dual-mode commitments significantly simplifies definitions and proofs. Since our constructions achieve this stronger security notion, we use it. More precisely, without a dual-mode commitment, we could not use the standard definition of witness encryption: witness encryption indeed just ensures that ciphertexts related to a false statement (about the committed value, in our setting) cannot be decrypted. Without the dual mode, because of equivocality of the commitments, it would be possible to open any commitment to any value. Hence any statement about a committed value would be always true or always false (independently of the committed value).

Definition 4 (Dual-Mode Commitments). A (dual-mode) commitment scheme COM has a *binding* mode and a *simulation* mode, each involves three polynomial-time algorithms.

- Binding Setup: $\mathsf{crs} \leftarrow \mathsf{CSetup}_{\mathsf{bind}}(1^\lambda)$ on input the security parameter λ generates a binding CRS crs.
- Commitment: $(c, d) \leftarrow \mathsf{CCom}(\mathsf{crs}, v)$ on input the CRS crs and a message v in some implicitly defined message set $\mathcal{V}$,[1] generates a commitment c of v and an associated decommitment (a.k.a., opening) d.

---

[1] The message set $\mathcal{V}$ may depend on the CRS crs. The only required constraints are that messages in $\mathcal{V}$ have polynomial size in the security parameter λ and that testing membership to $\mathcal{V}$ can be done in polynomial-time given crs. The reason to use messages spaces more complicated than $\{0,1\}^{\mathrm{poly}(\lambda)}$ is to allow messages to be elements of some finite field $\mathbb{Z}_p$ for the definition of bilinear commitments with proofs of quadratic relations.

- <u>Verification:</u> $b := \mathsf{CVer}(\mathsf{crs}, c, v, d)$ on input the CRS crs, a commitment c, a message $v \in \mathcal{V}$, and a decommitment d, outputs 1 if c indeed commits to v, and 0 otherwise.
- <u>Simulation Setup:</u> $(\mathsf{crs}, \tau) \leftarrow \mathsf{CSetup}_{\mathsf{sim}}(1^\lambda)$ on input the security parameter λ generates a simulation CRS crs and an associated trapdoor τ.
- <u>Commitment Simulation:</u> $(c, \mathsf{aux}) \leftarrow \mathsf{CSimCom}(\tau)$ on input a simulation trapdoor τ, generates a simulated commitment c and some auxiliary data aux.
- <u>Opening Simulation:</u> $d \leftarrow \mathsf{CSimOpen}(\tau, \mathsf{aux}, v)$ on input an auxiliary data aux and a message $v \in \mathcal{V}$, generates some decommitment d corresponding to an opening of the associated commitment c to v.

satisfying the following properties:

Perfect Correctness: For every security parameter $\lambda \in \mathbb{N}$, CRS crs $\leftarrow$ $\mathsf{CSetup}_{\mathsf{bind}}(1^\lambda)$ or $(\mathsf{crs}, \tau) \leftarrow \mathsf{CSetup}_{\mathsf{sim}}(1^\lambda)$, message $v \in \mathcal{V}$, and commitment $(c, d) \leftarrow \mathsf{CCom}(\mathsf{crs}, v)$, we have: $\mathsf{CVer}(\mathsf{crs}, c, v, d) = 1$.

Setup Indistinguishability: The following two distributions are computationally indistinguishable:

$$\left\{ \mathsf{crs} \leftarrow \mathsf{CSetup}_{\mathsf{bind}}(1^\lambda) \ : \ \mathsf{crs} \right\}_\lambda \approx \left\{ (\mathsf{crs}, \tau) \leftarrow \mathsf{CSetup}_{\mathsf{sim}}(1^\lambda) \ : \ \mathsf{crs} \right\}_\lambda .$$

Perfect Binding in Binding Mode: For every security parameter $\lambda \in \mathbb{N}$, binding CRS crs $\leftarrow$ $\mathsf{CSetup}_{\mathsf{bind}}(1^\lambda)$, message $v \in \mathcal{V}$, commitment $(c, d) \leftarrow$ $\mathsf{CCom}(\mathsf{crs}, v)$, message $v' \in \mathcal{V}$, bitstring d', if $v' \neq v$: $\mathsf{CVer}(\mathsf{crs}, c, v', d') = 0$.

Perfect Equivocality in Simulation Mode: For every security parameter $\lambda \in \mathbb{N}$, simulation CRS $(\mathsf{crs}, \tau) \leftarrow \mathsf{CSetup}_{\mathsf{sim}}(1^\lambda)$, message $v \in \mathcal{V}$, the following two distributions are identical:

$$\{(c, d) \leftarrow \mathsf{CCom}(\mathsf{crs}, v) \ : \ (c, d)\} \ ,$$
$$\{(c, \mathsf{aux}) \leftarrow \mathsf{CSimCom}(\tau), \ d \leftarrow \mathsf{CSimOpen}(\tau, \mathsf{aux}, v) \ : \ (c, d)\} \ .$$

We are interested in proving statements "in zero-knowledge" of the form: "c commits to some value v such that $G(v) = y$," where G is a circuit in some circuit class $\mathcal{G}$ and y is the expected output of the function. In our construction, the trapdoor of the NIZK will actually be the trapdoor of the commitment. That is why we cannot easily rely on a generic definition of NIZK and instead introduce the notion of dual-mode NIZK of commitments. The binding setup yields perfectly sound NIZK proofs, while the simulation setup yields zero-knowledge proofs.

Definition 5 (Dual-Mode NIZK of Commitments). Let COM be as in Definition 4, and $\mathcal{G}$ be a class of polynomial-size circuits. A dual-mode NIZK NIZK associated with COM for $\mathcal{G}$ consists of two polynomial-time algorithms:

- <u>Proof:</u> $\pi \leftarrow \mathsf{CProve}(\mathsf{crs}, c, G, v, d)$ on input the CRS crs, a commitment c, a circuit $G \in \mathcal{G}$,[2] the committed message $v \in \mathcal{V}$, the decommitment d, as defined by COM, generates a proof π that G on input the value v committed in c outputs $y = G(v)$. Refer to (c, G, y) as the statement and (v, d) the witness.

---

[2] We implicitly systematically assume that G has input size corresponding to the size of messages in the message set $\mathcal{V}$.

- <u>Proof Verification:</u> $b := \mathsf{CPVer}(\mathsf{crs}, c, G, y, \pi)$ on input the CRS crs, a statement (c, G, y), and a proof π, accepts or rejects the proof.

The algorithms satisfy the following properties:

Perfect Proof Correctness: For every security parameter $\lambda \in \mathbb{N}$, CRS crs $\leftarrow$ $\mathsf{CSetup}_{\mathsf{bind}}(1^\lambda)$ or $(\mathsf{crs}, \tau) \leftarrow \mathsf{CSetup}_{\mathsf{sim}}(1^\lambda)$, message $v \in \mathcal{V}$, circuit $G \in \mathcal{G}$, commitment $(c, d) \leftarrow \mathsf{CCom}(\mathsf{crs}, v)$ and proof $\pi \leftarrow \mathsf{CProve}(\mathsf{crs}, c, G, v, d)$, we have: $\mathsf{CPVer}(\mathsf{crs}, c, G(v), \pi) = 1$.

Perfect Soundness in Binding Mode: For every security parameter $\lambda \in \mathbb{N}$, binding CRS crs $\leftarrow \mathsf{CSetup}_{\mathsf{bind}}(1^\lambda)$, message $v \in \mathcal{V}$, commitment $(c, d) \leftarrow$ $\mathsf{CCom}(\mathsf{crs}, v)$, circuit $G \in \mathcal{G}$, incorrect output $y' \neq G(v)$, and bitstring π, $\mathsf{CPVer}(\mathsf{crs}, c, y', \pi) = 0$.

Zero-Knowledge in Simulation Mode: There exists a PPT simulator algorithm CPSim, such that for any PPT adversary $\mathcal{A}$, the quantity is negligible in λ:

$$\left| \Pr\left[\begin{array}{l} (\mathsf{crs}, \tau) \leftarrow \mathsf{CSetup}_{\mathsf{sim}}(1^\lambda),\ (\mathsf{st}, v) \leftarrow \mathcal{A}(\mathsf{crs}, \tau), \\ (c, \mathsf{aux}) \leftarrow \mathsf{CSimCom}(\tau),\ d \leftarrow \mathsf{CSimOpen}(\tau, \mathsf{aux}, v) \end{array} : \mathcal{A}^{\mathsf{Prove}}(\mathsf{st}) = 1 \right] \right.$$

$$\left. - \Pr\left[\begin{array}{l} (\mathsf{crs}, \tau) \leftarrow \mathsf{CSetup}_{\mathsf{sim}}(1^\lambda),\ (\mathsf{st}, v) \leftarrow \mathcal{A}(\mathsf{crs}, \tau), \\ (c, \mathsf{aux}) \leftarrow \mathsf{CSimCom}(\tau) \end{array} : \mathcal{A}^{\mathsf{Sim}}(\mathsf{st}) = 1 \right] \right|,$$

where $\mathsf{Prove}(G) := \mathsf{CProve}(\mathsf{crs}, c, G, v, d)$ and $\mathsf{Sim}(G) := \mathsf{CPSim}(\tau, \mathsf{aux}, G, G(v))$.

We remark that our notion of zero-knowledge allows the adversary to see the trapdoor τ but not the auxiliary data aux, that is why we let the adversary consider a single simulated commitment but as many simulated proofs as it wants. The reason that aux is not given to the adversary is because we need to store a PRF key in aux, to generate the randomness for simulation, to be sure to use the same randomness if the simulation is called twice with the same circuit G in the construction for P.

Definition 6 (Witness Encryption for NIZK of Commitments). Let COM, NIZK, and $\mathcal{G}$ be as in Definition 4 and 5. A Witness Encryption WE associated with COM, NIZK for $\mathcal{G}$ consists of two polynomial-time algorithms:

<u>Witness Encryption:</u> $\mathsf{ct} \leftarrow \mathsf{CWEnc}(\mathsf{crs}, c, G, y, \mathsf{m})$ on input the CRS crs, a statement (c, G, y) where $G \in \mathcal{G}$, and a bitstring m, encrypts m into a ciphertext ct, under that statement.

<u>Witness Decryption:</u> $\mathsf{m} := \mathsf{CWDec}(\mathsf{crs}, \mathsf{ct}, c, G, y, \pi)$ on input the CRS crs, a ciphertext ct, a statement (c, G, y), and a NIZK proof π, decrypts ct into the message m, or outputs $\bot$.

The algorithms satisfy the following properties:

Perfect Encryption Correctness: For every $\lambda \in \mathbb{N}$, CRS crs $\leftarrow \mathsf{CSetup}_{\mathsf{bind}}(1^\lambda)$ or $(\mathsf{crs}, \tau) \leftarrow \mathsf{CSetup}_{\mathsf{sim}}(1^\lambda)$, message $v \in \mathcal{V}$, circuit $G \in \mathcal{G}$, commitment $(c, d) \leftarrow$ $\mathsf{CCom}(\mathsf{crs}, v)$ and proof $\pi \leftarrow \mathsf{CProve}(\mathsf{crs}, c, G, v, d)$, bitstring m, and ciphertext $\mathsf{ct} \leftarrow \mathsf{CWEnc}(\mathsf{crs}, c, G, G(v), \mathsf{m})$, we have: $\mathsf{CWDec}(\mathsf{crs}, \mathsf{ct}, c, G, G(v), \pi) = \mathsf{m}$.

Semantic Security: For any PPT adversary $\mathcal{A}$, the following is negligible in λ:

$$\left| 2 \cdot \Pr \left[\begin{array}{l} (\mathsf{st}, \rho') \leftarrow \mathcal{A}(1^\lambda), \; \mathsf{crs} \leftarrow \mathsf{CSetup}_{\mathsf{bind}}(1^\lambda; \rho'), \\ (\mathsf{st}, v, \rho, G, y, \mathsf{m}_0, \mathsf{m}_1) \leftarrow \mathcal{A}(\mathsf{st}, \mathsf{crs}), \\ (c, d) := \mathsf{CCom}(\mathsf{crs}, v; \rho), \\ b \leftarrow \{0, 1\}; \; \mathsf{ct} \leftarrow \mathsf{CWEnc}(\mathsf{crs}, c, G, y, \mathsf{m}_b) \\ \mathsf{ct} := \bot \text{ if } G(v) = y \end{array} \; : \; \mathcal{A}(\mathsf{st}, \mathsf{ct}) = b \right] - 1 \right| \; ,$$

where ρ denotes the random tape used by CCom to generate the commitment c of the message v (ρ is provided by the adversary).

We remark that semantic security of our WE holds even when the binding CRS is generated semi-maliciously, i.e., the adversary chooses the random tape ρ'. This is important for our semi-malicious construction of mrNISC schemes, as the adversary generates itself the binding CRS. We also note that our construction for NC^1 actually achieves perfect semantic security for binding CRS, however, our transformation from NC^1 to P only achieves computational semantic security.

3.2 Bilinear Commitments with Proofs of Quadratic Relations

As a tool to construct witness encryption for NIZK of commitments, we first introduce the notion of bilinear commitments with proofs of quadratic relations. Such commitments essentially allow to "prove linearly and in a strong form of zero-knowledge" that one commitment $c_\times$ commits to the product of the values committed by two commitments c_1 and c_2 (quadratic proofs), and that one commitment c_+ commits to some linear combination of the values committed by two commitments c_1 and c_2 (linear proofs). These proofs are amenable to be verified by hash proof systems and can be combined to construct WE for NIZK of commitments.

Bilinear Groups and Notations. Denote by $(p, \mathbb{G}_1, \mathbb{G}_2, \mathbb{G}_t, e, g_1, g_2)$ a *bilinear group* where $e : \mathbb{G}_1 \times \mathbb{G}_2 \to \mathbb{G}_t$ is an efficiently computable bilinear map (called a pairing) such that $e(g_1, g_2) = g_T$ generates $\mathbb{G}_t$. We use the bracket notation $[a]_\iota$ to denote the element g_ι^a in group $\mathbb{G}_\iota$ for $a \in \mathbb{Z}_p$ and write $a[a']_\iota = [aa']_\iota$ as applying group exponentiation in $\mathbb{G}_\iota$ and $[aa']_t = [a]_1[a']_2$ as applying the pairing operation. This notation extends to vectors and matrices. We assume the *Symmetric External Diffie-Hellman assumption (SXDH)* assumption over asymmetric bilinear pairing groups, which requires the Decisional Diffie-Hellman (DDH) assumption to hold in each source group $\mathbb{G}_1$ and $\mathbb{G}_2$, namely, for any $\iota \in \{1, 2\}$, $\{[r]_\iota, [s]_\iota, [rs]_\iota\} \approx \{[r]_\iota, [s]_\iota, [t]_\iota\}$, where r, s, t are random scalars sampled from $\mathbb{Z}_p$. All vectors are denoted by bold letters and all matrices are denoted by uppercase letters.

Bilinear Commitments. Our construction starts from the SXDH-based commitment scheme used in Groth-Sahai NIZK [26]. This commitment scheme allows to commit values both in $\mathbb{G}_1$ and $\mathbb{G}_2$. The resulting commitments are dual-mode and called type-1 and type-2 commitments respectively. More formally we define:

- Binding Setup: crs ← $\mathsf{QSetup}_{\mathsf{bind}}(1^\lambda)$ generates a bilinear group $(p, \mathbb{G}_1, \mathbb{G}_2, \mathbb{G}_t, e, g_1, g_2)$, and for $\iota \in \{1, 2\}$, generates a random matrix $A_\iota \in \mathbb{Z}_p^{2\times2}$ *of rank 1* such that the vector $\mathbf{1} := (1, 1)^T \in \mathbb{Z}_p^2$ is not in the column span of A_ι, and outputs crs $= (p, \mathbb{G}_1, \mathbb{G}_2, \mathbb{G}_t, e, g_1, g_2, [A_1]_1, [A_2]_2)$.
- Simulation Setup: (crs, τ) ← $\mathsf{QSetup}_{\mathsf{sim}}(1^\lambda)$ is identical to binding setup except that A_1 and A_2 are chosen *of rank 2*. The trapdoor is $\tau = (A_1, A_2)$. Note that $\mathbf{1}$ is in the column spans of A_1 and A_2.
- Commitment: $(\mathbf{c}, \mathbf{d})$ ← $\mathsf{QCom}_\iota(\mathsf{crs}, v)$ generates a type-ι commitment of a message $v \in \mathcal{V} := \mathbb{Z}_p$ as follows:

$$\mathbf{d} \leftarrow \mathbb{Z}_p^2 \ , \qquad\qquad \mathbf{c} := [\tilde{\mathbf{c}}]_\iota := [A_\iota \cdot \mathbf{d} + v \cdot \mathbf{1}]_\iota \in \mathbb{G}_\iota^2 \ .$$

- Verification: $b := \mathsf{QVer}_\iota(\mathsf{crs}, \mathbf{c}, v, \mathbf{d})$ checks whether $\mathbf{c}$ is a valid type-ι commitment of v as follows: it returns 1 if and only if:

$$\mathbf{c} \overset{?}{=} [A_\iota \cdot \mathbf{d} + v \cdot \mathbf{1}]_\iota \ . \tag{7}$$

- Commitment Simulation: $(\mathbf{c}, \mathsf{aux})$ ← $\mathsf{QSimCom}_\iota(\tau)$ simulates a type-ι commitment as follows:

$$\mathsf{aux} \leftarrow \mathbb{Z}_p^2 \ , \qquad\qquad \mathbf{c} := [\mathsf{aux}]_\iota \in \mathbb{G}_\iota^2 \ . \tag{8}$$

- Opening Simulation: $\mathbf{d}$ ← $\mathsf{QSimOpen}_\iota(\tau = (A_1, A_2), \mathsf{aux}, v)$ opens the type-ι commitment corresponding to aux as follows:

$$\mathbf{d} := A_\iota^{-1} \cdot (\mathsf{aux} - v \cdot \mathbf{1}) \in \mathbb{Z}_p^2 \ . \tag{9}$$

We have the following lemma following directly from [26].

Lemma 2 (in [26]). *The two commitment schemes* ($\mathsf{QSetup}_{\mathsf{bind}}, \mathsf{QCom}_\iota, \mathsf{QVer}_\iota$, $\mathsf{QSetup}_{\mathsf{sim}}, \mathsf{QSimCom}_\iota, \mathsf{QSimOpen}_\iota$) *(for $\iota \in \{1, 2\}$) described above are both dual-mode commitments.*

Remark 1. Jumping ahead, for semi-malicious security of mrNISC in the plain model, we want the binding of COM, soundness of NIZK, and semantic security of WE to hold against every CRS in the support of $\mathsf{QSetup}_{\mathsf{bind}}$. This boils down to ensuring that the bilinear group generated by $\mathsf{QSetup}_{\mathsf{bind}}$ is always a valid one: p must be a prime number, g_1, g_2 generates the cyclic groups $\mathbb{G}_1$ and $\mathbb{G}_2$ of order p, and it is possible to check in polynomial time whether an element is in $\mathbb{G}_1$ or $\mathbb{G}_2$. This can be done, and we implicitly assume that this is the case.

Bilinear Commitments with Proofs of Linear Relations. We now show how to prove that a type-2 commitment $\mathbf{c}_+$ commits to a given linear combination of values committed in two type-2 commitments $\mathbf{c}_1$ and $\mathbf{c}_2$. Concretely, we want to prove that $\mathbf{c}_1, \mathbf{c}_2, \mathbf{c}_+$ respectively commit to values v_1, v_2, v_+ that satisfy the linear relation: $v_+ = \mu_1 v_1 + \mu_2 v_2$, where $\mu_1, \mu_2 \in \mathbb{Z}_p$ are some public parameters.

Statement: $(\mathsf{Linear}, \mathsf{crs}, \{\mu_i, \mathbf{c}_i\}_{i\in\{1,2\}}, \mathbf{c}_+)$,   Witness: $(v_1, \mathbf{d}_1, v_2, \mathbf{d}_2, \mathbf{d}_+)$

The main idea of the construction is to remark that the commitments are linearly homomorphic and the above statement is equivalent to proving that $[\tilde{c}_+ - \mu_1\tilde{c}_1 - \mu_2\tilde{c}_2]_2$ is a commitment of 0, where for $i \in \{1, 2, +\}$, $c_i = [\tilde{c}_i]_2$. Hence the proof π_+ is the opening of this commitment to the value $v = 0$:

$$[\tilde{c}_+ - \mu_1\tilde{c}_1 - \mu_2\tilde{c}_2]_2 = [A_2 \cdot \pi_+ + 0 \cdot 1]_2 .$$

Zero-knowledge comes from the fact that this value π_+ always exists and is unique in the simulation mode, as the matrix A_2 is full rank in that mode.

Formally, the construction is as follows:

- <u>Linear Proof:</u> QLinProve(crs, $\{\mu_i, c_i, v_i, d_i\}_{i \in [2]}, (c_+, d_+)$), given information of both statement and witness, outputs:

$$\pi_+ := d_+ - \mu_1 d_1 - \mu_2 d_2 \in \mathbb{Z}_p^2 . \tag{10}$$

- <u>Linear Proof Verification:</u> QLinVer(crs, $\{\mu_i, c_i\}_{i \in [2]}, c_+, \pi_+$) returns 1 iff:

$$[\tilde{c}_+ - \mu_1\tilde{c}_1 - \mu_2\tilde{c}_2]_2 \stackrel{?}{=} [A_2 \cdot \pi_+]_2 , \tag{11}$$

where $c_i = [\tilde{c}_i]_2$ for $i \in \{1, 2, +\}$.

Lemma 3. *For any security parameter* $\lambda \in \mathbb{N}$, *for any CRS* crs $\leftarrow$ $\mathsf{QSetup}_{\mathsf{bind}}(1^\lambda)$ *or* $(\mathsf{crs}, \tau) \leftarrow \mathsf{QSetup}_{\mathsf{sim}}(1^\lambda)$, *messages* $v_1, v_2, v_+ \in \mathbb{Z}_p$, *scalars* $\mu_1, \mu_2, \mu_+ \in \mathbb{Z}_p$, *bitstrings* $c_1, d_1, c_2, d_2, c_+, d_+$ *s.t.* $\forall i \in \{1, 2, +\}, \mathsf{QVer}_2(\mathsf{crs}, c_i, v_i, d_i) = 1$,

Perfect Correctness: If $v_+ = \mu_1 v_1 + \mu_2 v_2$, *a proof* $\pi_+ \leftarrow \mathsf{QLinProve}(\mathsf{crs}, \{\mu_i, c_i, v_i, d_i\}_i, (c_+, d_+))$ *passes verification:* $\mathsf{QLinVer}(\mathsf{crs}, \{\mu_i, c_i\}_{i \in [2]}, c_+, \pi_+) = 1$
Perfect Uniqueness: If $v_+ = \mu_1 v_1 + \mu_2 v_2$ *and the CRS is simulated, then there is a unique vector* $\pi_+ = (\tilde{c}_+ - \mu_1\tilde{c}_1 - \mu_2\tilde{c}_2)A_2^{-1} \in \mathbb{Z}_p^2$ *that passes verification.*
Perfect Soundness: If $v_+ \neq \mu_1 v_1 + \mu_2 v_2$ *and the CRS is binding, then no vector* $\pi_+ \in \mathbb{Z}_p^2$ *passes verification:* $\mathsf{QLinVer}(\mathsf{crs}, \{\mu_i, c_i\}_{i \in [2]}, c_+, \pi_+) = 0$ *for all* $\pi_+ \in \mathbb{Z}_p^2$.

Proof. **Perfect correctness** is straightforward. **Perfect uniqueness** follows from Eq. (11) and the fact that when the CRS is simulated, the matrix A_2 is full rank. **Perfect soundness** comes from the fact that:

$$[\mu_1\tilde{c}_1 + \mu_2\tilde{c}_2]_2 = [A_2 \cdot (\mu_1 d_1 + \mu_2 d_2) + (\mu_1 v_1 + \mu_2 v_2) \cdot 1]_2 \in \mathbb{G}_2^2$$

is a (perfectly binding) commitment of $\mu_1 v_1 + \mu_2 v_2 \neq v_+$. $\square$

Remark 2 (Zero-knowledge of the linear proof π_+ in simulation mode). Perfect uniqueness of the proof π_+ in simulation mode is a very strong form of witness indistinguishability: whatever witness $(v_1, d_1, v_2, d_2, d_+)$ is used, the proof is exactly the same $\pi_+ = (\tilde{c}_+ - \mu_1\tilde{c}_1 - \mu_2\tilde{c}_2)A_2^{-1}$. To show further that it is ZK, we need to argue that π_+ is also efficiently computable. This the case when the commitments $c_i = [\tilde{c}_i]_2$ are simulated with QSimCom, as the simulator can then equivocate c_1, c_2, c_+ to any v'_1, v'_2, v'_+ satisfying $v'_+ = \mu_1 v'_1 + \mu_2 v'_2$ with decommitments d'_1, d'_2, d'_+ using QSimOpen. This gives a valid witness $(v'_1, d'_1, v'_2, d'_2, d'_+)$ for the statement and a simulated proof can be generated by running the honest prover algorithm QLinProve with this witness.

Bilinear Commitments with Proofs of Quadratic Relations. We now show how to prove that a **type-2** commitment $c_\times$ commits to the product of values committed in a **type-1** commitment c_1 and a **type-2** commitment c_2. Concretely, we want to prove that c_1, c_2, c_+ respectively commit to values $v_1, v_2, v_\times$ that satisfy the quadratic relation $v_\times = v_1 \cdot v_2$.

$$\text{Statement: } (\mathsf{Mult}, \mathsf{crs}, \{c_i\}_{i \in \{1,2,\times\}}), \qquad \text{Witness:} (v_1, d_1, v_2, d_2, d_\times) \qquad (12)$$

The main idea of the construction is to construct from $c_1 = [\tilde{c}_1]_1$ and $c_2 = [\tilde{c}_2]_2$ a commitment of $v_1 \cdot v_2$. Remember that in the technical overview in Sect. 2.3, we could multiply commitments c_1 and c_2 directly (by using a pairing operation) to get a commitment of $v_1 \cdot v_2$, as commitments were a single group element. Intuitively, the equivalent of this multiplication to vector of group elements c_1 and c_2 is the tensor product operation $\otimes$. And we want to prove that $[\mathbf{1} \otimes \tilde{c}_\times - \tilde{c}_1 \otimes \tilde{c}_2]_t$ is a "commitment" of 0 in $\mathbb{G}_t$, where $\mathbf{1}$ is used as a type-1 commitment of 1.[3] Similar to multiplication of commitments in Sect. 2.3, computing these tensor products uses pairings.

The basic idea is then that the proof is a decommitment of this commitment $[\mathbf{1} \otimes \tilde{c}_\times - \tilde{c}_1 \otimes \tilde{c}_2]_t$ to 0. Unfortunately, this would not be zero-knowledge since there are multiple possible decommitments and choosing one may reveal information about the witness $(v_1, d_1, v_2, d_2, d_\times)$. To tackle this subtle issue (which does not happen with the commitments from the technical overview in Sect. 2.3 nor with proof of linear relations), the prover needs to rerandomize this decommitment, similarly to what is done in [26] to get perfect witness indistinguishability. This is the purpose of the vector ρ in Eq. (14).

TENSOR PRODUCTS. We first need to briefly recall the notion of tensor products. The tensor product of two matrices $M \in \mathbb{Z}_p^{k \times m}$ and $M' \in \mathbb{Z}_p^{k' \times m'}$ is the matrix $T = M \otimes M' \in \mathbb{Z}_p^{kk' \times mm'}$ defined as:

$$T = \begin{pmatrix} M_{1,1} \cdot M' & \cdots & M_{1,m} \cdot M' \\ \vdots & & \vdots \\ M_{k,1} \cdot M' & \cdots & M_{k,m} \cdot M' \end{pmatrix} .$$

We extensively use the following identity: if $M \in \mathbb{Z}_p^{k \times m}$, $M' \in \mathbb{Z}_p^{k' \times m'}$, $N \in \mathbb{Z}_p^{m \times n}$ and $N' \in \mathbb{Z}_p^{m' \times n'}$, then we have,

$$(M \otimes M') \cdot (N \otimes N') = (M \cdot N) \otimes (M' \cdot N') . \qquad (13)$$

CONSTRUCTION. Recall that the construction essentially consists of proving that $[\mathbf{1} \otimes \tilde{c}_\times - \tilde{c}_1 \otimes \tilde{c}_2]_t$ is a commitment of 0, which is what Eq. (15) below ensures.

---

[3] $[\mathbf{1} \otimes \tilde{c}_\times - \tilde{c}_1 \otimes \tilde{c}_2]_t$ is not a type-1 commitment (using the matrix A_1) nor a type-2 commitment (using the matrix A_2) but yet another type of commitment using another matrix B (formally defined in the proof in Eq. (17)). When the CRS is binding, this matrix B is such that the commitment is also binding.

To better understand how this value is computed (in term of group elements, pairings, and exponentiations), we explicitly write it down:

$$[1 \otimes \tilde{c}_\times - \tilde{c}_1 \otimes \tilde{c}_2]_t = \begin{pmatrix} e(g_1, c_{\times,1}) \cdot e(c_{1,1}, c_{2,1})^{-1} \\ e(g_1, c_{\times,1}) \cdot e(c_{1,1}, c_{2,2})^{-1} \\ e(g_1, c_{\times,2}) \cdot e(c_{1,2}, c_{2,1})^{-1} \\ e(g_1, c_{\times,2}) \cdot e(c_{1,2}, c_{2,2})^{-1} \end{pmatrix} \quad \text{where } c_i = \begin{pmatrix} c_{i,1} \\ c_{i,2} \end{pmatrix}$$

The construction is as follows:

- Quadratic Proof: $\pi_\times \leftarrow \mathsf{QQuadProve}(\mathsf{crs}, \{c_i, v_i, d_i\}_{i \in [2]}, c_\times, d_\times)$ picks $\rho \in \mathbb{Z}_p^4$ and outputs:

$$\pi_\times := \left(\begin{bmatrix} \tilde{\pi}_\times^\top \end{bmatrix}_2 \\ \begin{bmatrix} \tilde{\pi}_\times^\perp \end{bmatrix}_1 \right) = \left(\begin{matrix} [-v_2 \cdot d_1 \otimes 1 + (\mathsf{Id} \otimes A_2) \cdot \rho]_2 \\ [1 \otimes d_\times - \tilde{c}_1 \otimes d_2 - (A_1 \otimes \mathsf{Id}) \cdot \rho]_1 \end{matrix} \right), \quad (14)$$

where $\mathsf{Id} \in \mathbb{Z}_p^{2 \times 2}$ is the identity matrix. Recall that the vector ρ is used to randomize the proof so that it is uniformly random among the valid proofs, and hence is perfectly witness indistinguishable.
- Quadratic Proof Verification: $b := \mathsf{QQuadVer}(\mathsf{crs}, c_1, c_2, c_\times, \pi_\times)$ returns 1 if and only if:

$$[1 \otimes \tilde{c}_\times - \tilde{c}_1 \otimes \tilde{c}_2]_t = \left([A_1 \otimes \mathsf{Id}]_1 \quad [\mathsf{Id} \otimes A_2]_2 \right) \cdot \pi_\times , \quad (15)$$

where $\mathsf{Id} \in \mathbb{Z}_p^{2 \times 2}$ is the identity matrix. Note that computing $[\tilde{c}_1 \otimes \tilde{c}_2]_t$ involves pairing operations between elements of vectors $c_1 \in \mathbb{G}_1^2$ and $c_2 \in \mathbb{G}_2^2$. Computing the right hand side also involves pairing operations.

Remark 3. Quadratic proof verification just consists of checking a linear equation in $(c_2, c_\times, \pi_\times)$. Indeed, thanks to Eq. (13), Eq. (15) is equivalent to:

$$0 = \left([1 \otimes \mathsf{Id}]_1 \quad [-\tilde{c}_1 \otimes \mathsf{Id}]_1 \quad [A_1 \otimes \mathsf{Id}]_1 \quad [\mathsf{Id} \otimes A_2]_2 \right) \cdot \begin{pmatrix} [\tilde{c}_\times]_2 \\ [\tilde{c}_2]_2 \\ [\tilde{\pi}_\times^\top]_2 \\ [\tilde{\pi}_\times^\perp]_1 \end{pmatrix} .$$

Lemma 4. *For any security parameter $\lambda \in \mathbb{N}$, for any CRS $\mathsf{crs} \leftarrow \mathsf{QSetup}_{\mathsf{bind}}(1^\lambda)$ or $(\mathsf{crs}, \tau) \leftarrow \mathsf{QSetup}_{\mathsf{sim}}(1^\lambda)$, messages $v_1, v_2, v_\times \in \mathbb{Z}_p$, bitstrings $c_1, d_1, c_2, d_2, c_\times, d_\times$ such that $\forall i \in \{1, 2, \times\}, \mathsf{QVer}_i(\mathsf{crs}, c_i, v_i, d_i) = 1$, we have:*

Perfect Correctness: If $v_\times = v_1 v_2$, a proof $\mathsf{QQuadProve}(\mathsf{crs}, \{c_i, v_i, d_i\}_{i \in [2]}, (c_\times, d_\times))$ passes verification: $\mathsf{QQuadVer}(\mathsf{crs}, \{\mu_i, c_i\}_{i \in [2]}, c_\times, \pi_\times) = 1$
Perfect Uniformity: If $v_\times = v_1 v_2$ and the CRS is simulated, then the vector $\pi_\times$ generated by $\mathsf{QQuadProve}$ follows a uniform distribution among the solutions of Eq. (15).
Perfect Soundness: If $v_\times \neq v_1 v_2$ and the CRS is binding, then no $\pi_\times \in \mathbb{Z}_p^8$ passes verification: $\mathsf{QQuadVer}(\mathsf{crs}, c_1, c_2, c_\times, \pi_\times) = 0$ for all $\pi_\times \in \mathbb{Z}_p^8$.

Proof. To prove **perfect correctness**, we use Eqs. (13) and (14) and remark:

$$1 \otimes \tilde{c}_\times - \tilde{c}_1 \otimes \tilde{c}_2 = 1 \otimes (A_2 d_\times + v_\times \cdot 1) - \tilde{c}_1 \otimes (A_2 d_2 + v_2 \cdot 1)$$
$$= 1 \otimes (A_2 d_\times) + v_\times \cdot 1 \otimes 1 - \tilde{c}_1 \otimes (A_2 d_2) - (A_1 d_1 + v_1 \cdot 1) \otimes (v_2 \cdot 1)$$
$$= 1 \otimes (A_2 d_\times) - \tilde{c}_1 \otimes (A_2 d_2) - (A_1 d_1) \otimes (v_2 \cdot 1) + (v_\times - v_1 v_2) \cdot (1 \otimes 1)$$
$$= (\mathsf{Id} \otimes A_2) \cdot (1 \otimes d_\times) - (\mathsf{Id} \otimes A_2) \cdot (\tilde{c}_1 \otimes d_2)$$
$$-(A_1 \otimes \mathsf{Id}) \cdot (v_2 d_1 \otimes 1) + (v_\times - v_1 v_2) \cdot (1 \otimes 1) \ . \tag{16}$$

We conclude by remarking that $v_\times = v_1 v_2$ and that:

$$\begin{pmatrix} A_1 \otimes \mathsf{Id} & \mathsf{Id} \otimes A_2 \end{pmatrix} \cdot \begin{pmatrix} (\mathsf{Id} \otimes A_2) \cdot \rho \\ -(A_1 \otimes \mathsf{Id}) \cdot \rho \end{pmatrix} = 0 \ .$$

Perfect soundness follows from Eq. (16) and the fact that $1 \otimes 1$ is not in the subspace generated by the columns of the matrix

$$B := \begin{pmatrix} A_1 \otimes \mathsf{Id} & \mathsf{Id} \otimes A_2 \end{pmatrix} \in \mathbb{Z}_p^{4 \times 8} \ , \tag{17}$$

when the CRS is binding, because if $a_1, a_2 \in \mathbb{Z}_p^2$ are two vectors generating the column space of A_1 and A_2 respectively, then $(a_1 \otimes a_2, \ a_1 \otimes 1, \ 1 \otimes a_2, \ 1 \otimes 1)$ is a basis of $\mathbb{Z}_p^4$.

Finally, **perfect uniformity** comes from the fact that the kernel of the matrix B (from Eq. (17)) consists of all the vectors:

$$\begin{pmatrix} (\mathsf{Id} \otimes A_2) \cdot \rho \\ -(A_1 \otimes \mathsf{Id}) \cdot \rho \end{pmatrix} \ ,$$

for $\rho \in \mathbb{Z}_p^4$, since these elements are clearly in the kernel and form a subspace of dimension 4, and the kernel is of dimension 4 as $B \in \mathbb{Z}_p^{8 \times 4}$ is of rank 4 (because A_1 is full rank and hence $A_1 \otimes \mathsf{Id} \in \mathbb{Z}_p^{4 \times 4}$ is of full rank).

Remark 4 (Zero-knowledge of the quadratic proof $\pi_\times$ in simulation mode). Perfect uniformity in the simulation mode is a very strong form of witness indistinguishability: whatever witness is used, the proof follows exactly the same uniform distribution over solutions of Eq. 15. To show that $\pi_\times$ is zero-knowledge, it remains to argue that this distribution can be efficiently sampled. This can be done similarly as in Remark 2: for simulated commitments c_i, the simulator can equivocate $c_1, c_2, c_\times$ to any $v_1', v_2', v_\times'$ satisfying $v_\times' = v_1' v_2'$ with decommitment $d_1', d_2', d_\times'$ using QSimOpen. This gives a valid witness $(v_1', d_1', v_2', d_2', d_\times')$ for the statement and a simulated proof can be generated by running the honest prover algorithm QQuadProve with this witness.

3.3   WE for NIZK of Commitments for NC^1

We now describe our construction of WE for NIZK of commitments for NC^1. It follows the technical overview Sect. 2.3. The idea is to represent the function by a Restricted Multiplication Straight-line (RMS) Program [10,14], which only performs multiplications or quadratic operations between an intermediate variable and an input. We start with defining a variant of RMS where operations are done modulo some prime number p.

Definition 7 (RMS Programs). Let p be a prime. A Restricted Multiplication Straight-line (RMS) program modulo p with input $v = v_1 \| \cdots \| v_n \in \{0,1\}^n$ and output $y = y_1 \| \cdots \| y_m \in \{0,1\}^m$ is a sequence of the following instructions:

- Load a constant $\omega \in \mathbb{Z}_p$ into the memory value u_j: $(u_j \leftarrow \omega)$.
- Linearly combine memory values u_i and u_j into the memory value u_k: $(u_k \leftarrow \mu u_i + \mu' u_j \bmod p)$, with $(\mu, \mu') \in \mathbb{Z}_p^2 \setminus \{(0,0)\}$ a non-zero pair of constants.
- Multiply the input value v_i by the memory value u_j into the memory value u_k: $(u_k \leftarrow v_i \cdot u_j \bmod p)$.

where each memory value is written at most once and each memory value that is read was written before. The program aborts if one memory value u_k is not in $\{0,1\}$. If it does not abort, it outputs $y = y_1 \| \cdots \| y_m = u_1 \| \cdots \| u_m$.

The *size* of an RMS is the number of instructions. Furthermore, any NC^1 circuit G can be written as an RMS program of polynomial size, because deterministic branching programs can be encoded into RMS with constant overhead [10, Claim A.2]. The resulting RMS program outputs the correct value when evaluated modulo any prime number p, as when evaluated without modulo, all the memory values are in $\{0,1\}$.

Construction. Let $\mathsf{QC} = (\mathsf{QSetup}_{\mathsf{bind}}, \mathsf{QSetup}_{\mathsf{sim}}, \{\mathsf{QCom}_i, \mathsf{QVer}_i, \mathsf{QSimCom}_i, \mathsf{QSimOpen}_i\}_{i \in \{1,2\}}, \mathsf{QQuadProve}, \mathsf{QQuadVer})$ be the bilinear commitment scheme with proofs of quadratic relations from the previous section. We construct a witness encryption WE for NIZK of commitments for NC^1 below. To help differentiate type-1 and type-2 commitments, all type-ι commitments have subscript starting with ι, such as, $c_{\iota,k}$.

- <u>Commitment:</u> $(c, d) \leftarrow \mathsf{CCom}(\mathsf{crs}, v)$ for $v \in \mathcal{V} := \{0,1\}^n$, generates type-1 commitments for each bit of $v = v_1 \| \cdots \| v_n$. More formally, $c = (c_{1,1}, \ldots, c_{1,n})$ and $d = (d_{1,1}, \ldots, d_{1,n})$, where for $i \in [n]$, $(c_{1,i}, d_{1,i}) \leftarrow \mathsf{QCom}_1(\mathsf{crs}, v_i)$.
- <u>Verification, Commitment Simulation and Opening:</u> just consist in running the respective algorithms $\mathsf{QVer}_1, \mathsf{QSimCom}_1, \mathsf{QSimOpen}_1$ in parallel for each commitment $c_{1,i}$.
- <u>Proof</u> $\pi \leftarrow \mathsf{CProve}(\mathsf{crs}, c, G, v, d)$, for an NC^1 circuit G represented as an RMS program with n-bit input and m-bit output works as follows. Let S_ω, S_+, and $S_\times$ be the sets of memory indexes written by constant loading, linear, and multiplication instructions respectively. We suppose that the used memory values are $u_1, \ldots, u_L$. The proof π is a tuple $(\{c_{2,k}\}_{k \in [L]}, \{d_{2,k}\}_{k \in [m] \cup S_\omega}, \{\pi_k\}_{k \in S_+ \cup S_\times})$ where these values are generated as follows, for each instruction

- $(u_k \leftarrow \omega)$: generate $(c_{2,k}, d_{2,k}) \leftarrow \mathsf{QCom}_2(\mathsf{crs}, \omega)$.
- $(u_k \leftarrow \mu u_i + \mu' u_j \bmod p)$: compute

$$(c_{2,k}, d_{2,k}) \leftarrow \mathsf{QCom}_2(\mathsf{crs}, \mu u_i + \mu' u_j) \ ,$$
$$\pi_k := \mathsf{QLinProve}(\mathsf{crs}, (\mu, c_{2,i}, u_i, d_{2,i}), (\mu', c_{2,j}, u_j, d_{2,j}), (c_{2,k}, d_{2,k})) \ .$$

- $(u_k \leftarrow v_i \cdot u_j \bmod p)$: compute

$$(c_{2,k}, d_{2,k}) \leftarrow \mathsf{QCom}_2(\mathsf{crs}, v_i \cdot u_j) \ ,$$
$$\pi_k := \mathsf{QQuadProve}(\mathsf{crs}, (c_{1,i}, v_i, d_{1,i}), (c_{2,j}, u_j, d_{2,j}), (c_{2,k}, d_{2,k})) \ .$$

(Note that values v_i and u_j are known by the prover.)

– Proof Verification: just consists in verifying the provided openings and quadratic proofs. More formally, $\mathsf{CPVer}(\mathsf{crs}, c, G, y, \pi)$ where $y = y_1 \| \cdots \| y_m$ returns 1 if and only if all the following tests pass:
  - For every $i \in [m]$, check that $\mathsf{QVer}_2(\mathsf{crs}, c_{2,i}, y_i, d_{2,i}) \overset{?}{=} 1$.
  - For every instruction:
    * $(u_k \leftarrow \omega)$: check $\mathsf{QVer}_2(\mathsf{crs}, c_{2,k}, \omega, d_{2,k}) \overset{?}{=} 1$.
    * $(u_k \leftarrow \mu u_i + \mu' u_j \bmod p)$: check $\mathsf{QLinVer}(\mathsf{crs}, (\mu, c_{2,i}), (\mu', c_{2,j}),$ $c_{2,k}, \pi_k) \overset{?}{=} 1$.
    * $(u_k \leftarrow v_i \cdot u_j \bmod p)$: check $\mathsf{QQuadVer}(\mathsf{crs}, c_{1,i}, c_{2,j}, c_{2,k}, \pi_k) \overset{?}{=} 1$.

– Proof Simulation: $\pi \leftarrow \mathsf{CPSim}(\tau, \mathsf{aux}, c, G, y)$ where $c = (c_{1,1}, \ldots, c_{1,n})$ are simulated with auxiliary data $\mathsf{aux} = (\mathsf{aux}_{1,1}, \ldots, \mathsf{aux}_{1,n})$, simulates a proof $\pi = (\{c_{2,k}\}_{k \in [L]}, \{d_{2,k}\}_{k \in [m] \cup S_\omega}, \{\pi_k\}_{k \in S_+ \cup S_\times})$ as follows: Run through the instructions in RMS in order and for each instruction do:
  - $(u_k \leftarrow \omega)$: generate

$$(c_{2,k}, \mathsf{aux}_{2,k}) \leftarrow \mathsf{QSimCom}_2(\tau) \ , \quad d_{2,k} \leftarrow \mathsf{QSimOpen}_2(\tau, \mathsf{aux}_{2,k}, \omega) \ .$$

  - $(u_k \leftarrow \mu u_i + \mu' u_j \bmod p)$: set $u'_k := y_k$ if $k \in [m]$ or 0 otherwise, and let $u'_i, u'_j \in \mathbb{Z}_p$ be arbitrary scalars such that $\mu u'_i + \mu' u'_j = u'_k$ (which is possible as $(\mu, \mu') \neq 0$), and compute:

$$(c_{2,k}, \mathsf{aux}_{2,k}) \leftarrow \mathsf{QSimCom}_2(\tau) \ ,$$
$$d'_{2,\ell} \leftarrow \mathsf{QSimOpen}_2(\tau, \mathsf{aux}_{2,\ell}, u'_\ell) \quad \text{for } \ell \in \{i, j, k\} \ , \qquad (18)$$
$$\pi_k := \mathsf{QLinProve}(\mathsf{crs}, (\mu, c_{2,i}, u'_i, d'_{2,i}), (\mu', c_{2,j}, u'_j, d'_{2,j}), (c_{2,k}, d'_{2,k})) \ .$$

Note: values u'_i, u'_j, u'_k are local and may be different for different instructions.

  - $(u_k \leftarrow v_i \cdot u_j \bmod p)$: set $u'_k := y_k$ is $k \in [m]$ or 0 otherwise, as well as $u'_i := 1$ and $u'_j := u'_k$ (so that $u'_k = u'_i u'_j$—again values u'_i, u'_j, u'_k are local) and compute:

$$(c_{2,k}, \mathsf{aux}_{2,k}) \leftarrow \mathsf{QSimCom}_2(\tau) \ ,$$
$$d'_{1,i} \leftarrow \mathsf{QSimOpen}_1(\tau, \mathsf{aux}_{1,i}, u'_i) \qquad (19)$$

$$d'_{2,\ell} \leftarrow \mathsf{QSimOpen}_2(\tau, \mathbf{aux}_{2,\ell}, u'_\ell) \quad \text{for } \ell \in \{j, k\} \ , \tag{20}$$

$$\pi_k := \mathsf{QQuadProve}(\mathsf{crs}, (c_{1,i}, u'_i, d'_{1,i}), (c_{2,i}, u'_j, d'_{2,j}), (c_{2,k}, d'_{2,k})) \ .$$

– Witness Encryption: Looking at Eqs. (7) and (11) and Remark 3, we remark that the proof verification $\mathsf{CPVer}(\mathsf{crs}, c, G, y, \pi)$ is affine in the vector π. Concretely, there exists a matrix $[\Gamma_{\mathsf{crs},c,G,y}]_\star$ and a vector $[\theta_{\mathsf{crs},c,G,y}]_\star$ (both only depend on crs, c, G, y and can be efficiently computed from these three values—the star $\star$ denotes the fact that elements are not necessarily in the same group), such that, seeing π as a vector of elements in $\mathbb{Z}_p, \mathbb{G}_1, \mathbb{G}_2$ of length β, and denoting by $\tilde{\pi} \in \mathbb{Z}_p^\beta$ the vector derived from π by replacing every $\mathbb{G}_\iota$ element with its discrete logarithm, we have:

$$[\theta_{\mathsf{crs},c,G,y}]_t = [\Gamma_{\mathsf{crs},c,G,y} \cdot \tilde{\pi}]_t \ .$$

(Note: This is because: By Eq. 7 and 11, verification of opening and verification of a linear proof are both linear equations whose coefficients are either constants or elements in crs*. By Remark 3, verification of a quadratic proof is a linear equation whose coefficients are constants, or elements in* crs*, or commitments* $c_{1,i}$ *(as in Eq. 19) to the first operand in the multiplication. Since in RMS the first operand of multiplication is always an input bit,* $c_{1,i}$ *is contained in* c*.)*

The witness encryption then just uses hash proof systems from [1]. More formally, to encrypt a bit message $\mathsf{m} \in \{0, 1\}$, $\mathsf{CWEnc}(\mathsf{crs}, c, G, y, \mathsf{m})$ picks a uniformly random row vector $\boldsymbol{\alpha} \in \mathbb{Z}_p^{1 \times \nu}$, where ν is the number of rows of $\Gamma_{\mathsf{crs},c,G,y}$, and outputs the ciphertext $\mathsf{ct} = ([\gamma]_\star, [\delta]_t)$ where:

$$[\gamma]_\star := [\boldsymbol{\alpha} \cdot \Gamma_{\mathsf{crs},c,G,y}]_\star \ , \qquad [\delta]_t := [\boldsymbol{\alpha} \cdot \theta_{\mathsf{crs},c,G,y} + \mathsf{m}]_t \ .$$

– Witness Decryption: Using the notation from witness encryption, $\mathsf{CWDec}(\mathsf{crs}, \mathsf{ct}, c, G, y, \pi)$ outputs $\mathsf{m} \in \{0, 1\}$ satisfying

$$[\mathsf{m}]_t = [\delta - \gamma \cdot \tilde{\pi}]_t \ .$$

EFFICIENCY: The algorithms $\mathsf{CSetup}_{\mathsf{bind}}, \mathsf{CCom}, \mathsf{CVer}$ (as well as the simulators $\mathsf{CSetup}_{\mathsf{sim}}, \mathsf{CSimCom}, \mathsf{CSimOpen}$) of the resulting WE for NIZK of commitments run in time polynomial in their inputs. The algorithms $\mathsf{CProve}, \mathsf{CPVer}, \mathsf{CWEnc}, \mathsf{CWDec}$ run in time polynomial in their inputs and *exponential in the depth of the circuit* G. This exponential blow up is due to the representation by a RMS program and explains the restriction to NC^1.

Theorem 8. *Assuming SXDH over bilinear groups. The construction* Π *described above is a WE for NIZK of commitments for* NC^1*.*

Proof. **Perfect correctness** of the commitment, **setup indistinguishability**, **perfect binding**, and **perfect equivocality** follow directly from the fact that $(\mathsf{QSetup}_{\mathsf{bind}}, \mathsf{QSetup}_{\mathsf{sim}}, \mathsf{QCom}_1, \mathsf{QVer}_1, \mathsf{QSimCom}_1, \mathsf{QSimOpen}_1)$ is a dual-mode commitment scheme. **Perfect proof correctness** follows from perfect correctness of linear and quadratic proofs. **Perfect soundness** follows from perfect binding of type-1 and type-2 commitments as well as perfect soundness of linear and quadratic proofs. **Perfect encryption correctness** and **perfect semantic security** follow immediately from correctness and smoothness of the hash proof systems in [1]. It remains to prove the **perfect zero-knowledge property**. This is where the uniqueness of linear proofs (Remark 2) and the perfect uniformity (Remark 4) of the quadratic proofs are used. We give a proof by games:

- Game 0 corresponds to the zero-knowledge game where proofs are honestly generated.
- Game 1 is similar to Game 0 except that all the commitments are simulated but still opened to the value a real prover would use. This game is perfectly indistinguishable from the previous one by perfect equivocality of type-1 and type-2 commitments.
- Game 2 is similar to Game 1, except that the decommitments $d_{2,k}$ for $k \in (S_+ \cup S_\times) \setminus [m]$ (i.e., the ones which are not published) and $d'_{\star,\star}$ used to generate the linear and quadratic proofs (see Eqs. (18) to (20)) are generated as by CPSim. By perfect equivocality of type-1 and type-2 commitments, these values $d_{2,k}$ and $d'_{\star,\star}$ are valid decommitments. Hence by uniqueness of linear proofs and perfect uniformity of quadratic proofs, the resulting proofs π_k are perfectly indistinguishable between Game 1 and Game 2.

As Game 2 corresponds to the zero-knowledge game where proofs are simulated, this conclude the proof of perfect zero-knowledge. □

Acknowledgments. Huijia Lin was supported by NSF grants CNS-1528178, CNS-1514526, CNS-1652849 (CAREER), CNS-2026774, a Hellman Fellowship, a JP Morgan Research Award, the Defense Advanced Research Projects Agency (DARPA) and Army Research Office (ARO) under Contract No. W911NF-15-C-0236, and a subcontract No. 2017-002 through Galois. Part of the work was done while Huijia Lin was visiting the Simons Institute for the Theory of Computing, Berkeley. The views expressed are those of the authors and do not reflect the official policy or position of the Department of Defense, the National Science Foundation, or the U.S. Government.

References

1. Abdalla, M., Benhamouda, F., Pointcheval, D.: Disjunctions for hash proof systems: new constructions and applications. In: Oswald, E., Fischlin, M. (eds.) EUROCRYPT 2015. LNCS, vol. 9057, pp. 69–100. Springer, Heidelberg (2015). https://doi.org/10.1007/978-3-662-46803-6_3
2. Asharov, G., Jain, A., López-Alt, A., Tromer, E., Vaikuntanathan, V., Wichs, D.: Multiparty computation with low communication, computation and interaction via threshold FHE. In: Pointcheval, D., Johansson, T. (eds.) EUROCRYPT 2012. LNCS, vol. 7237, pp. 483–501. Springer, Heidelberg (2012). https://doi.org/10.1007/978-3-642-29011-4_29

3. Badrinarayanan, S., Jain, A., Manohar, N., Sahai, A.: Threshold multi-key FHE and applications to round-optimal MPC. Cryptology ePrint Archive, Report 2018/580 (2018). https://eprint.iacr.org/2018/580

4. Barak, B., et al.: On the (Im)possibility of obfuscating programs. In: Kilian, J. (ed.) CRYPTO 2001. LNCS, vol. 2139, pp. 1–18. Springer, Heidelberg (2001). https://doi.org/10.1007/3-540-44647-8_1

5. Beimel, A., Gabizon, A., Ishai, Y., Kushilevitz, E., Meldgaard, S., Paskin-Cherniavsky, A.: Non-interactive secure multiparty computation. In: Garay, J.A., Gennaro, R. (eds.) CRYPTO 2014. LNCS, vol. 8617, pp. 387–404. Springer, Heidelberg (2014). https://doi.org/10.1007/978-3-662-44381-1_22

6. Benhamouda, F., Krawczyk, H., Rabin, T.: Robust non-interactive multiparty computation against constant-size collusion. In: Katz, J., Shacham, H. (eds.) CRYPTO 2017. LNCS, vol. 10401, pp. 391–419. Springer, Cham (2017). https://doi.org/10.1007/978-3-319-63688-7_13

7. Benhamouda, F., Lin, H.: k-round multiparty computation from k-round oblivious transfer via garbled interactive circuits. In: Nielsen, J.B., Rijmen, V. (eds.) EURO-CRYPT 2018. LNCS, vol. 10821, pp. 500–532. Springer, Cham (2018). https://doi.org/10.1007/978-3-319-78375-8_17

8. Benhamouda, F., Lin, H.: Multiparty reusable non-interactive secure computation. Cryptology ePrint Archive, Report 2020/221 (2020). https://eprint.iacr.org/2020/221

9. Boyle, E., Gilboa, N., Ishai, Y.: Function secret sharing. In: Oswald, E., Fischlin, M. (eds.) EUROCRYPT 2015. LNCS, vol. 9057, pp. 337–367. Springer, Heidelberg (2015). https://doi.org/10.1007/978-3-662-46803-6_12

10. Boyle, E., Gilboa, N., Ishai, Y.: Breaking the circuit size barrier for secure computation under DDH. In: Robshaw, M., Katz, J. (eds.) CRYPTO 2016. LNCS, vol. 9814, pp. 509–539. Springer, Heidelberg (2016). https://doi.org/10.1007/978-3-662-53018-4_19

11. Canetti, R.: Security and composition of multiparty cryptographic protocols. J. Cryptol. **13**(1), 143–202 (2000)

12. Catalano, D., Visconti, I.: Hybrid trapdoor commitments and their applications. In: Caires, L., Italiano, G.F., Monteiro, L., Palamidessi, C., Yung, M. (eds.) ICALP 2005. LNCS, vol. 3580, pp. 298–310. Springer, Heidelberg (2005). https://doi.org/10.1007/11523468_25

13. Clear, M., McGoldrick, C.: Multi-identity and Multi-key leveled FHE from learning with errors. In: Gennaro, R., Robshaw, M. (eds.) CRYPTO 2015. LNCS, vol. 9216, pp. 630–656. Springer, Heidelberg (2015). https://doi.org/10.1007/978-3-662-48000-7_31

14. Cleve, R.: Towards optimal simulations of formulas by bounded-width programs. Comput. Complex. **1**(1), 91–105 (1991)

15. Cramer, R., Shoup, V.: Universal hash proofs and a paradigm for adaptive chosen ciphertext secure public-key encryption. In: Knudsen, L.R. (ed.) EUROCRYPT 2002. LNCS, vol. 2332, pp. 45–64. Springer, Heidelberg (2002). https://doi.org/10.1007/3-540-46035-7_4

16. Döttling, N., Garg, S.: Identity-based encryption from the Diffie-Hellman assumption. In: Katz, J., Shacham, H. (eds.) CRYPTO 2017. LNCS, vol. 10401, pp. 537–569. Springer, Cham (2017). https://doi.org/10.1007/978-3-319-63688-7_18

17. Feige, U., Kilian, J., Naor, M.: A minimal model for secure computation (extended abstract). In: 26th ACM STOC, pp. 554–563. ACM Press, May 1994

18. Garg, S., Gentry, C., Halevi, S., Raykova, M.: Two-round secure MPC from indistinguishability obfuscation. In: Lindell, Y. (ed.) TCC 2014. LNCS, vol. 8349, pp. 74–94. Springer, Heidelberg (2014). https://doi.org/10.1007/978-3-642-54242-8_4
19. Garg, S., Gentry, C., Sahai, A., Waters, B.: Witness encryption and its applications. In: Boneh, D., Roughgarden, T., Feigenbaum, J. (eds.) 45th ACM STOC, pp. 467–476. ACM Press, June 2013
20. Garg, S., Srinivasan, A.: Garbled protocols and two-round MPC from bilinear maps. In: Umans, C. (ed.) 58th FOCS, pp. 588–599. IEEE Computer Society Press, October 2017
21. Garg, S., Srinivasan, A.: Two-round multiparty secure computation from minimal assumptions. In: Nielsen, J.B., Rijmen, V. (eds.) EUROCRYPT 2018. LNCS, vol. 10821, pp. 468–499. Springer, Cham (2018). https://doi.org/10.1007/978-3-319-78375-8_16
22. Goldreich, O., Micali, S., Wigderson, A.: How to play any mental game or A completeness theorem for protocols with honest majority. In: Aho, A. (ed.) 19th ACM STOC, pp. 218–229. ACM Press, May 1987
23. Goldwasser, S., et al.: Multi-input functional encryption. In: Nguyen, P.Q., Oswald, E. (eds.) EUROCRYPT 2014. LNCS, vol. 8441, pp. 578–602. Springer, Heidelberg (2014). https://doi.org/10.1007/978-3-642-55220-5_32
24. Dov Gordon, S., Liu, F.-H., Shi, E.: Constant-round MPC with fairness and guarantee of output delivery. In: Gennaro, R., Robshaw, M. (eds.) CRYPTO 2015. LNCS, vol. 9216, pp. 63–82. Springer, Heidelberg (2015). https://doi.org/10.1007/978-3-662-48000-7_4
25. Groth, J., Ostrovsky, R., Sahai, A.: New techniques for non interactive zero-knowledge. J. ACM (JACM) 59(3), 11 (2012)
26. Groth, J., Sahai, A.: Efficient non-interactive proof systems for bilinear groups. In: Smart, N. (ed.) EUROCRYPT 2008. LNCS, vol. 4965, pp. 415–432. Springer, Heidelberg (2008). https://doi.org/10.1007/978-3-540-78967-3_24
27. Groth, J., Sahai, A.: Efficient non interactive proof systems for bilinear groups. SIAM J. Comput. 41(5), 1193–1232 (2012). https://doi.org/10.1137/080725386
28. Halevi, S., Ishai, Y., Jain, A., Komargodski, I., Sahai, A., Yogev, E.: Non-interactive multiparty computation without correlated randomness. In: Takagi, T., Peyrin, T. (eds.) ASIACRYPT 2017. LNCS, vol. 10626, pp. 181–211. Springer, Cham (2017). https://doi.org/10.1007/978-3-319-70700-6_7
29. Ishai, Y., Kushilevitz, E.: Private simultaneous message protocols with applications. In: Proceedings of ISTCS, pp. 174–184 (1997)
30. Ishai, Y., Kushilevitz, E., Ostrovsky, R., Prabhakaran, M., Sahai, A.: Efficient non-interactive secure computation. In: Paterson, K.G. (ed.) EUROCRYPT 2011. LNCS, vol. 6632, pp. 406–425. Springer, Heidelberg (2011). https://doi.org/10.1007/978-3-642-20465-4_23
31. Lin, H., Matt, C.: Pseudo flawed-smudging generators and their application to indistinguishability obfuscation. Cryptology ePrint Archive, Report 2018/646 (2018). https://eprint.iacr.org/2018/646
32. Lindell, Y.: An efficient transform from sigma protocols to NIZK with a CRS and non-programmable random Oracle. In: Dodis, Y., Nielsen, J.B. (eds.) TCC 2015. LNCS, vol. 9014, pp. 93–109. Springer, Heidelberg (2015). https://doi.org/10.1007/978-3-662-46494-6_5
33. Mukherjee, P., Wichs, D.: Two round multiparty computation via multi-key FHE. In: Fischlin, M., Coron, J.-S. (eds.) EUROCRYPT 2016. LNCS, vol. 9666, pp. 735–763. Springer, Heidelberg (2016). https://doi.org/10.1007/978-3-662-49896-5_26

Secure Massively Parallel Computation
for Dishonest Majority

Rex Fernando[1(✉)], Ilan Komargodski[2], Yanyi Liu[3], and Elaine Shi[3]

[1] UCLA and NTT Research, Los Angeles, USA
rex@cs.ucla.edu
[2] NTT Research and Hebrew University, Los Angeles, USA
ilan.komargodski@ntt-research.com
[3] Cornell University, Ithaca, USA
yl2866@cornell.edu, runting@gmail.com

Abstract. This work concerns secure protocols in the massively parallel computation (MPC) model, which is one of the most widely-accepted models for capturing the challenges of writing protocols for the types of parallel computing clusters which have become commonplace today (MapReduce, Hadoop, Spark, etc.). Recently, the work of Chan et al. (ITCS '20) initiated this study, giving a way to compile any MPC protocol into a secure one in the common random string model, achieving the standard secure multi-party computation definition of security with up to 1/3 of the parties being corrupt.

We are interested in achieving security for much more than 1/3 corruptions. To that end, we give two compilers for MPC protocols, which assume a simple public-key infrastructure, and achieve semi-honest security for all-but-one corruptions. Our first compiler assumes hardness of the learning-with-errors (LWE) problem, and works for any MPC protocol with "short" output—that is, where the output of the protocol can fit into the storage space of one machine, for instance protocols that output a trained machine learning model. Our second compiler works for any MPC protocol (even ones with a long output, such as sorting) but assumes, in addition to LWE, indistinguishability obfuscation and a circular secure variant of threshold FHE. Both protocols allow the attacker to choose corrupted parties based on the trusted setup, an improvement over Chan et al., whose protocol requires that the CRS is chosen independently of the attacker's choices.

1 Introduction

In the past two decades, the model of a sequential algorithm executing on a RAM machine with one processor has become increasingly impractical for large-scale datasets. Indeed, numerous programming paradigms, such as MapReduce, Hadoop, and Spark, have been developed to utilize parallel computation power in order to manipulate and analyze the vast amount of data that is available today. Starting with the work of Karloff, Suri, and Vassilvitskii [49], there have been several attempts at formalizing a theoretical model capturing such frameworks [3,33,47,49,52,54,57,70]. Today the most widely accepted model is called the *Massively Parallel Computation* (MPC) model. Throughout this

© International Association for Cryptologic Research 2020
R. Pass and K. Pietrzak (Eds.): TCC 2020, LNCS 12551, pp. 379–409, 2020.
https://doi.org/10.1007/978-3-030-64378-2_14

paper, whenever the acronym MPC is used, it means "Massively Parallel Computation" and not "Multi-Party Computation".

The MPC model is believed to best capture large clusters of Random Access Machines (RAM), each with a somewhat considerable amount of local memory and processing power, yet not enough to store the massive amount of available data. Such clusters are operated by large companies such as Google or Facebook. To be more concrete, letting N denote the total number of data records, each machine can only store $s = N^{\epsilon}$ records locally for some $\epsilon \in (0, 1)$, and the total number of machines is $m \approx N^{1-\epsilon}$ so that they can jointly store the entire dataset. One should think of N as huge, say tens or hundreds of petabytes, and ϵ as small, say 0.2[1]. In many MPC algorithms it is also okay if $m \cdot s = N \cdot \log^c N$ for some constant $c \in \mathbb{N}$ or even $m \cdot s = N^{1+\theta}$ for some small constant $\theta \in (0, 1)$, but not much larger than that (see, e.g., [1,4,49,54]).

The primary metric for the complexity of algorithms in this model is their *round complexity*. Computations that are performed within a machine are essentially "for free". The rule of thumb in this context is that algorithms that require $o(\log_2 N)$ rounds (e.g., $O(1)$ or $O(\log \log N)$) are considered *efficient*. With the goal of designing efficient algorithms in the MPC model, there is an immensely rich algorithmic literature suggesting various non-trivial efficient algorithms for tasks of interest, including graph problems [1,3–5,7–10,12,16–18], [30,33,38,41,43,53,54,62,68], clustering [13,15,35,42,73] and submodular function optimization [36,52,58,67].

Secure MPC. In a very recent work, Chan, Chung, Lin, and Shi [26] initiated the study of secure computation in the MPC model. Chan et al. [26] showed that any task that can be efficiently computed in this model can also be securely computed with comparable efficiency. More precisely, they show that any MPC algorithm can be compiled to a secure counterpart that defends against a malicious adversary who controls up to $1/3 - \eta$ fraction of machines (for an arbitrarily small constant η), where the security guarantee is similar to the one in *cryptographic secure multiparty computation*. In other words, an adversary is prevented from learning anything about the honest parties' inputs except for what the output of the functionality reveals. The cost of this compilation is very small: the compiled protocol only increases the round complexity by a constant factor, and the space required by each machine only increases by a multiplicative factor that is a fixed polynomial in the security parameter. Since round complexity is so important in the MPC setting, it is crucial that these cost blowups are small. Indeed, any useful compiler must preserve even a sublogarithmic round complexity. The security of their construction relies on the Learning With Errors (LWE) assumption and they further rely on the existence of a common random string that is chosen *after* the adversary commits to its corrupted set.

Why is secure MPC hard? Since there is a long line of work studying secure multiparty computation (starting with [19,45]), a natural first question is whether

---

[1] If N is one Petabyte (10^6 Gigabytes), then the storage of each machine in the cluster needs to be < 16 Gigabytes.

these classical results extend to the MPC model in a straightforward way. The crucial aspect of algorithms in the MPC model which makes this task non-trivial is the combination of the space constraint with the required small round complexity. Indeed, many existing techniques from the standard secure computation literature fail to extend to this model, since they either require too many rounds or they require each party to store too much data. For instance, it is impossible for any one party to store commitments or shares of all other parties' inputs, a common requirement in many secure computation protocols (e.g., [50, 65]). This also rules out naively adapting protocols that rely on more modern tools such as threshold FHE [6, 34, 59], as they also involve a similar first step. Even previous work that focused on large-scale secure computation [22] required one broadcast message *per party*, which either incurs a large space overhead or a large blowup in the number of rounds. Chan et al. [26] give an exciting feasibility result for secure protocols in this model, but their construction, as mentioned, has some significant limitations: (1) it only tolerates at most ≈1/3 corruptions, and (2) it relies on a trusted setup which must be chosen *after* the choice of the corrupted parties. Whether these limitations are inherent in this new model remains an intriguing open question.

This work. We consider the setting of *all-but-one corruptions*, where the computation is performed in the MPC model but security is required even for a single honest machine if all other players are controlled by an adversary. In the classical secure multi-party computation literature this setting is referred to as the *dishonest majority* setting and generic protocols tolerating such adversarial behaviour are well known (e.g., [45]). In contrast, in the MPC model, it is a-priori not even clear that such a generic result can be obtained with the space and round complexity constraints. This raises the following question, which is the focus of this work:

Is there a generic way to efficiently compile any massively parallel protocol into a secure version that tolerates all-but-one corruptions?

1.1   Our Results

We answer the above question in the affirmative. We give two compilers that can be used to efficiently compile any algorithm in the MPC model into an algorithm that implements the same functionality also in the MPC model, but now secure even in the presence of an attacker who controls up to $m - 1$ of the m machines. Both of our protocols handle *semi-honest* attackers who are assumed to follow the specification of the protocol.

In terms of trusted setup, in both of our protocols we assume that there is a public-key infrastructure (PKI) which consists of a $(\mathsf{pk}, \mathsf{sk}_1, \ldots, \mathsf{sk}_m)$: a single public key and m secret keys, one per machine. Machine $i \in [m]$ knows pk and sk_i, whose size is independent of N (and none of the other secret keys). Crucially, our protocols allow the adversary to choose the corrupted parties based on the setup phase, an improvement over the construction of [26], for which there is an obvious and devastating attack if the adversary can choose corrupted parties based on the common random string.

Notation and parameters. Let N denote the bit size of the data-set[2] and suppose that each machine has space $s = N^\epsilon$ for some fixed constant $\epsilon \in (0, 1)$. We further assume that the number of machines, m, is about $N^{1-\epsilon}$ or even a little bigger. The security parameter is denoted λ and it is assumed that $N < \lambda^c$ for some $c \in \mathbb{N}$ and $s > \lambda$.

Secure MPC with Short Outputs. Our first result is a compiler that fits best for tasks whose output is "short". By short we mean that it fits into the memory of (say) a single machine. The compiler blows up the number of rounds by a constant and the space by a fixed polynomial in the security parameter, which is identical to the efficiency of the compiler in [26]. For security, we rely on the LWE assumption [69].

While at first it may seem that this compiler is quite restricted in the class of algorithms it supports, in fact, there are many important and central functionalities that fit in this class. For instance, this class contains all graph problems whose output is somewhat succinct (like finding a shortest path in a graph, a minimum spanning tree, a small enough connected component, etc.). Even more impressively, all submodular maximization problems, a class of problems that captures a wide variety of problems in machine learning, fit into this class [67].

Theorem 1 (Secure MPC for Short Output, Informal). *Assume hardness of LWE. Given any massively parallel computation (MPC) protocol Π which after R rounds results in an output of size $\leq s$ for party 1 and no output for any other party, there is a secure MPC algorithm $\tilde{\Pi}$ that securely realizes Π with semi-honest security in the presence of an adversary that statically corrupts up to $m - 1$ parties. Moreover, $\tilde{\Pi}$ completes in $O(R)$ rounds, consumes at most $O(s) \cdot \mathsf{poly}(\lambda)$ space per machine, and incurs $O(m \cdot s) \cdot \mathsf{poly}(\lambda)$ total communication per round.*

As mentioned above, by security we mean an analogue of standard cryptographic multiparty computation security, adapted to the massively parallel computation (MPC) model. We use the LWE assumption to instantiate a secure variant of an n-out-of-n threshold fully-homomorphic scheme (FHE) [6,20] which supports "incremental decoding". This is an alternative to the standard decoding procedure of threshold FHE schemes which is suited to work in the MPC model. See Sect. 2 for details.

We prove that our construction satisfies semi-honest security where the attacker gets to choose its corrupted set *before* the protocol begins but *after* the public key is published. (In comparison, recall that [26] had their attacker commit on its corrupted set before even seeing the CRS.)

---

[2] We assume for simplicity that a data record takes up one bit.

Secure MPC with Long Outputs. Our second result is a compiler that works for *any* protocol in the MPC model. Many MPC protocols perform tasks whose output is much larger than what fits into one machine. Such tasks may include, for example, the task of sorting the input. Here the result of the protocol is that each machine contains a small piece of the output, which is considered to be the concatenation of all machines' outputs in order. Our second compiler can be used for such functionalities.

In this construction we rely, in addition to LWE, on a circular secure variant of the threshold FHE scheme from the short output protocol and also on indistinguishability obfuscation [14,39,71]. The compiler achieves the same round and space blowup as the short-output compiler.

Theorem 2 (Secure MPC for Long Output, Informal). *Assume the existence of an circular secure n-out-of-n threshold FHE scheme with incremental decoding, along with iO and hardness of LWE. Given any massively parallel computation (MPC) protocol Π that completes in R rounds, there is a secure MPC algorithm $\tilde{\Pi}$ that securely realizes Π with semi-honest security in the presence of an adversary that statically corrupts up to $m-1$ parties. Moreover, $\tilde{\Pi}$ completes in $O(R)$ rounds, consumes at most $O(s) \cdot \mathsf{poly}(\lambda)$ space per machine, and incurs $O(m \cdot s) \cdot \mathsf{poly}(\lambda)$ total communication per round.*

1.2 Related Work

The cryptography literature has extensively studied secure computation on parallel architectures, but most existing works focus on the PRAM model (where each processing unit has $O(1)$ local storage) [2,22,23,27–29,31,32,56,61]. Most real-world large-scale parallel computation is now done on large clusters which are much more accurately modeled by the MPC architecture, and the aforementioned works usually do not apply to this setting. Other distributed models of computations have been considered in cryptographic contexts. Parter and Yogev [63,64] considered secure computation on graphs in the so-called CONGEST model of computation (where each message is of size at most $O(\log N)$ bits).

Paper Organization

An overview of our constructions is given next in Sect. 2. Some standard preliminaries and the building blocks that we use in our construction are formally defined in Sect. 3. The MPC model is formally defined in Sect. 4. The compiler for short output protocols appears in Sect. 5 and the compiler for long output protocols is in Sect. 6.

2   Technical Overview

In this section we give the high-level overview of our protocols. Let us briefly recall the model. The total input size contains N bits and there are about

$m \approx N^{1-\epsilon}$ machines, each having space $s = N^\epsilon$. In every round, each machine can send and receive at most s bits since its local space is bounded (e.g., a machine cannot broadcast a message to everyone in one round). We are given some protocol in the MPC model that computes some functionality $f\colon (\{0,1\}^{l_{in}})^m \to (\{0,1\}^s)^m$, where $l_{in} \leq s$, and we would like to compile it into a secure version that computes the same functionality. We would like to preserve the round complexity up to constant blowup, and to preserve the space complexity as much as possible. Moreover, we want semi-honest security, which means there must exist a simulator which, without the honest parties' inputs, can simulate the view of a set of corrupted parties, provided the parties do not deviate from the specification of the protocol.

Since our goal is to use cryptographic assumptions to achieve security for MPC protocols, we introduce an additional parameter λ, which is a security parameter. One should assume that N is upper bounded by some large polynomial in λ and that s is large enough to store $O(\lambda)$ bits.

We first note that we can start by assuming that the communication patterns, i.e., the number of messages sent by each party, the size of messages, and the recipients, do not leak anything about the parties' inputs. We call a protocol that achieves this *communication oblivious*. A generic transformation for any MPC protocol was shown by [26], which achieved communication obliviousness with constant blowup in rounds and space.

2.1   The Short Output Protocol

We start with a protocol in the easier case where the underlying MPC results with a "short" output, meaning that it fits into the memory of a single machine (say the first one).

In a nutshell, the idea is as follows: we want to execute an encrypted version of the (insecure) MPC algorithm using a homomorphic encryption scheme. In the classical setting of secure computation this idea was extensively used in threshold/multi-key FHE based solutions, for instance, in [6,11,20,25,55,60,66] There, in a high-level, each party first broadcasts an encryption of its input. Then each party can (locally) homomorphically compute the desired function over the combined inputs of all parties, and finally all parties participate in a joint decryption protocol that allows them to decrypt the output. Moreover, this joint decryption protocol does not allow any party to decrypt any ciphertext beyond the output ciphertext. The classical joint decryption protocol is completely non-interactive: each party broadcasts a "partial decryption" value so that each party who holds partial decryptions from all other parties can locally decode the final output of the protocol.

Recall that in our setting each party has bounded space and so it is impossible for any party to store all partial decryptions and so the joint decryption protocol described above cannot work in the MPC model. To get around this, we relax the joint decryption protocol by allowing it to be *interactive*. To this end, we design a new joint decryption protocol that splits the process of "combining" partial decryption into many rounds (concretely, $\log_\lambda m \in O(1)$ rounds).

We use the additive-secret-sharing threshold FHE scheme of Boneh et al. [20] and modify their decryption procedure, as we explain next.

At a high-level, the ciphertext in the simplest variant of Boneh et al.'s [20] scheme is a GSW [40] ciphertext, and each party's secret key is a linear share of the GSW secret key. In addition, partial decryption works in the same way as the GSW decryption using the secret key share with an additional re-randomization, and then the final decryption phase is just a linear function that combines the partial decryptions and a final step of rounding[3]. We observe that the first part of final decryption, which is just a linear function, can be executed in a tree-like fashion, so that if each party has a partial decryption, no party will need to store more than a few partial decryptions at a time.

Our trick is to adjust the parameters of this tree to be aligned with the MPC model. We let each machine hold about λ different partial decryptions (causing a λ blow up in space) which causes the depth of the tree to be roughly $\log_\lambda m$. Since m is bounded by some fixed polynomial in λ this is still $O(1)$. Overall, this step adds $O(1)$ rounds of communication and results with a single party knowing the output. As a small technical note, to simulate the view of set of corrupted parties which do not learn the output, we require one additional property of the threshold FHE scheme: it must be possible to simulate partial decryptions of an incomplete set $I' \subsetneq [m]$ of parties without knowing even the output of the circuit. This requirement is not captured in the original definition of threshold FHE in [20], but we show that their construction satisfies it.

2.2 The Long Output Protocol

Here, we would like to support MPC protocols whose output is "long", namely, each party will have an output. Directly extending the short output protocol fails. Indeed, there, we used a tree-like protocol to gradually "aggregate" the sum of all partial decryption at a single machines's memory. In the current case, each party needs to do the same procedure to recover its own output. Since we have a bound on the total communication of each party, we cannot run all gradual decryptions in parallel, so this requires about m/ϵ rounds (which is way too much).

Recall that the goal of the decryption phase is for the parties to learn the decryption of its output, without learning the decryptions of any other cipher-text. If we can somehow construct a decryption phase where the communication is independent of the output size, we would have a valid long output protocol. This is non-trivial: what we essentially need is some "limited" master secret key, which somehow only decrypts a limited set of ciphertexts, and nothing else. Moreover, we need to be able to generate this key within the limitations of the MPC model: no single machine can even hold the complete set of ciphertext which this secret key is supposed to decrypt.

Let us define the functionality of this "limited" master secret key more formally. It will be convenient to describe it as a circuit. Ideally, the circuit has

---

[3] Note that although the Shamir-based TFHE scheme in [20] requires a field size which is polynomial in the number of parties n, the field size in the simpler additive-based scheme is independent of n, which is crucial in our construction.

hardwired the secret keys from all parties along with all ciphertexts which correspond to the output of the computation. Each party would be able to submit its output to the circuit, and the circuit would be able to check if this ciphertext is a member of the valid set, and decrypt if this is the case. Even ignoring security (namely, that a machine can learn all keys; we will address this later), there are two efficiency problems: first, the circuit contains m ciphertexts, and the second is that it contains m secret keys (and recall that $m \gg s$).

To solve the first problem, instead of storing the ciphertexts explicitly, we use a succinct commitment thereof. We need a way for the parties to collectively compute this commitment in the MPC model and without increasing the number of rounds too much. To this end, we use a variant of Merkle commitments with larger arity. We note that the tree structure of Merkle commitments suits our model very well: if a single machine is responsible for computing the label of a single node in the tree, we achieve a low-communication-complexity protocol relatively easily. Then, if we set the arity to be $O(\lambda)$, the number of rounds will be roughly $\log_\lambda m$, which is constant assuming m is at most a fixed polynomial in λ.

To solve the second problem, we observe an important property about the basic n-out-of-n threshold FHE scheme of Boneh et al. Namely, in this scheme, the public key is a GSW public key, each party's secret key is a linear share of the corresponding GSW secret key, and encryption under the threshold FHE scheme is simply a GSW encryption with this public key. This means that knowing the sum of all parties' secret keys is sufficient to decrypt, and this sum is compact.

So we have a feasible circuit with the functionality we need in order to implement a "limited" master secret key. We of course need a secure version of this circuit, which will not leak the master secret key hardcoded in the circuit. To do this we use indistinguishability obfuscation. We give a high-level overview of the techniques which we use in conjunction with obfuscation to achieve security. Since we want to be able to simulate the view of the corrupted parties, we need a simulated version of the circuit, which has no master secret key embedded but which can still produce the decrypted outputs. The main idea for how we overcome this is to exploit the fact that the simulator is allowed to set the randomness of the corrupted parties. We will use the Merkle commitment to force each party to input their randomness to the circuit, and when simulating we will embed the output in this randomness, padded with a PRF. The circuit can then unpad and use this as its output without knowing the secret key. This is a somewhat standard technique in iO literature first used by [46]. One technical detail is that since iO only guarantees indistinguishability against circuits which are functionally equivalent, we need a succinct commitment which can guarantee statistical binding for some indices. This type of primitive, a somewhere-statistically-binding (SSB) hash, was also constructed by [46] from the learning-with-errors (LWE) assumption. We observe that the construction of [46] also uses a tree structure similar to a Merkle tree, which allows the machines to collectively compute the commitment without too much communication or storage.

Now that we have a way to generate a "limited" secret key, the question is, how can the parties do this without leaking their secret key shares? We need to somehow assemble this obfuscated circuit, which has the master secret key embedded, even though no party is allowed to know the master secret key. Our key idea is to leverage our short-output secure MPC protocol for this purpose: we can use that protocol to securely compute the obfuscated circuit! The short-output protocol guarantees that parties learn nothing about the execution of the protocol beyond the output and their inputs, and this is exactly what we need in order to compute the obfuscated circuit without revealing the master secret key.

One final technical challenge we need to overcome is that an SSB hash commitment does not guarantee privacy; it may leak information about the committed values. In order to achieve output privacy, we introduce an extra step in the protocol where each party pads their encrypted output before committing. We refer to Sect. 6 for details.

On the necessity of a PKI. Our constructions require a public-key infrastructure (PKI); a trusted party must generate a (single) public key and (many) secret key shares which it distributes to each machine. We do not know if this is necessary, but at least we argue that known techniques from the classical secure computation literature do not work in the MPC model (and so drastically new ideas are needed). Indeed, classically, secure multi-party computation protocols avoid using a PKI by using threshold multi-key FHE (e.g., [6,11,25,55,60,66]), where each party generates its own key pair and uses the concatenation of all public keys as the master public key. This does not extend to our setting, since the number of machines is much larger than the space of each individual machine (and so a machines cannot even store all public keys). Of course, obtaining our results without a PKI is a natural open problem.

3 Preliminaries

For $x \in \{0,1\}^*$, let $x[a : b]$ be the substring of x starting at a and ending at b. A function $\mathsf{negl} \colon \mathbb{N} \to \mathbb{R}$ is *negligible* if it is asymptotically smaller than any inverse-polynomial function, namely, for every constant $c > 0$ there exists an integer N_c such that $\mathsf{negl}(\lambda) \leq \lambda^{-c}$ for all $\lambda > N_c$. Two sequences of random variables $X = \{X_\lambda\}_{\lambda \in \mathbb{N}}$ and $Y = \{Y_\lambda\}_{\lambda \in \mathbb{N}}$ are *computationally indistinguishable* if for any non-uniform PPT algorithm $\mathcal{A}$ there exists a negligible function negl such that $\left| \Pr[\mathcal{A}(1^\lambda, X_\lambda) = 1] - \Pr[\mathcal{A}(1^\lambda, Y_\lambda) = 1] \right| \leq \mathsf{negl}(\lambda)$ for all $\lambda \in \mathbb{N}$.

3.1 Threshold FHE with Incremental Decryption

We will use a threshold FHE scheme with an "incremental" decryption procedure, specialized for the MPC model. Our definition follows that of [48].

An n-out-of-n threshold fully homomorphic encryption scheme with incremental decryption is a tuple (TFHE.Setup, TFHE.Enc, TFHE.Eval, TFHE.Dec, TFHE.PartDec, TFHE.CombineParts, TFHE.Round) of algorithms which satisfy the following properties:

- TFHE.Setup($1^\lambda, n$) → ($pk, sk_1, \ldots, sk_n$): On input the security parameter λ and the number of parties n, the setup algorithm outputs a public key and a set of secret key shares.
- TFHE.Enc$_{pk}(m)$ → ct: On input a public key pk and a plaintext $m \in \{0,1\}^*$, the encryption algorithm outputs a ciphertext ct.
- TFHE.Eval($C, ct_1, \ldots, ct_k$) → $\hat{ct}$: On input a public key pk, a circuit C : $\{0,1\}^{l_1} \times \cdots \times \{0,1\}^{l_k} \to \{0,1\}^{l_o}$, and a set of ciphertexts $ct_1, \ldots, ct_k$, the evaluation algorithm outputs a ciphertext $\hat{ct}$.
- TFHE.Dec$_{sk}(ct)$ → m: On input the master secret key $sk_1 + \cdots + sk_n$ and a ciphertext ct, the decryption algorithm outputs the plaintext m.
- TFHE.PartDec$_{sk_i}(ct)$ → p_i: a ciphertext ct and a secret key share sk_i, the partial decryption algorithm outputs a partial decryption p_i for party P_i.
- TFHE.CombineParts(p_I, p_J) → $p_{I \sqcup J}$: On input two partial decryptions p_I and p_J, the combine algorithm outputs another partial decryption algorithm $p_{I \sqcup J}$
- TFHE.Round(p) → m: On input a partial decryption p, the rounding algorithm outputs a plaintext m.

Compactness of ciphertexts: There exists a polynomial p such that $|ct| \leq \mathsf{poly}(\lambda) \cdot |m|$ for any ciphertext ct generated from the algorithms of the TFHE, and $p_i \leq \mathsf{poly}(\lambda) \cdot |m|$ as well for all i^4.

Correctness with local decryption: For all $\lambda, n, C, m_1, \ldots, m_k$, the following condition holds. For ($pk, sk_1, \ldots, sk_n$) ← TFHE.Setup($1^\lambda, n$), ct_j ← TFHE.Enc$_{pk}(m_j)$ for $j \in [k]$, $\hat{ct}$ ← TFHE.Eval($C, ct_1, \ldots, ct_k$), and p_i ← TFHE.PartDec$_{sk_i}(\hat{ct})$, take any binary tree with n leaves labeled with the p_i, and with each non-leaf node v labeled with TFHE.CombineParts(p_l, p_r), where p_l is the label of v's left child and p_r is the label of v's right child. Let ρ be the label of the root; then

$$\Pr\left[\mathsf{TFHE.Round}(\rho) = C(m_1, \ldots, m_k)\right] = 1 - \mathsf{negl}(\lambda).$$

Correctness of MSK decryption: For all $\lambda, n, C, m_1, \ldots, m_k$, the following condition holds. For ($pk, sk_1, \ldots, sk_n$) ← TFHE.Setup($1^\lambda, n$), ct_i ← TFHE.Enc$_{pk}(m_i)$ for $i \in [k]$, $\hat{ct}$ ← TFHE.Eval($C, ct_1, \ldots, ct_k$),

$$\Pr\left[\mathsf{TFHE.Dec}_{sk}(\hat{ct}) = C(m_1, \ldots, m_k)\right] = 1 - \mathsf{negl}(\lambda),$$

where $sk = sk_1 + \cdots + sk_n$.

Semantic (and circular) security of encryption: We give two alternative definitions of semantic security, the standard one and a notion of circular security. For any PPT adversary $\mathcal{A}$, the following experiment $\mathsf{Expt}_{\mathcal{A}, \mathrm{TFHE,sem}}$ outputs 1 with $1/2 + \mathsf{negl}(\lambda)$ probability:

---

[4] As noted in the technical overview, although this does not hold for the Shamir-based TFHE scheme in [20], it *does* hold for the simpler additive-based TFHE scheme given in the same paper.

$\mathsf{Expt}_{\mathcal{A},\text{TFHE},\text{sem}}$:

---

1. The challenger runs $(pk, sk_1, \ldots, sk_n) \leftarrow \mathsf{TFHE.Setup}(1^\lambda, n)$ and provides pk to $\mathcal{A}$.
2. $\mathcal{A}$ outputs a set $I \subsetneq [n]$ and a message m; for circular security m can contain special symbols $\llcorner sk_i \lrcorner$.
3. The challenger provides $\{sk_i\}_{i \in I}$ to $\mathcal{A}$.
4. In circular security, the challenger computes m' by replacing every symbol $\llcorner sk_i \lrcorner$ with the secret key sk_i. In normal semantic security the challenger sets $m' = m$.
5. The challenger chooses $b \xleftarrow{\$} \{0,1\}$; if $b = 0$ then the challenger sends $\mathsf{TFHE.Enc}_{pk}(m')$, and if $b = 1$ then the challenger sends $\mathsf{TFHE.Enc}_{pk}(0^{|m'|})$.
6. $\mathcal{A}$ outputs a guess b'. The experiment outputs 1 if $b = b'$.

(Circular) Simulation security: There exists a simulator ($\mathsf{TFHE.Sim.Setup}$, $\mathsf{TFHE.Sim.Query}$) such that for any PPT $\mathcal{A}$, the following experiments $\mathsf{Expt}_{\mathcal{A},\text{TFHE},\text{real}}$ and $\mathsf{Expt}_{\mathcal{A},\text{TFHE},\text{ideal}}$ are indistinguishable:

$\mathsf{Expt}_{\mathcal{A},\text{TFHE},\text{real}}$:

---

1. The challenger runs $(pk, sk_1, \ldots, sk_n) \leftarrow \mathsf{TFHE.Setup}(1^\lambda)$ and provides pk to $\mathcal{A}$.
2. $\mathcal{A}$ outputs a set $I \subsetneq [n]$ and messages $m_1, \ldots, m_k$, along with $\{r_j\}_J$ for some subset $J \subset [k]$. In addition, for circular simulation security each m_i can contain special symbols $\llcorner sk_{i'} \lrcorner$.
3. In circular simulation security, for each $i \in [k]$, the challenger computes m_i' by replacing every symbol $\llcorner sk_{i'} \lrcorner$ with the secret key $sk_{i'}$. In normal simulation security, the challenger sets $m_i' = m_i$.
4. The challenger provides $\{sk_i\}_{i \in I}$ to $\mathcal{A}$ and $\{\mathsf{TFHE.Enc}_{pk}(m_i')\}_{i \in [k]}$ to $\mathcal{A}$. For each $i \in [k]$, if the adversary supplied randomness r_i, then this randomness is used as the randomness for encrypting m_i'.
5. $\mathcal{A}$ issues a polynomial number of adaptive queries of the form (I', C), and for each query the challenger computes $\hat{ct} \leftarrow \mathsf{TFHE.Eval}(C, ct_1, \ldots, ct_k)$ and responds with $\{\mathsf{TFHE.PartDec}_{sk_i}(\hat{ct})\}_{i \in I'}$.
6. At the end of the experiment, $\mathcal{A}$ outputs a distinguishing bit b.

$\mathsf{Expt}_{\mathcal{A},\mathrm{TFHE,ideal}}$:

---

1. The challenger runs $(pk, sk'_1, \ldots, sk'_n, \sigma_{sim}) \leftarrow \mathsf{TFHE.Setup}(1^\lambda)$ and provides pk to $\mathcal{A}$.
2. $\mathcal{A}$ outputs a set $I \subsetneq [n]$ and messages $m_1, \ldots, m_k$, along with $\{r_j\}_J$ for some subset $J \subset [k]$. In addition, for circular simulation security each m_i can contain special symbols $\llcorner sk_{i'} \lrcorner$.
3. In circular simulation security, for each $i \in [k]$, the challenger computes m'_i by replacing every symbol $\llcorner sk_{i'} \lrcorner$ with the secret key $sk_{i'}$. In normal simulation security, the challenger sets $m'_i = m_i$.
4. The challenger runs $(\{sk_i\}_{i \in I}, \sigma_{sim}) \leftarrow \mathsf{TFHE.Sim.Setup}(pk, I)$ and provides $\{sk_i\}_{i \in I}$ and $\{\mathsf{TFHE.Enc}_{pk}(m'_i)\}_{i \in [k]}$ to $\mathcal{A}$. For each $i \in [k]$, if the adversary supplied randomness r_i, then this randomness is used as the randomness for encrypting m'_i.
5. $\mathcal{A}$ issues a polynomial number of adaptive queries of the form (I', C), and the challenger runs the simulator $\{p_i\}_{i \in I'} \leftarrow \mathsf{TFHE.Sim.Query}(C, \{ct_i\}_{i \in [k]}, \{r_j\}_{j \in J}, C(m'_1, \ldots, m'_k), I', \sigma_{sim})$ and responds with $\{p_i\}_{i \in I'}$.
6. At the end of the experiment, $\mathcal{A}$ outputs a distinguishing bit b.

Simulation of incomplete decryptions: We additionally require that, for the above experiments, if $I \cup I' \neq [n]$, then it is possible to simulate partial decryptions without knowing the circuit output. In other words, if $I \cup I' \neq [n]$ then in the ideal world the challenger can compute

$$\{p_i\}_{i \in I'} \leftarrow \mathsf{TFHE.Sim.Query}(C, \{ct_i\}_{i \in [k]}, \{m'_j, r_j\}_{j \in J}, \bot, I', \sigma_{sim})$$

in step 4 above, and indistinguishability still holds.

Although this additional requirement is not explicit in the simulation security definition of [48], it follows implicitly from the fact that semantic security holds whenever the adversary does not have all secret keys sk_i. More specifically, assume the adversary requests an "incomplete" partial decryption set I' from the challenger, where $I \cup I' \neq [m]$. This means that for all $i \in [m] \setminus (I \cup I')$, the adversary receives no information at all about sk_i, so by TFHE semantic security it is possible to switch all encryptions for $i \notin J$ (i.e. where the adversary does not supply the encryption randomness) to 0. Thus to simulate partial decryptions for I', it is only necessary to know the output of C over the inputs $m'_i, i \in J$, and $0, i \notin J$. Since the TFHE simulator receives m'_i for all $i \in J$, it can thus simulate partial decryptions without knowing the output of C over the true inputs.

The next theorem states that a threshold FHE (TFHE) scheme with incremental decryption exists under the Learning with Errors (LWE) assumption.

Theorem 3. *Assuming LWE, there exists a threshold FHE (TFHE) scheme with incremental decryption satisfying the above requirements except for circular security.*

Proof sketch. We use the most basic construction of [20] and observe that it can be modified to satisfy the incremental decryption property as follows. In their decryption procedure, one gets all partial decryptions and they are added together and then a non-linear rounding is performed. We obtain incrementality by separating the two parts into two procedures. The first only performs the first part of adding up partial decryptions–this can be done incrementally since this is a linear operation. The second operation is the rounding operation which is executed in the end.

To see why the simulation of incomplete decryptions property holds, note that the secret keys of the parties are linear shares of a GSW secret key. This means that if $I \cup I' \neq [n]$ then the distribution of shares corresponding to $I \cup I'$ are identical to uniform. Thus the simulator can pick uniform random sk_i for each $i \in I'$ in order to simulate partial decryptions without knowing the circuit evaluation.

Remark 1. We note that we will use a plain threshold FHE (TFHE) scheme with incremental decryption in the protocol for short output functionalities (see Sect. 5) and so that one can be based on the hardness of LWE. However, the long output protocol (see Sect. 6) will require a circular secure version of threshold FHE (TFHE) scheme with incremental decryption (defined above) which we do not know how to base on any standard assumption, except by assuming that the construction from Theorem 3 satisfies it).

3.2 Somewhere Statistically Binding Hash

A somewhere statistically binding (SSB) hash [46] consists of the following algorithms, which satisfy the properties below:

- SSB.Setup($1^\lambda, L, d, f, i^*$) → h: On input integers L, d, f, and an index $i^* \in [f^d L]$, outputs a hash key h.
- SSB.Start(h, x) → v: On input h and a string $x \in \{0,1\}^L$, output a hash tree leaf v.
- SSB.Combine($h, \{v_i\}_{i \in [f]}$) → $\hat{v}$: On input h and f hash tree nodes $\{v_i\}_{i \in [f]}$, output a parent node $\hat{v}$.
- SSB.Verify($h, i, x_i, z, \{v\}$) → b: On input h, and index i, a string x_i, a hash tree root z, and a set $\{v\}$ of nodes, output 1 iff $\{v\}$ consists of a path from the leaf corresponding to x_i to the root z, as well as the siblings of all nodes along this path.

Correctness: For any integers L, d, and f, and any indices i^*, j, strings $\{x_i\}_{i \in [f^d]}$ where $|x_i| = L$, and any $h \leftarrow$ SSB.Setup($1^\lambda, L, d, f, i^*$), if $\{v\}$ consists of a path in the tree generated using SSB.Start($h, \cdot$) and SSB.Combine($h, \cdot$) on the leaf strings $\{x_i\}_{i \in [f^d]}$, from the leaf corresponding to x_j to the root z, along with the siblings of all nodes along this path, then SSB.Verify($h, j, x_j, z, \{v\}$) = 1.

Compactness of commitment and openings: All node labels generated by the SSB.Start and SSB.Combine algorithms are binary strings of size poly(λ) $\cdot L$.

Index hiding: Consider the following game between an adversary $\mathcal{A}$ and a challenger:

1. $\mathcal{A}(1^\lambda)$ chooses L, d, and f, and two indices i_0^* and i_1^*.
2. The challenger chooses a bit $b \leftarrow_\$ \{0,1\}$ and sets $h \leftarrow$ SSB.Setup$(1^\lambda, L, d, f, i_b^*)$.
3. The adversary gets h and outputs a bit b'. The game outputs 1 iff $b = b'$.

We require that no PPT $\mathcal{A}$ can win the game with non-negligible probability.

Somewhere statistically binding: For all λ, L, d, and f, i^*, and for any key $h \leftarrow$ SSB.Setup$(1^\lambda, L, d, f, i^*)$, there do not exist any values z, x, x', $\{v\}$, $\{v'\}$ such that SSB.Verify$(h, i^*, x, z, \{v\}) =$ SSB.Verify$(h, i^*, x', z, \{v'\}) = 1$.

Theorem 4 ([46, **Theorem 3.2**]). *Assume LWE. Then there exists an SSB hash construction satisfying the above properties.*

3.3   Indistinguishability Obfuscation for Circuits

Let $\mathcal{C}$ be a class of Boolean circuits. An obfuscation scheme for $\mathcal{C}$ consists of one algorithm iO with the following syntax.

$iO(C \in \mathcal{C}, 1^\lambda)$: The obfuscation algorithm is a PPT algorithm that takes as input a circuit $C \in \mathcal{C}$, security parameter λ. It outputs an obfuscated circuit.

An obfuscation scheme is said to be a secure indistingushability obfuscator for $\mathcal{C}$ [14,39,71] if it satisfies the following correctness and security properties:

- Correctness: For every security parameter λ, input length n, circuit $C \in \mathcal{C}$ that takes n bit inputs, input $x \in \{0,1\}^n$, $C'(x) = C(x)$, for $C' \leftarrow iO(C, 1^\lambda)$.
- Security: For every PPT adversary $\mathcal{A} = (\mathcal{A}_1, \mathcal{A}_2)$, the following experiment outputs 1 with at most $1/2 + \mathsf{negl}(\lambda)$:

EXPERIMENT $\mathsf{Expt}_{\mathcal{A}, iO}$:

---

1. $(C_0, C_1, \sigma) \leftarrow \mathcal{A}_1(1^\lambda)$
2. If $|C_0| \neq |C_1|$, or if either C_0 or C_1 have different input lengths, then the experiment outputs a uniformly random bit.
   Else, let n denote the input lengths of C_0, C_1. If there exists an input $x \in \{0,1\}^n$ such that $C_0(x) \neq C_1(x)$, then the experiment outputs a uniformly random bit.
3. $b \leftarrow \{0,1\}$, $\tilde{C} \leftarrow iO(C_b, 1^\lambda)$.
4. $b' \leftarrow \mathcal{A}_2(\sigma, \tilde{C})$.
5. Experiment outputs 1 if $b = b'$, else it outputs 0.

3.4   Puncturable Pseudorandom Functions

We use the definition of puncturable PRFs given in [72], given as follows. A puncturable family of PRFs F is given by a triple of turing machines PPRF.KeyGen, PPRF.Puncture, and F, and a pair of computable functions $n()$ and $m()$, satisfying the following conditions:

- **Functionality preserved under puncturing:** For every PPT adversary $\mathcal{A}$ such that $\mathcal{A}(1^\lambda)$ outputs a set $S \subseteq \{0,1\}^{n(\lambda)}$, then for all $x \in \{0,1\}^{n(\lambda)}$ where $x \notin S$, we have that:

$$\Pr\left[F(K,x) = F(K_S,x) \;\middle|\; \begin{array}{l} K \leftarrow \mathsf{PPRF.KeyGen}(1^\lambda), \\ K_S \leftarrow \mathsf{PPRF.Puncture}(K,S) \end{array}\right] = 1$$

- **Pseudorandom at punctured points:** For every PPT adversary $(\mathcal{A}_1, \mathcal{A}_2)$ such that $\mathcal{A}_1(1^\lambda)$ outputs a set $S \subseteq \{0,1\}^{n(\lambda)}$ and state σ, consider an experiment where $K \leftarrow \mathsf{PPRF.KeyGen}(1^\lambda)$ and $K_S \leftarrow \mathsf{PPRF.Puncture}(K,S)$. Then we have

$$\Big|\Pr\left[\mathcal{A}_2(\sigma, K_S, S, F(K,S)) = 1\right] - \Pr\left[\mathcal{A}_2(\sigma, K_S, S, U_{m(\lambda)|S|}) = 1\right]\Big| \leq \mathsf{negl}(\lambda)$$

where $F(K,S)$ denotes the concatenation of $F(K,x)$ for all $x \in S$ in lexicographic order and U_ℓ denotes the uniform distribution over ℓ bits.

Theorem 5 ([21, 24, 44, 51]). *If one-way functions exist, then for all efficiently computable $n(\lambda)$ and $m(\lambda)$ there exists a puncturable PRF family that maps $n(\lambda)$ bits to $m(\lambda)$ bits.*

4   Model

4.1   Massively Parallel Computation (MPC)

We now describe the Massively Parallel Computation (MPC) model. This description is an adaptation of the description in [26]. Let N be the input size in bits and $\epsilon \in (0,1)$ a constant. The MPC model consists of m parties, where $m \in [N^{1-\epsilon}, \mathsf{poly}(N)]$ and each party has a local space of $s = N^\epsilon$ bits. Hence, the total space of all parties is $m \cdot s \geq N$ bits. Often in the design of MPC algorithms we also want that the total space is not too much larger than N, and thus many works assume that $m \cdot s = \tilde{O}(N)$ or $m \cdot s = O(N^{1+\theta})$ for some small constant $\theta \in (0,1)$. The m parties are pairwise connected, so every party can send messages to every other party.

Protocols in the MPC model work as follows. At the beginning of a protocol, each party receives N/m bits of input, and then the protocol proceeds in rounds. During each round, each party performs some local computation bounded by $\mathsf{poly}(s)$, and afterwards may send messages to some other parties through pairwise channels. A well-formed MPC protocol must guarantee that each party sends and receives at most s bits each round, since there is no space to store more messages. After receiving the messages for this round the party appends them to its local state. When the protocol terminates, the result of the computation is written down by all machines, i.e., by concatenating the outputs of all machines. Every machine's output is also constrained to at most s bits. An MPC algorithm may be randomized, in which case every machine has a sequential-access random tape and can read random coins from the random tape. The size of this random tape is not charged to the machine's space consumption.

Communication Obliviousness: In this paper we will assume that the underlying MPC protocol discussed is *communication-oblivious*. This means that in each round, the number of messages, the recipients, and the size of each message are determined completely independently of all parties' inputs. More formally, we assume that there is an efficient algorithm which, given an index i and round number j, outputs the set of parties P_i sends messages to in round j, along with number of bits of each message. The work of [26] showed that this is without loss of generality: any MPC protocol can be compiled into an communication-oblivious one with constant round blowup. We also assume for simplicity that the underlying MPC protocol is given in the form of a set of circuits describing the behavior of each party in each round (one can emulate a RAM program with storage s with a circuit of width $O(s)$).

4.2 Secure Massively Parallel Computation

We are interested in achieving *secure* MPC: we would like protocols where, if a subset of the parties are corrupted, these parties learn nothing from an execution of the protocol beyond their inputs and outputs. We focus on semi-honest security, where all parties follow the protocol specification completely even if they are corrupted. We will also work in the PKI model, where we assume there is a trusted party that runs a setup algorithm and distributes a public key and secret keys to each party.

For an MPC protocol Π and a set I of corrupted parties, denote with $\mathsf{view}_I^\Pi(\lambda, \{(x_i, r_i)\}_{i \in [m]})$ the distribution of the view of all parties in I in an execution of Π with inputs $\{(x_i, r_i)\}$. This view contains, for each party $P_i, i \in I$, P_i's secret key sk_i, inputs (x_i, r_i) to the underlying MPC protocol, the random coins it uses in executing the compiled protocol, and all messages it received from all other parties throughout the protocol. We argue the existence of simulator S, a polynomial-time algorithm which takes the public key and the set I off corrupted parties and generates a view indistinguishable from $\mathsf{view}_I^\Pi(\lambda, \{(x_i, r_i)\}_{i \in [m]})$.

Definition 1. *We say that an MPC protocol Π is* semi-honest secure in the PKI model *if there exists an efficient simulator S such that for all $\{(x_i, r_i)\}_{i \in [m]}$, and all $I \subsetneq [m]$ chosen by an efficient adversary after seeing the public key, $S(\lambda, pk, I\{(x_i, r_i)\}_{i \in I}, \{y_i\}_{i \in I})$ is computationally indistinguishable from $\mathsf{view}_I^\Pi(\lambda, \{(x_i, r_i)\}_{i \in [m]})$.*

Note that in this definition we allow the simulator to choose each corrupted party's secret key and the random coins it uses.

5   Secure MPC for Short Output

In this section, we prove the following theorem:

Theorem 6 (Secure MPC for Short Output). *Assume hardness of LWE. Suppose that $s = N^\epsilon$ and that m is upper bounded by a fixed polynomial in N. Let λ denote a security parameter, and assume $\lambda \leq s$ and that $N \leq \lambda^c$ for some fixed constant c. Given any massively parallel computation (MPC) protocol Π that completes in R rounds where each of the m machines has s local space, and assuming Π results in an output of size $l_{out} \leq s$ for party 1 and no output for any other party, there is a secure MPC algorithm $\tilde{\Pi}$ in the PKI setting that securely realizes Π with semi-honest security in the presence of an adversary that statically corrupts up to $m - 1$ parties. Moreover, $\tilde{\Pi}$ completes in $O(R)$ rounds, consumes at most $O(s) \cdot \mathsf{poly}(\lambda)$ space per machine, and incurs $O(m \cdot s) \cdot \mathsf{poly}(\lambda)$ total communication per round.*

The rest of this section is devoted to the proof of Theorem 6.

5.1   Assumptions and Notation

We assume, without loss of generality, the following about the massively parallel computation (MPC) protocol which we will compile (these assumptions are essentially the same as in the previous section):

- The protocol takes R rounds, and is represented by a family of circuits $\{M_{i,j}\}_{i \in [m], j \in [R]}$, where $M_{i,j}$ denotes the behavior of party P_i in round j. In the proof of security we will also use the circuit M, the composition of all $M_{i,j}$, which takes in all parties' initial states and outputs the combined output of the protocol.
- The protocol is communication-oblivious: during round j, each party P_i sends messages to a prescribed number of parties, each of a prescribed number of bits, and that these recipients and message lengths are efficiently computable independent of P_i's state in round j.
- $M_{i,j}$ takes as input P_i's state $\sigma_{j-1} \in \{0,1\}^{\leq s}$ at the end of round $j - 1$, and outputs P_i's updated state σ_j. We assume σ_j includes P_i's outgoing messages for round j, and that these messages are at a predetermined location in σ_j. Let $\mathsf{MPCMessages}(i, j)$ be an efficient algorithm which produces a set $\{(i', s_{i'}, e_{i'})\}$, where $\sigma[s_{i'} : e_{i'}]$ is the message for $P_{i'}$.
- At the end of each round j, P_i appends all messages received in round j to the end of σ_j in arbitrary order.
- The parties' input lengths are all l_{in}, and the output length is l_{out}.

We assume the following about the Threshold FHE (TFHE) scheme:

- For simplicity, we assume each ciphertext ct has size blowup λ.
- If ct is a valid ciphertext for message m, then $ct[\lambda \cdot (i - 1) : \lambda \cdot i]$ is a valid ciphertext for the i-th bit of m.
- We assume the TFHE scheme takes an implicit depth parameter, which we set to the depth of M; we omit this in our descriptions for simplicity.

5.2   The Protocol

We now give the secure MPC protocol. The protocol proceeds in two phases: first, each party encrypts its initial state under pk, and the parties carry out an encrypted version of the original (insecure) MPC protocol using the TFHE evaluation function. Second, P_1 distributes the resulting ciphertext, which is an encryption of the output, and all parties compute and combine their partial decryptions so that P_1 learns the decrypted output. This second phase crucially relys on the fact that the TFHE scheme partial decryptions can be combined locally in a tree.

The formal description of the protocol is below. Note that we use two sub-protocols Distribute and Combine, which are given after the main protocol.

SHORT OUTPUT PROTOCOL

Setup: Each party P_i knows a public key pk along with a secret key sk_i, where $(pk, sk_1, \ldots, sk_m) \leftarrow \mathsf{TFHE.Setup}(1^\lambda, m)$.

Input: Party P_i has input x_i and randomness r_i to the underlying MPC protocol.

Encrypted MPC Phase: For the first R rounds, the behavior of each party P_i is as follows:

- **Before starting:** P_i computes $ct_{\sigma_{i,0}} \leftarrow \mathsf{TFHE.Enc}_{pk}((x_i, r_i))$, its encrypted initial state.
- **During round j:** P_i starts with a ciphertext $ct_{\sigma_{i,j-1}}$, and does the following:
  1. Compute $ct_{\sigma_{i,j}} \leftarrow \mathsf{TFHE.Eval}(M_{i,j}, ct_{\sigma_{i,j-1}})$
  2. For each $(i', s_{i'}, e_{i'}) \in \mathsf{MPCMessages}(i, j)$, send $ct_{\sigma_{i,j}}[\lambda \cdot s_{i'} : \lambda \cdot e_{i'}]$ to party $P_{i'}$.
  3. For each encrypted message ct_m received in round j, append to $ct_{\sigma_{i,j}}$.

Distributed Output Decryption Phase: At the end of the encrypted execution of the MPC protocol, P_1's resulting ciphertext $ct_{\sigma_{1,R}} = ct_o$ is an encryption of the output of the protocol, and the parties do the following:

1. **All parties:** Run $\mathsf{Distribute}(ct_o)$.
2. **Each party P_i:** Compute $ct_{o,i} \leftarrow \mathsf{TFHE.PartDec}_{sk_i}(ct_o)$.
3. **All parties:** Run $\mathsf{Combine}(\mathsf{TFHE.CombineParts}, \{c_{o,i}\}_{i \in [m]})$; P_1 obtains the resulting ρ.
4. **Output:** P_1 runs $\mathsf{TFHE.Round}(\rho)$ to obtain a decryption of the output of the underlying MPC protocol.

Distribute(x):

Parameters: Let the fan-in f be $s/(\lambda|x|)$. Let $t = \lceil \log_f m \rceil$.

Round k: In this round, the parents are all P_i such that $i \equiv 0$ (mod f^{t-k}), and the children are all P_j such that $j \equiv 0$ (mod f^{t-k+1}) but $j \not\equiv 0$ (mod f^{t-k}). Each parent P_i sends x to all its child nodes. The protocol stops after t rounds. After this point all nodes have x.

Combine(op, $\{x_i\}_{i \in [m]}$):

Parameters: Assume op is associative and commutative, $|x_i| = |x_j|$ for all i, j, and that $|x_i op x_j| = |x_i| = |x_j|$. Let the fan-in f be $s/(\lambda|x|)$.

Start: Each node P_i sets $x_{i,0} \leftarrow x_i$.

Round k: In this round, the parents are all P_i such that $i \equiv 0$ (mod f^k), and the children are all P_j such that $j \equiv 0$ (mod f^{k-1}) but $j \not\equiv 0$ (mod f^k). Each child P_j sends $x_{j,k-1}$ to its parent P_i. P_i sets $x_{i,k} \leftarrow x_{j_s,k-1} op x_{j_s+1,k-1} op \ldots op x_{j_e,k-1}$, where j_s is the index of the first child of P_i, and j_e is the index of the last child.

End: After $t = \lceil \log_f m \rceil$ rounds, P_1 has $x_{1,t} = x_1 op \ldots op x_m$.

5.3 Correctness and Efficiency

We refer to the full version of the paper [37] for the proofs of correctness and efficiency.

5.4 Security

To prove security, we exhibit a semi-honest simulator for the protocol given above. This simulator will generate a view of an arbitrary set of corrupted parties using only the corrupted parties' inputs and randomness and the output of the protocol, which will be indistinguishable from the view of the corrupted parties in an honest execution of the protocol. Note that the simulator receives the public key which is assumed to be generated honestly by the TFHE setup algorithm, and also receives the set I as input. This allows the corrupted set I to be chosen based on the public key.

The behavior of the simulator is described below.

SHORT OUTPUT SIMULATOR

Input: The simulator receives the corrupted set I, the public key pk, the corrupted parties' inputs and randomness $\{(x_i, r_i)\}_{i \in I}$, and, if $1 \in I$, the output y.

Simulated Setup: To generate the corrupted parties' secret keys, the simulator uses the TFHE simulated setup:
$(\{sk_{c,i}\}_{i \in I}, \sigma_{sim}) \leftarrow \mathsf{TFHE.Sim.Setup}(pk, I)$.
After initializing the PKI, the simulator carries out a virtual execution of the protocol to generate the corrupted parties' views.

Simulated Encrypted MPC Phase: For the first R rounds, the behavior of the simulator is as follows:
- **Before starting:**
    • **For each corrupted party P_i:** The simulator generates uniform randomness r_i and then encrypts P_i's inputs and randomness under the public key: $ct_{\sigma_{i,0}} \leftarrow \mathsf{TFHE.Enc}_{pk}((x_i, r_i))$.
    • **For each honest party $P_{i'}$:** The simulator computes an encryption of 0: $ct_{\sigma_{i,0}} \leftarrow \mathsf{TFHE.Enc}_{pk}((0^{|x_i|}, 0^{|r_i|}))$
- **During round j:** The simulator carries out round j in the same way as in the real world.

Distributed Output Decryption Phase: At the end of the encrypted execution of the MPC protocol, the simulator has P_1's resulting ciphertext $ct_{\sigma_{1,R}} = ct_o$. It then does the following:
1. **On behalf of all parties:** Run $\mathsf{Distribute}(ct_o)$.
2. **For each corrupted P_i:** Compute $ct_{o,i} \leftarrow \mathsf{TFHE.PartDec}_{sk_i}(ct_o)$.
3. Invoke the TFHE simulator to obtain simulated partial decryptions:
   $\{ct_{o,i'}\}_{i \notin I} \leftarrow \mathsf{TFHE.Sim.Query}(M, \{ct_{\sigma_{i,0}}\}_{i \in [m]}, y, [m] \setminus I, \sigma_{sim})$, or if $1 \notin I$,
   $\{ct_{o,i'}\}_{i \notin I} \leftarrow \mathsf{TFHE.Sim.Query}(M, \{ct_{\sigma_{i,0}}\}_{i \in [m]}, \bot, [m] \setminus I, \sigma_{sim})$.
4. Compute $ct_{o,i} \leftarrow \mathsf{TFHE.PartDec}_{sk_i}(ct_o)$.
5. **On behalf of all parties:** Run
   $\mathsf{Combine}(\mathsf{TFHE.CombineParts}, \{c_{o,i}\}_{i \in [m]})$; P_1 obtains the resulting ρ.
6. **Output:** P_1 runs $\mathsf{TFHE.Round}(\rho)$ to obtain a decryption of the output of the underlying MPC protocol.

We refer to the full version of the paper [37] for the proof of indistinguishability between the real and ideal worlds.

On the source of randomness. The massively parallel computation model states that a party should not incur a space penalty for the random coins it uses. For simplicity, we did not address this part of the model in our construction, but a simple modification allows our protocol to support arbitrarily many random coins. We can do this by having the randomness embedded in the circuit $M_{i,j}$ for each step of the underlying MPC protocol, and having each party rerandomize the ciphertexts encrypting the MPC messages before sending, the standard technique for circuit privacy in FHE, to hide this randomness.

6 Long Output

We now discuss our long-output result. The theorem we prove is below.

Theorem 7 (Secure MPC for Long Output). *Assume the existence of an n-out-of-n threshold FHE scheme with circular security, along with iO and LWE. Suppose that $s = N^\epsilon$ and that m is upper bounded by a fixed polynomial in N. Let λ denote a security parameter, and assume $\lambda \leq s$ and that $N \leq \lambda^c$ for some fixed constant c. Given any massively parallel computation (MPC) protocol Π that completes in R rounds where each of the m machines has s local space, and assuming Π results in each party having an output of size $l_{out} \leq s$, there is a secure MPC algorithm $\tilde{\Pi}$ that securely realizes Π with semi-honest security in the presence of an adversary that statically corrupts up to $m - 1$ parties. Moreover, $\tilde{\Pi}$ completes in $O(R)$ rounds, consumes at most $O(s) \cdot \mathsf{poly}(\lambda)$ space per machine, and incurs $O(m \cdot s) \cdot \mathsf{poly}(\lambda)$ total communication per round.*

The rest of this section is devoted to proving Theorem 7.

6.1 Assumptions and Notation

We assume, without loss of generality, the following about the massively parallel computation (MPC) protocol which we will compile:

- The protocol takes R rounds, and is represented by a family of circuits $\{M_{i,j}\}_{i \in [m], j \in [R]}$, where $M_{i,j}$ denotes the behavior of party P_i in round j. In the proof of security we will also use the circuit M, the composition of all $M_{i,j}$, which takes in all parties' initial states and outputs the combined output of the protocol.
- The protocol is oblivious: during round j, each party P_i sends messages to a prescribed number of parties, each of a prescribed number of bits, and that these recipients and message lengths are efficiently computable independent of P_i's state in round j.
- $M_{i,j}$ takes as input P_i's state $\sigma_{j-1} \in \{0,1\}^{\leq s}$ at the end of round $j - 1$, and outputs P_i's updated state σ_j. We assume σ_j includes P_i's messages for round j, and that these messages are at a predetermined location in σ_j. Let $\mathsf{MPCMessages}(i, j)$ be an efficient algorithm which produces a set $\{(i', s_{i'}, e_{i'})\}$, where $\sigma[s_{i'} : e_{i'}]$ is the message for $P_{i'}$.
- At the end of each round j, P_i appends all messages received in round j to the end of σ_j in arbitrary order.
- Each party's input is of size l_{in} and its output is of size l_{out}.

We assume the following about the TFHE scheme:

- For simplicity, we assume each ciphertext ct has size blowup λ.
- If ct is a valid ciphertext for message m, then we assume $ct[\lambda \cdot (i-1) : \lambda \cdot i]$ is a valid ciphertext for the i-th bit of m.
- We assume the TFHE scheme takes an implicit depth parameter, which we set to the maximum depth of M, SSBDistSetup, or GenerateCircuit; we omit this in our descriptions for simplicity.

6.2   The Protocol

We now give the secure MPC protocol. Recall that we are working under a PKI, so every party P_i knows the public key along with its secret key sk_i. At a high level, the protocol is divided into two main phases, as in the previous protocol, with the major differences occurring in the second phase. In the first phase, as in the short-output protocol, each party encrypts its initial state under pk, and the parties carry out an encrypted version of the original (insecure) MPC protocol using the TFHE evaluation function. In the second phase, the parties interact with each other so that all parties obtain an obfuscation of a circuit which will allow them to decrypt their outputs and nothing else. This involves carrying out a subprotocol CalcSSBHash in which the parties collectively compute a somewhere-statistically-binding (SSB) commitment to their ciphertexts along with some randomness. Recall that an SSB hash is a construction Merkle-tree which is designed specifically to enable security proofs when using iO.

We briefly explain CalcSSBHash. The purpose of this protocol is for all parties to know an SSB commitment z to their collective inputs, and for each party P_i to know an opening π_i for its respective input. We will perform this process over a tree with arity f (which we will specify later), mirroring the Merkle-like tree of the SSB hash. In the first round, the parties use SSB.Start, and then send the resulting label to the parties $P_{i'}$, $i' \equiv 0 \pmod{f}$ (call these nodes the parents). Each of these parties $P_{i'}$ then uses SSB.Combine on the labels $\{y_{i,0}\}$ of its children to get a new combined label $y_{i',1}$, and then all the $P_{i'}$ parties send their new labels to $P_{i''}$, $i'' \equiv 0 \pmod{f^2}$. In addition, since the string each party P_i' now has a part of its children's openings, namely $y_{i',1}$ and the set $\{y_{i,0}\}$ of sibling labels, it sends $\pi_{i,1} = (y_{i',1}, \{y_{i,0}\})$ to each of its children.

This process completes within $2\lceil \log_f m \rceil$ rounds, where in each round the current layer calculates new labels and sends them to the new layer of parents, and each layer sends any $\pi_{i,j}$ received from its parent to all its children. At the end, all parties will know z and π_i.

The formal description of the protocol is below. Note that we use the subprotocols Distribute and CalcSSBHash; Distribute was defined in the previous section, and CalcSSBHash is defined after the main protocol.

LONG OUTPUT PROTOCOL

Setup: Each party P_i knows a public key pk along with a secret key sk_i, where $(pk, sk_1, \ldots, sk_m) \leftarrow \mathsf{TFHE.Setup}(1^\lambda, m)$.

Input: Each party P_i has input x_i and randomness r_i to the underlying MPC protocol.

Encrypted MPC Phase: For the first R rounds, the behavior of each party P_i is exactly as in the encrypted MPC phase of the short output protocol.

Output Padding Phase: Assume without loss of generality each party's plaintext output in the underlying MPC protocol is of size L. After the R rounds of the encrypted MPC protocol are done, each party P_i does the following:

1. Compute a random string $pad_i \in \{0,1\}^{l_{out}}$.
2. Calculate $ct_{pad_i} \leftarrow \mathsf{TFHE.Enc}_{pk}(pad_i)$.
3. Calculate $ct_{o,i} \leftarrow \mathsf{TFHE.Eval}(\oplus, ct_{pad_i}, ct_{\sigma_{i,R}})$, the TFHE evaluation of the circuit which pads $\sigma_{i,R}$ with pad_i.

Output Circuit Generation Phase: At the end of the previous phase, each party P_i has an encryption $ct_{o,i}$ of their output padded with pad_i. The parties then coordinate with each other in a manner which is now described, so that at the end P_1 has an obfuscation of the circuit $C_{sk,z}$, defined below.

1. Each party P_i chooses a uniform random string $r_{h,i}$.
2. All parties run the short-output compiler from the previous section over the protocol $\mathsf{SSBDistSetup}(2l_{out}, 1, \{r_{h,i}\})$ defined below, so that P_1 obtains an SSB hash key h.
3. The parties run the protocol $\mathsf{Distribute}(h)$.
4. Each party chooses a uniform random string $r_{o,i}$ of size l_{out}, and the parties run the protocol $\mathsf{CalcSSBHash}(h, \{(ct_{o,i}, r_{o,i})\})$ defined below, so that each party P_i obtains an SSB commitment z and an opening π_i to $(ct_{o,i}, r_{o,i})$.
5. Each party chooses a uniform random string $r_{iO,i}$, and the parties run the short-output compiler over the protocol $\mathsf{GenerateCircuit}_{h,z}(\{(sk_i, r_{iO,i})\})$ defined below, so that P_1 obtains an obfuscation C' of the circuit $C_{z,sk}$, also defined below.
6. The parties run $\mathsf{Distribute}(C')$.

Offline Output Decryption Phase: Once every party knows C', each party P_i can run $C'(i, ct_{o,i}, \pi_i)$ to obtain y'_i, P_i's padded output under the original MPC protocol. P_i can then compute $y_i \leftarrow y'_i \oplus pad_i$.

CalcSSBHash($h, \{x_i\}_{i\in[m]}$):

Input: Each party P_i has a key h and x_i. In this protocol we will number the parties starting at 0 (so the first party will be P_0).

Parameters: Let $\lambda \leq s$. Assume h is an SSB hash which has been initialized with fan-in $f = s^{1/2}\lambda/|x|^{1/2}$ and $t = \lceil \log_f m \rceil$.

Before starting: Each party P_i first computes $\leftarrow$ SSB.Start(h, x_i) to obtain a string $y_{i,0}$ of size λ.

When carrying out the protocol, we will divide the parties into subsets. Let $S_r = \{P_i \mid i \equiv 0 \pmod{f^r}\}$ (and let $S_0 = \{P_i\}_{i\in[m]}$), let the set of children for i in S_r be $D_{i,r} = \{P_j \mid j \equiv 0 \pmod{f^{r-1}}$ and $i \leq j \leq i + f^r\}$, and let the parent of i in S_r be $q_{i,r} = f^r\lfloor i/f^r \rfloor$.

For $k = 1, \ldots, \lceil \log_f m \rceil + 1$, do the following:

Round k: In this round, the parties in the sets S_{k-t}, $t = 1, 3, \ldots, 2\lceil k/2 \rceil - 1$ will participate.

- Each party P_i in S_{k-1} does the following:
    1. If $k - 1 > 0$, receive $y_{j,k-2}$ from each $P_j \in D_{i,k-1}$
    2. If $k - 1 > 0$, calculate
       $y_{i,k-1} \leftarrow$ SSB.Combine$(h, \{y_{j,k-2}\}_{P_j\in D_{i,k-1}})$, and send
       $(y_{i,k-1}, \{y_{j,k-2}\}_{j\in D_{i,k-1}}$ to all parties P_j, $j \in D_{i,k-1}$.
    3. Send $y_{i,k-1}$ to P_{q_i}
- Each party P_j in S_r for $r = 0, \ldots, k - 2$ does the following:
    1. Check if received $\pi_{j,r'} = (y_{i,r'}, \{y_{j',r'-1}\}_{j'\in D_{i,r'}})$ from P_{q_j}
    2. If so, append $\pi_{j,r'}$ to π_j.
    3. If $r > 0$, send $\pi_{j,r'}$ to all $P_{j''} \in D_{j,r}$.

For $k' = \lceil \log_f m \rceil + 2, \ldots, 2\lceil \log_f m \rceil + 1$:

Round k': Each party P_j in S_r for $r = 0, \ldots, \lceil \log_f m \rceil$ does the following:
1. Check if received $\pi_{j,r'} = (y_{i,r'}, \{y_{j',r'-1}\}_{j'\in D_{i,r'}})$ from P_{q_j}
2. If so, append $\pi_{j,r'}$ to π_j.
3. If $r > 0$, send $\pi_{j,r'}$ to all $P_{j''} \in D_{j,r}$.

Output: The protocol stops after $2\lceil \log_f m \rceil$ rounds, and every party P_i knows the SSB tree root y and the opening π_i of x_i.

SSBDistSetup$(l, i^*, \{r_{h,i}\})$:

Parameters: Let $\lambda \leq s$. Let the fan-in f be $s^{1/2}\lambda/l^{1/2}$ and $d = \lceil \log_f m \rceil$.
1. Parties run $\mathsf{Combine}(+, \{r_{h,i}\})$ so that P_1 gets $r_h = \sum r_{h,i}$.
2. P_1 generates an SSB hash key $h \leftarrow \mathsf{SSB.Setup}(1^\lambda, l, d, f, i^*; r_h)$ with l as the block size and i^* as the statistically binding index.

Output: At the end of the protocol, P_1's output is defined as h. All other parties have blank output.

GenerateCircuit$_{h,z}(\{(sk_i, r_{iO,i})\}_{i \in [m]})$:

Input: P_1 the SSB commitment z; each party P_i has sk_i.
1. Parties run $\mathsf{Combine}(+, \{sk_i\})$ so that P_1 has the master secret key sk.
2. Parties run $\mathsf{Combine}(+, \{r_{iO,i}\})$ so that P_1 has $r_{iO} = \sum r_{iO,i}$.
3. P_1 calculates the obfuscation $C' \leftarrow iO(C_{sk,z}; r_{iO})$.

Output: At the end of the protocol, P_1's output is defined as C'. All other parties have blank output.

CIRCUIT $C_{h,sk,z}(i, ct_{o,i}, r_{o,i}, \pi_i)$:

---

1. If $\mathsf{SSB.Verify}(h, z, i, (ct_{o,i}, r_{o,i}), \pi_i) = 1$:
    (a) Output $\mathsf{TFHE.Dec}_{sk}(ct_{o,i})$.
1. Otherwise, output $\perp$.

6.3 Correctness and Efficiency

We refer to the full version of the paper [37] for the proofs of correctness and efficiency.

6.4 Security

Let $I \subset [m]$ be the set of corrupted parties. We describe the behavior of the simulator, which takes as input 1^λ, I, the public key, the parties' outputs $\{y_i\}_{i \in [m]}$, and the corrupted parties' inputs $\{x_i\}_{i \in I}$, and outputs the secret keys and the view of the corrupted parties. Note that as in the short output construction the construction of this simulator allows the corrupted set I to be chosen based on the public key.

LONG OUTPUT PROTOCOL SIMULATOR:

Input: The simulator receives the corrupted set I, the public key pk, the corrupted parties' inputs and randomness $\{(x_i, r_i)\}_{i \in I}$, and the corrupted parties' outputs $\{y_i\}_{i \in I}$.

Simulated Setup: To generate the corrupted parties' secret keys, the simulator uses the TFHE simulated setup:
$(\{sk_{c,i}\}_{i \in I}, \sigma_{sim}) \leftarrow \mathsf{TFHE.Sim.Setup}(pk, I)$.
After initializing the PKI, the simulator carries out a virtual execution of the protocol to generate the corrupted parties' views.

Simulated Encrypted MPC Phase: The simulator performs this phase in exactly the same way as in the short output simulator.

Output Padding Phase: After the R rounds of the encrypted MPC protocol are done, the simulator does the following on behalf of each P_i:
1. Compute a random string $pad_i \in \{0, 1\}^{l_{out}}$.
2. If $i \in I$, calculate $ct_{pad_i} \leftarrow \mathsf{TFHE.Enc}_{pk}(pad_i)$; otherwise calculate $ct_{pad_i} \leftarrow \mathsf{TFHE.Enc}_{pk}(0^{l_{out}})$.
3. Calculate $ct_{o,i} \leftarrow \mathsf{TFHE.Eval}(\oplus, ct_{pad_i}, ct_{\sigma_{i,R}})$, the TFHE evaluation of the circuit which pads $\sigma_{i,R}$ with pad_i.

Simulated Output Circuit Generation Phase: At the end of the encrypted execution of the MPC protocol, each party P_i has an encryption $ct_{o,i}$ of their output. The simulator then simulates the output circuit generation phase in the following manner, so that at the end P_1 has an obfuscation of the circuit $\tilde{C}_{h,k,z}$, defined below.
1. The simulator uses the short-output simulator from the previous section for the compiled SSBDistSetup protocol, where the protocol output is set to be $h \leftarrow \mathsf{SSB.Setup}(1^\lambda, 2l_{out}, f, d, m, r)$ for uniform random r.
2. The simulator runs the protocol Distribute(h) on behalf of all parties.
3. The simulator chooses a PRF key k.
4. The simulator sets $r_{o,i} = PRF_k(i) \oplus y_i \oplus pad_i$ for all $i \in I$, and $r_{o,i}$ uniformly random for $i \notin I$.
5. The simulator runs the protocol CalcSSBHash($h, \{(ct_{o,i}, r_{o,i})\}$) on behalf of all parties, so that each party P_i obtains an SSB commitment z and an opening π_i to $(ct_{o,i}, r_{o,i})$.
6. The simulator uses the short-output simulator from the previous section for the compiled GenerateCircuit protocol, where the protocol output is set to be the obfuscation $\tilde{C}' = iO(\tilde{C}_{h,k,z})$.
7. The simulator runs Distribute(C') on behalf of all parties.

CIRCUIT $\tilde{C}_{h,k,z}(i, ct_{o,i}, r_{i,c}, \pi_i)$:

---

1. If SSB.Verify$(z, i, (ct_{o,i}, r_{i,c}), \pi_i) = 1$:
   (a) Output $r_{i,c} \oplus PRF_k(i)$.
2. Otherwise, output $\perp$.

We refer to the full version of paper [37] for the proof of indistinguishability between the real and ideal worlds.

Acknowledgments. We would like to thank Shir Maimon and Wei-Kai Lin for helpful discussions. We gratefully acknowledge the TCC '20 reviewers for their thoughtful comments. We would like to thank Tatsuaki Okamoto for being supportive of this work.

References

1. Ahn, K.J., Guha, S.: Access to data and number of iterations: dual primal algorithms for maximum matching under resource constraints. ACM Trans. Parallel Comput. (TOPC) **4**(4), 17 (2018)
2. Ananth, P., Chen, Y., Chung, K., Lin, H., Lin, W.: Delegating RAM computations with adaptive soundness and privacy. In: Theory of Cryptography - 14th International Conference, TCC, pp. 3–30 (2016)
3. Andoni, A., Nikolov, A., Onak, K., Yaroslavtsev, G.: Parallel algorithms for geometric graph problems. In: Symposium on Theory of Computing, STOC, pp. 574–583 (2014)
4. Andoni, A., Song, Z., Stein, C., Wang, Z., Zhong, P.: Parallel graph connectivity in log diameter rounds. In: 59th IEEE Annual Symposium on Foundations of Computer Science, FOCS, pp. 674–685 (2018)
5. Andoni, A., Stein, C., Zhong, P.: Log diameter rounds algorithms for 2-vertex and 2-edge connectivity. In: 46th International Colloquium on Automata, Languages, and Programming, ICALP, pp. 14:1–14:16 (2019)
6. Asharov, G., Jain, A., López-Alt, A., Tromer, E., Vaikuntanathan, V., Wichs, D.: Multiparty computation with low communication, computation and interaction via threshold FHE. In: Pointcheval, D., Johansson, T. (eds.) EUROCRYPT 2012. LNCS, vol. 7237, pp. 483–501. Springer, Heidelberg (2012). https://doi.org/10.1007/978-3-642-29011-4_29
7. Assadi, S.: Simple round compression for parallel vertex cover. CoRR abs/1709.04599 (2017)
8. Assadi, S., Bateni, M., Bernstein, A., Mirrokni, V.S., Stein, C.: Coresets meet EDCS: algorithms for matching and vertex cover on massive graphs. In: Proceedings of the Thirtieth Annual ACM-SIAM Symposium on Discrete Algorithms, SODA, pp. 1616–1635 (2019)
9. Assadi, S., Khanna, S.: Randomized composable coresets for matching and vertex cover. In: Proceedings of the 29th ACM Symposium on Parallelism in Algorithms and Architectures, SPAA, pp. 3–12 (2017)
10. Assadi, S., Sun, X., Weinstein, O.: Massively parallel algorithms for finding well-connected components in sparse graphs. In: ACM Symposium on Principles of Distributed Computing, PODC, pp. 461–470 (2019)

11. Badrinarayanan, S., Jain, A., Manohar, N., Sahai, A.: Threshold multi-key FHE and applications to round-optimal MPC. IACR Cryptol. ePrint Arch. **2018**, 580 (2018)
12. Bahmani, B., Kumar, R., Vassilvitskii, S.: Densest subgraph in streaming and mapreduce. Proc. VLDB Endowment **5**(5), 454–465 (2012)
13. Bahmani, B., Moseley, B., Vattani, A., Kumar, R., Vassilvitskii, S.: Scalable k-means++. Proc. VLDB Endowment **5**(7), 622–633 (2012)
14. Barak, B., et al.: On the (im)possibility of obfuscating programs. J. ACM **59**(2), 6:1–6:48 (2012)
15. Bateni, M., Bhaskara, A., Lattanzi, S., Mirrokni, V.: Distributed balanced clustering via mapping coresets. In: Advances in Neural Information Processing Systems, pp. 2591–2599 (2014)
16. Behnezhad, S., et al.: Massively parallel computation of matching and MIS in sparse graphs. In: ACM Symposium on Principles of Distributed Computing, PODC, pp. 481–490 (2019)
17. Behnezhad, S., Derakhshan, M., Hajiaghayi, M., Karp, R.M.: Massively parallel symmetry breaking on sparse graphs: MIS and maximal matching. CoRR abs/1807.06701 (2018)
18. Behnezhad, S., Hajiaghayi, M., Harris, D.G.: Exponentially faster massively parallel maximal matching. In: 60th IEEE Annual Symposium on Foundations of Computer Science, FOCS, pp. 1637–1649 (2019)
19. Ben-Or, M., Goldwasser, S., Wigderson, A.: Completeness theorems for non-cryptographic fault-tolerant distributed computation (extended abstract). In: Proceedings of the 20th Annual ACM Symposium on Theory of Computing, STOC, pp. 1–10 (1988)
20. Boneh, D., et al.: Threshold cryptosystems from threshold fully homomorphic encryption. In: Shacham, H., Boldyreva, A. (eds.) CRYPTO 2018. LNCS, vol. 10991, pp. 565–596. Springer, Cham (2018). https://doi.org/10.1007/978-3-319-96884-1_19
21. Boneh, D., Waters, B.: Constrained pseudorandom functions and their applications. In: Sako, K., Sarkar, P. (eds.) ASIACRYPT 2013. LNCS, vol. 8270, pp. 280–300. Springer, Heidelberg (2013). https://doi.org/10.1007/978-3-642-42045-0_15
22. Boyle, E., Chung, K.-M., Pass, R.: Large-scale secure computation: multi-party computation for (parallel) RAM programs. In: Gennaro, R., Robshaw, M. (eds.) CRYPTO 2015. LNCS, vol. 9216, pp. 742–762. Springer, Heidelberg (2015). https://doi.org/10.1007/978-3-662-48000-7_36
23. Boyle, E., Chung, K.-M., Pass, R.: Oblivious parallel RAM and applications. In: Kushilevitz, E., Malkin, T. (eds.) TCC 2016. LNCS, vol. 9563, pp. 175–204. Springer, Heidelberg (2016). https://doi.org/10.1007/978-3-662-49099-0_7
24. Boyle, E., Goldwasser, S., Ivan, I.: Functional signatures and pseudorandom functions. In: Krawczyk, H. (ed.) PKC 2014. LNCS, vol. 8383, pp. 501–519. Springer, Heidelberg (2014). https://doi.org/10.1007/978-3-642-54631-0_29
25. Brakerski, Z., Perlman, R.: Lattice-based fully dynamic multi-key FHE with short ciphertexts. In: Robshaw, M., Katz, J. (eds.) CRYPTO 2016. LNCS, vol. 9814, pp. 190–213. Springer, Heidelberg (2016). https://doi.org/10.1007/978-3-662-53018-4_8
26. Chan, T.H., Chung, K., Lin, W., Shi, E.: MPC for MPC: secure computation on a massively parallel computing architecture. In: 11th Innovations in Theoretical Computer Science Conference, ITCS, pp. 75:1–75:52 (2020)

27. Chan, T.-H.H., Chung, K.-M., Shi, E.: On the depth of oblivious parallel RAM. In: Takagi, T., Peyrin, T. (eds.) ASIACRYPT 2017. LNCS, vol. 10624, pp. 567–597. Springer, Cham (2017). https://doi.org/10.1007/978-3-319-70694-8_20

28. Chan, T.-H.H., Nayak, K., Shi, E.: Perfectly secure oblivious parallel RAM. In: Beimel, A., Dziembowski, S. (eds.) TCC 2018. LNCS, vol. 11240, pp. 636–668. Springer, Cham (2018). https://doi.org/10.1007/978-3-030-03810-6_23

29. Hubert Chan, T.-H., Shi, E.: Circuit OPRAM: unifying statistically and computationally secure ORAMs and OPRAMs. In: Kalai, Y., Reyzin, L. (eds.) TCC 2017. LNCS, vol. 10678, pp. 72–107. Springer, Cham (2017). https://doi.org/10.1007/978-3-319-70503-3_3

30. Chang, Y., Fischer, M., Ghaffari, M., Uitto, J., Zheng, Y.: The complexity of $(\Delta+1)$ coloring in congested clique, massively parallel computation, and centralized local computation. In: ACM Symposium on Principles of Distributed Computing, PODC, pp. 471–480 (2019)

31. Chen, Y., Chow, S.S.M., Chung, K., Lai, R.W.F., Lin, W., Zhou, H.: Cryptography for parallel RAM from indistinguishability obfuscation. In: ACM Conference on Innovations in Theoretical Computer Science, ITCS, pp. 179–190 (2016)

32. Chung, K.-M., Qian, L.: Adaptively secure garbling schemes for parallel computations. In: Hofheinz, D., Rosen, A. (eds.) TCC 2019. LNCS, vol. 11892, pp. 285–310. Springer, Cham (2019). https://doi.org/10.1007/978-3-030-36033-7_11

33. Czumaj, A., Łącki, J., Mądry, A., Mitrović, S., Onak, K., Sankowski, P.: Round compression for parallel matching algorithms. In: Proceedings of the 50th Annual ACM SIGACT Symposium on Theory of Computing, STOC, pp. 471–484 (2018)

34. Dodis, Y., Halevi, S., Rothblum, R.D., Wichs, D.: Spooky encryption and its applications. In: Robshaw, M., Katz, J. (eds.) CRYPTO 2016. LNCS, vol. 9816, pp. 93–122. Springer, Heidelberg (2016). https://doi.org/10.1007/978-3-662-53015-3_4

35. Ene, A., Im, S., Moseley, B.: Fast clustering using mapreduce. In: Proceedings of the 17th ACM SIGKDD International Conference on Knowledge Discovery and Data Mining, pp. 681–689. ACM (2011)

36. Ene, A., Nguyen, H.: Random coordinate descent methods for minimizing decomposable submodular functions. In: International Conference on Machine Learning, pp. 787–795 (2015)

37. Fernando, R., Komargodski, I., Liu, Y., Shi, E.: Secure massively parallel computation for dishonest majority. IACR Cryptol. ePrint Arch. 2017. https://eprint.iacr.org/2020/1157

38. Gamlath, B., Kale, S., Mitrovic, S., Svensson, O.: Weighted matchings via unweighted augmentations. In: ACM Symposium on Principles of Distributed Computing, PODC, pp. 491–500 (2019)

39. Garg, S., Gentry, C., Halevi, S., Raykova, M., Sahai, A., Waters, B.: Candidate indistinguishability obfuscation and functional encryption for all circuits. In: 54th Annual IEEE Symposium on Foundations of Computer Science, FOCS, pp. 40–49 (2013)

40. Gentry, C., Sahai, A., Waters, B.: Homomorphic encryption from learning with errors: conceptually-simpler, asymptotically-faster, attribute-based. In: Canetti, R., Garay, J.A. (eds.) CRYPTO 2013. LNCS, vol. 8042, pp. 75–92. Springer, Heidelberg (2013). https://doi.org/10.1007/978-3-642-40041-4_5

41. Ghaffari, M., Gouleakis, T., Konrad, C., Mitrovic, S., Rubinfeld, R.: Improved massively parallel computation algorithms for mis, matching, and vertex cover. In: ACM Symposium on Principles of Distributed Computing, PODC, pp. 129–138 (2018)

42. Ghaffari, M., Lattanzi, S., Mitrović, S.: Improved parallel algorithms for density-based network clustering. In: International Conference on Machine Learning, pp. 2201–2210 (2019)
43. Ghaffari, M., Uitto, J.: Sparsifying distributed algorithms with ramifications in massively parallel computation and centralized local computation. In: Proceedings of the Thirtieth Annual ACM-SIAM Symposium on Discrete Algorithms, SODA, pp. 1636–1653 (2019)
44. Goldreich, O., Goldwasser, S., Micali, S.: How to construct random functions (extended abstract). In: 25th Annual Symposium on Foundations of Computer Science, FOCS, pp. 464–479 (1984)
45. Goldreich, O., Micali, S., Wigderson, A.: How to play any mental game or A completeness theorem for protocols with honest majority. In: Proceedings of the 19th Annual ACM Symposium on Theory of Computing, STOC, pp. 218–229 (1987)
46. Hubáček, P., Wichs, D.: On the communication complexity of secure function evaluation with long output. In: ITCS, pp. 163–172 (2015)
47. Im, S., Moseley, B., Sun, X.: Efficient massively parallel methods for dynamic programming. In: Proceedings of the 49th Annual ACM SIGACT Symposium on Theory of Computing, STOC, pp. 798–811 (2017)
48. Jain, A., Rasmussen, P.M.R., Sahai, A.: Threshold fully homomorphic encryption. IACR Cryptol. ePrint Arch. **2017**, 257 (2017)
49. Karloff, H.J., Suri, S., Vassilvitskii, S.: A model of computation for mapreduce. In: Proceedings of the Twenty-First Annual ACM-SIAM Symposium on Discrete Algorithms, SODA, pp. 938–948 (2010)
50. Katz, J., Ostrovsky, R., Smith, A.: Round efficiency of multi-party computation with a dishonest majority. In: Biham, E. (ed.) EUROCRYPT 2003. LNCS, vol. 2656, pp. 578–595. Springer, Heidelberg (2003). https://doi.org/10.1007/3-540-39200-9_36
51. Kiayias, A., Papadopoulos, S., Triandopoulos, N., Zacharias, T.: Delegatable pseudorandom functions and applications. In: 2013 ACM SIGSAC Conference on Computer and Communications Security, CCS, pp. 669–684 (2013)
52. Kumar, R., Moseley, B., Vassilvitskii, S., Vattani, A.: Fast greedy algorithms in mapreduce and streaming. TOPC **2**(3), 14:1–14:22 (2015)
53. Łącki, J., Mirrokni, V.S., Włodarczyk, M.: Connected components at scale via local contractions. CoRR abs/1807.10727 (2018)
54. Lattanzi, S., Moseley, B., Suri, S., Vassilvitskii, S.: Filtering: a method for solving graph problems in mapreduce. In: SPAA, pp. 85–94 (2011)
55. López-Alt, A., Tromer, E., Vaikuntanathan, V.: On-the-fly multiparty computation on the cloud via multikey fully homomorphic encryption. In: Proceedings of the 44th Symposium on Theory of Computing Conference, STOC, pp. 1219–1234 (2012)
56. Lu, S., Ostrovsky, R.: Black-box parallel garbled RAM. In: Katz, J., Shacham, H. (eds.) CRYPTO 2017. LNCS, vol. 10402, pp. 66–92. Springer, Cham (2017). https://doi.org/10.1007/978-3-319-63715-0_3
57. Mirrokni, V.S., Zadimoghaddam, M.: Randomized composable core-sets for distributed submodular maximization. In: STOC, pp. 153–162 (2015)
58. Mirzasoleiman, B., Karbasi, A., Sarkar, R., Krause, A.: Distributed submodular maximization: Identifying representative elements in massive data. In: Advances in Neural Information Processing Systems, pp. 2049–2057 (2013)

59. Mukherjee, P., Wichs, D.: Two round multiparty computation via multi-key FHE. In: Fischlin, M., Coron, J.-S. (eds.) EUROCRYPT 2016. LNCS, vol. 9666, pp. 735–763. Springer, Heidelberg (2016). https://doi.org/10.1007/978-3-662-49896-5_26

60. Mukherjee, P., Wichs, D.: Two round multiparty computation via multi-key FHE. In: EUROCRYPT, pp. 735–763 (2016)

61. Nayak, K., Wang, X.S., Ioannidis, S., Weinsberg, U., Taft, N., Shi, E.: GraphSC: parallel secure computation made easy. In: IEEE S & P (2015)

62. Onak, K.: Round compression for parallel graph algorithms in strongly sublinear space. CoRR abs/1807.08745 (2018)

63. Parter, M., Yogev, E.: Distributed algorithms made secure: a graph theoretic approach. In: Proceedings of the Thirtieth Annual ACM-SIAM Symposium on Discrete Algorithms, SODA, pp. 1693–1710 (2019)

64. Parter, M., Yogev, E.: Secure distributed computing made (nearly) optimal, pp. 107–116. PODC'2019 (2019)

65. Pass, R.: Bounded-concurrent secure multi-party computation with a dishonest majority. In: Babai, L. (ed.) STOC, pp. 232–241. ACM (2004)

66. Peikert, C., Shiehian, S.: Multi-key FHE from LWE, revisited. In: Hirt, M., Smith, A. (eds.) TCC 2016. LNCS, vol. 9986, pp. 217–238. Springer, Heidelberg (2016). https://doi.org/10.1007/978-3-662-53644-5_9

67. da Ponte Barbosa, R., Ene, A., Nguyen, H.L., Ward, J.: A new framework for distributed submodular maximization. In: FOCS, pp. 645–654 (2016)

68. Rastogi, V., Machanavajjhala, A., Chitnis, L., Sarma, A.D.: Finding connected components in map-reduce in logarithmic rounds. In: 29th IEEE International Conference on Data Engineering, ICDE, pp. 50–61 (2013)

69. Regev, O.: On lattices, learning with errors, random linear codes, and cryptography. J. ACM **56**(6), 34:1–34:40 (2009)

70. Roughgarden, T., Vassilvitskii, S., Wang, J.R.: Shuffles and circuits: (on lower bounds for modern parallel computation). In: Proceedings of the 28th ACM Symposium on Parallelism in Algorithms and Architectures, SPAA, pp. 1–12 (2016)

71. Sahai, A., Waters, B.: How to use indistinguishability obfuscation: deniable encryption, and more. In: Symposium on Theory of Computing, STOC, pp. 475–484 (2014)

72. Sahai, A., Waters, B.: How to use indistinguishability obfuscation: deniable encryption, and more. In: STOC, pp. 475–484. ACM (2014)

73. Yaroslavtsev, G., Vadapalli, A.: Massively parallel algorithms and hardness for single-linkage clustering under ℓ_p-distances. In: Proceedings of the 35th International Conference on Machine Learning (2018)

Towards Multiparty Computation Withstanding Coercion of All Parties

Ran Canetti[1]([⊠]) and Oxana Poburinnaya[2,3]

[1] Boston University, Boston, USA
canetti@bu.edu
[2] University of Rochester, Rochester, USA
[3] Ligero, Inc., Rochester, USA
oxanapob@bu.edu

Abstract. Incoercible multi-party computation [Canetti-Gennaro'96] allows parties to engage in secure computation with the additional guarantee that the public transcript of the computation cannot be used by a coercive external entity to verify representations made by the parties regarding their inputs to and outputs from the computation. That is, any deductions regarding the truthfulness of such representations made by the parties could be made even without access to the public transcript. To date, all incoercible secure computation protocols withstand coercion of only a fraction of the parties, or else assume that all parties use an execution environment that makes some crucial parts of their local states physically inaccessible even to themselves.

We consider, for the first time, the setting where *all parties* are coerced, and the coercer expects to see *the entire history of the computation.* In this setting we construct:

- A general multi-party computation protocol that withstands coercion of all parties, as long as none of the coerced parties cooperates with the coercer, namely they all use the prescribed "faking algorithm" upon coercion. We refer to this case as *cooperative incoercibility*. The protocol uses deniable encryption and indistiguishability obfuscation, and takes 4 rounds of communication.
- A general two-party computation protocol that withstands even the "mixed" case where some of the coerced parties cooperate with the coercer and disclose their true local states. This protocol is limited to computing functions where the input of one of the parties is taken from a small (poly-size) domain. This protocol uses deniable encryption with public deniability for one of the parties; when instantiated using the deniable encryption of Canetti, Park, and Poburinnaya [Crypto'20], it takes 3 rounds of communication.

Finally, we show that protocols with certain communication pattern cannot be incoercible, even in a weaker setting where only some parties are coerced.

R. Canetti—Boston University. Member of the CPIIS. Supported by NSF Awards 1931714, 1801564, 1414119, and the DARPA DEVE program.

O. Poburinnaya—University of Rochester and Ligero, Inc. The work was done in part while in Boston University.

R. Pass and K. Pietrzak (Eds.): TCC 2020, LNCS 12551, pp. 410–438, 2020.
https://doi.org/10.1007/978-3-030-64378-2_15

1   Introduction

Consider a tight-knit society whose members regularly meet behind closed doors and run their society's business with complete privacy. An external entity might be able to deduce information on the nature of the interactions that take place in the society's meetings from the external behavior of the society members, but no direct information on what really takes place at the meetings can be obtained. As long as the meetings are not directly monitored by the external entity, this continues to be the case even if the external entity has coercive power over the society's members and demand that they fully disclose the contents of the meetings: All that the coercive entity can obtain is the word of the members, which may or may not be truthful.

Can we reproduce this situation online, where the society members communicate over public channels that are accessible to the external entity? That is, can the society members engage in a multiparty computation that allows them to limit the power of the external coercive entity to the power that it had when they met behind closed doors? Furthermore, can they do so even in the case where *all* members are coerced, and the coercive entity now expects to have the complete history of the interaction and the local states of all parties, including all the local randomness used? Indeed, doing so essentially results in rewriting the entire history of a system, in a way that's undetectable to anyone that did not directly witness the events at the time and location where they took place.

This is a special case of the *incoercible multiparty computation* problem, first studied in [CG96]. In a nutshell, a multiparty protocol is *incoercible* if it enables the participants to preserve the privacy of their inputs and outputs even against coercive adversaries who demand to see the entire internal state of coerced parties[1]. Towards this end, each party is equipped with a "faking procedure" that enables it to run the protocol as prescribed on the given input x, obtain an output y, and then, given arbitrary values x', y', generate a "fake internal state" (or, equivalently, fake local randomness) r' such that the public communication transcript of the party is consistent with input x', output y' and randomness r'. Moreover, we would like to guarantee more global incoercibility properties. Specifically: (a) As long as the inputs and outputs claimed by the coerced parties are consistent with the evaluated function, the entire information reported by the parties should look like an honest execution of the protocol with these inputs and outputs; this should hold regardless of whether the inputs and outputs are true or fake or partially true and partially fake. (b) If the claimed inputs and outputs are not globally consistent with the evaluated function, the coercer should not be able to deduce any information which it cannot deduce given the inputs and outputs alone - such as, e.g., the identities of parties which reported fake values.

Incoercibility might indeed appear unobtainable at first. Still, [CG96] construct an incoercible general multi-party function evaluation protocol, for the case where only a minority of the parties are coerced, and furthermore the coercions takes place at the end of the interaction. The [CG96] protocol assumes sender-deniable encryption [CDNO96, SW14]. The works of [DKR14] and [CGP15] extend these results to the case where all but one of the parties are coerced. The works of [MN06, AOZZ15] consider the case where all parties are coerced - in fact they consider an even more adversarial setting of *active coercions*, where the coercer may force parties to deviate from the protocol, to

---

[1] In [AOZZ15] this is referred to as *semi-honest incoercibility*.

make it harder for them to deceive the coercer. However, they assume that the parties have access to secure hardware whose internals are not available *even to the parties themselves*.

Still, whether incoercibility is at all possible in a setting where all parties are coerced, the communication is public, and the parties have full access to the transcripts of their own internal computations, has remains open. Indeed, in this case the adversary obtains an entire transcript of a computation, which can be verified step by step. Still, it should be unable to tell a fake transcript from a real one.

Our Results. We consider the case where the parties have full access to the computing devices they use, all communication is public, and all parties are eventually coerced. Still, we concentrate on the case where coercions take place only at the end of the protocol. We consider two main settings, or levels, of incoercibility:

Cooperative Incoercibility. In the cooperative incoercibility setting, it is guaranteed that all parties "cooperate" with each other, in a sense that either they all present their real randomness (and real inputs and outputs), or they all present randomness computed via their faking algorithms, along with the corresponding input and output values (which may be either fake or real). This scenario corresponds to a standard setting where a group of participants wants to protect itself against an external coercer. (We stress that we assume no additional coordination between parties: each party runs its faking algorithm locally, only based on the information available to that party. Further, the inputs and outputs claimed by the parties need not necessarily be globally consistent with each other.)

Full Incoercibility. In this setting, there are no guarantees of behavior of the parties. In particular, upon coercion, some parties may decide to present their real randomness (and real inputs and outputs), and some parties may decide to present their fake randomness (and real or fake inputs and outputs). Further, the claimed inputs and outputs could even be globally inconsistent - and still the protocol has to hide everything which is not revealed by inputs and outputs alone (e.g., the identities of the liars could still remain hidden). This definition additionally gives protection in the setting where parties have conflicting insentives and might act against each other; we will refer to the case where parties present mixed (real and fake) randomness as *off-the-record* case. Thus, full incoercibility incorporates both cooperative incoerciblity and off-the-record incoercibility.

Moreover, in full incoercibility we even allow the environment to make standard (adaptive) corruption requests, in addition to coercion requests.[2]

We show:

- A cooperatively incoercible protocol for general secure multi-party function evaluation. Our protocol works in the common reference string (CRS) model and requires 4 rounds of communication.

---

[2] Note that the adversary receives the party's true internal state both in case of a corruption and in case of a coercion, if that party decides to tell the truth. However, in the former case the adversary knows that the given internal state is authentic, and in the latter it doesn't.

- A fully incoercible protocol for secure two-party function evaluation, for functions with poly-size input domains. For this protocol, we build an incoercible oblivious transfer (OT) from any deniable encryption with certain properties. In particular, our construction, instantiated with deniable encryption of [CPP20], yields a 3-message protocol in the CRS model.
- For $n \geq 3$, no n-party protocols with a certain communication pattern can be secure even against coercion of 2 parties, except for trivial functions.

On the Applicability of Off-the-Record/Full incoercibility. First, with cooperative incoercibility only, the adversarial parties may be able to provide an unequivocal proof that other parties are lying; thus, this type of incoercibility doesn't protect the participants against each other. In contrast, incoercibility in the off-the-record case guarantees that the coercer will not be able to use the protocol transcript to verify claims of parties—any deduction made by the coercer will be exclusively based on "taking the word" of the coerced parties.

Furthermore, cooperatively incoercible protocols may drop their security guarantees if some parties give real coins to the coercer, and other parties give fake coins. Because of that, cooperatively incoercible protocols impose a classical prisoner's dilemma onto the participants, due to the fact that the identities of liars could be revealed by such a protocol. Indeed, upon coercion, each party has to make a decision - whether to lie or tell the truth. On one hand, for each party it is better to tell the truth - otherwise it may get caught lying, if some other party tells the truth. On the other hand, all parties jointly are better off if they all present fake randomness - no one gets caught, and their inputs remain protected. In contrast, if a protocol remains incoercible even in the off-the-record setting, once parties have already decided on which inputs and outputs to disclose, for each party it is strictly better to disclose fake randomness (even if it still reports the true inputs and outputs). Indeed, no matter how other parties act, the protocol guarantees that nothing is revealed beyond inputs and outputs.

1.1   Related Work

Prior Work on Generic Incoercible MPC. The prior work on generic incoercible MPC can be split into two parts, depending on whether it focuses on *semi-honest* or *active* coercion (in the language of [AOZZ15]). Intuitively, a coercer is semi-honest if it lets the party participate in the protocol as prescribed (by following the instructions of the protocol), but after that demands to see the entire view of that party and checks whether it matches the claimed input of that party. In contrast, an *active* coercer assumes full control over the party and in particular may instruct the party to deviate from the protocol, in order to make it harder for the party to deceive the coercer.

As already noted in [BT94] in the context of secure voting, active coercion is clearly unachievable with cryptography alone: coerced parties have no hope of lying about their inputs if the adversary watches over their shoulder during the computation. As a result, security against active coercion requires some form of physical unaccessibility assumption. Indeed, to come up with the protocol secure against active coercion, [AOZZ15] makes use of a stateful hardware token which can generate keys, distribute them to all parties, and encrypt.

In contrast, semi-honest incoercibility is well within the reach of "digital cryptography", without the need to assume inaccessible hardware: sender-deniable encryption and encryption deniable for both parties was constructed by [SW14] and [CPP20], respectively, from indistinguishability obfuscation and one-way functions, and it was shown back in 1996 how to transform any sender-deniable encryption into incoercible MPC which withstands coercion of up to half participants [CG96]. The protocols of [CGP15, DKR14], originally devised as adaptively secure protocols withstanding corruption of all parties, can withstand coercion of a single party.

Note that, although from a practical standpoint active incoercibility is stronger and more desirable than semi-honest one, from theoretical perspective semi-honest and active incoercibility are two completely different and incomparable problems. Indeed, achieving semi-honest incoercibility requires solving the problem of "inverting the computation" - i.e. finding randomness which makes some computation appear to stem from a different input (note that this problem is also interesting on its own, without its connection to incoercibility). Active incoercibility, as discussed above, inherently requires inaccessible hardware to hide parts of the computation and thus avoids the inverting problem altogether; instead, the goal there is to ensure that the active coercer cannot force parties to output something committing, while making the underlying physical assumptions as realistic as possible.

Impossibility Results. [CG96] shows that semi-honest incoercible computation is not achievable against unbounded adversaries; this impossibility holds even in the presence of private channels. To the best of our knowledge, in the computational setting no impossibility results specific to incoercible MPC were known. However, the impossibility of non-interactive (i.e. 2-message) receiver-deniable encryption [BNNO11] immediately implies that 2-round incoercible MPC is impossible, even against coercion of a single party which receives the output[3] (in particular, the 2-round protocol of [CGP15] only withstands coercion of a party which doesn't receive the output); this impossibility holds for all functions which imply a bit transmission.

On the Difference Between the Definitions of Incoercible MPC in [CG96] *and* [CGP15]. In this work we use the definition of incoercible computation from [CGP15]. We briefly explain how it differs from the one in [CG96]. The definitions of [CG96] and [CGP15] are conceptually similar but differ in case when an environment instructs a party to fake, but sets its fake input and output to be exactly the same as its real input and output. In this case the definition in [CG96] instructs the party to output its true randomness, while the definition in [CGP15] instructs the party to run the fake algorithm anyways and output the resulting fake randomness.

---

[3] Indeed, any incoercible protocol for a message transmission functionality can be turned into a 2-message receiver-deniable encryption, by letting the party R which receives the output be a receiver of deniable encryption, and letting the sender run the MPC protocol on behalf of all other parties. In particular, the first message (sent by the receiver) will consist of all messages sent by R in the first round of the protocol, and the second message (sent by the sender) will consist of all messages sent to R in rounds 1 and 2. Messages sent by R in round 2 of MPC protocol do not have to be sent, since S doesn't receive the output, nor does S have to deny later.

This difference may appear minor - indeed, if a party is not going to lie about its inputs nor outputs, why fake the randomness? Nevertheless, there are situations when a party may want to fake its randomness anyways. Indeed, as we discuss in the technical overview, our incoercible MPC protocol only retains its incoercibility properties as long as *all* parties disclose their fake coins to the coercer. In particular, there may be a party which has no interest in lying about its own input, but which anticipates that other participants may need to lie about theirs, and which thus decides to give out its fake randomness to make sure its true randomness doesn't compromise other parties' security.

Deniable Encryption. Perhaps the most relevant prior work for us is the interactive deniable encryption of [CPP20], which we use as a building block in all our protocols. It is an encryption scheme which withstands coercion of both the sender and the receiver even in the off-the-record setting. The protocol requires a common reference string, takes 3 rounds, and assumes subexponential indistinguishability obfuscation and one way functions.

1.2   Technical Overview

On the Definition of Incoercible Computation. We use the definition of incoercible computation from [CGP15], which can be seen as the "UC equivalent" of the definition of [CG96], with one critical difference. (See Sect. 1.1 for the discussion of the difference between the two.) Specifically, this definition models coercion as the following special form of corruption: When a party is notified that it is coerced, it first contacts the its caller to ask whether to disclose true or fake randomness, and if fake, what value (input and output) to report to the coercer. The response can be either "fake" together with an input and an output, or "tell the truth". In the former case, the coerced party runs the faking algorithm with the prescribed value; in the latter case it reveals its actual internal state.

In the ideal process, when the simulator asks to coerce a party, the ideal functionality obtains from the environment either the value v to be presented, or the "tell the truth" directive. If the response was a value v, then the functionality forwards v to the simulator. If the response was "tell the truth", then the ideal functionality provides the actual input and output values of the coerced party to the simulator. *Crucially, the simulator isn't told if this value is true or fake.* Intuitively, the fact that the simulator can simulate the protocol without learning whether the inputs were real or fake, means that in the real world the adversary doesn't learn this information either.

This definition in particular means that the protocol must maintain the best possible incoercibility even when *claimed inputs and outputs are inconsistent*. For instance, even in case of clearly inconsistent inputs and outputs, the total number of liars or their identities may be still hidden; thus the real-world protocol is required to provide the same guarantee.

We note that we still allow standard adaptive corruption requests, in addition to coercion requests.

We refer to this setting as *full incoercibility*. The case of *cooperative* incoercibility is obtained from the above definition by restricting the environment in two ways: first, it must either provide "tell the truth" to *all* parties, or else provide it to *no* participant; second, we prohibit corruption operation.

As noted in [CG96], this definition of incoercibility immediately implies semi-honest adaptive security.

Obstacles to Incoercibility: Inversion and Coordination. We start by giving some intuition for why it is hard to build incoercible protocols. For instance, consider a two-party computation protocol based on Yao garbled circuits [Yao86], where the sender sends a garbled circuit, together with labels for the inputs of the sender and the receiver; the latter is sent via oblivious transfer (OT). If both the sender and the receiver become coerced and decide to lie about their inputs and outputs, then:

- the receiver should demonstrate the adversary how it receives (potentially incorrect) output of the OT corresponding to a different receiver bit. At the same time, the receiver shouldn't be able to obtain the *true* OT output for that bit - indeed, this would violate sender privacy.
- the sender should explain how the garbled circuit was generated, i.e. provide its generation randomness. The problem is, the sender has already "committed" to its own labels (by sending them over the public channel), and now it has to come up with different generation randomness such that those labels, initially corresponding to its true input, now represent a fake input.
- further, this generation randomness also has to be consistent with the labels of the receiver and fake input of the receiver, which the sender doesn't know.

This example already demonstrates two difficulties with designing incoercible protocols. One is the problem of *inversion*, where some or all parties have to invert some randomized function $f(x; r)$ with respect to a different x' (like the generation of a garbled circuit)[4]. The other is a problem of *coordination*, where parties have to lie about their intermediate states *in a consistent way*, even though parties do not know fake inputs and outputs of each other.

These problem are reminiscent of the problems arising in the context of adaptive security. However, incoercibility is much stronger than adaptive security. Indeed, in the setting of adaptive security fake randomness is only created by a simulator in the proof, as part of a mental experiment, and not by parties in the real protocol. In particular, the simulator may keep secret trapdoors to help with generating fake randomness (thus simplifying the problem of inversion), and the fact that all fake randomness is generated by the same entity eliminates the problem of coordination. In contrast, in incoercible protocols, the parties themselves should be able to fake their randomness, and they must do so independently of each other (after the protocol finishes).

These issues manifest themselves even in a simpler task of a message transmission function. To date, despite having a number of clean and modular constructions of adaptively secure (or, non-committing) encryption schemes [DN00, CDMW09, BH92, HOR15, HORR16, YKT19] we have only one construction of a deniable encryption

---

[4] Note that in the model where not everybody is coerced, it is easy to avoid the inversion problem altogether by, e.g., secret-sharing r across all parties, thus guaranteeing that the coercer never gets to see r.

scheme (withstanding coercion of both parties), and this construction is very non-modular: it is built from the ground up using obfuscation, and both the construction and its security proof are quite heavy [CPP20].

Thus, we have two potential approaches for designing incoercible MPC. One is to build the whole protocol from scratch, perhaps using obfuscation, similar to the construction of deniable encryption; needless to say, such a construction is likely to be even more complicated. The other approach is to use deniable encryption as a primitive and explore how much incoercibility can we obtain by composing it with other primitives.

In this work we take the latter approach. We show how to combine deniable encryption with adaptive security to obtain an incoercible protocol, and how to turn certain deniable encryption schemes into incoercible OT, thus yielding incoercible 2PC with short inputs.

Our Setting. We allow parties (and adversaries) to have an access to a common reference string (CRS), which has to be generated only once and is good for unboundedly many executions. However, we require that protocols should only rely on cryptographic assumptions (as opposed to inaccessible hardware assumptions). We consider the case where coercions and corruptions happen only after the execution has finished. Our two main settings are the setting of *cooperative incoercibility*, where security is guaranteed to hold only as long as partitipants lie or tell the truth simultaneously, and the setting of *full incoercibility*, which doesn't have such a restriction.

We present semi-honestly incoercible protocols, which withstand coercion of all participants. Faking procedure of each party is local: that is, each party fakes only based on its own real and fake inputs and outputs and the information made available by the protocol. In particular, neither party knows fake inputs of other parties, nor does it know whether other parties are corrupted or coerced, and if coerced, whether they tell the truth or li.e.

Deniable Encryption. A common building block in all our protocols is a deniable encryption scheme [CDNO96], which can be thought of as an incoercible protocol for the message transmission functionality. We require deniable encryption which remains deniable even when both parties are coerced, and even in the off-the-record setting; as of September 2020, the only such protocol is given by [CPP20]. Roughly, deniable encryption give the following security guarantee:

1. the adversary cannot distinguish whether it sees
   - real randomness s of the sender, real randomness r of the receiver, and the communication transcript for plaintext m, or
   - fake randomness of the sender s' consistent with fake m, fake randomness of the receiver r' consistent with fake m, and the communication transcript for plaintext m'.
2. (off-the-record setting) the adversary cannot distinguish whether it sees
   - real randomness s of the sender, fake randomness r' of the receiver consistent with m', and the communication transcript for plaintext m,
   - fake randomness of the sender s' consistent with m, real randomness of the receiver r consistent with m', and the communication transcript for plaintext m',

- fake randomness s' of the sender consistent with m, fake randomness r' of the receiver consistent with m', and the communication transcript for plaintext m''. This should hold for any, potentially equal, m, m', m''.

Incoercible Oblivious Transfer and 2PC with Short Inputs. Incoercible oblivious transfer has the functionality of a standard oblivious transfer - i.e. it allows the receiver to obtain exactly one value x_b (corresponding to its own input b), out of two values x_0, x_1 held by the sender. However, it additionally provides security guarantees against a coercer: that is, even if the coercer demands to see all randomness used by both parties in the protocol, parties can successfully lie about their inputs. That is, the sender can claim that it used any, possibly different inputs x_0', x_1' (and provide convincing randomness supporting this claim). Similarly, the receiver can claim it used a possibly different input bit b', and received a different output x' of its choice.

This primitive can be constructed from any receiver-oblivious deniable encryption (DE) with public receiver deniability. Here "public receiver deniability" means that the faking algorithm of the receiver doesn't take true receiver coins as input (thus anyone can fake on behalf of the receiver). "Receiver-oblivious" DE means that the adversary cannot tell if the receiver messages were generated honestly (following the algorithm of DE), or instead chosen at random (in this case, we say that these messages were generated obliviously); further, this indistinguishability should hold even given fake random coins of the sender. We note that deniable encryption of [CPP20] has public receiver deniability, and in the full version we show that it is also receiver-oblivious.

Theorem 1. *Any receiver-oblivious deniable encryption, which remains deniable even in the off-the-record setting and has public receiver deniability, can be converted into fully incoercible 1-out-of-m oblivious transfer, for any polynomial m, in a round-preserving way.*

The construction of incoercible OT is inspired by the construction of adaptively secure OT from non-committing (adaptively secure) encryption [CLOS02]. Namely, let x_0, x_1 be the inputs of the sender, and b be the input of the receiver. The parties should run in parallel two instances of DE: DE_0 and DE_1. The sender's input to each DE_i is x_i, for both $i = 0, 1$. The receiver should pick random r and generate messages of DE_b honestly (using r as randomness of the receiver in the protocol), while messages of DE_{1-b} should be generated by the receiver obliviously.

It is easy to see that the receiver can learn only x_b but not x_{1-b}, since the receiver knows r, which allows it to decrypt DE_b, but doesn't know randomness for DE_{1-b} and therefore cannot decrypt it. The sender, in turn, doesn't learn the receiver bit b, since it doesn't know which execution was generated obliviously by the receiver. Further, this OT is indeed incoercible: the sender can directly use deniability of DE to claim that different inputs x_0', x_1' were sent. The receiver can lie about its input b by claiming that DE_b was generated obliviously, and by presenting fake r' as randomness for DE_{1-b}. This fake r' can be generated by using the faking algorithm on DE_{1-b} and y', where y' is the desired fake output of the oblivious transfer. Note that the receiver doesn't know true coins for obliviously generated DE_{1-b}, but it can generate fake r' anyway due to the fact that receiver deniability is public.

This construction can be extended to 1-out-of-m incoercible OT in a straightforward way.

Incoercible 2PC for Short Inputs from incoercible OT. Recall that, when the number m of possible inputs of some party is polynomial, standard 1-out-of-m OT immediately implies general 2PC [GMW87]: The OT sender should input to the OT m possible values of $f(x, y)$, corresponding to m possible values of the receiver's input y, and a single sender's input x. Using incoercible 1-out-of-m OT in this protocol immediately makes the resulting 2PC protocol incoercible.

Incoercible MPC from OT? Despite the fact that standard OT implies general secure multi-party computation [GMW87], it is not clear whether *incoercible* OT implies *incoercible* MPC as well. In particular, simply plugging (even ideal) incoercible OT into the protocol of [GMW87] doesn't seem to result in an incoercible protocol, even just for two parties. The problem here is the following: recall that this protocol works by letting the parties compute additive secret shares of each wire of the circuit of $f(x_1, x_2)$. On one hand, since in the normal execution two shares add up to the value of the wire of $f(x_1, x_2)$, the same should hold in the fake case: fake secret shares should add up to the value of the wire of $f(x'_1, x'_2)$. However, it is not clear how, upon coercion, parties can compute these fake shares *locally*, without the knowledge of the other party's input.

Incoercible MPC. A natural starting point for building an incoercible MPC is to make parties run any secure MPC protocol, where each message is encrypted under a separate instance of deniable encryption. If in addition the parties are allowed to communicate outside of the view of the adversary - e.g. by meeting physically - and if they are comfortable sharing their fake inputs with each other, this method immediately gives incoercible MPC. Indeed, upon coercion parties can use their out-of-band channel to all agree on some transcript $\text{tr}' = \text{tr}(\{x'_i, r'_i\})$ of an underlying MPC executed on their fake inputs. When coerced, each party can use deniability of encryption to lie (by presenting consistent randomness and keys of deniable encryption) that it sent and received messages of tr'. In addition, each party should claim that x'_i, r'_i are the true input and randomness which it used to compute the messages of tr'.

However, this protocol fails when no out-of-band interaction is possible, since parties do not have means to agree on tr'. To fix this problem, we combine deniability with adaptive security. That is, we use MPC which is adaptively secure and has a special property called *corruption oblivious simulation* (defined in [BCH12] in a setting of leakage tolerance). Roughly, it means that there is a "main" simulator which simulates the transcript, and in addition each party has its own, "local" simulator which simulates the coins of that party, using that party's inputs only and the state of the "main" simulator (but not the inputs of other parties). If parties had a way to agree on the same simulation randomness r_{Sim}, then upon coercion, they could do the following: First they should run the main simulator on r_{Sim} to generate (the same) simulated transcript tr' of an underlying adaptive MPC, and then each party should use its own local simulator to locally compute fake coins consistent with this simulated transcript and its own input. Finally, as before, each party can use deniability of encryption to claim that the messages of tr' were indeed sent.

It remains to determine how the parties agree on the random coins r_{Sim} of the main simulator. A natural approach to do this is to let one of the parties (say, the first) choose r_{Sim} at random and send it, encrypted under deniable encryption, to each other party at the beginning of the protocol, for case that they need to fake later. However, this introduces another difficulty: now the adversary can demand to see r_{Sim}, and revealing it would allow the adversary to check that the transcript was simulated and thus detect a li.e. Therefore, instead of sending r_{Sim}, the first party should send randomly chosen seed s to all other parties. This seed is not used by parties in the execution of the protocol. However, upon coercion each party can use a pseudorandom generator to expand s into a string $r_{Sim}||s'$, where r_{Sim}, as before, is used to produce the same simulated transcript of an adaptive MPC, and s' is what parties will claim as their fake seed (instead of a true seed s). Note that it is safe to reveal s' to the adversary, since $s'||r_{Sim}$ is pseudorandom, and therefore s' cannot help the adversary to indicate in any way that tr$'$ was simulated.

We underline that security of this protocol is only maintains in the cooperative setting. As a result, this protocol is useful in scenarios where parties "work together" and are interested in keeping all their inputs secret, rather than turn against each other trying to make sure others get caught cheating. We note however that the protocol remains secure even if *inputs* of some parties are real and inputs of some other parties are fake - as long as *randomness* of all parties is fake. Indeed, it might happen so that a certain party is not interested in lying about its input, but still wishes the whole group of people to succeed in deceiving; then this party may provide fake randomness for its real input, thus not ruining the joint attempt to deceive, while achieving its own goals[5]. Further, this protocol maintains the best possible security even in the case when the claimed inputs and outputs are clearly inconsistent.

4-Round Protocol for Incoercible MPC. We now describe the same protocol more formally and in particular show how to achieve 4 rounds of communication:

Theorem 2. *It is possible to build cooperatively incoercible secure function evaluation protocol from deniable encryption and adaptively secure MPC protocol with a global CRS and corruption-oblivious simulator.*

We need the following ingredients for our protocol:

- 2-round adaptively secure MPC aMPC with global CRS[6] and corruption-oblivious simulator, e.g. that of [CPV17].
- 3-round delayed-input[7] deniable encryption DE, e.g. that of [CPP20]. While that construction is not delayed-input, we observe that it is easy to turn any deniable encryption into its delayed-input version. This can be done by letting the sender send a randomly chosen key k using deniable encryption, and also send $m \oplus k$ in the clear at the last round.

---

[5] Note that this scenario highlights a subtle but important difference between the modelling of coercion in [CG96] and [CGP15]. Indeed, in [CG96], if the party is given a real input, it has to provide its true randomness.

[6] The CRS of the protocol is said to be global, if the simulator can simulate the execution, *given* the CRS (as opposed to generating the CRS on its own, possibly from a different distribution, or with underlying trapdoors).

[7] That is, only the third message of the sender depends on the plaintext.

Then our protocol proceeds as follows:

1. In rounds $1 - 3$ parties exchange the messages of the *first* round of aMPC, encrypted under point-to-point deniable encryption.
2. In rounds $2 - 4$ parties exchange the messages of the *second* round of aMPC, encrypted under point-to-point deniable encryption. It is important that deniable encryption requires its input only by the last round, since parties receive the messages of the first round of aMPC only after round 3.
3. In rounds $2 - 4$ party 1 sends to each party randomly chosen seed, encrypted under point-to-point deniable encryption. Note that each party receives the same value of seed.

After round 4, parties learn all messages of aMPC and therefore can compute the output. Note that our protocol is delayed input, since inputs are required only by round 3. Upon coercion, each party first computes fake transcript tr′ of aMPC. tr′ is computed by running the "main" simulator of aMPC on r_{Sim}, where r_{Sim} is obtained by expanding seed into seed′$\|r_{\mathsf{Sim}}$ using a prg. (Note that parties use the same r_{Sim} and therefore obtain the same tr′ upon coercion). Next, each party can use its local simulator to produce fake coins consistent with tr′ and fake input x'. Therefore, each party can claim that the transcript of the underlying protocol was tr′, and this claim will be consistent with party's own fake input, and across different parties. Finally, each party should claim that the seed value sent by party 1 was in fact seed′.

Note that our construction crucially uses the fact that underlying adaptive MPC has *global* CRS. Indeed, this allows to put this CRS as part of the final CRS of the protocol, and lets parties simulate the transcript of underlying adaptive MPC with respect to that CRS. Had the CRS been local, parties would have to generate it during the protocol and thus eventually provide the adversary with the generation coins; yet, security of protocols with local CRS usually holds only as long as the generation randomness of this CRS remains private.

Impossibility of Incoercible MPC with Lazy Parties

Impossibility of Incoercible MPC with Lazy Parties. We show that unlike 2-party protocols, multiparty protocols with some communication structure cannot be incoercible (this holds even against coercion of only 2 parties). Concretely, let us say that a party is *lazy*, if it only sends its messages in the first and the last round of a protocol, but doesn't send anything in intermediate rounds (if any). In particular, in all 2 round protocols all parties are lazy by definition. We show that coercing a lazy party and some output-receiving party allows to learn information about inputs of other parties, therefore rendering the protocol insecure for most functions:

Theorem 3. *Assume there exists an n-party protocol withstanding 2 corruptions and 1 coercion for computing function f with a lazy party, where $n \geq 3$. Then the function f is such that for any inputs $x_1, \ldots, x_n$ it is possible, given x_1, x_n, and $f(x_1, \ldots, x_n)$, to compute $f(x, x_2, \ldots, x_n)$ for any x.*

We consider this negative result to be especially important in light of the fact that building fully incoercible protocols may require complicated obfuscation-based constructions. For instance, consider the following natural attempt to build a 3-round fully incoercible protocol. Take deniable encryption of [CPP20] which essentially lets the sender send an encryption of a plaintext together with some auxiliary information, which the receiver can decrypt using an obfuscated decryption program. This protocol features a "ping-pong" communication pattern, with a total of 3 messages sent between a sender and a receiver. One could attempt to turn it into MPC with a similar "ping-pong" communication pattern by letting $n-1$ senders $P_1, \ldots, P_{n-1}$ send its input to a single receiver P_n in a similar manner, and let the obfuscated evaluation program of the receiver decrypt the messages and evaluate the result. While this approach sounds very plausible and appealing in a sense that it potentially requires only minor modifications of the construction of deniable encryption, our impossibility result implies that such protocol cannot be incoercible.

Finally, it is interesting to note that this impossibility result is "tight" both with respect to the number of participants n, and with respect to coercion operation (as opposed to adaptive corruption). Indeed, there exists a 3-round *two-party* incoercible protocol (e.g. our OT-based protocol), and a 3-round multi-party *adaptively secure* protocol [DKR14], which features such a "ping-pong" communication pattern.[8]

To get an idea of why impossibility holds, consider standard MPC with a super-lazy party who only sends its messages in the very last round; clearly, such a protocol is insecure, since the adversary who corrupts this party together with some output-receiving party can rerun the protocol on many inputs of the lazy party and therefore infer some information about the inputs of uncorrupted parties.

Such an attack in the standard MPC case doesn't work when a lazy party sends messages in two rounds of the protocol. However, we show that in case of incoercible protocols there is a way for a lazy party to modify its last message such that the protocol now thinks that a different input is used - despite the fact that its first message still corresponds to the original input. With this technique in place we can mount the same attack as described before. This technique is based on the observation in [CPP20] that sender-deniability in any deniable encryption implies that a party can "fool" its own protocol execution into thinking that a different input is being used. We refer the reader to Sect. 5 for details.

Discussion, Open Problems, and Future Work. Our results naturally lead to the following open problems:

- *Round Complexity:* is it possible to build an incoercible protocol, withstanding coercion of all parties, for general functions in 3 rounds?
- *Full Incoercibility:* Is it possible to obtain a protocol which withstands coercion of all parties and remains incoercible even in the off-the-record setting - with any number of rounds?

---

[8] Note that formally speaking, the protocol of [DKR14] takes 4 rounds; however, the receiver learns the output already after round 3. The 4-th round is only required to send this output back to everyone.

The protocols in this paper follow a blueprint of composing deniable encryption with non-deniable primitives, resulting in a simple and clean protocol design. However, it could be problematic to use this approach for answering the questions listed above. The reason is the following. Since incoercible MPC implies deniable encryption, any construction of incoercible MPC:

- either has to use some construction of deniable encryption,
- or has to build deniable encryption from scratch, at least implicitly.

As we explain in more detail next, improving on our results would likely require the latter. This is a problem because the only known construction of encryption which is deniable for both parties [CPP20] is fairly complex and has lengthy proofs (the paper is more than 250 pages), and moreover, complex constructions could be inherent for deniable encrypion, because of a certain attack which can be done by the adversary (see the technical overview of [CPP20] for more details).

We now give more details about each open question separately.

Round Complexity. We show the existence of a 4-round deniable protocol, whereas 2-round incoercible protocols are ruled out by the impossibility of receiver-deniable encryption in 2 rounds [BNNO11]. This leads to a natural question of whether deniable computation can be done in 3 rounds generically.

It could be hard to achieve this by using deniable encryption as a building block. Since deniable encryption itself provably takes 3 rounds of communication, this means that only the last message in the protocol can be "protected" by deniability of encryption; yet, previous messages have to depend on the inputs as well and somehow have to be deniable. We leave it to future work to either extend this argument towards a lower bound, or to come up with a protocol which avoids this issue.

Off-the-Record Incoercibility. A natural attempt to build an off-the-record incoercible protocol is to combine deniable encryption (secure even in the off-the-record setting) with other, weaker-than-incoercible primitives (e.g. standard MPC). Unfortunately, this is unlikely to help. Indeed, a very simple argument made by [AOZZ15] shows that in any construction of off-the-record incoercible MPC with the help of secure channels, parties have to use these (perfectly deniable!) channels in an inherently non-deniable way: that is, if a party sends (receives) a message M via secure channel during the protocol, then its faking algorithm cannot instruct this party to lie about M[9]. This can be informally interpreted as follows: in any incoercible protocol which uses deniable encryption, deniable encryption can be replaced with standard encryption such that the protocol still remains incoercible[10]. This in turn indicates that such a protocol would have to be incoercible to begin with.

---

[9] Roughly, this is because said party doesn't know whether its peer is lying or telling the truth; it could be telling the truth, thus revealing true M, and from definition of off-the-record deniability, their joint state should look valid even in the case when the party is lying and its peer is telling the truth - as long as their inputs and outputs are consistent.

[10] We underline again that this is an informal statement - indeed, such a statement is tricky to even formalize, let al.one prove.

2   Preliminaries

2.1   Incoercible Computation

We use the definition of incoercible computation from [CGP15], which can be regarded as a re-formulation of the definition of [CG96] within the UC framework. (We note that the formulations of [MN06, AOZZ15] are similar to and consistent with the one we use, with the exception that they allow also Byzantine corruptions and incorporate modeling of ideally opaque hardware.) Specifically, we let the adversary send a special coercion message (in addition to standard corruption messages) to parties; upon receiving this message a party notifies a predetermined external entity (say, its "caller" via subroutine output) that it was coerced and expects an instruction to either "tell the truth", in which case it reveals its entire local state to the adversary, or "fake to input x and output y", in which case the party runs the faking algorithm provided as part of the protocol, on x, y and the current local state, and uses the output of the algorithm as the fake internal state reported to the adversary. We also restrict the parties to accept coercion/corruption messages from the environment only once the protocol execution ended. We refer to this setting as full incoercibility.

Cooperative Environments. If an environment is guaranteed to either instruct all coerced parties to "tell the truth", or else neither of the coerced/corrupted parties are instructed to "tell the truth" (in which case, each party is instructed to fake to some input x and output y, of the environment's choice), and in addition if standard corruptions are prohibited, then we say that it is cooperative.

Incoercible Ideal Functionalities. An ideal functionality can now guarantee incoercibility via the following mechanism: When asked by the adversary (or, simulator) to coerce a party P, the ideal functionality outputs a request to coerce P to the said external entity, in the same way as done by the protocol. If the response is "fake to input x and output y, then the pair x, y is returned to the adversary. If the response is "tell the truth" then the actual input x and output y are returned to the adversary. *Crucially, the simulator is not told whether the values received are real or fake.*

This behavior is intended to mimic the situation where the computation is done "behind closed doors" and no information about it is ever exposed, other than the inputs and outputs of the parties. In particular, such an ideal functionality does not prevent situations where the outputs of the parties are globally inconsistent with their inputs, or where a certain set of inputs of the parties are inconsistent with auxiliary information that's known outside the protocol execution. Indeed, the only goal here is to guarantee that any determination made by an external coercer (modeled by the environment) after interacting with the protocol, could have been done in the ideal model, given only the claimed inputs and outputs.

Figures 1, 2 and 3 depict incoercible variants of the standard ideal functionalities for secure message transmission, oblivious transfer, and multiparty function evaluation, respectively.

We say that π is a fully incoercible message transmission protocol if π UC-realizes $\mathcal{F}_{imt}$. If π UC-realizes $\mathcal{F}_{imt}$ only with respect to cooperative environments then π is a

---

Functionality $\mathcal{F}_{\text{IMT}}$

- Upon receiving input $(\texttt{Send}, sid, R, m)$ from party S, where R is an identity for the intended receiver, send $(sid, S, R, |m|)$ to the adversary. When receiving $\texttt{ok}$ from the adversary, output $(\texttt{Receive}, sid, S, m)$ to R.
- Upon receiving $(\texttt{Coerce}, sid, P)$ from the adversary, where $P \in \{S, R\}$, output $(\texttt{Coerce}, sid)$ to P. Upon receiving V from P do: If $V = (\texttt{tell-truth})$ then send m to the adversary. If $V = (\texttt{fake-to}, m')$ then send m' to the adversary.
- Upon receiving $(\texttt{Corrupt}, sid, P)$ from the adversary, where $P \in \{S, R\}$, output $(\texttt{Corrupt}, sid)$ to P, and send m to the adversary.

Fig. 1. The incoercible message transmission functionality $\mathcal{F}_{imt}$.

Functionality $\mathcal{F}_{\text{IOT}}$

- Upon receiving input $(\texttt{OT-Sender}, sid, R, (m_0, m_1))$ from party S, where R is an identity for the intended receiver, send (sid, S, R) to the adversary. When receiving $\texttt{ok}$ from the adversary, output $(\texttt{OT-Receiver}, sid, S)$ to R.
- Upon receiving input $(\texttt{OT-Receiver}, sid, b)$ from R, send sid to the adversary. When receiving $\texttt{ok}$ from the adversary, output $(\texttt{OT-Receiver}, sid, m_b)$ to R.
- Upon receiving $(\texttt{Coerce}, sid, P)$ from the adversary, where $P \in \{S, R\}$, output $(\texttt{Coerce}, sid)$ to P. Upon receiving V from P do: If $V = (\texttt{tell-truth})$ then send P's input and output to the adversary. If $V = (\texttt{fake-to}, v)$ then send v to the adversary.
- Upon receiving $(\texttt{Corrupt}, sid, P)$ from the adversary, where $P \in \{S, R\}$, output $(\texttt{Corrupt}, sid)$ to P, and send P's input and output to the adversary.

Fig. 2. The incoercible oblivious transfer functionality $\mathcal{F}_{iot}$.

Functionality $\mathcal{F}_{\text{IFE}}$

- Upon receiving input $(\texttt{Init}, sid, P_1, ..., P_n, f$ from party P_i, send $(sid, P_1, ..., P_n, f)$ to the adversary. When receiving $(\texttt{ok}, P_i)$ from the adversary, output $(\texttt{Init}, sid, P_1, ..., P_n, f)$ to P_i.
- Upon receiving input $(\texttt{Init}, sid, x_i)$ from P_i, record (P_i, x_i). Once (P_i, x_i) are recorded for all $i = 1..n$, compute $(y_1, ..., y_n) \leftarrow f(x_1, ..., x_n)$ and send $(\texttt{Output}, sid)$ to the adversary.
- When receiving $\texttt{output}$ from P_i, output y_i to P_i.
- Upon receiving $(\texttt{Coerce}, sid, P_i)$ from the adversary output $(\texttt{Coerce}, sid)$ to P_i. Upon receiving V from P_i do: If $V = (\texttt{tell-truth})$ then send P_i's input and output to the adversary. If $V = (\texttt{fake-to}, v)$ then send v to the adversary.
- Upon receiving $(\texttt{Corrupt}, sid, P_i)$ from the adversary output $(\texttt{Corrupt}, sid)$ to P_i, and send P_i's input and output to the adversary.

Fig. 3. The incoercible function evaluation functionality $\mathcal{F}_{ife}$.

cooperatively incoercible message transmission protocol. Incoercible oblivious transfer and function evaluation are defined analogously.

2.2 Other Preliminaries

Our protocols require deniable encryption with special properties, and adaptively secure MPC with corruption-oblivious simulator. An informal description of these primitives can be found in the introduction. We refer the reader to the full version for rigorous definitions.

3 Incoercible Oblivious Transfer

In this section we describe our construction of incoercible oblivious transfer. As noted in the introduction, such a protocol immediately implies incoercible 2PC for the case where one of the parties has polynomial input space.

3.1 Protocol Description

For simplicity, we consider 1-out-of-2 OT (the construction can be generalized to 1-out-of-n OT in a straightforward way), and we also assume that all inputs are bits. Our protocol is described on Fig. 4. It requires a special deniable encryption (DE) scheme, where deniability of the receiver is public (i.e. the faking algorithm of the receiver doesn't take receiver's true coins as input), and which satisfies receiver-obliviousness, i.e. the real transcript is indistinguishable from a transcript where receiver simply generated all its messages at random. As noted in [CPP20], their DE protocol satisfies public receiver deniability. In the full version we note that this protocol is also receiver-oblivious.

Before stating the theorem, we remind that we consider the model of semi-honest coercions of potentially all parties, and we assume that all coercions happen after the protocol finishes. We refer the reader to Sect. 2 for a description of our coercion model.

Theorem 4. *Assume* DE *is an interactive deniable encryption scheme which satisfies public receiver deniability and receiver obliviousness, and remains deniable even in the off-the-record scenario. Then the protocol on Fig. 2 is a semi-honest, fully incoercible oblivious transfer protocol.*

3.2 Proof of the Theorem

Correctness. Correctness immediately follows from correctness of deniable encryption.

Incoercibility. Consider the simulator depicted on Fig. 5, which essentially generates two transcripts of deniable encryption, each encrypting plaintext $m = 0$, and then uses faking algorithm of deniable encryption to simulate the coins. Note that the simulator generates the simulated coins in the same way (by using faking algorithm), no matter whether the party is corrupted or coerced.

Incoercible Oblivious Transfer

The CRS: CRS $=$ CRS$_{DE}$, where CRS$_{DE}$ is a CRS of deniable encryption with receiver-obliviousness, and public receiver deniability.

Inputs: inputs x_0, x_1 of the sender S; input bit b of the receiver R.

The protocol:

The sender chooses random coins s_0, s_1 for two executions of deniable encryption, where S acts as a sender. The receiver chooses randomness r for a single execution of deniable encryption where it acts as a receiver. The sender and the receiver run two instances of deniable encryption, DE$_0$ and DE$_1$, in parallel. Here:

- In each execution i, for $i = 0, 1$, the sender computes its messages by honestly running the code of deniable encryption on its input x_i, randomness s_i, and the transcript so far;
- In the execution b the receiver computes its messages by honestly running the code of deniable encryption on its randomness r and the transcript so far. In the execution $1 - b$ the receiver instead generates all its messages at random, using randomly chosen $\tilde{r}$.

At the end of both executions, the receiver sets its output in the protocol to be DE.Dec$(r; DE_b)$.

Faking procedure of the sender S

Inputs: fake inputs x_0', x_1' of the sender, true inputs and randomness x_0, s_0, x_1, s_1 of the sender, the protocol transcript (DE$_0$, DE$_1$), and the CRS.

In order to fake, the sender runs the faking algorithm of deniable encryption for each execution, i.e. computes $s_i' \leftarrow$ DE.SFake$(s_i, x_i, x_i', DE_i; \cdot)$ for both $i = 0, 1$. It gives s_0', s_1' to the adversary.

Faking procedure of the receiver R

Inputs: fake input b' and fake output x' of the receiver, true inputs and randomness $b, r, \tilde{r}$ of the receiver, the protocol transcript (DE$_0$, DE$_1$), and the CRS.

In order to fake, the receiver claims that messages of the receiver in execution $1 - b'$ were generated at random, and sets fake $\tilde{r}'$ to be the concatenation of these receiver messages. Next, it uses public deniability of the receiver to compute $r' \leftarrow$ DE.RFake$(x', DE_{b'}; \cdot)$. It gives $r', \tilde{r}'$ to the adversary.

Fig. 4. Incoercible oblivious transfer.

We need to show that for every pattern of corruptions and coercions, and every set of real and fake inputs and outputs, the real execution is indistinguishable from a simulated one. This boils down to showing indistinguishability in the following cases:

1. If claimed inputs and outputs are consistent, we should prove indistinguishability between the case where both the sender and the receiver show their true coins, the case where both the sender and the receiver show their fake coins, the case where the sender shows true coins and the receiver shows fake coins, and the case where the sender shows fake coins and the receiver shows true coins.

Simulation of communication

Inputs given to simulate the communication: CRS.
The simulator chooses random s_0, s_1, r_0, r_1, and computes $DE_i \leftarrow DE(s_i, r_i, 0)$ for both $i = 0, 1$, i.e. sets DE_i to be the transcript of the protocol for deniable encryption, computed with the sender input 0, sender randomness s_i, and receiver randomness r_i. (DE_0, DE_1) is a simulated transcript of the protocol.

Simulation of corruption and coercion of the sender S

Inputs additionally given to simulate the coercion of S: claimed inputs x_0', x_1' of S.
The simulator computes $s_i' \leftarrow DE.SFake(s_i, 0, x_i', DE_i; \cdot)$ for both $i = 0, 1$. It gives s_0', s_1' to the adversary.

Simulation of corruption and coercion of the receiver R

Inputs additionally given to simulate the coercion of R: claimed input b', claimed output x'.
The simulator claims that messages of the receiver in execution $1 - b'$ were generated at random, and sets fake $\tilde{r}'$ to be the concatenation of these receiver messages. Next, it computes $r_{b'}' \leftarrow DE.RFake(x', DE_{b'}; \cdot)$. It gives $r_{b'}', \tilde{r}'$ to the adversary.

Fig. 5. Simulation

2. If claimed inputs and outputs are inconsistent, we should prove indistinguishability between the case where the sender shows true coins and the receiver shows fake coins, the case where the sender shows fake coins and the receiver shows true coins, and the case where they both show fake coins.

The proof is very straighforward and uses two main steps - (a) switching between normally and obliviously generated execution of DE, using obliviousness and public receiver deniability of DE, and (b) switching randomness of DE of the sender between real and fake, using sender-deniability of DE.

Below we formally prove indistinguishability between the simulated execution (Hyb_{Sim}) and the real execution with consistent inputs x_0', x_1', b and output x_b', where both parties tell the truth (i.e. disclose their true coins) (Hyb_{Real}). Indistinguishability between other distributions can be shown in a very similar manner.

- Hyb_{Sim}. This is the execution from Fig. 5, where both the sender and the receiver are either corrupted or coerced, and the values reported to the simulator are the following: inputs x_0', x_1' of the sender, input b' of the receiver, output $x' = x_{b'}'$ of the receiver. The simulator gives the adversary $(DE_0, DE_1, s_0', s_1', r_{b'}', \tilde{r}')$.
- Hyb_1. In this hybrid the receiver generates messages in $DE_{1-b'}$ obliviously (instead of generating them honestly, using $r_{1-b'}$). Indistinguishability between this and the previous hybrid follows from obliviousness of the receiver of deniable encryption. Note that it is important for the reduction that the receiver deniability is public, since the reduction needs to compute fake randomness of execution $1 - b'$, $r_{1-b'}'$, for which it doesn't know the true coins $r_{1-b'}$.

- Hyb_2. In this hybrid the sender encrypts x_0' (instead of 0) in the execution $i = 0$. It also gives the adversary its true randomness s_0 instead of fake s_0'. Indistinguishability follows from bideniability of the encryption scheme DE_0.
- $\mathsf{Hyb}_{\mathsf{Real}}$. In this hybrid the sender encrypts x_1' (instead of 0) in the execution $i = 1$. It also gives its true randomness s_1 instead of fake s_1'. Indistinguishability follows from sender deniability of the encryption scheme DE_1.
  Note that this distribution corresponds to the real world where parties use x_0', x_1', b' as inputs.

4 4-Round Incoercible MPC

4.1 Description of the Protocol

In this section we describe our protocol achieving incoercibility even when all parties are coerced, but only in cooperative scenario. That is, as discussed in the introduction, the deception remain undetectable only as long as *all* parties lie about their randomness (however, then can still tell the truth about their inputs, if they choose so). We remind that in this work we only focus on coercions and corruptions which happen after the protocol execution.

Our protocol is presented on Fig. 6. As discussed more in detail in the introduction, the protocol essentially instructs parties to run the underlying adaptively secure protocol, where each message is encrypted under a separate instance of deniable encryption. In addition, party P_1 sends to everyone the same seed $seed$ of the prg, to be used in the faking procedure. Parties' faking algorithm instructs parties to use $seed$ to derive (the same for all parties) coins r_{Sim}, which are used to generate (the same for all parties) simulated transcript σ' of the underlying MPC. Next each party uses the local simulator of that MPC (recall that we need that MPC to have corruption-oblivious simulator) to simulate its own fake coins of the underlying MPC. Finally parties claim that they indeed exchanged messages of σ', using deniability of encryption.

Faking the Inputs vs Faking the Inputs and the Outputs. We note that it is enough for parties to be able to fake their inputs (as opposed to inputs and outputs), due to the standard transformation allowing parties to mask their output with a one time pad k: $f'((x_1, k_1), (x_2, k_2)) = f(x_1, x_2) \oplus k_1 || f(x_1, x_2) \oplus k_2$. Indeed, here faking the output can be achieved by faking inputs k_i instead. Thus, in the protocol, we only describe an input-faking mechanism.

Theorem 5. *Assume the existence of the following primitives:*

- $\mathsf{aMPC} = (\mathsf{aMPC.msg1}, \mathsf{aMPC.msg2}, \mathsf{aMPC.Eval}, \mathsf{aMPC.Sim}, \mathsf{aMPC.Sim}_i)$ *is a 2-round adaptively secure MPC with corruption-oblivious simulation, in a global CRS model;*
- $\mathsf{DE} = (\mathsf{DE.msg1}, \mathsf{DE.msg2}, \mathsf{DE.msg3}, \mathsf{DE.Dec}, \mathsf{DE.SFake}, \mathsf{DE.RFake})$ *is a 3-message, delayed-input deniable encryption protocol, in a CRS model;*
- prg *is a pseudorandom generator.*

Then the protocol iMPC *on Figs. 6, 7 is a 4-round semi-honest MPC protocol in a CRS model[11], which is cooperatively incoercible.*

We note that all required primitives can be built using subexponentially-secure indistinguishability obfuscation and one-way functions [CPP20, CPV17]. Therefore we obtain the following corollary:

Corollary 1. *Assume the existence of subexponentially secure indistinguishability obfuscation and subexponentially secure one-way functions. Then in a CRS model there exists a 4-round semi-honest MPC, which is cooperatively incoercible.*

Notation and Indexing. Subscript i, j on the message of the protocol means that the message is sent from P_i to P_j. Subscript i, j of the randomness means that this randomness is used as sender or receiver randomness in the protocol where i is the sender and j is the receiver.

For example, $M1_{i,j}$ is the first message of aMPC, sent from P_i to P_j. Our protocol transmits this message inside deniable encryption, which in turn consists of messages $a1_{i,j}$, $a2_{j,i}$, and $a3_{i,j}$. To compute these messages, party P_i uses its sender randomness $s_{i,j,1}$, and party P_j uses its receiver randomness $r_{i,j,1}$.

4.2   Proof of the Theorem

Correctness. Correctness of the protocol immediately follows from correctness of the underlying aMPC protocol and correctness of deniable encryption DE.

Incoercibility. We define a simulator which can simulate communication and internal states of all parties, given inputs and outputs only, but without knowing whether these inputs are real or fake.

We can assume that the simulator knows the output y before the protocol starts, due to the following standard transformation, where parties additionally choose OTP keys k_i and use it to mask the output: $f'((x_1, k_1), x_2, k_2) = f(x_1, x_2) \oplus k_1 || f(x_1, x_2) \oplus k_2$. Due to this transformation, the simulator can always choose output z of parties uniformly at random, and once the first coercion occurs and the true output y becomes known, set the corresponding k_i to be $z \oplus (y||y)$. From now on we assume that the simulator knows the output y ahead of time.

Simulation. The simulator is formally described on Fig. 8. Informally, the simulator uses the underlying simulator of aMPC to simulate communication between parties, σ'. It then encrypts messages of σ' under deniable encryption. It encrypts randomly chosen seed' under deniable encryption as well. This concludes the description of simulation of communication.

Upon coercion of a party, given an input x_i' (without knowing whether x_i is real or fake), the simulator computes fake random coins of aMPC by running the local simulator aMPC.Sim$_i$ on input x_i'. These are the only coins which are faked by the simulator; the simulator reveals true values of seed' and all randomness of DE.

---

[11] Note that our CRS is global (recall that the notion of deniability or incoercibility only makes sense in the global CRS model).

4-round incoercible MPC protocol iMPC:

The CRS: $\mathrm{CRS} = (\mathrm{CRS_{DE}}, \mathrm{CRS_{aMPC}})$, where $\mathrm{CRS_{DE}}$ is a CRS of deniable encryption, and $\mathrm{CRS_{aMPC}}$ is a CRS of adaptively secure MPC protocol.
Inputs: inputs $x_1, \ldots, x_n$ of parties $P_1, \ldots, P_n$, respectively;
Randomness: each party P_i generates the following random values:

1. $s_{i,j,1}, r_{i,j,1}, j \neq i$, which is sender and receiver randomness of DE, used to send and receive aMPC messages of round 1;
2. $s_{i,j,2}, r_{i,j,2}, j \neq i$, which is sender and receiver randomness of DE, used to send and receive aMPC messages of round 2;
3. $s_{\mathrm{aMPC},i}$, which is randomness of party P_i in the underlying aMPC protocol.

In addition, party P_1 chooses at random:

1. seed, which will be used by parties to generate coins of the simulator r_{Sim} and fake seed$'$;
2. $s_{1,j,3}, j \neq 1$, which is sender randomness of DE used to send seed;

Finally, parties P_i, $i \neq 1$ generate $r_{1,i,3}$, which is receiver randomness of DE, used to receive seed.
We denote all randomness generated by each party P_i by s_i.
The protocol:

1. **Round 1:** Each party P_i sends to each other party P_j, $j \neq i$, the following:
   $$a1_{i,j} = \mathrm{DE.msg1}(\mathrm{CRS_{DE}}; s_{i,j,1}).$$
2. **Round 2:** Each party P_i sends to each other party P_j, $j \neq i$, the following:
   - $a2_{i,j} = \mathrm{DE.msg2}(\mathrm{CRS_{DE}}; r_{i,j,1}, a1_{j,i}).$
   - $b1_{i,j} = \mathrm{DE.msg1}(\mathrm{CRS_{DE}}; s_{i,j,2}).$
   In addition, P_1 sends to each other party P_j, $j \neq 1$, the following:
   - $c1_{1,j} = \mathrm{DE.msg1}(\mathrm{CRS_{DE}}; s_{1,j,3}).$
3. **Round 3:** Each party P_i for each $j \neq i$ computes $\{M1_{i,1}, \ldots, M1_{i,n}\} \leftarrow \mathrm{aMPC.msg1}(\mathrm{CRS_{aMPC}}; x_i; s_{\mathrm{aMPC},i})$, and sends the following:
   - $a3_{i,j} = \mathrm{DE.msg3}(\mathrm{CRS_{DE}}; s_{i,j,1}, M1_{i,j}, a1_{i,j}, a2_{j,i}).$
   - $b2_{i,j} = \mathrm{DE.msg2}(\mathrm{CRS_{DE}}; r_{i,j,2}, b1_{j,i}).$
   In addition, each party P_i except P_1 sends to P_1 the following:
   - $c2_{i,1} = \mathrm{DE.msg2}(\mathrm{CRS_{DE}}; r_{1,i,3}, c1_{1,i}).$
4. **Round 4:** Each party P_i, for each $j \neq i$, computes $M1_{j,i} \leftarrow \mathrm{DE.Dec}(\mathrm{CRS_{DE}}; r_{j,i,1}, a1_{j,i}, a2_{i,j}, a3_{j,i}).$ Next for each $j \neq i$ it computes $\{M2_{i,1}, \ldots, M2_{i,n}\} \leftarrow \mathrm{aMPC.msg2}(\mathrm{CRS_{aMPC}}; x_i, M1_{1,i}, \ldots, M1_{n,i}; s_{\mathrm{aMPC},i})$, and sends the following:
   - $b3_{i,j} = \mathrm{DE.msg3}(\mathrm{CRS_{DE}}; s_{i,j,2}, M2_{i,j}, b1_{i,j}, b2_{j,i}).$
   In addition, P_1 sends to each other party P_j, $j \neq 1$, the following:
   - $c3_{1,j} = \mathrm{DE.msg3}(\mathrm{CRS_{DE}}; s_{1,j,3}, \mathrm{seed}, c1_{1,j}, c2_{j,1}).$
5. **Evaluation:** Each party P_i, for each $j \neq i$, computes $M2_{j,i} \leftarrow \mathrm{DE.Dec}(\mathrm{CRS_{DE}}; r_{j,i,2}, b1_{j,i}, b2_{i,j}, b3_{j,i}).$ Next for each $j \neq i$ it computes $y \leftarrow \mathrm{aMPC.Eval}(\mathrm{CRS_{aMPC}}; x_i, M1_{1,i}, \ldots, M1_{n,i}, M2_{1,i}, \ldots, M2_{n,i}; s_{\mathrm{aMPC},i})$. It sets y to be its output in the protocol.

By $\pi = \mathrm{iMPC}(\mathrm{CRS}, (x_1, s_1), \ldots, (x_n, s_n)) = (\{a1_{i,j}, a2_{i,j}, a3_{i,j}\}_{i \neq j}, \{b1_{i,j}, b2_{i,j}, b3_{i,j}\}_{i \neq j}, \{c1_{1,j}, c2_{j,1}, c3_{1,j}\}_{j \neq 1})$ we denote the transcript of our protocol.
By $\sigma = \mathrm{aMPC}(\mathrm{CRS_{aMPC}}, (x_1, s_{\mathrm{aMPC},1}), \ldots, (x_n, s_{\mathrm{aMPC},n})) = (\{M1_{i,j}, M2_{i,j}\}_{i \neq j})$ we denote the transcript of underlying adaptive MPC protocol aMPC.

Fig. 6. 4-round incoercible MPC protocol.

Faking procedure of party P_i, $i = 1, \ldots, n$

Inputs: P_i's true input x_i, fake input x_i', true output y, real random coins s_i, and the protocol transcript π.

1. **learning the seed:** P_1 knows the seed seed (which it generated). For $i \neq 1$, P_i computes seed $\leftarrow$ DE.Dec($\text{CRS}_{\text{DE}}; r_{1,i,3}, c1_{1,i}, c2_{i,1}, c3_{1,i}$).
2. **expanding the seed:** P_i computes prg(seed) and parses the result as $r_{\text{Sim}} \| \text{seed}'$, where $|\text{seed}| = |\text{seed}'|$.
3. **computing fake transcript:** P_i computes the fake transcript and state $(\sigma', \text{state}) \leftarrow$ aMPC.Sim($\text{CRS}_{\text{aMPC}}, y, r_{\text{Sim}}$) of the underlying 2-round MPC protocol. Let $\sigma' = (\{M1_{i,j}', M2_{i,j}'\}_{i \neq j})$.
4. **computing fake coins of the underlying MPC:** P_i computes the fake coins $s_{\text{aMPC},i}' \leftarrow$ aMPC.Sim$_i$($\text{CRS}_{\text{aMPC}}, \text{state}, x_i', y$) of the underlying MPC protocol, using the local simulator.
5. **computing fake coins of deniable encryption:** P_i computes the fake coins for each instance of deniable encryption as follows:

   $s_{i,j,1}' \leftarrow$ DE.SFake($\text{CRS}_{\text{DE}}, s_{i,j,1}, M1_{i,j}, M1_{i,j}', a1_{i,j}, a2_{j,i}, a3_{i,j}; \cdot$), to claim that it sent $M1_{i,j}'$ instead of $M1_{i,j}$;

   $s_{i,j,2}' \leftarrow$ DE.SFake($\text{CRS}_{\text{DE}}, s_{i,j,2}, M2_{i,j}, M2_{i,j}', b1_{i,j}, b2_{j,i}, b3_{i,j}; \cdot$), to claim that it sent $M2_{i,j}'$ instead of $M2_{i,j}$;

   $r_{i,j,1}' \leftarrow$ DE.RFake($\text{CRS}_{\text{DE}}, r_{i,j,1}, M1_{j,i}, M1_{j,i}', a1_{j,i}, a2_{i,j}, a3_{j,i}; \cdot$), to claim that it received $M1_{j,i}'$ instead of $M1_{j,i}$;

   $r_{i,j,2}' \leftarrow$ DE.RFake($\text{CRS}_{\text{DE}}, r_{i,j,2}, M2_{j,i}, M2_{j,i}', b1_{j,i}, b2_{i,j}, b3_{j,i}; \cdot$), to claim that it received $M2_{j,i}'$ instead of $M2_{j,i}$.

   Further, if $i = 1$, then for each $j \neq 1$ the party computes:

   $s_{1,j,3}' \leftarrow$ DE.SFake($\text{CRS}_{\text{DE}}, s_{1,j,3}, \text{seed}, \text{seed}', c1_{1,j}, c2_{j,1}, c3_{1,j}; \cdot$), to claim that it sent seed' instead of seed.

   If $i \neq 1$, then P_i computes

   $r_{1,i,3}' \leftarrow$ DE.RFake($\text{CRS}_{\text{DE}}, r_{1,i,3}, \text{seed}, \text{seed}', c1_{1,i}, c2_{i,1}, c3_{1,i}; \cdot$), to claim that it received seed' instead of seed.

The output of the faking procedure: Finally, P_i gives the adversary its fake internal state s_i', where:

- If $i \neq 1$, $s_i' = \{s_{i,j,1}'\}_{j \neq i}, \{r_{i,j,1}'\}_{j \neq i}, \{s_{i,j,2}'\}_{j \neq i}, \{r_{i,j,2}'\}_{j \neq i}, \{r_{1,i,3}'\}, s_{\text{aMPC},i}'$.
- If $i = 1$, $s_i' = \{s_{i,j,1}'\}_{j \neq i}, \{r_{i,j,1}'\}_{j \neq i}, \{s_{i,j,2}'\}_{j \neq i}, \{r_{i,j,2}'\}_{j \neq i}, \{s_{1,j,3}'\}_{j \neq 1}, s_{\text{aMPC},i}', \text{seed}'$.

(Note that all other information which P_i should know in the honest execution, e.g. seed' or $M1_{i,j}'$, can be derived by the adversary using random coins s_i', input x_i', the transcript π, and the CRS.)

Fig. 7. Faking procedure of party P_i, $i = 1, \ldots, n$

Let $x_1, \ldots, x_n$ and $x_1', \ldots, x_n'$ be some inputs to the protocol, and let y be some output. Consider the following distributions:

- Hyb_{Real}: this is the distribution corresponding to the real execution of the protocol with inputs $x_1', \ldots, x_n'$, where parties disclose their *true* inputs and randomness.

Simulation of communication

Inputs given to simulate the communication: CRS; output of the protocol y

1. **computing simulated transcript:** the simulator chooses r_{Sim} at random and computes the simulated transcript and state $(\sigma', \text{state}) \leftarrow \text{aMPC.Sim}(\text{CRS}_{\text{aMPC}}, y, r_{\text{Sim}})$ of the underlying MPC protocol. Let $\sigma' = (\{M1'_{i,j}, M2'_{i,j}\}_{i \neq j})$.

2. **computing messages of** π: the simulator chooses seed$'$ at random. It also chooses $\{s_{i,j,1}\}_{j \neq i}, \{r_{i,j,1}\}_{j \neq i}, \{s_{i,j,2}\}_{j \neq i}, \{r_{i,j,2}\}_{j \neq i}, \{r_{1,j,3}\}_{j \neq 1}, \{s_{1,j,3}\}_{j \neq 1}$ uniformly at random, and uses these randomness to compute messages of deniable encryption, $(\{a1_{i,j}, a2_{i,j}, a3_{i,j}\}_{i \neq j}, \{b1_{i,j}, b2_{i,j}, b3_{i,j}\}_{i \neq j}, \{c1_{1,j}, c2_{j,1}, c3_{1,j}\}_{j \neq 1})$, encrypting $M1'_{i,j}, M2'_{i,j}$, seed$'$, respectively.

3. **the output of the simulator:** The simulator outputs the simulated communication $\pi' = (\{a1_{i,j}, a2_{i,j}, a3_{i,j}\}_{i \neq j}, \{b1_{i,j}, b2_{i,j}, b3_{i,j}\}_{i \neq j}, \{c1_{1,j}, c2_{j,1}, c3_{1,j}\}_{j \neq 1})$.

Simulation of coercion of P_i

Inputs additionally given to simulate the coercion of the party P_i: P_i's input x'_i (without the information whether this input is real or fake)

1. **computing fake coins of the underlying MPC:** the simulator computes the fake coins $s'_{\text{aMPC},i} \leftarrow \text{aMPC.Sim}_i(\text{CRS}_{\text{aMPC}}, \text{state}, x'_i, y; \cdot)$ of the underlying MPC protocol, using the local simulator.

2. **The output of the simulator:** The simulator gives the adversary simulated internal state s'_i of P_i, where:
   - If $i \neq 1$, $s'_i = \{s_{i,j,1}\}_{j \neq i}, \{r_{i,j,1}\}_{j \neq i}, \{s_{i,j,2}\}_{j \neq i}, \{r_{i,j,2}\}_{j \neq i}, \{r_{1,i,3}\}, s'_{\text{aMPC},i}$.
   - If $i = 1$, $s'_i = \{s_{i,j,1}\}_{j \neq i}, \{r_{i,j,1}\}_{j \neq i}, \{s_{i,j,2}\}_{j \neq i}, \{r_{i,j,2}\}_{j \neq i}, \{s_{1,j,3}\}_{j \neq 1}, s'_{\text{aMPC},i}, \text{seed}'$.

   (Note that all other information which P_i should know in the honest execution, e.g. seed$'$ or $M1'_{i,j}$, can be derived by the adversary using random coins s'_i, input x'_i, the transcript π', and the CRS.)

Fig. 8. Simulation

- Hyb$_{\text{Fake}}$: this is the distribution corresponding to the real execution of the protocol with inputs $x_1, \ldots, x_n$, where parties disclose *fake* inputs $x'_1, \ldots, x'_n$, output y, and fake randomness.
- Hyb$_{\text{Sim}}$: this is the distribution corresponding to the simulation from Fig. 8, where the simulator is given output y and claimed inputs $x'_1, \ldots, x'_n$.

We need to show the following:

1. If $x'_1, \ldots, x'_n$ and y are consistent (i.e. $f(x'_1, \ldots, x'_n) = y$), then we need to show that Hyb$_{\text{Sim}} \approx$ Hyb$_{\text{Real}}$ and Hyb$_{\text{Sim}} \approx$ Hyb$_{\text{Fake}}$.
2. If $x'_1, \ldots, x'_n$ and y are not consistent, then we need to show that Hyb$_{\text{Sim}} \approx$ Hyb$_{\text{Fake}}$.

We show this below. First, we show indistinguishability between Hyb$_{\text{Sim}} \approx$ Hyb$_{\text{Fake}}$, for any values $x_1, \ldots, x_n, x'_1, \ldots, x'_n$, and y:

- $\mathsf{Hyb}_{\mathsf{Fake}}$. We start with the distribution corresponding to the real-world execution of the protocol, where parties fake their random coins upon coercion. In other words, the adversary sees CRS, π, and x_i', s_i' for each i, generated as in Figs. 6, 7. In particular, the truly sent transcript σ of the underlying MPC is a transcript on inputs x_i; however, parties claim that they instead sent (simulated) transcript σ', which appears consistent with fake inputs x_i'.
- Hyb_1. In this hybrid P_1 sends seed$'$ instead of seed inside $\{c1_{1,j}, c2_{j,1}, c3_{1,j}\}_{j \neq 1}$, and parties (both senders and receivers) give the adversary true randomness for this deniable encryption (instead of faking it to seed$'$). Indistinguishability between this and the previous distribution holds by $n-1$ invocations of bideniability of encryption for plaintexts seed and seed$'$.
- Hyb_2. In this hybrid we switch $r_{\mathsf{Sim}}\|$seed$'$ from prg(seed) to uniformly random. Indistinguishability holds by security of a prg. Note that seed is not used anywhere else in the distribution, thus the reduction is possible.
- $\mathsf{Hyb}_{\mathsf{Sim}}$. In this hybrid we set $\{a1_{i,j}, a2_{i,j}, a3_{i,j}\}_{i \neq j}$ to encrypt 1-round messages of simulated σ' (consistent with fake x_i'), instead of encrypting 1-round messages of real transcript σ (consistent with x_i). Also, all parties give true randomness $\{s_{i,j,1}\}_{j \neq i}$, $\{r_{i,j,1}\}_{j \neq i}$, instead of giving fake randomness consistent with σ'.

  Similarly, we change $\{b1_{i,j}, b2_{i,j}, b3_{i,j}\}_{i \neq j}$ to encrypt 1-round messages of simulated σ' (consistent with fake x_i'), instead of encrypting 1-round messages of real transcript σ (consistent with x_i). Also, all parties give true randomness $\{s_{i,j,2}\}_{j \neq i}$, $\{r_{i,j,2}\}_{j \neq i}$, instead of giving fake randomness consistent with σ'.

  Indistinguishability between this and the previous distribution holds by $2n(n-1)$ invocations of bideniability of encryption, where plaintexts are messages of σ and σ'.

  Note that this is the simulated distribution.

Further, for the case when $f(x_1', \ldots, x_n') = y$, in one last step we show that $\mathsf{Hyb}_{\mathsf{Sim}} \approx \mathsf{Hyb}_{\mathsf{Real}}$:

- $\mathsf{Hyb}_{\mathsf{Real}}$. Compared to $\mathsf{Hyb}_{\mathsf{Sim}}$, we switch the messages of aMPC, encrypted inside deniable encryption, from simulated σ' to real σ, which is the true transcript of aMPC on inputs x_i'. In addition, parties reveal their true randomness $s_{\mathsf{aMPC},i}$ instead of computing simulated $s_{\mathsf{aMPC},i}'$ consistent with x_i' using the local simulator aMPC.Sim$_i$.

  Indistinguishability between this and the simulation follows from adaptive security of aMPC. Note that indeed r_{Sim}, randomness of the simulator, is not used anywhere else in the distribution.

  This distribution corresponds to the real execution of the protocol on inputs x_i', where parties disclose their true randomness upon being coerced.

  This concludes the security proof.

5   Incoercible MPC with Lazy Parties is Impossible

In this section we describe our impossibility result for incoercible MPC protocols with a certain communication pattern. We consider the synchronous model of communication, where parties send their messages in rounds. We call a party *lazy*, if it sends its messages only in the first and in the last round of the protocol, but not in any other round[12]. We show that a protocol for 3 or more parties cannot be incoercible, as long as there is at least one lazy party Z, and there is another party (different from Z) which receives the output.

In particular, this impossibility rules out protocols with the following communication structure, which is a natural extention of a "ping-pong" communication of 3-message 2PC to a multiparty setting: assume just one party receives the output; we call this party the receiver, and call all other parties the senders. Then the communication proceeds as follows:

- In round 1 the senders send out their messages to everybody;
- In round 2 the receiver sends its messages to the senders;
- In round 3 the senders send out their messages to everybody[13].

Our impossibility is based on the fact that in an incoercible protocol with lazy party Z it is possible to do a variation of a residual function attack, similar to impossibility of standard (non-incoercible) non-interactive MPC. Concretely, we show that lazy party Z can always pick an input x' different from its real input x and generate a different last message of the protocol corresponding to new input x', such that the resulting transcript will be a valid transcript for this new input x', as if Z used x' even in the first message (despite the fact that in reality its first message was generated using x). As a result, the adversary may coerce (or even corrupt) Z together with some output-receiving party and evaluate the function on any possible input of Z, thus compromising security of other parties.

Theorem 6. *Let $n \geq 3$, and assume there exists an n-party protocol for evaluating function $f(x_1, \ldots, x_n)$, such that P_1 is lazy and P_n receives the output. Further, assume it is secure against up to one coercion and up to two corruptions. Then the function f is such that for any inputs $x_1, \ldots, x_n$ it is possible, given x_1, x_n, and $f(x_1, \ldots, x_n)$, to compute $f(x, x_2, \ldots, x_n)$ in polynomial time for any x of the same length as x_1.*

Note that, while the theorem statement also holds for the case of 2 parties, it doesn't imply any impossibility since for any 2-input function f it is always possible to compute $f(\cdot, x_2)$ given x_1, x_2, and thus the theorem doesn't impose any restrictions on functions f which can be computed incoercibly using 2-party protocols.

Proof of Theorem 6. Without loss of generality we assume that the lazy party is P_1, and party which receives the output is P_n. Further, we assume that P_1 is the first to send its messages in round 1, and the last to send its messages in round N.

Let us denote the randomness of P_1 by r_1, the concatenated randomness of all other parties by $R = r_2 || \ldots || r_n$, the input of P_1 by x_1, the concatenated input of all other parties by $X = x_2 || \ldots || x_n$. In addition, let X^0 denote some fixed set of inputs such

---

[12] In particular, when the protocol requires only 2 rounds, each party is lazy by definition.

[13] Note that in standard, non-deniable MPC the last message doesn't need to be sent to parties who don't receive the output. However, in deniable MPC parties who don't get the output may still need the last message in order to fake.

that $|X| = |X^0|$, e.g. all-zero inputs $0^{|X|}$. Let NMF_i denote the next message function of the protocol for party 1 in round i. Let $\mathsf{Eval}(x_n; transcript; r_n)$ denote the output evaluation function of party P_n which takes as input its randomness r_n, input x_n, and all communication in the protocol. Let $\alpha = \mathsf{NMF}_1(x_1; r_1)$ denote the concatenated messages sent by P_1 to all other parties in round 1, $, =, (\alpha; X; R)$ denote the concatenated messages sent by parties $P_2, \ldots, P_n$ in all rounds, $,_{N-1}$ denote , except for messages of the last round, and $\beta = \mathsf{NMF}_N(x_1, ,_{N-1}; r_1)$ denote the concatenated messages sent by P_1 to all other parties in round N. Finally, let $\mathsf{Fake}_1(r_1, x_1, x_1', , ; \rho)$ denote the faking algorithm of party P_1, which takes as input its true coins and input r_1, x_1, desired fake input x_1', and ,, all communication sent to P_1. Fake_1 could be deterministic or randomized; without loss of generality we assume that it is randomized using its own random coins ρ.

Consider the following algorithm NewMessage (Fig. 9) which for any x_1' allows P_1 to generate a different β' such that $(\alpha, , , \beta')$ is a valid transcript resulting in the output $f(x_1', X)$. The intuition behind this procedure is as follows: First, P_1 computes a transcript which starts with the same α but continues with a different $\tilde{,}$ (computed under freshly chosen randomness of other parties and fixed inputs X^0). Next, it runs its faking algorithm to generate fake coins r_1' which make this transcript look consistent with x_1' (in particular, this makes r_1', x_1' look like valid coins and input for α, even though α was generated under x_1). Finally, it uses fake r_1' to generate its last message β' using the original communication , and new input x_1'. In the following Lemma 1 we claim that β', together with the original communication $(\alpha,)$, forms a valid transcript for inputs x_1, X which will be evaluated correctly by the output-receiving party:

Algorithm NewMessage

$\mathsf{NewMessage}(x_1, r_1, x_1', \alpha, \mathsf{com}; \rho)$
Inputs: input x_1 and randomness r_1 of P_1 in the MPC protocol; new desired input x_1'; communication of P_1 in round 1 α, communication of all other parties com; local random coins $\rho = \rho_1 \| \rho_2$.
Constants: arbitrary fixed input X^0 of length $|X|$, e.g. all-zero input $X^0 = 0^{|X|}$.

- Compute $\widetilde{\mathsf{com}} = \mathsf{com}(\alpha; X^0; \rho_1)$.
- Compute $r_1' \leftarrow \mathsf{Fake}_1(r_1, x_1, x_1', \widetilde{\mathsf{com}}; \rho_2)$.
- Output $\beta' = \mathsf{NMF}_N(x_1', \mathsf{com}_{N-1}; r_1')$.

Fig. 9. Algorithm NewMessage to generate the last message consistent with a different x_1'.

Lemma 1. *Let* $\alpha, , , \beta'$ *be generated as described above, and let the protocol be secure against the coercion of* P_1. *Then for any* f, x_1, X, x_1', *with overwhelming probability over the choice of* r_1, R, ρ *it holds that* $\mathsf{Eval}(x_n; \alpha, , , \beta'; r_n) = f(x_1', X)$.

We defer the proof of Lemma 1 to the full version.

Now we finish the proof of the Theorem 6. We claim that the adversary who corrupts P_1 and P_n in the real world can compute $f(x, x_2, \ldots, x_n)$ for any input x (of the same length as x_1), where $x_1, \ldots, x_n$ are inputs of the parties in the protocol. Indeed, the adversary can do so in two steps: first it corrupts P_1 to learn r_1 and x_1 and runs $\beta' \leftarrow \mathsf{NewMessage}(x_1, r_1, x, \alpha, , ; \rho)$ for any desired input x and random ρ (as before, $\alpha, ,$ is the communication of P_1 in round 1 and of all other parties). Next it corrupts P_n to learn r_n and computes $\mathsf{Eval}(x_n; \alpha, , , \beta'; r_n)$, which is with overwhelming probability equal to $f(x, x_2, \ldots, x_n)$, as shown in the Lemma 1. Note that in the ideal world the adversary who only corrupts P_1 and P_n and learns x_1, x_n, and $f(x_1, \ldots, x_n)$ cannot compute residual function $f(\cdot, x_2, \ldots, x_n)$ (except for very special functions f), and therefore the adversary in the real world has strictly more power. This finishes the proof of the Theorem 6.

Finally, we note that a similar proof can be made in case when the adversary coerces P_1 and P_n, instead of corrupting them.

References

[AOZZ15] Alwen, J., Ostrovsky, R., Zhou, H.-S., Zikas, V.: Incoercible multi-party computation and universally composable receipt-free voting. In: Gennaro, R., Robshaw, M. (eds.) CRYPTO 2015. LNCS, vol. 9216, pp. 763–780. Springer, Heidelberg (2015). https://doi.org/10.1007/978-3-662-48000-7_37

[BCH12] Bitansky, N., Canetti, R., Halevi, S.: Leakage-tolerant interactive protocols. In: Cramer, R. (ed.) TCC 2012. LNCS, vol. 7194, pp. 266–284. Springer, Heidelberg (2012). https://doi.org/10.1007/978-3-642-28914-9_15

[BH92] Beaver, D., Haber, S.: Cryptographic protocols provably secure against dynamic adversaries. In: Rueppel, R.A. (ed.) EUROCRYPT 1992. LNCS, vol. 658, pp. 307–323. Springer, Heidelberg (1993). https://doi.org/10.1007/3-540-47555-9_26

[BNNO11] Bendlin, R., Nielsen, J.B., Nordholt, P.S., Orlandi, C.: Lower and upper bounds for deniable public-key encryption. In: Lee, D.H., Wang, X. (eds.) ASIACRYPT 2011. LNCS, vol. 7073, pp. 125–142. Springer, Heidelberg (2011). https://doi.org/10.1007/978-3-642-25385-0_7

[BT94] Benaloh, J.C., Tuinstra, D.: Receipt-free secret-ballot elections (extended abstract). In: Proceedings of the Twenty-Sixth Annual ACM Symposium on Theory of Computing, 23–25 May 1994, Montréal, Québec, Canada, pp. 544–553 (1994)

[CDMW09] Choi, S.G., Dachman-Soled, D., Malkin, T., Wee, H.: Improved non-committing encryption with applications to adaptively secure protocols. In: Matsui, M. (ed.) ASIACRYPT 2009. LNCS, vol. 5912, pp. 287–302. Springer, Heidelberg (2009). https://doi.org/10.1007/978-3-642-10366-7_17

[CDNO96] Canetti, R., Dwork, C., Naor, M., Ostrovsky, R.: Deniable encryption. IACR Cryptol. ePrint Archive **1996**, 2 (1996)

[CG96] Canetti, R., Gennaro, R.: Incoercible multiparty computation (extended abstract). In: 37th Annual Symposium on Foundations of Computer Science, FOCS '96, Burlington, Vermont, USA, 14–16 October 1996, pp. 504–513 (1996)

[CGP15] Canetti, R., Goldwasser, S., Poburinnaya, O.: Adaptively secure two-party computation from indistinguishability obfuscation. In: Dodis, Y., Nielsen, J.B. (eds.) TCC 2015. LNCS, vol. 9015, pp. 557–585. Springer, Heidelberg (2015). https://doi.org/10.1007/978-3-662-46497-7_22

[CLOS02] Canetti, R., Lindell, Y., Ostrovsky, R., Sahai, A.: Universally composable two-party and multi-party secure computation. In: Proceedings on 34th Annual ACM Symposium on Theory of Computing, May 19–21 2002, Montréal, Québec, Canada, pp. 494–503 (2002)

[CPP20] Canetti, R., Park, S., Poburinnaya, O.: Fully deniable interactive encryption. In: Micciancio, D., Ristenpart, T. (eds.) CRYPTO 2020. LNCS, vol. 12170, pp. 807–835. Springer, Cham (2020). https://doi.org/10.1007/978-3-030-56784-2_27

[CPV17] Canetti, R., Poburinnaya, O., Venkitasubramaniam, M.: Better two-round adaptive multi-party computation. In: Fehr, S. (ed.) PKC 2017. LNCS, vol. 10175, pp. 396–427. Springer, Heidelberg (2017). https://doi.org/10.1007/978-3-662-54388-7_14

[DKR14] Dachman-Soled, D., Katz, J., Rao, V.: Adaptively secure, universally composable, multi-party computation in constant rounds. IACR Cryptol. ePrint Archive **2014**, 858 (2014)

[DN00] Damgård, I., Nielsen, J.B.: Improved non-committing encryption schemes based on a general complexity assumption. In: Bellare, M. (ed.) CRYPTO 2000. LNCS, vol. 1880, pp. 432–450. Springer, Heidelberg (2000). https://doi.org/10.1007/3-540-44598-6_27

[GMW87] Goldreich, O., Micali, S., Wigderson, A.: How to play any mental game or A completeness theorem for protocols with honest majority. In: Proceedings of the 19th Annual ACM Symposium on Theory of Computing, 1987, New York, USA, pp. 218–229 (1987)

[HOR15] Hemenway, B., Ostrovsky, R., Rosen, A.: Non-committing encryption from Φ-hiding. In: Theory of Cryptography - 12th Theory of Cryptography Conference, TCC 2015, Warsaw, Poland, 23–25 March 2015, Proceedings, Part I, pp. 591–608 (2015)

[HORR16] Hemenway, B., Ostrovsky, R., Richelson, S., Rosen, A.: Adaptive security with quasi-optimal rate. In: Kushilevitz, E., Malkin, T. (eds.) TCC 2016. LNCS, vol. 9562, pp. 525–541. Springer, Heidelberg (2016). https://doi.org/10.1007/978-3-662-49096-9_22

[MN06] Moran, T., Naor, M.: Receipt-free universally-verifiable voting with everlasting privacy. In: Advances in Cryptology - CRYPTO 2006, 26th Annual International Cryptology Conference, Santa Barbara, California, USA, 20–24 August 2006, Proceedings, pp. 373–392 (2006)

[SW14] Sahai, A., Waters, B.: How to use indistinguishability obfuscation: deniable encryption, and more. In: Symposium on Theory of Computing, STOC 2014, New York, NY, USA, May 31 - June 03 2014, pp. 475–484 (2014)

[Yao86] Yao, A.C.: How to generate and exchange secrets. In: 27th Annual Symposium on Foundations of Computer Science (SFCS 1986), pp. 162–167 (1986)

[YKT19] Yoshida, Y., Kitagawa, F., Tanaka, K.: Non-committing encryption with quasi-optimal ciphertext-rate based on the DDH problem. IACR Cryptol. ePrint Arch. **2019**, 1151 (2019)

Synchronous Constructive Cryptography

Chen-Da Liu-Zhang$^{(\boxtimes)}$ and Ueli Maurer

ETH Zurich, Zürich, Switzerland
{lichen,maurer}@inf.ethz.ch

Abstract. This paper proposes a simple synchronous composable security framework as an instantiation of the Constructive Cryptography framework, aiming to capture minimally, without unnecessary artefacts, exactly what is needed to state synchronous security guarantees. The objects of study are specifications (i.e., sets) of systems, and traditional security properties like consistency and validity can naturally be understood as specifications, thus unifying composable and property-based definitions. The framework's simplicity is in contrast to current composable frameworks for synchronous computation which are built on top of an asynchronous framework (e.g. the UC framework), thus not only inheriting artefacts and complex features used to handle asynchronous communication, but adding additional overhead to capture synchronous communication.

As a second, independent contribution we demonstrate how secure (synchronous) multi-party computation protocols can be understood as constructing a computer that allows a set of parties to perform an arbitrary, on-going computation. An interesting aspect is that the instructions of the computation need not be fixed before the protocol starts but can also be determined during an on-going computation, possibly depending on previous outputs.

1 Introduction

1.1 Composable Security

One can distinguish two different types of security statements about multi-party protocols. *Stand-alone security* considers only the protocol at hand and does not capture (at least not explicitly) what it means to use the protocol in a larger context. This can cause major problems. For example, if one intuitively understands an r-round broadcast protocol as implementing a functionality where the sender inputs a value and r rounds later everybody learns this value, then one missed the point that a dishonest party learns the value already in the first round. Therefore a naive randomness generation protocol, in which each party broadcasts (using a broadcast protocol) a random string and then all parties compute the XOR of all the strings, is insecure even though naively it may look secure [17]. There are also more surprising and involved examples of failures when using stand-alone secure protocols in larger contexts.

The goal of *composable security* frameworks is to capture all aspects of a protocol that can be relevant in any possible application; hence the term *universal composability* [6]. While composable security is more difficult to achieve

© International Association for Cryptologic Research 2020
R. Pass and K. Pietrzak (Eds.): TCC 2020, LNCS 12551, pp. 439–472, 2020.
https://doi.org/10.1007/978-3-030-64378-2_16

than some form of stand-alone security, one can argue that it is ultimately necessary. Indeed, one can sometimes reinterpret stand-alone results in a composable framework. There exist several frameworks for defining and reasoning about composable security (e.g. [6,11,19,24,29,32,34]).

1.2   Composable Synchronous Models

One can classify results on distributed protocols according to the underlying interaction model. Synchronous models, where parties are synchronized and proceed in rounds, were first considered in the literature because they are relatively simple in terms of the design and analysis of protocols. Asynchronous models are closer to the physical reality, but designing them and proving their security is significantly more involved, and the achievable results (e.g. the fraction of tolerable dishonest parties) are significantly weaker than for a synchronous model. However, synchronous models are nevertheless justified because if one assumes a maximal latency of all communication channels as well as sufficiently well-synchronized clocks, then one can execute a synchronous protocol over an asynchronous network.

Most composable treatments of synchronous protocols are in (versions of) the UC framework by Canetti [6], which is an inherently asynchronous model. The models presented in [6,18,22,33] propose different approaches to model synchronous communication on top of the UC framework [6]. These approaches inherit the complexity of the UC framework designed to capture full asynchrony. Another approach was introduced with the Timing Model [12,14,21]. This model integrates a notion of time in an intuitive manner, but as noted in [22] fails to exactly capture the guarantees expected from a synchronous network. A similar approach was proposed in [2], which modifies the asynchronous reactive-simulatability framework [3] by adding an explicit time port to each automaton.

Despite the large number of synchronous composable frameworks, the overhead created when using them is still too large. For example, when using a model built on top of UC, one typically needs to consider clock/synchronization functionalities, activation tokens, message scheduling, etc. Researchers wish to make composable statements, but using these models often turn out to be a burden and create huge overhead. As a consequence, papers written in synchronous UC models tend to be rather informal: the descriptions of the functionalities are incomplete, clock functionalities are missing, protocols are underspecified and the proofs are often made at an intuitive level. This leaves the question:

Can one design a composable framework targeted to minimally capture synchronous protocols?

People have considered capturing composable frameworks for restricted settings (e.g. [7,36]), but to the best of our knowledge, there is no composable framework that is targeted to minimally capture any form of synchronous setting.

1.3 Multi-party Computation

In the literature on secure multi-party computation (MPC) protocols, of which secure function evaluation (SFE) is a special case, most of the results are for the synchronous model as well as stand-alone security, even though intuitively most protocols seem to provide composable security. To the best of our knowledge, the first paper proving the composable security of a classical SFE protocol is [8], where the security of the famous GMW-protocol [15] is proved. The protocol assumes trusted setup, and security is obtained in the UC framework. In [1], the security of the famous BGW-protocol [4] is proved in the plain model. With the results in [22, 23], one can prove security in the UC framework.

1.4 Contributions of this Paper

A guiding principle in this work is to strive for minimality and to avoid unnecessary artefacts, thus lowering the entrance fee for getting into the field of composable security and also bringing the reasoning about composable security for synchronous protocols closer to being tractable by formal methods.

Our contributions are two-fold. First, we introduce a new composable framework to capture settings where parties have synchronized clocks (in particular, traditional synchronous protocols), and illustrate the framework with a few simple examples. Our focus is on the meaningful class of information-theoretic security as well as static corruption. However, in Sect. 9, we discuss how one can further extend the framework.

As a second contribution, we prove the composable security of Maurer's simple-MPC protocol [27] and demonstrate that it perfectly constructs a versatile computer resource which can be (re-)programmed during the execution. Compared to [1, 8], our treatment is significantly simpler for two reasons. First, the protocol of [27] is simpler than the BGW-protocol. Second, and more importantly, the simplicity of our framework allows to prove security of the protocols without the overhead of asynchronous models: we do not deal with activation tokens, message scheduling, running time, etc.

Synchronous Constructive Cryptography. Our framework is an instantiation of the Constructive Cryptography framework [28–30], for specific instantiations of the resource and converter concepts. Moreover, we introduce a new type of construction notion, parameterized by the set Z of potentially dishonest parties, allowing to capture the guarantees for every such dishonest set Z. An often considered special case is that nothing is guaranteed if Z contains too many parties.

Synchronous resources are very simple: They are (random) systems where the alphabet is list-valued. That is, a system takes a complete input list and produces a complete output list. Parallel composition of resources is naturally defined. There is no need to talk about a scheduler or activation patterns.

To allow that dishonest parties can potentially make their inputs depend on some side information of the round, we let one round r of the protocol correspond to two rounds, $r.a$ and $r.b$ (called semi-rounds). Honest parties provide the

round input in semi-round $r.a$ and the dishonest parties receive some information already in the same semi-round $r.a$. In semi-round $r.b$, the dishonest parties
give their inputs and everybody receives the round's output.[1]

The framework is aimed at being minimal and differs from other frameworks
in several ways. One aspect is that the synchronous communication network is
simply a resource and not part of the framework; hence it can be modelled arbitrarily, allowing to capture incomplete networks and various types of channels
(e.g., delay channels, secure, authenticated, insecure, etc.).

We demonstrate the usage of our model with three examples: a two-party
protocol to construct a common randomness resource (Sect. 5), the protocol
introduced in [5] to construct a broadcast resource (Sect. A), and the simple
MPC protocol [27] as the construction of a computer resource (Sects. 7 and 8).

The Computer Resource. We introduce a system Computer which captures
intuitively what traditional MPC protocols like GMW, BGW or CCD [4,9,13,
15,27,35] achieve. Traditionally, in a secure function evaluation protocol among
n parties, the function to compute is modelled as an arithmetic circuit assumed
to be known in advance. However, the same protocols are intuitively secure even
if parties do not know in advance the entire circuit. It is enough that parties
have agreement on the next instruction to execute.

We capture such guarantees in an interactive computer resource, similar to a
(programmable) old-school calculator with a small instruction set (read, write,
addition, and multiplication in our case), an array of value-registers, and an
instruction queue. The resource has n interfaces. The interfaces $1, \ldots, n-1$ are
used to give inputs to the resource and receive outputs from the resource. Interface n is used to write instructions into the queue. A read instruction (INPUT, i, p)
instructs the computer to read a value from a value space $\mathcal{V}$ at interface i and
store it at position p of the value register. A write instruction (OUTPUT, i, p)
instructs the computer to output the value stored at position p to interface i. A
computation instruction (OP, p_1, p_2, p_3), OP $\in \{$ADD, MULT$\}$ instructs the computer to add or to multiply the values at positions p_1 and p_2 and store it at
position p_3. We then show how to construct the computer resource using the
Simple MPC protocol [27]. A similar statement could be obtained using other
traditional MPC protocols.

1.5 Notation

We denote random variables by capital letters. Prefixes of sequences of random variables are denoted by a superscript, e.g. X^i denotes the finite sequence
$X_1, \ldots, X_i$. For random variables X and Y, we denote by $\mathsf{p}_{X|Y}$ the corresponding conditional probability distribution.[2] Given a tuple t, we write the projection

---

[1] What is known as a rushing adversary in the literature is the special case of communication channels where a dishonest receiver sees the other parties' inputs of a
round before choosing his own input for that round.

[2] Conditional probability distributions are denoted by a small "p" because they are
defined without defining a random experiment. A capital P for probabilities is used
only if a random experiment is defined.

to the j-th component of the tuple as $[t]_j$. Given a sequence t^i of tuples $t_1, \ldots, t_i$, we write $[t^i]_j$ as the sequence $[t_1]_j, \ldots, [t_i]_j$. For a finite set X, $x \leftarrow_\$ X$ denotes sampling x uniform randomly from X.

2   Constructive Cryptography

The basic concepts of the Constructive Cryptography framework by Maurer and Renner [28–30] needed for this paper are quite simple and natural and are summarized below.

2.1   Specifications

A basic idea, which one finds in many disciplines, is that one considers a set Φ of objects and *specifications* of such objects. A specification $\mathcal{U} \subseteq \Phi$ is a subset of Φ and can equivalently be understood as a predicate on Φ defining the set of objects satisfying the specification, i.e., being in $\mathcal{U}$. Examples of this general paradigm are the specification of mechanical parts in terms of certain tolerances (e.g. the thickness of a bolt is between 1.33 and 1.34 mm), the specification of the property of a program (e.g. the set of programs that terminate, or the set of programs that compute a certain function within a given accuracy and time limit), or in a cryptographic context the specification of a close-to-uniform n-bit key as the set of probability distributions over $\{0,1\}^n$ with statistical distance at most ϵ from the uniform distribution.

A specification corresponds to a guarantee, and smaller specifications hence correspond to stronger guarantees. An important principle is to *abstract* a specification $\mathcal{U}$ by a larger specification $\mathcal{V}$ (i.e., $\mathcal{U} \subseteq \mathcal{V}$) which is simpler to understand and work with. One could call $\mathcal{V}$ an ideal specification to hint at a certain resemblance with terminology often used in the cryptographic literature. If a construction (see below) requires an object satisfying specification $\mathcal{V}$, then it also works if the given object actually satisfies the stronger specification $\mathcal{U}$.

2.2   Constructions

A *construction* is a function $\gamma : \Phi \to \Phi$ transforming objects into (usually in some sense more useful) objects. A well-known example of a construction useful in cryptography, achieved by a so-called extractor, is the transformation of a pair of independent random variables (say a short uniform random bit-string, called seed, and a long bit-string for which only a bound on the min-entropy is known) into a close-to-uniform string.

A construction statement of specification $\mathcal{S}$ from specification $\mathcal{R}$ using construction γ, denoted $\mathcal{R} \xrightarrow{\gamma} \mathcal{S}$, is of the form

$$\mathcal{R} \xrightarrow{\gamma} \mathcal{S} \quad :\Longleftrightarrow \quad \gamma(\mathcal{R}) \subseteq \mathcal{S}.$$

It states that if construction γ is applied to any object satisfying specification $\mathcal{R}$, then the resulting object is guaranteed to satisfy (at least) specification $\mathcal{S}$.

The composability of this construction notion follows immediately from the transitivity of the subset relation:

$$\mathcal{R} \xrightarrow{\gamma} \mathcal{S} \wedge \mathcal{S} \xrightarrow{\gamma'} \mathcal{T} \implies \mathcal{R} \xrightarrow{\gamma' \circ \gamma} \mathcal{T}.$$

2.3   Resources and Converters

The above natural and very general viewpoint is also taken in Constructive Cryptography, where the objects in Φ are systems, called *resources*, with interfaces to the parties considered in the given setting. If a party performs actions at its interface, this corresponds to applying a so-called *converter* which can also be thought of as a system or protocol engine. At its inside, the converter "talks to" the party's interface of the resource and at the outside it emulates an interface (of the transformed resource). Applying such a converter induces a mapping $\Phi \to \Phi$. We denote the set of converters as Σ.

Figure 1 shows a resource with four interfaces where converters are applied at two of the interfaces. The resource obtained by applying a converter π at interface j of resource $\mathbf{R}$ is denoted as $\pi^j \mathbf{R}$. Applying converters at different interfaces commutes.[3] The resource shown in Fig. 1 can hence be written

$$\pi^2 \rho^4 \mathbf{R},$$

which is equal to $\rho^4 \pi^2 \mathbf{R}$.

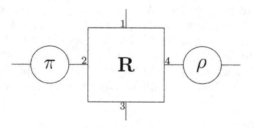

Fig. 1. Example of a resource with 4 interfaces, where converters π and ρ are attached to interfaces 2 and 4.

Several resources (more precisely a tuple of resources) can be understood as a single resource, i.e., as being composed in parallel. One can think that for each party, all its interfaces are merged into a single interface, where the original interfaces can be thought of as sub-interfaces.

---

[3] This is an abstract requirement, in the sense of an axiom, which for an instantiation of the theory, for example to the special case of discrete systems, must be proven to hold.

2.4   Multi-party Protocols and Constructions

Let us consider a setting with n parties, where $\mathcal{P} = \{1, \ldots, n\}$ denotes the set of parties (or, rather, interfaces).[4] A *protocol* consists of a tuple $\boldsymbol{\pi} = (\pi_1, \ldots, \pi_n)$ of converters, one for each party, and a construction consists of each party applying its converter. However, an essential aspect of reasoning in cryptography is that one considers that parties can either be honest or dishonest, and the goal is to state meaningful guarantees for the honest parties.[5] While an honest party applies its converter, there is no such guarantee for a dishonest party, meaning that a dishonest party may apply an arbitrary converter to its interface, including the identity converter that gives direct access to the interface.

In many cryptographic settings one considers a set of (honest) parties and a fixed dishonest party (often called the adversary). However, in a so-called multi-party context one considers each party to be either honest or dishonest. For each subset $Z \subseteq \mathcal{P}$ of dishonest parties one states a separate guarantee: If the assumed resource satisfies specification $\mathcal{R}_Z$, then, if all parties in $\mathcal{P} \setminus Z$ apply their converter, the resulting resource satisfies specification $\mathcal{S}_Z$. Typically, but not necessarily, all guarantees $\mathcal{R}_Z$ (and analogously all $\mathcal{S}_Z$) are compactly described, possibly all derived as variations of the same resource.

Definition 1. *The protocol* $\boldsymbol{\pi} = (\pi_1, \ldots, \pi_n)$ *constructs specifications* $\mathcal{S}_Z$ *from* $\mathcal{R}_Z$ *if*

$$\forall Z \subseteq \mathcal{P} \quad \mathcal{R}_Z \xrightarrow{\ \pi_{\mathcal{P} \setminus Z}\ } \mathcal{S}_Z.$$

A special case often considered is that one provides guarantees only if the set of dishonest parties is within a so-called adversary structure [16], for example that there are at most t dishonest parties. This simply corresponds to the special case where $\mathcal{S}_Z = \Phi$ if $|Z| > t$. In other words, if Z is not in the adversary structure, then the resource is only known to satisfy the trivial specification Φ.

2.5   Specification Relaxations

As mentioned above, that a party j is possibly dishonest means that we have no guarantee about which converter is applied at that interface. For a given specification $\mathcal{S}$, this is captured by relaxing the specification to the larger specification $\mathcal{S}^{*j}$:

$$\mathcal{S}^{*j} := \{\pi^j \mathbf{S} \mid \pi \in \Sigma \wedge \mathbf{S} \in \mathcal{S}\}.$$

If we consider a set Z of potentially dishonest parties, we can consider the set of interfaces in Z as being merged to a single interface with several sub-interfaces, and applying the above relaxation to this interface. The resulting specification

---

[4] In the literature, one often refers to parties with a name, say P_i for party at interface i, but we do not need explicit party names and can simply refer to party i.

[5] Note that in this view, the often used term "corruption" does not mean that a party switches from being honest to being dishonest, it rather means that a resource loses some guarantees, for example the memory resource of a party becomes accessible to some other parties.

is denoted $\mathcal{S}^{*Z}$. This corresponds to the viewpoint that all dishonest parties collude (or, as sometimes stated in the literature, are under control of a central adversary). It is easy to see that the described $*$-relaxation is idempotent: For any specification $\mathcal{S}$ and any set of interfaces Z, we have $(\mathcal{S}^{*Z})^{*Z} = \mathcal{S}^{*Z}$.

If one wants to prove that a given specification $\mathcal{U}$ is contained in $\mathcal{S}^{*Z}$, one can exhibit for every element $U \in \mathcal{U}$ a converter α such that $U = \alpha^Z S$ for some $S \in \mathcal{S}$. Here $\alpha^Z S$ means applying α to the interface resulting from merging the interfaces in Z. If the same α works for every U, then one can think of α as corresponding to a (joint) simulator for the interfaces in Z.

It should be pointed out that Constructive Cryptography [30] considers general specifications, and the above described specification type is only a special case. Therefore the construction notion does not involve a simulator. Indeed, this natural viewpoint allows to circumvent impossibility results in classical simulation-based frameworks (including the early version of Constructive Cryptography [28,29]) because the type of specifications resulting from requiring a single simulator is too restrictive. See [20] for an example.

3   Synchronous Systems

To instantiate the Constructive Cryptography framework at the level of synchronous discrete systems, we need to instantiate the notions of a resource $\mathbf{R} \in \Phi$ and a converter $\pi \in \Sigma$. We define each of them as special types of random systems [26,31]. We briefly explain the role of random systems in such definitions.

3.1   Random Systems

Definition 2. *An $(\mathcal{X}, \mathcal{Y})$-random system $\mathbf{R}$ is a sequence of conditional probability distributions* $\mathrm{p}^R_{Y_i|X^iY^{i-1}}$, *for $i \geq 1$. Equivalently, the random system can be characterized by the sequence* $\mathrm{p}^R_{Y^i|X^i} = \prod_{k=1}^i \mathrm{p}^R_{Y_k|X^kY^{k-1}}$, *for $i \geq 1$.*

As explained in [25], a random system is the mathematical object corresponding to the *behavior* of a discrete system. A deterministic system is a special type of function (or sequence of functions), and the composition of systems is defined via function composition. Probabilistic systems are often thought about (and described) at a more concrete level, where the randomness is made explicit (e.g. as the randomness of an algorithm or the random tape of a Turing machine). Hence a probabilistic discrete system (PDS) corresponds to a probability distribution over deterministic systems, and the definition of the composition of probabilistic systems is induced by the definition of composition of deterministic systems (analogously to the fact that the definition of the sum of real-valued random variables is naturally induced by the definition of the sum of real numbers, which are not probabilistic objects).

Different PDS can have the same behavior, which means that the behavior, i.e., a random system, corresponds to an equivalence class of PDS (with the same behavior). The fact that the composition of (independent) random systems corresponds to a particular product of the involved conditional distribution can be proved and should not be seen as the definition. However, in this paper, which only considers random systems (the actual mathematical objects of study), the product of distributions appears as the definition.

It is important to distinguish the *type* and the *description* of a mathematical object. An object of a given type can be described in may different ways. For example, a random system can be described by several variants of pseudo-code, and as is common in the literature we also use such an ad-hoc description language. The fact that a random system is defined via conditional probability distributions does not mean that they have to described in that way.

3.2   Resources

A resource (the mathematical type) is a special type of random system [26, 31].

Definition 3. *An $(\mathcal{X}, \mathcal{Y})$-random system $\mathbf{R}$ is a sequence of conditional probability distributions $\mathrm{p}^{R}_{Y_i|X^iY^{i-1}}$, for $i \geq 1$. Equivalently, the random system can be characterized by the sequence $\mathrm{p}^{R}_{Y^i|X^i} = \prod_{k=1}^{i} \mathrm{p}^{R}_{Y_k|X^kY^{k-1}}$, for $i \geq 1$.*

A resource with n interfaces takes one input per interface and produces an output at every interface (see Fig. 2). Without loss of generality, we assume that the alphabets at all interfaces and for all indices i are the same.[6] An $(n, \mathcal{X}, \mathcal{Y})$-resource is a resource with n interfaces and input (resp. output) alphabet $\mathcal{X}$ (resp. $\mathcal{Y}$).

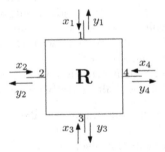

Fig. 2. An example resource with 4 interfaces. At each invocation, the resource takes an input $x_j \in \mathcal{X}$ at each interface j, and it outputs a value $y_j \in \mathcal{Y}$ at each interface j.

Definition 4. *An $(n, \mathcal{X}, \mathcal{Y})$-resource is an $(\mathcal{X}^n, \mathcal{Y}^n)$-random system.*

Parallel Composition. One can take several independent $(n, \mathcal{X}_j, \mathcal{Y}_j)$-resources $\mathbf{R}_1, \ldots, \mathbf{R}_k$ and form an $(n, \times_{j=1}^{k} \mathcal{X}_j, \times_{j=1}^{k} \mathcal{Y}_j)$-resource, denoted $[\mathbf{R}_1, \ldots, \mathbf{R}_k]$.

---

[6] The alphabets are large enough to include all values that can actually appear.

A party interacting with the composed resource $[\mathbf{R}_1, \ldots, \mathbf{R}_k]$ can give an input $\mathbf{a} = (a^1, \ldots, a^k)$, which is interpreted as giving each input $a^j \in \mathcal{X}_j$ to resource $\mathbf{R}_j$, and then receive an output $\mathbf{b} = (b^1, \ldots, b^k)$ containing the output from each of the resources.

In the following definition, we denote by $x_i = (\mathbf{a}_{1,i}, \ldots, \mathbf{a}_{n,i})$ the i-th input to the resource, and by $y_i = (\mathbf{b}_{1,i}, \ldots, \mathbf{b}_{n,i})$ the i-th output from the resource. We further let $[[x_i]]_j = ([\mathbf{a}_{1,i}]_j, \ldots, [\mathbf{a}_{n,i}]_j)$ be the tuple with the j-th component of each tuple $\mathbf{a}_{.,i}$; and let $[[x^i]]_j$ be the finite sequence $[[x_1]]_j, \ldots, [[x_i]]_j$. We let $[[y_i]]_j$ and $[[y^i]]_j$ be defined accordingly.

Definition 5. *Given a tuple of resources* $(\boldsymbol{R}_1, \ldots, \boldsymbol{R}_k)$, *where* $\boldsymbol{R}_j$ *is an* $(n, \mathcal{X}_j, \mathcal{Y}_j)$-*resource. The parallel composition* $\boldsymbol{R} := [\boldsymbol{R}_1, \ldots, \boldsymbol{R}_k]$, *is an* $(n, \times_{j=1}^{k} \mathcal{X}_j, \times_{j=1}^{k} \mathcal{Y}_j)$-*resource, defined as follows:*

$$\mathrm{p}_{Y_i \mid X^i Y^{i-1}}^{\boldsymbol{R}}(y_i, x^i, y^{i-1}) = \prod_{j=1}^{k} \mathrm{p}_{Y_i \mid X^i Y^{i-1}}^{R_j}([[y_i]]_j, [[x^i]]_j, [[y^{i-1}]]_j)$$

3.3   Converters

An $(\mathcal{X}, \mathcal{Y})$-converter is a system (of a different type than resources) with two interfaces, an outside interface **out** and an inside interface **in**. The inside interface is connected to the $(n, \mathcal{X}, \mathcal{Y})$-resource, and the outside interface serves as the interface of the combined system. When an input is given (an input at the outside), the converter invokes the resource (with an input on the inside), and then converts its response into a corresponding output (an output on the outside). When a converter is connected to several resources in parallel $[\mathbf{R}_1, \ldots, \mathbf{R}_k]$, we address the corresponding sub-interfaces with the name of the resource, i.e, **in.R1** is the sub-interface connected to $\mathbf{R}_1$.

More concretely, an $(\mathcal{X}, \mathcal{Y})$-converter is an $(\mathcal{X} \cup \mathcal{Y}, \mathcal{X} \cup \mathcal{Y})$-random system whose input and output alphabets alternate between $\mathcal{X}$ and $\mathcal{Y}$. That is,

- On the first input, and further odd inputs, it takes a value $x \in \mathcal{X}$ and produces a value $x' \in \mathcal{X}$.
- On the second input, and further even inputs, it takes a value $y' \in \mathcal{Y}$, and produces a value $y \in \mathcal{Y}$.

Definition 6. *An* $(\mathcal{X}, \mathcal{Y})$-*converter* π *is a pair of sequences of conditional probability distributions* $\mathrm{p}_{X_i' \mid X^i X'^{i-1} Y'^{i-1} Y^{i-1}}^{\pi}$ *and* $\mathrm{p}_{Y_i \mid X^i X'^i Y'^i Y^{i-1}}^{\pi}$, *for* $i \geq 1$. *Equivalently, a converter can be characterized by the sequence* $\mathrm{p}_{X'^i Y^i \mid X^i Y'^i}^{\pi} = \prod_{k=1}^{i} \mathrm{p}_{X_k' \mid X^k X'^{k-1} Y'^{k-1} Y^{k-1}}^{\pi} \cdot \mathrm{p}_{Y_k \mid X^k X'^k Y'^k Y^{k-1}}^{\pi}$, *for* $i \geq 1$.

Application of a Converter to a Resource Interface. The application of a converter π to a resource $\mathbf{R}$ at interface j can be naturally understood as the resource that operates as follows (see Fig. 3):

– On input $(x_1, \ldots, x_n) \in \mathcal{X}^n$: input x_j to π, and let x'_j be the output.
  Then, input $(x_1, \ldots, x_{j-1}, x'_j, x_{j+1}, \ldots, x_n) \in \mathcal{X}^n$ to $\mathbf{R}$.
– On output $(y_1, \ldots, y_{j-1}, y'_j, y_{j+1}, \ldots, y_n) \in \mathcal{Y}^n$ from $\mathbf{R}$, input y'_j to π, and let
  y_j be the output.
  The output is $(y_1, \ldots, y_n) \in \mathcal{Y}^n$.

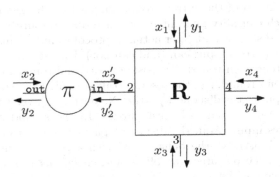

Fig. 3. The figure shows the application of a converter π to the interface 2 of a resource $\mathbf{R}$. On input a value $x_2 \in \mathcal{X}$ to interface out of π, the converter π outputs a value $x'_2 \in \mathcal{X}$ at interface in. The resource $\mathbf{R}$ takes as input $(x_1, x'_2, x_3, x_4) \in \mathcal{X}^4$, and outputs $(y_1, y'_2, y_3, y_4) \in \mathcal{Y}^4$. On input y'_2 to interface in of π, the converter outputs a value y_2 at interface out.

Given a tuple $a = (a_1, \ldots, a_n)$, we denote $a_{\{j \to b\}}$ the tuple where the j-th component is substituted by value b, i.e. the tuple $(a_1, \ldots, a_{j-1}, b, a_{j+1}, a_n)$. Moreover, given a sequence a^i of tuples $t^1, \ldots, t^i$ and a sequence b^i of values $b_1, \ldots, b_i$, we denote $a^i_{\{j \to b^i\}}$, the sequence of tuples $t^1_{\{j \to b_1\}}, \ldots, t^i_{\{j \to b_i\}}$.

Definition 7. *The application of an $(\mathcal{X}, \mathcal{Y})$-converter π at interface j of an $(n, \mathcal{X}, \mathcal{Y})$-resource $\mathbf{R}$ is the $(n, \mathcal{X}, \mathcal{Y})$-resource $\pi^j \mathbf{R}$ defined as follows:*

$$\mathrm{p}^{\pi^j \mathbf{R}}_{Y^i | X^i} (y^i, x^i) = \sum_{x'^i, y'^i} \mathrm{p}^{\pi}_{X'^i Y^i | X^i Y'^i} (x'^i, [y^i]_j, [x^i]_j, y'^i) \, \mathrm{p}^{\mathbf{R}}_{Y^i | X^i} \left(y^i_{\{j \to y'^i\}}, x^i_{\{j \to x'^i\}} \right)$$

One can see that applying converters at distinct interfaces commutes. That is, for any converters π and ρ, any resource $\mathbf{R}$ and any disjoint interfaces j, k, we have that $\pi^j \rho^k \mathbf{R} = \rho^k \pi^j \mathbf{R}$.

For a tuple of converters $\boldsymbol{\pi} = (\pi_1, \ldots, \pi_n)$, we denote by $\boldsymbol{\pi} \mathbf{R}$ the resource where each converter π_j is attached to interface j. Given a subset of interfaces I, we denote by $\boldsymbol{\pi}_I \mathbf{R}$ the resource where each converter π_j with $j \in I$, is attached to interface j.

4   Resources with Specific Round-Causality Guarantees

The resource type of Definition 4 captures that all parties act in a synchronized manner. The definition also implies that any (dishonest) party's input depends solely on the previous outputs seen by the party.

In practice this assumption is often not justified. For example, consider a resource consisting of two parallel communication channels (in a certain round) between two parties, one in each direction. Then it is typically unrealistic to assume that a dishonest party can not delay giving its input until having seen the output on the other channel. Such adversarial behavior is typically called "rushing" in the literature. More generally, a dishonest party's input can depend on partial information of the current round inputs from honest parties.

To model such causality guarantees, we introduce resources that proceed in two rounds (called semi-rounds) per actual protocol round.[7] This makes explicit what a dishonest party's input can (and can not) depend on.

More concretely, each round r consists of two semi-rounds, denoted $r.a$ and $r.b$. In the first semi-round, $r.a$, the resource takes inputs from the honest parties and gives an output to the dishonest parties. No output is given to honest parties, and no input is taken from dishonest parties. In the second semi-round, $r.b$, the resource takes inputs from the dishonest parties and gives an output to all parties. Figure 4 illustrates the behavior of such a resource within one round. When describing such resources, we often omit specifying the semi-round when it is clear from the context.

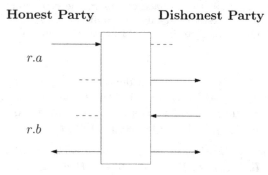

Fig. 4. Figure depicts a resource operating in a round. The dashed lines indicate that no value is taken as input to the resource, and is output from the resource. The honest (resp. dishonest) parties give inputs to the resource in the first (resp. second) invocation, and all parties receive an output in the second invocation. The dishonest parties receive in addition an output in the first invocation.

When applying a protocol converter to such a resource, we formally attach the corresponding converter that operates in semi-rounds, where round-r inputs are given to the resource at $r.a$, and round-r outputs are obtained at $r.b$.

---

[7] This type of resource is similar to the notion of *canonical synchronous functionalities* in [10].

5   A First Example

We demonstrate the usage of our model to describe a very simple 2-party protocol which uses delay channels to generate common randomness. The protocol uses a channel with a known lower and upper bound on the delay, and proceeds as follows: Each party generates a random value and sends it to the other party via a delay channel. Then, once the value is received, each party outputs the sum of the received value and the previously generated random value. It is intuitively clear that the protocol works because 1) a dishonest party does not learn the message before round r, and 2) an honest party is guaranteed to learn the message at round R.

Bounded-Delay Channel with Known Lower and Upper Bound. We model a simple delay channel $\overrightarrow{\mathcal{DC}}$ (resp. $\overleftarrow{\mathcal{DC}}$) from party 1 to party 2 (resp. party 2 to party 1) with known lower and upper bound on the delay. It takes a message at round 1, and is guaranteed to not deliver the message until round r to a dishonest party, but is guaranteed to deliver it at round R to an honest party. To model such a delay channel, we define a delay channel $\overrightarrow{\mathsf{DC}}_{r,R,Z}$ with message space $\mathcal{M}$ from party 1 to party 2 with fixed delay that takes a message at round 1 and delivers it at round r if the receiver is dishonest, and at round R if the receiver is honest. The set Z indicates the set of dishonest parties. The channel $\overleftarrow{\mathsf{DC}}_{r,R,Z}$ in the other direction is analogous.

Resource $\overrightarrow{\mathsf{DC}}_{r,R,Z}$

$\mathsf{msg} \leftarrow 0$
On input $m \in \mathcal{M}$ at interface 1 of round 1, set $\mathsf{msg} \leftarrow m$.
if $2 \in Z$ **then**
 Output msg at interface 2 at round r.
else
 Output msg at interface 2 at round R.
end if

To capture that the delay channel is not guaranteed to deliver the message to a dishonest receiver exactly at round r, we consider the $*$-relaxation $(\overrightarrow{\mathsf{DC}}_{r,R,Z})^{*z}$ on the delay channel at the dishonest interfaces Z. This specification includes resources with no guarantees at Z. For example, the resource may deliver the message later than r, or garbled, or not at all.

Common Randomness Resource. The sketc.hed protocol constructs a common randomness resource CRS that outputs a random string. We would like to model a CRS that is guaranteed to output the random string at round R to an honest party, but does not output the random string before r to a dishonest party. For that, we first consider a resource which outputs a random string to each honest (resp. dishonest) party at round R (resp. r).

Resource $\mathsf{CRS}_{r,R,Z}$

$\mathbf{rnd} \leftarrow_\$ \mathcal{M}$
For each party $i \in \{1,2\}$:
if $i \in Z$ **then**
    Output $\mathbf{rnd}$ at interface i at round r.
else
    Output $\mathbf{rnd}$ at interface i at round R.
end if

With the same idea as with the delay channels, we can model a common randomness resource that is guaranteed to deliver the randomness to the honest parties at round R but is not guaranteed to deliver the output to the dishonest parties at round r, by considering a $*$-relaxation on the resource over the dishonest interfaces Z, $(\mathsf{CRS}_{r,R,Z})^{*Z}$.

Two-Party Construction. We describe the 2-party protocol $\boldsymbol{\pi} = (\pi_1, \pi_2)$ sketc.hed at the beginning of the section and show that it constructs a common randomness resource.

Converter π_1

Local variable: rnd
Round 1
    $\mathbf{rnd} \leftarrow_\$ \mathcal{M}$
    Output $\mathbf{rnd}$ at $\mathbf{in.\overrightarrow{dc}}$. // $\mathbf{in.\overleftarrow{dc}}$ for π_2
Round R
    On input $v \in \mathcal{M}$ at $\mathbf{in.\overleftarrow{dc}}$, output $\mathbf{rnd} + v$ at **out**. // $\mathbf{in.\overrightarrow{dc}}$ for π_2

Lemma 1. $\boldsymbol{\pi} = (\pi_1, \pi_2)$ *constructs the specification* $(\mathsf{CRS}_{r,R,Z})^{*Z}$ *from the specification* $[(\overrightarrow{\mathsf{DC}}_{r,R,Z})^{*Z}, (\overleftarrow{\mathsf{DC}}_{r,R,Z})^{*Z}]$.

Proof. We prove each case separately.

1) $Z = \varnothing$: In this case, it is easy to see that $\pi_1 \pi_2 [\overrightarrow{\mathsf{DC}}_{r,R,\varnothing}, \overleftarrow{\mathsf{DC}}_{r,R,\varnothing}] = \mathsf{CRS}_{r,R,\varnothing}$ holds, since the sum of two uniformly random messages is uniformly random.

2) $Z = \{2\}$: Consider now the case where party 2 is dishonest (the case where party 1 is dishonest is similar). Let $\mathbf{S} := [\overrightarrow{\mathsf{DC}}_{r,R,Z}, \overleftarrow{\mathsf{DC}}_{r,R,Z}]$. It suffices to prove that $\pi_1 \mathbf{S} \in (\mathsf{CRS}_{r,R,Z})^{*Z}$ because:

$$\pi_1[(\overrightarrow{\mathsf{DC}}_{r,R,Z})^{*z}, (\overleftarrow{\mathsf{DC}}_{r,R,Z})^{*z}] \subseteq (\pi_1[\overrightarrow{\mathsf{DC}}_{r,R,Z}, \overleftarrow{\mathsf{DC}}_{r,R,Z}])^{*z}$$
$$= (\pi_1\mathsf{S})^{*z} \subseteq ((\mathsf{CRS}_{r,R,Z})^{*z})^{*z} = (\mathsf{CRS}_{r,R,Z})^{*z},$$

where the last equality holds because the $*$-relaxation is idempotent. Hence, we show that the converter σ described below is such that $\pi_1\mathsf{S} = \sigma^2\mathsf{CRS}_{r,R,Z}$.

Converter σ

Initialization

   $\mathbf{rcv} \leftarrow 0$.

Round 1.b

   On input $v \in \mathcal{M}$ at $\mathtt{out}.\overleftarrow{\mathtt{dc}}$, set $\mathbf{rcv} \leftarrow v$.

Round $r.a$

   On input $\mathbf{rnd}$ at $\mathtt{in}$, output $\mathbf{rnd} - \mathbf{rcv}$ at $\mathtt{out}.\overrightarrow{\mathtt{dc}}$.

Consider the system $\pi_1\mathsf{S}$. The system outputs at interface 1 of round $R.b$, a value $\mathbf{rnd} + v$, where $\mathbf{rnd}$ is a random value and v is the value received at interface 2 of round 1.b (and $v = 0$ if no value was received). Moreover, the system outputs at interface 2 of round $r.a$, the value $\mathbf{rnd}$.

Now consider the system $\sigma^2\mathsf{CRS}_{r,R,Z}$. The system outputs at interface 1 of round $R.b$, a random value $\mathbf{rnd}'$. Moreover, the system outputs at interface 2 of round $r.a$, the value $\mathbf{rnd}' - v$, where v is the same value received at interface 2 of round 1.b (and $v = 0$ if no value was received).

Since the joint distribution $\{\mathbf{rnd} + v, \mathbf{rnd}\}$ and $\{\mathbf{rnd}', \mathbf{rnd}' - v\}$ are exactly the same, we conclude that $\pi_1\mathsf{S} = \sigma^2\mathsf{CRS}_{r,R,Z}$. $\qquad\square$

6 Communication Resources

6.1 Point-to-Point Channels

We model the standard synchronous communication network, where parties have the guarantee that messages input at round k are received by round $k + 1$, and dishonest parties' round-k messages potentially depend on the honest parties' round-k messages. Let $\mathsf{CH}_{\ell,Z}(s,r)$ be a bilateral channel resource with n interfaces, one designated to each party $i \in \mathcal{P}$, and where two of the interfaces, s and r are designated to the sender and the receiver. The channel is parameterized by the set of dishonest parties $Z \subseteq \mathcal{P}$. The privacy guarantees are formulated by a leakage function $\ell(\cdot)$ that determines the information leaked to dishonest parties. For example, in an authenticated channel $\ell(m) = m$, and in a secure channel $\ell(m) = |m|$.

Resource $\mathsf{CH}_{\ell,Z}(s,r)$

Round $k, k \geq 1$

On input m at interface s, output m at interface r.
Output $\ell(m)$ at each interface $i \in Z$.

Let $\mathcal{N}_Z$ be the complete network of pairwise secure channels. That is, $\mathcal{N}_Z$ is the parallel composition of secure channels $\mathsf{CH}_{\ell,Z}(i,j)$ with $\ell(m) = |m|$, for each pair of parties $i, j \in \mathcal{P}$.

6.2   Broadcast Resource Specification

Broadcast is an important building block that many distributed protocols use. It allows a specific party, called the sender, to consistently distribute a message. More formally, it provides two guarantees: 1) Every honest party outputs the same value (consistency), and 2) the output value is the sender's value in case the sender is honest (validity).

The broadcast specification $\mathcal{BC}_{k,l,Z}(s)$ involves a set of parties $\mathcal{P}$, where one of the parties is the sender s. It is parameterized by the round numbers k and l indicating when the sender distributes the message and when the parties are guaranteed to receive it. The specification $\mathcal{BC}_{k,l,Z}(s)$, is the set of all resources satisfying both validity and consistency. That is, there is a value v such that the output at each interface j for $j \notin Z$ at round $l.b$ is $y_j^{l.b} = v$, and if the sender is honest, this value is the sender's input $x_s^{k.a}$ at round $k.a$. That is:

$$\mathcal{BC}_{k,l,Z}(s) := \left\{ \mathbf{R} \in \varPhi \ \middle| \ \exists v \left[\left(\forall j \in \overline{Z} \ y_j^{l.b} = v \right) \wedge \left(s \in \overline{Z} \rightarrow v = x_s^{k.a} \right) \right] \right\}$$

We show how to construct such a broadcast specification in Sect. A. Let $\mathcal{BC}_{\Delta,Z}(s)$ be the parallel composition of $\mathcal{BC}_{k,k+\Delta,Z}(s)$, for each $k \geq 1$, and let $\mathcal{BC}_{\Delta,Z}$ be the parallel composition of $\mathcal{BC}_{\Delta,Z}(s)$, for each party $s \in \mathcal{P}$.

7   The Interactive Computer Resource

In this section, we introduce a simple ideal *interactive computer* resource with n interfaces. Interfaces $1, \ldots, n-1$ are used to give input values and receive output values. Interface n allows to input *instruction commands*. The resource has a memory which is split into two parts: an array storing values S and a queue C storing instruction commands to be processed. We describe the functionality of the resource in two parts: Storing the instructions that are input at n, and processing the instructions.

Store Instructions. On input an instruction at interface n at round r, the instruction is stored in the queue C. Then, after a fixed number of rounds, the input instruction is output at each honest interface i, and at dishonest interfaces at round $r.a$.

Instruction Processing. The interactive computer processes instructions sequentially. There are three types of instructions that the resource can process. Each instruction type has a fixed number of rounds.

1. An input instruction (INPUT, i, p) instructs the resource to read a value from a value space $\mathcal{V}$ at interface i and store it at position p of the array S. If party i is honest, it inputs the value at the first round of processing the input instruction, otherwise it inputs the value at the last round. This models the fact that a dishonest party i can defer the choice of the input value to the end of processing the instruction.
2. An output instruction (OUTPUT, i, p) instructs the computer to output the value stored at position p to interface i. If party i is dishonest, it receives the value at the first round of processing the output instruction. Otherwise, the value is output at the last round of processing the instruction.
3. A computation instruction (OP, p_1, p_2, p_3)), OP $\in \{$ADD, MULT$\}$ instructs the computer to add or to multiply the values at positions p_1 and p_2 and store it at p_3.

One could consider different refinements of the interactive computer. For example, a computer that can receive lists of instructions, process instructions in parallel, or a computer that allows instructions to be the result of a computation using values from S. For simplicity, we stick to a simple version of the computer and leave possible refinements to future work.

Resource Computer$_Z$

Parameters: r_i, r_o, r_a, r_m, r_s. // #rounds to process an input, output, addition or multiplication instruction, and to store an instruction

Initialization
    $L \leftarrow$ empty array. // Store values
    $C \leftarrow$ empty queue. // Store instructions
    Next2Read $\leftarrow 1$. // Counter indicating when to read the next instruction
    Current $\leftarrow \bot$. // Contains the current instruction being processed

Round $k, k \geq 1$
    // Read next instruction
    if Next2Read $= k$ **then**
        Current $\leftarrow C$.pop()
        if Current $\neq \bot$ **then**
            Next2Read $\leftarrow k + r_j$, where r_j, for $j \in \{i, o, a, m\}$, is the round delay of the instruction in Current.
        else
            Next2Read $\leftarrow k + 1$
        end if
    end if
    // Process instruction

> **if** Current $= (\text{INPUT}, i, p)$ **then**
>> **if** $i \notin Z$ **then**
>>> Read $x \in \mathcal{V}$ at interface i at round Next2Read $- r_i$.
>>
>> **else**
>>> Read $x \in \mathcal{V}$ at interface i at round Next2Read $- 1$.
>>
>> **end if**
>> $L[p] \leftarrow x$
>
> **else if** Current $= (\text{OP}, p_1, p_2, p_3)$, OP $\in \{\text{ADD}, \text{MULT}\}$ **then**
>> $L[p_3] \leftarrow L[p_1] \text{ OP } L[p_2]$
>
> **else if** Current $= (\text{OUTPUT}, i, p)$ **then**
>> **if** $i \notin Z$ **then**
>>> Output $L[p]$ at interface i at round Next2Read $- 1$.
>>
>> **else**
>>> Output $L[p]$ at interface i at round Next2Read $- r_o$.
>>
>> **end if**
>
> **end if**
> Current $\leftarrow \perp$
> // Store instruction in queue
> Read instruction I at interface n.
> If I is a valid instruction, output I at each interface $i \in Z$. Then, at round
> $k + \Delta$ introduce the instruction in the queue $C.\text{push}(I)$, and output I at each
> interface $i \notin Z$. // If party n is honest, output to honest parties at $(k + \Delta).b$
> and dishonest parties at $k.a$. Otherwise, output to all parties at $(k + \Delta).b$

8   Protocol Simple MPC

We adapt Maurer's Simple MPC protocol [27], originally described for SFE in the stand-alone setting, to realize the resource Computer from Sect. 7, thereby proving a much stronger (and composable) statement. The protocol is run among a set $\mathcal{P} = \{1, \ldots, n\}$ of n parties. Parties $1, \ldots, n-1$ process the instructions, give input values and obtain output values. Party n has access to the instructions that the other parties needs to execute.

General Adversaries. In many protocols, the sets of possible dishonest parties are specified by a threshold t, that indicates that any set of dishonest parties is of size at most t. However, in this protocol, one specifies a so-called *adversary structure* $\mathcal{Z}$, which is a monotone[8] set of subsets of parties, where each subset indicates a possible set of dishonest parties. We are interested in the condition that no three sets in $\mathcal{Z}$ cover $[n-1]$, also known as $\mathcal{Q}^3([n-1], \mathcal{Z})$ [16].

8.1   Protocol Description

Let $\mathcal{Z}$ be an adversary structure that satisfies $\mathcal{Q}^3([n-1], \mathcal{Z})$. Protocol sMPC $= (\pi_1, \ldots, \pi_n)$ constructs the resource Computer$_{\mathcal{Z}}$, introduced in Sect. 7, for any $Z \in \mathcal{Z}$. For sets $Z \notin \mathcal{Z}$, the protocol constructs the trivial specification Φ.

---

[8] If $Z \in \mathcal{Z}$ and $Z' \subseteq Z$, then $Z' \in \mathcal{Z}$.

Assumed Specifications. The protocol assumes the following specifications: a network specification $\mathcal{N}_Z$ among the parties in $\mathcal{P}$ (see Sect. 6.1) and a parallel broadcast specification $\mathcal{BC}_{\Delta,Z}$ which is the parallel composition of broadcast channels where any party in $\mathcal{P}$ can be a sender and the set of recipients is $\mathcal{P}$ (see Sect. 6.2).

Converters. The converter π_n is the identity converter. It allows to give direct access to the flow of instructions that the parties need to process. Because the instructions are delivered to the parties in $\mathcal{P}$ via the broadcast specification $\mathcal{BC}_{\Delta,Z}(n)$, parties have agreement on the next instruction to execute.

We now describe the converters $\pi_1, \ldots, \pi_{n-1}$. Each converter π_i keeps an (initially empty) array L with the current stored values, and a queue C of instructions to be executed. Each time an instruction is received from $\mathcal{BC}_{\Delta,Z}(n)$, it is added to C and also output. Each instruction in C is processed sequentially.

In order to describe how to process each instruction, we consider the adversary structure $\mathcal{Z}' := \{Z \setminus \{n\} : Z \in \mathcal{Z}\}$. Let the maximal sets in $\mathcal{Z}'$ be $\max(\mathcal{Z}') := \{Z_1, \ldots, Z_m\}$.

Input Instruction (input, i, p), for $i \in [n-1]$. Converter π_i does as follows: On input a value s from the outside interface, compute shares $s_1, \ldots, s_m$ using a m-out-of-m secret-sharing scheme (m is the number of maximal sets in $\mathcal{Z}'$). That is, compute random summands such that $s = \sum_{j=1}^m s_j$. Then, output s_j to the inside interface in.net.ch$_{i,k}$, for each party $k \in \overline{Z_j}$.

Then each converter for party in $\overline{Z_j}$, echoes the received shares to all parties in $\overline{Z_j}$, i.e. outputs the received shares to in.net.ch$_{i,k}$, for each party $k \in \overline{Z_j}$. If a converter obtained different values, it broadcasts a complaint message, i.e. it outputs a complaint message at in.bc. In such a case, π_i broadcasts the share s_j. At the end of the process, the converters store the received shares in their array, along with the information that the value was assigned to position p. Intuitively, a consistent sharing ensures that no matter which set Z_k of parties is dishonest, they miss the share s_k, and hence s remains secret.

Output Instruction (output, i, p), for $i \in [n-1]$. Each converter π_l, $l \in [n-1]$, outputs all the stored shares assigned to position p at interface in.net.ch$_{l,i}$. Converter π_i does: Let v_j^l be the value received from party l as share j at in.net.ch$_{l,i}$. Then, converter π_i reconstructs each share s_j as the value v such that $\{l \mid v_j^l \neq v\} \in \mathcal{Z}$, and outputs $\sum_j s_j$.

Addition Instruction (add, p_1, p_2, p_3). Each converter for a party in $\overline{Z_j}$ adds the j-th shares of the values assigned to positions p_1 and p_2, and stores the result as the j-th share of the value at position p_3.

Multiplication Instruction (mult, p_1, p_2, p_3). The goal is to compute a share of the product ab, assuming that the converters have stored shares of a and of b respectively. Given that $ab = \sum_{p,q=1}^m a_p b_q$, it suffices to compute shares of each term $a_p b_q$, and add the shares locally. In order to compute a sharing of $a_p b_q$, the converter for each party $i \in \overline{Z_p} \cap \overline{Z_q}$ executes the same steps as the input instruction, with the value $a_p b_q$. Then, converters for parties in $\overline{Z_p} \cap \overline{Z_q}$ check that they all shared the same value by reconstructing the difference of every pair of shared values. In the case that all differences are zero, they store the shares of a fixed party (e.g. the shares from the party in $\overline{Z_p} \cap \overline{Z_q}$ with the smallest index). Otherwise, each term a_p and b_q is reconstructed, and the default sharing $(a_p b_q, 0, \ldots, 0)$ is adopted.

Theorem 1. *Let* $\mathcal{P} = \{1, \ldots, n\}$, *and let* $\mathcal{Z}$ *be an adversary structure that satisfies* $\mathcal{Q}^3([n-1], \mathcal{Z})$. *Protocol* sMPC *constructs* $(\mathsf{Computer}_Z)^{*z}$ *with parameters* $(r_i, r_o, r_a, r_m, r_s) = (2\Delta + 2, 1, 0, 2\Delta + 4, \Delta)$ *from* $[\mathcal{N}_Z, \mathcal{BC}_{\Delta,Z}]$, *for any* $Z \in \mathcal{Z}$, *and constructs* Φ *otherwise.*

Proof. **Case** $Z = \varnothing$: In this case all parties are honest. We need to argue that:

$$\mathcal{R}_\varnothing := \mathsf{sMPC}[\mathcal{N}_\varnothing, \mathcal{BC}_{\Delta,\varnothing}] = \mathsf{Computer}_\varnothing.$$

At the start of the protocol, the computer resource $\mathsf{Computer}_\varnothing$, and each protocol converter has an empty queue C of instructions and empty array L of values. Consider the system $\mathcal{R}_\varnothing$. Each time party n inputs an instruction I to $\mathcal{BC}_{\Delta,\varnothing}(n)$, because of validity, it is guaranteed that after Δ rounds each protocol converter receives I, stores I in the queue C and outputs I at interface out. Each converter processes the instructions in its queue sequentially, and each instruction takes the same constant amount of rounds to be processed for all parties. Hence, all honest parties keep a queue with the same instructions throughout the execution of the protocol.

Now consider the system $\mathsf{Computer}_\varnothing$. It stores each instruction input at interface n in its queue C, and outputs the instruction I at each party interface $i \in \mathcal{P}$ after Δ rounds. The instructions are processed sequentially, and it takes the same amount of rounds to process each instruction as in $\mathcal{R}_\varnothing$.

We then conclude that each queue for each protocol converter in $\mathcal{R}_\varnothing$ contains exactly the same instructions as the queue in $\mathsf{Computer}_\varnothing$.

We now argue that the behavior of both systems is identical not only when storing the instructions, but also when processing them.

Let us look at the content of the arrays L that $\mathsf{Computer}_\varnothing$ and each protocol converter in $\mathcal{R}_\varnothing$ has. Whenever a value s is stored in the array L of $\mathsf{Computer}_\varnothing$ at position p, there are values s_l, such that $s = \sum_{l=1}^m s_l$ and s_l is stored in each converter π_j such that $j \notin Z_l$. For each value s_l, the converters that store s_l, also stores additional information containing the position p and the index l.

Consider an input instruction, (INPUT, i, p) at round k, and a value x is input at the next round at interface i. In the system $\mathcal{R}_\varnothing$, the converter π_i computes values s_l, such that $s = \sum_{l=1}^m s_l$ and sends each s_l to each converter π_j such that $j \notin Z_l$. All broadcasted messages are 0, i.e. there are no complaints, and as a consequence s_l is stored in each converter π_j, where $j \notin Z_j$. In the system $\mathsf{Computer}_\varnothing$, the value x is stored at the p-th register of the array L.

Consider an output instruction, (OUTPUT, i, p). In the system $\mathcal{R}_\varnothing$, each converter π_j sends the corresponding previously stored values s_l associated with position p, and π_i outputs $s = \sum_{l=1}^{m} s_l$. In the system $\mathsf{Computer}_\varnothing$, the value x stored at the p-th register of the array L is output at interface i.

Consider an addition instruction, $(\text{ADD}, p_1, p_2, p_3)$. In the system $\mathcal{R}_\varnothing$ each converter adds, for each share index l, the corresponding values associated with position p_1 and p_2, and stores the result as a value associated with position p_3 and index l. In the system $\mathsf{Computer}_\varnothing$, the sum of the values a and b stored at the p_1-th and p_2-th positions is stored at position p_3.

Consider a multiplication instruction, $(\text{MULT}, p_1, p_2, p_3)$. In the ideal system $\mathsf{Computer}_\varnothing$, the product of the values a and b stored at positions p_1-th and p_2-th is stored at position p_3. In the system $\mathcal{R}_\varnothing$, let a_p (resp. b_q) be the value associated with position p_1 (resp. p_2) and with index p (resp. q), that each converter for party in $\overline{Z_p}$ (resp. $\overline{Z_q}$) has. For each $1 \leq p, q \leq m$, consider each protocol converter for party $j \in \overline{Z_p} \cap \overline{Z_q}$. (Note that since the adversary structure satisfies $Q^3(\mathcal{P}, \mathcal{Z})$, then, for any two sets $Z_p, Z_q \in \mathcal{Z}$, $\overline{Z_p} \cap \overline{Z_q} \neq \varnothing$.) The converter does the following steps:

1. Input instruction steps with the value $a_p b_q$ as input. As a result, each converter in $\overline{Z_u}$ stores a value, which we denote v_j^u, from $j \in \overline{Z_p} \cap \overline{Z_q}$.
2. Execute the output instruction, with the value $v_j^u - v_{j_0}^u$ and towards all parties in $[n-1]$. As a result, every party obtains 0, and the value $v_{j_0}^u$ is stored.
3. The value associated with position p_3 and index p, stored by each converter for party in $\overline{Z_p}$, is the sum $w_p = \sum_{j_0} v_{j_0}^p$.

As a result, each party in $\overline{Z_p}$ stores w_p, and $\sum_p w_p = ab$.

Case $Z \neq \varnothing$: In this case, the statement is only non-trivial if $Z \in \mathcal{Z}$, because otherwise the ideal system specification is $\mathcal{S}_Z = \Phi$, i.e. there are no guarantees.

We need to show that when executing sMPC with the assumed specification, we obtain a system in the specification $(\mathsf{Computer}_Z)^{*z}$. That is, for each network resource $\mathsf{N} \in \mathcal{N}_Z$ and parallel broadcast resource $\mathsf{PBC} = [\mathsf{BC}_1, \ldots, \mathsf{BC}_n] \in \mathcal{BC}_{\Delta, Z}$ we need to find a system σ such that:

$$\mathbf{R} := \mathsf{sMPC}_{\mathcal{P} \backslash Z}[\mathsf{N}, \mathsf{PBC}] = \mathbf{S} := \sigma^Z \mathsf{Computer}_Z.$$

Converter σ

Round k, $k \geq 1$

    // Dishonest party n

1: Emulate the behavior of the assumed broadcast resource BC_n, where honest parties' inputs are $\perp$, and dishonest parties' inputs are given at out.

2: On input an instruction at in, store it.

    // Instruction emulation

3: Read the next instruction I to execute.

4: **if** $I = (\text{INPUT}, i, p)$ **then**

5:     **if** $i \notin Z$ **then**

6:         Compute and output a random value s_q at each interface out.i, $i \in Z \cap \overline{Z_q}$. Store s_q, q and p.

7:         On input a complaint message on q at out.i, output the stored value s_q at interface out.bc.

8:     **else**

9:         If there is exactly one value received s_q for each $\overline{Z} \cap \overline{Z_q}$, then store the values s_q with q and p.

10:        Otherwise, emulate the behavior of BC_j for a complaint message, for each q such that there are zero or more than a different value, and for each $j \in \overline{Z} \cap \overline{Z_q}$.

11:        On input s_q at out, store it.

12:        Input at in the sum of values s_q stored.

13:     **end if**

14: **else if** $I = (\text{OUTPUT}, i, p)$ **then**

15:     Read $x \in \mathcal{V}$ at interface in.

16:     Output at out, random values s'_q such that $\sum_{q: Z \cap \overline{Z_q} = \varnothing} s'_q + \sum_{q: Z \cap \overline{Z_q} \neq \varnothing} s_q = x$. // The dishonest values s_q associated with position p are stored

17: **else if** $I = (\text{ADD}, p_1, p_2, p_3)$ **then**

18:     For each q, add the values s_q, s'_q associated with p_1 and p_2 respectively, and store the result as well as the position p_3.

19: **else if** $I = (\text{MULT}, p_1, p_2, p_3)$ **then**

20:     Consider, for each $1 \leq p, q \leq m$, two possible cases:

21:     **if** $Z \cap \overline{Z_p} \cap \overline{Z_q} \neq \varnothing$ **then**

22:         The values a_p and b_q, where a_p (resp. b_q) is the value associated with position p_1 (resp. p_2).

23:         For each $i \in Z \cap \overline{Z_p} \cap \overline{Z_q}$, follow the same steps as with the input instruction (Steps 9-11). // Check that the dishonest parties in $\overline{Z_p} \cap \overline{Z_q}$ input a consistent sharing

24:         Check that the values from party i add up to $a_p b_q$. If so, store the values from the party with the smallest index. Otherwise, define the sharing of $a_p b_q$ as $(a_p b_q, \ldots, 0)$, and output the corresponding shares to the dishonest parties.

25:     **else**

26:         If all parties in $\overline{Z_p} \cap \overline{Z_q}$ are honest, generate random values as shares of $a_p b_q$, store them and answer complaints, according to Steps 6-7.

27:        Output 0s as the reconstructed differences.

28:     **end if**

29: **end if**

We first argue that the instructions written at the queue C in resource $\sigma^Z \mathsf{Computer}_Z$ follow the same distribution as the instructions that the honest parties store in their queue in the system $\mathcal{R}_Z$. If party n is honest, this is true, as argued in the previous case for $Z = \varnothing$. In the case that party n is dishonest, the converter σ inputs (equally distributed) instructions as BC_n outputs to honest parties in $\mathcal{R}_Z$ by emulating the behavior of BC_n, taking into account the inputs from dishonest parties provided at the outside interface, and the honest parties' inputs are $\perp$.

Now we need to show that the messages that dishonest parties receive in both systems are equally distributed. We argue about each single instruction separately. Let I be the next instruction to be executed.

Input instruction: $I = (\text{INPUT}, i, p)$. We consider two cases, depending on whether party i is honest.

Dishonest party i. In the system $\mathbf{R}$, if a complaint message is generated from an honest party, the exact same complaint message will be output by σ in the system $\mathbf{S}$. This is because σ stores the shares received at the outside interface by the dishonest parties, and checks that the shares are consistent. Moreover, at the end of the input instruction it is guaranteed that all shares are consistent (i.e., all honest parties in each $\overline{Z_q}$ have the same share), and hence the sum of the shares is well-defined. This exact sum is input at $\mathsf{Computer}_Z$ by σ.

Honest party i. In this case, the converter σ generates and outputs random consistent values as the shares for dishonest parties. On input a complaint from a dishonest party, output at the broadcast interface its share to all dishonest parties. In the system $\mathbf{R}$, dishonest parties also receive shares that are randomly distributed. Observe that in this case, the correct value is stored in the queue of $\mathsf{Computer}_Z$, but σ only has the shares of dishonest parties.

Output instruction: $I = (\text{OUTPUT}, i, p)$. In this case, the emulation is only non-trivial if party i is dishonest. The converter outputs random shares such that the sum of the random shares and the corresponding shares from dishonest parties that are stored, corresponds to the output value x obtained from $\mathsf{Computer}_Z$. Observe that in the system $\mathbf{R}$, the shares sum up to the value x as well, because of the $\mathcal{Q}^3$ condition. Given that the correct value was stored in the queue in every input instruction, the same shares that are output by σ follow the same distribution as the shares received by dishonest parties in $\mathbf{R}$ (namely, random shares subject to the fact that the sum of the random shares and the dishonest shares is equal to x).

Addition instruction: $I = (\text{ADD}, p_1, p_2, p_3)$. The converter σ simply adds the corresponding shares and stores them in the correct location.

Multiplication instruction: $I = (\text{MULT}, p_1, p_2, p_3)$. Consider each $1 \leq p, q \leq m$. Consider the following steps in the execution of the multiplication instruction in $\mathbf{R}$:

1. Honest parties execute the input instruction steps with the value $a_p b_q$ as input. Dishonest parties can use any value as input. However, it is guaranteed that the sharing is consistent. That is, each converter for an honest party in $\overline{Z_u}$ stores a value, which we denote v_j^u, from $j \in \overline{Z_p} \cap \overline{Z_q}$.

2. Execute the output instruction, with the value $v_j^u - v_{j_0}^u$ and towards all parties in $\mathcal{P}$. If any dishonest party used a value different than $a_p b_q$ in the previous step, one difference will be non-zero, and the default sharing $(a_p b_q, 0, \ldots, 0)$ is adopted. Otherwise, the sharing from P_{j_0}, i.e. the values $v_{j_0}^u$, is adopted.

Case $Z \cap \overline{Z_p} \cap \overline{Z_q} \neq \varnothing$: If there is a dishonest party in $\overline{Z_p} \cap \overline{Z_q}$, then the converter σ has the values a_p and b_q stored.

Step 1: For each dishonest party $i \in \overline{Z_p} \cap \overline{Z_q}$, the converter σ checks whether the shares are correctly shared (it checks that the dishonest parties in $\overline{Z_p} \cap \overline{Z_q}$ input a consistent sharing), in the same way as when emulating the input instruction.

Step 2: After that, σ checks that the shares from party i add up to $a_p b_q$. If not, the converter σ defines the sharing of $a_p b_q$ as $(a_p b_q, 0, \ldots, 0)$, and outputs the corresponding shares to the dishonest parties.

Observe that given that the adversary structure satisfies the $\mathcal{Q}^3$ condition, there is always an honest party in $\overline{Z_p} \cap \overline{Z_q}$. Then, in the system $\mathbf{R}$, it is guaranteed that the value $a_p b_q$ is shared. Moreover, as in $\mathbf{S}$, the default sharing is adopted if and only if a dishonest party shared a value different from $a_p b_q$.

Case $Z \cap \overline{Z_p} \cap \overline{Z_q} = \varnothing$: If all parties in $\overline{Z_p} \cap \overline{Z_q}$ are honest, dishonest parties receive random shares in $\mathbf{R}$. Moreover, all reconstructed differences are 0, since honest parties in $\overline{Z_p} \cap \overline{Z_q}$ share the same value. In $\mathbf{S}$, σ generates random values as shares of $a_p b_q$ as well, and then open 0s as the reconstructed differences.

□

9   Concluding Remarks

The fact that the construction notion in Definition 1 states a guarantee for every possible set of dishonest parties, might suggest that our model cannot be extended to the setting of adaptive corruptions. However, the term adaptive corruption most often refers to the fact that a resource can be adaptively compromised, e.g. a party's computer has a weakness (e.g. a virus) which allows the adversary to take it over, depending on environmental events. This can be modeled by stating explicitly the party's resources with an interface to the adversary and with a so-called *free* interface on which the corruptibility can be (adaptively) initiated. If one takes this viewpoint, it is actually natural to consider a more fine-grained model of the resources (e.g. the computer, the memory, and the randomness resource as separate resources) with separate meanings of what "corruption" means. Note that the guarantees for honest parties whose resources have been (partially) taken over are (and must be) still captured by the constructed resource specification.

Appendix

A   Broadcast Construction

We show how to construct the broadcast resource specification introduced in Sect. 6.2, using the so-called *king-phase* paradigm [5]. The construction consists of several steps, each providing stronger consistency guarantees.

A.1   Weak-Consensus

Let Z be a set of parties. The primitive *weak-consensus* provides two guarantees:

- Validity: If all parties in $\overline{Z}$ input the same value, they agree on this value.
- Weak Consistency: If some party $i \in \overline{Z}$ decides on an output $y_i \in \{0,1\}$, then every other party $j \in \overline{Z}$ decides on a value $y_j \in \{y_i, \perp\}$.

A specification $\mathcal{WC}_{k,l,Z,t}$ capturing the guarantees of a weak-consensus primitive (up to t dishonest parties, and where parties input at round k and output at round l) can be naturally defined as the set of all resources satisfying validity and weak consistency. More concretely, for $|Z| \leq t$, $\mathcal{WC}_{k,l,Z,t}$, is the set of all resources which output a value at round $l.b$ that satisfy the validity and weak consistency properties, according to the inputs from round $k.a$. That is:

$$\mathcal{WC}_{k,l,Z,t} := \left\{ \mathbf{R} \in \Phi \;\middle|\; \exists v \left(\forall j \in \overline{Z} \; y_j^{l.b} \in \{v, \perp\} \right) \wedge \right.$$
$$\left. \left(\exists v' \; \forall j \in \overline{Z} \; x_j^{k.a} = v' \rightarrow \forall j \in \overline{Z} \; y_j^{l.b} = x_j^{k.a} \right) \right\}$$

And when $|Z| > t$, $\mathcal{WC}_{k,l,Z,t} = \Phi$.

Protocol $\Pi_{\mathtt{wc}}^k = (\pi_1^{\mathtt{wc}}, \ldots, \pi_n^{\mathtt{wc}})$ constructs specification $\mathcal{WC}_{k,k,Z,t}$ from $\mathcal{N}_Z$. The protocol is quite simple: At round k each party sends its input message to every other party via each channel. Then, if there is a bit b that is received at least $n - t$ times, the output is b. Otherwise, the output is $\perp$. At a very high level, the protocol meets the specification because, if a party i outputs a bit b, it received b from at least $n - t$ parties, and hence it received b from at least $n - 2t$ honest parties. This implies that every other party received the bit $1 - b$ at most $2t < n - t$ times (since $t < \frac{n}{3}$). Hence, no honest party outputs $1 - b$.

Converter $\pi_i^{\mathtt{wc}}$

Local Variable: y.

Round k

On input x_i at **out**, output x_i to each **in.net.ch**$_{i,j}$, where $j \in \mathcal{P}$.
On input values y_j at each **in.net.ch**$_{i,j}$:
if $\left| \{ j \in \mathcal{P} \mid y_j = 0 \} \right| \geq n - t$ **then**
$\quad y \leftarrow 0$

> **else if** $\left|\{j \in \mathcal{P} \mid y_j = 1\}\right| \geq n - t$ **then**
> $\quad y \leftarrow 1$
> **else**
> $\quad y \leftarrow \bot$
> **end if**
> Output y at out.

Theorem 2. *Let* $t < \frac{n}{3}$. Π_{wc}^{k} *constructs* $\mathcal{WC}_{k,k,Z,t}$ *from* $\mathcal{N}_Z$, *for any* $Z \subseteq \mathcal{P}$ *such that* $|Z| \leq t$, *and constructs* Φ *otherwise.*

Proof. Let $Z \subseteq \mathcal{P}$ such that $|Z| \leq t$. We want to prove that the system specification $\mathcal{R}_Z := (\Pi_{wc}^{k})_{\overline{Z}}\mathcal{N}_Z \subseteq \mathcal{WC}_{k,k,Z,t}$.

For that, all we need to prove is that at round $k.b$, the outputs from the honest parties satisfy both the weak-consistency and the validity property, where the inputs to be taken into account are those at round $k.a$. We divide two cases:

- If every party $i \in \overline{Z}$ had as input value b at round k (there was pre-agreement): In the system specification $\mathcal{WC}_{k,k,Z,t}$, the parties output the bit b by definition. In the system specification $\mathcal{R}_Z$, each party $i \in \overline{Z}$ receives the bit b at least $n - t$ times. Hence, each party $i \in \overline{Z}$ also outputs b.
- Otherwise, in $\mathcal{R}_Z$, either every party $i \in \overline{Z}$ outputs $\bot$ (in which case the parties meet the specification $\mathcal{WC}_{k,k,Z,t}$), or some party i outputs a bit b. In this case, we observe that it received b from at least $n - t$ parties, and hence it received b from at least $n - 2t$ honest parties. This implies that every other party received the bit $1 - b$ at most $2t < n - t$ times (since $t < \frac{n}{3}$). In conclusion, no honest party outputs $1 - b$, and the parties output a value $v_i \in \{\bot, b\}$.

$\qquad\qquad\qquad\qquad\qquad\qquad\qquad\qquad\qquad\qquad\qquad\qquad\qquad\qquad\square$

A.2 Graded-Consensus

We define *graded-consensus* with respect to a set of parties Z. In this protocol, each party inputs a bit $x_i \in \{0,1\}$ and outputs a pair value-grade $(y_i, g_i) \in \{0,1\}^2$. The primitive provides two guarantees:

- Validity: If all parties in $\overline{Z}$ input the same value, they agree on this value with grade 1.
- Graded Consistency: If some party $i \in \overline{Z}$ decides on a value $y_i \in \{0,1\}$ with grade $g_i = 1$, then every other party $j \in \overline{Z}$ decides on the same value $y_j = y_i$.

Specification $\mathcal{GC}_{k,l,Z,t}$ captures the guarantees of a graded-consensus primitive secure up to t dishonest parties, and where parties give input at round k and output at round l. If $|Z| \leq t$:

$$\mathcal{GC}_{k,l,Z,t} := \left\{ \mathbf{R} \in \Phi \ \Big| \right.$$

$$\forall v \ \left(\exists j \in \overline{Z} \ y_j^{l.b} = (v,1) \rightarrow \forall i \in \overline{Z} \ y_i^{l.b} = (v,g) \ \wedge \ g \in \{0,1\} \right) \wedge$$

$$\left. \left(\exists v \ \forall j \in \overline{Z} \ x_j^{k.a} = v \rightarrow \forall j \in \overline{Z} \ y_j^{l.b} = (x_j^{k.a},1) \right) \right\}$$

And when $|Z| > t$, $\mathcal{GC}_{k,l,Z,t} = \Phi$.

We show a protocol $\Pi_{\text{gc}}^k = (\pi_1^{\text{gc}}, \dots, \pi_n^{\text{gc}})$ that constructs specification $\mathcal{GC}_{k,k+1,Z,t}$ from the assumed specification $[\mathcal{WC}_{k,k,Z,t}, \mathcal{N}_Z]$: At round k, each party i invokes the weak consensus protocol on its input x_i. Then, at round $k + 1$, each party sends the output from the weak consensus protocol to every other party via the network. After that, each party i sets the output value y_i to be the most received bit, and the grade $g_i = 1$ if and only if the value was received at least $n - t$ times.

If any party i decides on an output y_i with $g_i = 1$, it means that the party received y_i from at least $n - t$ parties, where at least $n - 2t$ are honest parties. Hence, every other honest party received the value y_i at least $n - 2t$ times. Given that $n - 2t > t$, at least one honest party obtained y_i as output of $\mathcal{WC}_{k,k,Z,t}$. Therefore, by weak consistency, no honest party obtained $1 - y_i$ as output from $\mathcal{WC}_{k,k,Z,t}$, from which it follows that each honest party j received it at most $t < n - 2t$ times and therefore outputs $y_j = y_i$.

Converter π_i^{gc}

Local Variables: y, g.

Round k

    On input x_i at **out**, output x_i at **in.wc**. // Output the value to $\mathcal{WC}_{k,k,Z,t}$
    On input z_i at **in.wc**, store the value.

Round $k + 1$

    Output z_i at each interface **in.net.ch**$_{i,j}$, for $j \in \mathcal{P}$.
    On input a message z_j from each **in.net.ch**$_{j,i}$: // Value from each party j
    if $\left| \{ j \in \mathcal{P} \mid z_j = 0 \} \right| \geq \left| \{ j \in \mathcal{P} \mid z_j = 1 \} \right|$ **then**
        $y \leftarrow 0$
    else
        $y \leftarrow 1$
    end if
    if $\left| \{ j \in \mathcal{P} \mid z_j = y \} \right| \geq n - t$ **then**
        $g \leftarrow 1$
    else
        $g \leftarrow 0$
    end if
    Output (y, g) at **out**.

Theorem 3. *Let* $t < \frac{n}{3}$. Π_{gc}^k *constructs* $\mathcal{GC}_{k,k+1,Z,t}$ *from* $[\mathcal{WC}_{k,k,Z,t}, \mathcal{N}_Z]$, *for any* $Z \subseteq \mathcal{P}$ *such that* $|Z| \leq t$, *and constructs* Φ *otherwise.*

Proof. Let $Z \subseteq \mathcal{P}$ such that $|Z| \leq t$. We want to prove that the system specification $\mathcal{R}_Z := (\Pi_{gc}^k)_{\overline{Z}}[\mathcal{WC}_{k,k,Z,t}, \mathcal{N}_Z] \subseteq \mathcal{GC}_{k,k+1,Z,t}$.

For that, all we need to prove is that at round $(k+1).b$, the outputs from the honest parties satisfy both the graded-consistency and the validity property, where the inputs to be taken into account are those at round $k.a$.

At round $k.a$, each party $i \in \overline{Z}$ inputs the message x_i to $\mathcal{WC}_{k,k,Z,t}$. Then, it is guaranteed that at round $k.b$, honest parties obtain an output that satisfies validity and weak-consistency. At round $(k+1).b$, we divide two cases:

- If every party $i \in \overline{Z}$ had as input value b at round k (there was pre-agreement): In $\mathcal{GC}_{k,k+1,Z,t}$, the parties output the bit $(b,1)$ by definition. In $\mathcal{R}_Z$, each party $i \in \overline{Z}$ outputs the bit b as z_j because of the validity of $\mathcal{WC}_{k,k,Z,t}$. Then, party i receives at least $n - t$ times the bit b. Hence, each party $i \in \overline{Z}$ also outputs b.
- If an honest party i decides on an output y_i with $g_i = 1$, then it means that the party received y_i from at least $n - t$ parties, where at least $n - 2t$ are honest parties. This implies that every other honest party received the value y_i at least $n - 2t$ times. Given that $n - 2t > t$, at least one honest party obtained y_i as output of $\mathcal{WC}_{k,k,Z,t}$ at round $(k+1).b$. Therefore, by weak consistency, no honest party obtained $1 - y_i$ as output from $\mathcal{WC}_{k,k,Z,t}$, from which it follows that each honest party j received at most $t < n - 2t$ times and therefore outputs $y_j = y_i$.

$\square$

A.3   King-Consensus

We first define a specification that achieves *king-consensus* with respect to a set of parties Z. In the king-consensus primitive, there is a party K, the king, which plays a special role. The primitive provides two guarantees:

- Validity: If all parties in $\overline{Z}$ input the same value, they agree on this value.
- King Consistency: If party $K \in \overline{Z}$, then there is a value y such that every party $j \in \overline{Z}$ decides on the value $y_j = y$.

We describe a specification $\mathcal{KC}_{k,l,Z,t,K}$ that models a king-consensus primitive where K has the role of king, and is secure up to t dishonest parties, which starts at round k and ends at round l. If $|Z| \leq t$:

$$\mathcal{KC}_{k,l,Z,t,K} := \left\{ \mathbf{R} \in \Phi \,\middle|\, \left(K \in \overline{Z} \to \exists v \; \forall i \in \overline{Z} \; y_i^{l.b} = v \right) \wedge \right.$$
$$\left. \left(\exists v \; \forall j \in \overline{Z} \; x_j^{k.a} = v \to \forall j \in \overline{Z} \; y_j^{l.b} = x_j^{k.a} \right) \right\}$$

And when $|Z| > t$, $\mathcal{KC}_{k,l,Z,t,K} = \Phi$.

Protocol $\Pi_{kc}^{k} = (\pi_1^{kc}, \ldots, \pi_n^{kc})$ constructs specification $\mathcal{KC}_{k,k+2,Z,t,K}$ from the assumed specification $[\mathcal{GC}_{k,k+1,Z,t}, \mathcal{N}_Z]$: At round k, each party i invokes the graded consensus protocol on its input x_i. Then, at round $k+2$, the king K sends the output z_K from the graded consensus protocol to every other party. Finally, each party i sets the value $y_i = z_i$ to the output of graded consensus if the grade was $g_i = 1$, and otherwise to the value of the king $y_i = z_K$. Note that consistency is guaranteed to hold only in the case the king is honest: if every honest party i has grade $g_i = 0$, they all adopt the king's value. Otherwise, there is a party j with grade $g_j = 1$, and graded consistency ensures that all honest parties (in particular the king) have the same output.

Converter π_i^{kc}

Local Variable: y.

Round k

> On input x_i at **out**, output x_i at **in.gc**. // Output to $\mathcal{GC}_{k,k+1,Z,t}$

Round $k+1$

> On input (z_i, g_i) from **in.gc**, store the pair.

Round $k+2$

> If $i = K$, output z_K to each **in.net.ch**$_{K,j}$, for $j \in \mathcal{P}$. // Party i is the king
> On input z_K from **in.net.ch**$_{K,i}$:
> **if** $g_i = 0$ **then**
> > $y \leftarrow z_K$
>
> **else**
> > $y \leftarrow z_i$
>
> **end if**
> Output y at **out**.

Theorem 4. *Let* $t < \frac{n}{3}$. Π_{kc}^{k} *constructs* $\mathcal{KC}_{k,k+2,Z,t,K}$ *from* $[\mathcal{GC}_{k,k+1,Z,t}, \mathcal{N}_Z]$, *for any* $Z \subseteq \mathcal{P}$ *such that* $|Z| \leq t$, *and constructs* Φ *otherwise.*

Proof. Let $Z \subseteq \mathcal{P}$ such that $|Z| \leq t$. We want to prove that the system specification $\mathcal{R}_Z := (\Pi_{kc}^{k})_{\overline{Z}}[\mathcal{GC}_{k,k+1,Z,t}, \mathcal{N}_Z] \subseteq \mathcal{KC}_{k,k+2,Z,t,K}$.

At round $k.a$, each party $i \in \overline{Z}$ inputs the message x_i to $\mathcal{GC}_{k,k+1,Z,t}$. Then, it is guaranteed that at round $(k+1).b$, honest parties obtain an output that satisfies validity and graded-consistency. We divide two cases:

- If every party $i \in \overline{Z}$ had as input value b at round k (there was pre-agreement): In $\mathcal{KC}_{k,k+2,Z,t,K}$, the parties output the bit b at round $k+2$ by definition. In the system specification $\mathcal{R}_Z$, each party $i \in \overline{Z}$ receives the bit $(b,1)$ at round $k+1$, because of the validity of $\mathcal{GC}_{k,k+1,Z,t}$. Hence, each party $i \in \overline{Z}$ also outputs b at round $k+2$.

- Otherwise, assume the king is honest. If every honest party i obtains an output $(z_i, 0)$, then at round $(k+2).b$, every party takes the value of the king z_K. Otherwise, there is a party j that obtained an output $(z_j, 1)$ at round $(k+1).b$. In this case, graded consistency implies that all honest parties have the same output. In particular, this holds for the honest king. Thus, all parties decide on the same output. □

A.4   Consensus

We define a specification that achieves *consensus* with respect to a set of parties Z. The primitive provides two guarantees:

- Validity: If all parties in $\overline{Z}$ input the same value, they agree on this value.
- Consistency: There is a value y such that every party $j \in \overline{Z}$ decides on the value $y_j = y$.

We describe a specification $\mathcal{C}_{k,l,Z,t}$ that models consensus, secure up to t dishonest parties, which starts at round k and ends at round l. If $|Z| \leq t$:

$$
\mathcal{C}_{k,l,Z,t} := \left\{ \mathbf{R} \in \Phi \;\middle|\; \left(\exists v \; \forall i \in \overline{Z} \; y_i^{l.b} = v \right) \wedge \right.
$$
$$
\left. \left(\exists v \; \forall j \in \overline{Z} \; x_j^{k.a} = v \to \forall j \in \overline{Z} \; y_j^{l.b} = x_j^{k.a} \right) \right\}
$$

And when $|Z| > t$, $\mathcal{C}_{k,l,Z,t} = \Phi$.

Protocol $\Pi_{\text{cons}}^k = (\pi_1^{\text{cons}}, \dots, \pi_n^{\text{cons}})$ constructs specification $\mathcal{C}_{k,k+3(t+1)-1,Z,t}$ from the assumed specification $[\mathcal{KC}_{k,k+2,Z,t,1}, \dots, \mathcal{KC}_{k+3t,k+3(t+1)-1,Z,t,t+1}]$. The idea is simply to execute the king consensus protocol sequentially $t + 1$ times with different kings. More concretely, at round $k + 3j$, $j \in [0, t]$, parties execute the king consensus protocol, where the king is $j + 1$. If parties start with the same input bit, validity of king consensus guarantees that this bit is kept until the end. Otherwise, since the number of dishonest parties is at most t, one of the executions has an honest king. After the execution with the honest king, consistency is reached, and validity ensures that consistency is maintained until the end of the execution.

Converter π_i^{cons}

Local Variable: y.

On input x at round k, $y \leftarrow x$.
for $j = 0$ to t **do**
    Output y at **in.kc** at round $k + 3j$. // Output to $\mathcal{KC}_{k+3j,k+3j+2,Z,t,j+1}$
    On input x' at **in.kc** at round $k + 3j + 2$, set $y \leftarrow x'$.
end for
Output y at **out**.

Theorem 5. *Let $t < n$. Π^k_{cons} constructs $\mathcal{C}_{k,k+3t+2,Z,t}$ from $[\mathcal{KC}_{k,k+2,Z,t,1}, \ldots, \mathcal{KC}_{k+3t,k+3t+2,Z,t,t+1}]$, for any $Z \subseteq \mathcal{P}$ such that $|Z| \leq t$, and constructs Φ otherwise.*

Proof. Let $Z \subseteq \mathcal{P}$ such that $|Z| \leq t$. We divide two cases:

- If every party $i \in \overline{Z}$ had as input value b at round k (there was pre-agreement): After each input to $\mathcal{KC}_{k+3j,k+3j+2,Z,t,j+1}$, the parties obtain the bit b because of validity. This is the same in $\mathcal{C}_{k,k+3t+2,Z,t}$ by definition.
- Otherwise, given that there are up to t dishonest parties and there are $t + 1$ different kings, there is an honest king K. The output of any system in the specification $\mathcal{KC}_{k+3(K-1),k+3K-1,Z,t,K}$ is the same value v for all honest parties because of the king consistency. All the following invocations to king consensus keep the value v as the output because of the validity property. Thus, all parties decide on the same output.

$\square$

A.5   Broadcast

In Sect. 6.2 we introduced a broadcast resource specification. We show how to achieve such a specification from $\mathcal{C}_{k,l,Z,t}$, as long as $|Z| \leq t$, for any $t \leq \frac{n}{3}$.
We recall the broadcast specification resource secure up to t dishonest parties, which starts at round k and ends at round l. If $|Z| \leq t$:

$$\mathcal{BC}_{k,l,Z,t} := \left\{ \mathbf{R} \in \Phi \; \middle| \; \exists v \left[\left(\forall j \in \overline{Z} \; y^{l,b}_j = v \right) \wedge \left(s \in \overline{Z} \rightarrow v = x^{k,a}_s \right) \right] \right\}$$

And when $|Z| > t$, $\mathcal{BC}_{k,l,Z,t} = \Phi$.

Protocol $\Pi^k_{\text{bc}} = (\pi^{\text{bc}}_1, \ldots, \pi^{\text{bc}}_n)$ constructs specification $\mathcal{BC}_{k,k+3t+3,Z,t}$ from the assumed specification $[\mathcal{C}_{k+1,k+3t+3,Z,t}, \mathcal{N}_Z]$. The sender simply sends its input value x to every party, and then parties execute the consensus protocol on the received value from the sender.

Theorem 6. *Let $t < \frac{n}{2}$. Π^k_{bc} constructs $\mathcal{BC}_{k,k+3t+3,Z,t}$ from $[\mathcal{C}_{k+1,k+3t+3,Z,t}, \mathcal{N}_Z]$, for any $Z \subseteq \mathcal{P}$ such that $|Z| \leq t$, and constructs Φ otherwise.*

Proof. Let $Z \subseteq \mathcal{P}$ such that $|Z| \leq t$. We divide two cases:

- If the sender is honest, every honest party receives the sender's input x_s and inputs this value into the consensus resource. Because of the validity of consensus, every honest party obtains x_s from the consensus resource and outputs it. This is the same in $\mathcal{BC}_{k,k+3t+3,Z,t}$ by definition.
- Otherwise, the consistency of the consensus resource guarantees that every honest party receives the same value from the consensus resource, and hence every honest party outputs the same value. $\square$

As a corollary of composing all the previous protocols, we obtain that there is a protocol which constructs broadcast from a network of bilateral channels.

Corollary 1. *Let $t < \frac{n}{3}$. There is a protocol that constructs $\mathcal{BC}_{k,k+3t+3,Z,t}$ from $\mathcal{N}_Z$, for any $Z \subseteq \mathcal{P}$ such that $|Z| \leq t$, and constructs Φ otherwise.*

References

1. Asharov, G., Lindell, Y.: A full proof of the BGW protocol for perfectly secure multiparty computation. J. Cryptol. **30**(1), 58–151 (2017)
2. Backes, M., Hofheinz, D., Müller-Quade, J., Unruh, D.: On fairness in simulatability-based cryptographic systems. In: Proceedings of the 2005 ACM workshop on Formal methods in security engineering, pp. 13–22. ACM (2005)
3. Backes, M., Pfitzmann, B., Waidner, M.: The reactive simulatability (rsim) framework for asynchronous systems. Inf. Comput. **205**(12), 1685–1720 (2007)
4. Ben-Or, M., Goldwasser, S., Wigderson, A.: Completeness theorems for non-cryptographic fault-tolerant distributed computation (extended abstract). In: 20th ACM STOC, pp. 1–10. ACM Press, May 1988
5. Berman, P., Garay, J.A., Perry, K.J.: Towards optimal distributed consensus. In: FOCS, pp. 410–415. IEEE (1989)
6. Canetti, R.: Universally composable security: a new paradigm for cryptographic protocols. In: 42nd FOCS, pp. 136–145. IEEE Computer Society Press, October 2001
7. Canetti, R., Cohen, A., Lindell, Y.: A simpler variant of universally composable security for standard multiparty computation. In: Gennaro, R., Robshaw, M. (eds.) CRYPTO 2015, Part II. LNCS, vol. 9216, pp. 3–22. Springer, Heidelberg (2015). https://doi.org/10.1007/978-3-662-48000-7_1
8. Canetti, R., Lindell, Y., Ostrovsky, R., Sahai, A.: Universally composable two-party and multi-party secure computation. In: 34th ACM STOC, pp. 494–503. ACM Press, May 2002
9. Chaum, D., Crépeau, C., Damgård, I.: Multiparty unconditionally secure protocols (extended abstract). In: 20th ACM STOC, pp. 11–19. ACM Press, May 1988
10. Cohen, R., Coretti, S., Garay, J., Zikas, V.: Probabilistic termination and composability of cryptographic protocols. In: Robshaw, M., Katz, J. (eds.) CRYPTO 2016, Part III. LNCS, vol. 9816, pp. 240–269. Springer, Heidelberg (2016). https://doi.org/10.1007/978-3-662-53015-3_9
11. Datta, A., Küsters, R., Mitchell, J.C., Ramanathan, A.: On the relationships between notions of simulation-based security. In: Kilian, J. (ed.) TCC 2005. LNCS, vol. 3378, pp. 476–494. Springer, Heidelberg (2005). https://doi.org/10.1007/978-3-540-30576-7_26
12. Dwork, C., Naor, M., Sahai, A.: Concurrent zero-knowledge. In: 30th ACM STOC, pp. 409–418. ACM Press, May 1998
13. Gennaro, R., Rabin, M.O., Rabin, T.: Simplified VSS and fast-track multiparty computations with applications to threshold cryptography. In: Coan, B.A., Afek, Y. (ed.) 17th ACM PODC, pp. 101–111. ACM, June/July 1998
14. Goldreich, O.: Concurrent zero-knowledge with timing, revisited. In: 34th ACM STOC, pp. 332–340. ACM Press, May 2002
15. Goldreich, O., Micali, S., Wigderson, A.: How to play any mental game or A completeness theorem for protocols with honest majority. In: Aho, A. (ed.) 19th ACM STOC, pp. 218–229. ACM Press, May 1987

16. Hirt, M., Maurer, U.M.: Player simulation and general adversary structures in perfect multiparty computation. J. Cryptol. **13**(1), 31–60 (2000)
17. Hirt, M., Zikas, V.: Adaptively secure broadcast. In: Gilbert, H. (ed.) EURO-CRYPT 2010. LNCS, vol. 6110, pp. 466–485. Springer, Heidelberg (2010). https://doi.org/10.1007/978-3-642-13190-5_24
18. Hofheinz, D., Müller-Quade, J.: A synchronous model for multi-party computation and the incompleteness of oblivious transfer. Proc. FCS **4**, 117–130 (2004)
19. Hofheinz, D., Unruh, D., Müller-Quade, J.: Polynomial runtime and composability. J. Cryptol. **26**(3), 375–441 (2013)
20. Jost, D., Maurer, U.: Overcoming impossibility results in composable security using interval-wise guarantees. In: Micciancio, D., Ristenpart, T. (eds.) CRYPTO 2020. LNCS, vol. 12170, pp. 33–62. Springer, Cham (2020). https://doi.org/10.1007/978-3-030-56784-2_2
21. Kalai, Y.T., Lindell, Y., Prabhakaran, M.: Concurrent general composition of secure protocols in the timing model. In: Gabow, H.N., Fagin, R. (eds.) 37th ACM STOC, pp. 644–653. ACM Press, May 2005
22. Katz, J., Maurer, U., Tackmann, B., Zikas, V.: Universally composable synchronous computation. In: Sahai, A. (ed.) TCC 2013. LNCS, vol. 7785, pp. 477–498. Springer, Heidelberg (2013). https://doi.org/10.1007/978-3-642-36594-2_27
23. Kushilevitz, E., Lindell, Y., Rabin, T.: Information-theoretically secure protocols and security under composition. In: Kleinberg, J.M., (ed.) 38th ACM STOC, pp. 109–118. ACM Press, May 2006
24. Küsters, R., Tuengerthal, M.: The IITM model: a simple and expressive model for universal composability. IACR Cryptol. EPrint Archive **2013**, 25 (2013)
25. Lanzenberger, D., Maurer, U.: Coupling of random systems. In: Theory of Cryptography – TCC 2020, to appear, November 2020
26. Maurer, U.: Indistinguishability of random systems. In: Knudsen, L.R. (ed.) EUROCRYPT 2002. LNCS, vol. 2332, pp. 110–132. Springer, Heidelberg (2002). https://doi.org/10.1007/3-540-46035-7_8
27. Maurer, U.: Secure multi-party computation made simple. Discrete Appl. Math. **154**(2), 370–381 (2006)
28. Maurer, U.: Constructive cryptography – a new paradigm for security definitions and proofs. In: Mödersheim, S., Palamidessi, C. (eds.) TOSCA 2011. LNCS, vol. 6993, pp. 33–56. Springer, Heidelberg (2012). https://doi.org/10.1007/978-3-642-27375-9_3
29. Maurer, U., Renner, R.: Abstract cryptography. In: In Innovations in Computer Science, Citeseer (2011)
30. Maurer, U., Renner, R.: From indifferentiability to constructive cryptography (and back). In: Hirt, M., Smith, A. (eds.) TCC 2016, Part I. LNCS, vol. 9985, pp. 3–24. Springer, Heidelberg (2016). https://doi.org/10.1007/978-3-662-53641-4_1
31. Maurer, U., Pietrzak, K., Renner, R.: Indistinguishability amplification. In: Menezes, A. (ed.) CRYPTO 2007. LNCS, vol. 4622, pp. 130–149. Springer, Heidelberg (2007). https://doi.org/10.1007/978-3-540-74143-5_8
32. Micciancio, D., Tessaro, S.: An equational approach to secure multi-party computation. In: Kleinberg, R.D. (ed.) ITCS 2013, pp. 355–372. ACM, January 2013
33. Nielsen, J.B.: On Protocol Security in the Cryptographic Model. BRICS, Russia (2003)
34. Pfitzmann, B., Waidner, M.: Composition and integrity preservation of secure reactive systems. In: IBM Thomas J, Watson Research Division (2000)

35. Rabin, T., Ben-Or, M.: Verifiable secret sharing and multiparty protocols with honest majority (extended abstract). In: 21st ACM STOC, pp. 73–85. ACM Press, May 1989
36. Wikström, D.: Simplified universal composability framework. In: Kushilevitz, E., Malkin, T. (eds.) TCC 2016, Part I. LNCS, vol. 9562, pp. 566–595. Springer, Heidelberg (2016). https://doi.org/10.1007/978-3-662-49096-9_24

Topology-Hiding Communication
from Minimal Assumptions

Marshall Ball[1], Elette Boyle[2], Ran Cohen[3], Lisa Kohl[4], Tal Malkin[1],
Pierre Meyer[2,5(✉)], and Tal Moran[2,3,6]

[1] Columbia University, New York, USA
{marshall,tal}@cs.columbia.edu
[2] IDC Herzliya, Herzliya, Israel
elette.boyle@idc.ac.il, talm@idc.ac.il
[3] Northeastern University, Boston, USA
rancohen@ccs.neu.edu
[4] Technion, Haifa, Israel
lisa.kohl@cs.technion.ac.il
[5] École Normale Supérieure de Lyon, Lyon, France
pierre.meyer@ens-lyon.fr
[6] Spacemesh, Tel Aviv, Israel

Abstract. *Topology-hiding broadcast* (THB) enables parties communicating over an incomplete network to broadcast messages while hiding the topology from within a given class of graphs. THB is a central tool underlying general *topology-hiding secure computation* (THC) (Moran et al. TCC'15). Although broadcast is a privacy-free task, it was recently shown that THB for certain graph classes necessitates computational assumptions, even in the semi-honest setting, and even given a single corrupted party.

In this work we investigate the minimal assumptions required for topology–hiding communication—both *Broadcast* or *Anonymous Broadcast* (where the broadcaster's identity is hidden). We develop new techniques that yield a variety of necessary and sufficient conditions for the feasibility of THB/THAB in different cryptographic settings: information theoretic, given existence of key agreement, and given existence of oblivious transfer. Our results show that feasibility can depend on various properties of the graph class, such as *connectivity*, and highlight the role of different properties of topology when kept hidden, including *direction*, *distance*, and/or *distance-of-neighbors* to the broadcaster.

An interesting corollary of our results is a dichotomy for THC with a public number of at least three parties, secure against one corruption: information-theoretic feasibility if all graphs are 2-connected; necessity and sufficiency of key agreement otherwise.

1 Introduction

Reliable communication between a set of mutually distrustful parties lies at the core of virtually any distributed protocol, ranging from consensus tasks [15,19] to secure multiparty computation [5,9,11,21]. Classical protocols from the '80s

© International Association for Cryptologic Research 2020
R. Pass and K. Pietrzak (Eds.): TCC 2020, LNCS 12551, pp. 473–501, 2020.
https://doi.org/10.1007/978-3-030-64378-2_17

considered complete communication graphs between the parties, where each pair of parties is connected by a communication channel. However, in many real-life scenarios the parties are not pairwise connected; this raises the need for distributed interactive computations, and in particular communication protocols, over an incomplete graph. Often, the *network topology itself* may be sensitive information that should not be revealed by the protocol.

Topology–Hiding Broadcast. With this motivation, Moran et al. [18] formalized the concept of *topology–hiding computation (THC)*. Here, the goal is to allow parties who see only their immediate neighborhood (and possibly know that the graph belongs to some class), to securely compute arbitrary functions without revealing any additional information about the graph topology other than the output (computations on the graphs, e.g., establishing routing tables, are also supported). THC is of theoretical interest, but is also motivated by real-world settings where it is desired to keep the underlying communication graph private. These include social networks, ISP networks, ad hoc (or mesh) networks, vehicle-to-vehicle communications, and possible approaches for contact tracing.

Given the existence of general MPC protocols, achieving THC for arbitrary functions hinges on communicating in a topology–hiding way, rather than on keeping inputs private. In particular, a core bottleneck for achieving general THC is the special case of *topology–hiding broadcast (THB)*, where a designated party (the broadcaster) reliably sends its message to all other parties. Indeed, given an MPC protocol for a function f defined in the broadcast model (where *all* communication is sent via a broadcast channel, possibly encrypted),[1] the parties can replace the broadcast channel by a THB protocol to obtain a THC protocol for the function f.

Although broadcast is a privacy-free task, realizing THB turns out to be challenging, even in the semi-honest setting where all parties follow the protocol. This is in stark contrast to standard (topology-revealing) broadcast, which is trivially achievable in the semi-honest setting, e.g., simply "flooding" the network, forwarding received messages. For general semi-honest corruptions, the best THB constructions follow from a series of works [1,2,12,16,18], culminating in THB (as well as THC) protocols for all graphs. However, even for THB, all known protocols require structured public-key cryptographic assumptions, such as QR, DDH, or LWE.[2] The use of strong assumptions was justified by Ball et al. [3] who showed that without an honest majority, even THB implies oblivious transfer (OT).[3]

A central paradigm in standard (topology–revealing) secure computation is to exchange *cryptographic* assumptions with an *honest-majority* assumption [5,9,20]. A recent work of Ball et al. [4] asked whether such a paradigm can be applied in the

---

[1] Such protocols exist in the honest-majority setting assuming key agreement, and thus under this assumption, THB implies THC. In the information-theoretic setting THC can be strictly stronger, as we will see.

[2] That is, the *Quadratic Residuosity* assumption, the *Decisional Diffie-Hellman* assumption, and the *Learning With Errors* assumption, respectively.

[3] The lower bound of [3] holds for 4-party 2-secure THB with respect to a small class of 4-node graphs, namely, a square, and a square with any of its edges removed.

topology-hiding realm. The results of [4] demonstrated that answering this question is more subtle than meets the eye, even when considering the basic case of *one semi-honest corruption*. On the one hand, they showed that information-theoretic THB (IT-THB) can be achieved for the graph class of *cycles*, where the protocol hides the ordering of parties within the cycle. On the other hand, they identified that THB for *paths* of $n \geq 4$ nodes (again hiding ordering) implies key agreement.

This Work. In a sense, [4] unveiled the tip of the iceberg, revealing a range of questions: Which aspects of the topology can be hidden information theoretically, and which require cryptographic hardness? Is key agreement sufficient for 1-corruption THB, or are there graph classes that require stronger assumptions?

In this paper we study the cryptographic power of THB. The main question that we ask is:

> *What are the minimal cryptographic assumptions*
> *required for THB for a given class of graphs?*

We focus on a minimal setting, with a small number of parties and a single, or few, semi-honest corruptions, which we denote by t-THB for t corruptions. This makes our lower bounds stronger; and, as we demonstrate, even this simple setting offers a rich multi-layered terrain, and provides insights and implications for more general settings (including THC).

Before proceeding to state our results, we note that prior THB protocols actually achieved the stronger property of *topology-hiding anonymous broadcast* (THAB), where the identity of the broadcaster remains hidden [7,8]. From the definitions of these primitives, we have that

$$THC \implies THAB \implies THB.$$

Thus, all lower bounds for THB (such as the one from [4] and our own results) apply also for THAB and THC. As we will show, there are classes of graphs where THB is possible information theoretically, but THAB, and thus THC, require strong cryptographic assumptions. Understanding for which topologies the reverse implications hold is addressed here in part, but the full answer remains an interesting open question.

1.1 Our Results

This work makes significant strides in mapping the landscape of THB, THAB, and THC in minimal settings, in the process developing new techniques that may be useful to achieve a full understanding of its complexities. As standard in the THC literature, we consider a synchronous setting, where the protocol proceeds in rounds.[4]

---

[4] LaVigne et al. [17] recently studied THC in a non-synchronous setting, demonstrating many barriers.

New Lower Bounds and Techniques

- *THB.* We explore which properties of graph topology are "hard" to hide, in the sense of requiring cryptographic assumptions to do so. We show that hiding any one of the properties of *direction*, *distance*, and/or *distance-of-neighbors* to the broadcaster is hard—while revealing all three but nothing else (in fact, only revealing distance-of-neighbors) can always be achieved information theocratically, using the trivial flooding protocol.
- *THAB.* We observe that t-THAB for any graph class containing a graph that is not $(t + 1)$-connected[5] implies *key agreement*. We further show that hiding the *number of participants* in certain graph classes implies *infinitely often oblivious transfer*, even for 1-THAB.

Unconditional & KA-Based Upper Bounds.

- *Unconditional.* We provide a construction of 1-THAB for *all 2-connected graphs*, whose complexity grows with the number of potential graphs in the class (in particular, it is efficient for constant-size graphs), which achieves *statistical* information-theoretic security.
- *Key Agreement.* Assuming the existence of *key agreement*, we achieve 1-THB for *all graphs*, and 1-THAB for all graphs of ≥ 3 nodes.

Corollaries and Conclusions

- *Dichotomy for* 1-THC with ≥ 3 parties. An interesting corollary of our results is a dichotomy for 1-THC with a fixed and known set of at least three parties[6] (i.e., where all graphs share the same vertex set): if all graphs in a class are 2-connected, the class supports information-theoretic 1-THC; otherwise, key agreement is necessary and sufficient for 1-THC.
- *Dichotomy for* 1-THAB with ≥ 3 parties. A similar result holds for 1-THAB for a dynamic set of parties (i.e., the vertex set of every graph is a *subset* of $[n]$) as long as each graph contains at least three nodes: if all graphs in a class are 2-connected, the class supports information-theoretic 1-THAB; otherwise, key agreement is necessary and sufficient for 1-THAB.
- *Characterization of* 1-THB for small graphs. Our results introduce several new constructions and analysis techniques; as a demonstration of their wider applicability, we provide a characterization of the more complex case of 1-THB for all graph classes on four nodes or fewer. Note that the feasibility boundaries of 1-THB are more complex than 1-THAB since, as we show, certain lower bounds for 1-THAB do not apply to 1-THB.
- THB *without OT.* Our upper bounds constitute the first protocols using machinery "below" oblivious transfer,[7] aside from the specific graph class of cycles of fixed length (that was shown in [4]).

---

[5] A graph is k-connected if and only if every pair of nodes is connected by k *vertex-disjoint* paths.

[6] If the class of graphs contains a 2-path, then oblivious transfer is necessary for secure computation [14].

[7] Note that OT is strictly stronger than KA in terms of black-box reductions, since OT implies KA in a black-box way, but the converse does not hold [10].

We next describe these results in more detail.

Lower Bounds. We begin by investigating the conditions under which THB and THAB for a graph class $\mathcal{G}$ *necessitate* cryptographic assumptions.

THB: Hiding direction, distance, or distance-of-neighbors. Recall that restricting attention to a class of graphs $\mathcal{G}$ captures that a THB protocol hides *partial* information about a graph topology. For example, if all graphs in $\mathcal{G}$ have property P, then the THB protocol need not hide whether P is satisfied when providing indistinguishability within this class. Our question thus becomes: for which properties of a graph topology is it the case that hiding necessitates cryptography?

Consider as a baseline the trivial "flooding" protocol, which in general is *not* topology hiding. Parties flood the network: on receiving the broadcast message, a party forwards it to all neighbors from which it was not previously received. Indeed, this protocol reveals information; e.g., the round number in which a party first receives the message corresponds directly to its distance from the broadcaster. However, even for this simple protocol, the amount of information revealed is limited. The leakage can be quantified precisely: each party learns exactly the distance from the broadcaster of each of its neighbors,[8] or *"distance-of-neighbors."* In particular, this includes the information of (a) *direction* of the broadcaster (i.e., which neighbors are on a shortest path to the broadcaster), and (b) *distance* to the broadcaster. Since the flooding protocol can be executed unconditionally for any graph class $\mathcal{G}$, it can only be some combination of this leaked distance-of-neighbors information for which hiding requires cryptography.

Examining the lower bound of [4], we observe that it constitutes an example where hiding the *direction* of the broadcaster from a given party necessitates key agreement (KA). This is embodied via the class of two graphs $\mathcal{G}_{4-\text{path}} = \{(A-B-\mathbf{C}-D), (B-\mathbf{C}-D-A)\}$ on a path, where party C is unaware whether the broadcasting party A lies to its left or right. Indeed, broadcaster direction is central to their lower bound, where KA agents Alice and Bob emulate the THB parties B and D, respectively, and jointly emulate C. Each flips a (private) coin to decide whether to also emulate A on their corresponding side. The two parties can detect cases where both (or neither) party decided to emulate A. In the remaining cases both parties agree on which side the broadcaster appears: this will serve as the secret common key bit.

At a high level, the security of this KA protocol relies on the fact that the eavesdropper's view is essentially that of party C—who, by topology hiding, cannot distinguish the relative direction of A. Thus, one may naturally ask whether hiding the *direction* to the broadcaster captures the essence of the cryptographic power of THB.

---

[8] If the neighbor sends the message in the first round that the party learns it, then its distance is one less of the party's distance. If the neighbor sends after the party learned it, then its distance equals the party's distance. If the neighbor does not send, then its distance is one more than the party's distance.

Our first result shows that the direction to the broadcaster is not the complete answer. We present a class of graphs $\mathcal{G}_{oriented-5-path}$ for which any constant-round 1-secure THB implies *infinitely often key agreement*,[9] but for which the direction to the broadcaster is always known. Specifically, we consider the class of 5-path graphs where the broadcaster A is always on the left,[10] i.e.,

$$\mathcal{G}_{oriented-5-path} = \big\{(A-B-C-D-E), (A-E-B-C-D), (A-D-E-B-C), (A-C-D-E-B)\big\}.$$

Because of this structure, the lower-bound techniques of Ball et al. [4] do not apply. Proving a key-agreement implication for $\mathcal{G}_{oriented-5-path}$ requires a new, more subtle approach, which we discuss in Sect. 2. In particular, unlike [4], we must leverage the fact that topology hiding holds for *any* choice of corrupted party. For example, party C cannot distinguish between $(A-B-C-D-E)$ and $(A-E-B-C-D)$, and party B cannot distinguish between $(A-E-B-C-D)$ and $(A-D-E-B-C)$.

Taking a broader view of this example, we observe that while the *direction* of the broadcaster is public for $\mathcal{G}_{oriented-5-path}$, the information to be hidden corresponds directly to the *distance* of the given parties to the broadcaster. One may thus once again wonder whether revealing both the *direction and distance* to the broadcaster dictates unconditional THB feasibility.

Our second result reveals that the answer is even more intricate. We demonstrate a class of graphs for which each party publicly knows *both its direction and distance* to the broadcaster, but for which 1-THB still implies key agreement.

Specifically, we consider the class $\mathcal{G}_{triangle}$ consisting of a triangle, with possibly one of its edges missing (see Fig. 1). Interestingly, this is a very basic communication pattern: if a party has two neighbors it does not know if its neighbors are directly connected or not, but a party with one neighbor knows the entire topology. Notably, direction and distance from the broadcaster are both clearly identifiable to each party given just its neighbor set; the only information hidden from a party is *its neighbor's* distance to the broadcaster. We show that this is enough to imply KA (see Sect. 2 for details).

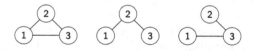

Fig. 1. The class $\mathcal{G}_{triangle}$.

To summarize, for each strict subset of the properties that are leaked by the flooding protocol (namely, *direction* and/or *distance* to the broadcaster), we

---

[9] An infinitely often key agreement guarantees correctness and security for infinitely many $\lambda \in \mathbb{N}$ (where λ stands for the security parameter).

[10] In particular, the "left/right" orientation can be deduced locally from each node's neighbor set.

demonstrate a graph class for which hiding only these properties implies public-key cryptographic assumptions. Complementarily, if all three properties (essentially, just the distance-of-neighbors) are known then one can use the flooding protocol to obtain THB information theoretically.

Theorem 1. (THB lower bounds, informal). *We consider THB with 1 semi-honest corruption.*

- *1-secure THB for the graph class $\mathcal{G}_{\text{oriented}-5-\text{path}}$ of 5-path graphs for which the broadcasting party is always in the leftmost direction (see above) implies infinitely often key agreement.*
- *1-secure THB for the graph class $\mathcal{G}_{\text{triangle}}$ (Fig. 1), for which the broadcasting party is always at a known distance and direction, implies key agreement.*

In contrast, for any class $\mathcal{G}$ such that for every party the distance of each of its neighbors to the broadcaster is fixed and known across all graphs, there exists an unconditionally 1-secure THB protocol.

THAB: Key Agreement and Beyond. We next turn to topology-hiding *anonymous* broadcast (THAB). As mentioned above, any lower bound for THB is also a lower bound for THAB; however, we show even stronger results for THAB.

The connection between anonymous communication and cryptographic hardness was previously studied by Ishai et al. [13]. They showed that in a communication network that provides *sender-anonymity* (under relatively strong adversarial observation), key agreement exists unconditionally; i.e., each pair of parties within the system can agree on a secret key. Our setting is slightly different, however, using the lower-bound technique from [4] a similar observation can be made: sender-anonymous communication over a path of three nodes implies the existence of standard Alice-Bob key agreement, where the eavesdropper can see which party sends which message.

This clear-cut impossibility of information-theoretic 1-THAB (in fact, 1-secure anonymous broadcast) on arbitrary incomplete networks stands in contrast to 1-THB, where the determination of when a graph class yields an implication to key agreement was demonstrably complex. Concretely, consider the following (singleton) class $\mathcal{G}_{\{a-b-c\}}$:

$$\mathcal{G}_{\{a-b-c\}} = \{(A - B - C)\}.$$

THB for this class is glaringly trivial (indeed, there is no information to hide because the topology is fixed); however, as discussed, 1-THAB on this class implies key agreement. For completeness, in Sect. 5.1 we prove this implication as a direct corollary of the key-agreement lower bound of Ball et al. [4], where the "direction" of the broadcaster (either A or C) in this case is hidden from the intermediate party B by anonymity.

At this moment, the reader may pause, ensnared in the underwhelming nature of the above class $\mathcal{G}_{\{a-b-c\}}$. However, by a standard player-partitioning argument ("projecting" a larger graph down onto the 3-path), the above result yields a much broader statement.

Proposition 1 (THAB lower bound 1, informal, [4,13]). *Let $\mathcal{G}$ be a class of graphs that contains a graph with at least $(t + 2)$ nodes that is not $(t + 1)$-connected. Then t-secure THAB for $\mathcal{G}$ implies KA.*

In our final lower-bound result, we demonstrate an even more extreme form of separation between THB and THAB. We consider the graph class $\mathcal{G}_{2-\text{vs}-3}$ that consists of all possible 2-path and 3-path graphs over three parties, i.e.,

$$\mathcal{G}_{2-\text{vs}-3} = \{(A - B), (A - C), (B - C), (A - B - C), (B - C - A), (C - A - B)\}.$$

In this class, for example, if A is only connected to B, it does not know whether B has a second neighbor or not. It is easy to see that 1-secure THB exists unconditionally (by the flooding protocol); however, we show that 1-secure THAB implies *infinitely often oblivious transfer*.[11] We emphasize that as opposed to other classes of graphs discussed thus far, the "hardness" of the class $\mathcal{G}_{2-\text{vs}-3}$ is based on hiding the *number of nodes* participating in the protocol. We refer the reader to Sect. 2 and 5.2 for further details on the lower bound.

Overall, we obtain the following theorem.

Theorem 2 (THAB lower bound 2, informal). *1-secure THAB for $\mathcal{G}_{2-\text{vs}-3}$ implies infinitely often OT.*

We remark that these results separate THB from THAB for very simple graph classes, where THAB requires computational assumptions whereas unconditional THB exists via the trivial flooding protocol. Later, in Section 1.1 we will show a more interesting separation via the "butterfly" graph, where the existence of information-theoretic THB itself is non-trivial.

Upper Bounds. Before stating our results, we recall the state-of-the-art for semi-honest THB and THAB with one corruption. Assuming oblivious transfer (OT), 1-THAB can be obtained for all graphs following the construction approach of Moran et al. [18].[12] Without assuming OT, the only previously known nontrivial[13] construction of THB or THAB is the information-theoretic 1-THAB for the specific graph class of cycles on a known number of nodes in [4].

We consider three settings of upper bounds: (1) with *information-theoretic* security, (2) assuming only *key agreement*, and (3) converting generically from THB to THAB.

---

[11] An infinitely often OT protocol guarantees correctness and security for infinitely many $\lambda \in \mathbb{N}$ (where λ stands for the security parameter).

[12] The result of [18] was limited to graphs of small diameter to allow an arbitrary number of corruptions. With a single corruption the same construction can support all graphs.

[13] THB exists trivially for any graph class in which each party's neighborhood uniquely identifies the graph topology.

Information-Theoretic Security. First, we consider protocols for achieving 1-THAB (and THB) in the *information-theoretic* setting, without cryptographic assumptions. Recall that the lower bound in Proposition 1 above rules out the possibility of 1-THAB for any graph class containing a graph that is not 2-connected. We show that conversely, if a class of graphs $\mathcal{G}$ contains only 2-connected graphs, then 1-THAB for $\mathcal{G}$ *is* feasible.

The protocol's communication grows polynomially in the *size* of the class $\mathcal{G}$ and its computation grows polynomially in the size of $\mathcal{G}$ and exponentially in the *maximal degree* of any $G \in \mathcal{G}$. However, our results are meaningful despite this caveat: First, the protocol is efficient when considering a constant number of parties (or appropriate graph classes of polynomial size). Second, since the protocol remains secure against computationally unbounded adversaries, it is still meaningful to consider protocols that are inefficient in the class.

Theorem 3 (1-IT-THAB for 2-connected, informal). *Let $\mathcal{G}$ be a class containing only 2-connected graphs. Then, there exists a statistical information-theoretic 1-THAB for $\mathcal{G}$ whose communication complexity is polynomial in the size of $\mathcal{G}$, and whose computation complexity is polynomial in the size of $\mathcal{G}$ and exponential in the maximal degree of $\mathcal{G}$.*

Combining Proposition 1 and Theorem 3 gives a characterization for information-theoretic 1-THAB: Namely, a protocol exists if and only if all graphs in the class are 2-connected (with the exception of the trivial class containing only the 2-path). For the case of 1-THB such dichotomy does not hold and, as we show, there exist graph classes with 1-connected graphs that still admit information-theoretic 1-THB protocols.

*Remark 1 (1-**IT-THB** for $\mathcal{G}_{\text{butterfly}}$).* Consider the 5-node, 1-connected butterfly graph (Fig. 2) and let $\mathcal{G}_{\text{butterfly}}$ contain all permutations of the nodes on the graph (where parties' positions are permuted). In Sect. 6.2, we show that although the simple flooding protocol does *not* directly hide topology, there exists a (perfectly secure) information-theoretic 1-THB protocol for $\mathcal{G}_{\text{butterfly}}$.

Fig. 2. The butterfly graph.

Upper bounds from KA. Recall that from the lower bounds presented above (see Sect. 1.1), key agreement is a necessary assumption for 1-THB and 1-THAB for many classes of graphs. This begs the question of when key agreement is also a *sufficient* assumption for 1-THB and 1-THAB. We show that assuming key agreement there exist 1-secure THB for all graphs, and 1-secure THAB for all graphs containing at least 3 nodes.

Theorem 4 (1-THAB and 1-THB from KA, informal).

- *Let $\mathcal{G}$ be a class consisting of graphs with at least three nodes. Assuming key agreement, there exist 1-THAB for $\mathcal{G}$.*
- *Let $\mathcal{G}$ be a class of graphs. Assuming key agreement, there exist 1-THB for $\mathcal{G}$.*

We note that in the first item of Theorem 4, removing the restriction of at least three nodes would require bypassing black-box separation results, due to Theorem 2 that asserts the necessity of (infinitely often) OT for the class $\mathcal{G}_{2-vs-3}$. On the other hand, by [18], assuming OT there exists 1-THAB for all graphs, essentially closing the gap in this regime.

THC Dichotomy. Upon closer inspection, we observe that our upper bounds—both the information-theoretic protocols for 2-connected graphs, as well as the results from KA above—give something even stronger than 1-THAB: they give topology-hiding *secure message transmission*, i.e., emulating pairwise secure point-to-point channels. In this case, assuming that the number of parties is fixed and known across all graphs, we can run the semi-honest "BGW" protocol [5], which only requires pairwise secure channels and works for an honest majority. Thus, together with our lower bounds, we arrive at the following dichotomy for 1-THC:

Corollary 1 (1-secure THC dichotomy, informal). *Consider a class of graphs $\mathcal{G}$ on $n \geq 3$ nodes. Then, the following hold regarding existence of THC for $\mathcal{G}$ secure against 1 semi-honest corruption:*

- *If all graphs $G \in \mathcal{G}$ are 2-connected, then there exists a statistically information-theocratically secure, 1-THC protocol for $\mathcal{G}$, whose communication is polynomial in the size of $\mathcal{G}$ and whose computation is polynomial in the size of $\mathcal{G}$ and exponential in the maximal degree of $\mathcal{G}$.*
- *If there exists $G \in \mathcal{G}$ that is not 2-connected, then KA is necessary and sufficient for 1-secure THC for $\mathcal{G}$.*

Generically converting THB to THAB. Our results have demonstrated a number of nontrivial separations between THB and THAB, identifying classes of t-connected graphs and computational assumptions which admit t-THB protocols but provably cannot obtain t-THAB. This includes, for example, $\mathcal{G}_{\{a-b-c\}}$ and $\mathcal{G}_{butterfly}$ for information theoretic vs. key agreement, as well as $\mathcal{G}_{2-vs-3}$ for information theoretic vs. oblivious transfer.

Finally, we show that graph connectivity is, indeed, a critical property for determining the relation between THB and THAB on a class of graphs. Specifically, we show that $(t + 1)$-connectivity is a sufficient condition for *equivalence* of the two notions against t corruptions.

Theorem 5 (t-THB$\Rightarrow$ t-THAB given (t+1)-connectivity, informal). *Let $n \in \mathbb{N}$ and let $\mathcal{G}$ be a class consisting of $(t + 1)$-connected graphs over n nodes. If there exists t-THB for $\mathcal{G}$ then there exists t-THAB for $\mathcal{G}$.*

Our reduction builds upon the "Dining Cryptographers" approach for anonymous broadcast due to Chaum [8]. Recall in THAB there exists a unique broadcaster who wishes to convey its input bit $x \in \{0, 1\}$ to all parties without revealing its identity (or the topology). To do so, each party first additively secret shares its input—defined to be 0 for any non-broadcaster—across its neighbors, locally sums all received shares to $s_i \in \{0, 1\}$, and then acts as broadcaster within the underlying (non-anonymous) THB with input value s_i. After this phase, all parties receive the vector of shares $(s_1, \ldots, s_n)$, which can be summed to yield the original input x. It was shown by [8] that if the graph is $(t + 1)$-vertex connected (so as to ensure that the adversary cannot corrupt a vertex cut), then the protocol is anonymous. We observe that the protocol further preserves the *topology hiding* of the underlying THB protocol. Indeed, given $(t + 1)$-connectivity, the vector of broadcasted shares $(s_1, \ldots, s_n)$ will be *uniform* conditioned on the necessary sum, independent of the graph structure.

Summary and Characterization of Graphs with up to Four Nodes. We summarize our combined contributions in Table 1, together with relevant prior results.

Table 1. Summary of Upper and Lower Bound Results. Read as "[row label] is necessary/sufficient for [column label]." E.g. the IT setting suffices to construct 1-THAB for any 2-connected family of graphs, whereas KA is needed to construct 1-THB for $\mathcal{G}_{\text{triangle}}$.

	1-THB		1-THAB	
	Sufficient	Necessary	Sufficient	Necessary
IT	$\mathcal{G}_{\text{cycle}}$ [4] $\mathcal{G}_{\text{butterfly}}$ (Remark 1) 2-connected (Theorem 3)	–	2-connected (Theorem 3)	–
KA	All graphs (Theorem 4)	$\mathcal{G}_{4-\text{path}}$ [4] $\mathcal{G}_{\text{oriented}-5-\text{path}}$ (Theorem 1) $\mathcal{G}_{\text{triangle}}$ (Theorem 1)	All graphs (≥ 3 nodes) (Theorem 4)	Not 2-connected (≥ 3 nodes) (Proposition 1)
OT	All graphs [18]	–	All graphs [18]	$\mathcal{G}_{2-\text{vs}-3}$ (Theorem 2)

In addition, and as a demonstration of the power and applicability of the techniques developed, in the full version of this work we provide a characterization of the feasibility of 1-THB and 1-THAB for all graph classes on up to 4 parties. The characterization uses a partition of the 4-node graphs into multiple classes, each of which can be handled by a separate technique.

Organization of the Paper. We proceed in Sect. 2 to provide an overview of the core new techniques toward proving our main results. In Sect. 3 we provide the necessary definitions and preliminaries. In Sect. 4 and Sect. 5 we present an abbreviated version of our THB and THAB lower bounds, respectively. And, in Sect. 6 and Sect. 7 we include a short version of our information-theoretic and KA-based upper bounds. We refer the reader to the full version of this paper for detailed treatment of these results, as well as corollaries and implications to characterization of 1-THB, 1-THAB, and 1-THC.

2   Technical Overview

We next highlight a selection of our new analysis and protocol-construction techniques, described in Sects. 2.1 and 2.4. We will describe two analysis techniques that are used in our lower bounds: *"phantom jump"* and *"artificial over-extension."* In addition, we will describe two protocol-design techniques that are used in our upper bounds: *"censored brute force"* and *"dead-end channels."*

2.1   Analysis Technique: "Phantom Jump"

The "phantom jump" technique is a means for proving indistinguishability of the transcript of messages sent across a given edge $A - B$ in THB executions on two different graphs, via a sequence of intermediate indistinguishability steps, each appealing to THB security for a different graph pair. In applications, the initial and final graphs will have a party "jump" from one side of the graph to the other, which will be used within the key-agreement implication analysis.

This technique is used within some of our key-agreement lower bounds. We focus here on a specific example for the class $\mathcal{G}_{\text{triangle}}$ (of a triangle graph with a potential edge missing). We point the reader to more elaborate examples on 4-node graph classes in the full version.

We start by recalling how a 1-THB protocol π for $\mathcal{G}_{4-\text{path}} = \{(A - B - C - D), (B - C - D - A)\}$ was used to construct key agreement in [4]. The idea is for Alice to choose two long random strings r_1 and r_2 and send them to Bob in the clear. Next, Alice and Bob continue in phases as follows:

- In each phase Alice and Bob locally toss coins x_{Alice} and x_{Bob}, respectively.
- They proceed to run two executions of π in which Alice always emulates B and C and Bob emulates D. In addition, if $x_{\text{Alice}} = 0$ then Alice emulates A (as a neighbor of B) broadcasting r_1 in the first run; otherwise she emulates A broadcasting r_2 in the second run. Similarly, if $x_{\text{Bob}} = 1$ then Bob emulates A (as a neighbor of D) broadcasting r_1 in the first run; otherwise he emulates A broadcasting r_2 in the second run.
- If parties B and D output r_1 in the first run and r_2 in the second, Alice and Bob output their bits x_{Alice} and x_{Bob}, respectively; otherwise, they execute another phase.

Clearly, if $x_{\text{Alice}} = x_{\text{Bob}}$ in some iteration then Alice and Bob will output the same coin, and by the assumed security of π, the eavesdropper Eve will not be able to learn who emulated A in the first run and who in the second. If $x_{\text{Alice}} \neq x_{\text{Bob}}$, then in at least one of the runs nobody emulates the broadcaster A, so with overwhelming probability Alice and Bob will detect this case.

We now show how to adjust this argument to $\mathcal{G}_{\text{triangle}}$. Constructing the KA protocol is rather similar, where Alice always emulates B and Bob always emulates C, and each party emulates the broadcaster A based on their local coins x_{Alice} and x_{Bob} (see Fig. 3). Proving correctness follows exactly as in the argument from [4]; however, proving security is more involved. Indeed, in $\mathcal{G}_{4-\text{path}}$ the view of Eve corresponds to a partial view of the intermediate node C who is never a neighbor of A, and so by the security of π, never learns its direction to A. When considering $\mathcal{G}_{\text{triangle}}$, the view of Eve consists of the communication between B and C, and one of them must be a neighbor of A.

This is where the new phantom-jump technique comes into play. As opposed to [4], we do not construct a reduction from Eve to the security of the THB protocol; rather, we use a direct indistinguishability argument. Notice that the KA construction required the use of only two graphs $(A-B-C)$ and $(B-C-A)$. The third graph (the triangle) is needed for the proof.

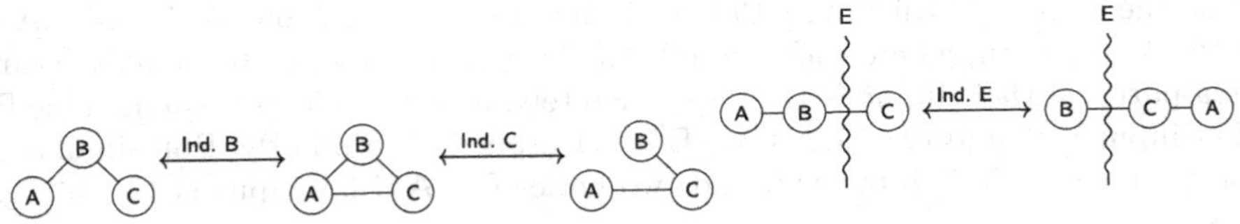

Fig. 3. 1-THB on $\mathcal{G}_{\text{triangle}}$ implies KA.

As depicted in Fig. 3, the view of Eve consists of the communication between B and C. By THB security B cannot distinguish between the 3-path $(A-B-C)$ and the complete triangle; in particular, the distribution of the messages on the channel between B and C is indistinguishable in both cases. Similarly, by THB security C cannot distinguish between the 3-path $(B-C-A)$ and the complete triangle; in particular, the distribution of the messages on the channel between B and C is indistinguishable in both cases. By a simple hybrid argument it follows that the messages between B and C are indistinguishable when communicating in $(A-B-C)$ and when communicating in $(B-C-A)$. It follows that the distinguishing advantage of Eve is negligible.

2.2 Analysis Technique: "Artificial Over-Extension"

The artificial over-extension technique is used for proving two of our lower bounds. First, Theorem 1 where 1-THB for $\mathcal{G}_{\text{oriented}-5-\text{path}}$ is used to construct infinitely often KA (see also Sect. 4.1); and second, Theorem 2 where 1-THAB for $\mathcal{G}_{2-\text{vs}-3}$ is used to construct infinitely often OT (see Sect. 5.2). In the following, we focus on the latter.

Recall that in the class $\mathcal{G}_{2-\text{vs}-3}$ a party (say A) that has a single neighbor (say B) does not know whether B has another neighbor C or not. This uncertainty is the source of the cryptographic hardness we present; indeed, if the parties know that an honest majority cannot be assumed (i.e., there are only two parties) then 1-THAB is trivial, whereas if an honest majority can be assumed (i.e., there are three parties) then 1-THAB exists assuming KA (by Theorem 4). We also note that without anonymity, 1-THB trivially exists in $\mathcal{G}_{2-\text{vs}-3}$ (via the flooding protocol).

We start with an intermediate goal, that of constructing oblivious transfer from a *two-round* 1-THAB protocol π for the graph class $\mathcal{G}_{2-\text{vs}-3}$,[14] and later explain how the novel "artificial over-extension" technique allows us to extend this construction to arbitrary constant-round protocols. Note that using this technique we can only construct *infinitely often* OT, and extending the implication to a full-blown OT is left as an interesting open question.

OT from two-round 1-THAB. Given a two-round 1-THAB protocol π we construct a secure two-party protocol for Boolean AND (which in turn implies OT [14]).

In the protocol, Alice and Bob will emulate an execution of the 1-THAB protocol on a path, where each extends the length of the path (by emulating an extra party) if their input is 1. More concretely, Alice simulates a single node B if her input is 0, and two nodes A − B if her input is 1. Similarly, Bob simulates a single node C if his input is 0 and two nodes C − A if his input is 1 (see Fig. 4). Next, Alice chooses a message $m \xleftarrow{R} \{0,1\}^\lambda$ at random, sends it to Bob in the clear, and initiates an execution of π on message m on the graph with her leftmost node (either B or A) as broadcaster. At the conclusion of π, Bob identifies whether his right-most emulated party (either C or A) correctly outputs m. If so, then Bob outputs 0; if not, he outputs 1.

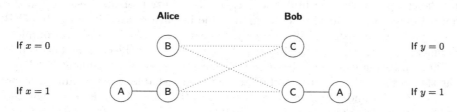

Fig. 4. Boolean AND from two-round 1-THAB for $\{B - C, A - B - C, B - C - A\}$

We show that this protocol securely computes AND of Alice and Bob's inputs.

---

[14] In fact, for this step we will only need for the smaller graph class $\{B - C, A - B - C, B - C - A\} \subset \mathcal{G}_{2-\text{vs}-3}$.

- For *security*, we exploit the fact that the only case where there is something to hide (namely, if a party holds input 0) is where the respective party has control over just a *single* node in π. Security therefore follows from the fact that π is a THAB protocol with security against one corruption. For example, the views of a corrupt Alice emulating B within executions over graphs $B - C$ (Bob has input 0) and $B - C - A$ (Bob has input 1) are indistinguishable. Note here that for security it is crucial that π is an *anonymous* broadcast protocol, because in case $x = 0$, Alice broadcasts from node B and in case $x = 1$ from node A. (In fact, as noted above, 1-THB can be achieved trivially on $\mathcal{G}_{2-\text{vs}-3}$.)
- For *correctness*, first note that when at least one party has input 0, the corresponding graph is an element of $\{B - C, A - B - C, B - C - A\} \subset \mathcal{G}_{2-\text{vs}-3}$, in which case proper delivery of m to Bob's right-most node is guaranteed by correctness of π. On the other hand, when $x \wedge y = 1$ (i.e., both Alice and Bob emulate node A) the parties effectively emulate π over an "invalid" length-4 path $A - B - C - A$. While behavior of π within such execution is unclear, since π runs in only 2 rounds, the message m simply cannot reach the right-most node emulated by Bob at distance 3. Thus, Bob will correctly output 1.

Infinitely often OT from constant-round 1-THAB. Note that correctness of the construction above crucially relies on efficiently detecting an execution of π on the graph $A - B - C - A$, leveraging its insufficient round complexity. However, this argument is no longer guaranteed when π completes in more than two rounds. This is where the "artificial over-extension" technique comes into play.

The insight is that *either* an execution of π on graph $A - B - C - A$ can indeed be efficiently detected, in which case the protocol above extends (and we are done), *or* π actually provides a stronger form of topology hiding that we can further leverage. Namely, if neither Alice nor Bob can identify when π is executed on $A - B - C - A$ as opposed to a legal graph, then in particular π provides 1-THAB for the larger graph class $\mathcal{G}_{2-\text{vs}-3}' := \mathcal{G}_{2-\text{vs}-3} \cup \{A - B - C - A\}$.

In this case, we can take a similar approach to above, but with the graphs $\{A - B, C - A - B, A - B - C - A\} \subset \mathcal{G}_{2-\text{vs}-3}'$, with Alice emulating A or $C - A$, and Bob emulating B or $B - C - A$, and hope that π identifiably breaks down on the "over-extended" path $C - A - B - C - A$ of length 5. If not, this argument repeats, until—via this artificial over-extension technique—ultimately we reach a graph class $\mathcal{G}$ for which:

- π *is* 1-THAB on $\mathcal{G}$, including $\{Y - Z, X - Y - Z, Y - Z - P\} \subset \mathcal{G}$
- π is *not* 1-THAB on $\mathcal{G} \cup \{X - Y - Z - P\}$,

where $X, Y, Z \in \{A, B, C\}$, and P is a path of length upper-bounded by the round complexity of π. Once we do, then the original secure-AND protocol approach will succeed, modulo some differences described below, with Alice emulating Y or $X - Y$, and Bob emulating Z or $Z - P$.

To argue that eventually we find a path $X - Y - Z - P$ for which π identifiably breaks down, we again appeal to its bounded round complexity, i.e., π must fail identifiably (with probability 1) once the length of the path exceeds the round complexity. The limitation of constant rounds is a subtle side effect of the corresponding hybrid argument, to argue that there must be some step where we jump sufficiently from indistinguishable to efficiently identifiable.

Consider the resulting secure-AND protocol, once an appropriate $\mathsf{X}, \mathsf{Y}, \mathsf{Z}, \boldsymbol{P}$ are found. The only modification from the simpler two-round version is how to detect the (over-extended) case $x \wedge y = 1$. When π was two rounds, identifying this event was immediate: Bob's right-most party simply will not receive the delivered message. Here, this is not necessarily the case, as the identifiable "breakdown" of π may occur before the length of $\mathsf{X} - \mathsf{Y} - \mathsf{Z} - \boldsymbol{P}$ exceeds π's round complexity. Thus, instead, the parties will run the distinguisher that—roughly speaking—exists from the fact that π is not 1-THAB on $\mathcal{G} \cup \{\mathsf{X} - \mathsf{Y} - \mathsf{Z} - \boldsymbol{P}\}$. This is the reason why our final protocol guarantees correctness only for infinitely many $\lambda \in \mathbb{N}$: All we can say is that *either* the protocol π is 1-THAB on $\mathcal{G} \cup \{\mathsf{X} - \mathsf{Y} - \mathsf{Z} - \boldsymbol{P}\}$ and we can continue with the extension argument, *or* π is not 1-THAB, i.e., there exists a distinguisher that efficiently detects the "too-long" path $\mathsf{X} - \mathsf{Y} - \mathsf{Z} - \boldsymbol{P}$ with noticeable advantage for *infinitely many* $\lambda \in \mathbb{N}$. Finally, in order to boost correctness towards negligible correctness error (for infinitely many λ), Alice and Bob simply run the protocol π and the distinguisher sufficiently many times, each time on input of a fresh message m, and take a corresponding majority vote.

2.3   Protocol Design: "Censored Brute Force"

This technique enables constructing unconditionally secure pairwise channels between each pair of parties which further guarantees sender anonymity. Such anonymous and private channels are used for proving Theorem 3 and Corollary 1, by constructing 1-THAB and 1-THC with information-theoretic security for any class $\mathcal{G}$ for which all graphs are 2-connected (see Sect. 6.1 for more details). Recall that the communication complexity of the resulting protocols is polynomial in the size of $\mathcal{G}$ (which could be superpolynomial) and the computation complexity is polynomial in the size of $\mathcal{G}$ and exponential in the maximal degree of $\mathcal{G}$.

The high-level idea is twofold: For any *single* 2-connected graph G, we show how to unconditionally perform sender-anonymous point-to-point communication on G with an ability for any party to (anonymously) "censor" the communication, i.e., yielding delivery of random garbage instead of the intended message. Then, for a given class of 2-connected graphs $\mathcal{G}$, the parties will simultaneously execute (in parallel) a separate anonymous-communication protocol for *every graph* $G \in \mathcal{G}$; for each such G-execution, a party will *censor* the execution if its true neighborhood is inconsistent with its neighborhood in G. As such, the only protocol execution that remains uncensored will be the one corresponding to the *correct* execution graph G (and the identity of which G this corresponds to can be made hidden to the receiving party). We elaborate on these two aims below.

Communicating Anonymously in a 2-Connected Graph. More concretely, suppose we have a *single* 2-connected graph G on vertex set $[n]$, and fix some designated source and target nodes $\sigma \neq \tau \in [n]$. Let $H_{\sigma\tau}$ denote an arbitrary

$\sigma\tau$-*orientation* of G,[15] i.e., a directed acyclic graph with unique sink τ and unique source σ formed by assigning a direction to each edge in G. Moreover, label all nodes $1, 2, \ldots, n$ according to a topologically consistent ordering of $H_{\sigma\tau}$ (beginning with σ and ending at τ). We consider the numbering/orientation of any graph G to be a public parameter, computed according to some deterministic procedure (see full version).

Now suppose node u wishes to send a message m to the target node τ anonymously and securely on the graph G. In the first round, the source σ (i.e., the node labeled 1) prepares additive shares of 0 (or of m if $\sigma = u$) for each of its outgoing edges in $H_{\sigma\tau}$. In round 2, the source σ sends the corresponding share to its neighbor node labeled 2, who then prepares secret shares of what it received ($+m$ if it is u) for each outgoing edge. More generally, in round $i < n$ all nodes with an edge to the ith node send their shares to the ith node. The ith node, having received shares on all incoming edges, then sums up what it receives (adds m if it is u) and prepares additive shares of the result for each of its outgoing edges. In round n, all nodes with edges to τ (the target node) send their shares to τ and τ outputs their summation.

Correctness follows from the homomorphic properties of additive secret sharing. To see why this protocol is secure (namely, that it hides u and m), note that the 2-connectivity of G implies that there are at least 2 vertex-disjoint $\sigma\tau$-paths in $H_{\sigma\tau}$. Thus, the messages any intermediate party (corresponding to $2, \ldots, n-1$) receives are uniformly random because that node is in some sense always missing at least one share (corresponding to a disjoint $\sigma\tau$-path); the source σ does not receive anything at all, and the view of the target τ is simply a random sharing of its output m.

This protocol enjoys some other useful properties. Most notably, any non-sink node can covertly "censor" communication by simply preparing (and sending) shares of a uniformly random message, instead of preparing shares corresponding to what they received (as per the protocol). The view of every other party is identically distributed, with the exception of τ who now receives secret shares of a uniformly random message in the final round.

Compiling to Hide Topology. Now, let $\mathcal{G}$ be a class of 2-connected graphs on vertex set $[n]$. Loosely speaking, the parties will simulate the above protocol for every possible graph in $\mathcal{G}$ simultaneously. Each node will covertly censor every protocol corresponding to a graph that is *not* locally consistent with their local neighborhood (sending random messages at the appropriate times). As a result, exactly one protocol (corresponding to the "real" graph) will give the correct output message and all others will give uniformly random output.

To be slightly more concrete, all nodes will execute the protocol above for each graph in the class in parallel. To keep track of which message is which, for every node but τ we will label the messages with the graph/protocol that the message corresponds to. If an edge is missing from the real graph, but present in

---

[15] The standard notation in the literature is st-orientation; to avoid confusion with the notation t that stands for the corruption threshold, we use $\sigma\tau$-orientation instead.

a graph corresponding to one of the simulated protocols, the corresponding message cannot be sent. However, the receiving node knows not to expect a message either. From this and the uniformly random nature of non-terminal messages in the above protocol, nothing is leaked locally by labeling the simulations. However, sending labeled messages to τ would clearly identify the "real" topology. So instead, all parties will send all final protocol messages in randomly permuted order. To enable τ identifying the real output, the sender will append a long checksum to the message. The target τ will try all message combinations (this is the reason for the exponential dependency in the maximal degree) and output the unique one with a correct checksum (or abort if more than one message has a valid checksum).

2.4   Protocol Design Technique: "Dead-End Channels"

The Dead-End Channels technique is used to obtain 1-THAB for all graphs of at least 3 nodes (and 1-THB for all graphs), assuming existence of *key agreement*. Recall that before the present work, such results were only known assuming oblivious transfer [18].

The high-level idea of our 1-THAB protocol, as in Moran et al. [18], is to broadcast the message via *flooding*, but in a way that hides from the parties at which round they received the broadcast message. This can be achieved by passing the message between *virtual parties*, each consisting of two real parties that hold additive secret shares of the message (depicted, e.g., as purple bars for each neighboring pair of parties below). Only in the final round will the parties exchange their secret shares and recover the message.

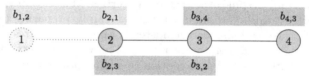

The challenge thus becomes passing the messages between virtual parties. In [18] this is solved by using oblivious transfer (OT) to run an MPC protocol realizing the virtual party, and allowing every adjacent pair of virtual parties to securely compute the *OR* of their messages.

In our setting, we do not have the ability to perform secure computations pairwise between parties without OT. Instead, we leverage the fact that given at least three nodes we are guaranteed an honest majority, and can therefore (once the parties establish secure channels using the key agreement protocol) build on techniques from information-theoretic secure computation to appropriately pass along the message.

However, this itself is not so straightforward. For example, in the image above, the neighboring parties $2 - 3 - 4$ would wish to jointly emulate a three-party secure computation to perform the secure transfer from $2-3$ to $3-4$. But, the issue is that parties cannot reveal whether they truly have neighbors with which to jointly compute: for example, party 2 above must then emulate a nonexistent neighbor 1 to hide its true degree. Thus grouping parties in three, including possibly a simulated neighbor, would allow the adversary to gain control over a majority. (On the other hand, building on secure computation including four our more neighbored parties, the same party could appear several times in the protocol and therefore potentially learn about the connectivity of its neighbors.)

Our approach builds on the following idea: We will give one party within each group of three the role of a *dealer* to deal *OT correlations*, which can be used to establish a secure OT channel between two other parties. This alone is not sufficient, as one of the parties could be simulated by the dealer (in the case that the dealer has degree one), and therefore allows the dealer to gain full control over the OT channel, and in particular learn the honest parties' inputs. To prevent this, we observe that—again using OT correlations—one can establish *dead-end channels* (i.e., information sent via such a channel cannot be read by anyone apart from the sender) if and only if the receiver is a simulated party. Therefore, even if the dealer simulates one of the parties, it does not learn anything about the honest parties' inputs. Note that it is crucial that dead-end channels are indistinguishable from secure channels from the view of the sender. Further, a key observation is that using OT correlations to establish dead-end channels does not leak anything about the topology, even if the dealer of the OT correlations has degree one. This is the case, because the only thing the dealer could potentially learn from the other party is whether its degree is one—but if the dealer has degree one it already knows that the degree of its neighbor must be at least two (as we are guaranteed a connected graph with a strict honest majority).

3   Preliminaries

Notations. For $n \in \mathbb{N}$ let $[n] = \{1, \cdots, n\}$. In our protocols we sometimes denote by B an upper bound on the number of participating parties, by n the number of actually participating parties, and by t an upper bound on the number of corrupted parties. The security parameter is denoted by λ.

Graph Notations and Properties. A graph $G = (V, E)$ is a set V of vertices and a set E of edges, each of which is an unordered pair $\{v, w\}$ of distinct vertices. A graph is *directed* if its edges are instead ordered pairs (v, w) of distinct vertices. An *oriented* graph is a directed graph having no symmetric pair of directed edges, and an *orientation* of an undirected graph is an assignation of a direction to each of its edges so as to make it oriented. A graph is k-*connected* if it has more than k vertices and remains connected whenever fewer than k vertices are removed. A graph class $\mathcal{G}$ is k-connected if every graph $G \in \mathcal{G}$ is k-connected. Throughout this paper we only consider *connected* graphs, even if we do not systematically make this explicit. The *(open) neighborhood* of a vertex v in an undirected graph G, denoted $\mathcal{N}_G(v)$, is the set of vertices sharing an edge with v in G. The *closed neighborhood* of v in G is in turn defined by $\mathcal{N}_G[v] := \mathcal{N}_G(v) \cup \{v\}$.

UC Framework. We work in the UC framework of Canetti [6]. Unless stated otherwise, we will consider computationally unbounded, static, and semi-honest adversaries and environments.

Topology-Hiding Computation (THC). We recall the definition of topology-hiding computation from [4,18]. The real-world protocol is defined in a model where all communication is transmitted via the functionality $\mathcal{F}^{\mathcal{G}}_{\text{graph}}$ (described in Fig. 5). The functionality is parametrized by a family of graphs $\mathcal{G}$, representing all possible network topologies (aka communication graphs) that the protocol supports. We implicitly assume that every node in a graph is associated with a specific *party identifier*, pid. To simplify the notation, we will consider that P_v in the protocol is associated with node v in the graph.

Initially, before the protocol begins, $\mathcal{F}^{\mathcal{G}}_{\text{graph}}$ receives the network communication graph G from a special graph party P_{graph}, makes sure that $G \in \mathcal{G}$, and provides to each party P_v with $v \in V$ its local neighbor-set. Next, during the protocol's execution, whenever party P_v wishes to send a message m to party P_w, it sends (v, w, m) to the functionality; the functionality verifies that the edge (v, w) is indeed in the graph, and if so delivers (v, w, m) to P_w.

Note that if all the graphs in $\mathcal{G}$ have exactly n nodes, then the exact number of participants is known to all and need not be kept hidden. In this case, defining the ideal functionality and constructing protocols becomes a simpler task. However, if there exist graphs in $\mathcal{G}$ that contain a *different* number of nodes, then the model must support functionalities and protocols that only know an *upper bound B* on the number of participants. In the latter case, the actual number of participating parties n must be kept hidden.

Given a class of graphs $\mathcal{G}$ with an upper bound B on the number of parties, we define a protocol π with respect to $\mathcal{G}$ as a set of B PPT interactive Turing machines (ITMs) $(P_1, \ldots, P_B)$ (the parties), where any subset of them may be activated with (potentially empty) inputs. Only the parties that have been activated participate in the protocol, send messages to one another (via $\mathcal{F}^{\mathcal{G}}_{\text{graph}}$), and produce output.

An ideal-model computation of a functionality $\mathcal{F}$ is augmented to provide the corrupted parties with the information that is leaked about the graph; namely, every corrupted (dummy) party should learn its neighbor-set. Note that the functionality $\mathcal{F}$ can be completely agnostic about the actual graph that is used, and even about the family $\mathcal{G}$. To augment $\mathcal{F}$ in a generic way, we define the wrapper-functionality $\mathcal{W}^{\mathcal{G}}_{\text{graph}-\text{info}}(\mathcal{F})$, that runs internally a copy of the functionality $\mathcal{F}$. The wrapper $\mathcal{W}^{\mathcal{G}}_{\text{graph}-\text{info}}(\cdot)$ acts as a shell that is responsible to provide the relevant leakage to the corrupted parties; the original functionality $\mathcal{F}$ is the core that is responsible for the actual ideal computation.

More specifically, the wrapper receives the graph $G = (V, E)$ from the graph party P_{graph}, makes sure that $G \in \mathcal{G}$, and sends a special initialization message containing G to $\mathcal{F}$. (If the functionality $\mathcal{F}$ does not depend on the communication graph, it can ignore this message.) The wrapper then proceeds to process messages as follows: Upon receiving an initialization message from a party P_v responds with its neighbor set $\mathcal{N}_G(v)$ (just like $\mathcal{F}^{\mathcal{G}}_{\text{graph}}$). All other input messages

---

The functionality $\mathcal{F}^{\mathcal{G}}_{\text{graph}}$

The functionality $\mathcal{F}^{\mathcal{G}}_{\text{graph}}$ is parametrized by a family of graphs $\mathcal{G}$; let B denote the maximal number of nodes in $G \in \mathcal{G}$. The functionality proceeds with a special graph party P_{graph} and with a subset of the parties $P_1, \ldots, P_B$ (to be defined by the graph received from P_{graph}) as follows.

Initialization Phase:
   Input: $\mathcal{F}^{\mathcal{G}}_{\text{graph}}$ waits to receive the graph $G = (V, E)$ from P_{graph}. If $G \notin \mathcal{G}$, abort.
   Output: Upon receiving an initialization message from P_v, verify that $v \in V$, and if so send $\mathcal{N}_G(v)$ to P_v.
Communication Phase:
   Input: $\mathcal{F}^{\mathcal{G}}_{\text{graph}}$ receives from a party P_v a destination/data pair (w, m) where $w \in \mathcal{N}_G(v)$ and m is the message P_v wants to send to P_w. (If $v, w \notin V$, or if w is not a neighbor of v, $\mathcal{F}^{\mathcal{G}}_{\text{graph}}$ ignores this input.)
   Output: $\mathcal{F}^{\mathcal{G}}_{\text{graph}}$ gives output (v, m) to P_w indicating that P_v sent the message m to P_w.

Fig. 5. The communication graph functionality

from a party P_v are forwarded to $\mathcal{F}$ and every message from $\mathcal{F}$ to a party P_v is delivered to its recipient.

Note that formally, the set of all possible parties V^* is fixed in advance. To represent a graph $G' = (V', E')$ where $V' \subset V^*$ is a subset of the parties, we use the graph $G = (V^*, E')$, where all vertices $v \in V^* \setminus V'$ have degree 0.

Definition 1 (Topology-hiding computation). We say that a protocol π securely realizes a functionality $\mathcal{F}$ in a topology-hiding manner with respect to $\mathcal{G}$ tolerating a semi-honest adversary corrupting t parties if π securely realizes $\mathcal{W}^{\mathcal{G}}_{\text{graph-info}}(\mathcal{F})$ in the $\mathcal{F}^{\mathcal{G}}_{\text{graph}}$-hybrid model tolerating a semi-honest adversary corrupting t parties.

Broadcast and Anonymous Broadcast. In this work we will focus on topology-hiding computation of two central functionalities. The first is the *broadcast* functionality (see Fig. 6), where a designated and publicly known party, named *the broadcaster*, starts with an input value m. Our broadcast functionality guarantees that every party that is connected to the broadcaster in the communication graph receives the message m as output. In this paper, we assume the communication graphs are always connected. However, the broadcaster may not be participating, in which case it is represented as a degree-0 node in the communication graph (and all the participating nodes are in a separate connected component.)

Parties that are not connected to the broadcaster receive a message that is supplied by the adversary (we can consider stronger versions of broadcast, but this simplifies the proofs).

We denote the broadcast functionality where the broadcaster is P_i by $\mathcal{F}_{\text{bc}}(P_i)$.

The functionality $\mathcal{F}_{\mathsf{bc}}(P_i)$

The broadcast functionality $\mathcal{F}_{\mathsf{bc}}(P_i)$ is parametrized by the broadcaster P_i and proceeds as follows.

Initialization: The functionality receives the communication graph G from the wrapper $\mathcal{W}_{\mathsf{graph\text{-}info}}$.

Input: Record the input message $m \in \{0, 1\}$ sent by the broadcaster P_i.

Output: Send the output m to every party that is in the same connected component as P_i in G. For every other party in G, the output delivered to that party is supplied by the adversary.

Fig. 6. The broadcast functionality

Definition 2 (t-THB). Let $\mathcal{G}$ be a family of graphs and let t be an integer. A protocol π is a t-THB protocol with respect to $\mathcal{G}$ if $\pi(P_v)$ securely realizes $\mathcal{F}_{\mathsf{bc}}(P_v)$ in a topology-hiding manner with respect to $\mathcal{G}$, for every P_v, tolerating a semi-honest adversary corrupting t parties.

The second is the *anonymous-broadcast* functionality (see Fig. 7). This functionality is similar to broadcast with the exception that the broadcaster is not known and its identity is kept hidden even after the computation completes. Namely, the environment will activate exactly one of the parties with an input value, informing this party that it is the broadcaster. We denote the anonymous broadcast functionality $\mathcal{F}_{\mathsf{anon-bc}}$.

The functionality $\mathcal{F}_{\mathsf{anon\text{-}bc}}$

The anonymous-broadcast functionality $\mathcal{F}_{\mathsf{anon\text{-}bc}}$ proceeds as follows.

Initialization: The functionality receives the communication graph G from the wrapper $\mathcal{W}_{\mathsf{graph\text{-}info}}$.

Input: Upon receiving an input message $m \in \{0, 1\}$ from one of the parties P_i, record it.

Output: If exactly one input message m from party P_i was received, Send the output m to every party that is in the same connected component as P_i in G. For every other party in G, the output delivered to that party is supplied by the adversary.

If more than one input was received, send G and all received inputs to the adversary, and for every party in G, the output delivered to that party is supplied by the adversary (i.e., there is no security guarantee if more than one input was received.)

Fig. 7. The anonymous-broadcast functionality

Definition 3 (t-THAB). Let $\mathcal{G}$ be a family of graphs and let t be an integer. A protocol π is a t-THAB protocol with respect to $\mathcal{G}$ if π securely realizes $\mathcal{F}_{anon-bc}$ in a topology-hiding manner with respect to $\mathcal{G}$, tolerating a semi-honest adversary corrupting t parties.

4   THB Lower Bounds

In this section we demonstrate that achieving broadcast while hiding certain graph properties necessitates cryptographic assumptions.

4.1   Hiding Distance Requires io-KA (The Oriented 5-Path)

In this section, we show that hiding the distance from the broadcaster, in constant rounds, requires infinitely-often Key Agreement (io-KA). In particular, we will show that any constant-round protocol for the class $\mathcal{G}_{oriented-5-path}$ (Fig. 8), implies io-KA.

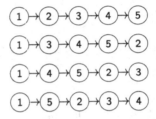

Fig. 8. The class $\mathcal{G}_{oriented-5-path}$ of oriented paths, rooted in P_1. Communication is bidirectional, arrows simply indicate that nodes can deduce the broadcaster's direction.

In this class the nodes ②,③,④,⑤ always know the direction of the broadcaster, ① (it's in the direction of their lowest-valued neighbor, mod 5), but cannot distinguish (from their local neighborhood) whether they are distance 2 or 3 from the broadcaster. E.g. ③ cannot distinguish between ①-②-③-④-⑤ and ①-⑤-②-③-④, as in both cases its local neighborhood is ②-③-④. Note that if just distance is leaked to this class, the trivial flooding protocol is secure.

Intriguingly, the resulting key agreement construction is not fully-black-box, nor is it even explicit. Further, our result critically requires the $\mathcal{G}_{oriented-5-path}$-THB to be efficient in *round* complexity. We remark that such a limitation is inherent, as we demonstrate that $\mathcal{G}_{oriented-5-path}$ *unconditionally* admits an ϵ-secure topology-hiding broadcast protocol that works in $O(1/\epsilon)$ rounds, for any $\epsilon > 0$.[16] In contrast, the key agreement construction of Sect. 4.2 *is* fully

---

[16] In fact, the upper bound holds for a large body of graph classes, where only distance need be hidden.

black-box and rules out the existence of such an upper bound for the class $\mathcal{G}_{\text{triangle}}$. It remains open whether an ϵ-secure $\mathcal{G}_{\text{oriented}-5-\text{path}}$-THB in $< 1/\epsilon$ rounds requires io-KA, or more generally whether negligible security in polynomial rounds requires io-KA.

Theorem 6 *If there exists a constant-round 1-THB protocol for the class $\mathcal{G}_{\text{oriented}-5-\text{path}}$, then infinitely-often key-agreement also exists.*

The proof introduces an argument called '*artificial over-extension*' (Sect. 2) which involves using the 1-THB on longer and longer graphs (outside of the scope of its correctness and security guarantees) until the protocol breaks in an identifiable way. Details are deferred to the full version of this paper.

4.2 Hiding Neighbor Distances Requires KA (The Triangle)

Consider the class $\mathcal{G}_{\text{triangle}} = \{G_{\text{tr}}^0, G_{\text{tr}}^1, G_{\text{tr}}^2\}$ as represented in Fig. 9, which we (abusively) call '*the Triangle*'. The players are P_1, P_2, P_3 with the broadcaster always being P_1; P_2 and P_3 are connected, and P_2 and/or P_3 is connected to P_1.

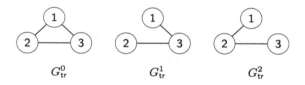

$$G_{\text{tr}}^0 \qquad\qquad G_{\text{tr}}^1 \qquad\qquad G_{\text{tr}}^2$$

Fig. 9. The class $\mathcal{G}_{\text{triangle}}$.

The *secret of the topology* can be summarized as follows: if one of the two non-broadcasting parties P_2 or P_3 is connected to the broadcaster, it does not know if the other is as well. Note that preserving the secret of the topology of $\mathcal{G}_{\text{triangle}}$ can also be reformulated as 'hiding the neighbor distances' from the parties. Indeed, for P_2 (resp. P_3) knowing the topology means knowing if P_3 (resp. P_2) is at distance one or two from the broadcaster.

Theorem 7 (Broadcast on 'The Triangle' requires KA) *If there exists a 1-THB(1) protocol for the class $\mathcal{G}_{\text{triangle}}$ then there exists a key-agreement protocol.*

In order to prove this theorem, we explicitly construct a key-agreement scheme from a 1-THB(1) protocol π on $\mathcal{G}_{\text{triangle}}$. The construction of this KA protocol follows very closely the proof of Theorem 3.1 (and the associated Protocol 3.2) in Ball et al. [4], but we use a novel technique (the *phantom jump* argument to reduce the security of the key-agreement scheme to the topology-hiding properties of π. See description in Sect. 2.1; the details of the proof are deferred to the full version of this paper.

5   THAB Lower Bounds

5.1   Low Vertex Connectivity Requires KA

In this section we show how t-THAB on a class which contains even a single graph with at least $t+2$ vertices and which is not $(t+1)$-connected implies Key-Agreement. It should be noted that this is a relatively weak result on its own, as testified by the fact that even non topology-hiding anonymous broadcast on such a class already implies KA, but we present it here for completeness' sake and because it matches the upper bound of Theorem 11.

Proposition 2 *t-THAB on a class containing a graph with at least $(t+2)$ vertices which is not $(t+1)$-vertex-connected implies KA.*

The result is similar in spirit to that of Ishai et al. [13]—who showed how *anonymity* can be leveraged to obtain *privacy*—. We show it using techniques from [4] however, which are more directly applicable as their setting is the same as ours. The proof is deferred to the full version of this paper.

5.2   Uncertain Honest Majority Requires io-OT (The 2-vs-3 Paths)

In the previous section we showed that, for a large number of graph classes, key-agreement is *necessary* to achieve 1-THAB. A natural follow-up question is to ask whether key agreement is sufficient to achieve 1-THAB *on all graphs* or not. We answer this question negatively by showing that constant-round 1-THAB on the class of paths of length two and three implies *infinitely often oblivious transfer*.

This is similar to the result of Ball et al. [3], who showed no honest majority can imply oblivious transfer in the 2-corruption setting. Note though that our result requires inherently different techniques, as in the one-corruption setting there exists only one graph with no honest majority, namely the path of length 2. 1-THAB on this graph only is trivial, as the only party that is not the broadcaster *knows* that the other party must be the broadcaster. But, adding the path of length 3 (where in fact there is always a honest majority), we can prove an implication to infinitely-often oblivious transfer (io-OT). From a certain point of view, we show that one cannot hide *how far* information travels, unless *always* guaranteed an honest majority.

Theorem 8 *Let π be a constant-round 1-THAB protocol for $\mathcal{G}_{2\text{-vs-}3}$. Then, there exists a uniform infinitely-often OT protocol secure in the presence of a semi-honest adversary.*

In order to prove this theorem, we show that a constant-round 1-THAB for $\mathcal{G}_{2\text{-vs-}3}$ can be used to build a secure two-party infinitely often AND functionality, which in turn implies infinitely often OT. The proof closely follows that of Theorem 6, which introduced the "artificial over-extension" technique, and is described in Sect. 2.2. The details are deferred to the full version of this paper.

6   Information-Theoretic Upper Bounds

In this section, we present our information-theoretic constructions: in Sect. 6.1, 1-IT-THAB for 2-connected graphs, and in Sect. 6.2, 1-IT-THB for the 1-connected butterfly graph.

6.1   2-Connectivity is Sufficient for 1-IT-THAB

On an intuitive level, $(t + 1)$-vertex-connectivity could be a sufficient condition to perform t-IT-THAB since messages exchanged between distant parties in the graph can be secret-shared among $t + 1$ vertex-disjoint paths. This way, privacy of communication can be ensured (since, with only t corruptions, an adversary cannot recover all the shares). The core challenge, however, is *how* to have the parties route message shares consistently on general, unstructured graphs, in a topology-hiding fashion (in particular, message routing can only be done locally). We prove this intuition to be true for $t = 1$, and provide a way for parties to route secret-shares in 2-connected graphs.

Theorem 9. *Let $n \in \mathbb{N}$, let $\mathcal{G}$ be a class of 2-connected graphs of vertex set size at most n, let d_{max} is the maximal degree of any graph in $\mathcal{G}$, and let $\delta > 0$. Then, there exists a protocol that securely realizes $\mathcal{F}_{\mathsf{anon-bc}}$ with security δ in a topology-hiding manner with respect to $\mathcal{G}$, tolerating a single semi-honest corruption.*

Moreover, the protocol completes within n rounds with total communication complexity $O(n^2 d_{\mathsf{max}} \cdot |\mathcal{G}| \cdot (\ell + \log(n/\delta) + d_{\mathsf{max}} \cdot \log |\mathcal{G}|))$ and computation complexity $O(|\mathcal{G}|^{d_{\mathsf{max}}})$ per node.

The proof revolves around a technique we call *"censored brute-force"* (see Sect. 2.3). Full details are deferred to the full version of this paper.

6.2   2-Connectivity is Not Necessary for 1-IT-THB (Butterfly Graph)

Section 5.2 shows a separation between 1-THAB and 1-THB, with the class $\mathcal{G}_{2-\mathsf{vs}-3}$: 1-THAB implies infinitely often OT, yet 1-THB is possible information-theoretically by flooding. In order to understand if the separation is really meaningful or due to an edge case of the definition of THB, we ask whether there is a class which separates the two functionalities and for which 1-THB is not trivial (i.e., cannot be achieved by simple flooding). To this end, we prove there exist graph classes on which 1-IT-THAB is impossible and flooding is not topology-hiding, but there still exist 1-IT-THB. One such class is the family of butterfly graphs (Fig. 10), on which 1-IT-THAB is impossible by Proposition 2.

Fig. 10. The class of butterfly graphs consists of all possible permutations of the graph depicted above with nodes in $\{1, 2, 3, 4, 5\}$.

Theorem 10 (IT-THB on butterfly). There exists a 1-IT-THB protocol with respect to $\mathcal{G}_{\text{butterfly}}$ with perfect security.

What makes this problem non-trivial is that the center node cannot learn which of its neighbors are connected, while the other nodes cannot learn which node is the center node. We present an information-theoretic protocol which runs in two phases. In the first, the broadcaster sends the message to all its neighbors which ensures the center node gets hold of it. In the second phase, the center node broadcasts the message in parallel on a bunch of subgraphs. Each of these is the graph induced by the center and any other two parties. Note that each of these subgraphs is either a triangle or a 3-path, much like in 'the Triangle', described in Sect. 6.1. Crucially, we ensure the center node does not learn which of them are triangles and which are 3-paths, while also preventing the other parties learning the identity of the center node. Now, every neighbor of the center—i.e., every party—knows the broadcast bit. The protocol is detailed in the full version of the paper.

7 Key-Agreement Upper Bounds

We show that key-agreement is sufficient to achieve 1-THAB on all graphs with *at least 3 nodes*—in other words, on all graphs where we are guaranteed an *honest majority*. As shown in Sect. 5.2 this is the best we can hope to achieve for general graph classes. This result can then be extended to 1-THB for *all graphs*.

Theorem 11 (KA is sufficient for 1-THAB on all graphs of size at least 3). If there exists a key-agreement protocol, there exists a 1-THAB protocol on the class of all graphs with at least 3 and at most B vertices.

Based on [18], the idea is to broadcast the message via *flooding*, but in a way that hides from the parties at which round they received the broadcast message. We leverage the fact there is a guaranteed honest local majority nearly everywhere in the network to run a protocol between locally simulated virtual parties.[17] The weakened assumption when compared to [18] (KA instead OT)

---

[17] In fact, we critically exploit the fact that if a party has a single neighbor (and thus no guaranteed local honest majority), she *knows* that neighbor's neighborhood is majority honest.

means we have to take extra steps to run secure protocols locally; to that effect we introduce the trick of *'dead-end channels'*. The details of this construction are deferred to the full version of this paper.

Theorem 12 (KA is sufficient for 1-THB on all graphs). If there exists a key-agreement protocol, there exists a 1-THB protocol on the class of all graphs with at most B vertices.

The proof of Theorem 12 follows almost immediately from that of Theorem 11, and only involves introducing a small step to handle the case of size-2 networks. Again, it is left to the full version.

Acknowledgments. We thank the anonymous reviewers of TCC 2020 for pointing to the connection between anonymous communication and key agreement in [13]. M. Ball's research is supported in part by an IBM Research PhD Fellowship.

M. Ball and T. Malkin's work is supported in part by JPMorgan Chase & Co. as well as the U.S. Department of Energy (DOE), Office of Science, Office of Advanced Scientific Computing Research under award number DE-SC-0001234. E. Boyle's research is supported in part by ISF grant 1861/16, AFOSR Award FA9550-17-1-0069, and ERC Starting Grant 852952 (HSS). R. Cohen's research is supported by NSF grant 1646671. L. Kohl's research is supported by ERC Project NTSC (742754). P. Meyer's research is supported in part by ISF grant 1861/16, AFOSR Award FA9550-17-1-0069, and ERC Starting Grant 852952 (HSS).

Any views or opinions expressed herein are solely those of the authors listed, and may differ from the views and opinions expressed by JPMorgan Chase & Co. or its affiliates. This material is not a product of the Research Department of J.P. Morgan Securities LLC. This material should not be construed as an individual recommendation for any particular client and is not intended as a recommendation of particular securities, financial instruments or strategies for a particular client. This material does not constitute a solicitation or offer in any jurisdiction.

References

1. Akavia, A., Moran, T.: Topology-hiding computation beyond logarithmic diameter. In: Coron, J.-S., Nielsen, J.B. (eds.) EUROCRYPT 2017. LNCS, vol. 10212, pp. 609–637. Springer, Cham (2017). https://doi.org/10.1007/978-3-319-56617-7_21
2. Akavia, A., LaVigne, R., Moran, T.: Topology-hiding computation on all graphs. In: CRYPTO'17, part I, pp. 176–227 (2019)
3. Ball, M., Boyle, E., Malkin, T., Moran, T.: Exploring the boundaries of topology-hiding computation. In: Nielsen, J.B., Rijmen, V. (eds.) EUROCRYPT 2018. LNCS, vol. 10822, pp. 294–325. Springer, Cham (2018). https://doi.org/10.1007/978-3-319-78372-7_10
4. Ball, M., Boyle, E., Cohen, R., Malkin, T., Moran, T.: Is information-theoretic topology-hiding computation possible? In: Hofheinz, D., Rosen, A. (eds.) TCC 2019. LNCS, vol. 11891, pp. 502–530. Springer, Cham (2019). https://doi.org/10.1007/978-3-030-36030-6_20
5. Ben-Or, M., Goldwasser, S., Wigderson, A.: Completeness theorems for non-cryptographic fault-tolerant distributed computation (extended abstract). In: Proceedings of the 20th STOC, pp. 1–10 (1988)

6. Canetti, R.: Security and composition of multiparty cryptographic protocols. J. Cryptology **13**(1), 143–202 (2000)
7. Chaum, D.: Untraceable electronic mail, return addresses, and digital pseudonyms. Commun. ACM **24**(2), 84–88 (1981)
8. Chaum, D.: The dining cryptographers problem: Unconditional sender and recipient untraceability. J. Cryptology **1**(1), 65–75 (1988)
9. Chaum, D., Crépeau, C., Damgård, I.: Multiparty unconditionally secure protocols (extended abstract). In: Proceedings of the Twentieth Annual ACM Symposium on Theory of Computing, pp. 11–19 (1988)
10. Gertner, Y., Kannan, S., Malkin, T., Reingold, O., Viswanathan, M.: The relationship between public key encryption and oblivious transfer. In: Proceedings 41st Annual Symposium on Foundations of Computer Science, pp. 325–335. IEEE (2000)
11. Goldreich, O., Micali, S., Wigderson, A.: How to play any mental game or a completeness theorem for protocols with honest majority. In: STOC, pp. 307–328 (1987)
12. Hirt, M., Maurer, U., Tschudi, D., Zikas, V.: Network-hiding communication and applications to multi-party protocols. In: Robshaw, M., Katz, J. (eds.) CRYPTO 2016. LNCS, vol. 9815, pp. 335–365. Springer, Heidelberg (2016). https://doi.org/10.1007/978-3-662-53008-5_12
13. Ishai, Y., Kushilevitz, E., Ostrovsky, R., Sahai, A.: Cryptography from anonymity. In: 47th Annual IEEE Symposium on Foundations of Computer Science (FOCS 2006), pp. 239–248. IEEE (2006)
14. Kilian, J.: A general completeness theorem for two-party games. In: Proceedings of the 23rd Annual ACM Symposium on Theory of Computing, pp. 553–560 (1991)
15. Lamport, L., Shostak, R.E., Pease, M.C.: The Byzantine generals problem. ACM Trans. Program. Lang. Syst. **4**(3), 382–401 (1982)
16. LaVigne, R., Liu-Zhang, C.-D., Maurer, U., Moran, T., Mularczyk, M., Tschudi, D.: Topology-hiding computation beyond semi-honest adversaries. In: Beimel, A., Dziembowski, S. (eds.) TCC 2018. LNCS, vol. 11240, pp. 3–35. Springer, Cham (2018). https://doi.org/10.1007/978-3-030-03810-6_1
17. LaVigne, R., Liu-Zhang, C.-D., Maurer, U., Moran, T., Mularczyk, M., Tschudi, D.: Topology-hiding computation for networks with unknown delays. In: Kiayias, A., Kohlweiss, M., Wallden, P., Zikas, V. (eds.) PKC 2020. LNCS, vol. 12111, pp. 215–245. Springer, Cham (2020). https://doi.org/10.1007/978-3-030-45388-6_8
18. Moran, T., Orlov, I., Richelson, S.: Topology-hiding computation. In: Dodis, Y., Nielsen, J.B. (eds.) TCC 2015. LNCS, vol. 9014, pp. 159–181. Springer, Heidelberg (2015). https://doi.org/10.1007/978-3-662-46494-6_8
19. Pease, M.C., Shostak, R.E., Lamport, L.: Reaching agreement in the presence of faults. J. ACM **27**(2), 228–234 (1980)
20. Rabin, T., Ben-Or, M.: Verifiable secret sharing and multiparty protocols with honest majority (extended abstract). In: Proceedings of the 21st Annual ACM Symposium on Theory of Computing, pp. 73–85 (1989)
21. Yao, A.C.: Protocols for secure computations (extended abstract). In: FOCS, pp. 160–164. IEEE (1982)

Information-Theoretic 2-Round MPC Without Round Collapsing: Adaptive Security, and More

Huijia Lin[1(✉)], Tianren Liu[1], and Hoeteck Wee[2,3]

[1] University of Washington, Seattle, USA
{rachel,tianrenl}@cs.washington.edu
[2] NTT Research, California, USA
[3] ENS, Paris, France
wee@di.ens.fr

Abstract. We present simpler and improved constructions of 2-round protocols for secure multi-party computation (MPC) in the semi-honest setting. Our main results are new information-theoretically secure protocols for arithmetic NC1 in two settings:
(i) the plain model tolerating up to $t < n/2$ corruptions; and
(ii) in the OLE-correlation model tolerating any number of corruptions.
Our protocols achieve adaptive security and require only black-box access to the underlying field, whereas previous results only achieve static security and require non-black-box field access. Moreover, both results extend to polynomial-size circuits with computational and adaptive security, while relying on black-box access to a pseudorandom generator. In the OLE correlation model, the extended protocols for circuits tolerate up to $n - 1$ corruptions.

Along the way, we introduce a conceptually novel framework for 2-round MPC that does not rely on the round collapsing framework underlying all of the recent advances in 2-round MPC.

1 Introduction

Secure multi-party computation (MPC) [5,12,18,23] allows a group of n mutually distrusting parties to jointly evaluate a function over their private inputs in a manner that reveals nothing beyond the output of the function. In this work, we focus on semi-honest two-round MPC protocols. The state of the art, following the recent breakthroughs in [6,17] may be broadly classified as follows:

H. Lin and T. Liu—Supported by NSF grants CNS-1528178, CNS-1514526, CNS-1652849 (CAREER), CNS-2026774, a Hellman Fellowship, a JP Morgan Research Award, the Defense Advanced Research Projects Agency (DARPA) and Army Research Office (ARO) under Contract No. W911NF-15-C-0236, and a subcontract No. 2017-002 through Galois. The views expressed are those of the authors and do not reflect the official policy or position of the Department of Defense, the National Science Foundation, or the U.S. Government.

H. Wee—Research supported in part by ERC Project aSCEND (H2020 639554).

© International Association for Cryptologic Research 2020
R. Pass and K. Pietrzak (Eds.): TCC 2020, LNCS 12551, pp. 502–531, 2020.
https://doi.org/10.1007/978-3-030-64378-2_18

- protocols for $\mathbf{NC^1}$ achieving information-theoretic security tolerating $t < n/2$ adversarial parties [2];
- protocols for polynomial-size circuits $\mathbf{P/poly}$ achieving computational security tolerating $t < n/2$ adversarial parties, assuming the existence of one-way functions [1,2];
- protocols for polynomial-size circuits $\mathbf{P/poly}$ achieving computational security tolerating $t < n$ adversarial parties, assuming the existence of oblivious transfer [6,17].

All of these constructions follow the same high-level "round collapsing" strategy introduced in [15]. In particular, they apply garbled circuits to the circuits of parties' algorithms of a multi-round MPC protocol, where the garbling is used to collapse the multi-round MPC protocol to a 2-round protocol.

1.1 Our Results

We present simpler and improved constructions of 2-round protocols for secure multi-party computation (MPC) in the semi-honest setting. Our main results are new information-theoretically secure protocols for arithmetic $\mathbf{NC^1}$ in two settings:

(i) the plain model tolerating up to $t < n/2$ corruptions; and

(ii) in the OLE-correlation model tolerating any number of corruptions. Two parties with an Oblivious Linear Evaluation (OLE) correlation hold respectively random elements $(a^{(1)}, b^{(1)})$ and $(a^{(2)}, b^{(2)})$ such that $a^{(1)}a^{(2)} = b^{(1)} + b^{(2)}$ over a field.

Our protocols achieve adaptive security [10,11] and require only black-box access to the underlying field, whereas previous results only achieve static security and require non-black-box field access. Moreover, both results extend to polynomial-size circuits with computational and adaptive security, while relying on black-box access to a pseudorandom generator. In the OLE correlation model, the extended protocols for circuits tolerate up to $n - 1$ corruptions. While the honest majority setting is a natural and well-established model, we believe that the OLE-correlation model is also very natural to study, especially for arithmetic computation: OLE correlations enable very efficient online computation, and the correlations themselve can be generated efficiently in the pre-processing phase [8,9]. We provide a comparison of our results with the state of the art in Fig. 1 and Fig. 2.

Along the way, we introduce a conceptually novel framework for 2-round MPC that does not rely on the round collapsing framework underlying all of the recent advances in 2-round MPC staring from [15].

Our Techniques. The crux of our protocols, following [2,19,20], is a way to "encode" degree-3 polynomials into randomized polynomials that have degree 2 after pre-processing of local inputs and randomness – known as multi-party randomized encodings (MPREs). Following the round-collapsing framework of 2-round MPC, prior MPRE schemes garble the next-step circuits of a multi-round MPC protocol, to reduce the degree from 3 to 2.

Reference	Class	IT/Comp	Corruption	Black-box field	Adaptive
[19,20,5]	arith-**NC^1**	IT	$t < n/3$	yes	yes
[13,4,23]	**P/poly**	Comp	$t < n/3$	–	yes
[16]	**NC^1**	IT	$t < n/2$	–	yes*
[2]	**NC^1**	IT	$t < n/2$	no	no
[2,1,16]	**P/poly**	Comp	$t < n/2$	–	no
this work	arith-**NC^1**	IT	$t < n/2$	yes	yes
this work	**P/poly**	Comp	$t < n/2$	–	yes

Fig. 1. Summary of semi-honest 2-round MPC protocols with a honest majority. All of the constructions for **P/poly** (starting with [13]) make black-box use of a PRG. The protocol by [16] handles only a constant number of parties. * They did not fully specify the adaptive simulator.

Reference	Class	Model	Assumptions	Adaptive
[6,17]	**P/poly**	standard	OT	no
[7]	**P/poly**	standard	adaptive OT	yes
[16]	**P/poly**	standard	NIOT	yes*
[21]	**P/poly**	n-ary correlations	OWF	yes
this work	arith-NC1	2-ary correlated randomness	IT	yes
this work	**P/poly**	2-ary correlated randomness	OWF	yes

Fig. 2. Summary of semi-honest 2-round MPC protocols with a honest minority (that is, any $t < n$). * They did not fully specify the adaptive simulator.

We construct MPRE directly without using "inner" multi-round MPC. We observe that the [20] randomizing polynomials give a way to replace the multiplication between two input elements with multiplication between two random elements. With an OLE-correlation, the product of two random elements are additively shared between two parties, immediately reducing the degree to 2. In the honest majority setting, we exploit a delicate interplay between the IK02 randomized polynomials and the 2-round BGW [5] protocol for computing degree-2 polynomials (or essentially Shamir's secret sharing scheme) to turn multiplication between two input elements into multiplication between two local random elements, again reducing the degree to 2. Our MPRE schemes and 2-round MPC protocols based on them enjoy simplicity and better efficiency.

Information-Theoretic Security vs Adaptive Security. The folklore belief is that any information theoretically secure protocol is also adaptively secure with an *inefficient* simulator. Therefore, to formally prove adaptive security, the technical issue is presenting an explicit efficient simulator. We systematically present and analyze efficient adaptive simulators for our protocols, taking into account different corruption schedules. The analysis benefits greatly from our simpler and modular approach.

2   Technical Overview

We present an overview of our constructions, focusing on the honest-majority 2-round MPC for arith-NC1, followed by a more detailed comparison with prior approaches.

Following [19,20], to construct 2-round MPC for arith-NC1, it suffices to construct a 2-round protocol for the 3-party functionality $(x_1, x_2, x_3) \mapsto x_1 x_2 x_3$. More precisely, we need the functionality $((x_1, s_1), (x_2, s_2), (x_3, s_3)) \mapsto x_1 x_2 x_3 + s_1 + s_2 + s_3$; for simplicity, we ignore the additive terms in this overview, as they are easy to handle. As with [2], the starting point of our construction is the BGW protocol for computing $x_1 x_2 x_3$. In BGW and also in ABT, the parties (i) multiply Shamir shares of x_2, x_3 for threshold t, (ii) perform degree reduction to obtain Shamir shares of $x_2 x_3$ for threshold t, (iii) multiply the ensuing shares by that of x_1 to obtain Shamir shares of $x_1 x_2 x_3$ for threshold $2t$, (iv) interpolate the shares to recover $x_1 x_2 x_3$. Our construction replaces steps (ii) and (iii) with a completely different gadget.

MPRE. A (n, t)-MPRE [2] for a n-party functionality $f(\mathbf{x}_1, \ldots, \mathbf{x}_n)$ is a randomized function $\hat{f}(\mathbf{x}_1, \ldots, \mathbf{x}_n; \mathbf{r}_1, \ldots, \mathbf{r}_n)$ with the following properties:

- (correctness). There exists an efficient decoder Dec such that for all $\mathbf{x} = (\mathbf{x}_1, \ldots, \mathbf{x}_n), \mathbf{r} = (\mathbf{r}_1, \ldots, \mathbf{r}_n)$,

$$\mathsf{Dec}(\hat{f}(\mathbf{x}; \mathbf{r})) = f(\mathbf{x})$$

- (security). We say that the MPRE is (selectively) secure against up to t corruptions if there exists a simulator Sim such that for any $\mathbf{x}_1, \ldots, \mathbf{x}_n$ and any subset $T \subseteq [N], |T| \le t$,

$$\mathsf{Sim}(f(\mathbf{x}_1, \ldots, \mathbf{x}_n), \mathbf{x}_T) \approx \left(\hat{f}(\mathbf{x}_1, \ldots, \mathbf{x}_n; \mathbf{r}_1, \ldots, \mathbf{r}_n), \mathbf{r}_T \right)$$

  by distribution, where $\mathbf{r}_1, \ldots, \mathbf{r}_n$ on the right side are random, and $\mathbf{x}_T := (\mathbf{x}_i : i \in T), \mathbf{r}_T := (\mathbf{r}_i : i \in T)$.
- (effective degree). We say that a MPRE has effective degree d if there exists functions $h_1, \ldots, h_n$ such that $\hat{f}$ can be expressed as a degree d function of $h_1(\mathbf{x}_1, \mathbf{r}_1), \ldots, h_n(\mathbf{x}_n, \mathbf{r}_n)$. The functions h_i capture pre-computation on the local input $\mathbf{x}_i$ and randomness $\mathbf{r}_i$ of party P_i.

In this work, we think of $\mathbf{x}_1, \ldots, \mathbf{x}_n, \mathbf{r}_1, \ldots, \mathbf{r}_n$ as vectors over some field $\mathbb{F}$. In addition, we define the following new properties:

- We say that an MPRE is adaptively secure if the adversaries can adaptively decide which party to corrupt next, based on the encoding and/or local input and randomness of previously corrupted parties. Correspondingly, simulation is done in an "online" fashion using the output and/or inputs of already corrupted parties.

- We extend MPRE security with leakage: Each party P_i is associated with a leakage function L_i. If P_i is corrupted, the simulator will get $L_i(\mathbf{x}_1, \ldots, \mathbf{x}_n)$ in addition to $\mathbf{x}_i$. Unless otherwise specified, the leakage function L_i simply outputs $\perp$.

MPRE with leakage is the key notion that captures our main gadget which uses preprocessing to reduce the degree of IK randomized polynomials from 3 to 2. This notion is also new to this work.

2.1 Our Basic Construction

Main gadget. Our main gadget is MPRE for the 4-party functionality

$$((x, \mu), a, b, \perp) \mapsto xab + \mu$$

with the following properties:

(I) it has effective degree 2;
(II) tolerates any number of corruptions with leakage $L_4((x, \mu), a, b, \perp) = (a, b)$.

To build this gadget, we start with the IK02 randomized encoding for $xab + \mu$ where

$$(x, a, b, \mu \; ; \; w_1, w_2, w_3, w_4, w_5) \mapsto$$
$$\begin{bmatrix} a - w_1 & \begin{pmatrix} aw_3 + xw_1 \\ -w_3 w_1 - w_2 \end{pmatrix} & \begin{pmatrix} w_2 b - w_2 w_5 - w_1 w_4 \\ + \boxed{w_1 w_5 x} + w_4 a + \mu) \end{pmatrix} \\ -1 & x - w_3 & -w_4 + w_5 x \\ & -1 & b - w_5 \end{bmatrix} \quad (1)$$

As a quick warm-up, observe that we can have P_4 sample all of the randomness w_1, w_2, w_3, w_4, w_5. This achieves effective degree 2, but with leakage $L_4((x, \mu), a, b, \perp) = (x, a, b, \mu)$. We show that by distributing the randomness more cleverly, we can reduce the leakage upon corruption of P_4 to just a, b while preserving effective degree 2.

In particular, we will crucially rely on the fact that the randomized encoding contains exactly one monomial $w_1 w_5 x$ of degree 3. In our MPRE,

- w_2, w_3, w_4 are shared additively, $w_i = w_i^{(1)} + w_i^{(4)}$, between P_1 and P_4 (if both P_1 and P_4 are corrupted, then the adversary already learns all inputs x, a, b, μ);
- P_4 samples w_1, w_5 and pre-computes $w_1 w_5$ so that the encoding has effective degree two.

In summary, the MPRE computes the following in effective degree 2:

$$\hat{f}((x, \mu), a, b, \perp \; ; \; \mathbf{w})$$
$$= g\Big(\big(x, \mu, w_2^{(1)}, w_3^{(1)}, w_4^{(1)}\big), \; a, \; b, \; \big(w_1 w_5, w_2^{(4)}, w_3^{(4)}, w_4^{(4)}\big)\Big) = (1)$$

To handle corruption of P_4 in the analysis of the MPRE, we crucially rely on the fact that we can simulate the randomized encoding together w_1, w_5 given $(xab + \mu, a, b)$. To see this, observe that given a simulated encoding Π and a, b, one can compute matching $w_1 = \Pi[1, 1] + a$ and $w_5 = \Pi[3, 3] + b$.

MPRE for $x_1 x_2 x_3$ with OLE correlations. A two-party OLE correlation over $\mathbb{F}$ is a pair

$$(w^{(1)}, b^{(1)}), (w^{(2)}, b^{(2)}) : b^{(1)} + b^{(2)} = w^{(1)} \cdot w^{(2)}$$

Observe that in the IK02 randomized encoding Eq. (1), multiplication of input elements a and b is replaced with multiplication of random elements w_1 and w_5. If assuming OLE correlation between P_2, P_3, the IK02 encoding can be computed in degree 2, without any leakage to P_4 (in fact there is no need for P_4 at all). This gives an effective degree 2 MPRE for computing the 3-party functionality

$$x_1, x_2, x_3 \mapsto x_1 x_2 x_3$$

- P_2 and P_3 hold $(w_1, b^{(1)}), (w_5, b^{(5)})$ such that $b^{(1)} + b^{(5)} = w_1 w_5$;
- w_2, w_3, w_4 are shared additively between P_1, P_2, P_3.

Then the encoding computes the following in effective degree 2:

$$\hat{f}(x_1, x_2, x_3 \; ; \; \mathbf{w}, \mathbf{b}) = g\Big(\big(x_1, w_2^{(1)}, w_3^{(1)}, w_4^{(1)} \big),$$
$$\big(x_2, w_1, b^{(1)}, w_2^{(2)}, w_3^{(2)}, w_4^{(2)} \big), \big(x_3, w_5, b^{(5)}, w_2^{(3)}, w_3^{(3)}, w_4^{(3)} \big) \Big) = (1)|_{\mu=0}$$

Since every degree-3 polynomial can be expanded into a sum of degree-3 monomials, we immediately obtain a degree-2 MPRE for computing general degree-3 polynomials, by computing independent MPRE for each degree-3 monomial.

Lemma 1 (MPRE for Degree-3, Honest Minority). *There exists an adaptively secure MPRE for degree-3 polynomials with effective degree 2 in the OLE-correlation model, for $t \leq n$.*

MPRE for $x_1 x_2 x_3$ for honest majority. Next, we build a n-party MPRE with effective degree 2 for

$$x_1, \; x_2, \; x_3, \; \underbrace{\perp, \ldots, \perp}_{n-3} \mapsto x_1 x_2 x_3$$

tolerating $t < n/2$ corruptions, as long as $|\mathbb{F}| > n$ (without any leakage). For simplicity, we consider the setting where P_1 is never corrupted. Following the overview,

- P_2 samples a random degree-t polynomial Q_2 such that $Q_2(0) = x_2$.
- Similarly, P_3 samples Q_3 with $Q_3(0) = x_3$.
- P_1 samples a random degree-$(n-1)$ polynomial Z such that $Z(0) = 0$.

Now, consider the polynomial

$$Y := x_1 Q_2 Q_3 + Z$$

Observe that Y has degree at most $n - 1$, and satisfies $Y(0) = x_1 x_2 x_3$. Then, for each $i = 1, 2, \ldots, n$, parties P_1, P_2, P_3, P_i run the gadget MPRE to compute

$$((x_1, Z(i)), Q_2(i), Q_3(i), \perp) \mapsto Y(i) = x_1 Q_2(i) Q_3(i) + Z(i)$$

The output party can recover $Y(0) = x_1 x_2 x_3$ given $Y(1), \ldots, Y(n)$ via polynomial interpolation. In summary, the MPRE is the parallel composition of n gadget MPRE and hence have effective degree 2.

$$\hat{F}(x_1, x_2, x_3, \underbrace{\perp, \ldots, \perp}_{P_4 \text{ to } P_n}; \mathbf{r}) = \left(\hat{f}\big(\underbrace{(x_1, Z(i))}_{P_1}, \underbrace{Q_2(i)}_{P_2}, \underbrace{Q_3(i)}_{P_3}, \underbrace{\perp}_{P_i} \big) \right)_{i \in [n]}$$

We can in fact prove security of this MPRE for up to $t < n/2$ corruptions, as long as P_1 is not corrupted. We sketc.h the security proof for the setting where the last t parties $P_{n-t+1}, \ldots, P_n$ are corrupted:

- We can simulate the encoding by sampling a random degree $n - 1$ polynomial Y whose constant term is $x_1 x_2 x_3$, thanks to the randomization via Z;
- To simulate the view of the last t parties, security of the gadget MPRE tells us that it suffices to simulate $Q_2(i), Q_3(i), i = n - t + 1, \ldots, n$. By the security of Shamir's secret sharing, these are just a collection of uniformly random field elements, and leaks no additional information to the adversary.

More generally, P_1 may be corrupted, at which point x_1 and the polynomial Z are revealed. To ensure privacy of x_2, x_3 in this case, we need to modify the polynomial to $Y := x_1 Q_2 Q_3 + Z + S$, with an additional random degree-$(n - 1)$ polynomial S jointly sampled by all parties, with P_i sampling $S(i)$ at random. To recover the output $x_1 x_2 x_3$, the parties additionally compute $S(0)$, which is a linear function over local inputs.

Since MPRE for computing degree-3 monomials gives MPRE for general degree-3 polynomials, we obtain

Lemma 2 (MPRE for Degree-3, Honest Majority). *There exists an adaptively secure MPRE for degree-3 polynomials with effective degree 2 in the plain model, for $t < n/2$.*

Handling Adaptive Corruptions. All our MPRE schemes introduced so far have perfect information theoretic security. In later sections, we construct an efficient and stateful simulator for simulating the view of adaptive adversaries. In particular, the simulator Sim can be decomposed into a stateful two-subroutine simulator $(\mathsf{SimO}, \mathsf{SimI})$ in which $\mathsf{SimO}(f(\mathbf{x}_1, \ldots, \mathbf{x}_n))$ simulates the encoding $\hat{f}(\mathbf{x}_1, \ldots, \mathbf{x}_n; \mathbf{r}_1, \ldots, \mathbf{r}_n)$, and $\mathsf{SimI}(i, \mathbf{x}_i)$ simulates $\mathbf{r}_i$, in the order that the adaptive adversary corrupts parties.

Putting Pieces Together for **NC¹**. Given an MPRE for computing degree-3 polynomials in a model (the OLE correlation model or in the plain model with honest majority), we can "lift" it to handle arithmetic **NC¹** computation in the same model, while preserving the effective degree. The IK02 randomized encoding [20] for arith-NC1 allows for transforming a function g in **NC¹** by a degree-3 polynomial $\hat{g}$, such that, $\hat{g}(\mathbf{x}_1, \cdots \mathbf{x}_n ; \mathbf{r})$ reveals only $g(\mathbf{x}_1, \cdots, \mathbf{x}_n)$ and nothing else. This means it suffices to compute the following n-party degree-3 functionality where randomness $\mathbf{r}$ is *additively* shared among all parties.

$$(\mathbf{x}_1, \mathbf{r}^{(1)}) \cdots (\mathbf{x}_n, \mathbf{r}^{(n)}) \; \mapsto \; \hat{g}(\mathbf{x}_1, \cdots \mathbf{x}_n ; \mathbf{r} = \textstyle\sum_i \mathbf{r}^{(i)}) \;. \tag{2}$$

The above is an effective-degree-3 MPRE for arithmetic **NC¹**. We further reduce the effective degree to 2, by computing the effective-degree-3 MPRE using the effective-degree-2 MPREs for degree 3 polynomials.

Lemma 3 (MPRE for Arith-NC1). *There exist adaptively secure MPRE for arith-NC1 with effective degree 2 in the OLE-correlation model for any number $t \leq n$ of corruptions, and in the plain model for $t < n/2$.*

Finally, to obtain 2-round MPC for arith-NC1, we compute the effective-degree-2 MPRE using 2-round MPC for degree-2 polynomials. In the honest majority model, the BGW protocol has only 2 rounds when computing degree-2 polynomials. In the OLE correlation model, we design a very simple 2-round protocol for computing degree-2 polynomials.

Extension to Circuits. Starting from Yao's garbled circuits, we can get a $(n-1)$-private MPRE for **P/poly** with effective degree 3 that makes black-box use of a PRG G, using the techniques introduced in [4,13]. For simplicity, consider garbling a single gate g with input wire u, v and output wire o. For each input/output wire j, each party P_i samples a pair of PRG seeds $s_{j,0}^{(i)}, s_{j,1}^{(i)}$ corresponding the wire having value 0 or 1; the two labels for wire j is then set to $\ell_{j,b} = s_{j,b}^{(1)} \| \cdots \| s_{j,b}^{(n)}$. To hide the labels of the output wire o, each party locally expands their seeds through G, and hide label $\ell_{o,g(a,b)}$ using the XOR of PRG outputs from all parties. For instance,

$$\ell_{o,g(a,b)} \oplus \left(\bigoplus_i G_d(s_{u,a}^{(i)}) \right) \oplus \left(\bigoplus_i G_{d'}(s_{v,b}^{(i)}) \right)$$

where G_d for $d = 0$ or 1 outputs the first or second half of the PRG output bits respectively, and d, d' are set so that the same output bit is never reused. These table entries are further randomly permuted using mask bits k_u, k_v which are additively shared among all parties. The computed encoding is secure as long as one party remains uncorrupted. The computation makes black-box use of the PRG and has effective degree 3 after pre-processing of form:

$$h(\mathbf{x}_i ; \mathbf{k}^{(i)}, \mathbf{s}^{(i)}) = (x_i, (k_j^{(i)}, s_{j,0}^{(i)}, s_{j,1}^{(i)}, G(s_{j,0}^{(i)}), G(s_{j,1}^{(i)}))_j)$$

We can then combine this with our MPRE for degree-3 polynomials with effective degree 2 (over a sufficiently large field extension of $\mathbb{F}_2$).

Lemma 4 (MPRE for P/poly). *There exist adaptively secure MPRE for* **P/poly** *with effective degree 2 in the OLE-correlation model for any number* $t \leq n - 1$ *of corruptions, and in the plain model for* $t < n/2$. *The scheme makes black-box use of a PRG.*

2-round MPC protocols for **P/poly** in the same models then follow.

3   Preliminaries and Definitions

For any positive integer n, define $[n] := \{1, 2, \ldots, n\}$. For any set $S \subseteq [n]$ and vector $\mathbf{x} = (\mathbf{x}_1, \ldots, \mathbf{x}_n)$, where $\mathbf{x}_i$ itself can be a vector, let $\mathbf{x}[S]$ denote the indexed set $(\mathbf{x}_i)_{i \in S}$. Let $\mathbb{F}$ denote a finite field, and $\otimes$ tensor product.

3.1   MPC Protocols

Definition 1 (Functionality). *An n-party functionality is a function* $f : \mathcal{X}_1 \times \ldots \times \mathcal{X}_n \to \mathcal{Y}$, *where* $\mathcal{X}_i$ *is the i-th party's input domain and* $\mathcal{Y}$ *is the output space.*

Definition 2 (MPC Protocol). *An r-rounds MPC protocol* Π *for a n-party functionality* f *consists of* n *algorithms* $(C_i)_{i \in [n]}$. *An execution of* Π *with inputs* $\mathbf{x} = (\mathbf{x}_1, \ldots, \mathbf{x}_n) \in \mathcal{X}_1 \times \ldots \times \mathcal{X}_n$ *and security parameter* 1^λ *proceeds as follows:*

Randomness. *Each party* P_i *samples local randomness* $\mathbf{r}_i \leftarrow \mathcal{R}_i$, *where* $\mathcal{R}_i$ *is the local randomness space of the* P_i. *It initializes its state as* $\mathsf{st}_i^{(0)} = (\mathbf{x}_i, \mathbf{r}_i)$.

Round. $1 \leq j \leq r$: *Every party* P_i *computes* $(m_{i \to 1}^{(j)}, \cdots, m_{i \to n}^{(j)}) \leftarrow C_i(1^\lambda, \mathsf{st}_i^{(j-1)})$. *For every* $i' \in [n] \setminus \{i\}$, P_i *sends message* $m_{i \to i'}^{(j)}$ *to party* $P_{i'}$, *and receives message* $m_{i' \to i}^{(j)}$ *from party* $P_{i'}$. *It updates its state* $\mathsf{st}_i^{(j)} = (\mathsf{st}_i^{(j-1)}, (m_{i' \to i}^{(j)})_{i' \in [n] \setminus \{i\}})$.

Output: *After* r *rounds, every party* P_i *computes* $\mathbf{y}_i \leftarrow C_i(1^\lambda, \mathsf{st}^{(r_i)})$, *and outputs* $\mathbf{y}_i$.

Define the view of party P_i *in the above execution to be* $\mathrm{VIEW}_\Pi(1^\lambda, \mathbf{x})[i] = \mathsf{st}_i^{(r)} = (\mathbf{x}_i, \mathbf{r}_i, (m_{i' \to i}^{(j)})_{i' \in [n] \setminus \{i\}, j \in [r]})$. *Let* $\mathrm{VIEW}_\Pi(1^\lambda, \mathbf{x})$ *denote the array of views of all parties.*

We also consider MPC protocol that relies on correlated *randomness. If the MPC protocol relies on correlated randomness, which is a distribution* $\mathcal{D}$ *over* $\mathcal{R}_1' \times \cdots \times \mathcal{R}_n'$, *then in each execution of the protocol,* $(\mathbf{r}_1', \ldots, \mathbf{r}_n') \leftarrow \mathcal{D}$ *is sampled by the beginning of the protocol, and each party* P_i *initialize its state as* $\mathsf{st}_i^{(0)} = (\mathbf{x}_i, \mathbf{r}_i, \mathbf{r}_i')$.

Below, we suppress the appearance of the security parameter 1^λ, which is assumed implicitly.

Remark 1. We remark that the above definition considers the same output for all parties. It can be generalized to the case where each party has a different output. From a protocol design point of view, it is without loss of generality to consider a common output: To compute function f mapping $\mathbf{x}_1, \ldots, \mathbf{x}_n$ to different outputs $\mathbf{y}_1, \ldots, \mathbf{y}_n$, every party P_i can sample a one-time pad $\mathbf{k}_i$ of appropriate length and jointly compute the augmented functionality mapping $(\mathbf{x}_1, \mathbf{k}_1), \ldots, (\mathbf{x}_n, \mathbf{k}_n)$ to $(\mathbf{y}_1 + \mathbf{k}_1), \ldots, (\mathbf{y}_n + \mathbf{k}_n)$, where $\mathbf{k}_i$'s and $+$ should be defined appropriately for the specific functionality f. For instance, if f is a Boolean computation, $\mathbf{k}_i$'s should be random strings and $+$ is XOR, and if f is an arithmetic computation over a finite field, $\mathbf{k}_i$'s should be random vectors and $+$ over the field.

Definition 3 (MPC Correctness). *A protocol Π for a functionality $f : \mathcal{X}_1 \times \ldots \times \mathcal{X}_n \to \mathcal{Y}$ is perfectly or statistically correct, if for every input tuple $\mathbf{x} \in \mathcal{X}_1 \times \ldots \times \mathcal{X}_n$ and every security parameter $\lambda \in \mathbb{N}$, the output of every party P_i equals $f(x_1, \ldots, x_n)$, with probability 1 or with overwhelming probability respectively.*

Definition 4 (Semi-honest Security Against Static Corruption). *A protocol Π for a n-party functionality f is perfectly, or statistically, or computationally semi-honest secure against t-corruption, if there is a PPT simulator Sim, such that for every subset $T \subseteq [n]$ of at most t parties, input tuple $\mathbf{x}$, it holds that the real views $\mathrm{VIEW}_\Pi(\mathbf{x})[T]$ of parties in T and the output of the simulator $\mathsf{Sim}(T, \mathbf{x}[T], f(\mathbf{x}))$ are identically distributed, or statistically close, or computationally indistinguishable respectively.*

Semi-honest Adaptive Security. In the adaptive corruption model, a semi-honest adversary is allowed to choose which party to corrupt next adaptively (up to t corruptions) depending on its current view, which includes the views of previously corrupted parties. Correspondingly, the simulator for adaptive adversaries is an interactive stateful algorithm that responds to adversary's corruption requests with simulated views, generated from the inputs and output of corrupted parties.

Definition 5 (Semi-honest Security Against Adaptive Corruption.). *A protocol Π for a n-party functionality f is perfectly, or statistically, or computationally semi-honest adaptively secure against t-corruption, if there is a PPT interactive and stateful simulator Sim, such that, for every adversary $\mathcal{A}$ (PPT in the computational setting, computationally unbounded otherwise), input tuple $\mathbf{x}$, the outputs of the following two experiments are identically distributed, or statistically close, or computationally indistinguishable respectively.*

- In the real world: *The challenger runs an execution of Π on input $\mathbf{x}$ using fresh randomness, obtaining parties' views $\mathrm{VIEW}_\Pi(\mathbf{x})$.*
  The adversary $\mathcal{A}$ adaptively and iteratively queries $\mathsf{Corrupt}(i)$, and receives P_i's view $\mathrm{VIEW}_\Pi(\mathbf{x})[i]$, up to at most t corruptions.
  Return $\mathcal{A}$'s output.
- In the simulation: *Proceed identically as in the real world, except that upon $\mathcal{A}$'s request $\mathsf{Corrupt}(i)$, invoke the simulator $(\widetilde{\mathrm{VIEW}}[i], \mathsf{st}) \leftarrow \mathsf{Sim}(i, \mathbf{x}_i, y, \mathsf{st})$ and sends $\widetilde{\mathrm{VIEW}}[i]$ to $\mathcal{A}$, where st is initialized to be empty.*

3.2   (Multi-party) Randomized Encoding

Definition 6 (Randomized Encoding [3,20]). *Let $f : \mathcal{X} \to \mathcal{Y}$ be some function. The* randomized encoding *of f is a function $\hat{f} : \mathcal{X} \times \mathcal{R} \to z\mathcal{Y}$, where $\mathcal{R}$ is the randomness space. A randomized encoding should be both correct and private.*

Correctness. *There is a decoding function* Dec *such that for all $x \in \mathcal{X}, r \in \mathcal{R}$, it holds that*
$$\mathsf{Dec}(\hat{f}(x;r)) = f(x).$$

Privacy. *There exists a efficient randomized simulation algorithm* Sim *such that for any $x \in \mathcal{X}$, the distribution of $\mathsf{Sim}(f(x))$ is identical to that of $\hat{f}(x;r)$. The privacy can be relaxed to statistical privacy (resp. computational privacy), if the $\mathsf{Sim}(f(x))$ and $\hat{f}(x;r)$ are statistically close (resp. computational indistinguishable).*

Definition 7 (Multi-party Randomized Encoding [2]). *Let $f : \mathcal{X}_1 \times \cdots \times \mathcal{X}_n \to \mathcal{Y}$ be some n-party functionality. A* multi-party randomized encoding *(MPRE) of f consists of*

- *Input space $\mathcal{X} = \mathcal{X}_1 \times \cdots \times \mathcal{X}_n$ and output space $\mathcal{Y}$;*
- *Local randomness space $\mathcal{R}_i$ for $i \in [n]$;*
  Correlated randomness space $\mathcal{R}'_1 \times \cdots \times \mathcal{R}'_n$ together with a distribution $\mathcal{D}$ over it;
- *Local preprocessing function $h_i : \mathcal{X}_i \times \mathcal{R}_i \times \mathcal{R}'_i \to \hat{\mathcal{X}}_i$;*
- *Encoding function $\hat{f} : \hat{\mathcal{X}}_1 \times \cdots \times \hat{\mathcal{X}}_n \to \hat{\mathcal{Y}}$, the degree of $\hat{f}$ is called the* effective degree *of this MPRE.*

Such that for any input $(x_1, \ldots, x_n)$, the encoding $\hat{f}(h_1(x_1, r_1, r'_1), \ldots, h_n(x_n, r_n, r'_n))$ represents $y = f(x_1, \ldots, x_n)$ in the following sense:

Correctness. There exists a decoding function Dec $: \hat{\mathcal{Y}} \to \mathcal{Y}$, *such that for any input $(x_1, \ldots, x_n) \in \mathcal{X}_1 \times \cdots \times \mathcal{X}_n$, randomness $(r_1, \ldots, r_n) \in \mathcal{R}_1 \times \cdots \times \mathcal{R}_n$ and correlated randomness $(r'_1, \ldots, r'_n)$ in the support of $\mathcal{D}$, the corresponding encodings $\hat{y} = \hat{f}(h_1(x_1, r_1, r'_1), \ldots, h_n(x_n, r_n, r'_n))$ satisfies that $f(x_1, \ldots, x_n) = \mathsf{Dec}(\hat{y})$.*

Semi-honest Adaptive t-Privacy. The MPRE is perfectly (resp. statistically or computationally) secure against t adaptive corruptions if there exists an adaptive simulator such that the following real world and ideal world are perfectly (resp. statistically or computationally) indistinguishable.

In both the real world and the ideal world, the distinguisher first chooses input $\mathbf{x} = (x_1, \ldots, x_n)$, and sends it to the challenger. Then the distinguisher can make queries and tries to guess which world it is.

- In the real world: *The distinguisher chooses input $\mathbf{x} = (x_1, \ldots, x_n)$, and sends it to the challenger. The challenger samples local randomness $r_i \leftarrow \mathcal{R}_i$ for each $i \in [n]$ and correlated randomness $(r'_1, \ldots, r'_n) \leftarrow \mathcal{D}$; computes*

$\hat{x}_i = h_i(x_i, r_i, r'_i)$ for $i \in [n]$ and $\hat{y} = \hat{f}(\hat{x}_1, \ldots, \hat{x}_n)$. In short, the challenger follows the protocol.

The challenger allows the distinguisher to adaptively query the following two oracles. The later one can be queried up to t times.

Upon CorruptO: Output $\hat{y}$

Upon CorruptI(i): Output r_i, r'_i.

- In the ideal world: The distinguisher chooses input $\mathbf{x} = (x_1, \ldots, x_n)$, and sends it to the challenger. The challenger does nothing other than stores the input. The queries are answered by the simulator, which is a randomized stateful algorithm $(\mathsf{SimO}, \mathsf{SimI})$.

The challenger allows the distinguisher to adaptively query the following two oracles. The later one can be queried up to t times.

Upon CorruptO: Compute $y = f(\mathbf{x})$ and output whatever $\mathsf{SimO}(y)$ outputs.

Upon CorruptI(i): Output what is output by $\mathsf{SimI}(i, x_i)$.

3.3   Composition of MPREs

If there is a MPRE for f whose encoding function is $\hat{f}$, together with a MPRE for $\hat{f}$ whose encoding function is $\hat{\hat{f}}$. Then Theorem 1 shows that they can be composed as a MPRE for f whose encoding function is $\hat{\hat{f}}$. Theorem 1 is adaptive version of Lemma 3.3 and 3.4 in [2]. Such composition is useful when $\hat{\hat{f}}$ is simpler than $\hat{f}$.

If there are MPREs for f_1, f_2. W.l.o.g., assume their input domain are the same. Then Theorem 2 shows that they can be composed as a MPRE for the functionality

$$f(x_1, \ldots, x_n) = (f_1(x_1, \ldots, x_n), f_2(x_1, \ldots, x_n))$$

while preserving the complexity.

Theorem 1 (Sequential Composition). *Assume there is a perfectly (resp. statistically or computationally) adaptively t-private MPRE for functionality f : $\mathcal{X}_1 \times \cdots \times \mathcal{X}_n \to \mathcal{Y}$, whose encoding function is $\hat{f} : \hat{\mathcal{X}}_1 \times \cdots \times \hat{\mathcal{X}}_n \to \hat{\mathcal{Y}}$. Assume there is a perfectly (resp. statistically or computationally) adaptively t-private MPRE for $\hat{f}$, whose encoding function is $\hat{\hat{f}} : \hat{\hat{\mathcal{X}}}_1 \times \cdots \times \hat{\hat{\mathcal{X}}}_n \to \hat{\hat{\mathcal{Y}}}$. Then there exists a perfectly (resp. statistically or computationally) adaptively t-private MPRE for f whose encoding function is $\hat{\hat{f}}$.*

Theorem 2 (Parallel Composition). *For each $j \in [m]$, assume there is a perfectly (resp. statistically or computationally) adaptively t-private MPRE for functionality $f^{(j)} : \mathcal{X}_1 \times \cdots \times \mathcal{X}_n \to \mathcal{Y}^{(j)}$, whose encoding function is $\hat{f}^{(j)} : \hat{\mathcal{X}}_1^{(j)} \times \cdots \times \hat{\mathcal{X}}_n^{(j)} \to \hat{\mathcal{Y}}^{(j)}$. Then there exists a perfectly (resp. statistically or computationally) adaptively t-private MPRE for f whose encoding function is $\hat{f}$, where f concatenate the outputs of $f^{(1)}, \ldots, f^{(m)}$*

$$f(x_1, \ldots, x_n) := (f^{(1)}(x_1, \ldots, x_n), \ldots, f^{(m)}(x_1, \ldots, x_n))$$

and $\hat{f}$ is the concatenation of $\hat{f}^{(1)}, \ldots, \hat{f}^{(m)}$.

Additionally, if the MPRE for $f^{(j)}$ has leakage $l_i^{(j)} : \mathcal{X}_1 \times \cdots \times \mathcal{X}_n \to \mathcal{L}_i^{(j)}$ to P_i for $i \in [n], j \in [m]$, then the resulting MPRE has leakage $l_i : \mathcal{X}_1 \times \cdots \times \mathcal{X}_n \to \mathcal{L}_i^{(1)} \times \cdots \times \mathcal{L}_i^{(m)}$,

$$l_i(x_1, \ldots, x_n) = (l_i^{(1)}(x_1, \ldots, x_n), \ldots, l_i^{(m)}(x_1, \ldots, x_n)),$$

to the i-th party.

The proof of composition theorems are defered to the full version.

4   MPRE for Degree-3 Polynomials

In this section, we build MPRE for degree-3 polynomials in two settings: (i) honest majority, and (ii) OLE correlations. Our road-map is as follows: In Sect. 4.1, we construct a 4-party gadget MPRE; in Sect. 4.2, we construct an MPRE for the 3-party functionality 3MultPlus$_3$ described below, which computes a degree-3 monomial shifted by some linear terms, in the OLE-correlation model; then in Sect. 4.3, we consider the n-party version of the functionality 3MultPlus$_n$ and construct an MPRE for it in the honest majority setting.

$$\text{3MultPlus}_3 \ : \ ((x_1, \alpha), (x_2, \beta), (x_3, \gamma)) \mapsto x_1 x_2 x_3 + \alpha + \beta + \gamma$$
$$\text{3MultPlus}_n \ : \ ((x_1, \alpha), (x_2, \beta), (x_3, \gamma), \underbrace{\bot, \ldots, \bot}_{n-3}) \mapsto x_1 x_2 x_3 + \alpha + \beta + \gamma$$

Finally, 3MultPlus is complete in the sense that MPRE for the 3MultPlus functionalities implies MPRE for general degree-3 functionalities. The proof can be found in the full version. All our MPRE have effective degree 2.

4.1   Our 4-Party Gadget MPRE with Leakage

Fix a field $\mathbb{F}$. We begin with a MPRE with leakage for the following 4-party gadget function

$$((x, \mu), a, b, \nu) \mapsto abx + \mu + \nu.$$

For randomly sampled $w_1, \ldots, w_5$, [19,20] show that $(\phi_1, \ldots, \phi_6)$ is a randomized encoding of $abx + \mu + \nu$, where $\phi_1, \ldots, \phi_6$ are defined as

$$
\begin{bmatrix} \phi_1 & \phi_2 & \phi_6 \\ -1 & \phi_3 & \phi_4 \\ & -1 & \phi_5 \end{bmatrix} := \begin{bmatrix} 1 & w_1 & w_2 \\ & 1 & \\ & & 1 \end{bmatrix} \begin{bmatrix} a & & \mu+\nu \\ -1 & x & \\ & -1 & b \end{bmatrix} \begin{bmatrix} 1 & w_3 & w_4 \\ & 1 & w_5 \\ & & 1 \end{bmatrix}
$$
$$
= \begin{bmatrix} a - w_1 & \begin{pmatrix} aw_3 + xw_1 \\ -w_3 w_1 - w_2 \end{pmatrix} & \begin{pmatrix} w_2 b - w_2 w_5 - w_1 w_4 \\ + w_1 w_5 x + w_4 a + \mu + \nu \end{pmatrix} \\ -1 & x - w_3 & -w_4 + w_5 x \\ & -1 & b - w_5 \end{bmatrix}. \tag{3}
$$

[19,20] guarantee that $\phi_1, \ldots, \phi_5$ are i.i.d. uniform despite the value of (a, b, x, μ, ν). We would like to transfer this randomized encoding into an effective degree-2 MPRE with leakage.

---

fully-private MPRE for the gadget functionality

Local randomness: P_1 samples $w_3, w_2', w_4' \leftarrow \mathbb{F}$; P_4 samples $w_1, w_5, w_2'', w_4'' \leftarrow \mathbb{F}$.

Preprocessing function h_i: P_4 locally computes $w_1 w_5$, i.e. let $h_4(w_1, w_5, w_2'', w_4'') = (w_1, w_5, w_1 w_5, w_2'', w_4'')$. Other parties simply outputs their local input and randomness, i.e., h_i for $i \neq 4$ is the identity function.

Encoding function g: On input the outputs of all h_i, output $(\phi_1, \ldots, \phi_6)$ as defined in Equation (3), with $w_2 := w_2' + w_2''$, $w_4 := w_4' + w_4''$.

Decoding function: On input $(\phi_1, \ldots, \phi_6)$, output $\det \begin{bmatrix} \phi_1 & \phi_2 & \phi_6 \\ -1 & \phi_3 & \phi_4 \\ & -1 & \phi_5 \end{bmatrix}$.

Fig. 3. Effective degree-2 MPRE for the gadget functionality

Lemma 5. *The scheme defined in Fig. 3 is an MPRE for the following 4-party gadget function*

$$((x, \mu), a, b, \nu) \mapsto abx + \mu + \nu$$

with the following properties:

(I) it has effective degree 2;

(II) tolerates any number of corruptions with leakage $L_4((x, \mu), a, b, \nu) = (a, b)$.

Proof. The correctness is straight forward. The decoding function is the determinant of the matrix in (3), thus

$$\mathsf{Dec}(\phi_1, \ldots, \phi_6) = \det \begin{bmatrix} \phi_1 & \phi_2 & \phi_6 \\ -1 & \phi_3 & \phi_4 \\ & -1 & \phi_5 \end{bmatrix} = \det \begin{bmatrix} a & & \mu + \nu \\ -1 & x & \\ & -1 & b \end{bmatrix} = abx + \mu + \nu.$$

For the adaptive privacy, we need to define the simulator.

- *In the real world:* For input x, a, b, μ, ν

  At the outset: Sample random $w_1, w_3, w_5, w_2', w_2'', w_4', w_4''$, compute $w_2 = w_2' + w_2''$, $w_4 = w_4' + w_4''$, compute $(\phi_1, \ldots, \phi_6)$ according to Eq. (3).

  CorruptO: Output $\phi_1, \ldots, \phi_6$.

  CorruptI(1): Output w_3, w_2', w_4'.

  CorruptI(2): Output $\perp$.

  CorruptI(3): Output $\perp$.

  CorruptI(4): Output w_1, w_5, w_2'', w_4''.

- *In the ideal world:*

  At the Outset: Sample random $\phi_1, \ldots, \phi_5$,

  Upon CorruptO, SimO(y): Let ϕ_6 be the unique value that $\det \begin{bmatrix} \phi_1 & \phi_2 & \phi_6 \\ -1 & \phi_3 & \phi_4 \\ & -1 & \phi_5 \end{bmatrix} = y$. Output $\phi_1, \ldots, \phi_6$.

Upon CorruptI(1), SimI(1, (x, μ)): Set w_3 as the unique value that $\phi_3 = x - w_3$.

If P_4 is not corrupted yet, sample w_2', w_4' at random.

If P_4 is already corrupted, subroutine SimI(4, ν, (a, b)) has learned a and has sampled the values of w_1, w_5. Then, set w_2, w_4 to satisfy $\phi_2 = aw_3 + xw_1 - w_3w_1 - w_2$, $\phi_4 = -w_4 + w_5x$, and set $w_2' = w_2 - w_2''$, $w_4' = w_4 - w_4''$. Output w_3, w_2', w_4'.

Upon CorruptI(2), SimI(2, a): Output $\perp$.

Upon CorruptI(3), SimI(3, b): Output $\perp$.

Upon CorruptI(4), SimI(4, ν, (a, b)): Set w_1, w_5 to satisfy $\phi_1 = a - w_1$, $\phi_5 = b - w_5$.

If P_1 is not corrupted yet, sample w_2'', w_4'' at random.

If P_1 is already corrupted, subroutine SimI(1, (x, μ)) has learned x and has sampled the value of w_3. Then, set w_2, w_4 to satisfy $\phi_2 = aw_3 + xw_1 - w_3w_1 - w_2$ and $\phi_4 = -w_4 + w_5x$, set $w_2'' = w_2 - w_2'$, $w_4'' = w_4 - w_4'$. Output w_1, w_5, w_2'', w_4''.

To formally show that adversary cannot distinguish between the real world and the ideal world, we introduce a middle world.

– *In the middle world:*
  At the Outset: Sample random $\phi_1, \ldots, \phi_5$.

  Let ϕ_6 be the unique value that $\det \begin{bmatrix} \phi_1 & \phi_2 & \phi_6 \\ -1 & \phi_3 & \phi_4 \\ & -1 & \phi_5 \end{bmatrix} = abx + \mu + \nu$.

  Solve $w_1, \ldots, w_5$ from Eq. (3). Sample w_2', w_2'' as additive sharing of w_2, Sample w_4', w_4'' as additive sharing of w_4.
  CorruptO: Output $\phi_1, \ldots, \phi_6$.
  CorruptI(1): Output w_3, w_2', w_4'.
  CorruptI(2): Output $\perp$.
  CorruptI(3): Output $\perp$.
  CorruptI(4): Output w_1, w_5, w_2'', w_4''.

The real world is indistinguishable from the middle world, due to the security of the randomized encoding in (3).

Comparing the ideal world with the middle world, the only difference is that the computation is deferred in the ideal world: Same as the real world, the simulator in the ideal samples random $\phi_1, \ldots, \phi_5$. But the simulator cannot compute $w_1, \ldots, w_5$ at the beginning as it doesn't know a, b, x, μ, ν at that moment. Instead, the simulator compute each of $w_1, \ldots, w_5$ once it has the necessary information, using exactly the method as the middle world (i.e. by solving (3)). Thus the ideal world is also indistinguishable from the middle world.

4.2 MPRE for 3-Party **3MultPlus** Using OLE Correlation

In this section, we construct an MPRE for the three party functionality

$$\mathsf{3MultPlus}_3 \ : \ ((x_1, \alpha), (x_2, \beta), (x_3, \gamma)) \mapsto x_1 x_2 x_3 + \alpha + \beta + \gamma$$

that has effective degree 2 and tolerates any number of corruptions in the OLE-correlation model.

For randomly sampled $w_1, \ldots, w_5$, [19,20] show that $(\phi_1, \ldots, \phi_6)$ is a randomized encoding of $x_1 x_2 x_3 + \alpha + \beta + \gamma$, where $\phi_1, \ldots, \phi_6$ are defined as

$$
\begin{bmatrix} \phi_1 & \phi_2 & \phi_6 \\ -1 & \phi_3 & \phi_4 \\ & -1 & \phi_5 \end{bmatrix} := \begin{bmatrix} 1 & w_1 & w_2 \\ & 1 & \\ & & 1 \end{bmatrix} \begin{bmatrix} x_1 & \alpha + \beta + \gamma \\ -1 & x_2 & \\ & -1 & x_3 \end{bmatrix} \begin{bmatrix} 1 & w_3 & w_4 \\ & 1 & w_5 \\ & & 1 \end{bmatrix}
$$
$$
= \begin{bmatrix} x_1 - w_1 & \begin{pmatrix} x_1 w_3 + x_2 w_1 \\ - w_3 w_1 - w_2 \end{pmatrix} & \begin{pmatrix} w_2 x_3 - w_2 w_5 - w_1 w_4 + w_4 x_1 \\ + w_1 w_5 x_2 + \alpha + \beta + \gamma \end{pmatrix} \\ -1 & x_2 - w_3 & -w_4 + w_5 x_2 \\ & -1 & x_3 - w_5 \end{bmatrix}.
$$
(4)

[19,20] guarantee that $\phi_1, \ldots, \phi_5$ are i.i.d. uniform despite the value of $(x_1, x_2, x_3, \alpha + \beta + \gamma)$. We would like to transfer this randomized encoding into an effective degree-2 MPRE using OLE correlated randomness.

Notice that $w_1 w_5 x_2$ is the only degree-3 monomial in the randomized encoding, and w_1, w_5 belong to the randomness of the randomized encoding. Thus if w_1, w_5 are sampled from OLE correlated randomness, monomial $w_1 w_5 x_2$ can be transferred into a degree-2 term. More precisely, let $(w_1, b^{(1)}, w_5, b^{(3)}) \in \mathbb{F}^4$ be sampled from OLE correlation, it holds that $w_1 w_5 = b^{(1)} + b^{(3)}$. The marginal distribution of (w_1, w_5) is still uniform; and $w_1 w_5 x_2$ equals $(b^{(1)} + b^{(3)}) x_2$, which is a degree-2 term. Then the randomized encoding has "effective" degree 2 as it can be computed from

$$
\begin{bmatrix} \phi_1 & \phi_2 & \phi_6 \\ -1 & \phi_3 & \phi_4 \\ & -1 & \phi_5 \end{bmatrix} = \begin{bmatrix} x_1 - w_1 & \begin{pmatrix} x_1 w_3 + x_2 w_1 \\ - w_3 w_1 - w_2 \end{pmatrix} & \begin{pmatrix} w_2 x_3 - w_2 w_5 - w_1 w_4 + w_4 x_1 \\ + (b^{(1)} + b^{(3)}) x_2 + \alpha + \beta + \gamma \end{pmatrix} \\ -1 & x_2 - w_3 & -w_4 + w_5 x_2 \\ & -1 & x_3 - w_5 \end{bmatrix}.
$$
(5)

MPRE for the 3-party functionality 3MultPlus₃

Local randomness: P_i samples $w_2^{(i)}, w_3^{(i)}, w_4^{(i)} \leftarrow \mathbb{F}$.

Correlated randomness: P_1 is given $(w_1, b^{(1)}) \in \mathbb{F}^2$, and P_3 is given $(w_5, b^{(3)}) \in \mathbb{F}^2$, for random $(w_1, b^{(1)}, w_5, b^{(3)}) \in \mathbb{F}^4$ satisfying $w_1 w_5 = b^{(1)} + b^{(3)}$.

Preprocessing function: Preprocessing is not necessary. I.e., h_i is the identity function for $i \in \{1, 2, 3\}$.

Encoding function: On input the outputs of all h_i, output $(\phi_1, \ldots, \phi_6)$ as defined in Equation (5), with $w_2 := \sum_{i \in [3]} w_2^{(i)}$, $w_3 := \sum_{i \in [3]} w_3^{(i)}$, $w_4 := \sum_{i \in [3]} w_4^{(i)}$.

Decoding function: On input $(\phi_1, \ldots, \phi_6)$, output $\det \begin{bmatrix} \phi_1 & \phi_2 & \phi_6 \\ -1 & \phi_3 & \phi_4 \\ & -1 & \phi_5 \end{bmatrix}$.

Fig. 4. Effective degree-2 MPRE for the 3MultPlus₃ functionality

Lemma 6. *The MPRE in Fig. 4 for the 3-party functionality* 3MultPlus$_3$ *has effective degree 2 and tolerates any number of corruptions, in the OLE-correlation model.*

Proof. The correctness is straight forward,

$$\mathsf{Dec}(\phi_1,\ldots,\phi_6) = \det \begin{bmatrix} \phi_1 & \phi_2 & \phi_6 \\ -1 & \phi_3 & \phi_4 \\ & -1 & \phi_5 \end{bmatrix} = \det \begin{bmatrix} x_1 & & \alpha+\beta+\gamma \\ -1 & x_2 & \\ & -1 & x_3 \end{bmatrix}$$

$$= x_1 x_2 x_3 + \alpha + \beta + \gamma.$$

For the adaptive privacy, we need to define the simulator.

– *In the real world:* For input $x_1, x_2, x_3, \alpha, \beta, \gamma$
  At the Outset: Sample random $w_1, w_5, w_2^{(1)}, w_2^{(2)}, w_2^{(3)}, w_3^{(1)}, w_3^{(2)}, w_3^{(3)}, w_4^{(1)},$
  $w_4^{(2)}, w_4^{(3)} \in \mathbb{F}$, sample random $b^{(1)}, b^{(3)}$ that $b^{(1)} + b^{(3)} = w_1 w_5$, compute $w_2 = \sum_{i \in [3]} w_2^{(i)}$, $w_3 = \sum_{i \in [3]} w_3^{(i)}$, $w_4 = \sum_{i \in [3]} w_4^{(i)}$, compute $(\phi_1, \ldots, \phi_6)$ according to Eq. (5).
  CorruptO: Output $\phi_1, \ldots, \phi_6$.
  CorruptI(1): Output $w_1, b^{(1)}, w_2^{(1)}, w_3^{(1)}, w_4^{(1)}$.
  CorruptI(2): Output $w_2^{(2)}, w_3^{(2)}, w_4^{(2)}$.
  CorruptI(3): Output $w_5, b^{(3)}, w_2^{(3)}, w_3^{(3)}, w_4^{(3)}$.
– *In the ideal world:*
  At the Outset: Sample random $\phi_1, \ldots, \phi_5$,
  Upon CorruptO, SimO(y): Let ϕ_6 be the unique value that $\det \begin{bmatrix} \phi_1 & \phi_2 & \phi_6 \\ -1 & \phi_3 & \phi_4 \\ & -1 & \phi_5 \end{bmatrix} = y$. Output $\phi_1, \ldots, \phi_6$.
  Upon CorruptI(1), SimI(1, (x_1, α)): Set w_1 to satisfy $\phi_1 = x_1 - w_1$.
   If P_3 is not corrupted yet, sample $b^{(1)}$ at random.
   If P_3 is already corrupted, subroutine SimI(3, (x_3, γ)) has set the values of $w_5, b^{(3)}$. Set $b^{(1)} = w_1 w_5 - b^{(3)}$.
   If both P_2 and P_3 are corrupted, subroutines SimI(2, (x_2, β)), SimI(3, (x_3, γ)) have set $w_j^{(2)}, w_j^{(3)}$ for $j \in \{2, 3, 4\}$. Then solve $w_2, w_3,$ w_4 from Eq. (4) and set $w_j^{(1)} = w_j - w_j^{(2)} - w_j^{(3)}$ for $j \in \{2, 3, 4\}$.
   If at least one of P_2, P_3 is not corrupted yet, sample $w_2^{(1)}, w_3^{(1)}, w_4^{(1)} \in \mathbb{F}$. Output $w_1, b^{(1)}, w_2^{(1)}, w_3^{(1)}, w_4^{(1)}$.
  Upon CorruptI(2), SimI(2, (x_2, β)): If both P_1 and P_3 are corrupted, subroutines SimI(1, (x_1, β)), SimI(3, (x_3, γ)) have set $w_j^{(1)}, w_j^{(3)}$ for $j \in \{2, 3, 4\}$. Then solve w_2, w_3, w_4 from Eq. (4) and set $w_j^{(2)} = w_j - w_j^{(1)} - w_j^{(3)}$ for $j \in \{2, 3, 4\}$.
   If at least one of P_1, P_3 is not corrupted yet, sample $w_2^{(2)}, w_3^{(2)}, w_4^{(2)} \in \mathbb{F}$. Output $w_2^{(2)}, w_3^{(2)}, w_4^{(2)}$.

Upon CorruptI(3), SimI(3, (x_3, γ)): Set w_5 to satisfy $\phi_5 = x_3 - w_5$.

If P_1 is not corrupted yet, sample $b^{(3)}$ at random.

If P_1 is already corrupted, subroutine SimI(1, (x_1, α)) has set the values of $w_1, b^{(1)}$. Set $b^{(3)} = w_1 w_5 - b^{(1)}$.

If both P_1 and P_2 are corrupted, subroutines SimI(1, (x_1, β)), SimI(2, (x_2, γ)) have set $w_j^{(1)}, w_j^{(2)}$ for $j \in \{2, 3, 4\}$. Then solve w_2, w_3, w_4 from Eq. (4) and set $w_j^{(3)} = w_j - w_j^{(1)} - w_j^{(2)}$ for $j \in \{2, 3, 4\}$.

If at least one of P_1, P_2 is not corrupted yet, sample $w_2^{(3)}, w_3^{(3)}, w_4^{(3)} \in \mathbb{F}$.

Output $w_5, b^{(3)}, w_2^{(3)}, w_3^{(3)}, w_4^{(3)}$.

To show the indistinguishability between the real world and the ideal world, we introduce a middle world.

- *In the middle world:* For input $x_1, x_2, x_3, \alpha, \beta, \gamma$

  At the Outset: Sample random $\phi_1, \ldots, \phi_5$.

  Let ϕ_6 be the unique value that det $\begin{bmatrix} \phi_1 & \phi_2 & \phi_6 \\ -1 & \phi_3 & \phi_4 \\ & -1 & \phi_5 \end{bmatrix} = y$.

  Solve $w_1, \ldots, w_5$ from Eq. (4).

  Sample random $b^{(1)}, b^{(3)}$ that $b^{(1)} + b^{(3)} = w_1 w_5$. For each of $j \in \{2, 3, 4\}$, sample random $w_j^{(1)}, w_j^{(2)}, w_j^{(3)}$ that $w_j^{(1)} + w_j^{(2)} + w_j^{(3)} = w_j$.

  CorruptO: Output $\phi_1, \ldots, \phi_6$.

  CorruptI(1): Output $w_1, b^{(1)}, w_2^{(1)}, w_3^{(1)}, w_4^{(1)}$.

  CorruptI(2): Output $w_2^{(2)}, w_3^{(2)}, w_4^{(2)}$.

  CorruptI(3): Output $w_5, b^{(3)}, w_2^{(3)}, w_3^{(3)}, w_4^{(3)}$.

The real world is indistinguishable from the middle world, due to the security of the randomized encoding in (3).

Comparing the ideal world with the middle world, the only difference is that the computation is deferred in the ideal world: Same as the real world, the simulator in the ideal samples random $\phi_1, \ldots, \phi_5$. But the simulator cannot compute $w_1, \ldots, w_5$ by solving (4) at the beginning as it doesn't know x_1, x_2, x_3, α, β, γ at that moment. Instead, the simulator compute w_1 once it knows x_1; compute w_5 once it knows x_3; and compute w_2, w_3, w_4 once it knows all the inputs. Thus the ideal world is also indistinguishable from the middle world.

4.3   MPRE for n-Party 3MultPlus with Honest Majority

We construct an MPRE (Fig. 5) for the n-party functionality

$$\text{3MultPlus}_n : ((x_1, \alpha), (x_2, \beta), (x_3, \gamma), \underbrace{\bot, \ldots, \bot}_{n-3}) \mapsto x_1 x_2 x_3 + \alpha + \beta + \gamma$$

that has effective degree 2 and tolerates minority corruptions. The construction requires $|\mathbb{F}| > n$.

Additional Notation. Let $\mathbb{F}$ be a field that $|\mathbb{F}| > n$, let $1, \ldots, n$ denote n distinct non-zero elements in $\mathbb{F}$. Denote by $\mathcal{P}(t, m)$ the set of degree-t polynomials P with constant term m over $\mathbb{F}$, so that $Q \leftarrow \mathcal{P}(t, m)$ refers to sampling a random degree-t polynomial Q whose constant term is m. In addition, $m = \mathrm{rec}(t, (i_1, \sigma_1) \ldots, (i_{t+1}, \sigma_{t+1}))$ denotes the procedure for reconstructing the constant term from $t + 1$ points on the polynomial via interpolation. For convenience, we also denote by $\mathcal{P}(t, m) \mid (i_1, \sigma_1) \ldots, (i_s, \sigma_s)$ the set of polynomials $Q \in \mathcal{P}(t, m)$ such that $Q(i_1) = \sigma_1, \ldots, Q(i_s) = \sigma_s$, for $s \leq t + 1$.

Protocol Overview. We decompose the computation of $x_1 x_2 x_3 + \alpha + \beta + \gamma$, into two parts $x_1 x_2 x_3 + z + s$ and $\alpha + \beta + \gamma - z - s$ where z is sampled by P_1 and s is jointly sampled by all n parties. Since the second term is linear, we focus on designing an MPRE for the first part.

- P_1 samples $z \leftarrow \mathbb{F}, Z \leftarrow \mathcal{P}(n - 1, z)$.
- P_2 samples $Q_2 \leftarrow \mathcal{P}(t, x_2)$ and P_3 samples $Q_3 \leftarrow \mathcal{P}(t, x_3)$.
- P_i samples $S(i) \leftarrow \mathbb{F}$, for every $i \in [n]$.
  Let $s = \mathrm{rec}(n - 1, (1, S(1)), \ldots, (n, S(n)))$.

Observe that

$$Y := x_1 Q_2 Q_3 + Z + S \in \mathcal{P}(n - 1, x_1 x_2 x_3 + z + s) \ .$$

Here, we rely on the fact that $2t \leq n - 1$. Then, for each $i = 1, 2, \ldots, n$, parties P_1, P_2, P_3, P_i can run the gadget MPRE described in Sect. 4.1 to compute $Y(i)$

$$((x_1, Z(i)), \ Q_2(i), \ Q_3(i), \ S(i)) \mapsto x_1 Q_2(i) Q_3(i) + Z(i) + S(i) = Y(i) \ ,$$

from which the output party can reconstruct Y and the constant term $x_1 x_2 x_3 + z + s$.

Security Intuition. We can prove security of this protocol for up to $t < n/2$ corruptions. Consider two cases: If P_1 is not corrupted, or corrupted. In the first case, the view of the output party consists of $\alpha + \beta + \gamma - z - s$, and a degree $n - 1$ polynomial Y with constant term $x_1 x_2 x_3 + z + s$, which is random thanks to the randomization via Z. Now, suppose the adversary additional corrupts t parties, excluding P_1; call this set of parties T. Then, security of the gadget MPRE tells us that the adversary also learns $\{Q_2(i), Q_3(i), S(i) : i \in T\}$. Suppose for now $2, 3 \notin T$. By the property of Shamir's secret sharing, this leaks no additional information about x_1, x_2, x_3 to the adversary. Now, if $2 \in T$, then the adversary also learns Q_2, but that is okay since it already learns x_2; the same argument applies to $3 \in T$.

In the second case that P_1 is corrupted and adversary learns x_1 and all $Z(i)$'s, the polynomial Y is still a random degree-$(n - 1)$ polynomial with constant term $x_1 x_2 x_3 + z + s$ thanks to the randomization via S. If the adversary corrupts at set T of t parties, including P_1, and learns $\{Q_2(i), Q_3(i), S(i) : i \in T\}$, Shamir's secret sharing, again protects x_2, x_3 from being leaked to the adversary.

Protocol Specification. In short, the MPRE $\hat{F}$ for $x_1x_2x_3 + \alpha + \beta + \gamma$ simply computes n 4-party gadget MPRE,

$$\hat{f}((x_1, Z(i)),\ Q_2(i),\ Q_3(i),\ S(i))\quad \text{for all } i \in [n]$$

together with the linear term $\alpha + \beta + \gamma + z + s$. A formal description is in Fig. 5. It is easy to see that $\hat{F}$ has effective degree 2 since $\hat{f}$ has effective degree ≤ 2.

MPRE $\hat{F}$ for the n-party gadget functionality

This scheme uses the following tools:

- $\hat{f}$ is the effective degree-2 MPRE for the 4-party gadget in Section 4.1.

Local Randomness and Preprocessing: Parties locally sample and do:
- P_1 samples $z \leftarrow \mathbb{F}, Z \leftarrow \mathcal{P}(n-1, z)$.
- P_2 samples $Q_2 \leftarrow \mathcal{P}(t, x_2)$.
- P_3 samples $Q_3 \leftarrow \mathcal{P}(t, x_3)$.
- $\forall i \in [n]$, P_i samples $S(i) \leftarrow \mathbb{F}$.
- $\forall i \in [n]$, P_1, P_2, P_3, P_i sample $\mathbf{r}_1^{(i)}, \mathbf{r}_i^{(i)}$ respectively and performs local preprocessing for the i'th invocation of MPRE $\hat{f}$ below.

Encoding: Compute the encoding function of $\hat{f}$ and output:

$$\forall i \ \hat{\mathbf{y}}_i = \hat{f}((x_1, Z(i)),\ Q_2(i),\ Q_3(i),\ S(i)\ ;\ \mathbf{r}_1^{(i)}, \perp, \perp, \mathbf{r}_i^{(i)})$$
$$\hat{y} = \alpha + \beta + \gamma - s - z\ ,$$

where $s = \mathrm{rec}(n-1, (i, S(i))_i)$.

Decoding: For every i, decode $\hat{\mathbf{y}}_i$ to obtain $Y(i) = x_1 Q_2(i) Q_3(i) + Z(i) + S(i)$. Output $\mathrm{rec}(n-1, (i, Y(i))_i) + \hat{y}$.

Fig. 5. Effective degree-2 MPRE $\hat{F}$ for the n-party gadget functionality

Lemma 7. *The MPRE scheme in Fig. 5 for the n-party functionality* 3MultPlus$_n$ *has effective degree 2 and satisfies t-adaptive privacy for $t < n/2$. The construction requires $|\mathbb{F}| > n$.*

Simulator. Observe that the MPRE $\hat{F}$ invokes the 4-party gadget MPRE $\hat{f}$ for n times and computes a linear function ℓ. By the adaptive security of $\hat{f}$ and Theorem 2, we have that the parallel composition of all n invokations of $\hat{f}$ and the linear function ℓ is an MPRE $\hat{G}$ for the following composed functionality G:

$$G: \Big((x_1, \alpha, (Z(i))_i, S(1)),\ (x_2, \beta, (Q_2(i))_i, S(2)),$$
$$(x_3, \gamma, (Q_3(i))_i, S(3)),\ \dots,\ S(i),\ \dots,\ S(n) \Big)$$
$$\mapsto \alpha + \beta + \gamma - s - z, (Y(i))_i\ .$$

The leakage function of $\hat{f}$ gives the leakage function of $\hat{G}$, which is L_i leaking $(Q_2(i), Q_3(i))$ to P_i for every i. $\hat{G}$ is secure against $t < n/2$ adaptive corruption. Let $(\mathsf{Siml}_G, \mathsf{SimO}_G)$ be its simulator. Below, we use this simulator to construct the simulator $(\mathsf{Siml}_F, \mathsf{SimO}_F)$ for $\hat{F}$.

Overview. The encoding of $\hat{F}$ consists of encoding of $\hat{f}$ and the output of ℓ with appropriate input / output. The job of $(\mathsf{Siml}_F, \mathsf{SimO}_F)$ is: *1)* simulate the input / output of calls to $\hat{G}$, i.e., calls to $\hat{f}$ and $\hat{\ell}$, and *2)* invoke $(\mathsf{Siml}_G, \mathsf{SimO}_G)$ to simulate the encoding and local randomness of all calls to $\hat{f}$ and ℓ. Task *1)* requires simulating $Y(i)$, a random n-out-of-n Shamir sharing of $x_1 x_2 x_3 + z + s$ belonging to the output of encoding, all $Z(i)$ belonging to P_1, each $S(i)$ belonging to P_i, and each $Q_2(i), Q_3(i)$ belonging to P_2, P_3 respectively, and leaked to P_i. Consistency between $Y(i)$ and $Z(i), S(i)$ is maintained by "programming" the variable that is simulated the last. This can be done as $S(i)$ $Z(i)$ are all marginally random and provide enough degree of freedom for programming even if all parties were corrupted. Consistency between simulating $Q_2(i), Q_3(i)$ when P_2, P_3 are corrupted and when P_i is corrupted can be maintained, thanks to the fact that at most t parties are corrupted and Q_2, Q_3 have degree t with constant term x_2, x_3.

Proof (Proof of Lemma 7). We start with the formal description of the simulator.

Upon CorruptO, $\mathsf{SimO}(y = x_1 x_2 x_3 + \alpha + \beta + \gamma)$:
- Sample $\tau \leftarrow \mathbb{F}$.
- $\forall i$, if P_1, P_i are already corrupted, $Y(i) = x_1 Q_2(i) Q_3(i) + Z(i) + S(i)$ is fixed.
- Sample $O \leftarrow \mathcal{P}(n-1, \tau) \mid (i_1, Y(i_1)), \ldots, (i_s, Y(i_s))$ conditioned on the list of fixed $(i_j, Y(i_j))$'s from previous step. (Note that $s \le t$ points are fixed.)

Send to adversary $\mathsf{SimO}_G(y - \tau, (Y(i))_i)$.

Upon CorruptI(1), $\mathsf{Siml}(x_1, \alpha)$:
- Sample $S(1) \leftarrow \mathbb{F}$.
- $\forall i$, if P_i and the output party are already corrupted, find the unique $Z(i)$ that satisfies the equation $Y(i) = x_1 Q_2(i) Q_3(i) + Z(i) + S(i)$.

Send to adversary $\mathsf{Siml}_G(x_1, \alpha, (Z(i))_i, S(1))$.

Upon CorruptI(2), $\mathsf{Siml}(x_2, \beta)$:
- $\forall i$, if P_i is already corrupted, $Q_2(i)$ is already fixed.
- Sample $Q_2 \leftarrow \mathcal{P}(t, x_2) \mid (i_1, Q_2(i_1)), \ldots, (i_s, Q_2(i_s))$, conditioned on the list of fixed $(i_j, Q_2(i_j))$. (Note that this can be done as $s \le t$ points are fixed, and Q_3 has degree t.)
- if P_1 and the output party are already corrupted, find the unique $S(2)$ that satisfies the equation $Y(2) = x_1 Q_2(2) Q_3(2) + Z(2) + S(2)$.

Send to adversary $\mathsf{Siml}_G(x_2, \beta, (Q_2(i))_i, S(2))$.

Upon CorruptI(3), $\mathsf{Siml}(x_3, \gamma)$: Same as in $\mathsf{Siml}(x_2, \beta)$:
- $\forall i$, if P_i is already corrupted, $Q_3(i)$ is already fixed.
- Sample $Q_3 \leftarrow \mathcal{P}(t, x_3) \mid (i_1, Q_3(i_1)), \ldots, (i_s, Q_3(i_s))$, conditioned on the list of fixed $(i_j, Q_3(i_j))$.

- if P_1 and the output party are already corrupted, find the unique $S(3)$ that satisfies the equation $Y(3) = x_1 Q_2(3) Q_3(3) + Z(3) + S(3)$.

Send to adversary $\mathsf{Sim}_G(x_3, \gamma, (Q_3(i))_i, S(3))$.

Upon CorruptI(i), Siml($\perp$)) for $i \notin \{1,2,3\}$:
- If P_2 and/or P_3 is already corrupted, Q_2 and/or Q_3 are fixed. Otherwise, sample $Q_2(i), Q_3(i) \leftarrow \mathbb{F}$.
- Sample $Q_3 \leftarrow \mathcal{P}(t, x_3) \mid (i_1, Q_3(i_1)), \ldots, (i_s, Q_3(i_s))$, conditioned on the list of fixed $(i_j, Q_3(i_j))$.
- if P_1 and the output party are already corrupted, find the unique $S(i)$ that satisfies the equation $Y(i) = x_1 Q_2(i) Q_3(i) + Z(i) + S(i)$.

Send to adversary $\mathsf{Sim}_G(S(i), Q_2(i), Q_3(i))$.

Correctness of Simulation. We argue that the view of the adversary in the real world and simulation are identically distributed following from the simulation security of $\hat{G}$ and the fact that the input/output of the invokation of $\hat{G}$ are simulated perfectly.

Hybrid. More formally, consider the following hybrid, where input/output of the invokation of $\hat{G}$ is generated at the beginning as in the real world, while the encoding of $\hat{G}$ is still simulated.

At the Outset: With knowledge of $x_1, x_3, x_3, \alpha, \beta, \gamma$.
- $\forall i$, sample $Z(i) \leftarrow \mathbb{F}$. Let $z = Z(0)$.
- Sample $Q_2 \leftarrow \mathcal{P}(t, x_2)$.
- Sample $Q_3 \leftarrow \mathcal{P}(t, x_3)$.
- $\forall i$, sample $S(i) \leftarrow \mathbb{F}$. Let $s = S(0)$.
- $\forall i$, compute $Y(i) = x_1 Q_2(i) Q_3(i) + Z(i) + S(i)$.
- Compute $\tau = x_1 x_2 x_3 + z + s$, and $y = x_1 x_2 x_3 + \alpha + \beta + \gamma$.

Upon Corrupt0: Send to adversary $\mathsf{SimO}_G(y - \tau, (Y(i))_i)$.
Upon CorruptI(1): Send to adversary $\mathsf{Sim}_G(x_1, \alpha, (Z(i))_i, S(1))$.
Upon CorruptI(2) Send to adversary $\mathsf{Sim}_G(x_2, \beta, (Q_2(i))_i, S(2))$.
Upon CorruptI(3): Send to adversary $\mathsf{Sim}_G(x_3, \gamma, (Q_3(i))_i, S(3))$.
Upon CorruptI(i): Send to adversary $\mathsf{Sim}_G(S(i), Q_2(i), Q_3(i))$.

The only difference between the above hybrid and the real world is whether the encoding of $\hat{G}$ is simulated or not, it follows from the security of $\hat{G}$ that the views of the adversary are identically distributed. The only difference between the hybrid and the simulation is whether the input/output of the call to $\hat{G}$ is generated at the beginning with knowledge of $x_1, x_2, x_3, \alpha, \beta, \gamma$ or generated in a delayed fashion. Since these two ways of generation yield the same distribution, the hybrid and simulation are also identically distributed. We conclude that the real world and simulation are identically distributed.

5   MPRE for $\mathbf{NC^1}$ and $\mathbf{P/poly}$

We lift our effective degree-2 MPRE for degree-3 functionalities constructed in the previous section, to MPRE for $\mathbf{NC^1}$ and $\mathbf{P/poly}$. The transformation uses the former MPRE to compute degree-3 randomized encodings for $\mathbf{NC^1}$ [20] and for $\mathbf{P/poly}$ [22], and preserves the effective degree. The resulting effective-degree-2 MPRE for $\mathbf{NC^1}$ is information theoretically secure and tolerates any adaptive corruptions, while the resulting MPRE for $\mathbf{P/poly}$ is computationally secure making black box access to a PRG, and tolerates $n - 1$ adaptive corruptions.

By our sequential composition theorem (Theorem 1), it is sufficient to construct degree-3 MPRE for $\mathbf{NC^1}$ and for $\mathbf{P/poly}$. The former is constructed in [2]. The later, a $(n-1)$-private degree-3 MPRE for $\mathbf{P/poly}$ that makes black-box use of PRG, has been implicitly constructed in [13]. We will formally analyze the adaptive security of our MPRE for $\mathbf{P/poly}$ in the rest of the section. The adaptive security of the our MPRE for $\mathbf{NC^1}$ is deferred to the full version.

5.1   Computational MPRE for P/poly based on Black-box PRG

Lemma 8. *The scheme in Fig. 6 is a MPRE for* $\mathbf{P/poly}$ *such that*
- *the MPRE uses PRG as a black-box;*
- *the MPRE is computationally secure against* $n - 1$ *adaptive corruptions;*
- *the MPRE has effective degree 3 over boolean field.*

Proof Overview. The construction is similar to Yao's garbled circuits. Yao's garbled circuits can be viewed as a degree-3 computational randomized encoding for $\mathbf{P/poly}$.

Recall that in Yao's garbled circuits, the construction involves many pairs of the form
$$(s_j, \hat{s}_j),$$
so that they need to satisfy the following properties
- s_j is uniformly random;
- $\hat{s}_j$ is longer than s_j and can be deterministically computed from s_j;
- if s_j is hidden, $\hat{s}_j$ is computationally indistinguishable from uniform distribution.

PRG exactly fits the requirements. In Yao's garbled circuits, s_j is sampled at random, and $\hat{s}_j := G(s_j)$, where G is a PRG.

To convert Yao's garbled circuit into a computational MPRE, the label s_j should be jointly sampled by all parties. For the MPRE to be secure, $\hat{s}_j$ should be indistinguishable from uniform randomness as long as at least one party's local randomness is hidden. Moreover, for the MPRE to have low effective degree, PRG should be only be used in the preprocessing phase.

A natural construction that satisfies all the requirements is
- $s_j := s_j^{(1)} \| \ldots \| s_j^{(n)}$, where $s_j^{(i)}$ is locally sampled by the i-th party;
- $\hat{s}_j := G(s_j^{(1)}) \oplus \cdots \oplus G(s_j^{(n)})$.

Denote the mapping from s_j to $\hat{s}_j$ by G^{MP}, i.e.
$$G^{\mathrm{MP}}(z^{(1)} \| \ldots \| z^{(n)}) := G(z^{(1)}) \oplus \cdots \oplus G(z^{(n)}).$$
Under the new notation, $\hat{s}_j = G^{\mathrm{MP}}(s_j)$.

Circuit Definition. To rigorously state our MPRE, we formalize the notations for functionality in **P/poly**. A boolean circuit is specified by a directed acyclic graph. The nodes in the graph are indexed by numbers in $[m]$, each represents a wire in the circuit.

- For any $j \in [m]$, let x_j denote the wire value of the j-th wire.
- Let $\mathcal{J}_i$ denote the input wires of the i-th party. For each $j \in \mathcal{J}_i$, the i-th party knows the value of x_j. Let $\mathcal{J}_{\text{in}} := \bigcup_i \mathcal{J}_i$ denote all the input wires.
- Any wire other than the input wires is the output of a gate. Let $j_1, j_2 < j$ denotes the input wires of the gate (j_1, j_2 are implicit functions of j), let $g_j : \{0,1\} \times \{0,1\} \to \{0,1\}$ be the corresponding gate function. Thus $x_j = g_j(x_{j_1}, x_{j_2})$.
- For each wire j, let $d(j)$ denote the fan-out of the wire.
- Let $\mathcal{J}_{\text{out}}$ denote all the output wires. Thus the circuit output consists of x_j for all $j \in \mathcal{J}_{\text{out}}$.

Proof (Proof of Lemma 8). Scheme is essentially Yao's garbled circuit which uses G^{MP} as PRG. k_j is the permutation bit of the j-th wire. $s_{j,0}, s_{j,1}$ are the wire keys of the j-th wire. $(w_{j,0,0}, w_{j,0,1}, w_{j,1,0}, w_{j,1,1})$ is the table associated with the j-th gate. Thus both the correctness and privacy can be proved in a similar fashion as garbled circuit.

The correctness is implied from the statement that

$$\bar{x}_j := x_j \oplus k_j, \quad \hat{z}_j := \hat{s}_{j,\bar{x}_j} \tag{6}$$

for all $j \in [m]$. The statement can be proved by induction. For any $j \in \mathcal{J}_{\text{in}}$, (6) is directly guaranteed by the encoding function. For any $j \notin \mathcal{J}_{\text{in}}$, assume the statement holds for j_1, j_2 – the two input wire of the j-th gate, then

$$
\begin{aligned}
\bar{x}_j \| z_j &= w_{j,\bar{x}_{j_1},\bar{x}_{j_2}} \oplus \hat{s}_{j_1,\bar{x}_{j_1}}[j, \bar{x}_{j_2}] \oplus \hat{s}_{j_2,\bar{x}_{j_2}}[j, \bar{x}_{j_1}] \\
&= (k_j \oplus g_j(\bar{x}_{j_1} \oplus k_{j_1}, \bar{x}_{j_2} \oplus k_{j_2}) \| s_{j,k_j \oplus g_j(\bar{x}_{j_1} \oplus k_{j_1}, \bar{x}_{j_2} \oplus k_{j_2})}) \\
&= k_j \oplus g_j(x_{j_1}, x_{j_2}) \| s_{j,k_j \oplus g_j(x_{j_1}, x_{j_2})} \\
&= k_j \oplus x_j \| s_{j,k_j \oplus x_j},
\end{aligned}
$$

thus $\bar{x}_j = k_j \oplus x_j$, $z_j = s_{j,k_j \oplus x_j} = s_{j,\bar{x}_j}$ and $\hat{z}_j = G^{\text{MP}}(z_j) = G^{\text{MP}}(s_{j,\bar{x}_j}) = \hat{s}_{j,\bar{x}_j}$. As the consequence, for each $j \in \mathcal{J}_{\text{out}}$, the decoding function will output $\bar{x}_j \oplus k_j$, which equals the right output x_j.

For adaptive privacy, the simulator in *the ideal world* works as the follows

At the Outset: Sample $\bar{x}_j \leftarrow \{0,1\}$ for all $j \in [m]$, sample random $\hat{z}_j$ for all $j \in \mathcal{J}_{\text{in}}$, sample random z_j and sets $\hat{z}_j = G^{\text{MP}}(z_j)$ all $j \notin \mathcal{J}_{\text{in}}$.
Upon Corruptl(i), Siml($i, (x_j)_{j \in \mathcal{J}_i}$): Sets $k_j = x_j \oplus \bar{x}_j$ for all $j \in \mathcal{J}_i$.
  Sample random $\hat{s}_{j,0}^{(i)}, \hat{s}_{j,1}^{(i)}$ for all $j \in \mathcal{J}_{\text{in}}$, sample random $k_j^{(i)}$ for all $j \notin \mathcal{J}_{\text{in}}$.
  Set $s_{j,\bar{x}_i}^{(i)}$ as the i-th part of z_j and sample random $s_{j,\bar{x}_i \oplus 1}^{(i)}$ for all $j \notin \mathcal{J}_{\text{in}}$.
  Output $\left(x_j, k_j\right)_{j \in \mathcal{J}_i}, \left(\hat{s}_{j,0}^{(i)}, \hat{s}_{j,1}^{(i)}\right)_{j \in \mathcal{J}_{\text{in}}}, \left(k_j^{(i)}, s_{j,0}^{(i)}, s_{j,1}^{(i)}\right)_{j \notin \mathcal{J}_{\text{in}}}.$

$(n-1)$-private MPRE for circuit C

Input P_i has x_j for each $j \in \mathcal{J}_i$.

Randomness For each $j \in \mathcal{J}_i$, the i-th party samples $k_j \in \{0,1\}$. For each $j \in \mathcal{J}_{\text{in}}$, the i-th party samples $\hat{s}_{j,0}^{(i)}, \hat{s}_{j,1}^{(i)} \in \{0,1\}^{2(\mu+1)\cdot d(j)}$. For each $j \notin \mathcal{J}_{\text{in}}$, the i-th party samples $k_j^{(i)} \in \{0,1\}$, $s_{j,0}^{(i)}, s_{j,1}^{(i)} \in \{0,1\}^{\mu}$.

Preprocessing function: The i-th party computes $\hat{s}_{j,0}^{(i)} = G(s_{j,0}^{(i)})$, $\hat{s}_{j,1}^{(i)} = G(s_{j,1}^{(i)})$ for all $j \notin \mathcal{J}_{\text{in}}$.

That is,

$$h_i\left((x_j, k_j)_{j \in \mathcal{J}_i}, (\hat{s}_{j,0}^{(i)}, \hat{s}_{j,1}^{(i)})_{j \in \mathcal{J}_{\text{in}}}, (k_j^{(i)}, s_{j,0}^{(i)}, s_{j,1}^{(i)})_{j \notin \mathcal{J}_{\text{in}}} \right)$$
$$:= \left((x_j, k_j)_{j \in \mathcal{J}_i}, (\hat{s}_{j,0}^{(i)}, \hat{s}_{j,1}^{(i)})_{j \in \mathcal{J}_{\text{in}}}, (k_j^{(i)}, s_{j,0}^{(i)}, s_{j,1}^{(i)}, G(s_{j,0}^{(i)}), G(s_{j,1}^{(i)}))_{j \notin \mathcal{J}_{\text{in}}} \right).$$

Encoding function: Define $k_j := \bigoplus_{i \in [n]} k_j^{(i)}$, $\hat{s}_{j,b} := \bigoplus_{i \in [n]} \hat{s}_{j,b}^{(i)}$ for $j \in [m]$; $s_{j,b} := s_{j,b}^{(1)} \| \dots \| s_{j,b}^{(n)}$ for $j \notin \mathcal{J}_{\text{in}}$. The encoding consists of

$$\bar{x}_j := x_j \oplus k_j, \quad \hat{z}_j := \hat{s}_{j,\bar{x}_j}$$

for each $j \in \mathcal{J}_{\text{in}}$; and

$$w_{j,b_1,b_2} := \hat{s}_{j_1,b_1}[j,b_2] \oplus \hat{s}_{j_2,b_2}[j,b_1]$$
$$\oplus \left(k_j \oplus g_j(b_1 \oplus k_{j_1}, b_2 \oplus k_{j_2}) \| s_{j,k_j \oplus g_j(b_1 \oplus k_{j_1}, b_2 \oplus k_{j_2})} \right)$$

for each $j \notin \mathcal{J}_{\text{in}}$, $b_1, b_2 \in \{0,1\}$; and k_j for each $j \in \mathcal{J}_{\text{out}}$.

Decoding function: For each $j \notin \mathcal{J}_{\text{in}}$, compute

$$\bar{x}_j \| z_j = w_{j,\bar{x}_{j_1},\bar{x}_{j_2}} \oplus \hat{z}_{j_1}[j,\bar{x}_{j_2}] \oplus \hat{z}_{j_2}[j,\bar{x}_{j_1}].$$

and $\hat{z}_j = G^{\text{MP}}(z_j)$. Output $k_j \oplus \bar{x}_j$ for each $j \in \mathcal{J}_{\text{out}}$.

Fig. 6. Computational MPRE for **P/poly** using Black-box PRG

Upon CorruptO, SimO$((x_j)_{j \in \mathcal{J}_{\text{out}}})$: Sets $k_j = x_j \oplus \bar{x}_j$ for all $j \in \mathcal{J}_{\text{out}}$.
For each $j \notin \mathcal{J}_{\text{in}}$, the simulator sets

$$w_{j,\bar{x}_{j_1},\bar{x}_{j_2}} = \hat{z}_{j_1}[j,\bar{x}_{j_2}] \oplus \hat{z}_{j_2}[j,\bar{x}_{j_1}] \oplus (\bar{x}_j \| z_j),$$

and samples random w_{j,b_1,b_2} for $(b_1, b_2) \neq (\bar{x}_{j_1}, \bar{x}_{j_2})$.
Output $(\bar{x}_j, \hat{z}_j)_{j \in \mathcal{J}_{\text{in}}}, (w_{j,b_1,b_2})_{j \notin \mathcal{J}_{\text{in}}, b_1, b_2 \in \{0,1\}}, (k_j)_{j \in \mathcal{J}_{\text{out}}}$ to the adversary.

In order to show the real world and the ideal world are computationally indistinguishable from the adversary's view, we define a sequence of $2m+1$ hybrid worlds. *In the t-th hybrid world ($t \in \{0, \frac{1}{2}, 1, \frac{3}{2}, \dots, m\}$):*

At the Outset: The adversary decides input $(x_j)_{j \in \mathcal{J}_{\text{in}}}$.
Sample $\bar{x}_j \in \{0,1\}$ for all $j \in [m]$, sample random $\hat{z}_j$ for all $j \in \mathcal{J}_{\text{in}}$, sample random z_j and sets $\hat{z}_j = G^{\text{MP}}(z_j)$ all $j \notin \mathcal{J}_{\text{in}}$.

For all $j \in [m]$, set $k_j = x_j \oplus \bar{x}_j$. For all $j \in \mathcal{J}_{\text{in}}$, set $\hat{s}_{j,\bar{x}_j} = \hat{z}_j$ and sample random $\hat{s}_{j,\bar{x}_j \oplus 1}$. For all $j \notin \mathcal{J}_{\text{in}}$, set $s_{j,\bar{x}_j} = z_j$, set $\hat{s}_{j,\bar{x}_j} = G^{\text{MP}}(s_{j,\bar{x}_j})$, $\hat{z}_j = G^{\text{MP}}(z_j)$, thus $\hat{z}_j = \hat{s}_{j,\bar{x}_j}$.
set $s_{j,\bar{x}_j} = z_j$, sample random $s_{j,\bar{x}_j \oplus 1}$.
For each $j \notin \mathcal{J}_{\text{in}}$ that $j \leq t$, sample random $s_{j,\bar{x}_j \oplus 1}, \hat{s}_{j,\bar{x}_j \oplus 1}$.
For each $j \notin \mathcal{J}_{\text{in}}$ that $j > t$, sample random $s_{j,\bar{x}_j \oplus 1}$, set $\hat{s}_{j,\bar{x}_j \oplus 1} = G^{\text{MP}}(s_{j,\bar{x}_j \oplus 1})$.

Upon CorruptI(i): Sample random $\hat{s}_{j,0}^{(i)}, \hat{s}_{j,1}^{(i)}$ for all $j \in \mathcal{J}_{\text{in}}$. Sample random $k_j^{(i)}$ for all $j \notin \mathcal{J}_{\text{in}}$. Set $s_{j,b}^{(i)}$ as the i-th part of $s_{j,b}$ for all $j \notin \mathcal{J}_{\text{in}}$.

Send $\left(x_j, k_j\right)_{j \in \mathcal{J}_i}, \left(\hat{s}_{j,0}^{(i)}, \hat{s}_{j,1}^{(i)}\right)_{j \in \mathcal{J}_{\text{in}}}, \left(k_j^{(i)}, s_{j,0}^{(i)}, s_{j,1}^{(i)}\right)_{j \notin \mathcal{J}_{\text{in}}}$ to the adversary.

Upon CorruptO: For each $j \notin \mathcal{J}_{\text{in}}$ that $j \leq t + \frac{1}{2}$, set

$$w_{j,\bar{x}_{j_1},\bar{x}_{j_2}} = \hat{z}_{j_1}[j, \bar{x}_{j_2}] \oplus \hat{z}_{j_2}[j, \bar{x}_{j_1}] \oplus (\bar{x}_j \| z_j),$$

and sample random w_{j,b_1,b_2} for $(b_1, b_2) \neq (\bar{x}_{j_1}, \bar{x}_{j_2})$.
For each $j \notin \mathcal{J}_{\text{in}}$ that $j > t + \frac{1}{2}$, set

$$w_{j,b_1,b_2} = \hat{s}_{j_1,b_1}[j, b_2] \oplus \hat{s}_{j_2,b_2}[j, b_1] \oplus (k_j \oplus g_j(b_1 \oplus k_{j_1}, b_2 \oplus k_{j_2}) \| s_{j,k_j \oplus g_j(b_1 \oplus k_{j_1}, b_2 \oplus k_{j_2})})$$

for $b_1, b_2 \in \{0, 1\}$.
The simulator sends $(\bar{x}_j, \hat{z}_j)_{j \in \mathcal{J}_{\text{in}}}, (w_{j,b_1,b_2})_{j \notin \mathcal{J}_{\text{in}}, b_1, b_2 \in \{0,1\}}, (k_j)_{j \in \mathcal{J}_{\text{out}}}$ to the adversary.

The ideal world is computationally indistinguishable from the real world, because 1) the real world is indistinguishable from the 0-th hybrid world; 2) the ideal world is indistinguishable from the m-th hybrid world; 3) the j-th hybrid world is computationally indistinguishable from the $(j-1)$-th hybrid world.

The Real World is Indistinguishable from the 0-th Hybrid World as they are essentially the same. E.g. in the real world, $k_j^{(1)}, \ldots, k_j^{(n)}$ are i.i.d. random boolean, and $k_j := k_j^{(1)} \oplus \cdots \oplus k_j^{(n)}$, $\bar{x}_j := k_j \oplus x_j$; while in the 0-th hybrid world, $\bar{x}_j$ and $k_j^{(i)}$ for all corrupted party i are randomly sampled, and $k_j := \bar{x}_j \oplus x_j$. There two methods of sampling yield the same distribution.

The Ideal World is Indistinguishable from the m-th Hybrid World. Compared with the m-th hybrid world, the only difference of the ideal world is that some computation is deferred. E.g. in the m-th hybrid world, it sets $k_j := \bar{x}_j \oplus x_j$ at the beginning; while in the ideal world, the simulator can only set k_j after x_j is given.

The the $(j-1)$-th hybrid world. is indistinguishable from the $(j-\frac{1}{2})$-th hybrid world. The only difference between them is how $w_{j,0,0}, w_{j,0,1}, w_{j,1,0}, w_{j,1,1}$ are generated.
As for $w_{j,\bar{x}_{j_1},\bar{x}_{j_2}}$, we have

$$w_{j,\bar{x}_{j_1},\bar{x}_{j_2}} \quad \text{(in the } (j - \tfrac{1}{2})\text{-th hybrid world)}$$
$$= \hat{z}_{j_1}[j, \bar{x}_{j_2}] \oplus \hat{z}_{j_2}[j, \bar{x}_{j_1}] \oplus (\bar{x}_j \| z_j)$$

$$= \hat{s}_{j_1, \bar{x}_{j_1}}[j, \bar{x}_{j_2}] \oplus \hat{s}_{j_2, \bar{x}_{j_2}}[j, \bar{x}_{j_1}] \oplus (\bar{x}_j \| s_{j, \bar{x}_j})$$

$$= \hat{s}_{j_1, \bar{x}_{j_1}}[j, \bar{x}_{j_2}] \oplus \hat{s}_{j_2, \bar{x}_{j_2}}[j, \bar{x}_{j_1}]$$
$$\oplus (k_j \oplus g_j(\bar{x}_{j_1} \oplus k_{j_1}, \bar{x}_{j_2} \oplus k_{j_2}) \| s_{j, k_j \oplus g_j(\bar{x}_{j_1} \oplus k_{j_1}, \bar{x}_{j_2} \oplus k_{j_2})})$$

$$= w_{j, \bar{x}_{j_1}, \bar{x}_{j_2}} \quad \text{(in the } (j-1)\text{-th hybrid world).}$$

For the other three terms, w_{j, b_1, b_2} for $(b_1, b_2) \neq (\bar{x}_{j_1}, \bar{x}_{j_2})$, we have

$$w_{j, b_1, b_2} \quad \text{(in the } (j-1)\text{-th hybrid world)}$$
$$= \hat{s}_{j_1, b_1}[j, b_2] \oplus \hat{s}_{j_2, b_2}[j, b_1] \oplus (k_j \oplus g_j(b_1 \oplus k_{j_1}, b_2 \oplus k_{j_2}) \| s_{j, k_j \oplus g_j(b_1 \oplus k_{j_1}, b_2 \oplus k_{j_2})}).$$

Notice that in the $(j-1)$-th hybrid world, $\hat{s}_{j_1, \bar{x}_{j_1} \oplus 1}$, $\hat{s}_{j_2, \bar{x}_{j_2} \oplus 1}$ are fresh randomness that are only used to generate $w_{j, \bar{x}_{j_1} \oplus 1, \bar{x}_{j_2} \oplus 1}, w_{j, \bar{x}_{j_1}, \bar{x}_{j_2} \oplus 1}, w_{j, \bar{x}_{j_1} \oplus 1, \bar{x}_{j_2}}$. Thus it's equivalent to sampling w_{j, b_1, b_2} for $(b_1, b_2) \neq (\bar{x}_{j_1}, \bar{x}_{j_2})$ at random as they are already one-time padded by fresh randomness, which is exactly how they are generated in the $(j - \frac{1}{2})$-th hybrid world.

The Last Piece is the Computational Indistinguishability between the j-th Hybrid World and the $(j - \frac{1}{2})$-th Hybrid World. The only difference between them is how $\hat{s}_{j, \bar{x}_j \oplus 1}$ is generated.

In the $(j - \frac{1}{2})$-th hybrid world, $s_{j, \bar{x}_j \oplus 1} = s^{(1)}_{j, \bar{x}_j \oplus 1} \| \dots \| s^{(n)}_{j, \bar{x}_j \oplus 1}$ are randomly sampled and $\hat{s}_{j, \bar{x}_j \oplus 1}$ is determined by $\hat{s}_{j, \bar{x}_j \oplus 1} = G^{\mathrm{MP}}(s_{j, \bar{x}_j \oplus 1}) = \bigoplus_i G(s^{(i)}_{j, \bar{x}_j \oplus 1})$. As we are proving $(n-1)$-privacy, the adversary cannot corrupts all parties. Let i^* denote a party currently not corrupted by the adversary. Notice that $s^{(i^*)}_{j, \bar{x}_j \oplus 1}$ is only used to generate $\hat{s}_{j, \bar{x}_j \oplus 1}$, thus it is computational indistinguishable if $G(s^{(i^*)}_{j, \bar{x}_j \oplus 1})$ is replaced by uniform randomness. Replacing $G(s^{(i^*)}_{j, \bar{x}_j \oplus 1})$ by uniform randomness is equivalent to sampling $\hat{s}_{j, \bar{x}_j \oplus 1}$ at random, which is how $\hat{s}_{j, \bar{x}_j \oplus 1}$ is generated in the j-th hybrid world.

6 Two-Round MPC

As what we are going to show in Lemma 9, an effective-degree-2 adaptive MPRE for functionality f and an adaptive 2-round MPC for any degree-2 functions will imply an adaptive 2-round MPC for the functionality f. In previous sections, we construct effective degree-2 MPRE for $\mathbf{NC}^1$ and $\mathbf{P/poly}$ under different settings. The last step is to construct adaptive 2-round MPC protocols for degree-2 functionalities in these settings, which are Sect. 6.1 and 6.2.

Lemma 9. *Let $(\hat{f}, h_1, \dots, h_n)$ be a MPRE for functionality f that tolerates t adaptive corruptions. Assume there is a MPC protocol for $\hat{f}$ that tolerates t adaptive corruptions. Then there exists a MPC protocol for f such that*

– *the resulting MPC protocol has the same round and communication complexity as the MPC protocol for $\hat{f}$;*

- the resulting MPC protocol tolerates t adaptive corruptions; the type of the simulation security (prefect, statistical or computational) align with that of the MPRE for f and MPC for $\hat{f}$;
- if the MPC for $\hat{f}$ or the MPRE for f uses correlated randomness, the resulting MPC uses the same correlated randomness.

The proof is deferred to the full version.

6.1   Honest Majority and Plain Model

In the honest majority setting, the BGW [5] protocol when restricted to computing degree-2 polynomials has only two rounds. The adaptive security of BGW is proved in [14].

Lemma 10. *For any degree-2 functionality f, the BGW protocol computes f in 2-round and tolerates adaptive minority corruptions.*

6.2   Honest Minority and OLE Correlations

We now construct a very simple adaptively secure MPC protocol using OLE-correlation for the following 2MultPlus functionality, which is sufficient for computing any degree-2 polynomials.

Input P_1 has $x_1, z_1 \in \mathbb{F}$; P_2 has $x_2, z_2 \in \mathbb{F}$.
OLE Correlation Sample random $a_1, a_2, b_1, b_2 \in \mathbb{F}$ such that $a_1 a_2 = b_1 + b_2$.
   P_1 has $a_1, b_1 \in \mathbb{F}$, P_2 has $a_2, b_2 \in \mathbb{F}$.
Round 1 P_1 sends $m_{1,1} := x_1 - a_1$ to P_2. P_2 sends $m_{2,1} := x_2 - a_2$ to P_1.
Round 2 P_1 sends $m_{1,1}$ and $m_{1,2} := m_{2,1} x_1 + b_1 + z_1$ to the receiver.
   P_2 sends $m_{2,1}$ and $m_{2,2} := m_{1,1} x_2 + b_2 + z_2$ to the receiver.
   The receiver outputs $m_{1,2} + m_{2,2} - m_{1,1} m_{2,1}$.

Fig. 7. 2-round MPC for 2MULTPlus in OLE correlation model

Lemma 11. *The 2-round MPC described in Figure 7 is a adaptive secure MPC protocol for the following functionality*

$$\text{2MultPlus} : ((x_1, z_1), (x_2, z_2)) \mapsto x_1 x_2 + z_1 + z_2$$

and it tolerates an arbitrary number of corruptions.

Proof Overview. The scheme can also be explained as a randomized encoding for branching program. As (b_1, b_2) is the additive secret sharing of $a_1 a_2$, the receiver essentially learns $m_{1,1}, m_{2,1}$ and $m_{1,2} + m_{2,2}$.

As
$$\begin{bmatrix} 1 & a_1 \\ & 1 \end{bmatrix} \begin{bmatrix} x_1 & z_1 + z_2 \\ -1 & x_2 \end{bmatrix} \begin{bmatrix} 1 & a_2 \\ & 1 \end{bmatrix} = \begin{bmatrix} m_{1,1} & m_{1,2} + m_{2,2} \\ -1 & m_{2,1} \end{bmatrix},$$

the message received by the receiver is a randomized encoding of $x_1 x_2 + z_1 + z_2$, and a_1, a_2 are the randomness of the randomness encoding. The formal proof is deferred to the full version.

Acknowledgements. We thank Yuval Ishai for insightful discussions. Part of this work was done while the authors were visiting the Simons Institute for the Theory of Computing.

References

1. Ananth, P., Choudhuri, A.R., Goel, A., Jain, A.: Round-optimal secure multiparty computation with honest majority. In: Shacham, H., Boldyreva, A. (eds.) CRYPTO 2018. LNCS, vol. 10992, pp. 395–424. Springer, Cham (2018). https://doi.org/10.1007/978-3-319-96881-0_14

2. Applebaum, B., Brakerski, Z., Tsabary, R.: Perfect secure computation in two rounds. In: Beimel, A., Dziembowski, S. (eds.) TCC 2018. LNCS, vol. 11239, pp. 152–174. Springer, Cham (2018). https://doi.org/10.1007/978-3-030-03807-6_6

3. Applebaum, B., Ishai, Y., Kushilevitz, E.: Cryptography in NC^0. SIAM J. Comput. **36**(4), 845–888 (2006)

4. Beaver, D., Micali, S., Rogaway, P.: The round complexity of secure protocols. In: Proceedings of the 22nd Annual ACM Symposium on Theory of Computing, pp. 503–513 (1990). https://doi.org/10.1145/100216.100287

5. Ben-Or, M., Goldwasser, S., Wigderson, A.: Completeness theorems for non-cryptographic fault-tolerant distributed computation. In: Providing Sound Foundations for Cryptography: On the Work of Shafi Goldwasser and Silvio Micali, pp. 351–371 (1988). https://doi.org/10.1145/62212.62213

6. Benhamouda, F., Lin, H.: k-round multiparty computation from k-round oblivious transfer via garbled interactive circuits. In: Nielsen, J.B., Rijmen, V. (eds.) EURO-CRYPT 2018. LNCS, vol. 10821, pp. 500–532. Springer, Cham (2018). https://doi.org/10.1007/978-3-319-78375-8_17

7. Benhamouda, F., Lin, H., Polychroniadou, A., Venkitasubramaniam, M.: Two-round adaptively secure multiparty computation from standard assumptions. In: Beimel, A., Dziembowski, S. (eds.) TCC 2018. LNCS, vol. 11239, pp. 175–205. Springer, Cham (2018). https://doi.org/10.1007/978-3-030-03807-6_7

8. Boyle, E., Couteau, G., Gilboa, N., Ishai, Y.: Compressing vector OLE. In: Lie, D., Mannan, M., Backes, M., Wang, X. (eds.) Proceedings of the ACM SIGSAC Conference on Computer and Communications Security, CCS 2018, Toronto, ON, Canada, October 15–19, 2018, pp. 896–912. ACM (2018). https://doi.org/10.1145/3243734.3243868

9. Boyle, E., Couteau, G., Gilboa, N., Ishai, Y., Kohl, L., Scholl, P.: Efficient pseudorandom correlation generators from ring-LPN. In: Micciancio, D., Ristenpart, T. (eds.) CRYPTO 2020. LNCS, vol. 12171, pp. 387–416. Springer, Cham (2020). https://doi.org/10.1007/978-3-030-56880-1_14

10. Canetti, R.: Security and composition of multiparty cryptographic protocols. J. Cryptology **13**(1), 143–202 (2000). https://doi.org/10.1007/s001459910006

11. Canetti, R., Feige, U., Goldreich, O., Naor, M.: Adaptively secure multi-party computation. In: Proceedings of the 28th Annual ACM Symposium on Theory of Computing, pp. 639–648. ACM (1996) https://doi.org/10.1145/237814.238015

12. Chaum, D., Crépeau, C., Damgård, I.: Multiparty unconditionally secure protocols. In: Proceedings of the twentieth Annual ACM Symposium on Theory of Computing, pp. 11–19. ACM (1988). https://doi.org/10.1145/62212.62214

13. Damgård, I., Ishai, Y.: Constant-round multiparty computation using a black-box pseudorandom generator. In: Shoup, V. (ed.) CRYPTO 2005. LNCS, vol. 3621, pp. 378–394. Springer, Heidelberg (2005). https://doi.org/10.1007/11535218_23

14. Damgård, I., Nielsen, J.B.: Adaptive versus static security in the UC model. In: Chow, S.S.M., Liu, J.K., Hui, L.C.K., Yiu, S.M. (eds.) ProvSec 2014. LNCS, vol. 8782, pp. 10–28. Springer, Cham (2014). https://doi.org/10.1007/978-3-319-12475-9_2

15. Garg, S., Gentry, C., Halevi, S., Raykova, M.: Two-round secure MPC from indistinguishability obfuscation. In: Lindell, Y. (ed.) TCC 2014. LNCS, vol. 8349, pp. 74–94. Springer, Heidelberg (2014). https://doi.org/10.1007/978-3-642-54242-8_4

16. Garg, S., Ishai, Y., Srinivasan, A.: Two-round MPC: information-theoretic and black-box. In: Beimel, A., Dziembowski, S. (eds.) TCC 2018. LNCS, vol. 11239, pp. 123–151. Springer, Cham (2018). https://doi.org/10.1007/978-3-030-03807-6_5

17. Garg, S., Srinivasan, A.: Two-round multiparty secure computation from minimal assumptions. In: Nielsen, J.B., Rijmen, V. (eds.) EUROCRYPT 2018. LNCS, vol. 10821, pp. 468–499. Springer, Cham (2018). https://doi.org/10.1007/978-3-319-78375-8_16

18. Goldreich, O., Micali, S., Wigderson, A.: How to play any mental game or A completeness theorem for protocols with honest majority. In: Providing Sound Foundations for Cryptography: On the Work of Shafi Goldwasser and Silvio Micali, pp. 218–229. ACM (1987). https://doi.org/10.1145/28395.28420

19. Ishai, Y., Kushilevitz, E.: Randomizing polynomials: a new representation with applications to round-efficient secure computation. In: Proceedings 41st Annual Symposium on Foundations of Computer Science, pp. 294–304. IEEE (2000). https://doi.org/10.1109/SFCS.2000.892118

20. Ishai, Y., Kushilevitz, E.: Perfect constant-round secure computation via perfect randomizing polynomials. In: Widmayer, P., Eidenbenz, S., Triguero, F., Morales, R., Conejo, R., Hennessy, M. (eds.) ICALP 2002. LNCS, vol. 2380, pp. 244–256. Springer, Heidelberg (2002). https://doi.org/10.1007/3-540-45465-9_22

21. Ishai, Y., Mittal, M., Ostrovsky, R.: On the message complexity of secure multiparty computation. In: Abdalla, M., Dahab, R. (eds.) PKC 2018. LNCS, vol. 10769, pp. 698–711. Springer, Cham (2018). https://doi.org/10.1007/978-3-319-76578-5_24

22. Yao, A.C.C.: Protocols for secure computations. In: 23rd Annual Symposium on Foundations of Computer Science (sfcs 1982), pp. 160–164. IEEE (1982). https://doi.org/10.1109/SFCS.1982.38

23. Yao, A.C.C.: How to generate and exchange secrets. In: 27th Annual Symposium on Foundations of Computer Science (sfcs 1986), pp. 162–167. IEEE (1986). https://doi.org/10.1109/SFCS.1986.25

On Statistical Security in Two-Party Computation

Dakshita Khurana[✉] and Muhammad Haris Mughees

University of Illinois Urbana-Champaign, Urbana, USA
{dakshita,mughees2}@illinois.edu

Abstract. There has been a large body of work characterizing the round complexity of general-purpose maliciously secure two-party computation (2PC) against probabilistic polynomial time adversaries. This is particularly true for zero-knowledge, which is a special case of 2PC. In fact, in the special case of zero knowledge, optimal protocols with unconditional security against one of the two players have also been meticulously studied and constructed.

On the other hand, general-purpose maliciously secure 2PC with *statistical* or unconditional security against one of the two participants has remained largely unexplored so far. In this work, we initiate the study of such protocols, which we refer to as 2PC with one-sided statistical security. We settle the round complexity of 2PC with one-sided statistical security with respect to black-box simulation by obtaining the following tight results:

- In a setting where only one party obtains an output, we design 2PC in 4 rounds with statistical security against receivers and computational security against senders.
- In a setting where both parties obtain outputs, we design 2PC in 5 rounds with computational security against the party that obtains output first and statistical security against the party that obtains output last.

Katz and Ostrovsky (CRYPTO 2004) showed that 2PC with black-box simulation requires at least 4 rounds when one party obtains an output and 5 rounds when both parties obtain outputs, even when only computational security is desired against both parties. Thus in these settings, not only are our results tight, but they also show that statistical security is achievable at no extra cost to round complexity. This still leaves open the question of whether 2PC can be achieved with black-box simulation in 4 rounds with statistical security against senders and computational security against receivers. Based on a lower bound on computational zero-knowledge proofs due to Katz (TCC 2008), we observe that the answer is negative unless the polynomial hierarchy collapses.

This material is based on work supported in part by DARPA under Contract No. HR001120C0024. Any opinions, findings and conclusions or recommendations expressed in this material are those of the author(s) and do not necessarily reflect the views of the United States Government or DARPA.

© International Association for Cryptologic Research 2020
R. Pass and K. Pietrzak (Eds.): TCC 2020, LNCS 12551, pp. 532–561, 2020.
https://doi.org/10.1007/978-3-030-64378-2_19

1   Introduction

Secure two-party computation allows two mutually distrustful participants to compute jointly on their private data without revealing anything beyond the output of their computation. Protocols that securely compute general functionalities have been constructed under a variety of assumptions, and with a variety of efficiency guarantees.

A fundamental question in the study of secure computation is *round complexity*. This question has been researched extensively, and even more so for the special case of zero-knowledge.

Zero-Knowledge. Computational zero-knowledge arguments with negligible soundness error can be achieved in 4 messages [19], under the minimal assumption that one-way functions exist [7]. This is tight: for languages outside BPP, with black-box simulation and without any trusted setup, zero-knowledge arguments require at least four messages [24].

For zero-knowledge with black-box simulation, different flavors have been studied depending on the level of soundness and zero knowledge achieved. Either property can be statistical or computational, meaning that it holds against unbounded or computationally bounded adversaries, respectively. Protocols that satisfy both properties statistically, known as statistical zero knowledge proofs, are only possible for languages in AM ∩ coAM [1,20]; however, once either property is relaxed to be computational, protocols for all of NP can be constructed assuming the existence of one way functions [11,25,26,40,41]. Specifically,

- *Statistical Zero-knowledge Arguments for* NP, where soundness is computational and zero-knowledge is statistical, are known to be achievable in 4 rounds with black-box simulation, assuming the existence of collision resistant hash functions [7].
- *Computational Zero-knowledge Proofs for* NP, that satisfy statistical soundness and computational zero-knowledge, are known to be achievable in 5 rounds with black-box simulation, assuming the existence of collision resistant hash functions [24].

Protocols that satisfy *statistical security*, either against a malicious prover or a malicious verifier, are more secure and therefore can be more desirable than protocols that are only computationally secure on both sides. For instance, statistical zero-knowledge arguments provide an unconditional privacy guarantee – even a verifier that runs an arbitrary amount of post-processing on the proof transcript, does not obtain any information that cannot be simulated efficiently.

Secure Computation of General Functionalities. While tight results for zero-knowledge with black-box simulation with statistical security against one party are known, the state of affairs is significantly lacking in the case of two-party secure computation of general functionalities. Specifically, in the two-party setting, it is natural to ask whether statistical or unconditional security can be achieved, against at least one of the parties.

In a setting where both parties are computationally bounded, Katz and Ostrovsky [33] showed how to securely compute general functionalities with black-box simulation, with only 4 messages of interaction, when one party receives the output, and 5 messages when both parties receive the output. They also demonstrate that this result is tight with respect to black-box simulation. There has been significant progress in the last few years, extending the results of Katz and Ostrovsky to obtain better round optimal secure protocols both in [15,44] and beyond the two-party setting [3,6,10,13,14,23].

Despite all this progress, there are significant gaps in our understanding of the round complexity of 2PC with one-sided statistical security, i.e. statistical security against one of the participants. While there are known techniques to achieve weaker notions such as super-polynomial simulation with statistical security [12,31,43], the (standard) setting of polynomial simulation is not well understood at all.

1.1   Our Results

In this paper, we settle the round complexity of two-party secure computation with black-box simulation and one-sided statistical security. This is the best possible security that can be achieved by any non-trivial two-party protocol in the plain model.

We now describe our results in some detail. First, we consider a setting where only one party receives the output of the computation. Without loss of generality, we call the party that receives the output, the receiver R, and the other party the sender S. We obtain a tight characterization with respect to black-box simulation, as follows.

Informal Theorem 1. *Assuming polynomial hardness of either DDH or QR or LWE, there exists a 4 round two-party secure computation protocol for general functionalities with black-box simulation, with statistical security against an adversarial receiver and computational security against an adversarial sender.*

Next, we recall a result due to Katz [32] who proved that 4 round computational zero-knowledge proofs for NP with black-box simulation cannot exist unless the polynomial hierarchy collapses. This helps rule out the existence of a 4 round two-party protocol for secure computation of general functionalities with black-box simulation, with statistical security against an adversarial sender and computational security against an adversarial receiver, unless the polynomial hierarchy collapses. A formal proof of this statement appears in the full version of the paper. We also match this lower bound with the following result.

Informal Theorem 2. *Assuming polynomial hardness of either DDH or QR or LWE, there exists a 5 round two-party secure computation protocol for general functionalities with black-box simulation, with statistical security against an adversarial sender and computational security against an adversarial receiver.*

We formalize and prove Informal Theorem 1 and Informal Theorem 2 by demonstrating a *single* 5 round protocol for symmetric functionalities (i.e. functionalities that generate identical output for both parties), where the receiver R obtains the output at the end of the 4th round, and the sender S obtains the output at the end of the 5th round. This protocol is unconditionally secure against malicious receivers, and computationally secure against malicious senders. Such a protocol can be unconditionally compiled (in a round-preserving way) to work for asymmetric functionalities using the following folklore technique: each participant additionally inputs a random key to the functionality, and the symmetric functionality masks each participant's output with their respective key.

We prove that our protocol provides statistical security against a malicious receiver R and computational security against a malicious sender S. We observe that Informal Theorem 1 follows from this protocol by simply eliminating the last message from the receiver R to the sender S. Informal Theorem 2 also follows from this protocol *by simply renaming the players: that is, we will now call the party S in our original protocol, R; and we will call R, S.* The resulting protocol, after renaming parties, is statistically secure against a malicious sender S and computationally secure against a malicious receiver R. Because both parties obtain the output by the end of the 5th round, the (re-named) receiver R is guaranteed to obtain the output at the end of round 5.

Together, these results completely characterize the round complexity of secure two-party computation with black-box simulation and statistical security against one participant. Along the way, we develop a toolkit for establishing statistical security that may be useful in other settings.

In the rest of this paper, in protocols where a single party gets the output – we will call the party that obtains an output the receiver, and the other party the sender. In protocols both parties get the output, we call the party that obtains its output first, the receiver and the party that obtains output second, the sender.

2   Our Techniques

We now provide an informal overview of our techniques. Our starting point is the simple case of security against semi-honest adversaries, with statistical security against one party and computational security against the other. A simple way to obtain round-optimal secure computation for general functionalities, in the semi-honest setting, is to rely on Yao's garbling technique. In this technique, one party, referred to as the garbler, computes a garbled circuit and labels for the evaluation of a circuit. The garbler sends the resulting circuit to the other party, the evaluator, and both parties rely on 2-choose-1 oblivious transfer (OT) to transfer the "right" labels corresponding to the input of the evaluator. The evaluator then executes a public algorithm on the garbled circuit and labels to recover the output of the circuit.

Limitations in the Semi-honest Setting. Even in the semi-honest setting, garbled circuits that provide security against unbounded evaluators are only known for circuits in NC1. In fact, whether constant round two-party *semi-honest* protocols secure against unbounded senders and unbounded receivers exist, even in the OT hybrid model, is an important unresolved open problem in information-theoretic cryptography. In the absence of such protocols, the best security we can hope to achieve even in the semi-honest setting, is when at least one party is computationally bounded. As a result, in the malicious setting also, the best we can hope for is security against unbounded senders and bounded receivers, or unbounded receivers and bounded senders.

As discussed in the previous section, we construct a *single* 5 round protocol for symmetric functionalities (i.e. functionalities that generate identical output for both parties), where the receiver R obtains the output at the end of the 4th round, and the sender S obtains the output at the end of the 5th round[1]. We prove that this protocol provides statistical security against an unbounded malicious receiver R* and security against a computationally bounded malicious sender S*. For simplicity, we discuss the first 4 rounds of this protocol in more detail: specifically, we discuss a 4 round protocol where R obtains the output (and S does not), that we prove is secure against an unbounded malicious R* and computationally bounded malicious S*.

R *must generate the garbled circuit, and* S *must evaluate it.* Garbled circuits form an important component of our protocol. Because garbled circuits for functions outside of NC1 are insecure against unbounded evaluators, when looking at all efficiently computable functions (which is the focus of this work), our de-facto strategy will be to have a malicious evaluator that is computationally bounded whereas a malicious garbler may be computationally unbounded.

Because we desire statistical security against R*, the receiver R must be the entity that generates the garbled circuit, and S will evaluate this circuit on labels obtained via a 2-choose-1 oblivious transfer (OT) protocol. Recall that we also require the receiver R to obtain the output by the end of round 4. Since S is the one evaluating the garbled circuit, this enforces that the garbled circuit must be evaluated by the sender by the end of round 3. In other words, R must output the garbled circuit and transfer labels to the sender by round 3.

This requires that labels for the garbled circuit be transferred from R to S via a 3 round OT protocol, in which R is the OT sender and S is the OT receiver. Naturally, this oblivious transfer protocol is also required to be statistically secure against malicious R* (who is the OT sender) and computationally secure against malicious S* (who is the OT receiver). Unfortunately, no OT protocols achieving malicious security are known in 3 rounds (in fact, the existence of such protocols with black-box simulation would contradict the lower bound of [33]). The fact that the OT must also be statistically secure against malicious senders complicates matters further. This brings us to our first technical barrier: *identifying and using weaker forms of OT to obtain full malicious security.*

---

[1] We note that this is without loss of generality, since any asymmetric functionality can be unconditionally computed from a symmetric one by having each party input a random value, and using it to mask the output.

Reconciling Three Round Oblivious Transfer. Here, it is appropriate to discuss known notions of oblivious transfer that are achievable in three rounds and provide some semblance of malicious security. A popular notion has been game-based security: roughly, this requires that the receiver choice bit be hidden from a malicious sender, and one of the sender messages remain hidden from the receiver. A further strengthening of this notion is security with superpolynomial simulation, commonly called *SPS*-security. Very roughly, this requires the existence of a *superpolynomial* simulator that simulates the view of a malicious sender/receiver only given access to the ideal functionality. There are known constructions of SPS-secure OT: in 2 rounds, SPS-secure OT was first constructed by [5] based on two-round game-based OT, which can itself be realized based on a variety of assumptions, including DDH, LWE, QR, and N^{th}-residuosity [2,9,27,30,42].

Here, recall that we also desire *statistical security* against an adversarial sender. Achieving this property requires at least three rounds [31], and [31] obtained 3 round OT with SPS security based on superpolynomial hardness of DDH, LWE, QR, and N^{th}-residuosity. Even more recently, [28] improved this result to rely only on polynomial hardness of any of the same assumptions. In fact, [28] achieve a notion in between SPS-security and standard security against malicious receivers: their protocol obtains distinguisher-dependent security [18,29] against malicious receivers. This relaxes the standard notion of malicious security by reversing the order of quantifiers, namely, by allowing the simulator to depend upon the distinguisher that is attempting to distinguish the real and ideal experiments. Importantly, unlike standard security, a distinguisher-dependent OT simulator is *not* guaranteed to efficiently extract the adversary's actual input, unless it has access to the distinguisher. On the other hand, we would like to achieve *full-fledged* malicious security in our 2PC protocol. This means that our 2PC simulator must nevertheless find a way to extract the adversary's input and cannot rely on the OT simulator for this purpose. Looking ahead, we will only rely on the OT protocol to obtain an indistinguishability-based guarantee, and our 2PC simulator will not use the OT simulator at all. Next, we describe additional components that we add to this protocol to enable full-fledged malicious security.

Immediate Pitfalls of the Current Template. Now as discussed previously, garbled circuits and an appropriate OT protocol do *not* by themselves guarantee meaningful security against malicious adversaries. A malicious garbler could generate the garbled circuit or labels so as to completely alter the output of an honest evaluator. As such, the sender must be convinced that the garbled circuit and labels that she obtained from the receiver were generated "correctly", before she evaluates the garbled circuit. In other words, R should convince S, *within three rounds*, that the garbled circuit and oblivious transfer messages were correctly generated, so that it is "safe" for the sender to evaluate the garbled circuit.

A naïve approach would entail the use of a *computational* zero-knowledge *proof*, where R proves to S that the garbled circuit, labels and OT messages sent by R were correctly generated. Unfortunately, *computational* zero-knowledge *proofs* are not known to exist in less than 4 rounds of interaction from standard assumptions, even assuming non-black-box simulation. This brings us to our second technical barrier.

We overcome this barrier with the help of a special conditional disclosure of secrets (CDS) protocol, that we will detail towards the end of this overview. This CDS protocol will help us compile protocols that are secure against adversaries that "promise to behave well" (that we will denote as *explainable adversaries* in line with [8]) into protocols secure against arbitrarily malicious adversaries, while retaining one-sided statistical security. An "explainable" adversary generates messages in the support of the distribution of all honestly generated messages.[2]

In fact, we take a modular approach to building 2PC with one-sided statistical security against fully malicious adversaries: first, we obtain a protocol secure against explainable adversaries alone, and next, we compile this protocol to one that is secure against arbitrary malicious adversaries. For now, we focus our attention towards achieving simulation-based security against explainable adversaries alone, instead of arbitrary malicious ones. Later, we discuss our CDS-based approach to achieve security against arbitrary malicious adversaries.

Extracting inputs of Explainable Adversaries. Recall that by definition of explainability, for every garbled circuit GC and OT message that an explainable R^* sends, there exists randomness r and input inp such that GC is generated as an output of the garbling algorithm for the circuit corresponding to the two-party function f, on input inp and with randomness r.

As already discussed, proving security requires establishing the existence of a *simulator* that interacts with an ideal functionality and with the adversary to output a view that is indistinguishable from the adversary's view in its interaction with the honest party. Importantly, this simulator must *extract* the input of a malicious R^* or S^*, and cannot use the 3-round OT for this purpose.

Therefore, to enable extraction from R^*, we modify the protocol to require the receiver to send a statistically binding extractable commitment (constructed, eg, in [45]) to its input, in parallel with the rest of the protocol. By definition, an *explainable* R^* is guaranteed to send an extractable commitment to the "right" input that is consistent with the garbled circuit, and a simulator Sim^{R^*} will be able to extract R^*'s input from the extractable commitment. Such extractable commitments are known to exist in 3 rounds by the work of Prabhakaran et al. [45].

Similarly, in order to enable the extraction of S^*'s input, we will modify the protocol to require S to send an extractable commitment to its input, in parallel with the rest of the protocol. The simulator Sim^{S^*} will be able to extract the

---

[2] Importantly, this is *different* from semi-malicious security [38,39] where the adversary in addition to generating messages in the support of the distribution of all honestly generated messages, outputs the input and randomness that it used, on a special tape. On the other hand, simulating an explainable adversary is much more challenging: since in this case the adversary does not output any such special tape, and therefore the input and randomness must still be extracted from an explainable adversary by the simulator.

sender's input from this extractable commitment. Since we require statistical security against R, the extractable commitment used by S should be statistically hiding. A simple modification to the extractable commitments of Prabhakaran et al. [45], replacing statistically binding computationally hiding commitments with statistically hiding computationally binding commitments yields the required extractable commitment in 4 rounds. Unfortunately, this also means that Sim^{S^*} can *only* send the input of S^* and obtain an output from the ideal functionality at the end of the 4th round. However, S^* evaluates the garbled circuit and may obtain an output before round 4 even begins, which would allow S^* to distinguish the real and ideal executions. Said differently, this would leave Sim^{S^*} with no opportunity to program the output of the ideal functionality in the view of S^*.

To provide Sim^{S^*} with such an opportunity and overcome this technical barrier, we modify the protocol as follows: instead of garbling the circuit corresponding to the function f, R samples the keys $(\mathsf{pk}, \mathsf{sk})$ for a public key encryption scheme, and garbles a circuit that computes $(\mathsf{Enc}_{\mathsf{pk}} \circ f)$. Here $\mathsf{Enc}_{\mathsf{pk}}$ denotes the encryption algorithm of an IND-CPA secure encryption scheme, and the randomness used for encryption is hardwired by R into the circuit. As a result, S on evaluating the garbled circuit, obtains a ciphertext that *encrypts* the output of the function under R's public key. It must then forward this ciphertext to R, who uses the corresponding secret key to decrypt the ciphertext and recover the output of the function[3]. This concludes the bare-bones description of our 5-round protocol with security against explainable adversaries.

In addition to proving that this protocol is secure against explainable PPT adversaries, we also establish an additional property, that will come in handy later. We prove that the protocol is *robust* in the first two rounds: meaning that even an adversary that behaves arbitrarily maliciously (and not necessarily explainably) in the first two rounds can only influence the function output, but not obtain any information about the private input of the other participant.

Simulating Explainable Adversaries. This completes a simplified overview of our protocol with security against explainable adversaries. But there are several subtleties that arise when formalizing the proof of security. We describe our simulators and discuss a few of these subtleties below.

First, we discuss how to build a simulator Sim^{S^*} that simulates the view of a malicious sender S^*. Recall that Sim^{S^*} must extract the input of a malicious S^*, query the ideal functionality, and program the resulting output in the view of S^*. The use of statistically hiding extractable commitments allows Sim^{S^*} to extract S^*'s input by the end of the fourth round. Therefore, Sim^{S^*} only obtains an output from the ideal functionality by the end of the fourth round. But Sim^{S^*} must send to S^* a garbled circuit in the third round, on behalf of R, *even before* learning the output. How should Sim^{S^*} construct this circuit? Sim^{S^*} cannot even

---

[3] Alternatively, R could withhold the garbled circuit decoding information, i.e. the correspondence between the output wire labels and the output of the circuit, from S until the 5th round. This would achieve the same effect, but leads to a more complex analysis. For simplicity of analysis, we choose to garble an encrypted circuit in our formal presentation.

invoke the simulator of the garbled circuit because it has not extracted S*'s input at this time. Instead, we have the simulator simply garble a circuit that outputs an encryption of the all zeroes string. Finally, the simulator extracts the input of S* from the fourth round message, and queries the ideal functionality to obtain an output. In the fifth round, it sends this output S* in the clear.

Recall that S* can behave arbitrarily maliciously while generating its OT message, and only provides a proof of correct behaviour in round 4. Therefore, we must use a careful argument to ensure that the result appears indistinguishable to S*. The indistinguishability argument heavily relies on *the distinguisher-dependent simulation* property of the OT protocol. In particular, we build a careful sequence of hybrids where we extract S*'s (who is the OT receiver) input to the OT protocol in a distinguisher-dependent manner, and use the extracted input to replace the actual garbled circuit with a simulated one. Next, we change the output of the garbled circuit from an encryption of the right output to an encryption of the all zeroes string, and finally we replace the simulated garbled circuit with a real circuit that always outputs an encryption of the all zeroes string. All intermediate hybrids in this sequence are distinguisher-dependent. A similar argument also helps prove *robustness* of our protocol against S* that behaves maliciously in the second round.

Next, we discuss how we simulate the view of an unbounded malicious R*. The simulator Sim^{R^*} uses the third round extractable commitment to obtain the input of R*, queries the ideal functionality to obtain an output, and in the fourth round message, sends an encryption under the receiver's public key pk of this output. Here, we carefully prove that for any explainable receiver R*, the simulated message (encrypting the output generated by the ideal functionality) is indistinguishable from the message generated by an honest sender.

This concludes an overview of how we achieve a protocol with security against explainable adversaries. Next, we discuss techniques to compile any explainable protocol with robustness in the first two rounds, into one that is secure against malicious adversaries. We also discuss a few additional subtleties that come up in this setting.

Security against Malicious Senders via Statistical ZK Arguments. In order to achieve security against arbitrary malicious S*, the protocol is further modified to require R and S to execute a *statistical zero-knowledge argument*, where S proves to R that S generated its OT messages correctly, and perform the garbled circuit evaluation correctly to obtain the result that it output to R. Because of a technical condition in the proof, we actually require the SZK argument to be an argument *of knowledge*. Such arguments of knowledge with delayed-input completeness and soundness, and requiring exactly 4 rounds can be obtained by instantiating the FLS paradigm with statistically hiding extractable commitments. These are executed in parallel with our 4 round explainable protocol described above. With these arguments in place, at the end of the fourth round R will decrypt the ciphertext to recover the output *only if* the verification algorithm applied to the zero-knowledge argument accepts. Otherwise R rejects. This helps argue security against malicious S*, but we point out one subtlety: the SZK argument can only be verified at the end of round 4, an unwitting receiver could send its round 3 message in response to an arbitrarily maliciously generated round 2 sender message. This is where we invoke the additional robustness property discussed earlier. Next, we discuss the somewhat more complex case of malicious receivers.

Security against Malicious Receivers via Statistical Conditional Disclosure of Secrets. So far, an arbitrary malicious R* could recover additional information about the sender's input based on the output of evaluation of incorrectly garbled circuits. Ideally, we would like to ensure that R* can obtain the sender's fourth round message if and only if R* generated its first and third round messages in an "explainable" manner.

As discussed at the beginning of this overview, using zero-knowledge proofs to enable this requires too many rounds: therefore, our next idea is to rely on a two-round conditional disclosure of secrets (CDS) protocol. This will allow R* to recover the message sent by S if and only if R* inputs a witness attesting to the fact that its first and third messages were explainable. Notably, the witness input by R* is hidden from S. Furthermore, when no such witness exists (i.e. when R* does not generate explainable messages), the CDS protocol computationally hides the message of S[4]. Clearly, such a protocol can be used to ensure that R* recovers the output of evaluation of the garbled circuit iff it behaved in an explainable fashion, and otherwise obtains no information.

However, because we desire statistical security against R*, we need the CDS protocol to provide *statistical* security against R*. Fortunately, a CDS protocol with statistical security can be obtained for the class of relations that are verifiable by NC1 circuits, by combining two round game-based OT (eg, Naor-Pinkas [42]) with information-theoretic garbled circuits for NC1. Specifically, the receiver generates OT receiver messages corresponding to each of the bits in his witness, and the sender garbles a circuit that outputs the original sender message if and only if the receiver's input is a valid witness. We also note that there exists a generic transform [21] that allows verifying (given the randomness and inputs of R*) that R* behaved in an explainable way – in logarithmic depth, or by an NC1 circuit.

Next, we rely on robustness of the underlying protocol to argue security against a receiver that may have behave arbitrarily maliciously in the first round of the protocol. Finally, to ensure that the receiver sends the correct output to the sender in the fifth round, we require the receiver to send a zero-knowledge proof asserting that it computed this final message explainably. This proof can be obtained in 5 rounds [24], and is executed in parallel with the rest of the protocol.

Another hurdle, and its Resolution. While CDS helps keep round complexity low, it leads to another technical barrier when simulating the view of a malicious sender. Specifically, the malicious simulator obtains messages from the

---

[4] Such protocols have been used previously in the literature, most recently in [8].

underlying simulator of the robust explainable protocol. Because it obtains these messages externally, there is no way for the malicious simulator to recover the sender's next message encoded within the CDS protocol. At the same time, the simulator needs to necessarily recover this next message in order to generate the final message of the protocol. To get around this issue, we require the statistical ZK argument provided by the simulator to be an *argument of knowledge* (AoK). As a result, the malicious simulator is able to use the AoK property of the sender's SZK argument to extract a witness, and we carefully ensure that this witness helps the simulator reconstruct the next message of the sender, and proceed as before.

Concluding Remarks. This completes an overview of our techniques. In summary, we obtain round optimal two-party computation with one-sided statistical security assuming the existence of public key encryption, collision resistant hash functions, and two round statistically sender-private OT. We also note that we depart from existing work by using OT protocols with distinguisher-dependent simulation to achieve an end goal of standard simulation security in a general-purpose two-party computation protocol. We believe that this application to statistically secure 2PC represents a meaningful new application domain for distinguisher-dependent simulation [29], beyond [16,17,29,34]. In addition, we rely on several other technical tools such as deferred evaluation of garbled circuits, and combining robust protocols with delayed-input proofs - that may be of independent interest.

Open Problems and Future Directions. Our work obtains feasibility results for round optimal *two-party* secure computation with one-sided statistical security, which is the best possible security that one can hope to achieve in two-party protocols in the plain model. A natural question is whether statistical security can be obtained against at least one of the participants in more general multi-party settings. It is also interesting to understand the minimal assumptions required to obtain 2PC with one-sided statistical security, in a round optimal manner, following similar investigations on assumptions versus round complexity in ZK with one-sided statistical security, perhaps via highly optimized cut-and-choose techniques. Another interesting question is whether it is possible to achieve one-sided statistically secure protocols that make black-box use of cryptography. Finally, it is also interesting to understand whether 4 rounds are *necessary* to obtain specialized statistically secure protocols, such as statistical ZAPs, from polynomial hardness assumptions (in light of the fact that recent constructions of statistical ZAPs in less that 4 rounds [4,28,37] rely on superpolynomial hardness assumptions).

Roadmap. We refer the reader to Sect. 4 for a detailed description of our protocol against explainable adversaries, and a sketch of the proof of its security; and to Sect. 5 for a description of our protocol against malicious adversaries, and a sketch of the proof of its security.

3   Preliminaries

In the rest of this paper, we will denote the security parameter by k, and we will use $\mathsf{negl}(\cdot)$ to denote any function that is aymtpotically smaller than the inverse of every polynomial.

3.1   Secure Two-Party Computation

Two Party Computation. A two-party protocol Π is cast by specifying a process that maps pairs of inputs to pairs of outputs (one for each party). We refer to such a process as a *functionality* and denote it by $\mathcal{F} = f_n : \{0,1\}^n \times \{0,1\}^n \to \{0,1\}^{\mathsf{poly}(n)} \times \{0,1\}^{\mathsf{poly}(n)}$. We restrict ourselves to symmetric functionalities, where for every pair of inputs (x, y), the output is a random variable $f(x, y)$ ranging over pair of strings.

Secure Two Party Computation. In this definition we assume an adversary that corrupts one of the parties. The parties are *sender* S and *receiver* R. Let $\mathcal{A} \in \{\mathsf{S}, \mathsf{R}\}$ denote a corrupted party and $\mathcal{H} \in \{\mathsf{S}, \mathsf{R}\}, \mathcal{H} \neq \mathcal{A}$ denote the honest party.

- **Ideal Execution.** An ideal execution for the computation of functionality $\mathcal{F}$ proceeds as:
  - **Inputs:** S and R obtain inputs $x \in X_n$ and $y \in Y_n$, respectively.
  - **Send inputs to trusted party:** $\mathcal{H}$ sends its input to $\mathcal{F}$. Moreover, there exists a simulator $\mathsf{Sim}^{\mathcal{A}}$ that has black box access to $\mathcal{A}$, that sends input on behalf of $\mathcal{A}$ to F.
  - **Trusted party output to simulator:** If $x \notin X_n$, $\mathcal{F}$ sets x to some default input in X_n; likewise if $y \notin Y_n$, $\mathcal{F}$ sets y equal to some default input in Y_n. Then the trusted party sends $f(x, y)$ to $\mathsf{Sim}^{\mathcal{A}}$. It waits for a special symbol from $\mathsf{Sim}^{\mathcal{A}}$, upon receiving which, it sends the output to $\mathcal{H}$. If it receives $\perp$ from $\mathsf{Sim}^{\mathcal{A}}$, it outputs $\perp$ to $\mathcal{H}$.
  - **Outputs:** $\mathcal{H}$ outputs the value it obtained from $\mathcal{F}$ and $\mathcal{A}$ outputs its view. We denote the joint distribution of the output of $\mathcal{H}$ and the view of $\mathcal{A}$ by $\mathsf{IDEAL}_{\mathcal{F},\mathsf{Sim},\mathcal{A}}(x, y, n)$.
  We let $\mathsf{IDEAL}_{\mathcal{F},\mathsf{Sim},\mathcal{A}}(x, y, n)$ be the joint distribution of the view of the corrupted party and the output of the honest party following an execution in the ideal model as described above.
- **Real Execution.** In the real world, the two party protocol Π is executed between S and R. In this case, $\mathcal{A}$ gets the inputs of the party it has corrupted and sends all the messages on behalf of this party, using an arbitrary polynomial-time strategy. $\mathcal{H}$ follows the instructions in Π.
  Let $\mathcal{F}$ be as above and let π be two-party protocol computing $\mathcal{F}$. Let $\mathcal{A}$ be a non-uniform probabilistic poly-time machine with auxiliary input z. We let $\mathsf{REAL}_{\Pi,\mathcal{A}}(x, y, n)$ denote the joint distribution the view of corrupted party and the output of the honest party, in the real execution of the protocol.

Definition 1. *A protocol* Π *securely computes* $\mathcal{F}$ *with computational security against a party if there exists a PPT simulator* Sim *such that for every non-uniform probabilistic polynomial time adversary* $\mathcal{A}$ *corrupting the party,*

$$\mathsf{IDEAL}_{\mathcal{F},\mathsf{Sim},\mathcal{A}}(x,y,n) \approx_c \mathsf{REAL}_{\Pi,\mathcal{A}}(x,y,n)$$

It securely computes $\mathcal{F}$ *with statistical security against a party if there exists a PPT simulator* Sim *such that for every non-uniform probabilistic polynomial time adversary* $\mathcal{A}$ *corrupting the party,*

$$\mathsf{IDEAL}_{\mathcal{F},\mathsf{Sim},\mathcal{A}}(x,y,n) \approx_s \mathsf{REAL}_{\Pi,\mathcal{A}}(x,y,n)$$

Definition 2 (Explainable transcript). *Let* $\Pi_{\mathsf{S}^*,\mathsf{R}^*}$ *be a protocol between an arbitrary sender* S^* *and arbitrary receiver* R^*. *We say that a transcript* T *of an execution* Π *between* S^* *and* R^* *is explainable for* S^* *if there exists an input* i *and coins* r *such that* T *is consistent with the transcript of an execution between* $\mathsf{S}_{i,r}$ *and* R^*, *until the point in* T *where* $\mathsf{S}_{i,r}$ *aborts. (Here* $\mathsf{S}_{i,r}$ *is the honest sender on input* i *using coins* r). *Similarly, we say that a transcript* T *of an execution* Π *between* S^* *and* R^* *is explainable for* R^* *if there exists an input* i *coins* r *such that* T *is consistent with the transcript of an execution between* $\mathsf{R}_{i,r}$ *and* S^*, *until the point in* T *that* $\mathsf{R}_{i,r}$ *aborts. (Here* $\mathsf{R}_{i,r}$ *is the honest receiver strategy using input* i *and coins* r).

Definition 3 (Explainable sender). *Let* $\Pi_{\mathsf{S}^*,\mathsf{R}^*}$ *be a protocol between an arbitrary sender* S^* *and arbitrary receiver* R^*. *A (possibly probabilistic) sender* $\mathsf{S}^* = \{\mathsf{S}_k^*\}_{k\in\mathbb{N}}$ *is explainable if there exists a negligible* $\mu(\cdot)$ *such that for any receiver* $\mathsf{R}^* = \{\mathsf{R}_k^*\}_{k\in\mathbb{N}}$, *and large enough* $k \in \mathbb{N}$,

$$\Pr_{\mathsf{S}_k^*}[T \text{ is explainable } | T \leftarrow \Pi_{\mathsf{S}_k^*,\mathsf{R}_k^*}] \geq 1 - \mu(k).$$

Definition 4 (Explainable receiver). *Let* $\Pi_{\mathsf{S}^*,\mathsf{R}^*}$ *be a protocol between an arbitrary sender* S^* *and arbitrary receiver* R^*. *A (possibly probabilistic) receiver* $\mathsf{R}^* = \{\mathsf{R}_k^*\}_{k\in\mathbb{N}}$ *is explainable if there exists a negligible* $\mu(\cdot)$ *such that for any sender* $\mathsf{S}^* = \{\mathsf{S}_k^*\}_{k\in\mathbb{N}}$, *and large enough* $k \in \mathbb{N}$,

$$\Pr_{\mathsf{R}_k^*}[T \text{ is explainable } | T \leftarrow \Pi_{\mathsf{S}_k^*,\mathsf{R}_k^*}] \geq 1 - \mu(k).$$

Definition 5 (Robust Explainable Secure Protocol). *We will say that a protocol is secure against explainable adversaries, if Definition 1 holds against explainable adversaries. Furthermore, such a protocol is robust if for every (arbitrarily) malicious* R^*, *the real view of an adversary conditioned on aborting after round 2 is indistinguishable from the adversary's simulated view, and for every (arbitrarily) malicious* S^*, *the real view of the adversary conditioned on aborting after round 3 is indistinguishable from the adversary's simulated view.*

3.2 Yao's Garbled Circuits

We will also rely on Yao's technique for garbling circuits [46]. In the following, we define the notation that we will use, and the security properties of Yao's garbling scheme.

Definition 6. *Let $p(\cdot)$ denote any fixed polynomial. We will consider a circuit family $\mathbb{C} : \{0,1\}^k \to \{0,1\}^{p(k)}$, that takes an input of size k bits and outputs $p(k)$ bits. Yao's garbled circuits consist of the following algorithms:*

- $\mathsf{GARBLE}(1^k, C; r)$ *obtains as input a circuit $C \in \mathbb{C}$ and randomness r, and outputs the garbled circuit $\mathsf{G_C}$ as well as a set of $2k$ keys corresponding to setting each of the k input bits to 0 and 1. We will denote this by:*

$$(\mathsf{G_C}, \{\mathtt{label}_{i,b}\}_{i \in [k], b \in \{0,1\}}) \leftarrow \mathsf{GARBLE}(1^k, C; r).$$

- $\mathsf{EVAL}(\mathsf{G_C}, \{\mathtt{label}_{i,x_i}\}_{i \in [k]})$ *obtains as input garbled circuit $\mathsf{G_C}$, and a set of k keys. It generates an output z. We will denote this by*

$$z \leftarrow \mathsf{EVAL}(\mathsf{G_C}, \{\mathtt{label}_{i,x_i}\}_{i \in [k]}).$$

We require these algorithms to satisfy the following properties:

- **Correctness:** *For all $C \in \mathbb{C}, x \in \{0,1\}^k$,*

$$\Pr\left[C(x) = z \; \middle| \; \begin{matrix} (\mathsf{G_C}, \{\mathtt{label}_{i,b}\}_{i \in [k], b \in \{0,1\}}) \leftarrow \mathsf{GARBLE}(1^k, C; r) \\ z \leftarrow \mathsf{EVAL}(G_C, \{\mathtt{label}_{i,x_i}\}_{i \in [k]}) \end{matrix} \right] = 1 - \mathsf{negl}(k)$$

- **Security:** *There exists a PPT simulator Sim such that for all non-uniform PPT $\mathcal{D}$, and all $C \in \mathbb{C}, x \in \{0,1\}^k$,*

$$\Big| \Pr[\mathcal{D}(\mathsf{G_C}, \{\mathtt{label}_{i,x_i}\}_{i \in [k]}) = 1] - \Pr[\mathcal{D}(\mathsf{Sim}(1^k, C(x))) = 1] \Big| = \mathsf{negl}(k)$$

where
$$(\mathsf{G_C}, \{\mathtt{label}_{i,b}\}_{i \in [k], b \in \{0,1\}}) \leftarrow \mathsf{GARBLE}(1^k, C; r).$$

3.3 Extractable Commitments

Definition 7 (Extractable Commitment). *A statistically binding and computationally hiding three round commitment scheme is said to be extractable if there exists a PPT extractor Ext such that for any PPT committer C and every polynomial $p(\cdot)$, If*

$$\Pr_{\substack{c_1 \leftarrow \mathsf{C}, \\ c_2 \leftarrow \mathsf{R}(c_1, 1^k), \\ c_3 \leftarrow \mathsf{C}(c_1, c_2)}} [\mathsf{R}(c_1, c_2, c_3) \neq \perp] \geq \frac{1}{p(k)}$$

then

$$
\Pr_{\substack{c_1 \leftarrow C \\ c_2 \leftarrow R(c_1, 1^k) \\ c_3 \leftarrow C(c_1, c_2)}}
\begin{bmatrix}
R(c_1, c_2, c_3) = 1 \wedge \\
d \leftarrow C(c_1, c_2, c_3) \wedge \\
s \leftarrow R(c_1, c_2, c_3, d) \wedge \\
s' \leftarrow \mathsf{Ext}^C(1^k, 1^{p(k)}) \wedge \\
s' \neq s \wedge s \neq \bot
\end{bmatrix}
\leq \mathsf{negl}(k)
$$

where R *denotes the honest receiver algorithm,* d *denotes a decommitment string (obtained from* $C(c_1, c_2, c_3)$ *at the start of the decommit phase), and* R *outputs* s *to be equal to the decommitted value if it accepts the decommitment, and* $\bot$ *otherwise.*

Three-message computationally hiding extractable commitments can be constructed from non-interactive commitments [45]. We will also consider statistically hiding extractable commitments, that satisfy the same extraction guarantee, except against computationally unbounded committers. These can be obtained in four rounds by substituting non-interactive commitments in the construction of [45] with two round statistically hiding commitments.

3.4 Zero-Knowledge Proofs and Arguments for NP

An n-round delayed-input interactive protocol $\langle P, V \rangle$ for deciding a language L with associated relation R_L proceeds in the following manner:

- At the beginning of the protocol, P and V receive the size of the instance and execute the first $n - 1$ rounds.
- At the start of the last round, P receives input $(x, w) \in R_L$ and V receives x. Upon receiving the last round message from P, V outputs 0 or 1.

We will rely on proofs and arguments for NP that satisfy delayed-input completeness, adaptive soundness and adaptive ZK.

Definition 8 (Statistical Zero Knowledge Argument). *Fix any language* L. *Let* $\langle P, V \rangle$ *denote the execution of a protocol between a PPT prover* P *and a (possibly unbounded) verifier* V, *let* V_{out} *denote the output of the verifier and let* $\mathsf{View}_{\mathcal{A}}\langle P, V \rangle$ *denote the transcript together with the state and randomness of a party* $\mathcal{A} \in \{P, V\}$ *at the end of an execution of a protocol. Then we say* $\langle P, V \rangle$ *is zero knowledge proof system for* L *if the following properties hold:*

- **Completeness:** For all $x \in L$,

$$
\Pr[V_{\mathsf{out}}\langle P, V \rangle = 1] = 1 - \mathsf{negl}(k),
$$

where the probability is over the random coins of P and V.
- **Adaptive Soundness:** For all polynomial size P^* and all $x \notin L$ sampled by P^* adaptively depending upon the first $n - 1$ rounds,

$$
\Pr[V_{\mathsf{out}}\langle P^*, V \rangle = 1] = \mathsf{negl}(k)
$$

- **Statistical Zero Knowledge:** There exists a PPT simulator Sim such that for all V^* and all $x \in L$,

$$\left| \Pr[V^*(\mathsf{View}_{V^*}\langle P(x,w), V^* \rangle) = 1] - \Pr[V^*(\mathsf{Sim}^{V^*}(x)) = 1] \right| = \mathsf{negl}(k)$$

These can be obtained by a simple modification to delayed-input ZK arguments based on the Lapidot-Shamir [35] technique, by relying on a two round statistically hiding commitent (that can itself be based on any collision-resistant hash functions), instead of a one-round statistically binding one.

Definition 9 (Zero Knowledge Proof). *Fix any language L. Let $\langle P, V \rangle$ denote the execution of a protocol between a (possibly unbounded) prover P and a PPT verifier V, let $\mathsf{V}_{\mathsf{out}}$ denote the output of the verifier and let $\mathsf{View}_{\mathcal{A}}\langle P, V \rangle$ denote the transcript together with the state and randomness of a party $\mathcal{A} \in \{P, V\}$ at the end of an execution of a protocol. Then we say $\langle P, V \rangle$ is zero knowledge proof system for L if following properties hold:*

- **Completeness:** For all $x \in L$,

$$\Pr[\mathsf{V}_{\mathsf{out}}\langle P, V \rangle = 1] = 1 - \mathsf{negl}(k),$$

where the probability is over the random coins of P and V.
- **Adaptive Soundness:** For all P^* and all $x \notin L$ sampled by P^* adaptively depending upon the first $n-1$ rounds,

$$\Pr[\mathsf{V}_{\mathsf{out}}\langle P^*, V \rangle = 1] = \mathsf{negl}(k)$$

- **Computational Zero Knowledge:** There exists a PPT simulator Sim such that for all polynomial size V^* and all $x \in L$,

$$\left| \Pr[V^*(\mathsf{View}_{V^*}\langle P(x,w), V^* \rangle) = 1] - \Pr[V^*(\mathsf{Sim}^{V^*}(x)) = 1] \right| = \mathsf{negl}(k)$$

Such proofs were first constructed by [24], and can be made complete and sound when the instance is chosen by the prover in the last round of the interaction, by relying on the work of [35].

Imported Theorem 1 *[24, 35]. Assuming the existence of collision-resistant hash functions, there exist 5 round zero-knowledge proofs for all languages in NP, satisfying Definition 9.*

3.5 Oblivious Transfer (OT)

Oblivious Transfer (OT) is a protocol between two parties, an (unbounded) sender S with messages (m_0, m_1) and a (PPT) receiver R with choice bit b, where R receives output m_b at the end of protocol. We let $\langle S(m_0, m_1), R(b) \rangle$ denote execution of the OT protocol with sender input (m_0, m_1) and receiver input b. We will rely on a three round oblivious transfer protocol that satisfies perfect correctness and the following security guarantee:

Definition 10 (Statistically Receiver-Private OT). *We will say that an oblivious transfer protocol is statistically receiver private if it satisfies the following properties.*

- *Statistical Receiver Security. For every unbounded S^* and all $(b, b') \in \{0, 1\}$, the following distributions are statistically indistinguishable:*

$$\mathsf{View}_{S^*}\langle S^*, R(b)\rangle \text{ and } \mathsf{View}_{S^*}\langle S^*, R(b')\rangle$$

- *Sender Security (Distinguisher-dependent Simulation Under Parallel Composition). For every polynomial $n = n(k)$, for every efficiently sampleable distribution over messages $\{\mathcal{M}_{0,i}, \mathcal{M}_{1,i}\}_{i \in [n]}$, there exists a PPT simulator Sim such that for every non-uniform PPT receiver R^* and non-uniform PPT distinguisher $\mathcal{D}$,*

$$|\Pr[\mathcal{D}(\mathsf{View}_{R^*}\langle S(\{m_{0,i}, m_{1,i}\}_{i \in [n]}), R^*\rangle) = 1]$$

$$- \Pr[\mathcal{D}(\mathsf{Sim}^{R^*, \mathcal{D}, \{\mathcal{F}_{\mathsf{OT},i}(m_{0,i}, m_{1,i}, \cdot)\}_{i \in [n]}}) = 1]| = \mathsf{negl}(k)$$

where the probability is over the randomness of sampling $\{(m_{0,i}, m_{1,i})\}_{i \in [n]} \xleftarrow{\$} \{(\mathcal{M}_{0,i}, \mathcal{M}_{1,i})\}_{i \in [n]}$, the randomness of the sender and the simulator, and where $\mathcal{F}_{\mathsf{OT}}$ is a single-query ideal OT functionality with $\{(m_{0,i}, m_{1,i})\}_{i \in [n]}$ hardwired, that on input $\{b_i\}_{i \in [n]}$ outputs $\{m_{b_i,i}\}_{i \in [n]}$ and then self-destructs.

Imported Theorem 2 *[28]. Assuming the existence of any two-round statistical sender-private OT (resp., polynomial hardness of CDH), there exists a three-round statistically receiver-private OT protocol in the plain model satisfying Definition 10.*

Here, we note that two-round statistical sender-private OT can in turn be based on the polynomial hardness of DDH [42], QR and N^{th} residuosity [27,30] and LWE [9]. We will represent the three messages of an OT protocol satisfying Definition 10 by $\mathsf{OT}_{\mathsf{S},1}, \mathsf{OT}_{\mathsf{R}}(\cdot), \mathsf{OT}_{\mathsf{S},3}(\cdot)$.

3.6 Conditional Disclosure of Secrets

Conditional disclosure of secrets for an NP language $\mathcal{L}$ [2] can be viewed as a two-message analog of witness encryption [22]. That is, the sender holds an instance x and message m and the receiver holds x and a corresponding witness w. If the witness is valid, then the receiver obtains m, whereas if $x \notin \mathcal{L}$, m remains hidden. We further require that the protocol hides the witness w from the sender.

Definition 11. *A conditional disclosure of secrets scheme* (CDS.R, CDS.S, CDS.D) *for a language $\mathcal{L} \in$ NP satisfies:*

1. **Correctness:** *For any $(x, w) \in R_{\mathcal{L}}$, and message $m \in \{0, 1\}^*$,*

$$\Pr\left[\mathsf{CDS.D}_K(c') = m \middle| \begin{array}{l} (c, K) \leftarrow \mathsf{CDS.R}(x, w) \\ c' \leftarrow \mathsf{CDS.S}(x, m, c) \end{array}\right] = 1$$

2. **Message Indistinguishability:** *For any* $x \in \{0,1\}^k \setminus \mathcal{L}$, c^*, *and two equal-length messages* m_0, m_1, *the following distributions are statistically indistinguishable:*

$$\mathsf{CDS.S}(x, m_0, c^*) \text{ and } \mathsf{CDS.S}(x, m_1, c^*)$$

3. **Receiver Simulation:** *There exists a simulator* $\mathsf{CDS.Sim}$ *such that for any polynomial-size distinguisher* $\mathcal{D}$, *there exists a negligible* μ *such that for any* $x \in \mathcal{L}$, $w \in R_{\mathcal{L}}(x)$ *and large enough security parameter* $k \in \mathbb{N}$,

$$|\Pr[\mathcal{D}(\mathsf{CDS.R}(x, w)) = 1] - \Pr[\mathcal{D}(\mathsf{CDS.Sim}(x)) = 1]| = \mu(k)$$

Instantiations. CDS schemes satisfying Definition 11 for relations that are verifiable in NC1 can be instantiated by combining information-theoretic Yao's garbled circuits for NC1 with any two-message oblivious transfer protocol where the receiver message is computationally hidden from any semi-honest sender, and with (unbounded) simulation security against malicious receivers. Such oblivious transfer schemes are known based on DDH [42], Quadratic (or N^{th}) Residuosity [27], and LWE [9].

3.7 Low-Depth Proofs

We will describe how any computation that is verifiable by a family of polynomial sized ciruits can be transformed into a proof that is verifiable by a family of circuits in NC1. Let R be an efficiently computable binary relation. For pairs $(x, w) \in R$ we call x the statement and w the witness. Let L be the language consisting of statements in R.

Definition 12 (Low-Depth Non-Interactive Proofs). *A low-depth non-interactive proof with perfect completeness and soundness for a relation* R *consists of an (efficient) prover* P *and a verifier* V *that satisfy:*

- **Perfect Completeness.** *A proof system is perfectly complete if an honest prover with a valid witness can always convince an honest verifier. For all* $(x, w) \in R$ *we have*
$$\Pr[V(\pi) = 1 | \pi \leftarrow P(x)] = 1$$

- **Perfect Soundness.** *A proof system is perfectly sound if it is infeasible to convince an honest verifier when the statement is false. For all* $x \notin L$ *and all (even unbounded) adversaries* $\mathcal{A}$ *we have*
$$Pr[V(x, \pi) = 1 | \pi \leftarrow \mathcal{A}(x)] = 0.$$

- **Low Depth.** *The verifier* V *can be implemented in* NC1.

We discuss a very simple construction of a low-depth non-interactive proof, that was outlined in [21]. The prover P executes the NP-verification circuit on the witness and generates the proof as the concatenation (in some specified order) of the bit values assigned to the individual wires of the circuit. The verifier V proceeds by checking consistency of the values assigned to the internal wires of the circuit for each gate. In particular for each gate in the NP-verification circuit the verifier checks if the wire vales provided in the proof represent a correct evaluation of the gate. Since the verification corresponding to each gate can be done independent of every other gate and in constant depth, we have that V itself is constant depth.

4   2PC with One-Sided Statistical Security Against Explainable Parties

4.1   Construction

As a first step, in Fig. 1, we describe a 5 round protocol with security against explainable adversaries (Definitions 3 and 4). In a nutshell, these adversaries are like malicious adversaries, but with an additional promise: explainable adversaries generate messages that are in the suport of honestly generated messages, except with negligible probability.

Our protocol uses the following building blocks:

- A 3 round statistically binding and computationally hiding commitment scheme satisfying extractability according to Definition 7, denoted by Ecom.
- A 4 round statistically hiding and computationally binding commitment scheme satisfying extractability according to Definition 7, denoted by SHEcom.
- A 3 round statistically receiver private oblivious transfer protocol satisfying Definition 10, denoted by OT.
- Garbled circuits satisfying Definition 6, with algorithms denoted by Garble, Eval.

4.2   Analysis

We demonstrate security of our protocol against explainable adversaries by proving the following theorem.

Theorem 1. *Assuming* 3 *round computationally hiding and* 4 *round statistically hiding extractable commitments according to Definition 7, garbled circuits satisfying Definition 6 and three round oblivious transfer satisfying Definition 10, there exists a robust* 5-*round secure two-party computation protocol with black-box simulation against unbounded explainable receivers and PPT explainable senders, where the receiver obtains its output at the end of round 4 and the sender obtains its output at the end of the fifth round*[5].

We observe that 3 round computationally hiding commitments can be based on any non-interactive commitment scheme [45], which can itself be based on any public-key encryption [36], and 4 round statistically hiding extractable commitments can be based on collision-resistant hash functions. Garbled circuits

---

[5] We point out that Informal Theorem 2 follows from this theorem by exchanging the roles of S and R.

Public Input: Function f that players wish to compute on their private inputs.
Private Inputs: The receiver R has private input A and sender S has private input B.

Round 1: R does the following.

1. Sample randomness $r_c, r_d, r_{enc}, \{r_{OT,i}\}_{i \in [k]} \xleftarrow{\$} \{0,1\}^*$. Set $(pk, sk) = \mathsf{KeyGen}(1^k)$.

2. Set $f' = \mathsf{Enc}_{pk}(f_A(\cdot); r_{enc})$ where $f_A(\cdot)$ denotes f with input A hardwired.

3. Garble f' to obtain a garbled circuit and labels $(G, \{\mathsf{label}_{i,b}\}_{i \in [k], b \in \{0,1\}} = \mathsf{Garble}(1^k, f')$. Compute OT sender messages for $i \in [k]$ as $o_{1,i} = \mathsf{OT}_{S,1}(\mathsf{label}_{i,0}, \mathsf{label}_{i,1}; r_{OT,i})$.

4. Set $c_1 = \mathsf{Ecom}_S((A \| r_{enc}); r_c)$ to be the first (committer) message of a statistically binding extractable commitment to $(A \| r_{enc})$. Additionally, set $d_1 = \mathsf{SHEcom}_R(r_d)$ to be the first (receiver) message of a statistically hiding extractable commitment.

5. Send $(pk, \{o_{1,i}\}_{i \in k}, c_1, d_1)$ to S. Note that R does not send G yet.

Round 2: S does the following.

1. Sample randomness $\{r'_{OT,i}\}_{i \in [k]}, r'_c, r'_d \xleftarrow{\$} \{0,1\}^*$.

2. Set $c_2 = \mathsf{Ecom}_{R,c_1}(r'_c)$ to be the second (receiver) message of the statistically binding extractable commitment, and $d_2 = \mathsf{SHEcom}_{S,d_1}(B; r'_d)$ to be the second (committer) message of the statistically hiding extractable commitment, committing to input B.

3. Compute OT receiver messages for every $i \in [k]$ as $o_{2,i} = \mathsf{OT}_R(o_{1,i}, B_i; r'_{OT,i})$.

4. Send $(c_2, d_2, \{o_{2,i}\}_{i \in [k]})$ to R.

Round 3: R does the following.

1. Compute the OT sender messages for indices $i \in [k]$ as $\{o_{3,i} = \mathsf{OT}_{S,3}(o_{2,i}, (\mathsf{label}_{i,0}, \mathsf{label}_{i,1}); r_{OT,i})\}_{i \in [k]}$.

2. Set $c_3 = \mathsf{Ecom}_{S,c_1,c_2}(A \| r_{enc}; r_c)$ to be the final (committer) message of the statistically binding extractable commitment and $d_3 = \mathsf{SHEcom}_{R,d_1,d_2}(r_d)$ to be the third (receiver) messages of the statistically hiding extractable commitment.

3. Send $(G, c_3, d_3, \{o_{3,i}\}_{i \in [k]})$ to S, where recall that G was computed in round 1.

Round 4: S does the following.

1. For $i \in [k]$, get lab_i from $o_{3,i}$. Evaluate the garbled circuit to obtain $z = \mathsf{Eval}(G, \{\mathsf{lab}_i\}_{i \in [k]})$.

2. Set $d_4 = \mathsf{SHEcom}_{S,d_1,d_2,d_3}(B; r'_d)$ to be the final message of the statistically hiding extractable commitment.

3. Send (z, d_4) to R.

Round 5: R outputs out $= \mathsf{DEC}_{sk}(z)$ and sends out to S.

Output: S outputs out.

Fig. 1. The protocol $\Pi_{exp}\langle S, R \rangle$ secure against explainable adversaries.

can be obtained only assuming the existence of one-way functions [46], and three round oblivious transfer satisfying Definition 10 can be based on any statistically sender-private 2 round OT. All of these primitives can be based on the hardness of the Decisional Diffie-Hellman assumption (DDH), or Quadratic Residuosity (QR), or the Learning with Errors assumption (LWE), and we therefore have the following corollary.

Corollary 1. *Assuming polynomial hardness of the Decisional Diffie-Hellman assumption (DDH), or Quadratic Residuosity (QR), or the Learning with Errors assumption (LWE), there exists a robust 5-round secure two-party computation protocol with black-box simulation against unbounded explainable receivers and PPT explainable senders, where the receiver obtains its output at the end of round 4 and the sender obtains its output at the end of round 5.*

Theorem 1 follows immediately from Lemma 1 that proves security against bounded explainable senders and Lemma 2 that proves security against unbounded explainable receivers.

Lemma 1. *Assuming computational hiding of* Ecom, *extractability of* SHEcom *according to Definition 7, security of garbled circuits according to Definition 6, and sender security of OT according to Definition 10, the construction in Fig. 1 satisfies robust simulation-based security against explainable PPT senders according to Definition 3.*

Proof. We prove that there exists a simulator Sim^{S^*} that with black-box access to a computationally bounded explainable sender S^*, outputs a simulated view that is indistinguishable from the real view of S^*. Our simulator is described in Fig. 2, with differences from the real protocol underlined.

In the full version of the paper, we prove via a sequence of hybrids, that the real and ideal distributions are indistinguishable.

Lemma 2. *Assuming statistical hiding of* SHEcom *and extractability of* Ecom *according to Definition 7 and receiver security of OT according to Definition 10, the construction in Fig. 1 satisfies robust statistical simulation security (Definition 1) against explainable unbounded receivers as per Definition 3.*

Proof. We prove that there exists a PPT simulator Sim^{R^*} that with black-box access to an unbounded explainable sender R^*, outputs a simulated view that is statistically indistinguishable from the real view of R^*. Our simulator is described in Fig. 3, with changes from the real protocol underlined.

In the full version of the paper, we prove via a sequence of hybrids, that the real and ideal distributions are indistinguishable.

5   From Explainable to Malicious One-Sided Statistical Security

In this section, we describe a compiler that compiles any robust two-party secure computation protocol against explainable adversaries, into one that

---

The simulator $\mathsf{Sim}^{\mathsf{S}^*}$ interacts with S^*, sending the following messages on behalf of R. It uses as subroutine $\mathsf{SHEcom}_{\mathsf{Ext}}$, which denotes the extractor for SHEcom.

Round 1: $\mathsf{Sim}^{\mathsf{S}^*}$ does the following.

1. Sample $r_k, r_c, , r_{enc}, \{r_{OT,i}\}_{i \in [k]} \xleftarrow{\$} \{0,1\}^*$, set $\mathsf{A} = 0^k$. Set $(pk, sk) = \mathsf{KeyGen}(1^k; r_k)$.

2. Set $f' = \mathsf{Enc}_{pk}(f_A(\cdot), r_k)$, $(G, \{label_{i,b}\}_{i \in [k], b \in \{0,1\}}) = \mathsf{Garble}(1^k, f')$.

3. Set $\{o_{1,i} = \mathsf{OT}_{\mathsf{S},1}(label_{i,0}, label_{i,1}; r_{OT,i})\}_{i \in [k]}$, and

4. Set $c_1 = \mathsf{Ecom}_{\mathsf{S}}((\mathsf{A}, 0^k); r_c)$, and obtain d_1 from $\mathsf{SHEcom}_{\mathsf{Ext}}$.

5. Send $(pk, \{o_{1,i}\}_{i \in [k]}, c_1, d_1)$ to S^*.

Round 3: $\mathsf{Sim}^{\mathsf{S}^*}$ does the following.

1. Obtain input $(c_2, d_2, \{o_{2,i}\}_{i \in [k]})$ from S^*. Send d_2 to $\mathsf{SHEcom}_{\mathsf{Ext}}$ and obtain d_3.

2. Set $\{o_{3,i} = \mathsf{OT}_{\mathsf{S},3}(o_{2,i}, (label_{i,0}, label_{i,1}); r_{OT,i})\}_{i \in [k]}$ and $c_3 = \mathsf{Ecom}_{\mathsf{S},c_1,c_2}(\mathsf{A}; r_c)$.

3. Send $(G, c_3, d_3, \{o_{3,i}\}_{i \in [k]})$ to S^*.

Round 5: $\mathsf{Sim}^{\mathsf{S}^*}$ does the following.

1. Obtain input (z, d_4) from S^* and send d_4 to $\mathsf{SHEcom}_{\mathsf{Ext}}$.

2. If $\mathsf{SHEcom}_{\mathsf{Ext}}$ rewinds, the execution automatically goes back to round 3. Otherwise, obtain B' from $\mathsf{SHEcom}_{\mathsf{Ext}}$.

3. Send B' to the ideal functionality $\mathcal{F}$ and obtain output out. Send out to S^*.

Fig. 2. Simulation strategy for an explainable adversarial sender S^*

is secure against arbitrary malicious adversaries. Assuming the hardness of DDH/LWE/QR, the resulting protocol is computationally secure against PPT malicious senders. In addition, we demonstrate that the resulting protocol is secure against unbounded malicious receivers if the underlying robust explainable protocol is secure against unbounded malicious receivers.

5.1   Construction

In Fig. 4, we describe a protocol compiler that compiles any 5 round robust explainable protocol into a fully malicious protocol while preserving round complexity. Our protocol uses the following building blocks:

- Any robust two-party protocol secure against explainable adversaries from Fig. 1 by $\Pi_{\mathsf{exp}}\langle \mathsf{S}, \mathsf{R} \rangle$. We denote the messages of this protocol where S uses input B and randomness r_S, and R uses input A and randomness r_R, by:

$$\left(\tau_{\mathsf{R},1} = \Pi_{\mathsf{exp},\mathsf{R},1}(\mathsf{A}; r_\mathsf{R}), \tau_{\mathsf{S},2} = \Pi_{\mathsf{exp},\mathsf{S},2}(\tau_{\mathsf{R},1}, \mathsf{B}; r_\mathsf{S}), \tau_{\mathsf{R},3} = \Pi_{\mathsf{exp},\mathsf{R},3}(\tau_{\mathsf{S},2}, \mathsf{A}; r_\mathsf{R}), \right.$$

$$\left. \tau_{\mathsf{S},4} = \Pi_{\mathsf{exp},\mathsf{S},4}(\tau_{\mathsf{R},1}, \tau_{\mathsf{R},3}, \mathsf{B}; r_\mathsf{S}), \tau_{\mathsf{R},5} = \Pi_{\mathsf{exp},\mathsf{R},5}(\tau_{\mathsf{S},2}, \tau_{\mathsf{S},4}, \mathsf{A}; r_\mathsf{R}) \right)$$

The simulator $\mathsf{Sim}^{\mathsf{R}^*}$ interacts with R^*, sending the following messages on behalf of S. It uses as subroutine Ecom, the extractor of Ecom.

Round 2: $\mathsf{Sim}^{\mathsf{R}^*}$ does the following.

1. Obtain input $(pk, \{o_{1,i}\}_{i\in[k]}, c_1, d_1)$ from R^*. Send c_1 to $\mathsf{Ecom}_{\mathsf{Ext}}$ and obtain c_2.

2. Sample $\{r'_{\mathsf{OT},i}\}_{i\in[k]}, r'_c, r'_d \xleftarrow{\$} \{0,1\}^*$. Set $\mathsf{B} = 0^k$.

3. Set $d_2 = \mathsf{SHEcom}_{\mathsf{S},d_1}(\mathsf{B}; r'_d)$ and $\{o_{2,i} = \mathsf{OT}_{\mathsf{R}}(\mathsf{B}_i; r'_{\mathsf{OT},i})\}_{i\in[k]}$.

4. Send $(c_2, d_2, \{o_{2,i}\}_{i\in[k]})$ to R^*.

Round 4: $\mathsf{Sim}^{\mathsf{R}^*}$ does the following.

1. Obtain input $(G, c_3, d_3, \{o_{3,i}\}_{i\in[k]})$ from R^*. Send c_3 to $\mathsf{Ecom}_{\mathsf{Ext}}$.

2. If $\mathsf{Ecom}_{\mathsf{Ext}}$ rewinds, the execution automatically goes back to the beginning of round 2. Otherwise, obtain $(\mathsf{A}, r_{\mathsf{enc}})$ from $\mathsf{Ecom}_{\mathsf{Ext}}$.

3. Send A to the ideal functionality. Obtain out and compute $z = \mathsf{Enc}_{pk}(\mathsf{out}; r_{\mathsf{enc}})$.

4. Set $d_4 = \mathsf{SHEcom}_{\mathsf{S},d_1,d_3}(\mathsf{B}; r'_d)$ where recall that B was set to 0^k.

5. Send (z, d_4) to R^*.

Fig. 3. Simulation strategy against an explainable unbounded adversarial receiver R^*

- A 4 round delayed-input adaptively sound and adaptively statistical ZK argument of knowledge according to Definition 8, with messages denoted by

$$\mathsf{SZKA.V}, \mathsf{SZKA.P}(\cdot), \mathsf{SZKA.V}(\cdot), \mathsf{SZKA.P}(\cdot, x, w),$$

and the output of the verifier denoted by $\mathsf{SZKA.out}(\cdot, x)$.
- A 5 round delayed-input adaptively sound and adaptively computational ZK proof according to Definition 9, with messages denoted by

$$\mathsf{ZKP.P}, \mathsf{ZKP.V}(\cdot), \mathsf{ZKP.P}(\cdot), \mathsf{ZKP.V}(\cdot), \mathsf{ZKP.P}(\cdot, x, w),$$

and the output of the verifier denoted by $\mathsf{ZKP.out}(\cdot, x)$.

Languages for the CDS protocol, SZK argument and ZK proof are defined as:

$$\mathsf{L}_{\mathsf{CDS}} = \{(\tau_{\mathsf{R},1}, \tau_{\mathsf{R},3}) : \exists (\mathsf{A}, r_{\mathsf{R}}, \mathsf{ldp}) \text{ s.t. } \mathsf{ldp} \text{ is for } (\tau_{\mathsf{R},1}, \tau_{\mathsf{R},3}) = \mathsf{R}(\mathsf{A}, r_{\mathsf{R}}, \tau_{\mathsf{S},2})\}$$

$$\mathsf{L}_{\mathsf{ZKP}} = \{(\tau_{\mathsf{R},1}, \tau_{\mathsf{R},3}, \tau_{\mathsf{R},5}) : \exists (\mathsf{A}, r_{\mathsf{R}}) \text{ s.t. } (\tau_{\mathsf{R},1}, \tau_{\mathsf{R},3}, \tau_{\mathsf{R},5}) = \mathsf{R}(\mathsf{A}, r_{\mathsf{R}}, \tau_{\mathsf{S},2}, \tau_{\mathsf{S},4})\}$$

$$\mathsf{L}_{\mathsf{SZKA}} = \{(\tau_{\mathsf{S},2}, c) : \exists (\mathsf{B}, r_{\mathsf{S}}) \text{ s.t. } (\tau_{\mathsf{S},2}, c) = \mathsf{S}(\mathsf{B}, r_{\mathsf{S}}, \tau_{\mathsf{R},1}, \tau_{\mathsf{R},3})\}$$

where $\mathsf{R}(\mathsf{A}, r_{\mathsf{R}}, \tau_{\mathsf{S},2}))$ denotes that the transcript $(\tau_{\mathsf{R},1}, \tau_{\mathsf{R},3})$ is generated using honest receiver strategy with input A and randomness r_{R}; $\mathsf{R}(\mathsf{A}, r_{\mathsf{R}}, \tau_{\mathsf{S},2}, \tau_{\mathsf{S},4}))$ denotes that the transcript $(\tau_{\mathsf{R},1}, \tau_{\mathsf{R},3}, \tau_{\mathsf{R},5})$ is generated using honest receiver strategy with input A and randomness r_{R}; and $\mathsf{S}(\mathsf{B}, r_{\mathsf{S}}, \tau_{\mathsf{R},1}, \tau_{\mathsf{R},3}))$ denotes that the transcript $(\tau_{\mathsf{S},2}, c)$ is generated using honest sender strategy with input B and randomness r_{S}, and ldp denotes a low-depth proof.

Public Input: Function f that players wish to compute on their private inputs.
Private Inputs: The receiver R has private input A and sender S has private input B.

Round 1: R does the following.

1. Sample $r_R \leftarrow \{0,1\}^*$, compute $\tau_{R,1} = \Pi_{\exp,R,1}(A; r_R)$ according to the explainable protocol.

2. Set $z_1 \leftarrow$ ZKP.P and $z_1' \leftarrow$ SZKA.V as the first messages of the ZK proof with R as prover, and SZK argument with R as verifier, respectively.

3. Send $(\tau_{R,1}, z_1, z_1')$ to S.

Round 2: S does the following.

1. Sample $r_S \leftarrow \{0,1\}^*$ and set $\tau_{S,2} = \Pi_{\exp,S,2}(\tau_{R,1}, B; r_S)$ according to the explainable protocol.

2. Set $z_2 \leftarrow$ ZKP.V(z_1), $z_2' \leftarrow$ SZKA.P(z_1') as the second message of the ZK proof with S as verifier, and SZK argument with S as prover, respecitvely.

3. Send $(\tau_{S,2}, z_2, z_2')$ to R.

Round 3: R does the following.

1. Set $\tau_{R,3} = \Pi_{\exp,R,3}(\tau_{S,2}, A; r_R)$. Set $x = (\tau_{R,1}, \tau_{R,3})$, $w = (A, r_R, \mathsf{ldp})$ where ldp is a low-depth proof of $(\tau_{R,1}, \tau_{R,3}) = R(A, \tau_R, \tau_{S,2})$.

2. Compute CDS message $(\mathsf{ct}, \mathsf{k}) \leftarrow$ CDS.R(x, w) and $z_3 \leftarrow$ ZKP.P(z_2), $z_3' \leftarrow$ SZKA.V(z_2'). Send $(\tau_{R,3}, \mathsf{ct}, z_3, z_3')$ to S.

Round 4: S does the following.

1. Set $\tau_{S,4} = \Pi_{\exp,S,4}(\tau_{R,1}, \tau_{R,3}, B; r_S)$, and CDS response $c \leftarrow$ CDS.S$(x, \tau_{S,4}, \mathsf{ct})$.

2. Set $x_1 = (\tau_{S,2}, c)$, $w_1 = (B, r_S)$, $z_4 \leftarrow$ ZKP.V(z_1, z_3), $z_4' \leftarrow$ SZKA.P(z_1', z_3', x_1, w_1). Send (c, z_4, z_4') to R.

Round 5: R does the following.

1. If SZKA.out$(z_1', z_2', z_3', z_4') = 0$, abort. Otherwise, recover $\tau_{S,4} =$ CDS.D$_k(c)$ and set $\tau_{R,5} = \Pi_{\exp,R,5}(\tau_{S,2}, \tau_{S,4}, A; r_R)$.

2. Set $x = (\tau_{R,1}, \tau_{R,3}, \tau_{R,5})$, $w = (A, r_R)$, $z_5 =$ ZKP.P(z_2, z_4, x_2, w_2).

3. Send $(\tau_{R,5}, z_5)$ to S, and output $\Pi_{\exp,R,\mathsf{out}}(\tau_{S,2}, \tau_{S,4}, A; r_R)$.

Sender Output: If ZKP.out$(z_1, z_2, z_3, z_4, z_5) = 0$, abort. Else output $\Pi_{\exp,S,\mathsf{out}}(\tau_{R,1}, \tau_{R,3}, \tau_{R,5}, B; r_S)$.

Fig. 4. Our two-party secure computation protocol $\Pi_{\mathsf{mal}}\langle S, R \rangle$ for general functionalities, with computational security against malicious S and statistical security against malicious R.

5.2   Analysis

We demonstrate one-sided statistical security of our protocol against arbitrary malicious adversaries by formally proving the following theorem.

Theorem 2. *Assume the existence of four round delayed-input adaptive statistical zero-knowledge arguments of knowledge with adaptive soundness according to Definition 8, five round delayed-input adaptive computational zero-knowledge proofs with adaptive soundness according to Definition 9, and two round statistical* CDS *for* NP *relations verifiable by* NC_1 *circuits according to Definition 11. Assume also that there exists a robust two-party secure computation protocol against explainable adversaries according to Definition 5. Then there exists a 5-round secure two-party computation protocol for general functionalities with black-box simulation against unbounded malicious receivers and PPT malicious senders, where the receiver obtains its output at the end of round 4 and the sender obtains its output at the end of round 5.*

Here, we note that the required proof systems can be based on two round statistically hiding commitments, which can themselves be based on the hardness of Decisional Diffie-Hellman (DDH), Quadratic Residuosity (QR) or the Learning with Errors (LWE) assumption. Furthermore, the requisite statistical CDS for NP relations verifiable by NC_1 circuits can be based on any two round statistically sender private OT, which can itself be based on DDH/QR/LWE. We also make use of a transform due to [21] that converts arbitrary proofs to low depth proofs (Definition 12) verifiable in NC_1 – this is done to ensure that the CDS relation of interest is verifiable in NC_1. In addition, we observe that the robust two-party secure computation protocol against explainable adversaries constructed in Sect. 4 satisfies Definition 5, and can be instantiated based on DDH/QR/LWE. This results in the following Corollary of Theorem 2.

Corollary 2. *Assuming polynomial hardness of the Decisional Diffie-Hellman (DDH) assumption, or Quadratic Residuosity (QR) or Learning with Errors (LWE), there exists a 5-round secure two-party computation protocol with black-box simulation against unbounded malicious receivers and PPT malicious senders, where the receiver obtains its output at the end of round 4 and the sender obtains its output at the end of round 5.*

The proof of Theorem 2 follows from Lemma 3 and Lemma 4, that prove security against malicious senders and unbounded malicious receivers respectively. These are formally stated and proved below.

Lemma 3. *Assuming* CDS *satisfies receiver simulation according to Definition 11,* SZKA *is adaptively sound according to Definition 8 and* ZKP *satisfies adaptive computational zero-knowledge according to Definition 9, and assuming Π_{exp} is a robust explainable protocol satisfying the additional property described in Theorem 2, the protocol $\Pi_{mal}\langle S, R \rangle$ in Fig. 4 is secure against PPT malicious senders according to Definition 1.*

Proof. We prove that there exists a simulator $\mathsf{Sim}^{\mathsf{S}^*}$ that with black-box access to a computationally bounded malicious sender S^*, outputs a simulated view that is indistinguishable from the real view of S^*. Our simulator is in Fig. 5, and the proof is deferred to the full version.

The simulator $\mathsf{Sim}^{\mathsf{S}^*}$ interacts with S^*, sending the following messages on behalf of R. It uses as subroutine the simulator $\mathsf{Sim}_{\mathsf{S},\mathsf{exp}}$ against an explainable sender S, the simulator CDS.Sim of the CDS protocol, the simulator ZKP.Sim of the 5 round zero-knowledge proof and the extractor SZKA.Ext of the 4 round statistical zero-knowledge argument of knowledge.

Round 1: $\mathsf{Sim}^{\mathsf{S}^*}$ does the following.
1. Obtain $\tau_{\mathsf{R},1}$ from $\mathsf{Sim}_{\mathsf{S},\mathsf{exp}}$.
2. Sample $z_1 \leftarrow \mathsf{ZKP.Sim}$, $z_1' \leftarrow \mathsf{SZKA.Ext}$.
3. Send $(\tau_{\mathsf{R},1}, z_1, z_1')$ to S^*.

Round 3:
1. Obtain $(\tau_{\mathsf{S},2}, z_2, z_2')$ from S^*.
2. Send $\tau_{\mathsf{S},2}$ to $\mathsf{Sim}_{\mathsf{S},\mathsf{exp}}$ and obtain $\tau_{\mathsf{R},3}$.
3. Set $x = (\tau_{\mathsf{R},1}, \tau_{\mathsf{R},3})$, $\mathsf{ct} \leftarrow \mathsf{CDS.Sim}(x)$.
4. Sample $z_3 \leftarrow \mathsf{ZKP.Sim}(z_2)$, $z_3' \leftarrow \mathsf{SZKA.Ext}(z_2')$.
5. Send $(\tau_{\mathsf{S},2}, \mathsf{ct}, z_3, z_3')$ to S^*.

Round 5:
1. Obtain (ct, z_4, z_4') from S^*.
2. Obtain $\tau_{\mathsf{S},4}$ from SZKA.Ext. Send $\tau_{\mathsf{S},4}$ to $\mathsf{Sim}_{\mathsf{S},\mathsf{exp}}$ and obtain $\tau_{\mathsf{R},5}$.
3. Set $x_2 = (\tau_{\mathsf{R},1}, \tau_{\mathsf{R},3}, \tau_{\mathsf{R},5})$, and $z_5 \leftarrow \mathsf{ZKP.Sim}(z_2, z_4, x_2)$.
4. Send $(\tau_{\mathsf{R},5}, z_5)$ to S^*.

Fig. 5. Simulation strategy against a PPT malicious sender S^*

Lemma 4. *Assuming* CDS *satisfies statistical message indistinguishability for NP relations verifiable by* NC_1 *circuits according to Definition 11, assuming* $\mathsf{L}_{\mathsf{CDS}}$ *is verifiable in* NC_1, *assuming* ZKP *is adaptively sound against unbounded provers according to Definition 9 and* SZKA *satisfies adaptive statistical zero-knowledge according to Definition 8, and assuming* Π_{exp} *is robust and statistically secure against unbounded explainable receivers, the protocol* $\Pi_{\mathsf{mal}}\langle\mathsf{S},\mathsf{R}\rangle$ *in Fig. 4 is statistically secure against unbounded malicious receivers according to Definition 1.*

Proof. We prove that there exists a simulator $\mathsf{Sim}^{\mathsf{R}^*}$ that with black-box access to a malicious receiver R^*, outputs a simulated view that is indistinguishable from the real view of R^*. Our simulator is described in Fig. 6, and the proof is deferred to the full version.

The simulator $\mathsf{Sim}^{\mathsf{R}^*}$ interacts with R^*, sending the following messages on behalf of S. It uses as subroutine the simulator $\mathsf{Sim}_{\mathsf{R}^*,\mathsf{exp}}$ against an explainable receiver R^* and the simulator $\mathsf{SZKA.Sim}$ of the 4 round zero-knowledge argument of knowledge.

Round 2: $\mathsf{Sim}^{\mathsf{R}^*}$ does the following.

1. Obtain $(\tau_{\mathsf{R},1}, z_1, z_1')$ from R^*.
2. Send $\tau_{\mathsf{R},1}$ to $\mathsf{Sim}_{\mathsf{R}^*,\mathsf{exp}}$ and obtain $\tau_{\mathsf{S},2}$.
3. Sample $z_2 \leftarrow \mathsf{ZKP.V}(z_1)$, $z_2' \leftarrow \mathsf{SZKA.Sim}(z_1')$.
4. Send $(\tau_{\mathsf{S},2}, z_2, z_2')$ to R^*.

Round 4: $\mathsf{Sim}^{\mathsf{R}^*}$ does the following.

1. Obtain input $(\tau_{\mathsf{R},3}, \mathsf{ct}, z_3, z_3')$ from R^*.
2. Send $\tau_{\mathsf{R},3}$ to $\mathsf{Sim}_{\mathsf{R}^*,\mathsf{exp}}$ and obtain $\tau_{\mathsf{S},4}$.
3. Set $x_1 = (\tau_{\mathsf{S},2}, c)$, where $c \leftarrow \mathsf{CDS.S}(x, \tau_{\mathsf{S},4}, \mathsf{ct})$ and $x = (\tau_{\mathsf{R},1}, \tau_{\mathsf{R},3})$.
4. Sample $z_4 \leftarrow \mathsf{ZKP.V}(z_3)$, $z_4' \leftarrow \mathsf{SZKA.Sim}(z_3', x_1)$.
5. Send (c, z_4, z_4') to R^*.

Output: Obtain $\tau_{\mathsf{R},5}, z_5$ from R^*. Allow the ideal functionality to release the output to honest party iff $\mathsf{ZKP.out}(z_1, z_2, z_3, z_4, z_5) = 1$.

Fig. 6. Simulation strategy against a malicious receiver R^*

Acknowledgement. We thank Giulio Malavolta, Akshayaram Srinivasan and the anonymous TCC reviewers for useful suggestions.

References

1. Aiello, W., Håstad, J.: Statistical zero-knowledge languages can be recognized in two rounds. J. Comput. Syst. Sci. **42**(3), 327–345 (1991)
2. Aiello, B., Ishai, Y., Reingold, O.: Priced oblivious transfer: how to sell digital goods. In: Pfitzmann, B. (ed.) EUROCRYPT 2001. LNCS, vol. 2045, pp. 119–135. Springer, Heidelberg (2001). https://doi.org/10.1007/3-540-44987-6_8
3. Ananth, P., Choudhuri, A.R., Jain, A.: A new approach to round-optimal secure multiparty computation. In: Katz, J., Shacham, H. (eds.) CRYPTO 2017. LNCS, vol. 10401, pp. 468–499. Springer, Cham (2017). https://doi.org/10.1007/978-3-319-63688-7_16
4. Badrinarayanan, S., Fernando, R., Jain, A., Khurana, D., Sahai, A.: Statistical ZAP arguments. In: Canteaut, A., Ishai, Y. (eds.) EUROCRYPT 2020. LNCS, vol. 12107, pp. 642–667. Springer, Cham (2020). https://doi.org/10.1007/978-3-030-45727-3_22
5. Badrinarayanan, S., Garg, S., Ishai, Y., Sahai, A., Wadia, A.: Two-message witness indistinguishability and secure computation in the plain model from new assumptions. In: Takagi, T., Peyrin, T. (eds.) Advances in Cryptology - ASIACRYPT 2017–23rd International Conference on the Theory and Applications of Cryptology and Information Security, Hong Kong, China, December 3–7, 2017, Proceedings, Part III. pp. 275–303 (2017)

6. Badrinarayanan, S., Goyal, V., Jain, A., Kalai, Y.T., Khurana, D., Sahai, A.: Promise zero knowledge and its applications to round optimal MPC. In: Shacham, H., Boldyreva, A. (eds.) CRYPTO 2018. LNCS, vol. 10992, pp. 459–487. Springer, Cham (2018). https://doi.org/10.1007/978-3-319-96881-0_16
7. Bellare, M., Jakobsson, M., Yung, M.: Round-optimal zero-knowledge arguments based on any one-way function. In: Advances in Cryptology - EUROCRYPT 1997, Proceeding. pp. 280–305 (1997)
8. Bitansky, N., Khurana, D., Paneth, O.: Weak zero-knowledge beyond the black-box barrier. In: Proceedings of the 51st Annual ACM SIGACT Symposium on Theory of Computing, STOC 2019, pp. 1091–1102, Phoenix, AZ, USA, June 23–26 (2019)
9. Brakerski, Z., Döttling, N.: Two-message statistically sender-private OT from LWE. In: TCC (2018)
10. Brakerski, Z., Halevi, S., Polychroniadou, A.: Four round secure computation without setup. In: Kalai, Y., Reyzin, L. (eds.) TCC 2017. LNCS, vol. 10677, pp. 645–677. Springer, Cham (2017). https://doi.org/10.1007/978-3-319-70500-2_22
11. Brassard, G., Chaum, D., Crépeau, C.: Minimum disclosure proofs of knowledge. J. Comput. Syst. Sci. **37**(2), 156–189 (1988)
12. Chongchitmate, W., Ostrovsky, R.: Circuit-private multi-key FHE. In: Fehr, S. (ed.) PKC 2017. LNCS, vol. 10175, pp. 241–270. Springer, Heidelberg (2017). https://doi.org/10.1007/978-3-662-54388-7_9
13. Choudhuri, A.R., Ciampi, M., Goyal, V., Jain, A., Ostrovsky, R.: On round optimal secure multiparty computation from minimal assumptions. IACR Cryptology ePrint Archive 2019, 216 (2019). https://eprint.iacr.org/2019/216
14. Ciampi, M., Ostrovsky, R., Siniscalchi, L., Visconti, I.: Delayed-input non-malleable zero knowledge and multi-party coin tossing in four rounds. In: Kalai, Y., Reyzin, L. (eds.) TCC 2017. LNCS, vol. 10677, pp. 711–742. Springer, Cham (2017). https://doi.org/10.1007/978-3-319-70500-2_24
15. Ciampi, M., Ostrovsky, R., Siniscalchi, L., Visconti, I.: Round-optimal secure two-party computation from trapdoor permutations. In: Kalai, Y., Reyzin, L. (eds.) TCC 2017. LNCS, vol. 10677, pp. 678–710. Springer, Cham (2017). https://doi.org/10.1007/978-3-319-70500-2_23
16. Döttling, N., Garg, S., Goyal, V., Malavolta, G.: Laconic conditional disclosure of secrets and applications. In: 60th IEEE Annual Symposium on Foundations of Computer Science, FOCS 2019, pp. 661–685, Baltimore, Maryland, USA, November 9–12 (2019). https://doi.org/10.1109/FOCS.2019.00046
17. Döttling, N., Garg, S., Hajiabadi, M., Masny, D., Wichs, D.: Two-round oblivious transfer from CDH or LPN. In: Canteaut, A., Ishai, Y. (eds.) EUROCRYPT 2020. LNCS, vol. 12106, pp. 768–797. Springer, Cham (2020). https://doi.org/10.1007/978-3-030-45724-2_26
18. Dwork, C., Naor, M., Reingold, O., Stockmeyer, L.J.: Magic functions. In: 40th Annual Symposium on Foundations of Computer Science, FOCS 1999, pp. 523–534, New York, USA October 17–18 (1999)
19. Feige, U., Shamir, A.: Witness indistinguishable and witness hiding protocols. In: Proceedings of the 22nd Annual ACM Symposium on Theory of Computing, pp. 416–426, Baltimore, Maryland, USA, May 13–17 (1990)
20. Fortnow, L.: The complexity of perfect zero-knowledge (extended abstract). In: Proceedings of the 19th Annual ACM Symposium on Theory of Computing, 1987, pp. 204–209, New York, USA (1987)
21. Garg, S., Gentry, C., Halevi, S., Raykova, M., Sahai, A., Waters, B.: Candidate indistinguishability obfuscation and functional encryption for all circuits. SIAM J. Comput. **45**(3), 882–929 (2016). https://doi.org/10.1137/14095772X

22. Garg, S., Gentry, C., Sahai, A., Waters, B.: Witness encryption and its applications. In: Symposium on Theory of Computing Conference, STOC 2013, pp. 467–476, Palo Alto, CA, USA, June 1–4, (2013). https://doi.org/10.1145/2488608.2488667
23. Garg, S., Mukherjee, P., Pandey, O., Polychroniadou, A.: The exact round complexity of secure computation. In: EUROCRYPT (2016)
24. Goldreich, O., Kahan, A.: How to construct constant-round zero-knowledge proof systems for NP. J. Cryptol. **9**(3), 167–189 (1996). https://doi.org/10.1007/BF00208001
25. Goldreich, O., Micali, S., Wigderson, A.: Proofs that yield nothing but their validity for all languages in NP have zero-knowledge proof systems. J. ACM **38**, 691–729 (1991)
26. Haitner, I., Nguyen, M., Ong, S.J., Reingold, O., Vadhan, S.P.: Statistically hiding commitments and statistical zero-knowledge arguments from any one-way function. SIAM J. Comput. **39**(3), 1153–1218 (2009)
27. Halevi, S., Kalai, Y.T.: Smooth projective hashing and two-message oblivious transfer. J. Cryptology **25**(1), 158–193 (2012)
28. Jain, A., Jin, Z., Goyal, V., Malavolta, G.: Statistical zaps and new oblivious transfer protocols, to appear. In: Eurocrypt (2020)
29. Jain, A., Kalai, Y.T., Khurana, D., Rothblum, R.: Distinguisher-dependent simulation in two rounds and its applications. In: Katz, J., Shacham, H. (eds.) CRYPTO 2017. LNCS, vol. 10402, pp. 158–189. Springer, Cham (2017). https://doi.org/10.1007/978-3-319-63715-0_6
30. Kalai, Y.T.: Smooth projective hashing and two-message oblivious transfer. In: Cramer, R. (ed.) EUROCRYPT 2005. LNCS, vol. 3494, pp. 78–95. Springer, Heidelberg (2005). https://doi.org/10.1007/11426639_5
31. Kalai, Y.T., Khurana, D., Sahai, A.: Statistical witness indistinguishability (and more) in two messages. In: Nielsen, J.B., Rijmen, V. (eds.) EUROCRYPT 2018. LNCS, vol. 10822, pp. 34–65. Springer, Cham (2018). https://doi.org/10.1007/978-3-319-78372-7_2
32. Katz, J.: Which languages have 4-round zero-knowledge proofs? In: Canetti, R. (ed.) TCC 2008. LNCS, vol. 4948, pp. 73–88. Springer, Heidelberg (2008). https://doi.org/10.1007/978-3-540-78524-8_5
33. Katz, J., Ostrovsky, R.: Round-Optimal secure two-party computation. In: Franklin, M. (ed.) CRYPTO 2004. LNCS, vol. 3152, pp. 335–354. Springer, Heidelberg (2004). https://doi.org/10.1007/978-3-540-28628-8_21
34. Khurana, D.: Round optimal concurrent non-malleability from polynomial hardness. In: Theory of Cryptography - 15th International Conference Proceedings, Part II, TCC 2017, pp. 139–171, Baltimore, MD, USA, November 12–15 (2017). https://doi.org/10.1007/978-3-319-70503-3_5
35. Lapidot, D., Shamir, A.: Publicly verifiable non-interactive zero-knowledge proofs. In: Advances in Cryptology - CRYPTO 1990, 10th Annual International Cryptology Conference Proceedings. pp. 353–365, Santa Barbara, California, USA, August 11–15 (1990). https://doi.org/10.1007/3-540-38424-3_26
36. Lombardi, A., Schaeffer, L.: A note on key agreement and non-interactive commitments. IACR Cryptol. ePrint Arch. 2019, 279 (2019). https://eprint.iacr.org/2019/279
37. Lombardi, A., Vaikuntanathan, V., Wichs, D.: Statistical ZAPR arguments from bilinear maps. In: Canteaut, A., Ishai, Y. (eds.) EUROCRYPT 2020. LNCS, vol. 12107, pp. 620–641. Springer, Cham (2020). https://doi.org/10.1007/978-3-030-45727-3_21

38. López-Alt, A., Tromer, E., Vaikuntanathan, V.: On-the-fly multiparty computation on the cloud via multikey fully homomorphic encryption. IACR Cryptol. ePrint Arch. **2013**, 94 (2013)
39. Mukherjee, P., Wichs, D.: Two round multiparty computation via multi-key FHE. In: Fischlin, M., Coron, J.-S. (eds.) EUROCRYPT 2016. LNCS, vol. 9666, pp. 735–763. Springer, Heidelberg (2016). https://doi.org/10.1007/978-3-662-49896-5_26
40. Naor, M.: Bit commitment using pseudorandomness. J. Cryptol. **4**(2), 151–158 (1991). https://doi.org/10.1007/BF00196774
41. Naor, M., Ostrovsky, R., Venkatesan, R., Yung, M.: Perfect zero-knowledge arguments for NP using any one-way permutation. J. Cryptology **11**(2), 87–108 (1998)
42. Naor, M., Pinkas, B.: Efficient oblivious transfer protocols. In: SODA (2001)
43. Ostrovsky, R., Paskin-Cherniavsky, A., Paskin-Cherniavsky, B.: Maliciously circuit-private FHE. In: Garay, J.A., Gennaro, R. (eds.) CRYPTO 2014. LNCS, vol. 8616, pp. 536–553. Springer, Heidelberg (2014). https://doi.org/10.1007/978-3-662-44371-2_30
44. Ostrovsky, R., Richelson, S., Scafuro, A.: Round-Optimal Black-Box Two-Party Computation. In: Gennaro, R., Robshaw, M. (eds.) CRYPTO 2015. LNCS, vol. 9216, pp. 339–358. Springer, Heidelberg (2015). https://doi.org/10.1007/978-3-662-48000-7_17
45. Prabhakaran, M., Rosen, A., Sahai, A.: Concurrent zero knowledge with logarithmic round-complexity. In: 43rd (FOCS 2002), pp. 366–375, Vancouver, BC, Canada, November 16–19 (2002)
46. Yao, A.C.: How to generate and exchange secrets (extended abstract). In: 27th Annual Symposium on Foundations of Computer Science, pp. 162–167, Toronto, Canada, October 27–29 (1986)

The Resiliency of MPC with Low Interaction: The Benefit of Making Errors (Extended Abstract)

Benny Applebaum[1], Eliran Kachlon[1(✉)], and Arpita Patra[2]

[1] Tel-Aviv University, Tel-Aviv, Israel
benny.applebaum@gmail.com, elirn.chalon@gmail.com
[2] Indian Institute of Science, Bangalore, India
arpita@iisc.ac.in

Abstract. We study information-theoretic secure multiparty protocols that achieve full security, including guaranteed output delivery, at the presence of an active adversary that corrupts a constant fraction of the parties. It is known that 2 rounds are insufficient for such protocols even when the adversary corrupts only two parties (Gennaro, Ishai, Kushilevitz, and Rabin; Crypto 2002), and that perfect protocols can be implemented in 3 rounds as long as the adversary corrupts less than a quarter of the parties (Applebaum, Brakerski, and Tsabary; Eurocrypt, 2019). Furthermore, it was recently shown that the quarter threshold is tight for any 3-round *perfectly-secure* protocol (Applebaum, Kachlon, and Patra; FOCS 2020). Nevertheless, one may still hope to achieve a better-thanquarter threshold at the expense of allowing some negligible correctness errors and/or statistical deviations in the security.

Our main results show that this is indeed the case. Every function can be computed by 3-round protocols with *statistical* security as long as the adversary corrupts less than third of the parties. Moreover, we show that any better resiliency threshold requires 4 rounds. Our protocol is computationally inefficient and has an exponential dependency in the circuit's depth d and in the number of parties n. We show that this overhead can be avoided by relaxing security to computational, assuming the existence of a non-interactive commitment (NICOM). Previous 3-round computational protocols were based on stronger public-key assumptions. When instantiated with statistically-hiding NICOM, our protocol provides *everlasting statistical* security, i.e., it is secure against adversaries that are computationally unlimited *after* the protocol execution.

To prove these results, we introduce a new hybrid model that allows for 2-round protocols with linear resiliency threshold. Here too we prove that, for perfect protocols, the best achievable resiliency is $n/4$, whereas statistical protocols can achieve a threshold of $n/3$. In the plain model, we also construct the first 2-round $n/3$-statistical verifiable secret sharing

The full version of this paper can be found in [7]. The first two authors are supported by the European Union's Horizon 2020 Programme (ERC-StG-2014–2020) under grant agreement no. 639813 ERC-CLC, and the Check Point Institute for Information Security. Arpita Patra would like to acknowledge financial support from SERB MATRICS (Theoretical Sciences) Grant 2020 and Google India AI/ML Research Award 2020.

R. Pass and K. Pietrzak (Eds.): TCC 2020, LNCS 12551, pp. 562–594, 2020.
https://doi.org/10.1007/978-3-030-64378-2_20

that supports second-level sharing and prove a matching lower-bound, extending the results of Patra, Choudhary, Rabin, and Rangan (Crypto 2009). Overall, our results refine the differences between statistical and perfect models of security, and show that there are efficiency gaps even for thresholds that are realizable in both models.

Keywords: Information-theoretic cryptography · Cryptographic protocols · Secure computation · Round complexity

1 Introduction

Interaction is a valuable and expensive resource in cryptography and distributed computation. Consequently, a huge amount of research has been devoted towards characterizing the amount of interaction, typically measured via round complexity, that is needed for various distributed tasks (e.g., Byzantine agreement [27,29,44], coin flipping [24,45], and zero-knowledge proofs [19,35]) under different security models. In this paper, we focus on two central cryptographic goals: secure-multiparty-computation (MPC) of *general* n-party functionalities and *verifiable secret sharing* (VSS) [23]. We strive for full information-theoretic security, including guaranteed output delivery, at the presence of a computationally-unbounded active (aka Byzantine or malicious) rushing adversary that controls up to t of the parties. In this setting, originally presented in the classical works of Ben-Or, Goldwasser, and Wigderson [17] and Chaum, Crépeau and Damgård [21], we assume that each pair of parties is connected by a secure and authenticated point-to-point channel and that all parties have access to a common broadcast channel, which allows each party to send a message to all players and ensures that the received message is identical.

The round complexity of information-theoretic MPC was extensively studied [2–5,8,12,16,28,31,32,34,37,39–41,43,46,52]. For passive perfect security, it was recently showed that optimal resiliency of $t = \lfloor (n-1)/2 \rfloor$ and optimal round complexity of two can be simultaneously achieved [4,31]. For active-security the picture is more complicated, and there seems to be a tradeoff between the number of rounds r and the resiliency threshold t. If the adversary is allowed to corrupt a single party ($t = 1$) then 2 rounds are sufficient whenever $n \geq 4$ [37]. Any larger resiliency threshold $t > 1$ requires at least three rounds [32,34]. For 3-round *error-free perfectly-secure* protocols, it was recently showed that a resiliency threshold of $t = \lfloor (n-1)/4 \rfloor$ is achievable [5] and that no better resiliency can be achieved [8]. The latter paper also shows that, for error-free perfectly-secure protocols, 4 rounds suffice for a threshold of $t_p = \lfloor (n-1)/3 \rfloor$ which is known to be optimal for perfect protocols regardless of their round complexity [17].

In this paper, we will be studying the other extreme point of this tradeoff. We fix a *minimal* model of communication (i.e., a round-complexity bound $r_{\min}$) for which linear resiliency is realizable, and try to characterize the best achievable *resiliency* t within this model. Since 2-round protocols cannot achieve resiliency larger than 1, we ask:

Q1: What is the best resiliency threshold t that can be achieved by a three-round protocol with full information-theoretic active security? Can we beat the $\lfloor(n-1)/4\rfloor$ perfect-MPC barrier by resorting to statistical security?

Q2: Can we formalize a meaningful two-round model in which a linear resiliency threshold is achievable ?

We provide a complete answer to the first question and show that statistical three-round protocols can achieve $\lfloor(n-1)/3\rfloor$ resiliency and nothing beyond that! We also answer the second question to the affirmative by presenting a new two-round hybrid model in which linear-resiliency is achievable. This model will serve as a stepping stone towards constructing three-round protocols. Along the way, we reveal new interesting differences between perfectly-secure error-free protocols to protocols that achieve perfect-secrecy but make errors with negligible probability. We continue with a detailed account of our results starting with the two-round hybrid model.

1.1   Two-Round Protocols in a Single-Input First-Round Hybrid Model

Single-Input First-Round Hybrid (SIFR) Model. We present a new *Single-Input First-Round Hybrid Model* (SIFR). In this model the communication network, which contains the usual peer-to-peer/broadcast channels, is augmented with some ideal n-party functionalities $\mathcal{F}$ that are restricted in two ways: (1) Every party P_i is allowed to invoke the functionalities multiple times but only during the *first round*; and (2) The ideal functionalities must be *single-input functionalities*, that is, when P_i invokes a functionality $\mathcal{F}^i_{\mathsf{si}} : \{0,1\}^* \to (\{0,1\}^*)^n$ the functionality delivers an output that depends only on the input of P_i. For example, both the authenticated-private channel functionality (that delivers a message from P_i to P_j) and the broadcast functionality (that delivers a message from P_i to all other parties) are simple instances of single-input functionalities. A more interesting example is the polynomial-VSS functionality that takes from P_i a degree-t polynomial Q over some finite field $\mathbb{F}$, and delivers to every party P_j an evaluation of Q in some canonical point $\alpha_j \in \mathbb{F}$. We refer to this model as the $\mathcal{F}$-SIFR model or simply as the SIFR model when we wish to keep the oracles $\mathcal{F}$ unspecified.

We will be interested in two-round protocols in the SIFR model. In such protocols, all the first-round messages depend solely on the input of a single party and the only "mixing" (between different inputs of different parties) occurs during the second round. Hence, two rounds are indeed essential for computing any non-trivial functionality. As an additional feature, we note that single-input functionalities can be trivially implemented with passive security via a single-round protocol, and so any two-round protocol in the SIFR model immediately translates into a two-round passively-secure protocol in the plain model.

Limitations of Perfect protocols in SIFR Model. To get a sense of the model, note that one can perfectly compute any degree-2 functionality over any finite field $\mathbb{F}$

of size larger than n with resiliency of $t = \lfloor (n-1)/4 \rfloor$. Roughly speaking, at the first round each party uses the single-input $\mathcal{F}_{\text{poly}}$ functionality to share each input via Shamir-based secret-sharing with polynomials of degree t; then each party locally computes the functionality over the shares (making an arbitrary number of additions and a single multiplication). At the end of this local computation, each party holds a share of the output that lies on a degree-$2t$ polynomial. At the second round, the parties broadcast the output shares and apply Reed-Solomon decoding to overcome the effect of at most t adversarial corruptions.[1] In fact, it was recently showed in [8] (building on [5]) that degree-2 functionalities over any binary extension field are *complete under non-interactive reductions* either with perfect resiliency of $\lfloor (n-1)/3 \rfloor$ or with statistical resiliency of $\lfloor (n-1)/2 \rfloor$. Therefore, the above observation yields an $\lfloor (n-1)/4 \rfloor$-perfect protocol in our model for an arbitrary functionality. In the full version [7], we prove that for perfect protocols this is the best achievable threshold.

Theorem 1 (perfect 2-round SIFR-protocols). *General n-party functionalities can be perfectly-computed in two rounds in the SIFR Model with resiliency of t if and only if $t \le \lfloor (n-1)/4 \rfloor$.*

The upper-bound holds in the $\mathcal{F}_{\text{poly}}$-SIFR model. The lower-bound holds relative to any (vector of) computationally-unbounded single-input functionalities and applies even when the adversary is non-rushing. In fact, the negative result shows that even the AND functionality cannot be computed in this model. As a corollary, for any $t \ge n/4$, the theorem rules out the existence of t-private secret sharing scheme that is *robustly-multiplicative* in the sense that parties can locally convert shares of x and shares of y to shares of xy that are t-*robust*, i.e., they are recoverable even at the presence of t-corruptions. (This notion of multiplicative secret-sharing is stronger than the standard variants of multiplicative and strongly-multiplicative secret sharing, see [26].) The negative part of Theorem 1 is proved by turning a two-round $n/4$-perfectly secure protocol for the AND-functionality in the SIFR hybrid model into a two-party protocol in the plain model for AND with perfect security against semi-honest adversaries, contradicting the impossibility result of [22].

Statistical Protocols in $\mathcal{F}_{\text{vsh}}$-SIFR Model. We show that the $n/4$ lower-bound can be bypassed by allowing the protocol to make negligible correctness errors while preserving perfect secrecy.[2] Our protocol makes use of the bivariate version of the VSS functionality, denoted by $\mathcal{F}_{\text{vsh}}$. Roughly speaking, this single-input

---

[1] The above description ignores some technical details such as output randomization which can be easily applied in the $\mathcal{F}_{\text{poly}}$-SIFR model; see for example [5].

[2] Formally, this means that, in addition to standard statistical security, the output distribution of the simulator $\mathcal{S}$ in the ideal world and the output distribution of the adversary $\mathcal{A}$ in the real world are identically distributed. This additional property (which is common to all our positive results) does not seem to be very useful as a feature, but it indicates more accurately what is needed in order to bypass the lower-bounds in the perfect setting.

functionality receives a symmetric bivariate polynomial $F(x, y)$ of degree less than or equal to t from a dealer and sends the polynomial $f_i(x) = F(x, i)$ to every party P_i. (See Fig. 2 in Sect. 3 for a formal definition.)

Theorem 2 (statistical 2-round SIFR-protocols). *Any n-party functionality f of degree-2 over some finite field $\mathbb{F}$ of cardinality larger than n can be computed by a two-round $\mathcal{F}_{\mathsf{vsh}}$-SIFR protocol with $\lfloor (n-1)/3 \rfloor$-resiliency, perfect-secrecy, statistical-correctness and complexity of $\mathrm{poly}(S, n, \log |\mathbb{F}|, \log(1/\epsilon))$ where S is the circuit size of f and ϵ is the error probability.*

Moreover, a similar result applies to any functionality f except that the complexity is also exponential in the depth of the Boolean circuit that computes f. The dependency in the depth can be avoided at the expense of downgrading security to computational and under the assumption that one-way functions exist.

The "Moreover" part follows from the first part by using the aforementioned completeness of degree-2 functionalities [8, Theorem. 5.23] whose overhead is exponential in the circuit's depth in the case of information-theoretic security. This makes the statistical variant of the theorem efficient only for NC^1 functionalities.[3] Similar limitations apply to all known constant-round protocols in the information-theoretic setting even for the case of passively-secure protocols. Let us further mention that even inefficient protocols are non-trivial since security holds against a computationally-unbounded adversary.

On the proof of Theorem. 2: Round Compression via Guards. The proof of Theorem 2 is based on several novel components. In a nutshell, following a blue-print suggested in [8], we derive a three-round protocol π in the SIFR-hybrid model. We then exploit the special structure of the last two-rounds and show how to *compress* them into a single round. In slightly more concrete terms, at the end of the first round, some party, say Alice, holds two values a and b and some other party, say Bob, also has a copy of b. (Think of b as a secret-share that was shared by Alice in the first round of π.) The purpose of the remaining rounds is to release to all parties a value $c = g(a, b)$ that depends on Alice's a and Bob's b while keeping b private. This is done by using two additional rounds: First Alice broadcasts a, and then Bob computes the value c based on (a, b) and broadcasts the result. The key observation is that all the relevant information (a and b) is known to Alice, and the role of Bob is to make sure that the outcome c is computed properly with respect to his own copy of b. (Other consistency mechanisms take care of the "correctness" of a). We abstract this notion via a new form of *Secure Computation with a Guard* (SCG) and show that if one is willing to tolerate *statistical errors*, then any function g can be realized (in the plain model) by a single-round protocol that employs correlated randomness. Furthermore, the correlated randomness can be sampled by Bob in a single preprocessing round. This allows us to collapse the last two rounds of π into a single round (plus an additional offline preprocessing that is being

---

[3] As usual in such settings, the exponential dependency in the depth can be replaced by an exponential dependency in the (non-deterministic) branching-program complexity of f.

handled during the first round.) Overall, our single-round SCG's allow us to compress the three-round SIFR-protocol into a two-round SIFR-protocol. The resulting protocol makes use of the $\mathcal{F}_{vsh}$ functionality and an additional single-input functionality $\mathcal{F}_{tsh}$ that essentially deals the shares of a random multiplicative triple $(a, b, c = ab)$. In order to remove the $\mathcal{F}_{tsh}$ oracle, we first implement it in three-rounds in the $\mathcal{F}_{vsh}$-SIFR model, and then compress the last round via an additional use of SCG. (See Sect. 3 for further details.) Our SCG constructions are based on a combination of message-authentication codes (MACs) and multiparty private-simultaneous-message protocols [28,38] (also known as fully-decomposable randomized encoding of functions [6,39]). (See Sect. 2 for details.)

1.2 Two-Round Verifiable Secret Sharing

Motivated by Theorem 2, our next goal is to realize the $\mathcal{F}_{vsh}$ functionality in the standard model within a minimal number of rounds. The round complexity of VSS was extensively studied in the literature [1,10,30,32,37,42,43,46,49]. In the perfect setting, we have a complete answer: In order to achieve a linear resiliency t, one must use a two-round protocol, and within this "budget" the best achievable resiliency is $t = \lfloor (n-1)/4 \rfloor$ [32]. Patra et al. [46] were the first to suggest that this bound may be bypassed by allowing negligible statistical errors. Specifically, they view VSS as a stand-alone two-phase primitive, and showed that the sharing phase of VSS with statistical error and perfect secrecy can be realized in two rounds if and only if $t \leq \lfloor (n-1)/3 \rfloor$.

Unfortunately, the resulting protocol does not implement the polynomial-based $\mathcal{F}_{vsh}$-functionality and so we cannot plug it into Theorem 2. Indeed, the existing protocol suffer from several caveats that make it less suitable for MPC applications. Specifically, after the sharing phase some of the honest parties may not hold a valid share, let alone a "second-level share". In addition, the sub-protocol needed for the "reconstruction" phase is relatively complicated and requires two rounds. In contrast, existing *perfect* VSS protocols [32,42] realize the $\mathcal{F}_{vsh}$ functionality, and correspondingly enable a trivial single-round reconstruction in which the parties broadcast their views. The possibility of an analogous statistical realization of $\mathcal{F}_{vsh}$ in two rounds and resiliency threshold of $\lfloor (n-1)/3 \rfloor$ was left open by previous works. We answer this question in the affirmative. (See Sect. 4 for further details.)

Theorem 3 (2-round statistical protocols for $\mathcal{F}_{vsh}$). *There exists a 2-round protocol that $\lfloor (n-1)/3 \rfloor$-securely realizes the n-party functionality $\mathcal{F}_{vsh}$ over an arbitrary finite field $\mathbb{F}$ with perfect-secrecy and statistical-correctness. The communication complexity is polynomial in $n, \log |\mathbb{F}|$ and $\log(1/\epsilon)$ where ϵ is the error-probability. The computational complexity is polynomial in $\log |\mathbb{F}|, \log(1/\epsilon)$ and exponential in the number of parties.*

The exponential dependency in the number of parties is due to the use of a clique finding algorithm over an "agreement graph" of size n. While this dependency is unfortunate, the protocol is still meaningful since it provides security against unbounded adversaries. The existence of a similar protocol with polynomial dependency in n is left as an interesting open question.

Resiliency Lower-bounds. We further strengthen the lower-bounds of [46] and show that any resiliency of $t \geq n/3$ cannot be achieved by a VSS with a two-round sharing phase even if both secrecy and correctness are statistical, and even if the adversary is non-rushing. This result applies to the more general setting where the VSS is viewed as a two-phase primitive, as opposed to an MPC functionality. (See the full version [7] for further details.) We also reveal an additional qualitative difference for the $t \geq n/3$ regime: No matter how many rounds are used in the sharing phase, the reconstruction phase cannot be implemented by letting the parties broadcast their local view. That is, even during the reconstruction some secrecy must be maintained. (See the full version [7] for further details.) Indeed, existing constructions in this regime [43,51], employ information-theoretic MACs or signatures and keep some of the secret-key information private even during reconstruction. Our lower-bound shows that this is inherent.

1.3 Three-Round MPC in the Standard Model

We can now get back to the case of three-round plain-model protocols for general functionalities. Recall that in **Q1** we asked what is the best resiliency that can be achieved by 3 rounds protocols. This question was recently resolved in the perfect setting. Specifically, it was shown that 3 rounds can achieve a resiliency of $t = \lfloor (n-1)/4 \rfloor$ [5][4], and that even a slightly better resiliency threshold of $t = \lfloor (n-1)/4 \rfloor + 1$ requires at least four rounds [8].[5]

Again, we show that a small statistical error allows us to bypass the lower-bound. Specifically, by taking the two-round $\mathcal{F}_{\mathsf{vsh}}$-SIFR protocol from Theorem 2 and instantiating the $\mathcal{F}_{\mathsf{vsh}}$ oracle with the two-round implementation from Theorem 3, we derive a three-round statistical protocol that remains secure as long as at most $\lfloor (n-1)/3 \rfloor$ of the parties are being corrupted. We further prove a matching lower bound on the resiliency of three-round statistical protocols by showing that a 3-round protocol with $(\lfloor (n-1)/3 \rfloor + 1)$-resiliency for an authenticated-VSS functionality can be collapsed into a VSS with a 2-round sharing phase,

---

[4] The positive result can now be obtained by combining the simple 2-round VSS-hybrid protocol for quadratic functions (Theorem 1) with the 2-round perfect-VSS of [32] and with the completeness of degree-2 arithmetic functionalities [8]. The original proof from [5] was significantly more complicated since it relied on a weaker degree-2 completeness result that was applicable only over the binary field.

[5] The impossibility of three-round plain-model perfect protocols with resiliency $t \geq \lfloor (n-1)/4 \rfloor + 1$ seems to be incomparable to the impossibility of two-round perfect SIFR-model protocols (Theorem 1). One could deduce the latter result from the former with the aid of two-round protocols for single-input functionalities with perfect resiliency of $t \geq \lfloor (n-1)/4 \rfloor + 1$. However, such protocols do not exist even for the special case of the VSS functionality [32].

contradicting our VSS negative results. (See full version [7] for further details.) Overall we derive the following theorem.

Theorem 4 (3-round protocols with optimal resiliency). *Every n-party functionality can be computed in three-rounds with statistical security against an active rushing computationally-unbounded adversary that corrupts at most $\lfloor (n-1)/3 \rfloor$ of the parties. The communication complexity of the protocol is polynomial in $n, 2^D$ and S and the computational complexity is polynomial in $2^n, 2^D$ and S where S and D are the size and depth of the Boolean circuit that computes f.*

Furthermore, the security threshold is tight for three-round protocols. That is, there is a finite functionality that cannot be computed in three rounds at the presence of an active (non-rushing) computationally-unbounded adversary that corrupts $\lfloor (n-1)/3 \rfloor + 1$ of the parties.

Theorem 4 fully characterizes the feasible security threshold of three-round protocols with information-theoretic active security. As already mentioned the exponential dependency in the depth is expected, and seems to be unavoidable given the current state of the art. The exponential dependency in n is derived from our VSS construction (Theorem 3), and we hope that future works will be able to improve it and get a polynomial overhead.

Downgrading to Computational Security. One way to bypass the exponential blow-up in n is to replace the two-round $\lfloor (n-1)/3 \rfloor$-statistical VSS with the cryptographic VSS of [10]. The latter achieves the same $\lfloor (n-1)/3 \rfloor$-resiliency against computationally-bounded adversaries assuming the existence of a non-interactive commitment (NICOM). Specifically, by plugging this VSS into the computational part of Theorem 2, we get the following theorem. (See full version [7] for further details.)

Theorem 5 (3-round computational MPC). *Assuming the existence of NICOM, every n-party functionality f admits a three-round protocol with computational security against a computationally-bounded adversary that actively corrupts up to $t \leq \lfloor (n-1)/3 \rfloor$ of the parties. The complexity is polynomial in n and in the circuit's size of f. Moreover, if f is a single-input functionality the round complexity can be reduced to 2.*

The optimality of three rounds for any $t > 1$ is owing to the two-round impossibility result of [34] that remains valid even in the cryptographic setting. For the special case of $t = 1$ and $n = 4$, [37] shows a two-round construction from any one-way function. Other existing round-optimal constructions [2,11] work with $t < n/2$, albeit rely on public-key encryption schemes and two-round witness indistinguishable proofs (ZAPs). These assumptions are believed to be strictly stronger than NICOM that can be based on injective one-way functions [18,36,55] or even on general one-way functions assuming standard complexity-theoretic de-randomization assumptions [13].

We further mention that if one employs a perfectly-hiding NICOM, then our protocol achieves *everlasting security*, i.e., it is secure against adversaries that are computationally unlimited *after* the protocol execution [54]. For this result one has to invoke the statistical variant of Theorem 2, and so the protocol is efficient only for NC^1 functionalities or general single-input functionalities. Perfectly-hiding NICOM can be based on collision-resistance hash functions at the CRS model. Even in this model, the round-complexity lower-bounds of [34] hold, and one cannot hope for two-round protocols.

The "moreover" part of the theorem covers an interesting family of "single-input" functionalities including important tasks such as distributed ZK, multiplication triple generation (modellled via $\mathcal{F}_{tsh}$) and VSS. Our two-round protocol complements the incomparable result of [34] that achieves a similar round-complexity with perfect-security, but with a smaller resiliency threshold of $t < n/6$. The proof of Theorem 5 of appears in the full version [7].

1.4   Discussion: The Benefit of Errors

Since the works of Rabin and Ben-Or [51] and Beaver [15], it is known that *statistical* protocols can achieve a resiliency threshold $t_s = \lfloor (n-1)/2 \rfloor$ that is strictly larger than the best resiliency threshold $t_p = \lfloor (n-1)/3 \rfloor$ that is achievable by *perfect* protocols [17,50]. Patra et al. [46] were the first to suggest that the statistical setting may lead to better round complexity even for thresholds of $t \leq t_p$ which are *perfectly realizable* (i.e., realizable with perfect security). Specifically, they showed that the sharing phase of statistical VSS with $t = \lfloor (n-1)/3 \rfloor$ can be carried in two rounds, bypassing a three-round lower-bound of [34]. Another indication for a possible advantage was given by [37] who showed that 4-party linear functions can be statistically computed in two rounds with threshold of $t = 1$ which is impossible in the perfect setting as shown by [33, Thm 8].[6] However, to the best of our knowledge, so far we did not have a single example of an infinite MPC functionality whose statistical round complexity is strictly smaller than its perfect round complexity under a perfectly-realizable threshold $t \leq t_p$. Theorem 4 settles this question in a strong way showing that, for any $n/4 \leq t \leq \lfloor (n-1)/3 \rfloor$, statistical t-security can be achieved for *all* functions in three rounds, whereas perfect t-security cannot be achieved in three rounds even for simple finite functionalities [8].

The separation proved in the SIFR model (Theorem 1 vs. Theorem 2) should be taken with more care. An immediate corollary of Theorem 1 asserts that for any perfect resiliency-threshold t that is larger than $\lfloor (n-1)/4 \rfloor$, one cannot transform an r-round perfect-VSS (modeled as some ideal sharing functionality) into an $r + 1$-round general MPC in a "black-box" way. Furthermore, since it is known that for $t_p = \lfloor (n-1)/3 \rfloor$ perfect VSS takes exactly 3 rounds, one can naively conclude that for such resiliency general perfectly-secure MPC cannot be implemented in less than $3 + 2 = 5$ rounds. Nevertheless, [8] constructed a 4-round perfectly-secure t_p-resilient MPC protocol in the plain model.

---

[6] We thank Yuval Ishai for pointing this out.

This construction is based on a 3-round implementation of the $\mathcal{F}_{\mathsf{vsh}}$ functionality in a fairly complicated way that exploits the concrete properties of the underlying $\mathcal{F}_{\mathsf{vsh}}$-*protocol*. Specifically, the transformation makes use of intermediate values that are available before the $\mathcal{F}_{\mathsf{vsh}}$-protocol terminates. The impossibility of perfect two-round $\mathcal{F}_{\mathsf{vsh}}$-SIFR protocol for general functionalities (Theorem 1) should therefore be interpreted as saying that such a complication is *inherent*! In contrast, the statistical relaxation allows us to obtain a significantly simpler reduction (i.e., two-round $\mathcal{F}_{\mathsf{vsh}}$-SIFR) as shown in Theorem 2.

We end up the introduction, by depicting in Fig. 1 the resiliency-vs-round landscape of MPC in various models.

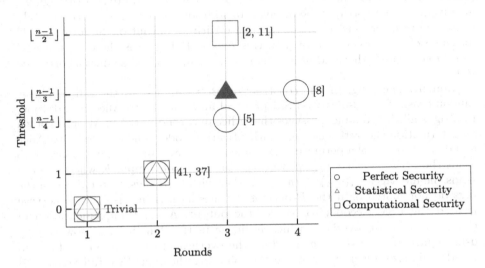

Fig. 1. The best trade-offs known between the thresholds t and the number of rounds r in the plain model. Circles, triangles and squares indicate perfect, statistical and computational security, respectively. Our results are marked with solid shapes. Each of the marked points is optimal in the sense that it cannot be moved up. That is, no better resiliency can be achieved under the corresponding model with the permitted round complexity.

Organization. In the extended abstract version, we present a succinct version of the upper bounds. Section 2 presents the high-level idea of the Secure-Computation-with-Guard primitive, which is being employed in Sect. 3 towards the construction of 2-round statistical $\mathcal{F}_{\mathsf{vsh}}$-SIFR Protocols. In Sect. 4 we construct 2-round VSS protocols.

2   Secure Computation with a Guard

In this section we present a new *Secure Computation with a Guard* (SCG) primitive that will be employed later in our constructions. In SCG, there are two *senders*, Alice and Bob, with asymmetric roles: Bob knows a single input $b \in B$ whereas Alice knows both inputs $a \in A$ and $b \in B$. The goal is to release the value of $f(a,b)$ to a receiver Carol who holds no input. (This can be formalized by the 3-party functionality $F((a,b), b, \perp) = (\perp, \perp, f(a,b))$.) Syntactically, the protocol consists of an offline phase, denoted scg.off, and an online phase, scg.on. In the offline phase, Bob sends a single message to Carol and a single message to Alice, these messages depend only on the randomness of Bob and do not depend on his input. In the online phase, both Alice and Bob send a single message to Carol based on the offline messages and on their inputs a, b. At the end Carol should output the value $f(a,b)$ or a special abort symbol. As in the setting of private simultaneous message (PSM) protocols [28], we require security against an adversary that corrupts the receiver. In addition, if Alice (resp., Bob) is malicious, the receiver must abort or terminate with an output of the form $f(a', b)$ for some $a' \in A$ (resp., $f(a', b)$). In this sense, "Bob guards the computation" against corrupted Alice and "Alice guards the computation" against a corrupted Bob.

Roughly speaking, in our construction Bob samples, in the offline phase, randomness r for a 2-party f-PSM protocol and sends it to Alice. In addition, Bob signs all the possible messages that Alice may send in the PSM protocol via an information-theoretic message authentication code, sends the tags to Alice and delivers to Carol a permuted version of all the keys. In the online phase, Bob sends the PSM message $s_B(b; r)$ that corresponds to his input b, whereas Alice sends the messages $s_A(a; r), s_B(b; r)$ together with their tags. Carol aborts if the tags do not match or if the B-part of the messages is inconsistent, otherwise it used the PSM decoder to recover the output. A naive implementation of this idea yields an overhead which is linear in the domain size, however, by using multiparty PSM, we can reduce the overhead to be poly-logarithmic in the domain-size. Overall, we prove the following theorem. (See full version [7] for a proof.)

Lemma 1 (Polynomial-time SCG Protocols). *Let $A = \mathbb{F}_2^{m_1}$, $B = \mathbb{F}_2^{m_2}$ and $C = \mathbb{F}_2^p$. Let $m = m_1 + m_2$ and let $f : A \times B \to C$ be a Boolean circuit with depth logarithmic in m, size polynomial in m and bounded fan-in and fan-out. Then, for every statistical parameter ϵ, there exists an SCG protocol with complexity $\mathrm{poly}(m) \cdot \log(1/\epsilon)$.*

3   A Two-Round Statistically-Secure $\mathcal{F}_{\mathsf{vsh}}$-SIFR Protocol

In this section, we prove Theorem 2. For an integer x, we use $\|x\|$ to denote the set $\{1, \ldots, x\}$. Let us denote the set of n parties by P.

3.1   Definitions

The following definitions are parameterized by a resiliency threshold t, a finite field $\mathbb{F}$ of size $q > n$, and a tuple of n non-zero elements in $\mathbb{F}$, one for each party in P, which are denoted (with a slight abuse of notation) by $1, \ldots, n$. Throughout this section, we fix t to $\lfloor (n-1)/3 \rfloor$.

Definition 1 ($\lfloor \cdot \rceil$-sharing). *A value s is said to be* committed *amongst* P, *denoted as $\lfloor s \rceil$, if there exists a polynomial $f(x)$ of degree at most t with $f(0) = s$ such that every honest party P_i either holds $f(i)$ or $\bot$ and at least $t + 1$ honest parties hold non-$\bot$ values.*

Definition 2 ($[\cdot]$-sharing). *A value s is said to be t-shared amongst* P, *denoted as $[s]$, if there exists a polynomial $f(x)$ of degree at most t with $f(0) = s$ such that every honest party P_i holds $f(i)$.*

Definition 3 ($[[\cdot]]$-sharing). *A value s is said to be* doubly t-shared *amongst* P, *denoted as $[[s]]$, if there exist polynomials $f(x), \{f_i(x)\}_{i \in \{1,...,n\}}$, all of degree at most t with $f(0) = s$ and $f(i) = f_i(0)$ for $i \in \{1, \ldots, n\}$ such that $f(0), \{f_i(0)\}_{i \in \{1,...,n\}}$ are t-shared via polynomials $f(x), \{f_i(x)\}_{i \in \{1,...,n\}}$ and every honest P_i holds $f_i(x)$.*

Definition 4 ($\langle \cdot \rangle$-sharing). *A value s is said to be* doubly $2t$-shared *amongst* P, *denoted as $\langle s \rangle$, if there exist a degree-$2t$ polynomial $f(x)$ and degree-t polynomials $\{f_i(x)\}_{i \in \{1,...,n\}}$ with $f(0) = s$ and $f(i) = f_i(0)$ for every honest party P_i such that $\{f_i(0)\}_{i \in \{1,...,n\}}$ are t-shared via polynomials $\{f_i(x)\}_{i \in \{1,...,n\}}$ and every honest P_i holds $f(i)$ and $f_i(x)$.*

Definition 5 (First-level and Second-level sharing, Shares and Share-shares). *In the double secret sharing definitions ($[[\cdot]]$ and $\langle \cdot \rangle$), the sharings done for the shares of the secret are referred as* second-level *sharings, while the sharing for the actual secret is termed as* first-level *sharing and the shares of the shares are termed as* share-shares. *The ith share of s is denoted as s_i (the context will make it clear whether the shares correspond to t or $2t$ sharing). The jth share-share of the ith share s_i of s is denoted as s_{ij}.*

The sharings $[\cdot], [[\cdot]]$ and $\langle \cdot \rangle$ are linear i.e. local addition of the shares of $[a]$ and $[b]$ results in $[a + b]$ (similarly for the other types of sharing). Furthermore, addition of $\langle a \rangle$ and $[[b]]$ results in $\langle a + b \rangle$.

3.2   The High-Level Idea

Our goal is to build a 2-round statistical protocol in the $\mathcal{F}_{\mathsf{vsh}}$-SIFR model, that can evaluate any n-party degree-2 functionality (over a field larger than n).

Prologue. Our starting point is the following completeness theorem from [8, Prop. 4.5 and Theorem. 5.23].

Proposition 1. *[8]. Let $\mathcal{F}$ be an n-party functionality that can be computed by a Boolean circuit of size S and depth D and let $\mathbb{F}$ be an arbitrary extension field of the binary field $\mathbb{F}_2$. Then, the task of securely-computing $\mathcal{F}$ non-interactively reduces to the task of securely-computing the degree-2 n-party functionality f over $\mathbb{F}$ that each of its outputs is of the form*

$$x^\alpha x^\beta + \sum_{j=1}^{n} r^j, \tag{1}$$

where x^α and x^β are the inputs of party P_α and P_β respectively and r^j is an input of party P_j for $j \in \{1, \ldots, n\}$.

The reduction preserves active perfect-security (resp., statistical-security) with resiliency threshold of $\lfloor (n-1)/3 \rfloor$ (resp., $\lfloor (n-1)/2 \rfloor$) and the complexity of the function f and the overhead of the reduction is $\mathrm{poly}(n, S, 2^D, \log |\mathbb{F}|)$. Furthermore, assuming one-way functions, one can get a similar reduction that preserves computational-security with resiliency threshold of $\lfloor (n-1)/2 \rfloor$ and complexity/security-loss of $\mathrm{poly}(n, S, \log |\mathbb{F}|)$.

Throughout this section we fix $\mathbb{F}$ to an $\mathbb{F}_2$-extension field of size larger than n, and assume that all the sharing functionalities are defined with respect to $\mathbb{F}$. (Specifically, we can take the smallest such field.) By Proposition 1, it suffices to focus on functionalities whose output can be written as (1). From now on, we focus on such a functionality f and construct a 2-round $\mathcal{F}_{\mathsf{vsh}}$-SIFR protocol whose complexity is polynomial n and in the description of f. For simplicity, we will discuss computation of one degree-2 term as above. The extension, guaranteeing that the same x values are used across different degree-2 terms, will follow easily.

2-round $\mathcal{F}_{\mathsf{vsh}}$-SIFR Protocol. Given access to an ideal VSS functionality, denoted $\mathcal{F}_{\mathsf{vsh}}$, that can generate a $[[\cdot]]$-sharing of a party's secret, we show how to construct a 2-round $\mathcal{F}_{\mathsf{vsh}}$-SIFR protocol for degree-2 computation. The $\mathcal{F}_{\mathsf{vsh}}$-SIFR protocol is efficient and statistically-secure for threshold $t < n/3$. Therefore, when the protocol is instantiated with a realisation of VSS, the security (statistical vs. cryptographic) and efficiency of the final MPC protocol reduce to that of underlying realisation of VSS.

Building on $\mathcal{F}_{\mathsf{vsh}}$, we first design a 2-round triple secret sharing (TSS) protocol in the $\mathcal{F}_{\mathsf{vsh}}$-SIFR model, that verifiably generates $[\cdot]$-sharing of a party's triple secrets a, b, c satisfying the product relation $c = ab$. The TSS completes the sharing in the first round, and the verification of the product relation is done in the second round. Subsequently, we use both the VSS functionality $\mathcal{F}_{\mathsf{vsh}}$ and the TSS protocol, in order to obtain a protocol for degree-2 computation in the $\mathcal{F}_{\mathsf{vsh}}$-SIFR model, which is both efficient and statistically secure.

Partial Degree-reduction. Traditionally, evaluating a degree-2 function involves secret-sharing the values and multiplying them distributively. The secret sharing takes the form of t-sharing and the share-wise multiplication results in a non-random $2t$-sharing of the product. The latter is transformed to a t-sharing via degree-reduction and randomization, and lastly the t-shared product is reconstructed robustly to complete degree-2 function evaluation. The degree-reduction in each step of multiplication seems necessary to keep the degree inflation in check when a sequence of multiplications needs to be performed. With degree-two functions as the end goal, we ditch full-fledged round-expensive degree-reduction. Rather we settle for generating a randomized *double* $2t$-sharing of the product which enables robust reconstruction via the second-level t-sharings. That is, we perform one-time degree reduction for the second-level sharings alone. This idea is borrowed from [8]. As we demonstrate in this work, the degree reduction is an easier task than the degree-reduction of the first-level sharing. The key idea is to have P_i monitor the degree reduction for the ith second-level sharings. We elaborate more below, starting with the description of a 3-round $\mathcal{F}_{\mathsf{vsh}}$-SIFR protocol, and then showing how to shave a round in order to obtain a 2-round protocol.

A 3-round $\mathcal{F}_{\mathsf{vsh}}$ -SIFR protocol. Our aim is to compute $\langle x^\alpha x^\beta + \sum_{k=1}^n r^k \rangle$ and reconstruct the output via robust reconstruction of its second-level t-sharings. For simplicity, we ignore the additive terms and focus on producing $\langle y \rangle = \langle x^\alpha x^\beta \rangle$ and reconstructing the product. First, the $\mathcal{F}_{\mathsf{vsh}}$ functionality is used to generate $[[x^\alpha]]$ and $[[x^\beta]]$ in the first round. A local multiplication over the shares generates a non-random 2t-sharing of the product $x^\alpha x^\beta$. Generating $\langle y \rangle$ is then done in two steps– randomization of the sharing and degree-reduction of the second-level sharing. The former requires generating a $\langle 0 \rangle$ and adding to the non-random second-level degree-reduced sharing of y. Generating a $\langle 0 \rangle$ requires producing t $[[\cdot]]$-sharing via the $\mathcal{F}_{\mathsf{vsh}}$ functionality and can be concluded in the first round. Next, the degree reduction for the ith second-level sharing is conducted under the supervision of P_i that produces an independent triple sharing $([a^i], [b^i], [c^i])$ which is then used to turn the t-sharing of the ith shares of x^α and x^β (respectively, x_i^α and x_i^β) to a t-sharing of their product via Beaver's circuit randomization technique [14]. The TSS generates the triple sharings in the first round via $\mathcal{F}_{\mathsf{vsh}}$ and completes the verification of product relation in the second round. Having all the material ready by the first round (except the verification of the product-relation), Beaver's technique can be initiated in the second round, and it requires the reconstruction of $u_i = (x_i^\alpha - a^i)$, $v_i = (x^\beta - b^i)$ to compute $[y_i] = [x_i^\alpha x_i^\beta]$ as $u_i v_i + u_i[b^i] + v_i[a^i] + [c^i]$. Subsequently, degree-2 computation requires reconstruction of y_i (the randomized version of it) which, if correct, is a share of the first-level 2t-sharing of the product $x^\alpha x^\beta$. The above approach leads to a 3-round protocol. We compress the two sequential reconstructions, each of which typically achieved via a single round communication followed by error correction, into a single-round affair.

Shaving a Round using 3-party Secure Computation with a Guard (SCG). Our approach takes note that the jth share-share y_{ij} is expressed as $u_i v_i + u_i b_j^i + v_i a_j^i + c_j^i$ (where a_j^i, b_j^i and c_j^i are the j-th shares of a^i, b^i and c^i), and the parties P_i, P_j jointly hold all the inputs before the start of round 2. Specifically, the two values u_i, v_i that can be publicly reconstructed earliest at round 2 are already available to P_i in the end of round 1 (as she herself generated the triples and $\mathcal{F}_{\mathsf{vsh}}$ instances for x^α, x^β conclude in round 1). The shares of a, b, c, on the other hand, is known to both P_i, P_j in the end of round 1 as soon as the relevant $\mathcal{F}_{\mathsf{vsh}}$ conclude. This perfectly creates a vacuum for a 3-party primitive between Alice, Bob and Carol. Alice holds inputs x, y respectively from sets X and Y and Bob holds y. Together, they would like to enable Carol to compute $f(\mathsf{x}, \mathsf{y})$ (and nothing else) with a one-shot communication. While Alice alone can do this, having Bob allows us to conduct a 'secure computation with a guard' (SCG). Between Alice and Bob, the honest party guards the computation ensuring certain level of correctness. Specifically, Carol outputs either $f(\mathsf{x}', \mathsf{y})$ or $\perp$ when Alice is corrupt, whereas

$f(x, y)$ or $\perp$ when Bob is corrupt. Using a SCG for a slightly tweaked function $g(x, y) = (x, f(x, y))$ and ensuring that correct x is made available to Carol in round 2, it is possible to make Carol output either $f(x, y)$ or $\perp$ in the Alice-corrupt case. We plug in an SCG, for every triple (i, j, k), with P_i in the shoes of Alice with inputs $x = (u_i, v_i)$, $y = (a_j^i, b_j^i, c_j^i)$, P_j in the shoes of Bob with input y, and the function g outputting (u_i, v_i, y_{ij}) to P_k (Carol). We reconstruct u_i, v_i from their t-sharing in round 2 to make them available with every P_k, to make sure that either $f(x, y)$ or $\perp$ are extracted from the reconstruction of the SCG of g. For an honest P_i, SCG with every honest P_j will disclose y_{ij}, while with that of a corrupt P_j is guaranteed to output either y_{ij} or $\perp$. Denoting a SCG leading to $\perp$ as a *silent* one, the reconstruction of y_i for an honest P_i reduces to fitting the unique t-degree polynomial over the disclosed y_{ij}. On the other hand, a corrupt P_i needs to keep at least $n - t$ SCGs non-silent (which is the case for an honest P_i), and consequently it must agree to the inputs fed by the $n - 2t$ honest parties. Furthermore, the SCG, together with the reconstructed u_i and v_i, ensure that nothing but y_{ij} or $\perp$ can make way to the output. Thus, if some value is reconstructed in this case, it will be y_i. Lastly, P_i can cheat by not ensuring $c^i = a^i b^i$ for its triple. However, TSS offers a mechanism to detect this mischief in round 2. Therefore, the reconstruction, if at all successful, results in the correct y_i for a corrupt P_i. Leveraging super-honest majority, we will always have enough y_i ($n - t \geq 2t + 1$) for the reconstruction of y.

Employing the SCGs. Recall that apart from the single-round communication, SCGs need an offline input-independent communication round. In our protocols, the offline can be run in round 1. Furthermore, we apply the SCG's only to functions whose formula size is polynomial in n, and our construct is polynomial-time. SCG also plays a key role in our TSS protocol.

Epilogue. For the degree-2 completeness, we need every party to output different y (yet with the same form). To ensure that the same x inputs are used for computation of all the y values, the same secret sharing of the x values needs to be used for computation of $\langle y \rangle$ as above for all y values. With the above high-level idea, we first present the notion of secure computation with a guard, and then use this notion to derive a 2-round statistically-secure degree-2 protocol in the $\mathcal{F}_{\text{vsh}}$-SIFR model.

3.3 $\mathcal{F}_{\text{vsh}}$-SIFR Protocol for Degree-2 Computation

For the $\mathcal{F}_{\text{vsh}}$-SIFR protocol, we use an idealized version of VSS given in Fig 2, which is used in the first round of the $\mathcal{F}_{\text{vsh}}$-SIFR protocol.

Functionality $\mathcal{F}_{\text{vsh}}$

$\mathcal{F}_{\text{vsh}}$ receives $F(x, y)$ from $D \in \mathsf{P}$. If $F(x, y)$ is not a symmetric bivariate polynomial of degree less than or equal to t in both x and y, then it replaces $F(x, y)$ with a default choice of such polynomial. Lastly, it sends $f_i(x) = F(x, i)$ to every P_i.

Fig. 2. Functionality $\mathcal{F}_{\text{vsh}}$

We further require a reconstruction protocol for $[s]$. We define two variants of reconstruction– rec for public reconstruction and rec_j for private reconstruction to party P_j. rec_j is given below and rec can be realized by running n copies of rec_j for every P_j. Both require one round. In rec_j, on holding s_i (ith share of s), P_i sends s_i to P_j who applies RS error correction to correct t errors and reconstruct the underlying polynomial $f(x)$ and output $s = f(0)$.

We now move on to present a TSS protocol and then building on it, a degree-2 computation protocol, both in the $\mathcal{F}_{\mathsf{vsh}}$-SIFR model.

Triple Secret Sharing. The goal of this protocol is to allow a dealer to share three values (a, b, c) via VSS such that $c = ab$ holds. Given access to an ideal VSS in the first round, we achieve our goal in 2 rounds. We abstract out the need in a functionality $\mathcal{F}_{\mathsf{tsh}}$ given in Fig. 3 and present our protocol subsequently.

Functionality $\mathcal{F}_{\mathsf{tsh}}$

$\mathcal{F}_{\mathsf{tsh}}$ receives $f^a(x), f^b(x), f^c(x)$ from $D \in \mathsf{P}$. If any of the polynomials is not a polynomial of degree less than or equal to t or $f^c(0) \neq f^a(0)f^b(0)$, then it sends $\bot$ to every P_i and $f^a(i), f^b(i), f^c(i)$ otherwise.

Fig. 3. Functionality $\mathcal{F}_{\mathsf{tsh}}$

Following the idea proposed in [17] and recalled in [9], the dealer chooses two polynomials of degree at most t, $f^a(x)$ and $f^b(x)$ with $f^a(0) = a$ and $f^b(0) = b$. It then picks a sequence of t polynomials $f^1(x), \ldots, f^t(x)$, all of degree at most t such that $f^c(x)$ which is equal to $f^a(x)f^b(x) - \sum_{\alpha=1}^{t} x^\alpha f^\alpha(x)$ is a random polynomial of degree at most t with the constant term equalling ab. Both [9,17] elucidate the idea of choosing the coefficients of $f^1(x), \ldots, f^t(x)$ in a way that simultaneously cancels out the higher order coefficients and randomizes the remaining coefficients of the product polynomial $f^a(x)f^b(x)$. The dealer hides these $t + 3$ polynomials in symmetric bivariate polynomials and invokes $t + 3$ instances of $\mathcal{F}_{\mathsf{vsh}}$. At the end of the first round the sharings are returned by the $\mathcal{F}_{\mathsf{vsh}}$ functionalities, and the check for the product relation $c = ab$ is enabled by letting every party P_i verify if $f^c(i) = f^a(i)f^b(i) - \sum_{\alpha=1}^{t} x^\alpha f^\alpha(i)$. Therefore, a complaint can be raised in round 2 and reconstruction of the shares of the complainant can be done in round 3 to enable public verification. To conclude the verification in round 2, we need to shave a round, or compress the rounds 2 and 3 into a single one. Given that, the complaint bit (indicating whether P_i's verification succeeds or not) is known to P_j and the jth share-shares are known to both P_i and P_j at the end of round 1, round 2 can be used for running (the online phase) of an SCG protocol to reveal the jth share-shares when the complaint bit is true. So the function of our interest is $f : \mathbb{F}_2 \times \mathbb{F}^{t+3} \to \mathbb{F}^{t+4}$ defined by

$$f(\mathsf{x}, \{\mathsf{x}^\alpha\}_{\alpha \in \|t+3\|}) = \begin{cases} (\mathsf{x}, 0, \ldots, 0) & \text{if } \mathsf{x} = 0, \\ (\mathsf{x}, \{\mathsf{x}^\alpha\}_{\alpha \in \|t+3\|}) & \text{otherwise,} \end{cases} \tag{2}$$

with $A := \mathbb{F}_2$, $B := \mathbb{F}^{t+3}$ and $C := \mathbb{F}^{t+4}$ (as per Lemma 1). To conduct P_i's verification, we plug in SCGs between every triple (i, j, k) varying over all j, k, with P_i as Alice P_j as Bob and P_k as carol. P_i and P_j together allow P_k to compute the jth share-shares of all the $t + 3$ $[[\cdot]]$-sharing if P_i's complaint bit is on. Precisely, P_i's inputs are the complaint bit and the share-shares, whereas P_j's input is just the share-shares. The offline of the SCGs are run during the first round, and the online in round 2. An SCG instance that leads to $\perp$ for a Carol, is labelled as *silent*.

For an honest P_i with genuine complaint, $n - t$ SCGs corresponding to the honest P_js will spit out the correct share-shares (via correctness), while the rest will either be silent or spit out correct share-shares (via correctness with a guard for honest-Alice case). This enables public reconstruction of the ith shares of all the $t + 3$ $[[\cdot]]$-sharing and so subsequent public verification will instate the compliant publicly. Thus an honest party can always convince others about its complaint and can ensure D's disqualification. A corrupt P_i, on the other hand, can only force the SCGs to output f on either $x = 0$ or 1, apart from turning them silent. A corrupt P_i needs to keep at least $n - t$ SCGs non-silent (which is the case for an honest P_i) for not to be disqualified. Among these, it must allow every P_k to receive at least $n - 2t$ correct share-shares corresponding to the SCGs with honest P_js. Therefore, the reconstruction, if at all successful, results in reconstructing the correct shares, ensuring a successful public verification and absolution of D. Therefore, a corrupt P_i cannot make a false allegation against an honest D. Protocol tsh is described in Fig. 4 and is proven to realize functionality $\mathcal{F}_{\mathsf{tsh}}$ (Lemma 2) in the full version [7]. Finally, note that the function, that is computed using SCG is a formula of constant multiplicative depth and therefore has an efficient realization.

Lemma 2 (Security). *Protocol* tsh *realises functionality* $\mathcal{F}_{\mathsf{tsh}}$, *except with probability* ϵ, *tolerating a static, active adversary* $\mathcal{A}$ *corrupting* t *parties, possibly including the dealer* D. *Moreover, it is a statistically-correct and perfectly-secret protocol. Assuming the error probability of protocols* scg *and* vsh, *as* ϵ_{scg} *and respectively* ϵ_{vsh}, *we have* $\epsilon \leq t(2t + 1)\epsilon_{\mathsf{scg}} + (t + 3)\epsilon_{\mathsf{vsh}}$.

Lemma 3 (Efficiency). *In* $\mathcal{F}_{\mathsf{vsh}}$-*SIFR model, protocol* tsh *has a complexity of* $O\Big(\mathsf{poly}(n \log |\mathbb{F}|) \log (1/\epsilon)\Big)$.

Simplifications in Cryptographic Setting. Protocol tsh can be simplified in the cryptographic setting significantly, using the specifics of the VSS realization. In particular, the SCGs can be avoided altogether and further two rounds are enough to complete theTSS protocol. In fact, we prove a stronger statement— VSS and any single-input functionality has the same round complexity in cryptographic setting. However, the latter uses the VSS in a non-black-box way (hence does not lead to a one-round protocol in $\mathcal{F}_{\mathsf{vsh}}$-SIFR model). We postpone these details to the full version [7].

Protocol tsh

Inputs: D has inputs (a, b, c) such that $c = ab$.
Output: By the end of **R1**, the parties output $[[a]], [[b]], [[c]]$ or discards D. If D is not discarded, then by the end of **R2**, the parties output $[a], [b], [c]$ where $c = ab$ holds or output $\perp$.

R1 D and the parties do the following
  - *(VSS calls)* D chooses $t + 3$ random polynomials $f^a(x), f^b(x), f^c(x), f^1(x), \ldots, f^t(x)$, each of degree t such that (a) $f^a(0) = a$, $f^b(0) = b$, $f^c(0) = c$ and (b) $f^c(x) = f^a(x)f^b(x) - \sum_{\alpha=1}^{t} x^\alpha f^\alpha(x)$ as discussed in [17, 9]. D

    picks $t + 3$ symmetric bivariate polynomials $F^a(x, y), F^b(x, y), F^c(x, y), F^1(x, y), \ldots, F^t(x, y)$ with $F^a(x, 0) = F^a(0, y) = f^a(x)$, $F^b(x, 0) = F^b(0, y) = f^b(x)$, $F^c(x, 0) = F^c(0, y) = f^c(x)$ and $F^\alpha(x, 0) = F^\alpha(0, y) = f^\alpha(x)$ for every $\alpha \in \{1, \ldots, t\}$ and invokes $t + 3$ instances of $\mathcal{F}_{\text{vsh}}$ with these bivariate polynomials.
  - *(SCG offline calls)* For every triple (i, j, k), P_i in the role of Alice, P_j in the role of Bob, and P_k in the role of Carol, run scg.off^{ijk}, an execution of the offline phase of an SCG instance scg^{ijk} for function f as given in Equation 2.
  - *(Local Computation)* Upon conclusion of the instances of $\mathcal{F}_{\text{vsh}}$, let the parties hold $t + 3$ $[[\cdot]]$-sharing $\{[[z^\alpha]]\}_{\alpha \in \|t+3\|}$ ready where $z^1 = f^a(0) = a$, $z^2 = f^b(0) = b$, $z^3 = f^c(0) = c$ and $z^\alpha = f^\alpha(0)$. Every P_i sets $\text{flag}_i = 0$, if $z_i^3 = z_i^1 z_i^2 - \sum_{\alpha=1}^{t} i^\alpha z_i^{\alpha+3}$ and 1 otherwise.

R2 The parties do the following.
  - *(SCG online calls)* For every triple (i, j, k), P_i, as Alice, inputs $\mathsf{x} = \text{flag}_i$ and $\mathsf{x}^\alpha = z_{ij}^\alpha$ (the jth share-share of z_i^α) and P_j, as Bob, inputs $\{\mathsf{x}^\alpha\}_{\alpha \in \|t+3\|}$ to the execution of scg.on^{ijk} (the matching online of scg.off^{ijk}).
  - *(Local Computation)* Every P_k acts as follows. For every i and j, execution scg^{ijk} is considered to be *silent* if the output of P_k is $\perp$. Let for a non-silent scg^{ijk}, P_k outputs $(\text{flag}_{ij}, \{z_{ij}^\alpha\}_{\alpha \in \{1, \ldots, t+3\}})$. P_k discards D and outputs $\perp$, if there exists a party P_i such that all the following are true.
    - At least $n - t$ executions of $\{\text{scg}^{ijk}\}_j$ are non-silent. Let L_i denote the set of all such js.
    - All $\{\text{flag}_{ij}\}_{j \in L_i}$ from non-silent executions are 1.
    - For every $\alpha \in \{1, \ldots, t+3\}$, there is a unique polynomial of degree at most t that passes through $\{z_{ij}^\alpha\}_{j \in L_i}$. Let z_i^α denote the constant term of the polynomial. The condition $z_i^3 = z_i^1 z_i^2 - \sum_{\alpha=1}^{t} i^\alpha z_i^{\alpha+3}$ is *not* satisfied.
    Otherwise, P_k outputs $[a], [b], [c]$ ignoring the second-level sharing.

Fig. 4. Protocol tsh

Degree-2 Computation. Here we show how to compute a degree-2 computation of the following form: $y = x^\alpha x^\beta + \sum_{k=1}^{n} r^k$, where x^α and x^β are the inputs of P_α and P_β respectively and r^k is an input of P_k for $k \in \{1, \ldots, n\}$. This extended computation was proven to be complete for any polynomial-time computation. The goal is abstracted as a functionality $\mathcal{F}_{\text{deg2c}}$ below and the protocol appears subsequently for the computation of a single y. We assume the output is given to everyone for simplicity. The functionality can be modified to take a random input from the rightful recipient P_γ and y can be sent out in blinded form using the randomness as the blinder. The realisation of this slightly modified functionality can obtained relying on the realisation of the below functionality and additionally asking P_γ to run a VSS on a random polynomial (with a uniform random element m^γ in the constant term). The value y is then reconstructed in blinded form to everyone with m^γ as the blinder, which only P_γ can unblind. Thus, we assume y be dispatched to all in $\mathcal{F}_{\text{deg2c}}$.

Recall that the high-level idea our protocol is to generate $\langle x^\alpha x^\beta + \sum_{\ell=1}^{n} r^\ell \rangle$ from $[[x^\alpha]], [[x^\beta]], \{[[r^\ell]]\}_{\ell \in \{1, \ldots, n\}}$ and reconstruct the secret $x^\alpha x^\beta + \sum_{\ell=1}^{n} r^\ell$ via its second-level t-sharings. A bunch of VSS instances are invoked to generate $[[x^\alpha]], [[x^\beta]], \{[[r^\ell]]\}_{\ell \in \{1, \ldots, n\}}$ in the first round. Ignoring the additive terms, the major task boils down to generating $\langle x^\alpha x^\beta \rangle$ from $[[x^\alpha]]$ and $[[x^\beta]]$. Local product of the shares and share-shares of these two sharings results in a non-randomized $2t$-sharing in both the first and second level. To compute a $\langle \cdot \rangle$-sharing, we (a)

Functionality $\mathcal{F}_{\text{deg2c}}$

$\mathcal{F}_{\text{deg2c}}$ receives x^α from P_α, x^β from P_β and r^k from $P_k \in \mathsf{P}$. It computes $y = x^\alpha x^\beta + \sum_{k=1}^n r^k$ and returns y to every party.

Fig. 5. Functionality $\mathcal{F}_{\text{deg2c}}$

use the Beaver's trick to compute t-sharing of the product-share $x_i^\alpha x_i^\beta$ from the t-sharing of shares x_i^α and x_i^β and then (b) randomize the first-level $2t$-degree product polynomial. For the latter, we use the existing techniques via VSS (for example see [8]). We only recall the functionality $\mathcal{F}_{\langle 0 \rangle}$ responsible for generating a $\langle 0 \rangle$, and mention that it can be implemented in one round in the $\mathcal{F}_{\text{vsh}}$-SIFR model. Let zsh denote a one-round $\mathcal{F}_{\text{vsh}}$-SIFR protocol for zero-sharing (these protocols are termed as ZSS protocols).

Functionality $\mathcal{F}_{\langle 0 \rangle}$

Given a set of parties $\mathsf{C} \subset \mathsf{P}$ that are controlled by ideal adversary $\mathcal{A}$, $\mathcal{F}_{\langle 0 \rangle}$ receives $\{s_i\}_{i \in \mathsf{C}}$ and $\{s_{ij}\}_{i \in \{1,\ldots,n\}; j \in \mathsf{C}}$. It picks a random polynomial of degree at most $2t$, $f(x)$, such that– (i) $f(0) = 0$ and (ii) $f(i) = s_i$ for $i \in \mathsf{C}$. It further picks a set of random polynomials $\{f_i(x)\}_{i \in \{1,\ldots,n\}}$ of degree at most t such that for each $f_i(x)$– (a) $f_i(0) = f(i)$ and (ii) $f_i(j) = s_{ij}$ for all $j \in \mathsf{C}$. It sends $(f(i), f_i(x))$ to every P_i.

Fig. 6. Functionality $\mathcal{F}_{\langle 0 \rangle}$

To achieve the former task, every P_i generates $([a^i], [b^i], [c^i])$ such that (a^i, b^i, c^i) are random and independent of the actual inputs and satisfy $c^i = a^i b^i$ using an instance of protocol tsh. Recall that while generating the sharings takes is done in the first round, the verification of the product relation takes place in the second round. Beaver's trick requires reconstruction of $u_i = (x_i^\alpha - a^i)$, $v_i = (x_i^\beta - b^i)$ first to compute $[y_i] = [x_i^\alpha x_i^\beta]$ as $u_i v_i + u_i [b^i] + v_i [a^i] + [c^i]$ and subsequently, degree-2 computation requires reconstruction of y_i (the randomized version of it) which, if correct, is a share of the first-level $2t$-sharing of the product $x^\alpha x^\beta$. Therefore, the above approach leads a 3 round protocol. To conclude within 2 rounds, we need a reconstruction mechanism that achieves– (a) for an honest P_i, the reconstruction is robust and y_i is the correct share (b) for a corrupt P_i, either the reconstruction fails or y_i is the correct share. This reconstruction is enabled via SCGs. For the reconstruction of y_i, P_i in the role of Alice, P_j in the role of Bob run an SCG to allow every P_k learn y_{ij}, the jth share-share of y_i. The input of P_i is (u_i, v_i) and the jth share-shares, a_j^i, b_j^i, c_j^i of a, b, c. The input of P_j is jth share-shares of a, b, c. The function f computes $y_{ij} = u_i v_i + u_i b_j^i + v_i a_j^i + c_j^i$ and outputs (u_i, v_i, y_{ij}). With all the inputs ready at the end of the first round, we compute the offline phase in the first round as well, while the online phase can be executed in the second round. During the online phase, we also make sure P_k, as Carol, holds u_i, v_i, by reconstructing these values from their t-sharing. This allows P_k to make sure that P_i used the values

u_i and v_i as an input to the SCG, thus making sure that the value extracted from the SCG is either y_{ij} or $\perp$, even when P_i is corrupt. The protocol appears in Fig. 7 and the proof that it realizes functionality $\mathcal{F}_{\mathsf{deg2c}}$ (Theorem 6) in the full version of the paper [7].

Protocol deg2c

Inputs: P_α and P_β input x^α and respectively x^β. In addition, P_ℓ inputs r^ℓ for $\ell \in \{1, \ldots, n\}$.
Output: Every party outputs $y = x^\alpha x^\beta + \sum_{\ell=1}^{n} r^\ell$.

R1 The parties do the following in parallel
- *(VSS calls)* P_α picks a symmetric bivariate polynomial of degree at most t in each variable $X^\alpha(x, y)$ with $X^\alpha(0,0) = x^\alpha$ and initiates an instance of $\mathcal{F}_{\mathsf{vsh}}$. P_β picks $X^\beta(x, y)$ with $X^\beta(0,0) = x^\beta$ and initiates an instance of $\mathcal{F}_{\mathsf{vsh}}$. Each P_ℓ picks $R^\ell(x, y)$ with $R^\ell(0,0) = r^\ell$ and initiates an instance of $\mathcal{F}_{\mathsf{vsh}}$ with input $R^\ell(x, y)$.
- *(TSS calls)* Every P_i initiates an instance of tsh, denoted as tsh^i, with inputs (a^i, b^i, c^i), randomly chosen, yet satisfying product relation $c^i = a^i b^i$.
- *(ZSS call)* The parties initiate an instance of zsh, which is concluded by the end of the round.
- *(SCG offline calls)* For every triple (i, j, k), P_i in the role of Alice, P_j in the role of Bob, and P_k in the role of Carol execute $\mathsf{scg.off}^{ijk}$ for function $f : \mathbb{F}^2 \times \mathbb{F}^{n+4} \to \mathbb{F}^3$ defined by

$$f\big((u, v), (a, b, c, o, \{w^\ell\}_{\ell \in \{1, \ldots, n\}})\big) = (u, v, uv + ub + va + c + o + \sum_{\ell=1}^{n} w^\ell). \qquad (3)$$

- *(Local computation)* At the end of this round, we have $[[x^\alpha]]$, $[[x^\beta]]$, $\{[[r^\ell]]\}_{\ell \in \{1, \ldots, n\}}$, $\{[a^i], [b^i], [c^i]\}_{i \in \{1, \ldots, n\}}$ from $\{\mathsf{tsh}^i\}_{i \in \{1, \ldots, n\}}$, and $\langle 0 \rangle$ (we denote the ith share as o_i and jth share-share of o_i as o_{ij}).

R2 The parties do the following:
- *(TSS completion)* The parties run **R2** of $\{\mathsf{tsh}^i\}_{i \in \{1, \ldots, n\}}$.
- *(SCG online calls)* For every pair (i, j), we assign the arguments of f of Equation 3 as: $\mathsf{u} = (x_i^\alpha - a^i)$, $\mathsf{v} = (x_j^\beta - b^i)$, $\mathsf{a} = a_j^i$ (jth share of a^i), $\mathsf{b} = b_j^i$ (jth share of b^i), $\mathsf{c} = c_j^i$ (jth share of c^i), $\mathsf{o} = o_{ij}$ (jth share-share of ith share of 0 corresponding to the generated $\langle 0 \rangle$), $\mathsf{w}^\ell = r_j^\ell$ (jth share of r^ℓ). For every (i, j, k) P_i, as Alice, inputs (u, v) and $(\mathsf{a}, \mathsf{b}, \mathsf{c}, \mathsf{o}, \{\mathsf{w}^\ell\})$, while P_j, as Bob, inputs $(\mathsf{a}, \mathsf{b}, \mathsf{c}, \mathsf{o}, \{\mathsf{w}^\ell\})$ to the execution of $\mathsf{scg.on}^{ijk}$.
- *(Recovering u, v for all)* For every P_i, the parties run two instances of rec for $[x_i^\alpha - a^i]$ and $[x_i^\beta - b^i]$ to recover the values for all.
- *(Local computation)* Every P_k initiates a set L to P and acts as follows. P_k runs the local computation steps of $\{\mathsf{tsh}^i\}_{i \in \{1, \ldots, n\}}$. For every (i, j, k), run the local computation for $\mathsf{scg.on}_{ijk}$ using the SCG output (u_{ij}, v_{ij}, y_{ij}) (which can be $\perp$). An scg^{ijk} is called *silent* if the output of P_k is $\perp$. For every $P_i \in \mathsf{L}$, P_k does the following.
  - Exclude P_i from L, if P_i is discarded, as a dealer, in tsh^i.
  - Exclude P_i from L if there exists some j such that $u_{ij} \neq (x_i^\alpha - a^i)$ or $v_{ij} \neq (x_i^\beta - b^i)$.
  - Exclude P_i from L, if at least $t+1$ executions of $\{\mathsf{scg}^{ijk}\}_j$ are silent. Otherwise let L_i denote the set of all js (which is at least $n-t$) for non-silent circuits.
  - Exclude P_i from L, if the values $\{y_{ij}\}_{j \in \mathsf{L}_i}$ do not lie on a polynomial of degree t.
  - $P_i \in \mathsf{L}$, let the the constant term of the unique polynomial defined by $\{y_{ij}\}_{j \in \mathsf{L}_i}$ be y_i.
  Finally, P_k uses $\{y_i\}_{P_i \in \mathsf{L}}$ to interpolate the $2t$-degree polynomial holding output y in the constant term and outputs y.

Fig. 7. Protocol deg2c

Theorem 6 (Security). *Protocol* deg2c *realises functionality* $\mathcal{F}_{\mathsf{deg2c}}$, *except with probability* ϵ, *tolerating a static adversary* $\mathcal{A}$ *corrupting* t *parties. Moreover, it is a statistically-correct and perfectly-secret protocol. Assuming the error probability of protocols* scg *and* vsh, *as* ϵ_{scg} *and respectively* ϵ_{vsh}, *we have* $\epsilon \leq (nt + 5n + 2)\epsilon_{\mathsf{vsh}} + (n+1)t(2t+1)\epsilon_{\mathsf{scg}}$.

Theorem 7 (Efficiency). *In* $\mathcal{F}_{\mathsf{vsh}}$-*SIFR model, protocol* deg2c *has a complexity of* $O\big(\mathsf{poly}(n \log |\mathbb{F}|) \log 1/\epsilon\big)$.

4   Verifiable Secret Sharing

Here, we introduce a new statistical VSS and recall the existing cryptographic VSS of [10]. In the latter section, we also suggest a simplified computational TSS protocol that is devoid of the SCGs.

In this section, the underlying field for sharing, $\mathbb{F}$, can be taken to be an arbitrary finite field of size $q > n$. We let κ denote a statistical security parameter that guarantees a correctness error of $2^{-\Omega(\kappa)}$ (and perfect secrecy), and always take κ to be super-logarithmic in the number of parties, i.e., $\kappa = \omega(\log n)$. We assume without loss of generality that $\log |\mathbb{F}| > \Omega(\kappa)$, and if this is not the case, we lift $\mathbb{F}$ up to a sufficiently-large extension field. Finally, we assume that basic arithmetic operations over $\mathbb{F}$ can be implemented with polynomial complexity in the $\log |\mathbb{F}|$. As usual, we fix the resiliency t to $\lfloor (n-1)/3 \rfloor$.

4.1   Statistical VSS

In this section, we construct the first 2-round statistical VSS that produces $[[s]]$ of D's secret from $\mathbb{F}$. The existing 2-round VSS of [1,46] does not generate $[[\cdot]]$-sharing and further the set of secrets that are allowed to be committed is $\mathbb{F} \cup \{\bot\}$. The latter implies that a corrupt D has the liberty of not committing to any secret or put differently, the committed secret can be $\bot$. A natural consequence of being able to produce $[[\cdot]]$-sharing is that the reconstruction turns to a mere one-round communication of shares followed by error correction, unlike the complicated approach taken in [1,46].

As a stepping stone towards a statistical VSS, we first build two weaker primitives–interactive signature and weak commitment.

Interactive Signature. An interactive signature protocol is a three-phase protocol (distribute, verify and open), involving four entities–a dealer $D \in \mathsf{P}$, an intermediary $I \in \mathsf{P}$, a receiver $R \in \mathsf{P}$ and a set of verifiers P. In the distribute phase, the dealer D, on holding a secret, *distributes* the secret and a signature on the secret to intermediary I and private verification information to each party P_i in P. In the verify phase, I and the verifiers P together verify if the secret and signature verify with the verification information. In the open phase, I opens the message and signature to R and the verifiers open verification information to R who verifies and accepts the message if it verifies correctly. Intuitively, we require four properties from the primitive–(a) *privacy* of the secret till the end of execution of the three phases when D, I, R are honest and at most t of the verifiers are corrupt; (b) *unforgeability* of honest D's secret in the open phase against the collusion of a corrupt I and at most t corrupt verifiers; (c) *nonrepudiation* of the secret after the verify phase succeeds against the collusion of a corrupt D and at most t corrupt verifiers, i.e. an honest R accepts an honest I's secret and signature after a successful verify phase and a corrupt D, colluding with t verifiers cannot repudiate to not have sent the message to I during distribute phase; and lastly (a) *correctness* i.e. R outputs D's secret when D and I are honest. We give the formal definition below.

Definition 6 (Interactive Signature Scheme (ISS)). *In an interactive signature scheme (ISS) amongst a set of n parties* P, *there is a distinguished party $D \in$ P that holds an input s picked over a field $\mathbb{F}$, referred to as a secret. The scheme involves three more entities apart from D, an intermediary $I \in$ P, a receiver $R \in$ P and a set of verifiers* P *and consists of three phases, a distribute, a verify and an open phase. In the beginning, D holds s and each party including the dealer holds an independent random input.*

- *Distribute: In this phase, D sends private information (computed based on its secret and randomness) to a designated intermediary $I \in$ P and to each of the verifiers in* P.
- *Verify: In this phase, I and the verifiers interact to ensure that the information received from D are consistent. This phase ends with a public accept or reject, indicating whether verification is successful or not.*
- *Open: Here, I and each verifier in* P *send the information received from D in distribute phase to a designated receiver $R \in$ P that applies a verification function to conclude if the message sent by I can be accepted or not. The output of this phase is considered only upon a successful execution of verify phase.*

A three-phase, n-party protocol as above is called a $(1-\epsilon)$-secure ISS scheme, if for any adversary $\mathcal{A}$ corrupting at most t parties amongst P, *the following holds:*

- *Correctness: If D and I are honest, the verify phase will complete with a success and an honest R accepts and outputs s in the open phase.*
- *ϵ-nonrepudiation: If I and R are honest and the verify phase has completed with a success, then R accepts and outputs s' sent by I in the open phase, except with probability ϵ.*
- *ϵ-unforgeability: If D and R are honest, then R accepts and outputs s' sent by I in the open phase only if $s' = s$, except with probability ϵ.*
- *Privacy: If D, I, R are honest, then at the end of the protocol the adversary's view is identical for any two secrets s and s'. Denoting $\mathcal{D}_s$ as $\mathcal{A}$'s view during the ISS scheme when D's secret is s, the privacy property demands $\mathcal{D}_s \equiv \mathcal{D}_{s'}$ for any $s \neq s'$.*

We would like to note that the existence of a similar primitive, known as information-checking protocol (ICP) [20,25,51]. ICP is played amongst three entities a dealer D, an intermmediary INT and a receiver R, where the verification information is held by R alone. In a variant of ICP [47,48], R is replaced with the set of parties P, similar to our definition, but the secret and the signature are disclosed in the public. We introduce the definition above that suits best for our protocols using ISS as the building block.

We now present an ISS scheme where the three phases will require one round each and importantly the verify and open phase can be run in parallel, making the whole scheme consume only two rounds. At a very high level, D hides its secret in a high-degree polynomial and gives out the polynomial as its signature to I. A bunch of *secret* evaluation points and evaluation of the signature polynomial on those points are given out as verification information to the verifiers. The idea of using secret evaluation points dates back to Tompa and Woll [53]. The verification is now enabled via cut-and-choose proof, though public disclosure of a padded form of the signature polynomial by I and evaluations of it by the verifiers on a set of randomly selected points. The high-degree of the polynomial and the padding ensure that the privacy of the secret and signature is maintained during the verification. Lastly, the opening simply involves revealing the signature polynomial and the remaining secret evaluation points and the evaluations to the designated receiver R that simply checks if the polynomial and the evaluations are consistent or not. It should be noted that a cheating I, exercising its rushing capability, may try to foil the cut-and-choose proof during the verify phase. Nevertheless, we show that such an adversary will be caught, with overwhelming probability, during the opening phase. We present our protocol iSig and state its properties below. For more details, see the full version of this paper [7].

Protocol iSig

Inputs: D has input s in the beginning of distribute phase. All parties share a statistical security parameter 1^κ.
Output: Every party outputs Success or Failure in the end of verify phase. R outputs s' or $\perp$ in the end of open phase and all other parties output nothing. If D is honest, then $s' = s$.

R1 (distribute phase): D does the following.
  - D chooses a random polynomial $f(x)$ over $\mathbb{F}$ of degree at most $n\kappa + 1$, where κ is the statistical security parameter, with $f(0) = s$. It further picks a random polynomial $r(x)$ over $\mathbb{F}$ of degree at most $n\kappa + 1$.
  - D picks $n\kappa$ random, non-zero, distinct elements from $\mathbb{F}$, denoted by $\alpha_{i1}, \ldots, \alpha_{i\kappa}$ for $i \in \|n\|$.
  - D sends $f(x)$ and $r(x)$ to I and $\{(\alpha_{ij}, f_{i,j} = f(\alpha_{ij}), r_{ij} = r(\alpha_{ij}))\}_{j \in \|\kappa\|}$ to P_i.

R2 (verify phase): The parties do the following.
  - I picks a random *non-zero* value $c \in \mathbb{F}$ and broadcasts polynomial $g(x) = f(x) + cr(x)$ and c. Each verifier P_i chooses a random subset of $\kappa/2$ indices $L_i \subset \{\kappa\}$ and broadcasts $\{(\alpha_{ij}, f_{ij}, r_{ij})\}_{j \in L_i}$.
  - We say P_i *accepts* I if $g(\alpha_{ij}) = f_{ij} + cr_{ij}$ for all $j \in L_i$. Every P_j (including D, I and R) outputs Success if at least $2t + 1$ P_i accepts and Failure otherwise.

R2 (open phase): The parties do the following.
  - I sends $f(x)$ to R. Let $\bar{L}_i := \|\kappa\| \setminus L_i$ denote the complement of L_i. Each verifier P_i sends to R the set $\{(\alpha_{ij}, f_{ij})\}_{j \in \bar{L}_i}$.
  - We say P_i *reaccepts* I if (a) it accepted I in verify phase and (ii) $f(\alpha_{ij}) = f_{ij}$ for at least $\kappa/8$ of the indices $j \in \bar{L}_i$.
  R outputs $s = f(0)$ if (a) at least $t + 1$ P_i reaccepts AND (b) it outputted Success in verify phase, and $\perp$ otherwise.

R2 (Public open phase for non-rushing adversaries): The parties act exactly as in the private open phase, execept that the informations are broadcasted. Every party P_k reaches at the same output as R would in the private open phase.

Fig. 8. Protocol iSig

Lemma 4. *The Protocol* iSig *is* $(1 - 2^{-\Omega(\kappa)})$-*secure ISS tolerating a static adversary* $\mathcal{A}$ *corrupting* t *parties, possibly including the dealer* D, I *and* R. *Moreover, the protocol achieves perfect privacy, and perfect correctness, and can be implemented in time* $\text{poly}(n, \kappa, \log |\mathbb{F}|)$.

Weak Commitment. As a stepping stone towards VSS, we first build a weaker primitive called weak commitment (WC) [8]. WC and opening are distributed information-theoretic variant of cryptographic commitment schemes. It also can be viewed as a (weaker) variant of the typical building block of VSS, known as Weak Secret Sharing (WSS). WC has a clean goal of ensuring that– for a unique secret s, at least $t + 1$ honest parties must hold the shares of the secret. WSS, on the other hand, ensures that a unique secret must be committed in the sharing phase so that either the secret or $\perp$ will be reconstructed latter during the distributed reconstruction phase. It is noted that a committed secret in WC needs the help of the dealer for its opening, unlike the secret committed in WSS. With a simpler instantiation, weak commitment and opening are sufficient to build a VSS scheme.

The dealer D starts with a polynomial of degree at most t and generates $\lfloor \cdot \rfloor$-sharing of its constant term through the input polynomial. For an honest D, WC in fact produces $[\cdot]$-sharing of the constant term. We abstract out the need in terms of a functionality $\mathcal{F}_{\mathsf{wcom}}$ given in Fig. 9 and present the protocol realizing the functionality below. The dealer sends a polynomial $g(x)$ and a set P$'$, indicating who should receive a share, to the functionality. An honest D will send $g(x)$ of degree at most t and P$' = $ P. When a corrupt D sends either a polynomial which is of degree more than t or a set of size less than $n - t$ (denying shares to at least $t + 1$ honest parties), all the parties receive $\perp$ from the functionality.

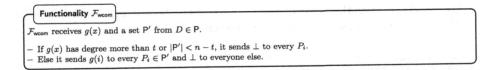

Fig. 9. Functionality $\mathcal{F}_{\mathsf{wcom}}$

At a high level, D, on holding a polynomial $g(x)$ of degree at most t, initiates the protocol by picking a *symmetric* bivariate polynomial $G(x, y)$ of degree t in both variables uniformly at random over $\mathbb{F}$ such that $G(x, 0)$ and $G(0, y)$ are the same as the input polynomial $g(x)$ (with change of variable for $G(0, y)$). Following some of the existing WSS/VSS protocols based on bivariate polynomials [32,42], D sends $g_i(x) = G(x, i)$ to party P_i and in parallel the parties exchange random pads to be used for pairwise consistency checking of their common shares. When a bivariate polynomial is distributed as above, a pair of parties (P_i, P_j) will hold the common share $G(i, j)$ via their respective polynomials $g_i(x)$ and $g_j(x)$. Namely, $g_i(j) = g_j(i) = G(i, j)$. A pair (P_i, P_j) is marked to be in conflict when the padded consistency check fails. In addition, D runs an ISS protocol for every ordered pair (i, j) with P_i as the intermediary and P_j as the receiver for secret $G(i, j)$. This allows D to pass a signature on $G(i, j)$ to P_i who can later use the signature to convince P_j of the receipt of $G(i, j)$. (D, P_i)

are marked to be in conflict when one of the n instances with P_i as the intermediary results in failure. Now a set of non-conflicting parties, W, of size $n - t$, including D, is computed (using a deterministic clique finding algorithm). Due to pair-wise consistency of the honest parties in W, their polynomials together define a unique symmetric bivariate polynomial, say $G'(x, y)$ and an underlying degree t univariate polynomial $g'(x) = G'(x, 0)$, the latter of which is taken as D's committed input. For an honest D, such a set exists and can be computed (in exponential time in n), albeit, it may exclude some honest parties. The possibility of exclusion of some of the honest parties makes this protocol different from existing 3-round constructions where D gets to resolve inconsistencies in round 3 and therefore an honest party is never left out of such a set. The honest parties in W output the constant term of their $g_i(x)$ polynomials received from D as the share of $g'(x)$. An honest outsider recomputes its $g_i'(x)$ interpolating over the non-$\perp$ outcomes from interactive signatures (as a receiver) corresponding to intermediaries residing in set W. When D is honest, the correct $g_i(x)$ can be recovered this way, thanks to the unforgeability of the signature and as a result, every honest party will hold a share of $g(x)$. For a corrupt D, while non-repudiation allows honest parties in W to convey and convince an honest outsider about their common share, the corrupt parties in W can inject any value as their common share. As a result, the interpolated polynomial may be an incorrect polynomial of degree more than t. In this case, an honest outsider may not be able to recover its polynomial $g_i'(x)$ and share of $g'(x)$. Protocol swcom, which realizes functionality $\mathcal{F}_{\mathsf{wcom}}$ (Lemma 5) is described in Fig. 10. For more details, see the full version of this paper [7].

We point out that the error in the outputs of the honest parties in WC are totally inherited from the underlying ISS instances.

Protocol swcom

Inputs: D has input $g(x)$. All parties share a statistical security parameter 1^κ.
Output: The parties output $[g(0)]$ if D is honest and $\lfloor g'(0) \rceil$ otherwise for some $g'(x)$ of degree at most t. The parties output $\perp$, if D is discarded.

R1: D and every party P_i do the following in parallel.
- D chooses a random symmetric bivariate polynomial $G(x, y)$ of degree at most t in each variable such that $G(x, 0) = g(x)$. D sends to each P_i the polynomial $g_i(x) = G(x, i)$.
- For every ordered pair (P_i, P_j), D initiates the distribute phase of one instance of iSig, denoted as iSig$_{ij}$, with P_i as the intermediary, P_j as the receiver and $G(i, j)$ as the secret (and with security parameter 1^κ).
- Each P_i picks a random polynomial $r_i(x)$ of degree at most t and sends $r_{ij} = r_i(j)$ to every P_j.

R2: Each P_i sets its share $s_i = g_i(0)$. For each ordered pair (i, j), the parties broadcast $m_i(x) = g_i(x) + r_i(x)$ and $m_{ij} = r_{ij} + g_j(i)$ respectively. For each ordered pair (i, j), the parties execute the verify and open phases of iSig$_{ij}$ and let P_j outputs g_{ij}' or $\perp$ in iSig$_{ij}$.

Local Computation: A pair (P_i, P_j) is called *conflicting* pair if $m_i(j) \neq m_{ij}$ or $m_j(i) \neq m_{ji}$. A pair (D, P_i) is called *conflicting* pair if any of the iSig$_{ij}$ instances for $j \in \|n\|$ results in Failure. Compute a set, W, of $n - t$ pairwise non-conflicting parties including D deterministically (a clique finding algorithm can be used). If no such set exists, then D is discarded and W is reset to $\varnothing$. Otherwise, every $P_i \notin$ W computes a polynomial $g_i'(x)$ interpolating over $\{g_{ji}'\}_{P_j \in \mathsf{W}}$. If degree of $g_i'(x)$ is more than t, then P_i resets s_i to $\perp$. Otherwise, P_i resets $g_i(x) = g_i'(x)$ and $s_i = g_i'(0)$.

Fig. 10. Protocol swcom

Lemma 5. *Protocol* swcom *realises functionality* $\mathcal{F}_{\text{wcom}}$, *except with probability* ϵ, *tolerating a static adversary* $\mathcal{A}$ *corrupting* t *parties, possibly including the dealer* D. *Moreover, it is a statistically-correct and perfectly-secret protocol. Assuming the error probability of protocol* iSig *as* ϵ_{iSig}, *we have* $\epsilon \leq (2t+1)^2 \epsilon_{\text{iSig}} = O(n^2 \epsilon_{\text{iSig}})$. *The communication complexity is* $\text{poly}(n, \kappa, \log|\mathbb{F}|)$, *and the computational complexity is exponential in* n *and polynomial in* κ *and* $\log|\mathbb{F}|$.

While we never need to reconstruct a $\lfloor \cdot \rfloor$-shared secret, non-robust reconstruction can be enabled by allowing D to broadcast the committed polynomial and the parties their shares. The D's polynomial is taken as the committed one if $n - t$ parties' share match with it. Clearly an honest D's opened polynomial will be accepted and a non-committed polynomial will always get rejected.

The Statistical VSS. VSS allows a dealer to distributedly commit to a secret in a way that the committed secret can be recovered robustly in a reconstruction phase. Our VSS protocol vsh allows a dealer D to generate double t-sharing of the constant term of D's input bivariate polynomial $F(x, y)$ of degree at most t and therefore allows robust reconstruction via Read-Solomon (RS) error correction, unlike the weak commitment scheme swcom.

At a high level, protocol svsh proceeds in the same way as the weak commitment scheme wcom, except that each blinder polynomial is now committed via an instance of swcom. A happy set, V, is formed in the same way. Two conflicting honest parties cannot belong to V, implying all the honest parties in V are pairwise consistent and together define a unique symmetric bivariate polynomial, say $F'(x, y)$ and an underlying degree t univariate polynomial $f'(x) = F'(x, 0)$, the latter of which is taken as D's committed input. A crucial feature that vsh offers by enforcing the W set of every party in V to have an intersection of size at least $n - t$ with V, is that the blinded polynomial of a corrupt party from V is consistent with $F'(x, y)$. This follows from the fact that the shares (pads) that the parties in W receive as a part of wcom remain unchanged, implying $n - 2t \geq t + 1$ of the honest parties in V ensure the consistency of the blinded polynomial of the corrupt party. This feature crucially enables an honest party P_i that lies outside V (in case of a corrupt dealer) to extract out her polynomial $f'_i(x) = F'(x, i)$ and thereby completing the double t-sharing of $f'(0)$. To reconstruct $f'_i(x)$, P_i looks at the blinded polynomial of all the parties in V who kept her happy in their respective weak commitment instances (implying her share did not change). For each such party, the blinded polynomial evaluated at i and subtracted from P_i's share/pad from the underlying wcom instance, allows P_i to recover one value on $f'_i(x)$. All the honest parties in V (which is at least $t + 1$) contribute to one value each, making sure P_i has enough values to reconstruct $f'_i(x)$. A corrupt party in V, being committed to the correct polynomial as per $F'(x, y)$, with respect to the parties in its W set, cannot inject a wrong value. Protocol vsh, which realizes functionality $\mathcal{F}_{\text{vsh}}$ (Theorem 8), is now described in Fig. 11. See the full version of this paper [7] for more details.

We point out that the error in the outputs of the honest parties in VSS are totally inherited from the underlying WC and in turn the ISS instances.

Protocol svsh

Inputs: D has input $F(x, y)$, a symmetric bivariate polynomial of degree at most t.
Output: The parties output $[[F(0,0)]]$ when D is honest and $[[F'(0,0)]]$ otherwise where $F'(x, y)$ is a bivariate polynomial of degree at most t.

R1 D and every party P_i do the following in parallel.
  - D sends to each P_i the polynomial $f_i(x) = F(x, i)$.
  - Each party P_i picks a random polynomial $h_i(x)$ of degree at most t and initiates an instance of swcom, denoted as swcom$_i$ as a dealer with polynomial $h_i(x)$.
R2 For each ordered pair (i, j), P_i and P_j broadcast $p_i(x) = f_i(x) + h_i(x)$ and $p_{ij} = h_{ij} + f_j(i)$ respectively, where h_{ij} is the share of P_j in swcom$_i$. In parallel, parties execute **R2** of swcom$_i$ for all $i \in \{1, \ldots, n\}$.
Local Computation The parties execute local computation step for every swcom$_i$ for $i \in \{1, \ldots, n\}$. A pair (P_i, P_j) is called *conflicting* pair if $p_i(j) \neq p_{ij}$ or $p_j(i) \neq p_{ji}$. Compute a set, V, of $n - t$ pairwise non-conflicting parties including D deterministically such that $|V \cap W_i| \geq n - t$ for every $P_i \in V$, where W_i denote the set of non-conflicted parties in swcom$_i$ (a clique finding algorithm can be used). If no such set exists, then D is discarded and a default sharing is assumed and reset V to P. Otherwise, every $P_i \notin V$ resets polynomial $f_i(x)$ to the degree t polynomial interpolated over the values $\{p_j(i) - h_{ji}\}_{P_j \in V; P_i \in W_j}$ (where $p_j(x)$ was broadcasted by P_j in **R2** and P_i has its share h_{ji} from swcom$_j$). Finally, every P_i outputs $f_i(0)$ and $f_i(x)$.

Fig. 11. Protocol svsh

Theorem 8. *Protocol* svsh *realises functionality* $\mathcal{F}_{\mathsf{vsh}}$, *except with probability* ϵ, *tolerating a static adversary* $\mathcal{A}$ *corrupting* t *parties, possibly including the dealer* D. *Moreover, it is a statistically-correct and perfectly-secret protocol. Assuming the error probability of protocol* iSig *as* ϵ_{iSig}, *we have* $\epsilon \leq n(2t+1)^2 \epsilon_{\mathsf{iSig}}$. *The communication complexity is* $\mathrm{poly}(n, \kappa, \log |\mathbb{F}|)$, *and the computational complexity is exponential in* n *and polynomial in* κ *and* $\log |\mathbb{F}|$.

It is easy to note that svsh generates $[[F(0,0)]]$ via the set of polynomials $\{F(x,0), \{f_i(x)\}_{i \in \{1,\ldots,n\}}\}$. Plugging in the above VSS in the deg2c protocol, we get a 3-round MPC for degree-2 computation.

4.2 Cryptographic VSS and Computation of Any Single-Input Functions

We briefly recall the construction of [10]. In Round 1, D publicly commits to a symmetric bivariate polynomial $F(x, y)$ using a NICOM and delivers the opening corresponding to $f_i(x) = F(x, i)$ to P_i. The commitments are computed in a way that simple public verification suffice for the checking of pairwise consistency between the common points (such as $f_i(j)$ and $f_j(i)$). To ensure that the commitments correspond to a polynomial of degree at most t in both x and y, it suffices if the honest parties (which are $n - t$ in number) confirm that their received polynomials are consistent with their commitments and they are of degree at most t. If this is not true, then P_i's goal is to make D publicly reveal the polynomial consistent with the commitments in the second round. Towards realizing the goal, P_i commits to a pad publicly and send the opening to D alone during Round 1. If D finds the opening inconsistent to the public commitment, then it turns unhappy towards P_i and opens the commitments corresponding to $f_i(x)$ publicly. Otherwise, it blinds the opening of $f_i(x)$ using the pad and makes it public. When P_i's check about $f_i(x)$ fails, she similarly turns unhappy with

D and opens the pad which in turn unmask the opening for $f_i(x)$. A corrupt P_i cannot change the pad and dismiss an honest D, owing to the binding property of NICOM. A corrupt D however may choose not to hand P_i the correct $f_i(x)$ in Round 1 and reveal $f_i(x)$ correctly in Round 2. The above technique therefore makes the $f_i(x)$ that is consistent with the public commitment of D publicly known when D and P_i are in conflict (and P_i is honest).

In the cryptographic setting, the VSS of [10] has the special feature of making the share (the entire univariate polynomial) of a party public when they are in conflict. We can tweak the TSS protocol (Sect. 3.3) so that the shares for all the $t+3$ instances are made public for party P_i in round 2, if P_i is in conflict with D (which also includes the reason that P_i's share do not satisfy the relation). This allows the public verification for corrupt parties in round 2 itself and thus TSS concludes in 2 rounds, like the VSS. We, in fact, can prove a stronger version of the result– any single-input function takes 2 rounds in cryptographic setting. TSS is a special case. We present this general result below. Plugging in the above VSS, and TSS in the deg2c protocol, we get a 3-round MPC for degree-2 computation.

Cryptographic MPC for Single-Input Functions. In this section, we obtain a 2-round protocol for every function whose outputs are determined by the input of a single party (single-input functions). This class of functions include important tasks such as distributed ZK and VSS. While a VSS protocol will be implied from our result from this section, we have separated out VSS in the previous section, as the VSS of [10] is used in a non-blackbox way for MPC for single-input functions.

[34] reduces secure computation of a single-input function to that of degree-2 polynomials and subsequently show a 2-round construct to evaluate the latter with perfect security and threshold $t < n/6$. In this work, we complement their reduction with a 2-round protocol to evaluate a degree-2 polynomial with threshold $t < n/3$ and relying on NICOMs. Let the sole input-owner be denoted as $D \in \mathsf{P}$, the inputs be $x^1, \ldots, x^m$ and the degree-2 polynomial be p (in most general form, there can be a vector of such polynomials). Broadly, the goal is to compute $2t$-sharing of $p(x^1, \ldots, x^m)$ and reconstruct the secret relying on the guidance of D in 2 rounds. The protocol starts with D sharing all the inputs using m instances of VSS. For the guided reconstruction, D locally computes the shares $p(x_i^1, \ldots, x_i^m)$ (p applied on the ith shares of the inputs) of the degree $2t$ polynomial holding $p(x^1, \ldots, x^m)$ in the constant term and broadcasts all the n points. In Round 2, apart from the checks P_i conducts inside the VSS instances, it also verifies if the broadcast of D is consistent with her received polynomials. If the check fails, then it becomes unhappy with D in all the instances and opens the pads distributed in the VSS instances to expose all the polynomials in her share. This allows public reconstruction of the correct $p(x_i^1, \ldots, x_i^m)$. The reconstruction in Round 2 is then achieved simply by fitting a degree $2t$ polynomial over the values $p(x_i^1, \ldots, x_i^m)$– (i) if P_i is not in conflict with D, this value is taken from D's broadcast (ii) otherwise, this value is publicly recomputed as

explained. If there is no such $2t$ degree polynomial, then D is concluded to be corrupt and is discarded. An honest D will always broadcast the correct values $p(x_i^1, \ldots, x_i^m)$ that lie on a $2t$ degree polynomial and a corrupt unhappy P_i cannot open a different value than this (due to binding property of NICOM). Lastly, since these values correspond to a non-random $2t$ degree polynomial, they are randomized using a $\langle 0 \rangle$ before broadcast. The $\langle 0 \rangle$ sharing is created by D by running t additional instances of VSS.

We present the functionality and the protocol below, the security proof of the latter (Lemma 6) is deferred to the full version of this paper [7]. We assume the output is given to everyone for simplicity. For a function that outputs distinct values for the parties, say y^i to P_i, the functionality can be modified to deliver y^i to P_i. This can be implemented by D t-sharing ($[\cdot]$-sharing) a random pad, pad^i for every party P_i, where the bivariate polynomial (used for sharing) and all the commitment opening are disclosed to P_i, who becomes unhappy when there is any inconsistency. D broadcasts masked values $p(x_j^1, \ldots, x_j^m) + pad_j^i$ so that $y^i + pad^i$ gets publicly reconstructed and y^i gets privately reconstructed by P_i alone.

Functionality $\mathcal{F}_{\mathsf{sif}}$

$\mathcal{F}_{\mathsf{sif}}$ receives $x^1, \ldots, x^m$ from D, computes $y = p(x^1, \ldots, x^m)$ and returns y to every party, where p is a degree-2 polynomial in the inputs of D.

Fig. 12. Functionality $\mathcal{F}_{\mathsf{sif}}$

Protocol sif

Inputs: D has input $x^1, \ldots, x^m$.
Output: The parties output $p(x^1, \ldots, x^m)$.

R1 D picks a symmetric and random bivariate polynomial $F^j(x, y)$ with $F^j(0,0) = x^j$ and initiates an instance of cvsh for $j \in \{1, \ldots, m\}$. It additionally picks a symmetric and random bivariate polynomial $M^j(x, y)$ and initiates an instance of cvsh for $j \in \{1, \ldots, t\}$ (used for randomization). Let D sends $\{f_i^j(x), m_i^j(x)\}_{j \in \{1, \ldots, t\}}$ to P_i in these cvsh instances. D further broadcasts $y_i = p(f_i^1(0), \ldots, f_i^m(0)) + \sum_{j=1}^t i^j m_i^j(0)$. All the parties participate in these instances and perform their respective steps.
R2 Run **R2** of all the instances. Further P_i checks if the value y_i broadcasted by D is consistent with the received polynomials. If this check fails, it becomes *unhappy* with D in all the VSS instances and opens the pads to publicly reconstruct $\{f_i^j(x), m_i^j(x)\}_{j \in \{1, \ldots, t\}}$ as per cvsh protocol. Every party recomputes y_i for every P_i in conflict with D. Let V be the set of parties who do not have conflict with D. Every party checks if $\{y_i\}_{i \in \{1, \ldots, n\}}$ lie on a $2t$ degree polynomial, where y_i is broadcasted by D when P_i is not in conflict with D and y_i is the publicly recomputed value otherwise. In case of yes, then every party outputs the constant term of the polynomial. Otherwise, D is discarded and p evaluated on default inputs is taken as output.

Fig. 13. Protocol sif

Lemma 6. *Protocol* sif *realizes* $\mathcal{F}_{\mathsf{sif}}$ *tolerating a static adversary* $\mathcal{A}$ *corrupting* t *parties, relying on NICOM.*

References

1. Agrawal, S.: Verifiable secret sharing in a total of three rounds. Inf. Process. Lett. **112**(22), 856–859 (2012). https://doi.org/10.1016/j.ipl.2012.08.003
2. Ananth, P., Choudhuri, A.R., Goel, A., Jain, A.: Round-optimal secure multiparty computation with honest majority. In: Advances in Cryptology - CRYPTO 2018–38th Annual International Cryptology Conference Proceedings, Part II. pp. 395–424, Santa Barbara, CA, USA, August 19–23 (2018)
3. Ananth, P., Choudhuri, A.R., Goel, A., Jain, A.: Two round information-theoretic MPC with malicious security. In: Advances in Cryptology - EUROCRYPT 2019–38th Annual International Conference on the Theory and Applications of Cryptographic Techniques Proceedings, Part II. pp. 532–561, Darmstadt, Germany, May 19–23(2019)
4. Applebaum, B., Brakerski, Z., Tsabary, R.: Perfect secure computation in two rounds. In: Theory of Cryptography - 16th International Conference Proceedings, Part I. TCC 2018, pp. 152–174, Panaji, India, November 11–14 (2018)
5. Applebaum, B., Brakerski, Z., Tsabary, R.: Degree 2 is complete for the round-complexity of malicious MPC. In: Advances in Cryptology - EUROCRYPT 2019–38th Annual International Conference on the Theory and Applications of Cryptographic Techniques Proceedings, Part II. pp. 504–531, Darmstadt, Germany, May 19–23(2019)
6. Applebaum, B., Ishai, Y., Kushilevitz, E.: Cryptography in NC^0. SIAM J. Comput. **36**(4), 845–888 (2006)
7. Applebaum, B., Kachlon, E., Patra, A.: The resiliency of mpc with low interaction: The benefit of making errors (2020)
8. Applebaum, B., Kachlon, E., Patra, A.: The round complexity of perfect mpc with active security and optimal resiliency. In: Proceedings of 61st FOCS (2020). https://eprint.iacr.org/2020/581
9. Asharov, G., Lindell, Y.: A full proof of the BGW protocol for perfectly secure multiparty computation. J. Cryptol. **30**(1), 58–151 (2017)
10. Backes, M., Kate, A., Patra, A.: Computational verifiable secret sharing revisited. In: Advances in Cryptology - ASIACRYPT 2011–17th International Conference on the Theory and Application of Cryptology and Information Security Proceedings. pp. 590–609, Seoul, South Korea, December 4–8 (2011)
11. Badrinarayanan, S., Jain, A., Manohar, N., Sahai, A.: Secure MPC: laziness leads to GOD. IACR Cryptology ePrint Archive **2018**, 580 (2018). https://eprint.iacr.org/2018/580
12. Bar-Ilan, J., Beaver, D.: Non-cryptographic fault-tolerant computing in constant number of rounds of interaction. In: Proceedings of the Eighth Annual ACM Symposium on Principles of Distributed Computing, pp. 201–209, Edmonton, Alberta, Canada, August 14–16 (1989)
13. Barak, B., Ong, S.J., Vadhan, S.P.: Derandomization in cryptography. SIAM J. Comput. **37**(2), 380–400 (2007). https://doi.org/10.1137/050641958
14. Beaver, D.: Efficient multiparty protocols using circuit randomization. In: Feigenbaum, J. (ed.) CRYPTO 1991. LNCS, vol. 576, pp. 420–432. Springer, Heidelberg (1992). https://doi.org/10.1007/3-540-46766-1_34

15. Beaver, D.: Multiparty protocols tolerating half faulty processors. In: Brassard, G. (ed.) CRYPTO 1989. LNCS, vol. 435, pp. 560–572. Springer, New York (1990). https://doi.org/10.1007/0-387-34805-0_49

16. Beaver, D., Feigenbaum, J., Kilian, J., Rogaway, P.: Security with low communication overhead. In: Advances in Cryptology - CRYPTO 1990, 10th Annual International Cryptology Conference, pp. 62–76, Santa Barbara, California, USA, August 11–15 (1990)

17. Ben-Or, M., Goldwasser, S., Wigderson, A.: Completeness theorems for noncryptographic fault-tolerant distributed computation (extended abstract). In: Proceedings of the 20th Annual ACM Symposium on Theory of Computing, pp. 1–10, Chicago, Illinois, USA, May 2–4 (1988)

18. Blum, M.: Coin flipping by telephone. In: Advances in Cryptology: A Report on CRYPTO 81, CRYPTO 81, IEEE Workshop on Communications Security, pp. 11–15, Santa Barbara, California, USA, August 24–26 (1981)

19. Canetti, R., Kilian, J., Petrank, E., Rosen, A.: Black-box concurrent zero-knowledge requires omega (log n) rounds. In: Proceedings on 33rd Annual ACM Symposium on Theory of Computing. pp. 570–579, Heraklion, Crete, Greece, July 6–8 (2001)

20. Canetti, R., Rabin, T.: Fast asynchronous byzantine agreement with optimal resilience. In: Proceedings of the Twenty-Fifth Annual ACM Symposium on Theory of Computing. pp. 42–51, San Diego, CA, USA, May 16–18 (1993)

21. Chaum, D., Crépeau, C., Damgård, I.: Multiparty unconditionally secure protocols (extended abstract). In: Proceedings of the 20th Annual ACM Symposium on Theory of Computing, pp. 11–19, Chicago, Illinois, USA, May 2–4 (1988)

22. Chor, B., Kushilevitz, E.: A zero-one law for boolean privacy. In: Proceedings of the Twenty-First Annual ACM Symposium on Theory of Computing. pp. 62–72. STOC 1989, Association for Computing Machinery, New York, USA (1989). https://doi.org/10.1145/73007.73013

23. Chor, B., Goldwasser, S., Micali, S., Awerbuch, B.: Verifiable secret sharing and achieving simultaneity in the presence of faults (extended abstract). In: 26th Annual Symposium on Foundations of Computer Science, Portland, Oregon, pp. 383–395 USA, October 21–23 (1985)

24. Cleve, R.: Limits on the security of coin flips when half the processors are faulty (extended abstract). In: Proceedings of the 18th Annual ACM Symposium on Theory of Computing, pp. 364–369, Berkeley, California, USA, May 28–30 (1986)

25. Cramer, R., Damgård, I., Dziembowski, S., Hirt, M., Rabin, T.: Efficient multiparty computations secure against an adaptive adversary. In: Advances in Cryptology - EUROCRYPT 1999, International Conference on the Theory and Application of Cryptographic Techniques, Prague, Czech Republic, pp. 311–326, May 2–6(1999)

26. Cramer, R., Damgård, I., Maurer, U.M.: General secure multi-party computation from any linear secret-sharing scheme. In: Advances in Cryptology - EUROCRYPT 2000, International Conference on the Theory and Application of Cryptographic Techniques, pp. 316–334, Bruges, Belgium, May 14–18 (2000)

27. Dolev, D., Reischuk, R.: Bounds on information exchange for byzantine agreement. J. ACM 32(1), 191–204 (1985)

28. Feige, U., Kilian, J., Naor, M.: A minimal model for secure computation (extended abstract). In: Proceedings of the Twenty-Sixth Annual ACM Symposium on Theory of Computing, pp. 554–563, Montréal, Québec, Canada, May 23–25 (1994)

29. Feldman, P., Micali, S.: Byzantine agreement in constant expected time (and trusting no one). In: 26th Annual Symposium on Foundations of Computer Science, pp. 267–276, Portland, Oregon, USA, October 21–23 (1985)

30. Fitzi, M., Garay, J.A., Gollakota, S., Rangan, C.P., Srinathan, K.: Round-optimal and efficient verifiable secret sharing. In: Theory of Cryptography, Third Theory of Cryptography Conference, TCC 2006, pp. 329–342, New York, USA, March 4–7 (2006)
31. Garg, S., Ishai, Y., Srinivasan, A.: Two-round mpc: information-theoretic and black-box. In: Beimel, A., Dziembowski, S. (eds.) TCC 2018. LNCS, vol. 11239, pp. 123–151. Springer, Cham (2018). https://doi.org/10.1007/978-3-030-03807-6_5
32. Gennaro, R., Ishai, Y., Kushilevitz, E., Rabin, T.: The round complexity of verifiable secret sharing and secure multicast. In: Proceedings on 33rd Annual ACM Symposium on Theory of Computing, pp. 580–589, Heraklion, Crete, Greece, July 6–8 (2001)
33. Gennaro, R., Ishai, Y., Kushilevitz, E., Rabin, T.: The round complexity of verifiable secret sharing and secure multicast. In: Proceedings of the thirty-third annual ACM symposium on Theory of computing. pp. 580–589. ACM (2001)
34. Gennaro, R., Ishai, Y., Kushilevitz, E., Rabin, T.: On 2-round secure multiparty computation. In: Advances in Cryptology - CRYPTO 2002, 22nd Annual International Cryptology Conference, pp. 178–193, Santa Barbara, California, USA, August 18–22 (2002)
35. Goldreich, O., Krawczyk, H.: On the composition of zero-knowledge proof systems. SIAM J. Comput. **25**(1), 169–192 (1996)
36. Goldreich, O., Levin, L.A.: A hard-core predicate for all one-way functions. In: Proceedings of the 21st Annual ACM Symposium on Theory of Computing, pp. 25–32, Seattle, Washington, USA May 14–17 (1989)
37. Ishai, Y., Kumaresan, R., Kushilevitz, E., Paskin-Cherniavsky, A.: Secure computation with minimal interaction, revisited. In: Gennaro, R., Robshaw, M. (eds.) CRYPTO 2015. LNCS, vol. 9216, pp. 359–378. Springer, Heidelberg (2015). https://doi.org/10.1007/978-3-662-48000-7_18
38. Ishai, Y., Kushilevitz, E.: Private simultaneous messages protocols with applications. In: Fifth Israel Symposium on Theory of Computing and Systems, ISTCS 1997, pp. 174–184, Ramat-Gan, Israel, June 17–19 (1997)
39. Ishai, Y., Kushilevitz, E.: Randomizing polynomials: A new representation with applications to round-efficient secure computation. In: 41st Annual Symposium on Foundations of Computer Science, FOCS 2000, pp. 294–304, Redondo Beach, California, USA, November 12–14 (2000)
40. Ishai, Y., Kushilevitz, E.: Perfect constant-round secure computation via perfect randomizing polynomials. In: Widmayer, P., Eidenbenz, S., Triguero, F., Morales, R., Conejo, R., Hennessy, M. (eds.) ICALP 2002. LNCS, vol. 2380, pp. 244–256. Springer, Heidelberg (2002). https://doi.org/10.1007/3-540-45465-9_22
41. Ishai, Y., Kushilevitz, E., Paskin, A.: Secure multiparty computation with minimal interaction. In: Rabin, T. (ed.) CRYPTO 2010. LNCS, vol. 6223, pp. 577–594. Springer, Heidelberg (2010). https://doi.org/10.1007/978-3-642-14623-7_31
42. Katz, J., Koo, C., Kumaresan, R.: Improving the round complexity of VSS in point-to-point networks. Inf. Comput. **207**(8), 889–899 (2009)
43. Kumaresan, R., Patra, A., Rangan, C.P.: The round complexity of verifiable secret sharing: the statistical case. In: Abe, M. (ed.) ASIACRYPT 2010. LNCS, vol. 6477, pp. 431–447. Springer, Heidelberg (2010). https://doi.org/10.1007/978-3-642-17373-8_25
44. Lamport, L., Fischer, M.: Byzantine generals and transaction commit protocols. Technical Report 62, SRI International (1982)
45. Moran, T., Naor, M., Segev, G.: An optimally fair coin toss. J. Cryptology **29**(3), 491–513 (2016). https://doi.org/10.1007/s00145-015-9199-z

46. Patra, A., Choudhary, A., Rabin, T., Rangan, C.P.: The round complexity of verifiable secret sharing revisited. In: Halevi, S. (ed.) CRYPTO 2009. LNCS, vol. 5677, pp. 487–504. Springer, Heidelberg (2009). https://doi.org/10.1007/978-3-642-03356-8_29

47. Patra, A., Choudhary, A., Rangan, C.P.: Simple and efficient asynchronous byzantine agreement with optimal resilience. In: Proceedings of the 28th Annual ACM Symposium on Principles of Distributed Computing, PODC 2009, pp. 92–101, Calgary, Alberta, Canada, August 10–12 (2009)

48. Patra, A., Rangan, C.P.: Communication and round efficient information checking protocol. CoRR abs/1004.3504 (2010). http://arxiv.org/abs/1004.3504

49. Patra, A., Ravi, D.: On the power of hybrid networks in multi-party computation. IEEE Trans. Inf. Theory **64**(6), 4207–4227 (2018)

50. Pease, M.C., Shostak, R.E., Lamport, L.: Reaching agreement in the presence of faults. J. ACM **27**(2), 228–234 (1980)

51. Rabin, T., Ben-Or, M.: Verifiable secret sharing and multiparty protocols with honest majority (extended abstract). In: Proceedings of the 21st Annual ACM Symposium on Theory of Computing, pp. 73–85, Seattle, Washigton, USA, May 14–17 (1989)

52. Sander, T., Young, A.L., Yung, M.: Non-interactive cryptocomputing for NC1. In: 40th Annual Symposium on Foundations of Computer Science, FOCS 1999, pp. 554–567, New York, USA, October 17–18 (1999)

53. Tompa, M., Woll, H.: How to share a secret with cheaters. In: Odlyzko, A.M. (ed.) CRYPTO 1986. LNCS, vol. 263, pp. 261–265. Springer, Heidelberg (1987). https://doi.org/10.1007/3-540-47721-7_20

54. Unruh, D.: Everlasting multi-party computation. J. Cryptology **31**(4), 965–1011 (2018). https://doi.org/10.1007/s00145-018-9278-z

55. Yao, A.C.: Theory and applications of trapdoor functions (extended abstract). In: 23rd Annual Symposium on Foundations of Computer Science, pp. 80–91, Chicago, Illinois, USA, November 3–5 (1982)

Revisiting Fairness in MPC: Polynomial Number of Parties and General Adversarial Structures

Dana Dachman-Soled[(⊠)]

University of Maryland, College Park, USA
danadach@umd.edu

Abstract. We investigate fairness in secure multiparty computation when the number of parties $n = \text{poly}(\lambda)$ grows polynomially in the security parameter, λ. Prior to this work, efficient protocols achieving fairness with no honest majority and polynomial number of parties were known only for the AND and OR functionalities (Gordon and Katz, TCC'09). We show the following:

- We first consider symmetric Boolean functions $F : \{0,1\}^n \to \{0,1\}$, where the underlying function $f_{n/2,n/2} : \{0,\ldots,n/2\} \times \{0,\ldots,n/2\} \to \{0,1\}$ can be computed fairly and efficiently in the 2-party setting. We present an efficient protocol for any such F tolerating $n/2$ or fewer corruptions, for $n = \text{poly}(\lambda)$ number of parties.
- We present an efficient protocol for n-party majority tolerating $n/2 + 1$ or fewer corruptions, for $n = \text{poly}(\lambda)$ number of parties. The construction extends to $n/2 + c$ or fewer corruptions, for constant c.
- We extend both of the above results to more general types of adversarial structures and present instantiations of non-threshold adversarial structures of these types. These instantiations are obtained via constructions of *projective planes* and *combinatorial designs*.

1 Introduction

In secure multiparty computation (MPC), parties compute the joint function of their inputs in a distributed fashion, while keeping their inputs private. Formally defining the security model for MPC is quite complex and there are various different flavors of security such as *computational* vs. *information-theoretic*, *security-with-abort* vs. *fairness* vs. *guaranteed output delivery*, *broadcast-channel* vs. *no broadcast channel*, *rushing* vs. *non-rushing*.

In this work, we focus on the setting of *computationally-secure*, n-party MPC in the presence of a *broadcast channel* with a *rushing* adversary. Further, we will require the *fairness* guarantee, which, informally, states that if one party

Supported in part by NSF grants #CNS-1933033, #CNS-1453045 (CAREER) and by financial assistance awards 70NANB15H328 and 70NANB19H126 from the U.S. Department of Commerce, National Institute of Standards and Technology.

R. Pass and K. Pietrzak (Eds.): TCC 2020, LNCS 12551, pp. 595–620, 2020.
https://doi.org/10.1007/978-3-030-64378-2_21

obtains the output of the function being computed, then all parties must obtain the output.

It is known how to securely compute every functionality in the above setting, assuming honest majority (i.e. more than half the parties are uncorrupted) [10, 12,17,18,37]. On the other hand, impossibility results, showing that there are n-party functionalities that cannot be computed fairly (even computationally and even with a broadcast channel), are known in the case of no honest majority. Negative results on fairness include the early work of Cleve [13], who showed that fair coin-tossing is impossible when $n/2$ out of n parties are fail-stop (i.e. behave in an honest-but-curious manner with the exception that they may abort early). In the 2-party case, non-trivial functions that can be computed fairly *without* honest majority, were first discovered in the seminal work of Gordon et al. [19]. By now, the 2-party setting is well-understood, with a full characterization of the necessary and sufficient conditions for fair computation of large classes of functionalities [2,3].

In this paper we focus on the n-party case, where $n = \text{poly}(\lambda)$ is any polynomial in λ, the security parameter. We will begin by considering threshold adversaries, these are adversaries who may corrupt up to some threshold th number of parties. In this case, Cleve's result [13] tells us that it is impossible to achieve fairness for all functionalities when $th \geq n/2$.

Threshold Adversaries. The relevant prior works that we are aware of are those of Gordon and Katz [21] and Asharov et al. [3]. Gordon and Katz [21] present fair protocols for 3-party majority and for the OR function (and by symmetry for the AND function) for any polynomial n number of parties and $n - 1$ or fewer corruptions. Asharov et al. [3] present n-party protocols with up to $n/2$ corruptions for functions F for which every $n/2$-size partition can be computed fairly in the 2-party setting. We emphasize, however, that the protocol of Asharov et al. [3] only scales to $O(\log \lambda)$ number of parties, regardless of the efficiency of the underlying fair 2-party protocol employed. Moreover, extending their results to more than $n/2$ out of n corruptions was considered an open problem in their work. Thus, prior to our work, AND and OR were the only functionalities for which efficient protocols achieving fairness with no honest majority for any $n = \text{poly}(\lambda)$ parties were known.

We also consider non-threshold adversaries. Specifically, we consider adversarial structures $\mathcal{A}_{\text{adv}}$ for which it is known to be impossible to achieve fairness for all functionalities. We ask whether for such adversarial structures there exist non-trivial functions that can be computed fairly.

Background on MPC with General Adversarial Structures. An adversarial structure $\mathcal{A}_{\text{adv}}$ on a set $[n]$—corresponding to n parties $P_1, \ldots, P_n$—is a monotone collection of non-empty sets S. We say that an MPC protocol is secure with fairness for adversarial structure $\mathcal{A}_{\text{adv}}$ if it is secure with fairness under any set of corruptions $S \in \mathcal{A}_{\text{adv}}$. In the seminal works of Hirt and Maurer [26,27], they defined a set of adversarial structures $Q^{(2)}$, which consists of adversarial structures $\mathcal{A}_{\sf adv}$ for which no two sets in $\mathcal{A}_{\sf adv}$ cover $[n]$. They presented an (inefficient) information-theoretic secure protocol for fail-stop adversaries for adversarial structures $Q^{(2)}$. They also gave a simple argument that it is impossible to achieve (even computational) fairness for adversarial structures not in $Q^{(2)}$ using the classical result of Cleve [13].

Fairness for $(\mathcal{A}_{\sf adv}, F)$-*pairs.* In this work, we initiate the research direction of achieving MPC protocols with fairness against—possibly non-threshold—adversarial structures $\mathcal{A}_{\sf adv}$ that are not in $Q^{(2)}$. While for any adversarial structure $\mathcal{A}_{\sf adv} \notin Q^{(2)}$, it is impossible (even computationally) to achieve MPC with fairness for all functionalities F, there can be some functionalities F for which it is possible to achieve MPC with fairness. We will investigate pairs of functionalities and adversarial structures $(\mathcal{A}_{\sf adv}, F)$ for which is it possible to achieve fairness in the multiparty setting. To the best of our knowledge, prior work on complete fairness in multiparty computation for adversarial structures outside $Q^{(2)}$ has considered only threshold adversarial structures.

1.1   Our Results

Consider a symmetric Boolean function[1] $F(\boldsymbol{w}) = F(\boldsymbol{x}, \boldsymbol{y})$, where $\boldsymbol{w} = \boldsymbol{x}\|\boldsymbol{y}$ and $\boldsymbol{x}, \boldsymbol{y} \in \{0,1\}^{n/2}$. We consider n-party MPC protocols for computing the function F. Note that since F is symmetric, there exists a two-input function f such that $F(\boldsymbol{x}, \boldsymbol{y}) = f_{n/2,n/2}(\sum_{i=1}^{n/2} x_i, \sum_{i=1}^{n/2} y_i)$. In our first result, we present a fair MPC protocol for functionalities F that are symmetric and for which the corresponding $f_{n/2,n/2}$ can be computed fairly in the 2-party setting. Importantly, our protocol handles any polynomial $n = \text{poly}(\lambda)$ number of parties (polynomial in security parameter λ) and is secure against $n/2$ or fewer corruptions. Recall that Asharov et al. [3] gave a transformation from fair 2-party protocols to fair n-party protocols, secure against $n/2$ or fewer corruptions. Their transformation, however, requires running the underlying protocol with all possible subsets $S \subseteq [n]$ of size $|S| = n/2$ playing the part of the two parties in the underlying 2-party protocol. This means that their protocol can only handle a number of parties n that is at most logarithmic in the security parameter $n = O(\log(\lambda))$. In this work, we show how to extend their construction to any number of parties n that is polynomial in the security parameter $n = \text{poly}(\lambda)$. However, the extension applies only to symmetric Boolean functions.

Theorem 1 (Informal). *Let* $F : \{0,1\}^n \to \{0,1\}$ *be a symmetric function, such that there is an efficient protocol for computing* $f_{n/2,n/2}$ *fairly in the two-party setting. Then for any* $n = \text{poly}(\lambda)$, *there is an efficient protocol for computing* F *fairly in the* n-*party setting with up to* $n/2$ *corruptions.*

We extend the above result to more general, non-threshold, adversarial structures outside of $Q^{(2)}$, which may include corrupted sets of parties of

---

[1] In this context, we mean a Boolean function whose output depends only on the number of ones in the input. See [36], Def. 2.8.

size greater than $n/2$. For symmetric F and any $n' \in [n-1]$, we consider $F(\boldsymbol{x}, \boldsymbol{y}) = f_{n',n-n'}(\sum_{i=1}^{n'} x_i, \sum_{i=1}^{n-n'} y_i)$, and require that for all $n' \in [n-1]$ there is an efficient protocol computing $f_{n',n-n'}$ fairly in the two-party setting. For any such F, we define a corresponding set of adversarial structures $Q^{(F)}$. Informally, $Q^{(F)}$ contains adversarial structures $\mathcal{A}_{\mathsf{adv}}$ such that $\mathcal{A}_{\mathsf{adv}}$ can be partitioned into $\mathcal{A}_{\mathsf{adv},1} \in Q^{(2)}$ and $\mathcal{A}_{\mathsf{adv},2} \notin Q^{(2)}$ such that for any pair of distinct sets $(T, T') \in \mathcal{A}_{\mathsf{adv},2}$, $T' \not\subseteq T$. Additionally, we require certain efficient secret sharing schemes corresponding to $\mathcal{A}_{\mathsf{adv},1}$ and $\mathcal{A}_{\mathsf{adv},2}$. See the full version for a formal definition of $Q^{(F)}$.

Theorem 2 (Informal). *Let $F : \{0,1\}^n \to \{0,1\}$ be a symmetric function, such that there is an efficient protocol for computing $f_{n',n-n'}$ fairly in the two-party setting for all $n' \in [n-1]$. Let $Q^{(F)}$ be defined as above. Then for any $n = \mathrm{poly}(\lambda)$, there is an efficient protocol for computing F fairly in the n-party setting under any adversarial structure $\mathcal{A}_{\mathsf{adv}} \in Q^{(F)}$.*

As an additional result of interest, we show that (ignoring efficiency requirements for the underlying secret-sharing schemes) any *projective plane* can be used to construct a non-threshold adversarial structure in $Q^{(F)}$. See the full version for additional details.

In our second main result, we present a fair MPC protocol for the majority function, for any polynomial $n = \mathrm{poly}(\lambda)$ number of parties, and $n/2+1$ or fewer corruptions.

Theorem 3 (Informal). *There is an efficient protocol for computing n-party Majority fairly for any $n = \mathrm{poly}(\lambda)$ (s.t. $n \geq 8$) with $n/2+1$ or fewer corruptions.*

The construction can be straightforwardly extended to work for $n/2 + c$ or fewer corruptions, where c is a constant.

As before, we extend the result to more general, non-threshold, adversarial structures outside of $Q^{(2)}$, by defining a set of adversarial structures $Q^{(\mathsf{Maj})}$. Informally, $Q^{(\mathsf{Maj})}$ contains adversarial structures $\mathcal{A}_{\mathsf{adv}}$ such that $\mathcal{A}_{\mathsf{adv}}$ can be partitioned into $\mathcal{A}_{\mathsf{adv},1} \in Q^{(2)}$ and $\mathcal{A}_{\mathsf{adv},2} \notin Q^{(2)}$ such that for any pair of distinct sets $(T, T') \in \mathcal{A}_{\mathsf{adv},2}$ such that $T' \subseteq T$, it is the case that $|T \backslash T'| \leq c$. Additionally, we require certain efficient secret sharing schemes corresponding to $\mathcal{A}_{\mathsf{adv},1} \in Q^{(2)}$ and $\mathcal{A}_{\mathsf{adv},2} \notin Q^{(2)}$. See the full version for a formal definition of $Q^{(\mathsf{Maj})}$.

Theorem 4 (Informal). *There is an efficient protocol for computing n-party Majority fairly for any $n = \mathrm{poly}(\lambda)$ under every adversarial structure $\mathcal{A}_{\mathsf{adv}} \in Q^{\mathsf{Maj}}$.*

As an additional result of interest, we show that (ignoring efficiency requirements for the underlying secret-sharing schemes) starting from an appropriate type of *combinatorial design* and adding certain sets to it, we obtain a non-threshold adversarial structure in $Q^{(\mathsf{Maj})}$. See the full version for additional details.

1.2   Technical Overview

Half (n/2) or Fewer Corruptions. Recall that [3] showed that, for $n = O(\log(\lambda))$ number of parties, a function $F(x_1, \ldots, x_n)$ is computable with fairness under $n/2$ corruptions if and only if for every partition (S_L, S_R) of $[n]$ of size $n/2$, $F([x_i]_{i \in S_L}, [x_i]_{i \in S_R})$ is computable with complete fairness in the two party setting, where one party holds input $[x_i]_{i \in S_L}$ and the other holds input $[x_i]_{i \in S_R}$. We begin by re-casting the protocol of [3] in a player-simulation model (similar to Hirt and Maurer [26,27]). The protocol of [3] considers all possible 2-partition (S_L, S_R) of $[n]$ of size $n/2$ (where S_L always contains 1) and for each partition, parties $P_i, i \in S_L$ simulate virtual party P_L and parties $P_i, i \in S_R$ simulate virtual party P_R in the fair two party protocol Π_F for functionality $F([x_i]_{i \in S_L}, [x_i]_{i \in S_R})$ that exists by assumption. WLOG, we can take the states of P_L and P_R in round r of Π_F to simply consist of "backup values" a^r, b^r, respectively. For simplicity, we first construct an n-party protocol in a "trusted dealer" model (later we will show how to get rid of the assumption). In each round r, the dealer secret shares the backup values of each virtual party P_L (resp. P_R) across the corresponding parties in S_L (resp. S_R). This is referred to as the *inner* secret sharing scheme in [3]. If at any time, all the real parties simulating a certain virtual party (say P_L) abort, the dealer stops handing out shares and the remaining real parties reconstruct virtual P_R's state to obtain the corresponding backup value. The above description relies on the fact that there are at most $n/2$ corruptions, since if exactly $n/2$ parties corresponding to some virtual party P_L abort there is a uniquely identifiable corresponding virtual party P_R, simulated by exactly the remaining set of $n/2$ parties (all of whom are honest). The remaining parties can therefore identify P_R and compute the correct backup value. On the other hand, if the protocol completes, any set of parties of size $n/2$ or more can reconstruct the correct value, since all subsets of size $n/2$ receive the output of the functionality in the final round. To implement the dealer and ensure that the protocol continues if less than $n/2$ parties abort, [3] additionally perform an $(n/2 + 1)$-out-of-n secret sharing of each real party's state during the preprocessing, called the *outer secret sharing*. In each round, the parties send their share of the outer-secret sharing to each party. In case at most $n/2 - 1$ parties abort, the remaining parties can continue the protocol by simulating the aborting parties using the $(n/2 + 1)$-out-of-n secret sharing. The number of simulated sub-protocols is essentially $\binom{n}{n/2} \approx 2^n/\sqrt{n}$. Thus, they can only handle at most $n = O(\log(\lambda))$ number of parties, where λ is security parameter.

In our first result we show that the above paradigm can be modified to work for symmetric functions $F : \{0,1\}^n \to \{0,1\}$ without requiring the blowup of running the protocol across each possible subset. Since F is symmetric, its value at all inputs is equivalent to the output of some $f_{n/2,n/2} : \{0, \ldots, n/2\} \times \{0, \ldots, n/2\} \to \{0,1\}$. Let us assume that there is a fair protocol $\Pi_{f_{n/2,n/2}}$ for computing $f_{n/2,n/2}$. We describe the constructed fair protocol for n-party functionality F in the "trusted dealer" setting: The dealer receives all the parties' inputs $x = x_1, \ldots, x_n$ and computes $N = \sum_{i=1}^{n} x_i$. For every $z \in \{0, \ldots, n/2\}$, the dealer runs protocol $\Pi_{f_{n/2,n/2}}(z, N-z)$ and $\Pi_{f_{n/2,n/2}}(N-z, z)$ "in the head" to obtain backup values for each party and each round.[2] Specifically, for virtual party P_L (resp. P_R), its share when running with input z (resp. $N-z$) in the r-th round is denoted $a^{r,z,N-z}$ (resp. $b^{r,z,N-z}$). We now use an appropriate type of secret sharing scheme to share $a^{r,z,N-z}$ (resp. $b^{r,z,N-z}$), which ensures that a set of corrupted parties can open only the backup values corresponding to *one of the virtual parties' views* in a *single execution* of the (at most) $n/2+1$ executions of the underlying 2PC protocol (i.e. corresponding to the view of P_L or P_R in a single $(z, N-z)$ pair). This is done by defining an augmented set $[n] \times \{0,1\}$ and defining access structures over this set. Specifically, a party P_i holding input bit b, will correspond to the element $(i, b) \in [n] \times \{0,1\}$. Thus, parties along with their inputs correspond to subsets S^+ of $[n] \times \{0,1\}$, and a share that a party receives from the dealer depends both on its index i as well as its input b. Let $S^0 := \{(i, 0) : i \in [n]\}$ and $S^1 := \{(i, 1) : i \in [n]\}$. We will use a secret sharing scheme to share $a^{r,z,N-z}$ (resp. $b^{r,z,N-z}$) so that its value can be reconstructed by any set S^+ that consists of party P_1 holding either input 0 or 1 (resp. does not include party P_1), z (resp. $N-z$) parties holding input 1 (i.e. $|S^+ \cap S^1| \geq z$, resp. $|S^+ \cap S^1| \geq N-z$) and $n/2 - z$ (resp. $n/2 - (N-z)$) parties holding input 0 (i.e. $|S^+ \cap S^0| \geq n/2 - z$, resp. $|S^+ \cap S^0| \geq n/2 - (N-z)$). If exactly $n/2$ parties abort, the remaining honest parties output the "backup" value corresponding to *the remaining party* in *the same* underlying protocol execution. E.g., if a set of $n/2$ parties, including P_1, holding z number of 1's, abort, the remaining parties can open $b^{r,z,N-z}$, since if the corrupt parties hold z number of 1's, the honest parties must hold $N-z$ number of 1's and $n/2 - (N-z)$ number of 0's. On the other hand, if less than $n/2$ parties abort, the *outer* secret sharing scheme is used to ensure that all the honest parties continue to receive their shares in each round.

Difficulty of a Generic Transformation for more than $n/2$ Corruptions. In the following, we provide some intuition on the difficulty of extending the above protocol to more than $n/2$ corruptions. We do not make any formal claims here. For concreteness, let us assume we want to handle $n/2 + 1$ corruptions. First, we must ensure that if $n/2 + 1$ parties abort, the remaining parties can output some backup value from the underlying protocol, as otherwise there is no hope of obtaining a fair protocol. But this means that any set of $n/2 - 1$ parties must be able to reconstruct a view from the underlying execution, which means that the set of $n/2 + 1$ corrupted parties will be able to reconstruct *multiple* views (since there are multiple subsets of size $n/2 - 1$—with distinct values of z— among the set of $n/2 + 1$ corrupted parties, and each must be able to open an underlying view). When using a generic protocol, it is not clear how to argue that if the underlying protocol is fair when a party sees a single view, it is still fair when a party sees multiple views of the protocol running in parallel with *correlated inputs*. Another difficulty is that if less than $n/2+1$ parties abort—say

---

[2] If $N - z$ is an invalid input (i.e. $N - z \notin \{0, \ldots, n/2\}$), then the dealer simply uses dummy values.

$n/2-1$ parties abort—then the remaining parties do not necessarily know which backup value to output. As before, there are multiple subsets of size $n/2 - 1$— with distinct values of z—among the set of $n/2 + 1$ remaining parties, and each may correspond to a different backup value. Further, note that the outer secret sharing can no longer be used when $n/2 - 1$ (or more) parties abort, since if the outer secret sharing scheme can be reconstructed by $n/2+1$ or fewer parties, then the set of corrupt parties can recover backup values for round r before round r is executed, thus negating the fairness guarantees of the underlying protocol. Our solution for $n/2 + 1$ or fewer corruptions will resolve each of these problems, but will use special properties of a specific protocol, and will not work generically for any underlying fair-2-PC protocol.

Direct Construction for Majority with $n/2 + 1$ or Fewer Corruptions. We next present our protocol for n-party computation of Maj assuming at most $n/2 + 1$ corruptions. As discussed above, the generic transformation techniques no longer work. Therefore, we extend the two-party protocol of Gordon et al. [19] and the analysis of Asharov et al. [2] to our setting. Specifically, recall that in the 2-party protocol of Gordon et al. [19], the dealer chooses a designated round r^*, drawn from a geometric distribution with parameter α (and with all but negligible probability is assured that $r^* \leq$ rounds, where rounds $= \omega(\log(\lambda)) \cdot 1/\alpha$ is the number of rounds in the protocol) in which to begin releasing the correct output of the functionality. In the rounds previous to this, each party receives the output of the functionality evaluated with its own input and a randomly chosen input for the other party. Now, in the n party case, we set $R := \{1, 2, 3\}$. In each round r, the dealer computes backup values $a^{r,R',n',z}$ for each $R' \subseteq R$, $n' \in \{n/2-1, n/2, n/2+1\}$ and each $z \in \{0, \ldots, n'\}$. For $r < r^*$, each value $a^{r,R',n',z}$ is chosen as $f_{n',n-n'}(z, \hat{x})$, where $\hat{x}$ is chosen uniformly from $\{0, \ldots, n-n'\}$, and $f_{n',n-n'}$ outputs 1 when the sum of its inputs is at least $n/2+1$. For $r \geq r^*$, each value $a^{r,R',n',z}$ is set to $f_{n',n-n'}(x, y)$, where x, y are the inputs of the corrupted and uncorrupted parties, respectively. Each $a^{r,R',n',z}$ is shared so that it can be opened by any set S that has a subset W of size n' such that $W \cap R = R'$ and has a subset W' of size n' consisting of z parties holding a 1 input and $n' - z$ parties holding a 0 input. We observe than any set of corrupt parties of size at most $n/2 + 1$ can open at most a constant number, deg, of backup values. Furthermore, if $n/2 - 1$ or more parties abort in round r, the remaining set of parties, S', which has size $n' \in \{n/2-1, n/2, n/2+1\}$ and for which $S' \cap R = R'$, run a secure computation protocol (with fairness and guaranteed output delivery, since when $n \geq 8$ we have an honest majority among the remaining parties) to recover $a^{r-1,R',n',z}$ for the appropriate values of R', n', and z. The set R' is needed since in the security proof, we will argue that the backup value opened by the remaining parties cannot be opened by the set of corrupt parties before aborting. If less than $n/2 - 1$ parties abort, then each remaining party can still recover its share in each round using the outer secret sharing scheme and so the protocol continues. By setting α correctly, the ideal adversary is able to skew the output appropriately (as in [19]), even though the corrupt parties see multiple random values in rounds $r < r^*$. Intuitively, this comes from the fact that the real adversary will with some $1/\text{poly}(n)$ probability obtain the same view in round r when $r = r^*$ or when $r < r^*$. In the case $r = r^*$, the honest parties output their backup value (which is distributed as described above) in the real world, but always output the correct output value in the ideal world. In the case that $r < r^*$, the honest parties still output their backup value in the real world. However, the simulator in the ideal world can lie about the corrupted parties' inputs and submit values from a carefully constructed distribution to the ideal functionality, since the ideal functionality has not yet been called in the simulation (it is only called in round r^*). Thus, it is possible that for a fixed adversarial view, the distribution of outputs of the honest parties is the same in the real and ideal worlds. To analyze the resulting distributions in the real and ideal world, we follow the techniques of Asharov [2], who explicitly computes the required probabilities as a vector and finds the sufficient conditions so that this vector falls within the convex hull of a set of vectors corresponding to the rows of the truthtable. Unfortunately, the proof of Asharov [2] works only for constant-size domain. Since we want to extend our case to any polynomial number of parties n, we necessarily require a polynomial domain (since the domain will be exactly $\{0, \ldots, n\}$). Specifically, Asharov's technique [2] fixed the domain size to be constant and used existence theorems to prove that α can be set sufficiently small so that the vector is contained in the convex hull. Instead, we consider the spectral norm of the matrix corresponding to the inverse of $M_{\tilde{f}}^{\pm}$, where $M_{\tilde{f}}$ is the truthtable corresponding to a function $\tilde{f}$ that is closely related to $f_{n',n-n'}$, and $M_{\tilde{f}}^{\pm}$ is equal to $M_{\tilde{f}}$ concatenated with a column of 1's, and show that it is upper bounded by a constant. This allows us to achieve the desired result. We note that the techniques outlined above can be straightforwardly extended to the case of $n/2 + c$ corruptions, where c is a fixed constant.

Extending to more General Adversarial Structures. Secret sharing schemes are used in two ways in the results for threshold adversarial structures described above: (1) The *outer secret sharing scheme*, which ensures that when certain sets of parties abort, the protocol can continue. We require that no set from the adversarial structure is an authorized set for the access structure corresponding to this scheme. (2) The *inner secret sharing scheme*, which ensures that if the surviving parties cannot continue the protocol using the outer secret sharing scheme, they can reconstruct a backup value using this scheme. We can no longer require that no set from the adversarial structure is an authorized set for the access structure corresponding to this scheme. Instead, we merely limit the number of instances of the inner secret sharing scheme that can be opened by the corrupt parties.

To achieve this, we view an arbitrary adversarial structure as the union of a $Q^{(2)}$ adversarial structure, $\mathcal{A}_{\mathsf{adv},1}$ and a non-$Q^{(2)}$ adversarial structure, $\mathcal{A}_{\mathsf{adv},2}$. The outer secret sharing scheme will correspond to access structure, $\mathcal{A}_{\mathsf{hon},1}$, which is equal to the complement of $\mathcal{A}_{\mathsf{adv},1}$. For the inner secret sharing scheme, we consider $\mathcal{A}_{\mathsf{hon},2} = \mathcal{A}_{\mathsf{adv},2}$ and we partition $\mathcal{A}_{\mathsf{hon},2}$ according to the size n' of the authorized sets, yielding sets $\mathcal{A}_{\mathsf{hon},2}^{n'}$. We then obtain monotone access structures

$\mathcal{A}_{\mathsf{hon},2}^{n',+}$ for all $n' \in [n]$, consisting of $\mathcal{A}_{\mathsf{hon},2}^{n'}$ and all supersets of sets in $\mathcal{A}_{\mathsf{hon},2}^{n'}$. We then construct a secret sharing scheme for each n' and each $z \in \{0, \ldots, n'\}$, which allows a set of parties to reconstruct the secret if the set of parties is contained in $\mathcal{A}_{\mathsf{hon},2}^{n',+}$ and the set of parties includes z number of parties holding a 1 and $n' - z$ number of parties holding a 0. For the first result (corresponding to fair computation of symmetric functions) we require that $\mathcal{A}_{\mathsf{adv},2}$ does not contain any two sets T, T' such that $T' \subsetneq T$. For the second result (corresponding to fair computation of Maj) we require that for any two sets $T, T' \in \mathcal{A}_{\mathsf{adv},2}$ if T is a superset of T', it can only contain c additional elements, where c is a constant.

1.3 Related Work

The 2-party Setting. Subsequent to the seminal paper of Gordon et al. [19], a large body of work has been dedicated to understanding which functionalities can be computed fairly in the two-party setting. Various works, culminating in a full characterization for symmetric, constant-size-domain functionalities, include [2,3].

The n-party Setting. Hirt and Maurer [26,27] characterized the set of access structures that are necessary and sufficient for fair n-party computation of *all functionalities*, and dubbed this set $Q^{(2)}$. The question remained of whether there are non-trivial functionalities that can be computed fairly for adversarial structures outside of $Q^{(2)}$. In particular, the works of [21] and [3], which have already been discussed above, considered threshold access structures outside of $Q^{(2)}$.

Partial Fairness and Other Notions. Another line of works has considered achieving partial fairness (also called $1/p$-fairness) guarantees for large classes of functionalities, even when there is no honest majority. Specifically, the goal is to obtain protocols for which the real and ideal world are distinguishable by at most $1/p$, for some polynomial $p = p(\lambda)$. Partial fairness has been studied in both the 2-party and multiparty setting [7,9,22]. Note that our focus in the current work is to achieve "complete" fairness, where the real and ideal world are computationally indistinguishable. "Best of both worlds" security has also been studied–where protocols are required to achieve fairness in the case of honest majority and security-with-abort in the case of honest minority [7,28,29]. We also mention other desirable security properties related to fairness that have been considered in the literature such as *guaranteed output delivery* [14,23] and *security with identifiable abort* [30,31].

Partial Fairness for Coin-Tossing. For the special case of coin-tossing, it is known by the classical result of Cleve [13] that complete fairness is impossible. However, there are several results in the two-party and multi-party settings that deal with achieving partial fairness—i.e. bias of $1/p$—for the best possible p [1,6,8,11,34,35].

Lower Bounds. Lower bounds on number of rounds or computational assumptions necessary to achieve (partially) fair protocols have also been studied [15,16,24,25]. Complete primitives for fairness and primitives that imply secure coin-tossing were studied in [4,20]. Further works have elucidated properties of protocols necessary to achieve fairness [33].

2   Notation, Definitions and Preliminaries

Definitions of MPC with full security (i.e. fairness) and security-with-abort are deferred to the full version. We follow [5] for the definitions of access structures and secret sharing schemes. Given a set $S \subseteq [n]$, denote by $\overline{S} := [n] \setminus S$ and by $\mathcal{P}(S)$ the power set of S.

Useful Access Structures. We consider access structures over the set $[n]$, as well as the set $[n] \times \{0, 1\}$. Let $S^0 := [n] \times \{0\}$ and $S^1 := [n] \times \{1\}$. Access structure $\mathcal{A}_{a,z,n'-z,2n}$, for $n' \in [n]$ and $z \in \{0, \dots, n'\}$, consists of sets $S^+ \subseteq [n] \times \{0, 1\}$ with corresponding $S := \{i : (i, 0) \text{ or } (i, 1) \in S^+\}$ that satisfy all of the following: (1) $1 \in S$; (2) $|S^+ \cap S^1| \geq z$; (3) $|S^+ \cap S^0| \geq n' - z$.

Access structure $\mathcal{A}_{b,z,n'-z,2n}$, for $n' \in [n]$ and $z \in \{0, \dots, n'\}$, consists of sets $S^+ \subseteq [n] \times \{0, 1\}$ with corresponding $S := \{i : (i, 0) \text{ or } (i, 1) \in S^+\}$ that satisfy all of the following: (1) $1 \notin S$; (2) $|S^+ \cap S^1| \geq z$; (3) $|S^+ \cap S^0| \geq n' - z$.

More generally, let R be a set of distinguished elements of $[n]$. Let $R' \subseteq R$ and let $R'' = R \setminus R'$. Access structure $\mathcal{A}_{R,R',z,n',2n}$, for $R' \subseteq R$, $n' \in [n]$ and $z \in \{0, \dots, n'\}$, consists of sets $S^+ \subseteq [n] \times \{0, 1\}$ with corresponding $S := \{i : (i, 0) \text{ or } (i, 1) \in S^+\}$ that satisfy all of the following: (1) $R' \subseteq S$; (2) $R'' \cap S = \emptyset$; (3) $|S^+ \cap S^1| \geq z$; (4) $|S^+ \cap S^0| \geq n' - z$.

See full version for constructions.

3   Symmetric Functions and $n/2$ Corruptions

Let $F : \{0, 1\}^{n/2} \times \{0, 1\}^{n/2} \rightarrow \{0, 1\}$ be a symmetric Boolean function. Then we have that for all $x \in \{0, 1\}^{n/2}$ and $y \in \{0, 1\}^{n/2}$, $F(x, y) = f_{n/2,n/2}(\sum_{i=1}^{n/2} x_i, \sum_{i=1}^{n/2} y_i)$, for some $f_{n/2,n/2}$. Assume that $f_{n/2,n/2} : \{0, \dots, n/2\} \times \{0, \dots, n/2\}$ can be fairly computed in the two-party setting and let $\Pi_{f_{n/2,n/2}}$ denote the two-party protocol (with parties P_L, P_R) that fairly computes $f_{n/2,n/2}(x, y)$. For $x, y \in \{0, \dots, n/2\}$, let $\Pi_{f_{n/2,n/2}}(x, y)$ denote an execution of $\Pi_{f_{n/2,n/2}}$, where P_L has input x and P_R has input y. Let $a_{f_{n/2,n/2}}^{x,y,r}$ denote the backup value of P_L in the r-th round of an execution of $\Pi_{f_{n/2,n/2}}(x, y)$ and let $b_{f_{n/2,n/2}}^{x,y,r}$ denote the backup value of P_R in the r-th round of the same execution of $\Pi_{f_{n/2,n/2}}(x, y)$. In the following, p is set to $p = 2 \cdot (n/2 + 1)$.

Theorem 5. *Let F, $f_{n/2,n/2}$ be as above. Assume there is an efficient protocol for computing $f_{n/2,n/2}$ fairly in the two-party setting. Then for any $n = \text{poly}(\lambda)$, the protocol presented in Fig. 1 (and Fig. 2) is an efficient protocol for computing F fairly in the n-party setting with $n/2$ or fewer corruptions.*

The protocol in Fig. 1 uses a secret sharing scheme for access structure $\mathcal{A}_{a,z,n/2-z,2n}$ and $\mathcal{A}_{b,z,n/2-z,2n}$, defined in Sect. 2.

1. The parties $P_1, \ldots, P_n$ hand their inputs, denoted $\boldsymbol{x} =_1, \ldots, _n \in \{0,1\}^n$, respectively, to the dealer. If a party P_j does not send an input, then the dealer selects $_j \in \{0,1\}$ uniformly at random. If half of the parties do not send an input, then the dealer sends $f_{n/2,n/2}(\sum_{i=1}^{n/2} i, \sum_{i=n/2+1}^{n} i)$ to the honest parties and halts. Let $N := \sum_{i=1}^{n} i$.

2. The dealer computes for $z \in \{\max\{0, N - n/2\}, \ldots, \min\{N, n/2\}\}$, $r \in$ [rounds], the backup outputs $a^{z,r} := a_{f_{n/2,n/2}}^{z,N-z,r} || 0^\lambda$, $b^{N-z,r} := b_{f_{n/2,n/2}}^{z,N-z,r} || 0^\lambda$ for an execution of $\Pi_{f_{n/2,n/2}}(z, N - z)$. The dealer also sends back to each P_i an authentication of its input $_i$.

3. If $N > n/2$, then for $z \in \{0, \ldots, N - n/2 - 1\}$, $r \in$ [rounds] set $a^{z,r} := \mathbf{0}$, $b^{z,r} := \mathbf{0}$.

4. If $N < n/2$, then for $z \in \{N+1, \ldots, n/2\}$, $r \in$ [rounds], set $a^{z,r} := \mathbf{0}$, $b^{r,z} := \mathbf{0}$.

5. For $r \in$ [rounds],

   (a) For $z \in \{0, \ldots, n/2\}$, the dealer secret shares $a^{z,r}$ using access structure $\mathcal{A}_{a,z,n/2-z,2n}$, producing (authenticated) shares $[\tilde{\boldsymbol{s}}_i^{b,z,r}]_{b \in \{0,1\}, i \in [n]}$. Each party P_i holding input b receives shares $[\tilde{\boldsymbol{s}}_i^{b,z,r}]_{z \in \{0,\ldots,n/2\}}$. If $n/2$ parties abort, including P_1, then the remaining parties (corresponding to set S) submit their (authenticated) inputs and shares from round $r - 1$ to $F_{\mathrm{Recon},S,p}^{\mathrm{th},n/2}$, output whatever it outputs and halt. Note that all parties in S are honest.

   (b) For $z \in \{0, \ldots, n/2\}$ the dealer secret shares $b^{r,z}$ using access structure $\mathcal{A}_{b,z,n/2-z}$, producing (authenticated) shares $[\tilde{\boldsymbol{s}}_i^{b,z,r}]_{b \in \{0,1\}, i \in [n]}$. Each party P_i holding input b receives shares $[\tilde{\boldsymbol{s}}_i^{b,z,r}]_{z \in \{0,\ldots,n/2\}}$. If $n/2$ parties abort, not including P_1, then the remaining parties (corresponding to set S) submit their (authenticated) inputs and shares from round r to ideal functionality $F_{\mathrm{Recon},S,p}^{\mathrm{th},n/2}$, output whatever it outputs and halt. Note that all parties in S are honest.

6. Otherwise, the remaining parties (set S) submit their (authenticated) inputs and shares to ideal functionality $F_{\mathrm{Recon},S,p}^{\mathrm{th},n/2}$, output whatever it outputs and halt. If some set $\widetilde{S}$ of parties abort, preventing the remaining parties from receiving output, the remaining parties: $S := S \setminus \widetilde{S}$ go back to the beginning of Step 6 and resubmit their shares to $F_{\mathrm{Recon},S,p}^{\mathrm{th},n/2}$. This continues until the honest parties receive the output from the ideal functionality.

Fig. 1. Fair, efficient, multiparty computation of F with n parties and $n/2$ or fewer corruptions.

Functionality $F_{\text{Recon},S,p}^{\text{th},n/2}$

- **Input:** Set $S \subseteq [n]$ of size n'. For $i \in S$, the i-th party's input is (authenticated) bit $_i$ and p shares $[\tilde{s}_i^k]_{k \in [p]}$. Let S' be the set of parties who submit input shares that are properly authenticated. We have that $|S'| \geq n/2$. We also assume WLOG that $|S'| = n/2$. If it is greater, then we just compute with some subset of the input shares. Let $z := \sum_{i \in S'} {}_i$.
- **Function Computation:** If $1 \in S'$ (resp. $1 \notin S'$), then for $k \in [p]$, run reconstruction algorithm **Recon** for secret-sharing scheme $\mathcal{A}_{a,z,n'-z,2n}$ (resp. $\mathcal{A}_{b,z,n'-z,2n}$) with input shares $[\tilde{s}_i^k]_{i \in S'}$ to obtain candidates $[\text{secret}^k = \text{secret}_1^k \| \text{secret}_2^k]_{k \in [p]}$.
- **Output:** secret_1^k corresponding to the first $k \in [p]$ such that $\text{secret}_2^k = 0^\lambda$.

Fig. 2. Reconstruction functionality with respect to p sets of secret shares.

Proof. Let $T \subseteq [n], |T| = n/2$ denote the set of corrupt parties. Assume WLOG that $1 \in T$. Sim applies the simulator $\text{Sim}_{f_{n/2,n/2}}$ of the two-party protocol $\Pi_{f_{n/2,n/2}}$.

- Sim constructs the following adversary $A_{f_{n/2,n/2}}$ for $\Pi_{f_{n/2,n/2}}$, playing the same role as A.
  - $A_{f_{n/2,n/2}}$ invokes A expecting its inputs $\boldsymbol{x}$.
  - $A_{f_{n/2,n/2}}$ sends inputs $x = \sum_{i \in T} x_i$ to the dealer of Π_f.
  - For $r = 1, \ldots,$ rounds, upon receiving backup value a^r, set $a^{x,r} = a^r \| 0^\lambda$ and $a^{z,r} = \boldsymbol{0}$ for $z \in \{0, \ldots, n/2\} \setminus \{x\}$. For $z \in \{0, \ldots, n/2\}$, secret share $a^{z,r}$ using access structure $\mathcal{A}_{a,z,n/2-z,2n}$, producing shares $[\tilde{s}_i^{b,z,r}]_{b \in \{0,1\}, i \in [n]}$. Each party P_i holding input b receives shares $[\tilde{s}_i^{b,z,r}]_{z \in \{0,\ldots,n/2\}}$.
  - If all the parties in T abort, then $A_{f_{n/2,n/2}}$ aborts, otherwise it continues.
  - If the final round rounds completes, $A_{f_{n/2,n/2}}$ submits shares for all remaining parties in T to the ideal functionality and simulates an output of out in return.
- Let $\text{Sim}_{f_{n/2,n/2}}$ be the simulator for $A_{f_{n/2,n/2}}$ in the hybrid model.
- The simulator Sim interacts with the two-party protocol simulator $\text{Sim}_{f_{n/2,n/2}}$ by invoking it on adversary A_f with input x. It then receives a simulated view for $A_{f_{n/2,n/2}}$, containing its random coins and backup outputs. Having received this view of $A_{f_{n/2,n/2}}$, the simulator S_f can extract from it the view of A in this execution, as it is implied by the view of $A_{f_{n/2,n/2}}$. Specifically, the randomness $A_{f_{n/2,n/2}}$ uses to share different secrets determines the shares that the corrupted parties see. If $A_{f_{n/2,n/2}}$ does not abort before the final reconstruction, $\text{Sim}_{f_{n/2,n/2}}$ obtains from $A_{f_{n/2,n/2}}$'s view any inputs to the functionality $F_{\text{Recon},S,p}^{\text{th},n/2}$. It uses the output out contained in the view (since the last round was reached) to simulate the output of the ideal functionality $F_{\text{Recon},S,p}^{\text{th},n/2}$. If some parties abort and the remaining parties re-submit their

inputs to the ideal functionality, $\mathrm{Sim}_{f_{n/2,n/2}}$ can still use out to simulate the output each time.

3.1 Implementing the Dealer and $F_{\mathrm{Recon},S,p}^{\mathrm{th},n/2}$

This is done similarly to Asharov et al. [3] and our exposition follows theirs. Following [3,7,8], we eliminate the trusted on-line dealer of our multiparty protocols in a few steps using a few layers of secret-sharing schemes. In the first step, we convert the on-line dealer to an off-line dealer. That is, we construct a protocol in which the dealer sends only one message to each party in an initialization stage; the parties then interact in rounds using a broadcast channel (without the dealer) and in each sub-round of round i each party learns its shares of the r-th round. Specifically, in round r, party P_j learns a share in a secret sharing scheme for access structure $\mathcal{A}_{a,z,n/2-z,2n}$, $\mathcal{A}_{b,z,n/2-z,2n}$, for every $z \in \{0,\ldots,n/2\}$ (we call these shares P_j's shares of the inner secret-sharing scheme).

For this purpose, the dealer computes, in a preprocessing phase, the appropriate shares for the inner secret-sharing scheme. For each round, the shares of each party P_j are shared in a *special* 2-out-of-2 secret-sharing scheme, where P_j gets one of the two shares (called the mask). In addition, all parties (including P_j) receive shares in a $n/2 + 1$-out-of-n secret-sharing scheme of the other share of the 2-out-of-2 secret sharing. We call the resulting secret-sharing scheme the *outer* $(n/2 + 1)$-out-of-n scheme ($n/2$ parties and the holder of the mask are needed to reconstruct the secret).

The use of the outer secret-sharing scheme with threshold $n/2 + 1$ plays a crucial role in eliminating the on-line dealer. On one hand, it guarantees that an adversary, corrupting at most $n/2$ parties cannot reconstruct the shares of round r before round r. On the other hand, at least $n/2$ parties must abort to prevent the reconstruction of the outer secret-sharing scheme. Note that $n/2$ aborting parties can prevent the remaining parties from receiving their shares and, indeed, in the description of the protocol, if $n/2$ parties abort, the remaining parties no longer receive shares from the dealer. Finally, we replace the off-line dealer by using a secure-with-abort and cheat-detection protocol computing the functionality computed by the dealer.

To prevent corrupted parties from cheating, by e.g., sending false shares and causing reconstruction of wrong secrets, every message that a party should send during (any possible flow of) the execution of the protocol is signed in the preprocessing phase (together with the appropriate round number and the party's index). In addition, the dealer sends a verification key to each of the parties. To conclude, the off-line dealer gives each party the signed shares for the outer secret-sharing scheme together with the verification key.

Whenever $F_{\mathrm{Recon},S,p}^{\mathrm{th},n/2}$ is run in Steps 5a and 5b, all parties are honest, so it can be trivially implemented. When $F_{\mathrm{Recon},S,p}^{\mathrm{th},n/2}$ is run in Step 6, there may *not* be an honest majority. In this case, however, it is the final round so the reconstruction protocol will output the same value, regardless of which subset of parties participate (as long as the subset includes all the $n/2$ honest parties). Thus, the adversary may get its output early and abort to prevent the honest parties to obtain output. The view of the adversary can be simulated since the ideal functionality has already been called at this time. Moreover, the protocol simply gets restarted until either no party aborts during the protocol (which happens in the worst case when only honest parties are remaining).[3] Therefore, the honest parties are guaranteed to obtain their output. We emphasize that the ideal functionality checks that the shares inputted by the parties are correctly authenticated (and are those same shares that were distributed by the "dealer"). Note also that corrupt parties may input an incorrect verification key for verifying the authenticated inputs and shares. In this case, the MPC functionality will partition the inputs according to the submitted verification key. Each party will receive as output the evaluation of the functionality with respect to the inputs of the set of parties who inputted the same verification key as it did.

4   Majority and $n/2 + 1$ Corruptions

We begin by presenting the protocol for computing n-party majority (Maj) in Figs. 3 and 4. The protocol in Fig. 3 uses a secret sharing scheme for access structure $\mathcal{A}_{R,R',z,n'-z,2n}$, defined in Sect. 2. In the following, p is set to $p = 8 \cdot (3n/2 + 3)$.

Notation. Let T be the set of corrupted parties with corresponding input $\boldsymbol{x}$, where $\boldsymbol{x}$ is indexed by the elements of T. Let $\overline{T} = [n] \backslash T$ be the set of uncorrupted parties with corresponding input $\boldsymbol{y}$, where $\boldsymbol{y}$ is indexed by the elements of $\overline{T}$. Let $x := \sum_{i \in T} x_i$ and $y := \sum_{i \in \overline{T}} y_i$. Let $T' \subseteq T$, $|T'| \geq n/2 - 1$ be the subset of parties who do not submit valid inputs in Step 4. Let $x^+ = \sum_{i \in T'} x_i$, $x^- = \sum_{i \in T \backslash T'} x_i$.

Define $f_{n_1,n_2}^{\mathsf{val}}(x,y)$ where $n_1 + n_2 = n$, $x \in \{0,\ldots,n_1\}, y \in \{0,\ldots,n_2\}$ and $\mathsf{val} \in \{0,\ldots,2\}$ to be the function that outputs 1 if $x + y + \mathsf{val} \geq n/2 + 1$ and outputs 0 otherwise. If $\mathsf{val} = 0$, we sometimes abbreviate by $f_{n_1,n_2}(x,y) = f_{n_1,n_2}^{\mathsf{val}}(x,y)$. Let $\boldsymbol{M}_{f_{n_1,n_2}^{\mathsf{val}}}$ be the truth table corresponding to $f_{n_1,n_2}^{\mathsf{val}}$. Define the distribution $\boldsymbol{X}_{Real,m}$ to be the uniform distribution over $\{0,\ldots,m\}$.

Let $\boldsymbol{a}$ be a vector of length $4n + 12$, indexed by tuples (R',n',z), where $R' \subseteq R = \{1,2,3\}$, $n' \in \{n/2 - 1, n/2, n/2 + 1\}$, $z \in \{0,\ldots,n'\}$. On input $\boldsymbol{x}$, We define a function $\phi(\boldsymbol{x})$ that outputs a set of triples (R',n',z), such that $(R',n',z) \in \phi(\boldsymbol{x})$ if there exists a subset $W \subseteq T$ of size $|W| = n'$ such that $W \cap R = R'$ and a subset $W' \subseteq T$ of size $|W'| = n'$ such that $z = \sum_{i \in W'} x_i$. For any set T of size $|T| \leq n/2 + 1$ and input $\boldsymbol{x} \in \{0,1\}^{|T|}$, $|\phi(\boldsymbol{x})|$ is at most

---

[3] We require an *identifiable abort* property to allow elimination of aborting/misbehaving parties and restarting of the protocol. Similar properties were needed in the work of [21]. They required secure computation with designated abort: If the output of the protocol is $\perp$, the parties restart without the lowest indexed party. Also, if the protocol outputs a set $\mathcal{S}$ (indicating those parties whose inputs were inconsistent), the set $\mathcal{S}$ is eliminated.

1. The parties $P_1, \ldots, P_n$ hand their inputs, denoted $\boldsymbol{x} = x_1, \ldots, x_n \in \{0,1\}^n$, respectively, to the dealer. If a party P_j does not send an input, then the dealer selects $x_j \in \{0,1\}$ uniformly at random. If $n/2 + 1$ of the parties do not send an input, then the dealer sends $f_{n/2-1,n/2+1}(\sum_{i=1}^{n/2-1} x_i, \sum_{i=n/2}^{n} x_i)$ to the honest parties and halts.

2. The dealer chooses a r^* from a geometric distribution with parameter α. For $r \in [\text{rounds}]$, $r < r^*$, $n' \in \{n/2 - 1, n/2, n/2 + 1\}$, $z \in \{0, \ldots, n'\}$ and for each subset $R' \subseteq R = \{1, 2, 3\}$, sample $\hat{x} \sim \boldsymbol{X}_{real, n-n'}$ and set $a^{r, R', n', z} := f_{n', n-n'}(z, \hat{x})$. For $r \in [\text{rounds}]$, $r \geq r^*$, $n' \in \{n/2 - 1, n/2, n/2 + 1\}$, $z \in \{0, \ldots, n'\}$, set $a^{r, R', n', z} := \text{out}$, where out denotes the output of the Majority function.

3. For $r \in [\text{rounds}]$, $r < r^*$, for $n' \in \{n/2 - 1, n/2, n/2 + 1\}$, $z \in \{0, \ldots, n'\}$, and for each subset $R' \subseteq R = \{1, 2, 3\}$, the dealer secret shares $a^{r, R', n', z} || 0^n$ using access structure $\mathcal{A}_{R, R', z, n'-z, 2n}$, producing shares $[\tilde{\boldsymbol{s}}_i^{b, R, R', n', z}]_{b \in \{0,1\}, i \in [n]}$. Each party P_i holding input b receives shares $[\tilde{\boldsymbol{s}}_i^{b, R, R', n', z}]$.

4. If $n/2 - 1$ or more parties abort, then the remaining parties (corresponding to set S) submit their shares from round $r - 1$ to ideal functionality $F_{\text{Recon}, S, p}^{th, n/2+1}$, output whatever it outputs and halt. Let S' denote the set of parties who submit properly authenticated shares to $F_{\text{Recon}, S, p}^{th, n/2+1}$. Note that S and S' contain an honest majority.

5. Otherwise, the remaining parties (set S) submit their final shares to ideal functionality $F_{\text{Recon}, S, p}^{th, n/2+1}$, output whatever it outputs and halt. If some set $\widetilde{T}$ of parties abort, preventing the remaining parties from receiving output, the remaining parties: $S := S \setminus \widetilde{T}$ go back to the beginning of Step 5 and resubmit their final shares to $F_{\text{Recon}, S, p}^{th, n/2+1}$. This continues until the honest parties receive the output.

Fig. 3. Fair, efficient, multiparty computation of Maj with n parties and $n/2 + 1$ or fewer corruptions.

Functionality $F_{\text{Recon}, S, p}^{th, n/2+1}$

- **Input Stage:** Set $S \subseteq [n]$ of size n'. For $i \in S$, the i-th party's input is (authenticated) bit x_i and p shares $[\tilde{\boldsymbol{s}}_i^k]_{k \in [p]}$. Let S' be the set of parties who submit input shares that are properly authenticated. Let $R' = S' \cap R$. We have that $|S'| \geq n/2 - 1$. We also assume WLOG that $|S'| \leq n/2 + 1$. If it is greater, then compute with some subset of the input shares. Let $z := \sum_{i \in S'} x_i$.
- **Function Computation:** For $k \in [p]$, run reconstruction algorithm Recon for secret-sharing scheme $\mathcal{A}_{R, R', z, n'-z, 2n}$ with input shares $[\tilde{\boldsymbol{s}}_i^k]_{i \in S'}$ to obtain candidates $[\text{secret}^k = \text{secret}_1^k || \text{secret}_2^k]_{k \in [p]}$.
- **Output:** secret_1^k corresponding to the first $k \in [p]$ such that $\text{secret}_2^k = 0^\lambda$.

Fig. 4. Reconstruction functionality with respect to p sets of secret shares.

a constant, deg, where deg $\leq 3 \cdot 8 \cdot 3 = 48$. Define $\boldsymbol{a}_0$ (resp. $\boldsymbol{a}_1$) such that all indeces in $\phi(\boldsymbol{x})$ are set to 0 (resp. 1) and all other indeces are set to $\perp$.

For $(R', n', z) \in \phi(\boldsymbol{x})$, define $p^{R',n',z}(x) := \Pr_{\hat{y} \sim \{0,\ldots,n-n'\}}[f_{n',n-n'}(z, \hat{y}) = 1]$ and $\overline{p}^{R',n',z}(x) := 1 - p^{R',n',z}(x)$. $p^{R',n',z}(x)$ denotes the probability that the corrupt parties, using sets $W, W' \subseteq T$, where $W \cap R = R'$, $|W'| = n'$, and $z = \sum_{i \in W'} x_i$, reconstruct a 1. For $(R', n', z) \notin \phi(\boldsymbol{x})$, define $p^{R',n',z}(x) := 1$ and $\overline{p}^{R',n',z}(x) := 1$.

Definition 1. *We say that a setting of parameters* $(T, t, \boldsymbol{x}, T', t', x^+, x^-, \boldsymbol{a})$ *is valid if:*

1. $T \subseteq [n]$, $n/2 - 1 \leq |T| = t \leq n/2 + 1$.
2. $T' \subseteq T$, $|T'| = t' \geq n/2 - 1$.
3. $\boldsymbol{x} \in \{0,1\}^{|T|}$
4. $x^+ = \sum_{i \in T'} x_i$. $x^- = \sum_{i \in T \setminus T'} x_i$,
5. *Indeces of* $\boldsymbol{a}$ *in* $\phi(\boldsymbol{x})$ *are set to* $0 \backslash 1$ *and all other indeces are set to* $\perp$.

We say that a setting of parameters $(T, t, \boldsymbol{x}, T', t', x^+, x^-)$ *is* valid *if all the above except (5) hold.*

For every valid $(T, t, \boldsymbol{x}, T', t', x^+, x^-)$, for $k \in \{0, \ldots, n-t\}$, define the probabilities $p^{x^-,t,t'}_{y=k} := \Pr_{\hat{x} \sim X_{Real,t'}}[f^{x^-}_{t',n-t}(\hat{x}, y = k) = 1]$. $p^{x^-,t,t'}_{y=k}$ corresponds to the probability the honest parties output a 1 in the Real execution in rounds prior to the designated round r^*, when the combined input of the honest parties is $y = k$, the input of the t' aborting parties is chosen from $X_{Real,t'}$, and the input of the $(t - t')$ corrupt but non-aborting parties is x^-.

For every valid $(T, t, \boldsymbol{x}, T', t', x^+, x^-)$, define the row vectors $\boldsymbol{Q}^{x^+,x^-,\boldsymbol{a}_0} = (q^{x^+,x^-,\boldsymbol{a}_0}_{y=n-t}, \ldots, q^{x^+,x^-,\boldsymbol{a}_0}_{y=0})$ and $\boldsymbol{Q}^{x^+,x^-,\boldsymbol{a}_1} = (q^{x^+,x^-,\boldsymbol{a}_1}_{y=n-t}, \ldots, q^{x^+,x^-,\boldsymbol{a}_1}_{y=0})$ indexed by $k \in \{0, \ldots, n-t\}$ as follows:

$$q^{x^+,x^-,\boldsymbol{a}_0}_{y=k} = \begin{cases} p^{x^-,t,t'}_{y=k} & \text{if } f^{x^-}_{t',n-t}(x^+, y = k) = 1 \\ p^{x^-,t,t'}_{y=k} + \frac{\alpha \cdot p^{x^-,t,t'}_{y=k}}{(1-\alpha) \cdot \prod_{(R',n',z)}(\overline{p}^{R',n',z}(x))} & \text{if } f^{x^-}_{t',n-t}(x^+, y = k) = 0 \end{cases}$$

$$q^{x^+,x^-,\boldsymbol{a}_1}_{y=k} = \begin{cases} p^{x^-,t,t'}_{y=k} & \text{if } f^{x^-}_{t',n-t}(x^+, y = k) = 0 \\ p^{x^-,t,t'}_{y=k} + \frac{\alpha \cdot (p^{x^-,t,t'}_{y=k} - 1)}{(1-\alpha) \cdot \prod_{(R',n',z)} p^{R',n',z}(x)} & \text{if } f^{x^-}_{t',n-t}(x^+, y = k) = 1 \end{cases}$$

For every valid $(T, t, \boldsymbol{x}, T', t', \boldsymbol{a}, x^+, x^-)$, such that $\boldsymbol{a} \notin \{\boldsymbol{a}_0, \boldsymbol{a}_1\}$, define the row vectors $\boldsymbol{Q}^{x^+,x^-,\boldsymbol{a}} = (q^{x^+,x^-,\boldsymbol{a}}_{y=n-t}, \ldots, q^{x^+,x^-,\boldsymbol{a}}_{y=0})$, indexed by $k \in \{0, \ldots, n-t\}$ as follows: $\boldsymbol{Q}^{x^+,x^-,\boldsymbol{a}} = (p^{x^-,t,t'}_{y=n-t}, \ldots, p^{x^-,t,t'}_{y=0})$.

Intuition. $q^{x^+,x^-,\boldsymbol{a}}_{y=k}$ corresponds to the probability that the Ideal honest parties receive an output of 1, when the simulator chooses its input to the Ideal functionality from distribution $X^{x^+,x^-,\boldsymbol{a}}_{ideal,t'}$, in the case that the adversary aborts in a round prior to the designated round r^*, the honest parties collectively hold input $y = k$, the aborting parties hold input x^+, the corrupted but non-aborting parties hold input x^-, and the view of the adversary consists of $\boldsymbol{a}$. Our goal is to set the values of $q_{y=k}^{x^+,x^-,a_0}$ so that the distributions in the Ideal and Real world are identical. Note, however, that the simulator does not know the value of y. Therefore, the simulator can only sample from a single probability distribution for all possible values of y, denoted $\boldsymbol{X}_{ideal,t'}^{x^+,x^-,a}$, and we must ensure that the resulting distribution over outputs, corresponding to $\boldsymbol{X}_{ideal,t'}^{x^+,x^-,a} \cdot \boldsymbol{M}_{f_{t',n-t}^{x^-}}$, produces the desired values of $\boldsymbol{Q}^{x^+,x^-,a} = (q_{y=n-t}^{x^+,x^-,a}, \ldots, q_{y=0}^{x^+,x^-,a})$.

In the upcoming theorem, we show that setting $\boldsymbol{Q}^{x^+,x^-,a} = (q_{y=n-t}^{x^+,x^-,a}, \ldots, q_{y=0}^{x^+,x^-,a})$ as described above, yields identical distributions in the Ideal/Real worlds. Then, we must show that there exists a probability vector $\boldsymbol{X}_{ideal,t'}^{x^+,x^-,a}$ such that $\boldsymbol{X}_{ideal,t'}^{x^+,x^-,a} \cdot \boldsymbol{M}_{f_{t',n-t}^{x^-}} = \boldsymbol{Q}^{x^+,x^-,a}$.

We observe that in some cases finding $\boldsymbol{X}_{ideal,t'}^{x^+,x^-,a}$ as above is easy. Specifically, for every valid $(T, t, \boldsymbol{x}, T', t', a, x^+, x^-)$, and for $a \notin \{a_0, a_1\}$, $\boldsymbol{X}_{ideal,t'}^{x^+,x^-,a} = \boldsymbol{X}_{real,t'}$ satisfies $\boldsymbol{X}_{ideal,t'}^{x^+,x^-,a} \cdot \boldsymbol{M}_{f_{t',n-t}^{x^-}} = \boldsymbol{Q}^{x^+,x^-,a}$.

Theorem 6. *Assume that for every valid setting of parameters $(T, t, \boldsymbol{x}, T',$ $t', x^+, x^-, a)$, there exists a probability vector $\boldsymbol{X}_{ideal,t'}^{x^+,x^-,a}$ such that*

$$\boldsymbol{X}_{ideal,t'}^{x^+,x^-,a} \cdot \boldsymbol{M}_{f_{t',n-t}^{x^-}} = \boldsymbol{Q}^{x^+,x^-,a}.$$

Then the protocol in Fig. 3 securely computes Maj *for any $n = \mathrm{poly}(\lambda)$ (s.t. $n \geq 8$) and $|T| \leq n/2 + 1$ corruptions.*

Proof. We begin with a description of the simulator Sim:

- Sim invokes A expecting its inputs $\boldsymbol{x}$, as sent to the dealer.
- Sim samples r^* from a geometric distribution with parameter α.
- For every $r = 1$ to $r^* - 1$
  - For $n' \in \{n/2 - 1, n/2, n/2 + 1\}$, $z \in \{0, \ldots, n'\}$, and $R' \subseteq R$, sample $\hat{x} \sim \boldsymbol{X}_{real,n-n'}$ and set $a^{r,R',n',z} := f_{n',n-n'}(z, \hat{x})$. Secret share each $a^{r,R',n',z}||0^n$ using access structure $\mathcal{A}_{R,R',z,n'-z,2n}$, producing shares $[\tilde{s}_i^{b,R',n',z,2n}]_{b \in \{0,1\}, i \in [n]}$. Each party $P_i \in T$ holding input b receives shares $[\tilde{s}_i^{b,R',n',z,2n}]$.
  - Fix the resulting view $\boldsymbol{a}$, consisting of the $a^{r,R',n',z}$ values that can be reconstructed by the adversary holding input $\boldsymbol{x}$.
  - If $n/2 - 1$ parties abort, Sim simulates the ideal functionality $F_{\mathrm{Recon},S,p}^{th,n/2+1}$. Recall that $S' \subseteq S$ submit valid inputs for $F_{\mathrm{Recon},S,p}^{th,n/2+1}$ to Sim. Let $T' = [n] \setminus S'$, where $|T'| = t'$. Let $x^+ = \sum_{i \in T'} \boldsymbol{x}_i$ and $x^- = \sum_{i \in T \setminus T'} \boldsymbol{x}_i$. Sim chooses $\hat{x} \sim \boldsymbol{X}_{Ideal,t'}^{x^+,x^-,a}$ and submits $\hat{x} + x^-$ to the ideal functionality,

receiving out in return. Note that the set S enjoys an honest majority, and so we can compute $F_{\text{Recon},S,p}^{\text{th},n/2+1}$ with fairness and guaranteed output delivery. Sim returns out as the output of $F_{\text{Recon},S,p}^{\text{th},n/2+1}$.

- For $r = r^*$
  - Sim sends input x to the ideal functionality computing $f_{t,n-t}$ and receives out $= f_{t,n-t}(x,y)$. For $n' \in \{n/2 - 1, n/2, n/2 + 1\}$, $z \in \{0, \ldots, n'\}$, and $R' \subseteq R$, set $a^{r,R',n',z} :=$ out. Secret share each $a^{r,R',n',z} \| 0^n$ using access structure $\mathcal{A}_{R,R',z,n'-z,2n}$, producing shares $[\tilde{s}_i^{b,R',n',z,2n}]_{b \in \{0,1\}, i \in [n]}$. Each corrupt party $P_i \in T$ holding input b receives shares $[\tilde{s}_i^{b,R',n',z,2n}]$.
- For $r > r^*$
  - For $n' \in \{n/2 - 1, n/2, n/2 + 1\}$, $z \in \{0, \ldots, n'\}$ and $R' \subseteq R$, set $a^{r,R',n',z} :=$ out. Secret share each $a^{r,R',n',z} \| 0^n$ using access structure $\mathcal{A}_{R,R',z,n'-z,2n}$, producing shares $[\tilde{s}_i^{b,R',n',z,2n}]_{b \in \{0,1\}, v \in [n]}$. Each party P_i holding input b receives shares $[\tilde{s}_i^{b,R',n',z,2n}]$.
- Final share reconstruction. At this point, Sim holds the output out from the ideal functionality. Furthermore, the same out will be reconstructed by any set of parties of size $n/2 - 1$ or more that remain. Sim also obtains from A any inputs to the functionality $F_{\text{Recon},S,p}^{\text{th},n/2+1}$ in the last stage. It uses out to simulate the output of the ideal functionality $F_{\text{Recon},S,p}^{\text{th},n/2+1}$. If some parties abort and the remaining parties re-submit their inputs to the ideal functionality, Sim_f can still use out to simulate the output each time.

In case the adversary aborts exactly at r^*, the simulator Sim sends the input x to the trusted party, and so both parties receive $f_{t,n-t}(x,y)$, unlike the real execution. Moreover, in case the adversary has aborted at round $r < r^*$, upon viewing a at round i, the simulator Sim chooses input $\hat{x}$ according to distribution $X_{ideal,t'}^{x^+,x^-,a}$ and submits $\hat{x} + x^-$ to the ideal functionality.

We show that the joint distribution of the view of the adversary and the output of the honest party is distributed identically in the hybrid and the ideal executions. This is done easily in the case where $n/2 - 1$ or more parties abort at some round $r > r^*$ (and thus, both parties receive the correct output $f_{t,n-t}(x,y)$). Now, we consider the case where $r \leq r^*$. The view of the adversary holding input x in the r-th round consists of: $a^{r,R',n',z}$ for all (R',n',z) such that $a_{(R',n',z)} \neq \bot$.

The view of the adversary until round i is distributed identically in both executions. Thus, all that is left to show is that the view of the adversary in the last round and the output of the honest party are distributed identically in both executions. That is, we show that for every (a,b), where $b \in \{0,1\}$ and a is such that all indeces in $\phi(x)$ are set to 0/1 and all other indeces are set to $\bot$, it is the case that:

$$\Pr[(\text{View}_{\text{hyb}}^r, \text{Out}_{\text{hyb}}) = (a,b) \mid r \leq r^*] = \Pr[(\text{View}_{\text{ideal}}^r, \text{Out}_{\text{ideal}}) = (a,b) \mid r \leq r^*].$$
$$(4.1)$$

Formally, $(\text{View}_{\text{hyb}}^r, \text{Out}_{\text{hyb}})$ and $(\text{View}_{\text{ideal}}^r, \text{Out}_{\text{ideal}})$ denote the entire view and output in the hybrid and ideal execution. Note that $\text{View}_{\text{hyb}}^r, \text{View}_{\text{ideal}}^r$ actually consist of secret shares, whereas a denotes the reconstructed values for the instances that can be opened by the adversary. We simplify our computations by assuming that the views $\text{View}_{\text{hyb}}^r, \text{View}_{\text{ideal}}^r$ consist only of the values the adversary can *reconstruct* given its set of shares, and not the shares themselves. Given the "perfect privacy" property of sharing schemes (see [5]), if the probabilities are the same with respect to the reconstructed values, then they will also be the same with respect to the original view.

Implicit in our argument, is that—in the hybrid execution—the output b of the honest parties in round $r < $ rounds is independent of the view of the adversary, represented by a. While this is trivially true in the two-party case, It is not as obvious in our protocol, since when $n/2$ or $n/2+1$ parties are corrupted, the adversary can open many instances of the secret sharing scheme. Specifically, we must show that for the instance used in Step 4 to reconstruct—identified by $(\overline{R}', n - t', *)$—it is always the case that $a_{(\overline{R}', n-t', *)} = \bot$.

This will follow from the following property that is straightforward to check:

Property 1. Let t be the number of corruptions. If for some $(R_1, n_1, z_1), (R_2, n_2, z_2)$, $a_{(R_1, n_1, z_1)} \neq \bot$ and $a_{(R_2, n_2, z_2)} \neq \bot$ then

$$|R_1 \cup R_2| + \max(n_1 - |R_1|, n_2 - |R_2|) \leq t.$$

Recall that the set of corrupted parties is denoted by T, and the set of parties who abort and/or do not submit valid input in Step 4 is denoted T'. Let $R' = T' \cap R$. Let $|T'| = t'$. Then parties reconstruct with $S' := \overline{T}'$, $n' = n - t'$, and $\overline{R}' = \overline{T}' \cap R$. Note that $\{R', \overline{R}'\}$ form a partition of R. Note that corrupted parties can open $(R', t', *)$, while the parties in S' can open $(\overline{R}', n-t', *)$. Assume towards contradiction that the adversary can also open $(\overline{R}', n - t', *)$. Note that $(t' - |R'|) + (n - t' - |\overline{R}'|) = n - |R| = n - 3$. Therefore, $\max(t' - |R'|, n - t' - |\overline{R}'|) \geq n/2 - 1$. Thus,

$$|R' \cup \overline{R}'| + \max(t' - |R'|, n - t' - |\overline{R}'|) \geq 3 + n/2 - 1 > n/2 + 1 \geq t,$$

which contradicts Property 1.

We now show that Eq. (4.1) holds by considering all possible values for (a, b). First, observe that

$$\Pr[r = r^* \mid r \leq r^*] = \alpha \text{ and } \Pr[r < i^* \mid r \leq i^*] = 1 - \alpha.$$

In the following we will consider only valid parameter settings $(T, t, \boldsymbol{x}, T', t', x^+, x^-, \boldsymbol{a})$.

In case $f_{t', n-t}^{x^-}(x^+, y) = 0$. Let $\boldsymbol{a}' \notin \{\boldsymbol{a}_0, \boldsymbol{a}_1\}$. Let $S_{\boldsymbol{a}'}$ be the set of positions in $\boldsymbol{a}'$ that are set to 0 and $S_{\boldsymbol{a}'}'$ be the set of positions in $\boldsymbol{a}'$ that are set to 1. $\boldsymbol{a}_0, \boldsymbol{a}_1$ are defined as before. For condensed notation, we let $\boldsymbol{a}_0, \boldsymbol{a}_1, \boldsymbol{a}'$ be indexed by $t = (R', n', z)$.

View	Real	Ideal
$(a_0,0)$	$\alpha \cdot (1 - p_y^{x^-,t,t'}) + (1-\alpha) \prod_t (\overline{p}_x^t) \cdot (1 - p_y^{x^-,t,t'})$	$\alpha + (1-\alpha) \prod_t (\overline{p}_x^t) \cdot (1 - q_y^{x^+,x^-,a_0})$
$(a_0,1)$	$\alpha \cdot p_y^{x^-,t,t'} + (1-\alpha) \prod_t (\overline{p}_x^t) \cdot p_y^{x^-,t,t'}$	$(1-\alpha) \prod_t (\overline{p}_x^t) \cdot (q_y^{x^+,x^-,a_0})$
$(a',0)$	$(1-\alpha) \prod_{t \in S_{a'}} (\overline{p}_x^t) \prod_{t \in S'_{a'}} (p_x^t) \cdot (1 - p_y^{x^-,t,t'})$	$(1-\alpha) \prod_{t \in S_{a'}} (\overline{p}_x^t) \prod_{t \in S'_{a'}} (p_x^t) \cdot (1 - q_y^{x^+,x^-,a'})$
$(a',1)$	$(1-\alpha) \prod_{t \in S_{a'}} (\overline{p}_x^t) \prod_{t \in S'_{a'}} (p_x^t) \cdot (p_y^{x^-,t,t'})$	$(1-\alpha) \prod_{t \in S_{a'}} (\overline{p}_x^t) \prod_{t \in S'_{a'}} (p_x^t) \cdot (q_y^{x^+,x^-,a'})$
$(a_1,0)$	$(1-\alpha) \prod_t (p_x^t) \cdot (1 - p_y^{x^-,t,t'})$	$(1-\alpha) \prod_t (p_x^t) \cdot (1 - q_y^{x^+,x^-,a_1})$
$(a_1,1)$	$(1-\alpha) \prod_t (p_x^t) \cdot (p_y^{x^-,t,t'})$	$(1-\alpha) \prod_t (p_x^t) \cdot (q_y^{x^+,x^-,a_1})$

In the table, we compute the probabilities of representative choices of (a,b) in the Real and Ideal worlds:

It can be seen that for $a' \notin \{a_0, a_1\}$ we get the following constraint: $q_y^{x^+,x^-,a'} = p_y^{x^-,t,t'}$. Thus, all constraints for $a' \notin \{a_0, a_1\}$ can be satisfied by setting $X_{ideal,t'}^{x^+,x^-,a} = X_{real,t'}$.

Additionally, we obtain the constraints:

$$q_y^{x^+,x^-,a_0} = p_y^{x^-,t,t'} + \frac{\alpha \cdot p_y^{x^-,t,t'}}{(1-\alpha) \cdot \prod_{(R',n',z)} (\overline{p}_x^{(R',n',z)})})$$

and

$$q_y^{x^+,x^-,a_1} = p_y^{x^-,t,t'},$$

which are satisfied according to our assumptions in the theorem.

In case $f_{t',n-t}^{x^-}(x^+,y) = 1$. Let $a' \notin \{a_0, a_1\}$. Let $S_{a'}$ be the set of positions in a' that are set to 0 and $S'_{a'}$ be the set of positions in a' that are set to 1. a_0, a_1 are defined as before. For condensed notation, we let a_0, a_1, a' be indexed by $t = (R', n', z)$.

In the table, we compute the probabilities of representative choices of (a,b) in the Real and Ideal worlds:

View	Real	Ideal
$(a_0,0)$	$(1-\alpha) \prod_t (\overline{p}_x^t) \cdot (1 - p_y^{x^-,t,t'})$	$(1-\alpha) \prod_t (\overline{p}_x^t) \cdot (1 - q_y^{x^+,x^-,a_0})$
$(a_0,1)$	$(1-\alpha) \prod_t (\overline{p}_x^t) \cdot p_y^{x^-,t,t'}$	$(1-\alpha) \prod_t (\overline{p}_x^t)(q_y^{x^+,x^-,a_0})$
$(a',0)$	$(1-\alpha) \prod_{t \in S_{a'}} (\overline{p}_x^t) \prod_{t \in S'_{a'}} (p_x^t) \cdot (1 - p_y^{x^-,t,t'})$	$(1-\alpha) \prod_{t \in S_{a'}} (\overline{p}_x^t) \prod_{t \in S'_{a'}} (p_x^t) \cdot (1 - q_y^{x^+,x^-,a'})$
$(a',1)$	$(1-\alpha) \prod_{t \in S_{a'}} (\overline{p}_x^t) \prod_{t \in S'_{a'}} (p_x^t) \cdot (p_y^{x^-,t,t'})$	$(1-\alpha) \prod_{t \in S_{a'}} (\overline{p}_x^t) \prod_{t \in S'_{a'}} (p_x^t) \cdot (q_y^{x^+,x^-,a'})$
$(a_1,0)$	$\alpha \cdot (1 - p_y^{x^-,t,t'}) + (1-\alpha) \prod_t (p_x^t) \cdot (1 - p_y^{x^-,t,t'})$	$(1-\alpha) \prod_t (p_x^t) \cdot (1 - q_y^{x^+,x^-,a_1})$
$(a_1,1)$	$\alpha \cdot p_y^{x^-,t,t'} + (1-\alpha) \prod_t (p_x^t) \cdot (p_y^{x^-,t,t'})$	$\alpha + (1-\alpha) \prod_t (p_x^t) \cdot (q_y^{x^+,x^-,a_1})$

It can be seen that for $a' \notin \{a_0, a_1\}$ we get the following constraint: $q_y^{x^+, x^-, a'} = p_y^{x^-, t, t'}$. Thus, all constraints for $a' \notin \{a_0, a_1\}$ can be satisfied by setting $X_{ideal, t'}^{x^+, x^-, a} = X_{real, t'}$.

Additionally, we obtain the constraints:

$$q_y^{x^+, x^-, a_1} = p_y^{x^-, t, t'} + \frac{\alpha \cdot (p_y^{x^-, t, t'} - 1)}{(1 - \alpha) \cdot \prod_{(R', n', z)} p_x^{(R', n', z)}}$$

and

$$q_y^{x^+, x^-, a_0} = p_y^{x^-, t, t'}.$$

Since $X_{ideal, t'}^{x^+, x^-, a} \cdot M_{f_{t', n-t}^{x^-}} = Q^{x^+, x^-, a}$, the above constraints are satisfied.

This concludes the proof of Theorem 6.

The following lemma concludes the analysis of the protocol in Fig. 3:

Lemma 1. *There exists $\alpha = 1/\text{poly}(n)$ such that for every valid setting of parameters $(T, t, \boldsymbol{x}, T', t', x^+, x^-, \boldsymbol{a})$, there exists a probability vector $X_{ideal, t'}^{x^+, x^-, a}$ such that $X_{ideal, t'}^{x^+, x^-, a} \cdot M_{f_{t', n-t}^{x^-}} = Q^{x^+, x^-, a}$.*

Proof. We begin by proving the lemma for the special case where $t = n/2 + 1$, $t' = n/2 - 1$ and $x^- = 1$.

Define $\boldsymbol{P}_y^{1, n/2+1, n/2-1} = (p_{y=n/2-1}^{1, n/2+1, n/2-1}, \ldots, p_{y=0}^{1, n/2+1, n/2-1})$.

Note that the output of the function $f_{n/2-1, n/2-1}^1$ is 1 in position $[x, y]$ if the sum of $x + y \geq n/2$. In the following example we set $n/2 - 1 = 3$. The truthtable of $f_{n/2-1, n/2-1}^1$ is as follows:

	$y = 3$	$y = 2$	$y = 1$	$y = 0$
$x = 0$	0	0	0	0
$x = 1$	1	0	0	0
$x = 2$	1	1	0	0
$x = 3$	1	1	1	0

And becomes the following in matrix form:

$$M_{f_{n/2-1, n/2-1}^1} = \begin{bmatrix} 0 & 0 & 0 & 0 \\ 1 & 0 & 0 & 0 \\ 1 & 1 & 0 & 0 \\ 1 & 1 & 1 & 0 \end{bmatrix}$$

Since the final column of the matrix is all 0, we can simply remove it, since $p_{y=0}^{1, n/2+1, n/2-1} = 0$, $q_{y=0}^{x^+, 1, a_0} = 0$, and $q_{y=0}^{x^+, 1, a_1} = 0$. Thus, $M_{f_{n/2-1, n/2-1}^1}$ denotes the above matrix with the final column deleted.

For every valid $(T, t = n/2 + 1, \boldsymbol{x}, T', t' = n/2 - 1, x^+, x^- = 1, \boldsymbol{a})$ we need to find a vector $\boldsymbol{s} \in \mathbb{R}^{n/2-1}$ such that $\boldsymbol{s} M_{f_{n/2-1, n/2-1}^1} = Q^{x^+, 1, a}$ and the vector

$s = s_0, \ldots, s_{n/2-1}$ further needs to correspond to a probability distribution–i.e. we require that $\sum_{k=0}^{n/2-1} s_k = 1$. In addition, we require that each s_k is non-negative.

Let $M^+_{f^1_{n/2-1,n/2-1}}$ denote the matrix obtained when a column vector of 1's is concatenated with the matrix $M_{f^1_{n/2-1,n/2-1}}$. For the case $n/2-1 = 3$, we obtain the following:

$$M^+_{f^1_{n/2-1,n/2-1}} = \begin{bmatrix} 1 & 0 & 0 & 0 \\ 1 & 1 & 0 & 0 \\ 1 & 1 & 1 & 0 \\ 1 & 1 & 1 & 1 \end{bmatrix}$$

We need to find a setting of α, such that $\alpha = 1/\operatorname{poly}(n)$ and such that the unique solution for s, where $sM^+_{f^1_{n/2-1,n/2-1}} = (1 || Q^{x,1,0,a})$ is non-negative. In the following, we argue that by setting α sufficiently small, but still $1/\operatorname{poly}(n)$ (yielding a protocol with $1/\alpha \cdot \omega(\log(\lambda)) = \operatorname{poly}(n,\lambda)$ rounds), we can find such a solution.

We know there is a non-negative solution s to $sM^+_{f^1_{n/2-1,n/2-1}} = (1 || P_y^{1,n/2+1,n/2-1})$. In fact, the solution is simply $s = (\frac{1}{n/2}, \ldots, \frac{1}{n/2})$, as this is the distribution $X_{real,t'=n/2-1}$ over inputs $\hat{x} \in \{0, \ldots, n/2-1\}$ that produces the real output distribution $P_y^{1,n/2+1,n/2-1}$. Note that s has distance at least $2/n$ from any vector with negative entries (since each coordinate of s has magnitude $2/n$). If $(1 || Q^{x-1,1,a}) = (1 || P_y^{1,n/2+1,n/2-1}) + w$, where w is a vector with magnitude at most d, we have that

$$(s + s')M^+_{f^1_{n/2-1,n/2-1}} = sM^+_{f^1_{n/2-1,n/2-1}} + s'M^+_{f^1_{n/2-1,n/2-1}} = (1 || P_y^{1,n/2+1,n/2-1}) + w,$$

where

$$s' = w(M^+_{f^1_{n/2-1,n/2-1}})^{-1}.$$

Now, the matrix $(M^+_{f^1_{n/2-1,n/2-1}})^{-1}$ has the following form:

$$(M^+_{f^1_{n/2-1,n/2-1}})^{-1} = \begin{bmatrix} 1 & 0 & 0 & 0 \\ -1 & 1 & 0 & 0 \\ 0 & -1 & 1 & 0 \\ 0 & 0 & -1 & 1 \end{bmatrix}$$

In other words, the diagonal entries are set to 1, the second diagonal entries are set to -1 and all other entries are set to 0. We upper bound the spectral norm of $(M^+_{f^1_{n/2-1,n/2-1}})^{-1}$ by $\sqrt{5}$ (see full version). Bounding the spectral norm of $(M^+_{f^1_{n/2-1,n/2-1}})^{-1}$ by $\sqrt{5}$ guarantees that since w has magnitude d, s' has magnitude at most $d' = \sqrt{5} \cdot d$. By choosing $d = \frac{2}{\sqrt{5} \cdot n}$, we have that $(s + s')$ has all non-negative entries. To ensure that w has magnitude at most d, it is sufficient to ensure that each coordinate of $\boldsymbol{w} = (1||\boldsymbol{Q}^{x-1,1,a}) - (1||\boldsymbol{P}_y^1)$ has magnitude at most $d/\sqrt{n}$. This can be achieved by setting $\alpha \leq 1/2$ such that

$$\frac{2\alpha}{\prod_{(R',n',z)} p_x^{(R',n',z)}} \leq d/\sqrt{n} \quad \text{and} \quad \frac{2\alpha}{\prod_{(R',n',z)} (\overline{p}_x^{(R',n',z)})} \leq d/\sqrt{n}. \quad (4.2)$$

Now, both $p_x^{(R',n',z)}$ and $\overline{p}_x^{(R',n',z)}$ must be at least $1/(n/2 + 2)$, since if they are not identically 0 (resp. identically 1), then there is at least one value of $\hat{y} \in \{0, \ldots, n - n'\}$ for which $f_{n',n-n'}(z, \hat{y}) = 1$ (resp. $f_{n',n-n'}(z, \hat{y}) = 0$) and since $n' \geq n/2 - 1$, $\mathrm{Pr}_{\hat{y} \sim \{0,\ldots,n-n'\}}[f_{n',n-n'}(z, \hat{y}) = 1] \geq 1/(n/2 + 2) > 1/n$ (resp. $\mathrm{Pr}_{\hat{y} \sim \{0,\ldots,n-n'\}}[f_{n',n-n'}(z, \hat{y}) = 0] \geq 1/(n/2 + 2) > 1/n$). Since, furthermore, $|\phi(\boldsymbol{x})| \leq \deg$, $\prod_{(R',n',z)} p_x^{(R',n',z)} \geq 1/n^{\deg}$ and $\prod_{(R',n',z)} (\overline{p}_x^{(R',n',z)}) \geq 1/n^{\deg}$. Thus, (4.2) is achieved by setting $\alpha \leq \frac{d}{2n^{\deg+0.5}}$. Finally, plugging in $d = \frac{2}{\sqrt{5} \cdot n}$, we have that $\alpha \leq \frac{1}{\sqrt{5}n^{\deg+1.5}}$. This results in a number of rounds $\omega(\log(\lambda)) \cdot 1/\alpha$, which is polynomial in the security parameter λ and in the number of parties n.

We now formalize the argument for any setting of $t = n/2 + 1$, $t' = n/2 - 1$ and $x^- = 1$. In fact, we see that the only thing that changes in the argument is $\boldsymbol{M}_{f_{n/2-1,n/2-1}^{+1}}$. We must prove that $\boldsymbol{M}_{f_{t',n-t}^{x^-}}^+$ is invertible and that the spectral norm of $(\boldsymbol{M}_{f_{t',n-t}^{x^-}}^+)^{-1}$ is bounded by $\sqrt{5}$.

In fact, we will show something slightly more general: For any m, n and any threshold th, consider the function $f_{m,n}^{th} : \{0, \ldots, m\} \times \{0, \ldots, n\}$ defined as: $f_{m,n}^{th}(x, y) = 1$ iff $x + y \geq th$. For non-triviality, we assume that $th > 0$ and that $m + n \geq th$. Consider the matrix $\boldsymbol{M}_{f_{m,n}^{th}}$.

We begin by removing from $\boldsymbol{M}_{f_{m,n}^{th}}$ columns that are all 0. I.e. columns $y = k$ such that $m + k < th$. The number of columns removed is $\ell_0 := th - m$, if $th - m \geq 1$ and 0 otherwise.

We next remove from $\boldsymbol{M}_{f_{m,n}^{th}}$ any columns ($y = k$) that are all 1 (this is ok since in this case $p_{y=k}^{x^+,x^-} = 1$, $q_{y=k}^{x^+,x^-,a_0} = 1$, and $q_{y=k}^{x^+,x^-,a_1} = 1$, and since the column will be added back at the end). Column $y = k$ will be all 1 if $k \geq th$. The number of columns removed is $\ell_1 := n - th + 1$, if $n - th + 1 \geq 1$ and 0 otherwise.

Now, we will show that the number of columns remaining $((n + 1) - \ell_1 - \ell_0)$ is at least one fewer than the number of rows $(m + 1)$. The number of columns remaining is

$$(n + 1) - \ell_1 - \ell_0 \leq (n + 1) - (th - m) - (n - th + 1)$$
$$= n + 1 - th + m - n + th - 1 = m.$$

Furthermore, if $m + 1 > (n + 1) - \ell_1 - \ell_0 + 1$, then there must be two identical rows, one of which can be removed. Therefore, after removing the columns, removing duplicate rows and adding a column of 1's, $\boldsymbol{M}_{f_{m,n}^{th}}^+$ has the form of a (non-singular) lower triangular matrix with 1's in each lower triangular entry and dimension $(n + 2 - \ell_1 - \ell_0) \times (n + 2 - \ell_1 - \ell_0)$.

4.1   Implementing the Dealer and $F_{\text{Recon},S,p}^{\text{th},n/2+1}$

Implementing the Dealer proceeds almost the same as the case of $n/2$ or fewer corruptions described in Sect. 3.1. The only differences are that we use a different access structure for the inner/outer secret-sharing schemes. Specifically, in round r, party P_j learns a share in a secret sharing scheme for access structure $\mathcal{A}_{R,R',n'-z,2n}$, for every $R' \subseteq R$, $n' \in [n]$, $z \in \{0, \ldots, n'\}$ (we call these P_j's shares of the inner secret-sharing scheme).

For each round, the shares of each party P_j are then shared in a *special* 2-out-of-2 secret-sharing scheme, where P_j gets one of the two shares (called the mask). In addition, all parties (including P_j) receive shares in a $n/2 + 2$-out-of-n Shamir secret-sharing scheme of the other share of the 2-out-of-2 secret sharing. We call the resulting secret-sharing scheme the *outer* $(n/2 + 2)$-out-of-n scheme (since $n/2 + 1$ parties and the holder of the mask are needed to reconstruct the secret).

To implement ideal functionality $F_{\text{Recon},S,p}^{\text{th},n/2+1}$, when $F_{\text{Recon},S,p}^{\text{th},n/2+1}$ is run in Step 4, not all parties remaining in the sets S and S' are necessarily honest. However, our restriction on $n \geq 8$ ensures that S and S' contains an honest majority. Therefore, $F_{\text{Recon},S,p}^{\text{th},n/2+1}$ can be implemented with a fully secure protocol (with fairness and guaranteed output delivery). When $F_{\text{Recon},S,p}^{\text{th},n/2+1}$ is run in Step 5, there may *not* be an honest majority, and the same approach from the previous section (Sect. 3.1) works.

References

1. Alon, B., Omri, E.: Almost-optimally fair multiparty coin-tossing with nearly three-quarters malicious. In: Hirt, M., Smith, A. (eds.) TCC 2016, Part I. LNCS, vol. 9985, pp. 307–335. Springer, Heidelberg (2016). https://doi.org/10.1007/978-3-662-53641-4_13

2. Asharov, G.: Towards characterizing complete fairness in secure two-party computation. In: Lindell [32], pp. 291–316

3. Asharov, G., Beimel, A., Makriyannis, N., Omri, E.: Complete characterization of fairness in secure two-party computation of boolean functions. In: Dodis, Y., Nielsen, J.B. (eds.) TCC 2015, Part I. LNCS, vol. 9014, pp. 199–228. Springer, Heidelberg (2015). https://doi.org/10.1007/978-3-662-46494-6_10

4. Asharov, G., Lindell, Y., Rabin, T.: A full characterization of functions that imply fair coin tossing and ramifications to fairness. In: Sahai, A. (ed.) TCC 2013. LNCS, vol. 7785, pp. 243–262. Springer, Heidelberg (2013). https://doi.org/10.1007/978-3-642-36594-2_14

5. Beimel, A.: Secret-sharing schemes: a survey. In: Chee, Y.M., Guo, Z., Ling, S., Shao, F., Tang, Y., Wang, H., Xing, C. (eds.) IWCC 2011. LNCS, vol. 6639, pp. 11–46. Springer, Heidelberg (2011). https://doi.org/10.1007/978-3-642-20901-7_2

6. Beimel, A., Haitner, I., Makriyannis, N., Omri, E.: Tighter bounds on multi-party coin flipping via augmented weak martingales and differentially private sampling. In: Thorup, M. (ed.) 59th FOCS, pp. 838–849. IEEE Computer Society Press, October 2018

7. Beimel, A., Lindell, Y., Omri, E., Orlov, I.: $1/p$-secure multiparty computation without honest majority and the best of both worlds. In: Rogaway, P. (ed.) CRYPTO 2011. LNCS, vol. 6841, pp. 277–296. Springer, Heidelberg (2011). https://doi.org/10.1007/978-3-642-22792-9_16

8. Beimel, A., Omri, E., Orlov, I.: Protocols for multiparty coin toss with dishonest majority. In: Rabin, T. (ed.) CRYPTO 2010. LNCS, vol. 6223, pp. 538–557. Springer, Heidelberg (2010). https://doi.org/10.1007/978-3-642-14623-7_29

9. Beimel, A., Omri, E., Orlov, I.: Secure multiparty computation with partial fairness. Cryptology ePrint Archive, Report 2010/599 (2010). http://eprint.iacr.org/2010/599

10. Ben-Or, M., Goldwasser, S., Wigderson, A.: Completeness theorems for non-cryptographic fault-tolerant distributed computation (extended abstract). In: STOC 1988 [39], pp. 1–10

11. Buchbinder, N., Haitner, I., Levi, N., Tsfadia, E.: Fair coin flipping: tighter analysis and the many-party case. In: Klein, P.N. (ed.) 28th SODA, pp. 2580–2600. ACM-SIAM, January 2017

12. Chaum, D., Crépeau, C., Damgård, I.: Multiparty unconditionally secure protocols (extended abstract). In: STOC 1988 [39], pp. 11–19

13. Cleve, R.: Limits on the security of coin flips when half the processors are faulty (extended abstract). In: 18th ACM STOC, pp. 364–369. ACM Press, May 1986

14. Cohen, R., Lindell, Y.: Fairness versus guaranteed output delivery in secure multiparty computation. In: Sarkar, P., Iwata, T. (eds.) ASIACRYPT 2014, Part II. LNCS, vol. 8874, pp. 466–485. Springer, Heidelberg (2014). https://doi.org/10.1007/978-3-662-45608-8_25

15. Dachman-Soled, D., Lindell, Y., Mahmoody, M., Malkin, T.: On the black-box complexity of optimally-fair coin tossing. In: Ishai, Y. (ed.) TCC 2011. LNCS, vol. 6597, pp. 450–467. Springer, Heidelberg (2011). https://doi.org/10.1007/978-3-642-19571-6_27

16. Dachman-Soled, D., Mahmoody, M., Malkin, T.: Can optimally-fair coin tossing be based on one-way functions? In: Lindell [32], pp. 217–239

17. Goldreich, O.: The Foundations of Cryptography - Volume 2: Basic Applications. Cambridge University Press, Cambridge (2004)

18. Goldreich, O., Micali, S., Wigderson, A.: How to play any mental game or a completeness theorem for protocols with honest majority. In: Aho, A. (ed.) 19th ACM STOC, pp. 218–229. ACM Press, May 1987

19. Gordon, S.D., Hazay, C., Katz, J., Lindell, Y.: Complete fairness in secure two-party computation. In: Ladner, R.E., Dwork, C. (eds.) 40th ACM STOC, pp. 413–422. ACM Press, May 2008

20. Gordon, D., Ishai, Y., Moran, T., Ostrovsky, R., Sahai, A.: On complete primitives for fairness. In: Micciancio, D. (ed.) TCC 2010. LNCS, vol. 5978, pp. 91–108. Springer, Heidelberg (2010). https://doi.org/10.1007/978-3-642-11799-2_7

21. Gordon, S.D., Katz, J.: Complete fairness in multi-party computation without an honest majority. In: Reingold [38], pp. 19–35

22. Gordon, S.D., Katz, J.: Partial fairness in secure two-party computation. In: Gilbert, H. (ed.) EUROCRYPT 2010. LNCS, vol. 6110, pp. 157–176. Springer, Heidelberg (2010). https://doi.org/10.1007/978-3-642-13190-5_8

23. Dov Gordon, S., Liu, F.-H., Shi, E.: Constant-round MPC with fairness and guarantee of output delivery. In: Gennaro, R., Robshaw, M. (eds.) CRYPTO 2015, Part II. LNCS, vol. 9216, pp. 63–82. Springer, Heidelberg (2015). https://doi.org/10.1007/978-3-662-48000-7_4

24. Haitner, I., Makriyannis, N., Omri, E.: On the complexity of fair coin flipping. In: Beimel, A., Dziembowski, S. (eds.) TCC 2018, Part I. LNCS, vol. 11239, pp. 539–562. Springer, Cham (2018). https://doi.org/10.1007/978-3-030-03807-6_20

25. Haitner, I., Tsfadia, E.: An almost-optimally fair three-party coin-flipping protocol. In: Shmoys, D.B. (ed.) 46th ACM STOC, pp. 408–416. ACM Press, May/June 2014

26. Hirt, M., Maurer, U.M.: Complete characterization of adversaries tolerable in secure multi-party computation (extended abstract). In: Burns, J.E., Attiya, H. (eds.) 16th ACM PODC, pp. 25–34. ACM, August 1997

27. Hirt, M., Maurer, U.M.: Player simulation and general adversary structures in perfect multiparty computation. J. Cryptol. 13(1), 31–60 (2000)

28. Ishai, Y., Katz, J., Kushilevitz, E., Lindell, Y., Petrank, E.: On achieving the best of both worlds in secure multiparty computation. Cryptology ePrint Archive, Report 2010/029 (2010). http://eprint.iacr.org/2010/029

29. Ishai, Y., Kushilevitz, E., Lindell, Y., Petrank, E.: On combining privacy with guaranteed output delivery in secure multiparty computation. In: Dwork, C. (ed.) CRYPTO 2006. LNCS, vol. 4117, pp. 483–500. Springer, Heidelberg (2006). https://doi.org/10.1007/11818175_29

30. Ishai, Y., Ostrovsky, R., Seyalioglu, H.: Identifying cheaters without an honest majority. In: Cramer, R. (ed.) TCC 2012. LNCS, vol. 7194, pp. 21–38. Springer, Heidelberg (2012). https://doi.org/10.1007/978-3-642-28914-9_2

31. Ishai, Y., Ostrovsky, R., Zikas, V.: Secure multi-party computation with identifiable abort. In: Garay, J.A., Gennaro, R. (eds.) CRYPTO 2014, Part II. LNCS, vol. 8617, pp. 369–386. Springer, Heidelberg (2014). https://doi.org/10.1007/978-3-662-44381-1_21

32. Lindell, Y. (ed.): TCC 2014. LNCS, vol. 8349. Springer, Heidelberg (2014)

33. Lindell, Y., Rabin, T.: Secure two-party computation with fairness - a necessary design principle. In: Kalai, Y., Reyzin, L. (eds.) TCC 2017, Part I. LNCS, vol. 10677, pp. 565–580. Springer, Cham (2017). https://doi.org/10.1007/978-3-319-70500-2_19

34. Moran, T., Naor, M., Segev, G.: An optimally fair coin toss. In: Reingold [38], pp. 1–18

35. Moran, T., Naor, M., Segev, G.: An optimally fair coin toss. J. Cryptol. 29(3), 491–513 (2016)

36. O'Donnell, R.: Analysis of Boolean Functions. Cambridge University Press, Cambridge (2014)

37. Rabin, T., Ben-Or, M.: Verifiable secret sharing and multiparty protocols with honest majority (extended abstract). In: 21st ACM STOC, pp. 73–85. ACM Press, May 1989

38. Reingold, O. (ed.): TCC 2009. LNCS, vol. 5444. Springer, Heidelberg (2009)

39. 20th ACM STOC. ACM Press, May 1988

On the Power of an Honest Majority in Three-Party Computation Without Broadcast

Bar Alon[1]([✉]), Ran Cohen[2], Eran Omri[1], and Tom Suad[1]

[1] Ariel University, Ariel Cyber Innovation Center (ACIC), Ariel, Israel
alonbar08@gmail.com, omrier@ariel.ac.il, tomsuad7@gmail.com
[2] Northeastern University, Boston, USA
rancohen@ccs.neu.edu

Abstract. Fully secure multiparty computation (MPC) allows a set of parties to compute some function of their inputs, while guaranteeing correctness, privacy, fairness, and output delivery. Understanding the necessary and sufficient assumptions that allow for fully secure MPC is an important goal. Cleve (STOC'86) showed that full security cannot be obtained in general without an honest majority. Conversely, by Rabin and Ben-Or (FOCS'89), assuming a broadcast channel and an honest majority enables a fully secure computation of any function.

Our goal is to characterize the set of functionalities that can be computed with full security, assuming an honest majority, but no broadcast. This question was fully answered by Cohen et al. (TCC'16) – for the restricted class of *symmetric* functionalities (where all parties receive the same output). Instructively, their results crucially rely on *agreement* and do not carry over to general *asymmetric* functionalities. In this work, we focus on the case of three-party asymmetric functionalities, providing a variety of necessary and sufficient conditions to enable fully secure computation.

An interesting use-case of our results is *server-aided* computation, where an untrusted server helps two parties to carry out their computation. We show that without a broadcast assumption, the resource of an external non-colluding server provides no additional power. Namely, a functionality can be computed with the help of the server if and only if it can be computed without it. For fair coin tossing, we further show that the optimal bias for three-party (server-aided) r-round protocol remains $\Theta(1/r)$ (as in the two-party setting).

Keywords: Broadcast · Point-to-point communication · Multiparty computation · Coin flipping · Impossibility result · Honest majority

B. Alon, E. Omri and T. Suad—Research supported by ISF grant 152/17, and by the Ariel Cyber Innovation Center in conjunction with the Israel National Cyber directorate in the Prime Minister's Office.

R. Cohen—Research supported by NSF grant 1646671.

R. Pass and K. Pietrzak (Eds.): TCC 2020, LNCS 12551, pp. 621–651, 2020.
https://doi.org/10.1007/978-3-030-64378-2_22

1   Introduction

In the setting of secure multiparty computation [9,16,28,38,39], a set of mutually distrustful parties wish to compute a function f of their private inputs. The computation should preserve a number of security properties even facing a subset of colluding cheating parties, such as: *correctness* (cheating parties can only affect the output by choosing their inputs), *privacy* (nothing but the specified output is learned), *fairness* (all parties receive an output or none do), and even *guaranteed output delivery* (meaning that all honestly behaving parties always learn an output). Informally speaking, a protocol π computes a functionality f with *full security* if it provides all of the above security properties.[1]

In the late 1980's, it was shown that every function can be computed with full security in the presence of malicious adversaries corrupting a strict minority of the parties, assuming the existence of a *broadcast communication channel* (such a channel allows any party to reliably send its message to all other parties, guaranteeing that all parties receive the same message) and pairwise private channels (that can be established over broadcast using standard cryptographic techniques) [9,38]. On the other hand, a well-known lower bound by Cleve [17] shows that if an honest majority is not assumed, then *fairness* cannot be guaranteed in general (even assuming a broadcast channel). More specifically, Cleve's result showed that given a two-party, r-round coin-tossing protocol, there exists an (efficient) adversarial strategy that can bias the output bit by $\Omega(1/r)$.

Conversely, a second well-known lower bound from the 1980's shows that in the plain model (i.e., without setup/proof-of-work assumptions), no protocol for computing broadcast can tolerate corruptions of one third of the parties [22,34,37].

This leads us to the main question studied in this paper:

What is the power of the honest-majority assumption
in a model where parties cannot broadcast?

Namely, we set to characterize the set of n-party functionalities that can be computed with full security over point-to-point channels in the plain model (i.e., without broadcast), in the face of malicious adversaries, corrupting up to t parties, where $n/3 \leq t < n/2$.

Cohen et al. [19] answered the above question for *symmetric functionalities*, where all parties obtain the same common output from the computation. They showed that, in the plain model over point-to-point channels, a function f can be computed with full security if and only if f is $(n - 2t)$-*dominated*, i.e., there exists a value y^* such that any $n - 2t$ of the inputs can determine the output of f to be y^* (for example, Boolean OR is 1-dominated since any input can be set to 1, forcing the output to be 1). They further showed that there is no n-party, $\lceil n/3 \rceil$-secure, δ-bias coin-tossing protocol, for any $\delta < 1/2$.

---

[1] The notion of full security is formally captured via the real vs. ideal paradigm, where the protocol is said to be secure if it emulates some ideal setting, in which the capabilities of the adversary are very limited.

The results in [19] leave open the setting of *asymmetric functionalities*, where each party computes a different function over the same inputs. Such functionalities include symmetric computations as a special case, but they are more general since the output that each party receives may be considered private and some parties may not even receive any output. Specifically, the lower bound from [19] does not translate into the asymmetric setting, as it crucially relies on a *consistency* requirement on the protocol, ensuring that all honest parties output the same value.

Asymmetric computations are very natural in the context of MPC in general, however, the following two use-cases are of particular interest:

Server-aided computation: Augmenting a two-party computation with a (potentially untrusted) server that provides no input and obtains no output has proven to be a very useful paradigm in overcoming lower bounds, even when the server may collude with one of the parties as in the case of optimistic fairness [6,14]. In the broadcast model, considering a *non-colluding* server is a real game changer, as it enables two parties to compute *any* function with full security. In our setting, where broadcast is not available, we explore to what extent a non-colluding server can boost the security of two-party computation. For the specific task of coin tossing we ask: "can two parties use a non-colluding third party to help them toss a coin?"

Computation with solitary output: Halevi et al. [32] studied computations in which only a single party obtains the output, e.g., a server that learns a function of the inputs of two clients. The focus of [32] was on the broadcast model with a dishonest majority, and they showed a variety of feasibility and infeasibility results. In this work we consider a model without broadcast but with an honest majority, which reopens the feasibility question. Fitzi et al. [25] showed that if the three-party solitary-output functionality *convergecast*[2] can be securely computed facing a single corruption, then so can the broadcast functionality; thus, proving the impossibility of securely computing convergecast in our setting. In this work, we extend the exploration of the set of securely computable solitary-output functionalities.

1.1 Split-Brain Simulatability

In this paper, we focus on general asymmetric three-party functionalities, where party A with input x, party B with input y, and party C with input z, compute a functionality $f = (f_1, f_2, f_3)$. The output of A is $f_1(x, y, z)$, the output of B is $f_2(x, y, z)$, and the output of C is $f_3(x, y, z)$. We will also consider the special cases of *two-output functionalities* where only A and B receive output (meaning that f_3 is degenerate), and of *solitary-output functionalities* where only A receives output (meaning that f_2 and f_3 are degenerate).

---

[2] Convergecast [25] is a three-party functionality where two of the parties start with a non-Boolean input, and the receiver learns exactly one of the input values. The receiver does not learn anything about the other input, and none of the senders learns the receiver's choice as well as the input of the other sender.

Our main technical contribution is adapting the so called *split-brain argument*, which was previously used in the context of Byzantine agreement [11,12,21] (where privacy is not required, but agreement must be guaranteed) to the setting of MPC. Indeed, aiming at full security, we are able to broaden the collection of infeasible functionalities. In particular, our results apply to the setting where the parties do not necessarily agree on a common output.

In Sect. 1.3 we provide a more detailed overview of the split-brain attack, however, the core idea can be explained as follows. Let $f = (f_1, f_2, f_3)$ be an asymmetric (possibly randomized) three-party functionality and let π be a secure protocol computing f over point-to-point channels, tolerating a single corruption. For the sake of simplicity of the presentation, in the remaining of this introduction we only consider perfect security and functionalities with finite domain and range. A formal treatment for general functionalities and computational security is given in Sect. 3.1. Consider the following two scenarios:

- A corrupted (split-brain) party C playing two independent interactions: in the *first* interaction, C interacts with A on input z_1 acting as if it never received any incoming messages from B, and in the *second* interaction, C interacts with B on input z_2, acting as if it never received any incoming messages from A.
- A corrupted party A internally emulating a first interaction of the above split-brain C: A interacts with B, ignoring all incoming messages from the honest C; instead, A emulates in its head the above (first-interaction) C on input z_1 (This part of the attack relies on the no-trusted-setup assumption, and on the fact that emulating C requires no interaction with B).

Clearly, the view of party B is identically distributed in both of these scenarios; hence, its output must be identically distributed as well. Note that by symmetry, an attacker B can be defined analogously to the above A, causing the output of an honest A to distribute as when interacting with the split-brain C.

By the assumed security of the protocol π, each of the three attacks described above can be simulated in an ideal world where a trusted party computes f for the parties. Since the only power the simulator has in the ideal world is to choose the input for the corrupted party, we can capture the properties that the functionality f must satisfy to enable the existence of such simulators via the following definition.

Definition 1 (CSB-simulatability, informal). *A three-party functionality* $f = (f_1, f_2, f_3)$ *is* C-*split-brain (CSB) simulatable if for every quadruple* (x, y, z_1, z_2), *there exist a distribution* P_{x,z_1} *over the inputs of* A, *a distribution* Q_{y,z_2} *over the inputs of* B, *and a distribution* R_{z_1,z_2} *over the inputs of* C, *such that*

$$f_1(x, y^*, z_1) \equiv f_1(x, y, z^*) \quad and \quad f_2(x^*, y, z_2) \equiv f_2(x, y, z^*),$$

where $x^* \leftarrow P_{x,z_1}$, $y^* \leftarrow Q_{y,z_2}$, *and* $z^* \leftarrow R_{z_1,z_2}$.

1.2   Our Results

Using the notion of split-brain simulatability, mentioned in Sect. 1.1, we present several necessary conditions for an asymmetric three-party functionality to be securely computable without broadcast while tolerating a single corruption. We also present a sufficient condition for two-output functionalities (including solitary output functionalities as a special case); the latter result captures and generalizes previously known feasibility results in this setting, including 1-dominated functionalities [18,19] and fair two-party functionalities [5]. Examples illustrating the implications of these theorems for different functionalities is provided in Table 1.

Impossibility Results. Our first impossibility result asserts that CSB simulatability is a necessary condition for securely computing a three-party functionality in our setting.

Theorem 1 (necessity of split-brain simulatability, informal). *A three-party functionality that can be securely computed over point-to-point channels, tolerating a single corruption, must be CSB simulatable.*

We can define A-split-brain and B-split-brain simulatability analogously, thus providing additional necessary conditions for secure computation. For a formal statement and proof we refer the reader to Sect. 3.1.

To illustrate the usefulness of the theorem, consider the two-output functionality where $f_1 = f_2$ are defined as $f_1(x, y, z) = (x \wedge y) \oplus z$. Note that since f_3 is degenerate, this functionality is not symmetric and therefore the lower bound from [19] does not rule it out. We next show that f is *not* CSB simulatable, and hence, cannot be securely computed. Clearly, input 0 for A and C will fix the output to be 0, whereas input 0 for B and input 1 for C will fix the output to be 1. The CSB simulatability of f would require that there exists distributions for sampling x^* and y^* such that

$$0 \equiv f_1(0, y^*, 0) \equiv f_1(x^*, 0, 1) \equiv 1.$$

This leads to a contradiction.

Our second result, is in the *server-aided* model, where only A and B provide input and receive output. We show that in this model, a functionality can be computed with the help of C if and only if it can be computed without C. In the theorem below we denote by λ the empty string.

Theorem 2 (server-aided computation is as strong as two-party computation, informal). *Let f be a three-party functionality where C has no input and no output. Then, f can be securely computed over point-to-point channels tolerating a single corruption if and only if the induced two-party functionality $g(x, y) = f(x, y, \lambda)$ can be computed with full security.*

An immediate corollary from Theorem 2 is that a non-colluding third party cannot help the two parties to toss a fair coin. In fact, if C cannot attack the protocol (i.e., C cannot bias the output coin), then the attack that is guaranteed by Cleve [17] (on the implied two-party protocol) can be directly translated to an attack on the three-party protocol, corrupting either A or B. Stated differently, either A or B can bias the output by $\Omega\left(1/r\right)$, where r is the number of rounds in the protocol. However, the above argument does not deal with protocols that allow a corrupt C to slightly bias the output. For example, one might try to construct a protocol where every party (including C) can bias the output by at most $1/r^2$. We strengthen the result for coin tossing, showing that this is in fact impossible.

Theorem 3 (implication to coin tossing, informal). *Consider a three-party, two-output, r-round coin-tossing protocol. Then, there exists an adversary corrupting a single party that can bias the output by $\Omega\left(1/r\right)$.*

As a result, letting A and B run the protocol of Moran et al. [36] constitutes an optimally fair (up to a constant) coin-tossing protocol.

We note that using a standard player-partitioning argument, the impossibility result extends to n-party r-round coin-tossing protocols, where *two* parties receive the output. Specifically, there exists an adversary corrupting $\lceil n/3 \rceil$ parties that can bias the output by $\Omega\left(1/r\right)$. Further, using [19, Lem. 4.10] we rule out any non-trivial n-party coin-tossing where *three* parties receive the output.

Another immediate corollary from Theorem 2 is that two-output functionalities that imply coin-tossing are not securely computable, even if C has an input. For example, the XOR function $(x, y, z) \mapsto x \oplus y \oplus z$ is not computable facing one corruption. For a formal treatment of server-aided computation, see Sect. 3.2.

Our third impossibility result presents two functionalities that are not captured by Theorems 2 and 3. Interestingly, unlike the previous results, here we make use of the *privacy* requirement on the protocol for obtaining the proof. We refer the reader to Sect. 1.3 below for an intuitive explanation, and Sect. 3.3 for a formal proof.

Theorem 4 (Informal). *Let f be a solitary-output three-party functionality where $f_1(x, y, z) = (x \wedge y) \oplus z$ (equivalently, $f_1(x, y, z) = (x \oplus y) \wedge z$). Then, f cannot be securely computed over point-to-point channels tolerating a single corruption.*

Feasibility Results. We proceed to state our sufficient condition. We present a class of two-output functionalities f that can be computed with full security. Interestingly, our result shows that if f is CSB simulatable, then under a simple condition that a related two-party functionality needs to satisfy, the problem is reduced to the two-party case. In the related two-party functionality, the first party holds x and z_1, while the second party holds y and z_2, and is defined as $f'((x, z_1), (y, z_2)) = f(x, y, z^*)$, where $z^* \leftarrow R_{z_1, z_2}$ is sampled as in the requirement of CSB simulatability.

Roughly, we require that there exist two distributions, for z_1 and z_2 respectively, such that the input z_1 can be sampled in a way that fixes the distribution of the output of f' to be independent of z_2, and similarly, that the input z_2

can be sampled in a way that fixes the distribution of the output of f' to be independent of z_1. Specifically, we prove the following.

Theorem 5 (Informal). *Let* $f = (f_1, f_2)$ *be a CSB simulatable three-party, two-output functionality. Define the two-party functionality* f' *as* $f'((x, z_1), (y, z_2)) = f(x, y, z^*)$, *where* $z^* \leftarrow R_{z_1, z_2}$.

Assume that there exists a randomized two-party functionality $g = (g_1, g_2)$ *and two distributions* R_1 *and* R_2 *over* C*'s inputs such that for every* $x, y, z \in \{0, 1\}^*$ *it holds that* $g(x, y) \equiv f'((x, z_1), (y, z)) \equiv f'((x, z), (y, z_2))$, *where* $z_1 \leftarrow R_1$ *and* $z_2 \leftarrow R_2$.

If g *can be securely computed with full security then* f *can be securely computed with full security over point-to-point channels tolerating a single corruption.*

The idea behind the protocol is as follows. First, by the honest-majority assumption, the parties can compute f with guaranteed output delivery *assuming a broadcast channel* [38]. By [18] it follows that they can compute f with *fairness* without using broadcast. If the parties receive an output, they can terminate; otherwise, A and B compute g using their inputs, *ignoring* C *in the process* (even if it is honest).

Intuitively, the existence of R_1 and R_2 allows the simulators of a corrupt A or a corrupt B, to "force" a computation of g in the ideal world of f; that is, the output will be independent of the input of C. To see this, consider a corrupt A and let $z_1 \leftarrow R_1$. Then, by the CSB simulatability assumption, sending $x^* \leftarrow P_{x, z_1}$ to the trusted party results in the output being

$$f(x^*, y, z) \equiv f(x, y, z^*) \equiv f'((x, z_1), (y, z)) \equiv g(x, y),$$

where $z^* \leftarrow R_{z_1, z}$.

In Sect. 1.3 below we give a more detailed overview of the proof. In Sect. 4 we present the formal statement and proof of the theorem.

We briefly describe a few classes of functions that are captured by Theorem 5. First, observe that the class of functionalities satisfying the above conditions contains the class of 1-dominated functionalities [19]. To see this, notice that x^*, y^*, and z^* can be sampled in a way that always fixes the output of f to be some value w^*. Then, any choice of R_1 and R_2 will do. Furthermore, observe that the resulting two-party functionality g will always be the constant function, with the output being w^*.

Another class of functions captured by the theorem is the class of fair two-party functionalities. For such functionalities the distributions R_{z_1, z_2}, R_1, and R_2 can be degenerate, as z^*, z_1, and z_2 play no role in the computation of f and f'. Additionally, taking $x^* = x$ and $y^* = y$ with probability 1 will satisfy the CSB simulatability constraint.

Next, we show that the class of functionalities satisfying the conditions of Theorem 5 includes functionalities that are *not* 1-dominated. Consider as an example the solitary XOR function $f(x, y, z) = x \oplus y \oplus z$. Note that for solitary-output functionalities the two-party functionality g can always be securely computed assuming oblivious transfer [33]. Furthermore, f is CSB simulatable since we can sample y^* and z^* uniformly at random. In addition, taking R_1 and R_2 to output a uniform random bit as well will satisfy the conditions of Theorem 5.

Finally, there are even two-output functionalities that are not 1-dominated, yet are still captured by Theorem 5. For example, consider the following three-party variant of the GHKL function [29], denoted 3P-GHKL: let $f = (f_1, f_2)$, where $f_1, f_2 : \{0,1,2\} \times \{0,1\} \times \{0,1\} \mapsto \{0,1\}$. The functionality is defined by the following two matrices

$$M_0 = \begin{pmatrix} 0 & 1 \\ 1 & 0 \\ 1 & 1 \end{pmatrix} \qquad M_1 = \begin{pmatrix} 1 & 0 \\ 0 & 1 \\ 1 & 1 \end{pmatrix}$$

where $f_1(x,y,z) = f_2(x,y,z) = M_z(x,y)$. That is, A's input determines a row, B's input determines a column, and C's input determines the matrix. For the above functionality, sampling y^* and z^* uniformly at random, and taking $x^* = x$ if $x = 2$ and a uniform bit otherwise, will always generate an output that is equal to 1 if $x = 2$ and a uniform bit otherwise. See Sect. 4.1 for more details.

Table 1. Summarizing the feasibility of interesting three-party functionalities tolerating one corruption. The second column considers the solitary case where only A receives the output, the third the two-output case where both A and B receive the same output, and the last column the case where all parties receive the same output.

functionality	A outputs	A, B output	A, B, C output
$x \wedge y \wedge z$	✓ [18]	✓ [18]	✓ [18]
$(x \wedge y) \oplus z$ $(x \oplus y) \wedge z$	✗ Theorem 4	✗ Theorem 1 (also 4)	✗ [19] (also Theorem 1, 4)
$x \oplus y \oplus z$ $x \wedge (y \oplus z)$ $x \oplus (y \wedge z)$	✓ Theorem 5	✗ Theorem 2	✗ [19] (also Theorem 2)
3P-GHKL	✓ Theorem 5	✓ Theorem 5	✗ [19]
δ-bias coin tossing	✓ $\delta = 0$ (trivial)	✓ $\delta = \Theta(1/r)$ [36] ✗ $\delta = o(1/r)$, Theorem 3	✗ $\delta < 1/2$ [19]

1.3 Our Techniques

We now turn to describe our techniques, starting with our impossibility results. The core argument in all of our proofs, is the use of an adaptation of the split-brain argument [11,12,21] to the MPC setting.

The C-split-brain argument. In the following, let f be a three-party functionality and let π be a protocol computing f with full security over point-to-point channels, tolerating a single corrupted party. Consider the following three attack-scenarios with inputs x, y, z_1, z_2 depicted in Fig. 1.

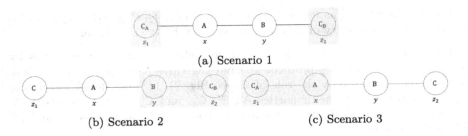

(a) Scenario 1

(b) Scenario 2   (c) Scenario 3

Fig. 1. Three adversaries of the C-split-brain attack. The shaded yellow areas in each scenario correspond to the (virtual) parties the adversary controls.

Scenario 1: Parties A and B both play honestly on inputs x and y respectively. The adversary corrupts C and applies the *split-brain attack*, that is, it emulates in its head two virtual copies of C, denoted C_A and C_B. C_A interacts with A as an honest C would on input z_1 as if it never received messages from B, and C_B interacts with B as an honest C would on input z_2 as if it never received messages from A.

By the assumed security of π, there exists a simulator for the corrupted C. This simulator defines a distribution over the input it sends to the trusted party. Thus, the outputs of A and B in this case must equal to $f_1(x, y, z^*)$ and $f_2(x, y, z^*)$, respectively, where z^* is sampled according to some distribution that depends only on z_1 and z_2.

Scenario 2: Party A plays honestly on input x and party C plays honestly on input z_1. The adversary corrupts party B, ignoring all incoming messages from C and not sending it any messages. Instead, the adversary emulates in its head the virtual party C_B as in Scenario 1, that plays honestly on input z_2 as if it never received any message from A. Additionally, the adversary instructs B to play honestly in this setting.

As in Scenario 1, by the assumed security of π, the output of A in this case must equal $f_1(x, y^*, z_1)$, where y^* is sampled according to some distribution that depends only on y and z_2.

Scenario 3: This is analogous to Scenario 2. Party B plays honestly on input y and party C plays honestly on input z_2. The adversary corrupts party A, ignoring all incoming messages from C and not sending it any messages. Similarly to Scenario 2, the adversary emulates in its head the virtual C_A, that plays honestly on input z_1 as if it never received any message from B, and instructs A to plays honestly in this setting.

As in the previous two scenarios, the output of B must equal $f_2(x^*, y, z_2)$, where x^* is sampled according to some distribution that depends only on x and z_1.

Observe that the view of the honest A in Scenario 1 is identically distributed as its view in Scenario 2; hence the same holds with respect to its output, i.e., $f_1(x, y^*, z_1) \equiv f_1(x, y, z^*)$. Similarly, the view of the honest B in Scenario 1 is identically distributed as its view Scenario 3; hence, $f_2(x^*, y, z_2) \equiv f_2(x, y, z^*)$. This proves the necessity of C-split-brain simulatability (i.e., Theorem 1).

The Four-Party Protocol. A nice way to formalize the above argument is by constructing a four-party protocol π' from the three-party protocol π, where two different parties play the role of C (see Fig. 2). In more detail, define the four-party protocol π', with parties A', B', C'_A, and C'_B, as follows. Party A' follows the code of A, party B' follows the code of B, and parties C'_A and C'_B follow the code of C.

The parties are connected on a path where (1) C'_A is the leftmost node, and is connected only to A', (2) C'_B is the rightmost node, and is connected only to B', and (3) A' and B' are also connected to each other. The second communication line of party C'_A is "disconnected" in the sense that C'_A is sending the messages as instructed by the protocol, but the messages arrive at a "sink" that does not send any messages back. Stated differently, the view of C'_A corresponds to the view of an honest C in π that never received any message from B. Similarly, the second communication line of party C'_B is "disconnected," and its view corresponds to the view of an honest C in π that never receives any message from A.

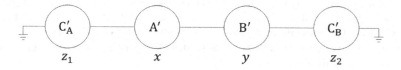

Fig. 2. The induced four-party protocol

Server-Aided Computation. We now make use of the four-party protocol to sketch the proof of Theorem 2. Recall that here we consider the server-aided model, where C (the server) has no input and obtains no output. Observe that under the assumption that π securely computes f, it follows that the four-party protocol π' correctly computes the two-output four-party functionality $f'(x, y, \lambda, \lambda) := f(x, y, \lambda)$, where λ is the empty string, as otherwise C could emulate C'_A and C'_B in its head and force A and B to output an incorrect value.

Next, consider the following *two-party* protocol $\widehat{\pi}$ where each of two pairs $\{\mathsf{A}', \mathsf{C}'_\mathsf{A}\}$ and $\{\mathsf{B}', \mathsf{C}'_\mathsf{B}\}$, is emulated by a single entity, $\widehat{\mathsf{A}}$ and $\widehat{\mathsf{B}}$ respectively, as depicted in Fig. 3. Observe that the protocol computes the two-party functionality $g(x, y) := f'(x, y, \lambda, \lambda) = f(x, y, \lambda)$. Furthermore, it computes g securely, since any adversary for the two-party protocol directly translates to an adversary for the three-party protocol corrupting either A or B. Moreover, since C does not have an input, the simulators of those adversaries in π can be directly translated to simulators for the adversaries in $\widehat{\pi}$. Thus, f can be computed with the help of C if and only if it can be computed without C.

The proof of Theorem 3, i.e., that the optimal bias for the server-aided coin-tossing protocol is $\Theta(1/r)$, extends the above analysis. We show that for any

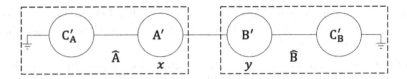

Fig. 3. The induced two-party protocol

r-round server-aided coin-tossing protocol π there exists a constant c and an adversary that can bias the output by at least $1/cr$. Roughly, assuming that party C cannot bias the output of π by more than $1/cr$, the output of A' and B' in the four-party protocol is a common bit that is $(1/cr)$-close to being uniform. Therefore, the same holds with respect to the outputs of $\widehat{\mathsf{A}}$ and $\widehat{\mathsf{B}}$ in the two-party protocol. Now, we can apply the result of Agrawal and Prabhakaran [1], which generalizes Cleve's [17] result to a general two-party sampling functionality. Their result provides an adversary for the two-party functionality that can bias by $1/dr$ for some constant d. Finally, we can emulate their adversary in the three party protocol as depicted in Scenarios 2 and 3. For sufficiently large c (specifically, $c > 2d$), the bias resulting from emulating the adversaries for the two-party protocol will be at least $1/cr$.

Impossibility Based on Privacy. We next sketch the proof of Theorem 4. That is, the solitary-output functionalities $f_1(x, y, z) = (x \wedge y) \oplus z$ and $f_1(x, y, z) = (x \oplus y) \wedge z$ cannot be computed in our setting. We prove it only for the case where the output of A is defined to be $f_1(x, y, z) = (x \wedge y) \oplus z$. The other case is proved using a similar analysis. The proof starts from the C-split-brain argument used in the proof of Theorem 1. Assume for the sake of contradiction that π computes f with perfect security. First, let us consider the following two scenarios.

- C is corrupted as in Scenario 1, i.e., it applies the split-brain attack with inputs z_1 and z_2. By the security of π, the output of A in this case is $(x \wedge y) \oplus z^*$, for some z^* that is sampled according some distribution that depends on z_1 and z_2.
- B is corrupted as in Scenario 2, i.e., it imagines that it interacts with C_B with input z_2 that does not receive any message from A. In this case, the output of A is $(x \wedge y^*) \oplus z_1$, where z_1 is the input of the real C, and y^* is sampled according some distribution that depends on y and z_2.

By Theorem 1 these two distributions are identically distributed for all $x \in \{0, 1\}$. Notice that setting $x = 0$ yields $z^* = z_1$ and that setting $x = 1$ yields $y^* \oplus z_1 = y \oplus z^*$, hence $y^* = y$. Therefore, the output of A in both scenarios is $(x \wedge y) \oplus z_1$.

Finally, consider an execution of π over random inputs y for B and z for C, where A is corrupted as in Scenario 2, and it emulates C_A' on input z_1. Since its view is exactly the same as in the other two scenarios, it can compute $(x \wedge y) \oplus z_1$. However, in this scenario A can choose $x = 1$ and $z_1 = 0$ and thus learn y. In the ideal world, however, A cannot guess y with probability better than $1/2$, as the output it sees is $(x \wedge y) \oplus z$ for random y and z. Hence, we have a contradiction to the security of π.

A Protocol for Computing Certain Two-Output Functionalities. Finally, We describe the idea behind the proof of Theorem 5. First, by the honest-majority assumption, the protocol of Rabin and Ben-Or [38] computes f assuming a *broadcast channel*; by [18] it follows that f can be computed with *fairness* over a point-to-point network. We now describe the protocol. The parties start by computing f with fairness. If they receive outputs, then they can terminate, and output what they received. If the protocol aborts, then A and B compute g with their original inputs using a protocol that guarantees output delivery (such a protocol exists by assumption), and output whatever outcome is computed. Clearly, a corrupt C cannot attack the protocol. Indeed, it does not gain any information in the fair computation of f; hence, if it aborts in this phase then the output of A on input x and B on input y will be $g(x,y) = f'((x, z_1), (y, z)) = f(x, y, z^*)$, where $z_1 \leftarrow R_1$ and $z^* \leftarrow R_{z_1, z}$.

We next consider a corrupt A (the case of a corrupt B is analogous). The idea is to take the distribution over the inputs used by the *two-party* simulator, and translate it into an appropriate distribution for the *three-party* simulator. That is, regardless of the input of C, the output of the honest party will be distributed exactly the same as in the ideal world for the two-party computation. To see how this can be done, consider a sample $z_1 \leftarrow R_1$ and let x' be the input sent by the two-party simulator to its trusted party. The three-party simulator will send to the trusted party the sample $x^* \leftarrow P_{x', z_1}$. Then, by the CSB simulatability constraint, it follows that the output will be $f(x^*, y, z) \equiv f(x', y, z^*)$, where $z^* \leftarrow R_{z_1, z}$. However, by requirement from the two-party functionality g, it follows that $g(x', y) \equiv f(x', y, z^*)$; hence, the output in the three-party ideal-world of f, is identically distributed as in the two-party ideal-world of g.

1.4 Additional Related Work

The split-brain argument has been used in the context of Byzantine agreement (BA) to rule out three-party protocols tolerating one corruption in various settings: over asynchronous networks [12] and partially synchronous networks [21], even with trusted setup assumptions such a public-key infrastructure (PKI), as well as over synchronous networks with weak forms of PKI [11]. The argument was mainly used by considering three parties (A, B, C) where party A starts with 0, party B starts with 1, and party C plays towards A with 0 and towards B with 1. By the *validity* property of BA it is shown that A must output 0 and B must output 1, which contradicts the *agreement* property. Our usage of the split-brain argument is different as it considers (1) *asymmetric* computations where parties do not agree on the output (and so we do not rely on violating agreement) and (2) *privacy-aware* computations that do not reveal anything beyond the prescribed output (as opposed to BA which is a privacy-free computation).

For the case of *symmetric* functionalities Cohen et al. [19] showed that $f(x, y, z)$ can be securely computed with guaranteed output delivery over point-to-point channels if and only if f is 1-dominated. Their lower bound followed the classical Hexagon argument of Fischer et al. [22] that was used for various consensus problems. Starting with a secure protocol π for f tolerating one corruption, they constructed a sufficiently large ring system where all nodes are guaranteed to output the same value (by reducing to the agreement property of f). Since the ring is sufficiently large (larger than the number of rounds in π), information from one side could not reach the other side. Combining these two properties yields an attacker that can fix some output value on one side of the ring, and force all nodes to output this value—in particular, when attacking π, the two honest parties participate in the ring (without knowing it) and so their output is fixed by the attacker. We note that this argument completely breaks when considering *asymmetric* functionalities, since it no longer holds that the nodes on the ring output the same value.

Cohen and Lindell [18] showed that any functionality that can be computed with guaranteed output delivery in the broadcast model can also be computed with *fairness* over point-to-point channels (using detectable broadcast protocols [23, 24]); as a special case, any functionality can be computed with fairness assuming an honest majority. Indeed, our lower bounds do not hold when the parties are allowed to abort upon detecting cheats, and rely on robustness of the protocol.

Recently, Garay et al. [26] showed how to compute every function in the honest-majority setting without broadcast or PKI, by restricting the power of the adversary in a proof-of-work fashion. This result falls outside our model as we consider the standard model without posing any restrictions on the resources of the adversary.

The possibility of obtaining fully secure protocols for non-trivial functions in the two-party setting (i.e., with no honest majority) was first investigated by Gordon et al. [29]. The showed that, surprisingly, such protocols do exist, even for functionalities with an embedded XOR. The feasibility and infeasibility results of [29] were substantially generalized in the works [4, 35]. The set of Boolean functionalities that are computable with full security was characterized in [5].

The breakthrough result of Moran et al. [36], who gave an optimally fair two-party coin-tossing protocol, paved the way to a long line of research on optimally fair coin-tossing. Positive results for the multiparty setting (with no honest majority) where given [2, 7, 13, 20, 30] alongside some new lower-bounds [8, 31].

Organization

In Sect. 2 we present the required preliminaries and formally define the model we consider. Then, in Sect. 3 we present our impossibility results. Finally, in Sect. 4 we prove our positive results.

2   Preliminaries

2.1   Notations

We use calligraphic letters to denote sets, uppercase for random variables and distributions, lowercase for values, and we use bold characters to denote vectors. For $n \in \mathbb{N}$, let $[n] = \{1, 2 \ldots n\}$. For a set $\mathcal{S}$ we write $s \leftarrow \mathcal{S}$ to indicate that s is selected uniformly at random from $\mathcal{S}$. Given a random variable (or a distribution) X, we write $x \leftarrow X$ to indicate that x is selected according to X. A PPT is probabilistic polynomial time, and a PPTM is a PPT (interactive) Turing machine. We let λ be the empty string.

A function $\mu \colon \mathbb{N} \to [0, 1]$ is called negligible, if for every positive polynomial $p(\cdot)$ and all sufficiently large n, it holds that $\mu(n) < 1/p(n)$. For a randomized function (or an algorithm) f we write $f(x)$ to denote the random variable induced by the function on input x, and write $f(x; r)$ to denote the value when the randomness of f is fixed to r. For a 2-ary function f and an input x, we denote by $f(x, \cdot)$ the function $f_x(y) := f(x, y)$. Similarly, for an input y we let $f(\cdot, y)$ be the function $f_y(x) := f(x, y)$. We extend the notations for n-ary functions in a straightforward way.

A *distribution ensemble* $X = \{X_{a,n}\}_{a \in \mathcal{D}_n, n \in \mathbb{N}}$ is an infinite sequence of random variables indexed by $a \in \mathcal{D}_n$ and $n \in \mathbb{N}$, where $\mathcal{D}_n$ is a domain that might depend on n. The statistical distance between two finite distributions is defined as follows.

Definition 2. *The statistical distance between two finite random variables X and Y is*

$$\mathrm{SD}\,(X, Y) = \frac{1}{2} \sum_a |\Pr\,[X = a] - \Pr\,[Y = a]| \,.$$

For a function $\varepsilon : \mathbb{N} \mapsto [0, 1]$, the two ensembles $X = \{X_{a,n}\}_{a \in \mathcal{D}_n, n \in \mathbb{N}}$ and $Y = \{Y_{a,n}\}_{a \in \mathcal{D}_n, n \in \mathbb{N}}$ are said to be ε-close, if for all large enough n and $a \in \mathcal{D}_n$, it holds that

$$\mathrm{SD}\,(X_{a,n}, Y_{a,n}) \leq \varepsilon(n),$$

and are said to be ε-far otherwise. X and Y are said to be statistically close, *denoted $X \overset{S}{\equiv} Y$, if they are ε-close for some negligible function ε. If X and Y are 0-close then they are said to be equivalent, denoted $X \equiv Y$.*

Computational indistinguishability is defined as follows.

Definition 3. *Let $X = \{X_{a,n}\}_{a \in \mathcal{D}_n, n \in \mathbb{N}}$ and $Y = \{Y_{a,n}\}_{a \in \mathcal{D}_n, n \in \mathbb{N}}$ be two ensembles. We say that X and Y are computationally indistinguishable, denoted $X \overset{C}{\equiv} Y$, if for every non-uniform PPT distinguisher D, there exists a negligible function $\mu(\cdot)$, such that for all n and $a \in \mathcal{D}_n$, it holds that*

$$|\Pr\,[\mathsf{D}(X_{a,n}) = 1] - \Pr\,[\mathsf{D}(Y_{a,n}) = 1]| \leq \mu(n).$$

2.2 The Model of Computation

We provide the basic definitions for secure multiparty computation according to the real/ideal paradigm, for further details see [27]. Intuitively, a protocol is considered secure if whatever an adversary can do in the real execution of protocol, can be done also in an ideal computation, in which an uncorrupted trusted party assists the computation. For concreteness, we present the model and the security definition for three-party computation with an adversary corrupting a single party, as this is the main focus of this work. We refer to [27] for the general definition.

The Real Model

A three-party protocol π is defined by a set of three PPT interactive Turing machines A, B, and C. Each Turing machine (party) holds at the beginning of the execution the common security parameter 1^κ, a private input, and random coins. The *adversary* Adv is a *non-uniform* PPT interactive Turing machine, receiving an auxiliary information $\mathsf{aux} \in \{0,1\}^*$, describing the behavior of a corrupted party $\mathsf{P} \in \{\mathsf{A}, \mathsf{B}, \mathsf{C}\}$. It starts the execution with input that contains the identity of the corrupted party, its input, and an additional auxiliary input aux.

The parties execute the protocol over a synchronous network. That is, the execution proceeds in rounds: each round consists of a *send phase* (where parties send their messages for this round) followed by a *receive phase* (where they receive messages from other parties). The adversary is assumed to be *rushing*, which means that it can see the messages the honest parties send in a round before determining the messages that the corrupted parties send in that round.

We consider a fully connected point-to-point network, where every pair of parties is connected by a communication line. We will consider the *secure-channels* model, where the communication lines are assumed to be ideally private (and thus the adversary cannot read or modify messages sent between two honest parties). We assume the parties *do not* have access to a broadcast channel, and no preprocessing phase (such as a public-key infrastructure that can be used to construct a broadcast protocol) is available. We note that our upper bounds (protocols) can also be stated in the *authenticated-channels* model, where the communication lines are assumed to be ideally authenticated but not private (and thus the adversary cannot modify messages sent between two honest parties but can read them) via standard techniques, assuming public-key encryption. On the other hand, stating our lower bounds assuming secure channels will provide stronger results.

Throughout the execution of the protocol, all the honest parties follow the instructions of the prescribed protocol, whereas the corrupted party receive its instructions from the adversary. The adversary is considered to be *malicious*, meaning that it can instruct the corrupted party to deviate from the protocol in any arbitrary way. Additionally, the adversary has full-access to the view of the corrupted party, which consists of its input, its random coins, and the messages it sees throughout this execution. At the conclusion of the execution, the honest parties output their prescribed output from the protocol, the corrupted party outputs nothing, and the adversary outputs a function of its view (containing the views of the corrupted party). In some of our proofs we consider *semi-honest* adversaries that always instruct the corrupted parties to honestly execute the protocol, but may try to learn more information than they should.

We denote by $REAL_{\pi,\mathsf{Adv}(\mathsf{aux})}(\kappa,(x,y,z))$ the joint output of the adversary Adv (that may corrupt one of the parties) and of the honest parties in a random execution of π on security parameter $\kappa \in \mathbb{N}$, inputs $x,y,z \in \{0,1\}^*$, and an auxiliary input $\mathsf{aux} \in \{0,1\}^*$.

The Ideal Model

We consider an ideal computation with *guaranteed output delivery* (also referred to as *full security*), where a trusted party performs the computation on behalf of the parties, and the ideal-world adversary *cannot* abort the computation. An ideal computation of a three-party functionality $f = (f_1, f_2, f_3)$, with $f_1, f_2, f_3 : (\{0,1\}^*)^3 \to \{0,1\}^*$, on inputs $x,y,z \in \{0,1\}^*$ and security parameter κ, with an ideal-world adversary Adv running with an auxiliary input aux and corrupting a single party P proceeds as follows:

Parties send inputs to the trusted party: Each honest party sends its input to the trusted party. The adversary Adv sends a value v from its domain as the input for the corrupted party. Let (x', y', z') denote the inputs received by the trusted party.

The trusted party performs computation: The trusted party selects a random string r, computes $(w_1, w_2, w_3) = f(x', y', z'; r)$, and sends w_1 to A, sends w_2 to B, and sends w_3 to C.

Outputs: Each honest party outputs whatever output it received from the trusted party and the corrupted party outputs nothing. The adversary Adv outputs some function of its view (i.e., the input and output of the corrupted party).

We denote by $IDEAL_{f,\mathsf{Adv}(\mathsf{aux})}(\kappa,(x,y,z))$ the joint output of the adversary Adv (that may corrupt one of the parties) and the honest parties in a random execution of the ideal-world computation of f on security parameter $\kappa \in \mathbb{N}$, inputs $x,y,z \in \{0,1\}^*$, and an auxiliary input $\mathsf{aux} \in \{0,1\}^*$.

Ideal Computation with Fairness. Although all our results are stated with respect to guaranteed output delivery, in our proofs in Sect. 4 we will consider a weaker security variant, where the adversary may cause the computation to prematurely abort, but only *before* it learns any new information from the protocol. Formally, an ideal computation with *fairness* is defined as above, with the difference that during the Parties send inputs to the trusted party step, the adversary can send a special abort symbol. In this case, the trusted party sets the output $w_1 = w_2 = w_3 = \bot$ instead of computing the function.

The Security Definition

Having defined the real and ideal models, we can now define security of protocols according to the real/ideal paradigm.

Definition 4 (security). *Let f be a three-party functionality and let π be a three-party protocol. We say that π computes f with 1-security, if for every non-uniform PPT adversary Adv, controlling at most one party in the real world, there exists a non-uniform PPT adversary Sim, controlling the same party (if there is any) in the ideal world such that*

$$\left\{ IDEAL_{f,\mathsf{Sim(aux)}}\left(\kappa, (x, y, z)\right) \right\}_{\kappa \in \mathbb{N}, x, y, z, \mathsf{aux} \in \{0,1\}^*}$$

$$\overset{C}{\equiv} \left\{ REAL_{\pi,\mathsf{Adv(aux)}}\left(\kappa, (x, y, z)\right) \right\}_{\kappa \in \mathbb{N}, x, y, z, \mathsf{aux} \in \{0,1\}^*} .$$

We define statistical and perfect 1-security similarly, replacing computational indistinguishability with statistical distance and equivalence, respectively.

The Hybrid Model

The *hybrid model* is a model that extends the real model with a trusted party that provides ideal computation for specific functionalities. The parties communicate with this trusted party in the same way as in the ideal models described above.

Let f be a functionality. Then, an execution of a protocol π computing a functionality g in the f-hybrid model involves the parties sending normal messages to each other (as in the real model) and in addition, having access to a trusted party computing f. It is essential that the invocations of f are done sequentially, meaning that before an invocation of f begins, the preceding invocation of f must finish. In particular, there is at most a single call to f per round, and no other messages are sent during any round in which f is called.

Let type $\in \{$g.o.d., fair$\}$. Let Adv be a non-uniform PPT machine with auxiliary input aux controlling a single party $\mathsf{P} \in \{\mathsf{A}, \mathsf{B}, \mathsf{C}\}$. We denote by $HYBRID_{\pi,\mathsf{Adv(aux)}}^{f,\mathsf{type}}(\kappa, (x, y, z))$ the random variable consisting of the output of the adversary and the output of the honest parties, following an execution of π with ideal calls to a trusted party computing f according to the ideal model "type", on input vector (x, y, z), auxiliary input aux given to Adv, and security parameter κ. We call this the (f, type)-hybrid model. Similarly to Definition 4, we say that π computes g with 1-security in the (f, type)-hybrid model if for any adversary Adv there exists a simulator Sim such that $HYBRID_{\pi,\mathsf{Adv(aux)}}^{f,\mathsf{type}}(\kappa, (x, y, z))$ and $IDEAL_{g,\mathsf{Sim(aux)}}(\kappa, (x, y, z))$ are computationally indistinguishable.

The sequential composition theorem of Canetti [15] states the following. Let ρ be a protocol that securely computes f in the ideal model "type". Then, if a protocol π computes g in the (f, type)-hybrid model, then the protocol π^ρ, that is obtained from π by replacing all ideal calls to the trusted party computing f with the protocol ρ, securely computes g in the real model.

Theorem 6 ([15]). *Let f be a three-party functionality, let $\mathsf{type}_1, \mathsf{type}_2 \in \{\mathsf{g.o.d.}, \mathsf{fair}\}$, let ρ be a protocol that 1-securely computes f with type_1, and let π be a protocol that 1-securely computes g with type_2 in the (f, type_1)-hybrid model. Then, protocol π^ρ 1-securely computes g with type_2 in the real model.*

3   Impossibility Results

In the following section, we present our impossibility results. The main ingredient used in the proofs of these results, is the analysis of a *four-party* protocol that is derived from the three-party protocol assumed to exist. In Sect. 3.1 we present the four-party protocol alongside some of its useful properties. Most notably, we show that if a functionality f can be computed with 1-security, then f must satisfy a requirement that we refer to as *split-brain simulatability*. Then, in Sect. 3.2 we show our second impossibility result, where we characterize the class of securely computable functionalities where one of the parties has no input. Finally, in Sect. 3.3 we present a class of functionalities where the impossibility of computing them follows from privacy.

3.1   The Four-Party Protocol

We start by presenting our first impossibility result that provides necessary conditions for secure computation with respect to the outputs of each *pair* of parties. Therefore, without loss of generality we will state and prove the results with respect to the outputs of A and B.

Fix a three-party protocol $\pi = (\mathsf{A}, \mathsf{B}, \mathsf{C})$ that is defined over secure point-to-point channels in the plain model (without a broadcast channel or trusted setup assumptions). Consider the split-brain attacker controlling C that interacts with A on input z_1 as if never receiving messages from B and interacts with B on input z_2 as if never receiving messages from A. The impact of this attacker can be emulated towards B by a corrupt A and towards A by a corrupt B. A nice way to formalize this argument is by considering a four-party protocol, where two different parties play the role of C. The first interacts only with A, and the second interacts only with B. The four-party protocol is illustrated in Fig. 2 in the Introduction.

Definition 5 (the four-party protocol). *Given a three-party protocol $\pi = (\mathsf{A}, \mathsf{B}, \mathsf{C})$ we denote by $\pi' = (\mathsf{A}', \mathsf{B}', \mathsf{C}'_\mathsf{A}, \mathsf{C}'_\mathsf{B})$ the following four-party protocol. Party A' is set with the code of A, Party B' with the code of B, and parties C'_A and C'_B with the code of C.*

The communication network of π' is a path. Party A' is connected to C'_A and to B', and party B' is connected to A' and to C'_B. In addition to its edge to A', party C'_A has a second edge that leads to a sink that only receives messages and does not send any message (this corresponds to the channel to B in the code of C'_A). Similarly, in addition to its edge to B', party C'_B has a second edge that leads to a sink.

We now formalize the above intuition, showing that an honest execution in π' can be emulated in π by any corrupted party. In fact, we can strengthen the above observation. Any adversary in π' corrupting A' and C'_A, can be emulated by an adversary in π corrupting A. Similarly, we can emulate any adversary corrupting B' and C'_B by an adversary in π corrupting B, and any adversary corrupting C'_A and C'_B by an adversary in π corrupting C.

Lemma 1 (mapping attackers for π' to attackers for π). *Let* $\pi = (A, B, C)$ *and* $\pi' = (A', B', C'_A, C'_B)$ *be as in Definition 5. Then*

1. *For every non-uniform* PPT *adversary* Adv'_1 *corrupting* $\{A', C'_A\}$ *in* π'*, there exists a non-uniform* PPT *adversary* Adv_1 *corrupting* A *in* π*, receiving the input* z_1 *for* C'_A *as auxiliary information, that perfectly emulates* Adv'_1*, namely*

$$\left\{REAL_{\pi, \mathsf{Adv}_1(z_1, \mathrm{aux})}\left(\kappa, (x, y, z_2)\right)\right\}_{\kappa, x, y, z_1, z_2, \mathrm{aux}}$$
$$\equiv \left\{REAL_{\pi', \mathsf{Adv}'_1(\mathrm{aux})}\left(\kappa, (x, y, z_1, z_2)\right)\right\}_{\kappa, x, y, z_1, z_2, \mathrm{aux}}.$$

2. *For every non-uniform* PPT *adversary* Adv'_2 *corrupting* $\{B', C'_B\}$ *in* π'*, there exists a non-uniform* PPT *adversary* Adv_2 *corrupting* B *in* π*, receiving the input* z_2 *for* C'_B *as auxiliary information, that perfectly emulates* Adv'_2*, namely*

$$\left\{REAL_{\pi, \mathsf{Adv}_2(z_2, \mathrm{aux})}\left(\kappa, (x, y, z_1)\right)\right\}_{\kappa, x, y, z_1, z_2, \mathrm{aux}}$$
$$\equiv \left\{REAL_{\pi', \mathsf{Adv}'_2(\mathrm{aux})}\left(\kappa, (x, y, z_1, z_2)\right)\right\}_{\kappa, x, y, z_1, z_2, \mathrm{aux}}.$$

3. *For every non-uniform* PPT *adversary* Adv'_3 *corrupting* $\{C'_A, C'_B\}$ *in* π'*, there exists a non-uniform* PPT *adversary* Adv_3 *corrupting* C *in* π*, receiving the input* z_2 *for* C'_B *as auxiliary information,[3] that perfectly emulates* Adv'_3*, namely*

$$\left\{REAL_{\pi, \mathsf{Adv}_3(z_2, \mathrm{aux})}\left(\kappa, (x, y, z_1)\right)\right\}_{\kappa, x, y, z_1, z_2, \mathrm{aux}}$$
$$\equiv \left\{REAL_{\pi', \mathsf{Adv}'_3(\mathrm{aux})}\left(\kappa, (x, y, z_1, z_2)\right)\right\}_{\kappa, x, y, z_1, z_2, \mathrm{aux}}.$$

Proof. We first prove Item 1. The proof of Item 2 is done using an analogous argument and is therefore omitted. Fix an adversary Adv'_1 corrupting $\{A', C'_A\}$. Consider the following adversary Adv_1 for π that corrupts A. First, it initializes Adv'_1 with input x for A', input z_1 for C'_A and auxiliary information aux. In each round, it ignores the messages sent by C, passes the messages it received from B to Adv'_1 (recall that Adv'_1 internally runs A' and C'_A), and replies to B as Adv'_1 replied. Finally, Adv_1 outputs whatever Adv'_1 outputs.

By the definition of Adv_1, in each round, the message it receives from B is identically distributed as the message received from B' in π'. Since it ignores the messages sent from the real C and answers as Adv'_1 does, it follows that the messages it will send to B are identically distributed as well. Furthermore, since Adv_1 does not send any message to C, the view of C will be identically distributed

---

[3] The choice of giving Adv_3 the input z_2 as auxiliary is arbitrary.

as well to that of C'_B in π'. In particular, the joint outputs of B and C in π are identically distributed as the joint outputs of B' and C'_B in π', conditioned on the messages received from Adv_1 and Adv'_1 respectively, hence

$$\left\{ REAL_{\pi,\mathsf{Adv}_1(z_1,\mathsf{aux})} \left(\kappa,(x,y,z_2)\right) \right\}_{\kappa,x,y,z_1,z_2,\mathsf{aux}}$$
$$\equiv \left\{ REAL_{\pi',\mathsf{Adv}'_1(\mathsf{aux})} \left(\kappa,(x,y,z_1,z_2)\right) \right\}_{\kappa,x,y,z_1,z_2,\mathsf{aux}}.$$

We next prove Item 3. Fix an adversary Adv'_3 corrupting $\{C'_A, C'_B\}$. The adversary Adv_3 corrupts C, initializes Adv'_3 with inputs z_1 and z_2 for C'_A and C'_B respectively, and auxiliary information aux. Then, in each round it passes the messages received from A and B to Adv'_3 and answers accordingly. Finally, it outputs whatever Adv'_3 outputs. Clearly, the transcript of π when interacting with Adv_3 is identically distributed as the transcript of π'. The claim follows.

As a corollary, it follows that if π securely computes some functionality f, then any adversary for π' corrupting $\{A', C'_A\}$, or $\{B', C'_B\}$, or $\{C'_A, C'_B\}$ can be simulated in the ideal-world of f.

Corollary 1. *Let* $\pi = (A, B, C)$ *be a three-party protocol that computes a functionality* $f : (\{0,1\}^*)^3 \mapsto (\{0,1\}^*)^3$ *with 1-security and let* $\pi' = (A', B', C'_A, C'_B)$ *be as in Definition 5. Then*

1. *For every adversary* Adv'_1 *for* π' *corrupting* $\{A', C'_A\}$ *there exists a simulator* Sim_1 *in the ideal world of* f *corrupting* A, *such that*

$$\left\{ IDEAL_{f,\mathsf{Sim}_1(z_1,\mathsf{aux})} \left(\kappa,(x,y,z_2)\right) \right\}_{\kappa,x,y,z_1,z_2,\mathsf{aux}}$$
$$\overset{C}{\equiv} \left\{ REAL_{\pi',\mathsf{Adv}'_1(\mathsf{aux})} \left(\kappa,(x,y,z_1,z_2)\right) \right\}_{\kappa,x,y,z_1,z_2,\mathsf{aux}}.$$

2. *For every adversary* Adv'_2 *for* π' *corrupting* $\{B', C'_B\}$ *there exists a simulator* Sim_2 *in the ideal world of* f *corrupting* B, *such that*

$$\left\{ IDEAL_{f,\mathsf{Sim}_2(z_2,\mathsf{aux})} \left(\kappa,(x,y,z_1)\right) \right\}_{\kappa,x,y,z_1,z_2,\mathsf{aux}}$$
$$\overset{C}{\equiv} \left\{ REAL_{\pi',\mathsf{Adv}'_2(\mathsf{aux})} \left(\kappa,(x,y,z_1,z_2)\right) \right\}_{\kappa,x,y,z_1,z_2,\mathsf{aux}}.$$

3. *For every adversary* Adv'_3 *for* π' *corrupting* $\{C'_A, C'_B\}$ *there exists a simulator* Sim_3 *in the ideal world of* f *corrupting* C, *such that*

$$\left\{ IDEAL_{f,\mathsf{Sim}_3(z_2,\mathsf{aux})} \left(\kappa,(x,y,z_1)\right) \right\}_{\kappa,x,y,z_1,z_2,\mathsf{aux}}$$
$$\overset{C}{\equiv} \left\{ REAL_{\pi',\mathsf{Adv}'_3(\mathsf{aux})} \left(\kappa,(x,y,z_1,z_2)\right) \right\}_{\kappa,x,y,z_1,z_2,\mathsf{aux}}.$$

One important use-case of Corollary 1 is when the three adversaries for π' are *semi-honest*. This is due to the fact that the views of the honest parties are identically distributed in all three cases, hence the same holds with respect to their outputs. Next, we consider the distributions over the outputs of A and B in the ideal world of f with respect to each such simulators. Recall that these simulators are for the *malicious* setting, hence they can send arbitrary inputs to the trusted party. Thus, the distributions over the outputs depend on the distribution over the input sent by each simulator to the trusted party. Notice that when considering semi-honest adversaries for π' that have no auxiliary input, these distributions would depend only on the security parameter and the inputs given to the semi-honest adversary. For example, in the case where $\{A', C_A'\}$ are corrupted, the simulator samples an input x^* according to some distribution P that depends only on the security parameter κ, the input x, and the input z_1, given to the semi-honest adversary corrupting A' and C_A'. We next give a notation for semi-honest adversaries, their corresponding simulators, and the distributions used by the simulators to sample an input value.

Definition 6. *Let* $\pi = (A, B, C)$ *be a three-party protocol that computes a three-party functionality* $f : (\{0,1\}^*)^3 \mapsto (\{0,1\}^*)^3$ *with 1-security. We let* $\mathsf{Adv}_1^{\mathsf{sh}}$ *be the semi-honest adversary for* π', *corrupting* $\{A', C_A'\}$. *Similarly, we let* $\mathsf{Adv}_2^{\mathsf{sh}}$ *and* $\mathsf{Adv}_3^{\mathsf{sh}}$ *be the semi-honest adversaries corrupting* $\{B', C_B'\}$ *and* $\{C_A', C_B'\}$, *respectively. Let* Sim_1, Sim_2, *and* Sim_3 *be the three simulators for the* malicious *ideal world of* f, *that simulate* $\mathsf{Adv}_1^{\mathsf{sh}}$, $\mathsf{Adv}_2^{\mathsf{sh}}$, *and* $\mathsf{Adv}_3^{\mathsf{sh}}$, *respectively, guaranteed to exist by Corollary 1.*

We define the distribution $P_{\kappa,x,z_1}^{\mathsf{sh}}$ *to be the distribution over the inputs sent by* Sim_1 *to the trusted party, given the inputs* x, z_1 *and security parameter* κ. *Similarly, we define the distributions* $Q_{\kappa,y,z_2}^{\mathsf{sh}}$ *and* $R_{\kappa,z_1,z_2}^{\mathsf{sh}}$ *to be the distributions over the inputs sent by* Sim_2 *and* Sim_3, *respectively, to the trusted party. Additionally, we let* $\mathcal{P}^{\mathsf{sh}} = \{P_{\kappa,x,z_1}^{\mathsf{sh}}\}_{\kappa \in \mathbb{N}, x, z_1 \in \{0,1\}^*}$, $\mathcal{Q}^{\mathsf{sh}} = \{Q_{\kappa,y,z_2}^{\mathsf{sh}}\}_{\kappa \in \mathbb{N}, y, z_2 \in \{0,1\}^*}$, *and* $\mathcal{R}^{\mathsf{sh}} = \{R_{\kappa,z_1,z_2}^{\mathsf{sh}}\}_{\kappa \in \mathbb{N}, z_1, z_2 \in \{0,1\}^*}$ *be the corresponding distribution ensembles.*

Now, as the simulators simulate the semi-honest adversaries for π', it follows that all the outputs of the honest parties in $\{A, B\}$ in the executions of the ideal-world computations are the same. This results in a necessary condition that the functionality f must satisfy for it to be securely computable. We call this condition C-split-brain *simulatability*. Similarly, we can define A-split-brain and B-split-brain simulatability to get additional necessary conditions. We next formally define the class of functionalities that are C-split-brain simulatable. We then show that it is indeed a necessary condition.

Definition 7 (C-split-brain simulatability). *Let* $f = (f_1, f_2, f_3)$ *be a three-party functionality and let* $\mathcal{P} = \{P_{\kappa,x,z_1}\}_{\kappa \in \mathbb{N}, x, z_1 \in \{0,1\}^*}$, $\mathcal{Q} = \{Q_{\kappa,y,z_2}\}_{\kappa \in \mathbb{N}, y, z_2 \in \{0,1\}^*}$, *and* $\mathcal{R} = \{R_{\kappa,z_1,z_2}\}_{\kappa \in \mathbb{N}, z_1, z_2 \in \{0,1\}^*}$ *be three ensembles of efficiently samplable distributions over* $\{0,1\}^*$. *We say that* f *is computationally* $(\mathcal{P}, \mathcal{Q}, \mathcal{R})$-C-*split-brain (CSB) simulatable if*

$$\left\{ f_1(x, y^*, z_1) \right\}_{\kappa \in \mathbb{N}, x, y, z_1, z_2 \in \{0,1\}^*} \overset{C}{\equiv} \left\{ f_1(x, y, z^*) \right\}_{\kappa \in \mathbb{N}, x, y, z_1, z_2 \in \{0,1\}^*}, \text{ and}$$

$$\left\{ f_2(x^*, y, z_2) \right\}_{\kappa \in \mathbb{N}, x, y, z_1, z_2 \in \{0,1\}^*} \overset{C}{\equiv} \left\{ f_2(x, y, z^*) \right\}_{\kappa \in \mathbb{N}, x, y, z_1, z_2 \in \{0,1\}^*},$$

where $x^* \leftarrow P_{\kappa,x,z_1}$, $y^* \leftarrow Q_{\kappa,y,z_2}$, and $z^* \leftarrow R_{\kappa,z_1,z_2}$. We say that f is computationally CSB simulatable, *if there exist three ensembles $\mathcal{P}$, $\mathcal{Q}$, and $\mathcal{R}$ such that f is $(\mathcal{P}, \mathcal{Q}, \mathcal{R})$-CSB simulatable.*

We define *statistically* and *perfectly* CSB simulatable functionalities in a similar way, replacing computational indistinguishability with statistical closeness and equivalence, respectively. In Sect. 3.1.1 we give several simple examples and properties of CSB simulatable functionalities.

We next prove the main result of this section, asserting that if a functionality is computable with 1-security, then it must be CSB simulatable. We stress that CSB simulatability is *not* a sufficient condition for secure computation. Indeed, the coin-tossing functionality is CSB simulatable, however, as we show in Sect. 3.2 below, it cannot be computed securely.

Theorem 7 (CSB simulatability – a necessary condition). *If a three-party functionality $f = (f_1, f_2, f_3)$ is computable with 1-security over secure point-to-point channels, then f is computationally CSB simulatable.*

Proof. Let $\pi = (\mathsf{A}, \mathsf{B}, \mathsf{C})$ be a protocol that securely realizes f tolerating one malicious corruption. Consider the four-party protocol $\pi' = (\mathsf{A}', \mathsf{B}', \mathsf{C}'_\mathsf{A}, \mathsf{C}'_\mathsf{B})$ from Definition 5, and let $\mathsf{Adv}_1^{\mathsf{sh}}$, $\mathsf{Adv}_2^{\mathsf{sh}}$, and $\mathsf{Adv}_3^{\mathsf{sh}}$, be three *semi-honest* adversaries corrupting $\{\mathsf{A}', \mathsf{C}'_\mathsf{A}\}$, $\{\mathsf{B}', \mathsf{C}'_\mathsf{B}\}$, and $\{\mathsf{C}'_\mathsf{A}, \mathsf{C}'_\mathsf{B}\}$, respectively, with no auxiliary information. We will show that f is $(\mathcal{P}^{\mathsf{sh}}, \mathcal{Q}^{\mathsf{sh}}, \mathcal{R}^{\mathsf{sh}})$-C-split-brain simulatable, where $\mathcal{P}^{\mathsf{sh}}$, $\mathcal{Q}^{\mathsf{sh}}$, and $\mathcal{R}^{\mathsf{sh}}$ are as defined in Definition 6.

We next analyze the output of the honest party B', once when interacting with $\mathsf{Adv}_1^{\mathsf{sh}}$ and once when interacting with $\mathsf{Adv}_3^{\mathsf{sh}}$. The claim would then follow since the view of B', and in particular its output, is identically distributed in both cases. The analysis of the output of an honest A' is similar and therefore is omitted. Let us first focus on the output of B' when interacting with $\mathsf{Adv}_1^{\mathsf{sh}}$. By Corollary 1 there exists a simulator Sim_1 for $\mathsf{Adv}_1^{\mathsf{sh}}$ in the ideal world of f, that is,

$$\left\{IDEAL_{f,\mathsf{Sim}_1(z_1)}\left(\kappa, (x, y, z_2)\right)\right\}_{\kappa,x,y,z_1,z_2} \overset{C}{\equiv} \left\{REAL_{\pi',\mathsf{Adv}_1^{\mathsf{sh}}}\left(\kappa, (x, y, z_1, z_2)\right)\right\}_{\kappa,x,y,z_1,z_2}.$$

In particular, the equivalence holds with respect to the output of the honest party B on the left-hand side, and the output of B' on the right-hand side. Recall that $P_{\kappa,x,z_1}^{\mathsf{sh}}$ is the probability distribution over the inputs sent by Sim_1 to the trusted party. Thus, letting $x^* \leftarrow P_{\kappa,x,z_1}^{\mathsf{sh}}$, it follows that the output of B in the ideal world is identically distributed to $f_2(x^*, y, z_2)$; hence, the output of B' in the four-party protocol is computationally indistinguishable from $f_2(x^*, y, z_2)$. By a similar argument, the output of B' when interacting with $\mathsf{Adv}_3^{\mathsf{sh}}$ is computationally indistinguishable from $f_2(x, y, z^*)$, where $z^* \leftarrow R_{\kappa,z_1,z_2}^{\mathsf{sh}}$, and the claim follows.

3.1.1 Properties of Split-Brain Simulatable Functionalities

Having defined C-split-brain simulatability, we proceed to provide several examples and properties of CSB simulatable functionalities. The proof and further generalizations of these properties appear in the full version [3]. To simplify the presentation, we consider deterministic two-output functionalities $f = (f_1, f_2)$ over a finite domain with $f_1 = f_2$. We denote it as a single functionality $f : \mathcal{X} \times \mathcal{Y} \times \mathcal{Z} \mapsto \mathcal{W}$. Furthermore, we only discuss *perfect* CSB simulatability, and where the corresponding ensembles are independent of κ.

In the Introduction (Sect. 1.2) we showed that the two-output three-party functionality $f : \{0,1\}^3 \mapsto \{0,1\}$ defined by $f(x, y, z) = (x \wedge y) \oplus z$ is not CSB simulatable. We next state a generalization of this example.

Proposition 1. *Let $f : \mathcal{X} \times \mathcal{Y} \times \mathcal{Z} \mapsto \mathcal{W}$ be a perfectly CSB simulatable two-output three-party functionality. Assume there exist inputs $x \in \mathcal{X}$, $y \in \mathcal{Y}$, and $z_1, z_2 \in \mathcal{Z}$, and two outputs $w_1, w_2 \in \mathcal{W}$, such that $f(x, \cdot, z_1) = w_1$ and $f(\cdot, y, z_2) = w_2$. Then, $w_1 = w_2$.*

We next show that for C-split-brain simulatable functionalities, if a pair of parties P and C, where $P \in \{A, B\}$, can fix the output to be some w, then P can do it by itself. In particular, if C can fix the output to be w, then A and B can do it as well, which implies that f must be 1-dominated.

Proposition 2. *Let $f : \mathcal{X} \times \mathcal{Y} \times \mathcal{Z} \mapsto \mathcal{W}$ be a perfectly $(\mathcal{P}, \mathcal{Q}, \mathcal{R})$-CSB simulatable two-output three-party functionality. Assume there exist $x \in \mathcal{X}$, $z \in \mathcal{Z}$, and $w \in \mathcal{W}$ such that $f(x, \cdot, z) = w$. Then, there exists an input $x^* \in \mathcal{X}$ such that $f(x^*, \cdot, \cdot) = w$. Similarly, assuming there exist $y \in \mathcal{Y}$ and $z \in \mathcal{Z}$ such that $f(\cdot, y, z) = w$, then there exists an input $y^* \in \mathcal{Y}$ such that $f(\cdot, y^*, \cdot) = w$.*

3.2   Server-Aided Two-Party Computation

In this section, we consider the server-aided model where two parties – A and B – use the help of an additional *untrusted* yet *non-colluding* server C that has no input in order to securely compute a functionality. The main result of this section is showing that the additional server does not provide any advantage in the secure point-to-point channels model. The proof of Theorem 8 can be found in the full version.

Theorem 8. *Let $f = (f_1, f_2, f_3)$ with $f_1, f_2, f_3 : \{0,1\} \times \{0,1\} \times \emptyset \mapsto \{0,1\}$ be a three-party functionality computable with 1-security over secure point-to-point channels. Then, the two-party functionality*

$$g(x, y) := \left(\left(f_1(x, y, \lambda), f_3(x, y, \lambda) \right), \left(f_2(x, y, \lambda), f_3(x, y, \lambda) \right) \right)$$

is computable with 1-security.

As a corollary of Theorem 8, a *two-output* server-aided functionality can be computed with C if and only if it can be computed without it. Formally, we have the following.

Corollary 2. *Let $f = (f_1, f_2)$ with $f_1, f_2 : \{0,1\} \times \{0,1\} \times \emptyset \mapsto \{0,1\}$ be a two-output three-party functionality and let $g(x, y) = (f_1(x, y, \lambda), f_2(x, y, \lambda))$ be its induced two-party variant. Then, f can be computed with 1-security if and only if g can be computed with 1-security.*

Observe that Theorem 8 only provides a necessary condition for secure computation, while Corollary 2 asserts that for two-output functionalities, the necessary condition is also sufficient. In other words, even when the induced two-party functionality g can be securely computed, if f_3 is non-degenerate, then f might not be computable with 1-security. Indeed, consider the functionality $(x, \lambda, \lambda) \mapsto (x, x, \lambda)$. Clearly, it is computable in our setting, however, the functionality where C also receive x is the broadcast functionality, hence it cannot be computed securely.

The proof of Theorem 8 is done by constructing a two-protocol for computing g. We next present the construction. The proof of security is deferred to the full version of the paper [3].

Definition 8 (the two-party protocol). *Fix a protocol* $\pi = (\mathsf{A}, \mathsf{B}, \mathsf{C})$ *and let* $\pi' = (\mathsf{A}', \mathsf{B}', \mathsf{C}'_\mathsf{A}, \mathsf{C}'_\mathsf{B})$ *be the related four-party protocol from Definition 5. We define the two-party protocol* $\widehat{\pi} = (\widehat{\mathsf{A}}, \widehat{\mathsf{B}})$ *as follows. On input* $x \in \{0,1\}^*$, *party* $\widehat{\mathsf{A}}$ *will simulate* A' *holding* x *and* C'_A *in its head. Similarly, on input* $y \in \{0,1\}^*$, *party* $\widehat{\mathsf{B}}$ *will simulate* B' *holding* y *and* C'_B. *The messages exchanged between* $\widehat{\mathsf{A}}$ *and* $\widehat{\mathsf{B}}$ *will be the same as the messages exchanged between* A' *and* B' *in* π', *according to their simulated random coins, inputs, and the communication transcript so far. Finally,* $\widehat{\mathsf{A}}$ *will output whatever* A' *and* C'_A *output, and similarly,* $\widehat{\mathsf{B}}$ *will output whatever* B' *and* C'_B *output.*

Similarly to the four-party protocol, we can emulate any malicious adversary attacking $\widehat{\pi}$ using the appropriate adversary for the three-party protocol π.

Lemma 2 (mapping attackers for $\widehat{\pi}$ to attackers for π). *For any non-uniform* PPT *adversary* $\widehat{\mathsf{Adv}}_1$ *corrupting* $\widehat{\mathsf{A}}$ *in* $\widehat{\pi}$, *there exists a non-uniform* PPT *adversary* Adv_1 *corrupting* A *in* π *that perfectly emulates* $\widehat{\mathsf{Adv}}_1$. *That is, the following two random variables are identically distributed:*

$$\left\{ REAL_{\pi, \mathsf{Adv}_1(\mathsf{aux})}\left(\kappa, (x,y)\right)\right\}_{\kappa, x, y, \mathsf{aux}} \equiv \left\{ REAL_{\widehat{\pi}, \widehat{\mathsf{Adv}}_1(\mathsf{aux})}\left(\kappa, (x,y)\right)\right\}_{\kappa, x, y, \mathsf{aux}}.$$
(1)

Similarly, for any non-uniform PPT *adversary* $\widehat{\mathsf{Adv}}_2$ *corrupting* $\widehat{\mathsf{B}}$ *in* $\widehat{\pi}$, *there exists a non-uniform* PPT *adversary* Adv_2 *corrupting* B *in* π, *that perfectly emulates* $\widehat{\mathsf{Adv}}_1$, *namely*

$$\left\{ REAL_{\pi, \mathsf{Adv}_2(\mathsf{aux})}\left(\kappa, (x,y)\right)\right\}_{\kappa, x, y, \mathsf{aux}} \equiv \left\{ REAL_{\widehat{\pi}, \widehat{\mathsf{Adv}}_2(\mathsf{aux})}\left(\kappa, (x,y)\right)\right\}_{\kappa, x, y, \mathsf{aux}}.$$
(2)

3.2.1 Coin-Tossing Protocols

Coin-tossing protocols [10] allow a set of parties to agree on uniform common random bit, such that even if some of the parties are malicious, the honest parties output a common bit close to being uniform. The seminal result of Cleve

[17] states that unless an honest majority is assumed, for any r-round protocol computing coin-tossing there is always an adversary that can bias the outcome by at least $\Omega(1/r)$ (even assuming a broadcast channel). In the honest-majority case without broadcast, the result of [19] rules out non-trivial n-party coin-tossing protocols (with any bias $\delta < 1/2$) that tolerate $\lceil n/3 \rceil$ corruptions, as long as *all* parties receive the output.

In this section, we consider three-party two-output coin tossing that tolerates one corruption; the results of [17,19] do not apply in this case since we assume an honest majority but not all parties learn the output. A direct implication of Corollary 2 together with [17] shows that this variation of coin tossing cannot be computed with negligible bias. Looking further into the proof, it follows that if we are given a protocol that is secure against a malicious C (i.e., C cannot bias the output coin), then Cleve's attackers (on the implied two-party protocol) can be directly translated to attackers for the three-party protocol, corrupting either A or B. Thus, either A or B can bias the output by $\Omega(1/r)$, where r is the number of rounds in the protocol. However, the above argument does not deal with protocols that allow a corrupt C to slightly bias the output. For example, one might try to construct a protocol where no party (including C) can bias the output by more than $1/r^2$.

We next prove a stronger result, showing that this is impossible. In particular, letting A and B execute the protocol of Moran, Naor, and Segev [36] results with an optimally fair protocol (up to a constant factor). We first formalize the security notion of the task at hand.

Definition 9 (coin-tossing protocol). *Let* $\gamma, \delta : \mathbb{N} \mapsto \mathbb{N}$ *be such that* $\gamma(r) \le \delta(r)$ *for all* $r \in \mathbb{N}$, *and let* $t, \ell, n \in \mathbb{N}$ *be such that* $t, \ell \le n$. *A polynomial-time n-party protocol* $\pi = (\mathsf{P}_1, \dots, \mathsf{P}_n)$ *is a* $(\gamma, \delta, t, \ell)$-*bias coin-tossing protocol, if the following holds.*

1. *In an honest execution, parties* $\mathsf{P}_1, \dots, \mathsf{P}_\ell$ *output a common bit that is γ-close to a uniform random bit. The rest of the parties do not output any value.*
2. *For any* PPT *adversary corrupting at most t parties, the honest parties in* $\{\mathsf{P}_1, \dots, \mathsf{P}_\ell\}$ *output a common bit that is δ-close to a uniform bit.*

We next state that in the three-party case, for every protocol there exists an adversary corrupting a single party that can bias the output by $\Omega(1/r)$. The proof of Lemma 3 can be found in the full version.

Lemma 3. *There exists* $c \in \mathbb{R}^+$, *for which there is no r-round three-party* $(0, 1/cr, 1, 2)$-*bias coin-tossing protocol.*

Using a standard player-partitioning argument, we can extend the impossibility of coin-tossing to the n-party case, assuming at least *two* parties receive the output. Specifically, we show that there exists an adversary biasing the output by $\Omega(1/r)$ if at least *two* parties receive the output, and there exists an adversary biasing the output by $1/2 - 2^{-\kappa}$ if at least *three* parties receive the output.

Corollary 3. *Fix $n \in \mathbb{N}$. Then, there is no r-round n-party $(0, 1/cr, \lceil n/3 \rceil, 2)$-bias coin-tossing protocol, where $c \in \mathbb{R}^+$ is as in Lemma 3. Moreover, there is no n-party $(0, 1/2 - 2^{-\kappa}, \lceil n/3 \rceil, 3)$-bias coin-tossing protocol.*

3.3 Impossibility Based on Privacy

In this section we present examples of functionalities that are C-split-brain simulatable yet are not securely computable tolerating one corruption.

Claim 9. *Let $f = (f_1, f_2, f_3)$ with $f_1, f_2, f_3 : \{0,1\}^3 \mapsto \{0,1\}$ be a functionality where A's output is defined as $f_1(x, y, z) = (x \wedge y) \oplus z$. Then f cannot be computed with 1-security.*

The proof of Claim 9 can be found in the full version. Using a similar argument, if we take $f_1(x, y, z) = (x \oplus y) \wedge z$ then f cannot be computed with 1-security.

Claim 10. *Let $f = (f_1, f_2, f_3)$ with $f_1, f_2, f_3 : \{0,1\}^3 \mapsto \{0,1\}$ be a functionality where A's output is defined as $f_1(x, y, z) = (x \oplus y) \wedge z$. Then f cannot be computed with 1-security.*

4   A Class of Securely Two-Output Computable Functionalities

In this section, we present a class of two-output functionalities that can be securely computed over point-to-point channels tolerating a single corruption. This class generalizes previously known feasibility results in this setting, namely, 1-dominated functionalities [18,19] and fair two-party functionalities [5].

Our result shows that if f is a two-output $(\mathcal{P}, \mathcal{Q}, \mathcal{R})$-CSB simulatable functionality, then under a simple condition that a related two-party functionality needs to satisfy, the problem is reduced to the two-party case. Given a two-output three-party functionality f we define the following related two-party functionality. Roughly, in addition to x and y, each of the two parties holds a possible input for C, denoted z_1 and z_2. The real input of C is then chosen according to some predetermined distribution that depends on z_1 and z_2, and output will be whatever is computed by f.

Definition 10. *Let $f : (\{0,1\}^*)^3 \mapsto (\{0,1\}^*)^2$ be a two-output three-party functionality and let $\mathcal{R} = \{R_{\kappa,z_1,z_2}\}_{z_1,z_2 \in \{0,1\}^*}$ be an ensemble of efficiently samplable distributions over $\{0,1\}^*$. Define the two-party functionality $h_\mathcal{R} : (\{0,1\}^* \times \{0,1\}^*)^2 \mapsto (\{0,1\}^*)^2$ as $h_\mathcal{R}((x, z_1), (y, z_2)) = f(x, y, z^*)$, where $z^* \leftarrow R_{\kappa,z_1,z_2}$.*

We now present a sufficient condition for f to be computable with 1-security. Roughly, we require that there exist two distributions, for z_1 and z_2 respectively, such that the input z_1 can be sampled in a way that fixes the distribution of the output of $h_\mathcal{R}$ to be independent of z_2, and furthermore, the same holds with respect to z_2. Specifically, we prove the following.

Theorem 11. *Let* f : $(\{0,1\}^*)^3$ $\mapsto$ $(\{0,1\}^*)^2$ *be a computationally* $(\mathcal{P}, \mathcal{Q}, \mathcal{R})$*-CSB simulatable two-output three-party functionality, and let* $h_\mathcal{R}$: $(\{0,1\}^* \times \{0,1\}^*)^2 \mapsto (\{0,1\}^*)^2$ *be the two-party functionality from Definition 10.*

Assume there exist a (randomized) two-party functionality $g : (\{0,1\}^*)^2 \mapsto (\{0,1\}^*)^2$ *and two ensembles of efficiently samplable distributions* $\mathcal{R}_1 = \{R_{1,\kappa}\}_{\kappa \in \mathbb{N}}$ *and* $\mathcal{R}_2 = \{R_{2,\kappa}\}_{\kappa \in \mathbb{N}}$ *over* $\{0,1\}^*$*, such that for every* $x, y, z \in \{0,1\}^*$*, and sufficiently large* $\kappa \in \mathbb{N}$*, it holds that*

$$g(x,y) \equiv h_\mathcal{R}((x,z_1),(y,z)) \equiv h_\mathcal{R}((x,z),(y,z_2)),$$

where $z_1 \leftarrow R_{1,\kappa}$ *and* $z_2 \leftarrow R_{2,\kappa}$*. Then,* f *can be computed with 1-security over secure point-to-point channels in the* $(g, \text{g.o.d.})$*-hybrid model.*

Stated differently, if the two-party functionality g can be computed with 1-security then the three-party f can be computed with 1-security as well.

In Sect. 4.1 below, we give another example of a non-solitary functionality where both A and B receive the same output, that can be securely computed.

We proceed by providing a general construction alongside the necessary and sufficient conditions for security to hold. The proof of Theorem 11 is deferred to the full version.

4.1 The Protocol

We proceed to describe a simple generic protocol $\pi_{\mathcal{R}^*}$ for computing an arbitrary two-output three-party functionality f. The protocol is parametrized by an ensemble of efficiently samplable distributions $\mathcal{R}^* = \{R_\kappa^*\}_{\kappa \in \mathbb{N}}$. Lemma 4 below describes the properties that f and $\mathcal{R}^*$ must satisfy in order for the protocol to be 1-secure.

To illustrate the main ideas behind the protocol and its proof of security, we first give a simple example. Consider the two-output functionality $f = (f_1, f_2)$, where $f_1, f_2 : \{0,1,2\} \times \{0,1\} \times \{0,1\} \mapsto \{0,1\}^2$ given by the following two matrices

$$M_0^A = M_0^B = \begin{pmatrix} 0 & 1 \\ 1 & 0 \\ 1 & 1 \end{pmatrix} \qquad M_1^A = M_1^B = \begin{pmatrix} 1 & 0 \\ 0 & 1 \\ 1 & 1 \end{pmatrix}$$

Stated differently, we let $f_1 \equiv f_2$ and let $M_z^A(x,y) = f_1(x,y,z)$, where A's input determines a row, B's input determines a column, and C's input determines the matrix. The protocol follows similar lines to that of [19]. First, the parties compute f with fairness (this can be done over point-to-point channels by the honest-majority assumption [18]). If the computation fails, then A and B compute the following symmetric randomized two-party functionality

$$\begin{pmatrix} 1/2 & 1/2 \\ 1/2 & 1/2 \\ 1 & 1 \end{pmatrix}$$

That is, if A's input is 2 the output is 1; otherwise, the output is a uniform bit. Note that this two-party functionality can be computed with guaranteed output delivery [5]. Clearly, as B and C have no affect over the distribution of the output of the two-party functionality, any adversary corrupting either party can be simulated by sending a uniformly random bit to the trusted party. The output of the honest parties will be 1 if A inputs 2 and a uniform bit otherwise, regardless of the other honest party's input – the same distribution is induced by the simulator for the two-party functionality. To simulate a corrupt A in the three-party protocol, the simulator will send input 2 with the same probability p that the two-party simulator sends input 2 to the trusted party; otherwise, the simulator will send a uniform random bit. Observe that regardless of the input of C, the output of B will be 1 with probability $\frac{1}{2}(1+p)$. Similarly to the previous cases, this is the same distribution as the one induced by the simulator for the two-party functionality.

We now generalize the above ideas. We next present the protocol in the $\{(f, \mathsf{fair}), (f_{\mathcal{R}^*}, \mathsf{g.o.d.})\}$-hybrid model.

Protocol 12 ($\pi_{\mathcal{R}^*}$).

Private input: party A holds $x \in \{0,1\}^*$, party B holds $y \in \{0,1\}^*$, and party C holds $z \in \{0,1\}^*$.
Common input: the parties hold the security parameter 1^κ.

1. *Each party invokes (f, fair) with its input. Let w_1 be the output of A and w_2 the output of B.*
2. *If $w_1, w_2 \neq \bot$ then A outputs w_1 and B outputs w_2.*
3. *Otherwise, A and B invoke $(f_{\mathcal{R}^*}, \mathsf{g.o.d.})$ on their inputs x and y, respectively, and output the result.*

We next intuitively explain the properties that f and $\mathcal{R}^*$ must satisfy for $\pi_{\mathcal{R}^*}$ to be secure. Since there are no messages exchanged between the parties, constructing a simulator amounts to defining an appropriate distribution over the inputs of the corrupted parties. In particular, simulating a corrupt C can be easily simulated by either sending the input it used when calling (f, fair), or sampling according to R_κ^*. Next, consider a corrupted A or B. Similarly to the above example, we first take the distribution given by the simulator for the two-party functionality $f_{\mathcal{R}^*}$, and construct a distribution for the three-party functionality f, so that the outputs of the honest party in both ideal-worlds are identically distributed, regardless of C's inputs. That is, A and B can each sample an input for the three-party functionality f in such a way that the distribution over the output is the same as if C sampled its input according to R_κ^*.

Lemma 4. *Let $f : (\{0,1\}^*)^3 \mapsto (\{0,1\}^*)^2$ be a two-output three-party functionality, and let $\mathcal{R}^*$ be an ensemble of efficiently samplable distributions over $\{0,1\}^*$. Assume that the following holds.*

1. *There exists an ensemble of efficiently samplable distributions* $\mathcal{P}^* = \{P^*_{\kappa,x}\}_{\kappa \in \mathbb{N}, x \in \{0,1\}^*}$ *over* $\{0,1\}^*$ *such that*

$$\left\{ f_{\mathcal{R}^*,2}(x,y) \right\}_{\kappa,x,y,z} \overset{C}{\equiv} \left\{ f_2(x^*,y,z) \right\}_{\kappa,x,y,z},$$

where $x^* \leftarrow P^*_{\kappa,x}$.

2. *There exists an ensemble of efficiently samplable distributions* $\mathcal{Q}^* = \{Q^*_{\kappa,y}\}_{\kappa \in \mathbb{N}, y \in \{0,1\}^*}$ *over* $\{0,1\}^*$ *such that*

$$\left\{ f_{\mathcal{R}^*,1}(x,y) \right\}_{\kappa,x,y,z} \overset{C}{\equiv} \left\{ f_1(x,y^*,z) \right\}_{\kappa,x,y,z},$$

where $y^* \leftarrow Q^*_{\kappa,y}$.

Then, $\pi_{\mathcal{R}^*}$ *computes* f *with 1-security in the* $\{(f, \mathsf{fair}), (f_{\mathcal{R}^*}, \mathsf{g.o.d.})\}$*-hybrid model.*

The proof of Lemma 4 can be found in the full version.

References

1. Agrawal, S., Prabhakaran, M.: On fair exchange, fair coins and fair sampling. In: Canetti, R., Garay, J.A. (eds.) CRYPTO 2013, Part I. LNCS, vol. 8042, pp. 259–276. Springer, Heidelberg (2013). https://doi.org/10.1007/978-3-642-40041-4_15
2. Alon, B., Omri, E.: Almost-optimally fair multiparty coin-tossing with nearly three-quarters malicious. In: Hirt, M., Smith, A. (eds.) TCC 2016-B, Part I. LNCS, vol. 9985, pp. 307–335. Springer, Heidelberg (2016). https://doi.org/10.1007/978-3-662-53641-4_13
3. Alon, B., Cohen, R., Omri, E., Suad, T.: On the power of an honest majority in three-party computation without broadcast. Cryptology ePrint Archive, Report 2020/1170 (2020). https://eprint.iacr.org/2020/1170
4. Asharov, G.: Towards characterizing complete fairness in secure two-party computation. In: Lindell, Y. (ed.) TCC 2014. LNCS, vol. 8349, pp. 291–316. Springer, Heidelberg (2014). https://doi.org/10.1007/978-3-642-54242-8_13
5. Asharov, G., Beimel, A., Makriyannis, N., Omri, E.: Complete characterization of fairness in secure two-party computation of boolean functions. In: Dodis, Y., Nielsen, J.B. (eds.) TCC 2015. LNCS, vol. 9014, pp. 199–228. Springer, Heidelberg (2015). https://doi.org/10.1007/978-3-662-46494-6_10
6. Asokan, N., Shoup, V., Waidner, M.: Optimistic fair exchange of digital signatures. In: Nyberg, K. (ed.) EUROCRYPT 1998. LNCS, vol. 1403, pp. 591–606. Springer, Heidelberg (1998). https://doi.org/10.1007/BFb0054156
7. Beimel, A., Omri, E., Orlov, I.: Protocols for multiparty coin toss with a dishonest majority. J. Cryptol. **28**(3), 551–600 (2015)
8. Beimel, A., Haitner, I., Makriyannis, N., Omri, E.: Tighter bounds on multi-party coin flipping via augmented weak martingales and differentially private sampling. In: FOCS, pp. 838–849 (2018)
9. Ben-Or, M., Goldwasser, S., Wigderson, A.: Completeness theorems for non-cryptographic fault-tolerant distributed computation (extended abstract). In: STOC, pp. 1–10 (1988)

10. Blum, M.: Coin flipping by telephone. In: CRYPTO 1981,.pp. 11–15 (1981)
11. Borcherding, M.: Levels of authentication in distributed agreement. In: Babaoğlu, Ö., Marzullo, K. (eds.) WDAG 1996. LNCS, vol. 1151, pp. 40–55. Springer, Heidelberg (1996). https://doi.org/10.1007/3-540-61769-8_4
12. Bracha, G., Toueg, S.: Asynchronous consensus and broadcast protocols. J. ACM **32**(4), 824–840 (1985)
13. Buchbinder, N., Haitner, I., Levi, N., Tsfadia, E.: Fair coin flipping: tighter analysis and the many-party case. In: Proceedings of the 28th Annual ACM-SIAM Symposium on Discrete Algorithms (SODA), pp. 2580–2600 (2017)
14. Cachin, C., Camenisch, J.: Optimistic fair secure computation. In: Bellare, M. (ed.) CRYPTO 2000. LNCS, vol. 1880, pp. 93–111. Springer, Heidelberg (2000). https://doi.org/10.1007/3-540-44598-6_6
15. Canetti, R.: Security and composition of multiparty cryptographic protocols. J. Cryptol. **13**(1), 143–202 (2000)
16. Chaum, D., Crépeau, C., Damgård, I.: Multiparty unconditionally secure protocols (extended abstract). In: STOC, pp. 11–19 (1988)
17. Cleve, R.: Limits on the security of coin flips when half the processors are faulty (extended abstract). In: STOC, pp. 364–369 (1986)
18. Cohen, R., Lindell, Y.: Fairness versus guaranteed output delivery in secure multiparty computation. J. Cryptol. **30**(4), 1157–1186 (2017)
19. Cohen, R., Haitner, I., Omri, E., Rotem, L.: Characterization of secure multiparty computation without broadcast. J. Cryptol. **31**(2), 587–609 (2018)
20. Cohen, R., Haitner, I., Omri, E., Rotem, L.: From fairness to full security in multiparty computation. In: Catalano, D., De Prisco, R. (eds.) SCN 2018. LNCS, vol. 11035, pp. 216–234. Springer, Cham (2018). https://doi.org/10.1007/978-3-319-98113-0_12
21. Dwork, C., Lynch, N.A., Stockmeyer, L.J.: Consensus in the presence of partial synchrony. J. ACM **35**(2), 288–323 (1988)
22. Fischer, M.J., Lynch, N.A., Merritt, M.: Easy impossibility proofs for distributed consensus problems. Distrib. Comput. **1**(1), 26–39 (1986)
23. Fitzi, M., Gisin, N., Maurer, U., von Rotz, O.: Unconditional byzantine agreement and multi-party computation secure against dishonest minorities from scratch. In: Knudsen, L.R. (ed.) EUROCRYPT 2002. LNCS, vol. 2332, pp. 482–501. Springer, Heidelberg (2002). https://doi.org/10.1007/3-540-46035-7_32
24. Fitzi, M., Gottesman, D., Hirt, M., Holenstein, T., Smith, A.D.: Detectable byzantine agreement secure against faulty majorities. In: PODC, pp. 118–126 (2002)
25. Fitzi, M., Garay, J.A., Maurer, U.M., Ostrovsky, R.: Minimal complete primitives for secure multi-party computation. J. Cryptol. **18**(1), 37–61 (2005)
26. Garay, J.A., Kiayias, A., Ostrovsky, R.M., Panagiotakos, G., Zikas, V.: Resource-restricted cryptography: revisiting MPC bounds in the proof-of-work era. In: Canteaut, A., Ishai, Y. (eds.) EUROCRYPT 2020, Part II. LNCS, vol. 12106, pp. 129–158. Springer, Cham (2020). https://doi.org/10.1007/978-3-030-45724-2_5
27. Goldreich, O.: Foundations of Cryptography - VOLUME 2: Basic Applications. Cambridge University Press, Cambridge (2004)
28. Goldreich, O., Micali, S., Wigderson, A.: How to play any mental game or a completeness theorem for protocols with honest majority. In: STOC, pp. 218–229 (1987)
29. Gordon, S.D., Hazay, C., Katz, J., Lindell, Y.: Complete fairness in secure two-party computation. In: STOC, pp. 413–422 (2008)
30. Haitner, I., Tsfadia, E.: An almost-optimally fair three-party coin-flipping protocol. SICOMP **46**(2), 479–542 (2017)

31. Haitner, I., Makriyannis, N., Omri, E.: On the complexity of fair coin flipping. In: Beimel, A., Dziembowski, S. (eds.) TCC 2018, Part I. LNCS, vol. 11239, pp. 539–562. Springer, Cham (2018). https://doi.org/10.1007/978-3-030-03807-6_20

32. Halevi, S., Ishai, Y., Kushilevitz, E., Makriyannis, N., Rabin, T.: On fully secure MPC with solitary output. In: Hofheinz, D., Rosen, A. (eds.) TCC 2019, Part I. LNCS, vol. 11891, pp. 312–340. Springer, Cham (2019). https://doi.org/10.1007/978-3-030-36030-6_13

33. Kilian, J.: Founding cryptography on oblivious transfer. In: STOC, pp. 20–31 (1988)

34. Lamport, L., Shostak, R.E., Pease, M.C.: The byzantine generals problem. ACM Trans. Program. Lang. Syst. (TOPLAS) 4(3), 382–401 (1982)

35. Makriyannis, N.: On the classification of finite boolean functions up to fairness. In: Abdalla, M., De Prisco, R. (eds.) SCN 2014. LNCS, vol. 8642, pp. 135–154. Springer, Cham (2014). https://doi.org/10.1007/978-3-319-10879-7_9

36. Moran, T., Naor, M., Segev, G.: An optimally fair coin toss. J. Cryptol. 29(3), 491–513 (2016)

37. Pease, M.C., Shostak, R.E., Lamport, L.: Reaching agreement in the presence of faults. J. ACM 27(2), 228–234 (1980)

38. Rabin, T., Ben-Or, M.: Verifiable secret sharing and multiparty protocols with honest majority (extended abstract). In: FOCS, pp. 73–85 (1989)

39. Yao, A.C.: Protocols for secure computations (extended abstract). In: FOCS, pp. 160–164 (1982)

A Secret-Sharing Based MPC Protocol for Boolean Circuits with Good Amortized Complexity

Ignacio Cascudo[1] and Jaron Skovsted Gundersen[2]

[1] IMDEA Software Institute, Madrid, Spain
ignacio.cascudo@imdea.org
[2] Aalborg University, Aalborg, Denmark
jaron@math.aau.dk

Abstract. We present a new secure multiparty computation protocol in the preprocessing model that allows for the evaluation of a number of instances of a boolean circuit in parallel, with a small online communication complexity per instance of 10 bits per party and multiplication gate. Our protocol is secure against an active dishonest majority, and can also be transformed, via existing techniques, into a protocol for the evaluation of a single "well-formed" boolean circuit with the same complexity per multiplication gate at the cost of some overhead that depends on the topology of the circuit.

Our protocol uses an approach introduced recently in the setting of honest majority and information-theoretical security which, using an algebraic notion called reverse multiplication friendly embeddings, essentially transforms a batch of evaluations of an arithmetic circuit over a small field into one evaluation of another arithmetic circuit over a larger field. To obtain security against a dishonest majority we combine this approach with the well-known SPDZ protocol that operates over a large field. Structurally our protocol is most similar to MiniMAC, a protocol which bases its security on the use of error-correcting codes, but our protocol has a communication complexity which is half of that of MiniMAC when the best available binary codes are used. With respect to certain variant of MiniMAC that utilizes codes over larger fields, our communication complexity is slightly worse; however, that variant of MiniMAC needs a much larger preprocessing than ours. We also show that our protocol also has smaller amortized communication complexity than Committed MPC, a protocol for general fields based on homomorphic commitments, if we use the best available constructions for those commitments. Finally, we construct a preprocessing phase from oblivious transfer based on ideas from MASCOT and Committed MPC.

Jaron Skovsted Gundersen wants to acknowledge the SECURE project at Aalborg University. Furthermore, he wants to thank IMDEA Software Institute for hosting a visit to Ignacio Cascudo in connection to this paper.

R. Pass and K. Pietrzak (Eds.): TCC 2020, LNCS 12551, pp. 652–682, 2020.
https://doi.org/10.1007/978-3-030-64378-2_23

1 Introduction

The area of secure multiparty computation (MPC) studies how to design protocols that allow for a number of parties to jointly perform computations on private inputs in such a way that each party learns a private output, but nothing else than that. In the last decade efficient MPC protocols have been developed that can be used in practical applications.

In this work we focus on secret-sharing based MPC protocols, which are among the most used in practice. In secret-sharing based MPC, the target computation is represented as an arithmetic circuit consisting of sum and multiplication gates over some algebraic ring; each party initially shares her input among the set of parties, and the protocol proceeds gate by gate, where at every gate a sharing of the output of the gate is created; in this manner eventually parties obtain shares of the output of the computation, which can then be reconstructed.

A common practice is to use the preprocessing model, where the computation is divided in two stages: a preprocessing phase, that is completely independent from the inputs and whose purpose is to distribute some correlated randomness among the parties; and an online phase, where the actual computation is performed with the help of the preprocessing data. This approach allows for pushing much of the complexity of the protocol into the preprocessing phase and having very efficient online computations in return.

Some secret sharing based MPC protocols obtain security against any static adversary which actively corrupts all but one of the parties in the computation, assuming that the adversary is computationally bounded. Since in the active setting corrupted parties can arbitrarily deviate from the protocol, some kind of mechanism is needed to detect such malicious behaviour, and one possibility is the use of information-theoretic MACs to authenticate the secret shared data, which is used in protocols such as BeDOZa [3] and SPDZ [14].

In SPDZ this works as follows: the computation to be performed is given by an arithmetic circuit over a large finite field $\mathbb{F}$. There is a global key $\alpha \in \mathbb{F}$ which is secret shared among the parties. Then for every value $x \in \mathbb{F}$ in the computation, parties obtain not only additive shares for that value, but also for the product $\alpha \cdot x$ which acts as a MAC for x. The idea is that if a set of corrupt parties change their shares and pretend that this value is $x + e$, for some nonzero error e, then they would also need to guess the correction value $\alpha \cdot e$ for the MAC, which amounts to guessing α since $\mathbb{F}$ is a field. In turn this happens with probability $1/|\mathbb{F}|$ which is small when the field is large.

The problem is that over small fields the cheating success probability $1/|\mathbb{F}|$ is large. While one can take a large enough extension field $\mathbb{L}$ of $\mathbb{F}$ (e.g. if $\mathbb{F} = \mathbb{F}_2$, then $\mathbb{L}$ could be the field of 2^s elements) and embed the whole computation into $\mathbb{L}$, this looks wasteful as communication is blown up by a factor of s.

An alternative was proposed in MiniMAC [15]. MiniMAC uses a batch authentication idea: if we are willing to simultaneously compute k instances of the same arithmetic circuit over a small field at once, we can bundle these computations together and see them as a computation of an arithmetic circuit over the ring $\mathbb{F}^k$, where the sum and multiplication operations are considered coordinatewise. Note the same authentication technique as in SPDZ does not directly work over this ring (if $|\mathbb{F}|$ is small): if we define the MAC of a data vector $\mathbf{x}$ in $\mathbb{F}^k$ to be $\boldsymbol{\alpha} * \mathbf{x}$ where the key $\boldsymbol{\alpha}$ is now also a vector in $\mathbb{F}^k$ and $*$ is the coordinatewise product, the adversary can introduce an error in a single coordinate with probability $1/|\mathbb{F}|$. Instead, MiniMAC first encodes every vector $\mathbf{x}$ as a larger vector $C(\mathbf{x})$ by means of a linear error-correcting code C with large minimum distance d, and then defines the MAC as $\boldsymbol{\alpha} * C(\mathbf{x})$. Now introducing an error requires to change at least d coordinates of $C(\mathbf{x})$ and the MAC can be fooled with probability only $1/|\mathbb{F}|^d$. However, when processing multiplication gates, the minimum distance d^* of the so-called Schur square code C^* also needs to be large. These requirements on the minimum distance of these two codes have an effect on the communication overhead of the protocol, because the larger d and d^* are, the worse the relation between the length of messages and the length of the encoding.

This same article shows how to adapt this technique for computing a *single* boolean "well-formed" circuit while retaining the efficiency advantages of the batch simultaneous computation of k circuits. The idea is that if the target boolean circuit is structured into layers of addition and multiplication gates, where each layer has a large number of gates and its inputs are outputs of previous layers, then we can organize them into blocks of k gates of the same type, which can be computed using the above method. We then need an additional step that directs each block of outputs of a layer into the right block of inputs of next layers; this uses some additional preprocessed random sharings, and some openings, which slightly increases the communication complexity of the protocol.

In this paper, we explore an alternative to the error-correcting codes approach from MiniMAC, using an idea recently introduced in the honest majority, information-theoretically secure setting [8]. The point is that we can embed the ring $\mathbb{F}_q^k$ in some extension field of $\mathbb{F}_q$ in such a way that we can make the operations of both algebraic structures, and in particular the products (in one case the coordinatewise product, in the other the product in the extension field), "somewhat compatible": i.e., we map $\mathbb{F}_q^k$ into a slightly larger field $\mathbb{F}_{q^m}$ with some dedicated linear "embedding" map ϕ, that satisfies that for any two vectors $\mathbf{x}, \mathbf{y}$ in $\mathbb{F}_q^k$ the field product $\phi(\mathbf{x}) \cdot \phi(\mathbf{y})$ contains all information about $\mathbf{x} * \mathbf{y}$, in fact there exists a "recovery" linear map ψ such that $\mathbf{x} * \mathbf{y} = \psi(\phi(\mathbf{x}) \cdot \phi(\mathbf{y}))$. The pair (ϕ, ψ) is called a (k, m)-reverse multiplication friendly embedding (RMFE) and was introduced in [5,8]. With such tool, [8] embeds k evaluations of a circuit over $\mathbb{F}_q$ (i.e. an evaluation of an arithmetic circuit over $\mathbb{F}_q^k$ with coordinatewise operations) into one evaluation of a related circuit over $\mathbb{F}_{q^m}$, which is securely computed via an information-theoretically secure MPC protocol for arithmetic circuits over that larger field (more precisely the Beerliova-Hirt protocol [2]). The use of that MPC protocol over $\mathbb{F}_{q^m}$ is not black-box, however, as there are a number of modifications that need to be done at multiplication and input gates, for which certain additional correlated information has to be created in the preprocessing phase. Note that the reason for introducing this technique was that Beerliova-Hirt uses Shamir secret sharing schemes and hyperinvertible matrices, two tools that are only available over large finite fields (larger than the number of parties in the protocol).

1.1 Our Contributions

In this paper we construct a new secure computation protocol in the dishonest majority setting that allows to compute several instances of a boolean circuit at an amortized cost.[1] We do this by combining the embedding techniques from [8] with the SPDZ methodology. As opposed to [8], where one of the points of the embedding was precisely to use Shamir secret sharing, in our construction vectors $\mathbf{x} \in \mathbb{F}_2^k$ are still additively shared in $\mathbb{F}_2^k$, and it is only the MACs which are constructed and shared in the field $\mathbb{F}_{2^m}$: the MAC of $\mathbf{x}$ will be $\alpha \cdot \phi(\mathbf{x})$ where ϕ is the embedding map from the RMFE. Only when processing a multiplication gate, authenticated sharings where the data are shared as elements in $\mathbb{F}_{2^m}$ are temporarily used. MACs are checked in a batched fashion at the output gate, at which point the protocol aborts if discrepancies are found.

By this method we obtain a very efficient online phase where processing multiplication gates need each party to communicate around 10 bits[2] per evaluation of the circuit, for statistical security parameters like $s = 64, 128$ (meaning the adversary can successfully cheat with probability at most 2^{-s}, for which in our protocols we need to set $m \geq s$).

Our protocol can also be adapted to evaluating a single instance of a boolean circuit by quite directly adapting the ideas in MiniMAC that we mentioned above, based on organizing the circuit in layers, partitioning the layers in blocks of gates and adding some preprocessing that allows to map each block into the appropriate one in the next layer. The reason is that the maps used between layers of gates are $\mathbb{F}_2$-linear, and essentially all we need to use is the $\mathbb{F}_2$-linearity of the map ϕ from the RMFE. The actual complexity added by this transformation is quite dependent on the topology of the circuit. Under some general assumptions one can expect to add 2 bits of communication per gate.

Our online phase follows a similar pattern to MiniMAC in the sense that, up to the output phase, every partial opening of a value in $\mathbb{F}_2^k$ takes place when a partial opening of a C-encoding occurs in MiniMAC. Respectively, we need to open values in $\mathbb{F}_{2^m}$ whenever MiniMAC opens C^*-encodings. At every multiplication gate, both protocols need to apply "re-encoding functions" to convert encodings back to the base authentication scheme, which requires a preprocessed pair of authenticated sharings of random correlated elements.

However, the encoding via RMFE we are using is more compact than the one in MiniMAC; the comparison boils down to comparing the "expansion factor" m/k of RMFEs with the ratio k^*/k between the dimensions of C^* and C for the best binary codes with good distances of C^* [7]. We cut the communication

---

[1] Our ideas can be extended to arithmetic circuits over other small fields.

[2] Here we assume that broadcasting messages of M bits requires to send M bits to every other player, which one can achieve with small overhead that vanishes for large messages [14, full version].

cost of multiplication gates by about half with respect to MiniMAC where those binary codes are used. We achieve even better savings in the case of the output gates since in this case MiniMAC needs to communicate full vectors of the same length as the code, while the input and addition gates have the same cost.

We also compare the results with a modified version of MiniMAC proposed by Damgård, Lauritsen and Toft [13], that allows to save communication cost of multiplication gates, by essentially using MiniMAC over the field of 256 elements, at the cost of a much larger amount of preprocessing that essentially provides authenticated sharings of bit decompositions of the $\mathbb{F}_{256}$-coordinates of the elements in a triple, so that parties can compute bitwise operations. This version achieves a communication complexity that is around 80% of that of our protocol, due to the fact that this construction can make use of Reed-Solomon codes. However, it requires to have created authenticated sharings of 19 elements, while ours need 5 and as far as we know there is no explicit preprocessing protocol that has been proposed for this version of MiniMAC.

Finally we compare the results with Committed MPC [16], a secret-sharing based protocol which uses (UC-secure) homomorphic commitments for authentication, rather than information-theoretical MACs. In particular, this protocol can also be used for boolean circuits, given that efficient constructions of homomorphic commitments [9,10,17] over $\mathbb{F}_2$ have been proposed. These constructions of homomorphic commitments also use error-correcting codes. We find that, again, the smaller expansion m/k of RMFE compared to the relations between the parameters for binary error-correcting codes provides an improvement in the communication complexity of a factor ~ 3 for security parameters $s = 64, 128$.

We also provide a preprocessing phase producing all authenticated sharings of random correlated data that we need. The preprocessing follows the steps of MASCOT [19] (see also [18]) based on OT extension, with some modifications due to the slightly different authentication mechanisms we have and the different format of our preprocessing. All these modifications are easily to carry out based on the fact that ϕ and ψ are linear maps over $\mathbb{F}_2$. Nevertheless, using the "triple sacrificing steps" from MASCOT that assure that preprocessed triples are not malformed presents problems in our case for technical reasons. Instead, we use the techniques from Committed MPC [16] in that part of the triple generation.

1.2 Related Work

The use of information-theoretical MACs in secret-sharing based multiparty computation dates back to BeDOZa (Bendlin et al. [3]), where such MACs where established between every pair of players. Later SPDZ (Damgård et al. [14]) introduced the strategy consisting of a global MAC for every element of which every party has a share, and whose key is likewise shared among parties. Tiny OT (Nielsen et al. [21]), a 2-party protocol for binary circuits, introduced the idea of using OT extension in the preprocessing phase. Larraia et al. [20] extended these ideas to a multi-party protocol by using the SPDZ global shared MAC approach. MiniMAC (Damgård and Zakarias, [15]), as explained above, used error-correcting codes in order to authenticate vectors of bits, allowing for efficient parallel computation of several evaluations of the same binary circuits on possibly different inputs. Damgård et al. [13] proposed several improvements for the implementation of MiniMAC, among them the use of an error correcting code over an extension field, trading smaller communication complexity for a larger amount of preprocessing. Frederiksen et al. [18] gave new protocols for the construction of preprocessed multiplication triples in fields of characteristic two, based on OT extension, and in particular provided the first preprocessing phase for MiniMAC. MASCOT (Keller et al. [19]) built on some of these ideas to create preprocessing protocols for SPDZ based on OT extension. Committed MPC (Frederiksen et al. [16]) is a secret-sharing based secure computation protocol that relies on UC-secure homomorphic commitments instead of homomorphic MACs for authentication, but other than that, it follows a similar pattern to the protocols above. Efficient constructions of UC-secure homomorphic commitments from OT have been proposed by Frederiksen et al. [17] and Cascudo et al. [10] based on error correcting codes. Later, in [9] a modified construction from extractable commitments, still using error-correcting codes, was proposed that presents an important advantage for its use in Committed MPC, namely the commitment schemes are multi-verifier.

The notion of reverse multiplication friendly embedding was first explicitly defined and studied in the context of secure computation by Cascudo et al. in [8] and independently by Block et al. in [5]. The former work is in the context of information-theoretically secure protocols, while the latter studied 2-party protocols over small fields where the assumed resource is OLE over an extension field. This is partially based on a previous work also by Block et al. [4] where (asymptotically less efficient) constructions of RMFEs were implicitly used.

2   Preliminaries

Let $\mathbb{F}_q$ denote a finite fields with q elements. Vectors are denoted with bold letters as $\mathbf{x} = (x_1, x_2, \ldots, x_n)$ and componentwise products of two vectors are denoted by $\mathbf{x} * \mathbf{y} = (x_1 \cdot y_1, x_2 \cdot y_2, \ldots, x_n \cdot y_n)$. Fixing an irreducible polynomial f of degree m in $\mathbb{F}_q[X]$, elements in the field $\mathbb{F}_{q^m}$ with q^m elements can be represented as polynomials in $\mathbb{F}_q[X]$ with degree $m-1$, i.e $\alpha = \alpha_0 + \alpha_1 \cdot X + \cdots + \alpha_{m-1} \cdot X^{m-1} \in \mathbb{F}_{q^m}$, where $\alpha_i \in \mathbb{F}_q$. The sums and products of elements are defined modulo f.

In our protocols we will assume a network of n parties who communicate by secure point-to-point channels, and an static adversary who can actively corrupt up to $n-1$ of these parties. Our proofs will be in the universal composable security model [6].

We recall the notion of reverse multiplication friendly embeddings from [8].

Definition 1. *Let $k, m \in \mathbb{Z}^+$. A pair of $\mathbb{F}_q$-linear maps (ϕ, ψ), where $\phi \colon \mathbb{F}_q^k \to \mathbb{F}_{q^m}$ and $\psi \colon \mathbb{F}_{q^m} \to \mathbb{F}_q^k$ is called a $(k, m)_q$-reverse multiplication friendly embedding (RMFE) if for all $\mathbf{x}, \mathbf{y} \in \mathbb{F}_q^k$*

$$\mathbf{x} * \mathbf{y} = \psi(\phi(\mathbf{x}) \cdot \phi(\mathbf{y}))$$

In other words, this tool allows to multiply coordinatewise two vectors over $\mathbb{F}_q$ by first embedding them in a larger field with ϕ, multiplying the resulting images and mapping the result back to a vector over $\mathbb{F}_q$ with the other map ψ.

Several results about the existence of such pairs can be found in [8], both in the asymptotic and concrete settings. For our results we will only need the following construction, which can be obtained via simple interpolation techniques:

Theorem 1 ([8]). *For all $r \leq 33$, there exists a $(3r, 10r - 5)_2$ -RMFE.*

However, we remark that for implementations, it might be more useful to consider the following constructions of RMFEs which can also be deduced from the general framework in [8] (also based on polynomial interpolation). They have worse rate k/m than those in Theorem 1, but they have the advantage that their image can be in a field of degree a power of two, e.g. $\mathbb{F}_{q^m} = \mathbb{F}_{2^{64}}$ or $\mathbb{F}_{2^{128}}$.

Theorem 2. *For any $r \leq 16$, there exists a $(2r, 8r)_2$-RMFE.*[3]

For our numerical comparisons we will mainly consider the constructions with better rate in Theorem 1 and point out that, should one want to use Theorem 2 instead, then some small overhead in communication is introduced.

It is important to understand some properties and limitations of the RMFEs. Because ϕ and ψ are $\mathbb{F}_q$-linear then

$$\phi(\mathbf{x} + \mathbf{y}) = \phi(\mathbf{x}) + \phi(\mathbf{y}), \quad \psi(x + y) = \psi(x) + \psi(y)$$

holds for all $\mathbf{x}, \mathbf{y} \in \mathbb{F}_q^k$ and $x, y \in \mathbb{F}_{q^m}$. However, for example

$$\phi(\mathbf{x} * \mathbf{y}) \neq \phi(\mathbf{x}) \cdot \phi(\mathbf{y})$$

in general. Likewise we will need to take into account that the composition $\phi \circ \psi : \mathbb{F}_{q^m} \to \mathbb{F}_{q^m}$ is a linear map over $\mathbb{F}_q$ but *not* over $\mathbb{F}_{q^m}$. Therefore

$$(\phi \circ \psi)(x + y) = (\phi \circ \psi)(x) + (\phi \circ \psi)(y) \text{ for all } x, y \in \mathbb{F}_{q^m}, \text{ but}$$
$$(\phi \circ \psi)(\alpha \cdot x) \neq \alpha \cdot (\phi \circ \psi)(x)$$

for $\alpha, x \in \mathbb{F}_{q^m}$ in general (it does hold when $\alpha \in \mathbb{F}_q$, but this is not too relevant).

These limitations on the algebra of ϕ and ψ posed certain obstacles in the information-theoretical setting [8], since processing multiplication gates required to compute gates given by the map $\phi \circ \psi$, and this cannot be treated as a simple linear gate over $\mathbb{F}_{q^m}$. The additivity of $\phi \circ \psi$ combined with certain involved preprocessing techniques saved the day there. For completion (and comparison to our paper) we sum up some of the main details of [8] in the full version of this paper [11]. In our case, we will again encounter problems caused by these limitations as we explain next, but can solve them in a different way.

---

[3] Specifically the result is obtained by noticing that the proof of Lemma 4 in [8] can also be used to show the existence of $(k, 2k)_q$-RMFE for any $q \leq k + 1$, and then composing $(2, 4)_2$ and $(r, 2r)_{16}$-RMFEs in the manner of Lemma 5 in the same paper.

3   The Online Phase

In this section we present our protocol for computing simultaneously k instances of a boolean circuit in parallel, which we can see as computing one instance of an arithmetic circuit over the ring $\mathbb{F}_2^k$ of length k boolean vectors with coordinatewise sum and product.

Our strategy is to have mixed authenticated sharings: inputs and the rest of values in the computation $\mathbf{x}$ are additively shared as vectors over $\mathbb{F}_2^k$ (we refer to this as data shares), but their MACs are elements $\alpha \cdot \phi(\mathbf{x})$ in the larger field $\mathbb{F}_{2^m}$, where $\alpha \in \mathbb{F}_{2^m}$ is (as in SPDZ) a global key that is additively shared among the parties from the beginning (with $\alpha^{(i)}$ denoting the share for party P_i), and parties hold additive shares of $\alpha \cdot \phi(\mathbf{x})$ also in the field $\mathbb{F}_{2^m}$ (the MAC shares). We will denote the authentication of $\mathbf{x}$ by $\langle \mathbf{x} \rangle$. That is

$$\langle \mathbf{x} \rangle = \left((\mathbf{x}^{(1)}, \mathbf{x}^{(2)}, \ldots, \mathbf{x}^{(n)}), (m^{(1)}(\mathbf{x}), m^{(2)}(\mathbf{x}), \ldots, m^{(n)}(\mathbf{x})) \right)$$

where each party P_i holds an additive share $\mathbf{x}^{(i)} \in \mathbb{F}_2^k$ and a MAC share $m^{(i)}(\mathbf{x}) \in \mathbb{F}_{2^m}$, such that $\sum_{i=1}^n m^{(i)}(\mathbf{x}) = \alpha \cdot \sum_{i=1}^n \phi(\mathbf{x}^{(i)}) = \alpha \cdot \phi(\mathbf{x})$.

The additivity of ϕ guarantees that additions can still be computed locally, and we can define $\langle \mathbf{x} \rangle + \langle \mathbf{y} \rangle = \langle \mathbf{x} + \mathbf{y} \rangle$ where every party just adds up their shares for both values. Moreover, given a public vector $\mathbf{a}$ and $\langle \mathbf{x} \rangle$, parties can also locally compute an authenticated sharing of $\mathbf{a} + \mathbf{x}$ as

$$\mathbf{a} + \langle \mathbf{x} \rangle = \left((\mathbf{x}^{(1)} + \mathbf{a}, \mathbf{x}^{(2)}, \ldots, \mathbf{x}^{(n)}), (\alpha^{(1)} \cdot \phi(\mathbf{a}) + m^{(1)}(\mathbf{x}), \ldots, \alpha^{(n)} \cdot \phi(\mathbf{a}) + m^{(n)}(\mathbf{x})) \right)$$

This allows to easily process addition with constants. Moreover, this also allows us to explain how inputs are shared in the first place. In the preprocessing phase parties have created for each input gate an authenticated random values $\langle \mathbf{r} \rangle$ where $\mathbf{r}$ is known to the party that will provide the input $\mathbf{x}$ at that gate. This party can just broadcast the difference $\epsilon = \mathbf{x} - \mathbf{r}$, and then parties simply add $\epsilon + \langle \mathbf{r} \rangle = \langle \mathbf{x} \rangle$ by the rule above.

As in SPDZ, parties in our protocol do not need to open any MAC until the output gate. At the output gate, the parties check MACs on random linear combinations of all values partially opened during the protocol, ensuring that parties have not cheated except with probability at most 2^{-m} (we need that $m \geq s$ if s is the statistical security parameter); then, they open the result of the computation and also check that the MAC of the result is correct.

A harder question, as usual, is how to process multiplication gates; given $\langle \mathbf{x} \rangle$, $\langle \mathbf{y} \rangle$ parties need to compute $\langle \mathbf{x} * \mathbf{y} \rangle$ which implies not only obtaining an additive sharing of $\mathbf{x} * \mathbf{y}$ but also of its MAC $\alpha \cdot \phi(\mathbf{x} * \mathbf{y})$. If we try to apply directly the well-known Beaver's technique [1] we encounter the following problem. Suppose we have obtained a random triple $\langle \mathbf{a} \rangle, \langle \mathbf{b} \rangle, \langle \mathbf{a} * \mathbf{b} \rangle$ from the preprocessing phase and, proceeding as usual, parties partially open the values $\epsilon = \mathbf{x} - \mathbf{a}$, $\delta = \mathbf{y} - \mathbf{b}$ (a partially opening is an opening of the shares but not the MAC shares). From here, computing data shares for $\mathbf{x} * \mathbf{y}$ is easy; however, the obstacle lies in computing shares of $\alpha \cdot \phi(\mathbf{x} * \mathbf{y})$. Indeed

$$\alpha \cdot \phi(\mathbf{x} * \mathbf{y}) = \alpha \cdot \phi(\mathbf{a} * \mathbf{b}) + \alpha \cdot \phi(\mathbf{a} * \boldsymbol{\delta}) + \alpha \cdot \phi(\boldsymbol{\epsilon} * \mathbf{b}) + \alpha \cdot \phi(\boldsymbol{\epsilon} * \boldsymbol{\delta}),$$

and the two terms in the middle present a problem: for example for $\alpha \cdot \phi(\mathbf{a} * \boldsymbol{\delta})$ we have by the properties of the RMFE

$$\alpha \cdot \phi(\mathbf{a} * \boldsymbol{\delta}) = \alpha \cdot \phi(\psi(\phi(\mathbf{a}) \cdot \phi(\boldsymbol{\delta}))) = \alpha \cdot (\phi \circ \psi)(\phi(\mathbf{a}) \cdot \phi(\boldsymbol{\delta}))$$

However, $\phi \circ \psi$ is only $\mathbb{F}_2$-linear, and not $\mathbb{F}_{2^m}$-linear, so we cannot just "take α inside the argument" and use the additive sharing of $\alpha \cdot \phi(\mathbf{a})$ given in $\langle \mathbf{a} \rangle$ to compute a sharing of the expression above. Instead, we use a two-step process to compute multiplication gates, for which we need to introduce regular SPDZ sharings on elements $x \in \mathbb{F}_{2^m}$. I.e. both x and its MAC $\alpha \cdot x$ are additively shared in $\mathbb{F}_{2^m}$. We denote these by $[x]$, that is

$$[x] = \left((x^{(1)}, x^{(2)}, \ldots, x^{(n)}), (m^{(1)}(x), m^{(2)}(x), \ldots, m^{(n)}(x)) \right),$$

where P_i will hold $x^{(i)}$ and $m^{(i)}(x) \in \mathbb{F}_{2^m}$ with $\sum_{i=1}^{n} m^{(i)}(x) = \alpha \cdot \sum_{i=1}^{n} x^{(i)}$.

To carry out the multiplication we need to preprocess a triple $(\langle \mathbf{a} \rangle, \langle \mathbf{b} \rangle, \langle \mathbf{c} \rangle)$ where $\mathbf{c} = \mathbf{a} * \mathbf{b}$, and a pair of the form $(\langle \psi(r) \rangle, [r])$ where r is a random element in $\mathbb{F}_{2^m}$. In the first step of the multiplication we compute and partially open

$$[\sigma] = [\phi(\mathbf{x}) \cdot \phi(\mathbf{y}) - \phi(\mathbf{a}) \cdot \phi(\mathbf{b}) - r]. \tag{1}$$

This can be computed from the $\boldsymbol{\epsilon}$ and $\boldsymbol{\delta}$ described above (details will be given later). In the second step, we create $\langle \mathbf{x} * \mathbf{y} \rangle$ from (1) by using the properties of the RMFE; namely, $\mathbf{x} * \mathbf{y} = \psi(\phi(\mathbf{x}) \cdot \phi(\mathbf{y}))$ and $\mathbf{a} * \mathbf{b} = \psi(\phi(\mathbf{a}) \cdot \phi(\mathbf{b}))$, so applying ψ on σ in (1) yields $\mathbf{x} * \mathbf{y} - \mathbf{a} * \mathbf{b} - \psi(r)$ because of the additivity of ψ. Adding $\langle \mathbf{a} * \mathbf{b} \rangle + \langle \psi(r) \rangle$ (the yet unused preprocessed elements) gives $\langle \mathbf{x} * \mathbf{y} \rangle$.

We still need to explain how to construct $[\sigma]$. For this we introduce some algebraic operations on the two types of authenticated sharings and public values. First given a public vector $\mathbf{a}$ and a shared vector $\mathbf{x}$ we define:

$$\mathbf{a} * \langle \mathbf{x} \rangle = \left((\phi(\mathbf{a}) \cdot \phi(\mathbf{x}^{(1)}), \ldots, \phi(\mathbf{a}) \cdot \phi(\mathbf{x}^{(n)})), (\phi(\mathbf{a}) \cdot m^{(1)}(\mathbf{x}), \ldots, \phi(\mathbf{a}) \cdot m^{(n)}(\mathbf{x})) \right)$$

Note that the data shares are shares of $\phi(\mathbf{a}) \cdot \phi(\mathbf{x})$, which is an element of $\mathbb{F}_{2^m}$, and the MAC shares also correspond to additive shares of $\alpha \cdot \phi(\mathbf{a}) \cdot \phi(\mathbf{x})$. However, the data shares are not distributed uniformly in $\mathbb{F}_{2^m}$ because ϕ is not surjective, so one cannot say this equals $[\phi(\mathbf{a}) \cdot \phi(\mathbf{x})]$. Nevertheless, given another $[z]$, with $z \in \mathbb{F}_{2^m}$, it is true that $\mathbf{a} * \langle \mathbf{x} \rangle + [z] = [\phi(\mathbf{a}) \cdot \phi(\mathbf{x}) + z]$ where the sum on the left is defined by just local addition of the data and MAC shares. We also define

$$\langle \mathbf{x} \rangle + [y] = \left((\phi(\mathbf{x}^{(1)}) + y^{(1)}, \ldots, \phi(\mathbf{x}^{(n)}) + y^{(n)}), \right.$$

$$\left. (m^{(1)}(\mathbf{x}) + m^{(1)}(y), \ldots, m^{(n)}(\mathbf{x}) + m^{(n)}(y)) \right) = [\phi(\mathbf{x}) + y]$$

Now, given $\langle \mathbf{x} \rangle, \langle \mathbf{y} \rangle$ and a triple $\langle \mathbf{a} \rangle, \langle \mathbf{b} \rangle, \langle \mathbf{a} * \mathbf{b} \rangle$, parties can open $\epsilon = \mathbf{x} - \mathbf{a}$, $\delta = \mathbf{y} - \mathbf{b}$ and construct

$$\epsilon * \langle \mathbf{y} \rangle + \delta * \langle \mathbf{x} \rangle - \phi(\epsilon) \cdot \phi(\delta) - [r] = [\phi(\epsilon) \cdot \phi(\mathbf{y}) + \phi(\delta) \cdot \phi(\mathbf{x}) - \phi(\epsilon) \cdot \phi(\delta) - r]$$
$$= [\phi(\mathbf{x}) \cdot \phi(\mathbf{y}) - \phi(\mathbf{a}) \cdot \phi(\mathbf{b}) - r],$$

where the latter equality can be seen by developing the expressions for ϵ and δ, and using the additivity of ϕ. The obtained sharing is the $[\sigma]$ we needed above. Summing up, the whole multiplication gate costs 2 openings of sharings of vectors in $\mathbb{F}_2^k$ and one opening of a share of an element in $\mathbb{F}_{2^m}$. Every multiplication gate requires fresh preprocessed correlated authenticated sharings $(\langle \mathbf{a} \rangle, \langle \mathbf{b} \rangle, \langle \mathbf{a} * \mathbf{b} \rangle)$ and $(\langle \psi(r) \rangle, [r])$ for random $\mathbf{a}, \mathbf{b}, r$.

We present formally the online protocol we just explained, the functionality it implements, and the functionalities needed from preprocessing. The functionality constructing the required preprocessed randomness is given in Fig. 2, and relies on the authentication functionality in Fig. 1. The latter augments the one in MASCOT [19] allowing to also authenticate vectors and to compute linear combinations involving the two different types of authenticated values and which can be realized by means of the $[\cdot]$- and $\langle \cdot \rangle$-sharings.

The functionality for our MPC protocol is in Fig. 3 and the protocol implementing the online phase is in Fig. 4.

Theorem 3. Π_{Online} *securely implements* $\mathcal{F}_{\text{MPC}}$ *in the* $\mathcal{F}_{\text{Prep}}$*-hybrid model.*

Proof. The correctness follows from the explanation above. For more details we refer to the full version, but we also note that the online phase from this protocol is similar to the online phases of protocols such as [14–16,19], except that in every multiplication we additionally need to use the pair $(\langle \psi(r) \rangle, [r])$ in order to transform a $[\cdot]$-sharing into $\langle \mathbf{x} * \mathbf{y} \rangle$. However, since r is uniformly random in the field $\mathbb{F}_{2^m}$, the opened value σ masks any information on $\mathbf{x}, \mathbf{y}$.

3.1   Comparison with MiniMAC and Committed MPC

We compare the communication complexity of our online phase with that of MiniMAC [15] and Committed MPC [16], two secret-sharing based MPC protocols which are well-suited for simultaneously evaluating k instances of the same boolean circuit. We will count broadcasting a message of M bits as communicating $M(n-1)$ bits (M bits to each other party). This can be achieved using point-to-point channels as described in the full version of [14].

Communication Complexity of Our Protocol. Partially opening a $\langle \cdot \rangle$-authenticated secret involves $2k(n-1)$ bits of communication, since we have one selected party receive the share of each other party and broadcast the reconstructed value. Likewise, partially opening a $[\cdot]$-authenticated value communicates $2m(n-1)$ bits. In our online phase, every input gate requires $k(n-1)$

Functionality $\mathcal{F}_{\text{Auth}}$

The functionality maintains two dictionaries Val and ValField, to keep track of authenticated values. We remark that we can store elements from $\mathbb{F}_2^k$ in Val and elements from $\mathbb{F}_{2^m}$ in ValField. Entries in the dictionaries cannot be changed.

1. **Input:** On input

$$(\text{Input}, (\text{id}_1, \text{id}_2, \ldots \text{id}_s), (\text{id}'_1, \text{id}'_2, \ldots \text{id}'_t), (\mathbf{x}_1, \mathbf{x}_2, \ldots, \mathbf{x}_s), (x_1, x_2, \ldots, x_t), P_i)$$

   from P_i and $(\text{Input}, (\text{id}_1, \text{id}_2, \ldots \text{id}_s), (\text{id}'_1, \text{id}'_2, \ldots, \text{id}'_t), P_i)$ from all other parties, set Val[id_j] = $\mathbf{x}_j$ for $j = 1, 2, \ldots, s$ and ValField[id'_j] = x_j for $j = 1, 2, \ldots, t$.

2. **Add:** On input $(\text{Add}, \bar{\text{id}}, \text{id}, a))$ from all parties. If a is an id store Val[$\bar{\text{id}}$] = Val[id] + Val[a]. If a is a vector in $\mathbb{F}_2^k$ store Val[$\bar{\text{id}}$] = Val[id] + a.

3. **LinComb:** On input

$$(\text{LinComb}, \bar{\text{id}}, (\text{id}_1, \text{id}_2, \ldots \text{id}_s), (\text{id}'_1, \text{id}'_2, \ldots \text{id}'_t), a_1, a_2, \ldots, a_{s+t}, a)$$

   from all parties, where a_j is in $\mathbb{F}_{2^m}$ or $\mathbb{F}_2^k$ and $t \geq 1$. Define $\tilde{a}_j$ to be a_j if $a_j \in \mathbb{F}_{2^m}$, and $\phi(a_j)$ if $a_j \in \mathbb{F}_2^k$, and store ValField[$\bar{\text{id}}$] = $\sum_{j=1}^{s} \tilde{a}_j \cdot \phi(\text{Val}[\text{id}_j]) + \sum_{j=1}^{t} \tilde{a}_{s+j} \cdot$ ValField[id'_j] + $\tilde{a}$.

4. **Open:** On input $(\text{Open}, \text{Dict}, \text{id}, S)$ from all parties, where S is a non-empty subset of parties. If Dict = Val and Val[id] $\neq \perp$ wait for an $\mathbf{x}$ from the adversary and send $\mathbf{x}$ to the honest parties in S. If Dict = ValField and ValField[id] $\neq \perp$ wait for an x from the adversary and send x to the parties in S.

5. **Check:** On input

$$(\text{Check}, (\text{id}_1, \text{id}_2, \ldots, \text{id}_s), (\text{id}'_1, \text{id}'_2, \ldots, \text{id}'_t), (\mathbf{x}_1, \mathbf{x}_2, \ldots, \mathbf{x}_s), (x_1, x_2, \ldots, x_t))$$

   from every party wait for an input from the adversary. If they input OK, Val[id_j] = $\mathbf{x}_j$ for $j = 1, 2, \ldots, s$ and ValField[id'_j] = x_j for $j = 1, 2, \ldots, t$ return OK to all parties. Otherwise abort.

Notation: We will use the notation $\langle \mathbf{x} \rangle$ to refer to a value $\mathbf{x} \in \mathbb{F}_2^k$ stored in Val, and the notation $[x]$ to refer to a value $x \in \mathbb{F}_{2^m}$ stored in ValField.

Fig. 1. Functionality – authentication

Functionality $\mathcal{F}_{\text{Prep}}$

This functionality has the same features as $\mathcal{F}_{\text{Auth}}$ along with the following commands.

1. **InputPair:** On input $(\text{InputPair}, \text{id}, P_i)$ from all parties let P_i choose $\mathbf{r} \in \mathbb{F}_2^k$ at random and call $\mathcal{F}_{\text{Auth}}$ with input $(\text{Input}, \text{id}, \mathbf{r}, P_i)$ to obtain $\langle \mathbf{r} \rangle$. Output $\langle \mathbf{r} \rangle$ to all parties and $\mathbf{r}$ to P_i.

2. **ReEncodePair:** On input $(\text{ReEncodePair}, \text{id}_1, \text{id}_2)$ sample a random field element $r \in \mathbb{F}_{2^m}$ and set Val[id_1] = $\psi(r)$ and ValField[id_2] = r.

3. **Triple:** On input $(\text{Triple}, \text{id}_a, \text{id}_b, \text{id}_c)$ from all parties, sample two random vectors $\mathbf{a}, \mathbf{b} \in \mathbb{F}_2^k$ and set $(\text{Val}[\text{id}_a], \text{Val}[\text{id}_b], \text{Val}[\text{id}_c]) = (\mathbf{a}, \mathbf{b}, \mathbf{a} * \mathbf{b})$.

Fig. 2. Functionality – preprocessing

Functionality $\mathcal{F}_{\mathrm{MPC}}$

1. **Initialize:** On input Init from all players setup an empty dictionary Val.
2. **Input:** On input $(\mathrm{Input}, \mathrm{id}, \mathbf{x}, P_i)$ from P_i and $(\mathrm{Input}, \mathrm{id}, P_i)$ from all other parties where $\mathbf{x} \in \mathbb{F}_2^k$ and $\mathrm{Val[id]} = \bot$ set $\mathrm{Val[id]} = \mathbf{x}$.
3. **Add:** On input $(\mathrm{Add}, \mathrm{id}_1, \mathrm{id}_2, \mathrm{id}_3)$ from all parties where $\mathrm{Val[id_1]} \neq \bot$ and $\mathrm{Val[id_2]} \neq \bot$, set $\mathrm{Val[id_3]} = \mathrm{Val[id_1]} + \mathrm{Val[id_2]}$.
4. **Multiply:** On input $(\mathrm{Mult}, \mathrm{id}_1, \mathrm{id}_2, \mathrm{id}_3)$ from all parties where $\mathrm{Val[id_1]} \neq \bot$ and $\mathrm{Val[id_2]} \neq \bot$, set $\mathrm{Val[id_3]} = \mathrm{Val[id_1]} * \mathrm{Val[id_2]}$.
5. **Output:** On input $(\mathrm{Output}, \mathrm{id})$ from all parties when $\mathrm{Val[id]} \neq \bot$ retrieve $z = \mathrm{Val[id]}$ and send z to the adversary. Wait for an input from the adversary, if the adversary inputs OK send z to the honest parties. Otherwise abort.

Fig. 3. Functionality – MPC

Protocol Π_{Online}

1. **Initialize:** The parties call the preprocessing functionality $\mathcal{F}_{\mathrm{Prep}}$ to obtain input pairs $(\mathbf{r}, \langle \mathbf{r} \rangle)$ for each party, re-encode pairs $(\langle \psi(r) \rangle, [r])$, and multiplication triples $(\langle \mathbf{a} \rangle, \langle \mathbf{b} \rangle, \langle \mathbf{c} \rangle)$.
2. **Input:** For an input gate for which P_i has input $\mathbf{x} \in \mathbb{F}_2^k$ the parties do the following
   (a) P_i takes a pair $(\mathbf{r}, \langle \mathbf{r} \rangle)$ and broadcasts $\epsilon = \mathbf{x} - \mathbf{r}$.
   (b) The parties compute $\langle \mathbf{x} \rangle = \epsilon + \langle \mathbf{r} \rangle$.
3. **Add:** To compute componentwise addition of $\langle \mathbf{x} \rangle$ and $\langle \mathbf{y} \rangle$ the parties locally compute $\langle \mathbf{x} + \mathbf{y} \rangle = \langle \mathbf{x} \rangle + \langle \mathbf{y} \rangle$.
4. **Multiply:** To compute a componentwise multiplication of $\langle \mathbf{x} \rangle$ and $\langle \mathbf{y} \rangle$, take the next available multiplication triple $(\langle \mathbf{a} \rangle, \langle \mathbf{b} \rangle, \langle \mathbf{c} \rangle)$ and pair $(\langle \psi(r) \rangle, [r])$.
   (a) Set $\langle \epsilon \rangle = \langle \mathbf{x} \rangle - \langle \mathbf{a} \rangle$ and $\langle \delta \rangle = \langle \mathbf{y} \rangle - \langle \mathbf{b} \rangle$ and partially open ϵ and δ.
   (b) Compute $[\sigma] = \epsilon * \langle \mathbf{y} \rangle + \delta * \langle \mathbf{x} \rangle - \phi(\epsilon) \cdot \phi(\delta) - [r] = [\phi(\mathbf{x}) \cdot \phi(\mathbf{y}) - \phi(\mathbf{a}) \cdot \phi(\mathbf{b}) - r]$ and partially open σ.
   (c) Compute $\psi(\sigma) + \langle \mathbf{c} \rangle + \langle \psi(r) \rangle = \langle \mathbf{x} * \mathbf{y} \rangle$ and output this value.
5. **Output:** This stage is entered when the players have an unopened sharing $\langle \mathbf{z} \rangle$ which they want to output. Let $\mathbf{x}_1, \mathbf{x}_2, \ldots, \mathbf{x}_s$ be all opened $\langle \cdot \rangle$-sharings, i.e. $\mathbf{x}_j \in \mathbb{F}_2^k$ and let $x_1, x_2, \ldots, x_t$ be all opened $[\cdot]$-sharings, i.e. $x_j \in \mathbb{F}_{2^m}$. The parties do the following:
   (a) Call $\mathcal{F}_{\mathrm{Auth.Check}}$ with inputs $(\mathbf{x}_1, \mathbf{x}_2, \ldots, \mathbf{x}_s)$ and $(x_1, x_2, \ldots, x_t)$.
   (b) If the check passes, partially open $\mathbf{z}$.
   (c) Call $\mathcal{F}_{\mathrm{Auth.Check}}$ with input $\mathbf{z}$.
   (d) If the check passes, output $\mathbf{z}$ to all parties.

Fig. 4. Online phase

bits of communication. Multiplication gates require the partial opening of two $\langle \cdot \rangle$-authenticated values and one $[\cdot]$-authenticated value, hence $(4k + 2m)(n - 1)$ bits of communication. An output gate requires to do a MAC-check on (a linear combination of) previously partially opened values, then partially opening the output, and finally doing a MAC check on the output. A MAC check require every party to communicate a MAC share in $\mathbb{F}_{2^m}$, for a total of mn bits communicated. Hence output gates require $2k(n - 1) + 2mn$ bits of communication.

MiniMAC. MiniMAC uses a linear error correcting code C with parameters $[\ell, k, d]$ (i.e., it allows for encoding of messages from $\mathbb{F}_2^k$ into $\mathbb{F}_2^\ell$ and has minimum distance d). Parties have additive shares of encodings $C(\mathbf{x})$, where the shares are also codewords, and shares of the MAC $\boldsymbol{\alpha} * C(\mathbf{x})$, which can be arbitrary vectors in $\mathbb{F}_2^\ell$. In addition, at multiplication gates C^*-encodings of information are needed, where C^* is the code $C^* = \text{span}\{\mathbf{x} * \mathbf{y} \mid \mathbf{x}, \mathbf{y} \in C\}$, the smallest linear code containing the coordinatewise product of every pair of codewords in C^*, with parameters $[\ell, k^*, d^*]$. We always have $d \geq d^*$, and the cheating success probability of the adversary in the protocol is 2^{-d^*}, so we need $d^* \geq s$ for the statistical parameter s. The online phase of MiniMAC has a very similar communication pattern to ours: a multiplication requires to open two elements encoded with C (coming from the use of Beaver's technique) and one encoded with C^*. Since shares of C-(resp C^*-)encodings are codewords in C (resp C^*), and describing such codewords require k bits (resp. k^* bits)[4] the total communication complexity is $(4k + 2k^*)(n - 1)$, so the difference with our protocol depends on the difference between the achievable parameters for their k^* and our m, compared below. Input gates require $k(n-1)$ bits, as in our case, and for output gates, since MAC shares are arbitrary vectors in $\mathbb{F}_2^\ell$, a total of $2k(n - 1) + 2\ell n$ bits are sent. See full version for more details on this.

Committed MPC. Committed MPC [16] is a secret-sharing based MPC protocol that relies on UC-secure additively homomorphic commitments for authentication, rather than on MACs. Efficient commitments of this type have been proposed in works such as [9,10,17] where the main ingredient[5] is again a linear error correcting code C with parameters $[\ell, k, d]$. In committed MPC, for every $\mathbf{x} \in \mathbb{F}_2^k$, each party P_i holds an additive share $\mathbf{x}_i \in \mathbb{F}_2^k$ to which she commits towards every other party P_j (in the multi-receiver commitment from [9], this can be accomplished by only one commitment). During most of the online phase there are only partial openings of values and only at output gates the commitments are checked. Multiplication is done through Beaver's technique. In this case only two values ϵ, δ are partially opened. In exchange, parties need to communicate in order to compute commitments to $\delta * \mathbf{a}$ (resp. $\epsilon * \mathbf{b}$) given δ, and commitments to $\mathbf{a}$ (resp. ϵ and commitments to $\mathbf{b}$) at least with current constructions for UC-secure homomorphic commitments. [16, full version, Fig. 16] provides a protocol where each of these products with known constant vectors requires to communicate one full vector of length ℓ and two vectors of k^* components (again ℓ is the length of C and k^* is the dimension of C^*). In total the communication complexity of a multiplication is $(4k + 2k^* + \ell)(n - 1)$ bits. Output gates require to open all the commitments to the shares of the output. Since opening commitments in [9,10,17] requires to send two vectors of length ℓ to every other party, which has a total complexity of $2\ell(n - 1)n$. Input gates have the same cost as the other two protocols.

---

[4] We observe that this is more lenient than the description of MiniMAC in [13,15] where it is implied that ℓ bits need to be sent in order to do these openings.

[5] The constructions rely also on OT (in the first two cases) and extractable commitments (in the third) but these primitives are only used in a preprocessing phase.

Concrete Parameters. Summing up we compare the communication costs of multiplication and output gates in Table 1 since these are the gates where the communication differs.

Table 1. Total number of bits communicated in the different gates in the online phases, when computing k instances of a boolean circuit in parallel. Communication per party is obtained dividing by n.

	MiniMAC	Committed MPC	Our protocol
Multiply	$(4k + 2k^*)(n - 1)$	$(4k + 2k^* + \ell)(n - 1)$	$(4k + 2m)(n - 1)$
Output	$2 \cdot \ell \cdot n + 2k(n - 1)$	$2 \cdot \ell \cdot (n - 1)n$	$2 \cdot m \cdot n + 2k(n - 1)$

The key quantities are the relation between m/k (in our case) and k^*/k and ℓ/k in the other two protocols. While the possible parameters ℓ, k, d of linear codes have been studied exhaustively in the theory of error-correcting codes, relations between those parameters and k^*, d^* are much less studied, at least in the case of binary codes. As far as we know, the only concrete non-asymptotic results are given in [7,12]. In particular, the parameters in Table 2 are achievable.

Table 2. Parameters for C and C^{*2} from [7].

ℓ	k	$d \geq$	k^*	$d^* \geq$	k^*/k	ℓ/k
2047	210	463	1695	67	8.07	9.75
4095	338	927	3293	135	9.74	12.11

Table 3. Parameters for RMFE from [8].

k	m	m/k
21	65	3.10
42	135	3.21

On the other hand, the parameters for our protocol depend on parameters achievable by RMFEs. By Theorem 1 for all $1 \leq r \leq 33$, there exists a RMFE with $k = 3r$ and $m = 10r - 5$. Some specific values are shown in Table 3.

This leads to the communication complexities *per computed instance of the boolean circuit* for security parameters $s = 64$ and $s = 128$ given in Table 4. For larger security parameter, the comparison becomes more favourable to our technique, since the "expansion factor" m/k degrades less than the one for known constructions of squares of error correcting codes.

If instead we want to use Theorem 2, so that we can define the MACs over a field of degree a power of two, then the last column would have complexities $12 \cdot (n - 1)$ and $8 \cdot n + 2(n - 1)$ in both the cases $s = 64$ and $s = 128$.

Comparison with an Online Communication-Efficient Version of Min-iMAC. In [13], a version of MiniMAC is proposed which uses linear codes over the extension field $\mathbb{F}_{256}$. The larger field enables to use a Reed-Solomon code, for which $k^* = 2k - 1$. However, because this only gives coordinatewise operations

Table 4. Total number of bits sent per instance at multiplication and output gates

Sec. par.	Phase	MiniMAC	Committed MPC	Our protocol
$s = 64$	Multiply	$20.14 \cdot (n - 1)$	$29.89 \cdot (n - 1)$	$10.2 \cdot (n - 1)$
	Output	$19.5 \cdot n + 2(n - 1)$	$19.5 \cdot (n - 1)n$	$6.2 \cdot n + 2(n - 1)$
$s = 128$	Multiply	$23.48 \cdot (n - 1)$	$35.58 \cdot (n - 1)$	$10.42 \cdot (n - 1)$
	Output	$24.22 \cdot n + 2(n - 1)$	$24.22 \cdot (n - 1)n$	$6.42 \cdot n + 2(n - 1)$

in $\mathbb{F}_{256}^k$, the protocol needs to be modified in order to allow for bitwise operations instead. The modified version requires the opening of two C^*-encodings at every multiplication gate and a more complicated and much larger preprocessing, where in addition to creating certain type of multiplication triple, the preprocessing phase needs to provide authenticated sharings of 16 other vectors created from the bit decompositions of the coordinates of the two "factor" vectors in the triple. As far as we know, no preprocessing phase that creates these authenticated elements has been proposed.

The amortized communication complexity of that protocol is of $8(n-1)$ bits per multiplication gate, per instance of the circuit, which is slightly less than 80% of ours. On the other hand, we estimate that the complexity of the preprocessing would be at least 4 times as that of our protocol and possibly larger, based on the number of preprocessed elements and their correlation.

Computation and Storage. In terms of storage, each authenticated share of a k-bit vector is $m + k$ bits, which is slightly over 4 bits per data bit. MiniMAC and Committed MPC require a larger storage of $\ell + k$ bits because the MAC shares/commitments are in $\mathbb{F}_2^\ell$. In [13] shares are also 4 bits per data bit because of using RS codes, but the amount of preprocessed data is much larger. In terms of computation, while our protocol does slightly better for additions (again because of the shorter shares, and since the addition in $\mathbb{F}_{2^m}$ is as in $\mathbb{F}_2^m$), and the same happens with additions required by multiplication gates, computing the terms $\epsilon * \langle \mathbf{y} \rangle$, $\delta * \langle \mathbf{x} \rangle$, $\phi(\epsilon) \cdot \phi(\delta)$ requires in total 5 multiplications in $\mathbb{F}_{2^m}$ which, being field multiplications, are more expensive than the coordinatewise ones required by MiniMAC, even if some of them are in a larger space $\mathbb{F}_2^\ell$.

4   From Batch Computations to Single Circuit Computations

We explain now how to adapt our protocol, which was presented as a protocol for the simultaneous secure evaluation of k instances of the same boolean circuit, into a protocol that computes a single evaluation of a boolean circuit with little overhead, as long as the circuit is sufficiently "well-formed". This is a quite straightforward adaptation of the ideas presented in [15]. The technique can be used in general for any boolean circuit but it works better when the circuit satisfies a number of features, which we can loosely sum up as follows:

- The circuit is organized in layers, each layer consisting of the same type of gate (either additive or multiplicative). We number the layers in increasing order from the input layer (layer 0) to the output layer.
- For most layers, the number of gates u is either a multiple of k or large enough so that the overhead caused by the need to add u' dummy gates to obtain a multiple of k and compute the gates in batches of k is negligible.
- For most pairs of layers i and j, where $i < j$, the number of output bits from layer i that are used as inputs in layer j is either 0 or sufficiently large so that they do not incur in much overhead by adding dummy outputs or inputs (again to achive blocks of size exactly k).

The idea from [15] is that given a layer of u gates, where we can assume $u = t \cdot k$ we organize the inputs of the layers in t blocks of k gates, and we will compute each block by using the corresponding subroutine in our protocol.

For that we need to have authenticated shared blocks of inputs $\langle \mathbf{x} \rangle$, $\langle \mathbf{y} \rangle$ where the i-th coordinates x_i, y_i are the inputs of the i-th gate in the block. This assumes gates are of fan-in 2. For the case of addition gates, we can also support of course arbitrary fan-in gates, but then we want to have the same fan-in in every gate in the same block, again to avoid overheads where we need to introduce dummy 0 inputs. In any case at the end of the computation of this layer we obtain t authenticated sharings $\langle \mathbf{z} \rangle$.

The question is how to now transition to another layer j. Let us assume that layer j takes inputs from l blocks $\langle \mathbf{x}_1 \rangle, \ldots, \langle \mathbf{x}_l \rangle$ of k bits each coming from some previous layer. Of course the issue is that we are not guaranteed that we can use these as input blocks for the layer j. We will likely need to reorganize the bits in blocks, we may need to use some of the bits more than once, and we may not need to use some of the bits of some output blocks. At first sight this reorganization may look challenging, because note that the bits of each $\mathbf{x}_i$ can be "quite intertwined" in the MAC $\alpha \cdot \phi(\mathbf{x}_i)$.

However in all generality, we can define l' functions $F_1, \ldots, F_{l'} : \mathbb{F}_2^{kl} \to \mathbb{F}_2^k$ such that if we write $\mathbf{X} = (\mathbf{x}_1, \mathbf{x}_2, \ldots, \mathbf{x}_l)$ the concatenation of the output blocks, then $F_1(\mathbf{X}), \ldots, F_{l'}(\mathbf{X})$ are the input blocks we need. These maps are $\mathbb{F}_2$-linear; in fact, each of the coordinates of each F_i are either a projection to one coordinate of the input or the 0-map. We assume that all these reorganizing functions can be obtained from the description of the function and therefore they are known and agreed upon by all parties.

Calling $F = (F_1, F_2, \ldots, F_{l'})$, suppose we can obtain by preprocessing

$$((\langle \mathbf{r}_1 \rangle, \langle \mathbf{r}_2 \rangle, \ldots, \langle \mathbf{r}_l \rangle), (\langle F_1(\mathbf{R}) \rangle, \langle F_2(\mathbf{R}) \rangle, \ldots, \langle F_{l'}(\mathbf{R}) \rangle)),$$

where $\mathbf{R} = (\mathbf{r}_1, \mathbf{r}_2, \ldots, \mathbf{r}_l)$ is again the concatenation in $\mathbb{F}_2^{kl}$. To ease the notation we will write $(\langle \mathbf{R} \rangle, \langle F(\mathbf{R}) \rangle)$ and call this a reorganizing pair.

Then, reorganizing is done in the following way. The parties compute $\langle \mathbf{x}_j \rangle - \langle \mathbf{r}_j \rangle$ and open these values for $j = 1, 2, \ldots, l$. Afterwards, they compute

$$F_j(\mathbf{x}_1 - \mathbf{r}_1, \ldots, \mathbf{x}_l - \mathbf{r}_l) + \langle F_j(\mathbf{r}_1, \ldots, \mathbf{r}_l) \rangle = \langle F_j(\mathbf{x}_1, \ldots, \mathbf{x}_l) \rangle$$

which holds by the linearity of F_j.

We can add this property to our setup above by including the supplements in Fig. 5 to $\mathcal{F}_{\text{Prep}}$, $\mathcal{F}_{\text{MPC}}$, and Π_{Online}. Apart from this we also need to point out that at the input layer, a party may need to add dummy inputs so that her input consists of a number of blocks of k bits.

Functionality $\mathcal{F}_{\text{Prep}}$ (supplement)

4. **ReOrgPair:** On input $(\text{ReOrgPair}, F, (\text{id}_1, \text{id}_2, \ldots, \text{id}_l), (\text{id}'_1, \text{id}'_2, \ldots, \text{id}'_{l'}))$ where $F = (F_1, F_2, \ldots, F_{l'})$, sample l random vectors $\mathbf{r}_1, \mathbf{r}_2, \ldots, \mathbf{r}_l$ and set $\text{Val}[\text{id}_j] = \mathbf{r}_j$ for $j = 1, 2, \ldots, l$ and $\text{Val}[\text{id}'_j] = F_j(\mathbf{r}_1, \mathbf{r}_2, \ldots, \mathbf{r}_l)$ for $j = 1, 2, \ldots, l'$.

Functionality $\mathcal{F}_{\text{MPC}}$ (supplement)

6. **Reorganize:** On input $(\text{ReOrg}, F, (\text{id}_1, \text{id}_2, \ldots, \text{id}_l), (\text{id}'_1, \text{id}'_2, \ldots, \text{id}'_{l'}))$ compute $F(\text{Val}[\text{id}_1], \text{Val}[\text{id}_2], \ldots, \text{Val}[\text{id}_l]) = (\mathbf{z}_1, \mathbf{z}_2, \ldots, \mathbf{z}_{l'})$. Set $\text{Val}[\text{id}'_j] = \mathbf{z}_j$ for $j = 1, 2, \ldots, l'$.

Protocol Π_{Online} (supplement)

6. **Reorganize:** To reorganize between the layers, take a corresponding reorganizing pair $(\langle \mathbf{R} \rangle, \langle F(\mathbf{R}) \rangle)$.
   (a) Compute $\langle \epsilon_j \rangle = \langle \mathbf{x}_j \rangle - \langle \mathbf{r}_j \rangle$ and open ϵ_j for $j = 1, 2, \ldots, l$.
   (b) Compute $F_j(\epsilon_1, \epsilon_2, \ldots, \epsilon_l) + \langle F_j(\mathbf{R}) \rangle = \langle F_j(\mathbf{x}_1, \mathbf{x}_2, \ldots, \mathbf{x}_l) \rangle$ for $j = 1, 2, \ldots, l'$ and input these to the next layer.

Fig. 5. Reorganizing supplement

Of course, it looks as though we have moved the problem to the preprocessing phase, as we still need to construct the reorganizing random pairs $(\langle \mathbf{R} \rangle, \langle F(\mathbf{R}) \rangle)$. But this will be easy because of the $\mathbb{F}_2$-linearity of the maps ϕ and F.

The communication complexity of each reorganizing round is that of opening l vectors in $\mathbb{F}_2^k$, therefore $2lk(n-1)$ bits of communication. Therefore, the efficiency of this technique clearly depends much on the topology of the circuit. For example if all the output bits of a given layer are used in the next layer and only there, then we can say that this technique adds roughly 2 bits of communication per party per gate.

5   Preprocessing

In this section, we present how to obtain the preprocessed correlated information we need in our online protocols. The implementation of authentication and construction of multiplication triples is adapted in a relatively straightforward way from MASCOT. This is because MASCOT is based on bit-OT extension, and working bit-by-bit is well suited for our situation because of the maps ϕ, ψ being $\mathbb{F}_2$-linear. For the preprocessing of multiplication triples we do need to introduce some auxiliary protocols with respect to MASCOT: one is the preprocessing of reencoding pairs $(\langle \psi(r) \rangle, [r])$ that we anyway need for the online protocol; another one creates $[r]$ for a random r in the kernel of ψ, which we need in order to avoid some information leakage in the sacrifice step. Both types of preprocessing can be easily constructed based on the $\mathbb{F}_2$-linearity of ψ. Finally, we use the sacrifice step in Committed MPC, rather than the one in MASCOT, because of some technical issues regarding the fact that the image of ϕ is not the entire $\mathbb{F}_{2^m}$ which creates problems when opening certain sharings.

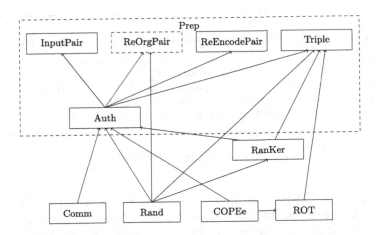

Fig. 6. Overview of dependency of the protocols needed for the preprocessing.

Aside from the aforementioned multiplication triples $(\langle a \rangle, \langle b \rangle, \langle c \rangle)$ where $c = a * b$, for the online phase we also need to generate input pairs $(r, \langle r \rangle)$, reencoding pairs of the form $(\langle \psi(r) \rangle, [r])$, and (in case we want to use the techniques in Sect. 4) layer reorganizing pairs $(\langle R \rangle, \langle F(R) \rangle)$.

To obtain an overview of the way the functionalities presented in this section are dependent on each consider Fig. 6. We use the following basic ideal functionalities: parties can generate uniform random elements in a finite set using the functionality $\mathcal{F}_{\mathrm{Rand}}$ (for the sake of notational simplicity we omit referring to $\mathcal{F}_{\mathrm{Rand}}$ in protocols). Moreover, parties have access to a commitment functionality $\mathcal{F}_{\mathrm{Comm}}$, see Fig. 7. We will also make use of a functionality $\mathcal{F}_{\mathrm{ROT}}^{n,k}$ that implements n 1-out-of-2 oblivious transfers of k-bit strings (Fig. 8).

We adapt the correlated oblivious product evaluation functionality $\mathcal{F}_{\mathrm{COPEe}}$ defined in MASCOT [19]. We recall how this functionality works: we again see the field $\mathbb{F}_{2^m}$ as $\mathbb{F}_2[X]/(f)$ for some irreducible polynomial $f \in \mathbb{F}_2[X]$. Then $\{1, X, X^2, \ldots, X^{m-1}\}$ is a basis for $\mathbb{F}_{2^m}$ as a $\mathbb{F}_2$-vector space. The functionality as described in [19] takes an input $\alpha \in \mathbb{F}_{2^m}$ from one of the parties P_B in the initialization phase; then there is an arbitrary number of extend phases where on input $x \in \mathbb{F}_{2^m}$ from P_A, the functionality creates additive sharings of $\alpha \cdot x$ for the two parties. However, if P_A is corrupted it may instead decide to input a vector of elements $(x_0, x_1, \ldots, x_{m-1}) \in (\mathbb{F}_{2^m})^m$, and in that case the functionality outputs a sharing of $\sum_{i=0}^{m-1} x_i \cdot \alpha_i \cdot X^i$ (where α_i are the coordinates

---

Functionality $\mathcal{F}_{\text{Rand}}$
1. Upon receiving (Rand, S) from all parties, where S is a finite set, choose a uniform random number $r \in S$ and send it to all parties.

Functionality $\mathcal{F}_{\text{Comm}}$
1. Upon receiving (Comm, x, P_i) from P_i and (Comm, P_i) from all other parties the functionality stores x. When receiving an opening command from all parties, the functionality sends x to all parties.

Fig. 7. Functionalities – randomness generation and commitment

---

Functionality $\mathcal{F}_{\text{ROT}}^{n,k}$
1. Upon receiving (ROT, P_i, P_j) from party P_i and (ROT, P_i, P_j, **b**) from party P_j, where $\mathbf{b} \in \{0,1\}^n$, the functionality chooses $\mathbf{r}_0^l, \mathbf{r}_1^l \in \{0,1\}^k$ uniformly at random and sends these to P_i, while it sends $\mathbf{r}_{b_l}^l$ to P_j for $l = 1, 2, \ldots, n$.

Fig. 8. Functionality – random OT

of α in the above basis). The honest case would correspond to all x_i being equal to x. This functionality from MASCOT corresponds to the steps Initialize and ExtendField in our version Fig. 10. We augment this by adding the step ExtendVector, where party P_A can input a vector $\mathbf{x} \in \mathbb{F}_2^k$ and the functionality outputs an additive sharing of $\alpha \cdot \phi(\mathbf{x}) \in \mathbb{F}_{2^m}$. If party P_A is corrupted it may instead input $(\mathbf{x}_0, \mathbf{x}_1, \ldots, \mathbf{x}_{m-1}) \in (\mathbb{F}_2^k)^m$. In that case the functionality outputs an additive sharing of $\sum_{i=0}^{m-1} \phi(\mathbf{x}_i) \cdot \alpha_i \cdot X^i$, and note that this is more restrictive for the corrupted adversary than ExtendField since the values $\phi(\mathbf{x}_i)$ are not free in $\mathbb{F}_{2^m}$ but confined to the image of ϕ. We define the functionality $\mathcal{F}_{\text{COPEe}}$ in Fig. 9 and present a protocol implementing the functionality in Fig. 10.

Proposition 1. Π_{COPEe} *securely implements* $\mathcal{F}_{\text{COPEe}}$ *in the* $\mathcal{F}_{OT}^{m,\lambda}$*-hybrid model.*

Proof. The commands Initialize and ExtendField are as in [19] (the latter being called Extend there). The proof for our ExtendVector command is analogous to the one for the ExtendField except, as explained, because the ideal functionality restricts the choice by a corrupt P_A of the element that is secret shared. We briefly show the simulation of ExtendVector together with Initialize.

If P_B is corrupted, the simulator receives $(\alpha_0, \ldots, \alpha_{m-1})$ from the adversary, and simulates the initialization phase by sampling the seeds at random, and sending the corresponding one to the adversary. It simulates the ExtendVector phase by choosing $\mathbf{u}_i$ uniformly at random in the corresponding domain, computes q as an honest P_B would do and inputs this to the functionality. Indistinguishability holds by the pseudorandomness of F, as shown in [19].

If P_A is corrupted then the simulator receives the seeds from the adversary in the Initialize phase, and from there it computes all the $\mathbf{t}_b^i$ in the ExtendVector phase. Then when the adversary sends $\mathbf{u}_i$, the simulators extract $\mathbf{x}_i = \mathbf{u}_i - \mathbf{t}_0^i + \mathbf{t}_1^i$

Functionality $\mathcal{F}_{\text{COPEe}}$

This functionality runs with two parties P_A and P_B and an adversary $\mathcal{A}$. The Initialize phase is run once first. The ExtendVector and ExtendField may be run an arbitrary number of times, in arbitrary order.

1. **Initialize:** On input $\alpha \in \mathbb{F}_{2^m}$ from P_B the functionality stores this value. We identify α by the vector $(\alpha_0, \alpha_1, \ldots, \alpha_{m-1}) \in \mathbb{F}_2^m$, s.t. $\alpha = \sum_{i=0}^{m-1} \alpha_i \cdot X^i$.

2. **ExtendVector:** P_A inputs a vector $\mathbf{x} \in \mathbb{F}_2^k$.
   (a) If P_A is corrupt receive $t \in \mathbb{F}_{2^m}$ and $(\mathbf{x}_0, \mathbf{x}_1, \ldots, \mathbf{x}_{m-1}) \in (\mathbb{F}_2^k)^m$ from $\mathcal{A}$, where the numbers indicate that $\mathbf{x}_i$ might be different from $\mathbf{x}$. Then compute q such that $q + t = \sum_{i=0}^{m-1} \phi(\mathbf{x}_i) \cdot \alpha_i \cdot X^i$.
   (b) If both parties are honest sample $t \in \mathbb{F}_{2^m}$ at random and compute q such that $q + t = \alpha \cdot \phi(\mathbf{x})$.
   (c) If only P_B is corrupt then receive $q \in \mathbb{F}_{2^m}$ from $\mathcal{A}$ and compute t such that $q + t = \alpha \cdot \phi(\mathbf{x})$.
   (d) Output t to P_A and q to P_B.

3. **ExtendField:** P_A inputs a field element $x \in \mathbb{F}_{2^m}$.
   (a) If P_A is corrupt receive $t \in \mathbb{F}_{2^m}$ and $(x_0, x_1, \ldots, x_{m-1}) \in (\mathbb{F}_{2^m})^m$ from $\mathcal{A}$, where the numbers indicate that x_i might be different from x. Then compute q such that $q + t = \sum_{i=0}^{m-1} x_i \cdot \alpha_i \cdot X^i$.
   (b) If both parties are honest sample $t \in \mathbb{F}_{2^m}$ at random and compute q such that $q + t = \alpha \cdot x$.
   (c) If only P_B is corrupt then receive $q \in \mathbb{F}_{2^m}$ from $\mathcal{A}$ and compute t s.t. $q + t = \alpha \cdot x$.
   (d) Output t to P_A and q to P_B.

Fig. 9. Functionality – correlated oblivious product evaluation with errors.

and inputs $t = -\sum_{i=0}^{m-1} \phi(\mathbf{t}_0^i) \cdot X^i$ and $(\mathbf{x}_1, \mathbf{x}_2, \ldots, \mathbf{x}_m)$ to $\mathcal{F}_{\text{COPEe}}$. In this case all outputs are computed as in the real world and indistinguishability follows.

5.1 Authentication

In protocol Π_{Auth} (Figs. 11, 12, and 13), we use $\mathcal{F}_{\text{COPEe}}$ to implement $\mathcal{F}_{\text{Auth}}$.

In the initialize phase each pair of parties (P_i, P_j) call the initialize phase from $\mathcal{F}_{\text{COPEe}}$ where P_i inputs a MAC key. Afterwards P_j can create authenticated sharings to the desired values, both of boolean vectors and of elements in the larger field: namely P_j constructs additive random sharings of the individual values and uses the appropriate extend phase of $\mathcal{F}_{\text{COPEe}}$ to obtain additive sharings of the MACs. At last, a random linear combination of the values chosen by P_j is checked. Here privacy is achieved by letting P_j include a dummy input x_{t+1} to mask the other inputs.

Proposition 2. Π_{Auth} *securely implements* $\mathcal{F}_{\text{Auth}}$ *in the* $(\mathcal{F}_{\text{COPEe}}, \mathcal{F}_{\text{Rand}}, \mathcal{F}_{\text{Comm}})$-*hybrid model*

Proof. Since the proof is similar to the proof of security for $\Pi_{[[\cdot]]}$ in [19], we point out the differences and argue why it does not have an impact on the security.

First of all note that our functionality, in contrary to $\Pi_{[[\cdot]]}$, has an Add command and a LinComb command. This is because we reserve the LinComb

---

Protocol Π_{COPEe}

The protocol is a two party protocol with parties P_A and P_B that uses PRFs $F\colon \{0,1\}^\lambda \times \{0,1\}^\lambda \to \mathbb{F}_2^k$ and $F_{\text{Field}}\colon \{0,1\}^\lambda \times \{0,1\}^\lambda \to \mathbb{F}_{2^m}$, has access to the ideal functionality $\mathcal{F}_{\text{ROT}}^{m,\lambda}$, and maintains a global counter $j := 0$. The Initialize phase is run once first, and then the ExtendVector and ExtendField may be run an arbitrary number of times, in arbitrary order.

1. **Initialize:** On input $\alpha \in \mathbb{F}_{2^m}$ from P_B:
   (a) The parties engage in $\mathcal{F}_{\text{ROT}}^{m,\lambda}$ where P_B inputs $(\alpha_0, \alpha_1, \ldots, \alpha_{m-1}) \in \mathbb{F}_2^m$ s.t. $\alpha = \sum_{i=0}^{m-1} \alpha_i \cdot X^i \in \mathbb{F}_{2^m}$. P_A receives $\{(\mathbf{k}_0^i, \mathbf{k}_1^i)\}_{i=0}^{m-1}$ and P_B receives $\mathbf{k}_{\alpha_i}^i$ for $i = 0, 1, \ldots, m-1$.

2. **ExtendVector:** On input $\mathbf{x} \in \mathbb{F}_2^k$ from P_A:
   (a) For $i = 0, 1, \ldots, m-1$:
      i. Define $\mathbf{t}_0^i = F(\mathbf{k}_0^i, j) \in \mathbb{F}_2^k$, $\mathbf{t}_1^i = F(\mathbf{k}_1^i, j) \in \mathbb{F}_2^k$ so P_A knows $(\mathbf{t}_0^i, \mathbf{t}_1^i)$ and P_B knows $\mathbf{t}_{\alpha_i}^i$.
      ii. P_A sends $\mathbf{u}_i = \mathbf{t}_0^i - \mathbf{t}_1^i + \mathbf{x}$ to P_B.
      iii. P_B computes $\mathbf{q}_i = \alpha_i \cdot \mathbf{u}_i + \mathbf{t}_{\alpha_i}^i = \mathbf{t}_0^i + \alpha_i \cdot \mathbf{x} \in \mathbb{F}_2^k$.
   (b) $j := j + 1$
   (c) P_B outputs $q = \sum_{i=0}^{m-1} \phi(\mathbf{q}_i) \cdot X^i$ and P_A outputs $t = -\sum_{i=0}^{m-1} \phi(\mathbf{t}_0^i) \cdot X^i$

3. **ExtendField:** On input $x \in \mathbb{F}_{2^m}$ from P_A:
   (a) For $i = 0, 1, \ldots, m-1$:
      i. Define $t_0^i = F_{\text{Field}}(\mathbf{k}_0^i, j) \in \mathbb{F}_{2^m}, t_1^i = F_{\text{Field}}(\mathbf{k}_1^i, j) \in \mathbb{F}_{2^m}$, so P_A knows (t_0^i, t_1^i) and P_B knows $t_{\alpha_i}^i$.
      ii. P_A sends $u_i = t_0^i - t_1^i + x$ to P_B.
      iii. P_B computes $q_i = \alpha_i \cdot u_i + t_{\alpha_i}^i$.
   (b) $j := j + 1$.
   (c) P_B outputs $q = \sum_{i=0}^{m-1} q_i \cdot X^i$ and P_A outputs $t = -\sum_{i=0}^{m-1} t_0^i \cdot X^i$.

Fig. 10. Correlated oblivious product evaluation with errors.

command for linear combinations which output $[\cdot]$-sharings, while Add outputs a $\langle\cdot\rangle$-sharing. In any case, the Add and LinComb command consist of local computations so it is trivial to argue their security. The Initialize command only invokes the Initialize command from the ideal functionality $\mathcal{F}_{\text{COPEe}}$, which is exactly the same as in [19]. Since the Open command lets the adversary choose what to open to there is not much to discuss here either.

Therefore, what we need to discuss is the Input and Check commands. The idea is that if the check in the input phase is passed and the adversary opens to incorrect values later on, then the probability to pass a check later on will be negligible. In comparison to [19], we have both values in $\mathbb{F}_{2^m}$ and vectors in $\mathbb{F}_2^k$, but we can still use the same arguments there, because the check in the Input phase and all further checks are in $\mathbb{F}_{2^m}$ and therefore the simulation and indistinguishability is following by the exact same arguments as in [19].

5.2   Input, Reencoding, and Reorganizing Pairs

The two functionalities $\mathcal{F}_{\text{COPEe}}$ and $\mathcal{F}_{\text{Auth}}$ are the building blocks for the preprocessing. They are very similar in shape to the MASCOT functionalities but

Protocol Π_{Auth} – Part 1

This protocol additively shares and authenticates elements in $\mathbb{F}_2^k$ or $\mathbb{F}_{2^m}$, and allows linear operations and openings to be carried out on these shares. Note that the **Initialize** procedure only needs to be called once, to set up the MAC key. We assume access to the ideal functionalities $\mathcal{F}_{\text{Rand}}$, $\mathcal{F}_{\text{Comm}}$, and $\mathcal{F}_{\text{COPEe}}$.

1. **Initialize:** Each party P_i samples a MAC key share $\alpha^{(i)} \in \mathbb{F}_{2^m}$. Each pair of parties (P_i, P_j) for $i \neq j$ calls $\mathcal{F}_{\text{COPEe.Initialize}}$ where P_i inputs $\alpha^{(i)}$.

2. **Input:** On input $\mathbf{x}_1, \mathbf{x}_2, \ldots, \mathbf{x}_s \in \mathbb{F}_2^k$ and $x_1, x_2, \ldots, x_t \in \mathbb{F}_{2^m}$ from P_j the parties do the following:

   (a) P_j samples random element $x_{t+1} \in \mathbb{F}_{2^m}$.

   (b) For $h = 1, 2, \ldots, s$, P_j generates additive sharing $\sum_{i=1}^{n} \mathbf{x}_h^{(i)} = \mathbf{x}_h$ and sends $\mathbf{x}_h^{(i)}$ to P_i. Similarly, for $l = 1, 2, \ldots, t+1$, P_j generates additive sharing $\sum_{i=1}^{n} x_l^{(i)} = x_l$ and sends $x_l^{(i)}$ to P_i.

   (c) For every $i \neq j$, P_i and P_j call $\mathcal{F}_{\text{COPEe.ExtendVector}}$ s times where P_j inputs $\mathbf{x}_1, \mathbf{x}_2, \ldots, \mathbf{x}_s$ and $\mathcal{F}_{\text{COPEe.ExtendField}}$ $t+1$ times with inputs $x_1, x_2, \ldots, x_{t+1}$.

   (d) P_i receives $q_h^{(i,j)} \in \mathbb{F}_{2^m}$ and P_j receives $t_h^{(j,i)} \in \mathbb{F}_{2^m}$ such that

$$q_h^{(i,j)} + t_h^{(j,i)} = \alpha^{(i)} \cdot \phi(\mathbf{x}_h), \qquad \text{for } h = 1, 2, \ldots, s$$

$$q_{l+s}^{(i,j)} + t_{l+s}^{(j,i)} = \alpha^{(i)} \cdot x_l, \qquad \text{for } l = 1, 2, \ldots, t+1$$

   (e) Each P_i, $i \neq j$ defines the MAC shares $m^{(i)}(\mathbf{x}_h) = q_h^{(i,j)}$ for $h = 1, 2, \ldots, s$ and $m^{(i)}(x_l) = q_{l+s}^{(i,j)}$ for $l = 1, 2, \ldots, t+1$. P_j computes MAC share

$$m^{(j)}(\mathbf{x}_h) = \alpha^{(j)} \cdot \phi(\mathbf{x}_h) + \sum_{i \neq j} t_h^{(j,i)} \qquad \text{for } h = 1, 2, \ldots, s$$

$$m^{(j)}(x_l) = \alpha^{(j)} \cdot x_l + \sum_{i \neq j} t_{l+s}^{(j,i)} \qquad \text{for } l = 1, 2, \ldots, t+1$$

   This implies that we have $\langle \mathbf{x}_h \rangle$ *for* $h = 1, 2, \ldots, s$ *and* $[x_l]$ *for* $l = 1, 2, \ldots, t+1$

   (f) The parties call $\mathcal{F}_{\text{Rand}}(\mathbb{F}_{2^m}^{s+t+1})$ to obtain $(r_1, \ldots, r_{s+t+1})$.

   (g) Compute $[y] = \sum_{h=1}^{s} r_h \cdot \langle \mathbf{x}_h \rangle + \sum_{l=1}^{t+1} r_{s+l} \cdot [x_l]$ by calling $\Pi_{\text{Auth.LinComb}}$ and open y by calling $\Pi_{\text{Auth.Open}}$.

   (h) Call $\Pi_{\text{Auth.Check}}$ on y. If the check succeeds output $\langle \mathbf{x}_h \rangle$ for $h = 1, 2, \ldots, s$, and $[x_l]$ for $l = 1, 2, \ldots, t$.

Fig. 11. Authenticated shares – part 1.

with some few corrections to include that sharings can be of vectors instead of field elements in $\mathbb{F}_{2^m}$. With these building blocks we can produce the randomness needed for the online phase. First of all, we produce input pairs with protocol $\Pi_{\text{InputPair}}$ in Fig. 14. Proposition 3 is straightforward.

Proposition 3. $\Pi_{\text{InputPair}}$ *securely implements* $\mathcal{F}_{\text{Prep.InputPair}}$ *in the* $\mathcal{F}_{\text{Auth}}$-*hybrid model.*

We also need to construct pairs to re-encode $[\cdot]$-sharings to $\langle \cdot \rangle$-sharings after a multiplication. A protocol $\Pi_{\text{ReEncodePair}}$ for producing the pairs $(\langle \psi(r) \rangle, [r])$ for random $r \in \mathbb{F}_{2^m}$ is shown in Fig. 15.

Protocol Π_{Auth} – Part 2

3. **Add:** On input $(\text{Add}, \bar{\text{id}}, \text{id}, a)$ the parties do the following. If a is an index of Val they retrieve shares and MAC shares $\mathbf{x}^{(i)}, \mathbf{y}^{(i)}, m^{(i)}(\mathbf{x}), m^{(i)}(\mathbf{y})$ where $\mathbf{x}$ corresponds to id and $\mathbf{y}$ corresponds to the index a in Val. P_i computes

$$\mathbf{x}^{(i)} + \mathbf{y}^{(i)} \quad \text{and} \quad m^{(i)}(\mathbf{x}) + m^{(i)}(\mathbf{y})$$

and stores these under $\bar{\text{id}}$. If a is a vector, i.e. $a = \mathbf{a}$, they retrieve the share and MAC share $\mathbf{x}^{(i)}, m^{(i)}(\mathbf{x})$ where $\mathbf{x}$ corresponds to id in Val. P_i computes

$$\mathbf{x}^{(i)} + \begin{cases} \mathbf{a} & \text{if } i = 1 \\ \mathbf{0} & \text{if } i \neq 1 \end{cases} \quad \text{and} \quad m^{(i)}(\mathbf{x}) + \alpha^{(i)} \cdot \phi(\mathbf{a}).$$

and stores these under Val[$\bar{\text{id}}$].

4. **LinComb:** On input $(\text{LinComb}, \bar{\text{id}}, (\text{id}_1, \text{id}_2, \ldots \text{id}_s), (\text{id}'_1, \text{id}'_2, \ldots \text{id}'_t), c_1, c_2, \ldots, c_{s+t}, c)$ where $t \geq 1$, the P_i retrieves its shares and MAC shares $\left\{ \mathbf{x}_j^{(i)}, m^{(i)}(\mathbf{x}_j) \right\}_{j=1,2,\ldots,s}$ corresponding to id_j in Val and $\left\{ x_j^{(i)}, m^{(i)}(x_j) \right\}_{j=1,2,\ldots,t}$ corresponding to id'_j in ValField. P_i computes

$$y^{(i)} = \sum_{j=1}^{s} c_j \cdot \phi(\mathbf{x}_j^{(i)}) + \sum_{j=1}^{t} c_{s+j} \cdot x_j^{(i)} + \begin{cases} c & \text{if } i = 1 \\ 0 & \text{if } i \neq 1 \end{cases}$$

$$m^{(i)}(y) = \sum_{j=1}^{s} c_j \cdot m^{(i)}(\mathbf{x}_j) + \sum_{j=1}^{t} c_{s+j} \cdot m^{(i)}(x_j) + c \cdot \alpha^{(i)}$$

and stores these under $\bar{\text{id}}$ in ValField.

Fig. 12. Authenticated shares – part 2.

Proposition 4. $\Pi_{\text{ReEncodePair}}$ *securely implements* $\mathcal{F}_{\text{Prep.ReEncodePair}}$ *in the* $(\mathcal{F}_{\text{Auth}}, \mathcal{F}_{\text{Rand}})$-*hybrid model with statistical security parameter* s.

Proof. First notice that at least one of the parties is honest and hence $r_j = \sum_{i=1}^{n} r_j^{(i)}$ is random because one of the terms is. Suppose that at the end of the Combine phase parties have created $(\langle s_j \rangle, [r_j])$, where possibly $s_j \neq \psi(r_j)$.

Let $\epsilon_j = s_j - \psi(r_j)$ for all j. By $\mathbb{F}_2$-linearity of ψ, $b_i - \psi(b_i) = \sum_{j=1}^{t+s} a_{ij}\epsilon_j$. Hence if all $\epsilon_j = 0$, the check passes for all i. While if there is some $\epsilon_j \neq 0$, $j = 1, \ldots, t$, then for every i the probability that $\sum_{j=1}^{t+s} a_{ij}\epsilon_j = 0$ is at most $1/2$.

Since the checks are independent we obtain that if some $\epsilon_j \neq 0$, $j = 1, \ldots, t$ then the protocol will abort except with probability at most 2^{-s}. Note also that $b_i = r_{t+i} + \sum_{j=1}^{t} a_{ij}r_j$, so opening the b_i reveals no information about the output values $r_1, \ldots, r_t$.

Finally, a protocol for producing reorganizing pairs is given in Fig. 16.

Protocol Π_{Auth} − Part 3

5. **Open:** On input $(\text{Open}, \text{Dict}, \text{id}, S)$ party P_i retrieves the share corresponding to the dictionary and index, sends the share to P_j (the party with lowest index in S) who sums the shares and sends the sum back to the other parties in S.

6. **Check:**
   (a) On input

$$(\text{Check}, (\text{id}_1, \text{id}_2, \ldots, \text{id}_s), (\text{id}'_1, \text{id}'_2, \ldots, \text{id}'_t), (\mathbf{x}_1, \mathbf{x}_2, \ldots, \mathbf{x}_s), (x_1, x_2, \ldots, x_t))$$

   parties sample a random vector $(r_1, r_2, \ldots, r_{s+t}) \in \mathbb{F}_{2^m}^{s+t}$. P_i retrieves its MAC shares $m^{(i)}(\mathbf{x}_j)$ for $j = 1, 2, \ldots, s$ corresponding to id_j in Val and $m^{(i)}(x_j)$ for $j = 1, 2, \ldots, t$ corresponding to id'_j in ValField. Define

$$y = \sum_{j=1}^{s} r_j \cdot \phi(\mathbf{x}_j) + \sum_{j=1}^{t} r_{s+j} \cdot x_j$$

   and let P_i compute

$$m^{(i)}(y) = \sum_{j=1}^{s} r_j \cdot m^{(i)}(\mathbf{x}_j) + \sum_{j=1}^{t} r_{s+j} \cdot m^{(i)}(x_j)$$

   (b) P_i calls $\mathcal{F}_{\text{Comm}}$ to commit to $\sigma^{(i)} = m^{(i)}(y) - \alpha^{(i)} \cdot y$ and afterwards open the commitment.
   (c) The parties check if $\sigma^{(1)} + \sigma^{(2)} + \cdots + \sigma^{(n)} = 0$ and abort otherwise.

Fig. 13. Authenticated shares − part 3.

Protocol $\Pi_{\text{InputPair}}$

The protocol generates $(\mathbf{r}, \langle \mathbf{r} \rangle)$ where $\mathbf{r} \in \mathbb{F}_2^k$ is chosen randomly by P_i, the party calling the protocol.

1. **Construct:**
   (a) P_i chooses $\mathbf{r} \in \mathbb{F}_2^k$ uniformly at random.
   (b) P_i calls $\mathcal{F}_{\text{Auth.Input}}$ to obtain $\langle \mathbf{r} \rangle$ and output this authenticated share.

Fig. 14. Creating input pairs.

Proposition 5. $\Pi_{\text{ReOrgPair}}$ *securely implements* $\mathcal{F}_{\text{Prep.ReOrgPair}}$ *in the* $(\mathcal{F}_{\text{Auth}}, \mathcal{F}_{\text{Rand}})$*-hybrid model with statistical security parameter* s.

The proof of this proposition is similar to that of Proposition 4.

5.3 Multiplication Triples

Our protocol Π_{Triple} for constructing triples is given in Figs. 17 and 18. We note that $\mathbf{c} = \mathbf{a} * \mathbf{b} = \sum_{i,j} \mathbf{a}^{(i)} * \mathbf{b}^{(j)}$ and hence sharings of $\mathbf{c}$ can be obtained by adding sharings of summands, where each of the summands only require two parties P_i

---

Protocol $\Pi_{\text{ReEncodePair}}$

The protocol generates $(\langle\psi(r_j)\rangle, [r_j])$ for $j = 1, 2, \ldots, t$, where r_j is random in $\mathbb{F}_{2^m}$ and unknown to all parties. We assume access to the functionalities $\mathcal{F}_{\text{Rand}}$ and $\mathcal{F}_{\text{Auth}}$.

1. **Construct:**
   (a) P_i chooses $r_j^{(i)}$ for $j = 1, 2, \ldots, t + s$ uniformly at random in $\mathbb{F}_{2^m}$.
   (b) P_i calls $\mathcal{F}_{\text{Auth.Input}}$ to obtain $[r_j^{(i)}]$ and $\langle\psi(r_j^{(i)})\rangle$.
   (c) Compute $[r_j] = \sum_{i=1}^{n}[r_j^{(i)}]$ and $\langle\psi(r_j)\rangle = \sum_{i=1}^{n}\langle\psi(r_j^{(i)})\rangle$ for $j = 1, 2, \ldots, t + s$.
2. **Sacrifice:**
   (a) Call $\mathcal{F}_{\text{Rand}}(\mathbb{F}_2^t)$ to obtain $\mathbf{a}_i'$ for $i = 1, 2, \ldots, s$ and define $\mathbf{a}_i = (\mathbf{a}_i', \mathbf{e}_i) \in \mathbb{F}_2^{t+s}$ where $\mathbf{e}_i$ is the i'th canonical basis vector of length s.
   (b) Compute $[b_i] = \sum_{j=1}^{t+s} a_{ij}[r_j]$ and $\langle b_i \rangle = \sum_{j=1}^{t+s} a_{ij}\langle\psi(r_j)\rangle$, where a_{ij} is the j'th entry of $\mathbf{a}_i$, and partially open b_i and $\mathbf{b}_i$.
   (c) If $\psi(b_i) \neq \mathbf{b}_i$ for some $i \in \{1, 2, \ldots, s\}$ then abort.
   (d) Call $\mathcal{F}_{\text{Auth.Check}}$ on the opened values $\mathbf{b}_i$ and b_i.
3. **Output:** Output $(\langle\psi(r_j)\rangle, [r_j])$ for $j = 1, 2, \ldots, t$.

Fig. 15. Re-encode pairs.

Protocol $\Pi_{\text{ReOrgPair}}$

The protocol generates $(\langle\mathbf{R}_h\rangle, \langle F(\mathbf{R}_h)\rangle)$ where $\mathbf{R}_h = (\mathbf{r}_{h,1}, \ldots, \mathbf{r}_{h,l})$ and $F = (F_1, \ldots, F_{l'})$ is a linear function $F \colon \mathbb{F}_2^{kl} \to \mathbb{F}_2^{kl'}$ for $h = 1, 2, \ldots, t$. Furthermore, $\mathbf{r}_{h,j}$ is random in $\mathbb{F}_2^k$ and unknown to all parties. We assume access to the functionalities $\mathcal{F}_{\text{Rand}}$ and $\mathcal{F}_{\text{Auth}}$.

1. **Construct:**
   (a) P_i chooses $\mathbf{r}_{h,j}^{(i)}$ for $j = 1, 2, \ldots, l$ and $h = 1, 2, \ldots t + s$ uniformly at random in $\mathbb{F}_2^k$.
   (b) P_i calls $\mathcal{F}_{\text{Auth.Input}}$ to obtain $\langle\mathbf{r}_{h,j}^{(i)}\rangle$ and $\langle F_{j'}(\mathbf{r}_{h,1}^{(i)}, \ldots, \mathbf{r}_{h,l}^{(i)})\rangle$ for $j = 1, 2, \ldots, l$, $j' = 1, 2, \ldots, l'$ and $h = 1, 2, \ldots, t + s$.
   (c) The parties compute $\langle\mathbf{r}_{h,j}\rangle = \sum_{i=1}^{n}\langle\mathbf{r}_{h,j}^{(i)}\rangle$ and $\langle F_{j'}(\mathbf{r}_{h,1}, \ldots \mathbf{r}_{h,l})\rangle = \sum_{i=1}^{n}\langle F_{j'}(\mathbf{r}_{h,1}^{(i)}, \ldots \mathbf{r}_{h,l}^{(i)})\rangle$. Thus we have $(\langle\mathbf{R}_h\rangle, \langle F(\mathbf{R}_h)\rangle)$ for $h = 1, 2, \ldots, t + s$.
2. **Sacrifice:**
   (a) Call $\mathcal{F}_{\text{Rand}}(\mathbb{F}_2^t)$ to obtain $\mathbf{a}_i'$ for $i = 1, 2, \ldots, s$ and define $\mathbf{a}_i = (\mathbf{a}_i', \mathbf{e}_i) \in \mathbb{F}_2^{t+s}$ where $\mathbf{e}_i$ is the i'th canonical basis vector of length s.
   (b) Compute $\langle\mathbf{B}_i\rangle = \sum_{h=1}^{t+s} a_{ih}\langle\mathbf{R}_h\rangle$ and $\langle\mathbf{D}_i\rangle = \sum_{h=1}^{t+s} a_{ih}\langle F(\mathbf{R}_h)\rangle$, where a_{ih} is the h'th entry of $\mathbf{a}_i$, and partially open $\mathbf{B}_i$ and $\mathbf{D}_i$.
   (c) If $F(\mathbf{B}_i) \neq \mathbf{D}_i$ for some $i \in \{1, 2, \ldots, s\}$ then abort.
   (d) Call $\mathcal{F}_{\text{Auth.Check}}$ on the opened values $\mathbf{B}_i$ and $\mathbf{D}_i$.
3. **Output:** Output $(\langle\mathbf{R}_h\rangle, \langle F(\mathbf{R}_h)\rangle)$ for $h = 1, 2, \ldots, t$.

Fig. 16. Re-organize pairs.

and P_j to interact. Again, the construction step is much like the construction step from the protocol Π_{Triple} in [19]. where we have modified the protocol such that it produces triples $(\langle\mathbf{a}\rangle, \langle\mathbf{b}\rangle, \langle\mathbf{c}\rangle)$ instead of $([a], [b], [c])$.

Protocol $\Pi_{\text{TripleConstruct}}$

The protocol produces N multiplication triples.

1. **Construction:**
    (a) P_i samples $\mathbf{a}_l^{(i)}, \mathbf{b}_l^{(i)} \in \mathbb{F}_2^k$ for $l = 1, 2, \ldots, N$. Denote by $a_{h,l}^{(i)}, b_{h,l}^{(i)}$ the h'th entry of $\mathbf{a}_l^{(i)}, \mathbf{b}_l^{(i)}$, respectively.
    (b) For $l = 1, 2, \ldots, N$ every ordered pair (P_i, P_j) does the following:
        i. The pair call $\mathcal{F}_{\text{ROT}}^{k,1}$ where P_i inputs $a_{h,l}^{(i)}$ for the h'th instance.
        ii. P_j receives $t_{0,h,l}^{(j,i)}, t_{1,h,l}^{(j,i)} \in \mathbb{F}_2$ and P_i receives $t_{a_{h,l}^{(i)},h,l}^{(j,i)}$ for $h = 1, 2, \ldots, k$.

        Denote by $\mathbf{t}_l^{(j,i)}$ the vector having $t_{0,h,l}^{(j,i)}$ as entries and $\mathbf{t}_{1,l}^{(j,i)}$ the vector having $t_{1,h,l}^{(j,i)}$ as entries for $h = 1, 2, \ldots, k$. Similarly, denote by $\mathbf{t}_{\mathbf{a}_l^{(i)}}^{(j,i)}$ the vector having $t_{a_{h,l}^{(i)},h,l}^{(j,i)}$ as entries.

        iii. P_j sends $\mathbf{u}_l^{(j,i)} = \mathbf{t}_l^{(j,i)} - \mathbf{t}_{1,l}^{(j,i)} + \mathbf{b}_l^{(j)}$.
        iv. P_i sets $\mathbf{q}_l^{(j,i)} = \mathbf{a}_l^{(i)} * \mathbf{u}_l^{(j,i)} + \mathbf{t}_{\mathbf{a}_l^{(i)}}^{(j,i)} = \mathbf{t}_l^{(j,i)} + \mathbf{a}_l^{(i)} \cdot \mathbf{b}_l^{(j)}$.
        v. P_i sets $\mathbf{c}_{i,j,l}^{(i)} = \mathbf{q}_l^{(j,i)}$ and P_j sets $\mathbf{c}_{j,i,l}^{(j)} = -\mathbf{t}_l^{(j,i)}$
    (c) Each party P_i computes $\mathbf{c}_l^{(i)} = \mathbf{a}_l^{(i)} * \mathbf{b}_l^{(i)} + \sum_{j \neq i} \mathbf{c}_{i,j,l}^{(i)} + \mathbf{c}_{j,i,l}^{(i)}$
        Now we have $\mathbf{c}_l = \sum_{i=1}^n \mathbf{c}_l^{(i)} = \sum_{i=1}^n \mathbf{a}_l^{(i)} * \sum_{i=1}^n \mathbf{b}_l^{(i)} = \mathbf{a}_l * \mathbf{b}_l$ *for* $l = 1, 2, \ldots, N$
2. **Authenticate:**
    (a) P_i calls $\mathcal{F}_{\text{Auth.Input}}$ to obtain $\langle \mathbf{a}_l^{(i)} \rangle$, $\langle \mathbf{b}_l^{(i)} \rangle$, and $\langle \mathbf{c}_l^{(i)} \rangle$.
    (b) Parties compute $\langle \mathbf{a}_l \rangle = \sum_{i=1}^n \langle \mathbf{a}_l^{(i)} \rangle$ and similarly to obtain $\langle \mathbf{b}_l \rangle$ and $\langle \mathbf{c}_l \rangle$.

Fig. 17. Construction of multiplication triples.

However, after authentication, we use techniques from Committed MPC [16] to check correctness and avoid leakage on the produced triples. Indeed using the combine and sacrifice steps in MASCOT presents some problems in our case: in the sacrificing step in MASCOT parties take two triples $([a], [b], [c])$ and $([\hat{a}], [b], [\hat{c}])$ and start by opening a random combination $s \cdot [a] - [\hat{a}]$ to some value ρ, so that they can later verify that $s \cdot [c] - [\hat{c}] - \rho \cdot [b]$ opens to 0. Since the second triple will be disregarded, and $s \cdot a - \hat{a}$ completely masks a since $\hat{a}$ is uniformly random, no information is revealed about a. In our case we would have triples $(\langle \mathbf{a} \rangle, \langle \mathbf{b} \rangle, \langle \mathbf{c} \rangle)$ and $(\langle \hat{\mathbf{a}} \rangle, \langle \mathbf{b} \rangle, \langle \hat{\mathbf{c}} \rangle)$ and sample a random $s \in \mathbb{F}_{2^m}$, it would not be the case that $\phi(\hat{\mathbf{a}})$ would act as a proper one-time pad for $s \cdot \phi(\mathbf{a})$[6]. A similar problem would arise for adapting the combine step in [19].

Therefore, we proceed as in [16]: in the protocol Π_{Triple} we start by constructing additive sharings of $N = \tau_1 + \tau_1 \cdot \tau_2^2 \cdot T$ triples. Then some of these triples are opened and it is checked that they are correct. This guarantees that most of the remaining triples are correct. The remaining triples are then organized in buckets and for each bucket all but one of the triples are sacrificed in order to guarantee that the remaining triple is correct with very high probability. In order to be

---

[6] Sampling $\mathbf{s} \in \mathbb{F}_2^k$ instead would not solve the problem since $\mathbf{s} * \langle \mathbf{a} \rangle - \langle \hat{\mathbf{a}} \rangle$ is not a proper $[\cdot]$-sharing as described in Sect. 3.

Protocol Π_{Triple}

The protocol generates T multiplication triples $(\langle \mathbf{a} \rangle, \langle \mathbf{b} \rangle, \langle \mathbf{c} \rangle)$ where $\mathbf{a}, \mathbf{b} \in \mathbb{F}_2^k$ are random vectors and $\mathbf{c} = \mathbf{a} * \mathbf{b}$. The integers τ_1, τ_2 are bucket sizes and are for security reasons. Let $N = \tau_1 + \tau_1 \cdot \tau_2^2 \cdot T$. We assume access to the functionalities $\mathcal{F}_{\text{Auth}}$, $\mathcal{F}_{\text{ROT}}^{m,k}$, $\mathcal{F}_{\text{Rand}}$, and $\mathcal{F}_{\text{RanKer}}$, and we call $\Pi_{\text{TripleConstruct}}$ as a subprotocol.

1. **Construction:** Call $\Pi_{\text{TripleConstruct}}$ to produce N multiplication triples.
2. **Cut-and-choose:**
   (a) Call $\mathcal{F}_{\text{Rand}}$ to obtain $(l_1, l_2, \ldots, l_{\tau_1})$, where $l_i \neq l_j$ when $i \neq j$.
   (b) Open $\langle \mathbf{a}_{l_j} \rangle$, $\langle \mathbf{b}_{l_j} \rangle$, and $\langle \mathbf{c}_{l_j} \rangle$ for $j = 1, 2, \ldots, \tau_1$. Abort if $\mathbf{c}_{l_j} \neq \mathbf{a}_{l_j} * \mathbf{b}_{l_j}$ for some j.
3. **Sacrifice:**
   (a) Use $\mathcal{F}_{\text{Rand}}$ to randomly divide the remaining $N - \tau_1$ triples into $\tau_2^2 \cdot T$ buckets with τ_1 triples in each.
   (b) In each bucket we denote the triples by $(\langle \mathbf{a}_l \rangle, \langle \mathbf{b}_l \rangle, \langle \mathbf{c}_l \rangle)$ for $l = 1, \ldots, \tau_1$ and call $\mathcal{F}_{\text{RanKer}}$ to obtain $[r_l]$, $l = 2, \ldots, \tau_1$ for each bucket.
      i. Compute $\langle \epsilon_l \rangle = \langle \mathbf{a}_l \rangle - \langle \mathbf{a}_1 \rangle$ and $\langle \delta_l \rangle = \langle \mathbf{b}_l \rangle - \langle \mathbf{b}_1 \rangle$ and open ϵ_l and δ_l for $l = 2, \ldots, \tau_1$.
      ii. Compute $[\sigma_l] = 1 * \langle \mathbf{c}_l \rangle - 1 * \langle \mathbf{c}_1 \rangle - \epsilon_l * \langle \mathbf{b}_1 \rangle - \delta_l * \langle \mathbf{a}_1 \rangle - \phi(\epsilon_l) \cdot \phi(\delta_l) + [r_l]$ and open σ_l for $l = 2, \ldots, \tau_2$. Abort if $\psi(\sigma_l) \neq \mathbf{0}$. Otherwise, call $(\langle \mathbf{a}_1 \rangle, \langle \mathbf{b}_1 \rangle, \langle \mathbf{c}_1 \rangle)$ a correct triple.
4. **Combine:**
   (a) Combine on $\mathbf{a}$: Use $\mathcal{F}_{\text{Rand}}$ to randomly divide the remaining $\tau_2^2 \cdot T$ non-malformed triples into $\tau_2 \cdot T$ buckets with τ_2 in each. Denote the triples in each bucket by $(\langle \mathbf{a}_l \rangle, \langle \mathbf{b}_l \rangle, \langle \mathbf{c}_l \rangle)$ for $l = 1, \ldots, \tau_2$ and call $\mathcal{F}_{\text{ReEncodePair}}$ to obtain one pair for each bucket. Combine the triples in each bucket as follows:
      i. Compute $\langle \mathbf{a}' \rangle = \sum_{l=1}^{\tau_2} \langle \mathbf{a}_l \rangle$ and $\langle \mathbf{b}' \rangle = \langle \mathbf{b}_1 \rangle$
      ii. For $l = 2, 3, \ldots \tau_2$: Compute $\langle \epsilon_l \rangle = \langle \mathbf{b}_1 \rangle - \langle \mathbf{b}_l \rangle$ and open ϵ_l
      iii. Compute $[\sigma'] = 1 * \langle \mathbf{c}_1 \rangle + \sum_{l=2}^{\tau_2} \epsilon_l * \langle \mathbf{a}_l \rangle + 1 * \langle \mathbf{c}_l \rangle - [r]$, where $[r]$ is from the reencoding pair.
      iv. Open σ' and set $\langle \mathbf{c}' \rangle = \psi(\sigma') + \langle \psi(r) \rangle = \langle \mathbf{a}' * \mathbf{b}' \rangle$ and call $(\langle \mathbf{a}' \rangle, \langle \mathbf{b}' \rangle, \langle \mathbf{c}' \rangle)$ a good triple.
   (b) Combine on $\mathbf{b}$: Use $\mathcal{F}_{\text{Rand}}$ to randomly divide the remaining $\tau_2 \cdot T$ non-malformed triples into T buckets with τ_2 in each. Denote the triples in each bucket by $(\langle \mathbf{a}_l \rangle, \langle \mathbf{b}_l \rangle, \langle \mathbf{c}_l \rangle)$ for $l = 1, \ldots, \tau_2$ and call $\mathcal{F}_{\text{ReEncodePair}}$ to obtain one pair for each bucket. Combine the triples in each bucket as follows:
      i. Compute $\langle \mathbf{b}' \rangle = \sum_{l=1}^{\tau_2} \langle \mathbf{b}_l \rangle$ and $\langle \mathbf{a}' \rangle = \langle \mathbf{a}_1 \rangle$
      ii. For $l = 2, 3, \ldots \tau_2$: Compute $\langle \epsilon_l \rangle = \langle \mathbf{a}_1 \rangle - \langle \mathbf{a}_l \rangle$ and open ϵ_l
      iii. Compute $[\sigma'] = 1 * \langle \mathbf{c}_1 \rangle + \sum_{l=2}^{\tau_2} \epsilon_l * \langle \mathbf{b}_l \rangle + 1 * \langle \mathbf{c}_l \rangle - [r]$, where $[r]$ is from the reencoding pair.
      iv. Open σ' and set $\langle \mathbf{c}' \rangle = \psi(\sigma') + \langle \psi(r) \rangle = \langle \mathbf{a}' * \mathbf{b}' \rangle$ and call $(\langle \mathbf{a}' \rangle, \langle \mathbf{b}' \rangle, \langle \mathbf{c}' \rangle)$ a good triple.
   (c) Call $\mathcal{F}_{\text{Auth.Check}}$ on all opened values so far. If the check succeeds output the T good triples.

Fig. 18. Multiplication triples.

Functionality $\mathcal{F}_{\text{RanKer}}$

This functionality is an extension to $\mathcal{F}_{\text{Prep}}$

1. **RanKer** On input (RanKer, id) sample a random field element $r \in \ker(\psi)$ and set ValField[id] $= r$.

Fig. 19. Functionality – authenticated random element in $\ker(\psi)$.

Protocol Π_{RanKer}

The protocol generates $[r_j]$ for $j = 1, 2, \ldots, t$, where $[r_j]$ is random in $\ker(\psi)$ and unknown to all parties. We assume access to the functionality $\mathcal{F}_{\text{Rand}}$.

1. **Construct:**
   (a) P_i chooses $r_j^{(i)}$ for $j = 1, 2, \ldots, t + s$ uniformly at random in $\ker(\psi)$.
   (b) P_i calls $\mathcal{F}_{\text{Auth.Input}}$ to obtain $[r_j^{(i)}]$.
   (c) Compute $[r_j] = \sum_{i=1}^{n} [r_j^{(i)}]$ for $j = 1, 2, \ldots, t + s$.
2. **Sacrifice:**
   (a) Call $\mathcal{F}_{\text{Rand}}(\mathbb{F}_2^t)$ to obtain $\mathbf{a}_i'$ for $i = 1, 2, \ldots, s$ and define $\mathbf{a}_i = (\mathbf{a}_i', \mathbf{e}_i) \in \mathbb{F}_2^{t+s}$ where $\mathbf{e}_i$ is the i'th canonical basis vector of length s.
   (b) Compute $[b_i] = \sum_{j=1}^{t+s} a_{ij} [r_j]$, where a_{ij} is the j'th entry of $\mathbf{a}_i$, and partially open b_i.
   (c) If $b_i \notin \ker(\psi)$ for some $i \in \{1, 2, \ldots, s\}$ then abort.
   (d) Call $\mathcal{F}_{\text{Auth.Check}}$ on the opened values b_i.
3. **Output:** Output $[r_j]$ for $j = 1, 2, \ldots, t$.

Fig. 20. Authenticated random element in $\ker(\psi)$.

able to open proper sharings in the sacrifice step we need to add authenticated sharings of an element in the kernel of ψ. We present a functionality serving that purpose in Fig. 19 and a protocol implementing it in Fig. 20.

Proposition 6. Π_{RanKer} *securely implements* $\mathcal{F}_{\text{RanKer}}$ *in the* $(\mathcal{F}_{\text{Auth}}, \mathcal{F}_{\text{Rand}})$-*hybrid model with statistical security parameter* s.

The proof of this proposition is similar to that of Proposition 4. The correctness follows from the additivity of ψ.

The sacrifice step opens the door for a selective failure attack, where the adversary can guess some information about the remaining triples from the fact that it has not aborted, so a final combining step is used to remove this leakage.

Proposition 7. Π_{Triple} *securely implements* $\mathcal{F}_{\text{Prep.Triple}}$ *in the* $(\mathcal{F}_{\text{Auth}}, \mathcal{F}_{\text{ROT}}^{m,k}, \mathcal{F}_{\text{Rand}}, \mathcal{F}_{\text{RanKer}})$-*hybrid model.*

The proof uses similar arguments as in [16] and can be found in the full version.

Proposition 8. $\Pi_{\text{InputPair}}$, $\Pi_{\text{ReEncodePair}}$, *and* Π_{Triple} *securely implements* $\mathcal{F}_{\text{Prep}}$ *in the* $(\mathcal{F}_{\text{Auth}}, \mathcal{F}_{\text{ROT}}^{m,k}, \mathcal{F}_{\text{Rand}})$-*hybrid model.*

Proof. This follows directly from Propositions 3, 4, and 7.

Complexity of Preprocessing

We briefly describe the communication complexity for producing the randomness needed for the online phase. Starting by considering the construction of an input pair the only communication we have to consider here is a single call to $\mathcal{F}_{\text{Auth.Input}}$. The main cost of authentication is the call to Π_{COPEe} where the parties needs to send $mk(n-1)$ bits for each vector authenticated. In the case where a field element is authenticated instead they need to send $m^2(n-1)$ bits. Furthermore, the party who is authenticating needs to send the shares of the vector authenticating but this has only a cost of $k(n-1)$ bits. At last, the check is carried out but we assume that the parties authenticate several vectors/values in a batch and hence this cost is amortized away.

For the re-encoding pairs we assume that t is much larger than s. This means that in order to obtain a single pair the parties need to authenticate n field elements and n vectors. Once again we assume that the check is amortized away, so this gives a total cost of sending $(m^2 + mk)n(n-1)$ bits.

The same assumption, that t is much larger than s, is made for the reorganizing pairs and the random elements in the kernel of ψ. This means that the amortized cost of producing a reorganizing pair is $(l+l')n$ vector-authentications and to obtain $[r]$ for $r \in \ker(\psi)$ costs n authentication amortized.

Regarding the communication for obtaining a single multiplication triple we ignore the vectors sent in the construction since the authentication is much more expensive. Besides authentication we make $\tau_1 \tau_2^2 n(n-1)$ calls to $\mathcal{F}_{\text{ROT}}^{k,1}$. We authenticate $3\tau_1 \tau_2^2 n$ vectors in the construction. Furthermore, we need $(\tau_2 - 1)\tau_2^2$ elements from $\mathcal{F}_{\text{RanKer}}$ and 2 reencoding pairs for the construction of the triple. The cost of the remaining steps is not close to be as costly, so we ignore these.

In [16] it is suggested to use $\tau_1 = \tau_2 = 3$. The cost of preparing a multiplication gate using these parameters is that of producing 3 reencoding pairs (2 for the preprocessing and 1 for the online phase), 18 authenticated elements in the kernel of ψ and the multiplication triple which yields 27 calls to $\mathcal{F}_{\text{ROT}}^{k,1}$ and $3 \cdot 27$ authentication of vectors. Thus using $m = 3.1k$ from Table 3 in order to obtain security $s \geq 64$ and ignoring the calls to $\mathcal{F}_{\text{ROT}}^{k,1}$ the communication becomes

$$3 \cdot (3.1^2 + 3.1)k^2 n(n-1) + 18 \cdot 3.1^2 k^2 n(n-1) + 3 \cdot 27 \cdot 3.1 \cdot k^2 n(n-1) \text{ bits}$$
$$= 462.21 \cdot k^2 n(n-1) \text{ bits}.$$

Similarly, in order to obtain $s \geq 128$ we use $m = 3.21k$ from Table 3 and the communication becomes $486.03 \cdot k^2 n(n-1)$ bits.

References

1. Beaver, D.: Efficient multiparty protocols using circuit randomization. In: Feigenbaum, J. (ed.) CRYPTO 1991. LNCS, vol. 576, pp. 420–432. Springer, Heidelberg (1992). https://doi.org/10.1007/3-540-46766-1_34

2. Beerliová-Trubíniová, Z., Hirt, M.: Perfectly-secure MPC with linear communication complexity. In: Canetti, R. (ed.) TCC 2008. LNCS, vol. 4948, pp. 213–230. Springer, Heidelberg (2008). https://doi.org/10.1007/978-3-540-78524-8_13

3. Bendlin, R., Damgård, I., Orlandi, C., Zakarias, S.: Semi-homomorphic encryption and multiparty computation. In: Paterson, K.G. (ed.) EUROCRYPT 2011. LNCS, vol. 6632, pp. 169–188. Springer, Heidelberg (2011). https://doi.org/10.1007/978-3-642-20465-4_11

4. Block, A.R., Maji, H.K., Nguyen, H.H.: Secure computation based on leaky correlations: high resilience setting. In: Katz, J., Shacham, H. (eds.) CRYPTO 2017. LNCS, vol. 10402, pp. 3–32. Springer, Cham (2017). https://doi.org/10.1007/978-3-319-63715-0_1

5. Block, A.R., Maji, H.K., Nguyen, H.H.: Secure computation with constant communication overhead using multiplication embeddings. In: Chakraborty, D., Iwata, T. (eds.) INDOCRYPT 2018. LNCS, vol. 11356, pp. 375–398. Springer, Cham (2018). https://doi.org/10.1007/978-3-030-05378-9_20

6. Canetti, R.: Universally composable security: a new paradigm for cryptographic protocols. In: Proceedings 42nd FOCS, pp. 136–145 (2001)

7. Cascudo, I.: On squares of cyclic codes. IEEE Trans. Inf. Theory **65**(2), 1034–1047 (2019)

8. Cascudo, I., Cramer, R., Xing, C., Yuan, C.: Amortized complexity of information-theoretically secure MPC revisited. In: Shacham, H., Boldyreva, A. (eds.) CRYPTO 2018. LNCS, vol. 10993, pp. 395–426. Springer, Cham (2018). https://doi.org/10.1007/978-3-319-96878-0_14

9. Cascudo, I., Damgård, I., David, B., Döttling, N., Dowsley, R., Giacomelli, I.: Efficient UC commitment extension with homomorphism for free (and applications). In: Galbraith, S.D., Moriai, S. (eds.) ASIACRYPT 2019. LNCS, vol. 11922, pp. 606–635. Springer, Cham (2019). https://doi.org/10.1007/978-3-030-34621-8_22

10. Cascudo, I., Damgård, I., David, B., Döttling, N., Nielsen, J.B.: Rate-1, linear time and additively homomorphic UC commitments. In: Robshaw, M., Katz, J. (eds.) CRYPTO 2016. LNCS, vol. 9816, pp. 179–207. Springer, Heidelberg (2016). https://doi.org/10.1007/978-3-662-53015-3_7

11. Cascudo, I., Gundersen, J.S.: A secret-sharing based MPC protocol for boolean circuits with good amortized complexity (full version). Cryptology ePrint Archive, Report 2020/162 (2020). https://eprint.iacr.org/2020/162.pdf

12. Cascudo, I., Gundersen, J.S., Ruano, D.: Squares of matrix-product codes. Finite Fields Appl. **62**, 101606 (2020)

13. Damgård, I., Lauritsen, R., Toft, T.: An empirical study and some improvements of the MiniMac protocol for secure computation. In: Abdalla, M., De Prisco, R. (eds.) SCN 2014. LNCS, vol. 8642, pp. 398–415. Springer, Cham (2014). https://doi.org/10.1007/978-3-319-10879-7_23

14. Damgård, I., Pastro, V., Smart, N., Zakarias, S.: Multiparty computation from somewhat homomorphic encryption. In: Safavi-Naini, R., Canetti, R. (eds.) CRYPTO 2012. LNCS, vol. 7417, pp. 643–662. Springer, Heidelberg (2012). https://doi.org/10.1007/978-3-642-32009-5_38

15. Damgård, I., Zakarias, S.: Constant-overhead secure computation of boolean circuits using preprocessing. In: Sahai, A. (ed.) TCC 2013. LNCS, vol. 7785, pp. 621–641. Springer, Heidelberg (2013). https://doi.org/10.1007/978-3-642-36594-2_35

16. Frederiksen, T.K., Pinkas, B., Yanai, A.: Committed MPC. In: Abdalla, M., Dahab, R. (eds.) PKC 2018. LNCS, vol. 10769, pp. 587–619. Springer, Cham (2018). https://doi.org/10.1007/978-3-319-76578-5_20

17. Frederiksen, T.K., Jakobsen, T.P., Nielsen, J.B., Trifiletti, R.: On the complexity of additively homomorphic UC commitments. In: Kushilevitz, E., Malkin, T. (eds.) TCC 2016. LNCS, vol. 9562, pp. 542–565. Springer, Heidelberg (2016). https://doi.org/10.1007/978-3-662-49096-9_23
18. Frederiksen, T.K., Keller, M., Orsini, E., Scholl, P.: A unified approach to MPC with preprocessing using OT. In: Iwata, T., Cheon, J.H. (eds.) ASIACRYPT 2015. LNCS, vol. 9452, pp. 711–735. Springer, Heidelberg (2015). https://doi.org/10.1007/978-3-662-48797-6_29
19. Keller, M., Orsini, E., Scholl, P.: MASCOT: faster malicious arithmetic secure computation with oblivious transfer. In: Proceedings of the 2016 ACM SIGSAC Conference on Computer and Communications Security, CCS 2016, pp. 830–842. ACM (2016)
20. Larraia, E., Orsini, E., Smart, N.P.: Dishonest majority multi-party computation for binary circuits. In: Garay, J.A., Gennaro, R. (eds.) CRYPTO 2014. LNCS, vol. 8617, pp. 495–512. Springer, Heidelberg (2014). https://doi.org/10.1007/978-3-662-44381-1_28
21. Nielsen, J.B., Nordholt, P.S., Orlandi, C., Burra, S.S.: A new approach to practical active-secure two-party computation. In: Safavi-Naini, R., Canetti, R. (eds.) CRYPTO 2012. LNCS, vol. 7417, pp. 681–700. Springer, Heidelberg (2012). https://doi.org/10.1007/978-3-642-32009-5_40

On the Round Complexity of the Shuffle Model

Amos Beimel[1], Iftach Haitner[2], Kobbi Nissim[3], and Uri Stemmer[4,5(✉)]

[1] Ben-Gurion University, Beersheba, Israel
amos.beimel@gmail.com
[2] Tel-Aviv University, Tel Aviv, Israel
iftachh@cs.tau.ac.il
[3] Georgetown University, Washington, D.C., USA
kobbi.nissim@georgetown.edu
[4] Ben-Gurion University, Beersheba, Israel
u@uri.co.il
[5] Google Research, Mountain View, USA

Abstract. The shuffle model of differential privacy [Bittau et al. SOSP 2017; Erlingsson et al. SODA 2019; Cheu et al. EUROCRYPT 2019] was proposed as a viable model for performing distributed differentially private computations. Informally, the model consists of an untrusted analyzer that receives messages sent by participating parties via a shuffle functionality, the latter potentially disassociates messages from their senders. Prior work focused on one-round differentially private shuffle model protocols, demonstrating that functionalities such as addition and histograms can be performed in this model with accuracy levels similar to that of the curator model of differential privacy, where the computation is performed by a fully trusted party. A model closely related to the shuffle model was presented in the seminal work of Ishai et al. on establishing cryptography from anonymous communication [FOCS 2006].

Focusing on the round complexity of the shuffle model, we ask in this work what can be computed in the shuffle model of differential privacy with two rounds. Ishai et al. showed how to use one round of the shuffle to establish secret keys between every two parties. Using this primitive to simulate a general secure multi-party protocol increases its round complexity by one. We show how two parties can use one round of the shuffle to send secret messages without having to first establish a secret key, hence retaining round complexity. Combining this primitive with the two-round semi-honest protocol of Applebaum, Brakerski, and Tsabary [TCC 2018], we obtain that every randomized functionality can be computed in the shuffle model with an honest majority, in merely two rounds. This includes any differentially private computation.

We hence move to examine differentially private computations in the shuffle model that (i) do not require the assumption of an honest majority, or (ii) do not admit one-round protocols, even with an honest majority. For that, we introduce two computational tasks: *common element*, and *nested common element with parameter* α. For the common element problem we show that for large enough input domains, no one-round

R. Pass and K. Pietrzak (Eds.): TCC 2020, LNCS 12551, pp. 683–712, 2020.
https://doi.org/10.1007/978-3-030-64378-2_24

differentially private shuffle protocol exists with constant message complexity and negligible δ, whereas a two-round protocol exists where every party sends a single message in every round. For the nested common element we show that no one-round differentially private protocol exists for this problem with adversarial coalition size αn. However, we show that it can be privately computed in two rounds against coalitions of size cn for every $c < 1$. This yields a separation between one-round and two-round protocols. We further show a one-round protocol for the nested common element problem that is differentially private with coalitions of size smaller than cn for all $0 < c < \alpha < 1/2$.

Keywords: Shuffle model · Differential privacy · Secure multiparty computation

1 Introduction

A recent line of work in differential privacy focuses on a distributed model where parties communicate with an analyzer via a random shuffle. The shuffle collects messages from the participating parties and presents them to the analyzer in a random order, hence potentially disassociating between messages and their senders [11, 16, 21]. The hope is that the shuffle model would be useful for the implementation of practical distributed differentially private statistical and machine learning analyses, and with accuracy comparable to that of centralized differential privacy solutions. The implementation of the shuffle itself is envisioned to be based on technologies such as secure enclaves, mix nets, and secure computation.

The theoretical work on the shuffle model has so far focused on developing protocols for the model formalized in [16]. In this synchronous one-round model, all the participating parties send their messages through the shuffle at once (parties may send one message or multiple messages). Already in this limited communication model there are fundamental statistical tasks for which differentially private shuffle model protocols exist with error comparable to that achievable in the (centralized) curator model of differential privacy [2, 4–6, 16, 23–25].

A model similar to the shuffle model was presented already in 2006 by Ishai, Kushilevits, Ostrovsky, and Sahai in the context of secure multiparty computation [27]. In particular, Ishai et al. presented a one-round secure summation protocol that has become one of the building blocks of noise efficient real summation differentially-private protocols, where each party holds a number $x_i \in [0, 1]$ and the analyzer's task is to estimate the sum $\sum x_i$ [4, 6, 23, 24]. Ishai et al. also presented a one-round protocol allowing any two parties to agree on a secret key, a step after which the parties can privately exchange messages. Combining this primitive with general constructions of secure multiparty computation protocols that rely on private or secure channels, Ishai et al. showed that it is possible to compute any (finite) function of the parties' joint inputs in a constant number of rounds. In particular, we observe that combining the key agreement protocol of

Ishai et al. [27] with the recent two-round secure multiparty protocol of Applebaum, Brakersky, and Tsabary [1] (denoted the ABT protocol), no more than three rounds suffice for computing any (finite) randomized function securely in the shuffle model, with semi-honest parties assuming an honest majority: one round for every pair of parties to setup a secret key, and hence private communication channels. Two more round to simulate the ABT protocol using these private channels. To conclude, the previous results imply that any randomized function (including, in particular, any curator model differential privacy computation) can be computed in the shuffle model with security against an honest majority.[1]

1.1 Our Results

In this work, we focus on the shuffle model with semi-honest parties. We ask what can be computed in the shuffle model with one and two rounds of communication, and at the presence of coalitions of semi-honest parties that can put together their inputs, randomization, and messages they receive during the computation with the goal of breaching the privacy of other parties. We present new techniques for constructing round-efficient protocols in the shuffle models as well as new lowerbound techniques for studying the limitations of one-round protocols. In more detail:

One-Round Private Message Transmission. In Sect. 3.1 we present a new building block for shuffle model protocols. This is a protocol that allows a party P_i to send a secret message to another party P_j in one round. In the key agreement protocol of Ishai et al. [27], mentioned above, to agree on a bit b of the key, each of P_i and P_j selects and sends through the shuffle a random element chosen from a large set. Denoting the elements sent by P_i, P_j as x, y resp., parties P_i and P_j can set the secret bit b to 0 if $x < y$ and to 1 if $x > y$. (The protocol fails if $x = y$.) The other parties cannot distinguish which of the two values is x and which is y and gain no information about the bit b. Using this protocol, party P_i learns the secret key only after the conclusion of one communication round, and only then can P_i use the key to encrypt a message. In contrast, our construction saves a round in the communication, as it allows P_i to encrypt a message without having to first establish a key.

Generic Two-Round Secure MPC for the Shuffle Model. Using the one-round message transmission protocol, we show in Sect. 3.2 how to simulate the two-round semi-honest secure multi-party computation protocol with information theoretic security of Applebaum et al. [1].[2] The result is a general construction in the shuffle model of two-round honest majority protocols for the

---

[1] Curator model computations returning real numbers, such as those resulting by adding Laplace or Gaussian noise, would need to be carefully truncated to finite precision.

[2] An alternative construction was given by Garg et al. [22]; the communication complexity of their protocol is exponential in the number of parties.

semi-honest setting, with information theoretic security. The construction is efficient in the size of the formula representing the functionality.

Our generic two-round construction shows that the shuffle model is extremely expressive: no more than two rounds suffice for computing any (finite) randomized function, including any curator level differential privacy computation, with semi-honest parties assuming an honest majority of players. We hence move to examine differentially private computations in the shuffle model that (i) do not require the assumption of an honest majority, or (ii) do not admit one-round protocols, even with an honest majority. To demonstrate our lowerbound and upperbound techniques, we introduce two computational tasks:

Common Element: Each of n parties holds an input x_i taken from a large finite domain $\mathcal{X}$. The parties communicate with an analyzer via the shuffle. If all the parties hold the same input $x \in \mathcal{X}$ then the analyzer's task is to output x. Otherwise, the analyzer's outcome is not restricted.

Nested Common Element with Parameter α: This is a variant of the common element problem, where parties $P_1, \ldots, P_{\lfloor \alpha n \rfloor}$ each holds an input $x_i \in \mathcal{X}$. The other parties $P_{\lfloor \alpha n \rfloor + 1}, \ldots, P_n$ each holds a vector of $|\mathcal{X}|$ elements taken from some finite domain $\mathcal{Y}$, i.e., $\boldsymbol{y}_i \in \mathcal{Y}^{|\mathcal{X}|}$. The parties communicate with an analyzer via the shuffle. If all the parties of the first type hold the same input $x \in \mathcal{X}$ and all the vectors held by parties of the second type have the same value z in their x-th entry, then the analyzer's task is to output z (otherwise, the analyzer's outcome is not restricted). We consider the case where $|\mathcal{X}|$ is polynomial in n, thus, the size of the inputs is polynomial in n even when $|\mathcal{Y}|$ is exponential in n.

Both tasks need to be performed with differential privacy, assuming semi-honest parties. We now describe the bounds we prove for these problems:

A Lowerbound on One-Round Shuffle Model Protocols for the Common Element Problem. In Sect. 4.1 we present a new lowerbound technique for one-round shuffle model protocols where the mutual information between input and output is high. Unlike other lowerbounds in the shuffle model of differential privacy that we are aware of, our lowerbound proof works for the multimessage setting, and does not require all parties to use the same randomizer.[3]

For the common element problem, we show a relationship between the message complexity ℓ, the input domain size $|\mathcal{X}|$, and the privacy parameters ε and δ. In particular, for constant ε and negligible δ, our bound yields that for constant number of messages ℓ and domain size $|\mathcal{X}| > 2^{n^{O(\ell)}}$ the common element problem does not admit a one-round shuffle model protocol. At the heart of the lowerbound proof is a transformation from a shuffle model protocol into a local differential privacy randomizer, for which bounds on the mutual information between the input and output are known (see, e.g., [29]).

The one-round lowerbound is contrasted in Sect. 4.2 with a two-round protocol for the common element problem where each party sends a *single* message in

---

[3] Three exceptions are the recent works of Balcer et al. [3], Cheu and Ullman [17], and Chen et al. [15], mentioned in Sect. 1.2.

each round. In this protocol, the parties need to communicate through the shuffle in only one of the rounds (and can either use the shuffle or a public channel in the other round).

An Impossibility Result for the Nested Common Element Problem. In Sect. 5.1 we show (for large enough $\mathcal{X}$, i.e., $|\mathcal{X}| = \tilde{\Omega}(n^2)$) that, regardless of the number of messages sent by each party, no one-round shuffle protocol exists for the problem that is secure against coalitions of αn semi-honest parties, even when the domain $\mathcal{Y}$ is binary. We observe that for every $c < 1$ the nested common element problem has a 2-round private protocol secure against a coalition of size cn. This gives a separation between what can be computed with coalitions of size up to αn in one- and two-round shuffle model protocols. Intuitively, the lowerbound follows from the fact that after seeing the shuffle outcome, a coalition covering $P_1, \ldots, P_{\lfloor \alpha n \rfloor}$ can simulate the protocol's execution for any possible value $x \in \mathcal{X}$ and hence learn all vector entries on which the inputs of parties $P_{\lfloor \alpha n \rfloor + 1}, \ldots, P_n$ agree. When $\mathcal{Y}$ is binary, Bun et al. [13] have used fingerprinting codes to show that this task is impossible when the dimension of the vectors is $\tilde{\Omega}(n^2)$, even in the curator model of differential privacy (in the setting of the nested common element the dimension corresponds to $|\mathcal{X}|$). [4]

A One-Round Protocol for the Nested Common Element Problem. A natural approach to solve the nested common element problem in two rounds is to execute a (one-round) protocol for the common element problem among parties $P_1, \ldots, P_{\lfloor \alpha n \rfloor}$, then, if a common element x is found, repeat the protocol with parties $P_{\lfloor \alpha n \rfloor + 1}, \ldots, P_n$ ignoring all but the x-th entry of their vectors. It may seem that any shuffle model protocol for the problem should require more than one round. We show that this is not the case. In fact, there is a one-round protocol that tightly matches the above impossibility result for $\alpha \leq 1/2$. For all $c < \min\{\alpha, 1 - \alpha\}$ there exist one-round shuffle model protocols for the nested common element problem that are secure in the presence of coalitions of size up to cn.

1.2 Other Related Work

Private protocols for the common element problem in the shuffle model are implied by protocols for histograms [2,16,23]. Specifically, for all $c < 1$, one-round shuffle model protocols for the common element problem that are secure in the presence of coalitions of size up to cn (provided that $n = \Omega(\frac{1}{\varepsilon^2} \log \frac{1}{\delta})$) are implied by the protocols of Balcer and Cheu [2]. While they only considered privacy given the view of the analyzer, their protocols are secure against coalitions containing a constant fraction of the parties.

   Lowerbounds on the error level achievable in the one-round single message shuffle model for the problems of frequency estimation and selection were provided by Ghazi et al. [23]. Robustness against adversarial behaviour in the shuffle

---

[4] Bun et al. [13] have considered a related problem, however their technique applies also to this task.

model was informally discussed by Balle et al. [6], when discussing the effect malicious parties can have on the accuracy guarantees in their protocols for addition of real numbers.

Closest to our interest are the recent lowerbounds by Balcer et al. [3]. They define robustly shuffle private one-round protocols, where privacy guarantees are required to hold if at least γn parties participate in the protocol. The other *malicious* parties avoid sending messages to the shuffle. While this model is equivalent to ours in the one-round setting, the lowerbound techniques in [3] are different from ours. In particular, they forge an interesting relationships between online pan-privacy [20] and robustly shuffle private one-round protocols and hence can use lowerbounds from pan-privacy to deduce lowerbounds for robustly shuffle private one-round protocols. Specifically, for estimating the number of distinct elements they prove that the additive error grows as $\Theta_\varepsilon(\sqrt{k})$, and for uniformity testing they prove that the sample complexity grows as $\tilde{\Theta}_{\varepsilon,\delta}(k^{2/3})$. In both cases k is the domain size. (These bounds also hold in our model.) As with our bounds, the lowerbounds by Balcer et al. hold in the case where different parties may use different randomizers, and send multiple messages.

Independent and parallel to our work, Cheu and Ullman [17] and Chen et al. [15] presented strong impossibility results for 1-round shuffle model protocols. In particular, Cheu and Ullman [17] showed that every 1-round shuffle model protocol for private agnostic learning of parity functions over d bits requires $\Omega(2^{d/2})$ samples, while $O(d)$ samples suffice in the (centralized) curator model. Our work shows, in particular, that private agnostic learning of parity functions using $O(d)$ samples can be done in the shuffle model in two rounds (with semi-honest parties assuming an honest majority). Hence, combined with our work, the results of [17] provide additional separations between one-round and two-round shuffle model protocols.

2   Preliminaries

2.1   The Communication Model

Let $\mathcal{X}$ be a data domain and let $\mathcal{M}$ be an arbitrary message domain (w.l.o.g., $\perp \in \mathcal{X}, \mathcal{M}$). We consider a model where the inputs and the computation are distributed among n parties $P_1, \ldots, P_n$ executing a protocol $\Pi = (\bar{R}, S)$, where $\bar{R} = (R_1, \ldots, R_n)$ are n stateful randomized functionalities and S is a stateless channel that acts either as a shuffle functionality or as a public channel. See Fig. 1 for a formal description of protocols in the shuffle model.

Definition 2.1. *Consider an execution of a protocol in the shuffle model as described in Fig. 1. The message complexity of Π is ℓ, the number of messages that each party sends to the shuffle in each round. The round complexity of Π is r. The shuffle complexity of Π is the number of rounds where S is used as a shuffle.*

Execution of a protocol $\Pi = ((R_1, \ldots, R_n), S)$ in the shuffle model

Initialization:

– All parties receive a public random string $w \in \{0,1\}^*$.
– Each party P_i receives its input $x_i \in \mathcal{X}$ and initializes the execution of $R_i(w, x_i)$.

Communication rounds $1 \leq j \leq r$:

1. If round j uses S as a shuffle:
   (a) Each party P_i invokes R_i to generate ℓ messages $(m_{i,j}[1], \ldots, m_{i,j}[\ell]) \in \mathcal{M}^\ell$ and sends $(m_{i,j}[1], \ldots, m_{i,j}[\ell]) \in \mathcal{M}^\ell$ to S.
   (b) Let $(\hat{m}_1, \ldots, \hat{m}_{n\ell}) = (m_{1,j}[1], \ldots, m_{1,j}[\ell], \ldots, m_{n,j}[1], \ldots, m_{n,j}[\ell])$ be the $n\ell$ messages received by S.
   (c) S chooses a permutation $\pi : [n\ell] \to [n\ell]$ uniformly at random.
   (d) S outputs $s_j = (\hat{m}_{\pi(1)}, \ldots, \hat{m}_{\pi(n\ell)})$ to all parties.
2. Otherwise (round j uses S as a public channel):
   (a) Each party P_i invokes R_i to generate a (single) message $m_{i,j} \in \mathcal{M}$, which it sends to S.
   (b) S outputs $s_j = (m_{1,j}, \ldots, m_{n,j})$.
3. P_i feeds s_j to R_i.

Output: Each party P_i invokes R_i to obtain its local output o_i.

Fig. 1. The communication model.

Remark 2.2. A protocol that uses a public random string w can always be converted into a protocol that does not use a public random string, at the cost of one additional communication round in which party P_1 sends the string w (in the semi-honest setting). This additional communication round can be thought of as an "offline" round, as it is independent of the inputs and the function.

2.2 Differentially Private Shuffle Model Protocols

Definition 2.3. *We say that input vectors $x = (x_1, \ldots, x_n) \in \mathcal{X}^n$ and $x' = (x'_1, \ldots, x'_n) \in \mathcal{X}^n$ are i-neighboring if they differ on exactly the i-th entry. We say that x and x' are neighboring if there exists an index i such that they are i-neighboring.*

Definition 2.4. *We say that two probability distributions $\mathcal{D}_0, \mathcal{D}_1 \in \Delta(\Omega)$ are (ε, δ)-close and write $\mathcal{D}_0 \approx_{\varepsilon,\delta} \mathcal{D}_1$ if for all events $T \subset \Omega$ and for $b \in \{0,1\}$,*

$$\Pr_{t \sim \mathcal{D}_b}[t \in T] \leq e^\varepsilon \cdot \Pr_{t \sim \mathcal{D}_{1-b}}[t \in T] + \delta.$$

Definition 2.5 (Differential privacy [18,19]). *An algorithm $\mathcal{A}$ is (ε, δ) differentially private if for all neighboring $\boldsymbol{x}, \boldsymbol{x}'$ we have that $\mathcal{A}(\boldsymbol{x}) \approx_{\varepsilon, \delta} \mathcal{A}(\boldsymbol{x}')$.*

We are now ready to define what it means for a protocol to be differentially private in the (semi-honest) shuffle model. Intuitively, this means that the view of every coalition $\mathcal{C}$ of up to t parties cannot depend too strongly on the input of a party $P_i \notin \mathcal{C}$. More formally,

Definition 2.6 (View in shuffle model). *The view of a coalition $\mathcal{C}$ on input $\boldsymbol{x}$ in protocol Π, denoted $\mathrm{View}_{\mathcal{C}}^{\Pi}(\boldsymbol{x})$, is the random variable consisting of the public randomness w, the inputs and local randomness of the parties in $\mathcal{C}$, and the output of the r rounds of Π when executed on $\boldsymbol{x}$, i.e., $s_1, \ldots, s_r$.*

Definition 2.7 (Multiparty semi-honest differential privacy[10,29]). *A protocol Π is (ε, δ)-differentially private against coalitions of size t if for all $i \in [n]$, for all coalitions $\mathcal{C}$ of t parties s.t. $P_i \notin \mathcal{C}$, and for all i-neighboring $\boldsymbol{x}, \boldsymbol{x}'$,*

$$\mathrm{View}_{\mathcal{C}}^{\Pi}(\boldsymbol{x}) \approx_{\varepsilon, \delta} \mathrm{View}_{\mathcal{C}}^{\Pi}(\boldsymbol{x}').$$

Observe that if a protocol is differentially private against coalitions of size t as in the definition above, then it also the case that $\mathrm{View}_{\mathcal{C}}^{\Pi}(\boldsymbol{x}) \approx_{\varepsilon, \delta} \mathrm{View}_{\mathcal{C}}^{\Pi}(\boldsymbol{x}')$ for all coalitions $\mathcal{C}$ of size less than t.

Remark 2.8.

1. **The shuffle functionality S.** It is not essential that the shuffle functionality S be randomized. The shuffle output s in Step (1d) of Protocol Π in Fig. 1 can be replaced with any canonical representation of the multiset $\{\hat{m}_1, \ldots, \hat{m}_{n\ell}\}$ (e.g., in lexicographic order) without affecting any of our results.
2. **Hybrid-shuffle model.** The shuffle model can equivalently be thought of as a hybrid model, where all parties have access to a shuffle functionality.
3. **The local randomizers R_i.** In deviation from most of prior work on the shuffle model, the randomizers $R_1, \ldots, R_n$ need not be identical. In particular, the execution of R_i may depend on the identity i of player P_i.
4. **Local model protocols.** An (ε, δ)-differentially private protocol Π with zero shuffle complexity satisfies local differential privacy [28,29].
5. **Shuffle model with an analyzer.** In prior work on the shuffle model one party, A, is an *analyzer*. The analyzer has no input ($x_A = \bot$) and does not send messages, i.e., $(m_{A,j}[1], \ldots, m_{A,j}[\ell]) = \bot^{\ell}$ for $1 \le j \le r$. In this setting the local output of parties $P_1, \ldots, P_n$ is $\bot$ and the outcome of the protocol is the local output of A. Sects. 4 and 5 consider the shuffle model with an analyzer.

2.3   Secure Computation Protocols with Semi-honest Parties

Let $f : \mathcal{X}^n \to \mathcal{Y}^n$ be a randomized functionality. We recall the definition from the cryptographic literature of what it means that a protocol Π securely computes $f(x_1, \ldots, x_n)$ with semi-honest parties. We will use this definition both in the shuffle model and in the setting where the parties communicate over a complete network of private channels. For the latter we define the view of a coalition as follows:

Definition 2.9 (View in a complete network of private channels). *The view of a coalition $\mathcal{C}$ on input $\boldsymbol{x}$ in protocol Π, denoted $\text{view}_{\mathcal{C}}^{\pi}(\boldsymbol{x})$, is the random variable consisting of the inputs and local randomness of the parties in $\mathcal{C}$ and the messages the parties in $\mathcal{C}$ receive from the parties in $\overline{\mathcal{C}} = \{P_1, \ldots, P_n\} \setminus \mathcal{C}$.*

Definition 2.10 (Secure computation in the semi-honest model). *A protocol Π is said to δ-securely compute f with coalitions of size at most t if there exists a simulator Sim^{Π} such that for any coalition $\mathcal{C}$ of at most t parties and every input vector $\boldsymbol{x} = (x_1, \ldots, x_n) \in \mathcal{X}^n$,*

$$\left(\text{Sim}^{\Pi}(\mathcal{C}, \boldsymbol{x}[\mathcal{C}], \boldsymbol{y}[\mathcal{C}]), \boldsymbol{y}[\overline{\mathcal{C}}]\right) \approx_{0,\delta} \left(\text{View}_{\mathcal{C}}^{\Pi}(\boldsymbol{x}), \text{Output}\left(\overline{\mathcal{C}}\right)\right),$$

where $\boldsymbol{y} = f(\boldsymbol{x})$ and $\text{Output}\left(\overline{\mathcal{C}}\right)$ is the output of the parties in $\overline{\mathcal{C}}$ in the protocol. The probability distribution on the left is over the randomness of f and the randomness of the simulator, and the probability distribution on the right is over the randomness of the honest parties and the adversary. When $\delta = 0$ we say that Π provides perfect privacy.

Remark 2.11. In the shuffle model, $\text{View}_{\mathcal{C}}^{\Pi}(\boldsymbol{x})$ also includes the public random string w (if exists), and the probability distribution on the right in Definition 2.10 is also over the public random string.

We next state a composition theorem for differentially private protocols using secure protocols.

Lemma 2.12. *Let Π be a protocol with one invocation of a black-box access to some function f (the f-hybrid model). Let Π_f be a protocol that δ'-securely computes f with coalitions of size up to t. Let Π' be as in Π, except that the call to f is replaced with the execution of Π_f. If Π is (ε, δ)-differentially private with coalitions of size up to t, then Π' is $(\varepsilon, (e^{\varepsilon} + 1) \cdot \delta' + \delta)$-differentially private with coalitions of size up to t.*

Proof. Consider a coalition $\mathcal{C}$ of up to t parties. The random variable $\text{View}_{\mathcal{C}}^{\Pi'}(\boldsymbol{x})$ consisting the view of coalition $\mathcal{C}$ in an execution of protocol Π' can be parsed into the view of $\mathcal{C}$ in protocol Π, i.e., $\text{View}_{\mathcal{C}}^{\Pi}(\boldsymbol{x})$, and the view of $\mathcal{C}$ in the execution of protocol Π_f, i.e., $\text{View}_{\mathcal{C}}^{\Pi_f}(\boldsymbol{y})$. In the latter $\boldsymbol{y}$ is the input to f in the execution of Π on input $\boldsymbol{x}$ (similarly, we will use $\boldsymbol{y}'$ to denote the input to f in the execution of Π on input $\boldsymbol{x}'$). Note that, by Definition 2.10, $\text{View}_{\mathcal{C}}^{\Pi_f}(\boldsymbol{y})$ can be simulated as $\text{Sim}^{\Pi_f}(\mathcal{C}, \boldsymbol{y}[\mathcal{C}], f_{\mathcal{C}}(\boldsymbol{y}))$ up to statistical distance δ'. Observe that $\text{View}_{\mathcal{C}}^{\Pi}$ contains the inputs $\boldsymbol{y}_{\mathcal{C}}$ sent to f as well as the outcome seen by the coalition, $f_{\mathcal{C}}(\boldsymbol{y})$. Hence, $\text{Sim}^{\Pi_f}(\mathcal{C}, \boldsymbol{y}[\mathcal{C}], f_{\mathcal{C}}(\boldsymbol{y}))$ is a post-processing of $\text{View}_{\mathcal{C}}^{\Pi}(\boldsymbol{x})$. To emphasize this fact, we write $\text{Sim}^{\Pi_f}(\text{View}_{\mathcal{C}}^{\Pi}(\boldsymbol{x}))$ instead of $\text{Sim}^{\Pi_f}(\mathcal{C}, \boldsymbol{y}[\mathcal{C}], f_{\mathcal{C}}(\boldsymbol{y}))$.

Let $P_i \notin C$. For all i-neighboring $\boldsymbol{x}, \boldsymbol{x}'$ and all T we have that

$$
\begin{aligned}
\Pr[\text{View}_C^{\Pi'}(\boldsymbol{x}) \in T] &= \Pr[(\text{View}_C^{\Pi}(\boldsymbol{x}), \text{View}_C^{\Pi_f}(\boldsymbol{y})) \in T] \\
&\leq \Pr[(\text{View}_C^{\Pi}(\boldsymbol{x}), \text{Sim}^{\Pi_f}(\text{View}_C^{\Pi}(\boldsymbol{x}))) \in T] + \delta' \\
&\leq e^{\varepsilon} \cdot \Pr[(\text{View}_C^{\Pi}(\boldsymbol{x}'), \text{Sim}^{\Pi_f}(\text{View}_C^{\Pi}(\boldsymbol{x}'))) \in T] + \delta + \delta' \\
&\leq e^{\varepsilon} \cdot (\Pr[(\text{View}_C^{\Pi}(\boldsymbol{x}'), \text{View}_C^{\Pi_f}(\boldsymbol{y}')) \in T] + \delta') + \delta + \delta' \\
&= e^{\varepsilon} \cdot \Pr[\text{View}_C^{\Pi'}(\boldsymbol{x}') \in T] + (e^{\varepsilon} + 1)\delta' + \delta.
\end{aligned}
$$

The second step in the analysis follows from the fact that differential privacy is preserved under post-processing.   □

2.4 Pairwise Independent Hash Functions

In our constructions We use pair pairwise independent hash functions, defined below.

Definition 2.13 (Pairwise independent hash functions). *A family of hash functions $H = \{h : \mathcal{X} \to R\}$ is said to be pairwise independent, if for any two distinct elements $x_1 \neq x_2 \in \mathcal{X}$, and any two (possibly equal) values $y_1, y_2 \in R$,*

$$
\Pr_{h \in H}[h(x_1) = y_1 \wedge h(x_2) = y_2] = \frac{1}{|R|^2},
$$

where h is chosen with uniform distribution from H independently of x_1, x_2.

In particular, if H is a pairwise independent family, then for every $x_1 \neq x_2 \in \mathcal{X}$ it holds that $\Pr_{h \in H}[h(x_1) = h(x_2)] = \frac{1}{|R|}$, and for every set $A \subseteq \mathcal{X}$ we have $\Pr_{h \in H}[\exists_{x_1 \neq x_2 \in A} h(x_1) = h(x_2)] \leq \frac{|A|^2}{|R|}$, in this case we say that A is perfectly hashed by h.

3 A Two-Round Secure MPC Protocol in the Shuffle Model

In this section we show that every functionality that can be computed with differential privacy in the centralized model can be computed with differential privacy in the shuffle model in two rounds assuming an honest majority. To achieve this result we first show a one-round protocol in the shuffle model for secure message transmission, that is, we show that how to emulate a private channel. This result together with an honest-majority two-round MPC protocol of [1] in the private channel model imply that every functionality (including differentially-private functionalities) can be securely computed in the shuffle model in two rounds assuming an honest majority.

3.1 A One-Round Secure Message Transmission Protocol

Assume that party P_i wants to send a message to party P_j using the shuffle such that any other party will not learn any information on the message. In [27] this was done in two rounds. In the first round P_i and P_j agree on a secret key, and in the second round P_i encrypts the message using this key as a one-time pad. We present a protocol such that P_i knows the key in advance and can encrypt the message already in the first round. The resulting protocol has statistical security.

We start by describing a variant of the protocol of [27] for key exchange. As a first step, we describe a key exchange protocol in which P_i and P_j agree with probability $1/2$ on a random bit (and with probability $1/2$ the output is "FAIL"). The protocol is as follows: Party P_i samples a uniformly distributed bit a and sends to the shuffle the message (i, j, a). Similarly, party P_j samples a uniformly distributed bit b and sends to the shuffle the message (i, j, b).[5] If $a = b$ the protocol fails. Otherwise, the joint key is a. As both parties P_i, P_j get the output of the shuffle, they both know if the protocol fails $(a = b)$ or not, and if the protocol does not fail $(a \neq b)$ they both know a – the common key. On the other hand, an adversary that sees the output of the shuffle when $a \neq b$, sees a shuffle of the two messages $\{(i, j, 0), (i, j, 1)\}$ and does not get any information on a. To generate a k-bit key, the above protocol is repeated $3k$ times in parallel with independent random bits a_ℓ, b_ℓ in each execution, and the shared key is the bits of P_i in the first k indices where $a_\ell \neq b_\ell$. By a simple Chernoff-Hoefding bound, the probability that there are no such k indices is exponentially small. See Fig. 2 for a formal description of the protocol.

Protocol KEYEXCHANGE

Inputs: P_i and P_j hold a security parameter 1^k.

1. P_i samples $3k$ uniformly distributed bits $(a_1, \ldots, a_{3k})$ and sends to the shuffle $3k$ messages $(i, j, 1, a_1), \ldots, (i, j, 3k, a_{3k})$.
2. P_j samples $3k$ uniformly distributed bits $(b_1, \ldots, b_{3k})$ and sends to the shuffle $3k$ messages $(i, j, 1, b_1), \ldots, (i, j, 3k, b_{3k})$.
3. The shuffle publishes a random permutation of the messages it got.
4. Let $\ell_1 < \ell_2 < \cdots < \ell_k$ be the first k indices such that $a_{\ell_j} \neq b_{\ell_j}$ (if there are no such k indices, output "FAIL"). The joint key is $(a_{\ell_1}, a_{\ell_2}, \ldots, a_{\ell_k})$.

Fig. 2. A one-round key exchange protocol.

To construct a one-round protocol for secure message transmission from P_i to P_j, we want P_i to know the key in advance so it can use the key to encrypt

---

[5] We add the prefix i, j to the messages sent by P_i and P_j to enable all pairs of parties to exchange keys in parallel. It is essential that both P_i and P_j list the identities i, j in the same order (e.g., lexicographic order).

the message at the same time it sends the messages for the key exchange. In Protocol KEYEXCHANGE, party P_i does not know the key in advance since it does not know the bits that $(a_1, \ldots, a_{3k})$ and $(b_1, \ldots, b_{3k})$ disagree. To overcome this problem P_i will use all the bits it generates as a pre-key K. In this case P_j will know all bits of the pre-key K whereas an adversary will learn only about half of the bits of K. Parties P_i and P_j wish to agree on a key generated from the pre-key K without interaction such that the adversary gets negligible information about the agreed key. This is an instance of the privacy amplification problem and a simple solution is to sample a pairwise independent hash function h and set the key as $h(K)$. It follows by the left-over hash lemma [26] that $h(K)$ is close to uniform given h and the knowledge of the adversary about the pre-key K.

Theorem 3.1 (The left-over hash lemma [26]). *Let m, n be integers and X be a random variable distributed over $\{0, 1\}^n$ such that $\Pr[X = x] \le 2^{-m}$ for every $x \in \{0, 1\}^n$. Let $\mathcal{H}$ be a family of pairwise independent hash functions from $\{0, 1\}^n$ to $\{0, 1\}^{m-2k}$. Then, for a random h uniformly distributed in $\mathcal{H}$ and independent of X,*

$$SD\left((h(X), h), (U, h)\right) \le 2^{-k},$$

where U is uniform over $\{0, 1\}^{m-2k}$ and independent of h, and where SD denotes the statistical distance (total variation distance) (Fig. 3).

Protocol SECUREMESSAGETRANSMISSION

Inputs: Party P_i holds a security parameter 1^k and a message M of length at most k, party P_j holds security parameter 1^k.

1. P_i samples $7k$ uniformly distributed bits $(a_1, \ldots, a_{7k})$ and sends to the shuffle $7k$ messages $(i, j, 1, a_1), \ldots, (i, j, 7k, a_{7k})$.
2. P_j samples $7k$ uniformly distributed bits $(b_1, \ldots, b_{7k})$ and sends to the shuffle $7k$ messages $(i, j, 1, b_1), \ldots, (i, j, 7k, b_{7k})$.
3. P_i samples a function h uniformly at random from a family of pairwise independent functions $\mathcal{H} = \left\{ h : \{0, 1\}^{7k} \to \{0, 1\}^k \right\}$ and sends to the shuffle the message $(i, j, \text{"message"}, h, h(a_1, \ldots, a_{7k}) \oplus M)$.
4. The shuffle publishes a random permutation of the messages it got.

Fig. 3. A one-round protocol for secure message transmission.

Theorem 3.2. *Protocol* SECUREMESSAGETRANSMISSION *is a correct and secure protocol for message transmission, that is (1) P_j can always recover M, (2) For every two messages M, M' the statistical distance between the views* of the referee and all parties except for P_i and P_j in an executions of Protocol SECUREMESSAGETRANSMISSION with M and Protocol SECUREMESSAGE-TRANSMISSION with M' is at most $3 \cdot 2^{-k}$.

Proof. For the correctness of the protocol, as P_j knows its messages, it can deduce for every ℓ the message (i, j, ℓ, a_ℓ) sent by P_i, hence compute the common key $h(a_1, \ldots, a_{7k})$ and compute M.

For the security of the protocol, first note that by a Chernoff-Hoefding bound, the probability that there are less than $3k$ indices ℓ such that $a_\ell \neq b_\ell$ is less than 2^{-k}, and such executions add at most 2^{-k} to the statistical distance. We continue the analysis assuming that such event did not occur.

We consider an execution of Protocol SECUREMESSAGETRANSMISSION in which is Step (3) party P_i sends the message $(i, j, \text{"message"}, h, u \oplus M)$ for a uniformly sampled $u \in \{0, 1\}^k$. In this case, the executions for M and M' are equally distributed (as u acts as a one-time pad). To prove the security it suffices to prove that for every message M, the statistical distance in the view in the executions of Protocol SECUREMESSAGETRANSMISSION and the modified Protocol SECUREMESSAGETRANSMISSION (both with M) is at most 2^{-k}. Fix a set $L \subset [7k]$ of size at least $3k$, and consider all executions in which $a_\ell \neq b_\ell$ if and only if $\ell \in L$. For every index $\ell \in L$, the view discloses no information on a_ℓ in these executions (since an adversary sees a random shuffle of the two messages $(i, j, \ell, 0), (i, j, \ell, 1)$ and does not get any information on a_ℓ). In other words, there are at least 2^{3k} strings $(a_1, \ldots, a_{7k})$ possible given the executions are consistent with L, and all strings are equiprobable. Thus, by Theorem 3.1, the statistical distance between u and $h(a_1, \ldots, a_{7k})$ is at most 2^{-k}. This completes the proof of security. $\qquad\square$

3.2   A Two Round MPC Protocol

We construct a two-round MPC protocol in the shuffle model for every functionality on inputs from a finite domain assuming an honest majority. The construction is via a combination of the two-round MPC protocol of Applebaum, Brakersky, and Tsabary [1] (Henceforth, Protocol ABT, see Theorem 3.3 below), which assumes private channels between every pair of parties, with Protocol SECUREMESSAGETRANSMISSION executed in the shuffle model. The latter is used for simulating the private channels.

Theorem 3.3 (Protocol ABT [1, Theorem 1.1]**).** *At the presence of honest majority, any function f can be computed with perfect privacy in a complete network of private channels in two rounds with polynomial efficiency in the number of parties and in the size of the formula that computes f.*

Theorem 3.4. *Let $f : \mathcal{X}^n \to \{0, 1\}$ be a function and $\gamma > 0$ (γ can depend on n and f). At the presence of honest majority, any function f can be computed with γ-statistical privacy in the shuffle model in two rounds with polynomial efficiency in the number of parties, in the size of the formula that computes f, and in $\log 1/\gamma$.*

Proof. In Fig. 4, we describe Protocol MPCinShuffle – the two round MPC protocol in the shuffle model.

Protocol MPCinShuffle

Protocol MPCinShuffle simulates (in the shuffle model) Protocol ABT of Theorem 3.3:

- In each of the two rounds of Protocol ABT:
  - For each $i, j \in [n]$:
    - Party P_i prepares the message that it would send to party P_j in Protocol ABT.
    - P_i and P_j execute Protocol SecureMessageTransmission with this message and security parameter 1^k.
  /* In each round, all $n(n-1)$ secure message transmission protocols are executed in parallel and using the same shuffle */
- At the end of the protocol, each party computes the output of f from the simulated messages of Protocol ABT.

Fig. 4. A two-round MPC protocol in the shuffle model for arbitrary functionalities.

As Protocol SecureMessageTransmission has perfect correctness, each party in Protocol MPCinShuffle can compute the messages it gets in Protocol ABT and compute f without any error.

For the security of the protocol, let $\mathcal{C}$ be a coalition of less than $n/2$ parties. We construct a simulator that generates a view for $\mathcal{C}$ that is $O(n^2 2^{-k})$ far from the view of $\mathcal{C}$ in the real-world execution of Protocol MPCinShuffle:

- Execute the simulator of Protocol ABT of Theorem 3.3 and generate a view for $\mathcal{C}$ that is identically distributed as the real view of $\mathcal{C}$ in Protocol ABT.
- For each round and for each pair P_i, P_j:
  - If at least one of P_i, P_j is in $\mathcal{C}$ then let $M_{i,j}$ be the message that P_i sends to P_j in the simulated view.
  - Otherwise, let $M_{i,j}$ be some fixed arbitrary message.
  - Execute Protocol SecureMessageTransmission with the message $M_{i,j}$ and generate the messages that P_i, P_j send to the shuffle.
- For each round, shuffle the messages generated by P_i, P_j for every $i, j \in [n]$.
- **Output:** The shuffled messages of round 1 and the shuffled messages of round 2, the randomness of every P_i generated by the simulator of Protocol ABT, and the randomness used by every $P_i \in \mathcal{C}$ in an execution of Protocol SecureMessageTransmission for which P_i is either the sender or the receiver.

By Theorem 3.2, for every $P_i, P_j \notin \mathcal{C}$, the messages generated in the simulation (i.e., the messages of Protocol SecureMessageTransmission for the fixed message $M_{i,j}$ and the message that P_i and P_j send to the shuffle in the real world for the real message of the Protocol ABT of Theorem 3.3 are only $O(2^{-k})$ far. Thus, the output of the simulator we constructed is at most $O(n2^{-k})$ far from the view of $\mathcal{C}$ in the real execution of Protocol MPCINSHUFFLE.   □

Remark 3.5.

1. In Protocol SECUREMESSAGETRANSMISSION we use the shuffle in both rounds as we execute Protocol SECUREMESSAGETRANSMISSION in each round. We can optimize the protocol and only use the shuffle in the first round. To achieve this, in the first round each ordered pair of parties P_i, P_j also executes Protocol KEYEXCHANGE in round 1 and generate a key, which is used by P_i to encrypt the message that it send to P_j in round 2. The encrypted messages is sent on the public channel.
2. In a setting with an analyzer as in Remark 2.8, the protocol can be simplified, with the expense that we now need to assume that the number of colluding parties in $P_1, \ldots, P_n$ is less than $(n-1)/2$. We execute Protocol ABT with $n + 1$ parties, where the $(n + 1)$-th party (i.e., the analyzer) has no input and is the only party that receives an output. Furthermore, we assume that the analyzer is always in the coalition, and, therefore, the messages that it sends and receives are public. As the analyzer cannot send messages to the shuffle, we use the public random string as the random string of the analyzer and the messages that the input-less analyzer sends in the first round to party P_j in Protocol ABT are generated by P_j without interaction using the random common string. Furthermore, in the second round each party only sends its message to the analyzer and this message is sent in the clear.
3. In Protocol SECUREMESSAGETRANSMISSION the shuffle receives $O(k)$ messages and shuffles them. We actually only need to shuffle every pair of messages $(i, j, \ell, a_\ell), (i, j, \ell, b_\ell)$, thus, we can use many copies of 2-message shuffle. The same is true for Protocol MPCINSHUFFLE.

Corollary 3.6. *Let f be an (ε, δ)-differentially private functional (in the centralized model) acting on inputs from a finite domain and using a finite number of random bits and $\gamma > 0$. At the presence of honest majority, the functionality f can be computed with $(\varepsilon, \delta + (e^\varepsilon + 1)\gamma)$-differential privacy in the shuffle model in two rounds with polynomial efficiency in the number of parties, in the size of the formula that computes f, and in $\log 1/\gamma$.*

Proof. We use Protocol MPCINSHUFFLE to compute the function f. By Lemma 2.12 the resulting protocol is private.   □

4   The Common Element Problem

In this section we study the following problem.

Definition 4.1 (The common element problem). *In the common element problem, there are n parties $P_1, \ldots, P_n$, where each party P_i gets an input $x_i \in \mathcal{X}$, and there is an analyzer P_0 (with no input). If all inputs are equal, i.e., $x_1 = x_2 = \cdots = x_n$, then with probability at least $3/4$ the analyzer must output x_1 at the end of the execution. The outcome is not restricted otherwise.*

4.1 An Impossibility Result for Single-Round Constant-Message Protocols

We present an impossibility result for 1-round protocols for the common element problem. Informally, we show that if the domain size $|\mathcal{X}|$ is large, then either the number of messages ℓ must be large, or else the privacy parameter δ must be "large". Before we state and prove this impossibility result, we introduce the following bound on the mutual information between the input of a party in a 1-round differentially protocol and the messages she submits to the shuffle. This bound holds for any 1-round differentially protocol (not only for protocols for the common element problem).

Theorem 4.2. *Let Π be a 1-round shuffle model protocol for n parties satisfying (ε, δ)-differential privacy for coalitions of size 1, with message complexity ℓ. Let $\mathcal{X}$ denote the input domain (i.e., the input of every party is an element of $\mathcal{X}$). Let $(Z_1, \ldots, Z_n) \in \mathcal{X}^n$ denote (possibly correlated) random variables. Consider the execution of Π on inputs $x_1 = Z_1, \ldots x_n = Z_n$, and for $i \in [n]$ let Y_i denote the vector of messages submitted by party P_i to the shuffle, in lexicographic order. Also let W be a random variable denoting the public randomness of the protocol. Then for every $i \in [n]$, if Z_i is uniformly distributed over $\mathcal{X}$ then*

$$I(Y_i, W; Z_i) = O\left((en)^\ell \cdot \left(\varepsilon^2 + \frac{\delta}{\varepsilon} \log |\mathcal{X}| + \frac{\delta}{\varepsilon} \log \frac{\varepsilon}{\delta} \right) + \ell \cdot \log(n) \right).$$

In words, the theorem states that the mutual information between Z_i (the input of party P_i), and (Y_i, W) (the messages submitted by party P_i and the public randomness) is bounded.

Before proving Theorem 4.2, we quote two basic results from information theory (see the full version of this work for the proofs of these lemmas, as well as additional preliminaries form information theory). Consider three random variables Y_1, Y_2, Z, where Y_1 and Y_2 are conditionally independent given Z. The following lemma shows that the amount of information that (Y_1, Y_2) give about Z, is at most the amount that Y_1 gives on Z plus the amount that Y_2 gives on Z. (This is not necessarily true without the conditionally independent assumption.)

Lemma 4.3. *Let Y_1, Y_2, Z be random variables, where Y_1 and Y_2 are conditionally independent given Z. Then, $I(Z; Y_1) + I(Z; Y_2) \geq I(Z; Y_1, Y_2)$.*

The following lemma shows that if $I(X; Y|Z)$ is high and if $H(Z)$ is low, then $I(X; Y)$ must also be high. That is, if X gives a lot of information on Y when conditioning on a random variable Z with low entropy, then X gives a lot of information on Y even without conditioning on Z.

Lemma 4.4. *Let X, Y, Z be three random variables. Then, $I(X; Y) \geq I(X; Y|Z) - H(Z)$.*

We are now ready to prove Theorem 4.2.

Proof of Theorem 4.2. Let $R_1, \ldots, R_n$ denote the randomizers in the protocol Π, and fix $i \in [n]$. We use Π and i to construct the following algorithm, which we call `LocalRandomizer`, that gets a single input x_i and a public random string w.

1. Compute $\widetilde{m}_i \leftarrow R_i(w, x_i)$. That is, $\widetilde{m}_i$ is the vector of ℓ messages chosen by R_i.
2. For $j \neq i$, sample $x_j \in \mathcal{X}$ uniformly at random, and let $\widetilde{m}_j \leftarrow R_j(w, x_j)$.
3. For $j \in [n]$, we write $\widetilde{y}_j$ to denote $\widetilde{m}_j$ after sorting it in lexicographic order.
4. Let $\widetilde{s}$ be a random permutation of the collection of all messages in $\widetilde{m}_1, \ldots, \widetilde{m}_n$.
5. Let $\widetilde{y}$ denote a (sorted) vector of ℓ messages chosen randomly (without repetition) from $\widetilde{s}$.
6. Return $\widetilde{y}, w$.

Consider the execution of `LocalRandomizer` on a uniformly random input $x_i = \widetilde{Z}$ with the public randomness $\widetilde{W}$. We will use $\widetilde{Y}, \widetilde{S}$ and $\left\{ \widetilde{M}_i \right\}_{i \in [n]}, \left\{ \widetilde{Y}_i \right\}_{i \in [n]}$ to denote the random variables taking values $\widetilde{y}, \widetilde{s}, \{\widetilde{m}_i\}_{i \in [n]}$, and $\{\widetilde{y}_i\}_{i \in [n]}$ during the execution.

Observe that $\widetilde{S}$ is identically distributed to the outcome of the shuffler in an execution of Π on random inputs, and observe that the outcome of `LocalRandomizer` is computed as a post-processing of $\widetilde{S}$ and $\widetilde{W}$. Algorithm `LocalRandomizer` is, therefore, (ε, δ)-differentially private (as a function of x_i). Since the mutual information between the input and the output of a differentially private algorithm is bounded (see, e.g., [8] or Theorem A.1), there exists a constant λ such that

$$I\left(\widetilde{Y}, \widetilde{W}; \widetilde{Z}\right) \leq \lambda \cdot \left(\varepsilon^2 + \frac{\delta}{\varepsilon} \log |\mathcal{X}| + \frac{\delta}{\varepsilon} \log(\varepsilon/\delta)\right). \tag{1}$$

We now relate $I\left(\widetilde{Y}, \widetilde{W}; \widetilde{Z}\right)$ to $I\left(\widetilde{Y}_i, \widetilde{W}; \widetilde{Z}\right)$. Intuitively, the connection is that with probability $\approx n^{-\ell}$ we get that $\widetilde{Y} = \widetilde{Y}_i$. Formally, let T be a random variable taking value 0 if $\widetilde{Y} = \widetilde{Y}_i$ and otherwise $T = 1$, and denote $p = \Pr[T = 0] = 1/\binom{\ell n}{\ell}$. By Lemma 4.4 and using standard bounds on the entropy of a binary random variable we get that

$$I\left(\widetilde{Y}, \widetilde{W}; \widetilde{Z}\right) \geq I\left(\widetilde{Y}, \widetilde{W}; \widetilde{Z} \middle| T\right) - H(T) \geq I\left(\widetilde{Y}, \widetilde{W}; \widetilde{Z} \middle| T\right) - p \log\left(\frac{4}{p}\right)$$

$$= \operatorname*{E}_{t \leftarrow T}\left[I\left(\widetilde{Y}, \widetilde{W}; \widetilde{Z} \middle| T = t\right)\right] - p \log\left(\frac{4}{p}\right)$$

$$\geq p \cdot I\left(\widetilde{Y}, \widetilde{W}; \widetilde{Z} \middle| T = 0\right) - p \log\left(\frac{4}{p}\right)$$

$$= p \cdot I(\widetilde{Y}_i, \widetilde{W}; \widetilde{Z}) - p \log\left(\frac{4}{p}\right). \tag{2}$$

So, combining Inequalities (1) and (2) we get that

$$I\left(\widetilde{Y}_i, \widetilde{W}; \widetilde{Z}\right) \leq \frac{\lambda}{p} \cdot \left(\varepsilon^2 + \frac{\delta}{\varepsilon} \log |\mathcal{X}| + \frac{\delta}{\varepsilon} \log(\varepsilon/\delta)\right) + \log\left(\frac{4}{p}\right)$$

$$\leq \lambda \cdot (en)^\ell \cdot \left(\varepsilon^2 + \frac{\delta}{\varepsilon} \log |\mathcal{X}| + \frac{\delta}{\varepsilon} \log(\varepsilon/\delta)\right) + \ell \cdot \log(4en).$$

Finally, observe that the input $\widetilde{Z}$, the public randomness $\widetilde{W}$, and the (sorted) vectors of messages $\widetilde{Y}_i$ in the execution of LocalRandomizer are identically distributed to these variables in the execution of Π on inputs $(Z_1, \ldots, Z_n)$ with the public randomness W. That is, the random variables $\left(\widetilde{Y}_i, \widetilde{W}, \widetilde{Z}\right)$ and (Y_i, W, Z_i) are identically distributed. Therefore,

$$I(Y_i, W; Z_i) \leq \lambda \cdot (en)^\ell \cdot \left(\varepsilon^2 + \frac{\delta}{\varepsilon} \log |\mathcal{X}| + \frac{\delta}{\varepsilon} \log(\varepsilon/\delta)\right) + \ell \cdot \log(4en).$$

$\square$

We next present our impossibility result for the common element problem.

Theorem 4.5. *There exists a constant $\lambda > 1$ such that the following holds. Let $\varepsilon \leq 1$, let $\ell \in N$, and let $\mathcal{X}$ be such that $|\mathcal{X}| \geq 2^{\lambda(4en)^{\ell+1}}$. Let Π be a 1-round protocol for the common element problem over the domain $\mathcal{X}$ with message complexity ℓ, such that Π is (ε, δ)-differentially private for coalitions of size 1. Then,*

$$\delta = \Omega\left((en)^{-\ell-1}\right).$$

Proof. We first give a short overview of the proof. Recall that if all inputs are equal to some element $x \in \mathcal{X}$, then the analyzer must output x with high probability. This also holds when the (common) input x is chosen uniformly at random from $\mathcal{X}$, which means that the mutual information between the (common) input and the output of the analyzer must be high. We show that this means that there must be at least one party P_{i*} such that mutual information between the random (common) input and the messages submitted by P_{i*} must be high, which will contradict Theorem 4.2.

Let $R_1, \ldots, R_n$ denote the randomizers in the protocol Π. Let Z be a uniformly random element of $\mathcal{X}$ and consider the execution of Π on inputs $x_1 = x_2 = \cdots = x_n = Z$ with a public random string W. For $i \in [n]$, let M_i denote a random variable representing the vector of ℓ messages submitted to the shuffler by party P_i, and let Y_i be the same as M_i after sorting it in lexicographic order. Let S be a random variable denoting the outcome of the shuffler. That is, S is a random permutation of all the messages in $M_1, \ldots, M_n$. Alternatively, S is a random permutation of all the messages in $Y_1, \ldots, Y_n$. We use A for the random variable denoting the outcome of the analyzer at the end of the execution.

Since $A = Z$ with probability at least $3/4$, the mutual information between A and Z must be high. Specifically, Let B be a random variable taking value 0 if $A = Z$ and otherwise $B = 1$. By Lemma 4.4

$$I(A; Z) \geq I(A; Z|B) - H(B) \geq I(A; Z|B) - 1 = \mathop{\mathbb{E}}_{b \leftarrow B} \left[I(A; Z|B = b) \right] - 1$$

$$\geq \frac{3}{4} \cdot I(A; Z|B = 0) - 1 = \frac{3}{4} \cdot I(Z; Z) - 1 = \frac{3}{4} \cdot H(Z) - 1$$

$$= \frac{3}{4} \cdot \log |\mathcal{X}| - 1 \geq \frac{1}{2} \cdot \log |\mathcal{X}|.$$

Recall that A is a (possibly randomized) function of the outcome of the shuffle S and the public randomness W. Hence, $I(S, W; Z) \geq I(A; Z) \geq \frac{1}{2} \cdot \log |\mathcal{X}|$. We now show that there must exist an index $i^* \in [n]$ such that

$$I(Y_{i^*}, W; Z) \geq \frac{1}{n} \cdot I(S, W; Z) \geq \frac{1}{2n} \cdot \log |\mathcal{X}|.$$

To that end, observe that since Π is a 1-round protocol, then conditioned on Z and on the public randomness W we have that the messages that party P_i sends are independent of the messages that party P_j, where $j \neq i$, sends. That is, the random variables $Y_1, \ldots, Y_n$ are conditionally independent given (Z, W). Therefore, by Lemma 4.3 we have that

$$\sum_{i \in [n]} I(Y_i, W; Z) = \sum_{i \in [n]} \left(I(W; Z) + I(Y_i; Z|W) \right)$$

$$= \sum_{i \in [n]} I(Y_i; Z|W)$$

$$\geq I(Y_1, \ldots, Y_n; Z|W)$$

$$\geq I(S; Z|W)$$

$$= I(S, W; Z) - I(W; Z)$$

$$= I(S, W; Z)$$

$$\geq \frac{1}{2} \cdot \log |\mathcal{X}|.$$

Hence, there must exist an index i^* such that

$$I(Y_{i^*}, W; Z) \geq \frac{1}{n} \cdot I(S, W; Z) \geq \frac{1}{2n} \cdot \log |\mathcal{X}|.$$

We are now ready to complete the proof. Observe that it suffices to prove the theorem assuming that $\varepsilon = 1$ and that $|\mathcal{X}| = 2^{\lambda(4en)^{\ell+1}}$. The reason is that any (ε, δ)-differentially private protocol with $\varepsilon \leq 1$ is also $(1, \delta)$-differentially private, and that a protocol for the common element problem over a domain $\mathcal{X}$ is, in particular, a protocol for the common element problem over subsets of $\mathcal{X}$. By Theorem 4.2 (our bound on the mutual information between the input and the messages submitted by any single party in a 1-round protocol), there exists a constant $\lambda > 1$ such that

$$\frac{1}{2n} \cdot \log |\mathcal{X}| \leq I(Y_{i^*}, W; Z)$$

$$\leq \lambda \cdot (en)^\ell \cdot \left(\varepsilon^2 + \frac{\delta}{\varepsilon} \log |\mathcal{X}| + \frac{\delta}{\varepsilon} \log(\varepsilon/\delta) \right) + \ell \cdot \log(4en).$$

Substituting $\varepsilon = 1$ and $|\mathcal{X}| = 2^{\lambda(4en)^{\ell+1}}$, and solving for δ, we get that $\delta \geq \frac{1}{8\lambda(en)^{\ell+1}}$. $\qquad\square$

4.2   A Two-Round Protocol with Message Complexity 1

Intuitively, Theorem 4.5 shows that in any 1-round protocol for the common element problem, we either have that the message complexity is large, or we have that δ cannot be too small. In Fig. 5 we present a two round protocol for the common element problem, in which the message complexity is 1 and δ can be negligible. Our protocol, which we call Protocol COMMONTWOROUND, uses the shuffle channel in only one of the two rounds, and the communication in the second round is done via a public channel.

Theorem 4.6. *Let* $\delta \in (0,1)$. *Protocol* COMMONTWOROUND, *described in Fig. 5, is* $(O(1), O(\delta))$-*differentially private against coalitions of size $0.9n$ that solves the common element problem. The protocol uses two rounds (one via a public channel and one via the shuffle) and has message complexity 1.*

We begin with the privacy analysis of Protocol COMMONTWOROUND.

Lemma 4.7. *Protocol* COMMONTWOROUND *is* $(O(1), O(\delta))$-*differentially private against coalitions of size $0.9n$.*

Proof. Fix an index $i \in [n]$, fix two i-neighboring input vectors $\boldsymbol{x}$ and $\boldsymbol{x}'$, and fix a coalition $\mathcal{C}$ of size $|\mathcal{C}| = 0.9n$ such that $P_i \notin \mathcal{C}$. We need to show that $\text{View}_{\mathcal{C}}^\Pi(\boldsymbol{x}) \approx_{\varepsilon,\delta} \text{View}_{\mathcal{C}}^\Pi(\boldsymbol{x}')$. First observe that with probability at least $1 - \delta$ over the choice of the hash function h, we have that h perfectly hashes all the different inputs in $\boldsymbol{x}, \boldsymbol{x}'$ (note $\boldsymbol{x}, \boldsymbol{x}'$ span at most $n + 1$ different values). We proceed with the analysis after fixing such a hash function h.

We write $\boldsymbol{x}_{\mathcal{C}} = \boldsymbol{x}'_{\mathcal{C}}$ to denote the inputs of the parties in $\mathcal{C}$, and fix the internal randomness $r_{\mathcal{C}}$ of the parties in $\mathcal{C}$. Now let S_1 and S_2 be random variables representing the output of the public channel and the shuffle, respectively, during the execution on $\boldsymbol{x}$, where we denote $S_2 = \perp$ if the execution halted on Step (3). Similarly, S_1', S_2' denote the outputs of these channels during the execution on $\boldsymbol{x}'$. With these notations we have that

$$\text{View}_{\mathcal{C}}^\Pi(\boldsymbol{x}) = (h, r_{\mathcal{C}}, \boldsymbol{x}_{\mathcal{C}}, S_1, S_2) \quad \text{and} \quad \text{View}_{\mathcal{C}}^\Pi(\boldsymbol{x}') = (h, r_{\mathcal{C}}, \boldsymbol{x}_{\mathcal{C}}, S_1', S_2').$$

Observe that S_1 and S_1' are computed using an $(\varepsilon, 0)$-differentially private protocol in the local model (see Theorem A.2), and hence,

$$(h, r_{\mathcal{C}}, \boldsymbol{x}_{\mathcal{C}}, S_1) \approx_{(\varepsilon,0)} (h, r_{\mathcal{C}}, \boldsymbol{x}_{\mathcal{C}}, S_1').$$

Protocol COMMONTWOROUND

Inputs: Each party P_i (for $i \in [n]$) holds an input $x_i \in \mathcal{X}$. The analyzer P_0 has no input. All parties have access to a hash function $h : \mathcal{X} \to [n^2/\delta]$ chosen with uniform distribution from a pairwise independent family (defined, e.g., using a public random string).

1. Every party P_i computes $y_i \leftarrow h(x_i)$.
2. The parties use the public channel to execute a 1-round $(\varepsilon, 0)$-differentially private protocol in the local model for histograms over the (distributed) database $Y = (y_1, y_2, \ldots, y_n)$ with failure probability δ (see e.g., [12], or Theorem A.2). This results in a data structure D (known to all parties) that gives estimations for the multiplicities of elements in Y. That is, for every $y \in [n^2/\delta]$ we have that $D(y) \approx |\{i \in [n] : y_i = y\}|$.
3. Let $y^* \in [n^2/\delta]$ be an element that maximizes $D(y)$. If $D(y) < \frac{98 \cdot n}{100}$ then all parties terminate, and the analyzer outputs $\perp$.
4. Otherwise, each party P_i prepares a single message m_i as follows:
   (a) If $y_i \neq y^*$ then $m_i = \perp$.
   (b) Otherwise, $m_i = \perp$ with probability $1/2$ and $m_i = x_i$ with probability $1/2$.
5. Each party P_i sends the message m_i to the shuffle. All parties receive a permutation s of $(m_1, \ldots, m_n)$.
6. The analyzer outputs the element $x^* \neq \perp$ with the largest number of appearances in s (the analyzer fails if all elements of s are equal to $\perp$).

Fig. 5. A two-round protocol in the shuffle model for the common element problem with message complexity 1.

We next argue about S_2 and S_2'. For an element $x \in \mathcal{X}$ we write $f_x(x)$ to denote the number of occurrences of x in the input vector $\boldsymbol{x}$. Also, let $x^* \in \mathcal{X}$ denote the most frequent element in $\boldsymbol{x}$, that is, an element such that $f_{\boldsymbol{x}}(x^*)$ is maximized.

Case (a) $f_{\boldsymbol{x}}(x^*) \leq \frac{96 \cdot n}{100}$: By the utility guarantees of the protocol for histograms (executed on Step (2)), each of the two executions terminates in Step (3) with probability at least $(1 - \delta)$. This is because if $n = \Omega(\frac{1}{\varepsilon^2} \log(\frac{1}{\varepsilon\delta}))$ then with probability at least $(1 - \delta)$ all of the estimates given by $D(\cdot)$ are accurate to within $\pm 0.01n$ (see Theorem A.2). Therefore, in case (a) we have

$$\text{View}_{\mathcal{C}}^{\Pi}(\boldsymbol{x}) = (h, r_{\mathcal{C}}, \boldsymbol{x}_{\mathcal{C}}, S_1, S_2) \approx_{(0,\delta)} (h, r_{\mathcal{C}}, \boldsymbol{x}_{\mathcal{C}}, S_1, \perp)$$
$$\approx_{(\varepsilon, \delta)} (h, r_{\mathcal{C}}, \boldsymbol{x}_{\mathcal{C}}, S_1', \perp) \approx_{(0,\delta)} (h, r_{\mathcal{C}}, \boldsymbol{x}_{\mathcal{C}}, S_1', S_2') = \text{View}_{\mathcal{C}}^{\Pi}(\boldsymbol{x}').$$

Case (b) $f_{\boldsymbol{x}}(x^*) > \frac{96 \cdot n}{100}$: Fix any value s_1 for the outcome of the public channel, such that all the estimates given by the resulting data structure $D(\cdot)$ are accurate to within $\pm 0.01n$ w.r.t. $\boldsymbol{x}$. We first show that conditioned on such an s_1 we have that

$$(h, r_\mathcal{C}, \boldsymbol{x}_\mathcal{C}, s_1, S_2) \approx_{(\varepsilon, \delta)} (h, r_\mathcal{C}, \boldsymbol{x}_\mathcal{C}, s_1, S_2').$$

To see this, observe that once we condition on s_1 then either both executions terminate on Step (3), or in the two executions we have that $y^* = h(x^*)$ (because $f_x(x^*) > 0.96n$). If s_1 is such that the two executions terminate on Step (3), then (conditioned on s_1) we have $S_2 = S_2' = \perp$ and so

$$(h, r_\mathcal{C}, \boldsymbol{x}_\mathcal{C}, s_1, S_2) \equiv (h, r_\mathcal{C}, \boldsymbol{x}_\mathcal{C}, s_1, S_2').$$

Now suppose that the two executions do not halt prematurely, and that $y^* = h(x^*)$. In that case, the outcome of the shuffle contains (randomly permuted) copies of $\perp$ and copies of x^*. Note that since the outcome of the shuffle is randomly permuted, then the outcome distribution of the shuffle is determined by the number of occurrences of x^*.

Note that if x_i and x_i' are both equal to x^*, or are both different from x^*, then S_2 and S_2' are identically distributed, which would complete the proof. We, therefore, assume that exactly one of x_i, x_i' is equal to x^*. Suppose without loss of generality that $x_i = x^*$ and $x_i' \neq x^*$.

Since $f_x(x^*) > 0.96n$ and since $|\mathcal{C}| = 0.9n$, there is a set of parties $\mathcal{I}$ of size $|\mathcal{I}| = 0.05n$ such that

1. $\mathcal{I} \cap (\mathcal{C} \cup \{i\}) = \emptyset$.
2. For every $j \in \mathcal{I}$ we have that $x_j = x_j' = x^*$.

We show that the outcome of the shuffle preserves differential privacy (over the randomness of the parties in $\mathcal{I}$ and the randomness of the shuffle). Fix the randomness of all parties except for parties in $\mathcal{I}$. Note that this fixes the messages that these parties submit to the shuffle, and suppose that party P_i submits x^* during the first execution and submits $\perp$ during the second execution (if party P_i submits $\perp$ during both execution then the outcome of the shuffle is, again, identically distributed). Let k denote the number of parties among the parties not in $\mathcal{I}$ that submitted x^* to the shuffle during the execution on $\boldsymbol{x}$. (So during the execution on $\boldsymbol{x}'$ exactly $k - 1$ such parties submitted x^*.)

Let us denote by Z the number of parties from $\mathcal{I}$ that submits x^* to the shuffle. Note that $Z \equiv \mathrm{Binomial}\left(|\mathcal{I}|, \frac{1}{2}\right)$. By the Hoeffding bound, assuming that $n = \Omega(\ln(1/\delta))$ (large enough), with probability at least $1 - \delta$ we have that $\frac{9}{20} \cdot |\mathcal{I}| \leq Z \leq \frac{11}{20} \cdot |\mathcal{I}|$. In addition, by the properties of the Binomial distribution, for every $\frac{9}{20} \cdot |\mathcal{I}| \leq z \leq \frac{11}{20} \cdot |\mathcal{I}|$ we have that

$$\frac{\Pr[Z = z]}{\Pr[Z = z + 1]} = \frac{2^{-|\mathcal{I}|} \cdot \binom{|\mathcal{I}|}{z}}{2^{-|\mathcal{I}|} \cdot \binom{|\mathcal{I}|}{z+1}} = \frac{z + 1}{|\mathcal{I}| - z} \in e^{\pm 1}.$$

Let us denote the number of occurrences of x^* at the output of the shuffle during the two executions as $|S_2|$ and $|S_2'|$, respectively. So $|S_2| \equiv k + Z$ and $|S_2'| \equiv k - 1 + Z$. Fix a set $F \subseteq [n]$ of possible values for $|S_2|$, and denote

$$T = \{(f - k) : f \in F\} \qquad \text{and} \qquad T' = \{(f - k + 1) : f \in F\}$$

We have that

$$\Pr\left[|S_2| \in F\right] = \Pr[Z \in T] \le \delta + \Pr\left[Z \in T \cap \left\{z : \frac{9|\mathcal{I}|}{20} \le z \le \frac{11|\mathcal{I}|}{20}\right\}\right]$$

$$\le \delta + e^1 \cdot \Pr\left[Z - 1 \in T \cap \left\{z : \frac{9|\mathcal{I}|}{20} \le z \le \frac{11|\mathcal{I}|}{20}\right\}\right]$$

$$\le \delta + e^1 \cdot \Pr\left[Z - 1 \in T\right] = \delta + e^1 \cdot \Pr\left[Z \in T'\right]$$

$$= \delta + e^1 \cdot \Pr\left[|S_2'| \in F\right].$$

A similar analysis shows that $\Pr\left[|S_2'| \in F\right] \le \delta + e^1 \cdot \Pr\left[|S_2| \in F\right]$. This shows that conditioned on an output of the public channel s_1 such that $D(\cdot)$ is accurate for $\boldsymbol{x}$, we have that

$$(h, r_C, \boldsymbol{x}_C, s_1, S_2) \approx_{(1,\delta)} (h, r_C, \boldsymbol{x}_C, s_1, S_2').$$

So far, we have established that the outcome of the first round (that uses the public channel) preserves $(\varepsilon, 0)$-differential privacy, and, conditioned on the outcome of the first round being "good" (i.e., the resulting data structure D is accurate) we have that the outcome of the second round (that uses the shuffle) preserves $(1, \delta)$-differential privacy. Intuitively, we now want to use composition theorems for differential privacy to show that the two rounds together satisfy differential privacy. A small technical issue that we need to handle, though, is that the privacy guarantees of the second round depend on the success of the first round. As the outcome of the first round is "good" with overwhelming probability, this technical issue can easily be resolved, as follows.

Consider two random variables $\tilde{S}_1$ and $\tilde{S}'_1$ that are identical to S_1 and S_1', except that if the resulting data structure $D(\cdot)$ is *not* accurate, then the value is replaced such that the resulting data structure $D(\cdot)$ is exactly correct. Since the protocol for histograms fails with probability at most δ, we have that

$$\left(h, r_C, \boldsymbol{x}_C, \tilde{S}_1\right) \approx_{(0,\delta)} (h, r_C, \boldsymbol{x}_C, S_1) \approx_{(\varepsilon,\delta)} (h, r_C, \boldsymbol{x}_C, S_1') \approx_{(0,\delta)} \left(h, r_C, \boldsymbol{x}_C, \tilde{S}'_1\right).$$

In words, consider an imaginary protocol in which the outcome distribution of the first round during the two executions is replaced by $\tilde{S}_1$ and $\tilde{S}'_1$, respectively. The statistical distance between the outcome distribution of this imaginary protocol and the original protocol is at most δ. In addition, for every possible fixture of the outcome of the first (imaginary) round we have the second round preserves differential privacy. Therefore, composition theorems for differential privacy show that the two rounds together satisfy differential privacy. Formally,

$$\mathrm{View}_C^{\Pi}(\boldsymbol{x}) = (h, r_C, \boldsymbol{x}_C, S_1, S_2) \approx_{(0,\delta)} \left(h, r_C, \boldsymbol{x}_C, \tilde{S}_1, S_2\right)$$

$$\approx_{(1+\varepsilon,\delta)} \left(h, r_C, \boldsymbol{x}_C, \tilde{S}'_1, S_2'\right) \approx_{(0,\delta)} (h, r_C, \boldsymbol{x}_C, S_1', S_2') = \mathrm{View}_C^{\Pi}(\boldsymbol{x}').$$

$\square$

Lemma 4.8. *Protocol* COMMONTWOROUND *solves the common element problem.*

Proof. Fix an input vector $x = (x_1, \ldots, x_n) \in \mathcal{X}^n$ such that for every i we have $x_i = x$. By the utility guarantees of the locally-private protocol for histograms, with probability at least $1 - \delta$ it holds that all of the estimates given by $D(\cdot)$ are accurate to within $\pm 0.01n$. In that case, we have that y^* (defined in Step (3)) satisfies $y^* = h(x)$. Thus, every message submitted to the shuffle in the second round is equal to x with probability $1/2$, and otherwise equal to $\perp$. Therefore, the analyzer fails to output x in Step (6) only if all of the parties submitted $\perp$ to the shuffle. This happens with probability at most 2^{-n}. Overall, with probability at least $(1 - \delta - 2^{-n})$ the analyzer outputs x.   □

Theorem 4.6 now follows by combining Lemma 4.7 and Lemma 4.8.

5   Possibility and Impossibility for the Nested Common Element Problem

In this section we define a nested version of the common element problem of Definition 4.1. This problem has a parameter $0 < \alpha < 1$. We show that this problem cannot be solved in the shuffle model in one round with differential privacy against coalitions of size αn (regardless of the number of messages each party can send). In contrast, we show that it can be solved with differential privacy in one round against coalitions of size cn for any constant $c < \min\{\alpha, 1 - \alpha\}$ and in two rounds against coalitions of size cn for any constant $c < 1$. The impossibility result for one round and the two round protocol imply a strong separation between what can be solved in one round and in two rounds.

Definition 5.1 (Nested common element problem with parameter α).
Let $0 < \alpha < 1$. Consider n parties $P_1, \ldots, P_n$ and an analyzer P_0 (as in Remark 2.8). The input of each party in $P_1, \ldots, P_{\lfloor \alpha n \rfloor}$ is an element $x_i \in \mathcal{X}$ and the input of each party $P_{\lfloor \alpha n \rfloor + 1}, \ldots, P_n$ is a vector y_i of $|\mathcal{X}|$ elements from some finite domain $\mathcal{Y}$. The analyzer P_0 has no input. If all inputs of $P_1, \ldots, P_{\lfloor \alpha n \rfloor}$ are equal (i.e., $x_1 = x_2 = \cdots = x_{\lfloor \alpha n \rfloor}$) and the x_1-th coordinate in all inputs of $P_{\lfloor \alpha n \rfloor + 1}, \ldots, P_n$ are equal (i.e., $y_{\lfloor \alpha n \rfloor + 1}[x_1] = y_{\lfloor \alpha n \rfloor + 2}[x_1] = \cdots = y_n[x_1]$), then the analyzer P_0 must output $y_{\lfloor \alpha n \rfloor + 1}[x_1]$ with probability at least $3/4$. The output is not restricted otherwise.

Remark 5.2. When $|\mathcal{X}| = \text{poly}(n)$ and $|\mathcal{Y}|$ is at most exponential in n, then the length of the inputs of all parties is polynomial in n. Our impossibility result for the nested common element problem holds in this regime (specifically, when $|\mathcal{X}| = \tilde{\Omega}(n^2)$ and $|\mathcal{Y}| = 2$). Our protocols are correct and private regardless of the size of $\mathcal{X}$ and $\mathcal{Y}$.

We prove the following three theorems.

Theorem 5.3. *Let* $|\mathcal{X}| = \tilde{\Omega}(n^2)$. *There is no one-round* $(1, o(1/n))$-*differentially private protocol in the shuffle model against coalition of size* $\lfloor \alpha n \rfloor$ *for the nested common element problem with parameter* α *(regardless of the number of messages each party can send).*

Theorem 5.4. *For every* $0 < c < 1$, $\varepsilon, \delta \in [0,1]$, *and* $n \geq \frac{200}{(1-c)n} \ln \frac{4}{\delta}$ *there exists a two-round* (ε, δ)-*differentially private protocol against coalitions of size* cn *that with probability at least* $1 - 1/2^{n-1}$ *solves the nested common element problem with parameter* α.

Theorem 5.5. *For every constants* c, α *such that* $0 < c < \min\{\alpha, 1 - \alpha\} < 1$, *there exists a constant* ε_0 *such that there exits a one-round* (ε_0, δ)-*differentially private protocol against coalitions of size* cn *that with probability at least* $3/4$ *solves the nested common element problem with parameter* α, *where* $\delta = 2^{-O(\min\{\alpha, 1-\alpha\}-c)n)}$ *and* $n \geq 6 \cdot \max\{1/\alpha, 1/(1-\alpha)\}$.

In the rest of this section we prove Theorem 5.3. The proofs of Theorems 5.4 and 5.5 are given in the full version of this paper.

5.1 An Impossibility Result for Private One-Round Protocols for the Nested Common Element Problem

We next show that the nested common element problem with parameter α cannot be solved privately against coalitions of size αn when $\mathcal{X}$ is large enough, namely, when $|\mathcal{X}| = \tilde{\Omega}(n^2)$. The proof of the impossibility result is done by using an impossibility result to the vector common element problem (in the centralized model) defined below.

Definition 5.6 (The vector common element problem). *The input of the problem is a database containing* n *vectors* $(\boldsymbol{y_1}, \ldots, \boldsymbol{y_n}) \in (\{0,1\}^d)^n$. *For a given set of vectors* $\boldsymbol{y_1}, \ldots, \boldsymbol{y_n}$, *define for every* $b \in \{0,1\}$

$$I_b = \{j : \boldsymbol{y_1}[j] = \cdots = \boldsymbol{y_n}[j] = b\}.$$

To solve the the vector common element problem, an analyzer must output with probability at least $1 - o(1/n)$ *sets* J_0 *and* J_1 *such that* $I_0 \subseteq J_0$, $I_1 \subseteq J_1$, *and* $J_0 \cap J_1 = \emptyset$.

In words, the task in the vector common element problem is to identify the coordinates in which the inputs vectors agree, that is, for each coordinate if all the vectors agree on the value of the coordinate then the algorithm should return this coordinate and the common value; if the vectors do not agree on this coordinate then the algorithm can say that this is either a zero-coordinate, a one-coordinate, or none of the above.

The following theorem is implied by the techniques of [14] (i.e., the reduction to fingerprinting codes).

Theorem 5.7 ([14]). *For every* $d \in \mathbb{N}$, *any* $(1, o(1/n))$-*differentially private algorithm in the centralized model for the vector common element problem with vectors of length* d *has sample complexity* $\tilde{\Omega}(\sqrt{d})$.

We next prove our impossibility result, i.e., prove Theorem 5.3.

Proof of Theorem 5.3. We show that if for $|\mathcal{X}| = \tilde{\Omega}(n^2)$ there is an n-party protocol, denoted Π, in the shuffle model for the nested common element problem with parameter α that is private against the coalition of parties holding the x-inputs, namely, $\mathcal{C} = \{P_1, \ldots, P_{\lfloor \alpha n \rfloor}\}$, then there is an algorithm in the centralized model for the vector common element problem with database of size $O(n^2 \log n)$ violating Theorem 5.7.

As a first step, consider the following algorithm $\mathcal{A}_1$ for the vector common element problem in the centralized model, whose inputs are $\boldsymbol{y}_{\lfloor \alpha n \rfloor + 1}, \ldots, \boldsymbol{y}_n$ (each vector of length $|\mathcal{X}|$).

1. The analyzer chooses a public random string w.
2. For each $i \in \{\lfloor \alpha n \rfloor + 1, \ldots, n\}$, the analyzer simulates party P_i in protocol Π with the input $\boldsymbol{y}_i$ and the public random string w, generating a vector of messages $\boldsymbol{m}_i$.
3. The analyzer shuffles the messages in $\boldsymbol{m}_{\lfloor \alpha n \rfloor + 1}, \cdots, \boldsymbol{m}_n$, denote the output of the shuffle by $\tilde{\boldsymbol{m}}$.
4. For every $x \in \mathcal{X}$ do:
   (a) For each $i \in \{1, \ldots, \lfloor \alpha n \rfloor\}$, the analyzer simulates party P_i in protocol Π with the input x and the public random string w, generating a vector of messages $\boldsymbol{m}_i$.
   (b) The analyzer shuffles the messages in $\tilde{\boldsymbol{m}}, \boldsymbol{m}_1, \ldots, \boldsymbol{m}_{\lfloor \alpha n \rfloor}$, gives the shuffled messages to the analyzer of Π, and gets an output z_x.
5. The analyzer returns $I_b = \{x : z_x = b\}$ for $b \in \{0, 1\}$.

First we argue that $\mathcal{A}_1$ is $(1, o(1/n))$-differentially private: The coalition $\mathcal{C}$ sees the output of the shuffle in Π and can remove the messages it sent to the shuffle in Π, therefore computing $\tilde{\boldsymbol{m}}$ from the view is a post-processing of an $(\varepsilon, o(1/n))$-differentially private output. Second, notice that for every $x \in \mathcal{X}$, the shuffled messages that the analyzer of Π gets in Step (4b) are distributed as in Π, thus, if $\boldsymbol{y}_{\lfloor \alpha n \rfloor + 1}[x] = \cdots = \boldsymbol{y}_n[x] = b$, then $z_x = b$ with probability at least $3/4$ (however for $x \neq x'$ these events might be independent).

The success probability of $\mathcal{A}_1$ is not enough to violate Theorem 5.3 and we repeat it $O(\log |\mathcal{X}|)$ times. This is done in $\mathcal{A}_2$, which preserves the privacy using sub-sampling:

1. **Inputs:** vectors $\boldsymbol{y}_1, \ldots, \boldsymbol{y}_t$, where $t = O(n \ln |\mathcal{X}|)$.
2. For $\ell = 1$ to $4 \ln |\mathcal{X}|$ do:
   (a) Sample a set $T \subset [t]$ of size $\frac{t}{(3+\exp(1)) 4 \ln |\mathcal{X}|} = n$ and execute $\mathcal{A}_1$ on the vectors $(\boldsymbol{y}_i)_{i \in T}$ and get sets J_0^ℓ, J_1^ℓ.
3. For $b \in \{0, 1\}$, let $J_b = \{j : j \in J_b^\ell$ for more than $4 \ln |\mathcal{X}|$ indices $\ell\}$.

By Theorem A.3 (i.e., sub-sampling) and since $\mathcal{A}_1$ is $(1, o(\frac{1}{n}))$-differentially private, each execution of Step (2a) is $(\frac{1}{4 \ln |\mathcal{X}|}, o(\frac{1}{n \ln |\mathcal{X}|}))$-differentially private. By simple composition, algorithm $\mathcal{A}_2$ is $(1, o(1/n))$-differentially private.

We next argue that with probability at least $1 - o(1/n)$ algorithm $\mathcal{A}_2$ outputs disjoint sets J_0, J_1 such that $I_0 \subseteq J_0$ and $I_1 \subseteq J_1$. Fix j such that $\boldsymbol{y}_1[j] = \cdots =$

$y_t[j] = b$ for some b. By the correctness of $\mathcal{A}_1$, for every $\ell \in [4 \ln |\mathcal{X}|]$ it holds that $j \in J_b^\ell$ with probability at least $3/4$ and these events are independent. Thus, by the Hoeffding inequality, $j \in J_b^\ell$ for more than half of the values of ℓ with probability at least $1 - 1/|\mathcal{X}|^2$. By the union bound, the probability that the algorithm errs for some coordinate for which all vectors y_i agree is at most $1/|\mathcal{X}| = \tilde{O}(1/n^2) = o(1/n)$.

To conclude, assuming that Π as above exits, we constructed a $(1, o(1/n))$-differentially private algorithm $\mathcal{A}_2$ with database of size $O(n^2 \log n)$ and $d = |\mathcal{X}| = \tilde{\Omega}(|\mathcal{X}|^2)$, contradicting Theorem 5.7. $\square$

Acknowledgments. The authors thank Rachel Cummings and Naty Peter for discussions of the shuffle model at an early stage of this research. Work of A. B. and K. N. was supported by NSF grant No. 1565387 TWC: Large: Collaborative: Computing Over Distributed Sensitive Data. This work was done when A. B. was hosted by Georgetown University. Work of A. B. was also supported by Israel Science Foundation grant no. 152/17, a grant from the Cyber Security Research Center at Ben-Gurion University, and ERC grant 742754 (project NTSC). I. H. is the director of the Check Point Institute for Information Security. His research is supported by ERC starting grant 638121 and Israel Science Foundation grant no. 666/19. Work of U. S. was supported in part by the Israel Science Foundation (grant 1871/19), and by the Cyber Security Research Center at Ben-Gurion University of the Negev.

A   Additional Preliminaries from Differential Privacy

The following theorem bounds the mutual information between the input and the output of a differentially private algorithm (that operates on a database of size 1).

Theorem A.1 ([8]). *Let X be uniformly distributed over $\mathcal{X}$. Let $\mathcal{A}$ be an (ε, δ)-differentially private algorithm that operates on a single input (i.e., a database of size 1) from $\mathcal{X}$. Let Z denote $\mathcal{A}(X)$. Then,*

$$I(X; Z) = O\left(\varepsilon^2 + \frac{\delta}{\varepsilon} \log |\mathcal{X}| + \frac{\delta}{\varepsilon} \log(\varepsilon/\delta)\right).$$

In our protocols we will use the following protocol in the local model for computing histograms.

Theorem A.2 (Histogram protocol [7,8,12]**).** *Let $\beta, \varepsilon \leq 1$ and $\mathcal{X}$ be some finite domain. There exists a 1-round $(\varepsilon, 0)$-differentially private protocol in the local model for n parties with message complexity 1, in which the input of each agent is a single element from $\mathcal{X}$ and the outcome is a data structure $D : \mathcal{X} \rightarrow [n]$ such that for every input to the protocol $x \in \mathcal{X}^n$, with probability at least $1 - \beta$, for every input vector $x = (x_1, \ldots, x_n) \in \mathcal{X}$ we have*

$$\left| D(x) - |\{i : x_i = x\}| \right| \leq O\left(\frac{1}{\varepsilon} \cdot \sqrt{n \cdot \log\left(\frac{|\mathcal{X}|}{\beta}\right)}\right).$$

We next recall the sub-sampling technique from [9,28].

Theorem A.3 (Sub-sampling [9,28]). *Let $\mathcal{A}_1$ be an (ε^*, δ)-differentially private algorithm operating on databases of size n. Fix $\varepsilon \leq 1$, and denote $t = \frac{n}{\varepsilon}(3 + \exp(\varepsilon^*))$. Construct an algorithm $\mathcal{A}_2$ that on input a database $D = (z_i)_{i=1}^t$ uniformly at random selects a subset $T \subseteq \{1, 2, ..., t\}$ of size n, and runs $\mathcal{A}_1$ on the multiset $D_T = (z_i)_{i \in T}$. Then, $\mathcal{A}_2$ is $\left(\varepsilon, \frac{4\varepsilon}{3 + \exp(\varepsilon^*)}\delta\right)$-differentially private.*

Secure Addition Protocols in the Shuffle Model. Ishai et al. [27] gave a protocol where $n \geq 2$ parties communicate with an analyzer (as in Remark 2.8) to compute the sum of their inputs in a finite group G, in the semi-honest setting and in the presence of a coalition including the analyzer and up to $n - 1$ parties. In their protocol, each participating party splits their input into $\ell = O(\log|G| + \log n + \sigma)$ shares and sends each share in a separate message through the shuffle. Upon receiving the $n\ell$ shuffled messages, the analyzer adds them up (in G) to compute the sum. Recent work by Ghazi et al. [24] and Balle et al. [6] improved the dependency of the number of messages on the number of participating parties to $\ell = O(1 + (\log|G| + \sigma)/\log n)$.

Theorem A.4 ([6,24,27]). *Let G be a finite group. There exist a one-round shuffle model summation protocol with n parties holding inputs $x_i \in G$ and an analyzer. The protocol is secure in the semi-honest model, and in the presence of coalitions including the analyzer and up to $n - 1$ parties.*

References

1. Applebaum, B., Brakerski, Z., Tsabary, R.: Perfect secure computation in two rounds. In: Beimel, A., Dziembowski, S. (eds.) TCC 2018. LNCS, vol. 11239, pp. 152–174. Springer, Cham (2018). https://doi.org/10.1007/978-3-030-03807-6_6
2. Balcer, V., Cheu, A.: Separating local & shuffled differential privacy via histograms. In: Kalai, Y.T., Smith, A.D., Wichs, D. (eds.) 1st Conference on Information-Theoretic Cryptography, ITC 2020. LIPIcs, vol. 163, pp. 1:1–1:14. Schloss Dagstuhl - Leibniz-Zentrum für Informatik (2020). https://doi.org/10.4230/LIPIcs.ITC.2020.1
3. Balcer, V., Cheu, A., Joseph, M., Mao, J.: Connecting robust shuffle privacy and pan-privacy. CoRR abs/2004.09481 (2020)
4. Balle, B., Bell, J., Gascón, A., Nissim, K.: Differentially private summation with multi-message shuffling. CoRR abs/1906.09116 (2019)
5. Balle, B., Bell, J., Gascón, A., Nissim, K.: The privacy blanket of the shuffle model. In: Boldyreva, A., Micciancio, D. (eds.) CRYPTO 2019. LNCS, vol. 11693, pp. 638–667. Springer, Cham (2019). https://doi.org/10.1007/978-3-030-26951-7_22
6. Balle, B., Bell, J., Gascón, A., Nissim, K.: Private summation in the multi-message shuffle model. CoRR abs/2002.00817 (2020)
7. Bassily, R., Nissim, K., Stemmer, U., Thakurta, A.G.: Practical locally private heavy hitters. In: Advances in Neural Information Processing Systems 30: Annual Conference on Neural Information Processing Systems 2017, pp. 2285–2293 (2017)

8. Bassily, R., Smith, A.D.: Local, private, efficient protocols for succinct histograms. In: Proceedings of the Forty-Seventh Annual ACM on Symposium on Theory of Computing, STOC 2015, pp. 127–135 (2015)
9. Beimel, A., Brenner, H., Kasiviswanathan, S.P., Nissim, K.: Bounds on the sample complexity for private learning and private data release. Mach. Learn. **94**(3), 401–437 (2013). https://doi.org/10.1007/s10994-013-5404-1
10. Beimel, A., Nissim, K., Omri, E.: Distributed private data analysis: simultaneously solving how and what. In: Wagner, D. (ed.) CRYPTO 2008. LNCS, vol. 5157, pp. 451–468. Springer, Heidelberg (2008). https://doi.org/10.1007/978-3-540-85174-5_25
11. Bittau, A., et al.: Prochlo: strong privacy for analytics in the crowd. In: Proceedings of the 26th Symposium on Operating Systems Principles, pp. 441–459. ACM (2017). https://doi.org/10.1145/3132747.3132769
12. Bun, M., Nelson, J., Stemmer, U.: Heavy hitters and the structure of local privacy. ACM Trans. Algorithms **15**(4), 51:1–51:40 (2019). https://doi.org/10.1145/3344722
13. Bun, M., Ullman, J., Vadhan, S.P.: Fingerprinting codes and the price of approximate differential privacy. In: Symposium on Theory of Computing, STOC 2014, pp. 1–10 (2014)
14. Bun, M., Ullman, J., Vadhan, S.P.: Fingerprinting codes and the price of approximate differential privacy. SIAM J. Comput. **47**(5), 1888–1938 (2018). https://doi.org/10.1137/15M1033587
15. Chen, L., Ghazi, B., Kumar, R., Manurangsi, P.: On distributed differential privacy and counting distinct elements. CoRR abs/2009.09604 (2020), https://arxiv.org/abs/2009.09604
16. Cheu, A., Smith, A., Ullman, J., Zeber, D., Zhilyaev, M.: Distributed differential privacy via shuffling. In: Ishai, Y., Rijmen, V. (eds.) EUROCRYPT 2019. LNCS, vol. 11476, pp. 375–403. Springer, Cham (2019). https://doi.org/10.1007/978-3-030-17653-2_13
17. Cheu, A., Ullman, J.: The limits of pan privacy and shuffle privacy for learning and estimation. CoRR abs/2009.08000 (2020)
18. Dwork, C., Kenthapadi, K., McSherry, F., Mironov, I., Naor, M.: Our data, ourselves: privacy via distributed noise generation. In: Vaudenay, S. (ed.) EUROCRYPT 2006. LNCS, vol. 4004, pp. 486–503. Springer, Heidelberg (2006). https://doi.org/10.1007/11761679_29
19. Dwork, C., McSherry, F., Nissim, K., Smith, A.: Calibrating noise to sensitivity in private data analysis. In: Halevi, S., Rabin, T. (eds.) TCC 2006. LNCS, vol. 3876, pp. 265–284. Springer, Heidelberg (2006). https://doi.org/10.1007/11681878_14
20. Dwork, C., Naor, M., Pitassi, T., Rothblum, G.N., Yekhanin, S.: Pan-private streaming algorithms. In: Yao, A.C. (ed.) Innovations in Computer Science - ICS 2010, pp. 66–80. Tsinghua University Press (2010)
21. Erlingsson, Ú., Feldman, V., Mironov, I., Raghunathan, A., Talwar, K., Thakurta, A.: Amplification by shuffling: from local to central differential privacy via anonymity. In: Chan, T.M. (ed.) Proceedings of the Thirtieth Annual ACM-SIAM Symposium on Discrete Algorithms, SODA 2019, pp. 2468–2479. SIAM (2019). https://doi.org/10.1137/1.9781611975482.151
22. Garg, S., Ishai, Y., Srinivasan, A.: Two-round MPC: information-theoretic and black-box. In: Beimel, A., Dziembowski, S. (eds.) TCC 2018. LNCS, vol. 11239, pp. 123–151. Springer, Cham (2018). https://doi.org/10.1007/978-3-030-03807-6_5
23. Ghazi, B., Golowich, N., Kumar, R., Pagh, R., Velingker, A.: On the power of multiple anonymous messages. IACR Cryptol. ePrint Arch. **2019**, 1382 (2019)

24. Ghazi, B., Manurangsi, P., Pagh, R., Velingker, A.: Private aggregation from fewer anonymous messages. In: Canteaut, A., Ishai, Y. (eds.) EUROCRYPT 2020. LNCS, vol. 12106, pp. 798–827. Springer, Cham (2020). https://doi.org/10.1007/978-3-030-45724-2_27

25. Ghazi, B., Pagh, R., Velingker, A.: Scalable and differentially private distributed aggregation in the shuffled model. CoRR abs/1906.08320 (2019)

26. Håstad, J., Impagliazzo, R., Levin, L.A., Luby, M.: A pseudorandom generator from any one-way function. SIAM J. Comput. 28(4), 1364–1396 (1999). https://doi.org/10.1137/S0097539793244708

27. Ishai, Y., Kushilevitz, E., Ostrovsky, R., Sahai, A.: Cryptography from anonymity. In: 47th Annual IEEE Symposium on Foundations of Computer Science (FOCS), pp. 239–248. IEEE Computer Society (2006). https://doi.org/10.1109/FOCS.2006.25

28. Kasiviswanathan, S.P., Lee, H.K., Nissim, K., Raskhodnikova, S., Smith, A.D.: What can we learn privately? SIAM J. Comput. 40(3), 793–826 (2011)

29. Vadhan, S.: The complexity of differential privacy. Tutorials on the Foundations of Cryptography. ISC, pp. 347–450. Springer, Cham (2017). https://doi.org/10.1007/978-3-319-57048-8_7

Author Index

Printed in the United States
By Bookmasters